[Books preserve] the principles which led to the formation of the church. Preachers and people may backslide; but the literature remains to remind them of what they once were.

B. T. ROBERTS, 1886

POPULIST SAINTS

B. T. and Ellen Roberts
and the First Free Methodists

Howard A. Snyder

WILLIAM B. EERDMANS PUBLISHING COMPANY
GRAND RAPIDS, MICHIGAN / CAMBRIDGE, U.K.

Published 2006 by

Wm. B. Eerdmans Publishing Co.

2140 Oak Industrial Drive, Grand Rapids, Michigan 49505 /

P.O. Box 163, Cambridge CB3 9PU U.K.

www.eerdmans.com

Printed in the United States of America

11 10 09 08 07 06   7 6 5 4 3 2 1

Library of Congress Cataloging-in-Publication Data

Snyder, Howard A.

Populist saints: B. T. and Ellen Roberts and the first Free Methodists /
Howard A. Snyder.

p.   cm.

ISBN-10 0-8028-2884-1 / ISBN-13 978-0-8028-2884-2 (cloth: alk. paper)

1. Free Methodist Church of North America — History. 2. Free Methodist
Church of North America — Biography. 3. Roberts, Benjamin Titus, 1823-1893.
4. Roberts, Ellen Lois Stowe.   I. Title

BX8413.S69   2006

287′.2 — dc22

2006021874

Permission to quote from Clarence Howard Zahniser, *Earnest Christian: Life and Works of Benjamin Titus Roberts* (Circleville, Ohio: Advocate Publishing House, 1957), has generously been granted by the author's son, Marvin R. Zahniser.

Permission to quote from Peter H. Argersinger, *Populism and Politics: William Alfred Peffer and the People's Party* (Lexington: University Press of Kentucky, 1974), has generously been granted by the University Press of Kentucky.

Reprinted by permission of the publisher from *Merchants, Farmers, and Railroads: Railroad Regulation and New York Politics, 1850-1887* by Lee Benson, pp. vii, 9, 80, 81, 82, 83, 87, 92-93, 94-95, 98-99, 102-103, 108-109, 110, 111, 112, 114, 250, 275, 277-278, Cambridge, Mass.: Harvard University Press, Copyright © 1955 by the President and Fellows of Harvard College.

Permission to reproduce the antislavery icon *"Am I not a man and a Brother?"* . . . (1820). Annual Report 1863, Edinburgh Ladies' Emancipation Society, has generously been granted by Boston Athenæum.

Permission to reproduce the image of the Wesleyan Grove Camp Meeting (1852) has generously been granted by the Drew University Library.

Dedicated to the memory of

Leslie R. Marston, Mark D. Ormston,
Charles V. Fairbairn, and J. Paul Taylor

Men of God and bishops in the church

Contents

━━━⬿⬿⬿━━━

II. LIMINALITY (1855-60)

III. MISSION (1860-1908)

Acknowledgments

Hundreds of people contributed to this book in more ways than can be acknowledged here. I am especially grateful to the following who assisted with ideas, leads, data, insights, research, encouragement, or critique: Donald W. Dayton, David Bundy, William B. Eerdmans, Jr., Cathy Fortner, Kate McGinn, Gerald Bates, Charles Cannon, Doug Newton, Bill Kostlevy, Bernard W. Osborne, Melvin Dieter, Susie Stanley, John Martin, Matt Zahniser, Barry Callen, LaVerne Blowers, Gregory Smith, Gerry Coates, Louise Campbell, Evelyn Marston Mottweiler, Jeanne Acheson Munos, Ken Kinghorn, Milo and Helen Kaufmann, Joe Culumber, Randy Maddox, and Donald Demaray. Marvin Zahniser, historian and son of B. T. Roberts's biographer C. H. Zahniser, kindly supplied me with copies of dozens of Roberts letters and other documents that were not included in the Library of Congress collection of the B. T. Roberts family, though they now have been added to that collection.

    I want to say thank you also to Asbury Theological Seminary (particularly the B. L. Fisher Library staff and the E. Stanley Jones School of World Mission and Evangelism) for support in multiple ways, and to the Marston Memorial Historical Center, Roberts Wesleyan College, and Free Methodist Communications for the assistance and support I received from them. Without these friends and collaborators the book simply would not have been possible.

Introduction

When we all get to heaven, if we do, we will find a million or more saints there who would not have made it if it hadn't been for the shared life and ministry of B. T. and Ellen Roberts.

That would meet Benjamin and Ellen Roberts's standard for success. Benjamin wrote in 1878, when he was fifty-five, "He is a successful minister who is successful in saving souls. If he fails in this — no matter in what else he may succeed — he fails in the one important thing." Success in life is to be measured by living in "devotion to God, in being instrumental, directly or indirectly, in turning many to righteousness, who shall live as imperishable memorials of [God's] fidelity and wisdom when earthly monuments shall have crumbled into dust."[1]

But B. T. Roberts wasn't quite as focused on the life to come as these statements might suggest.

A New York City businessman looking through the *New York Times* on Thursday, January 29, 1874, would likely have seen an article on page 2 entitled "Town Bonds for Railroads." It was signed "A Farmer. North Chili, Monroe County, N.Y." The reader would not know that the farmer was in fact Benjamin Titus Roberts, general superintendent of the Free Methodist Church and editor of the *Earnest Christian*. The piece appeared in the "Letters from the People" section. "Farmer" argued that new state legislation permitting railroads to finance construction through raising bonds in towns across the state was inherently unjust. It was based on the myth that railroads were of "public benefit." In reality railroads "are built and run to make money for those who control them"; any public benefit is "purely incidental." "For every service the railroad renders us we are required to pay a full equivalent." The

---

1. B. T. Roberts, *Fishers of Men; or, Practical Hints to Those Who Would Win Souls* (1878; reprint, Chicago: W. B. Rose, 1918), pp. 15-16.

new law permitted not only men property owners, but also women who owned property, "to whom the ballot is denied," to sign bonding issues. Women couldn't vote, but they "may have a voice for the purpose of putting bonds upon us."[2]

This book is the story of Benjamin Titus Roberts (1823-93) and Ellen Lois (Stowe) Roberts (1825-1908) and their life and ministry together. Benjamin necessarily occupies a larger place in the narrative than does Ellen, just as he did in their ministry, for reasons we will explore. Yet their life was a remarkable collaboration. At key points the story is seen better as a partnership than as the story of two separate persons.

B. T. Roberts's accomplishments were considerable. He was the principal founder of the Free Methodist Church; he began and with great consistency edited and published a monthly magazine, the *Earnest Christian,* which continued for half a century; he founded the institution that is now Roberts Wesleyan College and shaped the key initial leaders of Seattle Pacific University, Spring Arbor University, and Greenville College. He advocated for and helped found the New York Farmers' Alliance, the model for the National Farmers' Alliance that played a key role in the rise of the Populist movement. He encouraged women to fulfill their call to preach, opening many doors for them, and he helped launch a global missions program that has spawned churches, hospitals, educational institutions, and other ministries in dozens of countries around the world. Yet today he is virtually unknown outside a fairly small circle.

The Roberts narrative is part of the larger story of the nineteenth-century Methodist movement. Viewing Methodism's remarkable growth prior to the Civil War, sociologists Roger Finke and Rodney Stark make an intriguing comment about Benjamin Roberts. "Roberts and his Free Methodists were entirely correct that the Methodists in 1850 were no longer the church of the Wesleys or of Bishop Asbury." It was true that "the glory of the Methodist 'miracle' was not based on appealing to the 'proud and fashionable,'" as Roberts argued. Finke and Stark believe Roberts "was wrong to suppose that he could generate a return to higher tension Methodism," but his protest was on target and the formation of the Free Methodist Church in 1860 was "a valid portent of troubles to come."[3]

Despite considerable published research on nineteenth-century Methodism, the midcentury Methodist crisis remains relatively unexplored. Most histories reflect a "mainline" perspective that tends to discount the role of key reformers. Focusing on B. T. and Ellen Roberts helps balance the story.

As Finke and Stark argue, Roberts put his finger on a major shift within Methodism. The controversy Roberts provoked in western New York signaled broader changes. Yet the story of B. T. and Ellen Roberts themselves remains obscure. Despite two older biographies (one by his son Benson in 1900, and C. H. Zahniser's *Earnest*

---

2. A Farmer [B. T. Roberts], "Town Bonds for Railroads," *New-York Times,* January 29, 1874, p. 2. Roberts's diary confirms that he wrote this article.

3. Roger Finke and Rodney Stark, *The Churching of America, 1776-1990: Winners and Losers in Our Religious Economy* (New Brunswick, N.J.: Rutgers University Press, 1992), pp. 152-53.

Christian: Life and Works of Benjamin Titus Roberts, 1957), no critical biography has been written that sets Roberts's life and ministry within the broader religious and cultural context; deals with the matrix of revivalism, abolitionism, and perfectionism that formed Roberts and shaped his later ministry; or sufficiently highlights the key role of Ellen, his partner in home and ministry. This book gives particular attention to the early, formative period before 1860, a period largely overlooked in previous studies. It is important to understand currents and influences that shaped the later story. Each period in the life of Benjamin and Ellen Roberts has its own integrity and its own reasons, of course. But to see their lives whole we must understand the roots and the soil that nourished them.

Though best known as principal founder of the Free Methodist Church, Benjamin Titus Roberts was also a reform voice in such causes as abolitionism, farmers' rights, and women in ministry. Ellen Stowe Roberts, linked to a prominent Methodist family, shared her husband's passion for holiness, for "preaching the gospel to the poor," and for urban ministry. Telling their story illuminates the "crisis of Methodism" that gave rise to the Free Methodist Church and signaled numerous changes within the tradition. The lives of these two intriguing figures thus make a useful case study in nineteenth-century American religious and social history.

I refer to B. T. and Ellen Roberts as "populist saints." I am not claiming, of course, that these two very human persons were spotless saints, nor that they were populists in an ideological sense. But they advocated and sought to live a life of freedom, holiness, and justice that was for *all the people*, and especially for the poor — because that is what they saw in Jesus Christ. In this sense they were populist saints, proclaiming a holy, if radical, populism.

Of course, such populism was already in their Methodist bones. David Hempton points out in his perceptive *Methodism: Empire of the Spirit* that Methodism itself was essentially "a populist religious movement."[4] Methodism was always most populist when it was most radical. Benjamin Roberts was passionate about preserving this populist commitment and sensitivity.

The populist theme illuminates Roberts's promotion of the Farmers' Alliance in the 1870s (the subject of chapter 35). But his work in behalf of farmers and his concurrent advocacy of women's ordination were consistent with his whole pilgrimage. Roberts's early abolitionism, his advocacy of farmers' and women's rights, and his arguments in favor of inheritance taxes with an appeal to the biblical Jubilee are of one piece. God is creator and just governor of all, with special concern for the poor and oppressed, and this essential truth must be reflected in the church and in the political-economic order. Thus a pronounced biblical populism, influenced also of course by American democratic ideals, runs throughout the lives of B. T. and Ellen Roberts.

Today the term "populist" is often used negatively, sometimes linked with ex-

---

4. David Hempton, *Methodism: Empire of the Spirit* (New Haven: Yale University Press, 2005), p. 9.

tremism, anti-intellectualism, nativism, even racism and anti-Semitism. But of course, people movements ever are only as good or bad as their ideals, the character of their leaders, and their steadfastness in the face of both attackers and compromisers. Both the gospel and American democracy claim to be *for* the people — that is, *all* the people — yet church and state often favor elites of special interests over "the general welfare." The story of B. T. and Ellen Roberts is virtually a case study in the populist passion for all the people, not neglecting the poor.

In her biography of the colorful reformer Carry Nation, Fran Grace caught something of Roberts's biblical populism as she documented Free Methodist influence on Mrs. Nation: "B. T. Roberts unceasingly criticized the prosperity theology common in the Gilded Age. His alternative 'liberation' theology provided Nation with the connection between asceticism and reform."[5] If Roberts in fact taught a "liberation theology," it was really a kind of holy populism based in his understanding of God as revealed graciously for all people in creation, in Jesus Christ, and in the present work of the Holy Spirit.

My first objective here is to give a vivid sense of B. T. and Ellen Roberts as people — then to show their part in (and the reasons for) the formation of the Free Methodist Church. I narrate their personal, spiritual, intellectual, and relational pilgrimage. Compared to previous biographies, mine gives relatively more attention to marriage and family life and to Roberts as a reformer.

Benjamin and Ellen Roberts are best seen within the web of relationships they maintained. Mostly these have to do with Methodist and then Free Methodist circles. However, in the story we learn also of the Robertses' direct or indirect connection with such notable men as Charles Finney, Peter Cartwright, Stephen Olin, Gilbert Haven, Daniel Steele, James Caughey, A. B. Simpson, Frederick Douglass, Henry Ward Beecher, William Taylor, J. Hudson Taylor, William Booth, and Jonathan and Charles Blanchard (father-and-son presidents of Wheaton College) — and such remarkable women as Phoebe Palmer, Harriet Beecher Stowe, Frances Willard, Susan B. Anthony, Hannah Whitall Smith, and India's Pandita Ramabai. We see also B. T. Roberts's contact with such reform movements and issues as abolitionism, temperance, economic and monetary policy, and the rights of women, farmers, and Native Americans. We learn of his interest in Judaism and Islam. Particularly remarkable as part of the larger tale is the previously untold story of his catalytic role in the rise of the Populist movement in the 1870s.

Acts in the Drama

Benjamin Roberts's seventy-year life was a drama in three acts. In the first period Roberts became a Methodist, in the third a Free Methodist — identities important

---

5. Fran Grace, *Carry A. Nation: Retelling the Life* (Bloomington: Indiana University Press, 2001), p. 97.

to him. The middle period was transitional and decisive, a liminal (that is, an in-between "crossing-over") time filled with meaning. His wife Ellen was his companion through nearly the whole drama and thus passed through similar experiences.

B. T. Roberts's expulsion from the Methodist Episcopal Church occurred at the midpoint of his earthly journey. He was thirty-five years old when put on trial in 1858 and lived another thirty-five years, dying just months before his seventieth birthday. His ecclesiastical trial and expulsion was the central decisive drama in his ministerial career. It is the fulcrum of the story.

The conjoined lives of B. T. and Ellen Roberts thus fall naturally into three phases:

> *Grounding* — the period until 1855, when storm clouds began gathering in the Genesee Conference of the Methodist Episcopal Church.
> *Liminality* — 1855-60, the period of the "Nazarite" controversy, Roberts's trial and expulsion, and the birth of Free Methodism.
> *Mission* — 1860-1908, from the birth of the new denomination and the founding of the *Earnest Christian* through the years of Benjamin and Ellen's ministry, his death in 1893, and Ellen's last years.

The middle period, which I call "Liminality," receives much attention in the book (nine of forty chapters). Liminality, a concept from cultural anthropology, is a time of transition, but it is more. The term comes from the word for threshold — passing over from one place to another, a sort of rite of passage. It is an in-between time of "antistructure" in which, through some sort of ritual process, a person is changed and emerges into a new reality.

For Benjamin and Ellen Roberts, the six-year period from early 1855 to late 1860 was such a liminal time. "Liminality" highlights the ordeal Benjamin and Ellen endured, especially in 1857-58. I use the liminality model somewhat metaphorically, however. I do not argue that B. T.'s experience fits the liminal or rite of passage model in every respect, but simply that this model clarifies B. T. and Ellen Roberts's life and pilgrimage, not only during this middle passage but also in the long period that followed. It is instructive to view Roberts's two trials, and especially that of 1858, as ritual process — a course that meant more than anyone intended or understood at the time.[6]

---

6. Victor and Edith Turner (following the French ethnographer Arnold van Gennep) defined rites of passage as "transitional rituals accompanying changes of place, state, social position, and age" in a particular social context. These rites have three stages. The first "detaches the ritual subjects from their old places in society; the last installs them, inwardly transformed and outwardly changed, in a new place in society." The first phase, separation, consists of "symbolic behavior signifying the detachment of the individual" from "a relatively stable set of cultural conditions." This leads to "the intervening liminal phase" marked by ambiguity. The person "passes through a realm or dimension that has few or none of the attributes of the past or coming state"; is "betwixt and between all familiar lines of classification." In B. T. Roberts's case, his dramatic 1858 trial functioned as "symbolic behavior signify-

Following his expulsion from the Methodist Episcopal Church, Roberts led in founding the Free Methodist Church and began publishing the *Earnest Christian.* He and Ellen now had new identities as Free Methodists. Rather than being reintegrated into the Methodist Episcopal Church, they found a fruitful and increasingly accepted role within the new Free Methodist community and, with time, much more broadly.

Liminality implies not only change but also new opportunities and possibilities. Roberts's expulsion from the Methodist Episcopal Church, and thus from his well-defined role as a Methodist preacher, brought uncertainty but also opened new possibilities and potentialities. How would he respond to the challenge? This was the major question facing him after his 1858 trial. In a two-year journey through uncharted waters, he found the answers.

Benjamin experienced these dynamics of liminality during his ministry from 1855 to 1860. The Nazarite controversy and Roberts's trial and expulsion did not abolish *all* his socially sanctioned identities, statuses, and roles, but they did strip him of his denominational identity and role. He had to find a new, deeper sense of identity and mission, independent of the community and structure of his (former) denomination.

The story shows that this liminal transition did indeed spark fresh creativity. It also deepened his sense of common humanity, particularly his identification with the poor and oppressed. It tuned his antennae even more toward all forms of injustice.

Roberts was thrust from the Methodist Episcopal Church in 1858. No "rite of reincorporation" brought him back, though he sought reinstatement.[7] And yet the Laymen's Conventions, made up of Methodists who were not yet Free Methodists, in effect played this role for Roberts. As will be shown, these conventions served as catalyst and midwife in the birth of the new denomination — in the process affirming B. T. and Ellen Roberts and giving them new roles. This was incorporation into Methodism of a new type — *Free* Methodism — that Roberts and his colleagues saw as a hopeful reconstitution of what Methodism had been initially and was called to be.

As Free Methodists, beginning in 1860 Benjamin and Ellen fully entered into their life's mission. This was the third (and in Ellen's case, the longest) period of the story. It was the last stage of the pilgrimage, the final act in the drama. In the life of Ellen and of the Roberts children we trace the story up until 1908, when Ellen died.

Why did B. T. Roberts run into such strong, politicized antagonism in the

---

ing [his] detachment" from his previous role and status. Roberts's trial became a rite of separation that in fact brought a change of "place, state, [and] social position." Finally, "in the third phase the passage is consummated, and the subject returns" to a defined and stable life, though in some sense now transformed. The Turners suggest that "liminality is not only *transition* but also *potentiality,* not only 'going to be' but also 'what may be.'" Victor Turner and Edith Turner, *Image and Pilgrimage in Christian Culture: Anthropological Perspectives* (New York: Columbia University Press, 1978), pp. 2-3, 249.

7. Upon his expulsion from the Genesee Conference, Roberts did join the local Pekin ME congregation, where he had been the appointed preacher. But this step, which Ellen thought was a mistake, was not accepted or recognized by the conference or denomination. The story is told in chapter 22.

Genesee Conference in the 1850s when other pastors who were writing similar criticisms did not? Several reasons may be cited here in an introductory way, as they illuminate the story to follow. First, Roberts wrote very well, forthrightly, and persuasively. Second, the Genesee Conference was at the time already much more politicized than were other conferences in the denomination. Third, Roberts was young and was viewed as not having enough seniority to make the charges he did. Fourth, he attacked fairly directly some of the leading pastors in his conference (though not by name). Finally and perhaps most importantly, Roberts combined several issues into a sustained argument about Methodist decline: slavery (slaveholding/abolitionism), pew rental (a kind of elitism), secret societies, wealth and ostentation (fashion), decline in spirituality and discipline, and doctrinal drift regarding entire sanctification. He was perhaps unique in the way he put these together. His contemporary William Hosmer, for instance, editor of the *Northern Christian Advocate* and later of the reformist *Northern Independent,* was as outspoken an abolitionist but was not as concerned about pew rental and some other issues that Roberts saw as crucial.

Sources

The most important source for this biography has been the B. T. Roberts Family Papers, housed in the Library of Congress and available on microfilm at Asbury Theological Seminary, Roberts Wesleyan College, and the Marston Memorial Historical Center in Indianapolis.[8] This collection of sources has been supplemented by the published biographies of B. T. and Ellen Roberts, the *Earnest Christian* magazine (1860-1909), Ellen Roberts's diaries in the Roberts Wesleyan College Archives, the manuscript autobiography of evangelist John Wesley Redfield, and many other sources. I have done archival research at the Library of Congress and many public and institutional libraries and archives. My wife Jan and I have visited and researched cemeteries in several cities and states, also.

Nineteenth-century Methodism and Free Methodism are very extensively documented through both primary and secondary sources. This is particularly true for

---

8. These papers were collected and to some degree sorted by Clarence H. Zahniser as a part of his doctoral research, which became his biography of B. T. Roberts. Zahniser acquired the extensive collection from Dr. George Washington Garlock, president of A. M. Chesbrough Seminary at the time of Benson Roberts's death, and his wife, who apparently acquired them from Benson Roberts's family following Benson's death in 1930. The papers remained in the possession of C. H. Zahniser's widow but eventually were deposited with the Library of Congress. The collection consists of thirty-seven cartons (thirty-four microfilm reels) plus some eighty additional letters and documents, originally a part of the collection, which remained in the possession of Mrs. Zahniser until 2005, when they were transferred to the Library of Congress. See Zahniser, p. iv; Kostlevy, pp. 55-56; Douglas Russell Cullum, "Gospel Simplicity: Rhythms of Faith and Life among Free Methodists in Victorian America" (Ph.D. diss., Drew University, 2002), pp. xviii-xix.

the Genesee Conference of the Methodist Episcopal Church. I have relied on many sources that were unknown or unavailable to Clarence Zahniser and Benson Howard Roberts in their biographies of B. T. Roberts. I was surprised to find how little of the story is actually told in the published biographies. While Zahniser's fine book is indispensable, it omits major parts of the tale. Benson Roberts's biography of his father makes only the most limited use of sources outside B. T. Roberts's own writings.

The Roberts Family Papers contain many hundreds of letters. Much of this storehouse is personal correspondence between B. T. and Ellen Roberts and among other family members. Perhaps a word should be said about the ethics of using and quoting from letters that were intended to be personal and private. I use this material primarily to corroborate or amplify other sources and employ direct quotations where these help narrate the story. I believe this use is justified because this material is now part of the public record, it rounds out the picture of Benjamin and Ellen as real persons, and it often provides essential information. Here I follow the precedent of Clarence Zahniser and Benson Roberts in their biographies of B. T. Roberts, and Adella Carpenter in her *Ellen Lois Roberts: Life and Writings.*

I have used an inductive approach in interpreting B. T. and Ellen Roberts. I have sought to emphasize the things that were important to them and to follow the data (the story) wherever it led. Most of my own theological analysis comes in the later chapters, particularly chapters 34 and 36.

This is not a history of the Free Methodist Church. Several useful denominational histories exist, ranging from the earliest by B. T. Roberts and Elias Bowen to more recent ones by Leslie Marston and David McKenna.

Nor is this book the last word on B. T. and Ellen Roberts. Many areas deserve further research and analysis. I hope this book opens doors for others, as earlier research has for me.

Abbreviations and Conventions

Primary sources quoted in the book frequently contained italics, small caps, or other forms of emphasis. I have reproduced these as in the original. Where I have (infrequently) added my own emphasis, I have so indicated in the reference notes.

Correspondence of B. T. and Ellen Roberts quoted or cited is from the letters contained in the B. T. Roberts Family Papers, Library of Congress, unless otherwise indicated. I have frequently corrected misspelled words in these and other cited documents.

Membership statistics for the Genesee Conference of the Methodist Episcopal Church are taken from the annually published minutes for the years indicated. Membership and other statistical data on the Free Methodist Church are taken from the appropriate minutes or yearbooks of the denomination unless otherwise indicated.

The following abbreviations are used:

In the text:

AME	African Methodist Episcopal
FM	Free Methodist
ME	Methodist Episcopal
MEC	Methodist Episcopal Church

In the reference notes:

AAR	Anna Ackley (Rice) Roberts, first wife of George L. Roberts
ARH	*American Rural Home*, Rochester, N.Y.

BHR	Benson Howard Roberts, third son of B. T. and Ellen
BHR, *BTR*	Benson H. Roberts, *Benjamin Titus Roberts: Late General Superintendent of the Free Methodist Church; A Biography* (North Chili, N.Y.: "The Earnest Christian" Office, 1900)
BTR	Benjamin Titus Roberts
BTRD	Diary, Benjamin Titus Roberts
Carpenter	Adella P. Carpenter, *Ellen Lois Roberts: Life and Writings* (Chicago: Free Methodist Church, Woman's Missionary Society, 1926)
Chesbrough, *Defence*	Samuel K. J. Chesbrough, *Defence of the Rev. B. T. Roberts, A.M. Before the Genesee Conference of the Methodist Episcopal Church, at Perry, N.Y., Oct. 13-21, 1858* (Buffalo: Clapp, Matthews and Co., 1858)
COM	Matthew Simpson, ed., *Cyclopaedia of Methodism*, rev. ed. (Philadelphia: Louis H. Everts, 1880)
Conable	F. W. Conable, *History of the Genesee Annual Conference of the Methodist Episcopal Church, 1810-1872* (New York: Nelson and Phillips, 1876)
DCA	Daniel G. Reid, ed., *Dictionary of Christianity in America* (Downers Grove, Ill.: InterVarsity, 1990)
EC	*Earnest Christian* magazine
ELR	Ellen Lois (Stowe) Roberts (after marriage)
ELRD	Diary, Ellen Lois (Stowe) Roberts
ELS	Ellen Lois Stowe (before marriage to BTR)
ELSD	Diary, Ellen Lois Stowe
FM	*Free Methodist* magazine
GL	George Lane, uncle of ELS
GLR	George Lane Roberts, son of B. T. and Ellen
Hogue, *HFMC*	Wilson T. Hogue, *History of the Free Methodist Church of North America*, 2 vols. (Chicago: Free Methodist Publishing House, 1915)
JWR	John Wesley Redfield
Kostlevy	William C. Kostlevy, ed., *Historical Dictionary of the Holiness Movement* (Lanham, Md.: Scarecrow Press, 2001)
Kysor	Kenneth Kysor, *At Evening It Shall Be Light: Benjamin Titus Roberts and the Free Methodist Church* (Cattaraugus, N.Y.: By the author, 1976)
LBL	Lydia Bunting Lane (wife of George)
LBLD	Diary, Lydia Bunting Lane
Marston	Leslie R. Marston, *From Age to Age a Living Witness: A Historical Interpretation of Free Methodism's First Century* (Winona Lake, Ind.: Light and Life Press, 1960)
MMHC	Marston Memorial Historical Center, Free Methodist World Ministries Center, Indianapolis
NCA	*Northern Christian Advocate*, Auburn, N.Y.
NI	*Northern Independent*, Auburn, N.Y.

Redfield Autobiography	Redfield's manuscript autobiography, located in MMHC, which was the main source of Terrill's biography
RFP	B. T. Roberts Family Papers, Library of Congress
Smail	E[lmer] S. Smail, comp., "Forebears of Some Roberts Cousins" (n.p., 1959, mimeographed)
SO	Stephen Olin
Terrill, *Redfield*	Joseph Goodwin Terrill, *The Life of Rev. John Wesley Redfield, M.D.* (Chicago: Free Methodist Publishing House, 1889, 1912)
TR	Titus Roberts, father of BTR
WAS	B. T. Roberts, *Why Another Sect: Containing a Review of Articles by Bishop Simpson and Others on the Free Methodist Church* (Rochester, N.Y.: "The Earnest Christian" Publishing House, 1879)
WCKD	William C. Kendall, Pocket Diary for 1857, Marston Memorial Historical Center
Zahniser	Clarence Howard Zahniser, *Earnest Christian: Life and Works of Benjamin Titus Roberts* (Circleville, Ohio: Advocate Publishing House, 1957)

PART I

GROUNDING
(1823-55)

CHAPTER 1

"A Symmetrical Man"

"Let us become symmetrical Christians. Grace can make us such, whatever our peculiarities of temperament or education."

B. T. Roberts[1]

"He was always characterized by the most unaffected simplicity both in private and public life."[2]

Benjamin Titus Roberts "was, by nature, what we rarely find — a *symmetrical* man." So wrote Wilson T. Hogue, Roberts's colleague in Free Methodist ministry, shortly after Roberts's death on February 27, 1893.

Hogue was referring to Roberts's character and "natural endowments." He wrote, "Nature bestowed on him many of her rarest gifts. He was a man of strong physique and robust health; of vigorous personality and indomitable energy; of intellectual keenness and strength combined with a high degree of conscientiousness; of the finest sensibilities united with all the noble characteristics of large-hearted manhood. . . . All his natural endowments were directed to better ends and made the more fully to adorn his character through the influence of wholesome and Godly training in early life."[3]

1. B. T. Roberts, "The Essentials," *EC* 30, no. 1 (July 1875): 6. In 1882 Benjamin wrote to his wife, "I would like to be a symmetrical Christian, perfectly developed in every particular." BTR to ELR, June 28, 1882. Quoted in Zahniser, p. 311. He wrote in 1885, "In every thing act consistently with your profession. Let there be symmetry in your life. Dress plainly; but do not neglect to visit the sick in their affliction." B. T. Roberts, "Signs of Life," *EC* 50, no. 4 (Oct. 1885): 103.

2. Hogue, *HFMC*, 2:202.

3. W. T. Hogg [Hogue], "A Tribute to the Memory of Rev. B. T. Roberts, A.M.," *EC* 65, no. 4

Hogue, forty years old and about to become the first president of Greenville College, had known Roberts for twenty years. "The longer I knew him the higher my estimate of him became," Hogue wrote. "He held no grudges. He harbored no ill will. I never knew an uncharitable word to escape his tongue or pen concerning those who did him the greatest injury in connection with the mock trial of an earlier day which deprived him of all his ecclesiastical rights."

Looking to the future, Hogue wrote, "His enemies will pass into the shades, and be no more remembered, except so far as the accidental association of their names with his may preserve them from utter oblivion. But his name will live through many generations, and to thousands yet unborn will be as ointment poured forth."[4]

Hogue's prediction proved, and is still proving, to be precisely accurate.

B. T. Roberts's Last Journey

Though Hogue spoke of Roberts's stamina and "robust health," by 1890 Roberts was in fact unwell. He was suffering from overwork. (Perhaps the major exception to his "symmetry" was his tendency in later years to push himself too hard.) In December 1888 Roberts put an uncharacteristic personal item among his editorials in the *Earnest Christian*:

> After years of unceasing toil your Editor finds himself obliged to call a halt. His travels and incessant labors attending conferences, preaching from five to seven times a week, with tedious night journeyings, rendered more hard by the frequent necessity of changing [railroad] cars, often several times in one night, the constant demand of editorial work, all this has proved too much for a body that has been strong and faithful for many years. To appearances health is not lost; yet a slight exertion, often merely walking a few rods, brings severe pains in the chest and a sense of weariness and weakness all through the upper part of the body, caused, physicians say, by impaired action of the heart, the result of overwork. God has kindly given a sound body that may serve us yet faithfully for many years, if it be His will, if proper rest and care is given to it. In all this Divine peace is given. We hope to gain much in strength by a season of rest. May we not have your prayers?[5]

Roberts did not however "call a halt," even if he paced himself somewhat better. He was only halfway through a four-year term as editor of the weekly *Free Methodist*, was editing the *Earnest Christian*, was continuing his expanding duties as general su-

(Apr. 1893): 119-20. In 1900 Hogg and his family changed the spelling of the name to Hogue, according to the way it "has always been pronounced" ("Brevities," *FM*, Aug. 7, 1900, p. 9). Hogue, a prominent member of the FM Genesee Conference, became the first president of Greenville (Ill.) College in 1892. (The college was founded in 1892 and incorporated in 1893.)

4. Hogg, "Tribute," p. 122.

5. B. T. Roberts, "Personal," *EC* 61, no. 6 (Dec. 1888): 191.

perintendent of the Free Methodist Church, and was still supervising the farm at Chesbrough Seminary in New York. Roberts learned to live with the pain. He apparently got some medical help, but did not commit himself to the extended rest that likely would have prolonged his life another ten or twenty years.

Roberts was suffering from angina pectoris — coronary insufficiency. That is the too-late diagnosis of a twentieth-century physician and surgeon after reviewing Roberts's symptoms.[6]

By February 1893 Roberts's editorial duties with the *Free Methodist* were over; the trying 1890 General Conference was behind him. He was busy in the round of travel, preaching, writing, and decision making that had marked his duties as denominational leader and editor of the *Earnest Christian* for over thirty years. In 1891 he and Ellen had completed a 6,500-mile transcontinental trip to California, Oregon, and Washington, returning through Canada on the Canadian Pacific Railroad, and in 1892 Roberts made a tour by train of the South. In 1888 he had journeyed across the Atlantic to England.

Roberts had promised to lead a quarterly meeting at Cattaraugus, New York, forty miles south of Buffalo, on Saturday and Sunday, February 25-26, 1893. Cattaraugus was only fifteen miles by train from his old home of Gowanda, where his elderly mother still lived, so on Friday the twenty-fourth Roberts "took the cars" west from his home in North Chili, near Rochester, to visit her and spend the night. Benjamin's father Titus had died twelve years earlier at age seventy-seven, but his mother Sally Roberts, almost ninety, was still vigorous.[7]

Early Saturday morning Roberts, "in noticeably good spirits," said good-bye to his mother and boarded the train for the short ride to Cattaraugus. Four miles south, at Dayton, he had to change trains. As he hurried down the platform, suddenly a piercing pain gripped his chest. He managed to find his seat on the Cattaraugus-bound train, but the pain worsened during the twenty-minute trip. With difficulty Benjamin walked off the train and up the platform to meet Rev. George Allen, the Free Methodist pastor at Cattaraugus.[8]

"Why Brother Roberts, you look sick," Allen said.

"Yes — I am very sick," Roberts replied. Allen took him into the depot to rest

---

6. C. Albert Snyder, e-mail note to author, May 31, 2001. Dr. Snyder, a retired Free Methodist medical missionary, elaborated: "Unquestionably the diagnosis is angina pectoris, which is coronary insufficiency." *Taber's Cyclopedic Medical Dictionary* defines angina pectoris as "Severe pain around the heart caused by a relative deficiency of oxygen supply to the heart muscle. It occurs most often after increased activity, exercise, or a stressful event. Pain or numbness typically radiates to the left shoulder and down the left arm and may also radiate to the back or jaw. . . . Symptoms include steady, severe pain in the region of the heart; great anxiety, fear, and fixation of the body; and a pale, ashen, or livid face. . . . Attacks usually last less than 30 min and are relieved by rest or medication" (Clayton L. Thomas, ed., *Taber's Cyclopedic Medical Dictionary*, 18th ed. [Philadelphia: F. A. Davis Co., 1997], p. 104).

7. BHR, "Entered Into Rest. Rev. Benjamin T. Roberts, A.M.," *EC* 65, no. 3 (Mar. 1893): 94.

8. BHR, "Entered Into Rest," p. 94; Hogue, *HFMC*, 2:201.

while they waited for a sleigh to take them to the home of Brother and Sister Phillips, where Roberts was to lodge.[9]

At the Phillips home, Brother and Sister Phillips and Roberts's warm friends Brother and Sister Allen tried to ease Roberts's pain. He had recovered from similar attacks before, Roberts said, and with some rest would be all right. His friends suggested sending word to his wife Ellen, but Roberts said no. He didn't want to alarm his family, and figured he would improve enough to return home Sunday.

But B. T. Roberts did not improve. "By vigorous efforts the impeded circulation was quickened somewhat, but never again became normal," his son Benson wrote.[10] Dr. Amelia Tefft, a "trusted friend and medical advisor" to Roberts, lived about ten miles away, so Roberts's friends sent for her.[11] But Dr. Tefft didn't arrive until about eleven o'clock that night. When she did arrive, she examined Benjamin and told him his condition was critical. He had better attend to any last-minute legal or personal matters while he still could, she said, and so he did.[12]

Roberts remained at the Phillips home on Sunday, dressed and peaceful but very ill. "In the midst of his pain . . . he kept praying almost constantly," but when the pain lessened he talked cheerfully with George Allen. "You will have a good meeting," he assured Pastor Allen, referring to the quarterly meeting at the Cattaraugus church.[13]

Roberts bore the pain all Sunday night, attended by his friends. Through the night and in the early Monday morning he quoted Scriptures. At 5:00 A.M. Mrs. Allen found him lying on the couch, praying, "Oh! Jesus, take this pain away, take it away for Jesus' sake. Amen. Praise the Lord! Praise the Lord!" Later he repeated some of the Beatitudes — "Blessed are they which do hunger and thirst after righteousness: for they shall be filled. Blessed are the merciful: for they shall obtain mercy. Blessed are the pure in heart: for they shall see God." Turning to George Allen, he said, "Brother Allen, these are precious promises. The Bible is full of precious promises, if we only meet the conditions."[14]

An hour or so later Roberts quoted a verse from Charles Wesley's "O for a Thousand Tongues":

Jesus! the name that charms our fears,
That bids our sorrows cease;
'Tis music to the sinner's ears,
'Tis life, and health, and peace.

9. Zahniser, p. 343; BHR, "Entered Into Rest," p. 94.

10. BHR, "Entered Into Rest," p. 94.

11. Hogue (*HFMC*, 2:201) gives her name as Dr. Anstice Tefft. She was part of the Tefft family of East Otto, several of whom were Free Methodists.

12. Hogue, *HFMC*, 2:201; Zahniser, p. 343; BHR, "Entered Into Rest," pp. 94-95.

13. BHR, "Entered Into Rest," p. 94.

14. "Last Words. Notes made by Mrs. Rev. George Allen," *EC* 65, no. 3 (Mar. 1893): 95; Zahniser, p. 343. I have combined the two accounts, which differ slightly.

"Oh! Jesus, give life, and health, and peace," Roberts prayed. "Give it to me now, for Jesus sake. Praise the Lord! Amen!"

A few minutes later when Brother Phillips came in, Roberts greeted him: "Good morning! How are you this morning? Praise the Lord!" And Roberts repeated a phrase from Charles Wesley's hymn "O for a heart to praise my God": "So freely spilt for me." From time to time he quoted other Scriptures and snatches of hymns.[15]

The Allens and Phillipses felt Ellen Roberts really should know her husband's condition, despite Benjamin's wishes. So early Monday morning, apparently, his friends sent word — probably a telegram — to Roberts's family in North Chili. Ellen and their son Benson immediately set out for Cattaraugus by train, via Buffalo. They pulled into Buffalo about noon, but had to wait two hours for the connection to Cattaraugus.[16]

Dr. Tefft had stayed the night, perhaps sitting up with the patient. About 7:30 A.M. Roberts thought he should get up and get dressed. Dr. Tefft asked him, "What are you going to do today?" (probably meaning, "Just what do you think you're doing?!").

"Oh, I am going to direct you today," Roberts joked. He got up, dressed, and shaved himself.[17]

When his friends had family prayers at 10:00 A.M., reading from Psalms 108 and 110, Roberts responded to almost every verse, "Praise the Lord! Amen!" The day proved to be sunny, and Benjamin thought a walk outside would do him good. Mrs. Allen noted that Roberts "Sent the Doctor to bed so he could get away." He probably did not actually go out, however, though Mrs. Allen does not say.[18]

Through the rest of the morning Roberts rested in a chair or on the couch. At noon he washed his face and hands. Brother F. R. Ballard, a local preacher in the Cattaraugus congregation, had come into the kitchen, so about 12:45 Roberts walked into the kitchen and shook hands with him, but said little. He evidently still was in pain.

Roberts went back to his chair and sat down, but then, taken with a fresh spasm of pain, he knelt at the couch and prayed, "Jesus, take away this pain." The agony lessened and he lay on the couch and was heard to say, "Praise the Lord! Amen!"

Moments passed. Roberts groaned a few more times — then quietly passed to the next life. It was about 1:00 P.M. Ellen and Benson were still at the Buffalo train station, awaiting their connection to Cattaraugus. They learned of Roberts's death en route, probably at a station along the way. Benson wrote, "My father, our father, a loving, tender husband, a father in the Lord to many souls, adviser, counsellor to how many, only God knows, had gone to his home. He died at his post, clothed, ready for action, had strength been given."[19]

---

15. "Last Words," p. 95. As Mrs. Allen noted, this hymn was no. 433 in the (1883) *Free Methodist Hymn Book*.

16. BHR, "Entered Into Rest," pp. 94-95.

17. "Last Words," p. 95.

18. "Last Words," p. 95.

19. "Last Words," p. 95; BHR, "Entered Into Rest," p. 95. I have combined the two accounts, which vary slightly in detail.

Why couldn't Benjamin have survived until his family arrived, Ellen asked. "Why should he die away from home" among "comparative strangers"? And yet, Benson added, "they were not strangers, nor could any have shown more tender love. A thousand questions will arise. But we were not left comfortless." Ellen and her son arrived at the Allen home "at dusk to find only the body, lifeless, cold in death."[20] In the midst of their grief they took care of arrangements for conveying the body back to North Chili.[21]

"Oh, how bitter that I could not have been with him!" Ellen cried. But she recalled that in the Old Testament God had sent Moses away to die alone, and Aaron to die "away from the people and his dear ones." Sunday morning while Benjamin, unknown to her, lay suffering in Cattaraugus, Ellen had in fact read the passage about the death of Moses and had thought at the time: how different are God's ways from our ways.[22]

The Funeral

B. T. Roberts died on Monday, February 27, 1893; his funeral was held the following Thursday afternoon, March 2. The service took place at Chesbrough Seminary, the school he founded at North Chili, near Rochester. Cox Memorial Hall had just been completed, and the funeral was held in its fine auditorium. The large folding or sliding doors into the auditorium were opened for the first time to accommodate the crowd.[23]

The day was bitterly cold, the ground covered with a deep blanket of snow. A while before the funeral, forty Free Methodist preachers gathered at the Roberts home to escort the casket the two hundred or so yards across the whitened campus to Cox Hall. They formed a procession, the preachers first, then the casket, draped in black, on an open horse-drawn hearse. Family and friends followed in sleighs — a stark scene of black grief and white snow. Preachers who had formerly been Roberts's students served as pallbearers.[24]

The family asked Roberts's old friend Sam Chesbrough, Free Methodist publishing agent, to come from Chicago and preach the funeral sermon. Word reached him late; Chesbrough did not arrive in time to preach but did make it in time to give a tribute. The Reverend A. F. Curry of the Susquehanna Conference, "a man of much dignity," led the service and preached from Revelation 14:13, "Blessed are the dead which die in the Lord." The service opened with the hymn "The Redeemed in Heaven":

20. ELRD, Feb. 27, 1901.

21. BHR, "Entered Into Rest," p. 95.

22. Ellen L. Roberts, "In Loving Memory," *EC* 65, no. 4 (Apr. 1893): 136.

23. J. G. Terrill, "The Funeral," *EC* 65, no. 4 (Apr. 1893): 129; Neil E. Pfouts, *A History of Roberts Wesleyan College* (North Chili, N.Y.: Roberts Wesleyan College, 2000), p. 36.

24. Zahniser, p. 344; Terrill, "The Funeral," p. 129.

Lo! Round the throne, a glorious band,
The saints in countless myriads stand;
Of every tongue redeemed to God,
Arrayed in garments washed in blood.[25]

Symbolic of the "countless myriads" of "every tongue," two "heathen-born boys," probably students at the seminary, openly expressed their grief at Roberts's bier.[26]

Curry commended Roberts in his sermon. "To convince him that a thing was of God would cause him to take his position for it, no matter how few stood with him or how many stood against him," he noted. "Brother Roberts lived to raise the church to the Christian standard. The churches of America are better to-day for his having lived." J. G. Terrill in his tribute said, "The breadth of [Roberts's] thinking took in the wants of the present and the future of the church, of the State, of society and of the individual."[27] In this book we will see the multiple ways this was in fact true.

Gray-haired Sam Chesbrough, tall and spare at age sixty-seven, walked to the pulpit for his tribute. He recalled the day in 1857 when he heard that Roberts, "voted guilty of unchristian and immoral conduct," had been appointed as his pastor in Pekin, New York. But once he met Roberts, and heard him pray, he knew there was some mistake, for this was a man of God. When Roberts was expelled from the Methodist Episcopal Church in 1858, Chesbrough told him, "You are welcome to one-half of my house, and I'll share the last loaf with you."

"If I needed a friend in time of affliction and sorrow I would run into B. T. Roberts' arms," Chesbrough said. Roberts "was known outside the Free Methodist Church. The influence of his writings was felt throughout the land." He "worked until he dropped in the harness and died a martyr to the work."[28]

Wilson Hogue also rose to add his tribute. He felt he had "lost a father." "I have shed my tears along the way," traveling from Greenville, Illinois. Older preachers might mourn Roberts as a brother; we "younger brethren . . . mourn him as a father." Hogue concluded, "Brother Roberts has built his own monument. This school; the multiplication of the conferences; and the churches that dot the land from the Atlantic to the Pacific, are his monument. I think of him as our Moses who has led us out of the wilderness to the land of promise where we are to-day."[29]

The funeral service ended shortly after 5:00 P.M. The winter sun was already waning, casting slanted shadows across the snow, as the funeral procession passed

---

25. Terrill, "The Funeral," p. 129; Hogue, *HFMC*, 1:339; BHR, *BTR*, p. 563; *The Hymn Book of the Free Methodist Church* (1883; Chicago: Free Methodist Publishing House, 1906), hymn 736, "The Redeemed in Heaven," by M. L. Duncan.

26. BHR, *BTR*, p. 564.

27. Terrill, "The Funeral," p. 129.

28. Terrill, "The Funeral," p. 130.

29. Terrill, "The Funeral," p. 131.

through long lines of students, faculty, and friends. Roberts's casket was borne from Cox Hall to the nearby cemetery, followed by his widow Ellen and the Roberts family. Chesbrough led the graveside service while men and women wept openly. "None seemed to feel more deeply than the students of the seminary, and of these none more so than the Japanese youth, who while others were dropping sprigs of evergreen in the grave, dropped a coin according to the custom of his people," wrote Terrill.[30]

Benson Roberts later recalled the scene: "As the last rays of the sun lit up the overhanging branches of the pines, shedding a golden glory over all, the spot indeed seemed 'hallowed ground.' The loving ones turned reluctantly away, with sad and sorrowing hearts; yet even in this sorrowing hour, came the comforting words: 'I am the resurrection, and the life: he that believeth in me, though he were dead, yet shall he live.'"[31]

Some weeks later Ellen reflected on her loss. "The heaven side of this sorrow is full of blessed comfort, but the earth side has heavy shadows and lonely hours," she confessed. "The wound is a deep one, and while for a time, I was wonderfully upheld before the people, my tears flow in the lone places. I am afflicted yet comforted."[32]

Several years before his death, on May 26, 1883, B. T. Roberts was participating in a Saturday evening service at the Brooklyn, New York, Free Methodist Church. Just as the meeting began, an elderly gentleman died of a heart attack as he arose from kneeling to pray. Roberts commented, "If death must come, which comes to all, at what more desirable time could it be met than that in which it visited our aged brother." He added, "Death comes at all times, in all places, to all ages. We should live in constant readiness to exchange worlds."[33]

The Man and the Story

Benjamin Titus Roberts stood about five feet nine inches tall. During most of his adult life he weighed about 180 pounds. His son Benson described him as "well built." Benson wrote, "His features were large but not coarse, a hazel eye, a high, towering forehead, bald in later life. . . . His countenance was ruddy, bespoke good health. He wore a fringe of a beard as a protection for his throat. Benevolence and kindness [were] written on his face. Women traveling alone and children appealed to him for guidance never in vain."[34]

After his father's death, Benson — Benjamin and Ellen's third son, and Benjamin's truest successor — began work on a biography of his father. Benson recalled an incident thirty years earlier that captured his father's character.

30. BHR, *BTR*, p. 564; Zahniser, p. 344; Pfouts, *History*, p. 36; Terrill, "The Funeral," pp. 131-32.
31. BHR, *BTR*, p. 564.
32. Ellen L. Roberts, "In Loving Memory," p. 136.
33. [B. T. Roberts], "Death in a Church," *EC* 45, no. 6 (June 1883): 191.
34. BHR, *BTR*, p. 564-65.

Roberts was traveling by train, as he frequently did. At one stop a group of about ten well-dressed young African Americans boarded and entered his car. One of the passengers was incensed to see these black youth and insisted the conductor put them in second class.

"They have first-class tickets," the conductor explained.

The passenger grew irate and said he shouldn't have to ride with "niggers." At this point Roberts intervened, defending the young men and women. He "urged their cause convincingly, as he well could do," Benson wrote. The youth took their seats and the train went on.

When the train reached their stop, the youth gathered around Roberts and "thanked him in cultivated language." Then the group sang him "a most beautiful song" — a private concert. Roberts learned that these young men and women were the famed Jubilee Singers from Fisk University in Nashville, Tennessee. Formed in 1871, the Jubilee Singers won international acclaim, introducing white audiences to Negro spirituals like "Steal Away" and "Swing Low, Sweet Chariot." Their music "stirred the nation to an appreciation of what the black man [and woman] could do who had the school-master instead of the overseer for a guide," Benson Roberts wrote. But B. T. Roberts was their defender simply as a matter of equality and justice. "He would take the part of the oppressed."[35]

This incident occurred probably in the mid-1870s, when Roberts was in his fifties.[36] But it captures the tenor of Roberts's whole life, as this book will show.

Shortly after Roberts's death his colleague in the general superintendency, Edward Payson Hart, wrote from Alameda, California: "Our brother was manifestly raised up to head a movement inaugurated to maintain the Bible standard of Christianity and to preach the Gospel to the poor." Roberts's death, Hart concluded, was a loss not just to his family, his denomination, and "the church at large." The world itself lost "a man of God and a friend to humanity."[37] One acquaintance was convinced that Roberts "had the ability to fill the office of President of the United States."[38]

In his tribute to Roberts, Wilson Hogue said: "I always admired this saintly man because of his forgiving spirit. Having suffered much from oppression himself, he always inclined to favor the oppressed. Nor can I doubt that sometimes the compassion of his heart made him lenient toward such as deserved severity. How often have

---

35. This incident is given in BHR, *BTR*, pp. 565-66, and also in Zahniser, pp. 340-41 (citing Benson Roberts). Fisk University was founded by Clinton Bowen Fisk, a Methodist who, like Roberts, was born in western New York (in Livingston County, south of Rochester). See *COM*, pp. 362-63. The story of the Jubilee Singers is eloquently told in Andrew Ward, *Dark Midnight When I Rise: The Story of the Jubilee Singers, Who Introduced the World to the Music of Black America* (New York: Farrar, Straus and Giroux, 2000).

36. Benson Roberts does not give the date, but says this group was "one of the first troupes of Jubilee Singers," which would place the incident in the mid-1870s.

37. E. P. Hart, "In Memoriam," *EC* 65, no. 4 (Apr. 1893): 104.

38. Quoted by Clyde B. Ebey, "Heart Purity and Symmetrical Holiness," *EC* 97, no. 5 (May 1909): 134.

I heard him plead when some brother's alleged wrong or inconsistency was being urged as a bar to his further employment by the church, 'Brethren, we must *forgive*, FORGIVE, **FORGIVE!**'"[39]

Had that spirit prevailed in 1858 at the time of Roberts's trial, probably there would never have been a Free Methodist Church.

To understand the making of this man, and of his wife Ellen Stowe Roberts, we must first search out their radical roots.

39. Hogg, "Tribute," p. 121.

CHAPTER 2

Radical Roots

"The Bible is a Radical book. It never proposes half-way measures."

B. T. Roberts, 1869[1]

"The revivals which these men promoted were much more thorough than the popular revivals of [today]. The preachers did not hesitate to attack prevailing sins."

B. T. Roberts, describing his father's conversion[2]

B. T. Roberts was born in 1823 and died nearly seventy years later, in 1893. His life spanned most of the political, social, economic, and technological revolutions of the nineteenth century, including the Civil War. It stretched from the revivals of Charles Finney in the 1820s to those of Dwight L. Moody toward the end of the century. Roberts was born and raised in the days when the nation was still young, and some of the founding fathers still living. B. T. was almost three when Thomas Jefferson and John Adams both died on July 4, 1826, the fiftieth anniversary of the Declaration of Independence.

"In the uplands of Cattaraugus county, among the hills of Western New York, rich in well-timbered farms, Benjamin Titus Roberts was born in July, 1823."[3] So wrote Benson Roberts in the earliest biography of his father, *Benjamin Titus Roberts: Late General Superintendent of the Free Methodist Church.* Perhaps B. T. Roberts was

---

1. B. T. Roberts, "Radicalism of the Bible," *EC* 17, no. 2 (Feb. 1869): 37.
2. "Rev. Titus Roberts," *EC* 41, no. 4 (Apr. 1881): 130.
3. BHR, *BTR*, p. 1.

in fact born in Cattaraugus County, but he may have been born across the county line in or near Forestville, Chautauqua County, where his parents were married and first lived.[4] Four years after Benjamin's birth his parents moved east to Lodi (later named Gowanda), in Cattaraugus County, and there young Roberts grew up.

Behind these details lies the engaging story of a young couple, Titus and Sally Roberts.

The Big Walnut Tree

Twenty-two-year-old Titus Roberts stood gazing at the just-completed Erie Canal. Visiting Lockport, New York, Titus was intrigued by this feat of human ingenuity — the canal, and the towns already springing up along its course.

But Titus's mind was irked by money problems. He wrote his wife Sally, back home in Chautauqua County, "We have had very bad luck. . . . Our money is almost gone. . . . We intend to try to show here tomorrow and if we don't get any money here I don't know what we shall do."[5] The canal locks at Lockport were "worth seeing," he said, but he and his friend Halsey Stearns were worried about their next moves.

The date was October 3, 1825. The shimmering Erie Canal, winding westward across the state and rising 550 feet through a series of locks, was complete from Albany on the Hudson to Buffalo on Lake Erie. The official opening was just three weeks away.[6] The canal was an immediate success, linking Manhattan's bustling port with America's expanding frontier. Within a year of opening, some seven thousand horse- or mule-drawn boats were moving back and forth on the waterway. Construction costs were paid off in about twelve years, and the operation returned a tidy profit to investors and the state. The canal marked something of a transportation revolution, foreshadowing the much greater one railroads would bring a generation later.[7]

---

4. Kenneth Kysor assembled a number of census and real estate records that support Forestville as Roberts's birthplace; see Kysor, pp. 18-23. This is supported also by the fact of Titus and Sally's marriage in Forestville in 1823. However, the *Alumni Record of Wesleyan University* gives the birthplace as Leon, N.Y., fourteen miles south of Gowanda in Cattaraugus County (Frank W. Nicolson, ed., *Alumni Record of Wesleyan University, Middletown, Conn.*, centennial [6th] ed. [Middletown, Conn.: Pelton and King, 1931], p. 125). I have found no evidence that Titus and Sally Roberts ever lived in Leon. However, because the information in the *Alumni Record* may originally have come from B. T. Roberts, one wonders whether Sally may have given birth to Benjamin at Leon, either because she and Titus happened to be visiting there or lived there briefly or because she had intentionally gone there to be with friends or family for the birth. If so, the family tradition that Roberts was born in Cattaraugus County would be correct.

5. Titus Roberts to Sally Roberts, Lockport, N.Y., Oct. 3, 1825 (spelling and grammar corrected).

6. The canal was opened in stages; some sections were already in operation.

7. Peter L. Bernstein, *Wedding of the Waters: The Erie Canal and the Making of a Great Nation* (New York: Norton, 2005), pp. 325, 343-63.

With entrepreneurial flair, Titus Roberts and Halsey Stearns, like many others, hoped to ride the waterway to financial fortune. Raised southwest of Buffalo near the shores of Lake Erie, Titus remembered a huge black walnut tree that was toppled by a storm three years earlier. A local curiosity and landmark, the walnut was supposedly the largest tree east of the Rockies, measuring thirty-one feet around. When it blew over, local residents cut a twelve-foot section of the hollow trunk, roofed it over, and used it for a store. On its side, the trunk was large enough for a man to ride a horse through; upright, "20 people could sit comfortably inside the shell."

When the owner decided to sell this marvel, Titus Roberts saw a business opportunity. He and Stearns scraped together $200 and bought the tree in September 1825. Tying it on a wagon, they started an exhibition tour, heading northeast toward Buffalo and the Erie Canal. Curiosity would bring out the crowds. Young Titus and his friend would make a tidy sum.

It didn't turn out that way, however. Roberts and Stearns reached Lockport, north of Buffalo, but ran out of money. Bad weather dampened the crowds, and the entrepreneurs had to borrow money. Roberts and Stearns gave up the tree to their creditor and returned home. Titus was welcomed home by his wife Sally and their two little ones, baby Florilla and two-year-old Benjamin Titus. Meanwhile, other venturers took up where Roberts left off. In the spring the walnut trunk was shipped to Manhattan via the Erie Canal (it had to be cut in two to fit the narrow canal boats) and put on display. Some ten thousand gawking New Yorkers paid to see the tree before it was sold for $3,000, shipped to England, and put on display in a London museum that later burned, ending the story.[8]

Roberts Family Roots

Titus Roberts was born June 14, 1803, and his future wife, Sally Ellis, just two months later. The Roberts family traced its roots to Connecticut, "the land of steady habits," and earlier to England. Titus's father, Benjamin Roberts (one source says Benjamin Franklin Roberts),[9] was born in Hartford (later East Hartford), Connecticut, in 1771. With his wife Polly and three little girls Benjamin moved some 150 miles northwest to Hamilton, New York, about 1800. Here Titus and four other children were born. In 1811 Benjamin moved his family to far western New York, settling at Sheridan near the shores of Lake Erie.[10] In moving from the Connecticut River valley to western New York, the Robertses were part of a wave of New Englanders who migrated west and "opened up" the land for "settlement," displacing the Seneca and other Indians who long had called the area home.

8. From accounts collected by Kenneth Kysor. Kysor, pp. 44-47.

9. Kysor, pp. 27, 44. One of this Benjamin's sons was named Benjamin Franklin (a younger brother of Titus). Smail, p. 8.

10. Smail, p. 8.

"The land of steady habits" may have fit Connecticut, but it hardly described the adventurous spirit of frontier western New York in the 1820s. Yet most of the multiplying inhabitants of the frontier and along the shores of Lake Erie were only recent transplants from Connecticut or other New England states. They migrated as far west as one could; the next stage was either to cross over into Ontario, Canada, or move southwest into Ohio territory. The Roberts and Ellis families were among this flood of emigrants from back east who settled in far western New York.

Not only Titus Roberts's father but also his grandfather and great-grandfather were named Benjamin. Great-grandfather Benjamin (ca. 1698-1774), the son of William Roberts, was baptized in the Second Congregational Church of Hartford in August 1698.[11] His son Benjamin was born in 1741, a year and a half after his second wife, Jerusha, gave birth to twin girls.[12] The Roberts family continued to live in the Hartford area until Titus's parents, Benjamin and Polly, and others of their kin moved on to New York about 1800, leaving behind a goodly number of Roberts cousins in Connecticut and Massachusetts.[13]

William Roberts (ca. 1660–ca. 1735), the father of the first Benjamin, was born either in England or Connecticut. His parents emigrated from England sometime in the mid-1600s, probably from the Norwich area.[14] It appears that they settled at Saybrook, at the mouth of the Connecticut River, and then migrated upriver to Middletown and Hartford.

Who were these Connecticut Robertses? Religiously they were Congregationalists, like nearly everyone else in the area. They were fairly prominent socially. Benjamin Roberts, William's son and Titus's great-grandfather, acquired considerable land across the Connecticut River from Hartford in what became East Hartford. He owned several small ships that navigated the Connecticut River down to the coast and then to the West Indies, where he bought rum and molasses that he stored in large rooms under his house. Two of his descendants were Connecticut governors.[15] His son Benjamin, born in 1741, was a farmer and in 1777 enlisted in the Revolutionary army. When he and his wife Dorothy had a son in November 1771, after two daughters, they called him Benjamin after his father and grandfather. Five more children were born, including Thankful and Susannah.

This younger Benjamin grew up in (East) Hartford and married Polly Risley.

---

11. Edwin Pond Parker, *History of the Second Church of Christ in Hartford (1670-1892)* (Hartford: Belknap and Warfield, 1892), p. 308.

12. Smail, p. 5. The twins were Jerusha and Catherine, born nine months after Benjamin married Jerusha Pratt. One of Catherine's sons, Richard Dudley Hubbard, was later the Democratic governor of Connecticut, 1877-79 (Smail, p. 5; *World Book Encyclopedia* [1976], Ci:774).

13. Smail, p. 6.

14. William Roberts married Dorothy Forbes. Smail's genealogy traces the family back to Catherine Leeke and her husband, named Roberts or Robards, who may have come from around Norwich, England. These were the parents of William (ca. 1660–ca. 1735). Catherine died in Middletown, Conn., leaving a number of descendants in the area where B. T. Roberts would later attend university.

15. Smail, pp. 5-6.

When about thirty, he and Polly moved northwest into New York, as noted above, where presumably he farmed and where Titus and other children were born. The family then moved on to far western New York in 1811. Here Benjamin farmed for a while, bought and sold land, and in 1815 acquired a small inn at Pomfret, Chautauqua County, which he expanded into "quite a spacious 'hostelry'" that he ran until his death in 1836.[16] Titus Roberts doubtless grew up helping in his father's inn, acquiring business skills and learning something of the family history.

Benjamin Roberts, B. T. Roberts's grandfather, seems to have been a man of integrity and good character, if not particularly religious. He saw a business opportunity in running an inn. The frontier provided few places to stay, and people often passed through on their way to Ohio territory or farther west. One woman journeying with her husband's family from Worcester, Massachusetts, to Lake Chautauqua in 1818 remembered traveling southwest from Buffalo along the beach through Indian territory and coming to Roberts Inn. "Last evening we crossed Cattaraugus Creek in a ferry into Chautauqua County," she wrote, "and the first building we saw was a large elegant framed house. . . . 11 a.m. at Roberts' Inn, Pomfret. We this morning saw the big tree at Hanover [that] is upwards of 27 feet in circumference."[17] Four years later the storm that uprooted this great tree would rip through, leading to Titus Roberts's walnut tree adventure.

Frontier New York

Western New York was still frontier in the 1820s, though many settlers were moving farther west into the Ohio and Mississippi Valleys. Both New York and Massachusetts claimed rights to western New York due to conflicting land grants by England's King James I and the duke of York in the 1600s. After the Revolutionary War this dispute was settled, opening the door to private land sales and development. A group of wealthy Dutch investors formed the Holland Land Company and bought over three million acres in far western New York. Known thereafter as the Holland Purchase, this great tract of forests and rolling hills reached from Lake Ontario south to Pennsylvania and west to Lake Erie, including what later became Chautauqua, Cattaraugus, and Erie Counties.[18]

Before this wilderness could be settled by intruding whites from the east, however, long-standing Indian claims had to be faced. In treaties of 1788 and 1797 the

16. Smail, p. 10; Obed Edson, *History of Chautauqua County, New York* (Boston: W. A. Fergusson, 1894), p. 619.

17. From an article by Joyce Swan, *Buffalo Evening News*, March 1976, quoted in Kysor, p. 44. It is not clear whether or not the "large elegant framed house" was the Roberts Inn. Pomfret is the township in Cattaraugus County where Fredonia and Dunkirk are located. Sheridan and Hanover are adjoining townships northeast along the lakeshore from Pomfret.

18. Lockwood R. Doty, ed., *History of the Genesee Country (Western New York)* (Chicago: S. J. Clark Publishing Co., 1925), 1:389-95, 405-9.

Seneca Nation ceded its land to the United States but negotiated several reservations, including forty-two square miles along Cattaraugus Creek near its mouth at Lake Erie.[19] This reservation still winds southeast from Lake Erie along Cattaraugus Creek, ending at the edge of Gowanda.[20]

The Holland Land Company at first had difficulty selling its acreage because cheaper land was available from the U.S. government farther west. However, Joseph Ellicott, the company's hardworking agent, eventually pushed through some primitive roads, induced a few settlers to open inns for travelers in exchange for free land, and promoted the building of sawmills and gristmills, keys to settlement. Buffalo was founded in 1801, and over the next two decades many settlers, like the Roberts and Ellis families, ventured west from Connecticut and Massachusetts. Though New York State west of the Genesee River had only 23,000 white inhabitants in 1810 and less than eighteen people per square mile in 1820, the stage was set for the flood of immigration and development released by the opening of the Erie Canal in 1825.[21]

Titus and Sally Roberts

Titus Roberts and Sally Ellis grew up in this frontier setting. They fell in love, married, and gave birth to Benjamin Titus Roberts on July 25, 1823. They first made their home in or near the village of Forestville in northern Chautauqua County. Perhaps they lived awhile with Sally's parents. In 1827 they moved twelve miles east to the young village of Lodi, nestled in the valley created by Cattaraugus Creek as it winds northwest to empty into Lake Erie, thirty miles away.[22] The village was named Lodi in 1823, the name of the town in northern Italy where about twenty-five years earlier Napoleon won a decisive battle that convinced him he was destined to be a great conqueror.[23]

Sally Ellis, second child of Elnathan and Hannah Allen Ellis, was born August 18, 1803.[24] The family probably came originally from Massachusetts or Connecticut, but

19. Doty, *History,* 1:395-96. The latter pact, the Big Tree Treaty of September 1797, was attended by fifty-two Indians representing the Six Nations Confederacy (the ancient Iroquois League), of which the Senecas were one.

20. The Senecas earlier had a village along Cattaraugus Creek, just a few miles from Lodi. See Lewis Henry Morgan, *League of the Iroquois* (1851; Secaucus, N.J.: Citadel Press, 1962), maps in app. I.

21. Doty, *History,* 1:396-404; William Chazanof, *Joseph Ellicott and the Holland Land Company: The Opening of Western New York* (Syracuse: Syracuse University Press, 1970), p. 209; Ellen Semple, *American History and Its Geographic Conditions* (Boston: Houghton Mifflin, 1903), map, p. 152a.

22. A. A. Burgess, "Rev. Titus Roberts," *FM* 14, no. 18 (May 11, 1881): 2. Settled about 1816, Lodi was called Aldrich's Mills until 1823 and had a local school as early as 1817. I. R. Leonard, comp., *Historical Sketch of the Village of Gowanda, N.Y. in Commemoration of the Fiftieth Anniversary of its Incorporation* (Buffalo: Matthews-Northrup, 1898), p. 11; Doty, *History,* 2:1199. Thus, in a sense B. T. Roberts and his hometown of Lodi were born the same year.

23. Erasmus Briggs, *History of the Original Town of Concord . . . , Erie, New York* (Rochester, N.Y.: Union and Advertiser Co., 1883), p. 562.

24. Or possibly Aug. 22. See the obituary, "Mrs. Titus Roberts," *EC* 71, no. 5 (May 1896): 158-59.

at the time of Sally's birth her parents were living on Grand Island in Lake Champlain, Vermont. Later the family moved west to Chenango County, New York (north of present-day Binghamton), and about 1815 on to Chautauqua County. Here Elnathan bought a farm and built a log house near Forestville. One source describes Elnathan as "a true pioneer, always living on the edge of settled districts."[25]

Elnathan and Hannah Ellis were pioneers in another sense. In December 1817 they joined about thirty others to form the Forestville Baptist Church under the leadership of the Reverend James Bennett.[26] How or where Titus Roberts met young Sally Ellis we don't know, but neither was yet twenty when their romance bloomed. A notice in the Fredonia *Censor* for July 9, 1823, says Titus and Sally were married by Bennett but does not give the wedding date.[27] Apparently the marriage took place in the Ellis home.[28]

The records of Titus and Sally's marriage seem deliberately vague. The likely reason is that Benjamin Titus Roberts's birth came just two weeks after the published marriage announcement. Though Titus and Sally could have been married some months earlier, more probably the wedding occurred a week or two before the newspaper notice, perhaps around June 25, and thus only about a month before Benjamin's birth.[29] This accords with Titus Roberts's obituary in the *Free Methodist,* which states that Titus married Sally when he was twenty years of age, and also with Sally's obituary, which says "both bride and groom [were] 20 years old" when they married.[30] Titus turned twenty on June 14, 1823, six weeks before Benjamin's birth. Sally actually did not turn twenty until August 18, almost a month *after* the birth.[31]

It seems that Titus and Sally suppressed their marriage date to avoid embarrassment.[32] However, it is possible that, in these frontier conditions, the couple was living together as husband and wife though not yet officially married. They would have wanted to regularize their union before the baby arrived. In any case, pregnancy before marriage was fairly common during this period of American history.[33]

25. Smail, p. 63.

26. Edson, *History,* p. 644.

27. *New York Censor,* Fredonia, N.Y., July 9, 1823, marriage notice.

28. Smail says the marriage was performed "in a log cabin" on the Ellis farm — presumably that of Sally's parents (p. 63). Forestville Baptist Church did not have a church edifice until 1825 (Edson, *History,* p. 644), and home weddings were then common in any case.

29. Usually marriage notices were published within two weeks of the wedding and generally included the date of the marriage — but not in this case. The Forestville Baptist Church lost many of its records in a fire in 1859, and I have not been able to verify whether any original record of the Roberts-Ellis marriage survives. At this early period county governments were not yet recording marriages, so church records and newspaper notices are usually the only sources available, beyond family papers.

30. Burgess, "Rev. Titus Roberts."

31. Obituary, "Mrs. Titus Roberts," *EC* 71, no. 5 (May 1896): 158-59.

32. The assumption by B. T. and his later family that he was born in Cattaraugus rather than Chautauqua County may trace to the same deliberate vagueness about these early years. Is the fact that B. T. Roberts's tombstone in North Chili erroneously gives 1824 as his birth year related to the same circumstances?

33. Speaking of the decades immediately following the American Revolution, Jack Larkin ob-

Titus perhaps worked for his father until about the time he married Sally. As he grew up he likely would have helped out in his father's inn. Shortly after Titus and Sally were married, it appears, the couple began operating an inn in Forestville, and soon also started buying and selling property.[34] Real estate records show several transactions in the names of Titus and Sally Roberts between 1823 and 1825.[35] A daughter, Florilla, was born in 1825 while the family was still living in Forestville.

With their two little ones, Titus and Sally moved across the county line to Lodi in 1827.[36] Perhaps the opportunity to manage an inn in that village was the incentive. Some sources say Titus and Sally operated the Mansion House, "an inn for travelers," in Lodi during this period.[37] If so, the inn was probably their residence, as they apparently did not at first own property in Lodi. Before long Titus was also operating a store and had a thriving business, supplemented by continuing real estate transactions. On June 28, 1827, Sally gave birth to their third child, Caroline. About 1830 Titus's twelve-year-old nephew Ashbel Sellew, son of Titus's older sister, came to live with the Roberts family and presumably helped in Titus's store.[38]

Titus and Sally prospered sufficiently to make additional land deals. In September 1832 they bought their first real estate in Lodi, paying $50 for a lot on Main Street across the street from property that would later be their home for many years.[39] In November of the same year Titus bought fifty acres directly from the Holland Land Company for $200, a tract of land located across Cattaraugus Creek in Erie County.[40]

---

serves: "For many couples, sexual relations were part of serious courtship. Premarital pregnancies in late eighteenth-century Dedham, Massachusetts, observed the local historian Erastus Worthington in 1828, were occasioned by 'the custom then prevalent of females admitting young men to their beds, who sought their company in marriage.' Pregnancies usually simply accelerated a marriage that would have taken place in any case, but community and parental pressure worked strongly to assure it." He adds, "Most rural communities simply tolerated the early pregnancies that marked so many marriages." Jack Larkin, *The Reshaping of Everyday Life, 1790-1840* (New York: Harper and Row, 1989), pp. 193-94.

34. Kysor says the Robertses "owned and operated, or simply operated, an inn in Forestville" at this time (p. 44) but cites no sources.

35. Kysor, p. 23. Kysor cites other evidence that Titus Roberts owned "several properties" in Forestville (from the assessor's office in Silver Creek), but doesn't give dates (p. 43).

36. Obituary, "Mrs. Titus Roberts," p. 159.

37. Kysor, p. 44.

38. Smail, pp. 10, 175. Later Ashbel's daughter Emma would marry B. T.'s son Benson (they were second cousins).

39. Kysor, pp. 21-23. Later, in 1875, Titus Roberts deeded this property and the house on it in trust to the Free Methodist Church for parsonage use, Kysor notes.

40. Briggs, *History*, p. 552. The date of the sale was Nov. 19, 1832. Cf. Smail, p. 11.

Titus's Conversion

Titus Roberts eventually became fairly well-to-do through his varied business ventures, buying and selling over 150 properties between 1823 and his death in 1881.[41] Occasionally he assisted his son financially when B. T. was in pastoral work.

Titus was converted when he was about thirty-one — the key turning point in his life. B. T. recalled after Titus's death: "My father was converted to God while engaged in the mercantile business. It was in a meeting held by evangelists who had been raised up under Mr. Finney's labors. The revivals which these men promoted were much more thorough than the popular revivals of [today]. The preachers did not hesitate to attack prevailing sins. In the village [of Lodi], every merchant in the village — some half dozen or so — and most of the leading men were converted. There was in them an immediate, striking and permanent change."[42]

Titus's conversion was thus associated with the revival campaigns of the famous Charles Grandison Finney (1792-1875), a man eleven years older than Titus who likewise had roots in New England. A series of revivals under the young Finney's leadership broke out in upstate New York in 1824 and continued for several years, sparking controversy in the East. Finney described one area as "what in the western phrase would be called, 'a burnt district'" because of earlier revivals in the region led by Methodists and others that Finney considered extravagant and spurious.[43] But that's precisely how some of Finney's eastern critics saw *his* work. Lyman Beecher, the famous Boston preacher, called the areas of upstate New York where Finney conducted his 1826-27 revivals "burned over," giving rise eventually to the term "Burned-Over District" to designate the broad swath of upstate and western New York that witnessed repeated revivals and the rise of such movements as the Mormons and varieties of spiritualists, millenarians, and communitarians in the mid-1800s.[44] Titus and Sally Roberts lived at the far western edge of the Burned-Over District.

By 1834 the first wave of Finney's revivals had passed.[45] Yet revival fires still swept western New York, some of them sparked by itinerant evangelists converted under or influenced by Finney. A loose-knit group of Finney associates, sometimes

---

41. Kysor, p. 23.

42. "Rev. Titus Roberts," *EC*, p. 130.

43. Garth Rosell and Richard A. G. Dupuis, eds., *The Memoirs of Charles G. Finney: The Complete Restored Text* (Grand Rapids: Zondervan, 1989), pp. 78-79.

44. Rosell and Dupuis, *Memoirs of Charles G. Finney*, p. 78; Whitney R. Cross, *The Burned-Over District: The Social and Intellectual History of Enthusiastic Religion in Western New York, 1800-1850* (Ithaca, N.Y.: Cornell University Press, 1950; New York: Harper Torchbooks, 1965).

45. James Bratt argues that in fact the great period of Anglo-American revivals was 1735-1835 and that widespread revivals largely ceased after 1835 (the 1857-58 revival being a limited exception) — and that in general revivalism failed to achieve its objectives. James D. Bratt, "The Reorientation of American Protestantism, 1835-1845," *Church History* 67, no. 1 (March 1998): 52-82. "While Presbyterian and Congregational revivals dropped off after 1835, the Methodists' [revivals] did not flag for another ten years" (p. 64).

called Finney's "Holy Band," carried on a zealous form of revivalism beginning in late 1826.[46] Much revival and church-planting work was conducted also by Presbyterian/Congregational missionaries sponsored by the American Home Missionary Society as well as by Methodist itinerants and Baptist preachers. Methodists were among the early settlers in western New York, and the Methodist Episcopal Church began appointing missionary circuit riders to the Holland Purchase in 1807. One of these early missioners was George Lane, B. T. Roberts's future uncle by marriage, who as a young man of twenty-four was sent to the area in 1808 and who held the first Methodist camp meeting west of the Genesee River.[47]

Revivals continued throughout the region, including many in and around Lodi. James H. Hotchkin in his 1848 history of the Presbyterian Church in western New York reports that 1833 was "more distinguished by revivals in the churches" than the previous year and adds, "During the year 1834, the work of the Spirit, in a considerable degree, was continued." He notes specifically that in the fall of 1835 four churches in the Buffalo Presbytery (which included Lodi) "enjoyed . . . extensive revivals, in which about two hundred and fifty individuals were believed to have been converted unto God."[48] The story was similar with the Methodists, who reported a stirring revival in Lodi about 1833. "The labors of Salmon Judd and David Nichols on the Lodi charge, on the Cattaraugus, were greatly blessed," noted the Genesee Conference historian, F. W. Conable. Revival there produced a "wonderful reformation of the people of the village in matters of morality and religion."[49]

Titus Roberts was converted during this period, probably in 1833, 1834, or 1835.[50] Perhaps it happened during one of the revivals reported by Hotchkin. Whether the revival that transformed Titus was held under Presbyterian or Methodist auspices or was some sort of union meeting is not clear, though as B. T. noted, it had some connection to Finney and his associates. Sally Roberts may have been converted about the same time; throughout her long marriage to Titus she was a partner with him in his earnest faith.

Benjamin would have been a boy of about eleven when his father was converted — old enough to remember and be marked by the event. Though B. T.'s own conver-

---

46. Keith J. Hardman, *Charles Grandison Finney, 1792-1875* (Grand Rapids: Baker, 1987), pp. 460-61.

47. George Peck, *Early Methodism Within the Bounds of the Old Genesee Conference from 1788 to 1828* (New York: Carlton and Porter, 1860), pp. 234-35, 255, 346. This first camp meeting was held at Caledonia, southwest of Rochester. Lane's appointment to the Holland Purchase apparently was for one year only.

48. James H. Hotchkin, *A History of the Purchase and Settlement of Western New York and of the Rise, Progress, and Present State of the Presbyterian Church in That Section* (New York: M. W. Dodd, 1848), p. 152.

49. Conable, p. 360. Conable thus substantiates B. T. Roberts's description.

50. The obituary by A. A. Burgess says he was converted at about the age of thirty-one and soon felt that he should preach the gospel. Burgess, "Rev. Titus Roberts"; cf. Smail, p. 11. Titus turned thirty-one on June 14, 1834.

sion was still ten years off, his life and certainly his conception of revivals were marked by these Burned-Over District revivals of 1834-35.[51] Nearly fifty years later Benjamin wrote, "In a revival of God's work souls are born of the Spirit. They do not merely feel better; they are made better. There is a real change in their dispositions. The passionate become patient; the ambitious lowly, the proud humble and self-denying. People are converted, not simply to a belief, but to God. There is in them a great, and marked and obvious change. They become new creatures."[52] This is what Benjamin as a child saw in his own father's life.

Methodists were preaching in Lodi as early as 1830.[53] When the Lodi Methodist Episcopal Church was officially organized, Titus Roberts was one of its early members. He appears to have joined the Methodists about 1836, and in 1839 was granted a local preacher's license.[54] Methodist conference minutes show rapid growth in the Lodi charge from 150 members in 1831 to 307 in 1833, and to 410 a year later. Membership in 1836 was reported to be 399.[55] These figures do indeed suggest revival in the 1833-34 period.

There is no evidence that Titus had any connection with the Methodist church prior to his conversion. His wife Sally's family were Baptists. Evidently the revival fires of 1833-35 brought a good many Lodi citizens into the churches, including Titus and Sally Roberts into the Methodist fold.

Soon Titus began thinking about full-time itinerant ministry. In 1839 he sold his business, became a local preacher, and in September was admitted into the Genesee Conference on trial, the first step toward ordination.[56] He was appointed to assist John Shaw on the Gainesville charge, some fifty miles east of Lodi.[57] It is uncertain how actively he was involved at Gainesville during the conference year, though B. T. later noted that Titus "preached for one year."[58]

Apparently the buyers of Titus's business were not able to make good on the deal, and by the following March Titus was back in business. B. T. later wrote, "[H]is business coming into his hands again, he left the Conference, and from that time labored till near the close of his life as a Local Preacher."[59]

---

51. The *New York Evangelist* reported several revivals in Cattaraugus County and the surrounding area, and one specifically in Lodi, in 1834. *New York Evangelist*, May 17, 1834, p. 79; Nov. 8, 1834, p. 179; Dec. 27, 1834.

52. [B. T. Roberts], "A Revival of God's Work," *EC* 45, no. 1 (Jan. 1883): 33.

53. *Minutes of the Annual Conferences of the Methodist Episcopal Church, for the Years 1773-1828* (New York: T. Mason and G. Lane, 1840), 1:73.

54. Leonard, *Historical Sketch*, p. 89.

55. *Minutes . . . 1773-1828*, 1:111, 212, 273, 399.

56. Conable notes that "Titus Roberts [was recommended from the] Pike Station; [and with others] admitted on trial in the traveling connection." Conable, pp. 444-45.

57. *Minutes . . . 1773-1828*, 1:658.

58. "Rev. Titus Roberts," *EC*, p. 130.

59. "Rev. Titus Roberts," *EC*, p. 130. Titus's trial membership in the conference was discontinued in 1840, probably at his request. See Ray Allen, *A Century of the Genesee Annual Conference of the Methodist Episcopal Church, 1810-1910* (Rochester, N.Y.: By the author, 1911), p. 115.

During the interval between Titus's conversion and his short-lived venture in the Methodist ministry, the abolitionists came to town. Abolition fever was boiling. The American Anti-Slavery Society was formed in 1833, and the high point of its campaign in western New York (and throughout much of the North) was in the late 1830s. Abolitionist organizer Theodore Weld trained "The Seventy," activist agents of the American Anti-Slavery Society, in New York City in November 1836. These firebrands fanned out across the North in late 1836 and during 1837.[60] At least two of these, James Blakesley and Henry Bowen, were active in Chautauqua County in 1837, sometimes working together. Between December 1836 and mid-March 1837 Blakesley organized fifteen societies in Erie and Chautauqua Counties, each averaging around 100 members. He found the churches very open to the antislavery message, reporting that "nearly all of the region's clergymen were abolitionists."[61]

Annual reports of the American Anti-Slavery Society show that an abolitionist society was organized in Lodi in February 1837, with 112 members. A juvenile antislavery society was formed the following December with 123 members.[62] Halsey Stearns, Titus's old partner in the walnut tree adventure, was secretary of the Lodi Anti-Slavery Society in 1838.[63]

Titus Roberts (and young Benjamin) likely participated in these antislavery activities. In any case, they surely were influenced by them. B. T., at age fifteen, may well have been a member of the juvenile antislavery society.[64] No doubt this was one source, at least, of his strong abolitionist convictions.

Titus's conversion at thirty-one was a dramatic about-face. There is no evidence of any religious interest prior to this. Though his wife's parents were charter members of the Forestville Baptist Church and Titus may have participated nominally, he seems not to have exhibited any spiritual concern or attachment prior to the revival that changed his life.

Titus Roberts's Character

What sort of man was Titus Roberts, B. T.'s father? Like his forebears, he seems to have been a man of upright character, yet essentially irreligious until his conversion.

---

60. John Lytle Myers, "The Agency System of the Anti-Slavery Movement, 1832-1837, and Its Antecedents in Other Benevolent and Reform Societies" (Ph.D. diss., University of Michigan, 1960). Myers lists the names of "The Seventy" (actually sixty-five), pp. 401-2. The list includes James Birney, Charles Stuart, Orange Scott (later a founder of the Wesleyan Methodist Church), Jonathan Blanchard (later president of Wheaton College), and of course Weld.

61. Myers, "Agency System," p. 524.

62. *Fourth Annual Report of the American Anti-Slavery Society* (New York: William Dorr, 1837), p. 132; *Fifth Annual Report of the American Anti-Slavery Society* (New York: William Dorr, 1838), p. 141. The former presumably was organized by Blakesley (cf. Myers, "Agency System," pp. 523-24).

63. *Fifth Annual Report*, p. 141.

64. To my knowledge, no records survive of either of these Lodi antislavery societies.

From his youth he was something of an entrepreneur, and this trait continued throughout life. He became well known in the community, in 1851 serving on the Gowanda Board of Trustees.[65] Sometime before 1850 he bought a farm, and the censuses for 1850 and 1860 list him as a farmer. Yet he continued to buy and sell property throughout his life. In the spring of 1853 he bought a dairy farm. B. T., then pastoring, noted in his diary that due to this purchase Titus couldn't help him out financially. (In a laconic comment on the times, B. T. adds, "The spirit rapping mania is prevailing at Gowanda.")[66]

Some of Titus's character traits are already visible in the incident of the old walnut tree. The story illustrates at least three things about him: his entrepreneurial spirit, his optimism in the face of difficulties, and his ability to learn from setbacks and move on — qualities later visible in his son. Curiously, an adventurous, entrepreneurial spirit seems to run backward and forward through the Roberts generations — from B. T.'s great-great-grandfather Benjamin Roberts, the Connecticut landowner and shipping merchant, to his father Titus, to his own sons, who became entrepreneurs in their own ways.

These traits of B. T.'s father in turn raise the key issue of *character*. What is the stuff that character is made of? Where does it come from? How is it built and transmitted? And what is its relationship to Christian discipleship, to holy living? This question, illustrated in B. T.'s life, was also raised by him in his writing. It forms a recurring theme in exploring the lives of B. T. and Ellen Roberts.

Through the years Titus Roberts exhibited Christian character in a number of ways. His obituary noted, "As a business man he was active, energetic and successful, and would have been a man of wealth were it not that he gave away thousands of dollars. In him the poor and needy always found a friend. He had great sympathy for his debtors. He never would sue any one, for fear of distressing him." Titus died with over $3,000 owed him that he never used legal means to collect.[67]

Young B. T. Roberts

The story of Titus and Sally Roberts's life together sets the stage for Benjamin's early years. B. T. grew up in Lodi; there he got his earliest education and formed many of his deepest convictions. (It was not until the fall of 1848, after B. T. had graduated from Wesleyan University, that the town's name was changed to the more Indian-sounding Gowanda to avoid confusion with another Lodi in the state.)

Lying at the far western edge of the Burned-Over District, Lodi was just fifteen miles from the eastern shores of Lake Erie and about thirty miles directly south of

---

65. Leonard, *Historical Sketch*, pp. 19, 33.

66. BTRD, Apr. 4, 1853. B. T. notes that in June 1852 his parents had just moved into a new house; BTRD, June 22, 1852.

67. Burgess, "Rev. Titus Roberts."

the little city of Buffalo. Today, driving west toward Lake Erie from Gowanda, one can catch glimpses of the Buffalo skyline, but in the 1820s and 1830s a trip to the growing city was a major undertaking. Buffalo was the western terminus of the Erie Canal, completed just two years after B. T.'s birth, and the canal gave major impetus to the city's growth and importance.

Lodi had a couple of hotels and thirty-odd stores, shops, and businesses crowded along the main street that crossed Cattaraugus Creek. Until the great fire of 1856, the creek was spanned by a covered wooden bridge. Three times weekly a stage-coach brought the mail to town.[68] Newspapers were started from time to time, often in support of political causes. They thrived or struggled, one being replaced by another. One fall day when B. T. was a lad of seven a young journeyman printer named Horace Greeley walked into town, looking for work. Greeley found a job briefly with the *Lodi Pioneer,* the town's first newspaper. He was paid eleven dollars per month, but in six weeks his employer ran out of money and had to let him go. About New Year's Day 1831, Greeley walked out of town the way he had come in, going south to his parents' home across the state line in Erie County, Pennsylvania. Later that year Greeley moved to Manhattan to seek his fortune. There he founded the *New York Tribune,* one of New York's most influential newspapers.[69] Roberts probably wouldn't have known Greeley then, but he certainly came to know of him later when Greeley became a major voice for abolition, temperance, and other reforms. As editor of the *Tribune,* Greeley popularized the advice, "Go West, young man!" But at this point the young man went east to the big city.

Raised in Lodi, Benjamin Roberts doubtless helped out in his father's business and, sometime after his eleventh birthday, witnessed the sweeping revival that brought his father's life-changing conversion. Benjamin seems to have formed a close relationship with his parents and his two younger sisters, Florilla and Caroline. He was especially close to Florilla, two years younger than he. The two used to spend an hour or two together on Sundays, following the afternoon service, talking and reading to each other.[70] In these early years the Roberts home may have been the inn Titus and Sally ran, or some other rented property, as it appears that Titus and Sally didn't yet have their own house.[71]

Roberts's early education meant mastering "such books as were taught in the district school." His son Benson later pictured B. T. studying "by the flickering light of the candle, or the flaring blaze of the fire-place." According to Benson, the boy "soon became the best scholar, and as champion speller . . . went from school to

68. Briggs, *History,* p. 568.

69. Leonard, *Historical Sketch,* p. 22; Horace Greeley, *Recollections of a Busy Life* (New York: J. B. Ford and Co., 1868), pp. 79-84; William Harlan Hale, *Horace Greeley, Voice of the People* (New York: Harper and Brothers, 1950), p. 12; William M. Cornell, *The Life and Public Career of Hon. Horace Greeley* (Boston: D. Lothrop and Co., n.d.), pp. 63-68.

70. BHR, *BTR,* p. 17.

71. Kysor (p. 44) says Titus and Sally "moved into the house that was to be their home . . . for twenty-six years" in 1855, but as B. T.'s diary shows, this was not their first house in Gowanda.

school to spell down any competitors in the frequent spelling matches. He also held himself ready to solve any problem in any of the arithmetics in common use, that might be given him. He mastered algebra before he saw anyone who understood the science."[72]

Eager to learn, Benjamin began studying Latin, first on his own[73] and then probably with the Presbyterian pastor, John B. Preston, a missionary with the American Home Missionary Society who had been installed as the Lodi Presbyterian Church pastor in June 1835.[74] During his pastorate Preston "taught a flourishing school" in the basement of the Presbyterian church building,[75] probably with B. T. as one of the pupils.

The Presbyterians early organized a Sunday school in Lodi. Typically Presbyterian Sunday schools in the area were at first interdenominational, and this was probably true in Lodi. Benjamin Roberts and many other children attended.

John Preston was probably the Presbyterian pastor Roberts later mentioned as having a strong influence on him. "A Presbyterian minister came to me one day when a boy and invited me to go to Sabbath School. I went. I committed many chapters of the Bible to memory. At one lesson I recited the whole of the epistle of James."[76] Benjamin often showed up at Sunday school with more Scriptures memorized than there was time to recite. He always felt this early training gave him an important grounding in Scripture.[77]

Later when Roberts was about fifteen the Presbyterian pastor offered to educate him for his church's ministry. Benjamin replied, "I cannot accept it, as I have not yet been converted."[78]

Clarence Zahniser writes, "Little is known of this period except as it carried over into [Roberts's] later years in his love of precision of speech and in the clarity of his ideas."[79] However, a key part of Benjamin's early formation must have been the antislavery agitation of the early 1830s, noted above. Though B. T. makes no explicit reference to the antislavery societies formed in Lodi in 1837, it is clear that about this time he was converted to abolitionist views — well before his conscious conversion

72. BHR, *BTR*, p. 2.

73. Benson Roberts (BHR, *BTR*, p. 2) says B. T. began studying Latin "without a teacher," while another source says he studied Latin under the local Presbyterian minister (interview with Mrs. Bula Lincoln Palcic, B. T.'s great-grandniece, Apr. 22, 1997). Probably both are correct.

74. Leonard, *Historical Sketch*, p. 117. On Preston, see the *Home Missionary* (published by the American Home Missionary Society), Jan. 1835, p. 159; Feb. 1, 1836, p. 180. The January 1835 *Home Missionary* contains a report "From the Rev. J. B. Preston, Lodi, Erie County, N.Y." (p. 157).

75. Leonard, *Historical Sketch*, p. 117. A Presbyterian Sunday school was started in Lodi in 1826, and the church was organized in 1828 with eleven members. (The Presbyterian church building was on the Erie County side of the county line.) William Adams, ed., *Historical Gazetteer and Biographical Memorial of Cattaraugus County, N.Y.* (Syracuse: Lyman, Horton and Co., 1883), p. 982.

76. B. T. Roberts, "A Running Sketch," *EC* 9, no. 1 (Jan. 1865): 5; cf. Zahniser, p. 14; BHR, *BTR*, p. 2.

77. BHR, *BTR*, p. 2.

78. BHR, *BTR*, p. 3.

79. Zahniser, p. 13.

to Christianity. Zahniser says that later as a law student "One of his first speeches . . . was an abolition speech," and also that during this early period Roberts "began to champion the temperance cause," becoming a speaker at local temperance meetings.[80]

By age sixteen Benjamin had completed sufficient education to begin teaching others. Benson notes that at this time B. T. became a schoolmaster, "often teaching boys and girls older than himself, yet maintaining the dignity and respect of his office. His schools were uniformly well taught and governed. He retained the respect and esteem of his scholars, receiving many testimonies of the same when advanced in years and the former pupils of the red school house had become gray with age."[81]

B. T. Roberts was becoming an adult and making life decisions. But he was not yet a Christian.

80. It is not clear what Zahniser's sources are here. Regarding temperance, he cites BHR, *BTR*, pp. 1-2, but that reference contains nothing about temperance. Still, it would be very much in character for Roberts to have championed both temperance and abolitionism at this time and in this context.

81. BHR, *BTR*, p. 3.

CHAPTER 3

"A Duty to Be a Christian"

"I felt it was my duty to become a Christian."

B. T. Roberts[1]

"God's Spirit from my earliest recollections strove with me and restrained me."

B. T. Roberts, 1865[2]

Religious excitement stirred the United States, and especially New York State, in the early 1840s. Phoebe Palmer was beginning her ministry in New York City. Revivals were widespread and social reform efforts were gaining strength. The *Oberlin Evangelist* editorialized in early 1841, "The Millennium is at hand," and said in June 1841, "[B]eyond all doubt the preparation for the promised Millennium has begun."[3] Similar hopes were expressed by other publications, such as the *New York Evangelist*. In January 1843 William Miller announced that Christ would return to earth not later than March 21, 1844.[4] Mormonism, born in New York State the previous decade, was becoming increasingly controversial. On June 27, 1844, Joseph Smith and his brother were killed by a mob in Illinois.[5]

Douglas Strong writes of this period,

1. B. T. Roberts, "A Running Sketch," *EC* 9, no. 1 (Jan. 1865): 5.
2. B. T. Roberts, "A Running Sketch," p. 5; cf. BHR, *BTR*, p. 4; Zahniser, p. 14.
3. *Oberlin Evangelist* 3 (Feb. 17, 1841): 2; (June 23, 1841): 101. Quoted in Douglas Mark Strong, "Organized Liberty: Evangelical Perfectionism, Political Abolitionism, and Ecclesiastical Reform in the Burned-Over District" (Ph.D. diss., Princeton University, 1990), p. 263.
4. *DCA*, p. 740.
5. *DCA*, p. 1098.

The increasing millennial expectations of the early 1840s reached a fevered pitch in the autumn of 1844. More than a decade of urgent revivalistic preaching had conditioned the people of the burned-over district to be particularly receptive to the proposition of an immediate consummation of history. This excitement was partly a result of the Millerite predictions of a cataclysmic apocalypse, but even those who did not accept Miller's specific chronology were convinced that the coming reign of God, in some form, was right on the horizon.[6]

B. T. Roberts was converted during this period. Benjamin does not seem to have been much caught up in the religious excitement, however; for him conversion was a matter of rational choice. One day a woman "long known as a devoted saint of God" told him, "I know the world is coming to an end in March next; the Lord showed it to me plainly, as I was on my knees reading the Bible." Benjamin was not impressed. "She was pious, but mistaken," he later wrote.[7]

Benjamin apparently attended a Millerite meeting or two, however. Years later he wrote,

At first, their meetings were among the most deeply spiritual that we ever attended. But when the time they had fixed upon for the second-coming of Christ passed by without his making his appearance, many could not admit that there had been any mistake in their calculations. To save themselves from the mortifying confession that they had not fully understood "all mysteries, and all knowledge" they resorted to various expedients. Some held that time was really passed — that we were now in eternity — some held to the annihilation of the wicked — some went to the Shakers — and many made shipwreck of faith and of good conscience.[8]

This early exposure to Millerism may have forever immunized Roberts against millennial and apocalyptic excitement, though not against millennial hope.[9]

Benjamin's Conversion

As for his own experience, the young Benjamin Roberts of the early 1840s knew he was not a Christian. His focus was on himself and his own future. What career should he follow? What should be his aspirations? Though he had obvious teaching gifts, law sparked his interest. He began legal study, probably at first on his own while he continued teaching. Perhaps through Chester Howe, a lawyer in Lodi, Roberts heard of attorney Henry Link in Little Falls, New York, near Utica. Link

6. Douglas M. Strong, *Perfectionist Politics: Abolitionism and the Religious Tensions of American Democracy* (Syracuse: Syracuse University Press, 1999), p. 118.

7. [B. T. Roberts], "Led by the Spirit," *EC* 4, no. 1 (July 1862): 28.

8. [B. T. Roberts], "Mistaken," *EC* 4, no. 2 (Aug. 1862): 62.

9. See the discussion of Roberts's theology in later chapters.

(1811-91), German by descent, was a prominent Herkimer County citizen active in Democratic politics.[10] In April of 1842 Roberts traveled the two hundred miles east to Little Falls and began a legal apprenticeship with Link. For a little over two years he studied with Link while also teaching school on the side.[11]

Benjamin returned to Lodi in May 1844 and continued his legal training, studying with Howe.[12] Living again in Lodi gave B. T. a chance to renew acquaintances and spend time with his family. One pleasant June day he took a clean sheet of paper and wrote a poem to his sisters with the inscribed invitation: "B. T. Roberts presents his compliments to Misses Florilla and Caroline Roberts and solicits the pleasure of their company in a walk this evening." The poem itself breathes of summer life in Lodi and suggests an eye for nature.

> The evening sun is waning low,
>   Anxious to sleep behind the hills,
> The Zephyr cool begins to blow,
>   And the soft air with fragrance fills
>
> The birds in sweet and touching notes
>   Their joy at Eve's return proclaim
> And with their native untaught throats
>   Filling ungrateful man with shame
>
> Abroad in Nature's ample field
>   Together Sisters let us roam
> A walk such pleasures pure will yield
>   As nought can furnish us save Home[13]

The summer of 1844 was to be momentous for Benjamin (already calling himself "B. T."). He expected soon to be admitted to the bar and probably would have become a successful attorney. But God changed the course of his life.

Titus and Sally had been praying for Benjamin, and they saw his return to Lodi in May as answered prayer. "God's Spirit from my earliest recollections strove with me and restrained me," Benjamin said. As he studied law he became "ambitious, proud and worldly. At times I was powerfully convicted, but I thought it was a part of manliness to resist as long as possible. Conviction left me and my heart became

---

10. Information provided by the Little Falls Historical Society and the Little Falls Public Library. Link "was twice elected president of the village of Little Falls, and in 1871 ran on the Democratic ticket for county judge but was defeated by Judge Amos H. Prescott." George A. Hardin, *History of Herkimer County, N.Y.* (Syracuse: D. Mason and Co., 1893), p. 151.

11. BHR, *BTR,* pp. 3-4. Passing through Little Falls in 1849, after their marriage, Ellen wrote in her diary, "Little Falls — a romantic spot among the rocky hills where Benjamin spent some two years studying law." ELRD, May 15-16, 1849.

12. BHR, *BTR,* p. 4; Zahniser, p. 13. Howe was the Whig candidate for county judge in 1851. *Cattaraugus Chronicle* (Gowanda, N.Y.) 1, no. 32 (Oct. 23, 1851).

13. Original manuscript in the possession of Mrs. Bula Palcic, Gowanda.

hard."[14] Yet his grounding in Scripture kept him "from infidelity" and enabled him "to expose and refute [the] sophistical objections" of his friends and associates. He intellectually accepted Christian views, in other words, but had not personally committed himself to Christ and his way. Now, however, his life was coming to a crisis, a point of personal decision.

Benjamin Roberts was not a bad person, but he was strong-willed and perhaps a little self-righteous. "I never drank wine but once, and that was at a New Year's call. Tobacco I never used, and profanity I abhorred." His life was largely centered in himself and the legal career he envisioned.

Benjamin experienced a clear Christian conversion, however, in July 1844, around the time of his twenty-first birthday. One warm Sunday afternoon some friends invited him to attend a prayer meeting, probably at the Methodist church. It was a fairly routine gathering, but midway through the service God spoke to Benjamin's heart. An illiterate barrel maker stood and through halting, stammering lips told how God had changed his life. Somehow the words cut to Benjamin's heart. Something about the simplicity and humility of this man touched B. T. He saw that he was a lost sinner in need of God's grace. Then and there he was convinced that "it was my duty to become a Christian." But this conviction didn't settle the matter; it actually set up three weeks of intense struggle for control of his life and ambition.[15]

Benjamin tried negotiating with God, using his best arguments. He was ready to be converted so long as he could follow the legal career his heart was set on. The saints in the church could see the struggle Benjamin was going through and prayed earnestly.

Finally Benjamin saw that it came down to a decision between the law and God. "Christ demanded an unconditional surrender," he said. "I made it. The joys of pardon and peace flowed into my soul. My cup was full, my happiness was unspeakable."[16] Many years later Benjamin described his conversion: "God calls by his Spirit, he called me; in the still hours of the night he talked to me. God had kept me very moral, yet his Spirit came to me in such convincing power that I had to start to seek him when there was nothing like a religious revival in the place."[17]

This was the decisive turning point in Benjamin Roberts's life. He immediately abandoned his legal apprenticeship and began training for the Methodist ministry. In his son Benson's words, he felt that if it was necessary to "make careful preparation for pleading at the bar cases involving [people's] temporal interests . . . , he should make no less careful preparation for pleading at the bar of the human conscience, the interests of God's kingdom and the truths of Christ's Gospel."[18]

14. B. T. Roberts, "A Running Sketch," p. 5; cf. BHR, *BTR*, p. 4; Zahniser, p. 14.

15. B. T. Roberts, "A Running Sketch," p. 5.

16. B. T. Roberts, "A Running Sketch," p. 5. Cf. BHR, *BTR*, p. 4.

17. B. T. Roberts, "Sermon," *EC* 45, no. 1 (Jan. 1883): 7. This sermon was delivered at the 1882 FM General Conference.

18. BHR, *BTR*, p. 6. Charles Finney similarly gave up a legal career for Christian ministry twenty-three years earlier.

The first step was to attend Genesee Wesleyan Seminary near Rochester to get ready for college. Benjamin probably taught school in the fall of 1844, saving his money. Then he entered Genesee Wesleyan in April 1845 for the fifteen-week summer term.[19]

The Young Abolitionist

About this time Caroline Roberts, the younger of Benjamin's two sisters, married David Brown of Lodi. They wed in September 1844, when Caroline was only seventeen; David, a Lodi native, was five years older. David operated a store for several years until the great fire of 1856 wiped out several businesses in downtown Gowanda, including his own.[20]

Caroline's marriage left just Florilla at home with Titus and Sally when Benjamin went to Genesee Seminary. On Thursday, March 20, 1845, Benjamin spent time with Florilla (eighteen at the time) and gave her a remarkable poem, apparently his own composition, that is strongly abolitionist in tone. Tucked into the folded poem was an abolitionist coin or token with the inscription "Am I Not a Woman and a Sister" and the date 1838, and on the other side, "United States of America" and "Liberty." Such tokens were widely used at the time to promote the antislavery cause. The year 1838 may commemorate the burning of Liberty Hall in Philadelphia by an anti-abolitionist mob in May of that year.[21] British abolitionists used the image of a kneeling slave, his shackled arms upraised, with the inscription "Am I Not a Man

---

19. Richard R. Blews, *Master Workmen: Biographies of the Late Bishops of the Free Methodist Church during Her First Century, 1860-1960*, centennial ed. (Winona Lake, Ind.: Light and Life Press, 1960), p. 19; *Catalogue of the Officers and Students of the Genesee Wesleyan Seminary, 1844* (Rochester, N.Y.: David Hoyt, 1844), p. 29. The school had a twenty-nine-week "winter term" running from September through March, and a fifteen-week "summer term," April-July.

20. Kysor, p. 29; Cattaraugus County NY Biographies Forum (Internet). Benjamin commented on this fire in a letter to his father in May 1856. "It does seem to me as if [the fire] might have been stopped [at the river] by blowing up the bridge, but perhaps not. . . . I fear that the place will not be able to recover from the shock. David I suppose will rebuild. I hope he is not discouraged, though of course he will feel the blow. May it lead him to lay up for himself treasures in Heaven, where the fire consumes not, and where thieves steal not!" BTR (Albion, N.Y.) to TR, May 9, 1856.

21. Antislavery tokens of this type were used first in England and later in the United States. An Emancipation Jubilee Medal bearing the date of Aug. 1, 1834, was struck in Birmingham, England, for distribution in the United States bearing the inscriptions "Am I Not a Man and a Brother" and "A Voice from Great Britain to America." These metal tokens were distributed through the Anti-Slavery Office, 130 Nassau Street, New York, for 25¢ each (*New York Evangelist* 6, no. 1 [Jan. 3, 1835]: 1). In this case the 1838 Liberty medal may suggest that Roberts had some affinity with the "Liberty Men" who founded the abolitionist Liberty Party in April 1840. The Liberty Party garnered only 15 of 194 total votes cast in the town of Persia (which included Lodi) in the presidential election of 1844 (Strong, "Organized Liberty," p. 345; see also Vernon L. Volpe, *Forlorn Hope of Freedom: The Liberty Party in the Old Northwest, 1838-1848* [Kent, Ohio: Kent State University Press, 1990], p. 24).

and a Brother." To this famous icon American activists added the image of a female
slave and the motto, "Am I Not a Woman and a Sister."[22]

The token echoed the sentiments of B. T.'s poetry. He begins his poem to Florilla
— a piece of brotherly affection and moral instruction — with the abolitionist slogan.

To my dear Sister

> The voice of a Female Slave
> "Am I not a woman and a sister"?

Though curly locks my head adorn,
Though darkly sable be my face,
    Yet courses not within my veins
    The purple blood of Adams race?

Though with the invader's ruthless hand,
From friends and home I'm torn away,
    To be a slave in Christian's land,
    Deprived of Freedom's genial ray;

Though Master's whip hath torn my back,
And made the crimson current flow,
    In torrents down my quivering flesh,
    Till Death had almost eased my wo;

Though Tyrant's galling chains enclose
My mangled limbs in dire embrace,
    Though marks of bruises, and of blows,
    Eternity can ne'er efface;

Yet have I not that form divine
Which God to all mankind hath given?
    Is not that soul immortal mine
    Which e'er must dwell in hell or Heaven?

Abides there not within my breast
Devotion pure Affection deep?
    Oppression's rod can ne'er arrest
    Those powers of soul that never sleep.

As then if you were made a slave
You'd others have to feel for you,
    Deeply within your heart engrave,
    For me such feeling deep and true.

22. Henry Mayer, *All on Fire: William Lloyd Garrison and the Abolition of Slavery* (New York: St.
Martin's Press, 1998), p. 232 n.

Dear Sister keep the [*sic*] within as an amulet for the
repulsion of that evil Spirit the Genius of Slavery

> Your affectionate brother
> B T Roberts
> Lodi March 20th 1845[23]

This poem is remarkable on several counts — its passion and strong sentiment, its forthright identification with the abolitionist cause, and, not incidentally in the light of Roberts's later concerns, its implicitly feminist tone.

Such sentiment shortly after B. T.'s conversion and just when he was preparing for the Methodist ministry naturally raises the question: In what sense was B. T. Roberts an abolitionist? And where did the antislavery cause fit in his sense of priorities?

As we have seen, the years 1831-40 were the high point of the great antislavery crusade that grew partly out of revivalism. Abolitionism was then considered a radical movement, and Roberts was to some degree influenced by this radicalism. Zahniser is quite right that at this time "the word abolition was a term of severe reproach, a verbal stigma, and in many communities a precursor of physical persecution."[24]

The abolitionism of the 1830s owed much to the revivalism of the 1820s, as a number of scholars have pointed out. Two key figures were Charles Stuart and Theodore Dwight Weld, early converts of Finney who soon became leaders in the "immediate abolitionism" of the 1830s.[25]

The revivalism of the 1820s and earlier was rooted in hope for the reform and perfecting of both church and society, and also fueled such hope. Revival fires were in fact a key catalyst in the rise of the abolitionist movement beginning in 1831. But there were other contributing causes — particularly the British antislavery movement and England's abolishing of slavery in the West Indies in 1833. From 1831 on American abolitionism was a distinct and growing movement. Finney denounced slavery as "a great national sin" and William Lloyd Garrison published the first issue of the *Liberator* in Boston in January 1831. The New England Anti-Slavery Society was organized in 1832, and, as noted above, the American Anti-Slavery Society the next year.

The story of B. T.'s early years shows that he was "converted" to abolitionism well before his conversion to Christ. As his poem to Florilla and his later life show, he continued to be a firm opponent of slavery. He must have accepted the revivalist-abolitionist consensus: just as Christian discipleship meant no compromise with sin of any form in society or church, so abolitionism meant no compromise with popu-

---

23. Original manuscript in the possession of Mrs. Bula Palcic, Gowanda.

24. Zahniser, p. 13.

25. See especially Benjamin P. Thomas, *Theodore Weld, Crusader for Freedom* (New Brunswick, N.J.: Rutgers University Press, 1950; reprint, New York: Octagon Books, 1973); and Robert H. Abzug, *Passionate Liberator: Theodore Dwight Weld and the Dilemma of Reform* (New York: Oxford University Press, 1980).

lar toleration of slavery. For the antislavery radicals — and no doubt for Roberts — abolitionism and revivalism were twin moral crusades.

Here we begin to understand the currents that shaped B. T. Roberts. Since Benjamin clearly was an abolitionist from at least the late 1830s, the connection between revivalism and the rise of "immediate" abolitionism after 1830 is significant for understanding the "radical" nature of his formation as an older child, teen, and young adult (roughly from 1830 to 1848). Abolitionism apparently had a radicalizing effect on Roberts, or perhaps reinforced tendencies already present. The antislavery crusade intensified his determination to take the side of the oppressed, the downtrodden, and those most in need of God's mercy and grace. It helped convince him that "The Bible is a Radical book. It never proposes half-way measures. The word radical comes from radix[,] root — and the Bible always goes to the root of the matter."[26] Together with the Finneyite revivalism that changed his father's life, abolitionism was a force that molded Roberts's lifelong views concerning the gospel, pastoral ministry, and the role of the church in society.

The abolitionist cause was about ending slavery, of course, and so it focused on the plight of suffering African slaves. There was little parallel concern about the plight of displaced American Indians, many of whom were confined to reservations or forcibly marched west to Oklahoma Territory in the "Trail of Tears" of 1838-39.[27] What B. T. Roberts thought about Indian concerns is unclear, but it is not an idle question because while growing up he came into frequent contact with Native Americans. Seneca Indians lived nearby and often came to town on business. The Seneca reservation outside town, in fact, was only a mile from the Roberts home on Main Street. Yet Benjamin makes no reference to them during these early years, though many years later he did comment on injustices done to Indians.[28] Whatever sympathy Roberts may have felt for Native Americans, their concerns clearly did not weigh as heavily upon him as did the plight of African slaves and the evils of slaveholding. We do know that the influential abolitionist William Lloyd Garrison publicized to some extent the plight of the Indians in the *Liberator,* his antislavery paper, and Roberts may well have been sympathetic with these concerns.[29]

On the slavery issue, B. T. Roberts was a convinced abolitionist and remained so until the Civil War settled the matter. Yet his calling was to the church, not to the antislavery crusade. He opposed slavery and spoke for immediate abolition. But as he entered Genesee Wesleyan Seminary, his life focus was on serving the church and working as an instrument of revival.

26. B. T. Roberts, "Radicalism of the Bible," *EC* 17, no. 2 (Feb. 1869): 37.

27. Some 13,000 Cherokees were forced west from Georgia along the "Trail of Tears" in 1838-39 as a result, ultimately, of the Indian Removal Act of 1830 during the presidency of Andrew Jackson. See Anthony F. C. Wallace, *The Long, Bitter Trail: Andrew Jackson and the Indians* (New York: Hill and Wang, 1993), pp. 93-94. Wallace notes that evangelical missionaries to the Indians were among the few who opposed these acts of the U.S. government.

28. See chapter 37.

29. Mayer, *All on Fire,* pp. 138, 273.

CHAPTER 4

Genesee Wesleyan Student

"God would keep us while we honestly sought to be better qualified for useful-ness in His service."

B. T. Roberts, referring to his Wesleyan Seminary days, 1868[1]

"Religion grows more lovely to me the more I know of it; and I hope and expect to live religion while I live, that when I die I may meet all the saints of God around the throne."

B. T. Roberts, 1845[2]

Genesee Wesleyan Seminary was not a theological school but rather a liberal arts college-preparatory institution located in the village of Lima, New York, about twenty miles south of Rochester.[3] The seminary's main building sat atop a knoll on the north side of the village. About 1851 a classical Greek edifice fronted with six tall columns was built as the school was expanding into a college program. These build-ings still stand, now part of the campus of Elim Bible College. The college program itself was later moved to Syracuse, becoming Syracuse University.

1. B. T. Roberts, "Rev. Loren Stiles," *EC* 16, no. 1 (July 1868): 6.
2. Quoted in BHR, *BTR*, p. 7.
3. BHR, *BTR*, p. 6. The Methodist "seminary" or preparatory school at Lima was established by action of the Genesee Conference at its 1830 and 1831 sessions, a step prompted by the formation of the Oneida Conference from the eastern portion of the Genesee Conference in 1828, which left the Genesee Conference without such a school. Conable, pp. 311, 323, 331. Such Methodist seminaries were founded "to fit their students for admission to the best colleges in the United States, or to prepare them by mental training and knowledge to engage in the various industrial pursuits of life." M. L. Scudder, *American Methodism* (Hartford: S. S. Scranton, 1867), p. 400.

Founded by the Genesee Conference in 1831, Genesee Wesleyan was coeducational and "from the first a seminary of high grade . . . at a time when the modern high-school was almost unknown."[4] The school had a classical curriculum including science and mathematics.[5] It boasted "Apparatus . . . fully adequate to the illustration of the courses of lectures in the experimental sciences," including various magnets and batteries, "an Electrical Machine," "Morse's Telegraph," and "a valuable Achromatic Telescope, imported from Germany." Enrollment in 1844-45 was about 485, two-thirds men and one-third women.[6]

As a Methodist institution, Genesee Wesleyan was of course closely connected with the Genesee Conference. A key figure in the school was thirty-six-year-old Thomas Carlton, a Genesee Conference pastor of growing influence who was secretary of the seminary board of trustees at the time Roberts was a student.[7] He was the Methodist preacher in Lima in 1844-45, so presumably Roberts frequently sat under his preaching. He would later be a key figure in Roberts's own relationship with the Methodist Episcopal Church.

Having already taught school for a while, Roberts was well grounded academically when he went to Genesee Wesleyan. The fifteen-week summer term was sufficient to prepare him to enter Wesleyan University as a sophomore in the fall of 1845.[8] School records don't show precisely which subjects he studied, but the main divisions of the curriculum were moral science and belles lettres (including composition, logic, and philosophy), languages (principally Latin and Greek), mathematical and experimental science, natural science, and English (including penmanship, history, and astronomy).[9]

Benjamin, now nearly twenty-one, excelled at his studies. Genesee Wesleyan had a system of merits and demerits based on a five-point scale ranging from "Superior recitation" (5) to "Very good" (4) and "Good" (3), down to "Failure" (-1). The record book shows that in fact students almost never were given a five, and rarely a four. Demerits were marked for absence from class, tardiness, and absence from church. A

---

4. Ray Allen, *History of the East Genesee Annual Conference of the Methodist Episcopal Church* (Rochester, N.Y.: By the author, 1908), p. 26.

5. Emma Freeland Shay, *Mariet Hardy Freeland: A Faithful Witness; A Biography by Her Daughter* (Winona Lake, Ind.: Women's Missionary Society of the Free Methodist Church, [1913] 1937), p. 41. This book has a photo of the main Genesee Wesleyan building following p. 42. "It was the custom for many of the students to form clubs and board themselves, bringing much of their provisions from home" (p. 42).

6. Allen, *History*, pp. 26-27; *Catalogue of the Officers, Faculty, and Students of the Genesee Wesleyan Seminary, 1845* (Rochester, N.Y.: S. Hamilton, 1845), p. 24. The school actually opened on May 1, 1832. In 1850 a college program was added that was indirectly the predecessor of Syracuse University (founded in 1870-71). Allen, pp. 28-29.

7. *Catalogue . . . 1845*, p. 3. Carlton was born in 1808. He also served as board treasurer.

8. Zahniser says Benjamin spent two terms there (Zahniser, p. 15), but school records show he was there just for the spring term (April through July).

9. *Catalogue of the Officers, Faculty, and Students of the Genesee Wesleyan Seminary, 1844* (Rochester, N.Y.: S. Hamilton, 1844), pp. 25-28.

running tally was updated weekly, averaging the various classes. At the end of the term the scores were totaled, averaged, and multiplied by ten, yielding a two-digit "general standing for the term" of all students.[10] Roberts averaged 3.4, with no demerits. Thus when merits and demerits were calculated for the term, his score was 34 — the highest any student attained. The record book shows that Roberts and three others achieved the top standing of 34.[11]

Roberts and other outstanding students were recognized by being given speaking assignments at the year-end academic exercises in July, called the Anniversary. Sixteen students (all males) were chosen to speak, including William Kendall and Loren Stiles.[12]

Presumably B. T. participated in the normal round of school activities over the term, including classes and recitations, the literary societies, weekly prayer meetings, and Sunday services at the local Methodist church.[13] These spring and summer months were a time not only of academic preparation but also of spiritual deepening. He wrote his sister on July 1, "[T]he more I know of myself the more do I feel my incapacity for standing as a watchman on the walls of Zion. Had I that humility of soul, that spiritual wisdom, that constant, unremitting flow of love, that purified, sanctified heart that should . . . abound in every child of God, then could I work the mighty works whereto I am sent."[14] Clearly Roberts early had a strong sense of mission and vocation.

At Genesee Wesleyan Roberts became fast friends with his classmate Loren Stiles, later one of the first Free Methodists and a close associate.[15] Another future Free Methodist in Roberts's class was William Kendall.[16]

Though enjoying his studies, Roberts worried that academics might lead him away from the Lord. He discussed this with Stiles, and the two agreed that "learning was good, but salvation was better."[17]

What should they do? Should they continue their studies? Benjamin and Loren

---

10. Faculty Minutes, Genesee Wesleyan Seminary, Oct. 21, 1844. Archives and Special Collections, Syracuse University.

11. Record Book, "Names of Students and Points for D and M [Demerits and Merits] 1844-1848," Genesee Wesleyan Seminary, pp. 24-42. Archives and Special Collections, Syracuse University. In contrast to Roberts, W. C. Kendall's score was 30, as was Loren Stiles's.

12. Faculty Minutes, Genesee Wesleyan Seminary, June 5, 1845. The selection seems to have been based primarily but not exclusively on academic standing. Archives and Special Collections, Syracuse University.

13. Shay, *Mariet Hardy Freeland*, pp. 42-48. Shay notes that there were "various literary societies for the young ladies, as well as for the young men" during the time Mariet Hardy was a student at Genesee Wesleyan in 1851-53 (p. 44).

14. Quoted in BHR, *BTR*, pp. 6-7.

15. B. T. Roberts, "Rev. Loren Stiles," p. 6.

16. Carpenter, p. 38; B. T. Roberts, "Rev. William C. Kendall," *EC* 2, no. 4 (Apr. 1861): 117. Kendall was in fact converted while a student at Genesee Wesleyan Seminary during a "general awakening" there (Roberts, p. 117).

17. B. T. Roberts, "Rev. Loren Stiles," p. 6.

walked out into the woods one summer day to wrestle with the question. Kneeling beside a large log, they prayed the matter through. "We had both intended to prosecute our studies farther than through the Academic course; but seeing the formality of the Seminary professors, we were afraid to go farther for fear that we should lose our first love and become cold and formal."

This was a critical decision. "We wept and prayed before the Lord," B. T. wrote. "We consecrated ourselves anew to Him, to be His for time and eternity. The Holy Spirit came down, and Divine assurance was given that God would keep us while we honestly sought to be better qualified for usefulness in His service."[18]

With this new assurance, Roberts finished out the term at Genesee Wesleyan, earning enough credits to permit his transfer to Wesleyan University in Connecticut as a sophomore in the fall. Meanwhile Stiles went on to Methodist Theological Seminary at Concord, New Hampshire.[19] Toward the end of his time in Lima Benjamin wrote his mother, "O, mother, I long to know more of God — to enjoy more of His love shed abroad in my heart. Tell me how to crucify myself to the world and live wholly to God. Religion grows more lovely to me the more I know of it; and I hope and expect to live religion while I live, that when I die I may meet all the saints of God around the throne."[20]

Meanwhile, Benjamin was proceeding through the conference process toward ordination. On June 16, 1845, his local Methodist church licensed him to exhort.[21]

*   *   *

During B. T. Roberts's growing-up years in Lodi, in a small town along the Susquehanna River, two hundred miles back east, a girl named Ellen Stowe was born and grew to girlhood. Two years younger than B. T., Ellen spent her early years in Windsor, New York. Unlike Benjamin, however, Ellen's critical teenage years passed not in a small town but in the bustling metropolis of New York City.

---

18. B. T. Roberts, "Rev. Loren Stiles," p. 6.
19. BHR, *BTR*, p. 6; B. T. Roberts, "Rev. Loren Stiles," p. 6.
20. Quoted in BHR, *BTR*, p. 7.
21. BHR, *BTR*, p. 6.

CHAPTER 5

The Stows of Windsor

". . . to pray, strictly to observe the Sabbath, and to attend the Presbyterian church."

Ellen Lois (Stowe) Roberts, 1861[1]

". . . a lasting impression on my mind."

Ellen Lois (Stowe) Roberts, describing her first
experience of a Methodist meeting[2]

Ellen Lois Stowe was born in Windsor, New York. Though her critical teenage years would be spent in New York City, her personality was first shaped by her childhood in upstate New York. A key influence was her uncle, George Lane.[3]

The Lanes and the Stows

George Lane was a true pioneer of American Methodism. He was born in 1784, converted in 1803, and ordained by Francis Asbury in 1807. Thus his roots went deep in frontier Methodist revivalism. As a preacher and church planter he had traveled many frontier circuits. But in 1836 he ended up in New York City, sent there to serve as assistant book agent (assistant publisher) in the Methodist publishing enterprise.

1. Ellen L. Roberts, "Religious Experience," *EC* 2, no. 9 (Sept. 1861): 282.
2. Ellen L. Roberts, "Religious Experience," p. 282.
3. Mary Alice Tenney provides a biographical sketch of Ellen Lois Roberts in *Adventures in Christian Love* (Winona Lake, Ind.: Light and Life Press, 1964), pp. 26-48.

Lane was born about a hundred miles north of New York City, not far from the Hudson River. His parents, Nathan and Dorcas Lane, had come originally from Massachusetts. When George was a child the family moved west to Windsor, on the Susquehanna River, just north of the Pennsylvania state line.[4] The Lanes were among the earliest white settlers in the area, though an Onaquaga Indian village (part of the Iroquois League) had been located nearby. In fact, Jonathan Edwards in 1753 had selected the area for a mission outpost to the Indians as part of the work of his Stockbridge Mission, and several of his descendants settled in the area.[5]

Like many another frontiersman, Nathan Lane built first a sawmill and later a gristmill to support his family and provide lumber and flour for newly arriving settlers.[6] When the Windsor Presbyterian Church was organized in 1793, Nathan's wife, Dorcas, was one of the ten founding members, though not Nathan himself. Meanwhile in 1791 the Lanes' ninth and last child was born — a girl who was given her mother's name, Dorcas. This wee one, George's youngest sister, would grow up to become Ellen Stowe's mother.[7]

Probably the Lanes had been Congregationalists in Massachusetts. George Lane's obituary says "a strong moral influence was exerted upon him by his Puritan mother" but also notes that he "was destitute to a great extent of the public means of grace" during his growing-up years.[8] Apparently Nathan Lane was not a religious man, and young George was following in his footsteps.

Before long, however, George met the Methodists. He worked on farms during the summer and taught school in wintertime. The summer of 1802, when eighteen, George worked for a Methodist, Putnam Catlin, who had a large farm along the river. Living with the Catlins over the summer, George encountered a number of Methodists and was struck by their vibrant faith.

One day three well-worn Methodist circuit riders arrived, en route to the annual conference in Philadelphia. Mr. Catlin often entertained traveling Methodist preachers, and these stalwarts, Benjamin Bidlack, Ebenezer White, and John Husselkus, spent the night at the Catlins'.

Shortly after arriving the three preachers walked out to the barn for an impromptu prayer meeting. Later they returned, "full of the spirit of praise." They sat

---

4. Information on George Lane and the Lane family is drawn primarily from Smail, pp. 126-29; obituary of George Lane in *Minutes of the Annual Conferences of the Methodist Episcopal Church*, 1860 (New York: Carlton and Porter, 1860), pp. 40-41; *The National Cyclopaedia of American Biography* (New York: James T. White and Co., 1907), 5:522; George Peck, *Early Methodism Within the Bounds of the Old Genesee Conference from 1788 to 1828* (New York: Carlton and Porter, 1860), pp. 447-49, 492-95; and Bernard W. Osborne, town historian, Windsor, N.Y., interview with author, July 11, 1998.

5. Marjory B. Hinman, *The Creation of Broome County, New York* (Windsor, N.Y.: By the author, 1981), p. 23.

6. Marjory B. Hinman and Bernard Osborne, comps. and eds., *Historical Essays of Windsor Township and Village, Broome County, New York* (Windsor, N.Y.: Town of Windsor, Broome County, N.Y., 1976), p. 59.

7. H. P. Smith, ed., *History of Broome County* (Syracuse: D. Mason, 1885), p. 291.

8. *Minutes*, p. 40.

on the stoop and began singing. "And such singing as that was! They had great voices, splendid voices, and they made the whole neighborhood ring with heavenly melody, occasionally interrupted with shouts of praise."[9]

In later life George recalled the witness of these three "extraordinary men" as God's means of awakening him spiritually. He had joked with Mr. Catlin, "I am going to be a Methodist preacher, and I'll make the tears roll out of the old women's eyes!" But behind the levity George was feeling the weight of sin. Some months later he was converted and immediately joined the Methodists. Before long he began preaching and was admitted into the Philadelphia Conference on trial in 1805.[10] Three years later he was preaching Methodist revivals in the Holland Purchase in far western New York.

Stoddard and Dorcas Stow

George Lane's young sister Dorcas was raised in Windsor, more or less growing up with the town. Probably under the influence of her mother she eventually became a "strict Presbyterian" and firm Sabbath observer.[11] Ellen Roberts later recalled that her "Presbyterian grandmother," presumably Dorcas's mother, trained her as a little girl "never to overload Saturday with work, as with the setting sun we must be in readiness for the coming Sabbath."[12]

Growing up in the same small village, Dorcas Lane and Stoddard Stow probably knew each other from childhood. Several Stow families lived in the area, all of them at this time spelling their name Stow, without the *e*.[13]

With time Dorcas Lane and Stoddard Stow's friendship blossomed into romance. Tall and lean, Stoddard Stow was the same age as Dorcas; they were born only weeks apart in 1791. The two were married in October 1813, when both were twenty-two. Seven children were born to the couple over the next twenty years; the fifth was Ellen Lois, born on March 4, 1825.[14]

Like the Lanes, the Stows traced their roots back to Massachusetts, and before that to England. The Stows of Windsor were descendants of John Stow (born about 1500) of Kent, England. A grandson, also named John, emigrated to America in 1634 with his wife Elizabeth (Bigg), six children, and Elizabeth's mother. The family settled in Roxbury, Massachusetts, where John Stow was said to be "a man of education and property."[15] John and Elizabeth Stow were the ancestors of numerous promi-

---

9. George Peck recounts the story in *Early Methodism*, p. 448, having heard it from Lane himself.

10. Peck, *Early Methodism*, pp. 448-49, 492.

11. Carpenter, p. 19.

12. Ellen Roberts, "In Everything Give Thanks," *EC* 31, no. 5 (May 1876): 160.

13. Since Ellen spelled her name "Stowe" at least from the time she lived in New York, I use that spelling throughout the book when referring to her. But I have retained "Stow" for Stoddard and his ancestors, as this was the spelling they used.

14. Smail, pp. 129, 195; Carpenter, p. 19.

15. Smail, pp. 191-92.

nent eighteenth- and nineteenth-century Americans including Sarah Pierpont (wife of Jonathan Edwards), the financier J. Pierpont Morgan, and the infamous Aaron Burr, grandson of Jonathan and Sarah Edwards.[16] One of their sons, Nathaniel, lived in Concord, Massachusetts, and apparently his son, Ebenezer (1668-1722), moved to Connecticut. Ebenezer's son Daniel (1708-50), who married Elizabeth Adkins, lived most of his life in Middletown, Connecticut, and was the great-great-grandfather of Ellen.[17]

Given the family roots in colonial New England, Ellen's ancestry was intertwined with that of a number of prominent New Englanders. Many of the families that came from Britain were already interrelated, and these connections multiplied over the generations in America. With time nearly all Americans with New England roots were more or less related to each other, at least as distant cousins. So it is neither surprising nor particularly significant to find family connections between the Stows and many "famous families," though the connections are an interesting curiosity.

Was Ellen Stowe related to Harriet Beecher Stowe, famous author of *Uncle Tom's Cabin*? Some have claimed that Ellen and Harriet were close cousins through Harriet Beecher's marriage to Calvin Stowe.

Calvin Stowe and Ellen apparently were related, but only distantly — perhaps as seventh cousins. They probably didn't know each other and hardly even knew *of* each other. In fact, Ellen was actually one generation closer in relationship to Harriet Beecher (and her brother, Henry Ward Beecher) than she was to Calvin Stowe. Both Ellen and Harriet were descendants of John and Elizabeth Stow. Stoddard Stow, Ellen's father, was a fifth cousin to Lyman Beecher, Harriet's father, and thus Ellen and Harriet were sixth cousins. The connection is through Hope Stow (second cousin of Stoddard Stow's great-grandfather Daniel), who married Jehiel Hawley, a maternal great-grandfather of Lyman Beecher (according to Smail's genealogy of John Stow). The two did not know each other, though they may possibly have met at some point.

By the early 1800s a number of Stows had settled in Windsor. The oldest and youngest sons of Daniel Stow, Josiah (1735-1820) and Samuel (1749-1831), moved to the area around 1790, and both had descendants. Josiah was born in Middletown and lived there until he was thirteen, when his father bought land in Waterbury and moved the family there. His father dying soon afterward, Josiah at twenty-one inherited part of his land. He may also have inherited slaves from his father; Josiah certainly owned slaves, for the death of one of them in July 1771 is on record in Waterbury.[18] It is unlikely that Ellen Stowe ever knew that her great-grandfather was a slave owner.

Josiah Stow was a veteran of the French and Indian War and served as a major in the Revolutionary War. He married Esther Judd in 1760, and in 1765 Daniel, their fourth child (Stoddard's father), was born. At the age of nineteen Daniel married Lois

16. Smail, pp. 191-94, and genealogical charts.
17. Smail, pp. 191-93.
18. Smail, pp. 193-94.

Hickock, then only fifteen. Three years later, the Revolutionary War over, Daniel, Lois, and their infant daughter accompanied Josiah when he moved west into New York State.[19] Daniel helped his father survey a 14,720-acre tract in 1788 (the same year New York ratified the U.S. Constitution and entered the Union as the eleventh state). Apparently Josiah and Daniel then "took up homes on the surveyed land."[20] Josiah's younger brother Samuel and his family then came to Windsor in 1793.

The township of Windsor was created in 1807 (named no doubt after Windsor, Connecticut), and eventually comprised a number of towns and villages. The Stows settled on the west bank of the Susquehanna River, better suited for farming than the hilly eastern side. They lived just opposite Oquaga Island, where shallow water made fording possible.[21] The Stow homestead was thus just a mile north of the later village of Windsor. In fact, the earliest stores and businesses were mostly located in the area where the Stows lived, though the town developed a bit farther south.

Daniel Stow, Ellen's grandfather, ran a store and later a wayside inn. His wife Lois, small and quick, was famous for her cooking, contributing much to the success of the inn. She died in 1838, and the inn apparently passed into the hands of Daniel's son-in-law when Daniel himself died in 1852.[22]

Daniel and Lois Stow had eight children, four boys and four girls. Stoddard (born May 5, 1791, two months after John Wesley's death) was the second child and first son. He seems not to have had any particular religious upbringing or strong spiritual influence in the home; later his daughter Ellen would describe him as "decidedly irreligious."[23] Some of his relatives were Presbyterians; his great-uncle and great-aunt, Samuel and Elizabeth Stow, were at least nominal members of the Windsor Presbyterian Church, and his brother Hiram's infant son was baptized in the Presbyterian church in 1824.[24]

Stoddard and Dorcas Stow struggled financially as they raised a family of seven children. Their first child, Alzina Jeanette, was born at the end of August 1814, the year after their marriage. But months earlier, at the end of 1813, Stoddard was appointed guardian of two Stow boys aged sixteen and nine, David and Philemon, whose father had died.[25] Stoddard and Dorcas gave birth to a second daughter, Mary

---

19. Smail, pp. 99, 193-94; gravestone inscriptions, Windsor, N.Y.

20. Hinman and Osborne, *Historical Essays*, pp. 1-2. The record lists "Josiah Stow" and "Josiah Stow, Jr.," but the latter must have been Daniel, as Josiah had no son of the same name whereas Daniel accompanied his father to the Windsor area. See Smail, pp. 193-94.

21. Hinman and Osborne, *Historical Essays*, p. 7 (maps).

22. Smail, pp. 99, 194; Carpenter, p. 19; Hinman and Osborne, *Historical Essays*, p. 3. Both Daniel and Lois, Ellen Lois Stow's grandparents, are buried near their homestead in a tiny cemetery along the Susquehanna River. On her tombstone Lois's name is misspelled Louis.

23. Carpenter, p. 26.

24. Windsor Presbyterian Church Records, copy in the personal collection of Bernard Osborne.

25. Notice recorded in *Tree Talks* 16, no. 2 (June 1976): 86. The father was David S. Stow, but it is not clear what his relationship was to Stoddard. He was not his brother. However, Stoddard had an uncle David S. Stow who had died three years previously; the boys may have been his. Cf. Smail, pp. 193-94.

Ann, in 1816, and then to George Washington and Caroline, before Ellen appeared in 1825. Later Catherine and Charles Lane were born. The Stows suffered the loss of their young children George and Caroline to scarlet fever in 1830, when Ellen was five.[26]

Stoddard experienced a couple of business failures, first in some type of partnership and then in lumbering. (By contrast his younger brother, Hamilton, prospered in the lumber business.) It is not clear what the earlier business was, but Stoddard placed a notice of insolvency in the *Broome Republican,* the area newspaper, on August 29, 1828, when little Ellen was three and a half.[27] Stoddard kept a running account at Elias Whitemore's general store, where he bought such items as rice, salt, tea, fish, dishes, a broom, and wine and whiskey. On February 8, 1830, he bought some brandy, probably as medicine for his ailing children. Stoddard settled up his account with Elias Whitemore every year or two. On September 27, 1831, he paid a debt of a little over eight pounds, fourteen shillings (roughly equivalent to three hundred dollars today), partly by taking out a note at interest. The following August he settled his account by haying for Mr. Whitemore for four days at six shillings a day and by returning an item he had bought earlier.[28]

These trials and business reverses were likely the major reason Stoddard Stow set out for the Illinois frontier when Ellen was about thirteen.[29] They no doubt contributed also to the decision to have Ellen move to New York to live with her uncle some months later.

Ellen Stowe in Windsor

Ellen enjoyed growing up in Windsor. She must have relished the view through the trees, looking out on the flowing Susquehanna and the wooded hills beyond. She delighted in the sights and sounds of nature.

Ellen probably received some basic schooling as she was growing up. Though her parents were not particularly religious, Ellen was taught also "to pray, strictly to observe the Sabbath, and to attend the Presbyterian church," she said.[30] Her mother,

26. Smail, p. 195.

27. John J. Tyne, *Index of Names Appearing in the History of Broome County, New York* (Binghamton, N.Y., 1973), p. 356. Broome County Public Library, Binghamton.

28. Photocopies of pages from Elias Whitemore's account book 5, p. 269, in the possession of Bernard Osborne, Windsor, N.Y. On May 6, 1820, Stoddard settled an account of about £6 (Whitemore account book 2). The records of settlement of accounts are signed by Elias Whitemore and Stoddard Stow. (The accounts at this time were kept in pounds sterling, but also partly in dollars. In 1831 £1 was equivalent to about $2.35.)

29. Smail, pp. 194-95.

30. The Presbyterian congregation divided in 1840 over the Old School–New School controversy, and the two groups built rival buildings practically side by side overlooking the village green in Windsor. When the two branches reunited in 1852, the congregation sold the building to the north to a Baptist congregation that in 1866 sold it to the Free Methodists. This picturesque white building on the

Dorcas, made no public profession of faith but was "not a stranger to saving grace," Ellen thought.[31]

While still very small, Ellen and her sister managed to get into a Methodist love feast, and that left "a lasting impression on my mind," she later recalled.[32] Ellen thus received some religious formation as a child but had no deep personal encounter with God.

By the 1830s Ellen's father Stoddard was seriously considering a move farther west. Stoddard's younger brother Hiram had migrated to Boone County, Illinois, northwest of Chicago and just south of the Wisconsin territory, around 1834. Perhaps through his brother, Stoddard learned that good land was available from the government for $1.25 an acre at a place called Bonus Prairie (a thirty-six-square-mile township in Boone County), near where Hiram had settled. Stoddard bought some land there in 1836 and moved to his new stake about 1838, leaving his family in Windsor. He made the trip mostly by water, taking the newly completed Chenango Canal north to the Erie Canal, then continuing west by canal boat to Buffalo and traveling from Buffalo to Chicago by boats on the Great Lakes.[33] Dorcas Stow eventually joined her husband there, and the two spent their remaining years at Bonus Prairie.[34]

This was a time of transition for Ellen — a major upheaval. Her grandmother Stow died on July 14, 1838, her father had gone west, and the possibility arose of Ellen moving to New York City to live with her uncle George Lane. Ellen later explained, "My uncle was better off financially than we were and used to assist in bearing his mother's expenses, and in this way, visiting her often, he became well acquainted with our family."[35]

Possibly Ellen's stay with the Lanes was initially intended to be brief; she says she went to New York "to visit" the Lanes, not to live with them. But the initial visit turned into Ellen's becoming part of the Lane family for the next ten years.

After years of pioneer circuit riding, George Lane's health broke and he became a merchant for a while. Later he served with great success as a pastor and presiding elder in the Philadelphia Conference. For nine years he went back into business due to his wife's ill health, but after she died in 1832 he returned to the itinerancy. In 1836 he was elected assistant book agent, requiring a move to New York.

George married Lydia Bunting of Mount Holly, New Jersey, in January 1837. His job and his keen interest in Methodist missions meant many guests in the Lane

green is still in use by the Free Methodists. See Henry P. Smith, ed., *History of Broome County* (Syracuse: D. Mason, 1885), pp. 291-93.

31. Ellen L. Roberts, "Religious Experience," p. 282.

32. Ellen L. Roberts, "Religious Experience," p. 282.

33. Smail, p. 195; "Binghamton," in *Grolier Multimedia Encyclopedia,* 1998. Since the Chenango Canal linking the Windsor area to the Erie Canal wasn't completed until 1837, it seems likely that Stoddard's trip west occurred in late 1837 or during 1838.

34. Carpenter, p. 49; Smail, pp. 129, 195.

35. Quoted in Carpenter, p. 24.

home, so Lydia was busy entertaining. This may be one of the reasons Ellen was invited to live with George and Lydia Lane in their home at 12 Crosby Street, just a block off Broadway and near the Methodist Book Concern on Mulberry Street.[36]

Ellen was about to exchange life in rural New York for the big city, already being called Gotham.

36. Peck, *Early Methodism*, pp. 492-93; *Minutes*, pp. 40-41; Smail, p. 129.

CHAPTER 6

Ellen in New York City

"She grew up in the heart of New York Methodism."

Lois Ellen Roberts (Ellen Lois Roberts's granddaughter), 1908[1]

"We landed at Gotham."

Ellen Lois Stowe, July 13, 1844[2]

Fourteen-year-old Ellen Stowe sat down at her table, opened her diary, and began in a tight, neat script: "I left my home to visit my Uncle residing in New-York in company with Mr. and Mrs. Orcut. I had never been absent from home but few days — and my feelings were therefore rather indifferent on leaving the land of my birth, and friends of my childhood."[3]

She was about to enter a new world.

Ellen left her home in Windsor on Thursday, May 2, 1839. The following Monday she arrived in busy Manhattan and moved in with her uncle and aunt, George and Lydia Lane, at 12 Crosby Street.[4] New York was to be her home for the next ten years, until she married B. T. Roberts in 1849.

---

1. Lois Ellen Roberts, "A Grand-Daughter's Tribute," *EC* 95, no. 3 (Mar. 1908): 92.

2. ELSD, July 13, 1844.

3. ELSD, 1839-1845, May 2, 1839. As was common among diarists at the time, Ellen frequently ran sentences together with little punctuation, separating thoughts by a simple dash. For ease of reading, I have at times silently added punctuation or capitalization to make Ellen's meaning clear. Also, for many years Ellen spelled words like "having" and "coming" as "haveing" and "comeing." I have corrected these and other misspellings (since they occur frequently).

4. ELSD, May 2, 1839.

Ellen in New York

Traveling with friends, Ellen made the 200-mile, four-day journey from Windsor southeast to New York with anticipation. At some point she would have crossed the Hudson River, or perhaps sailed downriver by steamboat to New York City, as was common in those days. If so, she would have steamed past West Point where young Ulysses S. Grant would arrive by steamer three weeks later to begin his cadet training.[5] Earlier she would have passed near the farm where Angela Grimké Weld and her older sister Sarah had recently completed the research for Theodore Weld's dramatic *Slavery as It Is,* an indictment based largely on Southern newspaper accounts. Weld had published the book anonymously several weeks earlier; it quickly sold 100,000 copies, touching Harriet Beecher Stowe in Cincinnati along with many other readers and becoming the most influential antislavery tract until *Uncle Tom's Cabin* appeared in 1852.[6]

Ellen experienced culture shock when she saw Manhattan. In addition to the hustle and bustle of business and commerce and the streets full of new immigrants and dockworkers, New York was stirring socially and spiritually. The day after Ellen's arrival the American Anti-Slavery Society convened its sixth annual meeting at Broadway Tabernacle, the massive church edifice built for Charles Finney four years earlier in the heart of New York and eight blocks from the Lane home.[7] Within Methodism, the Holiness movement was just getting under way. Phoebe Palmer had recently been sanctified (July 26, 1837) and the next year would take over from her sister, Sarah Lankford, the leadership of the Tuesday Meeting for the Promotion of Holiness.

New York at this time counted 300,000 inhabitants — up 50 percent from a decade earlier. "No other place in the country was growing so fast."[8] This mixed multitude was concentrated on lower Manhattan Island; the city reached north only about as far as Twenty-first Street, above which were still farms.[9] The city's explosive growth and a disastrous fire in December 1835, however, had encouraged a building boom "uptown."[10] Central Park, above Fifty-ninth Street, didn't exist; it wouldn't be built for another twenty years. In the 1840s that remote site was home to a group of

5. Geoffrey Perret, *Ulysses S. Grant: Soldier and President* (New York: Random House, 1997), p. 21.

6. *Slavery as It Is* was published in March 1839 and sold 100,000 copies the first year. Benjamin P. Thomas, *Theodore Weld, Crusader for Freedom* (New Brunswick, N.J.: Rutgers University Press, 1950; reprint, New York: Octagon Books, 1973), p. v; *DCA,* p. 1241.

7. *Sixth Annual Report of the Executive Committee of the American Anti-Slavery Society* (New York: William S. Dorr, 1839), p. 3.

8. Edwin G. Burrows and Mike Wallace, *Gotham: A History of New York City to 1898* (New York: Oxford University Press, 1999), p. 434.

9. Burrows and Wallace, *Gotham,* p. 580; Paul E. Cohen and Robert T. Augustyn, *Manhattan in Maps, 1527-1995* (New York: Rizzoli International Publications, 1997), pp. 116-21.

10. Eric Homberger, *The Historical Atlas of New York City* (New York: Henry Holt, 1994), p. 78.

former slaves living in an area called Seneca Village.[11] Brooklyn, a ferry ride across the East River, was a separate city.

Burrows and Wallace, in their book *Gotham: A History of New York City to 1898*, paint a lively picture of New York as an international "reception center" at this time.

> By the early 1840s up to forty passenger ships might drop anchor off Manhattan every day, the biggest carrying as many as a thousand men, women, and children in steerage. As lighters and steamboats shuttled their cargoes to shore, bedlam engulfed the waterfront. Clattering wagons careened around heaps of boxes and crates. Newsboys, peddlers, apple sellers, and hot-corn girls elbowed noisily through the crowds. Throngs of bewildered newcomers milled about, searching for friendly faces and familiar voices. "Runners" wearing bright green neckties and speaking in thick accents competed to channel their "fellow countrymen" to boardinghouses along Greenwich Street — charging them exorbitantly or robbing them outright — or booked them passage to points further west at rates that were the envy of swindlers everywhere. Hundreds, penniless and half starved, wandered into town, where they begged for food and hunkered in doorways.[12]

Mushrooming growth triggered a city water crisis in the 1830s. When Ellen moved to New York, a municipal water system that would bring fresh water from the Croton River, forty miles north, was under construction. Temperance reformers had campaigned for a water system so the poor would have a safe alternative to alcohol and polluted groundwater. City water started flowing in June 1842, and soon many of the better New York homes enjoyed the novelty of running water. It would take half a century for the whole city to be connected.[13]

With its surging growth, New York was becoming a world center of trade, finance, publishing, and journalism. By 1839 the Harper brothers, stout Methodists, were prospering as one of New York's, and the nation's, leading publishers. Newspapers were booming and starting to reach the people on the street. James Gordon Bennett founded the *New York Herald*, the first penny paper to reach the masses, in 1835; by 1839 it had become the best-selling newspaper in the world, reporting everything from crime to stocks to church affairs with "brevity, variety, point, piquancy, and cheapness." Horace Greeley successfully founded the *New York Tribune* in 1841, two years after Ellen's arrival, to provide not only news but also moral uplift. Daily circulation soon hit 10,000.[14]

In short, Ellen Stowe reached New York City during one of its most dynamic periods. And her new home was pretty much in the center of the city. The Crosby

---

11. Burrows and Wallace, *Gotham*, p. 854.
12. Burrows and Wallace, *Gotham*, p. 737.
13. Homberger, *Historical Atlas*, pp. 82-83; Cohen and Augustyn, *Manhattan in Maps*, p. 118.
14. Burrows and Wallace, *Gotham*, pp. 441, 526-27, 641.

Street neighborhood where she lived with the Lanes was ethnically mixed; the imposing Shearith Israel Jewish synagogue, built in 1834, was just up the street a ways.

Ellen's life in New York centered in the Lane home and in the circle of Methodists that filled George and Lydia's life. George's two sons by his first marriage, Harvey and George Washington, were by this time married and away from home. Harvey became a professor at Wesleyan University in Middletown, Connecticut, the same year Ellen moved to New York.[15] So when Ellen arrived the Lane household at first consisted of George, Lydia, and Ellen, plus frequent guests, mostly Methodist leaders and missionaries. A girl named Matilda also lived with the Lanes during most of the years Ellen was there, apparently a hired girl who helped with household chores and child care. Then in January 1842 Lydia gave birth to a baby girl, Sarah. During most of her ten years in Manhattan, Ellen helped care for George and Lydia's little daughter.[16]

Living in Manhattan, Ellen felt herself far from her picturesque home in Windsor, and her thoughts often turned there. Her older sister Mary Ann paid a visit in October 1839, bringing welcome news from home.[17]

Ellen quickly bonded with Lydia, who was then about thirty-eight. Lydia wrote that Ellen was "like a dear child to me," "feeling all that grieves me, more than any one beside my husband."[18] Both George and Lydia Lane had a shaping influence on Ellen, though in different ways. George modeled the life of a Christian gentleman — a man of acumen, integrity, deep spirituality, and genuine humility. Lydia became both a mother and a sister to Ellen. She devoted her life to the church, ministry to the poor, and constant contact with Methodist missionaries passing through New York or writing to her from the field. As B. T. Roberts later wrote, "During the many years that her husband was treasurer of the Missionary Society, [Lydia] rendered great service to the Church. Her house was the home of the missionaries while they staid in New York, on their way to their distant fields of labors, or returning from them. She entertained them with Christian hospitality, encouraged them to trust in God, aided them in securing their necessary outfits, and corresponded with them while they were toiling among the heathen in far-off lands."[19]

Adella Carpenter described Lydia as "a most capable, methodical and cultured woman" who gave Ellen "the education in manners and domestic affairs that she

15. Carl F. Price, *Wesleyan's First Century* (Middletown, Conn.: Wesleyan University, 1932), p. 64.

16. Sarah Lane was born on Jan. 10, apparently in 1842. LBLD, Jan. 10 and Nov. 21, 1852; "Mrs. Lydia B. Lane," *EC* 12, no. 2 (Aug. 1866): 65. This obituary says the daughter died "some thirteen years ago," but we know from LBLD and Ellen Roberts's diary that she actually died Nov. 21, 1851, fifteen years before the obituary was published. If Sarah died at "ten years of age," as the obituary says, then she was born in 1841, but references in Lydia Lane's letters suggest she was born in 1842.

17. ELSD, undated entry, circa April 1840.

18. LBLD, Oct. 29, 1852; June 24, 1852. These entries are after Ellen was married, during the year following the death of Lydia's baby daughter.

19. "Mrs. Lydia B. Lane," p. 65.

would have imparted to one of her own daughters. She was adept with the needle and Ellen was a ready scholar, learning to do finest handwork when sewing machines were a thing of future days. Sewing became one of the fine arts." Ellen later wrote of Lydia, "How she would pray! She would bring heaven down. She was considered very gifted in prayer and in writing. She dressed very plainly. She wore a fine leghorn hat with a satin ribbon on it, no bows, no loops; a turndown linen collar, but there was no lace edge on it."[20]

During the summers Lydia sometimes made extensive trips with her husband George as he visited Methodist annual conferences on behalf of the Book Concern. Wherever she was, Lydia kept in touch with Ellen by letter. In early September 1840 Lydia described their trip to Michigan, telling of the people they met, the variety of wild flowers, the snakes, and their travel hazards. Near Marshall, Michigan, Lydia witnessed the Indian removals then in progress. Visiting a U.S. Army encampment, she wrote, "The commanding officer came out and invited us within their lines, we had an opportunity of viewing their tents and seeing the Indian families they are collecting. They have orders to gather all the Pottowattimy [*sic*] Indians, and remove them from the state of Michigan. Poor creatures they are unwilling to be removed and I do not wonder, for this was their father's land, and is also their home, which they will love with an everlasting love."[21]

In New York Ellen helped care for the house and the occasional guests while Lydia and George were traveling. Ellen grew culturally and in social graces during these years in New York City, not only spiritually. About the time she moved to New York, if not before, she began writing her last name "Stowe" rather than "Stow."[22]

George and Lydia Lane were well acquainted with most of the key figures of New York City Methodism. Dr. Walter Palmer was their family physician.[23] Lydia was often busy hosting Methodist bishops and other leaders in town on church business, but her real passion was the poor. Her 1852 diary is full of entries like these: "I visited many poor families." "Had many calls from the Poor." "Today attended to my poor as usual." "Called on many poor." "Went after meeting with Miss Maynard to visit a poor sick man, a very distressed family." "[W]ent to visit the family of a Polish Exile. Relieved their wants."[24]

The cramped conditions of the poor in lower Manhattan were particularly appalling at this time. The notorious Five Points area was just twelve blocks south of the Lane home, and many other neighborhoods also were crowded with the poor. In the 1830s, writes Eric Homberger, "Disturbing changes were taking place in New York. . . . Sickness and ill-health, crime, poverty, intemperance, and social disorder aroused fears that the moral fiber of the republic had been eroded. The poor lived in over-

20. Carpenter, p. 25.

21. LBL to ELS, Sept. 2, 1840.

22. In the class lists from Allen Street Methodist Church, Ellen's name is clearly given as "Ellen L. Stowe."

23. LBL to ELS, Aug. 22 and Sept. 14, 1842.

24. LBLD, 1852, passim.

crowded homes which lacked light and ventilation, and where sanitary facilities were unknown. Their streets were awash with filth. As the victims [of these conditions] were the poor, however, there was little inclination to confront the causes of so much misery."[25] In many places conditions were appalling, and yet Lydia once noted after visiting several poor homes, "Some families were so neat and clean, I was charmed."[26]

Charles Dickens arrived in the United States and visited Five Points while touring Manhattan about this time, in 1842. He described it as a place of "narrow ways diverging to the right and left, and reeking every where with dirt and filth . . . coarse and bloated faces at the doors. . . . Debauchery has made the very houses prematurely old. See how the rotten beams are tumbling down, and how the patched and broken windows seem to scowl dimly, like eyes that have been hurt in drunken frays." He described "lanes and alleys paved with mud knee-deep; under-ground chambers where they dance and game; . . . hideous tenements which take their name from robbery and murder: all that is loathsome, drooping and decayed is here."[27]

Some years later, in 1850, the Ladies' Home Missionary Society of the Methodist Episcopal Church responded to such poverty, social chaos, and human suffering by founding Five Points Mission.[28] Phoebe Palmer, active in the Allen Street Methodist Church located less than a mile from Five Points, supported the work of the mission.[29]

Methodism in New York City

In many respects New York City at this time was the center of American Methodism. Many of its leading preachers lived and worked there, in part because it was the main center of Methodist publishing and of growing Methodist missions. The Book Concern had been moved from Philadelphia to New York in 1804, and soon Methodist books and periodicals were pouring forth, including the *Methodist Magazine and Quarterly Review* and the *Christian Advocate and Journal,* a weekly newspaper covering general as well as church news. Started in 1826, the *Christian Advocate and Journal* was the first official weekly publication of the denomination. A large press building was erected at 200 Mulberry Street in 1833. Though completely destroyed by fire in February 1836, it was rebuilt; Mulberry Street was the site of the Book Concern during the years George Lane was book agent.[30] The location was an easy walk from the Lane home on Crosby Street and about four blocks east of Broadway.

25. Homberger, *Historical Atlas*, p. 80.

26. LBLD, Jan. 10, 1852.

27. Quoted in the Ladies of the Mission, *The Old Brewery, and the New Mission House at the Five Points* (New York: Stringer and Townsend, 1854), pp. 17-20.

28. Burrows and Wallace, *Gotham*, pp. 775-76; Ladies of the Mission, *The Old Brewery, and the New Mission House at the Five Points.*

29. Charles Edward White, *The Beauty of Holiness: Phoebe Palmer as Theologian, Revivalist, Feminist, and Humanitarian* (Grand Rapids: Francis Asbury Press/Zondervan, 1986), pp. 217-27.

30. COM, p. 119; W. F. Whitlock, *The Story of the Book Concerns* (Cincinnati: Jennings and Pye,

Lane brought his business skills to the management of the growing Book Concern. He successfully updated the enterprise so that during his tenure it achieved "the strongest credit the business possessed in all its history."[31] Lane had to shepherd the business through the major legal headache of the North/South church split in 1844 that eventually resulted in the division of Book Concern property between the two branches. Despite the difficulties, the enterprise thrived.

Serving as book agent gave Lane considerable prominence in the denomination. Books were published in the names of the book agent and assistant agent, rather than of the church, and the weekly, widely circulated *Christian Advocate and Journal* printed the publishers' names on the masthead of each issue. So, for instance, the December 28, 1842, issue, which carried the first two installments of Phoebe Palmer's "'The Way of Holiness': Is There Not a Shorter Way?" displayed right under the paper's name the line, "Published by G. Lane and P. P. Sandford, For The Methodist Episcopal Church." All across the denomination people would recognize the name George Lane.

From their beginning, Methodist missions were closely connected with the Book Concern — largely because Nathan Bangs, book agent from 1820 to 1828, had a vision for missions and combined the work of Missionary Society treasurer with his job as book agent. Subsequent book agents also served as missions treasurers, and this was true of Lane as well. The first American Methodist missions were among American Indians and southern blacks, but the Missionary Society established work in Liberia in 1833. The first Methodist missionaries to China were sent out in 1847, while Lane was treasurer.[32]

Ellen's lifelong missionary interest traces to this time. Years later she noted that the Lane home "was a constant stopping place for missionaries as they departed for their various fields. I used to accompany them to the stores as a guide when they went to do their shopping. I was especially interested in the first party sent to China."[33]

1903), pp. 26-27, 46; Samuel A. Seaman, *Annals of New York Methodism Being a History of the Methodist Episcopal Church in the City of New York from A.D. 1766 to A.D. 1890* (New York: Hunt and Eaton, 1892), p. 495.

31. H. C. Jennings, *The Methodist Book Concern: A Romance of History* (New York: Methodist Book Concern, 1924), p. 83.

32. W. H. Daniels, *The Illustrated History of Methodism in Great Britain and America, From the Days of the Wesleys to the Present Time* (New York: Methodist Book Concern, 1880), p. 723; Wade Crawford Barclay, *Early American Methodism, 1769-1844. Volume One: Missionary Motivation and Expansion,* History of Methodist Missions, vol. 1 (New York: Board of Missions and Church Extension of the Methodist Church, 1949), pp. 205-7, 325-26; Wade Crawford Barclay, *The Methodist Episcopal Church, 1845-1939. Volume Three: Widening Horizons, 1845-95,* History of Methodist Missions, vol. 3 (New York: Board of Missions of the Methodist Church, 1957), pp. 367-69. "The beginnings of the Liberia Mission were closely tied in with the organization and development during its formative years, of the American Colonization Society," formed in 1816 (Barclay, *Missionary Motivation and Expansion,* p. 325).

33. Carpenter, p. 126.

In 1840 there were twelve Methodist Episcopal congregations scattered through-out the thirteen wards of New York City, all located south of Twenty-first Street, plus the interdenominational Mariners' Church for seamen, with which the Methodists cooperated. Most Methodist congregations were known by their street locations — for example, the Allen Street, John Street, or Second Street ME churches. In 1840 these dozen Methodist congregations reported a total membership of 6,175 (6,140 "White" and 35 "Colored").[34] The largest congregation was Allen Street Church with 1,005 members; the average size was 515. Allen Street Church grew to 1,225 members in 1843 and then declined, reporting 750 members in 1850.[35] In all of the New York City area, including Brooklyn, the Methodist Episcopal Church counted 10,866 members in 1840, about 3.5 percent of the city's population. Ten years later, in 1850, total ME membership in the expanding city was almost the same, though there were more congregations; average congregational size had dropped to 310.[36] Clearly the Methodists were not keeping up with population growth during this period.

Methodist congregational life had been changing in the two decades before El-len moved to New York. Preachers had rotated among the churches on the circuit; they were not yet the "pastors" of local congregations, as developed later. Church buildings were plain, with uncarpeted wood floors, and were lit by sperm-oil lamps. By the time Ellen arrived in New York men and women no longer sat on opposite sides of the sanctuary, though that change had come into general practice (not with-out controversy) only recently. Typically Methodist churches in New York had three Sunday services, at 10:30 A.M., 3:00 P.M., and 7:30 P.M. (or 6:30 in winter), plus Sunday school at 9:00 A.M. and 1:30 P.M. Generally there were a Wednesday-night prayer meeting, a lecture or sermon Saturday night or some other evening, and vari-ous class meetings on other nights. At worship services "congregations were gener-ally large, benches being often needed in the aisles, and the pulpit stairs and altar filled, and the kneeling-board around the altar occupied by children."[37]

For Ellen Stowe, the most familiar Methodist congregations in New York were the Allen Street and Greene Street churches. Allen Street Church was located about twelve blocks (less than a mile) from the Lane home on Crosby Street. Greene Street was closer, just three blocks away, and Ellen occasionally visited there, but most of her church life initially centered at Allen Street.

Allen Street was also the home church of Walter and Phoebe Palmer, who in

34. *Minutes of the Annual Conferences of the Methodist Episcopal Church,* 1840-41 (New York: Thomas Mason and G. Lane, 1841), p. 46. There were of course other Methodist congregations in New York, including those of the African Methodist Episcopal and African Methodist Episcopal Zion de-nominations.

35. The decline was no doubt affected by the Methodist North/South split in 1844, plus members transferring to newly established Methodist churches.

36. *Minutes of the Annual Conferences,* 1840-1850. The New York East Conference was formed in 1848 from part of the New York Conference. The above figures combine the New York City member-ships for the two conferences.

37. Seaman, *Annals,* p. 470.

1836 had moved to 54 Rivington Street, nearby. It was here (in a house shared with Phoebe's elder sister Sarah and her husband, Thomas Lankford) that the Tuesday Meetings for the Promotion of Holiness were held.[38] As Charles White notes, "From 1840 to 1874, Mrs. Palmer was the central figure in the Tuesday Meeting for the Promotion of Holiness, which met in her home." These meetings were "the focus of the early Holiness movement and by 1886 had spawned at least 238 similar weekly meetings in places as far away as India and New Zealand."[39]

The Palmers were among the many whose lives were deepened spiritually in a great two-year revival at the Allen Street Church beginning in 1831 that became "historic in American Methodism" and saw the conversion of hundreds, including about twenty who became Methodist preachers.[40] Walter Palmer had taken a leading role in the revival.

Phoebe Palmer began to serve as a class leader (for the first time) in 1839, and was given a class of young women. Ellen Stowe was not in this group, as she came to New York just about this time and wasn't involved in class meetings until later.

Ellen's Conversion

Ellen fit naturally into the rhythms the Lanes had established in New York. George went daily to his office a few blocks away at 200 Mulberry Street, and he and Lydia were active in local Methodist church life. George was promoted to book agent for the denomination in 1841 when his predecessor, Thomas Mason, was relieved of the job, and served in that capacity until 1852.[41] George's large circle of friends and associates naturally became Ellen's as well. She was especially close to Mary Martindale and Mary Coles, Methodist young women about her age.[42]

Though Ellen only occasionally met Methodists before moving to New York, most of her life was now lived within the city's Methodist community. And she was soon influenced by it. "I had not been in [George Lane's] family long," she wrote, "before I was deeply convinced of my need of religion. My first convictions were caused by seeing him spend so much of his time in secret prayer."[43] During Ellen's first winter in New York she stayed for several weeks with the Coles family (probably

---

38. White, *The Beauty of Holiness*, p. 7. Burrows and Wallace describe Rivington Street as a "working-class" neighborhood in the 1840s. After the mid-1840s this area would come to be known as "Little Germany" because of the large influx of German immigrants, and by the end of the century, as the Lower East Side. Burrows and Wallace, *Gotham*, pp. 745, 1117-18.

39. White, *The Beauty of Holiness*, p. xvi.

40. Richard Wheatley, *The Life and Letters of Mrs. Phoebe Palmer* (New York: W. C. Palmer, 1881; New York: Garland, 1984), pp. 25-26.

41. *Minutes*, 1841, pp. 139, 141; *COM*, p. 117.

42. Mary Martindale was the daughter of the Reverend Stephen Martindale, presiding elder of the Long Island District of the New York Conference from 1840 to 1844. Mary Coles was probably the daughter of George Coles, assistant editor of the *Christian Advocate and Journal*.

43. Ellen L. Roberts, "Religious Experience," *EC* 2, no. 9 (Sept. 1861): 282.

the home of George Coles, assistant editor of the *Christian Advocate*) while George and Lydia Lane made an extended trip south. The "godly walk and conversation" of the Coles family "had an influence upon my mind," she said. "I saw plainly that I was walking in darkness — and at times was exceedingly troubled because of my sinful condition."[44]

Now fifteen, Ellen began seriously to seek God. "I saw myself a sinner, and often used to plead with the Lord to spare my life from day to day and I would seek religion. I prayed in secret and sought forgiveness," she later wrote.[45] Her aunt Lydia encouraged her in a letter, "Look every day for the divine blessings to rest upon you, and be not satisfied unless you feel that you are heard when you call on the Lord in secret. You know well that all this world cannot satisfy the desires of an immortal mind. . . . Let your affections be placed on God and heavenly things. Then, and only then can you expect to prosper and be happy in those things which relate to the present life."[46]

Attending a "protracted meeting" at the Greene Street Church one night, Ellen went to the altar, thinking "I could get religion if I would." But she got no help. "Being exceedingly timid," she wrote, "I feared to open my mind to any one, and thus did not receive the help I might have had. After a little I gave up seeking in a public way the forgiveness of my sins. Some of my friends then thought it would be well for me to join the church on probation as a seeker, but I would not consent. I felt I ought not to belong to a church until I met with a change of heart."[47]

The following September, 1841, Ellen went to a Saturday night service at Allen Street where Charles Pitman, corresponding secretary of the Methodist Missionary Society, preached from Psalm 126:6, "He that goeth forth and weepeth, bearing precious seed, shall doubtless come again with rejoicing, bringing his sheaves with him."[48] After the sermon John Poisal, the Allen Street preacher, exhorted and invited seekers to the altar. Later that night Ellen wrote, "The sermon and what [Mr. Poisal] said had a powerful effect upon my mind. I felt that the time had come when I must no longer 'halt between two opinions,' but choose which I would serve, 'God or Mammon.' I resolved at once to give up all and seek the forgiveness of my sins, for it appeared to me, were I again to quench the spirit — the anger of the Lord would be kindled against me. I went forward for prayers — but experienced no change of feelings."[49] At the altar she "besought the Lord with tears and entreaties to save me."[50] Though she received no assurance, she continued seeking.

The next day was Sunday, September 13. Ellen attended church (probably again

44. ELSD, undated entry, circa April 1840.
45. Ellen L. Roberts, "Religious Experience," p. 282.
46. LBL to ELS, Aug. 13, 1840, quoted in Zahniser, p. 34.
47. Ellen L. Roberts, "Religious Experience," p. 282.
48. ELSD, Sept. 12, 1841. (All biblical quotations are from the King James Version unless otherwise indicated.)
49. ELSD, Sept. 12, 1841.
50. Quoted in Carpenter, p. 27.

at Allen Street) both morning and evening. But her spiritual breakthrough came during the afternoon as she was praying alone.

> [T]he language of my heart was "I know Lord that thou art willing and will bless me even now." Then at that moment it seemed as if something had slid off of me — the weight that had rested upon me was removed and almost in audible language I heard a voice saying <u>peace</u> — <u>peace</u>. These lines were suggested, though I have no recollection of ever repeating them before —
>
> My God is reconciled,
>   His pardoning voice I hear;
> He owns me for his child,
>   I can no longer fear.[51]

For Ellen, at sixteen and a half years of age and after living with the Lanes for over two years, this was a clear conversion experience. Years later she remembered, "I was enabled to believe He does now for Jesus' sake forgive my sins. The load was removed, peace and joy sprang up in my heart. . . . The world looked new to me. I loved the things I once hated and found in my heart a love for individuals who had been particularly disagreeable before."[52]

Ellen grew in her newfound faith, trying to understand all it meant. She was helped by reading *The Convert's Guide*, Wesley's *Letters*, and other literature, and by the services at Allen Street. On Sunday morning, October 10, 1841, four weeks after her conversion, she witnessed the communion service after John Poisal preached but did not feel she should participate. "I would like to have been one of the number, but not having been baptised, or joined the church, I thought it would not be right."[53] She continued attending services but was not immediately baptized. But then she notes in her diary for April 5, 1842, "This morning I was baptized in Allen Street by Mr. Poisal — may it not be with water only, but with the <u>Holy spirit</u>."[54] Her frame of mind during this period may be judged from some of her diary entries.

Monday, October 25, 1841: "For some days my mind has been distressed the cause I hardly know — perhaps, I have neglected some duty. While praying the Lord showed me the cause of my feelings — I have not been self-denying enough."

Wednesday, November 3, 1841: "How sweet a few moments to spend in communion with my Heavenly Father after being busily employed all day — but in how many ways do I come short of doing the will of God — to whom I owe all and more than all. What is there below the skies, here on earth worth one thought or fear, but how I may escape the death that never, never dies."

Saturday, November 6, 1841: "I am troubled because my mind is so continually

51. ELSD, Sept. 13, 1841 (punctuation corrected).
52. Ellen L. Roberts, "Religious Experience," p. 282.
53. ELSD, Oct. 18, 1841; Oct. 10, 1841.
54. ELSD, Apr. 5, 1842.

wavering. May it be steadfastly fixed on the Lord — immoveable and let not the triv-ial things of this world tend for one moment to draw my mind from thee."

Sunday, November 7, 1841: "What a privilege to hear the gospel preached. I feel somewhat tried by outward circumstances, but oh! what are these little trials and troubles compared with immortality and eternal life. In heaven there will be no anx-ious cares, nothing to mar the happiness."

Sunday, November 21, 1841: "I have been reflecting upon my past & present life and feel truly that the goodness of the Lord has been with me from my earliest in-fancy to the present day — and how grateful ought I to be that the [Lord] did not cut me off in my sins but spared my unprofitable life to seek my happiness in religion. Fifteen years of my life have been devoted to this world exclusively."

Wednesday, November 24, 1841: "Attended love-feast in Allen St. Mr. Poisal re-lated his experience. . . . He was my spiritual father — and I love him much — per-haps too much.

> Is there a thing beneath the sun
> That strives with thee my heart to share?
> Ah, tear it hence and reign alone,
> The Lord of every motion there."

Saturday, January 1, 1842: "Another year has gone. Some of its precious time has been wasted — or spent to no purpose. Still it has been a happy one — yea, the hap-piest of my life. May the coming year be one of devoted [sic] to God!"

Thursday, June 2, 1842: "I have not that clear witness of my acceptance of God that I once had — in order to spiritual improvement we must watch and pray."

Monday, June 6, 1842: "My mind has been calm and peaceful though I have not been sensible of any distinct blessing. My heavenly Parent is able infinitely to do more for me than I can ask — not only able but willing — then why do I remain in this state of mind?"

Ellen took Communion for the first time, apparently, on Sunday, June 12, 1842. She wrote, "This day was communion and [I] ventured to my Masters table. I went feeling my unworthiness and sinfulness — but in [the] blood of Christ we have re-demption."[55]

Spiritual Growth, 1841-44

This first year following her conversion brought two significant new social experi-ences into Ellen's life. One was her participation in the Methodist class meeting. The other was attending Rutgers Female Institute.

Though Allen Street was a large congregation, like all ME churches at the time it had an extensive network of "class meetings," small groups for nurture and spiritual

55. ELSD, June 12, 1842.

discipline that were actually the portals to church membership. There were about forty class meetings at Allen Street in the early 1840s, ranging in size from a dozen to as many as forty members (larger than in early Methodism). Most were groups either of men or of women, though some were mixed.[56]

Immediately after her conversion in September 1841, Ellen began attending a class (though she may occasionally have visited one earlier). On the Monday evening following her conversion she wrote, "I went to a class-meeting with M____ [perhaps Mary Coles]. The meeting was a good one to me. I told them my feelings and what the Lord had done for me — felt that I was blest in so doing."[57]

It was in this connection that Ellen first met Mrs. Phoebe Palmer, just then becoming well-known for her leadership in the emerging Holiness movement. On Tuesday, October 26, Ellen went to a class meeting conducted by the preacher, John Poisal. She commented in her diary, "Have been to Mr. Poisal's class — part of which was led by Mrs. Palmer — she is deeply pious I think. I gave my name to be classed among the people of God."[58]

Having thus indicated her interest in church membership, Ellen was initially assigned to a class that met on Wednesdays. On November 17 she writes, "[O]ur class was led to-day by Mr. Ketcham — we had a good meeting — surely there is no place like class-meeting, this side of heaven. I was blessed and covenanted anew with my Heavenly Father, to be more devoted in his service — that I would strive to live neare[r] to him — that I may at last enter in at the strait gate." And again on December 29: "What a privilege in class-meetings — we were met to-day by Mr. Poisal. It is pleasant to retire from this busy world and hold communion with God — to meditate on his merciful dealings toward us."[59]

In early 1842, probably around the time of her baptism, Ellen was assigned to class number 20, led by Valentine Flaglor. The class consisted of about thirty women, including Mary Coles. It met on Tuesday (later Thursday) afternoons, probably at the Allen Street Church building. Ellen's name appears on the class list as "Ellen L. Stowe" at the address of 12 Crosby Street.[60]

Later this same year, 1842, Phoebe Palmer published "Is There Not a Shorter Way?" in the *New York Christian Advocate and Journal*, which became the opening chapter in her best-selling *The Way of Holiness*, published by Piercy and Reed in New

56. Class Records, Allen Street ME Church, 1838-45. Methodist Collection, Manuscript Division, New York Public Library.

57. ELSD, Sept. 14, 1841.

58. ELSD, Oct. 26, 1841. This was not one of the Tuesday Meetings for the Promotion of Holiness that Phoebe Palmer was now conducting but a regular class meeting at the Allen Street Church.

59. ELSD, Nov. 17 and Dec. 29, 1841.

60. Class list, Class no. 20, Allen Street ME Church, 1838-45. Methodist Collection, Manuscript Division, New York Public Library. The class list says, "Tuesday Afternoon — No. 11," probably meaning classroom number 11 at Allen Street. "Thursday" is crossed out and "Tuesday" written above; according to Ellen's diary, it was meeting on Thursdays in 1843. It is not clear from the records when this group began or just when Ellen was assigned to it, but early 1842 seems most consistent with Ellen's comments about her class-meeting participation.

York City in 1843, and then reprinted many times by Lane and Tippett (and later Methodist publishers).[61]

Ellen continued in the same class for about two years, until it was disbanded.[62] Along with Mary Coles and one or two others, Ellen was then assigned to class number 33, led by Dr. Walter C. Palmer, Phoebe's husband. She notes in her diary for March 7, 1844, "I went to Dr. Palmers class to which I have been assigned — mine having been broken up. I felt bad that it was so, as I had belonged to it since I first joined the church and was strongly attached to the members. I felt almost like a stranger as there was but one familiar face there. But God was with us — the all important thing."[63] The "familiar face" may have been that of Mary Coles, or perhaps she knew someone else in the group. This was a large group of around fifty, hardly a "class" in the original sense, so understandably Ellen felt the loss of her prior group. All but two of the members were women.[64]

These class meetings were no doubt important to Ellen, but she actually says little about them in her diary, especially after transferring to the larger group. The Allen Street classes at this time were no longer the small, intimate groups of earlier Methodism, and Ellen apparently did not develop the depth of openness and intimacy that marked the original Methodist class meetings, which were smaller and usually met in homes. Thus Ellen never experienced the class meeting the way it was originally designed by Wesley, and as it had functioned in Methodism's early decades — a fact of some significance for later Free Methodism. In his study of the class meeting in New York City Methodism, Philip Hardt notes that by the early 1800s the classes began "to reach extremely large levels, which weakened their effectiveness," and there was resistance to female class leaders, in contrast to early British Methodism under Wesley.[65]

Education at Rutgers Female Institute, 1841-43

The other major new experience in Ellen's life during this time was her schooling at the Rutgers Female Institute. She began her studies on December 1, 1841, noting in

61. *Phoebe Palmer: Selected Writings,* ed. Thomas C. Oden (New York: Paulist, 1988), p. 11.

62. The group was disbanded and most of the members assigned to other groups, probably because it was not functioning well. After Valentine Flaglor's name is the notation, "Remov'd by certif," probably indicating that he left Allen Street, perhaps transferring to another church. The fact that about half the class members were removed when the group disbanded, rather than assigned to other groups, likely indicates that they had not been attending for some time.

63. ELSD, Mar. 7, 1844.

64. Class list, Class no. 33, Allen Street ME Church, 1838-45. Methodist Collection, Manuscript Division, New York Public Library.

65. Philip F. Hardt, "'A Prudential Means of Grace': The Class Meeting in Early New York City Methodism" (Ph.D. diss., Fordham University, 1998), pp. 56-62. Utilizing New York City class records, Hardt documents several divergences from "the original Wesleyan model," including single-sex rather than mixed classes and the gradual tendency to move most class meetings to Sunday.

her diary, "I hope while engaged in the pursuit of the knowledge of the world, the desire for heavenly knowledge will not be lessened."[66] She attended Rutgers during the winters of 1841-42 and 1842-43.

George Lane was concerned that has niece, now a young lady of sixteen, receive the best education possible. Rutgers Female Institute was a new and well-respected academy. Incorporated in 1838, it opened for classes on April 27, 1839, in a new building on Madison Avenue near Clinton Street on the East Side, some twenty blocks (about a mile) from the Lane home.[67] Intended for "the higher education of women," the school was founded by the Reverend Isaac Ferris, pastor of the Market Street Reformed Dutch Church, who had previously served as president of the Albany Female Academy in Albany, New York.[68] The institute was nominally Presbyterian and Reformed, but nonsectarian. Phoebe Palmer's daughter Sarah, eight years younger than Ellen, attended the school some years later, after it had added a college program.[69]

Rutgers Female Institute set up "a progressive system of education" for the purpose of "developing the female mind in strength and understanding; and, by rigid and systematic training, . . . bringing it to that high culture, for which it had been thought incapable or unfitted."[70] The school "grew out of an increasing sense of the importance of the duties of women, and of the need that her work should be well done," according to its later president, Henry Miller Pierce.[71] Typical of the times, Pierce believed that "The sphere of woman differs widely from that of man" and argued, "The Church, the State, and the Family, are alike ordained of God. The ordering of the Family pertains to woman; of the State, to man; of the Church, to the Lord Jesus Christ," and each was "sovereign" in its own sphere.[72]

The school taught literature ("belles lettres"), philosophy, mathematics, and history.[73] Burrows and Wallace note wryly in *Gotham* that such schools "were not intended to prepare graduates for careers or roles in the public realm, . . . but rather to help them attract and later assist the right kind of husband."[74]

66. ELSD, Dec. 1, 1841.

67. Isaac Ferris, "History of Rutgers Female Institute," handwritten manuscript of an address by Isaac Ferris (1798-1873), the founder of the institute, July 2, 1856. Isaac Ferris Papers, Manuscript Division, New York Public Library. In 1863 the school became Rutgers Female College. It had no connection with Rutgers University in New Jersey other than benefaction from the Rutgers family.

68. Ferris, "History of Rutgers Female Institute." The school was given the name Rutgers to honor Col. Henry Rutgers, a prominent Dutch American New Yorker through whom the donor of the property, his nephew William Crosby, had inherited the land, which had once been part of the Rutgers estate.

69. White, *The Beauty of Holiness*, p. 58. Sarah graduated from Rutgers College, perhaps after first attending the institute.

70. Rutgers Female Institute, *Mathematics in Female Education. Abstracts from the Archives of Rutgers Female Institute* (New York: John A. Gray, 1860), p. 5.

71. Henry M. Pierce, *Address to the First Graduating Class of Rutgers Female College; delivered in the Fourth Avenue Presbyterian Church*, June 2, 1867 (New York: Agathynian Press, 1867), p. 9.

72. Pierce, *Address*, pp. 9, 10.

73. Burrows and Wallace, *Gotham*, p. 799.

74. Burrows and Wallace, *Gotham*, p. 799.

Ellen's courses that winter included such subjects as mental philosophy and English history. She learned all about the kings of England and the periods of English history, neatly outlining the facts in her notebook. Much later her granddaughter, Lois Roberts Hallet, saw Ellen's careful class notes as "evidence that she was learning to study, to think, and to put into clear, accurate form, the results of her reading" and could "think intelligently on abstruse subjects."[75]

Attending such a school devoted to rigorous study and "high culture" was quite a leap for a country girl like Ellen, even though she had been in the city for a couple of years. To Ellen Rutgers was "a fashionable school," an environment that clashed with the values of plainness and simplicity emphasized by many of her Methodist friends.[76] She found her studies exhausting, often demanding her time from 4:00 A.M. to 11:00 P.M. and depriving her of needed sleep,[77] and the twenty-block walk long and tiring. Her teacher was good, she thought, but "very homely."[78] On Thursday afternoons she was excused from school to attend her Methodist class meeting, and she noted, "[A]s all the students knew why I left, I had to take my cross as I walked out before them."[79]

Ellen felt conflict between her school life and her spiritual life. She wrote after her first week of classes, "O the weakness of human nature! — my studies demand my constant attention, and I fear lest my soul's interest is neglected."[80] Similarly in February, just a month before her seventeenth birthday, she wrote, "All I have to record from time to time is my unfaithfulness. I see it and I feel it. Being so constantly engaged as I am with my studies . . . I know is a draw back — but it should not be."[81] She cast her struggle in spiritual terms, not yet having the perspective to see that she was keeping an impossible schedule. Ellen was never a great student, though on her own she read widely, and Rutgers was more than she could handle. Yet she was sustained by her newfound faith, the encouragement of George and Lydia Lane, and her church life. It was toward the end of her first winter at Rutgers, in April 1842, that she was baptized in the Allen Street Church.

Ellen was glad to have the summer off from classes. In addition to helping in the Lane home, she attended many Methodist events and heard prominent Methodist preachers such as Jesse T. Peck, holiness advocate and later bishop.[82]

Ellen was especially busy toward the end of May when the annual sessions of the

75. Lois Ellen Roberts, "A Grand-Daughter's Tribute," p. 92.

76. Ellen described Rutgers as "a fashionable school" in her spiritual autobiography twenty years later. Ellen L. Roberts, "Religious Experience," p. 282.

77. ELSD, Feb. 4, 1842.

78. Carpenter, p. 29.

79. Quoted in Carpenter, p. 29. Carpenter's account gives the impression that Ellen began classes at Rutgers in 1843 and attended only a short time, but according to her diary she attended in both 1841-42 and 1842-43.

80. ELSD, Dec. 7, 1841.

81. ELSD, Feb. 4, 1842.

82. ELSD, May 22, 1842.

New York Conference brought many guests into the Lane home.[83] In July she relished a Sunday school excursion outside the metropolis: "It seemed very delightful to spend even one day, away from the noise of the city."[84]

Death of a Sister

After more than three years away from Windsor, Ellen was able to make a trip back home to visit her family in August 1842. The sojourn started joyfully but ended tragically.

Ellen traveled with her uncle George, who planned to attend the Methodist conference in Oxford, New York, about thirty miles north of Windsor. On Monday, August 8, the two traveled up the beautiful Hudson by steamboat to Albany, then west by train to Utica. The railroad revolution was just under way; a railway paralleling the Erie Canal had been pushed west from Albany since Ellen had journeyed to New York three years earlier. The trip between New York and Windsor was thus reduced from four days to three or less. George and Ellen clattered and creaked along through the night in wooden cars over dangerous iron strap-rails nailed to pine tracks. The strap ends had a nasty tendency to spring loose, forming "snakeheads" that would shoot up through the floorboards, injuring passengers.[85] But Ellen and her uncle arrived safely at Utica the next morning, though Ellen was "tolerably sleepy" since she'd been unable to sleep on the train.[86]

After an hour's rest, but no sleep, Ellen clambered aboard a crowded stagecoach with George and they rumbled south toward Oxford. With stops at towns along the way, the sixty-mile trip took all day and all night. They arrived in Oxford late Wednesday morning. Ellen said good-bye to her uncle, who arranged a ride for her on to Windsor, and arrived home later that day.

Ellen writes, "As we advanced nearer my home I seemed to be living over again my earliest days . . . each well known house I recognized, was like meeting an old friend. We came to the very door of my home. I was almost spell bound — for I could but just move. Catheron [her younger sister] first met me then Charles [her ten-year-old brother], then my dear mother."[87] Her father, Stoddard, had already gone west to Illinois. Since Mary Ann was now married, her mother's household consisted of only the two younger children and herself.

When Ellen first arrived there was "a general gathering in to see me," she said.

---

83. ELSD, May 25, 1842.

84. ELSD, July 13, 1842.

85. Charles Frederick Carter, *When Railroads Were New,* centenary ed. (New York: Simmons-Boardman Publishing Co., 1926), p. 165; Oliver Jensen, *The American Heritage History of Railroads in America* (New York: Bonanza Books, 1981), pp. 25, 36.

86. ELSD, Aug. 8, 1842.

87. ELSD, Aug. 9, 1842. (The entry is dated Aug. 9, but no doubt was written some days afterward; the actual date was the tenth.)

She spent "many a happy hour" the next few weeks making the rounds of family and friends. Her first weekend home she stayed with her sister Mary Ann and family. Mary Ann had married Stephen Swezey, a carpenter, eight years earlier, and the two now had children. Attending the Presbyterian church that Sunday, Ellen noted, "There seems great coldness and apathy among professing Christian[s]. I felt it when in church. How dead to their best and eternal interest!"[88]

Ellen spent part of her time in Windsor sewing, probably in company with one or both of her sisters. Lydia Lane wrote her from New York: "I do not want you to distress yourself about me, or any thing else, but try and enjoy yourself, while you are with your friends. Do not sew too constantly, and be sure to fix all your own clothes before you make your uncle's shirts, take pains with your dress and do not be in too much of a hurry to get it done. Many friends have enquired after you, and when you were coming home."

Lydia encouraged Ellen to "strive to draw near to God in fervent prayer, both for yourself and your friends," and to read the Bible daily, which is essential for "teaching us the way to heaven; we must read with prayer, that the Holy Spirit will apply what we read to our hearts, to cheer and comfort us, amid the sorrows and trials of life."[89]

Despite her joy in being back in Windsor, Ellen had a sense of uneasiness and foreboding. Mary Ann was reluctant to have Ellen leave. "Ellen, you must not go back to New York," she insisted. "I shall be so lonely without you."[90] And then Mary Ann got sick.

Mary Ann's illness started out as a cold but quickly developed into something much more serious, probably some sort of undiagnosed infectious disease. Medicines did no good as Mary Ann suffered from high fever and head pain. Ellen, still a teenager, cared constantly for her twenty-five-year-old sister, making her as comfortable as possible. "I walked around her bed day and night and tried to administer to her temporal wants. I watched too the sinking of nature — and oh! the agony I felt words cannot express. She thought she would not live, and expressed great concern about her children — she desired to live only for them, but said she would commit them into the hands of the Lord. Several times toward her last end she spoke to me about dying, but I could only express what I felt in tears, at which she would say to me Ellen you must not feel so."[91]

The whole experience overwhelmed Ellen. "It seemed to me a stroke I could not bear," she said, "yet I tried to submit to the will of the Lord."[92]

Mary Ann grew worse and became delirious, as Ellen noted during the night of October 8. She passed into unconsciousness and died the following Thursday, October 13, two months after Ellen arrived in Windsor. The following Tuesday, just a few

88. ELSD, Aug. 9 and 11, 1842; undated entry, probably about Nov. 1, 1842; Smail, p. 195.
89. LBL to ELS, Aug. 22, 1842.
90. ELSD, undated entry, probably about Nov. 1, 1842.
91. ELSD, undated entry, probably about Nov. 1, 1842.
92. ELSD, undated entry, probably about Nov. 1, 1842.

days after the funeral, Ellen sadly said good-bye to her Windsor family. "I left for home or rather for New York," she wrote. "It was hard to part with my dear Mother[;] much more painful than when I first left her, but the conviction that it was for the best prompted me to go. Everything around was clad in the habiliments of sorrow — and I felt indeed that one strong tie to earth was severed. I felt <u>alone</u> wherever I went."[93]

Ellen wrote no more in her diary that year. Soon she was back into the routines of the Lane household and the Allen Street Church, and again attending Rutgers Female Institute.

Spiritual Victory and Defeat and Visits to Middletown

The pressures of schooling and the death of her sister took their toll. Not until the following May did Ellen again pick up her diary, and then she wrote, "My studies have occupied my whole time so much so that I have not been able to keep a <u>minute of my proceedings</u> [i.e., write in her diary]. The state of my mind has been . . . too cold — I have spent too much time with my books, and not enough in prayer." She finally discontinued her schooling, simply recording, "My health would not admit of my attending longer therefore I left."[94] She stopped attending Rutgers Institute sometime in the spring of 1843, apparently. This would be the last of Ellen's formal education.

Reflecting back eighteen years later, Ellen described this period as a time of spiritual struggle and frequent defeat. In her testimony published in the September 1861 *Earnest Christian,* she said she "lost the evidence of [her] acceptance with God" during this period,[95] and apparently for some months wandered in a spiritual wilderness.

At the end of May 1843 Ellen traveled by steamboat to Middletown, Connecticut, for a two-month visit. She probably journeyed to Middletown with Harvey Lane and his family, who had come to New York for the annual meeting of the New York Conference. Leaving Manhattan in the afternoon, the group arrived at Middletown, on the Connecticut River, at 3:00 A.M. Ellen described the trip: "I rather reluctantly on some accounts while on others very gladly left the noisy busy city to abide a little season with my friends in the quiet 'land of steady habits.' . . . The sunset I enjoyed — it was a rare sight to me. I stood unmolested and gazed on it while my thoughts wandered back to the sunny days of my childhood, till the last ray had passed the reach of my vision."[96]

As on previous summer visits, Ellen enjoyed her time in the college town. "I

93. ELSD, undated entry, probably about Nov. 1, 1842.

94. ELSD, May 1843 (specific day not given). Cf. Carpenter, p. 29. It is not clear whether Ellen completed the winter 1843 term or dropped out before it ended.

95. Ellen L. Roberts, "Religious Experience," p. 282.

96. ELSD, May 24, 1843.

arose this morning in Paradise comparatively speaking," she said of her first day there. In a typical comment she wrote, "Where can I find words to express my feelings on being once more permitted to see the Country — the beautiful glorious works of my Creator. . . . How much better one can appreciate the beauties of the Country after having been shut up in the city."[97]

Ellen apparently stayed with Harvey Lane and his family during these weeks and was soon caught up in the social life of the Wesleyan University campus. She attended the local Methodist church on Sundays and at other times, and made or renewed acquaintance with university professors such as Joseph Holdich, August William Smith, and John Johnston and their wives and families. She also met William Bagnall and Edmund Longley, recent graduates who were serving as university tutors. Here also she first got acquainted with Mary Martindale, also visiting from New York, who was to become a fast friend. "The first impression I had of Miss. M[artindale] was that of entire ease and composure," Ellen wrote. "There is something very sweet and prepossessing in her appearance and manners."[98]

Ellen roamed around Middletown, either with friends or alone. From the top of the chapel she could look out over the town and see the winding Connecticut River and mountains in the distance. "The view from there exceeds anything I ever saw."[99] She liked to visit the cemetery where Willbur Fisk, the university's founding president who had died five years earlier, was buried. Nearby was the grave of Aaron Hurd, a Wesleyan University student who had died in 1836 at the beginning of his senior year and whose life and Christian witness had been commemorated by Professor Holdich in *The Wesleyan Student; or, Memoirs of Aaron Haynes Hurd*, a book Ellen read some months later.[100] "I have so much admired the character" of Hurd, she wrote, "that I felt as if I had known him personally. I hope to meet him in heaven. Oh! that we may remember when visiting the resting places of the long departed that we too must lie as low as they — that soon we will return to dust, and to the God who gave us! And above all let us be prepared to meet that God!"[101]

Ellen so enjoyed her time in Middletown that she sometimes feared she enjoyed herself too much. On June 7, 1843, she wrote, "I rose as usual at five. The mornings are delightful — they who spend them in bed lose the pleasanter part of the 24 hours. The air is vocal with the music of birds."[102] She went walking with Mary Martindale; they picked flowers. "Being somewhat inspired we made poetry as we onward went."[103] Ellen also enjoyed reading and copying poetry.[104] Yet one Saturday night she wrote, "Another week has passed by and what have I done to glorify my

97. ELSD, May 25, 1843.
98. ELSD, May 30, 1843.
99. ELSD, May 30, 1843.
100. ELSD, Oct. 1, 1843.
101. ELSD, June 2, 1843.
102. ELSD, June 7, 1843.
103. ELSD, June 12, 1843.
104. ELSD, July 7, 1843.

Maker. I enter too deeply into the spirit of the world. Oh! that I had more decision. Now I will read a chapter, commit myself to God and retire."[105]

In Middletown Ellen also met Dr. Stephen Olin, the respected president of Wesleyan University, and his wife. Olin was made president-elect in 1839 upon the death of Fisk, but for health reasons was not able to assume his duties until September 1842, so he had been in office less than a year when Ellen visited Middletown. She very likely had met him previously, however, or heard him preach, either in Middletown or New York. She noted on June 14 that Dr. Olin had arrived in Middletown, and the next evening she attended a gathering of the faculty with the Olins.[106] Visiting Professor Smith's home on a very hot day a week later, Ellen found President Olin there resting. "Dr. Olin was lying on the sofa," she noted. "He is better, but not well"[107] — a witness to Olin's continuing health problems.

Ellen returned to New York City on Saturday, July 8. Friends saw her off on the stagecoach. She sat alone in the stage, clutching two bouquets given her as she left and pondering her two months in Middletown. At Meriden she took the train to New Haven on the coast, then traveled on to New York, probably by steamer. "At six we landed at the great emporium [New York City]. I was too sensible of the change from country to city — but I was going home, and that was enough to dispel all discontent."[108]

Ellen was going to miss Connecticut, however. She left behind "the beautiful country — Middletown which I so much admired and all the pleasant walks around her." And she was leaving "friends who had become endeared to me during my sojourn with them — and one in particular was I leaving whose affections had entwined themselves around my heart. But this is what we must expect and look for in this world."[109]

Ellen doesn't identify this "one in particular." It could have been Mary Martindale, but that seems unlikely since she would later be in contact with her in New York. More likely it was the tutor Edmund Longley.

During her two months in Middletown both Bagnall and Longley, the two university tutors, showed some interest in the attractive eighteen-year-old Ellen. Longley in particular went out of his way to spend time with her. Ellen met him soon after her arrival in Middletown, as noted above.[110] He came by the Lane house on Monday evening, June 5, to talk with her and two weeks later took her on an evening walk to Pameacha Grove — for Ellen, a favorite romantic spot.[111] He called again on Friday,

---

105. ELSD, June 3, 1843.

106. ELSD, June 14-15, 1843.

107. ELSD, June 22, 1843.

108. ELSD, July 8, 1843.

109. ELSD, July 8, 1843.

110. She might have met him on earlier visits to Middletown when Longley was a student at the university, but her diary does not give that impression.

111. ELSD, June 5 and 19, 1843; June 13, 1845. In most of the diary references Longley is identified simply as "Mr. L.," and once as "Tutor L." Some of these references could conceivably refer to someone other than Longley, but since several references clearly refer to him, it is likely that the others do too. Ellen is deliberately vague in her diary references.

July 7, on the eve of Ellen's departure for New York, and walked with her as she went to bid good-bye to several friends. Ellen reflected, "I begin to wonder what his attentions mean. I hope there is no secret intention in all this."[112] Quite likely he was the unnamed one who showed up the next morning and handed her a bouquet as she was about to board the stage; she says, "Mr. _____ brought me a bouquet and cousin M. gave me one."[113]

The attentions of Longley birthed a conflict in Ellen's heart in more ways than one. Was he interested in her romantically? If so, that was unsettling, because Ellen at this stage had very ambivalent feelings about marriage. And yet she began to feel attracted to him. How would a romantic relationship affect her love for God? She wrote in her diary on October 3, 1843, "I saw this evening what is to me one of the saddest sights on earth. A couple married. There is something in it so forbidding to me. I could not envy her — or even think of it."[114] Marriage and romance were both appealing and appalling.

From May 1843 when Ellen first met him until February 1845, Ellen had intermittent contact with Longley. They apparently exchanged a number of letters. A friendship developed that Ellen alternatively hoped and feared might blossom into a proposal for marriage.

Ellen is very guarded about this relationship in her diary, but she says enough so that a clear picture emerges. It is a picture of a struggle of heart and mind, of ultimate loyalties and of natural hopes for marriage. For almost two years her relationship with Longley was intimately intertwined with her struggle over holiness and purity of heart — not unlike John Wesley's relationship with Sophy Hopkey in Georgia a century earlier.

A month after Ellen's return to New York, Longley stopped to see her on his way to Virginia where he apparently had found a teaching job at Emory and Henry College.[115] "Greatly to my surprise Mr. Longley called this evening," Ellen notes in her diary. "After talking over matters and things for awhile I went with him to call on Mary. We returned and had quite a conversation."[116] She apparently saw him again the next day. She writes, "Mr. L____ has left here this evening with the intention of sailing to-morrow for Virginia. He leaves in good spirits. I shall very probably never meet him again in this world."[117]

Over the next months Ellen continued her routine activities. In early 1844 she

112. ELSD, July 7, 1843.

113. ELSD, July 8, 1843.

114. ELSD, Oct. 3, 1843.

115. Longley became a professor at Emory and Henry College (founded by the Methodists in Emory, Va., in 1836) from 1844 (or possibly 1845) until near the time of his death. He died in 1906 in Emory, and is listed in the Wesleyan University *Alumni Record* as "College professor" (Frank W. Nicolson, ed., *Alumni Record of Wesleyan University, Middletown, Conn.*, centennial [6th] ed., 1931 [Middletown, Conn.: Pelton and King, 1931], p. 96). (Information provided by Robert J. Vejnar II, archivist, Emory and Henry College, e-mail to author, Sept. 29, 1999.)

116. ELSD, Aug. 9, 1843. This is one of two places where Ellen gives the name "Longley." The other is July 23, 1844.

117. ELSD, Aug. 10, 1843.

heard Stephen Olin preach in several Methodist churches in New York City as he was promoting Wesleyan University. She was very impressed with Olin and visited various churches where she knew he would be speaking. She "went over to hear Dr. Olin in Bedford St." on Thursday, February 22, and found his sermon "good like all his sermons. I never heard any one preach like him, or equal him. They are all characterised by plainness and simplicity. There is more meaning and truth in some four words he says, than in some whole sermons of others." Referring to an earlier Olin sermon, she wrote, "I felt profited while listening to it — and more than ever convinced that I knew nothing of religion, comparatively speaking. It was to me like a voice from another world."[118]

Ellen had physical as well as spiritual struggles during this period. She notes on February 20, 1844, "For a long time past I have not regularly recorded my feelings in this book. In the first place my health was never so poor as it has been for the past winter. I have been troubled in mind from outward circumstances, and all my thoughts and feelings have been clad in one garb of loneliness. My religious employment has been quite below <u>par</u> and though I have said nothing upon the subject I have felt keenly. But I purpose to begin anew to try and live differently."[119]

On March 1 she recorded that the past winter had been "a sorrowful one," and three days later, on her nineteenth birthday, she was "almost constrained to cry that this was the last year in my teens. But let me rather take another view of the subject," she wrote, "and weep that I do not grow better as I grow older."[120] Yet she was cheered by the promise of spring, and noted the next day, "A peace and happiness like the calm of a spring day seems to pervade all things and I have been rejoicing that though we could see nothing but brick walls with our natural eyes — that our minds were not pent up here but that we could soar above and beyond all these encumbrances and mentally enjoy the beautiful works of our Creator. Yes, and above all we may enjoy his presence here."[121]

It was this same week, on Thursday, that Ellen first went to Walter Palmer's class meeting, noted earlier. Her health continued to be rather poor, and toward the end of the month she came down with scarlet fever (from which her brother and sister had died as children). The disease kept her in bed for two weeks. "This has been the most severe spell of sickness I ever had," she noted.[122] During her recovery she was much cheered by Mary (Mary Martindale, apparently), her "best friend." "I love her as I never expect to love another," she wrote.[123] In her reading she came across in a book the words "God chastens his children for their profit; that they may be partak-

118. ELSD, Feb. 22, 1844.
119. ELSD, Feb. 20, 1844. She had recorded nothing substantial in her diary since mid-October 1843.
120. ELSD, Mar. 1 and 4, 1844.
121. ELSD, Mar. 5, 1844.
122. ELSD, Mar. 6, 1844; cf. Apr. 1, 1845.
123. ELSD, Mar. 8, 1844.

ers of his holiness." "By this chastisement [i.e., illness] though light shall I not partake more largely of the spirit of holiness?" she mused.[124]

In the midst of these struggles came the contentious 1844 Methodist General Conference that led to the formation of the Methodist Episcopal Church, South. The opening session on Wednesday, May 1, was held in the Greene Street Church, near the Lane home. Ellen attended the opening service and several of the sessions over the next few weeks; the conference did not end until June 10. She felt that a "cloud of darkness" hung over the conference, and when the critical vote was taken on Saturday, June 1, "there was stillness like that of death." That evening "Bishop [James] Andrew & [Bishop Thomas] Morris with many others dined here. Oh! I shall never forget that day. It was sorrowful in the extreme."[125] The General Conference debate had swirled around the case of Bishop Andrew of Georgia, who had acquired slaves through marriage and was not able legally to manumit them. Now Bishops Andrew and Morris would be leaders in separate denominations.

The following Saturday, June 8, as the conference drew to a close, George Lane was formally elected book agent for the first time, though he had functioned as such since 1841 (as noted earlier).[126]

The trials of the church mixed with Ellen's own. The day after the conference ended and everyone had gone home, Ellen reflected, "There is a loneliness in my feeling I cannot describe as sorrow because of the state of the church. . . . But the Lord will do all things well. He will not leave Zion in this trying hour."[127]

Ellen often enjoyed nighttime, especially the moonlight and the stars and planets when they were visible. One clear evening later in the month she noted, "Mars looks more beautiful than usual," and thought of "other times while gazing at that bright planet. I thought of the walk I took through paradise. I thought too of the little girl who wished to know if the stars were not places as holes for the glory to shine through. It was a bright idea."[128] She does not identify her "walk through paradise," but it likely was her evening walk with Longley in Middletown a year earlier.

At the end of the month Ellen accompanied her aunt Lydia Lane on a two-week visit to Lydia's friends and family in New Jersey.[129] They spent some time in Mount Holly, Lydia's childhood home, and with Lydia's sister made a visit to Philadelphia. Once again Ellen was delighted to get away from New York. She was glad to again be "leaving the 'wilderness of bricks and mortar'" and "away from the contaminating influence of vice."[130]

---

124. ELSD, Mar. 9, 1844. Ellen apparently did not recognize the quotation as an allusion to Heb. 12:10.

125. ELSD, May 5 and June 1, 1844.

126. ELSD, June 8, 1844. Ellen notes that her uncle received 160 votes to Leroy Swormstedt's 153.

127. ELSD, June 11, 1844.

128. ELSD, June 18, 1844. Perhaps the "little girl" was herself as a child.

129. They were also accompanied by "little Sarah," Lydia and George Lane's two-year-old daughter.

130. ELSD, June 28, 1844.

Ellen especially enjoyed the village of Mount Holly. Largely a Quaker town in its early years, it had been the home of John Woolman (1720-72), the Quaker saint and abolitionist. There is no mountain at Mount Holly; the town was named for a hill nearby, which Ellen visited, as had Woolman years earlier. John Greenleaf Whittier wrote of Mount Holly: "The name of the place is derived from the highest hill in the county, rising two hundred feet above the sea, and commanding a view of a rich and level country, of cleared farms and woodlands. Here, no doubt, John Woolman often walked under the shadow of its holly-trees, communing with nature and musing on the great themes of life and duty."[131]

At Mount Holly Ellen enjoyed morning and evening walks, listening to the sounds of crickets and whip-poor-wills. "I took a fine walk and heard the birds sing so sweetly their morning songs," she wrote on July 4. "I drink in the spirit of nature — my eyes feast on its beauties — it is food for Body and soul."[132] On this trip she also attended a Friends meeting for the first time and found it not to her liking.[133]

Ellen returned to New York City with Lydia on July 13, traveling by train and then steamboat. "We landed at Gotham just dark and found cousin C. ready to receive us."[134]

Longley reappeared on Ellen's doorstep ten days later, on Tuesday, July 23. "A great stranger called on me this morning and a very unexpected one[—]Mr. Longley. It seemed hardly like a reality — indeed I cannot realize it yet."[135] He returned in the afternoon, and together they paid a visit on Ellen's friend Mary. Longley was on his way to Middletown, probably traveling from Emory and Henry College in Virginia. He continued on his way the next day; obviously he had arranged his travel so he could see Ellen.

Ellen says nothing more about Longley at this point, but she met him again in Middletown a couple of weeks later. On August 1 she left with her friends "the two Marys" (Mary Martindale and Mary Coles) for Middletown to spend commencement week at Wesleyan University. The three friends sailed overnight by steamboat from New York to Middletown. Mary Martindale was "full of life and humor and wit." "There is no such thing as keeping a straight face" around her, Ellen noted. The night was warm; it was too hot in her berth, so Ellen went on deck. She sat on a barrel and enjoyed the night. "The moon shone very dimly on the wide waters. It was an hour of indelible impressions."[136]

---

131. John Greenleaf Whittier, introduction to *The Journal of John Woolman* (London: Headley Brothers, [1908]), p. 8. Ellen's description was similar: "In the evening I visited the cemetery and mount. The sun was just about setting when we reached the place. The view from the Mt. is certainly very beautiful. There is [*sic*] no hills or mountains to be seen — but one broad area of level country — well cultivated, covered with patches of trees, and a variety of shades of green" (ELSD, July 10, 1844).

132. ELSD, July 4, 1844.

133. ELSD, June 30, 1844. There was a Friends meetinghouse just half a block away from the ME church building.

134. ELSD, July 13, 1844.

135. ELSD, July 23, 1844.

136. ELSD, Aug. 1, 1844.

In Middletown Ellen had a chat with Longley (apparently) Saturday night at a social gathering, and the next morning heard President Olin give the baccalaureate address on "Young men exhort to be sober-minded" (Titus 2:6). She attended the commencement exercises on Wednesday and the next day, August 8, with a number of others, boarded the steamboat at 3:00 P.M. for New York. "Mr. L____ [Longley] came just in time to get on board," she noted. "He says he is always in a hurry and a friend told me he was living too fast. That is the case with too many."[137] She doesn't say how much she talked with him, but when the boat arrived in New York at sunrise, Longley "went directly on his lonely, winding way to Virginia," she noted. "May the smiles of Heaven go with him. I feel that I can sympathize with him — that I can understand — even comprehend his feelings. May God be more to him than all earthly friends!"[138]

She doesn't say how she felt about Longley, though the above comments may give some hints. But Friday she made this enigmatic entry in her diary: "Smiles often may, and do, conceal the sorrows they cannot express. I know why I feel sad and sorrowful. Yet I cannot feel otherwise. I would fain commit my cause into the hands of him who doeth all things well — but where is my faith? Oh! when I look at the 'inner man' my sorrow is aggravated rather than appeased. Willful disobedience to Him who has kindly kept me from my earliest infancy rises up before me. 'A guilty conscience! ah, who can bear'! The great deep of my heart is troubled."[139]

What does this mean? Her diary gives no hint of willful sin. It could well be that she was feeling romantically drawn to Longley but felt this was contrary to God's will, or in conflict with her quest for holiness. She remarks a few days later, "It is sometimes quite hard for me to act from principle — I prefer impulse, and this should not be. I was constrained to go out to tea when I desired much more to stay at home. I think I ought to have been a hermitess."[140] Thursday night she went to class meeting, which she had "longed for," but "did not enjoy it" as she usually did.[141]

Longley was still on Ellen's mind. Saturday evening she mused rather candidly, "I feel weary in body and indifferent in mind. I wish I felt more buoyant. Mr. L____ must have reached his lonely home ere this. I would like to see him & know what he is doing. But why wish for that which is impossible."[142] The following Thursday she remarked, "This is a lovely day. The Proff. commences his labors to day."[143] In context, this probably refers to the beginning of Longley's teaching at Emory and Henry College.

Ellen's heart was divided. She was headed for a crisis of affection, of loyalty and life direction.

137. ELSD, Aug. 8, 1844.
138. ELSD, Aug. 8, 1844.
139. ELSD, Aug. 9, 1844.
140. ELSD, Aug. 14, 1844.
141. ELSD, Aug. 15, 1844. A photocopy of a Methodist class ticket made out to "Ellen Stowe" for the third quarter 1844 (i.e., third quarter of the conference year, January-March), signed by "R Seney," the pastor at Allen Street, is on file in the Roberts Wesleyan College Archives.
142. ELSD, Aug. 17, 1844.
143. ELSD, Aug. 22, 1844.

CHAPTER 7

The Shadow of Phoebe Palmer

"How many deaths there are for the affections."

Ellen Stowe, quoting the poet Felicia Hemans, 1848[1]

"You must have your mind fixed on being wholly the Lord's."

Phoebe Palmer's advice to Ellen Stowe, 1845[2]

At nineteen years of age, Ellen Stowe was growing into young adulthood. By the time B. T. Roberts was converted in the summer of 1844, she had been a conscious believer for nearly three years. But Ellen was struggling to find a deep, abiding sense of God's peace.

The next three years were critical in Ellen's spiritual journey and in her life's direction.

Sing Sing Camp Meeting, 1844

The first week in September 1844, about the time B. T. Roberts's sister Caroline was married and he himself was preparing to attend Genesee Wesleyan Seminary, Ellen had the opportunity to spend a few days at the Sing Sing, New York, camp meeting, several miles up the Hudson. She traveled by steamboat with Mr. and Mrs. Bunting (probably Lydia Lane's parents). Part of the time traveling upriver she was lost in rev-

1. ELSD, July 2, 1848.
2. ELSD, Mar. 13, 1845.

erie; and she was fascinated by the scenery. "The Hudson is one of the grandest rivers in the world," she reflected. "What could be more sublime than its lofty Palisades covered with evergreens? There is every variety of scenery there. I gazed on its bold cliffs, the high rocks, and on its softer features with a silent admiration and awe."[3]

The days at Sing Sing were a significant spiritual experience for Ellen. She apparently referred to the occasion later in her spiritual autobiography: "The next year [after leaving Rutgers Institute] I attended a camp-meeting and was reclaimed, and immediately convicted of the need of having my heart cleansed from all sin. I saw I could not retain a justified state unless I sought and obtained the blessing of entire sanctification."[4]

In her diary Ellen doesn't specifically mention being "reclaimed" at the Sing Sing camp meeting, but clearly it was a time of spiritual renewal. This probably was her first camp meeting ever. "I had never before witnessed such a scene," she said. "It seemed to me, it was as if a spirit disembodied had just entered the land of paradise, and for the first time the music of the heavenly fell upon their ears. They were singing in the circle gathered to listen to preaching. What heaven-like music. I stood 'amazed and wondering I gazed and gazed.'"[5]

Ellen attended the prayer and preaching services over the next two and a half days and was deeply moved by both the spiritual and the natural atmosphere. She reflected on the Wednesday evening outdoor service: "As I seated myself and looked about at the charming scene (for I never saw a lovelier one) I raised my eyes above and thought to my self that I could not say the Maker of this Beautiful World was mine, or that I was his, for I felt that everything by which I was surrounded belonged to him — tears filled my eyes, and I thought I could there sit and weep my life, . . . and never feel that he was mine."[6]

She felt separated from God; yet she was seeking. Phoebe Palmer was ministering at the camp from a tent she had set up for teaching holiness. Ellen went to meetings in Palmer's tent three times on Thursday. At the morning meeting she "felt that the burden was in a measure removed. Dr. [Nathan] Bangs was there — said we must be thankful for a little and God will give us more." The Allen Street Church also had a tent, and Ellen went to a meeting there after the Palmer meeting. "[S]ome there professed to be sanctified. I did not feel satisfied. My soul still pined for an absent God. My faith was very weak. I desired a great work to be wrought within."[7]

The next morning, Friday, Ellen found some encouragement in the services. "I felt more peace — but not satisfied." She hated to leave the camp. "That 'tented

---

3. ELSD, Sept. 3, 1844.

4. Ellen L. Roberts, "Religious Experience," *EC* 2, no. 9 (Sept. 1861): 282. It is difficult to synchronize her 1861 recollections with her diary. The diary makes no mention of attending a camp meeting earlier, however, and this sequence seems to fit best with the tone of her diary entries before and after this time.

5. ELSD, Sept. 3, 1844.

6. ELSD, Sept. 4, 1844.

7. ELSD, Sept. 5, 1844.

grove' was to me a dear place." Before sailing for New York about 12:30 P.M. she wandered off into the woods, looking for some memento to take back. She found a pretty piece of moss and carried it back to the tent but found that it soon withered. "I looked at it in silence. I thought it a 'silent preacher' indeed. It preached to me an effectual sermon — it seemed to say get a memento that you can carry fresh and green with you, to your home — one that will not wither."[8]

A group of preachers was on the steamer, and their singing lifted Ellen's spirits on the five-hour trip back to New York. She prayed that God would be with her, and "I found in proportion as my faith increased, my peace of mind was greater."[9]

Ellen was now consciously seeking holiness. A week later she recalled that it was the third anniversary of her conversion and noted, "I praise God that I now am where I am — though I have made many crooked paths since I resolved to serve God, I have not gone entirely astray. To God be all the glory." Yet she was dissatisfied. "I feel the remains of inbred sin," she noted. "'Dead indeed unto the world, but alive unto Christ' is constantly ringing in my ears. I feel that this is required of me to make a full and entire surrender of all my powers to God for time and eternity. The sacrifice to be made is a great one, but not too great. O! the sacrifice that was made for me." She added, "I was thinking to-night what a relief it would be if I could feel free to open my mind to some one — and I wished for one that I would express all my mind to. In an instant a voice seemed to say there is <u>One</u> and he will heal all our wounds. I rejoice that I have a High-Priest above and one who is 'touched with the feelings of my infirmities.'"[10] These remarks show clearly that Ellen's class meeting at Allen Street was not fulfilling the original purpose, which was precisely to provide an intimate community that encouraged such open sharing. At this point Ellen found it difficult to talk about the deepest concerns of her heart, even with close friends and her aunt Lydia.

Ellen's search for holiness continued over the next months as the New York winter set in. Repeatedly she writes of her spiritual quest. September 15: "I long for full redemption in the blood of Christ. Then I can better bear the ills of life." She wants to make a full commitment, "and yet I hold back the idol." On September 20 she quoted,

'Tis worse than death my God to love
    And not my God alone.

She was experiencing a divided heart. The quotation here echoes Phoebe Palmer, who quotes these lines in her journal and may have used them on other occasions.[11] Was the "idol" Edmund Longley, or perhaps more generally the question

---

8. ELSD, Sept. 6, 1844.

9. ELSD, Sept. 6, 1844.

10. ELSD, Sept. 13, 1844.

11. Phoebe Palmer's journal for Nov. 24, 1827, quoted in Richard Wheatley, *The Life and Letters of Mrs. Phoebe Palmer* (New York: W. C. Palmer, 1881; New York: Garland, 1984), p. 24.

of marriage versus a single life, or something less specific? Though an inward, intro-spective person, Ellen felt and feared loneliness, despite all the people around her.

Ellen continued attending the Allen Street Church, though she was absent from class meeting for some weeks due to poor health. On January 4, 1845, she wrote, "I feel my mind distracted by wandering thoughts, and do not enjoy that nearness of access to God I have often enjoyed. I fear that I am retrograding in divine life instead of going forward." It was a struggle between earth and heaven: "Afflictions are indeed necessary in this life, we need something to wean us from earth. Our hearts and af-fections naturally centre here — and God sees it necessary often to break the ties one after another that bind us to earth and place them above, that our hearts may be raised to things above, that we may be led to contemplate the end of life and to pre-pare for an endless existence."[12]

She received "a fresh impulse" from the Saturday evening service: "I longed for purity of heart."[13]

On January 6 she reflected, "I feel an inward peace though not in the degree I desire to." And again two days later, "I would try to press forward but the past haunts me still. I feel like giving up all, leaving all behind and following Jesus only. Oh! that I could forget everything — that I could yield my will, my all to God."

Ellen attended Walter Palmer's class meeting again on Thursday, January 9, walk-ing over to Allen Street. "Dr. Palmer is a very spiritual man — and he urges holiness of heart upon his members in a way that I think he will be the means of doing much," she commented. "I am well assured that this is the only sure path to heaven."[14]

The next Tuesday Ellen wrote, "Yesterday I suffered more in mind [than] I could describe. I pray God that this subject may never be permitted to distress me so again. It is one upon which I fain would never think, but circumstances will sometimes bring it to mind. To-day I have felt that I could cast all on Jesus — a wonderful change has been wrought in my feelings — that which did trouble me I now scarcely think of — to God be all the praise. I feel in body very weak — my prospects for health are anything but f[l]attering, and here I fear I am not resigned."[15]

Ellen's quest during this time included reading. She read a biography of Felicia Hemans, the British poet, who was very popular at the time and whose poetry she enjoyed.[16] She began Joseph Holdich's *Life of Willbur Fisk,* the founding president of Wesleyan University. "I long [for] pure devotion of all to God — this desire has been fed and increased by my reading in Dr. Fisk's Life to-day," she wrote on Janu-ary 22. She desired to love God supremely, but "sometimes I think I can never do

12. ELSD, Jan. 4, 1845. Ellen may be reflecting here on some of her devotional reading.
13. ELSD, Jan. 4, 1845.
14. ELSD, Jan. 9, 1845.
15. ELSD, Jan. 14, 1845.
16. ELSD, Jan. 22, 1845. Among Mrs. Hemans's books was *Records of Woman,* published in 1828. The volume Ellen had access to was perhaps *The Poetical Works of Mrs. Felicia Hemans: Complete in One Volume* (Philadelphia: Thomas T. Ash, 1836), which included an unsigned "critical preface" that related Hemans's life.

this, for I am so wedded to earthly objects." She had not really forgotten Longley, for she noted on January 15 that this was the day he began his vacation. "I pray God to be with Him [*sic*] always and that <u>he</u> will be more to him than any earthly friend would be."[17] Here Ellen reflects her own feelings more than Longley's, whom she really didn't know intimately.

Conversations with Mary Martindale encouraged Ellen spiritually. After talking with her on January 18, Ellen felt "more and more the need of this holy religion to possess the soul in all its fulness."[18]

Stephen Olin was in New York again, and Ellen went to hear him on Sunday, January 19.

> This morning which was all bright and beautiful I went with the many up to hear the good Dr. Olin. It was very familiar-like to see him again in the pulpit. His text was "And Felix trembled and said On thy way, till a more convenient season." Like all his sermons it was <u>good</u>, <u>good</u>, <u>good</u> — though I did not think he had the liberty that he has on some occasions. He dwelt long on man's acting contrary to the requirements of the gospel and the conviction of his own heart, and conscience. I felt more than ever while listening to him like giving up self and all else for God — <u>his</u> name to glorify.[19]

The next days were busy with routine activities, but the spiritual struggle continued. She wrote on Tuesday: "My mind is still troubled, but for one object I think I would yield everything to God and I feel determined though it cost me my life this one object shall be wholly given to <u>God</u> even though all my prospects of future happiness be centered there. <u>God</u> claims all our affections — and all <u>God must</u> have."[20] The references to "one object" and "prospects of future happiness" suggest a spiritual struggle concerning her affection for Longley.

Ellen's struggle was reaching a crisis. Despite some pain from a dental appointment earlier in the day, she went to her class meeting on Thursday night, January 23, which was led partly by Phoebe Palmer. "Her exercises are very profitable to me — what she said was good and worth remembering," Ellen recorded.[21] But the next day Ellen was thrown into despair by news about Longley. She writes,

> Yes, this is the 24th[,] a day that will be enstamped on memory throughout time. The news of this morning has blasted my every earthly prospect — and while I try to write my heart bleeds at every pore[.] Alone! Alone!! a sound to me so dismal rings constantly in my ears. <u>The One</u> whom I had (vainly) thought cared for me — in whom I had placed implicit confidence — I have reason to think has been a trifler with my better feelings. . . . O! how I have longed for this day to pass away

17. ELSD, Jan. 15 and 22, 1845.
18. ELSD, Jan. 18, 1845.
19. ELSD, Jan. 19, 1845.
20. ELSD, Jan. 21, 1845.
21. ELSD, Jan. 23, 1845.

— how can I spend many such days? God only knows. I try to pray — but I cannot. I have neither words nor thoughts, nor desire.

The next day, Saturday, Ellen's "mourning was in a measure turned to joy" when she received a letter from Longley (though she doesn't reveal the contents). But the following Wednesday, January 29, she was

by other news . . . convinced that what I had heard was true and for a time I endured all the anguish I had felt before and a thousand times more. I could say or think nothing. But "oh! that I had never lived." ["]Oh! that I could now die." I felt that death would have been far preferable. As I raised my eyes everything was to me a barren waste. I said "what can I do. What shall I do" — I felt like I had been suddenly and unconsciously transplanted to the middle of a desert surrounded on all sides by vast, dreary, dismal extent.[22]

Ellen endured this "agony of mind" for two hours. But as she reflected more, "hope like a grain of mustard seed sprang up, and I said 'God reigns' — it is of Him that this thing has happened — and I began to exclaim 'Glory to God!' This I repeated times without number. I then felt that I could pray and that though friends all forsook the Lord would take me up. I have laid my case before Him — he will hear, and answer prayer."

Ellen recorded these feelings and events not at the time but a week later, on February 5. She wrote that the previous days had been "a season fraught with suffering both physically and mentally." She had been too upset to write in her diary. Even now, a week later, she felt she couldn't trust her jumbled feelings but she recalled the line, "earth has no sorrows that heaven cannot heal." And yet, she says,

when I revert again to the subject I say it cannot be — I can never realize it. The wound bleeds afresh — but I have been supported by grace above anything I could have believed. I feel that His grace is sufficient for me now. I have now only to live for God — for eternity. May this trial effectually wean me from all things earthly. I dare not for a moment look back. It has been the most severe trial of my life, and but for my sympathizing friends I am led to ask, what would I have done!

This is emphatically a "vale of tears" — there are disappointments all the way — but not one too many — they are designed for our good. This is the first day I have felt anything like myself.[23]

Ellen doesn't say precisely what she learned on January 29 that so upset her. Probably the news had to do with Longley's marriage plans, for in fact Longley married Mary Hammond of Middletown on February 16, two and a half weeks later.[24]

22. ELSD, Feb. 5, 1845.
23. ELSD, Feb. 5, 1845.
24. Information on Longley's marriage to Mary Hammond provided by Robert J. Vejnar, archivist, Emory and Henry College, e-mail of Sept. 30, 1999, and Suzy Taraba, archivist, Wesleyan University, e-mail of Oct. 14, 1999.

Apparently the letter Ellen received from Longley on January 25 gave no hint of this, and she felt deceived. She never again directly mentions Longley in her diary.[25]

Seeking Holiness

This crisis of the heart led Ellen to deeper spiritual commitment. Her spirit began to heal, though her struggle was not fully ended. The day after the above diary entry (on Thursday, February 6, 1845), Ellen went again to her class meeting and "felt sweet peace of mind. Oh! how can I praise <u>God</u> enough for this holy religion, which raises us above the ills of life — supports us under trials," she reflected. "May the remnant of my days be spent in serving God with a single heart — <u>Live for God and act for eternity</u>, has been in my mind all day." She found comfort also in poetry and in her friendship with Mary Martindale. She stayed overnight with Mary on February 11 and accompanied her to school the next morning, where Ellen read Elizabeth Barrett's poems. At lunchtime she and Mary talked over Felicia Hemans's life and poetry "and many other subjects," then Ellen spent the afternoon alone while Mary returned to school. "I had a glorious time reading, writing and doing all number of things," she says, before Mary returned and Ellen walked home. On parting Mary "observed to me this will be a bright spot to remember. So are all the little spots of time we spend together."[26]

Attending class meeting again on Thursday evening (though apparently not feeling well and "half inclined to stay home"), Ellen drew fresh courage. At the meeting "one sister . . . prayed that we might attain to all the heights and depths of humble love." Ellen "seemed to see more clearly than ever before that Christ was a full Savior, though I did not realize it." Saturday she spent partly in reading. She commented, "How swiftly the weeks pass by — 'Time' Mr. Wesley says 'is a fragment of eternity broken off at both ends.' I am reading Miss Barrett's Poems — they are very unique in style — Her '<u>Drama of Exile</u>' is very beautiful." Then she adds, "I long to lose my own will in the will of God[—]there is no other state of happiness here."[27]

During worship the next Sunday "all the feelings of the late past rushed upon my mind — and I could not refrain from tears." In the afternoon she went to hear "Mr. Poisal my spiritual father," though she doesn't say where he was preaching.

---

25. Ellen's correspondence with Longley (and his with her) apparently has not survived, so the story must be reconstructed primarily from her diary. There is perhaps a chance that something other than her relationship with Longley was causing her distress at this time, but it seems clear that her feelings regarding Longley lie behind these diary entries.

26. ELSD, Feb. 6 and 11, 1845. Elizabeth Barrett (1806-61) had published her popular *Poems* the previous year; it was this work that brought her to the attention of the poet Robert Browning and led to their marriage in 1846, and this is the work Ellen would have been reading. See *The Complete Works of Elizabeth Barrett Browning, Cambridge Edition* (Boston and New York: Houghton Mifflin, 1900), p. 67.

27. ELSD, Feb. 13 and 15, 1845. "A Drama of Exile" was the first poem in Barrett's *Poems* of 1844.

"Again I suffered such anguish of mind as I can not describe, but he turned my thoughts from the scene of trials to the home beyond the skies."[28]

At class meeting the following Thursday Ellen again received some help through Phoebe Palmer.

> Through much bodily effort I went to my class and was fully compensated in going, as we had one of the best of meetings. I was met by Mrs. P____ [Palmer]. I love her for her very quietness — she talks long to us but is not tedious. Her remarks are applicable[,] close and to the point. She dwelt much on our taking earnest heed lest we let slip the grace we have obtained — and on sacrificing for Christ — that he required the greatest sacrifice we could make — and on our doing many things that we may not offend others, indulging in that which though not hurtful to us, is an injury to others — and on educating ourselves for eternity.[29]

Apparently Ellen talked with Phoebe Palmer after the meeting, for she adds,

> Mrs. P____ repeats these word[s] to me, which I was struck with as they had no bearing on anything I said

> "Through much distress and pain,
> Through many a conflict here,
> Through blood ye must the entrance gain
> Yet, O disdain to fear;
> 'Courage,' your Captain cries,
> (Who all your toil foreknew,)
> Toil ye shall have, yet all despise,
> I have o'ercome for you."[30]

Ellen was encouraged by these words from the Methodist hymnbook.[31] Mrs. Palmer must have perceived something of Ellen's struggle, and this was her discerning counsel. Ellen was helped and eventually did experience entire sanctification, as recorded later in her "Religious Experience" testimony. It is unclear, however, when this breakthrough (related below) occurred; it seems to have been a year or two later. For several years Ellen was seeking holiness, and her struggles were many.

Teaching Sunday School at Greene Street

About this time in early 1845 Ellen was asked to begin teaching Sunday school at the nearby Greene Street Church, where Dr. Nathan Bangs was the appointed preacher.

28. ELSD, Feb. 16, 1845.

29. ELSD, Feb. 20, 1845. (The word given here as "quietness" is practically illegible; it could possibly be "gentleness.")

30. ELSD, Feb. 20, 1845.

31. The quotation is stanza 5 of Charles Wesley's hymn "Jesus, the Conqueror, Reigns."

She wasn't excited about it but felt it was her duty. "I tried to go in the spirit of my Master," she wrote.[32] She began teaching a girls class on February 23, and from this point was actually involved more at Greene Street than at Allen Street, though she continued her Allen Street class meeting.[33] By this time the Greene Street neighborhood was changing as prostitution was moving "uptown" from seamier environs farther south. Greene Street was becoming "one long string of whorehouses" in the 1850s.[34] Ellen may have walked by some of them on her way to and from services. Whatever she thought of these changes, she doesn't mention them in her diary.

Ellen continued reading Elizabeth Barrett. In a reflective moment on Monday evening, February 24, she wrote that some of Miss Barrett's poems "just suit my taste. The moon is shining brightly into my room. She always seems to speak to me of my sister, who is an inhabitant of the spirit-land — I think I feel stronger in spirit, than I have sometimes."[35]

In this mellow mood Ellen the next day visited a daguerreotype gallery. Daguerreotyping, a recently invented, early form of photography, had come to New York City in 1839 and from there spread across the country. In 1844 Matthew Brady opened probably the first photo gallery in New York, Brady's Daguerrean Miniature Gallery, at Broadway and Fulton, across the street from P. T. Barnum's museum and about sixteen blocks south of the Lane home.[36] Ellen probably strolled down to Brady's where, gazing at the photos, she wandered "among the great ones of the earth, or rather great ones of our Country." At Thorburn's Gallery she "stood before Abbotsford the residence of Sir Walter Scott — how many associations connected with that place arose in my mind, particularly Mrs. Hemans — her visit to that place. I lingered long before it — and how I would love to visit those Highlands of Scotland — and the Alps in Switzerland."[37] From Hemans's biography and poems Ellen knew of her visit to Scott's residence in Scotland in 1829 and of her poetic descriptions of Switzerland and other exotic places.[38]

At the end of the week Ellen finally answered the letter she had received three weeks earlier from Edmund Longley. She doesn't mention him by name but writes, "I have to day answered the letter that has rested with so much weight on my mind. But oh! when I think of the past . . . tears again fill my eyes — they come as ever to

32. ELSD, Feb. 23, 1845.

33. A photocopy of Ellen's class ticket, dated April 1846 and signed by the pastor, Leonard Vincent (on file at the Roberts Wesleyan College Archives), shows that Ellen was actively attending her Allen Street class meeting at that time.

34. Allan Keller, *Scandalous Lady: The Life and Times of Madame Restell, New York's Most Notorious Abortionist* (New York: Atheneum, 1981), p. 87.

35. ELSD, Feb. 24, 1845.

36. Edwin G. Burrows and Mike Wallace, *Gotham: A History of New York City to 1898* (New York: Oxford University Press, 1999), pp. 688-89. "By 1850 there were seventy-one daguerreotype studios" in New York City, "ready to take one's picture" (p. 689).

37. ELSD, Feb. 25, 1845.

38. See Paula Feldman, introduction to Felicia Hemans, *Records of Woman, with Other Poems*, ed. Paula R. Feldman (Lexington: University Press of Kentucky, 1999), p. xix.

my relief; when will they be dried up — I cannot, I will not let my mind dwell on the present circumstances. The wound inflicted would bleed afresh. How coldly I look upon earth — 'tis not my home! And yet I have seen much of happiness here."[39]

Saturday evening, March 1, Ellen went to the evening service (apparently at Allen Street) for "the first time in a long while." "I bore the cross and tried to speak" in the meeting, she noted. "My mind went back to the days of last summer spent in the 'tented grove' [the Sing Sing camp meeting] — I almost wished that I could hide myself away from this world somewhere, where I could hold uninterrupted communion with God." She was keeping up her Bible reading, for she notes on Sunday, March 2, that she had just finished 2 Chronicles.[40]

Ellen celebrated her twentieth birthday on March 4, 1845. This put her again in a pensive mood. "This is quite an era in my history; I am to day twenty years old — I feel to mourn somehow that I am out of my teens. I have felt an ardent desire on this day to begin my life anew." She prayed "that the coming years of my life may be devoted to God alone — and that I might stand higher in a moral sense and cultivate those virtues that adorn the sex; but this reform must begin in the heart. [L]et that first be right." She also noted that this was the day James Polk was inaugurated as president of the United States.[41]

Early spring was coming to New York. Ellen spent part of Saturday, March 8, visiting a greenhouse with her aunt Lydia — "a rich feast to my very soul" — and accompanied Lydia to the Saturday evening service, noting that Phoebe Palmer was also there. At Communion the next afternoon she "felt a strong desire for a fresh baptism from on high." She recorded: "I seemed to doubt whether the Lord was with me, whether I was His or not, when it was suggested to me that if He was not with me I would not have the desire — my fears were then put to flight. I could no longer doubt."[42]

Class meeting the next Thursday, March 13, was again helpful to Ellen. For several days she had felt "an unusual peace of mind." Though without "a bright witness, I have no condemnation." Mrs. Palmer led the meeting and spoke directly to Ellen. "You must have your mind fixed on being wholly the Lord's," she said. "You must be definite in your petitions, ask the Lord for holiness." Ellen took this advice as "a word in season." She wrote, "I have tried from that moment to feel that I must and did give up everything for God. May I feel that no sacrifice is too great." She still experienced "great heaviness" over the next days. Yet, she said, "I have felt as if one great point was gained, since I fully resolved to give up all for God."[43]

Palmer herself tells of counseling a young woman whose situation was similar to Ellen's. The incident occurred some years earlier, so the person involved was not Ellen. Still, it gives some insight into how Mrs. Palmer might have talked with Ellen. Palmer writes,

39. ELSD, Feb. 28, 1845.
40. ELSD, Mar. 1-2, 1845.
41. ELSD, Mar. 4, 1845.
42. ELSD, Mar. 8-9, 1845.
43. ELSD, Mar. 13 and 15, 1845.

On Tuesday evening, Miss _____, an amiable young lady, called to see me. Her mind has been deeply interested for some time on the subject of holiness. I lifted my heart to the Lord for a word in season, and God gave an immediate answer. I was quite unacquainted with her circumstances in life, and consequently unapprised of the temptations peculiar to her case, but began to assure her of the faithfulness of God, in the speedy performance of his own part of the work, as soon as she was willing to comply with the conditions. I then related to her the experience of a young lady, with whom I had been familiar, who seemed greatly to desire the blessing of holiness; but on trying to pray with her for a present bestowment of the blessing, I could feel no liberty, and became assured in my own mind that some insuperable barrier was standing between God and her soul. With much hesitation, she afterward informed me that she was contemplating a marriage engagement with a young gentleman not professing religion. The mystery was at once solved, and I assured her that unless it was already made, her aspirations for present holiness and future felicity also would be futile, if she persisted in the prosecution of the affair. She received the statement of my views with a heavy heart, and I feared that this important crisis in her experience was to be but the turning point for a fearful plunge into the fatal vortex of mere worldly-minded profession. But grace ordered it otherwise; the struggle ended the next evening — the idol was given up, and the victory was, beyond expectation, glorious. . . .

While I was giving this recital to the interesting young friend, her countenance bespoke a heart greatly disquieted, and, with much embarrassment, she informed me that a case of precisely the same interest was pending with herself. At once I saw that the Lord had indeed, in answer to prayer, given "a word in season." The advice was made instrumental in frustrating the designs of the tempter, — her feet were turned from the vortex, which had been well nigh reached, and she also became a happy, and useful, and deeply-interesting traveler in the King's highway.[44]

Ellen was still — or again — struggling to believe and to receive the inward witness of holiness. After a day in Sunday school and church on March 16, including a sermon by her uncle, George Lane, she wrote: "I can hold out no longer[—]there must be a change wrought within."

The next day, following the advice and the language of Phoebe Palmer, Ellen tried to enter into the experience of holiness but was not satisfied. She wrote, "I give myself away to God and try to rest there, believing that <u>he</u> will receive and sanctify the gift — but I have not the witness of the Spirit that I am cleansed from all sin — perhaps I look to myself too much — may the work be a thorough one."[45]

---

44. Phoebe Palmer, *The Way of Holiness, with Notes by the Way* (New York: G. Lane and C. B. Tippett, 1848), pp. 221-23.

45. ELSD, Mar. 17, 1845. She was also this day "sorely grieved by a notice that appears in this week's paper" — perhaps the notice of Edmund Longley's marriage four weeks earlier. "I did not think I would be so affected by it," she wrote, "but the last struggle methinks is past."

Ellen's life was not all taken up with her spiritual struggles, however. On Tuesday, March 25, she went with her cousin to watch the launching of the steamship *Henry Clay*, "the largest packet on the Liverpool line." Ellen was fascinated: "It was a grand sight, to see it move off so majestically into the water. I can now say that one desire of my heart has been gratified."[46] (Seven years later this great steamer burned in the North River at a loss of seventy lives, B. T. Roberts noted in his 1852 diary.)[47]

Later the same day she was "greatly profited" by reading some from Phoebe Palmer's *The Way of Holiness*, which had gained quick popularity since its publication two years earlier and had spread Mrs. Palmer's influence.[48] Ellen's uncle George Lane about this time published the first Methodist edition of *The Way of Holiness* at the Methodist Book Concern.[49] Reading Palmer, Ellen "resolved in the strength of God that the desire for holiness should be all absorbing" until she attained it.[50]

Ellen was making progress. She wrote the next day, "My mind is not yet at rest, but I think faith is increasing. It is suggested to me to believe though I have not one evidence that sin is all removed. Is this what I am called to do? I will try and believe but if I were to look to myself for an evidence of the work, I should doubt in a moment. I should lose my hold and again be involved in deep distress. It is suggested just that if I am given up into the hands of the Lord I need not look [for] an evidence — that I am His and this is sufficient for one to know just now."[51]

Thus Ellen in her diary is dialoguing with God and with herself. From time to time she uses the phrase "It is suggested to me," indicating thoughts that come to mind that she feels come from God's Spirit — and that also, as here, sometimes echo Phoebe Palmer's advice.

On March 27 at her class meeting she felt "more peace and more joy," and the next day she noted, "It has been made very clear to me that I am to live by faith in the love of God, and believe on him for full salvation." Yet after worship the next Sunday she was "exceeding troubled that sin still exists within." She was still struggling to believe and to *know* that God had done his cleansing work. She wrote, "O that I might prove the full salvation of God in my soul! And it is suggested to me just now 'had you a child that desired a gift in your power to bestow — as earnestly you desire freedom from sin would you not have it? And your Heavenly father is more willing to give you everlasting life!['] Can I doubt longer that he will — that he does?"[52] But still the assurance did not come.

46. ELSD, Mar. 25, 1845.

47. BTRD, Aug. 7, 1852.

48. ELSD, Mar. 25, 1845.

49. Phoebe Palmer, *The Way of Holiness: With Notes by the Way; Being a Narrative of Religious Experience Resulting from a Determination to be a Bible Christian* (New York: G. Lane and C. B. Tippett, 1845), p. 288. The Methodist Book Concern published a second edition in 1848, and the book went through many editions over the years.

50. ELSD, Mar. 25, 1845.

51. ELSD, Mar. 26, 1845.

52. ELSD, Mar. 27, 28, and 30, 1845.

The next Tuesday, April 1, recalling that it was the anniversary of her being desperately ill with scarlet fever a year earlier, Ellen was thankful that she had been spared and now enjoyed "comparative health." She was still "sorely grieved to find so much of sin" in her heart; yet she was encouraged to have a great High Priest "who is touched with the feeling of our infirmities." She continued praying and seeking. "I felt this morning while praying that I could give myself to God as I had never done before — that is that it should be a complete sacrifice and entire surrender of self," she noted on April 2. "I feel that I have no claims — 'tis no longer me, but Christ that liveth in me. I do not still feel satisfied, but I want the assurance all is <u>God's</u>, that sin is taken away." In her Thursday night class meeting she "tried to feel that I was not my own," she said, and that her one goal should be to glorify God. But she added, "I too often find myself asking what will this one think and that one."[53]

Friday night Ellen was troubled that she had spent a social time with friends too frivolously. "I feel as if my eye was not single to the glory of God continually. I did not think there was so much of evil in my heart before." But the next day she read some from Mrs. Fletcher and received help. "O for a heart from the least & last remains of sin set free! I can only stand fast while my eye is fixed on Jesus. As Mrs. Fletcher says it is only 'by simple and naked faith' that sanctification is to be attained."[54] But how could she exercise such faith?

Sunday, April 6, Ellen awoke to a beautiful spring morning and was cheered that "yonder is a tree in bloom." She went to church at Greene Street and heard Nathan Bangs preach from John 10:14-15 on Jesus the Good Shepherd.[55] Returning home, she renewed her covenant with God and signed her name to it: "I have anew covenanted with God that I would from henceforth reckon myself dead indeed unto <u>sin</u>, the <u>world</u>, and alive as unto Him. I would give myself to Him for <u>time</u> and for <u>eternity</u> — never more to take back any part of the price or gift, and I believe that the offering is accepted."[56]

This was her total commitment, putting her all on the altar and trusting in God. But two days later she was troubled that she yielded to anger, and she wondered "whether a temptation to anger in case we resisted would be incompatible with a sanctified state." The next Sunday, April 13, Ellen decided to go to the worship service at Allen Street, "my own home," rather than Greene Street, and heard Robert Seney preach. But she felt she "gave way to temptation in conversation & thought" and was

---

53. ELSD, Apr. 1-3, 1845.

54. ELSD, Apr. 5, 1845. See Henry Moore, *The Life of Mrs. Mary Fletcher, Consort and Relict of Rev. John Fletcher, Vicar of Madeley, Salop* (New York: Hunt and Eaton, n.d.): "I was now assured the blessing of sanctification (or, in other words, a heart entirely renewed) could not be received but by simple, naked faith" (p. 36). Cf. Phoebe Palmer's reference to "naked faith in a naked promise" in Wheatley, *Life and Letters*, p. 42.

55. ELSD, Apr. 6, 1845. She writes, "Listened to Dr. Bangs from John 10. 14.15," without specifying which church, but Bangs was the appointed pastor at Greene Street at this time, and Ellen was still teaching Sunday school there.

56. ELSD, Apr. 6, 1845.

troubled in her inability to resist temptation.[57] And on Monday she wrote, echoing and perhaps quoting Phoebe Palmer,

> I never saw the depravity of my own heart as I do now, but I am determined to lay all upon the altar though that <u>all</u> should be as dear as a right eye or hand. It was discovered to me to-night where the difficulty lay in my past vacillation, by this passage of Holy Writ — "I beseech, you, brethren, by the mercies of God, that ye present your bodies a <u>living sacrifice</u>, holy, acceptable, which is your reasonable service." "This blessing is <u>obtained</u> by [']<u>laying all on the altar</u>' and retained by keeping all on the altar a 'living sacrifice.'"[58]

Still, victory did not come. She wrote no more in her diary until the following Sunday when, after attending worship and again hearing Bangs, she confessed that she had "wandered far from God," allowing "the enemy to gain great victory." Why, she asked, should she "expect, or anticipate, pleasure in anything apart from the service of God"? Then she lay her diary aside for three weeks as she was busy getting ready for a two-month visit to Middletown. "In my experience of late I think I have lost — I say it in humility," she wrote on May 11.[59]

Visit to Middletown, 1845

As always, Ellen's mood changed when she arrived in Middletown. The language of spiritual struggle nearly disappeared from her diary, replaced by the whirl of social activities among her Middletown friends. It is as though she had nearly exhausted herself in her spiritual quest and was glad for a respite among the green hills of Connecticut. Her feelings about New York City are clear as she describes her early morning steamer trip to New Haven on Tuesday, May 13: "We left Babylon at 5 1/2 o'clock." Accompanied by friends, she left New York in a drizzling rain, and by train and stagecoach from New Haven reached Middletown about 3:00 P.M. She was glad to be back in Middletown, among friends, staying again in the home of her cousin Harvey Lane. Still, painful memories "would rise before me and it was in vain I tried to live only in the present." The rain picked up again after arriving at the Lanes. "[A]n everlasting rain set in and I spent the rest of the day in a dream."[60]

Ellen's diary for her three weeks in Middletown is detailed, tracing daily her activities and feelings. Cold rain continued for the first few days, dampening her spirits. "But shall I depend upon outward circumstances for happiness — shall I expect anything from this world but disappointment and sorrows? does not my own experience teach me to look for nought besides in this world? Look O my soul within!"

---

57. ELSD, Apr. 8 and 13, 1845.
58. ELSD, Apr. 14, 1845. (A quote from Palmer's *The Way of Holiness*.)
59. ELSD, Apr. 20 and May 11, 1845.
60. ELSD, May 13, 1845.

When the weather cleared a few days later, she wrote, "Welcome to the bright sun and clear blue sky! May they dispel the clouds that have dimmed the horizon of my mind. . . . About sunset I awoke to the reality that I was in Middletown. My former self returned and I felt the beauty of everything upon which my eyes rested."[61]

Ellen resumed her friendly interaction with her cousins and with Wesleyan University faculty such as the Johnstons, Holdichs, and Olins. She attended social events and occasional lectures on science and other topics. On Wednesday, May 21, she attended the wedding of her friend Hannah, performed by Stephen Olin, but found the next day "long weary and lonely." "I was as dull as grammar on an Eve of holiday," she mused half-humorously at the end of the day. Edmund Longley still crossed her mind from time to time. On a walk to Pameacha Grove south of the campus on the evening of June 13 with her cousin Elam, she recalled that this was "where I went once before with a friend, now far away. It was the 18th of June two years ago. The associations were at once too pleasant and too powerful." It was in fact just two years earlier that Ellen had her evening walk with Longley.[62]

Ellen again enjoyed pleasant walks around Middletown, but occasionally dark thoughts of the past would intrude. She found one Saturday walk so "intimately associated with the past, that it made me feel sad! sad! Oh! that I could forget. 'Every heart knoweth its own bitterness'[—]how true."[63]

Thursday, May 29, found Ellen reading *Hyperion* with her friend Mary (probably Longfellow's *Hyperion, a Romance* rather than Keats's poem *Hyperion*). One warm June evening she called at Dr. Olin's and later enjoyed gazing at the moon through a telescope with her young cousin Emily. She attended the "Horticultural meeting" where she was "nominated a life-member." One Saturday she enjoyed an afternoon of sailing on the Connecticut River with a group from the university, returning as the sun was setting behind the hills.[64] She again visited the graves of Willbur Fisk and "sweet-spirited Aaron Hurd. What a lovely young man."[65]

Wesleyan University enrolled only men at this time, and some of the students and young tutors showed interest in Ellen. But she was not much impressed with most of them. She became acquainted with "Mr. Garretson" (probably Francis Garrettson, then a student at Wesleyan) and with a "Mr. Thomison" who walked her home one night; "I did not seem to admire him much from some cause."[66]

As usual, Ellen attended the Methodist services in Middletown. These led her at times to reflect on her spiritual state. After one "excellent" prayer meeting she commented, "I could only bewail my unfaithfulness. When will I cease to wander from

---

61. ELSD, May 17 and 19, 1845.

62. ELSD, May 22; June 13 and 19, 1843.

63. ELSD, May 24, 1845. Cf. Prov. 14:10, "The heart knoweth his own bitterness."

64. ELSD, May 31, 1845.

65. ELSD, May 29; June 9, 7, and 1, 1845.

66. ELSD, June 6, 1845. The diary entry looks like "Thomison" but is hard to make out. John K. Thompson was one of the 1845 graduates, but there was no student or tutor named Thomison at this time.

the living and true God." On June 8 she "felt glad though unworthy to kneel at the table of the Lord" and was "pleased to see so large a number of the students present, and go forward to commune."[67]

As the time drew near to leave, Ellen increasingly enjoyed the neat, fresh beauty of Middletown and the surrounding area. On a Saturday outing, June 21, she found the view "sublime and beautiful." "The dwelling[s] in general present such a neat appearance — the fences white-washed[,] shrubbery and flowers not overlooked. Oh! who could help 'falling in love' with New-England?" The next day she reflected, "Soon I must leave these pleasant hills this delightful air and indeed all that is lovely and dear to me here. My fine view I must exchange for brick walls. Nature I must leave behind — her green grass — her bright blooming flowers — and not hear the birds I so dearly love."[68]

Saturday, June 28, Ellen accompanied the "ladies of the Faculty and some of the students" on an excursion to Hartford, some twenty miles north. Through "fine weather and a plenty of dust" they made the journey and saw a number of sights. In addition to several places of historical interest, the group stopped at a home for the insane and at the Deaf and Dumb Asylum. On their return they visited a prison where Ellen was "sad to see what was the effects of crime." The place was "dreadful," but with a poet's eye for detail and contrast she noted, "I saw a rose bush blooming in one corner of the yard — it looked as if in some foreign clime. I wonder what the poor prisoners think."[69]

The time had come to return to New York. Ellen said her friends were "pleading with me to stay till after the fourth"; she found this "quite amusing." Her uncle, George Lane, arrived July 1 to take her back, but it was arranged to extend her stay another week or so. She participated in Independence Day festivities that included bells, banners, the firing of cannon, orations, a Sunday school outing, and an evening fireworks display.[70]

Finally on Wednesday, July 9, Ellen returned to New York City. She left Middletown by steamboat about 3:00 P.M., traveling with Mary (Martindale, probably) and perhaps others.[71]

Spiritual Pilgrimage

Back in Manhattan, Ellen was very busy with her domestic duties over the next weeks and months, helping to care for the Lane household. She remained in New York while the Lanes went up to Middletown for the Wesleyan University commencement in early August. On August 5 a friend, "Dear Mrs. Wilcox" (probably a young woman Ellen

67. ELSD, May 29 and June 8, 1845.
68. ELSD, June 21-22, 1845.
69. ELSD, June 28, 1845.
70. ELSD, June 30 and July 4, 1845.
71. ELSD, July 9, 1845.

knew), stopped in and read her two of Felicia Hemans's popular poems, "The Graves of a Household" and "The Land of Dreams."[72] George and Lydia soon returned.

As usual, friends and church acquaintants were coming and going at the Lane household. After one friend left on August 15 Ellen wrote, "[I]t is all parting in this world. I have been sitting long under the grape vine, alone with the crickets thinking of my mother." Later in the month she attended the camp meeting at Rye, New York, where she "felt blessed" to join in singing "O for a Thousand Tongues" but "miserable" when she awoke in the night and heard people praising God at the all-night prayer meeting that she had left early to go to bed. "I shall never forget the sensations of that hour."[73]

Ellen was saddened in September when her friend Mrs. Wilcox left for the "far west"; "tears were the only words I could express." She had grown close to this friend with whom she had shared many conversations. "To her I could say everything and know that my feelings were appreciated. We have parted — perchance to meet no more on earth. I longed to keep her near me. But 'the dearest friends are doomed to part, The fondest ties must sever.'" She continued also her friendship with Mary Martindale and Mary Coles.[74]

Ellen says little about her spiritual journey during these weeks following her return from Middletown. She notes on Friday, September 12, "A peace that passeth all understanding has filled my mind to-day — a resting in Christ." She does not mention attending her class meeting on Thursday evenings, though her diary entries at this time are rather intermittent. Presumably she continued attending, as this was a duty of Methodist church membership.[75]

Ellen's diary stops on September 26, 1845, and starts again on Sunday, June 18, 1848, when Ellen was twenty-three years old, shortly before she first met Benjamin Roberts.[76] Ellen may have been a member of a class led by Phoebe Palmer in the period 1846-47, when there is no diary record.[77]

Though the diary does not pick up again until June 1848, at the beginning of 1858 Ellen recorded, "Will try to remember the text from which the first sermon to which I listened on the first Sabbath of 1848 was preached. The words addressed to Lot — 'Escape for thy life; look not behind thee — neither stay thou in all the plain; escape to the mountain lest thou be consumed.'"[78]

---

72. ELSD, Aug. 5, 1845.

73. ELSD, Aug. 15 and 29, 1845.

74. ELSD, Sept. 9, Aug. 6, and Sept. 26, 1845.

75. ELSD, Sept. 12, 1845. It was still true at this time that "attendance on class-meeting was a necessary condition of membership, and the names of those who neglected this were soon removed from the record." Samuel A. Seaman, *Annals of New York Methodism Being a History of the Methodist Episcopal Church in the City of New York from* A.D. *1766 to* A.D. *1890* (New York: Hunt and Eaton, 1892), p. 482.

76. It seems likely that Ellen kept a diary for the intervening two years and eight months, but if so it is apparently now lost.

77. Note *Phoebe Palmer: Selected Writings*, ed. Thomas C. Oden (New York: Paulist, 1988), p. 214.

78. ELRD, Jan. [1 or 2], 1858.

It was apparently about this time in 1845, though perhaps somewhat later, that Ellen entered into the experience of holiness she described in her 1861 testimony. "I read upon the subject, and prayed, and groaned, for weeks," she later wrote.[79] Then in class meeting one day the leader (possibly Phoebe Palmer), after speaking to her, began singing:

> Nay, but I yield, I yield,
> I can hold out no more.[80]

Ellen later testified, "I did 'yield,' I did 'sink,' and Jesus saved me to the uttermost — the inbred corruption was washed away in the blood of the Lamb. Heaven seemed begun below to me then. I felt so quiet, so calm; and afterwards, undisturbed by any provocation, I bore the cross; I loved it, though heavy. I testified definitely to what Jesus had done for me and was greatly blessed in doing it."[81]

Ellen's experience was clear and definite. She understood it as the experience of entire sanctification, as her 1861 testimony shows. Unfortunately, her assurance of the experience didn't last long. Hearing a while later that a minister's wife who was unsympathetic to the holiness emphasis had remarked snidely that Ellen "was getting along very fast," Ellen decided to keep quiet about it.

> The enemy took advantage of this remark in making me fearful of being too forward. I thought, I will be very careful in future and not speak of this blessing except when the Lord requires it. I was *so careful* as not again to testify to this work *definitely,* and soon consciousness of purity began to leave my soul, — that rest in Jesus was gone, and I dared not say my heart was clean. There came an aching void, a sense of loss and want, followed by condemnation. If I had then opened my heart to some faithful Christian I might have been saved years of wandering in the wilderness of sin and unbelief. I wept and prayed in secret, and longed to be all given up to God and his work. At times my desire to be useful in the world, — a Bible Christian, set apart for the work of the Lord — was unutterable. I often felt the blessing of God and his approving smile, but failing to make the consecration I saw I must, and not consenting to be singular for Christ's sake, and unlike the mass of professing Christians, I did not retain long at a time a consciousness of pardon.[82]

Ellen's assurance not only of sanctification but also of justification slipped away. Though she "did not neglect the means of grace nor secret prayer," Ellen had little spiritual victory — yet she continued to experience "untold longing after God and his work."[83] This lack of spiritual victory continued into Ellen's early married years, though she maintained an active spiritual quest.

---

79. Ellen L. Roberts, "Religious Experience," p. 282.

80. From Charles Wesley's hymn "When Shall Thy Love Constrain?" The next line is, "I sink, by dying love compell'd."

81. Ellen L. Roberts, "Religious Experience," p. 282.

82. Ellen L. Roberts, "Religious Experience," pp. 282-83.

83. Ellen L. Roberts, "Religious Experience," p. 283.

Since there are no surviving diaries for 1846-47, the precise chronology of Ellen's "religious experience" as she recollected it in 1861 is uncertain. It is not clear whether the loss of "a consciousness of pardon" occurred in 1845 or during 1846 or 1847.[84] Her lack of a vital, steady sense of God's presence, however, continued for some years.

Who Was Ellen Stowe?

Who was this young woman, Ellen Lois Stowe? What was she like, in personality and character?

From her diary one could get the impression that Ellen was very serious, overly introspective, and not very social. But this would be misleading. True, many of Ellen's diary entries focus inward, for here, she said, she "recorded my feelings."[85] But the diary also gives hints of an active social life, a sometimes playful spirit, and a subtle sense of humor. Ellen seldom indulges these qualities in her diary; sometimes in fact she feels she is too lighthearted, not solemn enough. Her life in New York was a shifting pattern of joy and sadness; of spiritual growth and unfulfilled longing; of rich associations and a few close friendships; and of a sense of loss of the home and family she had left back in Windsor, along the sloping banks of the Susquehanna. In other words, hers was the normal life of a quiet, small-town girl plunged into the whirl of New York City and passing from an uncertain teenager to a mature young woman of twenty-four.[86]

There seemed to have been a sort of quiet charisma to Ellen, even in her early days — something she herself was likely unaware of. She was of medium height, with naturally wavy brown hair. Her wide-set blue eyes gave her a look of quiet, thoughtful charm. Physically she was quite attractive — certainly more so than her distant cousin, Harriet Beecher Stowe, if contemporary photographs are to be believed. She was introverted or "retiring" (to use the term of the time), loving to spend time alone. To some degree this reflected a Stowe family trait; Benson Roberts later said Ellen "sprang from a family not much given to talk, reserved, quiet people, more likely to be taciturn than to be talkative" — and likely to enjoy long life.[87]

Yet Ellen had many friends. Like most people of her temperament, she preferred intimate conversation with one or two friends over larger social gatherings. One friend, Samuel Howe, sent her a poem in which he said he wished he could "portray thy beauteous mien," and added,

---

84. An August 1846 letter from Lydia Lane to Ellen shows that Ellen spent some weeks that summer with her mother and family in Windsor. LBL (New York City) to ELS (Windsor), Aug. 26, 1846.

85. ELSD, Feb. 20, 1844.

86. At one point in the 1970s when it was proposed that Ellen's diaries be published, the Free Methodist publisher at the time reportedly dismissed them as "too introspective" for publication. Letter to the author from Louise Campbell, May 19, 1999.

87. BHR, "My Mother," *EC* 95, no. 3 (Mar. 1908): 71.

Why should you doubt, endowed with graces
That may with other fair ones vie.
Your figure's good! and your face is
Not without its sparkling eye.[88]

Mariet Hardy Freeland described Ellen in 1849 as "a lovely woman to look upon," "naturally retiring in her manner, but pleasant and cheerful," her hair "naturally waved and . . . put up in the French twist."[89] Many years later Ellen's granddaughter, Lois Ellen Roberts, reading Ellen's diaries and looking at her early daguerreotype photo, pictured Ellen as follows: "a beautiful girlish face, oval-shaped, with features delicately but firmly cut, the mouth, wonderfully sweet in expression, the broad, spiritual brow shaded by heavy waves of soft, brown hair, and eyes from whose clear, blue depths shone forth all the beauty of her soul."[90]

By 1848 Ellen was firmly committed to the Christian faith and the Methodist Episcopal Church, but she lacked the clear inner witness that she had experienced for a time. She kept following the Lord and continued faithful in the church, sensing a comforting measure of God's presence from time to time, as her diaries show (though her later testimony describes this period more negatively). Her spiritual struggle and lack of complete victory were in fact quite parallel to what Phoebe Palmer herself went through when about the same age, before her experience of entire sanctification.[91]

The main influences on Ellen's life at this time, beyond her close friends and her daily interaction with George and Lydia Lane, were the Methodist preachers she heard weekly and the women who were in effect her mentors. She frequently heard the "greats" among New York Methodist preachers, including Stephen Olin and Dr. Nathan Bangs. Bangs was the appointed preacher at Greene Street for two years (1844-46), during which time, in February 1845, Ellen began teaching Sunday school there. So Ellen heard Dr. Bangs almost every Sunday for over a year.

First among the women who touched Ellen's life (other than her aunt Lydia) was Phoebe Palmer. But they included also the poets Felicia Hemans and Elizabeth Barrett (soon to be Elizabeth Barrett Browning).

Ellen had repeated and frequent contact with Palmer from 1841 to 1849. She heard her speak in class and camp meetings, as noted above, and read her book *The Way of Holiness* shortly after it was published. She conversed with Palmer personally on one or two occasions, though they seem never to have developed a personal rela-

---

88. Letter from Samuel Howe to ELS, Oct. 1, 1840[?], quoted in Zahniser, p. 35.

89. Mrs. M. H. Freeland, tribute to Ellen Roberts in *EC* 95, no. 3 (Mar. 1908): 87, describing her recollections from 1849. Rev. J. B. Freeland, Mariet's husband, similarly described Ellen as "naturally timid and retiring," but also as "cultured and intellectual" and "a spiritual power in all departments of the work of God, frequently breaking through formalism and ecclesiastical proprieties." J. B. Freeland, tribute to Ellen Roberts in *EC* 95, no. 3 (Mar. 1908): 88-89.

90. Lois Ellen Roberts, "A Grand-Daughter's Tribute," *EC* 95, no. 3 (Mar. 1908): 93.

91. See Oden, *Phoebe Palmer*, pp. 59-60.

tionship. To Palmer, Ellen Stowe was probably just one of many young women she helped (Ellen was about seventeen when she first heard Palmer speak; Palmer was thirty-three), but to Ellen Palmer was, at this early time, truly a "Mother in Israel."

Poets, particularly Barrett and Hemans, were important to Ellen. Barrett was just becoming known, and Ellen read her *Poems* of 1844 shortly after they were published. Hemans's poetry was very popular at this time; there was then a sort of literary community of female poets that included Hemans, Barrett, the Connecticut poet Lydia Sigourney,[92] and others. One of these was "L. E. L.," the pen name of Letitia Elizabeth Landon, who had died in 1838 at the age of about thirty-six. In May 1845 Ellen was reading a biography of her. Both Barrett in her *Poems* and Hemans refer to "L. E. L." in inscriptions to their own poems.[93]

Clearly Ellen identified with these women who put into words the feelings of her own heart. She especially appreciated the depictions of nature in Hemans's and Barrett's poetry, and the sense of longing for far-off places. In a sense Ellen felt exiled in New York, and Barrett's "Drama of Exile" spoke to her heart. Hemans, "one of the most influential and widely read poets of the nineteenth century,"[94] similarly wrote poetry full of bittersweet sentiment and nostalgia; of exotic places and of "the domestic affections."[95] "Swept to a full height of popularity by a strong undercurrent of sentimentality that her own works helped to create, [Mrs. Hemans's] reputation reached a peak during the Victorian age," notes Peter Trinder, and then rapidly declined.[96]

Hemans's best-known work was her 1828 volume *Records of Woman*, in which new interest was sparked in the 1990s and which was recently reprinted.[97] In *Records of Woman* Hemans pictured women in traditional roles showing great strength of character. As Paula Feldman writes, Hemans's poems "document the courage, nobility, and tragedy of women's lives; embedded in their painful situations lies a critique of the domestic ideal." Her poetry "undercuts, even while it reinforces, conventional views of women. Placed in intensely trying situations, her heroines evince uncommon strength of character, courage, and nobility of spirit. They are determined, proud, and gutsy, not servile or helpless. Several, such as Joan of Arc, are leaders of men."[98]

92. Ellen comments on Lydia Sigourney, and on the June 28, 1845, excursion from Middletown to Hartford (mentioned above) visited "Mrs. Sigourney's place" (ELSD, June 28, 1845). Sigourney was sometimes called "the American Hemans."

93. See Barrett's poem "L. E. L.'s Last Question," and the inscription to Hemans's poem "The Sicilian Captive," which was among the poems in the volume of Hemans's poetry that Ellen read. "L. E. L." is identified in Hemans, *Records of Woman*, p. 188, and elsewhere.

94. Feldman in Hemans, *Records of Woman*, p. xi.

95. One of Hemans's books was *The Domestic Affections, and Other Poems*.

96. Peter W. Trinder, *Mrs. Hemans* (Cardiff: University of Wales Press, 1984), p. 2.

97. Hemans, *Records of Woman, with Other Poems*. Paula Feldman, the editor of this volume, notes that the rediscovery of Hemans's work has even sparked a lively Internet discussion and debate (pp. xiii, xxvii).

98. Feldman in Hemans, *Records of Woman*, pp. xviii, xx.

A central theme of Hemans's poetry is captured in the lines,

Alas! too deep, too fond, is woman's love.
Too full of hope, she casts on troubled waves
The treasures of her soul![99]

Hemans's was one of the voices Ellen especially listened to during her New York City days. Ellen felt that in Mrs. Hemans she had met a kindred spirit. How much fortitude she drew from the strong women Hemans depicted is hard to say. How much were her ideals of womanhood shaped by Hemans's litanies of women's courage in trying situations? In any case, Ellen often could identify with the strength and sentiment of Hemans's verses. She would later quote the poet's comment, "O how many deaths there are in the world for the affections!"[100]

Ellen repeatedly experienced such "deaths" — the breaking of home ties with her family in Windsor; her disappointment with Edmund Longley; the Middletown friends she made and missed. But her faith in God remained strong, and she soon would meet the one who would be her lifelong companion.

99. *Poetical Works of Mrs. Felicia Hemans*, p. 146 ("The Vespers of Palermo").

100. ELSD, July 2, 1848: "How many deaths there are for the affections." The quote is from an 1828 letter by Mrs. Hemans, not from her poetry. Ellen no doubt found it in the biography of Hemans that she read. See Feldman in Hemans, *Records of Woman*, pp. xxiii, xxix.

CHAPTER 8

Wesleyan University

"To have a well regulated, well balanced mind is of great worth. To gain it is my ambition."

B. T. Roberts, 1846[1]

"I am happier than I ever was before, for I enjoy more religion."

B. T. Roberts, 1846[2]

With a "Divine assurance . . . that God would keep [him] while [he] honestly sought to be better qualified for usefulness,"[3] B. T. Roberts made the 600-mile trip east to Middletown in the fall of 1845 to begin his college work. He was twenty-two and had finished his preparatory studies at Genesee Wesleyan Seminary and been licensed as a Methodist exhorter. Roberts would spend three years at Wesleyan University. He told his father, "I am resolved to make the interests of my soul of first importance, my bodily health second, and the improvement of my mind third."[4]

Benjamin's father Titus and sister Florilla accompanied him as far as New York City, a considerable adventure for them. There Benjamin bid farewell and took a steamboat up Long Island Sound and the Connecticut River to Middletown, the same route Ellen Stowe took several times.[5]

1. BTR to his sister Florilla, Nov. 16, 1846.
2. BTR to his sister, Jan. 20, 1846, from Middletown. Quoted in BHR, *BTR*, p. 18.
3. B. T. Roberts, "Rev. Loren Stiles," *EC* 16, no. 1 (July 1868): 6.
4. BTR to his sister, Sept. 5, 1845, in BHR, *BTR*, pp. 9-12.
5. Zahniser, p. 16.

This may not have been his first visit to the big city. Years later he recalled that in May 1845 he heard the great New England abolitionist orator Wendell Phillips speak at the annual American Anti-Slavery Society (AAS) meeting, held in New York's Broadway Tabernacle.[6] Though it is possible that Roberts misremembered the year — it might have been a later trip to New York; perhaps in 1849 — it is in character with his lifelong antislavery convictions that he would attend the meeting of the AAS[7] and be impressed by Phillips — "the most radical of the abolitionists," according to the *Cambridge Dictionary of American Biography*.[8] Roberts later recalled, "We shall never forget some of [Phillips's] telling utterances. In meeting the objection that the Constitution protected slavery, he said, 'No matter how honored may be that conspiracy against human rights which men denominate a constitution, I trample it under my feet and I call upon you to do the same.'"[9]

Phillips had come to this position in the years just prior to 1845, and in that year he published two tracts on the subject, *The Constitution a Pro-slavery Compact* and *Can Abolitionists Vote or Take Office under the United States Constitution?*[10]

Wesleyan University

Benjamin entered Wesleyan University as a sophomore[11] the first week in September 1845, joining a student body of about 120 men.[12] Just four weeks earlier, at a student-sponsored lecture following the 1845 commencement, Ralph Waldo Emerson had addressed the graduating class with a speech entitled "Function of a Scholar." President Stephen Olin, who disapproved of Emerson's transcendentalism

6. [B. T. Roberts], "Wendell Phillips," *EC* 47, no. 2 (Feb. 1884): 66. Phillips died Feb. 3, 1884; Roberts's editorial is a tribute to him and consists largely of an extract from the *New York Evening Post*. Phillips was active in the American Anti-Slavery Society all through this period; Roberts presumably could have heard him in 1845 or later.

7. As will be noted in chapter 11, we know that Roberts attended the meeting of the AAS at Broadway Tabernacle on May 8, 1849, and that Wendell Phillips spoke on that occasion. It is not clear, however, whether Benjamin heard Phillips both in 1845 and in 1849 or (if he misremembered the year) only in 1849. See Oscar Sherwin, *Prophet of Liberty: The Life and Times of Wendell Phillips* (New York: Bookman Associates, 1958), pp. 154-55, 689.

8. John S. Bowman, ed., *The Cambridge Dictionary of American Biography* (Cambridge: Cambridge University Press, 1995), p. 571.

9. [B. T. Roberts], "Wendell Phillips," p. 67.

10. Sherwin, *Prophet of Liberty*, pp. 148-49. The first pamphlet was published a couple of months before the May AAS meeting; the second was published anonymously.

11. The *Catalogue of the Officers and Students of the Wesleyan University, 1845-6* (Middletown, Conn.: W. D. Starr, 1845) lists Roberts as a freshman (p. 23), but he had enough credits to be a sophomore, and the following year is listed in the catalogue as a junior.

12. Total enrollment in the fall of 1845 was 119, and remained around 120 during the three years Roberts was there. David B. Potts, *Wesleyan University, 1831-1910: Collegiate Enterprise in New England* (New Haven: Yale University Press, 1992), p. 238.

and its "unfruitful speculations," sharply attacked Emerson's views in his baccalaureate sermon a few days before Emerson's arrival on campus.[13]

University classes began on Thursday, September 4, at 9:00 A.M. The next day Benjamin wrote a long letter to Florilla, describing the place and revealing much about his state of mind and his brotherly affection.

My Dear Sister:

The recollection that your daily prayers are ascending in unison to a throne of grace in my behalf, and the remembrance of the mercy of God in sparing my life, converting my soul, and calling me to the holy work of the ministry, and opening the way for my preparation to that sacred office, came to my relief, and banished, if not the sadness of my soul, at least all repining thoughts, and made me willing to acquiesce in the will of God. Much as I love learning for itself, greatly as I desire to become versed in human lore, nothing but clear convictions of duty, brought to my mind by Providential interferences in opening the way, can ever induce me to spend three years within these gloomy walls. . . .

Middletown is certainly, without exception, the pleasantest place I ever was in. It lies on the west bank of the Connecticut river, some thirty miles from its mouth, and sixteen miles below Hartford. The land from the river ascends back with a gradual and even rise. Some of the streets run parallel with the river, and these are intersected by others crossing them at right angles, thus forming some beautiful squares. The houses are all of them good, many of them very elegant and costly. I have not seen a poor dwelling in the place. Almost every house is surrounded by a large and well-cultivated garden, containing many choice fruit trees, and many situations have a fine, large yard in front filled with ornamental trees and shrubs. This gives the city an appearance of elegance and comfort. Did my friends reside here, I should think it a most delightful place. Did a sister's presence enliven my feelings, I might not think these college halls so gloomy and irksome. But why should I give vent, or even give way to such feelings? I know that the period has now arrived when we must be separated. The calls of duty are more imperious than the feelings of affection. We ought to feel "at home," ought to feel happy when pursuing the paths that our own conscience and the Spirit of God points [*sic*] out to us to walk in. And so I endeavor, so I trust, I shall be enabled by Grace Divine to feel. You are still permitted to enjoy the society of friends who love and cherish you. Love them, as you do, fervently in return. Suffer no opportunity of adding to their happiness to pass unimproved. Cultivate a cheerful temper, a smiling aspect, a habit of being pleased. Remember, we are all fast passing away, and at the hour of death we shall never regret the pains we may have taken to increase the happiness of others. Above everything else, live at the foot of the Cross;

13. Potts, *Wesleyan University*, pp. 60-61, 270; William Gravely, *Gilbert Haven, Methodist Abolitionist: A Study in Race, Religion, and Reform, 1850-1880* (Nashville: Abingdon, 1973), p. 22. See Stephen Olin, "Resources and Duties of Christian Young Men," in *The Works of Stephen Olin, D.D., LL.D., Late President of the Wesleyan University* (New York: Harper and Brothers, 1852), 2:125-62, hereafter Olin, *Works.*

maintain a nearness to the Throne of Grace. Make the Word of God your study, doing His will your chief delight; go often to the Fountain of Wisdom, and you will find fresh and continual supplies. And in your wrestling before the Throne, forget not the absent brother. And I, too, will endeavor, with all my weakness, with humility, to improve to the utmost the advantages with which I am blessed. I will strive to act in all things to the acceptance of my Heavenly Father and the approbation of my friends at home. I thank God that He ever enables me to remember you in my feeble supplications. And delightful to me are the seasons of prayer. Christ our Saviour is blessing a simple mortal with His love.[14]

Like other new students arriving in Middletown, Benjamin was delighted with the city but found the university "gloomy." One of his early friends at Wesleyan was John Ivanhoe Morrow from Paterson, New Jersey, an incoming freshman. Morrow told his friends back home, "The houses here are aristocratic; the college looks more like a prison than an institution of learning." Apparently Morrow's views didn't change much over the ensuing months; he left Wesleyan for good at the end of his freshman year.[15]

There was good reason for such aversion to the physical appearance of the campus because the university's two main buildings, North College and South College, were fairly nondescript structures built originally to serve a military academy located on the site before the Methodists acquired it in 1830.[16]

Middletown on the busy Connecticut River was a natural place for an aspiring new university. In the 1790s it was Connecticut's largest city, due largely to trade in rum, molasses, and slaves with the West Indies.[17] In 1792, "Main street stretched its quiet length . . . with its hatters, saddlers[,] apothecaries; its silversmiths, rope walks, and barbers; its taverns, slave markets and churches."[18] Before long, however, Middletown was overtaken by Hartford and New Haven. Yale College (not called Yale University until 1887) in New Haven was only thirty miles away. Though in 1831 Middletown was "a thrifty, pious, smug community with muddy streets, frame

14. BTR to his sister (presumably Florilla), Sept. 5, 1845, in BHR, *BTR*, pp. 9-12.

15. BTR to his sister (quoting Morrow), Sept. 5, 1845, in BHR, *BTR*, p. 10. Roberts simply says "my friend Morrow," but presumably this was John Morrow, who was about Roberts's age and, like Roberts, had probably just arrived in Middletown — though it could possibly have been John's brother Cornelius, a junior in 1845-46. Frank W. Nicolson, ed., *Alumni Record of Wesleyan University, Middletown, Conn.,* centennial (6th) ed. (Middletown, Conn.: Pelton and King, 1931), pp. 122, 130.

16. Carl F. Price, *Wesleyan's First Century with an Account of the Centennial Celebration* (Middletown, Conn.: Wesleyan University, 1932), pp. 19-27; W. H. Daniels, *The Illustrated History of Methodism in Great Britain and America, From the Days of the Wesleys to the Present Time* (New York: Methodist Book Concern, 1880), p. 555.

17. Potts, *Wesleyan University,* p. 2; Leta Pittman, "A Black Profile of Middletown, Connecticut," in *Black Perspectives on Middletown: A Collection of Writings about the Black Experience in Middletown, Connecticut,* ed. the Black Women's League of Middletown (Middletown, 1976), p. 3.

18. Earle Christie, "Impact of Early Ministers Was Great on Lives of Parishioners of Long Ago," *Middletown Press,* Tercentenary Supplement: *The Story of Middletown,* Sept. 9, 1950, p. 7.

houses, six churches," and a ferry, it had much natural beauty.[19] In fact, in 1717 it had briefly been considered as a possible location for Yale.[20] Passing through the area in the 1820s, President John Quincy Adams pronounced Middletown "the most beautiful" of Connecticut's towns, with its overarching elms and maples and its "stately mansions" on High Street.[21] It certainly charmed Ellen Stowe on her repeated summer visits from noisy Manhattan.

In choosing Wesleyan University, Benjamin Roberts was opting for the crown jewel of Methodist higher education at the time. "The first of the long list of Methodist colleges in America,"[22] Wesleyan was one of the early fruits of growing Methodist concern for higher learning. Its founding owed much to the influence of Dr. Willbur Fisk, its illustrious first president. In the 1820s Fisk had become the leading advocate for Methodist higher education. At the 1828 General Conference he chaired the Committee on Education, which called for establishing a college to meet the needs of young men graduating from the many new Methodist secondary schools. Although Fisk felt that colleges should be nonsectarian (and no "religious test" required of students or faculty, as the original Wesleyan University charter specified), he advocated high-quality Christian colleges that would maintain a vital religious environment. Failing this, he said, graduates would "depart from the University more learned, but frequently more corrupted, if not wholly ruined."[23] It was natural that the New York and New England Conferences, which cooperatively founded the new school, would turn to Fisk as its first president in 1831.[24]

Though sponsored jointly by New York and New England Methodists, Wesleyan University had especially close ties to New York City Methodism. Middletown was within the New York Conference, and its ministers who were connected with the university, including Stephen Olin and Joseph Holdich, were under conference appointment to the school.[25] Heman Bangs and Stephen Martindale, who had served churches in New York City, were part of the original committee that explored the possibility of founding Wesleyan University.[26]

There were many personal links to New York, as well. Professor Harvey Lane

---

19. Price, *Wesleyan's First Century,* p. 19.

20. Potts, *Wesleyan University,* p. 248.

21. Price, *Wesleyan's First Century,* pp. 19-20.

22. Daniels, *Illustrated History,* p. 555.

23. Price, *Wesleyan's First Century,* pp. 9-18.

24. According to Phoebe Palmer, Fisk enjoyed the blessing of holiness, or entire sanctification. See Phoebe Palmer, *The Way of Holiness, with Notes by the Way* (New York: G. Lane and C. B. Tippett, 1848), pp. 250-51.

25. For example, Olin and Holdich are listed in the 1845 minutes as under appointment to Wesleyan University (*Minutes* [1845], New York Conference, p. 579). Middletown became part of the New York East Conference when it was formed in 1849.

26. Price lists Heman Bangs and "S. Martindale" as members of the joint committee representing the New England and New York Conferences; Martindale at the time was a member of the New England Conference (and was the father of Mary Martindale, as noted in chapter 2). Price, *Wesleyan's First Century,* p. 24.

was the son of Methodist book agent George Lane, as already noted. One of Wesleyan's early graduates (1835), Harvey joined the Wesleyan faculty in 1839. He taught mathematics, natural philosophy, civil engineering, and later, Greek and Latin.[27]

The cost of a year at Wesleyan, excluding room and board, was about forty-two dollars during Roberts's time there. Room and board, if taken at the college, might run another fifty to sixty.[28] Most of the students covered part of their college expenses by teaching in area schools during the winter, especially during the eight-week vacation from early December to late January, and this was true of Roberts as well.[29] Students received about five dollars a week for this arduous labor while often lodging with neighboring families.[30]

The faculty consisted of five at this time, including Lane and Holdich. When classes were in session, the schedule was rigorous. "Students coming from families where they were 'brought up to work' followed a schedule of required chapel services, recitations, and study hours that filled each weekday from before sunrise until about nine in the evening."[31] With the other young men, Roberts filed into chapel each morning at 6:00, and perhaps welcomed the schedule change to 7:45 in March of his first year.[32] President Olin usually conducted the daily evening worship. Professor Holdich remarked especially on Olin's praying: "[H]is prayers on those occasions were a treat" and "had wonderful power in bringing other spirits with his own immediately before the mercy-seat. It was like talking to the Divinity."[33]

Though Wesleyan was a Methodist school, not all the students were Methodists or professing Christians. During these early years the number of "religious students" (self-avowed Christians) usually ranged between one-third and one-half of the student body, according to Holdich. As an ordained Methodist minister, Prof. Holdich was "the recognized pastor of the Wesleyan University," though students and faculty attended the local Methodist congregation where John Gilder was the appointed preacher in 1845-46.[34]

As a convinced abolitionist, Roberts was decidedly in the minority at Wesleyan. Among the handful of students who shared his views, however, was Gilbert Haven, later to become a Methodist bishop. Haven was a senior during Roberts's first year at

27. Price, *Wesleyan's First Century,* p. 64. "In 1861 he entered business in New York and at one time was editor of the famous *American Agriculturist* [*sic*]" (p. 64).

28. *Catalogue,* Wesleyan University, 1847-48, p. 22.

29. In the 1850s three-fourths of Wesleyan University students taught school in the winter to help pay expenses. Potts, *Wesleyan University,* p. 45.

30. The usual pay was five dollars per week in the 1840s and up to fifteen dollars in the 1850s. Potts, *Wesleyan University,* p. 263.

31. Potts, *Wesleyan University,* p. 45.

32. Price, *Wesleyan's First Century,* p. 79.

33. *The Life and Letters of Stephen Olin, D.D., LL.D., Late President of the Wesleyan University,* 2 vols. (New York: Harper and Brothers, 1853), 2:88, hereafter Olin, *Life and Letters.*

34. Joseph Holdich, letter to the editors, "Revival in The Wesleyan University," *Christian Advocate and Journal* 20, no. 33 (Mar. 25, 1846): 130; *Minutes of the Annual Conferences,* 1845, p. 577.

Wesleyan; at the end of the year he stood third in his graduating class and thus was assigned the prestigious philosophical oration at the 1846 commencement.[35]

Roberts's First Year at Wesleyan, 1845-46

Benjamin worked heartily at his studies throughout the fall term, which ran until December 3. He was assigned room 48, south section, in the dormitory.[36]

The course of study for the fall term for sophomores, heavy in Latin and Greek literature, was:

Plane Trigonometry, Navigation, Surveying, and Heights and Distances
One of Woolsey's Greek Tragedies
Agamemnon of Æschylus, begun
Captives of Plautus
Cicero *de Officiis*, begun
Latin Exercises

The winter and spring terms continued the same emphases:

Winter Term
Spherical Trigonometry
Analytical Geometry, begun
Agamemnon of Æschylus, finished
Demosthenis Orationes Philippicæ, begun
Greek Prose Composition
Cicero *de Officiis*, finished
Hercules Furens of Seneca

Spring Term
Analytical Geometry, finished
Demosthenis Orationes Philippicæ, finished
Tacitus, begun.[37]

As part of the set curriculum Roberts would also have had Monday morning recitations in Robinson's *Greek Harmony of the Gospels* and on alternate Saturdays "Compositions and Declamations."[38]

---

35. Gravely, *Gilbert Haven*, p. 22.
36. *Catalogue*, Wesleyan University, 1845-46, p. 23.
37. *Catalogue*, Wesleyan University, 1847-48, p. 18.
38. *Catalogue*, Wesleyan University, 1847-48, p. 18. Presumably Roberts took the standard sophomore course of studies, though some adjustment might have been made because of his transfer from Genesee Wesleyan Seminary.

Roberts enjoyed his studies and did very well. In a letter to his sister at the end of his first semester, he outlined his educational philosophy in words that echoed Olin's: "The grand object in studying is to discipline the mind, expand its faculties, and prepare it for grappling with and overcoming obstacles. Our object in studying is not so much the acquisition of useful, practical knowledge, as to fit ourselves for skillfully culling that knowledge in future not only from books, but from the common occurrences of every-day life. This grand desideratum will be better attained by completely mastering one branch of science than by curiously skipping over a score."[39]

This was precisely Olin's view, and the reigning philosophy at Wesleyan. Discipline of the mind was the central theme. In "Academic Teaching," an address he gave at the opening of Genesee Wesleyan Seminary in Lima, New York, in January 1843, Olin had said, "Mental discipline . . . is the fundamental principle, the *beau ideal* of education, on which both teacher and learner should fix a steadfast eye" — more important than specific knowledge gained.[40] Olin decried educational innovations in which education "instead of being mental discipline, is coming to mean a smattering of all sorts of knowledge" rather than grounding in the classical disciplines.[41] Benjamin concurred, and worked hard to apply it to himself.

Benjamin began teaching in a district school the first week in November, four weeks before the end of the fall term, in order to support himself. He started with fifty-six pupils, but the number grew as the weather turned colder. "Going to the school-house, I found that the walls had been white-washed, and the floor and seats scoured about as white as the walls," he wrote. "It looked much neater than I am accustomed to see district school-houses look." The scholars were neat, nearly all of them showing up promptly at 9:00 A.M.[42] Class ran from Monday morning through Saturday afternoon. His teaching went well, and Roberts used the opportunity also to spiritual advantage. On Thursday evening, January 15, he conducted a public evangelistic meeting in the schoolhouse, inviting the neighborhood to attend. "Our large school-room was filled, and a more attentive audience I never saw together. The Lord was with us, His presence was felt by all, a solemn seriousness was manifested by all. My soul longs to see a gracious effusion of the Spirit in this place, and immortal souls brought into the fold of Christ."[43]

Overall, Roberts was not much impressed with Connecticut's district schools. He found most of the simple buildings used in the rural schools to be "wretched

---

39. BTR to his sister, Dec. 20, 1845, quoted in BHR, *BTR*, p. 15, and Zahniser, p. 27.

40. Olin, *Works*, 2:314.

41. Olin, *Life and Letters*, 2:445. On the history of mental discipline as "the foundation for a superior education," a major concern at Yale and other places in the late 1820s, see Potts, *Wesleyan University*, pp. 18-19.

42. BHR, *BTR*, pp. 14-15.

43. BTR to his sister, in BHR, *BTR*, p. 18. Roberts does not specify the exact nature of this meeting or whether he preached, but he describes it in such a way as to suggest it was an evangelistic or revival service.

apologies" for schoolhouses. They were often located in some "triangular nook be-tween three roads," and the seats and benches within were usually "exquisite instru-ments of torture." He noted that in many school districts the "cider mills, distilleries and grog shops" were in much better shape. The teacher, "like a parasite, is obliged to board round" with area families, as Roberts did. Since the biggest expense in run-ning a school was the teacher's pay, some districts resorted to "letting him out to keep as they do their paupers, to the lowest bidder."[44]

Benjamin attended the Methodist services in Middletown on Sundays and at other times, and taught a young ladies Sunday school class there.[45] But by January 1846 he became involved also at the Cross Street African Methodist Episcopal Zion Church. This congregation had a building just west of the campus. Fiery, red-haired Gilbert Haven, a senior and a key leader among the handful of abolitionists on cam-pus, became head teacher in the Cross Street Church Sabbath school about this time, and perhaps recruited Roberts to help out.[46] Haven told his mother about his class of young black women and jested about intermarriage: "The class is a fine, large col-lection of ladies of various ages, colors, and faces. Some are handsome and some are not; of all shades, from the color of this ink to nearly that of this paper. I shouldn't wonder if I should bring one of them home with me next August as a bride."[47]

Roberts began teaching a girls class at the AME Zion church. The class met on Sunday afternoons. "I feel very much interested in" the young ladies, he wrote, "and strive and pray to be the means of doing them good. They are both attentive and in-telligent."[48] Benson Roberts comments, "He was already ardently enlisted in the cause of the slave," and this participation in a black church was "at some risk" since in these "days of anti-slavery agitation . . . to befriend a negro was to be branded an abolitionist and to become an outcast in many circles."[49] Benjamin wrote his sister that there was so much "of the slavery spirit even here among the descendants of the Puritans" that they were unwilling "to worship the Universal Father in the same tem-ple with their sable brethren," and thus there were "negro churches, negro preachers, presiding elders, and conference."[50]

Benson Roberts doesn't exaggerate in saying that such white student involvement with blacks was risky. Middletown counted very few abolitionists. Those citizens who theoretically opposed slavery and viewed it as an evil saw "colonization" as the answer

44. B. T. Roberts, "Connecticut," an essay quoted in Zahniser, pp. 24-26.

45. BHR, *BTR*, p. 17.

46. Linda Walton, "The Black Church in Middletown," in *Black Perspectives on Middletown*, pp. 23-24; Gravely, *Gilbert Haven*, pp. 22-25. Possibly Roberts was involved in the church before Haven was, however.

47. George Prentice, *The Life of Gilbert Haven, Bishop of the Methodist Episcopal Church* (New York: Phillips and Hunt, 1883), p. 70; Gravely, *Gilbert Haven*, p. 23.

48. BHR, *BTR*, p. 17. The sources on Roberts do not identify the "African Church" that Benjamin participated in, but the information in Gravely, Pittman, and Walton make it clear that it was the Cross Street AME Zion Church.

49. BHR, *BTR*, pp. 16-17.

50. BHR, *BTR*, p. 17.

— freeing the slaves gradually and sending them "back" to Africa. This was the position of Wesleyan's first president, Fisk, who upon coming to Middletown in 1831 supported the colonizationist cause there. In an Independence Day address in 1835 he celebrated the fact that the local colonization society was "the earliest in Connecticut, if not in New England." "African Colonization," he argued, "is predicated on the principle that there is an utter aversion in the public mind, to an amalgamation and equalization of the two races." Colonization therefore "lifts up the man of color . . . and places him beyond the influence of the shackles of prejudice."[51]

Like Fisk, most Methodist opponents of slavery were "colonizationists," not abolitionists (whom many prominent Methodists viewed as radicals and "ultras"). Fisk, "the most respected and outstanding colonizationist in the Methodist Episcopal Church,"[52] thus represented the dominant view among Wesleyan's faculty, students, and trustees. Fisk argued that the American Colonization Society had "indirectly liberated more slaves, probably, than all the anti-slavery societies" in America and "by a successful experiment [of transporting freed slaves to Liberia], makes fair promise of giving to the world a convincing and extended exhibition of negro elevation, moral, intellectual, and social"[53] (and, of course, safely away from any possible "amalgamation and equalization" in America). Fisk felt that "high-wrought emotion" had led the abolitionists astray and threatened to divide both church and nation.[54]

Abolitionism was particularly disdained in Middletown, whose thriving textile industry in the 1830s depended on Southern cotton.[55] Due primarily to the earlier slave trade, Middletown had a black population almost from its beginning in the mid-1600s and was known as "one of the most lucrative slave trading posts in Connecticut." Some of its leading families traced their wealth to the slave trade. In the 1700s Middletown had twenty or more sea captains, and about a third of these were involved in the slave trade.[56]

When Roberts arrived in Middletown, the town had a black population of about two hundred.[57] The Cross Street AME Zion Church, possibly the first black Methodist church in New England, had been organized in 1828, just three years before the founding of Wesleyan University.[58] Jehiel Beman pastored the church from

51. Horatio T. Strother, *The Underground Railroad in Connecticut* (Middletown, Conn.: Wesleyan University Press, 1962), pp. 37, 153; cf. Pittman, "Black Profile," p. 7.

52. Donald G. Matthews, *Slavery and Methodism: A Chapter in American Morality, 1780-1845* (Princeton: Princeton University Press, 1965), p. 106.

53. Joseph Holdich, *The Life of Willbur Fisk, D.D., First President of the Wesleyan University* (New York: Harper and Brothers, 1842), p. 330.

54. Holdich, *Fisk*, p. 403.

55. Pittman, "Black Profile," pp. 8-9; Strother, *Underground Railroad in Connecticut*, p. 86; Peter Hall, *Middletown: Streets, Commerce, and People, 1650-1981*, Sesquicentennial Papers no. 8 (Middletown, Conn.: Wesleyan University, 1981), p. 25.

56. Pittman, "Black Profile," pp. 1-3.

57. Pittman, "Black Profile," pp. 7, 11; Walton, "Black Church in Middletown," p. 29.

58. Walton, "Black Church in Middletown," pp. 23-24.

1831 until about 1848. His father, a former slave, had chosen the name Beman because he wanted to "Be a man," not someone's property. He and his wife Clarissa were both active abolitionists; Mrs. Beman organized the Colored Female Anti-Slavery Society in Middletown in 1834, said to be only the second women's abolition society in the country.[59] Touring Connecticut in the 1840s, William Lloyd Garrison (who had founded the *Liberator* in 1831) was entertained by the Bemans.[60]

Middletown's small band of black Christian abolitionists was harassed and sometimes mobbed both for their skin color and for their antislavery activities. In general, "Middletown's Negroes found comparatively few of the citizens who cared in the least about their welfare. In fact, the temper of the city was predominantly sympathetic to slavery and opposed to abolition or anything that smacked of it." In 1831 a Middletown editor, denouncing Garrison, lamented the blight of slavery but said slaves could not simply be freed because they "know not the value of liberty . . . and any external interference, while it has no influence in meliorating their condition, exasperates their masters, and weakens our bond of Union."[61]

While the few abolitionist students at Wesleyan sympathized with blacks and helped out at the Cross Street Church, antiblack feeling was strong at the school, especially during these early days of the abolitionist movement. The enrollment of a black student, Charles Ray, in 1832 raised such student protest that the university's Joint Board voted in October of that year that "none but White male persons shall be admitted as students."[62] Though this action was rescinded in 1835, in practice blacks were unwelcome at Wesleyan until well after the Civil War. The controversy brought widespread criticism of Wesleyan in the abolitionist press; the school "gained national notoriety for being anti-abolitionist and openly excluding Blacks."[63] Garrison denounced the university in the pages of the *Liberator*.[64]

Amos Beman, son of the Cross Street Church's pastor, wanted to attend Wesleyan in 1833 but couldn't because of the school's all-white policy. However, a sympathetic Wesleyan freshman, Sam Dole, offered to tutor Amos privately. For a while Amos went to Dole's room three times weekly, though harassed and called names by other Wesleyan students.[65] He was undeterred by the hostility until he received a threatening letter on October 5, 1833:

59. Strother, *Underground Railroad in Connecticut*, pp. 153-54; Pittman, "Black Profile," p. 7; Walton, "Black Church in Middletown," pp. 26-27.

60. Walton, "Black Church in Middletown," p. 27; Strother, *Underground Railroad in Connecticut*, p. 154.

61. Strother, *Underground Railroad in Connecticut*, p. 153.

62. Price, *Wesleyan's First Century*, p. 50; Janet Franklin and Valerie Hazelton, "Wesleyan's Impact and Image in the Black Community," in *Black Perspectives on Middletown*, p. 72.

63. Franklin and Hazelton, "Wesleyan's Impact," p. 71.

64. Potts, *Wesleyan University*, pp. 54, 267. See the *Liberator*, Jan. 12 and 26, and Nov. 2, 1833.

65. Strother (based on the Beman papers at Yale University) says Beman was tutored by Dole for six months, but it seems more likely it was about six weeks, as Dole enrolled at Wesleyan, apparently, at the beginning of September 1833 and left at the end of the semester. Strother, *Underground Railroad in Connecticut*, p. 154; Nicolson, *Alumni Record* (1931), p. 85.

To Beman, Junior:

Young Beman: — A number of students of this University deeming it deroga-
tory to themselves, as well as to the University, to have you and other colored students recite here, do hereby warn you to desist from such a course; and if you fail
to comply with this peaceable request, we swear, by the Eternal God, that we will
resort to forcible means to put a stop to it.

Twelve of Us[66]

Amos took the threat seriously and left Middletown — as did his tutor, Dole,
abandoning his studies at the university.[67] Amos went on to become a well-known
minister and abolitionist leader.[68] This incident occurred twelve years before
Benjamin Roberts came to Middletown, but Roberts may have met Amos when he
visited his parents there.

While Roberts was at Wesleyan, Middletown was part of the network for runaway slaves that became famous as the Underground Railroad. Jesse Baldwin, a
successful businessman who moved to Middletown in 1833, was an active abolitionist and occasional "conductor" on the railroad. Two ships of his, built in 1848,
were thought to have carried fugitive slaves along with their regular cargoes.
Baldwin was the chief benefactor of the Middletown Anti-Slavery Society, which
he helped organize in 1834. In October 1837 the group met at the First Methodist
Episcopal Church and adopted resolutions declaring slavery to be opposed both to
Scripture and to the Methodist tradition. They resolved: "That the great and rapidly increasing number of slave holders in the M.E. Church is cause of grief and
alarm," and called upon "every friend of the purity and prosperity of the Church
to raise their united voices in remonstrance against it and their persevering efforts
for its overthrow."[69]

Very few from the Wesleyan University community were involved with the
Anti-Slavery Society, but at least one student was: Richard S. Rust. In 1839, while a
sophomore at Wesleyan, Rust pledged three dollars monthly to the society. Rust
graduated from Wesleyan in 1841, became a Methodist minister, and after the Civil
War served as secretary for the Freedman's Aid Society of the ME Church.[70] People

66. Strother, *Underground Railroad in Connecticut*, p. 155.

67. Strother, *Underground Railroad in Connecticut*, p. 155. It was Dole who reported to Garrison's
Liberator the ill treatment Charles Ray received when he tried to enroll at Wesleyan.

68. Strother, *Underground Railroad in Connecticut*, p. 155; Pittman, "Black Profile," pp. 27-28;
Franklin and Hazelton, "Wesleyan's Impact," pp. 72-74; Potts, *Wesleyan University*, pp. 54, 267; Henry
Mayer, *All on Fire: William Lloyd Garrison and the Abolition of Slavery* (New York: St. Martin's Press,
1998), pp. 138, 647. Charles Ray also became a prominent black leader and abolitionist. On the Beman
family and Ray, see the many references in David E. Swift, *Black Prophets of Justice: Activist Clergy before the Civil War* (Baton Rouge: Louisiana State University Press, 1989).

69. Strother, *Underground Railroad in Connecticut*, pp. 137, 156-59.

70. Strother, *Underground Railroad in Connecticut*, p. 158; Nicolson, *Alumni Record* (1931), p. 100;
COM, p. 770.

like Rust, Haven, and the various Wesleyan students who helped out in the AME Zion church had thus set a precedent for Roberts's own abolitionism at Wesleyan, but they represented a distinct minority within the university community.

With his studies, teaching, and helping at the AME Zion congregation, Benjamin had his hands full during the 1845-46 school year. When the fall term ended on December 3, he had already been teaching in the district school for four and a half weeks. The winter term began Thursday, January 29. A week earlier he wrote his sister, "[H]aving charge of a school of seventy scholars, and studying to keep up with my class in college, and reading and leading class-meeting one evening, and prayer-meeting another evening in the week, with two Bible-classes [at the ME and AME Zion churches], and boarding around from house to house, affords me quite constant employment."[71]

Benjamin asked his sister's prayers "that I may act well my part as a Christian, discharge every duty to the acceptance of my Heavenly Father." He added, "I am happier than I ever was before, for I enjoy more religion."[72] "I have proven by experience the truth of that quotation, found in the excellent little treatise, 'Watts on the Mind,' '*orasse est bene studiesse*' — 'praying is the best studying.' When my heart is often lifted up to God in secret prayer I meet with the greatest success studying. When I am happy in Christ my mind acts with vigor."[73]

Benjamin wrapped up his teaching probably about the end of January. When the winter term got under way, he was back on campus, ready to again immerse himself in his studies.

---

71. BTR to his sister, Jan. 20, 1846; BHR, *BTR,* p. 19.
72. BTR to his sister, Jan. 20, 1846; BHR, *BTR,* p. 18.
73. BTR to his sister, Nov. 23, 1845; BHR, *BTR,* p. 14.

CHAPTER 9

Stephen Olin and the Life of the Mind

"We never knew a professor or president half so idolized by his students, one-half so fitted to impress the great lineaments of his own character on the susceptible minds of young men."

Bishop William Wightman[1]

"The world is to be evangelized before another generation shall perish."

Stephen Olin, 1835[2]

President Stephen Olin (1797-1851) was the dominant figure at Wesleyan University during Roberts's time there. Olin headed the university from 1842 until his premature death in 1851. Roberts's three years at Wesleyan covered the middle third of Olin's nine-year tenure. Olin struggled all his adult life with illness, but his Wesleyan presidency was "the most productive nine years of [his] career."[3]

1. Quoted in Albert Deems Betts, *History of South Carolina Methodism* (Columbia, S.C.: Advocate Press, 1952), p. 298.

2. Stephen Olin, "Duties of the Church — Missions," *Christian Advocate and Journal* 9, no. 23 (Jan. 30, 1835): 89.

3. Carl F. Price, *Wesleyan's First Century with an Account of the Centennial Celebration* (Middletown, Conn.: Wesleyan University, 1932), p. 76. Olin died in Middletown (of typhoid fever, according to David B. Potts, *Wesleyan University, 1831-1910: Collegiate Enterprise in New England* [New Haven: Yale University Press, 1992], p. 28) on Aug. 16, 1851, two weeks after his younger son, James Lynch, died of dysentery. Within three years of his death Harper and Brothers in New York published his *Works* and his *Life and Letters* in matching two-volume sets edited by Julia Olin, his widow. Not long after Olin's death, a spiritualist published a book claiming to be from Olin! *Methodist Quarterly Review* 35 (Oct. 1853): 601.

Olin was impressive in both ability and appearance; "his intellectual proportions, like his physical, were colossal."[4] Over six feet tall, his head was so large that he had to have hats made to order.[5] John Quincy Adams, hearing him preach before the U.S. House of Representatives in January 1845, described Olin as "framed for a ploughman or a wood cutter with an anxious, deeply thoughtful, not unpleasing countenance, sprawling limbs and great awkwardness of gesticulation. But he preaches without notes, with uninterrupted fluency, plain but very appropriate language, close argument, well-chosen and at times elegant elocution." His audience was "chained in attention for an hour and a quarter."[6] Olin spoke rapidly but distinctly, and generally amazed his audience by his eloquent torrent of words.[7] Hearing him preach was "like standing under Niagara," one listener remarked. Another described Olin's preaching as "argument and sentiment, emotion and burning words — rolling and thundering, and fused together like lava down a mountain side."[8]

Olin had a pronounced influence on Benjamin Roberts.[9] A comprehension of Olin the man, the Methodist, and the scholar helps one understand Roberts's own later ministry. Olin's story and his assessment of Methodism also illuminate the context in which Roberts ministered and in which the Free Methodist Church came to be.

Olin's Methodist Formation

Stephen Olin was born in 1797 in Leicester, Vermont, the son of a state supreme court justice. Like Roberts, he briefly studied law before entering the Methodist ministry.[10] Olin graduated from Vermont's Middlebury College with top honors in 1820,[11] but without personal faith in Jesus Christ. In fact, his intellectual questioning gave him a rather inaccurate reputation as an atheist.

Though a New Englander, Olin spent several years in the South, gaining considerable sympathy with Southern ways and views. His Southern exposure gave him more the aspect of a Dixie gentleman than of a Northern reformer. After a couple of years in the South he wrote, "I am much reconciled to Southern life. The little invec-

---

4. John McClintock, "Stephen Olin," *Methodist Quarterly Review* 36 (Jan. 1854): 12. McClintock (later the president of Drew University) was editor of the *Quarterly Review* at this time.

5. Price, *Wesleyan's First Century,* p. 74.

6. Quoted in Potts, *Wesleyan University,* pp. 25, 27.

7. Price, *Wesleyan's First Century,* p. 74.

8. *The Life and Letters of Stephen Olin, D.D., LL.D., Late President of the Wesleyan University,* 2 vols. (New York: Harper and Brothers, 1853), 2:104, 1:98, hereafter Olin, *Life and Letters.*

9. A measure of Olin's influence within the Methodism of his day is the fact that a "host" of Methodists "honored him by naming their sons for him." Betts, *South Carolina Methodism,* pp. 187, 298.

10. Price, *Wesleyan's First Century,* p. 73.

11. Potts, *Wesleyan University,* p. 27.

tives in which my Northern friends sometimes indulge wound me almost as much as if I had been born in Carolina."[12]

It was in the South that Olin was converted and became a Methodist preacher. In November 1820 he became principal of Tabernacle Academy in Abbeville, South Carolina, near the Georgia border. "Here he fought out the battle of his religious difficulties, and emerged with a radiant Christian experience" that "at once altered the whole course of Olin's life."[13] Through the influence of James Glenn, a remarkable Methodist local preacher in whose home Olin boarded, Olin came under conviction and was clearly converted on September 20, 1821, three weeks before Charles Finney's conversion.[14] He wrote, "It was a glorious moment — a happy moment! I passed from hell to paradise! I was filled with speechless exultation, and a considerable time elapsed before I could believe that I was in my right mind. Blessed be God! I still feel the sacred flame glowing within me." His conversion "fully convinced me of the truth of the doctrine of a particular Providence, which I did not formerly believe."[15] Under his influence Tabernacle Academy twice experienced a powerful "outpouring of the Spirit" in which many students were converted.[16]

After his conversion Olin initially thought he would become an Episcopalian. The Episcopal Church was "on the whole, more congenial in principle and practice with my feelings and opinions" and less tainted with the "peculiarities" of the Methodists, he thought.[17] But a year later Olin wrote to a friend, "I have become a Methodist in good earnest, and shall never quit them for the Episcopalians. My prejudices have gradually melted away, and, though I still see some things that I deem extravagant, I believe that . . . there is more of the power of godliness among them than any other people."[18] "The humiliations, the labors, the poverty, the reproaches" of Methodist ministry "do not terrify me," he wrote a friend.[19]

Olin now decided definitely to give up law and to cast his lot among the Methodists. He wrote to his father, "You already know that I am a Methodist preacher. My life has taken an unlooked-for direction. With it, however, I am more than content, and only regret that my weak lungs are likely to keep me out of the itinerancy — a field of action in which I have a great desire to be engaged."[20]

Olin joined the South Carolina Conference in 1824 and was appointed to Charleston. Ill health forced him to give that up six months later, however, and he returned to Vermont. He was ordained deacon in 1826, but due to continued ill health he finally abandoned pastoral ministry (always his first love).

---

12. Olin, *Life and Letters*, 1:49.
13. Price, *Wesleyan's First Century*, p. 73.
14. Olin, *Life and Letters*, 1:42-45, 63, 67, 84; Betts, *South Carolina Methodism*, pp. 174-75.
15. SO to Charles D. Mallory, Dec. 14, 1821, Olin, *Life and Letters*, 1:63.
16. Olin, *Life and Letters*, 1:71; cf. 1:82, 87.
17. Olin, *Life and Letters*, 1:77-78.
18. SO to J. Merriam, Sept. 19, 1822, Olin, *Life and Letters*, 1:73.
19. SO to Charles Mallory, Sept. 26, 1822, Olin, *Life and Letters*, 1:78.
20. Olin, *Life and Letters*, 1:45-46.

Olin's time in Charleston, though brief, was fruitful. He shared with another Methodist preacher the responsibility for Charleston's four Methodist congregations. He wrote in June 1824, "God's Spirit has been poured out upon us, and during the last three months we have received between forty and fifty white persons, and about two hundred colored into our Church. . . . I feel my heart especially drawn out toward" the blacks.[21]

Olin became acquainted with James O. Andrew, Methodist pastor and presiding elder (and later bishop), also living in Charleston. The two became fast friends. Olin sometimes accompanied Andrew on horseback as he visited the churches in his district, and during several months of illness he stayed with the Andrews and was cared for by Mrs. Andrew. After he went north, Olin kept in touch with Bishop Andrew by letter.[22]

Forced to give up pastoral ministry, Olin concluded that God wanted him to serve as an educator. He was appointed professor of ethics and belles lettres at the University of Georgia in Athens in 1826. The same year he married Mary Ann Bostick, "a distinguished belle" from Milledgeville, Georgia, who had recently been converted and who years earlier, as a child, had been influenced toward Christ by the young James Andrew. Olin was ordained elder in 1828.[23]

Revivals stirred Georgia Methodism during Olin's time there, as Olin notes in his correspondence. In a letter to Charles Mallory in January 1827, Olin writes, "You have probably heard of the great revival in Washington, Wilkes county, Georgia. I have never witnessed such a scene before. About one hundred persons are professed converts in that place, and only two or three persons in the town are left unconcerned. This has been a glorious year for many parts of Georgia. What is singular, the subjects or the work are generally the first in their wealth and standing in the community."[24]

After teaching seven years at the University of Georgia, Olin became in 1834 the first president of Randolph-Macon College, a school founded by Virginia Methodists in 1832. The college prospered under Olin's leadership. Poor health forced him to give up this position after only three years, but his scholarly reputation grew steadily.[25] In 1834 Middlebury College (his alma mater), Wesleyan University, and the University of Alabama all honored him with doctor of divinity degrees, and a year later Yale conferred on him the honorary doctor of laws degree.[26]

---

21. Olin, *Life and Letters,* 1:104. Olin wrote later of this period, "The few months which I was permitted to spend in the ministry in early life were much devoted to an immense congregation of slaves. I mingled freely in their religious meetings and exercises" (1:104).

22. Olin, *Life and Letters,* 1:99-100, 2:169.

23. Price, *Wesleyan's First Century,* p. 75; Potts, *Wesleyan University,* p. 27; COM, p. 680; Olin, *Life and Letters,* 1:92-94, 137-41, 260. At the time of Olin's appointment the school was called Franklin College (named after Benjamin Franklin); it later became the University of Georgia.

24. Olin, *Life and Letters,* 1:138.

25. Potts, *Wesleyan University,* p. 27.

26. Price, *Wesleyan's First Century,* p. 76; Olin, *Life and Letters,* 1:164, 2:101. Price gives 1832 as the year of the Middlebury honorary degree.

When he married, Olin unwittingly became a slave owner. Though details are sketchy, he apparently did not manumit (free) his slaves but rather adapted to the system while in the South. One writer notes that Olin's involvement with slavery

> was to the last of his life, a source of no little uneasiness; . . . he was "not able to feel that he did wrong," but at the same time not satisfied that he had done right; for, under the influence of the prevailing customs, he had been induced both to buy and to sell his fellow-men. "All this," says he, "I have prayerfully reviewed many, many times, and with emotions not to be described, yet have I not been able to feel that I sinned in being the owner of slaves. Yet I the more humbly and patiently endure reproach from a feeling that I may have misjudged in this business."[27]

Olin sold his slaves at some point before assuming the presidency of Wesleyan University in 1842. Later, at the 1844 General Conference in New York City, where Olin was torn between North and South over his friend Bishop James Andrew's case, he freely admitted his slaveholding and gave his perspective. He could not agree with the abolitionists — they were extreme and divisive and moved more by outside influences than by true Methodist convictions, he felt.

Olin ended up voting with the General Conference majority in its request that Bishop Andrew withdraw from the episcopacy because of his slaveholding, but he had great sympathy for his old friend and thought he had done no wrong. Thus Olin managed to alienate friends in both North and South.[28] In his speech before the General Conference he argued that the denomination had no disciplinary restriction against bishops holding slaves and noted that most U.S. presidents to date had been slaveholders. "I believe we are all prepared to recognize the right of Southern brethren to hold slaves under the provision of the Discipline."[29] He added,

> I here declare that if I ever saw the graces of the Christian ministry displayed or its virtues developed, it has been among slaveholders. . . . I would not conceal — I avow that I was a slaveholder, and a minister at the South, and I never dreamed that my right to the ministry was questionable, or that in the sight of God I was less fitted to preach the Gospel on that account. And if the state of my health had not driven me away from that region, I should probably have been a slaveholder to this day. . . . I do not believe the slave fares worse for having a Christian master.[30]

Olin explained his views on abolitionism: "I have never thought it a good thing to introduce agitation into the Church. . . . The New York Conference . . .

---

27. John McClintock, ed., *Sketches of Eminent Methodist Ministers* (New York: Carlton and Phillips, 1854), p. 338.

28. The night before the vote Olin visited Bishop Andrew and explained his dilemma and his decision — the lesser of two evils, as he saw it. Betts, *South Carolina Methodism*, p. 276.

29. Olin, *Life and Letters*, 2:164, 167.

30. Olin, *Life and Letters*, 2:168-69.

was never an abolition Conference," and in fact suspended "some young preachers" for their abolitionist activities. A number of "Northern Conferences have firmly opposed the abolition movement." Most Northern Methodists "regard slavery as a great evil, though not necessarily a sin"[31] — a sentiment with which Olin apparently agreed.

Olin wrote to his wife on June 5, "The South, in effect, declined all compromise; they thought they could bear none. I think, as I all along have thought, that we shall be compelled to divide."[32]

Olin's View of Methodism

In late 1834 and early 1835, shortly after beginning his presidency at Randolph-Macon College, Olin published a series of articles in the (New York) *Christian Advocate and Journal* in which he discussed "the condition, prospects, wants, and duties of the Methodist Episcopal Church."[33] Among Methodism's "delinquencies" he cited its relative ineffectiveness in Bible and tract distribution, though he said nothing about slaveholding.

Olin's first article, "The Obligations of the Church," scolded the denomination for being "positively deficient in missionary zeal" and in general in its ministry to society, despite having over 600,000 members. Olin felt the ME Church lacked "vigorous and well directed efforts . . . [for] the prosecution of those comprehensive and enlightened plans of Christian benevolence which aim at the improvement, the extension, and the final and speedy triumph of the Redeemer's kingdom."[34]

Olin's second article spoke of Methodism's calling to exert "efficient influence in the promotion of enlightened and saving piety in this great country, and in carrying the Gospel to the heathen world." Methodism's concern should be "the happiness and salvation of the human race." Methodism possessed great resources that, if "properly directed," could "accomplish the noblest objects of Christian benevolence" in the interests of God's kingdom. The ME Church should be engaged effectively "in the work of evangelizing the world." The task of Methodism was to "promote the great objects of Christianity — personal holiness and the salvation of the species."[35]

31. Olin, *Life and Letters*, 2:173-74.

32. Olin, *Life and Letters*, 2:169.

33. Olin, *Life and Letters*, 1:164. For earlier and later expressions of Olin's views, see Stephen Olin, "An Address Delivered at the anniversary meeting of the South-Carolina Conference Missionary Society, in Charleston, January, 1824," *Methodist Magazine* 7 (Aug. 1824): 301-10, and [Stephen Olin], "Religious Training," *Methodist Quarterly Review* 31 (Apr. 1849): 303-31.

34. Stephen Olin, "The Obligations of the Church," *Christian Advocate and Journal* 9, no. 14 (Nov. 28, 1834): 53.

35. Stephen Olin, "Obligations and Resources of the Church," *Christian Advocate and Journal* 9, no. 17 (Dec. 19, 1834): 67.

In his third article, "Duties and Delinquencies of the Church," Olin wrote:

The spirit of the Gospel is essentially aggressive. Perfection is the Christian's goal, and he knows no resting place but heaven. Christ is a "prince" and a "conqueror." He is "straitened" and will not be "satisfied," until he "see the travail of his soul," until "the heathen become his inheritance, and the uttermost parts of the earth his possession." In proportion as the Church has the spirit of Christ, . . . it will chiefly value internal strength and prosperity as they may be made the instruments of subjecting other individuals and other nations of this revolted world to their rightful potentate. The great purpose of the Christian dispensation, and the objects of Christian duty, are summarily expressed in Titus ii, 14: "Who gave himself for us, *that he might redeem us from all iniquity,* AND PURIFY TO HIMSELF A PECULIAR PEOPLE, ZEALOUS OF GOOD WORKS." Our own safety requires that we be holy. "Our heavenly Father is glorified if we bear much fruit." . . . Benevolence, gratitude to God, "the love of Christ, constrain us" to seek the conversion of the world. . . . The man who has learned to care for his own soul will be anxious for the salvation of others. The missionary zeal of a Church is commonly a true index of its spiritual condition.[36]

Olin's fourth article was entitled "Duties of the Church — Tracts, Sunday Schools." Here Olin noted the good work being done but called for more successful efforts. For lack of effective educational enterprises, Olin argued, Methodism was losing some of its most promising youth — "often the children of our most useful and respectable members." He added, "It is our glory as well as our duty to preach the Gospel to the poor; yet God has been pleased to mingle together in society the unlettered and the learned, the poor and the rich, and that Church is the strongest and readiest for every good work in which these elements, sanctified by grace, are combined."[37]

Olin focused on missions in his fifth article. "The great enterprise of 'preaching the Gospel to every creature'" has often been neglected by the Christian church. Yet "The spirit of the Gospel is essentially missionary"; the "primitive Church was little else than a missionary camp." "The missionary enterprise" is "the conspicuous theatre for the exhibition of our love and loyalty to Christ," calling Christians "to merge self and selfish ends in the higher interests of the Redeemer's glory and the world's salvation."[38]

Olin noted that the Methodist itinerancy is itself "a missionary system." "What by other Churches are denominated domestic missions, constitute, to a large extent, the regular field of labor of the Methodist ministry in the new states and territories."

---

36. Stephen Olin, "Duties and Delinquencies of the Church," *Christian Advocate and Journal* 9, no. 21 (Jan. 16, 1835): 81.

37. Stephen Olin, "Duties of the Church — Tracts, Sunday Schools," *Christian Advocate and Journal* 9, no. 22 (Jan. 23, 1835): 85.

38. Olin, "Missions," p. 89.

He noted that "The conversion of the slaves has likewise been effected by the ordinary operation of the [itinerant] system."[39]

Like Methodist John R. Mott half a century later, Olin was confident that the task of world evangelization could be completed in short order if the church were properly mobilized. "Judging of the probabilities of the future from past experience, no sober-minded Christian . . . can doubt that [with sufficient prayer and mobilization] the world may be converted in thirty years. Ten years would suffice for the establishment of schools and churches, and for the translation of the Scriptures into every human dialect. . . . Fifteen or twenty years would raise up a native ministry . . . fully competent to do whatever might remain to be done toward uprooting idolatry and subjugating the nations to Christ."

In terms remarkably similar to the famous "watchword" of the Student Volunteer Movement fifty years later, Olin wrote: *The Church must familiarize itself with the stupendous apprehension that the world is to be evangelized before another generation shall perish.*[40] To this end the ME Church must devise workable plans and deploy the necessary resources.

In his final article, "Wants and Duties of the Church," Olin recognized that Methodism might not be up to such a task. He quoted Bishop William McKendree: "There are now symptoms of spiritual decay abroad. The love of the world. The work of the Lord is not now attended to. Discipline is neglected. The classes are not watched over by the preachers. The standard of holiness is not raised." Olin felt that "while as a denomination we neglect our duties, no extensive religious improvement may be expected." He called therefore for "speedy reformation." How? Olin had a specific proposal:

> If each conference would appoint one or a few preachers, chosen with strict reference to qualifications, to travel at large throughout their boundaries, to arouse the ministry and its membership, to diffuse the missionary spirit, and aid the preachers in the formation of Sunday schools, and of missionary, Bible and tract societies, it would be the dawning of a new era. If, in addition . . . , one or two general secretaries were appointed, who should devote their time to the correspondence and other interests of the parent societies in New-York, and to visiting the annual conferences and principal stations, . . . it is reasonable to conclude that the fruits of our benevolent exertions would be doubled in a single year.

Olin added that key to any such "speedy reformation" would be substantial increase in the number of genuinely called and adequately trained preachers.[41]

Over the next few years Olin continued to urge the priority of evangelism. In 1839 he wrote to Nathan Bangs,

39. Olin, *Life and Letters,* 1:172-73.
40. Olin, "Missions," p. 89.
41. Stephen Olin, "Wants and Duties of the Church," *Christian Advocate and Journal* 9, no. 24 (Feb. 6, 1835): 93.

I think it is the first duty of our Church to be more zealous and diligent in saving souls. This is its proper work; and in proportion as it is lost sight of, the Church will become useless. Let us remember that Christ died, not primarily to establish schools and colleges, and Bible and missionary societies, but to save souls from hell. . . . We are bound before God, as we love Christ, to spread the Gospel at home and in heathen lands. We must become more and more aggressive and missionary. We can do it. We are numerous and rich, and Christ will hold us responsible for the souls of a perishing world.[42]

Olin believed that God had established the church to be the agent of "the Redeemer's kingdom" on earth, and that its work was to be carried out primarily through evangelism and missions, the preaching and experience of Christian holiness, and a broad range of benevolent enterprises.

Olin was always a strong advocate of preaching the gospel to the poor. In "The Adaptation of the Gospel to the Poor" (a sermon Roberts later quoted), Olin said,

Sometimes we hear men prate about "preaching that may do for common people, while it is good for nothing for the refined and the educated." This is a damning heresy. It is a ruinous delusion. All breathe the same air. All are of one blood. All die. There is precisely one Gospel for all; and that is the Gospel that the poor have preached to them. The poor are the favored ones. They are not called up. The great are called down. They may dress, and feed, and ride, and live in ways of their own choosing; but as to getting to heaven, there is only God's way — the way of the poor.[43]

Olin was a keen observer of contemporary Methodism. "I believe that our system has not worked well in large cities, and that, relatively, we are losing strength in these 'great centres of influence,'" he wrote in 1842. "To what peculiarity of doctrine or economy these effects should be attributed is not, perhaps, quite obvious. . . . Perhaps, too, the general adoption of pewed churches and an abandonment of class-meetings, especially the former, [are] changes [that] leave us little or nothing distinctive but the name, since others have adopted our doctrines already."[44]

Olin's Pilgrimage

Olin continued as president of Randolph-Macon College only until 1837, due to worsening health. In May of 1837 he and Mary Ann sailed for Europe, feeling that the sea and time abroad would strengthen him. For three years he traveled in Europe

42. SO to Nathan Bangs, Aug. 6, 1839, in Olin, *Life and Letters*, 1:314.

43. *The Works of Stephen Olin, D.D., LL.D., Late President of the Wesleyan University* (New York: Harper and Brothers, 1852), 1:345, hereafter Olin, *Works*. Roberts quotes this passage in "Gospel to the Poor," *EC* 8, no. 3 (Mar. 1864): 72.

44. SO to "the Rev. Dr. _____," Mar. 27, 1842, in Olin, *Life and Letters*, 2:55.

and the Middle East in an attempt to recover his health. Though often ill, he made extensive notes and produced the book *Travels in Egypt, Arabia, Petraea, and The Holy Land* (1843). Olin did in a measure recover his health — but lost his wife. Mary Ann died in Naples in May 1839.[45]

While in Vienna in October 1839, Olin received word that he had been elected president of Wesleyan University. He "reluctantly complied" with the appointment, though "With more health I should prefer preaching," he noted.[46] He returned to America in 1840, but due to continued health problems he did not actually assume the presidency until September 1842.[47]

Olin showed remarkable resignation to God's will during all his health struggles. He often sensed God's strengthening presence, even when weakness kept him from attending public worship for months at a time. Apparently he passed through a crisis regarding his understanding and experience of holiness while in Egypt in early 1840, about the time of his forty-third birthday. For years he had been "at least sceptical" about the Methodist teaching on holiness.[48] Now, however, he entered into this deeper experience. Later, in 1845, he told the story to Abel Stevens. Stevens recalled Olin saying, "[I]t pleased God to *lead* me into the truth. My health failed, my official employments had to be abandoned; I lost my children, my wife died, and I was wandering over the world alone, with scarcely any thing remaining but God. I lost my hold on all things else, and became, as it were, lost myself in God. My affections centered in Him. My will became absorbed in His. I *sunk*, as it were, into the blessing of His perfect love, and found in my own consciousness the reality of the doctrine which I had theoretically doubted."[49]

Similarly Olin's friend Joseph Holdich, professor at Wesleyan University, recalled Olin "saying that it was during his wanderings in Egypt, and while engaged in deep meditation and mental prayer on the banks of the Nile, that he first *felt* that 'perfect love casteth out fear.'"[50]

This apparently is the occasion Olin refers to in his journal entry for March 2, 1840: "I am this day forty-three years old. I wish to consecrate myself anew to God. . . . I commit soul and body to his mercy and providence. To-day I begin my journey through the desert [in Egypt]. This enterprise I especially commit to God, as I do myself unreservedly for time and eternity, through Jesus Christ. S. Olin." Although Olin had made similar commitments before, his later conversations with Stevens and Holdich suggest that this was the occasion when Olin "found in [his] own consciousness the reality of the doctrine" that he had before doubted. Stevens added, "He lived through the remainder of his career in the spirit and power of the

---

45. Olin, *Life and Letters*, 1:208-67.

46. Olin, *Life and Letters*, 1:339, 361.

47. Price, *Wesleyan's First Century*, p. 76. Because of his ill health Olin resigned from the presidency after his initial election, but he was reelected in 1842. Nathan Bangs served briefly in the interim.

48. McClintock, "Stephen Olin," p. 17.

49. Olin, *Life and Letters*, 2:207-8.

50. Olin, *Life and Letters*, 2:91.

great doctrine of holiness. His views on it were remarkable for their simplicity. . . . He saw the simple, perfect standard of evangelical holiness; . . . he gave himself entirely to it by laying his whole being on the altar of consecration, where he daily kept it by faith and watchfulness."[51]

Olin's correspondence with Walter and Phoebe Palmer after his return to the United States suggests, however, that he still had questions about his experience. He wrote to the Palmers on November 29, 1841:

> I cordially believe in the doctrine of Christian holiness, and my highest aspiration is that I may live without sin, perfecting holiness in the fear of the Lord. God is my witness how fervently and incessantly I strive and pray for this. And yet, when I ask for the witness that I am now in the enjoyment of this high spiritual state, I feel something like a rebuke. I am thrown back upon the peace I enjoy — the sweet repose in Christ which I feel to be mine. . . . What more should I ask? Only that these things may remain in me and bring forth their proper fruits.[52]

On Sunday, March 13, 1842, he wrote in his journal, "I have been led strongly to desire a deeper experience in true vital religion. I have endeavored to make a *new* and solemn offering of soul and body to Christ, and am earnestly seeking for the experience of perfect love."[53] A week later he wrote to the Palmers, "I trust that I am trying to press forward toward the mark. I am sure God wills us to be holy in this life."[54] Phoebe Palmer was encouraging Olin on to a definite experience and testimony of entire sanctification, though it is not clear that Olin came to the clear witness to the present experience of holiness that Palmer hoped he would know.

In any case, during the three years between the death of his first wife and his taking up of the Wesleyan University presidency, Olin's spiritual life deepened considerably. He certainly became convinced theologically of the Methodist doctrine of holiness and experienced life in the Spirit to a profound degree, even though he still questioned his own experience and felt unable or reluctant to give a clear witness to entire sanctification. In August 1842 he speaks of his "still unsanctified nature." And yet he felt, after careful self-examination, that he had no "disposition to do or to love any thing that is not well-pleasing" to God.[55] He endorsed the ministry of Phoebe Palmer, feeling that God had called her to an important work in the church.

51. Olin, *Life and Letters*, 1:353, 2:208.

52. SO to Walter C. Palmer and Phoebe Palmer, Nov. 29, 1841, in Olin, *Life and Letters*, 2:44. The original letter is in the Methodist Collection, Manuscript Division, New York Public Library.

53. Olin, *Life and Letters*, 2:34.

54. SO to Walter C. Palmer and Phoebe Palmer, Mar. 20, 1842, in Olin, *Life and Letters*, 2:52.

55. Olin, *Life and Letters*, 2:36.

Olin at Wesleyan University

Olin was forty-five when he came to the Wesleyan presidency in 1842. By this time he had "a widespread reputation for extraordinary mental powers"[56] and strong convictions that Christian young men, properly instructed, were to be "agents and co-workers with Divine Providence in all His gracious and benevolent operations."[57] His health, though still precarious, improved to the point where he was able to enter vigorously into academic leadership. During his second year at Wesleyan he married Julia Lynch, daughter of Judge James Lynch of Rhinebeck, New York.[58]

When Olin arrived at Wesleyan in 1842, he found morale low, finances desperate, and faculty salaries in arrears. Olin brought needed discipline and direction, raising $60,000 and streamlining the curriculum, reducing the number of departments from nine to five. Though "an unusually strict disciplinarian," he was "loved by his students as few college presidents" ever were.[59] During Roberts's years at Wesleyan the five curricular departments were mathematics and astronomy, moral science and belles lettres, natural science, Greek and Latin literature, and law.[60]

Though stronger than he had been, Olin still was repeatedly incapacitated by pulmonary problems, and this, together with frequent fund-raising trips, meant he seldom taught or preached on campus. Yet, as Potts notes, "Olin's informal encounters with students and his occasional sermons and addresses made him 'eternally influential' in the lives of many graduates." In Olin's view, "Wesleyan had an evangelical mission to serve church and country," notes Potts, and during his tenure Olin "effectively sustained and strengthened the evangelical dimension of Wesleyan established by Willbur Fisk."[61]

When Benjamin Roberts arrived on campus in 1845, he was the beneficiary of Olin's leadership and reforms. Roberts appreciated Olin's strong leadership, and it is clear that he admired him and that Olin cast a long shadow in Roberts's own life.

A critical event in Roberts's time at Wesleyan, and in Olin's presidency, was a stirring 1846 revival sparked by the preaching of John Wesley Redfield.

---

56. Potts, *Wesleyan University,* p. 27.
57. Olin, *Works,* 2:106.
58. Olin, *Life and Letters,* 2:115. The marriage took place on Oct. 18, 1843.
59. Price, *Wesleyan's First Century,* pp. 76-77.
60. *Catalogue,* Wesleyan University, 1847-48, p. 14; Price, *Wesleyan's First Century,* p. 77.
61. Potts, *Wesleyan University,* pp. 27-28.

CHAPTER 10

John Wesley Redfield and the Power of Revival

"When I am happy in Christ my mind acts with vigor."

B. T. Roberts, 1845[1]

"Dr. Redfield's preaching created a profound sensation."

B. T. Roberts[2]

The highlight of the 1846 winter term at Wesleyan University was a rousing revival. Revivals had occurred several times in the university's brief history, most recently in 1843.[3] But the revival that now swept the town and campus was especially remarkable.

The key figure was evangelist John Wesley Redfield.

In many ways Redfield provides the counterpoint to Stephen Olin. Though both men were committed to maintaining the vitality of Methodism, they understood that challenge in quite different ways. To comprehend B. T. and Ellen Roberts and their ministry as well as the new denomination that arose through them, one must understand Redfield.

---

1. BTR to his sister, Nov. 23, 1845, from Middletown. Quoted in BHR, *BTR*, p. 14.

2. B. T. Roberts, "Dr. Redfield's Labors," *EC* 7, no. 2 (Feb. 1864): 37.

3. David B. Potts, *Wesleyan University, 1831-1910: Collegiate Enterprise in New England* (New Haven: Yale University Press, 1992), p. 265; Joseph Holdich, letter to the editors, *Christian Advocate and Journal* 17, no. 36 (Apr. 19, 1843): 142; Andrew A. Bushko, "Religious Revivals at American Colleges, 1783-1860: An Exploratory Study" (Ed.D. diss., Columbia University, 1974), p. 57.

Redfield the Evangelist

John Wesley Redfield was a sort of John the Baptist figure within 1840s and 1850s Methodism. Roberts called him "the most wonderful evangelist of his day,"[4] and Wilson Hogue considered him "among the greatest evangelists of the nineteenth century."[5] Yet he was a quixotic and controversial figure.

Redfield was a self-taught medical doctor and Methodist local preacher. Like Stephen Olin and Willbur Fisk, he was a New Englander. He was born June 23, 1810, probably in or near Claremont, New Hampshire.[6] His arrival was portentous: the day of his birth a woman appeared at the Redfields' door and told the new mother that in a dream an angel had told her the baby must be named John Wesley. Mrs. Redfield concurred. "By that unlucky name was I baptized and have been known through life," said Redfield.[7]

Redfield was converted in a Methodist camp meeting around the age of fourteen, but years earlier, as a child, he felt a call to Christian ministry. When he was eight he tried writing a sermon but was dismayed when he compared it with one of Wesley's published sermons![8] For many years he struggled over his call to preach.

At age thirteen he felt so deeply convicted of sin that he thought he was past hope. However, he went to a Methodist camp meeting where he heard Fisk, then the presiding elder, and others. He sought God at the altar, but the commotion was so great among the crowd of seekers that he was distracted and repulsed — until he saw that many were being saved. He went off into the woods alone and gave himself fully to Jesus. "Instantly, as I ventured on Jesus, my burden was gone. I was filled with inexpressible delight, and before I was aware of what I was doing, I was on my feet shouting, 'Glory to God'! . . . My burden was all gone. Everything around seemed vocal with the praises of God. . . . All nature seemed in harmony, like a beautiful and well-tuned harp, and sang praises to the Most High."[9]

---

4. B. T. Roberts, introduction to Terrill, *Redfield*, p. 3.

5. Hogue, *HFMC*, 1:267. Hogue placed a portrait of Redfield as the frontispiece of volume 2 of his history (corresponding to the picture of Roberts in vol. 1), thus portraying Redfield as the cofounder of the denomination.

6. B. T. Roberts, "Rev. J. W. Redfield, M.D.," *EC* 7, no. 1 (Jan. 1864): 1. Terrill gives Clarendon, N.H., as the birthplace, but there has never been a town in New Hampshire by that name (William Copeley, head librarian, New Hampshire Historical Society, e-mail to author, Jan. 7, 2000). There is, however, a Claremont, and a number of Redfields lived there. Probably Redfield was born in or near Claremont. "Clarendon" does not seem to have been a Methodist appointment in either New Hampshire or neighboring Vermont, but there was and is a Methodist church in Claremont. Although Terrill gives January as the birth month, Redfield's manuscript autobiography clearly has June.

7. Terrill, *Redfield*, p. 17. The principal sources on Redfield are this biography by Terrill and Redfield's manuscript autobiography (located in MMHC), which was the main source of Terrill's biography (cited as Redfield Autobiography). This has now been published as *"Live While You Preach": The Autobiography of Methodist Revivalist and Abolitionist John Wesley Redfield (1810-1863)*, ed. Howard A. Snyder (Lanham, Md.: Scarecrow Press, 2006), 412 pages.

8. Terrill, *Redfield*, p. 17.

9. Terrill, *Redfield*, pp. 19-20.

Redfield didn't know what had happened to him. He hadn't expected such joy. Returning to the campground, he told an elderly sister what had happened.

"Why, you are converted, and this is religion," she said.

"But I thought that religion would make me feel gloomy!"

"Oh, no! It makes people feel happy," she replied.

The youth said to himself, "Well, if this is religion, the world will now soon be converted; for I shall tell it so plain that everybody will certainly believe and seek, and find it." He began to share his faith. In coming weeks he went "from house to house and from town to town" witnessing. While some responded, he found that many people did not want to hear the message.[10]

Fisk was a friend of the Redfield family and took interest in this unusual youth. He suggested that Redfield go to Wesleyan Academy, which had just been opened at Wilbraham, Massachusetts. After several years of preaching, Fisk became the founding principal of the coeducational academy in 1825 and successfully launched the school before going on to become the founding president of Wesleyan University. Fisk thought the academy was the perfect place for the young Redfield.[11]

One of the great imponderables of history is what would have happened had Redfield taken Fisk's advice and gone to Wilbraham, where solid learning was punctuated with periodic revivals. He didn't, and never received much education. Terrified at "the awful responsibility of a Christian minister" and fearful of following human direction rather than God's, Redfield turned away from his call and began to wander spiritually.[12]

God intervened in his life in a number of remarkable ways, including dreams and visions. On one occasion, leaving a preacher's home where he had stayed overnight, Redfield saw the preacher's wife before him in the road, blocking his way. She said nothing, but every time Redfield tried to proceed she stepped in front of him. Terrified, he ran back to the house — and found the woman quietly sitting there, waiting. "I expected you would come back," she said, "for I prayed God to put my image before you as the angel appeared before Balaam." The next day a man appeared at the door as Redfield was about to leave and told him, "Stop, Jonah! for you are running away from God."[13]

After intense struggles and suffering, Redfield gave in to God and began assisting on a Methodist circuit. A while later, however, he turned down a local preacher's license and again rebelled. He abandoned his faith and, between the ages of twenty and thirty, studied medicine, dabbled in philosophy and spiritualism, and entered into a disastrous marriage.[14]

10. Terrill, *Redfield*, pp. 20-22.

11. Terrill, *Redfield*, p. 21; Potts, *Wesleyan University*, pp. 7-8, Joseph Holdich, *The Life of Willbur Fisk, D.D., First President of the Wesleyan University* (New York: Harper and Brothers, 1842), pp. 151, 164-70.

12. Terrill, *Redfield*, pp. 23-33.

13. Terrill, *Redfield*, pp. 26-27.

14. Terrill, *Redfield*, pp. 34-54.

After more years of struggle and separation from his wife, Redfield rededicated his life to Christ and entered a fruitful evangelistic ministry. He was licensed as a Methodist local preacher in Lockport, New York, despite his forthright declaration, when asked about his views on slavery: "I am an abolitionist of the strongest type." If given a license to preach, he added, "I shall certainly use it for God and the slave."[15] Eventually he was divorced from his wife and years later, in 1856, remarried.[16]

Redfield had already proved himself an ardent abolitionist. After his wife abandoned him about 1837, he went to Cleveland, supporting himself there by painting portraits and occasionally preaching and helping with revivals. He was asked to lecture on abolitionism. Despite mob opposition, he gave an eloquent lecture and organized an antislavery society.[17] Redfield took the time to become "acquainted with certain facts relating to slavery which would give my theme a better commendation" to those who mistakenly opposed the abolitionists. He "procured a synopsis of all the slave codes in each slave state" and "copied enough for my purpose of setting before them the true state as seen in the confessions & enactments of the wicked laws of . . . the American house of bondage. I then gave them the preambles & enactments which were passed by their respective legislatures to ameliorate the condition of the poor bond men of the South."[18]

Redfield also helped a runaway slave escape to Canada, an act of civil disobedience. "But what had I to do in protecting my own rights," he wrote, "when there stood my suffering Jesus in the person of this poor outcast. I seemed to hear his voice still ringing in my ears[:] in as much as ye have done it unto one of the least of these my brethren ye have done it unto *me*. Yes & I would do it again if I knew I must pay the whole penalty by imprisonment & fine."[19] This was characteristic of Redfield, who always felt great anguish at the suffering of God's creatures. "Suffering in others he could not witness, unless he could assist in relieving it." Killing animals bothered

15. Terrill, *Redfield*, pp. 60-61; Hogue, *HFMC*, 1:266-67. Redfield secretly hoped that his strong abolitionism would prevent his being licensed.

16. Terrill, *Redfield*, pp. 165-66, 292-93. Though never ordained in the MEC, Redfield was licensed as a local preacher at different times in various Methodist churches. A handwritten certificate signed by James Floy, presiding elder of the East New York District of the New York East Conference, dated June 5, 1855, indicates that Redfield had been given a local preacher's license by the Twenty-seventh Street Church on Apr. 13, 1855, where his membership apparently was at the time. In the early 1850s he lived in Harlem, farther to the north in Manhattan.

17. Terrill, *Redfield*, pp. 62-65. Terrill says this was the first antislavery society in Cleveland, but this is probably incorrect. A local society affiliated with the American Anti-Slavery Society was organized in 1834 or 1835, whereas Redfield seems to have been in Cleveland about 1840. See *Second Annual Report of the American Anti-Slavery Society* (New York: William S. Dorr, 1835), p. 84.

18. Redfield Autobiography, p. 72. Redfield probably secured a copy of Theodore Weld's influential *American Slavery As It Is: Testimony of a Thousand Witnesses* (New York: American Anti-Slavery Society, 1839), based largely on an exhaustive collection of clippings from Southern newspapers that his wife Angelina Grimké Weld and her sister Sarah had compiled. The book includes excerpts from laws in slave states. But as the book itself indicates, there were other published sources, and Redfield might have consulted some other publication.

19. Redfield Autobiography, p. 88; cf. Terrill, *Redfield*, p. 71.

him so much that when he visited a farm where an animal was being slaughtered, he paced his room in anguish.[20]

Shortly after this time in Cleveland, apparently, Redfield began earnestly to seek entire sanctification. He became very ill with "consumption" and spent several months in New York City, recuperating at the home of a friend. Apparently this was during the winter of 1841-42, though the chronology is difficult to determine. Struggling both with illness and his duty to preach, Redfield finally received the word from the Lord, "You may live while you preach, but no longer." He consecrated himself fully to do God's will. "This single sentence [from God] has kept me moving for more than twenty years at my own expense to toil in the face of all opposition," he later wrote.[21]

The home where Redfield stayed in Manhattan was across the street from a Methodist church building — likely the Bedford Street ME Church at the corner of Bedford and Morton Streets on the west side, across town from the Allen Street Church.[22]

Despite his illness, Redfield preached some in the local Methodist church. The pastor insisted that he make use of his preacher's license, and God used this insistence to confirm Redfield's renewed dedication. Redfield's health improved, and soon he was preaching in various New York City ME congregations with "great manifestations of divine power."[23] He was still seeking holiness, but was warned not to attend the Palmers' Tuesday Meeting, "for they will tell you to believe that you already have the blessing."[24] However, that summer (1842, apparently) Redfield attended a camp

20. Terrill, *Redfield*, p. 11.

21. Terrill, *Redfield*, pp. 81-87.

22. Redfield mentions a public cemetery to the rear of the Methodist church property, and that fits the Bedford Street MEC (Paul E. Cohen and Robert T. Augustyn, *Manhattan in Maps, 1527-1995* [New York: Rizzoli International Publications, 1997], pp. 116, 119). Very likely this was the church Redfield was involved in for a period of time. (See Terrill, *Redfield*, pp. 81, 85, 102-3.) "The Old Bedford Church in Greenwich Village was called 'The Eel Pot' because so many repentant sinners were made to squirm there at revivals" (Historical Committee of the New York Annual Conference, *The Onward Way: The Story of the New York Annual Conference of the Methodist Church* [Saugerties, N.Y.: Catskill Mountains Publishing Corp., 1949], p. 60); it probably acquired such notoriety about this time.

23. Terrill, *Redfield*, p. 88. Redfield was in New York City at the same time Ellen Stowe was, though she makes no reference to him in her diary. Methodist membership in New York City increased dramatically between 1841 and 1843 (from 6,722 to 9,780), and several new congregations were started. Redfield's ministry may have contributed to this growth; in any case, it is consistent with what he reports. See Terrill, *Redfield*, p. 103; Samuel A. Seaman, *Annals of New York Methodism Being a History of the Methodist Episcopal Church in the City of New York from A.D. 1766 to A.D. 1890* (New York: Hunt and Eaton, 1892), pp. 496-97. This was a time of unusual revival activity and millennial expectations generally. Leonidas Hamline wrote in 1842, two years before becoming bishop, "In this region [Ohio, apparently] nothing has ever been witnessed like the present revivals of God's work. Whether the millennium or the judgment is coming I know not, nor am anxious; but God has come forth in his power among the people." And to his son he wrote about the same time, "Great revivals of religion are going on all over America, and the millennium, I doubt not, is near at hand. Should you live to be old, I think you would see it. But many great and fearful events will transpire before it fully arrives." F. G. Hibbard, *Biography of Rev. Leonidas L. Hamline, D.D., Late One of the Bishops of the Methodist Episcopal Church* (Cincinnati: Walden and Stowe, 1881), pp. 274-75.

24. Terrill, *Redfield*, p. 92.

meeting where the Palmers were ministering in a tent set up especially for the promotion of holiness.[25] Here Redfield heard Phoebe Palmer for the first time. Mrs. Palmer "showed the reasonableness of believing that God meant what he said," Redfield noted, "and that our faith must rest mainly on his promise." God has promised holiness, Palmer said, "and faith consists in taking him at his word."[26]

Well, Redfield thought, "I have tried everything else but faith; I will now go out and make an experiment." Alone outside the campgrounds, Redfield continued to struggle over the faith question, but finally received the blessing of holiness by faith alone. He discovered that "Continuously acting faith brings a continuous supply. Faith to the soul is what breathing is to the body." Returning to the camp, he gave public testimony to what God had done for him, and this "seemed to settle and establish" him in his experience.[27]

From this point on Redfield "was marvelously used of God in the conversion of sinners, in the sanctification of believers, in the quickening of the Church, and in the general promotion of the work of God."[28] He began to travel, conducting revival meetings in New York and New England. He became acquainted with Leonidas Hamline about the time Hamline was elected bishop in 1844. According to Terrill, "For many years after [becoming bishop, Hamline] was the confidential adviser of Mr. Redfield, and, to a great extent, guided his labors, as to place and time."[29]

The 1846 Middletown Revival

Continuing to hold revivals in the East, Redfield arrived in Middletown in February 1846, apparently at the invitation of John Gilder, the Methodist pastor. At first blush, the presence of a character like Redfield in a cultured place like a university community would seem to be a total mismatch. "My heart dreaded the conflict which I knew must follow if I did not lower the standard of gospel truth, unless there were those who would take a stand for God," Redfield wrote. "But I had promised to go, and I made up my mind to meet the worst."[30]

Redfield began a series of revival meetings at the Middletown ME Church on

25. In 1842 Phoebe Palmer ministered in camp meetings at Bethlehem, Pa., Newark, N.J., and Newburgh, Ramapo Valley, and Sing Sing, N.Y. (Charles Edward White, *The Beauty of Holiness: Phoebe Palmer as Theologian, Revivalist, Feminist, and Humanitarian* [Grand Rapids: Francis Asbury Press/Zondervan, 1986], p. 237). Redfield doesn't specify which camp meeting he attended, other than that it was held the week after another one he attended "within the bounds of an adjoining conference" (Terrill, *Redfield*, pp. 92, 95). It seems likely that it was the Sing Sing camp meeting. If so, Redfield visited this camp meeting two years before Ellen Stowe likewise encountered the Palmers there.

26. Terrill, *Redfield*, pp. 95-96. Redfield later carried on some correspondence with the Palmers.

27. Terrill, *Redfield*, pp. 97, 99.

28. Hogue, *HFMC*, 1:267.

29. Terrill, *Redfield*, p. 113. Presumably Terrill got this information directly from Redfield. I have not been able to confirm it otherwise.

30. Terrill, *Redfield*, p. 162.

Sunday, February 15.[31] He preached almost daily for two weeks, addressing the church in the afternoons and sinners in the evenings.[32] "The church was crowded, and the people seemed amazed," Roberts later wrote. "For some eight or ten weeks, the altar was crowded with penitents — from fifty to a hundred coming forward at a time."[33] At the university, some who experienced entire sanctification formed prayer bands in which they prayed for specific students, many of whom were converted.[34] Both town and campus were stirred as a revival began and in fact continued for several weeks after Redfield left.[35]

This was the first time Benjamin Roberts had heard John Wesley Redfield, and he was mightily impressed. He was moved by Redfield's "deep-toned piety" and "unearthly, overpowering eloquence." "Dr. Redfield's preaching created a profound sensation," he wrote.[36] Roberts could see that the local Methodist church and the university needed revival. "The state of religion in the church was extremely low. Professing Christians were chiefly distinguished for their conformity to the world. The Methodists had ceased to be persecuted, and were fast becoming a proud and fashionable people. In the university, intellectual rivalry had well nigh supplanted zeal for the cause of God. But a small proportion of the students professed religion, and these exhibited but too little of the power of godliness."[37]

A degree of religious quickening was already stirring before Redfield arrived, however. Phoebe Palmer visited Middletown in early September, shortly after the beginning of the fall term. She talked with Prof. Holdich and other faculty and urged holiness as a "solemn *duty*," not just a privilege, in her private conversations and in the weekly university class meeting. Some students as well as faculty were present at this class meeting, but whether Roberts was among them is unknown. Palmer "endeavored to present Holiness as the duty of the *present* moment." She noted that several people "became deeply awakened to the importance of holiness" as a present experience. One of the professors admitted to her that "he had been faulty" in viewing holiness as merely optional, and felt too many at the university had a similar view. A number of people in the university community were affected by Palmer's visit, sowing seeds of the coming awakening.[38]

---

31. Mrs. Julia Olin to Mary R. Garrettson, Mar. 11, 1846 (Wesleyan University Archives). Apparently Feb. 15 was the beginning date, as Mrs. Olin says the revival continued for "a fortnight," and that Redfield "left ten days ago" (probably on Sunday, Mar. 1).

32. B. T. Roberts, introduction to Terrill, *Redfield*, p. 4.

33. B. T. Roberts, "Dr. Redfield's Labors," *EC* 7, no. 2 (Feb. 1864): 37. This article is the main source of the account of the Middletown revival in Terrill and in the Zahniser and B. H. Roberts biographies of B. T. Roberts. Prof. Holdich reported "thirty to fifty . . . at the altar night after night." Joseph Holdich, letter to the editors, "Revival in the Wesleyan University," *Christian Advocate and Journal* 20, no. 33 (Mar. 25, 1846): 130.

34. Terrill, *Redfield*, p. 164.

35. B. T. Roberts, "Dr. Redfield's Labors," p. 37.

36. B. T. Roberts, "Dr. Redfield's Labors," p. 37.

37. B. T. Roberts, "Dr. Redfield's Labors," p. 37.

38. Richard Wheatley, *The Life and Letters of Mrs. Phoebe Palmer* (New York: W. C. Palmer, 1881;

Through the fall term faculty members noticed "a sensible increase of [religious] interest and feeling" among the students. Some students held special prayer times for revival, including a Friday noon meeting for prayer and fasting; Roberts may have participated in these. Prof. Holdich saw signs of a potential "general awakening." As the winter term got under way at the end of January, religious fervor increased both on campus and in the local church. "[M]any were crying earnestly, 'O Lord, revive thy work!'"[39] Gilder, the Methodist pastor, noted that for some months "the blessed doctrine of entire holiness [had been] exciting much interest" in the local congregation and that during January, while most students were away for the winter vacation, "there were evident indications of awakening among the irreligious."[40] Thus Redfield found a fertile field when he began preaching on February 15.

Within a week of Redfield's arrival a powerful revival was under way. Though physically weak, Stephen Olin went to the Sunday morning service on February 22, only the second time he had been able to attend Sunday worship since the previous August.[41] He wanted to hear Redfield for himself, as some people were criticizing the revival.[42] Olin had "inquired at every opportunity as to the progress of the work, and became deeply interested in several cases that were related to him."[43] Hearing Redfield, he was convinced that a genuine work of God was under way. Olin's "candid hearing satisfied him both of the sincerity and the soundness of the preacher," Roberts noted. The thing young Benjamin most remembered from President Olin's remarks was the comment, "This, brethren, is Methodism, and you must stand by it." Olin's "word was law," and with Olin's affirmation "the faculty, the official members, and the church received and endorsed the truth." University professors of "outwardly blameless lives, saw they were not right with God, frankly confessed it, and, laying aside their official dignity, went forward for prayers."[44]

New York: Garland, 1984), pp. 273-74. "We have seldom felt more sure of going at the bidding of the Saviour, any where," said Palmer of her visit to Middletown. A few weeks earlier Palmer had visited Julia Olin's aunt, Mrs. Catharine Garrettson (widow of Freeborn Garrettson), and cousin Mary Garrettson in Rhinebeck, N.Y.; in March Mrs. Olin wrote to this cousin, telling her of the Middletown revival. The networks of friendship and family relationship thus are an important part of the story.

39. Holdich, "Revival in the Wesleyan University."

40. J. L. Gilder, letter to the editors, *Christian Advocate and Journal* 20, no. 31 (Mar. 11, 1846): 122.

41. SO to J. R. Olin, Mar. 1, 1846, in *The Life and Letters of Stephen Olin, D.D., LL.D., Late President of the Wesleyan University*, 2 vols. (New York: Harper and Brothers, 1853), 2:272, hereafter Olin, *Life and Letters*.

42. B. T. Roberts speaks of "a spirit of opposition" that prompted Olin to get "up from his bed and [go] out to hear him" (B. T. Roberts, introduction to Terrill, *Redfield*, p. 4; cf. B. T. Roberts, "Dr. Redfield's Labors," p. 37). Olin conceivably could have heard Redfield speak later that week during the Feb. 26 concert of prayer, but it seems more likely that Redfield did not speak at that service (which was an annual college event, not a revival service; see below).

43. Olin, *Life and Letters*, 2:89.

44. B. T. Roberts, "Dr. Redfield's Labors," p. 37. It is not clear whether Olin's comment, "This, brethren, is Methodism," was made at the Feb. 26 concert of prayer or at the church service the following Sunday. From Roberts's description, it seems more likely that the prayer meeting was the occasion.

Despite his delicate health, President Olin did what he could to encourage the revival, going "beyond his strength in exhorting the students and praying with them," Roberts noted. "This great man never seemed so great as in prayer."[45]

Thursday, February 26, was the annual concert of prayer for colleges,[46] and President Olin decided to attend.[47] Most of the campus community were present, including students and faculty with their families. They all watched the tall president as he made his way into the crowded classroom (where prayer meetings were usually held) shortly after the meeting began. After a couple of prayers and hymns Olin stood and addressed the group. He intended to speak only briefly, but his heart was full and he continued well over an hour. He spoke on "the simplicity of faith," noted his wife, and "seemed to feel the influence of the prepared audience before him — with their earnest faces, some joyful & bright others sad & serious, others full of solemn thoughts"; "the address seemed to appeal most powerfully to the feelings of all."[48] To Prof. Holdich, Olin's talk was "a deeply-thought, clearly-conceived, and well-reasoned oration, full of religious as well as intellectual power, that profoundly moved the entire company," leaving "few dry eyes."[49] "It was entrancing."[50] Ellen Stowe's friend "Emilie" was there and fired off an account to Ellen in Manhattan: "Oh, Ellen, here is where I must fail to give you any idea of the *power*, the *mighty power* in [Olin's] speech. The whole College seemed moved. . . . After speaking of . . . the great importance of educated men being pious men, he addressed himself particularly to those who had made up their minds to seek religion. Oh! what power!! Why, Ellen, tears streamed from all eyes and convulsive *sobs of joy* were heard from all sides."[51]

During the Sunday morning service a few days later, on March 1, forty-four new converts, "a goodly company of young men & maidens," came forward and were received into church membership as probationers. Twenty of these were "young gentlemen of the University," noted Gilder.[52] After the Lord's Supper, Olin gave a "long exhortation" that, he felt, did good.[53] In a letter to his brother, Olin wrote,

45. B. T. Roberts, "Dr. Redfield's Labors," p. 37.

46. About 1815, students at a number of New England colleges began holding "concerts of prayer for a revival of religion" in America's educational institutions. This grew into something of a movement, sparking a number of collegiate revivals. Many schools observed the last Thursday of January, or the last Thursday of February, "as a season of fasting and special prayer that God will pour out his spirit on the colleges of our country." Clarence P. Shedd, *Two Centuries of Student Christian Movements: Their Origin and Intercollegiate Life* (New York: Association Press, 1934), pp. 81-82, 164-65.

47. It is noteworthy that Joseph Holdich, Julia Olin, Stephen Olin, "Emilie," and B. T. Roberts all give accounts of this remarkable meeting (as noted in specific references, below).

48. Olin to Garrettson, Mar. 11, 1846.

49. Joseph Holdich, "Dr. Olin at the Wesleyan University," in Olin, *Life and Letters*, 2:89.

50. Holdich, "Revival in the Wesleyan University."

51. "Emilie" to ELS, Feb. 27 [1846], quoted in Zahniser, p. 20. "Emilie" was a friend of Ellen's at Middletown; no last name given.

52. Gilder, letter to the editors; Olin to Garrettson, Mar. 11, 1846. (Julia Olin gives the number taken into membership as forty-five.)

53. SO to J. R. Olin, Mar. 1, 1846, in Olin, *Life and Letters*, 2:272.

I have reason to believe that my extempore observations on the way of coming to Christ [at the February 26 prayer meeting] were made a blessing. Several of our students profess to have found peace while I was speaking. Twenty of them have become professed converts within the last ten days, and more are inquiring the way. Nearly fifty converts are also numbered in our town congregation. It is truly a wonderful time. About three fourths of our students profess religion, and I never saw a more hopeful company of young men. I think there are many preachers of righteousness among them, from whom the world will hear by-and-by.[54]

Overall, Redfield's ministry in Middletown was well received. Gilder said Redfield had "rendered us efficient and acceptable service."[55] Holdich found Redfield's ministry "very acceptable and useful, both in the city and the University." "There has been nothing of what any one could call extravagance," he reported. "The convictions have been deep, sound, and Scriptural. There has been little that could be set down to mere animal excitement," and "the conversions seemed clear and satisfactory." Holdich rejoiced in the "delightful scenes" of the believing students, including new converts, gathering around and praying with seekers at the altar.[56]

Though Redfield left for New Jersey after two weeks, the revival continued on, with Holdich and others preaching.[57] On Wednesday, March 11, about ten days after Redfield left, Mrs. Olin sent her cousin an account of the revival. At that point 108 persons had professed conversion, she noted. "A Mr. Redfield from Brooklyn has been here, preaching nearly every evening for a fortnight to crowded congregations, & the altar was every night crowded with penitents. . . . Upwards of twenty students[,] the most conspicuous & gayest young men in college[,] now speak at the class meetings & prayer meetings of the work of God in their souls. It was really wonderful in the general class meeting to hear more than sixty young men rise in rotation, & tell of their joys & prospects."[58] She added, "the meetings which are held every evening are rather losing their interest, but how much has already been accomplished — & the influence seems to have come in answer to prayer & faith, & not from any eloquent preaching — 4 or five young men in the college have met for an hour every Wednesday evening to pray especially for a revival, & their prayer has indeed been answered. . . . There are but twenty two or three young men who are not

54. SO to Olin, Mar. 1, 1846, in Olin, *Life and Letters*, 2:272.

55. Gilder, letter to the editors.

56. Holdich, "Revival in the Wesleyan University."

57. Olin to Garrettson, Mar. 11, 1846. Mrs. Olin's reference to Redfield leaving "ten days ago" suggests that the evangelist left on Sunday, Mar. 1.

58. Olin to Garrettson, Mar. 11, 1846. The "general class meeting" was a monthly or bimonthly church meeting in which all the classes and their leaders met together under the leadership of the preacher in charge. Class leaders reported on the progress of their classes, and new class members were introduced. It was usually held the week before the Lord's Supper was to be observed. James A. Porter, *A Compendium of Methodism: Embracing the History and Present Condition of Its Various Branches in All Countries; With a Defence of Its Doctrinal, Governmental, and Prudential Peculiarities* (Boston: Charles H. Peirce and Co., 1851), p. 461.

pious now in the college. It seemed at one time as if not a student would be left unconverted."[59]

A week later Holdich sent a report to the *Christian Advocate and Journal* in
New York, noting that as of that date *"twenty-five students have professed faith in
Christ, leaving only about twelve irreligious students"* on campus, and some of
these were under deep conviction.[60] Gilder noted that of the students converted,
several were "the sons of Methodist preachers."[61] Among the converts in the larger
campus community was the Holdichs' own daughter, Josephine.[62] Students were
sanctified as well; "the doctrine of entire holiness has not been overlooked, and several students have been made happy partakers of this high privilege in Christ Jesus,"
noted Prof. Holdich, and Gilder noted on March 3, "most of our people have been
baptized with the Holy Spirit."[63] William Kendall, Roberts's classmate and close
friend and later an early Free Methodist leader, received the blessing of holiness
during the revival.[64]

Despite the religious excitement, the faculty wisely decided not to suspend
classes. The only adjustment made was moving the "early morning recitation" from
six to eight o'clock to make it easier for students to attend the evening services. "Recitations were omitted only once or twice for special reasons," Holdich noted.[65] The
university had learned from the 1843 revival that maintaining the normal academic
routine actually extended the revival and increased its effectiveness. Without exception, earlier revivals had been "rapid and transient," Holdich noted — partly because
of the disruption in schedule. "The studies were suspended, meetings were held day
and night, and religion became the all-absorbing topic." But this could not be maintained, and once the normal schedule resumed, "religion was, in a great measure,
laid aside." The 1843 revival, which was more gradual and largely student-led, had a
longer-lasting effect. Holdich and his colleagues became convinced that "religion
may advance in connection with our daily routine of college duties." Through
"faithful personal effort . . . a state of uniform religious prosperity," empowered by
the Holy Spirit, could be maintained.[66] This approach was followed in the Redfield
revival, with good results: "the work has probably continued longer, greatly to the
benefit of the recently converted," Holdich observed.[67]

This was the most powerful revival Roberts had witnessed since the one in

59. Olin to Garrettson, Mar. 11, 1846.
60. Holdich, "Revival in the Wesleyan University."
61. Gilder, letter to the editors.
62. Olin to Garrettson, Mar. 11, 1846.
63. Holdich, "Revival in the Wesleyan University"; Gilder, letter to the editors.
64. BHR, *BTR*, p. 21. Roberts gives a summary of Kendall's experience at Wesleyan University in
EC 2, no. 4 (Apr. 1861): 118-19.
65. Holdich, "Revival in the Wesleyan University."
66. Joseph Holdich, letter to the editors, *Christian Advocate and Journal* 17, no. 36 (Apr. 19, 1843):
142.
67. Holdich, "Revival in the Wesleyan University."

which his father had been converted a dozen years earlier. Though already an earnest Christian, Benjamin Roberts drew closer to the Lord during the revival. He did not at this time enter into the experience of entire sanctification, but his commitment and experience were deepened. "Emilie" reported on the revival in her February 27 letter to Ellen Stowe: "of the students[,] Roberts and Brigham you may remember. They have both come out decidedly for the Lord," though they were already Christians.[68] For Roberts and the later story of Free Methodism, one of the most important results of the revival was his becoming acquainted with Redfield. Here "the acquaintance . . . [began] that led to the subsequent union of the two in the work of the Lord."[69]

By the time the revival ended toward the last of the spring term, some 400 people had been converted, about 300 from the city and 100 in the university community — 26 of whom became preachers.[70] Membership in the local Methodist church increased by 88, from 427 in 1845 to 515 a year later.[71] Holdich, a sober judge and a veteran of many revivals, said, "this is certainly the most remarkable revival of religion I have ever seen."[72]

Revival fervor cooled as the end of term approached, with its examinations and Junior Exhibition in early May. But many lives had been changed forever.

Spring term ended on May 6, and after two weeks' vacation classes resumed on Thursday, May 21, for the summer term, leading to commencement the first week of August. In June, Stephen and Julia Olin departed on a five-month trip to Europe. President Olin had been invited to participate in the founding of the Evangelical Alliance, scheduled for August in London. He took an active part in the proceedings, helping to defeat abolitionist efforts to commit the Alliance to a strong antislavery stance. Olin felt that would mean injecting a uniquely American issue into the Alliance and would sink the whole effort.[73] The Olins arrived back in Middletown in early November, toward the end of the fall term.

Roberts's academic load probably was lighter during summer term, as the curriculum prescribed only three courses: analytical geometry, Latin readings in Demosthenes, and beginning the Roman historian Tacitus.[74] As part of his physical

---

68. "Emilie" to ELS, Feb. 27 [1846], quoted in Zahniser, p. 20. This suggests that Ellen may possibly have already met Benjamin a time or two. If so, she had not yet really become acquainted with him.

69. BHR, *BTR*, p. 19.

70. Terrill, *Redfield*, pp. 4, 163-64; B. T. Roberts, "Dr. Redfield's Labors," p. 38.

71. *Minutes*, 1845, p. 577; 1846, p. 25. Membership for 1845 in the local church was 364, plus an additional 63 at the university (a total of 427). Beginning in 1846, Methodist members in the university were apparently included on the local church roll rather than listed separately, so in making a comparison it seems more accurate to use 427 for 1845 rather than 364. Membership decreased to 426 in 1847 (*Minutes*, 1847, p. 118).

72. Holdich, "Revival in the Wesleyan University."

73. Potts, *Wesleyan University*, p. 27; Olin, *Life and Letters*, 2:275-79, 293-99, 304-5.

74. BTR to unidentified recipient, June 27, 1846, quoted in BHR, *BTR*, p. 22; *Catalogue*, Wesleyan University, 1847-48, p. 18. In this letter Roberts doesn't mention the specific courses he was taking, but these are the courses that were prescribed for the summer term of the sophomore year.

regimen Benjamin walked an hour or two daily, and he took advantage of the university's "excellent library" to do extra reading.[75]

On Saturday, June 27, about halfway through the summer term, Roberts summarized his life at the time in a letter written probably to his parents or his sister.

> Commencement exercises come off now in about five weeks. I wish you could be here at that time, as it is expected to be an interesting occasion, though, from the absence of our much-loved president, there will probably be . . . less than ordinary interest. By taking the Gospel standard, and, with due reliance on the good Spirit of God for assistance, constantly endeavoring to come up to that standard, it is comparatively easy to live a Christian. As for myself, I am still enjoying a high and altogether unmerited degree of the goodness of God. Surrounded as I am by temptations of the most seducing kind, and taking into view my own natural weakness, I am led to wonder at that grace which has thus kept me from falling. I need as much as ever continual remembrance in your prayers, that I may bear every burden, perform every duty as becometh the disciple of Jesus Christ.[76]

Roberts's schoolwork included writing essays on various topics. In a flowery, stylized essay entitled "Self Reliance," Benjamin wrote, "We should study to know our own capabilities. The history of the achievements of prowess and genius is chiefly useful as it informs us of what we are capable of accomplishing." Comparing the present age with its "greater demands" but also "better instrumentalities" with the past, he wrote, "[I]f we but open our hearts to the inspiration which may be granted to us, . . . we may like [great men of the past] set in motion influences which shall be felt long after the bell of eternity has mournfully wrung the knell of the departure of earth." By disciplined self-improvement "in spite of public opinion," we may surmount "every obstacle that can be presented in the pathway of duty." Yet not without effort and "a desperate struggle can we break the charm around us thrown by the short lived pleasures of sensual enjoyment." The demands of duty and conscience call one to determined action: "Unmoved by the trumpet voice of popular applause that often lures to swift destruction, undaunted by the loud asseverations of an infatuated people rushing with mad impetuosity to the brink of ruin, he is neither attracted nor driven from the orbit in which a higher than earthly potentate has commanded him to move."[77]

At points Roberts almost echoes Ralph Waldo Emerson's 1841 essay "Self-Reliance," which he must have read. Emerson's major theme is "Trust thyself." Roberts writes, "[I]f we with strong hearts rise above all doubt, and trust in ourselves and in the power that always sustains the good and true," we can do our duty. Roberts wanted to make clear that one must not "forsake the path his conscience and his

---

75. BTR to unidentified recipient, June 27, 1846, quoted in BHR, *BTR*, p. 22.

76. BTR to unidentified recipient, June 27, 1846, quoted in BHR, *BTR*, pp. 21-22.

77. B. T. Roberts, "Self Reliance," quoted in Zahniser, pp. 21-22. It is not clear whether this essay was written at this time or later.

God made for him to tread," whereas Emerson's individualism was much more radical and humanistic. "It is only as a man puts off from himself all external support, and stands alone, that I see him to be strong and to prevail," Emerson wrote. Roberts agreed on the necessity to "stand alone," but precisely *with* God and his purposes against an erring world, not in independence of him. Roberts would have agreed with Emerson's emphasis on character, and perhaps that "An institution is the lengthened shadow of one man; . . . all history resolves itself very easily into the biography of a few stout and earnest persons." But he would not have agreed that "No law can be sacred to me but that of my nature" or that "Nothing can bring you peace but yourself," as Emerson affirmed.[78]

In another essay, "Beauty," Roberts wrote, "Anything that excites in me this sensation of beauty is beautiful to me, though it be unable to produce the same feeling in any other individual. Whether it does excite in me this sensation or not, I alone can determine."[79] He also wrote an essay entitled "Slavery," arguing that it must be rooted out. "We are only waiting for the time to come when the blow may be struck and the deadly tree may fall."[80]

Roberts's Junior Year

The 1846 summer vacation came and went. Benjamin resumed classes on September 3, beginning his junior year. His roommate was William Clarke from Rochester, New York, also a junior. The two shared room 54 in the middle section of the dormitory.[81]

That fall Benjamin's sister Florilla married William Smallwood in Lodi.[82] Weeks went by and Benjamin did not hear from Florilla, so he sent her a playfully chiding poem:

Have cares upon you come so fast
Since you have come together
That you can find no time to write
To a poor lonely brother?
    Perhaps you think it matters not.
But I will sure tell Mother
That you have quite refused to write
To your e'er scribbling brother.
And in my anger I will give

78. B. T. Roberts, "Self Reliance," quoted in Zahniser, pp. 21-22; Ralph Waldo Emerson, *Self-Reliance* (New York and Boston: H. M. Caldwell, 1900).

79. B. T. Roberts, "Beauty," quoted in Zahniser, p. 21. Emerson's essay "Beauty" was not published until 1860.

80. B. T. Roberts, "Slavery," quoted in Zahniser, p. 26.

81. *Catalogue*, Wesleyan University, 1846-47, p. 10.

82. Kysor (p. 27) gives the date of marriage as Sept. 20, 1846, but a Nov. 16, 1846, letter to Florilla from BTR suggests that the wedding had not yet occurred. Letter in RFP.

My love all to another;
And then I guess you'll wish you had
Been prompt to write your brother.[83]

Benjamin told his sister that he was enjoying his time at Middletown and was feeling "lively." Reflecting on his past, he wrote, "I believe that my health formerly suffered much from melancholy. A correct adjustment of our feelings & deportment in this respect is no unimportant, no easy part of our Christian experience. To have a well regulated, well balanced mind is of great worth. To gain it is my ambition."[84]

Roberts again taught school in the late fall and early winter. This time he found a school in the little town of Oxford, thirty-six miles southeast of Middletown and fifteen miles from New Haven. Roberts had heard that the people of the area were only nominal Christians — "Saturday-night Presbyterians" — but as their schoolmaster he determined to "live as devoted and useful a life among them as I can," walking in the presence of God.[85] The school was "orderly," he said, and easy to govern. He soon had the scholars studying algebra, geometry, Latin, and Greek. When word spread through the area that a Wesleyan University student was the schoolmaster, families from neighboring districts sent their children to study under Roberts. "I do not punish," Benjamin wrote, "and yet I do not hear a whisper from Monday morning to Saturday night."[86]

Roberts apparently continued living and teaching at Oxford into February 1847, past the beginning of the spring term at Wesleyan. University classes resumed on January 28, but a letter to a relative dated February 12 is marked "Oxford."[87] Like other students, Roberts probably obtained permission to return to campus a couple of weeks after the start of the spring term in order to wrap up his teaching.[88] He was soon back on campus, working hard on such subjects as philosophy, natural history, logic, and mechanics.[89]

Roberts's February 12 letter was an earnest, thoughtful appeal to a relative who was planning to marry an unconverted young man. He asked her how she, raised in a family that was "accustomed, evening and morning, to surround the family altar, and offer to the God of our fathers thanksgiving and praises," could "think of forming the joined head of a house, your own house, where no domestic altar is reared, where the blessing of God is not asked, and His very existence is not acknowledged."[90] Here already is a hint of Roberts's views on marriage. Not only should it be

---

83. Zahniser, p. 23.

84. BTR to his sister Florilla, Nov. 16, 1846. Cf. Zahniser, p. 27.

85. BTR to his sister Florilla, Nov. 16, 1846; BHR, *BTR*, pp. 22-23. Zahniser confuses the chronology a bit here, giving the impression that Roberts taught in the winter of 1846-47 but not 1845-46. He thus conflates references to two different teaching experiences. Zahniser, pp. 24-25.

86. BHR, *BTR*, p. 23.

87. BHR, *BTR*, p. 24.

88. See Potts, *Wesleyan University*, p. 45.

89. *Catalogue*, Wesleyan University, 1847-48, p. 19.

90. BHR, *BTR*, p. 24.

the union of two believers, but the marriage partners together form "the joined head" of the household, rather than the man being the head of the house.

About this time Roberts seems to have applied for a teaching position in his hometown of Lodi. Perhaps he hoped to teach there the following winter (1847-48) in order to be near his family.[91] To his surprise, he was turned down. His reaction, in a letter to his father on March 14, 1847, reveals something of Benjamin's personality and character. "I should like an opportunity to show the good people of Lodi to their satisfaction that though young, I am not inexperienced." He reminded his father that he had taught school practically every year since he was sixteen, and with good results. "So you will pardon my egotism, I trust, when I say that I think your village has lost a fine opportunity of securing an excellent school!" he concluded. "They do not know me yet at Lodi, but if I live, with the blessing of God, they shall hear from me in such a way that they shall not be ashamed to say, 'He was from our place.'"[92]

One day while teaching at Oxford Benjamin made an outing to the scenic Housatonic River nearby, an important source of power for New England factories. He walked through trees "naked and leafless from the winter's blast." On the rocky cliffs above the river he stood looking at "the torrent . . . roaring below." Seeing a woolen factory along the river, he clambered down and walked through it. He was impressed with the speed of the water-powered looms that had replaced the older hand looms — a sign of progress, he thought.[93] Roberts admired industry and deplored indigence. In a college essay entitled "Poverty," he argued that poverty was an enormous crime to be avoided at all costs. "It will disqualify thee from all honorable avocations, unfit thee for filling any post of importance or trust, stamp deep upon thee the insignia of thy dishonor and disgrace."[94] So he liked what he saw in the factory.

But as he continued exploring the mill, he found "a little girl, of about 10 or 12," tending two or three carding machines. He was struck by her "beautiful eyes, and the most intelligent expressive countenance" he had ever seen in a young girl. "She was pale from her long & unwholesome confinement." He stopped to talk with her, and his sense of injustice was aroused when she told him "with a voice of great sweetness" that she had been working constantly in the factory for two years, and that her father was the mill owner. "This is much against our factories," he wrote. "Children are put into them at an age when they ought to be at school."[95] This was probably Roberts's first encounter with child labor.

Soon Roberts was back in Middletown, hard at work on his studies. Winter

91. Zahniser, p. 25. Presumably the reference here is to teaching during the winter of 1847-48, during the university vacation. It is possible, however, that it applies to the winter just ending; possibly Roberts had applied to teach at Lodi during the 1846-47 winter vacation.

92. BTR to TR, Mar. 14, 1847, quoted in Zahniser, p. 25.

93. B. T. Roberts, "A Ramble to the Housatonic" (RFP, Microfilm Reel 10); see also Zahniser, pp. 22-23. The essay is undated, but this outing likely was made while Roberts was teaching in Oxford in the winter of 1846-47.

94. B. T. Roberts, "Poverty," quoted in Zahniser, p. 24.

95. Roberts, "A Ramble to the Housatonic."

gradually melted away and spring came beautifully to Connecticut. The Hartford District of the New York Conference held its quarterly meeting in Middletown on April 19, under the leadership of Bartholomew Creagh, the presiding elder, and there Roberts was licensed to preach, the next step on the path toward ordination.[96]

At the university, a highlight of the end of the spring term was always the "literary exercises" known as the Junior Exhibition. This was held on Wednesday evening, the last day of term. Roberts knew his grades were good, and he wondered whether he would be among the juniors chosen to speak at this much-anticipated event. He wrote to his father, "I have endeavored not to be swayed" by "college honors," but he was aware that they did influence him to some degree. "I would study because it is my duty to improve the faculties of mind which God has given me and to prepare myself for laboring in the cause of God and humanity," he wrote, not to gain recognition.[97]

In preparation for the exhibition, the faculty ranked the juniors by academic standing and assigned a series of orations to the top students. Meeting March 6, the faculty voted that all juniors with an academic standing over 300 would give orations at the exhibition, and those with a standing over 400 would be given "special appointments" among the orations. With a standing of 405, Roberts stood fifth in his class and so was assigned the Modern Classical Oration. The Latin Oration, the top honor, went to James Latimer (with a standing of 440). Edwin Keyes was assigned the Philosophical Oration, while Daniel Steele, with a standing of 412, was given the Metaphysical Oration and William Clarke the Classical Oration.[98] Benjamin's friend William Kendall, who apparently had a score between 300 and 400, was among the orators, choosing as his topic "Mission of the American Scholar."[99]

Benjamin sent a copy of the Junior Exhibition printed program to his sister, writing her a note on the back. The program shows that his topic was "Genius of Saxon Literature," while Steele's was "The Moral, the Perfection of the Intellectual."[100] In his oration Roberts argued rather ethnocentrically that due entirely to the influence of Christianity, Anglo-Saxon literature "in purity of expression, and devotion to the great interests of humanity, stands incomparably above that of any other age or nation," despite its flaws.[101]

The term over, Benjamin remained in Middletown during the two-week spring vacation, reading, sailing, and enjoying the more leisurely pace. The second vacation week coincided with the annual meetings of the American Bible Society and other philanthropic, missionary, and reform societies in New York City. Many Wesleyan students went to New York to attend, but Roberts remained in Middletown. In their

96. BHR, *BTR,* pp. 26-27.

97. BTR to TR, Mar. 17, 1847, quoted in Zahniser, p. 26.

98. Faculty Minutes, Wesleyan University, Mar. 6, 1847 (Wesleyan University Archives). Here also Zahniser confuses the chronology, implying that Roberts participated in the Junior Exhibition in 1848 (when he was a senior) rather than in 1847. Zahniser, p. 27.

99. BHR, *BTR,* p. 26; Zahniser, p. 27.

100. BHR, *BTR,* p. 26; Zahniser, pp. 27-28.

101. B. T. Roberts, "Genius of Saxon Literature," quoted in Zahniser, p. 28.

absence Benjamin found the town to be a lonely place, and was glad to be back in classes the next week.[102]

Benjamin began the eleven-week summer term on May 20, 1847. The next day he wrote his sister. "Study and toil are again the order of the day," he said, but the "fine spring air of New England makes me feel vigorous and buoyant." He added,

> I wish you were here by my side this morning, that you might look out from my window on the most delightful prospect you ever beheld. I have looked at it a thousand times, and it seems more beautiful than ever. The trees are finely leaved out, the meadows and the fields are clothed in their brightest green, the curving river rolls gently and gracefully along, bearing on its bosom, and plainly in sight, several sun-reflecting sails, the birds are gaily chanting their most cheerful lays, and lilacs and lilies and pinks are filling the air with the most grateful fragrance.[103]

The summer term ended with commencement on Wednesday, August 4, 1847. It is not clear whether Benjamin remained in Middletown during the four-week summer vacation or returned home to Lodi. In any case, his senior year began on Thursday, September 2.

Roberts's Senior Year

Roberts's last year at Wesleyan University followed much the same pattern of his previous two years. It ended, however, with the surprise of meeting Ellen Stowe.

Benjamin's studies included optics, astronomy, geology, moral philosophy, rhetoric, and political economy. Study of the U.S. Constitution was a part of his last term. His roommate again was William Clarke; this year they shared room 40 in the north section of the dormitory.[104] However, Benjamin was again off-campus teaching school during the winter break. He continued to do well academically, and was elected to membership in Phi Beta Kappa.[105]

Spring passed into summer, and after the usual two-week spring vacation, Roberts began his last term on Thursday, May 18. In June the faculty made the appointments for student participation in commencement. As Benjamin was still fifth in his class of twenty-six, he was assigned the Metaphysical Oration. James Latimer was valedictorian, and Daniel Steele, second in the class, was assigned the salutatory address.[106]

Just after these appointments were announced, Roberts gave his father the news.

---

102. BTR to his sister (probably Florilla), May 21, 1847, quoted in BHR, *BTR*, p. 25.

103. BTR to his sister, May 21, 1847, quoted in BHR, *BTR*, pp. 25-26.

104. *Catalogue*, Wesleyan University, 1847-48, pp. 20, 9.

105. BHR, *BTR*, p. 27. The 1931 *Alumni Record* does not however list Roberts as Phi Beta Kappa. Frank W. Nicolson, ed., *Alumni Record of Wesleyan University, Middletown, Conn.*, centennial (6th) ed., 1931 (Middletown, Conn.: Pelton and King, 1931), p. 32.

106. Faculty Minutes, Wesleyan University, June 20, 1848 (Wesleyan University Archives). William Kendall, who ranked lower, was assigned an English oration.

"In little more than five weeks graduation will come," he wrote. "I have one of the first honors assigned to me, the metaphysical oration."[107]

With graduation approaching, Roberts was of course thinking about the future. He was "rather anxious than otherwise" to take his first regular preaching appointment, he told his father. The Genesee Conference was to meet September 16, about six weeks after his graduation. "I tremble when I think of the responsibility and my own unfitness, but I know that it is my duty to preach, or I have rather the firmest conviction that it is, and since God has so condescended as to call me to this high and holy work, and the Saviour has promised to be with and support those who endeavor to do it in reliance upon Him, why should I shrink?"[108]

About this time another door opened up, however. Should he preach or go into education? Roberts received an invitation to serve as principal of Wyoming Seminary, a school near Wilkes-Barre, Pennsylvania, founded four years earlier by the Wyoming Conference of the ME Church. The school sought "to prepare students for the active duties of life or for a course of professional or collegiate study," much like Genesee Wesleyan Seminary.[109] Benjamin gave the matter some thought and asked President Olin's opinion. "There are more who are ready to teach than to preach," Olin said, and advised him to keep to his calling.[110] This made sense to Roberts, and he turned down the offer.

As Benjamin was ending his time at Wesleyan, Ellen Stowe continued her busy life in New York. Still living with George and Lydia Lane, she assisted with the housekeeping and the frequent entertaining of guests. When her diary resumes in June 1848, she reports spending time occasionally with Mary Martindale and other friends, and attending the Greene Street Church. In her opening diary entry on June 18, she mentions attending services three times on a warm Sunday and confesses, "I have sinned to-day in thought." She goes to the Missionary Meeting from time to time, and is again attending her Methodist class on Thursdays. She notes on June 22 that "through much tribulation" she went to class; "it was small but profitable." At the end of the week she wrote, "All in confusion — yet within calmness reigns — oh, the blessedness of keeping the mind stayed on God!" Her spiritual life seems to be stable, if still incomplete. She was kept busy with assorted household tasks, such as cleaning and "put[ting] the parlors in order."[111]

Poetry continued to be important in Ellen's life. While accompanying children on a Sunday school outing to Staten Island, she spent some time reading Long-

---

107. BTR to TR, June 24, 1848, quoted in BHR, *BTR*, p. 27.

108. BTR to TR, June 24, 1848, quoted in BHR, *BTR*, pp. 27-28.

109. *COM*, p. 968.

110. BHR, *BTR*, p. 29; Zahniser, p. 28; Carpenter, p. 43. Benson Roberts, Zahniser, and Carpenter say Benjamin was "offered the presidency" of the seminary, but the school was headed by a principal, not a president (unless there was some thought at this time of adding a president). Olin himself went into education, of course, but he always said his preference would have been preaching if his health could have stood it.

111. ELSD, June 18, 22, 24; Sept. 27, 1848.

fellow's *Evangeline*, talked with friends, and "roamed through the woods." Returning home late in the evening (delayed because of a broken rudder on the steamboat), she remarked, "I felt . . . the better for having spent a day in the wild woods."[112] Henry Wadsworth Longfellow had published his long narrative poem *Evangeline* the previous year. Ellen says she read "Evangeline in May," probably referring to part 2, section 2, which begins, "It was the month of May."[113]

On Sunday, July 2, Ellen said a sad good-bye to Mary, who was moving out of New York. It is not clear whether this was Mary Coles or Mary Martindale since in both cases their fathers, Methodist ministers, were given new assignments in 1848 outside the city. More likely it was Mary Martindale, Ellen's closest friend. Her father, Stephen Martindale, was appointed presiding elder of the Delaware District at this time.[114] It was "hard to part" with "my Mary," Ellen said. "Tears filled my eyes as I wended my way homeward. I felt sadly."[115] But she looked forward to a visit to Middletown for the July Fourth weekend.

The Independence Day festivities, just a month before the Wesleyan graduation, briefly interrupted Roberts's school schedule. Ellen traveled to Middletown on Monday, July 3, with her aunt Polly and her cousins to spend the holiday with her Connecticut friends. Benjamin may have seen her, but the two didn't become acquainted. Ellen saw many of her friends and acquaintances, including Prof. Holdich and Dr. and Mrs. Olin. She returned home the next day in a happy mood: "Nature seemed so glad and happy," she noted. "The world looked beautiful to me. I felt thankful that I lived, and felt that I had something to live for. A high and holy object. May I ever remember that this is but a probationary state."[116]

Ellen was in New York for only two weeks. On Thursday, July 6, she put "duty before pleasure," turning down an invitation to "go and ride" in order to attend her class meeting. Afterward she was glad she had done so. Friday morning she did some shopping, then spent the afternoon alone sewing. "I love to be alone," she noted in her diary — and then added as an afterthought, "perhaps too well." Saturday she enjoyed an outing to the beach on Long Island. "I was really lost in admiration as I looked upon the great waters. The wind blew furiously, which added much to the scene."[117]

The following week Ellen suffered from severe toothache. Her dentist filled several teeth, but the pain only increased. "I have suffered much with my teeth day and night," she wrote. Apparently she had an abscess. On Monday, July 17, "The Dr. lanced my face," she wrote, and in a few days the problem went away.[118]

Ellen returned to Middletown the next Thursday, July 20, to be there for all the

---

112. ELSD, Sept. 28, 1848.

113. Henry Wadsworth Longfellow, *Evangeline* (New York: Houghton, Mifflin, 1883), p. 60.

114. *Minutes*, 1847, p. 1848.

115. ELSD, July 2, 1848. (Ellen often used an adverbial form where an adjective would typically be grammatically more appropriate — as here, "sadly" for "sad.")

116. ELSD, July 5, 1848.

117. ELSD, July 6-8, 1848.

118. ELSD, July 10-17, 1848.

end-of-term activities at Wesleyan and the wedding of her friend Emilie Hamilton on August 3, the day after commencement.[119] She again took the overnight steamer from New York and was delighted to be back so soon "in my little room" at her cousin Harvey Lane's home. She spent five weeks in Middletown, staying through the commencement and returning to New York City in late August. On her first day in Middletown she wrote, "Oh how I enjoy nature. My cup of joy seems full to the brim, so beautiful, beautiful everything is. I cannot take in enough, of all this I feel — My God is here[;] I see Him in his works. I feel his presence, 'His presence makes my paradise.' I love to think of that paradise above." She enjoyed talking with the professors and others in the university community. She seems to have been comfortable in one-to-one conversations with both children and adults. One evening she had an "agreeable talk" with Prof. Holdich, "though he seems hard to draw out often."[120]

The Middletown summer was hot as July ended, ushering in commencement at the beginning of August. Graduation week was a "round of receptions, literary exercises, re-union and parting calls," with many meetings and social events.[121] It proved to be an especially significant time for both Benjamin Roberts and Ellen Stowe.

Commencement and Romance

One of the first events of commencement week was the annual declamation, held in the university chapel on Friday evening, July 28. Ellen attended; Benjamin no doubt was there also. The chapel was filled with university faculty, guests, and "students and their ladies," Ellen noted. She enjoyed the music and the declamation by junior John Pegg, "The Atheism of Shelley."[122]

For both Ellen and Benjamin, however, the most significant event of that warm Friday happened a few hours earlier. Harvey and Maria Lane invited Benjamin and his roommate, William Clarke, to tea. Perhaps they wanted Ellen to meet Benjamin; in any case, Roberts and Clarke had frequently been guests in the Lane home.

Benjamin and Ellen were introduced and began to talk. Ellen was immediately impressed with Benjamin — and he also with her. She later wrote in her diary, "I had a few words of conversation with Mr. Roberts. I liked the *tone* of his mind."[123] This

119. ELSD, Aug. 3, 1848. Benson Roberts says Ellen "had come from her home in New York with her uncle, Rev. George Lane, . . . to attend the wedding of a friend at Middletown where she was to act as bridesmaid" (BHR, *BTR*, p. 28). Ellen's diary, however, makes no mention of George Lane being with her either en route to Middletown or at the wedding, though he may in fact have been there. Ellen refers to her aunt Lydia as being in New York at this time.

120. ELSD, July 20, 21, 26, 1848.

121. BHR, *BTR*, p. 28.

122. ELSD, July 28, 1848.

123. ELSD, July 28, 1848; cf. BHR, *BTR*, pp. 28-29; Carpenter, p. 39. Carpenter says this first encounter was at the Holdich home, where Ellen dined the same day, but she misunderstands Ellen's diary. Ellen mentions dining at Holdichs', but then says, "Mr. Clarke and Roberts were here to tea," refer-

contrasts with the rather dismissive comments she made of other students she occasionally met. Ellen was now twenty-three, and Benjamin was twenty-five.

This was probably Ellen and Benjamin's first real encounter, though they no doubt had met on Ellen's earlier Middletown visits. Her diary makes it plain that this was the first time she had gotten acquainted with Benjamin or really conversed with him.

On Sunday Stephen Olin preached a powerful two-hour sermon to the graduating class with both Ellen and Benjamin in attendance. Entitled "The Relation of Christian Principle to Mental Culture" and based on Proverbs 23:7, "As a man thinketh in his heart, so is he," the address was soon published in New York as a small book by Lane and Scott.[124] A "powerful sermon," Ellen thought, that would "have a good effect upon all who heard it."[125]

The next two days Ellen helped out with commencement preparations — trimming the diplomas, making bouquets for the alumni dinner, helping fashion wreaths to adorn Willbur Fisk's monument. Roberts no doubt was preparing to give his brief commencement oration; Ellen and her friends encountered Kendall rehearsing his piece in the cemetery, near Fisk's grave.[126]

Ellen ran into Benjamin late Tuesday evening at the Alumni Collation, a reception for present and former graduates. She met Steele, whom she found "solemn as death," and had "a little talk" with Roberts — their second encounter.[127]

Wednesday, August 2, was the big day. The long commencement exercises were filled with speeches, senior orations, and music by a brass band. Ellen especially liked Ralza Manly's piece entitled "Silence."[128] Benjamin's essay was titled "Confidence," in which he adapted his earlier essay "Self Reliance" to the occasion.[129] We tend to overestimate the abilities of history's great men and underestimate our own, he said. Yet everyone is created in God's image. "In every human form there is a spark of the Infinite." Even "the most degraded" have received "a portion of [God's] own essence." He concluded, "The powers of every one, properly improved and employed, are adequate to the surmounting of every obstacle" that stands in the way of duty, if everyone but relies on God — whether that duty lies in science, in bearing "the word of life" to those in darkness, in working for peace and against war, or in "break[ing] the chains, that with impious hands have been riveted on the divine form of our brother."[130]

---

ring to the Lane home. On Sunday Ellen also met Roberts's friend and classmate William Kendall at tea at the Lane home and "was pleased with [his] piety and honesty" (ELSD, July 30, 1848).

124. Stephen Olin, *The Relation of Christian Principle to Mental Culture* (New York: Lane and Scott, 1850), 83 pages.

125. ELSD, July 30, 1848.

126. ELSD, Aug. 1, 1848.

127. ELSD, Aug. 1, 1848.

128. ELSD, Aug. 2, 1848.

129. B. T. Roberts, "Confidence," Metaphysical Oration delivered at the Wesleyan University Commencement, Aug. 2, 1848. The manuscript (or a copy of it) and a typed transcription are found in Roberts Wesleyan College Archives. Several of the passages in both pieces are virtually identical.

130. Roberts, "Confidence."

The long event finally ended, and Ellen took a nap. During an evening walk she talked with a number of people and again met Benjamin. She had "a few words with 'brother Roberts.'" Earlier she had remarked about "the tone of his mind"; now she recorded, "I like his spirit." She added that she "felt badly about one little circumstance" but doesn't say what it was. A relationship was being born. Clearly Benjamin was much taken by Ellen, "whose quiet ways and sweet face had been found attractive" by others as well.[131] He planned to leave Middletown the next day, but made up his mind to spend some time with Ellen before he left.

The next day, Thursday, August 3, was to be the wedding day of Ellen's friend Emilie, with Ellen serving as bridesmaid at the evening nuptials. Benjamin planned to take the afternoon steamer to New York, but in the morning he walked over to the Lane house to see Ellen. He invited her for a walk, and she accepted. They walked together south of the campus down to Pameacha Grove, one of Ellen's favorite spots. They came to a large old tree that was special to Ellen, a place where she and her friend Mary used to talk together, sitting side by side on a large branch. Benjamin climbed up on the branch and stood there, reciting "some beautiful lines" of poetry by the British poet Henry Kirke White.[132] The two had "some very pleasant and congenial conversation," Ellen noted. They crossed a bridge and walked along the stream near Pameacha Pond and continued talking.

Benjamin probably did not know it, but he could hardly have found a more romantic spot to get better acquainted with Ellen and win her affections. She remembered that she had once strolled these very paths "with a friend now far away! how time changes people & things!"[133] Very likely she was thinking of her walk in Pameacha Grove with Edmund Longley five years earlier, and all the memories and feelings that had evoked.

Ellen spent part of the afternoon at the home of John Johnston, Wesleyan's professor of natural science, talking with her good friend Mrs. Johnston, while Benjamin prepared to leave Middletown. Ellen "felt sadly sad," she later told her diary. "Everything looked so to me." Benjamin and many of Ellen's friends were leaving, and she herself would be returning to New York later in the month and saying good-bye to all her Middletown friends.[134]

That evening everyone had a "merry time" at Emilie's wedding supper, and later

131. BHR, *BTR*, p. 29.
132. ELSD, Aug. 3, 1848. Ellen writes, "Mr. R. stood upon its old branches where M. and I sat side by side, and repeated from Kirke White some beautiful lines." Cf. Carpenter, p. 40. Henry Kirke White (1785-1806) was a British poet who, though dying at twenty-one, left a body of poetry that was later published (1807; 2 vols.) by Robert Southey, who was something of a mentor to White. See Robert Southey, *The Complete Works of Henry Kirke White, of Nottingham, Late of St. John's College, Cambridge. With an Account of His Life* (New York: E. Kearny, [1848]). Roberts later included hymns by White in the 1883 Free Methodist hymnbook. See *The Hymn Book of the Free Methodist Church* (Chicago: Free Methodist Publishing House, 1883, 1906), nos. 36, 84.
133. ELSD, Aug. 3, 1848.
134. ELSD, Aug. 3, 1848.

many faculty and friends were present as Joseph Holdich performed the ceremony in the back parlor. "I always had a horror of attending weddings," Ellen had confided to her friend Hannah Maria Bunting when first invited to serve as Emilie's bridesmaid. "I would sooner go to a funeral — I wonder why it is, can't you tell me?"[135] But the wedding went well and Ellen seemed to enjoy it. Ellen doesn't identify the groom, but says, "Mr. Childs and I [stood] beside the happy pair."[136]

Ellen was not sure she'd ever see Benjamin Roberts again, but the next day he showed up at the Lane home. He had set off by steamboat the previous afternoon, but a dense fog on the Connecticut River forced the boat to return to Middletown.[137]

Benjamin probably saw this unexpected change in his plans as providential. Around noon he walked over to the Lane home and asked for Ellen. She had gone up to Emilie's to see the couple off and stayed to help "put up cake to send off," but her cousin summoned her. She was surprised to see Benjamin and thought he "looked quite sad." She mused, "It must be hard to leave such a place as [Middletown] after spending four pleasant years here" (actually three in Roberts's case). But if Benjamin was sad, that wasn't the reason. He had a serious talk with Ellen and she agreed to begin a correspondence with him. That afternoon he left Middletown.[138]

In the evening Ellen visited friends and then "came home in the gray twilight alone." Typically projecting her own feelings on her surroundings, she thought "a veil of sadness covered everything." She closed her diary entry that night, as Benjamin sailed down Long Island Sound toward Manhattan: "This has been a day I shall long remember — ."[139]

Ellen remained in Middletown at Harvey Lane's home for most of August, finally returning to New York on August 26. Middletown was quiet as the warm weeks of August vacation passed. Ellen enjoyed the weather and quiet walks around the town. She spent her leisure time reading, sewing, and writing letters.[140]

Ellen spent time with her friends, and visited the Olins and other faculty. On Sunday evening, August 6, she attended the missionary prayer meeting. It "was good to be there," she said. "Oh, the heathen! They need our prayers." Monday she spent some time with the Johnstons, reading to her friend Mrs. Johnston from *Life in Earnest* and in the evening talking with Prof. Johnston "out on the grass" at the Johnston home. "He thinks I will make a good '*Bugologist*,'" she told her diary. On Tuesday she took tea with Ruth Peck Fisk, President Fisk's widow. "One would think she might be happy," Ellen mused. "But mournfully she looks into the past and future and dwells

---

135. ELS to Hannah Maria Bunting (Mount Holly, N.J.), May 25, 1848.

136. ELSD, Aug. 3, 1848. (Probably the best man was Perry Childs, an 1846 graduate of Wesleyan University.)

137. BHR, *BTR*, p. 29.

138. ELSD, Aug. 4, 1848; BHR, *BTR*, p. 29.

139. ELSD, Aug. 4, 1848.

140. ELSD, Aug. 14, 1848. Ellen had planned to return home on Aug. 11, but a letter from Lydia Lane suggested she stay longer.

upon her own woes." Ellen was glad to see her friend Emilie when she and her husband returned from their wedding trip on August 19, though she found Emilie to be "quite sick."[141]

Ellen reveled in the long, warm August evenings and moonlit nights. "Long shall I remember these nights of unclouded beauty," she wrote. "I think I never saw so many such brilliant nights before. Oh, for the spirit of a friend! one altogether congenial, and how strong we would grow these nights. I commune with far away ones." Much as she enjoyed Middletown, she reminded herself: "My home is in Heaven — I am glad 'tis not here — 'I am a pilgrim and a stranger' and oh, I must live as such — I feel anxious about some things which I desire to throw off." After a Wednesday evening prayer meeting she recalled the lines from Charles Wesley,

Oh may it all my powers engage
to do my Masters will.[142]

On Monday, August 21, Ellen received a letter from her aunt Lydia and another from "Mr. _____" — probably a letter from Benjamin that Lydia had sent on from New York. Getting the letters was "really a treat." She had hardly dared to believe Benjamin really would write to her. "Has not my Father ever been better to me than my fears?" The next day she wrote to Benjamin ("my friend in western N. York") — "a shallow letter," she feared. She went out to mail it and "came home with a violent head-ache, and was obliged to go to bed." She was in some turmoil, not knowing just how she should respond to Benjamin and how much she dare reveal of her own feelings.[143]

Thursday Ellen took a final sentimental journey down to Pameacha Grove before her return to New York. Accompanied by her cousins, she "had a joyous happy childish time" in the woods — "climbed trees we did, ran down steep banks, leaped over ravines &c."[144]

Friday Ellen packed her trunk, said good-bye to her friends, and waited at the river for the three o'clock steamer. When it arrived, it was in such a "broken state" that Ellen's friends persuaded her to wait until the next day. So she sailed to New York on Saturday, arriving home in the evening. The next day she went to Greene Street Church and was pleased to hear her Sunday school girls say, "Oh, it was so lonely while you were gone!"[145]

Meanwhile Benjamin Roberts was back in Lodi (apparently), visiting his family after being gone for most of three years and awaiting his first pastoral appointment. Ellen was in New York, the busy metropolis that had been her home for nearly a decade. Though separated by four hundred miles, Benjamin and Ellen had begun a

---

141. ELSD, Aug. 6, 7, 9, 19, 1848. Mrs. Fisk died in 1884 (Potts, *Wesleyan University*, p. 191).
142. ELSD, Aug. 13, 15, 16, 1848.
143. ELSD, Aug. 21, 22, 1848.
144. ELSD, Aug. 24, 1848.
145. ELSD, Aug. 25-27, 1848.

friendship that swiftly blossomed into love. After her bitter disappointment with Edmund Longley three years earlier, however, Ellen was fearful of putting too much hope in Benjamin and his interest in her. Perhaps she would never hear from him again, she told herself. Roberts probably knew nothing of this, and he certainly was interested in Ellen. He did write, and she responded. They hardly knew each other, but their relationship grew as the letters flew back and forth between Manhattan and western New York. They did not see each other again, however, until their wedding day the following May.[146]

As Benjamin and Ellen became better acquainted and learned each other's stories, they discovered they had much in common. Most importantly, they were committed Christians and Methodists, devoted to the Methodist Episcopal Church and its mission. Also, as their writings make clear, they shared a deep love of nature. And though they probably didn't know it, they were distant cousins.[147] All told, they shared a common gene pool — biologically, culturally, and religiously.

Character: Duty, Earnestness, Justice

The account of Roberts's years at Wesleyan University suggests a number of things about his personality, character, and sense of calling.

Two themes recur frequently in his letters and other writings: *duty* and *earnestness*. These qualities thoroughly marked Benjamin's character, as they did also Ellen Stowe's. But these qualities were by no means unique to Benjamin and Ellen. They were the "vital air" of early Methodism. References to duty are constant in the writings of Olin and other Methodists of this period. As noted above, Phoebe Palmer urged upon Methodists the *duty* as well as the privileges of holiness. Similarly, as Wesley himself had stressed, Methodists were Christians *in earnest*. The Methodist evangelist James Caughey published *Methodism in Earnest* in 1850, relating his revival work in England, and in 1856 *Earnest Christianity Illustrated,* based on his journal.[148] In England, the playwright Oscar Wilde later parodied such earnestness in his 1895 play, *The Importance of Being Earnest.*[149]

It is impossible to understand the character of Benjamin Titus Roberts without appreciating this sense of duty and deep earnestness. These themes would mark the

146. Carpenter, p. 40.

147. According to Smail's genealogical research, Benjamin and Ellen were seventh cousins (through the Treat family) and double sixth cousins (through the Judd and Hopkins families). Smail, p. 13.

148. James Caughey, *Methodism in Earnest: Being the History of a Great Revival in Great Britain . . .* (Boston: Charles H. Peirce, 1850); *Earnest Christianity Illustrated; or, Selections from the Journal of the Rev. James Caughey* (Boston: J. P. Magee, 1856). Both volumes were edited by Daniel Wise.

149. Louis Kronenberger, ed., *Atlantic Brief Lives: A Biographical Companion to the Arts* (Boston: Little, Brown, 1971), p. 872.

rest of Benjamin's and Ellen's lives, especially over the next few years as they perceived the slippage of these virtues among the Methodist people.

Another insight into Benjamin's character arises from comparing the two persons who probably most influenced him while he was in Middletown: John Wesley Redfield and Stephen Olin. Redfield and Olin present fascinating contrasts. Despite their common New England ancestry, temperamentally and culturally the two were worlds apart. They agreed on the need to maintain old-time Methodism with its emphasis on holiness and the gospel to the poor. They saw this concern, however, in quite different ways. Redfield was always an "immediatist," whether the issue was revival, the abolition of slavery, or reform in the church. Roberts later noted that Redfield "generally encountered, wherever he labored, fierce opposition from ecclesiastics" because of his call for radical discipleship and opposition to "the gospel of expediency."[150] Olin on the other hand was more urbane and patient, though no less concerned. And though he came to despise slavery, Olin was never an abolitionist. In his view the abolitionists were doing more harm than good.

In contrast to Redfield's meager education, Olin affirmed education as well as the priority of the gospel to the poor. Despite his strong affirmation of ministry to the poor, he was convinced that a well-educated ordained ministry was necessary for Methodists to keep their own children as Methodists became more prosperous and better educated. As early as 1834 he argued that the Methodists "must educate our ministry better, or sink. We may boast of preaching to the poor, but without the due intermixture of the rich and influential, we can not fulfill our destiny as a Church. Nothing can save us but an able ministry, and this can not be had but by thorough education."[151]

Redfield and Olin represent two sides of B. T. Roberts's own personality: Redfield the "radical" revivalist, not much concerned about education; Olin the scholar and educator. Roberts could identify with both. Though temperamentally Roberts was perhaps more like Olin, he affirmed Redfield's radicalism. Redfield and Roberts, as they later worked together, made an interesting pair. Redfield was as "eccentric" as Roberts was "symmetrical."

Olin was Roberts's role model as a scholar, intellectual leader, and perhaps as a preacher, but Redfield was his model as a firebrand for revival. In Roberts's later ministry, and in the birth of Free Methodism, Redfield was to Roberts in a sense what Whitefield was to Wesley — a sort of John the Baptist, evangelizing, awakening, preparing the way, stirring things up, but not consolidating or preserving the work. Olin was a consolidator, and Roberts could see that need as well.

One notes in Roberts also an early sensitivity to issues of justice and injustice regarding both himself and others. He does not want to be treated unfairly or unjustly, and he is aroused when he sees injustice in society or the church — whether the issue is slavery or a small girl in a mill. The roots of this seem to be partly tempera-

---

150. B. T. Roberts, introduction to Terrill, *Redfield*, p. 5.
151. SO to the Rev. Mr. Landon, Sept. 4, 1834, in Olin, *Life and Letters*, 1:182.

mental and partly grounded in his cultural and church background. He is an abolitionist, and he immediately becomes concerned also about child labor when he
encounters it and, later, with the plight of farmers in the face of railroad monopolies.
His sensitivity to justice issues is a characteristic that runs throughout his life.

Relatedly, Roberts is ready to stand alone for God and righteousness. Like
Gilbert Haven, at Wesleyan Roberts was a part of the "tiny minority of students who
supported the antislavery cause."[152] There was a kind of individualism and "self-
reliance" in Roberts, a willingness to stand alone for the right, which was not however antisocial nor opposed to community or mutual interdependence. It was actually a consequence of a deep sense of God-reliance.

Roberts's intelligence and breadth of knowledge and interests are also manifest
during his time at Wesleyan. In this he had good mentors and models in people like
Olin, Joseph Holdich, and others. Roberts was not primarily a scholar, but he was an
excellent student; he was a quick learner and a firm believer in "mental discipline."
He never ceased his devotion to the life of the mind as well as the soul.

---

152. William Gravely, *Gilbert Haven, Methodist Abolitionist: A Study in Race, Religion, and Reform,
1850-1880* (Nashville: Abingdon, 1973), p. 23.

CHAPTER 11

First Pastorate and Marriage

". . . this happy art of serving <u>God</u>."

B. T. Roberts[1]

"I feel to lean upon God as a child upon an earthly parent."

Ellen Stowe, contemplating marriage, 1848[2]

B. T. Roberts began his pastoral ministry in 1848 at a key time of transition in Methodism as well as within American culture. The Methodist Episcopal Church underwent dramatic changes in the decades before 1860. From a dynamic movement mainly of the common people it was becoming, especially in the growing cities, a church of the newly prosperous and influential. It was transforming itself from a small movement into America's largest Protestant denomination. In the cities, ornate stone and brick church edifices were rising, prompting more formal and professionalized worship and new fund-raising techniques like pew rentals or auctions. Some of the more prominent pastors were becoming Masons or Odd Fellows.

James Revell sets this Methodist transition in its larger cultural context.

Methodism, along with much of mainstream America, was in the process of a large-scale cultural change in the years before the Civil War. The republican values and virtues of the early national period, augmented by those of revivalistic evan-

---

1. B. T. Roberts, manuscript sermon on Matt. 5:8.
2. ELSD, Nov. 7, 1848.

gelicalism so dominant in the wake of the Second Great Awakening, were being challenged by the cultural ideals of an emerging urban middle class. Among the most evident of these values [was] an enhanced sensitivity and proclivity to fashionable physical elements of culture which were at odds with virtue as defined by both republicanism and evangelical culture.[3]

This transition was most obvious in prospering Methodist churches in cities like New York, Buffalo, and Boston. Yet the great majority of Methodists in city, town, and country and on the frontier were comparatively poor. This contrast prompted divisions over the very nature and identity of Methodism and its theological core. Further agitating this picture was the unresolved issue of slavery and slaveholding.

Sociologists Roger Finke and Rodney Stark note that at this time well-placed Methodists were making "strong efforts to abandon their sectarian origins" as American society itself was changing. "Together, the privileged laity and the 'well-trained' clergy [began] to lift restrictions on behavior and to soften doctrines" that had set Methodism apart. "By the middle of the nineteenth century the Methodist church was no longer staffed by local amateurs [i.e., class leaders, principally] supervised by professional circuit riders — most of the circuit riders had dismounted and were now 'settled' pastors. It is no surprise that clergy would prefer this arrangement."[4]

Finke and Stark comment specifically on the situation in the ME Genesee Conference around 1850, suggesting that it shows clear "early signs of Methodist secularization."[5] The contrasts and divisions within Methodism were especially acute in western New York, where Buffalo's growing prominence and affluence contrasted with the surrounding countryside, only a generation removed from frontier days. Lively debate swirled around several interwoven issues: simplicity versus "propriety" in worship, pew rental, secret societies (Masons and Odd Fellows especially), slavery, wealth versus poverty, and the meaning of conversion and sanctification.

Inevitably, the role of the Methodist preacher was also changing at this time. As Roberts began his preaching ministry, he stood at about midpoint in the decades-long shift within Methodist clergy from frontier circuit rider to settled professional pastor.

Like the earlier circuit riders, Roberts was primarily an evangelist and revivalist, charged with organizing and regulating classes; he was liable to be moved from year

3. James Alan Revell, "The Nazirites: Burned-Over District Methodism and the Buffalo Middle Class" (Ph.D. diss., University of New York at Buffalo, 1993), pp. 4-5, citing A. Gregory Schneider, "Social Religion, the Christian Home, and Republican Spirituality in Antebellum Methodism," *Journal of the Early Republic* 10 (Summer 1990): 163-69.

4. Roger Finke and Rodney Stark, *The Churching of America, 1776-1990: Winners and Losers in Our Religious Economy* (New Brunswick, N.J.: Rutgers University Press, 1992), pp. 147-53.

5. Finke and Stark, *Churching*, p. 153.

to year. Like the professional pastor, however, he served one congregation (though perhaps with outlying preaching points), was a recognized "minister" in the community, had a parsonage, and received a stipulated salary more or less reliably. Unlike the circuit rider, he stayed in one place (though perhaps speaking and holding revivals elsewhere) and had a stable family life. Unlike the professional pastor, however, Roberts still saw himself primarily as an evangelist, revivalist, and maintainer of traditional Methodist discipline (in his own life and in the congregation) rather than as one called simply to nurture a settled congregation. He was always focused on outreach and fidelity to primitive Methodism as he understood it.

These shifting role expectations and the growing conflict within the conference shaped B. T. Roberts's early pastoral ministry.

As Roberts began his first year of preaching in 1848 and the first year of his two-year probationary conference membership leading to ordination, troubles in his own Genesee Conference were already surfacing. Concerned about drift in doctrine and practice, some pastors began calling for renewed fidelity to the Methodist *Discipline.* The decline of class meetings and love feasts, the introduction of choirs and instrumental music, and the fact that some prominent Methodist preachers were joining "secret societies" like the Masons and Odd Fellows deeply disturbed many rank-and-file Methodists. The preachers of the Rushford District met in May 1848 and passed resolutions calling for renewed emphasis on class meetings, love feasts, and congregational singing and the banning of choirs and instrumental music. They wanted all Methodists to be given a copy of the *Discipline* and the General Rules to be read in every congregation, along with Wesley's sermons "Advice on Dress" and "Cure of Evil Speaking," as called for in the *Discipline.*[6]

Similarly, several of the quarterly conferences sent petitions concerning secret societies to the annual conference. One of the preachers, Charles D. Burlingham, circulated a pamphlet against secret societies. The pamphlet caused a stir that F. W. Conable, a preacher who later wrote the conference history, dismissed as "a harmless, half-amusing bit of bluster." The 1848 conference assigned a committee to examine Burlingham's pamphlet and tried to make peace by dodging the specific issues. It passed a resolution recommending "to the ministry and membership . . . on both sides of the question, [that they] cease all action on the subject of secret societies which is calculated to alienate affection and create agitation among us."[7] Another resolution essentially defended those pastors who had joined secret societies. It read:

> *Whereas,* Certain members of this body feel themselves aggrieved by the statements [in Burlingham's pamphlet]; therefore,

6. Zahniser, p. 30; Conable, p. 570. Eleazar Thomas, the presiding elder, chaired this meeting. The preachers called for "the instant dismission of all choirs" and the "immediate introduction of congregational singing." Conable comments on a series of such unofficial preachers meetings held about this time, and their importance (which he evaluates both positively and negatively).

7. Conable, pp. 564-55. Conable says, "[T]hus was the whole matter disposed of."

> *Resolved,* That whether the tendency of secret societies be or be not such as is stated in said pamphlet, we do not believe that the said brethren joined said societies, or that they continue in them, believing the tendency to be such as aforesaid, and that we have undiminished confidence in the integrity and uprightness of the said brethren, and also in the author of said pamphlet, and that we continue to extend to them as heretofore the hand of Christian and ministerial fellowship.[8]

Thus all was not well as Benjamin Roberts began his preaching career in the Methodist Episcopal Church. The immediate controversy was only the tip of the iceberg. It didn't take a prophet to see that these were troubled times and that, one way or another, Roberts would find himself in the midst of controversy if he exercised any significant leadership and remained true to his convictions.

The fires of controversy in the Genesee Conference were just starting to build as Roberts prepared to receive his first appointment. The conference would meet in early September, so Benjamin had time to visit his family in Lodi beforehand. He was glad to be back among family and friends, spending time with his parents and his sisters Florilla and Caroline, now both married. Benjamin had to get used to his hometown's new name: Gowanda. The local newspaper changed its name from the *Western Democrat* to the *Gowanda Democrat* in September 1848, honoring the name change. About this time Florilla's husband, William Smallwood, was running newspaper ads for leather, boots, and shoes, and also advertising for "HIDES & VEAL SKINS, [to be] delivered at my Tannery in the village."[9] Benjamin's father also frequently ran ads, like the following:

TITUS ROBERTS,
DEALER IN DRY GOODS, GROCERIES,
Drugs, Medicines, Dye-woods, Paints, Oils, &c. &c.
No. 6, Main Street

Titus advertised regularly in the local paper; an ad the week Benjamin graduated from college hawked "a good Assortment of Dry Goods, Groceries, Hardware, Crockery, Dye woods and stuffs, Drugs and Medicines" recently "received direct from New York." Apparently Titus's business was booming; he was buying and selling large quantities of wheat, corn, butter, feathers, beans, and other items "at Buffalo prices." "My Motto is CHEAP FOR CASH OR READY PAY," he added.[10] His medications included Sweet's Linament [*sic*], Dr. Faulkner's Vegetable Elixer [*sic*], and Brant's Purifying Extract.[11]

Benjamin's home visit was brief, as he needed to attend the annual conference

---

8. Conable, p. 565.

9. *Lodi Western Democrat* 2, no. 4 (Apr. 26, 1848).

10. *Lodi Western Democrat* 2, no. 19 (Aug. 9, 1848). The same ad, along with others, ran in the paper for several weeks.

11. *Lodi Western Democrat* 2, no. 23 (Sept. 6, 1848).

sessions in nearby Buffalo. The conference met from September 6 to 14 at the Swan Street ME Church, and was chaired by Bishop Beverly Waugh.[12]

Though Benjamin was thinking of the first preaching appointment he would soon receive, Ellen Stowe was also on his mind, and he wrote her several letters.[13]

Benjamin was ready to begin preaching. He officially joined the Genesee Conference, probably at its opening session on Wednesday, September 6.[14] When the appointments were read at the end of conference, he found he was being sent to Caryville, in Genesee County, about thirty-five miles east of Buffalo and several miles northwest of Batavia — an area relatively new to Roberts.[15] Methodism was still growing in western New York, and this year the Genesee Conference was divided in two, the eastern part taking the name East Genesee Conference.[16]

At this conference Benjamin's friend William Kendall also received his first preaching appointment. Kendall was sent to Cambria, in Niagara County, where he soon became known as a staunch advocate of holiness. He was deeply impressed by a remark he had heard Bishop Leonidas Hamline make. When someone complained to him about some preachers making a hobby of holiness, Hamline replied, "Woe to that Methodist preacher, that son of perdition, who does not make holiness his hobby."[17] Kendall took this to heart.

Among those gathered in Buffalo for the annual conference were George Lane, present from New York City representing the Book Concern, and his wife Lydia. The Lanes had departed New York on September 4, leaving Ellen to care for the house. They were eager to meet Benjamin, whom Ellen had been telling them about. In a letter to Ellen on September 11, Lydia teasingly remarked that among those admitted into conference on trial was "a young man by the name of <u>Benjamin Titus Roberts</u>, a graduate of the Wesleyan University. . . . he seemed to be well thought of, and was admitted without a moment's hesitation. . . . Your Uncle was introduced to him last week, but I have not seen him."[18]

---

12. Ray Allen, *A Century of the Genesee Annual Conference of the Methodist Episcopal Church, 1810-1910* (Rochester, N.Y.: By the Author, 1911), p. 11; Conable, p. 564. Born in 1789, Waugh was elected bishop in 1836 and died in 1858 (*COM*, pp. 903-4).

13. BHR, *BTR*, p. 30.

14. Benson Roberts gives the date as Sept. 16, apparently an error, as the conference closed on the fourteenth. BHR, *BTR*, p. 30.

15. BHR, *BTR*, p. 30.

16. Zahniser, p. 29; Allen, *Century*, p. 9; Conable, p. 564. Conable notes, "The Conference having been divided, T. Carlton was appointed a committee to 'co-operate with a committee of the East Genesee Conference to obtain an act of incorporation for each Conference.'"

17. "Rev. Wm. C. Kendall, A.M. — His First Charge," *EC* 2, no. 6 (June 1861): 181. It is not clear when or where Kendall heard this remark, as Bishop Hamline presided at the Genesee Conference only in 1844. (This series of unsigned articles on Kendall was "written mostly" by Kendall's widow, Martha Francis Kendall, according to her son, William Kendall La Due. See John La Due, *The Life of Rev. Thomas Scott La Due . . .* [Chicago: Free Methodist Publishing House, 1898], p. 337. They were however edited and probably revised and/or expanded by Roberts.)

18. LBL to ELS, Sept. 11, 1848, from Buffalo; cf. Zahniser, p. 29. This letter confirms that the Lanes were not present at the Wesleyan University commencement in August.

Back in New York, Ellen passed quiet but busy days attending to her duties, resuming her Sunday school teaching and class meeting attendance, and reading Longfellow's *Evangeline* with friends. "My days pass pleasantly — happily, have time to think," she confided.[19] The Lanes returned on September 15, and Benjamin went to Caryville to begin his pastoral responsibilities.

About this time Ellen went to visit the popular American Art Union gallery on Broadway and "was greatly entertained with some of the paintings."[20] On Friday, September 22, she received a letter from Benjamin that no doubt told of his appointment. Ellen wrote back to him on October 2.[21] She was ill for some weeks during this period, not getting out much.

On Friday, October 13, Ellen recalled that it was the anniversary of her sister Mary Ann's death six years earlier. "How I love her memory! I would not have her back much as I miss her in this world," she wrote. "I have dwelt much on that future state and a fitness for it since I have felt so unwell. 'Tis all disappointment here!" But attending church services the following Sunday lifted her spirits.[22]

Later in the month Ellen was feeling much better. Saturday, October 28, she "swept in the morning" and later again visited the Art Union. "It has such a good and happy effect on my mind to look at paintings that I love to go often there." In the evening she again wrote to Benjamin. Tuesday, October 31, Aunt Lydia left for a brief visit to Middletown, probably for her health. Ellen wrote in her diary that night, reflecting a tension she often felt: "I am trying to live for my God. I think much of eternity, but I think far too much of this world."[23]

Caryville Appointment, 1848-49

Methodist preachers at this time served a maximum of two years at each appointment, and often only one.[24] Consistent with this pattern, Roberts served seven churches in ten years of pastoral ministry in the Methodist Episcopal Church. Appointment of preachers in each conference was made by the presiding bishop, but by the 1840s bishops were increasingly pressured to accede to the wishes of both preachers and more prominent congregations in making appointments. This led

19. ELSD, Sept. 6-8, 1848.

20. ELSD, Sept. 20, 1848. The American Art Union gallery had some half a million visitors in 1848. See Edwin G. Burrows and Mike Wallace, *Gotham: A History of New York City to 1898* (New York: Oxford University Press, 1999), pp. 687-88.

21. ELSD, Sept. 22 and Oct. 2, 1848. She may have written to him also the previous week, though in her diary she doesn't mention any other letter to Benjamin between Sept. 22 and Oct. 2.

22. ELSD, Oct. 13 and 15, 1848.

23. ELSD, Oct. 28 and 31, 1848. She says on Oct. 28, "Evening wrote to R___ and cousin Maria"; in context, "R___" seems to be Roberts.

24. The 1804 General Conference had set the two-year limit. It was extended to three years in 1864 and in 1888 raised to five years. Wade Crawford Barclay, *History of Methodist Missions*, vol. 3, *Widening Horizons, 1845-95* (New York: Board of Missions of the Methodist Church, 1957), p. 43.

Bishop Hedding to write in 1842, "The difficulties attending this duty [of appointing preachers] are increasing every year; and unless there be an abatement of the
claims of some, both of the preachers and people, for certain places and certain
men, it is impossible to see how the itinerant system can be long maintained in
some parts of the country."[25]

As a new, young conference preacher, Roberts had been given an appointment
that Bishop Waugh, no doubt in consultation with the presiding elders, thought represented a good match between preacher and congregation. Roberts began his work
at Caryville as soon as conference ended in September. He arrived there about noon
on Saturday, September 16, and made a quick assessment of the town and the local
Methodist society. Fortunately Brother Buck, the previous preacher, had not yet left
town, so Roberts had a chance to talk with him. Buck had served the church for two
years. He introduced Benjamin to Brother March, one of the church stewards, who
invited Roberts to stay with him for the time being.[26]

Roberts began preaching the next day, Sunday, September 17, 1848. Brother Buck
was present and Roberts tried to get him to preach, but he wisely refused. Roberts
was now in charge, and it was his duty to conduct the services. He preached Sunday
morning and afternoon and led a prayer meeting in the evening.[27] He wrote his parents the next day, "I never had such feelings when attempting to preach as I did in
the morning. . . . I felt that most were sitting as critics, comparing me with their former preacher. In the afternoon I had a much better time, and was greatly assisted
from on high." People listened "with marked attention and with outward manifestation of feeling." The congregation was large for both services, he said, and appeared
"respectable and intelligent."[28]

The Sunday evening prayer meeting gave Roberts a chance to gauge the spiritual
temperature of the congregation. While "a good number" attended, he felt the
prayers showed "a low state of piety." He wrote his parents, "A general coldness and
stupor prevail among the members, as far as I can learn; but they are said to be
united, and in each other's confidence." Officially there were 108 members, but only
80 or 90 seemed to be active, Roberts said.[29] "I think the prospect on the whole is
very favorable," Benjamin wrote. "I do not mean to spare hard labor or study to sustain myself and make myself useful to this people. I am trying hard to give myself up
wholly to the work of the Lord, to be a man of one calling, of one work." He sensed
his need of God's help and asked for his parents' prayers.[30]

The next morning the Presbyterian preacher stopped by to welcome Benjamin
to Caryville. Roberts learned that the town was home to Cary Collegiate Institute,

25. Elijah Hedding, *A Discourse on the Administration of Discipline* (New York: G. Lane and P. P.
Sandford, 1842), p. 75. Quoted in Barclay, *Widening Horizons*, p. 43.
26. BHR, *BTR*, p. 30.
27. BHR, *BTR*, p. 31.
28. BTR to his parents, Sept. 18, 1848, quoted in BHR, *BTR*, p. 31; Zahniser, p. 31.
29. The 1848 *Minutes* give the Caryville membership as 106.
30. BTR to his parents, Sept. 18, 1848, quoted in BHR, *BTR*, pp. 31-32.

"quite a flourishing academy." It made him feel more at home to know that he could "now and then run into a literary institution."[31]

Caryville was a prosperous farming community six miles northwest of Batavia, with stands of oak nearby. The land was fertile and especially good for growing grain. Roberts's first week there he found the farmers all busy sowing their wheat.[32]

The Caryville church had a parsonage, but rather than moving in, Roberts boarded with a family in the church.[33] The congregation owed a debt on the parsonage, and the house may have been in poor repair, or rented out. Also, since the pastor was single, the congregation may well have thought it best for Roberts to board with a church family.[34]

Roberts applied himself to his ministry and soon won people's confidence. "Between the people and pastor a deep friendship sprang up, that made this a happy year," Benson Roberts later wrote.[35] Benjamin worked conscientiously, following the expected Methodist pattern of devoting mornings to study and afternoons primarily to visitation.[36] He conducted a winter revival, with mixed results: "It did not survive the spring fashions," he said.[37]

Much of Benjamin's study time was devoted to sermon preparation, as his duties called for him to speak several times each week. Throughout the years of his pastoral ministry, in fact, Roberts commonly preached half a dozen or more times weekly, and he considered this his normal duty. Many years later, at sixty-one, he wrote, "More preachers die through preaching too little than through preaching too much. Want of work kills more preachers than overwork. . . . A preacher who runs down in health from preaching two or three times on the Sabbath will come up, and grow strong, by preaching as he should, six or seven times a week."[38] Roberts was young and strong and set a high standard of duty for himself, but he was also liable to wear himself out.

Among his papers is a nineteen-page manuscript based on Matthew 5:8 annotated in his hand — "My first Sermon." This may be the sermon Roberts preached his first Sunday at Caryville (September 17, 1848), although it could be an earlier sermon.[39] It

31. BTR to his parents, Sept. 18, 1848, quoted in BHR, *BTR,* p. 32.

32. BTR to his parents, Sept. 18, 1848, in BHR, *BTR,* pp. 31-32.

33. He initially stayed in the home of Brother March, one of the stewards, for a week or so until he could arrange "a permanent boarding place," which apparently was the home of the Menck family. BTR to his parents, Sept. 18, 1848, in BHR, *BTR,* p. 31; see ELSD, May 30, 1849.

34. The sources do not make clear why Roberts did not occupy the parsonage.

35. BHR, *BTR,* p. 36.

36. Presumably here Roberts followed this daily pattern, which he mentions in his diaries for 1852 and subsequent years.

37. BHR, *BTR,* p. 33.

38. [B. T. Roberts], "Work," *EC* 49, no. 2 (Feb. 1885): 59-60.

39. Zahniser (p. 31) assumes this was Roberts's first sermon at Caryville, though no place is indicated on the manuscript and it possibly dates from earlier. Nothing in the sermon suggests the context, other than that it apparently was a public worship service. The original manuscript is in the Roberts Wesleyan College Archives.

has no title other than the Scripture verse, "Blessed are the pure in heart for they shall see God."[40]

In this sermon Roberts, like Wesley, defines heart purity as "a restoration of the individual to the moral image and likeness of his maker, . . . a concurrence of his will with the will of God," so that all his actions are governed by "universal love to man and supreme love to God." In elaborating this theme Roberts notes, "Man is by nature a social being [who always] seeks someone to whom he may communicate his hopes and fears[,] his joys and sorrows. And his social happiness is always greatest when in company with those whose religion, education, inclinations, habits, modes of thinking and ways of acting approximate nearest to his own." The sermon is filled with Scripture and logic, including the meaning of two Greek terms. Roberts refers to "this happy art of serving <u>God</u>." Salvation is by faith, he notes, but he stresses that one may experience all that God has promised if one wills to do so, since the human being is "a free moral agent" with "a self determining self acting will." It is therefore a matter of duty: "If you know your duty you have all the conviction you need."[41]

The sermon ends with a strong evangelistic appeal and a warning about the agonies of hell.

Pastoring alone at Caryville as fall turned to winter, Benjamin's thoughts often turned to Ellen in New York. He wrote her several letters, and was pleased to get her replies.

Over the often dreary fall days in New York, Ellen frequently felt unwell. Her diary hints that part of her problem was depression. She stayed home on Sunday, November 5, because of a violent storm, and though she felt God's presence, she was low in spirit. "I would commit my ways, my all into His hands," she wrote. "What would I do without religion I often ask myself, without this hope of heaven? 'It lifts my fainting spirits up,' it gives me joy when other hopes lie low. There will be no sickness, no sorrow there." Monday morning she "felt quite miserable in body" but was buoyed after attending the sewing meeting in the afternoon and having "pleasant talk" with her friends there. That night she reflected, "I came home feeling much better. I am convinced my disease is of the nerves — my mind so affects my body. My thoughts are often on my better home."[42]

The next day Ellen was forced to think very much of her home in *this* world. A letter arrived from Benjamin, proposing marriage. Though the proposal probably wasn't totally unexpected, it threw Ellen into deep soul-searching. What was God's will? And what were her own true feelings? "Scarce could I speak of the feelings of this day. A memorable one t'will be. Oh, for divine direction, and I feel strange to

40. The sermon has a four-part outline:
    1. What is meant by purity of heart.
    2. Consider the necessity of being thus pure in heart.
    3. Endeavor to show that this moral purity is attainable.
    4. Advance some reasons why we should immediately strive to possess it.
41. B. T. Roberts, manuscript sermon on Matt. 5:8, pp. 5-12. Cf. Zahniser, pp. 31-33.
42. ELSD, Nov. 5 and 6, 1848.

myself, as if I had but one thing to do[.] I feel no hesitation. I seem to be assured 'tis my Father's will, yet awfully important seems the step. I long to do my Father's will even if [it] be not my own, if I do violence to my own feelings. How dependent I feel in view of anything so important[,] so responsible[,] on divine strength. I feel to lean upon God as a child upon an earthly parent."[43]

The Lane house was full of company the next day — Nathan Bangs; Bishop Elijah Hedding and his wife; Daniel Kidder, editor of Methodist Sunday school literature and early Methodist missionary to Brazil. But Ellen was preoccupied with her big decision. "My thoughts have been serious solemn, and my tears have flowed freely." In the evening she had a chance to talk things over with Aunt Lydia.[44]

Ellen had said on receiving Benjamin's proposal that she felt "no hesitation"; she wanted to be sure marriage to Benjamin, and the life of a Methodist preacher's wife, was God's will. Thursday she took pen and paper and answered Benjamin's letter. Apparently her response was yes — or perhaps a qualified yes, with some questions added. She confided to her diary: "I have tried [to] act right. I [am] relieved that I have written. I <u>feel</u> no doubts or fears, yet perhaps I have cause to. I will try and give all into the hands of my Father, and myself too. I need to pray much, that my mind and heart [not] be too much upon earth. There is great danger I am aware. May I be on my watch and leave no point unguarded."[45]

Over the remaining busy weeks of 1848, Ellen adjusted to the new reality that she was to be married. She felt some anxiety but tried to trust her way fully to the Lord. On November 14 she went to Phoebe Palmer's Tuesday Meeting and "enjoyed it much." She was glad to see Mrs. Holdich there, and she "felt better than usual" after her long walk home. "Felt like casting my care on God, and an assurance that he cared for me." She continued attending her Thursday class meeting, noting on November 16 that she had a new class leader.[46]

Benjamin wasted no time in replying to Ellen's letter. On Saturday, November 18, Ellen was "agreeably surprised" to get his reply. "Give to the winds thy fears," she quoted. "Shall I ever learn to trust my God." Given her disappointment with Edmund Longley some years earlier, she may have been worried about how Benjamin would respond to her letter.[47]

The next week Ellen was down with the flu, but she wrote to Benjamin on Saturday, the twenty-fifth. She continued unwell over the next couple of weeks. "I feel quite miserable in body from over-exertion," she commented on December 9, and

---

43. ELSD, Nov. 7, 1848. While Ellen does not say explicitly that Roberts's letter was a proposal for marriage, her diary entries make it clear that this was the case.

44. ELSD, Nov. 8, 1848; cf. *COM*, pp. 513-14.

45. ELSD, Nov. 9, 1848.

46. ELSD, Nov. 14 and 16, 1848. Her new class leader was "Mr. Creigh" — probably Bartholomew Creagh (mentioned earlier), who was appointed to the Allen Street Church in 1847.

47. ELSD, Nov. 18, 1848. This assumes that Roberts's letter that Ellen received on Nov. 18 was a response to her Nov. 9 letter. Due to the short time lapse, however (eight days), it is possible Benjamin's letter was in response to an earlier one from Ellen.

she suffered from "another touch of influenza" the next week. She made it to her class meeting on Thursday, however, led by Brother Creagh. She noted that this was her "last class meeting in Allen St. where I have always held my membership," as she had decided to transfer to Greene Street. "I felt sad to leave, but the distance is so long, and it seemed not quite consistent to go to class in one place while all my interests are in another." She added, "What sorrowful days these last few have been to me. I am childish to be so troubled about that I cannot help. But I know myself better than before. I believe all will be made plain to me. Yet suspense is not pleasant."[48]

The correspondence with Benjamin continued, and on December 15 Ellen received a very positive letter from him. "The long expected, white winged bird came," she wrote, "and I say, 'Why did I not give to the winds my fears?' Oh, what heart-stirring emotions it has caused! What thoughts. The assurance that I am in the hands of God calms my fears, and bids this tumult of soul <u>hush</u>!"[49]

With this exchange of letters, Ellen Stowe and Benjamin Roberts agreed to marry. They began planning a spring wedding.

Sunday, December 17, was "a serious day to me," Ellen wrote, as she thought about the big change coming. "Oh to trust in God how precious! I should exceedingly fear and tremble if I had not a strong arm to lean upon — tears often come to my eyes, and I cannot force them back."[50] From this point on she was looking forward to her life with Benjamin, yet already anticipating the loss of her close relationship with George and Lydia Lane.

Ellen wrote to Benjamin the next day, probably confirming the initial wedding plans. She confided to her diary, "I wrote to <u>my friend</u> and now feel so happy in my mind, as if I had more fully given myself to my God." Apparently Benjamin had shared with her that he had some thoughts of being a missionary, for she added, "Could I not would I not make any sacrifice for Christ? And if it should be his duty to go to distant lands to preach Christ, ought not I to rejoice to be permitted to share his self-denials?"[51]

The letters and planning continued, and though Ellen wrote on December 26 that she could "not quite comply with [Benjamin's] wishes," perhaps concerning the date of the wedding, their mutual commitment had been made. Stephen Olin and his wife spent the night of December 27 with the Lanes, and no doubt heard the news of the coming wedding.[52]

Ellen concluded this eventful year in a time of reflection. "Last day of 1848 — a day I trust it has been of serious solemn self-examination," she wrote. "I did not go out this evening, but tried to think at home. Was profited by reading in the hymn-book." For the new year she took the motto:

48. ELSD, Dec. 9, 11, and 14, 1848.
49. ELSD, Dec. 15, 1848.
50. ELSD, Dec. 17, 1848.
51. ELSD, Dec. 18, 1848.
52. ELSD, Dec. 26-27, 1848.

Act — act in the living present
Heart within and God o'erhead.[53]

January 1849 was bitterly cold in New York City. Lydia Lane became very ill, and Ellen was concerned about her. Friday, January 12, was a fast day at the Greene Street Church. Ellen went to the sunrise prayer meeting and then "visited a poor woman in Houston St.," perhaps because her aunt Lydia was too ill to make the call. "My heart ached for her." Ellen went to a meeting of the Assistance Society and called on two other women before returning home. Stomping in from the cold about two o'clock, she was delighted to find a letter from Benjamin awaiting her.[54]

Later in the month the Greene Street Church was having "excellent meetings," Ellen noted. "Oh, how happy I have felt sometimes of late. I find so much to be thankful for. Oh, that I were better!"[55] Ellen was not satisfied with her spiritual condition, particularly in light of her approaching marriage.

The letters continued coming from Benjamin. She received one on January 26. The next day she went to see a woman named Emily and told her of her marriage plans. "I felt sadly and my tears flowed freely as I walked through the dimly lighted streets to my home. There is much to make one sad as well as glad in this world."[56]

About this time Ellen went to a daguerreotype studio and had her picture taken so she could send it to Benjamin. Presumably this is the photo of her as a young woman that appears at the beginning of Adella Carpenter's biography.[57] It shows her in a dark long-sleeved dress with a plain white collar and narrow waist, pensive but attractive, with just a hint of mischief. In these early days of photography it was not yet the custom for people to smile when photographed, but Ellen, though unsmiling, wears a slightly bemused expression due partly to her wide-set, clear eyes.

On February 12, a stormy day in Manhattan, Ellen mailed the photograph to Benjamin. "Wrote to my friend, and sent my likeness to him," she noted. At the end of the week, on Saturday, she spent time in prayer for Benjamin and herself. She had "sweet access" to the "throne of grace, and much liberty in praying for my beloved — I long to be made fit for usefulness, to be prepared for all the future." The following Thursday Ellen received "an excellent letter" from Benjamin — "like a sunbeam to me."[58]

Benjamin wasted no time in getting his own photo taken so he could send it to Ellen. Ellen received it on February 26. "A pleasure truly — The reality seems to rush

---

53. ELSD, Dec. 31, 1848, and Jan. 1, 1849.

54. ELSD, Jan. 12, 1849.

55. ELSD, Jan. 23, 1849.

56. ELSD, Jan. 27, 1849.

57. ELSD, Feb. 12, 1849. This seems to be the only surviving photograph of her as a young woman.

58. ELSD, Feb. 12, 17, and 22, 1849. Cf. Carpenter, p. 41. Carpenter conflates Ellen's diary entries for Feb. 22, Feb. 26, and Mar. 29, 1849, altering the wording slightly, which somewhat confuses the chronology.

upon me for a moment and I felt it in all its force, and yet how can I realize it?"[59] The photo shows Benjamin with high forehead; dark, somewhat unruly hair; and beard under his chin.

Marriage of Benjamin and Ellen

Benjamin and Ellen agreed to be married on May 3. Once the date was fixed, Ellen shared the news with her friends. In February she wrote Mary Martindale, then in Prattsville, New York, asking her to be maid of honor. Mary readily consented. "Who will be the groomsman?" she asked. "Some congenial brother, I trust, one of our kind. Still it would not make the least difference to me if he should be an icicle, only have him somewhat taller than I." Affecting the "thee's" and "thou's" that were still in vogue in poetic writing of the day, Mary assured Ellen, "Thou wilt be happy, darling. I know thou wilt. Thou shalt grow strong, thou wilt care for souls, the timid will look to thee and find sympathy. The sinner will gaze upon thee and learn to love Him whom thou servest. Thou wilt have none the fewer trials, but thou wilt have a strong arm to lean upon, a loving human heart to feel for thee."[60] From Ellen's hometown of Windsor another friend, Mary Bronson, wrote, "I trust your hopes and aspirations are one and you may find in him a complete assemblage of all that a woman's heart could wish to love and honor."[61]

On March 4, a Sunday and her twenty-fourth birthday, Ellen attended preaching twice and enjoyed the coming of spring weather. "'[T]is passing strange to see how I have got so old. . . . A sweet bright day it has been[,] the sky so blue, the air so springy. . . . Sarah and I have been singing." On March 29 she was cheered by another letter from "my beloved Benjamin." For the first time in her diary she calls him "Benjamin," rather than "Mr. Roberts" or "my friend."[62]

Stephen Olin again came to town and on Sunday, April 1, preached a sermon on the Lord's Supper. Ellen found it "a great and good sermon. . . . He dwelt upon Christ having left the symbol of his death — not in words, but the symbol. All could understand it."[63]

Ellen was deeply conscious that her days in New York City were dwindling down to a precious few. On April 8 she wrote, "We are not forbidden I think to indulge pleasant hopes of the future" (perhaps quoting something she heard in church that day).[64] She spent precious moments with friends from whom she knew she would soon be parted. While Ellen was having a quiet talk with her friend Emilie on Thurs-

---

59. ELSD, Feb. 26, 1849. Presumably this is the photograph that appears opposite p. 38 in Carpenter.

60. Mary Martindale to ELS, Feb. 24, 1849, quoted in Zahniser, p. 35.

61. Mary S. Bronson to ELS, April 12, 1849, quoted in Zahniser, p. 35.

62. ELSD, Mar. 4 and 29, 1849.

63. ELSD, Apr. 1, 1849.

64. ELSD, Apr. 8, 1849. The sentence is in quotation marks in the diary.

day, April 12, Mary Martindale arrived unexpectedly and Ellen was "quite overcome" to see her. "We sat long together, we three," Ellen apparently skipping class meeting to spend this time with her special friends.[65]

Ellen was especially glad to be with Mary Martindale again. They spent Friday night together; "We talked till near morning of the past, present, & future." The next Sunday she was brutally honest in her assessment of the morning preaching: "I heard a poor sermon from a pale stranger." She spent the afternoon catching up on her sleep.[66]

Saturday evening, April 21, Ellen again visited the Art Union, this time with her friends Emily and Mary,[67] and on Monday she and Mary (probably Mary Martindale) went shopping, presumably getting ready for the wedding. She was shopping again later in the week, and "went over in the Bowery with Aunt Lydia." Saturday, April 28, was a pleasant day — "'A green day' as Mrs. Hemans would say."[68]

Ellen was concerned about her Sunday school girls, whom she soon would be leaving. After shopping on Monday, April 23, she visited some of them. She met her girls' class for the final time the following Sunday and later recorded in her diary, "The last time my little bright faced girls will gather around. They looked so sorrowful I scarce could speak to them. The familiar faces I have been in the habit of seeing Sabbath after Sabbath for a long time, will be exchanged for strange ones. Yet 'tis well."[69]

Monday, April 30, Ellen made a few calls on friends, "contrary to the customs of people in general." With the wedding just days away, many friends and acquaintances stopped by the Lane home to see her. "'Tis amusing to hear the people ask me <u>how I feel</u>. I feel so many ways, that I really have no feeling, at all," she wrote. In fact, she still had conflicting emotions, and on Tuesday morning, two days before the wedding, she "felt really sick."[70]

Wednesday, the day before the wedding, was to Ellen "a great day surely." Mary Martindale came, and Ellen spent most of the day with her. The two friends "talked pleasantly and profitably together, about religion and <u>getting married</u>," and went to the Art Union. Various friends stopped by the Lane home, including Mary Sennick, who came "to take a last look at <u>Ellen Stowe</u>," Ellen commented in her diary. "We parted in silence, we parted in tears," she wrote, quoting one of her favorite poets. Late in the evening Mary Martindale and Ellen talked some more as a bright moon climbed the night sky. "We will long remember this night," she mused. "Thoughts of the absent one filled my mind as I looked upon the brightness without." She was filled with wonder at this major life transition. "How strangely one feels at a time like this, How varied the emotions! I am happy and glad, and yet I am sad. Not many hours will pass ere I leave my maidenhood — no longer a girl but a married

65. ELSD, Apr. 12, 1849.

66. ELSD, Apr. 14-15, 1849.

67. ELSD, Apr. 21, 1849. Emily seemed to be different from Emilie, and Ellen doesn't specify which Mary this was.

68. ELSD, Apr. 23, 27, and 28, 1849.

69. ELSD, Apr. 23 and 29, 1849.

70. ELSD, Apr. 30 and May 1, 1849.

woman."[71] Meanwhile Benjamin was probably already in New York, or perhaps approached Manhattan by train.

Benson Roberts notes that his parents' wedding occurred during "anniversary week" — the week in which several Methodist societies and committees met, bringing many of the denomination's leaders to New York City.[72] This was traditionally the time also when a number of missionary and philanthropic societies held their annual meetings or "anniversaries" (as noted earlier).[73] It is not clear why Benjamin and Ellen chose this week for their wedding, but they probably intentionally chose "anniversary week."[74] For one thing, this would give Benjamin the opportunity to sit in on various meetings and get a sense of what was going on within Methodism and in the churches more broadly. Also many Methodist leaders, George Lane's colleagues, would be able to attend the wedding.

Benjamin showed up at the Lane home early on Thursday morning, his wedding day. Probably he had arrived in Manhattan the day before, traveling by train from Caryville. He walked up Crosby Street through the morning sun to the Lane home. Ellen was seated at the breakfast table with the Lanes. Hearing Benjamin at the front door, she hurried to let him in. "We met him at the door, with what feelings!"[75] This was the first she had seen him since they parted in Middletown nine months earlier.

Apparently Benjamin and Ellen spent most of the day talking, greeting friends, and preparing for the wedding. "The day passed pleasantly," Ellen said in her under-

71. ELSD, May 2, 1849.

72. BHR, *BTR*, p. 34.

73. See Garth M. Rosell, "Charles Grandison Finney and the Rise of the Benevolence Empire" (Ph.D. diss., University of Minnesota, 1971). Rosell notes that most of the evangelical reform societies were centered in New York City, including the American Bible Society, the American Colonization Society, the American Tract Society, and the American Temperance Society. All these organizations "held their annual meetings, what they called 'anniversaries,' each May [in New York City] in the Chatham Street Chapel. Finney's church became the operational center for national evangelical action" (p. 153). He adds, "Caught up in a general spirit of unity, evangelicals of many denominational worked together to establish an empire of benevolence on the earth," though the predominant leadership was Presbyterian. "Charles Finney, while declining to accept an office in any of the societies, gave his wholehearted support to these endeavors." In May 1832 Finney spelled out his views. "He specified, in terms of personal duty and social postmillennialism, the kind of motivation which was necessary for the task. Also, he suggested a broad national policy under which Americans could unite in such an effort. Drawing on the old Edwardsean [and Wesleyan, one might add] concept of 'universal benevolence,' . . . Finney pictured America as the center of a divinely ordered universe, a nation ruled by the moral government of God. . . . Everything should be estimated by 'its bearing upon Christ's Kingdom.' Duty thrusts the Christian into useful service" (pp. 154-56). "What really moved Finney and his colleagues was their desire to bring the nation under God's law, the rule of benevolence. Finney thought his blending of the millennial vision with the sense of national destiny would operate above the mundane affairs of parties and electioneering. Christian ideology should cut across political barriers, as it had already cut across denominational and class lines" (p. 160). Roberts was very much interested in these matters.

74. Carpenter erroneously says the Methodist General Conference was in session at this time (Carpenter, p. 41). In fact, the General Conference had met a year earlier, in 1848.

75. ELRD, May 3, 1849. (From this point on, Ellen's diary is cited as ELRD rather than ELSD. Ellen generally referred to herself as "Ellen Lois Roberts" following her marriage.)

stated way. In the evening everyone went to the Greene Street Church where George Lane performed the ceremony. "I never felt more calm or composed, and perhaps never more solemn," Ellen wrote. "My nearest friends and many others witnessed the solemn rite." Mary Martindale stood at Ellen's side; Ellen doesn't say who the groomsman was.[76]

A wedding dinner followed at the Lane home.[77] "The evening passed very pleasantly with several of the clergy and two of the bishops and their wives," Ellen wrote, but she does not name them.[78] According to Benson Roberts, the wedding guests included four of the five Methodist bishops: Thomas Morris, Elijah Hedding, Beverly Waugh, and Edmund Janes.[79] Probably four of the bishops attended the wedding, but just two of them and their wives joined in the supper at the Lane home afterward. Benjamin's marriage to the niece of the Methodist book agent "made Roberts suddenly a well-connected young preacher," comments James Revell.[80]

The newlyweds spent nearly two weeks in New York City as a sort of honeymoon, sharing a room at the Lane home, before heading for western New York.[81] A year earlier while still at Wesleyan University Benjamin had written an essay entitled "New York" that suggests the fascination the city had for him as for so many thousands of others. He remarked on "the interminable crowds of human beings of every hue & every language" that thronged Manhattan and on "Broadway that traverses like a vertebral column its entire length." He observed "the markets, filled with every thing that can minister to the wants or luxury of man, the huge printing establishments, . . . the rooms of the Bible & Missionary societies." He had noted "the parks, the fountains, the waterworks" of the city and "the ships of every nation" with their "thousand sails fluttering in the breeze," that filled its docks along both sides of lower Manhattan.[82] Now he was seeing the sights in company with his wife.

Friday, the day after the wedding, many friends called to congratulate Benjamin and Ellen and wish them well, and no doubt to see what sort of man Ellen had married. Ellen spent part of the day with Mary Martindale, and in the evening the newlyweds attended a gathering in their honor at the Skidmore home. "[N]early all my

76. ELRD, May 3, 1849. Ellen says "we went to the church" for the wedding but doesn't specify which one. Presumably it was Greene Street, where Ellen now had her membership, which may also have been the Lanes' home church.

77. Carpenter, p. 41.

78. ELRD, May 3, 1849.

79. BHR, *BTR*, pp. 33-34; Zahniser, pp. 35-36; Carpenter, p. 41. Benson Roberts has "Jones," apparently a misprint for Janes, as there was no Bishop Jones at this time. Carpenter claims that the bishops present were "Morris, Hedding, James [*sic*] and Scott" (p. 41). Levi Scott probably was present, but at the time he was assistant book agent, and was not elected bishop until 1852. The only bishop not present was Leonidas Hamline.

80. Revell, "The Nazirites," p. 117.

81. ELR to BTR, Feb. 14, 1851.

82. B. T. Roberts, essay, "New York," RFP, Microfilm Reel 10, dated May 30, 1848 (cf. Zahniser, p. 36). The essay is actually on New York State, but much of it is a description of Manhattan. Its detailed depiction suggests that Roberts had become quite familiar with New York City and was a keen observer.

most intimate friends" were there, Ellen noted. "I have seldom spent a pleasanter evening."[83]

During their days in New York, no doubt Ellen showed Benjamin some of her favorite places. They would have visited the Methodist Book Room at 200 Mulberry Street and other sites familiar to Ellen after living for a decade in ever-changing New York. Benjamin took advantage of the opportunity to pursue some of his own interests. Saturday, May 5, he walked through the rain to visit a Jewish synagogue and then went on downtown in the afternoon while Ellen remained at home, talking with Aunt Lydia. The rain continued on Sunday, so Ellen remained indoors, reading "the Memoirs of Mrs. Smith." Presumably Benjamin attended worship at Greene Street or one of the other Methodist churches in Manhattan. On Monday Ellen again visited the Art Union; she does not mention Benjamin accompanying her. She attended the Missionary Meeting in the evening with some of her friends.[84]

On Tuesday, May 8, "a dark day," Benjamin went down to Broadway Tabernacle to sit in on the opening session of the seventeenth annual meeting of the American Anti-Slavery Society.[85] On Thursday Ellen and Benjamin attended "the tract Anniversary" — that is, the anniversary session of the American Tract Society, also then meeting in New York.[86] The next day Benjamin wrote to his sister Florilla and her husband, telling them of his plans. With Ellen leaning on his shoulder, Benjamin wrote, "I am happy as the day is long, attending the various anniversaries in company with my better half, or in other words my wife!" He added a few lines of poetry:

> Domestic bliss has dearer names
> And finer ties and sweeter claims
> Than e'er unwedded hearts can feel
> Than wedded hearts can e'er reveal.[87]

83. ELRD, May 4, 1849.

84. ELRD, May 5-7, 1849.

85. ELRD, May 8, 1849. This was probably the opening session of the Annual Meeting of the American Anti-Slavery Society, which usually met at Broadway Tabernacle beginning on the first Tuesday in May, rather than the meeting of the more moderate, newer American and Foreign Anti-Slavery Society. Wendell Phillips spoke on this occasion, and (as noted in chapter 8) this may have been when Benjamin heard Phillips, to which he referred in 1884. See Oscar Sherwin, *Prophet of Liberty: The Life and Times of Wendell Phillips* (New York: Bookman Associates, 1958), pp. 154-55, 689.

86. ELRD, May 9, 1849.

87. BTR to W. T. Smallwood, May 10, 1849. Cf. Zahniser, pp. 36-37. The poetry is quoted from "The Lovers," by the Scottish poet Michael Bruce (1746-67), with slight alteration. The original reads:

> Connubial love has dearer names,
> And finer ties, and sweeter claims,
> Than e'er unwedded hearts can feel,
> Than wedded hearts can e'er reveal;
> Pure, as the charities above,
> Rise the sweet sympathies of love;
> And closer cords than those of life
> Unite the husband to the wife.

On Saturday the newlyweds enjoyed an outing to High Bridge, the spectacular 1,450-foot-long granite aqueduct across the Harlem River near the northern tip of Manhattan that since 1842 had supplied water to the city.[88] Ellen found it "quite a curiosity." They had lunch "among the trees" before returning home to the Lanes'. The next day was Ellen's last Sunday in New York, but she again remained indoors due to rainy weather.[89]

Ellen spent Tuesday, the fifteenth, getting ready for the long trip to her new home — "A sad day." Benjamin wanted to take his bride home to meet his parents in Gowanda before the couple settled in at Caryville, so they planned to go there first.

Ellen said good-bye to many of her friends; "none did I cling to as [to] my Uncle and Aunt."[90] In the evening she and Benjamin boarded the steamboat for the overnight trip up the Hudson River to Albany, the first leg of their journey west.[91] George Lane, Emilie, and other friends accompanied the couple to the dock to say good-bye. "And then we were wafted far away — then I felt as if I was married, when alone with my B____," Ellen wrote.[92]

Benjamin and Ellen had "good sleeping accommodation, only very hard beds" on the steamer up the Hudson River, Ellen noted. Arriving in Albany at 5:00 A.M., they had just time enough to catch the 6:00 train for Syracuse. "At some place we stopped long enough to take a cup of coffee and some crackers."[93]

This was the first time Ellen had traveled farther west than her hometown of Windsor. The train stopped in Little Falls, where several years earlier Benjamin had studied law with Henry Link. Benjamin had sent word to the Links about his marriage, and they had been expecting him and his bride when they passed through Little Falls. Mrs. Link boarded the train and traveled with the couple as far as Utica. Ellen was "very much pleased" with Mrs. Link; "she was so warm-hearted."[94]

The train pulled into Syracuse later in the day. Benjamin and Ellen had to wait for the next train west, so they had time to eat and to walk around the city a bit. They then continued their journey, passing through Auburn (where they "could see little, save the prison," Ellen noted), Geneva, and Rochester. When they arrived in Batavia, "quite a home feeling came over" Ellen as she realized this was the area where she and Benjamin would make their first home.[95]

The train huffed and screeched into the Buffalo station about nine o'clock Wednesday night. "What an uproar the hackmen make!" Ellen noted — worse than in New York. The weary couple got a ride to Bennett's Temperance House, where

---

88. Burrows and Wallace, *Gotham,* p. 625; Eric Homberger, *The Historical Atlas of New York City* (New York: Henry Holt, 1994), pp. 82-83. Roberts mentions the water system in his "New York" essay.

89. ELRD, May 12 and 13, 1849.

90. ELRD, May 15, 1849.

91. Zahniser, p. 36; BHR, *BTR,* pp. 34-35.

92. ELRD, May 15, 1849.

93. ELR to LBL, May 18, 1849, quoted in BHR, *BTR,* p. 34.

94. ELR to LBL, May 18, 1849, quoted in BHR, *BTR,* p. 35.

95. ELR to LBL, May 18, 1849, quoted in BHR, *BTR,* p. 35.

they dined and finally retired about midnight.[96] Ellen found the "accommodations good enough, but only tolerable in comparison with other places where I have been."[97] She was used to more refined places like Manhattan and Middletown; now she was in western New York, rapidly passing from frontier to bustling center of agriculture and commerce.

The next morning was less rushed. The newlyweds took a stagecoach at 9:00 for Gowanda, thirty miles distant. The rough roads made Ellen feel seasick, but she felt better when she and Benjamin changed to outside seats for the last twenty miles, and she enjoyed the scenery.[98]

The trip took all day. It was 6:00 P.M. when the stage finally pulled into Gowanda. "Our Father Roberts met us at the gate," Ellen wrote, "and our Mother Roberts and sister [probably Florilla and her husband William] at the door. The meeting was warm and kindly."[99] Ellen enjoyed some "pleasant conversation with my new Mother."[100] This was Titus and Sally Roberts's first opportunity to meet their daughter-in-law, and they seemed pleased.

Benjamin and Ellen spent almost two weeks in Gowanda so Ellen could get acquainted with Benjamin's family and friends. They visited both Florilla and Caroline and spent the night at Florilla's on May 23. Benjamin took Ellen to see the local sites, including the Seneca Indian reservation, and they visited Titus's farm outside Gowanda.[101]

Shortly after arriving in Gowanda Ellen wrote her aunt Lydia, thanking her and George for the home they had given her. "Your motherly care over me, and uncle's fatherly care, your thousand kindnesses to me, your forbearance toward me, will never be forgotten," she wrote. "For many days before I left, when I thought of these things, . . . and remembered how I would miss your society, your counsel and advice, I felt how hard it was —

'To smile when one would weep,
To speak when one would silent be.'"[102]

Ellen kept a frequent correspondence with Lydia Lane until Mrs. Lane died in 1866, at age sixty-five.[103]

Benjamin and Ellen attended the Methodist services both Sundays they were in Gowanda. Eleazar Thomas, presiding elder, came to Gowanda and preached Saturday

---

96. The Bennett Temperance House or hotel was run by the Methodist D. B. Hull, who was also a trustee of the Swan Street ME Church in Buffalo. A "Temperance House" was "a sort of inn or hotel with no alcohol or other vices allowed." Revell, "The Nazirites," pp. 215-16.

97. ELR to LBL, May 18, 1849, quoted in BHR, *BTR*, p. 35.

98. ELR to LBL, May 18, 1849, quoted in BHR, *BTR*, pp. 35-36.

99. ELR to LBL, May 18, 1849, quoted in BHR, *BTR*, p. 36.

100. ELRD, May 17, 1849.

101. ELRD, May 18-26, 1849.

102. ELR to LBL, May 18, 1849, quoted in BHR, *BTR*, p. 34.

103. See obituary, "Mrs. Lydia B. Lane," *EC* 12, no. 2 (Aug. 1866): 65-66.

afternoon, May 19, and on Sunday held a love feast, preached, and served Communion.[104] Ellen had a "good talk with Brother Thomas" following the meeting on Saturday.[105] The next Sunday Ellen heard Benjamin preach for the first time, as he accepted the invitation to be guest preacher. He took as his text 1 Corinthians 15:49, "And as we have borne the image of the earthy, we shall also bear the image of the heavenly."[106]

After visiting Gowanda, Benjamin took his bride back with him to Caryville. The couple left Gowanda Monday morning, May 28, taking a scenic journey north along the picturesque shore of Lake Erie. They stayed overnight with friends at Sheridan, then at Dunkirk boarded a boat that took them on to Buffalo. Ellen noted, "I had a long talk with a young woman who looked forsaken, who had never been from home before."[107]

Arriving in Buffalo a little after 5:00 P.M., Benjamin and Ellen again stayed overnight at Bennett's hotel. They got an early start the next day (Wednesday), taking the train to Batavia where they breakfasted before continuing on by stagecoach to Caryville. Arriving there midmorning, Ellen got her first glimpse of her new home.[108]

Ellen moved her things into the room at the Menck home where Benjamin was boarding. "Was glad to find myself in my own rather our own room, with none near save my loved Benjamin." The room was a little crowded for two people, so a couple of days later the newlyweds moved to a larger upstairs room that Ellen found "far more congenial." "I feel much more at home," she wrote.[109]

Benjamin agreed to pay the Mencks for his room and board, but found his income from the church was not sufficient for all his expenses. He ended the conference year "sixty dollars in debt for board," he noted.[110]

Ellen quickly became acquainted with the church people. She accompanied Benjamin on his calls or made some on her own. One of the class meetings met on Tuesday evenings, and Ellen became a member. "There seemed a good spirit prevailing among the brethren & sisters," she noted. In June she and Benjamin spent two days at a camp meeting at Parma, New York, where Ellen especially enjoyed the singing. "The people prayed and sung with the spirit." Independence Day, July 4, Benjamin and Ellen spent a quiet time alone together, walking out into the woods where they found a pleasant spot and sat reading a book. Then they walked on out to visit the Reed family, where they were invited to stay for tea.[111]

---

104. On Eleazar Thomas, see *COM*, p. 859; Sandford Hunt, *Methodism in Buffalo From Its Origin to the Close of 1892* (Buffalo: H. H. Otis and Sons, 1893), pp. 76-78. Hunt describes him as "a man of great force of character and an able and efficient minister" (p. 76).

105. ELRD, May 19-20, 1849. Eleazar Thomas was presiding elder in the Rushford District (called the Olean District after 1850) for two years (1848-50). Allen, *Century*, p. 20.

106. ELRD, May 27, 1849. (All biblical quotations are from the KJV.)

107. ELRD, May 29, 1849.

108. ELRD, May 30, 1849.

109. ELRD, May 30 and June 1, 1849.

110. BHR, *BTR*, p. 37.

111. ELRD, June 3-5, 21, and July 4, 1849.

From the very first, Benjamin and Ellen's marriage seems to have been unusually happy. They enjoyed each other and their life together, and of course they were both deeply committed to God and the work of ministry. After spending a day with Benjamin making calls and visiting "the sour springs," Ellen wrote, "Our ride was very pleasant. Indeed all our time together passes away so delightfully."[112] On August 3 she penned a snapshot of her new life as a Methodist preacher's wife: "Three months [ago] to-day we were married. A happy three months they have been. A year ago this morning we took a walk in P[ameacha] grove. This is <u>fast day</u>, appointed on account of the Cholera which is sweeping thousands from our land. Mr. R____ has gone to Batavia with some others to meeting. Have written to Mary. Afternoon at sewing society at Oakfield. Evening at prayer-meeting — a moon-light walk afterwards."[113]

Ellen pictured her new life with Benjamin also in a letter to Mary Martindale. Mary wrote back with her usual humor: "I am inclined to think that the one who could make married life as delightful to me as you describe yours to be is either dead or married — most likely dead." Yet she was happy for Ellen and her "dark eyed" husband, and pictured Ellen "sitting near the Woodbine window with thy friend by thy side, thou busy with the needle or pen, and he with his books."[114]

On August 12 Ellen wrote, "Heard two excellent sermons from my beloved B____." Perhaps these sermons spoke to her in some way, for the next day she resolved to be more intentional about her life. Though happily married, Ellen was not satisfied with her spiritual progress. She resolved to be more careful about keeping up her diary, "particularly in recording the exercises of my mind spiritually, believing it will be a benefit to me."[115]

Benjamin had gone to Rochester for the day, so Ellen spent part of the afternoon studying German and made some calls. But she felt unsatisfied with herself. "Came to my room and found it looking desolate — deserted — was fearful I loved Earth too well. I would not[;] I would love God supremely. O, that I may be enabled to give myself constantly to God and <u>live</u> for him." A couple of days later she wrote, "My own happiness depends too much upon the happiness of those around me. I sometimes fear I am thinking more of this world than I used to. Such is my nature that I need constantly to watch lest I love too well earthly objects. God must be supremely loved. I must not lean too much upon an <u>Arm</u> of flesh."[116]

Ellen still missed her New York friends, and this contributed to her sense of unease. "Thoughts of <u>Home</u> come to me," she wrote. "I never understood the meaning of these words 'I am a pilgrim, I'm a stranger' as since I left New York. Beyond the skies is a Home for the good. I've been thinking of the Christian warfare."[117]

112. ELRD, July 24, 1849.

113. ELRD, Aug. 3, 1849.

114. Martindale, Mount Kalmia [N.Y.?], to ELR, Aug. 1849, quoted in Zahniser, p. 37. Apparently Mary is recalling a time in the Lane home following the wedding, or perhaps is imagining the scene.

115. ELRD, Aug. 12-13, 1849.

116. ELRD, Aug. 13 and 15, 1849.

117. ELSD, Aug. 20, 1849.

Meanwhile Benjamin faithfully continued his duties as a Methodist preacher. His first year of pastoral ministry was fruitful, relatively free from problems. Under his leadership attendance increased at Caryville and the church prospered. Benjamin conducted well-attended prayer meetings on Thursday and Sunday evenings and watched over the several class meetings. Ellen generally found her Tuesday night class profitable; her leader was "a very zealous, good brother, who can sing."[118]

The church building was repaired and enlarged, and an old debt on the parsonage was settled. Benjamin received about 40 new members and at conference reported a total membership of 119, an increase of 13.[119] The only serious difficulty Roberts encountered was financial. The church paid a meager salary ("which they knew to be insufficient to meet his expenses," Ellen confided to Lydia Lane), and even that was sometimes slow in coming. This was the only drawback to an otherwise very pleasant situation, Ellen said. She felt the church's "remissness" in paying the preacher was due not to inability; rather "the official brethren are so inefficient."[120]

Summer came and went, and the conference year drew to a close. The good-hearted Caryville people naturally wondered whether they would get their preacher back — and hoped they would. "We would not have Brother Roberts go away for nothing," one elderly sister said. Everyone agreed that "the church is in a very different and far better state" than when Roberts came, Ellen told her aunt Lydia — adding, "I like the preaching much."[121] Benjamin wrote in his diary, "I had a pleasant year at Caryville. Was favored with some success. . . . The people expressed a strong desire for our return."[122] He later described his year at Caryville as "a prosperous one" with "a gracious revival, a large increase in the membership, and a general quickening among the people. The church edifice was enlarged and filled with an attentive congregation."[123]

Benjamin prepared to attend the annual conference in September, not knowing where he would be sent next. He intended to devote his life to the ministry of the church, whether as a pastor or as a missionary. Toward the end of his year at Caryville an inquiry came as to whether he would be willing to accept a missionary appointment to the Oregon Territory. Roberts was open to the possibility.

Interest in the Oregon mission was stirring in eastern Methodism at this time. Gustavus Hines, a prominent pastor in the Genesee Conference, had been appointed as missionary to the Oregon Territory in 1839. His work was successful, and in 1848

---

118. ELR to LBL, June 16, 1849, quoted in BHR, *BTR*, p. 37.

119. BHR, *BTR*, p. 37. The 1849 *Minutes* list 78 members and 41 probationers, for a total of 119. The 1848 *Minutes* give a total membership of 106, not divided between full and probationary members. Presumably Roberts removed around 27 inactive members, thus accounting for the overall increase of 13.

120. ELR to LBL, Sept. 22, 1849, quoted in Zahniser, p. 38, and BHR, *BTR*, pp. 38-39.

121. ELR to LBL, June 16, 1849, quoted in BHR, *BTR*, p. 37.

122. BHR, *BTR*, p. 37.

123. B. T. Roberts, "No Wrong Intention," *EC* 47, no. 2 (Feb. 1884): 38.

he published *A Voyage Round the World; with a History of the Oregon Mission* . . . , which sold very well.[124] Hines's book was recommended at the Genesee Annual Conference in 1850, and Roberts's own interest was kindled by reports of the Oregon work.[125] Yet he was uncertain, and Ellen's health was not robust. Ellen expressed some anxiety about the Oregon possibility in a letter to Lydia Lane.[126]

About this time there was also some thought of going as missionaries to China. Ellen later wrote, "After my marriage, there was talk of sending my husband and me to China as missionaries, but the Missionary Board decided that my health was not sufficiently good."[127]

124. *COM*, p. 445.
125. Conable, p. 585; Zahniser, pp. 40-41.
126. See Zahniser, p. 40.
127. Carpenter, p. 126.

CHAPTER 12

Two Years at Pike

"The great object of divine grace is to destroy our selfishness."

B. T. Roberts, 1883[1]

"The blessing came. The Spirit fell upon me in an overwhelming degree. I received a power to labor such as I had never possessed before."

B. T. Roberts[2]

Benjamin left Caryville on Monday, September 10, to attend the Genesee Annual Conference, not knowing whether he would be returned to Caryville, given a different church, or sent to Oregon. Conference that year was held from September 12 to 18 (Wednesday through Tuesday) at the Methodist Episcopal Church building at Albion, with Bishop Thomas Morris presiding. This was the conference at which Loren Stiles, Roberts's friend from Genesee Seminary days, and Joseph McCreery, Jr., became full members of conference and were ordained deacons.[3] Both would later be Roberts's colleagues in the conflicts that rocked the conference.

Ellen stayed home in Caryville, expecting to spend much of the week in "my lone room" while Benjamin was away. But on Wednesday Benjamin returned and the next day took her back with him to Albion so she could attend the conference activities — "an unexpected pleasure," she noted. She enjoyed being in Albion, situated

1. [B. T. Roberts], "Stagnant," *EC* 46, no. 2 (Aug. 1883): 64.
2. B. T. Roberts, "A Running Sketch," *EC* 9, no. 1 (Jan. 1865): 6.
3. Zahniser, p. 38; Conable, p. 575. McCreery's name is spelled McCreary or M'Creery in some sources. See Ray Allen, *A Century of the Genesee Annual Conference of the Methodist Episcopal Church, 1810-1910* (Rochester, N.Y.: By the Author, 1911), p. 105.

on the Erie Canal and thus connected to the New York she had left behind. Ellen found Albion "a pretty place — so tasty." Their hosts in Albion were "refined and intelligent people without [being] quite aristocratic." Thursday evening she walked over to the Erie Canal and watched the boats arriving. "The bustle[,] the quantity of people, the number of foreigners all seemed very New-Yorkish."[4]

Saturday Levi Scott arrived from New York City, representing the Methodist Book Concern, of which he was now assistant agent. Ellen was glad for the chance to talk with a friend from Manhattan. "I could scarce keep my tears when he asked me if I was weaned from N.Y.," she said. George Lane sent Benjamin and Ellen a letter and a book. "The letter made me sad," Ellen wrote. "It was about Oregon."[5] She doesn't say more, but apparently Lane's letter indicated that an Oregon appointment was still possible.

Ellen rode back to Caryville with friends on Monday while Benjamin remained for the final day of conference and the reading of the appointments.[6] When the appointments were given out, Roberts found that he was sent to Pike, almost fifty miles south of Caryville in hilly Wyoming County. Benjamin hurried home to tell Ellen, arriving about dark. "We are to go to Pike," Ellen wrote resignedly in her diary. "May God go with us."[7]

Even as Benjamin and Ellen prepared to move, the Oregon question was still on their minds. Lydia Lane wrote to Ellen, "I am sorry you are again agitated about Oregon. I could wish that you might remain in your native land until your health was better."[8] Benjamin had written to George Lane, who as treasurer of the Missionary Society would know the status of the Oregon mission, to see if he could give more definite word. But then he was fearful (Ellen confided as she answered Lydia's letter) that his letter might be misunderstood. Benjamin "did not wish to convey the idea that his mind was changed in regard to going there"; he simply wanted "to know something certain."[9] Lydia suggested that Benjamin contact Bishop Morris to get some definite word.[10]

Oregon remained an open question for a year or so, leaving Benjamin and Ellen

4. ELRD, Sept. 10-14, 1849.

5. ELRD, Sept. 15, 1849; COM, p. 790. The General Conference elected Levi Scott assistant book agent (thus George Lane's assistant) in 1848 and bishop in 1852.

6. ELRD, Sept. 17, 1849. In her diary Ellen notes, "called on the Bishop" in the morning. It is not clear whether she is speaking of herself only, or of both her and Benjamin. Perhaps the two of them wanted to talk with Bishop Morris about their future ministry, and the possibility of missionary service.

7. ELRD, Sept. 18, 1849.

8. LBL to ELR, Sept. 14, 1849, quoted in Zahniser, p. 40.

9. ELR to LBL, Sept. 22, 1849, quoted in BHR, BTR, p. 38.

10. LBL to ELR, Sept. 14, 1849, quoted in Zahniser, p. 40. As noted, Ellen in fact made it a point to talk with Bishop Morris on Monday, Sept. 17, before she returned to Caryville, probably to inquire about the Oregon possibility (ELRD, Sept. 17, 1849). It is not clear whether this was before or after she had received Lydia's letter, which was dated Sept. 14, but it probably was before. She found a letter from Lydia awaiting her when she returned to Caryville on the seventeenth.

a bit uncertain as they began their ministry at Pike. In the end, Benjamin was not appointed to Oregon and decided to remain in the Genesee Conference.[11]

The day after he returned from conference, Benjamin and Ellen packed up their few belongings and prepared to move. "This is the <u>itinerancy</u> — in real earnest," Ellen wrote. "But I feel that all is right, and will work together for good. It may not look so now, but I believe we will yet see it so. My spirits are quite good, yet I regret leaving here on some accounts — and not on others."[12] They left Caryville Thursday evening amid "great lamentation among the people," Ellen said.[13] They traveled south toward Pike, Sister March from Caryville accompanying them. They stayed Thursday night with Mrs. March's parents in Bethany. Arriving in Pike Friday afternoon, they met what to Ellen "seemed a cool reception." "We both felt a touch of home-sickness."[14]

First Year at Pike

Saturday, Benjamin and Ellen looked over their new home. They wandered around Pike, "feeling like strangers in a strange place, not looking for a bright side to the picture," Ellen said.[15] However, in the afternoon William Cooley, the Methodist preacher at nearby Portageville, stopped by.[16] Benjamin and Ellen found that they were to lodge temporarily with the Olin family. They discovered that Brother Olin was a cousin of Stephen Olin.[17]

Pike was larger than Caryville; it was more a small city than a farm town. Ellen described it as "quite a village, rather an old place."[18] It had three churches, and the families living on both sides of the Methodist parsonage were Presbyterians. The nearest railroad was twenty-four miles north at Attica, so one needed to take a stage-coach first to travel east or west by rail.[19]

Benjamin preached morning and afternoon on Sunday, September 23, at his new charge and led the evening prayer meeting. The day was cold and rainy, and few attended. The next day he and Ellen traveled to Gowanda and spent about ten days with Titus and Sally Roberts. Ellen was glad for the chance to get better acquainted with Benjamin's parents and his sisters Florilla and Caroline and their husbands.

Benjamin returned to Pike on Thursday, October 4, and Ellen the next day. He

11. BHR, *BTR*, pp. 36-37.

12. ELRD, Sept. 19, 1849.

13. ELR to LBL, Sept. 22, 1849, quoted in BHR, *BTR*, p. 38.

14. ELRD, Sept. 20-21, 1849.

15. ELRD, Sept. 22, 1849.

16. William Cooley, like Roberts, was later expelled from the Genesee Conference (in 1859) and became a Free Methodist. Allen, *Century*, p. 79.

17. ELRD, Sept. 22, 1849. Roberts was later to refer to some serious financial and ethical difficulties that Olin fell into.

18. ELR to LBL, Sept. 22, 1849, quoted in BHR, *BTR*, p. 39.

19. ELR to LBL, Sept. 22, and to unspecified recipient (LBL?), Oct. 24, 1849, quoted in BHR, *BTR*, pp. 39-41.

probably returned by horse; about this time (perhaps while visiting Gowanda) he bought a horse named Bill so he and Ellen would have their own transportation.[20]

Ellen rode to Pike by stagecoach, leaving Gowanda on a cold, dark morning, waving good-bye to Florilla, who stood in her doorway, "hair still in papers" but her face "bright and shining." Florilla blew a good-bye kiss, and Ellen was on her way. From Springville to Pike Ellen was the only passenger, and she fell into conversation with the driver, who recounted the history of the area. He "exercised a fatherly care over me, [and] fearing I was not sufficiently clad for the evening dews, he borrowed a cloak on the way, and as night came on he wrapped it around me, and then drew the buffalo skin over me, so I did not suffer with the cold." She reached the Olins around 8:30, glad to be reunited with Benjamin.[21]

Roberts now began his pastoral work at Pike in earnest. He preached on Sunday, October 7 — another rainy day, with small congregations.[22] Though Benjamin had expected to return to Caryville, he accepted the Pike assignment as God's will. He wasn't sent back to Caryville, he later learned, because an older pastor wanted to go there so his children could attend Cary Collegiate Institute.[23]

Pike was "an exceedingly dilapidated circuit" that "scarcely suited the preacher," Benson Roberts wrote. Many in the congregation wanted someone older and did not especially welcome Benjamin and Ellen.[24] Officially the church had 106 members, including 3 probationers, compared with Caryville's 119 when Roberts left. But weekly attendance was far below that. Benjamin and Ellen again faced a major rebuilding job.

Though the young preacher and his wife "were not expected nor wanted" at Pike, the church "received us, though coldly," Benjamin said.[25] But he and Ellen set to work. "We will try to be good and do good," Ellen wrote to Florilla.[26]

The first question whenever a Methodist preacher arrived at a new charge was: Where will he live? Some of the Methodist circuits had parsonages; others did not. While Pike had a large parsonage, it was unpainted and run-down, surrounded by a dilapidated fence. "A more forlorn and neglected-looking place I hope Methodist preachers will not often find," Ellen wrote her aunt Lydia. Still, it had a nice front yard and a garden plot behind. The house was located on a narrow backstreet, a rather quiet and peaceful spot.[27]

At first Benjamin and Ellen were undecided about living arrangements. The church wanted them to move into the parsonage, but that would require lots of re-

---

20. See BHR, *BTR*, p. 48.

21. ELR to Florilla Smallwood, Oct. 25, 1849, quoted in BHR, *BTR*, pp. 43-44.

22. ELRD, Sept. 24–Oct. 7, 1849. Benjamin must have arranged for someone else (perhaps a local preacher) to conduct the services on Sept. 30, while he was away.

23. B. T. Roberts, "No Wrong Intention," *EC* 47, no. 2 (Feb. 1884): 38.

24. BHR, *BTR*, p. 38.

25. B. T. Roberts, "No Wrong Intention."

26. ELR to Smallwood, Oct. 25, 1849, quoted in BHR, *BTR*, p. 45.

27. ELR to unspecified recipient (LBL?), Oct. 24, 1849, quoted in BHR, *BTR*, p. 41.

pair and buying furniture. The couple was reluctant, partly because missionary work in Oregon was still possible and they might have to move again. They continued to live temporarily with the Olins while deciding what to do.[28]

A solution to the housing question came through a kindly Methodist couple who lived in a nearby town, Stephen Bronson (a local preacher) and his wife. They had come to the area three years earlier from Connecticut. These "old-fashioned saints, with love for men and power with God," took pity on the young pastoral couple and volunteered to move into the parsonage with their sixteen-year-old son and keep house for Benjamin and Ellen, at least temporarily.[29] This seemed ideal, and the Robertses gratefully accepted.[30] "I long to get settled," Ellen confided.[31]

Benjamin and Ellen fixed up two large second-floor rooms in the parsonage and moved in. One room was their bedroom and the other, which was bigger and had two large windows, became their all-purpose living room. Benjamin and Ellen cleaned, wallpapered, whitewashed, painted, and soon had a comfortable, attractive place. Ellen discovered that her husband was handy with tools; Benjamin built a sort of lounge seat, which they upholstered, and started work on a bookcase. "If he only had conveniences for working, I think he might make all the furniture we would need," Ellen wrote admiringly to Aunt Lydia. Trying to keep the floors clean, she longed for a good old "New York scrubbing brush."[32]

At first the only furniture were their trunks and three wooden chairs, one with no back. Ellen said the chairs "made me feel when sitting upon them as perched upon a high rail fence, my feet hanging down."[33] But they were glad to have their own place. "We have enjoyed being once more where we could feel it was home, though it has not looked homelike much," Ellen wrote. One of the church members had recently lost his wife and "broken up house-keeping," so he lent Benjamin and Ellen a table, rocking chair, stove, and washstand, which helped considerably.[34] Ellen wrote to Florilla,

> Soon we will have a bed and carpet come, and then we will live like other people. Yet this primitive style of bare floors and open fires I rather like, only for its novelty, I reckon, though. I wish you could see our window curtains — so scant in size, neither wide enough nor long enough; but we dream of better ones soon. Yet we are happy here. The sun, when it shines, looks in upon us the livelong day, and our little birds fill our rooms with the sweetest music. We are so retired [back from the main street] that we will never be annoyed by the din of the world without, will

---

28. BHR, *BTR*, pp. 39, 43-44.

29. Apparently Bronson had some kind of business. Carpenter says, "[O]ne good brother moved his business from an adjoining town purposely to help make a home" for Benjamin and Ellen. Carpenter, p. 44.

30. BHR, *BTR*, pp. 38-40.

31. ELRD, Oct. 8, 1849.

32. ELR to unspecified recipient (LBL?), Oct. 24, 1849, quoted in BHR, *BTR*, pp. 40-42.

33. ELR to Smallwood, Oct. 25, 1849, quoted in BHR, *BTR*, p. 44.

34. BHR, *BTR*, pp. 40-44.

never long while here "for a lodge in some vast wilderness." Neither will we long for the multitude. Our hearts shall be a spring of ceaseless pleasures deep and pure.[35]

Ellen rather enjoyed the contrast with the bustle and noise of New York City. She also noticed cultural differences between Pike and Manhattan. "The men seem very slow and easy, and the women I see nothing of, save at church and a few places where we have called." Only one sister stopped by to see her during the first month. The fall was cold and rainy, and Ellen was told that the "summers are so short and cold" that supposedly "tomatoes never ripen."[36]

On October 22, as she and Benjamin were settling into the parsonage, Ellen wrote in her diary, "I feel the need of more religion." She didn't pick up her diary again until early December. She had become pregnant and perhaps was not feeling well. On December 9 she wrote, "I feel miserably in body and my mind not clear — troubled with temptations."[37]

This was a hard time for Benjamin, too. With the Bronsons occupying the rest of the house and providing the meals, Benjamin could give full attention to the church. He found the prospects discouraging. Many of the members were backslidden, and the church quite lifeless. By the middle of November Benjamin was feeling sorry for himself. But this led to renewed dedication.

A letter from Titus Roberts helped him regain perspective. In response, Benjamin wrote very candidly to his father on November 20:

> I have been quite too much dissatisfied with my station. . . . I have felt down, clear down most of the time since I came here. I never thought of preaching for the purpose of making money, and I used to think I should not be at all particular about the support I received as a preacher. But when I saw my class-mates, whose qualifications, it is modest to say, are not superior to mine, receiving from four to six hundred a year, for labors not as severe as [mine], and myself receiving at the same time but a bare subsistence, and not even that, while the churches, I believe, possess the ability to give their minister a respectable support, I felt like repining. It seemed as if our people [thought it] proper to get out of their preachers as much as possible of both labor and money, and to pay them in return as little as possible. I have been looking the wrong way altogether. I should have looked at the Saviour more and at the people less. As a necessary consequence I have not been able to preach with any degree of satisfaction. Till last Sabbath, I have hardly had a comfortable time preaching. But I am trying now to give myself up wholly to the Lord, repenting of my sin, and I feel better, and I believe preach better. Prospects are rather promising. Our congregation is increasing. Class and prayer meeting are better attended, and there is, I hope, an increasing spirituality among the members.[38]

35. ELR to Smallwood, Oct. 25, 1849, quoted in BHR, *BTR*, pp. 44-45.
36. ELR to unspecified recipient (LBL?), Oct. 24, 1849, quoted in BHR, *BTR*, pp. 41-42.
37. ELRD, Oct. 22 and Dec. 9, 1849.
38. BTR to TR, Nov. 20, 1849, quoted in BHR, *BTR*, pp. 45-46; cf. Zahniser, p. 39.

In January Benjamin conducted a revival, with good fruit. Services were held nearly every night. Benjamin wrote to Lydia Lane on January 17, 1850, reporting some twenty conversions, "most of them very clear," backsliders reclaimed, and "the members generally greatly revived." Class and prayer meetings were thriving, and special meetings were continuing every other night.[39]

Roberts had again won his way into the hearts of the people, as he did at Caryville. In February the church conducted its annual "donation" for the pastor and his wife, bringing gifts to the parsonage ranging from a study table and washstand and a bit of cash to handmade calico quilts of green and red, a barrel of meat, bushels of potatoes and corn, and some yards of muslin and calico. Ellen received two pairs of stockings and a nightcap. There was even a harness for horse Bill, plus hay and oats. The donations included "an order from the wool factory, which we will take in flannel for one or two pair of blankets. . . . They are all useful articles," Ellen said, "and mostly what we would need." One "very peculiar sister" brought "a yard of coarse, un-bleached muslin and two straight collars, such as men wore some time ago." In the evening the children "sung, played, and had supper," and offered their little gifts.[40]

By the end of March it was clear that Benjamin and Ellen would not be going to Oregon. With Ellen expecting her first child, the Bronsons moved out of the parson-age, and Benjamin and Ellen took over the whole house. Ellen wrote, "We have com-menced house-keeping in the Parsonage, which looks quite pleasant[,] comfortable & home-like. I enjoy myself well — O how much better than when we first came here."[41]

William Titus Roberts, Benjamin and Ellen's first child, was born at home on June 21, 1850. Apparently the birth was normal, and the proud parents were de-lighted. A few weeks after the birth Ellen said of the baby, "He is a treasure. The care of a little child is a new era in my life. I am weak in body & feeble[,] which has its ef-fect upon my mind."[42]

Another very significant event occurred during that same summer of 1850. In August Benjamin and Ellen decided to spend a week in Gowanda, which would give Ellen and baby Willie a chance to visit the grandparents and aunts and Benjamin the opportunity to attend the nearby Collins camp meeting. Ellen and Willie stayed with Florilla while Benjamin attended the camp meeting sessions. "He was greatly blessed while there," Ellen noted in her diary.[43]

Eleazar Thomas, presiding elder of the Rushford District, apparently was in charge of the camp meeting and had arranged for Phoebe Palmer to come.[44] As

---

39. BTR to LBL, Jan. 17, 1850, quoted in BHR, *BTR*, p. 47.

40. ELR to LBL, Feb. 21, 1850, quoted in BHR, *BTR*, pp. 47-49.

41. ELRD, Apr. 1850 (exact date not given).

42. ELRD, July 1850 (exact date not given). There are only four more entries in Ellen's diary for 1850 — one in August, two in September, and one in December. Ellen apparently was quite unwell dur-ing this time.

43. ELRD, Aug. 1850 (exact date not given).

44. Thomas was presiding elder for two years, 1848-49 and 1849-50, according to the conference minutes.

Roberts attended and listened to Mrs. Palmer, God did a deeper work in his own heart. He later wrote:

> The subject of holiness received special attention. Rev. Eleazar Thomas, presiding elder of the District was then a flame of fire. Mrs. Palmer attended the meeting and labored for the promotion of holiness with great zeal and success. While I was at [Wesleyan University in] Middletown, Dr. Redfield held a protracted meeting in the Methodist church. Such scenes of spiritual power I never had witnessed. The convictions I there received never left me. At the [Collins] camp meeting they were greatly increased. Two paths were distinctly marked out before me. I saw that I might be a popular preacher, gain applause, do but little good in reality, and at last lose my soul. Or I saw that I might take the narrow way, declare the whole truth as it is in Jesus, meet with persecution and opposition, but see a thorough work of grace go on, and gain Heaven. Grace was given to make the better choice. I deliberately gave myself anew to the Lord, to declare the whole truth as it is in Jesus, and to take the narrow way. The blessing came. The Spirit fell upon me in an overwhelming degree. I received a power to labor such as I had never possessed before. This consecration has never been taken back. I have many times had to humble myself before the Lord for having grieved his Spirit. I have been but an unprofitable servant. It is by grace alone that I am saved. Yet the determination is fixed, to obey the Lord and take the narrow way, come what will.[45]

Thus Benjamin recalled this key event in his spiritual pilgrimage fifteen years later, in an article in the *Earnest Christian*. This was his experience of entire sanctification — though he later passed through times of spiritual struggle, as we will see. Thirty-six years later, when Roberts was in his sixties, he still looked back to this consecration at the Collins camp meeting as a turning point in his walk with God and credited Phoebe Palmer for her part. In 1886 George Hughes published *Fragrant Memories of The Tuesday Meeting and The Guide to Holiness, and Their Fifty Years' Work for Jesus* as a testimonial to the ministry of Mrs. Palmer. Hughes solicited testimonies from those who had been blessed by Palmer's ministry, and Roberts responded: "We feel life-long obligations to Dr. and Mrs. Palmer, and hold their memories in the highest veneration. In the year 1849, the second year of my ministry, I experienced the blessing of holiness through the labors of Mrs. Palmer, at a camp-meeting held in Collins, Erie Co., N.Y. Mrs. Roberts, before she was married, was for four or five years a member of Dr. Palmer's class in the old Allen Street Church, New York, and he was instrumental in leading her to full salvation."[46]

This statement, written more than three decades after the fact, requires some clarification. While this event did in fact occur during Roberts's second year of pas-

---

45. B. T. Roberts, "A Running Sketch," p. 6. With some minor alterations in punctuation and capitalization, this testimony is found also in BHR, *BTR*, pp. 50-51.

46. George Hughes, *Fragrant Memories of The Tuesday Meeting and The Guide to Holiness, and Their Fifty Years' Work for Jesus* (New York: Palmer and Hughes, 1886), p. 147.

toral ministry, as he says (1849-50, his first year at Pike), the camp meeting mentioned took place in 1850, not 1849.[47] It is significant also that while in his 1865 "running sketch" Roberts gives due credit to Phoebe Palmer, he also mentions Eleazar Thomas and John Wesley Redfield as important influences. In his 1886 tribute to Phoebe Palmer, Benjamin notes that Ellen had for some time been in Dr. Walter Palmer's class in New York, and that he had been "instrumental in leading her to full salvation." Ellen's own testimony gives a somewhat different picture, however. She says she did not enter into "full salvation" until some years later — as we will see.

Nevertheless, Roberts's testimony makes it clear that Phoebe Palmer did play a key part in his experience of holiness. His basic understanding of holiness and of its relationship to abolitionism, preaching the gospel to the poor, and a range of social issues had already been shaped by his upbringing and experiences prior to the encounter with Palmer. But through her ministry, he notes, he entered into the experience of holiness. The Palmers' influence on Ellen was in some ways longer and more formative, though it is clear from Ellen's diaries that her conception of holiness and the Christian life was shaped also by George and Lydia Lane, including Lydia's missionary interest and involvement and her extensive ministry among the poor, as noted earlier.

Following the Collins camp meeting Ellen noted in her diary the blessing Benjamin had received. "Thank God," she added. "Nothing can exceed [Benjamin's] tenderness and kindness to me. O, that I may be a help and not a hindrance to him. I still feel very miserable in body."[48]

William Kendall was this year (1849-50) serving his second year at Cambria and was also growing in his experience of and convictions about holiness. Still single, he wrote to his fiancée on May 1, 1850, "My convictions have been a long time deepening, that holiness is the only doctrine which can save the church, and through her the world. Without it no man shall see the Lord; I love to think of it. I love to talk and preach it, and best of all, I love to *enjoy* it. With God's help it shall be my theme throughout life, and my watch-word at the gates of death."[49]

To help Ellen during this period of ill health, a Christian sister, "Maria B___," came and lived with the Robertses for a while. Perhaps this was Maria Bronson, Stephen Bronson's wife, who with her husband had kept house for Benjamin and Ellen earlier. Maria came sometime in August 1850 and stayed several weeks, until she herself took ill. Ellen wrote at the end of October, "Maria was nearly sick and has gone away. I am no better and Mr. R. is in search of a girl. Cold weather is coming truly."[50]

---

47. Roberts misremembers the year, both here and in his 1865 article, "A Running Sketch." This is clear from Ellen's diary. August of 1849 would have in fact been during Roberts's *first* year of pastoral ministry. Also, White's *Beauty of Holiness* lists Phoebe Palmer among the attendees of the Collins camp meeting in 1850, but not in 1849 (Charles Edward White, *The Beauty of Holiness: Phoebe Palmer as Theologian, Revivalist, Feminist, and Humanitarian* [Grand Rapids: Francis Asbury Press/Zondervan, 1986], p. 238). Zahniser incorrectly places this camp meeting in 1851 (Zahniser, pp. 45-46).

48. ELRD, Aug. 1850 (exact date not given).

49. "Rev. Wm. C. Kendall, A.M. — His First Charge," *EC* 2, no. 6 (June 1861): 183.

50. ELRD, "Last of the month" (apparently Oct. 31), 1850.

By this time annual conference had come and gone, and Roberts had been re-appointed to Pike. His first year at Pike had been very successful, despite the unpromising beginnings. Many people were converted, and clear signs of spiritual deepening among the members brightened the prospects for the coming year. Officially, church membership decreased from 106 in 1849 to 98 in 1850, showing that Roberts had to drop many names from the roll in order to have an up-to-date list.[51]

The 1850 annual conference, which met from September 25 to October 2 at Rushford with Bishop Beverly Waugh presiding, was a significant milestone in Roberts's ministerial career. He was admitted into full conference membership and on Sunday, September 29, was ordained deacon, along with Kendall and others.[52] Roberts and the other candidates had to pass a written examination before conference began, and Benjamin did very well on it. Most of the candidates passed, though one was rejected for having copied his essay word-for-word from the *Pulpit Reporter*. "I would not be in his place for all the world," Roberts wrote to Ellen.[53] Kendall passed but didn't do as well as he might have. He had recently married.[54] Benjamin commented wryly to Ellen, "I should judge from his examination that he has spent considerable time in courting."[55]

Thomas Carlton, presiding elder in the Buffalo District, chaired the examining committee. He was especially impressed with Roberts's examination, reportedly saying it was "perfect, the best he had ever attended." Carlton invited Benjamin to have dinner with him Tuesday noon, the day before conference began.[56] Roberts was thus becoming acquainted with one of the most influential pastors in the conference, and in fact the denomination — and later, one of his chief opponents.

Benjamin participated in the conference sessions until they ended on October 2. He appreciated Brother James Fuller's sermon Tuesday evening, and felt that "With a deeper baptism of the Holy Ghost he would be a useful preacher."[57] The next morning, the first full day of conference, Benjamin got up a little after 5:00 and walked a

---

51. *Minutes*, 1849 and 1850. The report for 1849 showed 103 full members and 3 probationers, compared with 86 full members and 12 probationers in 1850.

52. *Minutes*, 1850, p. 520; BHR, *BTR*, p. 51.

53. BTR to ELR, Sept. 25, 1850, quoted in BHR, *BTR*, p. 53.

54. Kendall married Martha Francis Wallace, the daughter of John H. Wallace, on Sept. 19, 1850, traveling to Clinton County, Mich., for the wedding. "Rev. Wm. C. Kendall, A.M. — His First Charge," p. 185. Martha Kendall later became Mrs. Thomas LaDue, or La Due. See her memoir, "Mrs. Martha Francis La Due," in John La Due, *The Life of Rev. Thomas Scott La Due* (Chicago: Free Methodist Publishing House, 1898), pp. 325-50.

55. BTR to ELR, Sept. 25, 1850, quoted in BHR, *BTR*, p. 52.

56. BTR to ELR, Sept. 25, 1850, quoted in BHR, *BTR*, pp. 54, 52. As chairman of the Examining Committee, Carlton perhaps arranged to meet separately with each candidate. Or he may have chosen to meet only with Roberts.

57. BTR to ELR, Sept. 25, 1850, quoted in BHR, *BTR*, p. 54. There were three Fullers in the conference at this time, but since James Fuller was secretary of the conference and an influential minister, presumably it was he who preached.

couple of miles. "I feel very well indeed," he wrote Ellen. "I want to work more faith-fully than I ever yet have done for the Lord."[58]

Benjamin remarked in his letter, "Father has not come yet."[59] Apparently Benjamin expected him, and he likely was present for his son's ordination on Sunday.[60]

Benjamin was quite impressed with Bishop Waugh's remarks when he examined the candidates for ordination. One of the disciplinary questions was, "Are you in debt?" Bishop Waugh said he would "rather go to conference or into the pulpit with a rusty, or patched coat, than wear a good one and be in debt for it." Once his coat had gotten so worn that he had it turned, since he couldn't afford a new one without incurring debt. Benjamin could identify with this, as his own clothes left something to be desired. "My hat seems to have incurred the displeasure of the preachers," he noted wryly. "Yesterday afternoon Brother Woodworth charged it with being deficient in ministerial dignity." Benjamin reminded him of the bishop's remarks. Brother Woodworth took out his wallet and said if Roberts wore his old hat because he couldn't afford a new one, he'd give him the money for it. "I thanked him, but could not, of course, accept," Benjamin told Ellen.[61] Whether Woodworth's comment was in jest or not, it shows the growing Methodist concern with "ministerial dignity," especially in cities like Buffalo, in contrast with the days when most Methodist preachers were frontier circuit riders. In fact, as James Revell notes, "Woodworth had just finished an assignment to Buffalo Niagara Street and was aware of the need for 'ministerial dignity' in the new social order."[62]

Second Year at Pike

Having laid a foundation the previous year, and with a renewed sense of God's presence, Roberts continued his ministry at Pike. He again conducted revivals, his principal method of evangelism. During the year he held meetings at East Pike and at Eagle, in addition to Pike, and at Eagle witnessed "quite a revival."[63] Roberts's new

---

58. BTR to ELR, Sept. 25, 1850, quoted in BHR, *BTR*, p. 52.

59. BTR to ELR, Sept. 25, 1850, quoted in BHR, *BTR*, p. 54.

60. In his letter to Ellen, Benjamin says his father was approved when the "admission of local preachers to deacon's orders was considered." Apparently he is referring to his approval as local deacon, since Titus Roberts was not a member of conference at this time and there is no mention of him in the minutes. See BHR, *BTR*, p. 54; Zahniser, p. 44.

61. BTR to ELR, Sept. 25, 1850, quoted in BHR, *BTR*, pp. 53-54. Philo Woodworth was the preacher at Niagara Street, Buffalo, and was appointed this year to Yates, Niagara District. He was about forty-nine at this time. *Minutes*, 1850; Allen, *Century*, p. 131.

62. James Alan Revell, "The Nazirites: Burned-Over District Methodism and the Buffalo Middle Class" (Ph.D. diss., University of New York at Buffalo, 1993), p. 235.

63. BHR, *BTR*, pp. 54-55. Benson Roberts says the revival at Eagle "resulted in building a church." However, the minutes list no appointment to Eagle in the immediately ensuing years, although Eagle Village appears in 1859. East Pike is listed as an appointment connected with Portageville in 1853, 1854, and 1856, and then with Pike in 1858 and 1859.

presiding elder in the district, Albert Wilbor, came and preached a few evenings for Benjamin in December, following the district quarterly meeting. "[W]e like Bro. Wilbor well," Ellen noted.[64]

In conducting and promoting revivals, Benjamin was following the classic Methodist way of evangelism and church growth. William Hosmer, at this time editor of the *Northern Christian Advocate*, published in Auburn, argued the importance of revivals in a February 1851 article. Revivals, he said, "are not an incident in Methodism; it is itself a revival, and a constant promoter of revivals. It is Christianity so much in earnest, both in the ministry and in the laity, and with such appropriateness of doctrine and discipline, that it must be successful in the work of evangelizing the world."[65] This was essentially Roberts's view as well.

As Benjamin attended to his pastoral work, he was concerned about Ellen and her health. When Maria left, he tried to find a girl to come and live with them and help with the care of the house. In November Ellen's niece, Mary Swezey, moved down from Windsor to help out. The daughter of Ellen's deceased sister Mary Ann, Mary would have been around fourteen at the time.[66] She apparently lived with the Robertses for three years or so.[67]

Ellen enjoyed watching young William Titus develop. "Little Willie grows more and more interesting. I fear loving him too well," Ellen observed in December. She was still not strong physically. In January she noted, "My eyes trouble me so much that I cannot use them scarcely any."[68]

Ellen traveled to New York City in February 1851 to visit the Lanes and her friends there, and so George and Lydia could see little Willie.[69] She took the night train so Willie would be sleeping much of the time and be less trouble. At first Willie would "jump and squeal as usual, much to the amusement of the people around him," but at dark he fell asleep on the seat beside Ellen and slept most of the night. After changing trains twice, she and Willie arrived at Jersey City about dawn and then took the ferry across to Manhattan. Willie got very fussy the last hour on the train, and Ellen was much relieved to find George Lane waiting for them when they stepped off the ferry in New York.[70]

This was Ellen's first visit back to her New York home since her marriage.[71] She was glad to see old friends, and took advantage of her time in the big city to get some

64. ELRD, Dec. 1850 (exact date not given).

65. William Hosmer, *NCA*, Feb. 27, 1851, p. 2. Quoted in Zahniser, p. 44.

66. ELRD, Dec. 1850 (exact date not given).

67. Ellen mentions Mary a few times in her diary and in May 1853 noted, "Mary has gone home." However, Ellen had so many friends named Mary that it's hard to be sure of the identification. Mary Swezey may not have lived continuously with the Robertses during this time, but she was still with them when Benjamin was pastoring in Buffalo in 1852-53.

68. ELRD, Dec. 1850 (exact date not given); Jan. 1851 (exact date not given).

69. She apparently arrived in New York about Feb. 12. On the thirteenth George Lane sent a telegram to Benjamin telling of Ellen and Willie's safe arrival. ELR to BTR, Feb. 14, 1851.

70. ELR to BTR, Feb. 14, 1851.

71. This apparently was the visit to New York referred to in Carpenter, p. 44.

medical attention for her eyes and teeth. She had Willie vaccinated a few days after arriving at the Lanes.[72]

Ellen wrote to Benjamin frequently during the weeks she was in Manhattan and welcomed each letter from him. This was the longest the couple had been separated since their marriage, and Benjamin missed his wife keenly. She wrote him, "Be assured it is the first and last time I'll leave thee."[73] On February 14, a couple of days after her arrival, she wrote Benjamin an account of her trip while Willie played nearby. "Willie is sitting on the floor playing with Sarah's large doll — he laughs over it and acts as if he thought it a living child."[74]

Ellen's letters give a vivid sense of the love that had developed between her and Benjamin during their two years of marriage. She told him, "Don't get lonely if you can help it. Ever remember how deeply and constantly I love you."[75] Her letter of February 25 is full of endearing words: "I am with you every night in my sleep." "Dearest, how I would [love] to throw my arms around you this morning." "Beloved, I love you so dearly, so truly, that I cannot bear to be separated from you."[76] And again, three days later: "O how I love you — yes, 'better than ever.' Thou art dearer to me, and I feel that I need Thee more and more. What a blessed relation! I am thankful that I am not a stranger to the joys of married life. I would not be a maiden again. I would not change situations with any person on earth. And oh, it seems to me when we are together again, that we will be more nearly <u>one</u> than ever before."[77]

Ellen was concerned about Benjamin's ministry and his studies, and prayed for his spiritual well-being.

> If my poor prayers can avail, you will find in your heart "no melancholy void," but you will be happy all the day long, and find your spiritual strength "renewed like the eagle's." Your soul will be filled with light and life, with power and love.
>
> How ardently do I desire that <u>my Husband</u> should be an all-devoted minister of the cross. I ask not for him popularity, but that he may be such an one as our Heavenly Father will delight to own and bless in all his labors. And <u>dearest</u> I would be a <u>help</u> and not a hindrance to you.[78]

Ellen worried also about Benjamin's health. "I am afraid you are preaching too often," she wrote. "When you do preach, do be very short, not over thirty minutes."[79]

---

72. ELR to BTR, Feb. 14 and 28, 1851.

73. ELR to BTR, Mar. 10, 1851, quoted in Zahniser, p. 45.

74. ELR to BTR, Feb. 14, 1851.

75. ELR to BTR, Feb. 14, 1851. She adds, "Let us know when you send the butter and how much it is. Give love to Mary and other friends."

76. ELR to BTR, Feb. 25, 1851.

77. ELR to BTR, Feb. 28, 1851.

78. ELR to BTR, Feb. 25, 1851.

79. ELR to BTR, Mar. 3, 1851, quoted in Zahniser, p. 44.

Ellen herself was still having eye trouble and sought help in New York. "Were it not for my eyes I should begin to think of coming to you soon," she wrote Benjamin on February 28, two weeks after her arrival. "But I feel desirous to give Homeopathy a fair trial, and have my eyes helped if possible — this I know you would have me do." She added, "I have not had anything done to my teeth yet, if I should have, and pay what is due on your books I shall be under the necessity of calling on you for some more money."[80]

One day during her New York visit Thomas Carlton, the prominent Genesee Conference minister who the next year would succeed George Lane as book agent, came to dinner at the Lane home. Ellen learned that Carlton had reportedly told Bishop Waugh that he "was not a member of any Secret Society in the world, but did not wish the fact to be known." If Carlton in fact said this, what did he mean? Was he being truthful, or had he perhaps become a Mason or Odd Fellow but did not consider these "secret societies"? The remark shows again that the issue of secret societies was agitating the church.[81] Carlton was influential in denominational politics, and years later Roberts accused him of using "secret society influence in the General Conference" to get elected book agent. It is not clear, however, that Carlton was ever himself a Mason or Odd Fellow.[82]

Ellen had intended to return to Pike early in March, but a severe snowstorm hit New York and the Lanes convinced her to wait. She wrote Benjamin on March 10, apologizing for the delay. One senses in the letter her anxiety to get back home. "Though I am a long distance from you, how I cling to you, and lean upon you in spirit." But "I must not love my husband too well, or my Father will take him from me. That would be a trial which I feel I could not bear." She added, "Love to my friends. Beg of them not to think I have run away from you," and closed with "an ocean of love."[83] On finally arriving home Ellen wrote in her diary, "I enjoyed my visit, but felt severely the separation from my dear B____."[84]

Little Willie was developing nicely. He "has quite an idea of walking," Ellen wrote shortly after her return from New York. "The little darling was such a comfort

---

80. ELR to BTR, Feb. 28, 1851. Ellen also mentions a number of domestic things in her letter. She writes, "I am glad you are thinking about a cow again — it does not seem to me we could live without one even one summer. Yet if you should think best to do so, I am willing to try." On Feb. 25 she wrote, "If you have much damp and rainy weather I should think it would be well occasionally when you are home to make a fire in the cook-stove, on account of the roof above leaking — it would be better for things that are in the Buttery [i.e., pantry] too."

81. ELR to BTR, Feb. 20, [1851], quoted in Zahniser, p. 42. Zahniser gives the date as Feb. 20, 1850, but this cannot be correct, as Ellen was in Pike at this time (BHR, BTR, p. 47). Ellen's diary has no entries for February 1850 (when she was pregnant), but her diary and other letters show she was in New York for much of February and March 1851.

82. WAS, p. 53. I have not been able to find any evidence that Carlton was a Mason or Odd Fellow. There is no reference to either society in his obituary notices, nor any fraternal order insignia on his tombstone near Elizabeth, N.J.

83. ELR to BTR, Mar. 10, 1851, quoted in Zahniser, p. 45.

84. ELRD, Mar. 1851 (exact date not given).

to me while travelling alone, with none to protect us. Yet we were protected by a kind Providence."[85]

In April Ellen complained of not being very well. About this time she became pregnant a second time. Toward the end of the month Willie took sick, and Ellen became increasingly concerned. A doctor came to see him on Sunday, April 27.[86] Willie did not improve, however, but instead grew steadily worse. Despite medical attention and the loving care of his anguished parents, Willie died on June 5, two weeks before his first birthday. Ellen tells the story in her diary:

> After an illness of six weeks and one day our darling child was taken to a home "in the skies" June 5th[,] just eleven months and fifteen days old. It was hard to see him suffer so long — it was hard to give him up. None but a parent who has passed through a similar trial can know the anguish it causes to lose a little one — an only one taken away. I feel thankful that he was permitted to leave this world so quietly, so easily to all appearances. The Physician said he had never seen a child die so easy. Again & again in his last moments he would [try] to put his little finger in his mouth. It did seem as if this would break my heart. My darling child was lovely in death, very lovely. He looked as if asleep. We buried him in Gowanda near his Father's early home, where he spent the first years of his life. We planted the green myrtle on his grave, and reluctantly left the place where we laid our lovely boy. We have friends there who will not pass carelessly by that spot. Now we are in our lonely home. Oh, it seems lonely — there is nothing I see but what tells me of the departed one. Yet I have blessings left. I have the best of husbands to go to with all my sorrows, Praise God for this blessing — May he be spared to me. I am much of the time harassed and troubled with the fear of his being taken away too. But I'll try to give all into the hands of Him who cannot err.[87]

Benjamin arranged to have the baby interred in the Presbyterian cemetery in Gowanda, and the sad parents took Willie there for the burial. After a few days with Benjamin's parents, they returned to their "lonely home" in Pike. Later Ellen wrote to Titus Roberts, "I never knew till since my little Willie died what it was to feel lonely, and I never knew either what it was to confide in Christ, to feel that I have one Friend always nigh as I have since then." She hoped through this trial to be "made better, for I feel so sure some greater trial will come upon me if this fails of accomplishing the end for which it was sent."[88]

Ellen received a consoling letter from Lydia Lane and replied,

> O how I have felt to turn to you, Aunt Lydia, for weeks that are past, for that comfort which I received, and which, it seems to me, no one else could give. I felt thus because of the comfort you had been to me in days past, when tried, and because I

---

85. ELRD, Mar. 1851 (exact date not given).
86. ELRD, Apr. 9 and 27, 1851.
87. ELRD, June 18, 1851.
88. ELR to TR[?], quoted in BHR, *BTR*, p. 57.

knew you loved our little Willie, and because I knew you did not think it a small thing to have a little child removed by death. . . . O, it seems sometimes as if my heart would break. The longer I am separated from him, the more it seems to me I love him and want to see him. I cannot say that I desire to have him back again, for that I know is not my Heavenly Father's will. His will is best for me. . . . I loved our dear little one too well, and while I feel that our Father has done all things well, I cannot control my nature. Pardon me for saying so much to you about my sorrows. I seldom speak of them to anyone except my husband. I strive to be cheerful, and to live for others. How differently everything seems to me from what it used to.[89]

Despite their sorrow, Benjamin and Ellen continued their ministry in Pike. At the end of June they attended a camp meeting for a week or so and found it a great blessing. As Ellen was preparing to leave on Wednesday, June 25, she wrote, "Of the past I can only say my heart most of the time has been full of sorrow. I think I feel resigned, yet I feel afflicted, wounded, my loss is constantly before me. I believe there is grace which can enable me to rise above these afflictions. I desire to profit by this chastening to the extent which my Father would have me. And to feel all the time, [']good is the will of the Lord.'"[90]

The camp meeting continued into the first few days of July. Walter and Phoebe Palmer were there part of the time. This appears to have been the camp meeting held near Cuba, New York, about thirty miles south of Pike, that Phoebe Palmer refers to in a letter dated July 3, 1851. This is uncertain, however, as the Palmers visited several camp meetings in western New York about this time, traveling on the Erie Railroad.[91]

"We spent a happy week in the grove," Ellen recorded. "My own soul was abundantly blessed, strengthened and encouraged. I have found it hard to give my own will up in some respects — but after I did it I had solid peace and much greater liberty in doing my duty."[92] A number of people from Pike attended the camp, along with Benjamin and Ellen. "We had two board tents, and one very large cloth tent in which we had some excellent meetings," Ellen wrote Titus Roberts. "Dr. and Mrs. Palmer were there a few days. . . . My own soul was greatly blessed. Not in several years have I enjoyed myself as well as I have since the camp-meeting. I have a more abiding assurance of the favor of God and feel that I am His entirely, and what I have realized of the power of grace to sustain, to comfort and cheer amid sore affliction, I have no words to express. While I feel keenly my loss, I do not dwell upon it as I did."[93]

Rather than returning home after the camp meeting, Benjamin took Ellen away from Pike for a couple of weeks of travel and visiting friends. Probably he saw this as a sort of therapy. They went first to Lima, where they heard Benjamin Tefft give his

---

89. ELR to LBL (undated), quoted in BHR, *BTR*, pp. 55-56.
90. ELRD, June 25, 1851.
91. Richard Wheatley, *The Life and Letters of Mrs. Phoebe Palmer* (New York: W. C. Palmer, 1881), p. 294.
92. ELRD, July 1851 (exact date not given).
93. ELR to TR, Aug. 6, 1851, quoted in BHR, *BTR*, p. 56.

inaugural address as president of Genesee College.[94] They also spent a day or two in the Caryville area, "visiting many of our old friends and calling on many." Then they traveled west to Niagara Falls, staying overnight with William Kendall and his wife at Royalton, near Lockport, where Kendall pastored a Methodist church of some 250 members.

Ellen found the view of Niagara Falls refreshing. "I was greatly pleased with Niagara — it far exceeded my largest anticipations," she wrote. "The River — the Rapids[,] all was so much grander, more sublime than I expected."[95]

Benjamin and Ellen then visited friends and acquaintances in Buffalo and did some shopping before returning to Pike. Finally arriving back home, Ellen wrote, "I enjoyed myself well spiritually. My home seemed less desolate. I thought not so much of my absent one as I did of trying to live so that I might be prepared to see him again. Yet at times my heart seemed more than full of grief."[96]

The summer of 1851 passed into early fall, meaning that the conference year was coming to an end. "I enjoy myself well spiritually. My peace much of the time is like a river," Ellen wrote early in September.[97]

When Benjamin prepared his annual report, he found that total membership during the year had increased from 98 to 116.[98] Given the loss the previous year due to removing inactive members, the total membership of 116 represented an increase of 10 over the two years that Roberts pastored at Pike. Though the numerical increase was not large, the church was much more vital than two years previously.

On September 8 Benjamin left for annual conference, leaving Ellen and her niece Mary at home. "I miss my little W____ most when my B. T. is gone," Ellen noted. She spent much of the time visiting parishioners while Benjamin was away, and stayed nights with the Brayton family. "I have not enjoyed myself very well," she wrote. "I have felt much of the time so distracted[,] so disturbed spiritually. Mary and I are alone."[99]

This year the annual conference was held September 10-16 at LeRoy, Bishop Edmund Janes presiding. Benjamin went to conference knowing that he would receive a new assignment. Arriving at LeRoy, he immediately sent off a letter to Ellen, which she received the day conference began. When conference ended the following week, he hurried home to tell Ellen that they were moving to Rushford, and that

94. Genesee Wesleyan Seminary added a college program in 1850. Benjamin Tefft was the first president, taking office in 1851. Ray Allen, *History of the East Genesee Annual Conference of the Methodist Episcopal Church* (Rochester, N.Y.: By the Author, 1908), pp. 28-29.

95. ELRD, July 1851 (exact date not given).

96. ELRD, July 1851 (exact date not given).

97. ELRD, Sept. 1851 (exact date not given).

98. *Minutes*, Genesee Conference, 1851. In this year the Genesee Conference began listing local preachers in a separate (third) column, as some other conferences had begun to do earlier. Thus total membership was made up of "members," "probationers," and "local preachers." Pike's total of 116 included 104 members, 11 probationers, and 1 local preacher.

99. ELRD, Sept. 8 and 13, 1851. Ellen says on Sunday, Sept. 14, "Been quite unwell." She was about five months pregnant at this time.

Kendall would replace him at Pike. Rushford, about twenty miles farther south, was a much larger church, with a total membership (officially) of 244, including five local preachers.[100] Statistically, it was the twelfth-largest church in the conference (out of seventy-six) and the fifth-largest in the district, in total membership.

1851 Portraits of Benjamin and Ellen

Shortly before moving from Pike to Rushford, Benjamin and Ellen had their portraits painted. The artist was Carlos L. Stebbins, a portrait painter living in Pike. Six months younger than Benjamin, Stebbins (1824-1914) was then in his beginning years as a portraitist. Benjamin and Ellen no doubt became acquainted with Stebbins and his wife Eleanor during their time in Pike, and, like many other local families, they asked him to do their portraits.

Carlos Leonard Stebbins went on to have a long career in Pike as artist, inventor, surveyor, banker, teacher, maker of violins, and repairer of anything. He became something of a living legend; the true Renaissance man of Pike. His mother had named him Carlo Leonardo at birth, honoring her Italian immigrant parents' family. The Stebbins family migrated to western New York from Massachusetts.

A number of Stebbins's portraits, drawings, and inventions can still be found in the Pike area. He came to have a substantial reputation regionally; an 1882 article in the *Buffalo Express* reported, "He has painted some very fine portraits of the wife and daughter of the late Chief Judge Sanford E. Church. . . . He has orders from New York, Chicago, Rochester and other places, the subjects coming to his studio in Pike for sittings. Many of his works have been on exhibition in the art galleries of New York, and received high awards of merit. Added to his studio he has a work shop where his mechanical genius finds full scope."[101]

For years Stebbins was also an active Mason and Odd Fellow, which Roberts may or may not have known.[102]

On Christmas Day 1851 Benjamin and Ellen went back to Pike from Rushford "on business about the Portrait," Ellen noted in her diary.[103] Probably this was to view the portraits and perhaps approve them or make suggestions. A month later Benjamin noted that he "brought home our portraits" from Pike, paying twelve dollars for them.[104] Neither Benjamin nor Ellen comment. . . . in their diaries on the

---

100. ELRD, Sept. 10 and 16, 1851; *Minutes,* 1851.

101. Quoted in Robert M. French, "Carlos Leonardo Stebbins," *Historical Wyoming* 17, no. 1 (Oct. 1963): 3.

102. *Biographical Review . . . The Leading Citizens of Livingston and Wyoming Counties, New York* (Boston: Biographical Review Publishing Co., 1895), p. 241. It is not clear whether Stebbins was already a Mason or Odd Fellow at the time Roberts knew him.

103. ELRD, Dec. 25, 1851.

104. BTRD, Jan. 26, 1852. Four years earlier, in 1847, another patron paid ten dollars for two portraits. French, "Carlos Leonardo Stebbins," p. 4.

quality of the paintings, nor of the frames. Stebbins customarily painted from photographs, not from sittings, and made his own frames.[105] For Benjamin and Ellen he may have used as his models the photos they had taken a couple of years earlier.[106]

These rare color portraits of Benjamin and Ellen, painted on linen, remained for two or three generations in the Roberts family, but eventually were lost. In 2002 they surfaced through an antique dealer in Indiana. The portraits were acquired by Roberts Wesleyan College and placed on display in the president's home, where they remain.

Artistically, the portraits are not especially impressive, but Stebbins was still in the early days of his career. Photographs of Benjamin and Ellen taken both before and after 1851 give more realistic depictions. Yet these portraits, made in the age before color photography, are historically significant for their portrayal of the young couple after about two and a half years of married life. Ellen was five months pregnant at the time. Her portrait shows her with blue eyes, black hair, and a black dress or jacket and a thin white ruffled collar. Her only adornment is a brown comb holding her hair at the back. She has the slightest hint of a smile, as in her photo from about three years earlier.

Benjamin is dressed in the same type of black coat, black tie, and high-collar white shirt as in the photograph he had taken a few years earlier. His high forehead and black hair are also similar to the photo. Unlike existing photos of Benjamin, he is clean shaven, without the long sideburns and beard. The main difference between the photographs and the portraits is that the faces in the latter appear somewhat narrower and more rounded at the chin.

These portraits are included in the photo section of this book.

105. French, "Carlos Leonardo Stebbins," p. 7.

106. Information on Carlos Stebbins was provided by Bonita A. Speer, deputy county historian, County of Wyoming, Warsaw, N.Y., Dec. 3, 2002. In addition to the sources cited above, see *History of Wyoming County, N.Y. with Illustrations, Biographical Sketches and Portraits of Some Pioneers and Prominent Residents* (New York: F. W. Beers and Co., 1880), p. 262.

CHAPTER 13

Life and Death at Rushford

"[T]o visit the people from house to house and converse with them closely about their religious state, requires grace."

B. T. Roberts, 1883[1]

"Uncle Tom's Cabin excites my sympathies so that I can neither read it or let it alone. I will make a thorough abolitionist I imagine."

Ellen Roberts, 1852[2]

Benjamin, Ellen, and Mary immediately began packing for the move to Rushford. They traveled there on Saturday so they could spend Sunday at the new charge. "Was quite well pleased," Ellen noted. "The people seem like warm-hearted Methodists."[3] Monday they returned to Pike for their belongings, and moved to Rushford on Wednesday. Ellen reflected, "I might feel sadly about leaving Pike and making my home again among strangers if I had not resolved to <u>think</u> and <u>feel</u> no more than I could possibly help."[4]

Despite Ellen's brave spirit, moving was hard — though Benjamin noted that it wasn't as difficult as it might have been since they had no heavy furniture.[5] By the end of the week Benjamin and Ellen (and presumably Mary) were settling into the

1. [B. T. Roberts], "Pastoral Visiting," *EC* 45, no. 2 (Feb. 1883): 65-66.
2. ELR to BTR, Sept. 17(?), 1852, quoted in Zahniser, p. 51. Possibly the correct date is Sept. 12, as Benjamin was back home by the seventeenth.
3. ELRD, Sept. 20, 1851.
4. ELRD, Sept. 22, 1851 (entry dated Sept. 22; obviously written the twenty-fourth or later).
5. BTR to TR, Sept. 29, 1851, quoted in BHR, *BTR*, p. 58.

Rushford parsonage. "To-day we take dinner in our home for the first time," Ellen wrote. "I have had some rather homeless, itinerant feelings since I came here in spite of myself. But no matter!"[6]

Benjamin had been told that the parsonage would be furnished, but they found it wasn't. The previous pastor, Charles Shelling, had some old furniture "that had been moved as long as it was worth moving." Shelling wanted Roberts to take the furniture and have the church reimburse him (Shelling) for it. Benjamin felt he couldn't do this without first consulting the church. He said that if Shelling would make a list of the furniture, with prices, he'd take that to the church, and they could decide what to buy. Shelling was "quite vexed" that Roberts wouldn't simply take the furniture, Benjamin reported, "and in his vexation went off and sold it. We felt glad to have it go."[7] However, the matter prompted the story that "Bro. Roberts was too proud to take Br. S's. old furniture," so Benjamin had to deal with that. The matter was resolved once the Rushford people learned the facts. At an official meeting the church agreed to go ahead and furnish the parsonage. Some opposed this, but Albert Wilbor, presiding elder, told the church that "unless they furnished the parsonage comfortably and promptly" he would send Roberts to a different church that would properly take care of him![8] So Benjamin and Ellen for the first time moved into a furnished home.

Benjamin noted in a letter to his father on September 29 that Rushford had "a good congregation and things look[ed] favorable." Yet there was great need for revival and awakening in the congregation and in the community.[9] "There were more old-fashioned Methodists" at Rushford than at any of Roberts's other appointments, writes Adella Carpenter. "Many were staunch and honored members of the community."[10]

Benjamin quickly made the transition to his new assignment and soon was hard at work. He continued the pattern he had established earlier of rising at 5:00 A.M., spending his mornings in study, and giving his afternoons to pastoral calls. Most mornings he spent time reading the Hebrew Bible and the Greek New Testament.[11] It may have been about this time also that he began what became a lifelong practice of reading the Bible through every year. He recommended this practice. He wrote years later,

> The Bible is a wonderful book. . . . The more we read it, the more we enjoy it. We always find in it something new. It is a field, the fertility of which increases the longer, and the more thoroughly it is cultivated. The more there is taken from it,

6. ELRD, Sept. 27, 1851.

7. BTR to TR, Sept. 29, 1851, quoted in BHR, *BTR*, pp. 58-59.

8. BTR to TR, Sept. 29, 1851, quoted in BHR, *BTR*, p. 59.

9. BTR to TR, Sept. 29, 1851, quoted in BHR, *BTR*, p. 58. Benson Roberts adds, "To lift up a church from a state of apathy and coldness into a condition of spiritual life, to awaken the ungodly in a community where indifference largely characterises church members, requires no little determination and perseverance coupled with spiritual strength" (pp. 59-60).

10. Carpenter, p. 44.

11. BHR, *BTR*, p. 60, citing Benjamin's 1851 diary.

the more it is capable of yielding. It is a mine which grows richer and richer the deeper it is worked. We lose our interest in other books, after reading them a few times. It is not so with the Bible. . . . It was adapted to every period of the world's history in the past; it is especially adapted to our times.[12]

Early in his ministry Roberts became convinced also of the value of pastoral calling, though it was hard work, and this he practiced faithfully at Rushford. He later wrote, "Men can preach who have been educated to do it, whether they enjoy religion or not. But to do pastoral work — to visit the people from house to house and converse with them closely about their religious state, requires grace. If one has the love of souls that the Spirit gives those in whom it [sic] dwells, he will do all he consistently can for their salvation."[13]

In addition to his work at Rushford, Roberts also went back to Pike several times to assist William Kendall with revival efforts there.

Meanwhile, Ellen continued to struggle with the adjustment of the move. After a month in their new home she was "feeling quite homesick. I am not living as near the Lord as I did a few weeks since."[14]

Ellen was comforted by her ongoing correspondence with Lydia Lane in New York. However, a letter from Lydia on November 7 brought fresh anxiety. Lydia's daughter Sarah, Ellen learned, was very ill.[15] "I fear she will not live," Ellen confided in her diary. She recalled a recent dream in which Sarah "was very, very ill and had dreadful spasms and died." The dream had "made a strong impression on my mind at the time."[16] Ellen soon learned that nine-year-old Sarah did in fact die on Friday, November 21. This was a hard blow for Ellen, who had cared for Sarah in the Lane home. "It seems a trial I can hardly bear — O how severe for her Parents."[17]

Ellen continued to struggle emotionally and spiritually during these last months of 1851. On Sunday, November 16, she noted, "Heard my Husband preach this morning from 'Examine yourselves.' It was a heart-searching sermon. I sat in tears under it, and felt to take it to myself." The next Sunday she remained indoors and "had a good day at home alone." On Thanksgiving Day, November 27, after hearing Benjamin preach and visiting friends, she enjoyed herself better spiritually. She wrote on December 10, after visiting revival services at Pike, "I have had great trials about praying before people."[18]

Ellen's niece Mary was still with her, but about this time Mary began attending school. Ellen was busy with household chores and the concerns of the church. "I find

12. [B. T. Roberts], "Editorial Notes," *FM* 20, no. 44 (Nov. 2, 1887): 1.

13. [B. T. Roberts], "Pastoral Visiting," pp. 65-66.

14. ELRD, Oct. 29, 1851.

15. Sarah Lane was born to George and Lydia Lane on Jan. 10, apparently in 1842. See chapter 6, and reference in LBLD, Jan. 10, 1852.

16. ELRD, Nov. 7, 1851.

17. ELRD, Nov. 25, 1851.

18. ELRD, Nov. 16, 23, and 27, and Dec. 10, 1851.

use for all the strength I have," she wrote. "We washed to-day, and baked," and then attended a church meeting. "I have had a good day. Have been enabled in patience to possess my soul, amid some little outward perplexities." Yet the next day she confided to her diary, "I have no good thing to write of myself to-day, I yielded to impatience and brought sorrow upon myself. I grieved my Husband and more than that, my Heavenly Father. When will I learn not to yield to sinful inclinations?"[19]

The next Sunday Ellen stayed home and read articles on holiness in the *Northern Christian Advocate*. Ellen was now eight months pregnant and often not feeling well. With Benjamin gone to Pike to help with the revival there, she wrote on Monday, December 15, "I have worked to-day more than I ought[,] written to my Aunt and my dear Husband. I miss him much. I have been trying to search my heart, to see if I love him too well. I do not think I do, but perhaps I lean on him too much. Enjoy myself quite well — yet I do not exercise faith as I desire and as I once could."[20]

With Benjamin away at Pike, Ellen did what she could to assist with the ministry at Rushford. She realized on Tuesday, December 16, that class meetings should be held and decided to take the initiative herself. She resolved, "if the Brethren have not life enough to meet the Sisters must have. I found on enquiry that [a meeting] had been appointed. So we met at Bro. B's and had an excellent meeting. I have not in months felt so much of the presence of the Lord and aid of the spirit [*sic*] as at this meeting. I do believe we shall have a revival in Rushford. I never felt the same anxiety for any place. I never felt so much of that faith which will take no denial as I do when praying for this church."[21]

Thursday Ellen felt "extremely nervous all day," with little spiritual desire, but was cheered by Benjamin's arrival back from Pike. "The clouds are passing over," she wrote. "My thoughts were turned into another channel and I began to feel more like myself. I cannot account for the state of mind I have experienced to-day unless it be occasioned by nervousness."[22]

During these weeks a significant revival was continuing at Pike through the preaching of Roberts's friend William Kendall, whom Zahniser describes as a "natural revivalist."[23] In December Benjamin spent "two Sabbaths and most of three weeks" assisting with the Pike revival.[24] Ellen accompanied Benjamin to Pike for the first week, but then returned to Rushford.[25]

19. ELRD, Dec. 10, 11, 1851.
20. ELRD, Dec. 14, 15, 1851.
21. ELRD, Dec. 16, 1851.
22. ELRD, Dec. 18, 1851.
23. Zahniser, p. 47.
24. BTR to LBL, Jan. 1, 1852, quoted in Zahniser, p. 47.
25. ELRD, Dec. 2 and 10, 1851. Ellen went with Benjamin to Pike on Tuesday, Dec. 2, and returned with him to Rushford on Dec. 9. Benjamin went back to Pike on Saturday, Dec. 13, leaving Ellen at Rushford. Ellen writes on Dec. 2, "I had not thought of going myself [to Pike] till a short time before we left. I believe it was right for I endured the ride far better than I could have expected — scarcely any fatigued."

The revival at Pike extended Roberts's work there from the previous year. "A good foundation for a genuine and extensive revival had been laid, and the work was already commenced" when Kendall arrived, Benjamin noted.[26] Kendall built on this, using his natural gifts as a singer. In addition to regular church services, Kendall began a public "singing school" so everyone could "learn to sing." He used this as a means of outreach, giving an evangelistic exhortation at the end of each evening's session. Many youth came out to these meetings on cold winter nights, and the Lord began to awaken them spiritually.[27] Some of the youth "were soon heard to cry aloud for mercy," Roberts notes. "Conviction deepened, [revival] meetings were appointed, and the work rapidly spread on every side. There was quite a general confession, and breaking down on the part of the church, and the tide of salvation rolled on day and night for many weeks."[28] During much of this time, special meetings were held both morning and evening.[29]

As a result of this winter revival, the Pike church gained one hundred new members and "many [were added] to other churches" as well.[30] Roberts adds, "A multitude already belonging to the churches were reclaimed and saved, who were before living in sin." Kendall "strongly and constantly insisted on both inward and outward holiness, *entire sanctification,* while he endeavored to keep the standard of justification as high as God's word has placed it," Roberts noted. While this brought solid fruit in "clear and strong conversions, and converts pressing into the enjoyment of entire holiness," it also provoked opposition to Kendall's ministry. Some members asked him "not to preach so much on holiness, for the present at least, lest he should 'drive away men of influence *needed in the church!'"[31]

At first Kendall followed this advice, but "he soon saw the entire church backsliding" and realized he must continue to hold to the high standard of holiness. In Roberts's words, Kendall "resolved to preach not only now and then on holiness, but to preach it, as Asbury said he was divinely impressed to do, 'in every sermon.' The Spirit returned, and some again sought and found the second rest."[32] The church prospered, but the controversy affected Kendall's reputation. According to Roberts, "From this time Brother Kendall, began to acquire the reputation of being 'self-willed,' 'indiscreet,' and 'unsafe,' because he would not — *dare* not offend God to save ease, influence or friends."[33]

Roberts assisted Kendall in the revival efforts through both visitation and

---

26. "Rev. W. C. Kendall," *EC* 2, no. 7 (July 1861): 204.

27. "Rev. W. C. Kendall," p. 204. Roberts does not say specifically that the singing meetings were held in the evening, but this seems likely.

28. "Rev. W. C. Kendall," p. 204.

29. ELRD, Dec. 10, 1851. Ellen mentions attending "one of the morning meetings."

30. "Rev. W. C. Kendall," p. 204. According to the Genesee Conference minutes, total membership at Pike went from 115 in 1851 to 217 in 1852 (a gain of 102) and back down to 141 in 1853.

31. "Rev. W. C. Kendall," p. 204.

32. "Rev. W. C. Kendall," pp. 204-5.

33. "Rev. W. C. Kendall," p. 205. On the Pike revival, see also Zahniser, pp. 46-47.

preaching. Philo Brown, the presiding elder, also came and helped.[34] On Wednesday, December 3, the day after arriving from Rushford, Benjamin "[v]isited among the unconverted most of the day" and preached at night. Many came forward to pray and some were converted. "The Spirit of God [was] powerfully manifest," Roberts noted. He preached also on Sunday morning, sensing God's help, and that day "[b]etween twenty and thirty [were] received into the Church."[35]

A few weeks later Roberts returned to Pike for the Friday night service to see how the revival was progressing. "Bro. Kendall in the opinion of many of the brethren is urging holiness upon the younger converts to the injury of the work of God," Roberts noted in his diary. "O how we need the wisdom of Serpents, the harmlessness of doves."[36]

Inspired by the Pike revival, Benjamin was soon promoting similar efforts at Rushford. He conducted a watch-night service on New Year's Eve — a "very solemn and interesting" time, and a sign of hope.[37] The next day, as "snow and ice upon the trees gave everything . . . a pure unearthly appearance,"[38] Benjamin wrote to Lydia Lane, assessing the prospects at Rushford. "We have a membership strong in numbers, wealth and social influence," Roberts noted, "and a stranger would imagine that they enjoyed a good degree of the life and power of religion." That was true in the past, but Benjamin felt that now the life had departed. "The words that then expressed their feelings they still use, but the feelings are gone"; the prayers seemed stereotyped. "I have been endeavoring to arouse them, but fear that I am no more than half awake myself," he wrote. He prayed that a revival like that in Pike would "break out in Rushford, and in the regions about."[39]

Roberts continued to follow the recommended Methodist pattern of rising early and devoting most of the morning to study. On New Year's Day 1852 he read in the Hebrew Bible and the Greek Septuagint, and also from Josephus. He had spent two dollars for a copy of Josephus (presumably the *Jewish Antiquities*) a year earlier.[40] The next day, Friday, he read two chapters in the Greek New Testament and took some notes from Josephus before visiting in the afternoon. On Saturday he spent most of the day in his study, reading and preparing for Sunday. He noted in his diary, "Rose at 5. Read Hebrew Bible and Greek. Compared their chronology with Josephus. Josephus and Septuagint agree in the main." He again read two chapters in the Greek New Testament.[41] Similarly the next week, he noted on

34. ELRD, Dec. 10, 1851.

35. BTRD, Dec. 3 and 7, 1851, quoted in BHR, *BTR*, p. 60. Roberts's text on Sunday morning was Matt. 1:21. Benson Roberts's account gives the impression that this ministry was at Rushford, but Ellen's diary makes clear the reference is to Pike and the revival there.

36. BTRD, Jan. 9, 1852.

37. BTR to LBL, Jan. 1, 1852, quoted in BHR, *BTR*, p. 60.

38. ELRD, Jan. 1, 1852.

39. BTR to LBL, Jan. 1, 1852, quoted in BHR, *BTR*, p. 61, and Zahniser, p. 47.

40. BTRD, Jan. 1, 1852, and "Book Account," p. 108 of 1852 diary.

41. BTRD, Jan. 3, 1852.

Monday that he rose at 4:00 and "Had a good time reading Greek & Hebrew" (though he felt he "Did but little after that"), and on Tuesday, "Rose at 5. Hebrew & Greek." On January 16 he wrote, "It seems I accomplish but little though always busy."[42]

During these years as a Methodist pastor, Roberts used the small pocket diary printed annually by George Lane and the Methodist Book House in New York. The diary doubled as a handy reference book of Methodist statistics (listed each year at the beginning of the diary) and included pages for membership data, subscriptions to Methodist periodicals, financial accounts, and similar information. The diary was bound in a black leatherette wraparound cover with a small flap that fit into a slot on the front when the diary was closed. The front cover carried the words "POCKET DIARY" in gold, and the year.

Benjamin used the diary not only to record his activities but also occasionally to make notes on various subjects. At the front of his 1852 diary he wrote, "Benton says that over 100,000,000 have been expended mostly since 1836 to make slave states of free territory." The slavery issue and the national debate over whether new territories would be slave or free were much on his mind during this period.[43]

At the end of the snowy first week of January 1852, George Lane Roberts was born. Ellen gave birth to him on Wednesday, January 7, presumably in the Rushford parsonage.[44] She and Benjamin named him after her uncle; George and Lydia Lane were much on Ellen's mind during this period. Sometime later Ellen wrote to Lydia, "Little G. L. (George Lane) is a great comfort to me. I love the name we have given him. Mr. Roberts talks to him much about being as good as his Uncle. He thinks there never was a better man than 'Uncle.'"[45]

To help keep house Miss E. Corre came to live with Benjamin and Ellen for some weeks. It may be that Mary Swezey, Ellen's niece, had returned to Windsor for a while, though she was with them later.[46]

On Saturday, January 10, Benjamin noted in his diary, "Bought a cutter . . . paid

---

42. BTRD, Jan. 5, 6, and 16, 1852.

43. Probably the reference is to Senator Thomas Hart Benton (1782-1858), U.S. senator from Missouri, an opponent of slavery, though considered a moderate.

44. ELRD, 1852. Exact date of entry not given, but apparently written toward the end of the year. The entry begins, "The 7th of this month [January, based on previous entry] our little George Lane was born." Smail inaccurately gives the birth date as Jan. 17 (Smail, pp. 12, 14). An undated (apparently 1920) University of Rochester "Alumni Catalogue Blank" completed by George Lane Roberts also gives the birthdate as Jan. 7, 1852.

Two days before George's birth, Ellen's grandfather Daniel Stow died in Windsor (Smail, p. 194; Daniel Stow tombstone, Windsor). Benjamin did not record the birth in his diary; his first mention of George is his notation on Feb. 24 that the baby was sick.

45. ELR to LBL, 1852, from Rushford. Precise date not given. Quoted in Zahniser, p. 51. (It is not clear whether the parenthetical "George Lane" was in the original or was added by Zahniser.)

46. BTRD, Jan. 7, 1852. The name seems to be "E Corre," though it is difficult to make out. Cf. ELRD, 1852 (exact date not given), where Ellen refers again to Mary. Possibly Mary remained with the Robertses but was busy with school.

for it $38.00."[47] With a new baby in the family, he needed better transportation than just his horse Bill. The cutter, a small sleigh that could be pulled easily by one horse, was the best answer for getting around in the winter.[48]

January continued snowy, blustery, and very cold — though the snow meant good sleighing. Benjamin and Ellen were delighted to again have a child in the home, but Ellen was not very well. "My health continued poor till March," she noted.[49]

Throughout January Benjamin was studying, writing, visiting, and praying for revival. Sunday, January 11, there was "a full house" at worship and Benjamin "had some liberty" in preaching, but he remarked, "Oh how little do I feel the awfulness of God's truths." The next Wednesday evening he set out to preach at nearby Fairview but had to turn back because the road was blocked with snowdrifts.[50]

Sunday the eighteenth many of the roads were blocked with snow, though Roberts was able to hold services and the congregation was large.[51] The following week, during his morning study time, he did some writing in addition to reading.[52] "Passed the day not very profitably," he noted on Monday, January 19, though he read several articles and wrote to his mother. On Thursday he had "comparatively a profitable day," including some visitation and a good prayer meeting in the evening, with some signs of spiritual awakening. Wednesday he felt he was making only "slow progress in Hebrew," but Friday he had "a profitable time in meditation" and "Read Hebrew with good success" in the morning before his afternoon calling. His self-evaluation for Saturday, January 24: "Not a very profitable day. Interrupted by many calls. . . . How and when shall I learn to redeem the time? I sometimes fear not till time with me shall be no more."[53]

Despite the wintry weather, Benjamin began planning a series of revival services. He was encouraged by the spirit at the general class meeting he conducted on Sunday, January 25, and announced a series of special meetings, beginning Tuesday night.

The revival effort continued for four weeks.[54] Often meetings were held both

---

47. BTRD, Jan. 10, 1852.

48. The cutter, "also known as the country cutter, [was] the most popular sleigh in America before the Civil War. It resembled the early tin bathtub and was sometimes referred to as a bathtub sleigh." Marc McCutcheon, *The Writer's Guide to Everyday Life in the 1800s* (Cincinnati: Writer's Digest Books, 1993), pp. 8-59.

49. BTRD, Jan. 12, 1852; ELRD, 1852 (exact date not given, but apparently written toward the end of the year).

50. BTRD, Jan. 11 and 14, 1852.

51. BTRD, Jan. 18, 1852.

52. Roberts's reading included the *Methodist Quarterly Review,* edited at this time (1848-56) by John McClintock. Roberts says on Jan. 16, "Read in the Quarterly a good article by the editor on Methodist preaching that will mak[e] McClintock Bishop." McClintock never did become bishop, but toward the end of his life was president of Drew Theological Seminary (*COM,* p. 73). Roberts was keenly aware of denominational politics.

53. BTRD, Jan. 19-24, 1852. The title page of his 1852 diary includes the printed verse from Eph. 5:16, "Redeeming the time, because the days are evil."

54. See BTRD, Jan. 28–Feb. 8. On Monday, Jan. 26, Benjamin rode up to Pike to pick up the portraits mentioned in the previous chapter.

morning and evening. Attendance and interest grew quickly. Benjamin noted on Thursday, January 29, "Omens of good seem increasing. Sinners are attentive to the word, but oh, they will not come to Christ. Laura Davis thinks she has passed from death into life."[55]

Soon people began to be converted in the services and at home. Kendall came and preached on Monday, February 2, helping Benjamin with the revival effort. By Thursday of that week Benjamin could say, "Congregation increasing. Interest deepening. . . . This was the most powerful meeting we have had as yet. More feeling among all."[56]

That night and Saturday night Brother J. Thomas preached.[57] Benjamin himself probably preached during the day. The weather moderated some and the end of the week was rainy, but people were being converted. Benjamin was not yet satisfied with the meetings, however. "Oh, for a break in the ranks of the impenitent," he wrote on January 30.[58]

Sunday, February 8, was "a glorious day," and Tuesday evening Benjamin considered "One of the most powerful meetings . . . I ever was at." Many people came forward to pray and several were converted.[59]

Other preachers came and helped, including Brother Pratt,[60] Elder Scott,[61] and Brother Gillam, a Presbyterian. Brother Pratt, Benjamin said, though a good preacher, did not "seem to have that power which one of his piety ought to have. He seems much like the Moravians." Brother Gillam preached Sunday morning, February 15. Benjamin preached in the afternoon and evening, though with a sore throat. Monday night his throat was worse, and Brother Pratt again preached.[62] The following Sunday Charles Woodward brought "a very good sermon" in the morning. In the afternoon Benjamin preached a missionary sermon and took up an offering in pledges totaling ninety dollars. That evening Roberts went to preach at Lindon, as he did regularly, while Brother Woodward delivered the sermon at Rushford.[63]

On Tuesday, February 24, Benjamin sent Lydia Lane a report on the revival.

---

55. BTRD, Jan. 29, 1852.

56. BTRD, Feb. 5, 1852.

57. BTRD, Feb. 5, 1852. J. Thomas may possibly have been a local preacher, as there was no one of that name listed among the ordained preachers of the Genesee Conference. Or he could have been a preacher of another denomination, or from a different ME conference.

58. BTRD, Jan. 30, 1852.

59. BTRD, Feb. 8 and 10, 1852.

60. Probably Edward B. Pratt, who the previous year had been the preacher at Smethport but was located (i.e., assigned membership in a local congregation rather than continuing in the itinerancy) in 1851. *Minutes*, Genesee Conference, 1850, 1851.

61. Perhaps Milo Scott, the preacher at Alexander. *Minutes*, Genesee Conference, 1851.

62. BTRD, Feb. 12-16, 1852.

63. BTRD, Feb. 22, 1852. Though Roberts does not give Woodward's first name, presumably this was Charles M. Woodward, agent this year for Genesee College and previously the preacher at Attica (*Minutes*, Genesee Conference, 1850, 1851; Ray Allen, *A Century of the Genesee Annual Conference of the Methodist Episcopal Church, 1810-1910* [Rochester, N.Y.: By the Author, 1911], p. 130).

Our meetings are still progressing with a good degree of interest. Our brethren say it is the best meeting they have had for many years. About thirty have thus far passed from death unto life, and among them are some of the most substantial citizens. The conversions are more marked and clear than is common in these days. I have thus far endured the labor very well.

How few persons we find are consistent followers of Jesus. I sometimes almost give way to discouragement arising from the unholy walk of professed Christians. But we must labor on to do all we can to get right ourselves and persuade others to become so.[64]

Though Benjamin wrote that the revival was progressing well, that evening he decided to stop the meetings for the time being. The reason may have been family illness. Roberts noted in his diary, "Meeting discontinued for the present. Little George L. taken sick." He spent most of the next day, Wednesday, caring for the baby and for Ellen, who also was unwell. He wrote, "George seemed so much like little Willie when taken sick that we felt some alarmed about him. Dr. Ripley called to see him." George was quite a bit better, however, by the end of the week.[65]

Roberts did not let up in his pastoral efforts, however. Friday evening he attended a service at the Baptist church. "They had a pretty cold time," he thought. The next morning, Saturday, he got up at 4:00 to read from Wesley's *Plain Account of Christian Perfection*. But he was too tired, and by 7:00 he found he had read only three pages! "Slept over it," he noted. He wrote at the end of the day, "I am very dull most of the time. Accomplished but little in my study. Poor preparation for the Sabbath."[66]

Roberts resumed the revival effort during the week of March 1, with nightly meetings culminating in the district quarterly conference at Rushford on Saturday and Sunday. Tuesday evening he preached on "Cursed is everyone that continueth not in all things to do them" and noted, "There seemed to be an unusual degree of feeling. I do not think that the claims of the law are sufficiently enforced."[67] Sunday, March 7, there was an "immense congregation" due in part to the quarterly conference and "One of the best love feasts we have had here."[68]

---

64. BTR to LBL, Sept. 24, 1852, quoted in BHR, *BTR*, pp. 61-62.

65. BTRD, Feb. 24-26, 1852.

66. BTRD, Feb. 27-28, 1852.

67. BTRD, Mar. 2, 1852.

68. BTRD, Mar. 6-8, 1852. On Friday, Mar. 5, Roberts noted that "Bro. Terry" was at Rushford — probably Albert G. Terry, one of the preachers at nearby Belfast (though there was also a George Terry in the conference). Roberts writes of Terry, "He has been led away like Bro. [Edward B.] Pratt but now sees that this is a delusion from the devil." Roberts notes on Mar. 9 that he talked with Brother Pratt and adds, "He is in a strange way. His interpretation of Scripture is fanciful in the extreme." Conable says Pratt "began well in the Conference, but he imbibed the erroneous opinions of his father, who was one of the New England 'Perfectionists,' left the Methodist Episcopal Church, and led a few astray with him." Conable, p. 95. Albert Terry later became a Free Methodist (1861). Allen, *Century*, p. 123; *Minutes*, Genesee Conference, 1850-52.

Roberts Begins Writing

Roberts had shown himself an excellent, clear writer while at Wesleyan University. Now, as a pastor, he began writing for publication. He mentions writing on January 15, 1852, and occasionally at other times. He was beginning his long writing career, though it is not always clear from his diary just what projects he was working on. He notes in his diary for Monday, February 23, however: "Sent an article to the N.A. [Northern Christian Advocate] against Theological Schools, in reply to Prof. Vail."[69] This publication (often called simply the Northern Advocate) was at this time a strong voice for both revivalism and abolitionism. Roberts would later be associated with its editor, William Hosmer, in writing and publishing for several years.

Continuing Pastoral Work

After the quarterly conference on March 6 and 7, Roberts shifted his focus for the time being from revival to the need for larger facilities. Among the Rushford people there now was talk of "building a new church," he noted. He began securing pledges or "subscriptions" from the members for a new building. One member signed up for $100, but Roberts noted, "This is a hard place to raise money. The people are well off but very close." Some opposed the project, though "All see its necessity." He managed to secure pledges of $400 on March 11.[70]

Over the next two months Roberts devoted himself to his studies, preaching, visitation, and raising money for the new building — occasionally interrupted by domestic chores: "Repaired the Kitchen in doing which I pounded my thumb very badly."[71] He received a package of books from the Methodist Book Room and was soon reading Headley's Life of Kossuth, about the Hungarian patriot Lajos Kossuth, who had visited New York City the previous year.[72]

Sunday, March 28, Roberts exchanged pulpits with the Baptist pastor for the afternoon service. The end of the next week he was preparing his Thanksgiving Day sermon for publication "at the urgent request of many" and also reading in Josephus and Wesley.[73] Other reading over these weeks included Townley's Illustrations of Biblical Literature, Mosheim's Ecclesiastical History, Ruter's Church History, and Homer.[74] Most of his reading was part of the required Course of Study for ordination as elder.[75]

---

69. BTRD, Feb. 23, 1852.

70. BTRD, Mar. 8, 10, 11, and 12, 1852.

71. BTRD, Mar. 18, 1852.

72. BTRD, Mar. 19, 29, and 31, 1852; Edwin G. Burrows and Mike Wallace, Gotham: A History of New York City to 1898 (New York: Oxford University Press, 1999), p. 822.

73. BTRD, Mar. 28 and Apr. 2, 1852.

74. BTRD, Apr. 4 and 8, 1852. Several of the books Roberts read had been published by the Methodist Book Concern.

75. The Doctrines and Disciplines of the Methodist Episcopal Church (New York: Lane and Scott, 1849), pp. 215-18.

Roberts continued to spend a lot of time visiting, especially in the afternoons. Sometimes Ellen accompanied him. On April 6 they visited Brother Ely Woods, and Benjamin noted that with six inches of snow on the ground, "The sleighing is about as good as I ever saw."[76]

Benjamin spent most of the next day visiting with his horse and cutter, calling at some fourteen homes and talking with about forty persons. "Passed the day profitably to myself, and hope some good was done," he wrote. Most of Friday and Saturday he spent in his study. Noting on Friday that he made "some preparation for the Sabbath," he commented that he intended "hence forth to do something towards this every day." Friday afternoon he took Ellen out for a ride. Signs of spring were in the air. "It is quite pleasant now though the roads are yet very muddy."[77]

Spring proved slow in coming, however. Yet the church was doing well. Roberts preached to "a very good and attentive congregation" Sunday morning, April 11, on the character of a Christian, and in the afternoon on the topic of Sunday as the Christian Sabbath. The next day he attended early to various errands, intending to begin work in his study at 9:00 A.M. But "the devil kept me out all day," he lamented. In the afternoon he went to hear a funeral sermon in a neighboring church; getting there was "a muddy affair."[78] Over these spring weeks Roberts attended a number of funerals — ten between March 25 and April 29; some for children. Most of these were funerals where he himself preached, though he also attended funerals of other denominations, including Baptist and Universalist.[79]

Friday, April 16, Roberts went over the class meeting lists at Rushford, making some revisions. "Our classes have contained from forty to sixty members," he noted.[80] He doesn't say how many classes there were, so it is unclear whether he means a total of about sixty persons were enrolled in classes, or that membership in the individual classes ranged between forty and sixty. Probably it was the latter. Since class membership was still a condition of Methodist membership[81] and membership at Rushford was over two hundred, presumably there were four or five classes meeting at various times during the week. Membership of forty or fifty is much too large for an effective class meeting, however, even if not everyone attends regularly. (If, alternatively, Roberts means only about fifty people were involved in the classes — less than a quarter of the members — that also was a bad sign.) The situation of the classes at Rushford was symptomatic of the general decline of the class meeting within Methodism during this period. In fact, it is unlikely that Roberts himself ever experienced the class meeting in its original form of small-group accountability — something of considerable significance for later Free Methodism. Roberts tried to

76. BTRD, Apr. 6, 1852.

77. BTRD, Apr. 7 and 9, 1852.

78. BTRD, Apr. 11-12, 1852.

79. BTRD, Mar. 25–Apr. 29, 1852.

80. BTRD, Apr. 16, 1852.

81. *Doctrines and Disciplines*, pp. 19-20; 73-74. The *Discipline* still included Wesley's General Rules, requiring class attendance.

make the class meeting system effective; he noted on December 7 that he presented a "financial plan making the leaders responsible for their class assessments."[82]

Roberts continued to struggle with the effective use of his time, and often did not measure up to his own ideal. He noted on Monday, April 19, "This has been the most profitably spent of any Monday in some time. I hope every hour of this week may be improved." But on Saturday he reflected, "Have got in a bad way of putting off too long my preparation for Sunday." He again resolved to do better, as he had in the past, but with a note of realism: "[W]hat weak things are human resolutions." He continued a vigorous round of visitation but concluded, "I am not I fear as useful in my pastoral visits as I ought to be."[83]

Meanwhile, money was scarce and Benjamin and Ellen were running out of food. Their contributions from the church were insufficient to live on; Benjamin's income for the second quarter was only sixty dollars.[84] April 22 Benjamin went "to hunt up some butter," paying sixteen cents a pound for it and one dollar a bushel for potatoes. He settled up a furniture bill the next Monday, leaving him and Ellen nearly broke. He noted on April 30, "Reduced to a state of starvation I called on Bro. Wm. Gordon and made my wants known. With no ado he took out his pocket book and gave me five [dollars], saying he had plenty of money." So the family needs were met for the moment, and a few weeks later Benjamin was able to plant his garden.[85]

On April 28 Roberts rose early and did some outside work. Benjamin used to "draw his wood and cut it," Ellen said — that is, he would buy logs and cut them up to burn in the stove.[86] This Wednesday morning as he was splitting a long log, the wedge bounced up and struck his face, badly cutting his nose and cheek. Benjamin was grateful he didn't lose an eye in the mishap. He was to conduct a funeral the next afternoon, but because of his injury Brother Nobles came over and filled in. That Saturday, May 1, Roberts worked hard getting ready for the Sabbath. "Seemed to have less wandering of mind than I have had sometimes," he noted. "My face is better though it still looks bad."[87]

Spring finally came, and with it spring cleaning. Benjamin helped around the house some the first two weeks in May, in addition to planting his garden. On May 5 he helped Ellen with housecleaning, including whitewashing some stones and shaking out the carpets. "[I have] no commission and no taste for such business," he complained, yet felt it was his duty. He spent Monday, May 10, also working around the house, making soap, helping with the washing, and building a henhouse with the aid of Brother Worthington. "It seems as if I was ready to make any thing a pretext

---

82. BTRD, Dec. 7, 1852.
83. BTRD, Apr. 19, 20, and 24, 1852.
84. BHR, *BTR*, p. 60 (apparently based on Roberts's 1851 diary).
85. BTRD, Apr. 22, 26, 30; May 11-13, 1852.
86. ELR to Lucy Coleman, undated, from North Chili, N.Y. Quoted in Zahniser, p. 48. Ellen added, "It is a great thing to be saved from laziness." Presumably Benjamin bought his wood, or it may at times have been donated to him.
87. BTRD, Apr. 28-29; May 1, 1852.

for leaving my study," he noted, still conflicted over his use of time. Meanwhile he received his first issue of *Zion's Herald,* dated May 3, and read it.[88] By this time Ellen's health was better, though she was busy caring for little Georgie. Apparently Miss Corre had left, but Ellen's niece Mary was still with them.[89]

Visit to 1852 General Conference in Boston

Roberts kept up with denominational news through the various Methodist publications. He was interested in the upcoming General Conference, to be held at the Bromfield Street ME Church in Boston. He wanted very much to attend. The conference convened on May 1, and George and Lydia Lane traveled from New York to be there. George didn't know whether he would be reelected book agent or not, but at age sixty-eight he apparently had some inkling he might not be. Lydia wrote a long letter to Ellen on May 12, two weeks before the election. "The future is all uncertainty to me," she told her diary.[90]

Roberts longed to attend the General Conference but lacked the money. On May 7 he talked to Brother Walter Gordon about it, and perhaps Walter or William Gordon provided the funds so he could make the trip.[91]

The third week in May Benjamin, Ellen, and little Georgie traveled to New York. Ellen and the baby stayed at the Lane home while Benjamin went on to Boston, arriving there on Saturday morning, May 22. The Lanes were surprised but pleased to see him.[92]

Roberts heard that Peter Cartwright[93] and "Father" E. T. Taylor, two of the most colorful characters of nineteenth-century Methodism, were both going to preach at the Mariners' Church on Sunday, so he went to hear them.[94] Father Taylor was famous for his colorful, spontaneous oratory — in fact, he was the model for Father

---

88. BTRD, May 5-10, 1852. *Zion's Herald,* a semi-independent Methodist periodical published in Boston, had been in existence since the 1820s. Gilbert Haven became editor of the paper in 1867. William Gravely, *Gilbert Haven, Methodist Abolitionist: A Study in Race, Religion, and Reform, 1850-1880* (Nashville: Abingdon, 1973), p. 158.

89. ELRD, 1852 (exact date not given).

90. LBLD, May 7 and 12, 1852.

91. BTRD, May 7, 1852. Walter Gordon was one of the conference preachers, serving this year at Somerset, in the Niagara District. He preached for Roberts on May 9. Perhaps he was the son of William Gordon, who previously lent money to Benjamin. Conable notes: "William Gordon was for many years a prominent member and useful local preacher at Rushford" (Conable, p. 304).

92. BTRD, May 23, 1852; ELRD, 1852 (exact date not given); LBLD, May 22, 1852.

93. Peter Cartwright (1785-1872), pioneer Methodist preacher in Kentucky, Illinois, and Ohio, "a man peculiar in his manners, and yet an acknowledged leader of the church in his day," was known for his physical strength and confrontational style. *COM,* p. 170.

94. BTRD, May 23, 1852. Edward Thompson Taylor (1793-1871), missionary and sailor, became a Methodist minister in 1819, and ministered in Boston from 1830 until his death. See Gilbert Haven and Thomas Russell, *Life of Father Taylor, the Sailor Preacher* (Boston: Boston Port and Seamen's Aid Society, 1904).

Mapple in Herman Melville's recently published *Moby Dick*.[95] "With a Bible under his arm Taylor paced his quarterdeck of a pulpit exhorting his crew to bend their shoulders to the capstan and weigh anchor for heaven," wrote Justin Kaplan.[96]

As a boy, Taylor, an orphan, ran off to sea. Converted in a Methodist revival while on shore leave in Boston at about age eighteen, he became a Methodist minister-evangelist. For years he pastored under Methodist appointment the non-denominational Mariners' Church in Boston (better known as the Seamen's Bethel — part of the worldwide network of Seamen's Bethel missions).[97] Ralph Waldo Emerson liked to listen to Taylor, savoring his picturesque speech drawn from the sea — though he said Taylor was "like a cannon, better on the Common than in the parlour."[98] Walt Whitman went to hear Taylor several times in 1859-60 and pronounced him the only "essentially perfect orator" he ever heard. "[W]hen Father Taylor preached or prayed, the rhetoric and art, the mere words, . . . seemed altogether to disappear, and the *live feeling* advanced upon you and seized you with a power before unknown."[99] Father Taylor once told a young Harvard divinity student who preached at the Seamen's Bethel on a Sunday morning, "My dear young Brother, if your text had the small-pox, your sermon never would have caught it."[100]

Roberts no doubt admired Father Taylor; he probably didn't know that Taylor, though a Methodist, was also an enthusiastic Mason.[101] Roberts was less impressed with Cartwright, and was not much taken with Daniel Webster, whom he heard at Faneuil Hall.[102]

Roberts divided his time in Boston between General Conference and sightseeing. He spent Monday afternoon with Lydia, visiting the Mount Auburn area. "[H]ad a profitable conversation with Mr Roberts," Lydia noted.[103] Mrs. Lane was not satisfied with the spiritual tone of the General Conference, however. "I do not feel that there is as much prayer among the Ministers as would be for their good or for the benefit and prosperity of the church," she confided to her diary.[104]

---

95. Justin Kaplan, *Walt Whitman: A Life* (New York: Simon and Schuster, 1980), p. 253. Melville had probably heard Taylor preach in 1849, if not before. See Hershel Parker, *Herman Melville: A Biography*, vol. 1, *1819-1851* (Baltimore: Johns Hopkins University Press, 1996), pp. 184, 614. Melville and B. T. Roberts were about the same age.

96. Kaplan, *Walt Whitman*, p. 253.

97. Roald Kverndal, *Seamen's Missions: Their Origin and Early Growth; A Contribution to the History of the Church Maritime* (Pasadena, Calif.: William Carey Library, 1986), pp. 493-99.

98. Quoted in Carlos Baker, *Emerson among the Eccentrics: A Group Portrait* (New York: Penguin Books, 1997), p. 80. Baker gives an excellent portrait of Taylor and his admirers in his chapter "Father Taylor," pp. 70-80.

99. Walt Whitman, "Father Taylor and Oratory," reprinted in Haven and Russell, *Life of Father Taylor*, pp. lxvii, lxix. This brief essay first appeared in the *Century*, Feb. 1887.

100. Haven and Russell, *Life of Father Taylor*, p. vii.

101. Baker, *Emerson among the Eccentrics*, p. 73.

102. BHR, *BTR*, p. 63.

103. LBLD, May 24, 1852.

104. LBLD, May 22, 1852.

Tuesday, May 25, Benjamin was present at General Conference for the election of four new bishops: Matthew Simpson, Edward Ames, Osmon Baker, and Levi Scott, the assistant book agent. All were elected on the first ballot. "There was much interest manifested and excitement also," Lydia commented.[105] Bishop Hedding had died shortly before the General Conference, and Bishop Hamline had resigned due to ill health. With bishops Waugh, Morris, and Janes continuing in office, the total number of Methodist bishops now increased from five to seven.

Roberts sat through the conference sessions but later in the day visited an art gallery to see "the Dusseldorf paintings," which he pronounced "very fine."[106]

Two issues came before the 1852 General Conference that were of importance for later Free Methodism: pewed churches and "lay" representation. The 1820 General Conference had added to the earlier rule that all church buildings must be "plain" and "not more expensive than is absolutely unavoidable," the requirement "and with free seats." By 1852, however, many new Methodist church buildings, especially in urban centers, had begun renting or selling pews as a fund-raising technique. Catching up with reality, the 1852 General Conference undercut the requirement of free seats by adding, "wherever practicable."[107]

Regarding "lay" representation, a convention meeting in Philadelphia earlier in 1852 had drawn up a petition asking the General Conference to include "laymen" as well as clergy in the church's governing structure.[108] The 1852 General Conference "decided that the introduction of lay delegation at that time was not expedient"[109] but left the door open to what would eventually become a successful reform — a decade or so after the Free Methodist Church built equal "lay" and clergy representation into its own structure.

For George and Lydia Lane the critical day was Wednesday, May 26, when the agent and assistant agent for the Book Concern in New York were elected. The balloting put Thomas Carlton into the office of book agent, replacing Lane. Zebulon Phillips was elected assistant agent, replacing Levi Scott. Thus George Lane effectively moved into retirement, while his assistant became bishop.

Lydia, still grieving the loss of her little daughter Sarah, wrote in her diary: "At

---

105. LBLD, May 25, 1852.

106. BTRD, May 25, 1852. The same day Benjamin noted, "Cut my thumb quite badly while preparing to shave. Thankful it was not my throat."

107. *COM*, pp. 399, 710.

108. The Philadelphia meeting was one of a series of conventions that constituted a broader "lay" movement in Methodism seeking increased participation of members and more democratic process in the church, and particularly "lay" representation in annual conferences and General Conferences. A number of Laymen's Conventions were held in various places during the 1850s. See Donald B. Marti, "Rich Methodists: The Rise and Consequences of Lay Philanthropy in the Mid-19th Century," in *Rethinking Methodist History*, ed. Russell E. Richey and Kenneth E. Rowe (Nashville: Kingswood, 1985), pp. 164-65. Marti's essay is reprinted in Russell E. Richey, Kenneth E. Rowe, and Jean Miller Schmidt, eds., *Perspectives on American Methodism: Interpretive Essays* (Nashville: Kingswood, 1993), pp. 265-76.

109. *COM*, p. 399.

twelve o'clock I learned that our fate was sealed, and that my dear husband was released from the Book Concern, and that our pleasant home in N. York is to be broken up. Father into thy hands alone I have my all restored." If Lydia was disappointed, George seemed relieved. "The great change in his situation does not make
him sad," Lydia wrote. "He seems happy and cheerful trusting in God."[110]

The evening of the election Lydia left for New York, accompanied by Benjamin,
while George remained at General Conference.[111] Traveling all night, Lydia and
Benjamin arrived at the Lane home at six o'clock the next morning. They were glad
to see Ellen and little George, who was still nursing, and to find them well.[112]

Benjamin, Ellen, and Georgie spent a week at the Lane home before returning to
Rushford. Ellen was glad for the chance to see Mary Martindale and other friends, if
only briefly, but saddened to learn that Mary's brother Stephen had just died.[113]
Meanwhile Benjamin spent his time walking around New York (catching a cold in
the process), reading books and newspapers, and visiting the Methodist Book Room.
At the Book Room he ran into Abel Stevens, editor of *Zion's Herald*, who had just
been appointed founding editor of the short-lived *National Magazine*. The denomination had mandated the new periodical as "a monthly magazine for popular reading."[114] Roberts commented on Stevens, "Should not think that he ever suffers from
diffidence."[115]

Benjamin preached at the ME Greene Street Church on Sunday morning, May
30. His text was 2 Corinthians 8:9, "For ye know the grace of our Lord Jesus Christ,
that, though he was rich, yet for your sakes he became poor, that ye through his
poverty might be rich." This was Lydia's first opportunity to hear Roberts preach. "I
was happy to have this privilege," she wrote. "May the Lord own and bless his labors, and finally bring him with those saved through his instrumentality to
heaven."[116]

The next day Benjamin had a chance to visit the Five Points Mission, a mile or
so south of the Lane home. He saw the mission school and heard the children sing.
"Much good has been done in this awfully wicked locality," he observed. On Tuesday
he "Walked about the city till I was so tired that I could scarcely get home." He went

110. LBLD, May 26 and June 2, 1852.

111. George Lane returned to New York on June 2, two days before the Robertses left for Rushford.
LBLD, June 2, 1852.

112. LBLD, May 27, 1852; BTRD, May 26, 1852; ELRD, 1852 (exact date not given).

113. ELRD, 1852 (exact date not given). Stephen Martindale, a young attorney and an 1838 graduate of Wesleyan University, died on May 28 (Frank W. Nicolson, ed., *Alumni Record of Wesleyan University, Middletown, Conn.*, centennial [6th] ed., 1931 [Middletown, Conn.: Pelton and King, 1931],
p. 88).

114. W. F. Whitlock, *The Story of the Book Concerns* (Cincinnati: Jennings and Pye, 1903), p. 170.
The magazine was discontinued in 1859 for "lack of proper support." Roberts wasn't much impressed
with the first issue when it came out in August: "Have read most of the first No. of National Magazine.
It does not meet my expectations. The style is too juvenile" (BTRD, Aug. 12, 1852).

115. BTRD, June 2, 1852; see May 29, 1852.

116. LBLD, May 30, 1852. In his diary Roberts does not mention preaching on this occasion.

to see the steamship *Great Briton,* a marvel at 330 feet long, and also walked to the Palmer home and attended Mrs. Palmer's Tuesday Meeting.[117]

George Lane arrived home from Boston on Tuesday morning, perhaps traveling together with Thomas Carlton, his successor. He invited Carlton to dinner the next day, just a day or so before the Robertses were to depart. Thus Benjamin and Ellen again had contact with Carlton, who was increasingly influential in the denomination and in the Genesee Conference.[118]

This was the period when so-called spirit rappings were causing excitement in New York and elsewhere. A few weeks after Benjamin and his family left Manhattan, Lydia commented on this in her diary. "Saw a Lady who is called a medium of spiritual rappings," she noted on Sunday, July 4. "This subject is troubling the people here. I am thankful that I have not been in the company of those occupied with it."[119]

Thursday, June 3, Benjamin and Ellen were busy getting ready for the trip back to Rushford and savoring the remaining hours with the Lanes. Lydia noted in her diary, "This morning I walked out with my dear Ellen."[120] Later Benjamin did some shopping with Ellen and then visited "the [Methodist] mission rooms and also . . . the book room," probably to pick up some literature.[121]

Benjamin, Ellen, and little George left New York early on Friday, June 4, to return home. Saturday they were back in the Rushford parsonage, and Benjamin resumed his pastoral work after an absence of two and a half weeks.[122]

As Benjamin and Ellen left for Rushford, Lydia was thinking of the fact that she and George had to move, also. They found a house in Mount Holly, New Jersey, Lydia's old home, and moved there in early July. Lydia wrote on June 24, as she was visiting Mount Holly making arrangements for the move, "I feel it to be a great privation now that my dear Sarah has gone, to be so widely separated from Ellen. She has always been like a loving Child to me[,] feeling all that grieves me, more than any one beside my husband. I hope her life may be spared. Her sympathy under my affliction has been highly prized. I pray the Lord to reward her."[123]

---

117. BTRD, May 31 and June 1, 1852. Roberts gives no description of or reaction to Palmer's meeting. The name of the ship appears to be *Great Briton,* but the writing of the second word is not clear.

118. BTRD, June 1 and 2, 1852; LBLD, June 2, 1852. Lydia Lane says George arrived home on June 2 (Wednesday) but Benjamin says Tuesday, June 1, which is more likely correct.

119. LBLD, July 4, 1852.

120. LBLD, June 3, 1852.

121. BTRD, June 3, 1852.

122. BTRD, June 4, 1852. They went "up the Delaware, down the Susquehannah, up the Chenang[o] & Chemung and down the Genesee to Belvidere," where they stayed overnight — apparently traveling by train through these river valleys, since they traveled "very rapidly" a distance of about 400 miles in one long day.

123. LBLD, June 24, 1852.

Last Months in Rushford

Benjamin continued his routine of devoting mornings to study and afternoons to visitation, with of course the usual interruptions. He was finishing up his reading in church history, often reading fifty pages a day — but "My progress in Church History is not very rapid." Another summer day he read till noon, "But my reading does not do me as much good as it ought." Ellen's health was somewhat better, but Benjamin noted on June 12 that her eyes were again getting inflamed. Georgie had had an eye inflammation, but it was now about gone.[124]

Benjamin took Ellen, Georgie, and Mary to Gowanda by horse and buggy to visit his family for the last ten days of June. He found his parents now "pleasantly situated in [their] new house." Benjamin visited a number of old friends and after one visit noted, "Social visits ought to be closed with prayer."[125] The New York and Erie Railroad, with its terminus at Dunkirk on Lake Erie, twenty-five miles west of Gowanda, had been completed the previous year with great fanfare, and Benjamin went with his father to see it. "The whistle of the engine and the rattling of the cars echos among the hills & forests, where but yesterday the deer roamed undisturbed."[126] For the first time linking "the ocean with the Lakes," the Erie line "marked an epoch in the history of railroads," noted Charles Frederick Carter. "The first great trunk line was now ready for traffic."[127] It soon became a favorite moneymaker for the Methodist businessman and financier Daniel Drew, who multiplied his profits through manipulating the railroad's stock.[128]

A circus came to town the last weekend in June, bringing crowds of up to four thousand to Gowanda. Roberts did not approve. A "great day here for the Indians

---

124. BTRD, June 10, 12, and 15, 1852.

125. BTRD, June 21-22 and 30, 1852.

126. BTRD, June 22-24, 1852. Benjamin later gave a warm commendation of the Erie Railroad in the *Earnest Christian*. See "The Erie Railway," *EC* 12, no. 2 (Aug. 1866): 67.

127. Charles Frederick Carter, *When Railroads Were New,* centenary ed. (New York: Simmons-Boardman Publishing Co., 1926), p. 95. Better known as the Erie Railroad, or simply the Erie, the New York and Erie Railroad was organized in 1833 and began construction west from New York City in 1839. Its completion at Dunkirk in May 1851 was celebrated with the presence of such honored guests as President Fillmore and Daniel Webster, then secretary of state (Carter, pp. 80, 83, 95-97). The Erie soon became the stuff of legend; see, for example, Horatio Alger, Jr., *The Erie Train Boy* (New York: Hurst and Co., 1900), first published in 1891.

128. Oliver Jensen, *The American Heritage History of Railroads in America* (New York: Wings Books, 1975), p. 138; James D. McCabe, Jr., *Great Fortunes, and How They Were Made: Struggles and Triumphs of Our Self-Made Men* (Cincinnati and Chicago: E. Hannaford and Co., 1871), pp. 200-208; *COM*, pp. 311-12. A nominal Methodist earlier, in 1841 Drew (1797-1879) became an active member of the Mulberry Street Methodist Church in New York City after a "narrow escape from death" by lightning (McCabe, p. 207). Though a major Methodist benefactor, trustee of Wesleyan University, and founder of Drew Theological Seminary, he went bankrupt after the Panic of 1873 (John S. Bowman, ed., *The Cambridge Dictionary of American Biography* [Cambridge: University of Cambridge Press, 1995], p. 201).

and rustics," he noted. "Fools are not all dead."[129] When he got back to Rushford, he wrote an article for the *Gowanda Chronicle* against circuses.[130]

During Roberts's visit to Gowanda, a Brother Blackmore offered to sell him 325 acres of land in Pennsylvania for $1,000, apparently as an investment. Benjamin talked it over with Ellen, and they decided against the deal.[131]

Back in Rushford at the beginning of July, Benjamin resumed his studies and his pastoral work. Ellen continued unwell; "to my surprise [she] is not sick abed," Benjamin noted. Again he was not happy with his use of time: "Felt dull and so do not attempt much and succeed." "I am troubled with an unnatural sleepiness this summer."[132]

Nevertheless, attendance continued to grow at the Rushford church. Roberts decided to preach on Sunday, July 4, on missions in the morning and temperance in the afternoon.

Benjamin attended the Methodist camp meeting at Portville (twenty miles south of Rushford, near the Pennsylvania border) from July 7 to 14 (Wednesday to Wednesday), leaving Ellen and Georgie at home. The crowds grew to some four thousand over the weekend, and Roberts felt the camp meeting was "the most powerful meeting [he] ever attended." Roberts himself was one of the preachers. He preached Wednesday, the first night of the camp, on "Work out your own salvation" (Phil. 2:12), and Saturday on "God's willingness to save all men." He had "only a passable time," he said, in preaching. "I have never yet had a good time preaching at Camp-Meeting." Friday he fasted and prayed and was blessed in doing so. "I suffer loss when I neglect this duty. I long for a deeper baptism of the Holy Spirit."[133]

Various conference preachers took turns at the stand throughout the camp meeting. A. D. Wilbor, the presiding elder, preached "an excellent sermon" Sunday morning following the love feast, and Joseph McCreery, then pastor at Ogden, preached Tuesday morning from 1 John 1:7. Roberts described McCreery's message as "one of the greatest sermons I ever heard. Its effect was mighty. Preachers and people almost lost themselves."[134]

Benjamin pronounced this camp meeting the best he'd experienced. "I never saw the power of God so manifest. One evening as many as a dozen fell and lay strengthless for a long time." Some sixty people were converted, including a number

---

129. BTRD, June 25, 1852.

130. BTRD, July 6, 1852. This may have been the article that appeared on July 24, 1852, in the *Gowanda Independent Chronicle,* accusing circuses of "planting the seeds of vice, licentiousness and crime; poizoning [*sic*], and demoralizing the mind . . . and ruining the youth by inspiring them with a fondness and an irresistable taste for unhallowed revelry, and low amusement" (p. 2). The article is unsigned, however, and stylistically it is more florid than Roberts's usual writing, so it may have been written by someone else.

131. BTRD, June 28, 1852.

132. BTRD, July 2 and 5, 1852.

133. BTRD, July 7, 9-11, and 14, 1852.

134. BTRD, July 13, 1852. Roberts here uses the spelling "McCreary."

of children. "The conversions were very marked and clear. Many were sanctified, and the members generally were very much quickened."[135]

Roberts sent an account to the *Northern Christian Advocate,* signing it "Titus."[136] "The meeting commenced in the spirit, progressed in power, and closed in triumph," he reported. During the camp "the woods almost constantly reverberated with the cries of the saints, the groans of the penitent and the shouts of the redeemed." People were slain in the Spirit. "Strong men were shorn of their strength, and left as powerless as if they lay in the arms of death." Some seekers "in their agony lay upon the open ground all night, groaning and praying for pardon."

Roberts turned his report into an editorial, arguing that camp meetings were needed to cure Methodism's "prevailing tendency to formality." When many churches "say in effect to the rich sit thou here in this good pew for thou art able to pay for it and to the poor 'here take this bench, or go get a seat in the gallery,' we are in danger of forgetting that in the presence of God, worldly distinctions are lost. But at the camp-meeting, the rich and poor meet together and feel as they cannot in many of our sanctuaries that 'the Lord is Maker of us all.'" Roberts concluded his report: "Long live camp-meetings!"[137] It is easy to see how reports such as this could raise eyebrows among decorous, newly rich Methodists in Buffalo and other cities, and among preachers eager to receive their benefactions.

Over the remaining weeks before annual conference Roberts continued his pastoral work, consolidating the gains of the year. He baptized several people on August 8, including Ellen's niece, Mary Swezey.[138]

Roberts was still trying to break his "bad way" of leaving his Sunday preparation to Saturday.[139] But Sunday services were packed, people sitting in the aisles. In addition to pastoral work, Benjamin attended to the everyday chores of living, picking red raspberries with Mary and searching for his horse, Bill, which he had put out to pasture.[140] He completed his assigned readings and began reviewing in preparation for his ordination examination (including the fourth part of Watson's *Theological Institutes,* prescribed for the fourth year of the Course of Study).[141]

Roberts attended a preachers association meeting at Olean on August 3 and 4 (Tuesday evening and all day Wednesday). Attendance was large, and "Reading and criticising Sketches and Essays were the chief order of the day," in addition to

135. BTRD, July 12, 1852; BHR, *BTR,* pp. 63-64. The quotations, found in Benson Roberts, seem to be from one of Benjamin's letters.

136. Benjamin started using "Titus" as a pen name about this time. See Zahniser, p. 49.

137. Titus [B. T. Roberts], "Portville Camp Meeting," *NCA* 12, no. 30 (July 28, 1852): 1. The report is dated July 16, 1852. See Zahniser, pp. 49-50. Zahniser incorrectly gives the date of publication as July 20, 1852.

138. BTRD, Aug. 8, 1852.

139. BTRD, July 17, 1852. On Aug. 1 he preached morning and afternoon on baptism, after consulting F. G. Hibbard's book on the subject the previous day. (Hibbard's book on baptism was recommended in the Course of Study.)

140. BTRD, July 18-20, 1852.

141. BTRD, July 21, 1852. See *Doctrines and Disciplines,* p. 217.

preaching.[142] This may have been another in the series of ad hoc preachers meetings such as the one in May 1848 in the Rushford District, mentioned in chapter 11.[143]

With annual conference approaching, Roberts held an official meeting in his congregation on Friday afternoon, August 13. The members were now convinced they needed a new building and "resolved with great unanimity to make an effort to build one," he noted. So the next week Roberts tried again getting subscriptions. Brother Stone signed up for $130, but still Roberts was doubtful that he could raise sufficient funds.[144]

Ellen's health continued to be poor over the summer months. In August a problem with her face flared up. "Her upper lip is swollen very much and she is in great pain." On Sunday evening, August 15, he stayed home from the prayer meeting because his "family were so unwell." He spent most of the next Wednesday trying to find a "hired girl," apparently to relieve him of some of the care of the house and family.[145] In September Ellen decided to wean Georgie, then eight months old, because "my own health was so poor."[146] Benjamin noted in his diary, "The doctor says we must wean our boy[;] Ellen is very poor," and again on August 27, "Drs. Minard and McCall say she must wean her boy before she can get well."[147] Weaning Georgie proved to be a trial, however. "Our dear little boy does not like at all to be weaned," Benjamin said. "He moans especially just at dark for his nurse. He is a precious child and I do most earnestly hope that he may be spared to us."[148] Ellen later noted, "Georgie has been very sick ever since I weaned him."[149] This was a trying time for the family.

Benjamin had nearly finished his assigned readings and was engaging in additional reading on his own. He seems to have been working out his theology of church vitality and revival. On August 21 he "examined the opinions of many eminent men upon religion." He concluded that most eminent authors "agree in conceding the excellency and the truth of the Christian religion. Would that more of the great ones had been consistent followers of the meek & lowly Jesus." The previous day he read some in James Caughey's recently published *Revival Miscellanies,* concluding that the "great success" of the Methodist evangelist "in saving souls is owing more to his entire devotion to the work than to any other cause."[150]

---

142. BTRD, Aug. 4, 1852.

143. See Conable, pp. 69-70. On July 26 Roberts wrote to "Bros. Williams[,] Thomas, Kendall and J. K. Miller. We are trying to arouse a sense of our individual responsibility" (BTRD, July 26, 1852). This may have been in connection with the Aug. 3-4 preachers association meeting.

144. BTRD, Aug. 13 and 16, 1852.

145. BTRD, Aug. 14, 15, and 18, 1852. It isn't clear whether Mary Swezey was leaving about this time, or would have less time at home due to school, or whether Benjamin and Ellen were simply finding her help insufficient.

146. ELRD, 1852 (exact date not given; written toward end of year).

147. BTRD, Aug. 18 and 27, 1852.

148. BTRD, Aug. 30, 1852.

149. ELRD, 1852 (exact date not given; written toward end of year).

150. BTRD, Aug. 20-21, 1852. See James Caughey, *Helps to a Life of Holiness and Usefulness; or,*

Toward the end of August, a couple of weeks before his own conference sessions, Roberts left Ellen and Georgie at Pike and traveled with Kendall to Honeoye Falls (south of Rochester, near Lima) to attend the last day's sessions of the East Genesee Conference. On Wednesday, August 25, the day after conference ended, Roberts went to Lima for the dedication of the new building to house Genesee College; the college had been started two years earlier as an expansion of Genesee Wesleyan Seminary. Roberts thought the address, given by Dr. Thompson, was "neat and perspicuous in style but sophistical in its reasonings. He labored to produce an impression favorable to Theological Schools."[151] The motive for Roberts's trip to East Genesee and to Lima is not clear, but it probably had to do with his concern about theological schools and, more generally, the direction the denomination was heading.

On his way back to Rushford, Benjamin spent most of Thursday, August 26, with Ellen at Pike. He found her "nearly tired out," but was moved by the warmth of the good folk there. "The Lord has given me a place in the hearts of this dear people," he wrote. "They are full of affection."[152] He returned with Ellen and Georgie to Rushford the next day.

The trip to Honeoye Falls and Lima put Roberts behind in his Sunday preparation, so he was again frustrated on Saturday over his time use. "It seems to me as if the devil was determined to have me," he wrote. "I squander and more than squander so much of my time. My preparations are put off till a late hour and then they are but poorly made."[153]

Benjamin's sister Florilla and her husband William Smallwood visited Benjamin and Ellen at the end of August. Florilla was about eight months pregnant at the time.[154] "Sister does not seem to grow old any," Benjamin observed.[155]

Roberts had now been at Rushford for nearly a year, and the people had come to appreciate his ministry. "I never saw a people that seemed so attached to a preacher as they do to Mr. Roberts," Ellen commented in a letter to Aunt Lydia. "It is a com-

---

Revival Miscellanies . . . (Boston: Magee, 1852), selected and edited by Ralph W. Allen and Daniel Wise. The book was reprinted many times. Caughey (1811-91) was born in Ireland, became an American Methodist, and held revivals in Quebec, the United States, and the United Kingdom. He had some contact with Phoebe Palmer and was an early, significant influence on William and Catherine Booth. Caughey emphasized *earnestness* in religion, as indicated in the book titles *Methodism in Earnest: Being the History of a Great Revival in Great Britain* . . . , ed. R. W. Allen and Daniel Wise (Boston: Charles H. Peirce, 1850), and *Earnest Christianity Illustrated; or, Selections from the Journal of the Rev. James Caughey*, ed. Daniel Wise (Boston: J. P. Magee, 1856). See *Phoebe Palmer: Selected Writings*, ed. Thomas C. Oden (New York: Paulist, 1988), pp. 226-27, 250-51; Melvin Easterday Dieter, *The Holiness Revival of the Nineteenth Century* (Metuchen, N.J.: Scarecrow Press, 1980), p. 60.

151. BTRD, Aug. 25, 1852. The speaker was probably Edward Thomson (not Thompson), president of Ohio Wesleyan University and later bishop. *COM*, p. 860.

152. BTRD, Aug. 26, 1852.

153. BTRD, Aug. 28, 1852.

154. See Kysor, p. 27.

155. BTRD, Aug. 31, 1852.

156. ELR to LBL, Aug. 30, 1852, quoted in Zahniser, p. 50.

fort to me that people like instead of dislike him." She added, "Our Presiding Elder says if they build a church here next year we will be returned; if they do not we will go to some other place." So Ellen knew they might be moving. Benjamin was given "materials for a very nice coat," Ellen noted, and with it "the young people are making a handsome coat for us."[156]

As annual conference approached, Benjamin updated the church records for his report. "Some forty or fifty more members were reported last year than ought to have [been]," he noted, so he had to remove many names. "Though I have received 30 or 40 more than I have dismissed yet I shall report a decrease in the number of members."[157] The Genesee Conference minutes show a membership at Rushford of 195, plus 20 probationers and 4 local preachers, a decrease of 1.[158] The total membership of 219 (combining full members, probationers, and local preachers) represented in fact a loss of 25 for the year. Roberts noted on Saturday, September 4, during the quarterly conference at Rushford, "Our finances are in a good state. . . . All seem very anxious to build a new house [of worship]. This has been a prosperous year for this charge."[159]

On Monday, September 6, Benjamin got up at 4:00 and left at 5:30 for the annual conference sessions at Lockport, to begin on Wednesday. He went a day early in order to take his examination for elders orders on Tuesday afternoon. "Passed through the examination in two hours," he noted. Presumably he also turned in the sermon or essay required by the Course of Study.[160]

Sunday morning, September 12, toward the end of conference, Bishop Thomas Morris preached on "Ye have not chosen me but I have chosen you," in the course of the sermon explaining the meaning of ordination.[161] In the afternoon Morris led the service in which Roberts was ordained elder, along with Kendall, Loren Stiles, Jr., and three others.[162] Roberts wrote in his diary, "O what solemn vows are upon me!"[163]

Benjamin wrote to Ellen on September 10, during the conference: "There is a strong talk now of our going to Niagara Street, Buffalo. I would rather not go there now; but the will of the Lord be done. Several have said, and among them a Presiding Elder, they wished I was three or four years older[;] they would put me on a District [as presiding elder]. But you need not feel concerned. This of course to you. I cannot

---

157. BTRD, Sept. 2, 1852.

158. On the membership record page of his diary Roberts lists 195 members, 20 probationers, and 5 local preachers, rather than 4. BTRD, p. 185.

159. BTRD, Sept. 4, 1852.

160. BTRD, Sept. 7, 1852; *Discipline*, 1849, p. 218.

161. BTRD, Sept. 12, 1852. Roberts outlined Morris's sermon on some unused subscription-list pages at the end of his diary (pp. 193 and 194). Morris said ordination is a "recognition of a previous call" and "a prudential regulation" in the church.

162. *Minutes*, 1852.

163. BTRD, Sept. 12, 1852.

164. BTR to ELR, Sept. 10, 1852, quoted in BHR, *BTR*, pp. 65-66; Zahniser, p. 51.

tell where our lot may be the coming year. We may have to stay at Rushford. If so we will do it cheerfully, and do the best we can. The Lord is good to me."[164]

Ellen was not at all cheered by this letter. She was still unwell, and little Georgie was very ill. Meanwhile she was reading Harriet Beecher Stowe's *Uncle Tom's Cabin*, just recently published.[165] She wrote back to Benjamin, reacting to the possible Buffalo appointment and reflecting her frustration:

> I cannot think appointments which are called first in the Conference are always most desirable. Sometimes since you left home I have felt like sending a petition to the Bishop to please send us where there are hired girls a plenty and a Homeopathic Physician. It is not best, nor right to be anxious about what may be[,] but occasionally I have ventured to wonder how we could move if obliged to, in our helpless state. . . . Uncle Tom's Cabin excites my sympathies so that I can neither read it or let it alone. I will make a thorough abolitionist I imagine.[166]

Ellen asked Benjamin to buy a gift for Mary, her niece, in appreciation for all her help — maybe "a port-folio, or a fan, or a silver top thimble."[167] Her reference to Mary, and to wanting a place where hired girls were plentiful, suggests she was feeling overwhelmed. Perhaps Mary was about to leave, for Benjamin had hired a girl named Martha to help Ellen.[168]

Benjamin apparently felt quite strongly that he should not go to Niagara Street, a prominent church in the conference. At some point, either before or after receiving Ellen's letter, he went to Bishop Morris and "entreated [him] not to send us there." Roberts "felt deeply [his] lack of ability, experience and grace, to fill so important a position," he recalled later. "But when we were sent, we resolved to do our duty faithfully."[169]

The appointments were given out on Tuesday, September 14, and Roberts was indeed appointed to Buffalo's Niagara Street Church.[170] This meant a major move for the family, not only geographically but also culturally and in terms of church politics. The 1852 sessions of the Genesee Conference were stormy, presaging things to come.

Conference over, Benjamin started for home Tuesday evening. "It was dark and rainy. Staid at Smaly's Tavern on Buffalo Road."[171] Traveling fifty-five miles over

---

165. The story began running as a serial in the *National Era* magazine in June 1851 and appeared as a book about March 1852. The book was an instant best seller. See Lyman Beecher Stowe, *Saints, Sinners, and Beechers* (New York: Blue Ribbon Books, 1934), pp. 182-83.

166. ELR to BTR, Sept. 17(?), 1852, quoted in Zahniser, p. 51. Possibly the correct date is Sept. 12, as Benjamin was back home by the seventeenth.

167. ELR to BTR, Sept. 17, 1852, quoted in Zahniser, p. 51.

168. BTRD, Sept. 16, 1852.

169. *WAS*, pp. 194-95. This was "the only appointment made for us with which we ever tried to interfere," Roberts noted. In his diary Roberts does not mention this conversation with Morris.

170. BTRD, Sept. 14, 1852.

171. BTRD, Sept. 14, 1852.

172. BTRD, Sept. 17, 1852.

muddy roads the next day, he reached home late in the evening. He found little Georgie very sick and Ellen stressed. Martha, the hired girl, had quit the day after Benjamin left for conference, despite her promise to stay. Ellen had been "wonderfully sustained," he noted, but "She has not had her clothes off a night since I left" due to Georgie's illness. Benjamin was worried about Georgie. "I do most earnestly pray that he may be spared to us. He does not look like himself he has grown so very thin."[172] In the midst of these stresses, Benjamin and Ellen faced an immediate move to Buffalo.

Benjamin had now completed four years of pastoral ministry, and Ellen had been with him for all but the first eight months of that time. He and Ellen had sought to be faithful, and in spite of her health problems these were fruitful years in the three churches they had served.

Zahniser concludes this chapter in Benjamin's life: "It was in Rushford that his devotion appears to have been enhanced; the church there had progressed under his labors so that a recognition of his ability was given in his promotion to Buffalo; there his revival work became more marked; his rising criticism of formalism and his antipathy to the pew system were becoming evident; and also his power of literary endeavor were evidenced by his writings in the *Northern Christian Advocate*."[173]

Zahniser notes also the significance of Roberts's association with Kendall and McCreery, in light of later developments.[174]

Benjamin Roberts was now twenty-nine years old, and Ellen was twenty-seven. Little George Lane Roberts, though not in robust health, had survived his first eight months of life and seemed to be regaining his strength as the Roberts family prepared to move to Buffalo.

173. Zahniser, p. 52.
174. Zahniser, p. 52.

CHAPTER 14

Showdown in Buffalo

"We have been raising monuments to the victories of our fathers, when we ought to have been achieving still greater conquests."

B. T. Roberts, 1853[1]

"I loved to please Jesus, to bear the cross, to help others in the way to heaven. I was in, to me, a new world."

Ellen Roberts, 1861[2]

B. T. Roberts hurried home to Rushford after the 1852 annual conference to tell Ellen that he was the newly appointed pastor at Niagara Street, Buffalo.

Benjamin knew that controversy lay ahead. Conference sessions had been stormy. Though as a young pastor he was only marginally involved, he knew which side he would have to be on as the conference became increasingly divided.

As noted in the previous chapter, the 1852 Genesee Conference met September 8-14 in Lockport, with Bishop Thomas Morris presiding. Roberts's diary gives a running account of the conference sessions. On Wednesday, the first day, Benjamin noted that one preacher from each district was appointed to each of the "more prominent commit-tees," and that he himself was appointed to the committee on slavery. "Things seem to be going right thus far," he commented. Yet he noted that John Kent, the preacher at Parma, "said in open conf. that Bro. [Asa] Abell was not the man for Presiding Elder."[3]

---

1. B. T. Roberts, "Genesee Conference — Causes of Its Decline," *NCA* 13, no. 10 (Mar. 9, 1853): 2.
2. Ellen L. Roberts, "Religious Experience," *EC* 2, no. 9 (Sept. 1861): 283.
3. BTRD, Sept. 8, 1852. Abell was, nonetheless, reappointed presiding elder of the Genesee District, which included Parma. See *Minutes*, Genesee Conference, 1851 and 1852.

The next day erupted in open controversy. "There is a falling out in the camp of the Greeks," Roberts noted. "Slaughter has preferred charges against Houghton and H. against De Pew [i.e., De Puy]."[4] William Slaughter, the outgoing pastor at Niagara Street, charged Daniel C. Houghton, a professor at the new Genesee College, with wrongdoing and insubordination, while Houghton pressed charges against William De Puy, principal of the Teachers' Department at Genesee Wesleyan Seminary (and later a prominent pastor in Buffalo and author).[5] "The charges originated probably in a personal quarrel," Benjamin wrote to Ellen.[6] His mention of "the camp of the Greeks" suggests that he saw Slaughter, Houghton, and De Puy as all representing the denominational drift away from traditional Methodism. (Roberts noted in his diary in early December, "Bro. Houghton who two years ago was one of the first ministers among us has been tried[,] found guilty and suspended from the ministry," and Roberts reflected, "Take heed to thyself.")[7] These charges and countercharges, though minor annoyances in the overall business of conference, reveal the undercurrent of contentiousness that existed within the Genesee Conference.

In his account of the conference Roberts notes that on Friday, September 10, the agent for the American Colonization Society spoke and quickly raised $150.[8] As a convinced abolitionist, Roberts was not especially sympathetic with the colonization cause, which proposed to transfer freed slaves to Africa but not directly to interfere with slavery itself. Nevertheless, he apparently contributed $2 to the offering.[9]

On Saturday Roberts wrote, "We remonstrated against taking Bro. Wilbor off the Dist."[10] Roberts doesn't clarify who the "we" are — presumably himself and some others of the Olean District. At the end of conference, however, A. D. Wilbor was assigned to the Swan Street Church in Buffalo.

During Monday's conference session, John E. Robie asked for supernumerary relationship, but was denied (presumably by Bishop Morris).[11] According to the Methodist *Discipline,* supernumerary status was for preachers "so worn out in the itinerant service as to be rendered incapable of preaching constantly."[12] Robie,

---

4. BTRD, Sept. 9, 1852.

5. See manuscript minutes of the Genesee Conference, *Journal of the Genesee Annual Conference of the Methodist Episcopal Church, Vol. IV,* p. 74 (Western New York Conference Archives, Buffalo), and Conable, p. 610. The minutes do not specify who brought the charges against Houghton. On De Puy, see *COM,* pp. 292-93.

6. BTR to ELR, Sept. 10, 1852, quoted in Zahniser, p. 51.

7. BTRD, Dec. 1, 1852. The 1853 Genesee Conference minutes show that Houghton made a sort of apology at that conference, and his character was then passed, in effect reversing the action Roberts refers to. The published minutes for 1853 list Houghton as "located." Conable (p. 610) notes that he subsequently joined the Presbyterians.

8. BTRD, Sept. 10, 1852. Conable (p. 601) says the total amount was $161.

9. BTRD, 1852, "Cash Account," p. 207.

10. BTRD, Sept. 11, 1852.

11. BTRD, Sept. 13, 1852.

12. *The Doctrines and Disciplines of the Methodist Episcopal Church* (New York: Lane and Scott, 1849), p. 67.

forty-one years old and actively editing the *Buffalo Christian Advocate,* was hardly "worn out."

Robie later played a key role in events leading to the formation of the Free Methodist Church. He had served churches in the Oneida Conference from 1834 to 1846, including in Auburn. A "practical printer and a good financier," he founded the *Northern Christian Advocate* in Auburn in 1841 as an independent weekly and then sold it to the Methodist General Conference in 1844.[13] Robie then began the *Genesee Evangelist* in Rochester, and after selling it to Presbyterians in 1849, moved on to Buffalo and founded the *Buffalo Christian Advocate* in 1850, which he owned and edited. His aim was "to establish in the more rapidly growing city of Buffalo a more pretentious sheet, hoping to make it [eventually] a member of the great Christian Advocate family" of Methodist papers.[14] Initially he lived and had his office in the Niagara Temperance House.[15]

Robie has been described as "a born journalist [who] possessed peculiar skill in the preparation of editorial paragraphs, and [whose] skill as a practical printer was seen in the mechanical appearance of the paper." He was also something of an entrepreneur and networker, preaching "in all the Methodist pulpits of the city" and thus coming "into contact with the people whom he desired to secure on his subscription list."[16] The *Buffalo Christian Advocate* was a financial success, and Robie a person of growing influence.

As a resident of Buffalo, Robie was now within the bounds of the Genesee, rather than the East Genesee, Conference. He was admitted to the Genesee Conference in 1851 and appointed to Buffalo's tiny Elk Street Church.[17] Always more interested in journalism and publishing than in serving churches, Robie requested supernumerary relationship but instead was "located" — that is, his membership assigned to a local church rather than the conference, since he really wasn't interested in itin-

---

13. Sandford Hunt, *Methodism in Buffalo From Its Origin to the Close of 1892* (Buffalo: H. H. Otis and Sons, 1893), p. 207. Allen notes, "On March 12, 1841, the Rev. John E. Robie, of the Oneida Conference, a practical printer, began the publication of an independent paper at Auburn, which he called the Northern Advocate. He arranged with the Rev. Freeborn C. [actually G.] Hibbard, of the Genesee Conference, to act as editor while serving as pastor at Penn Yan. After a year and a half Dr. Hibbard resigned, on account of the pressure of other duties, and the Rev. William Hosmer, also of the Genesee Conference, was secured as editor. The paper made encouraging progress, and in 1844 the proprietor [Robie] sold out to the Methodist Book Concern, and it became an official paper of the church, under the name now of the Northern Christian Advocate." Ray Allen, *History of the East Genesee Annual Conference of the Methodist Episcopal Church* (Rochester, N.Y.: By the Author, 1908), p. 32.

14. Hunt, *Methodism,* p. 208. That is, Robie hoped again to sell a paper he founded to the denomination, no doubt at some considerable profit. In this case it did not happen, however.

15. Hunt, *Methodism,* p. 208; cf. pp. 36-37.

16. Hunt, *Methodism,* p. 208.

17. John Edward Robie was born in New Hampshire on June 19, 1811 (not "about 1817," as Simpson has it in *COM,* p. 761). He owned and controlled the *Buffalo Christian Advocate* until his death in 1872, except for the period 1861-65, when he served as a Civil War chaplain. He was presiding elder of the Buffalo District from 1866 to 1870. Ray Allen, *A Century of the Genesee Annual Conference of the Methodist Episcopal Church, 1810-1910* (Rochester, N.Y.: By the Author, 1911), p. 115; *COM,* p. 761.

erant ministry. (He was later readmitted into the Genesee Conference in 1859 and assigned to assist at the Niagara Street Church.)[18]

After noting that Robie's supernumerary request was denied, Roberts commented, "Some personal feeling was excited by remarks which I made."[19] He doesn't explain. However, Robie soon became a principal antagonist of Roberts through his writings in the *Buffalo Christian Advocate*. If Roberts's "remarks" were in opposition to Robie's request for supernumerary relationship, this may have been a factor in Robie's later antagonism.

As conference progressed, Benjamin was "very busy" writing the report for the Slavery Committee.[20] The report was given on Tuesday, September 14, the last day of conference, and strongly denounced the Fugitive Slave Act. It was ordered to be published.[21]

Though Roberts does not mention it in his diary, during the conference sessions he was appointed to the Committee on Examination for first-year Course of Study candidates for 1853, and was elected to the Board of Visitors to Genesee Wesleyan Seminary, the conference committee charged with overseeing the relationship between the school and the conference.[22]

Preacher at Niagara Street

Saturday morning, September 18, Benjamin left Rushford early to make his first visit to his new charge. The fifty-mile trip cost him $2.50 in train fare. Roberts stayed

18. *Minutes*, Genesee Conference, 1851, 1852, 1859; Allen, *Century*, p. 115. Robie previously had been "located" from 1846 to 1851.

19. BTRD, Sept. 13, 1852.

20. BTR to ELR, Sept. 10, 1852, quoted in Zahniser, p. 51.

21. Manuscript Minutes of the Genesee Conference, 1852, p. 114. It is not clear whether Roberts or someone else presented the report. It was later published in *NCA* 12, no. 39 (Sept. 29, 1852). The last item read: "Resolved 7. That we view the Fugitive Slave Law with painful solicitude, deep mortification and unutterable detestation as an enactment, too vile for any nation, Christian or Pagan, civilized or savage and that we cannot in any case assist in remanding a fellow-being to Slavery. [Signed:] J. H. Wallace, P. Woodworth, A. Steel, B. T. Roberts, G. Benedict."

The report was also published in the *Buffalo Christian Advocate*. The Sept. 30, 1852, issue carried on page 1, first the "Report of the Committee on Colonization," then the "Report of the Committee on Slavery," listing the committee members, including Roberts. Robie chaired the Committee on Colonization, and its report included the resolution, "that the American Colonization Society is deserving of its high appreciation and respect, for the momentous results, already accomplished by its instrumentality." *Buffalo Christian Advocate* 3, no. 40 (Sept. 30, 1852): 1. Interestingly, Robie specifically commended the Committee on Slavery report on page 2: "It is clear and sound, and is unlike the action of three other conferences in Western New York, as light is from darkness. It is sufficiently decided to meet the full and responsible claims of the anti-slavery feeling of the State, without being fanatical and misguided." [John E. Robie], "Conference Matters," *Buffalo Christian Advocate* 3, no. 40 (Sept. 30, 1852): 2.

22. Manuscript Minutes of the Genesee Conference, 1852, pp. 105-6, 114.

overnight at the Niagara Temperance House, and noted in his diary that he met Brothers Robie, Wilbor, and Rufus Cooley.[23] A. D. Wilbor, Roberts's former presiding elder, had just been assigned to the 200-member Swan Street Church, then Buffalo's largest Methodist congregation, located about eight blocks from the Niagara Street Church. Cooley, a new member of the conference, was appointed to succeed Robie at Elk Street.[24]

Roberts preached at Niagara Street for the first time the next morning, choosing as his text Ezekiel 33:7, "Son of man, I have set thee a watchman" — thus signaling his perceived mission at the new charge. He preached again in the evening and noted in his diary, "Congregation very small. This charge has been running down for four years. I had rather a poor time."[25] The conference minutes show that Niagara Street had in fact declined sharply from a high of 375 members in 1848, when it had been the largest church in Buffalo and the third largest in the conference, to 135 members when Roberts arrived. The largest decline (158 members) had been in 1848-49, when Thomas Carlton was the pastor. Meanwhile the Swan Street Church had remained fairly constant at about 230 to 250 members. Lydia Lane remarked on Roberts's appointment to Niagara Street that he "has charge of an important station. May he be wise to win souls to Christ and live long to do good."[26]

Niagara Street, "the mother of Buffalo Methodism,"[27] was the city's oldest Methodist congregation. Its "very substantial stone building,"[28] built twenty years earlier, was located just a block off Niagara Square, the center of the city.[29]

The Niagara Street congregation had given birth to the Swan Street (later Grace) Church in the early 1840s and yet continued growing. But when the Pearl Street (later Asbury) congregation was formed from Niagara Street in 1848, reducing Niagara Street by well over 100 as members transferred north to Pearl Street, the congregation was thrown into crisis. Sandford Hunt notes that by 1849 the "financial affairs of [Niagara Street] were in a very unsatisfactory condition, and the church was struggling with a heavy debt. The 'mother church' had been depleted by removals, and the 'uptown' tide had already set in." A socioeconomic factor was at work as "a class of population of the city of Buffalo in easy circumstances drifted, in a quiet but strong current, 'uptown.'"[30]

23. BTRD, Sept. 18, 1852.

24. *Minutes*, Genesee Conference, 1852.

25. BTRD, Sept. 19, 1852.

26. LBLD, Oct. 29, 1852.

27. Hunt, *Methodism*, p. 43. Roberts summarized the history of the Niagara Street Church in 1861, tracing it back to the pioneering ministry of George Lane in the area in 1808. [B. T. Roberts], "Niagara Street M.E. Church," *EC* 2, no. 8 (Aug. 1861): 256-58.

28. *WAS*, p. 105.

29. B. T. Roberts, "Niagara Street M.E. Church," p. 257. See David A. Gerber, *The Making of an American Pluralism: Buffalo, New York, 1825-60* (Urbana: University of Illinois Press, 1989), p. 17.

30. Hunt, *Methodism*, pp. 34-44, 59, 76, 121. James Alan Revell, "The Nazirites: Burned-Over District Methodism and the Buffalo Middle Class" (Ph.D. diss., University of New York at Buffalo, 1993), provides additional information.

As Roberts prepared to move to Buffalo, then, he faced a declining congregation with a large building and a heavy debt. The most immediate issue, however, was finding a home. The house the church had "selected as a parsonage" was too far from the church building, Benjamin felt, and had no study. On Monday, September 20, following his first Sunday in Buffalo, he took a look at this house, then traveled back to Rushford to prepare for the move.[31]

Benjamin and Ellen spent the next couple of days packing. "This is one of the hardships of the itinerancy," Benjamin noted. "But our Master had not where to lay his head." Since the housing situation was unresolved, Benjamin and Ellen decided that Ellen would stay with Benjamin's parents in Gowanda while he arranged for a house. Benjamin preached both morning and evening at Gowanda on Sunday, September 26, and then returned to Buffalo the next Tuesday.[32]

It took a while for Benjamin to find a house in Buffalo. Ellen noted in her diary, "Spent several weeks in October at Father Roberts — They could not find a house sooner."[33] On Monday, October 4, Benjamin wrote, "Spent most of the day [in Buffalo] in running around to no purpose. . . . Can do nothing till we get settled." Meanwhile he rented box 141 at the post office (paying fifty cents for it) and bought some furniture at an auction house.[34]

Roberts apparently boarded with various church members during these days of transition while Ellen and Georgie were still in Gowanda. Monday night, October 4, he stayed with Judge Peter Vosburgh, a leading member of the church (and a trustee) who lived on Maryland Avenue, a little over a mile northwest of the church building. An "interesting family," Roberts observed.[35] Later (November 1) he called on Brother Vosburgh at his office, and on November 17 he notes, "Dined at Bro. Vosburgh's."[36] Peter Vosburgh had become a prominent businessman and attorney in Buffalo, serving from 1845 until 1851 as surrogate judge for Erie County, and was influential in the Niagara Street Church. He was elected county clerk in 1855 and served as the city comptroller in 1861-62. A contemporary described him as "slow and candid in forming opinions and firm in his own convictions of right and justice."[37]

---

31. BTRD, Sept. 20, 1852. This perhaps is the house on Sixth Street that he mentions on Sept. 29 as being unsatisfactory.

32. BTRD, Sept. 23-28, 1852.

33. ELRD, 1852 (precise date not given). "They" here presumably refers to Benjamin and the Niagara Street congregation. Zahniser says Ellen and Georgie stayed in Gowanda "until such time as the cholera, which was raging in Buffalo, should subside," but gives no source for this, and neither Ellen nor Benjamin give this as a reason in their diaries. Buffalo suffered cholera epidemics in 1832 and 1849, but apparently not in 1852. Still, because of the earlier epidemic and Georgie's poor health, Benjamin and Ellen may have been fearful of exposure to cholera or other diseases.

34. BTRD, Oct. 1, 2, and 4, 1852.

35. BTRD, Oct. 5, 1852.

36. BTRD, Nov. 1 and 17, 1852. It is not clear whether Ellen was with him on this latter occasion.

37. H. Perry Smith, ed., *History of the City of Buffalo and Erie County* (Syracuse: D. Mason and Co., 1894), 2:141-42, 472.

Roberts hurried back to Gowanda on Tuesday, October 5, because he received word that little Georgie had gotten worse. He found that Georgie was in no immediate danger, but spent the rest of the week with the family in Gowanda, returning to Buffalo on Saturday. While in Gowanda he bought peaches and sugar so Ellen and his mother could make preserves, and helped his father some. He noted that his father had sold Bill for $125; apparently Benjamin had decided not to take the horse with him to Buffalo. "I bought him 3 [years] ago for $70.00. He has been a serviceable horse, and it seems like parting with an old friend to let him go."[38]

While in Gowanda Benjamin also wrote to John Wesley Redfield, perhaps broaching the possibility of his coming to Niagara Street for a revival.[39]

Before returning to Buffalo for the weekend, Benjamin went with Ellen to visit the grave of "our dear Willie" in the Presbyterian cemetery. "We planted a weeping willow at the foot of his grave and Ellen set out some violets and other flowers."[40]

It took about a month for Benjamin to find a suitable house in Buffalo, at 46 South Division Street, about four blocks southwest of the Niagara Street church building, and near the end of October he moved his family to Buffalo.[41] Apparently Ellen's niece, Mary Swezey, was still with them, for Benjamin mentions her on January 4, 1853.[42]

Though Roberts was familiar with New York, this was the first time he lived and pastored in a dynamic, growing city. Ellen was more accustomed to city life, having spent ten of her twenty-seven years in Manhattan. "I like living in Buffalo quite well," she commented that January.[43]

Buffalo had a population of about fifty thousand at this time and was growing about 10 percent annually.[44] The city had a rapidly expanding German and Irish immigrant population, adding both dynamism and tensions — including religious tensions, since the majority of the new arrivals were Roman Catholics. David Gerber notes that in the 1840s and 1850s Buffalo's population grew markedly diverse and pluralistic. The major "source of this new social pluralism was the arrival of the first wave of mass immigration in American national history," consisting of Irish and German "peasants, small farmers, artisans, and petty traders." Benjamin and Ellen arrived in the middle of this immigrant explosion and ethnic diversification. By 1855 nearly 75 percent of Buffalo's population was foreign-born,

38. BTRD, Oct. 5-7, 1852.
39. BTRD, Oct. 7, 1852.
40. BTRD, Oct. 8, 1852.
41. Benjamin inscribed his 1853 diary, "B. T. Roberts, 46 South Division St., Buffalo"; presumably this was the house he and Ellen moved into at the end of October. It must have proved unsatisfactory, however, for in early 1853 he and Ellen were looking for a house they could buy. (Roberts's 1852 diary is largely blank from Oct. 16 to 30, which covers the period of the move.)
42. BTRD, Jan. 4, 1853. Benjamin speaks of her as being "at school," apparently meaning that she was living with the Robertses but not able to help Ellen much because of her schooling. He mentions her again on June 15, 1853.
43. ELRD, Jan. 1853 (exact date not given).
44. J. H. French, *Gazetteer of the State of New York* (Syracuse: R. Pearsall Smith, 1860), pp. 284-88.

a reversal of the situation only a decade earlier, when new immigrants were a distinct minority.[45]

Benjamin soon discovered that crime was a fact of life in Buffalo. "Crime abounds in this city," he observed. "One man has been recently killed. One has been stabbed seriously and another assaulted and beaten most outrageously. A boy 17 yrs old set fire to Mr. Wm Bennet's barn. He was sworn clear by prostitutes."[46] Buffalo was quite a contrast to Pike or Rushford.

During the weeks of arranging for the family's move, Roberts began his ministry at Niagara Street. "The brethren received me very kindly," he noted when he met several of them on Monday, September 20, after his first Sunday at the new church. He held an "official meeting" of the members on Wednesday night, September 29. "Brethren seem disposed to take hold and try to do something."[47]

On Thursday, September 30, Benjamin went calling with Eleazar Thomas, newly appointed as presiding elder of the Buffalo District. Thomas, preacher at Niagara Street from 1846 to 1848 during its period of rapid growth, knew the community well, and had previously been Roberts's presiding elder in the Rushford District.[48] Roberts found the people "kind & cordial," and noted that at the evening prayer meeting, with about forty present, "The Sisters took hold good and prayed."[49]

In some respects the initial prospects at Niagara Street looked promising. Preaching Sunday morning, October 10, on "O Lord, revive thy work" and then again in the afternoon, Roberts noted that the congregation "was much larger than it has been before since I came here. Had a very good time."[50] Benjamin was optimistic. He wrote to Ellen, "I dreaded coming here but I am glad now that I am sent to this people. I believe the Lord will use me for their good." He added, "I am expecting an outpouring of the Spirit. God is willing to grant it. The people desire it."[51]

Benjamin was concerned, however, about Ellen and her own readiness spiritually for the new challenge. He wrote, "How, darling, do you enjoy yourself now? Have you received any special spiritual blessings of late? You will need much grace to meet the duties that await you. You will have a wider field of usefulness than you have ever had before. . . . But I have no fears on your account. If you will only have

---

45. Gerber, *American Pluralism*, pp. 113-14, 172. According to Gerber, 39 percent of household heads in 1855 were German-born and 18 percent were born in Ireland. "In that year, too, one person in three among household heads was not a citizen," compared to one in six in 1846 (p. 114). The city's black population was small, numbering only about seven hundred in 1853 (p. 17).

46. BTRD, Mar. 4, 1853.

47. BTRD, Sept. 20 and 29, 1852.

48. As pastor at Niagara Street, Thomas "preached holiness, after the pattern of Asbury, in the power of the Holy Ghost," Roberts noted in *WAS*, p. 104.

49. BTRD, Sept. 30, 1852. Thomas had pastored the nearby Pearl Street Church for the previous two years (1850-52).

50. BTRD, Oct. 10, 1852.

51. BTR (Buffalo) to ELR (Gowanda), 1852, quoted in Zahniser, pp. 53-54.

better health, you will, I do not doubt, enjoy yourself much, and fully meet the high expectations."[52]

Ellen wrote back, expressing a deep sense of inadequacy and spiritual need. "Surely religion can make me more useful, if I only had more," she said. "I dread somewhat, yes a great deal, going to Buffalo, and should even more if I had not just such a husband as I have to lean upon." She advised Benjamin to be prudent if he bought a cookstove, and to "not buy anything we can do without." She wanted things to be plain and simple "when I come to Buffalo, if I ever do."[53]

The 1852 U.S. presidential election campaign was in full swing at this time, though voters generally were apathetic. The only reference Roberts makes to the campaign is to note that he saw General Winfield Scott, the Whig candidate, on Wednesday, October 13. "There does not seem to be much enthusiasm," he commented.[54] A few weeks later Franklin Pierce, the Democratic candidate, was elected president with an unusually low voter turnout.[55]

The district preachers association met at Niagara Street Church on October 12-13, and Roberts noted that most of the twenty or so preachers in the district attended. C. D. Burlingham, now stationed at Tonawanda, preached Tuesday evening on "Is there no balm in Gilead?"[56] At the end of the month (Sunday, October 31), Roberts noted that in the afternoon he "preached at the Bethel" — the mission to Great Lakes seamen in Buffalo that had been started some years earlier.[57]

Benjamin, Ellen, and little Georgie were now settled in their rented house on Division Street. Benjamin could again spend his mornings in his study.[58] On November 9 he read the Hebrew Bible "as usual" and noted, "Am making some proficiency in Hebrew."[59] Wednesday, November 3, after reading Hebrew and doing some writing in the morning, he called on some of his members. He wasn't encouraged as he got better acquainted with them. "Every body seems dead without know-

---

52. BTR (Buffalo) to ELR (Gowanda), 1852, quoted in Zahniser, p. 54.

53. ELR (Gowanda) to BTR (Buffalo), undated but written in Oct. 1852. Quoted in Zahniser, p. 54.

54. BTRD, Oct. 13, 1852.

55. See Michael F. Holt, *The Rise and Fall of the American Whig Party: Jacksonian Politics and the Onset of the Civil War* (New York: Oxford University Press, 1999), pp. 726-27.

56. BTRD, Oct. 12-13, 1852. See "Buffalo District Association," *Buffalo Christian Advocate* 3, no. 44 (Oct. 28, 1852): 2, a report submitted by A. D. Wilbor as secretary. "A respectable number were present," and Roberts was elected to the Standing Business Committee (apparently as chair) along with John Bowman and E. R. Keyes. Bowman later figured in Roberts's 1857 and 1858 trials.

57. BTRD, Oct. 31, 1852. The American Bethel Society was founded in Buffalo in 1836 as an inland counterpart to the American Seamen's Friend Society, based in New York City. Both societies were part of the worldwide Bethel mission to seamen. See Roald Kverndal, *Seamen's Missions: Their Origin and Early Growth; A Contribution to the History of the Church Maritime* (Pasadena, Calif.: William Carey Library, 1986), pp. 479-80.

58. Apparently they moved to the house at 46 South Division Street the last week in October, as noted above.

59. BTRD, Nov. 9, 1852. On Nov. 30 he noted, "Find it necessary to read some [Hebrew] every day to get along well."

ing it," he remarked. "Unless the Lord in His Almighty power help there is no deliverance for us."[60]

Roberts had to do something about the financial crisis at Niagara Street. The church building, rather imposing and "for that age a very commodious one," had been completed in 1835 and was valued at $15,000 in 1850. But the diminished congregation was struggling under a remaining debt of several thousand dollars.[61] On Friday, November 5, Roberts met with the church's leaders and "proposed to form a board of responsible stewards and trust the finances to them." He also took steps to meet the spiritual need of the church. The next day, a cold, rainy Saturday, he wrote to John Wesley Redfield and Fay H. Purdy, "inviting them to come and assist us in a meeting."[62] Purdy was a young Methodist lawyer-evangelist who "had received a mighty baptism of the Spirit" and was working "for the awakening of formal churches . . . with remarkable success."[63]

About this time Benjamin sent a letter to his father, assessing the situation. "Things are beginning to assume a much more favorable appearance," he wrote. "Our congregations are much larger than at first and there seems to be more interest. You have no idea of the low state of Methodism in this city. Nothing but the power of the Lord can save us."[64] Years later Roberts recalled, "The temptation to lower the standard was strong, but God kept us from compromising. The congregations began to increase. The preaching was of a character to arrest attention and the preacher was in earnest. By November it became apparent that ordinary methods would not avail to bring the Church up to the scriptural level."[65]

Benjamin sensed the weight of his new charge and the responsibility it brought. He tried especially to prepare himself well for Sundays. He noted on Saturday, November 13: "Passed the day chiefly in preparing for the Sabbath. Have succeeded better in my preparation than I have sometimes done. Have read carefully a chapter in the Hebrew Bible during the past week." He spent a considerable amount of time visiting, sometimes accompanied by Ellen, and devoted Friday, November 19, to fasting and prayer. "Have not experienced that growth in grace that I ought," he observed.[66]

Winter was coming on, and Roberts noted on Sunday, November 21, that the church building was "very cold & smoky." He came down with a severe cold "which unfits me for almost every thing," he noted on Saturday, November 27. Yet he "enjoyed [himself] very well" in preaching the next day and recorded that 108 were present for Sunday school and the morning congregation was "very good."[67]

60. BTRD, Nov. 3, 1852.

61. Hunt, *Methodism*, pp. 31-34, 253. A (somewhat later) picture of the Niagara Street Church building is found facing p. 34.

62. BTRD, Nov. 5-6, 1852.

63. *WAS*, p. 53.

64. BTR to TR, Nov. 8, 1852, quoted in BHR, *BTR*, p. 67.

65. Quoted in BHR, *BTR*, pp. 67-68.

66. BTRD, Nov. 13 and 19, 1852.

67. BTRD, Nov. 21, 27-28, 1852.

Roberts's sermon topics during this period give a sense of what he thought the church needed. Normally he preached Sunday morning and afternoon and conducted a prayer meeting Sunday evening, in typical fashion. His sermons included these topics:

October 3: "The word [of the LORD] is tried" (2 Sam. 22:31)
October 10: "O LORD, revive thy work" (Hab. 3:2)
  "Ephraim is a cake not turned" (Hos. 7:8)
October 17: "Riches and poverty of Christ" (2 Cor. 8:9)
  "He is able to save them to the uttermost" (Heb. 7:25)
October 24: "The path of the just" (Prov. 4:18)
  "Present your bodies a living sacrifice" (Rom. 12:1)
October 31: "Like fullers' soap" (Mal. 3:2)
November 7: "Examine yourselves, whether ye be in the faith" (2 Cor. 13:5)
  "Dead faith" (probably James 2:26)[68]

Clearly, Roberts thought the church needed to be awakened and revived![69]

Over the last week in November Benjamin read Isaac Taylor's new book, *Wesley, and Methodism*.[70] He felt that Taylor "leans too strongly to Calvinism" and "does not do full justice to Wesley," though he "looks for the advent of a new Methodism."[71] In December Roberts began reading Bishop Joseph Butler's classic *Analogy of Religion*, a book listed for the third year in the Course of Study, but which Roberts apparently hadn't read earlier.[72]

Family finances were very tight during this period, and Benjamin had to borrow money. The church fixed his salary at $500 (about $15,000 in today's dollars), a reasonable amount, but the cost of living in Buffalo was high.[73] On November 29 Benjamin borrowed $10 from Brother Bond and paid Brother Nash $25 he had borrowed earlier.[74] The next week he had to "[r]un around . . . to borrow some money to pay for borrowed money. I feel much embarrassed."[75]

The district quarterly meeting was held at the Niagara Street Church the first

---

68. BTRD for these dates. Roberts doesn't always record what his text and/or topic was.

69. Robie commented in the Dec. 9 issue of the *Buffalo Christian Advocate* on what he saw as "the prevalence of the revival power and influence among us." He saw "encouraging signs in several of the churches" that "seem to predict the approach of the time when the spirit in fuller dispensations shall be enjoyed. . . . In some of the Methodist churches, an increasing interest is manifested." [John E. Robie], "Religious Interests in Buffalo," *Buffalo Christian Advocate* 3, no. 50 (Dec. 9, 1852): 2.

70. BTRD, Nov. 23, 1852. The book was Isaac Taylor (1787-1865), *Wesley, and Methodism* (New York: Harper and Brothers, 1852), first published in London in 1851.

71. BTRD, Nov. 29, 1852.

72. BTRD, Dec. 3, 1852. See *Doctrines and Disciplines,* p. 217.

73. See BTR to TR, Oct. 18, 1853; BHR, *BTR,* p. 79.

74. BTRD, Nov. 29, 1852. Page 204 of Roberts's 1852 diary indicates that he had borrowed thirty-five dollars from Brother Nash on Nov. 10.

75. BTRD, Dec. 2, 1852.

weekend in December.[76] In preparation for this, Roberts held a fast prayer meeting on Friday, as instructed by the *Discipline*.[77] Nine members attended. "I find self denial most difficult when I try hardest to practice it," he commented.[78]

Eleazar Thomas, the presiding elder, conducted the quarterly meeting. He preached on Saturday and both morning and evening on Sunday, as well as speaking to the Sunday school children in the morning and giving Communion in the afternoon. "The Lord was present," Roberts noted.[79] The quarterly conference was followed by a Monday morning preachers meeting that included Thomas, Robie, and Brother Magill, probably a local preacher. The preachers then went together to visit the orphan asylum where, Roberts observed, some sixty-seven children were well cared for.[80]

As Roberts continued his pastoral work, he tried to be more disciplined with his time and his sermon preparation. "Had an unusually profitable time in my study this morning," he noted on Friday, December 17. "I find fasting an excellent means of grace." The next day he again had a "profitable time" in his study. He noted that Sunday morning attendance was good both December 12 and 19, though less so on December 26 due to stormy weather.[81]

Throughout the year in Buffalo Benjamin kept up his reading and Bible study. He noted on March 17, "I find more delight than ever in studying the Bible, in the original. O, May I find grace to obey it!"[82] A few days later he read some of Caesar's commentary in Latin and remarked admiringly that Caesar was "a man of remarkable industry."[83] Again, he noted on Thursday, March 24, "Studied as usual today. I am making good proficiency in the Hebrew."[84] The breadth of Roberts's mind and interests can be seen also in his visit to the Jewish synagogue in Buffalo on Saturday, March 26, his reading of Washington Irving's two-volume *Mohammed and His Successors*, and his attending lectures on public speaking.[85]

Roberts felt his commission was to preach the gospel to the poor, and so didn't confine his efforts to his own congregation. As at previous appointments, he went to the people who needed and were willing to hear. As Benson Roberts wrote, "At each of his previous stations he opened and maintained several preaching appointments outside of the stated church services. School-houses and private houses were thus

76. "Quarterly Meeting at the Niagara Street Church," *Buffalo Christian Advocate* 3, no. 49 (Dec. 2, 1852): 2.

77. *Doctrines and Disciplines*, p. 56.

78. BTRD, Dec. 3, 1852.

79. BTRD, Dec. 5, 1852.

80. BTRD, Dec. 6, 1852. Magill is not listed in the Genesee Conference minutes as a traveling preacher, so he must have been a local preacher.

81. BTRD, Dec. 12, 17-19, and 26, 1852.

82. BTRD, Mar. 17, 1853.

83. BTRD, Mar. 22, 1853. Note the character issue: though Caesar was not a Christian, one could still admire the virtue of industry he displayed.

84. BTRD, Mar. 24, 1854.

85. BTRD, Mar. 24, 30-31, and Apr. 4, 1853.

utilized at Rushford, Pike and Caryville. In Buffalo we find him repeatedly preaching in the jail, and occasionally at the hydraulics [i.e., the city waterworks]."[86]

Roberts's outreach efforts included helping to organize a Sunday school at the Ninth Street mission on May 29.[87]

Nor had Roberts forgotten the antislavery cause. On Sunday afternoon, November 14, he allowed Hannah Pierson, "a Quakeress," to preach at Niagara Street and took up an offering of seventeen dollars for "Bro. Basil Hall," a former slave who had been able to buy his freedom.[88] The next day Benjamin made some calls with Brother Hall, helping raise money to free Hall's wife and two children. They called on the mayor of the city and another gentleman.[89] Later, Roberts filled two and a half diary pages with notes on the peaceful abolition of slavery in the British West Indies in 1838 and subsequent developments there.[90] In May he sat in on some sessions of the New School Presbyterian General Assembly, which was meeting in Buffalo, and was intensely interested in the hot debate over the slavery issue. Roberts concluded, "Most of the speakers are apparently apologists for Slavery."[91]

Roberts also kept in touch with his friend Loren Stiles during his year in Buffalo. Stiles had been appointed to the nearby Pearl Street Church when Roberts went to Niagara Street. He remained there for two years and saw the membership grow from 169 to 206. Pearl Street had been organized out of the Niagara Street Church in 1848 (as noted earlier), and a "plain, substantial structure of brick, two stories," was built at the corner of Pearl and Chippewa Streets, just four blocks north of the Niagara Street building.[92]

Roberts saw Stiles regularly at the Buffalo District preachers meetings, held on Monday mornings, usually about twice a month. Roberts and Stiles exchanged pulpits at least once, and Stiles preached at the Niagara Street Church on Saturday, February 19. "He preached more plainly than I ever heard him before," Benjamin commented. "We need much grace to speak boldly as we ought to."[93] Following the preachers meeting on March 7, Roberts noted hopefully that revival was "in

86. BHR, *BTR*, p. 74. According to his diary, Benjamin preached in the jail at least on Feb. 27 and Mar. 27, and on May 31 visited a convicted murderer who was to be hung.

87. BTRD, May 29, 1853. According to the 1852 minutes, the Ninth Street work was attached to Elk Street, where Rufus Cooley was the appointed preacher.

88. BTRD, Nov. 14, 1852. Mrs. Basil Hall is mentioned in Martin Duberman, ed., *The Antislavery Vanguard: New Essays on the Abolitionists* (Princeton: Princeton University Press, 1965), p. 306 n. 14.

89. BTRD, Nov. 15, 1852.

90. BTRD, Apr. 25-29, 1853. These notes apparently were added later (probably in July, when Roberts was reading Charles Elliott, *Sinfulness of American Slavery*, a two-volume work published in 1851 by the Methodist book agents in Cincinnati, Swormstedt and Power), using pages Benjamin had earlier left blank. The following several pages (Apr. 30 through May 14) are blank.

91. BTRD, May 30-31, 1853.

92. Hunt, *Methodism*, p. 76. Niagara Street membership dropped from 375 to 217 (including probationers) when the Pearl Street congregation was organized. Pearl Street first appears in the minutes in 1849, reporting a total membership of 138, nearly all of which must have come from Niagara Street.

93. BTRD, Feb. 19, 1853.

progress in all our churches," and that "Bro. Stiles has received some forty into his Church."[94] Though Pearl Street apparently was a "stock church," Stiles did not feel led to protest pew rental the way Roberts did, though he eventually sided with Roberts.

Revival with Redfield

Now that Roberts was into the swing of his pastoral work, his major concern was revival. He had invited John Wesley Redfield and Fay Purdy to come and conduct special meetings, as already noted. Purdy apparently couldn't come, but Redfield arrived about January 1, 1853. Benjamin got John H. Wallace, an older preacher assigned to the Clarkson church, to help as well. Wallace had preached in the Sunday afternoon service at conference on September 12, when Benjamin was ordained, and Roberts must have been impressed with him.[95]

Roberts, of course, knew of Redfield and his ministry, but until this point the two men were not personally acquainted. Benjamin no doubt met Redfield during the 1846 revival at Wesleyan University, but Redfield did not remember him. Redfield later wrote,

> I had enquired of a good old preacher about [Roberts] & learned that I had nothing to fear in trying to go straight for he was a man who dared to identify himself with right[,] however unpopular. I found him to be one of the students whom I saw but made no acquaintance with at [Middletown] & his wife a very unassuming lady but very conscientious.
>
> I learned from Bro. [Roberts] & the principal man in the church that this once flourishing cradle of Methodism was almost run out & that it had been a hard matter to sustain prayer meetings for a year or two. Bro. R was at his post & ready to remain in.[96]

The Niagara Street revival effort under Redfield and Wallace began the first Sunday in January 1853. "Now begins the assault on sin and indifference in the Church," wrote Benson Roberts.[97] Redfield went to Buffalo after holding revivals in the Rochester and Elmira areas, expecting a difficult struggle. Even as he focused on Buffalo, he was concerned about the fate of Methodism generally. "It seems to me that such is the condition of the churches, that some unusual effort must be made to

94. BTRD, Mar. 7, 1853. In fact, Pearl Street reported a gain of 45 for the year (from 168 to 213) but a decrease of 13 the following year.

95. BTRD, Sept. 12, 1852. Wallace arrived on Saturday, Jan. 1 (BTRD, Jan. 1, 1853), and Redfield either that day or the next.

96. Redfield Autobiography, MMHC, p. 314 (spelling corrected). Terrill, *Redfield,* omits this sentence, which is important in establishing the significant relationship between Redfield and B. T. and Ellen Roberts.

97. BHR, *BTR,* p. 68.

check the progress of approaching ruin, and extend the borders of Zion to fields as yet unoccupied," Redfield wrote to Charles Hicks.[98]

Redfield and Wallace now applied themselves to "the work of confession, reclaiming, converting and sanctifying grace" at Niagara Street.[99] On Sunday, January 2, Wallace preached morning and evening, and Roberts in the afternoon. Wallace's morning topic was "Strengthen the things that remain," while Roberts preached on "Come out from among them" (2 Cor. 6:17), one of his favorite texts.[100] Redfield exhorted in the evening, following Wallace's sermon on "Ye are the light of the world."[101]

The revival with Redfield lasted through the four weeks of January. Though Redfield left on January 28, Roberts conducted special services almost every night for the next two months, and saw a number of conversions.

The critical period of the revival, however, was the first two or three weeks. Buffalo weather was cold and at times snowy, but special meetings were held almost every night and most afternoons as well.[102] And in the midst of this period, the weekend of January 23, came the Missionary Anniversary celebration, a major event that this year was held at the Niagara Street Church.

On January 13, after Redfield had been preaching for a little over a week, the *Buffalo Christian Advocate* took note of the meetings. A brief item commented that "Rev. Dr. Redfield . . . , celebrated as a revivalist, is now holding a protracted meeting" at Niagara Street. John Robie, presumably the writer, likely had attended some of the meetings, and he gave this assessment of Redfield: "He is talented as a speaker, of engaging appearance, and has, no doubt, a kind and christian [*sic*] heart. He labors with great zeal, and pours truth, hot and fiery, upon the conscience. We certainly have sympathy for the meeting, and can but wish him and the cause abundant success. If he had more reliable information, we judge, he would succeed better. As it is he will create an excitement, and it is to be hoped that something good and great may grow out of the movement. We shall see."[103]

98. Redfield (Henrietta, N.Y.) to Charles Hicks (Syracuse), Nov. 11, 1852, quoted in Terrill, *Redfield*, p. 269. Charles T. Hicks was an attorney and county clerk in Syracuse who had been sanctified under Redfield and Purdy's labors. A Methodist, Hicks later became a prominent leader in the Free Methodist Church. See Hogue, *HFMC*, 1:374-77; Terrill, *Redfield*, pp. 268-70.

99. Redfield Autobiography, p. 314 (corrected); cf. Terrill, *Redfield*, p. 279.

100. BTRD, Jan. 2, 1853. Roberts preached repeatedly on this text in later years.

101. BTRD, Jan. 2, 1853.

102. Benjamin's diary for January shows that evening services were held almost every evening and that frequent weekday afternoon services were also held. Since he apparently doesn't mention every service held, it is uncertain whether the afternoon services were intermittent or were conducted daily. Afternoon and evening services were a common revival pattern at least since the days of Charles Finney. One may see such revivals as an adaptation of camp meeting methodology to a local church situation.

103. "Rev. Dr. Redfield," *Buffalo Christian Advocate* 4, no. 2 (Jan. 13, 1853): 2.

A Deeper Experience for Ellen

For Ellen Roberts, the most significant event during these days was her experience of entire sanctification on Friday, January 14. This was a key turning point in her spiritual pilgrimage. Redfield preached that evening on "What things soever ye desire, when ye pray, believe that ye receive them, and ye shall have them" (Mark 11:24). Ellen responded and, as Benjamin wrote in his diary, "received the blessing of perfect love."[104] In her diary Ellen recorded, "We are having quite an interest awakened in our church. My own soul has been abundantly blessed even with full salvation. Praise God, I do feel that I am a new creature in Christ Jesus, [']old things are done away and all things are become new.'"[105]

Ellen related this experience at some length in her 1861 "Religious Experience" article. In her three and a half years of married life, she said, she had not had spiritual victory. She felt totally "unqualified" for the work God had given her as a pastor's wife, though she longed to do it. "I began to resolve to be better — only to fail." She felt that the Lord had used "severe means" to bring her to full commitment. "He took from us a lovely child [William], and soon after my health began to grow very feeble. I felt that my Father dealt with me in justice and mercy — my heart had begun to cling closer to the world, and I found little time or disposition to work for God."[106]

Ellen then relates the move to Buffalo and the revival at Niagara Street under Redfield, whom apparently she heard for the first time. "There was to me an irresistible power accompanying his words, a something that took hold of me as nothing ever had done. I began to feel encouraged, and to believe it possible for me to *get right*. I resolved to be thorough, cost what it might. The spirit [*sic*] began to lead me. I had first to confess to my family that while I had professed religion I had not lived as a Christian ought, — I had often yielded to *impatience*. This was a cross, but I was humbled and blessed in doing it."

At one of the revival services Ellen confessed her need and "told of [her] determination" to experience God's fullness. "I soon found justifying grace, and a few nights after, while listening to a sermon from 'what things soever ye desire *when ye pray*, believe that ye receive them and ye shall have them,' I was enabled to believe the cleansing blood applied to my heart." As with Phoebe Palmer, this had been the crux of her struggle, going back to her days at Allen Street Church before her marriage: to receive full salvation by faith in God's Word, regardless of other evidence. Ellen elaborated:

> I had made a thorough consecration of all to God, and now while I prayed I believed I received, [and] I continued to believe thus for some hours with no evidence but God's word, — the enemy constantly accusing me of presumption. I

104. BTRD, Jan. 14, 1853.

105. ELRD, Jan. 1853 (exact date not given). Surprisingly, Carpenter does not mention this in her biography of Ellen. See Carpenter, p. 45.

106. Ellen L. Roberts, "Religious Experience," p. 283.

had many times come to this point in the last few years, and because I did not realize at once the evidence that the work was wrought I let go and sunk back. Now, to doubt I saw was to sink. I said, if I never have any evidence but the word of the Lord, I will believe. After a few hours, and when I seemed to be emptied of sin, my soul began to be filled with light and glory and joy unspeakable, so that sleep departed from my eyes. The evidence that the work was wrought was clearer than it was the first time I experienced full salvation, though preceded by a greater trial of my faith. Blessed be God! how glad I was to get back to my Father's house where there was bread enough and to spare!

This new experience of God made an immediate difference in Ellen's behavior, though she still sometimes had spiritual struggles. "I loved to please Jesus, to bear the cross, to help others in the way to heaven. I was in, to me, a new world." The Scripture "whether ye eat or drink, or whatsoever ye do, do all to the glory of God" was "written upon my heart," she noted, adding: "I saw I must in my dress seek to please Jesus, and gladly laid aside some useless articles. I began to learn some lessons on being led by the Spirit, which have been of great value to me, also in reference to holding on to Jesus by faith in the absence of emotion. The latter has been a hard lesson for me to learn, especially when my health was poor and my nerves weak, as was often the case."[107]

From this point on Ellen became more fully a partner in the gospel with Benjamin. Although she had helped him before, her lack of spiritual victory and her physical problems and domestic responsibilities had kept much of her focus on herself. Benjamin spent considerable effort helping and supporting her in various ways. Now he and Ellen became a team, working together in the ministry.

The January revival effort had meant extra work for Ellen. Redfield and Wallace lodged with the Robertses for at least part of this time, and with meal preparation, the care of little Georgie (still not well), and no domestic help, Ellen had difficulty coping. Benjamin notes on January 4, "Assisted my dear wife to take care of our little boy. We have Br. R. and W. in the family — no girl and Mary at school." With Mary not able to help much because of her schooling, Benjamin tried unsuccessfully to find a girl he could hire.[108] Yet in the midst of these trying circumstances, Ellen sought and found deeper spiritual resources through the revival effort and the ministry of John Wesley Redfield.

Turning Point

Ellen's experience of full salvation came at the end of the second week of the revival. The two weeks following this were the critical period in the whole revival effort. Much

107. Ellen L. Roberts, "Religious Experience," pp. 283-84.

108. Benjamin notes on Jan. 3, "Spent most of the morning in looking for a girl. Unsuccessful" (BTRD, Jan. 3, 1853). His diary does not indicate whether he eventually found someone or not.

of what happened at Niagara Street and in B. T. Roberts's ministry over the following weeks and months hinged on developments the last two weeks in January 1853, and in particular on the Missionary Anniversary held at Niagara Street on January 23 and 24.

By coincidence, the celebration of the Methodist Missionary Society Anniversary — a major denominational event — was held at Niagara Street in the middle of the revival with Redfield.[109] Nathan Bangs and Joshua Soule had formed the Missionary Society in 1819 in New York City, and the next year by General Conference action it became the denominational missionary organization, though it continued to function as a voluntary society until it was made a church board in 1872. Its primary focus was initially on missionary extension within the United States. By 1853, however, it had initiated mission work in Liberia, South America, Europe, and China, and the work of missions was being broadly promoted in the denomination.[110] One of the chief ways to do this was by holding Missionary Anniversary rallies in various places. The vigorous John Price Durbin, a Kentuckian, was elected missionary secretary at the 1852 General Conference, and he brought new energy to missionary fund-raising with his stirring oratory as he traveled to many of the annual conferences.[111] Durbin came to Buffalo for the missions rally at Niagara Street,

---

109. Redfield, however, did not see this as a coincidence. He wrote, "But word soon reached the ears of the men who have been known as the regency & they came on in mass to hold a missionary meeting & appointed one meeting at the N. St. Church" (Redfield Autobiography, p. 315). Terrill says, a bit more evenhandedly: "In the midst of this revival the meetings of the General Missionary Society came on, and one service was appointed to be held in the Niagara Street church" (Terrill, *Redfield*, pp. 279-80). In fact, the *Buffalo Christian Advocate* had already announced on Dec. 16, 1852, that the "Anniversary of the Missionary Society of the Methodist Episcopal Church, . . . will be held in Buffalo, near the middle of January," though exact date and place were not yet determined. "The anniversaries of the society have hitherto been held in the city of New York, and have generally created great interest." "Missionary Society Anniversary," *Buffalo Christian Advocate* 3, no. 51 (Dec. 16, 1852): 2. The Jan. 6, 1853, issue announced the dates but not the place. "Anniversary of the Missionary Society," *Buffalo Christian Advocate* 4, no. 1 (Jan. 6, 1853): 2. An item in the Jan. 20 issue indicated that the anniversary would be "held at the Niagara street M.E. church, . . . on Monday evening the 24th." "Anniversary of the Parent Missionary Society of the M.E. Church," *Buffalo Christian Advocate* 4, no. 3 (Jan. 20, 1853): 2.

110. *COM*, p. 621. The summary for the "Missionary Society of the M.E. Church" at the front of the Methodist Diary for 1853 notes, "The Society has 4 missionaries in China, 20 in Africa, 1 in South America, 18 in Oregon, 29 in California, 5 (and three helpers) in Germany, among [the U.S.] German population 140, among French 3, among Swedes, Norwegians, and Danes 7, among the Welsh 5, among the Indians 22 (and 12 assistants,) among the destitute population 426."

111. See Wade Crawford Barclay, *History of Methodist Missions*, vol. 3, *Widening Horizons, 1845-95* (New York: Board of Missions of the Methodist Church, 1957), pp. 117-23; *COM*, pp. 318-19; John A. Roche, *The Life of John Price Durbin, D.D., LL.D., with An Analysis of His Homiletic Skill and Sacred Oratory* (New York: Phillips and Hunt, 1889). Durbin had been chaplain of the U.S. Senate (1831) and president of Dickinson College. Barclay notes, "He was generally recognized as one of the great preachers of Methodism" (Barclay, p. 123). Methodist missionary giving increased substantially over the ensuing decades, as the foreign missions work expanded. Abel Stevens thought that this "extraordinary increase of missionary zeal" was proof of Methodism's "increasing vitality" as well as of "its greatly increasing resources." Abel Stevens, *Supplementary History of American Methodism* (New York: Eaton and Mains, 1899), p. 60.

along with Thomas Carlton (who as book agent was also treasurer of the Missionary Society), Bishop Edmund Janes, and Abel Stevens, now serving as corresponding secretary of the recently organized Tract Society of the Methodist Episcopal Church.[112]

Two weeks earlier Roberts had written to all the preachers in the Buffalo District (there were about twenty), inviting them to attend the special missionary meetings. He noted in his diary that Janes, Durbin, and Stevens arrived in Buffalo on Friday night, January 21, for the weekend rally.[113] Since Roberts was to host these guests at his church on Sunday and Monday, he went to see them the next morning, and had dinner with Dr. Durbin.[114]

The main missions rally — billed as the Thirty-fourth Anniversary of the Methodist Missionary Society — was held Monday evening, January 24, at Niagara Street, though the Sunday services there and in other Methodist churches throughout the city were also given to the missions emphasis.[115] John Durbin preached at Niagara Street on Sunday morning, Bishop Janes in the afternoon, and William Slaughter in the evening.[116] Roberts was not impressed with Durbin's oratory; he found the missionary secretary's sermon from John 4:35 to be "a clear intellectual discourse [lacking] spirituality and life." Similarly, he thought Slaughter's sermon showed "Great deficiency of life and power." Bishop Janes preached from Acts 9:31, and Roberts found the sermon "Rich in instruction on spiritual life."[117]

The Niagara Street sanctuary was packed for the anniversary rally on Monday night. Janes, Durbin, and Stevens all spoke during the long service. Robie reported,

112. The Methodist Tract Society was organized in November 1852. During Stevens's first year as corresponding secretary he "gave a large part of his time to Annual Conference visitation" and formed auxiliaries in most of the conferences (Barclay, *Widening Horizons*, p. 108).

113. In the Jan. 20 issue of his *Buffalo Christian Advocate,* just days before the event, Robie tried to drum up enthusiasm for the rally. He wrote, "The anniversary is to be held in this city. — There must be no failure — there need be none. But to give the occasion the credit and importance which it demands, a general enthusiasm should be created. We hope that the place of meeting may be flooded. . . . A score of years may pass before another anniversary of the kind will be celebrated in Buffalo. — Let the present one be handsomely and triumphantly sustained." Editorial comment following "Anniversary of the Parent Missionary Society of the M.E. Church," p. 2.

114. BTRD, Jan. 10 and 22, 1853. Roberts notes, "Went with Dr. Durbin to James Evans' and took dinner." This may have been James C. Evans, a prominent Buffalo businessman and a director of the Board of Trade, who may also have been a member of the Niagara Street Church; see Smith, *History,* 2:211, 270. John R. Evans, a businessman engaged in shipping and banking and a city alderman in 1853, was a trustee at Niagara Street (Revell, "The Nazirites," pp. 221-22).

115. Roberts says on Monday, Jan. 24, "The anniversary of the Miss. Society held in our Church" in the evening. The Sunday services at Niagara Street were also part of the event, while some of the guest preachers spoke at other Methodist churches in Buffalo. Roberts's diary gives the impression that the Saturday night service at Niagara Street was part of the revival effort, not the missions celebration, so if a special missions event was held that evening, it must have been held elsewhere. See [John E. Robie], "Missionary Anniversary," *Buffalo Christian Advocate* 4, no. 4 (Jan. 27, 1853): 2.

116. BTRD, Jan. 23, 1853. Slaughter had been the Niagara Street pastor the previous year but was now "located," as noted above.

117. BTRD, Jan. 23, 1854.

"The church was crowded to its utmost capacity. A most happy state of feeling animated the large audience from the beginning. It was evident that the missionary fire was already in a blaze on the altars of devoted and philanthropic hearts."[118]

Carlton, as Missionary Society treasurer, took up the offering at the end, and Robie commended him. "He was after the money, and most adroitly he managed the question during the evening. It came in abundance. We propose that the bishop always take the Treasurer with him wherever he pleads for missions. One will move the heart, the other, the dollars." According to Robie, nearly $100 was received in cash and another $800 in pledges — a total of about $1,200, including Sunday's offerings.[119]

Roberts noted in his diary that about $1,000 was raised for missions and added, "I was made a Life Director by our church." In other words, a $150 contribution or pledge was made to the Missionary Society in Roberts's name, perhaps by members of the Niagara Street congregation.[120] Robie reported that "propositions for Life Directors" were "set on foot" during the rally as a fund-raising technique at $150 each and that five clergymen, including Roberts and Stiles, were thus made Life Directors. The other three were Thomas, Wilbor, and the venerable Micah Seager, the preacher at Churchville and Chili. Thus the five honored as Life Directors were the presiding elder, the pastors of Buffalo's three largest ME churches (Wilbor, Stiles, and Roberts), and a visiting older pastor (Seager) from the Genesee District.

All this activity came as something of an interruption in the Niagara Street revival with Redfield. Zahniser sees the schedule conflict as a complication that "a more experienced pastor" would have avoided, and suggests that Roberts might have avoided "the difficulties that arose from this situation . . . if this conflict in date had not occurred."[121] Roberts probably did not foresee the controversy that soon arose. In fact, he may have thought that the missions emphasis would actually give a boost to the revival. As it turned out, he was very disappointed with the whole Missionary Anniversary effort. He wrote later, "For several days, including the Sabbath, the aid of eloquence and wit, and personal, and church rivalry was invoked to raise money. A spirit of levity prevailed, and conviction was dissipated. Ministers occupying a prominent official position, who had come to attend the anniversary, exerted among the members an influence very damaging to the work of God, which had been commenced. When we resumed our meetings, we found that the wheels of the car of salvation were effectually blocked."[122]

Roberts did continue the special meetings with Redfield after the Monday night missions rally. On Tuesday Benjamin called on Brothers Vosburgh, Hill, Wormwood,

---

118. [Robie], "Missionary Anniversary," p. 2. Robie gave a full account of this service and the related events.

119. [Robie], "Missionary Anniversary."

120. BTRD, Jan. 24, 1853; see Conable, p. 602. One became a "Life Member" by contributing $20 to the denominational Missionary Society and a "Life Director" by contributing $150.

121. Zahniser, p. 56.

122. B. T. Roberts, "Dr. Redfield's Labors," *EC* 7, no. 2 (Feb. 1864): 38. Though Roberts says "several days," according to his diary the special missions meetings at Niagara Street were held on Sunday and Monday only, though there may have been special meetings at other churches.

and Newkirk, the first three being prominent members and trustees of the Niagara Street Church.[123] The meetings on Tuesday and Wednesday were uneventful, but a flare-up occurred in the Thursday afternoon meeting. Roberts relates, "Bros. Vosburg[h], Cowing and Hill came out openly and opposed us. V. thought the standard of religion too high. He objected to measures. C. [said] we should grow up into holiness."[124] By "measures" Vosburgh probably meant the special revival meetings and the way they were conducted. He and Harrison Cowing[125] clearly objected to the standard of holiness Redfield was preaching, and probably also to the manner.

Provoked by this opposition, Redfield left the next day for New York City. "The church did not offer even to pay Bro. Redfield's expenses," Roberts noted. Yet most of the people "seemed anxious that he should stay." Roberts continued to hold special services for a few more days but concluded that the revival effort was dead. "I fear 'Ichabod' is written on our walls," he wrote.[126] Ellen's summary was, "Much good has been done since [Redfield] has been with us and many have shown themselves to be enemies to spirituality — they choose to live in sin, yet want their names upon the Church book."[127]

Benjamin saw the real culprits in opposing the revival efforts as being "ungodly ministers" who had negatively influenced church members like Vosburgh and Cowing. "The opposition of [preachers] Robie, Carlton, Fuller etc. has defeated the efforts for the salvation of souls," he wrote the day Redfield left.[128] Robie, as editor of the *Buffalo Christian Advocate*, had considerable influence among Buffalo Methodists, as did also book agent Carlton, who belonged to the nearby Swan Street Church. James M. Fuller had long been a key figure in the conference; he had served as conference secretary several times and had pastored the influential Swan Street Church from 1848 to 1850.

Roberts was convinced that the Methodist leaders who had come to Niagara Street for the Missionary Anniversary had prejudiced his members against the Redfield revival, and against Redfield himself.[129] According to Redfield, even Bishop Janes took a stand against the revival.

123. BTRD, Jan. 25, 1853. See list of Niagara Street trustees in Revell, "The Nazirites," p. 221. An Isaac W. Newkirk was among those who petitioned to form a new Masonic lodge in Buffalo in 1844; whether this is the same Newkirk who was a Niagara Street member is unclear. See Smith, *History*, 2:359.

124. BTRD, Jan. 27, 1853. Benson Roberts and Zahniser (following Benson Roberts) incorrectly give Jan. 23 as the date; BHR, *BTR*, p. 71; Zahniser, p. 57.

125. Samuel M. Welch, *Home History: Recollections of Buffalo During the Decade from 1830 to 1850, or Fifty Years Since* (Buffalo: Peter Paul and Bro., 1891), p. 186, gives Cowing's first name as Harrison.

126. BTRD, Jan. 28, 1853.

127. ELRD, Feb. 1853 (exact date not given).

128. BTRD, Jan. 27 and 28, 1853.

129. Roberts gave this summary in 1861: "Just as the battle began to turn in favor of truth and holiness, the general missionary anniversary was held in this church. Several ministers of high official position, some of whom had been pastors of that church, came to the city, mingled with the members, and took a decided stand against the work which had commenced. It was impossible again to rally. The revival was killed in its incipiency. However, a very good interest was kept up during the year, and several were converted." B. T. Roberts, "Niagara Street M.E. Church," p. 257.

I saw the Bishop and to gain his influence in favor of Methodism I asked him if he could give a word in favor of Methodism, for we had [strong] opposition to contend [with], and to prepare him to appreciate our wants I told him how <u>God</u> had saved some of the people with power and [of] the two local preachers who had been reclaimed. I then told him what the principal members told me of the low state of the church. He turned upon me and abruptly said, I shall not believe a word of it.

I saw he had been engaged for the other side, and of course I must now prepare myself for trouble. When the Bishop preached he must needs go out of his way to make his flings against sour <u>godliness</u> and leave the people to infer that he was giving me a special benefit. Then A S [Abel Stevens], the Editor of the *Christian Advocate,* made his hits by giving the straight way his special note of rebuke and declared to them that Christianity is not inconsistent with the luxuries or the Elegances of life. [Meanwhile] old ministers sat nearby and seemed to enjoy the fun of hearing old Methodism put under foot.[130]

Stevens's comment hints where the key issue lay: Redfield's and Roberts's opposition to the growing fashionableness and fashion consciousness of urban Methodists, which both saw as inconsistent with biblical holiness and as a defection from genuine Methodism. Prominent and well-connected Methodists in Buffalo were eager to shed the plainness and boisterousness of traditional Methodism.[131] This offended Roberts's and Redfield's sense of the gospel itself. James Revell notes, "Expectations of wealth, behavior, and dress were conspiring to make even Methodist churches a foreign and hostile environment for ordinary working-class Buffalonians. . . . [Thus] when it became evident [to Roberts] how the fashion barrier affected the life of the church, his democratic Christianity was offended."[132]

Bishop Janes and the others who came to Niagara Street for the Missionary Anniversary no doubt immediately heard reports of how Redfield and Roberts were troubling the waters of Buffalo Methodism's growing urbanity. Redfield reports, "A sister B., one of the most fashionable Methodists of Niagara Street Church, was covered over with jewelry. She took off a large amount of ornaments and then went from house to house among the fancy Methodists and upon her knees confessed her great wrong in following their example, and then she came out a flaming simple disciple of <u>Jesus</u>."[133]

130. Redfield Autobiography, p. 315 (corrected); cf. Terrill, *Redfield,* p. 280. Terrill clarifies Redfield's comment: "When the bishop preached he seemed to take especial pains to impress the congregation that he did not approve of Mr. Redfield's work" (p. 280).

131. See the discussion in Revell, "The Nazirites," chap. 6.

132. Revell, "The Nazirites," p. 237.

133. Redfield Autobiography, pp. 314-15 (corrected); cf. Terrill, *Redfield,* p. 279. Roberts does not mention this specifically but says on Jan. 13, "Sister Perce came out with a very honest and frank confession." Perhaps "Sister B____" was in fact Sister Perce, probably the wife of Hiram W. Perce, grocer, a Niagara Street trustee whom Welch includes in his list of men "foremost in their vocations or occupations, prominent in the professional or business world and in social intercourse" (Welch, *Home History,* pp. 187-91).

This and similar incidents provoked opposition from some of the church's socially prominent members. It was just at this point that a number of Methodist pastors and denominational leaders arrived at Niagara Street for the Missionary Anniversary. As Terrill puts it, "Now there crowded into the Niagara Street church the leading opposers of [Methodist simplicity], and mingling among the membership, who were being graciously moved by the revival in progress, they circulated scandalous reports that had a tendency to stop the work."[134] Roberts later summarized, "Dr. Redfield was with us several weeks, and held a protracted meeting. A great interest in the community was excited; but we met with unexpected opposition from ministers occupying a high official position in the church, and the progress of the revival was stayed."[135]

Janes, Stevens, and others probably had heard scandalous rumors about Redfield, as negative stories had circulated about him for years. At a church where Redfield had previously ministered a committee came to him, saying, "We have heard that you are worth $300,000 and that you own a most splendid mansion in New York and that it is carpeted with tapestry carpeting from the top all the way down. That you have a splendid livery and carriage and waiters, and that you carry a splendid gold watch. Then you come out here and pounce upon us for our paltry 2 and 6 penny gold rings, and we think this ought to be corrected."[136]

In his typical style Redfield had responded, "Well, I do not hold myself responsible to use up my time in trying to settle all the lies which may be invented, for I should soon have my hands full & no time to work for God." Then he pulled out his plain silver watch and said,

This is all the watch I have. (They admitted that to be all right.) About that mansion, that is true, only they have not located it in the right place, and about the $300,000, I would not sell it for that sum. Indeed I do not think I ought to be blamed for the possession of it, for I did not build it nor purchase it, but it was willed to me by my Elder Brother when He died. And as for my describing it to please the fastidious, I shall not do it. Only this much I will say, that the fences around it are walls made of Diamonds, Amethyst, Beryl, Topaz and other like precious stones, and the walks are all paved with gold — and you may judge from that what the mansion must be.[137]

Redfield was present when Peter Vosburgh and other leading Niagara Street members openly opposed him the week following the missions rally. According to Redfield, Vosburgh "came into one of our afternoon meetings to carry out the wishes of these opposers of Methodism." Redfield quotes him as saying, in substance, that the Niagara Street Church "has long enough been annoyed and dis-

---

134. Terrill, *Redfield*, p. 280.
135. B. T. Roberts, "A Running Sketch," *EC* 9, no. 1 (Jan. 1865): 6.
136. Redfield Autobiography, pp. 309-10 (corrected); cf. Terrill, *Redfield*, p. 274.
137. Redfield Autobiography, p. 310 (corrected); cf. Terrill, *Redfield*, pp. 274-75.

gusted with this man Redfield, and now we shall have an end of these matters, for this meeting can no longer be endured."[138] Since Vosburgh, Cowing, and John Davidson Hill were all trustees, they carried considerable authority as to what would be allowed in the church.

When Vosburgh had finished, Redfield asked him what he had said that was contrary to the Bible or the Methodist discipline. Vosburgh replied, "It is all true enough, but we won't endure it here anyway."[139] "Is not my preaching according to the Bible?" Redfield asked. "Yes," his opponents replied, "but we cannot live up to it."[140]

With Redfield and Wallace gone, the revival effort was effectively dead. Redfield's account lends some weight to Roberts's view that Methodist leaders who came to Niagara Street for the Missionary Anniversary prejudiced some of the more prominent congregational leaders against Redfield and his preaching of holiness. Whether Robie, Carlton, and Fuller were specifically responsible, as Roberts believed, is hard to prove, though certainly they all represented and endorsed the very changes in Methodism that Roberts opposed, and all were present at Niagara Street for the missions rally.[141] James Revell makes the point, however, that socially prominent Niagara Street members such as Vosburgh and Cowing hardly needed outside influence to oppose Redfield. "Middle class laymen [were] more important to the development of the . . . conflict than either the principals or later interpreters understood. Churchmen of the period focussed disproportionately on the clergy in their analysis of developing problems, and Roberts was no exception. In fact, the ministers were not the only decisive element. The movement Roberts [later] labelled 'New school Methodism' would not have succeeded without a receptive medium in the Buffalo churches, especially among the middle class lay leadership."[142]

Or to state the matter somewhat differently, *both* pastors and their leading members in cities such as Buffalo were experiencing a social transformation into a middle-class professional culture that was uncomfortable and impatient with the simplicity, plainness, emotional freedom (or excess!), and lack of social sophistication of earlier Methodism. This reality underlies the whole story of B. T. and Ellen Roberts's ministry and the birth of the Free Methodist Church, as will become increasingly clear as the story unfolds.

Roberts stressed that those in his congregation who opposed the revival were a distinct minority. "A few — less than half a dozen — composed of secret society men,

---

138. Redfield Autobiography, pp. 316-17; cf. Terrill, *Redfield,* p. 280.

139. As quoted in Terrill, *Redfield,* p. 281.

140. Quoted in BHR, *BTR,* p. 71.

141. Zahniser comments regarding the opposition of some key Niagara Street members to the revival: "Roberts attributed this open opposition to the effect of the influence of certain of the visiting ministers who were attending the Missionary Convention. Whether this judgment be correct or not, it does seem certain that this revival meeting with Redfield, with the opposition that developed, was probably a key to some of the [difficult] situations [Roberts faced] in the future." Zahniser, p. 57.

142. Revell, "The Nazirites," p. 210.

and one or two proud women, encouraged by a former, secret society pastor, held out and opposed the work," he later wrote.[143] The "former pastor" presumably was Carlton. Roberts here is claiming that Carlton and leading members such as Vosburgh, Cowing, and Hill were lodge members, either Masons or Odd Fellows. This seems likely but may or may not be true, as will be discussed later. Roberts's claim is that their secret society membership connected them in a competing fraternity that directly undercut the work of the Spirit in the church. (Roberts noted in March that Chauncey Baker, the Methodist preacher at Pike, had joined the Odd Fellows.)[144]

Initially, Roberts was devastated by the seeming failure of the revival. The Sunday following the Missionary Anniversary, after Redfield had left, he preached in the morning on James 2:10, "For whosoever shall keep the whole law, and yet offend in one point, he is guilty of all," and in the afternoon on 1 Timothy 4:10, "For therefore we both labour and suffer reproach, because we trust in the living God, who is the Saviour of all men, specially of those that believe." He had "a very good time" in preaching. He conducted a society meeting following the afternoon service, but "we had quite a flare up," he reported. "Attempts were made to compose quarrels among the members. But matters were made worse."[145]

Clearly there was now deep division in the church between those who supported Roberts and his leadership and those who opposed him. In the Monday evening service, January 31, Charles Wormwood (also a trustee) expressed concern about "the bickering etc." in the church. Roberts noted, "[Brother] Newkirk said there was rottenness at heart etc. Devils are beginning to show themselves."[146] The next day Roberts wrote, "The indifference of some of our brethren and the active opposition of others have defeated our efforts for a revival. These are busy now in hunting up pretexts. Every thing that I have said that is capable of misconstruction is repeated. Doubtful whether I or Dr. Campbell [one of the Niagara Street members] will be the scapegoat."[147]

Roberts was deeply discouraged with the church. He spent most of the rest of the week in his study, noting on Wednesday, "I feel so bad at the failure of our meetings that I cannot do any thing. It seems as if Satan was about to hold undisputed sway here." Yet he reported "a very good prayer meeting" Thursday evening, though few attended, and "a very pleasant leaders' meeting" on Friday night. All was not dark. But on Saturday he reflected, "How hard to stand by Christ when all forsake him." He had a talk with Wormwood, who seemed "ashamed that he had made a start to get right." Two weeks earlier Wormwood, who ran a tailor shop, had told

143. WAS, p. 105.

144. BTRD, Mar. 12, 1853.

145. BTRD, Jan. 30, 1853.

146. BTRD, Jan. 31, 1853. Roberts noted that his parents had spent the weekend with him, and left on Monday for home.

147. BTRD, Feb. 1, 1853. Roberts "Heard many complaints against Doctor Campbell," one of his members, while calling on Sister Gilbert on Jan. 21, but does not indicate what the complaints were (BTRD, Jan. 21, 1853).

Roberts that God had showed him he was a sinner. He had passed a sleepless night in great "agony of mind." Now, apparently, Brother Wormwood was having second thoughts. "He is afraid of losing caste," Roberts wrote.[148]

Despite Benjamin's disappointment with the revival and the opposition it provoked, there were positive signs. Sunday congregations continued to be large, Roberts preached with freedom, and a number of people were converted.

In Roberts's view, while some of his members were paying the cost of discipleship and living out biblical Christianity, others were settling into a compromised culture Christianity that was a betrayal of original Methodism. The fact that one of his members, Sister Hathaway, had "put on her jewelry again" was one sign of the drift.[149] With the January revival behind him, Benjamin reflected on this situation by writing a significant series of articles while continuing his normal pattern of pastoral work.

Meanwhile, four hundred and some miles away in New York City, Redfield reflected on the state of Methodism in light of his experience in Buffalo. In Roberts, Redfield saw a ray of hope. Perhaps Roberts in time "would by his merits fill the Episcopal chair." Redfield was sure, he wrote, that Roberts

> would dare to speak favorably of salvation that saves. I was sure and so stated when I returned to N. York that I had seen one man who I believed would if raised to his true stand in the church be one of our bishops. I did not then know what wire pulling was practiced in making bishops & how utterly impossible it would be for so fearless and honest a man as B. T. R. was ever to get to a position which was gained not so much by merit as by management. . . . Little did I then dream that even B. T. R. would dare in after years to beard the Lion in his den. . . . I know he saw the wants of the church when I left him. But I dared not tell him how my heart was moved towards him.[150]

Were Roberts and Redfield Right?

Roberts and Redfield were sure they were upholding historic Methodism and, more importantly, the biblical standard of Christianity. They knew in what specific places they had to draw the line in order to be faithful to God. But were they right? Some of

---

148. BTRD, Jan. 20 and Feb. 2-5, 1853. Revell notes that a number of Buffalo Methodists were merchants. "Buffalo Methodists were not only a part of a fashion-conscious society, they were also substantially involved in the fashion industry" ("The Nazirites," p. 234). "Aside from social standing, there was potential business to be lost" if they too strongly adhered to traditional Methodist plainness. "If the Methodists were to lose the respect of upper levels of Buffalo's economy, businesses such as Wormwood's tailor shop or any of the merchants attending Swan Street might suffer" (p. 224).

149. BTRD, Feb. 24, 1853.

150. Redfield Autobiography, pp. 316-17 (corrected). Redfield later added, on Roberts's involvement with the ministry in St. Louis that Redfield had initiated: "I now saw why it was that I was so impressed on my first acquaintance with him when at Niagara St. Church, that he was a man bearing the mark of a high commission from God to do a great work" (pp. 353-54, corrected).

the issues involved — particularly dress, pew rental, and lodge membership — will be discussed more fully later. There are, of course, both the specific issues themselves and the question of how Roberts handled these issues.

Perhaps if Roberts had been more diplomatic and a bit more patient, he might have accomplished his purposes and still remained true to his convictions. But this was not his character. Seeing where Methodism was headed, he was terribly afraid of compromise. He felt duty-bound to speak out, and to draw the line at those points where Methodist declension could be specifically identified. So he took a stand. What he lacked in tact he made up in courage. Throughout his ministry he would have to find the right balance between uncompromising fidelity to the gospel and patient dealing with people who did not see things his way — which is also part of the gospel.

Roberts's Assessment of Methodism

Thursday, February 10, was a cold, blustery day in Buffalo. Benjamin worked in his study, beginning an article for the *Northern Christian Advocate,* the official Methodist weekly for upstate and western New York. The article was "on the State of the Church," he noted in his diary, and then added with some pleasure, "Georgie all at once began to run all about the house."[151] Little George Lane Roberts, now thirteen months, had survived into his second year, unlike Benjamin and Ellen's firstborn, William Titus.

Benjamin quickly finished his 700-word article and sent it off to William Hosmer, editor of the *Northern Christian Advocate* at Auburn. He was soon at work on the second, which he finished and mailed on February 26.[152] He completed his third article, about twice as long as the first, on March 25. These analytical pieces, the first of this type he had attempted, were published on February 16, March 9, and April 6, 1853.[153] His titles indicate the scope of his concern:

"Genesee Conference — Its Prosperity, Its Decline"
"Genesee Conference — Causes of Its Decline"
"Causes of Religious Declension"

As Zahniser notes, these hard-hitting articles "were the first publications which brought the young pastor into conflict with his ministerial brethren."[154]

Roberts began diplomatically by noting the prosperity of western New York and

151. BTRD, Feb. 10, 1853.
152. BTRD, Feb. 26, 1853.
153. Peck in *Early Methodism* notes, "An old rule of the Discipline prohibited a traveling preacher from publishing anything without first obtaining the leave of his conference," and Genesee Conference accordingly set up a committee in 1810 to deal with this matter (George Peck, *Early Methodism Within the Bounds of the Old Genesee Conference from 1788 to 1828* [New York: Carlton and Porter, 1860], p. 496). This rule had fallen by the wayside well before Roberts's time, however.
154. Zahniser, p. 58. Zahniser refers, however, to only the first two articles.

of Methodism in the region. The people generally, "moral, intelligent, and energetic," are "rapidly increasing in wealth." "Splendid mansions, elegantly furnished, rear their proud fronts, where but a few years ago stood the humble log house of the hardy pioneer. . . . The unmistakable evidences of an astonishing prosperity, are everywhere apparent" — an accurate picture of Buffalo, especially, in the 1850s. The area boasts "fertile meadows and well cultivated plains," now traversed by railroads.

And the Methodist Church was prospering materially. Roberts noted that the Genesee Conference led the denomination in per capita missions giving the previous year. "Our Church edifices are numerous, commodious, and some of them elegant." Many of the churches had fine, well-appointed parsonages.

But Roberts argued that this material prosperity masked serious spiritual decline. He made a study of conference statistics and found the data disturbing. Population in the region had increased by 25 percent, or some 67,000, in the past decade, Roberts calculated. If Methodism had grown proportionately, the conference would now have over 15,000 members. But the actual total membership in 1852 was 11,312 — about 1,000 less than in 1842![155] "To have simply maintained our ground, we ought to have increased with the increase of the population," he argued. And "to have only maintained our ground would have been failing of our duty." He then elaborated, making his key point:

> The spirit of Christianity in general, and of Methodism in particular, is aggressive. Every disciple of Christ is bound to *"gather with Him."* And who, if he had *"that mind which was in Christ,"* could not by the blessing of God, in the course of a year, bring at least one soul to the Savior? If every Christian *could* do this he is under *obligation* to do it. Hence the Church instead of diminishing in number should have "added to it daily of such as shall be saved."
>
> This great declension in numbers is *prima facie* evidence that our spiritual condition is not very good. We are a Conference low in spirituality. There is great want of the power and even of the form of godliness. In many and perhaps most of our charges, probably not one half of our members are enjoying justifying grace, according to the scriptural and the Methodist standard.

Here was a serious charge — that probably less than half the Methodists in the conference were really Christians, according to Methodist standards. Roberts concluded his article in the tones of a biblical prophet: "The Discipline is a dead letter. The Bible, where it forbids fashionable vices, and enjoins duties irksome to the carnal heart, is virtually repealed. The conscience is seared. Many living in open violation of God's commands, profess to feel no condemnation. A tide of worldliness threatening to sweep away the boundaries between the Church and the world, is setting in."[156]

---

155. Roberts worked out some of these calculations in the "General Memoranda" section of his 1853 diary (p. 216).

156. B. T. Roberts, "Genesee Conference — Its Prosperity, Its Decline," *NCA* 13, no. 7 (Feb. 16, 1853): 2.

"There must be causes for the existence of this state of things," Roberts wrote, indicating that he would address these in the next article.

The week after the first article appeared in the *Northern Christian Advocate*, Robie commented in the *Buffalo Christian Advocate*: "There is a spirit of religious fanaticism prevailing in some portions of Western New York, which, unless curbed, will work ruin in many churches. There will be more maniacs in the future than there have been!"[157] The comment may have been sparked partly by Roberts's article, though Robie probably had others in mind as well. In any case, in an article on the same page entitled "A Great Moral Waste," Robie took direct aim at Roberts. He quoted a passage from Roberts's article in which Roberts said the conference was "low in spirituality" and was being engulfed in a "tide of worldliness." Robie commented, "As we are inclined to doubt, to some extent, at least, both the practicability and correctness of the writer's statements, we may be permitted to look at them a little hereafter."[158]

Roberts may have complained to Robie that the extract he printed missed the main point of Roberts's article. In any case, in the next issue, a week later, Robie published a longer extract, giving Roberts's analysis of Methodist growth in comparison to population growth. Robie prefaced the quotation with this statement: "We publish cheerfully, the following additional remarks from the communication of Rev. B. T. Roberts, an extract only of which we inserted last week. From the data herein contained, he drew his conclusions, which we considered at the time very objectionable."[159]

Perhaps as a counterpoint to Roberts's argument, Robie followed Roberts's extract with a brief item entitled "Revivals in This City" in which he commented favorably on "an interesting revival" in two Presbyterian churches and added that "in the Pearl and Swan st. Methodist churches, the revival influence has been enjoyed for some time past. In each, souls have been converted."[160] A week later he published "Revivals in Western New York," suggesting that in the region "including the City of Buffalo there has never been a time of greater religious interest than the present." Revival was occurring in all the denominations. "Our columns might be filled with reports full of encouragement to the friends of Zion. . . . We shall greatly mistake if the present season does not witness the ingathering of thousands to the fold of the Church, and if the savor of life does not act more powerfully than ever on the morals and habits of the masses. It is the day of triumph."[161]

Meanwhile Roberts's second article, a bit longer than the first, appeared on Wednesday, March 9. Here Benjamin has one central thesis: the numerical decline in

157. [John E. Robie], editorial comment, *Buffalo Christian Advocate* 4, no. 8 (Feb. 24, 1853): 2.

158. [John E. Robie], "A Great Moral Waste," *Buffalo Christian Advocate* 4, no. 8 (Feb. 24, 1853): 2. Robie apparently intended the title "A Great Moral Waste" sarcastically.

159. [John E. Robie], editorial comment, *Buffalo Christian Advocate* 4, no. 9 (Mar. 3, 1853): 2.

160. [John E. Robie], "Revivals in this City," *Buffalo Christian Advocate* 4, no. 9 (Mar. 3, 1853): 2.

161. [John E. Robie], "Revivals in Western New York," *Buffalo Christian Advocate* 4, no. 10 (Mar. 10, 1853): 2.

the Genesee Conference is due above all to *"the want of entire devotion in the ministry."* Pastors and preachers are primarily responsible to see that Methodism fulfills its mission "to spread Scripture holiness over these lands"; therefore the lack of growth signals a failure in leadership.[162]

Roberts began this article with a small correction in the statistics he reported earlier. But he restated his main point about Methodist decline in western New York relative to the overall population. Ten years ago, *"one person out of every twenty was a member of our Church, now only one out of every twenty-seven."*

Roberts acknowledged that Methodism's failure to keep pace with population growth could be attributed to multiple causes. But he was convinced that the chief factor was the failure of the ordained leadership.

People still remembered the Millerite excitement of ten years earlier, and that had affected church growth, Roberts suggested. William Miller, an unordained Baptist preacher, had predicted that Jesus Christ would return to earth within the year following March 21, 1843. This created great public excitement. As F. W. Conable noted in his history of the Genesee Conference, with "appeals of warning and alarm being circulated in various printed forms, and sounded in the ears of multitudes by public lectures, with huge, staring pictures of 'the great red dragon having seven heads and ten horns, and seven crowns upon his heads,' and other similar illustrations," it was little wonder that many should "be awakened to some concern for their souls."[163] Roberts acknowledged this but discounted it as a factor in the ten-year growth pattern of the conference. He noted, "In 1843 the minds of the people were greatly agitated by predictions of the speedy coming of the end of the world. A general religious interest was awakened. Multitudes were added to the Church. The increase for 1843, in what was then the Genesee Conference, was over six thousand."

Roberts cited Nathan Bangs's recent book, *The Present State, Prospects, and Responsibilities of the Methodist Episcopal Church* (1850), to show that the vast majority of those added to the Methodist church during the Millerite excitement had remained faithful.[164] There was no great falling away that could explain the relatively low numbers nine years later. Factors more internal to Methodism must be sought.

---

162. B. T. Roberts, "Genesee Conference — Causes of Its Decline," p. 2.

163. Conable, p. 496.

164. See Nathan Bangs, *The Present State, Prospects, and Responsibilities of the Methodist Episcopal Church. With an Appendix of Ecclesiastical Statistics* (New York: Lane and Scott, 1850). Bangs noted that although there was some dip in membership after the Millerite excitement, still overall Methodist Episcopal membership in the United States grew from 1,068,525 in 1843 to 1,114,509 in 1849 (combining North and South). Methodists had increased from "one member for every sixty of the [U.S.] population" in 1795 to "at least one church-member to every twenty of the population." Bangs thus drew the opposite conclusion from Roberts. Despite "the hue and cry about the want of zeal and skill in the ministry, and the lukewarmness and backsliding of the membership," Methodism continued to grow. "Instead, therefore, of lamenting over our deficiencies," Bangs argued, Methodists should praise God that the church had continued to grow, without "any permanent departure from our ancient landmarks, either in doctrine, discipline, or practical piety" (pp. 19-21). But Bangs was speaking of American Methodism generally, while Roberts was describing the Genesee Conference

Methodist ministers were to preach and profess holiness, Roberts noted. "Yet how few of us ever profess to have attained to this perfection of love. . . . Thus because we have not trod the way ourselves, we have not been able to lead the Church up the hills of difficulty to the fair plane of holiness." Picking up the military metaphor, Roberts argued that rather than the church effectively attacking "the world with our spiritual weapons," instead "the world has been the assailant." The result was a devastating tide of worldliness within Methodism:

> Splendid houses, elegant furniture, parties of pleasure, ornaments of gold, and costly apparel have been offered her sons and daughters, if they would cease to be *"a peculiar people, zealous of good works,"* and the offer has been, in too many instances, accepted. And no wonder. Accredited ambassadors of Him who enjoined self-denial upon all his followers, have assured them, that they need not give up any of the elegancies of life, to aid in carrying on the mighty work of the redemption of the world, for the promoting of which, He who *was rich became so poor, that he had not where to lay his head.*[165]

Methodist ministers "have allowed the Church to rest in winter quarters," Roberts charged, rather than taking up "the stern duties of a soldier of Christ." He concluded, "We have been raising monuments to the victories of our fathers, when we ought to have been achieving still greater conquests. We have, ourselves yielded to too great an extent, to the spirit of the world. Some of us have labored these years past, with greater success, in saving property, than in saving souls. For these things we are responsible. With a deeper spirituality, our example would have been better, our words would have been accompanied with greater power, and God would have worked mightily by us."[166]

Roberts promised in a final article to discuss the "other causes" that had "contributed to this leading one" in bringing about Methodist decline.

The most striking thing about this second article is Roberts's reference to Jesus Christ as the one who was rich but became so poor that he had nowhere to lay his head (combining references to Luke 9:58 [or Matt. 8:20] and 2 Cor. 8:9, one of Roberts's favorite texts). Roberts appeals not primarily to the doctrine of holiness but to the example of Christ. Genuine holiness is measured by the example of Christ, especially in identifying with the poor. This is a key theological point that will recur in Roberts's writing.

---

only. Bangs's discussion is a reminder that Roberts's was but one voice among many warning of Methodist declension. "Much has been written, of late, respecting the state and prospects of the Methodist Episcopal Church," Bangs noted, and some had argued that the church had "abused its trust" and was "no longer an agent in the hand of God for effecting good for the human family" (p. 15).

165. Here Roberts is no doubt thinking of Abel Stevens and other Methodist leaders who spoke at Niagara Street during the Missionary Anniversary.

166. Roberts, "Genesee Conference — Causes of Its Decline." See the discussion in Zahniser, pp. 58-61.

Benjamin's third article — much longer than the other two — was published on April 6. Here he identified several causes of Methodist decline. In his diary he described this as "an article against pewed Churches," and this was in fact its main theme.[167] The 1,500-word article appeared on page 1 of the *Northern Christian Advocate* under the title "Causes of Religious Declension."

Roberts argued that one of the main reasons for Methodist decline was "*the prevailing custom of selling or renting the seats in our houses of worship.* Pewed churches are all the fashion. There are but few free Methodist churches in any of the villages, and none in the cities of western New York. The consequence is, multitudes do not attend our ministry who otherwise would. The people are virtually shut out of our churches."

This was perhaps the first time Roberts used the phrase "free Methodist" church or churches in his published writing. Here it means, of course, church buildings whose seating is open to all.

Roberts argued that while some "are too poor to buy a seat," others stay away because "their American pride" does not permit them to "intrude upon privileges" purchased by others for cash. "Not owning a seat, they seldom visit the church. And when they do, they are not at home. They feel like intruders. They are liable to be turned out of the pew. Therefore they stay at home, or saunter about on the Sabbath. They do not hear our preaching, and are not saved by it."

In the first article Roberts had charged that in many Methodist churches fewer than half the members were really Christians. This problem is compounded by renting the pews. "Unawakened pew-owners . . . are rarely converted," he suggested.

Roberts argued that renting and selling pews was really self-defeating. Methodists buy seats for their families, only to discover with time that "their children, who are to inherit" them, either become "indifferent to religion" or go to churches of other denominations that have grander buildings or better music. Pew rental plays into competition on worldly grounds, and here Methodists are bound to lose out: "We cannot yet, in outside splendor and tinseled gewgaws, vie with older Churches. Our edifices are not as magnificent. The '*performances*' of our pulpit and orchestra do not exhibit as much artistical skill. But by aping them, we base our claims to a hearing upon the same ground. The entertainment we offer is the same in kind, but poorer in quality."

Thus, Roberts argued, "we neither keep our children nor save the people." This is totally the wrong approach. A true church is built on fundamentally spiritual dynamics, not on fine buildings and professional music. "If the power of the Lord was manifest among us, . . . [then] old and young, rich and poor, would flock to our churches, not to admire the architecture and listen to the fine performances, *but to save their souls.*"

Roberts argued that pew rental also had a subtle influence in lessening the church's zeal for winning people for Christ. Members become more concerned with

---

167. BTRD, Mar. 25, 1853.

gaining the well-to-do than with winning the poor. "They do not feel like laboring for the conversion of the poor, for these cannot be received into our Churches as brethren entitled to equal privileges with all." Thus "there is not *always* joy in the Church on earth over *every* sinner that repenteth, but over the rich sinner coming into the Church there is great rejoicing." Here is the problem, Roberts argued: "Rich men have become necessary to us."

Roberts buttressed these arguments with the scriptural indictment of showing partiality to the rich, quoting from the Letter of James. When "we bind ourselves by our hand and seal, to him who is able and willing to pay the most, to give him, his heirs and assigns forever, the undisputed and exclusive possession of the best seat in the house," we violate God's Word. Roberts appealed also, as he typically did, to the example of Jesus Christ. Jesus drove the "buyers and sellers" of sacrificial animals out of the temple. *"What would he have done if he had found them there selling by auction to the highest bidder parts of the temple itself?"*

Roberts linked pew rental to a growing tendency to value financial considerations over spiritual ones. If the pew system functions properly, the financial security of the church is secured, and then "we shall not need much religion to have, financially, a very pleasant and prosperous state of things. Instead of protracted meetings, we may then have social parties." He added, in a dig at theological seminaries: "When this system shall be perfected, we shall only need a good establishment for the manufacturing to order, of genteel and graceful preachers, and the Church can then get along . . . without the agency or interposition of God."

In this system, naturally the most prominent and valued preachers will be those who are expert financial managers.

[A] Church sets the highest estimate on what she honors most. In our Conference, the reputation of possessing great financial ability is the highest to which a minister can attain. Piety, devotion to the work, and learning, are ranked below this. — The financier wields a controlling influence in all our councils. Whoever fails in this department, brings upon himself speedy and certain disgrace. We may preach from year to year without revivals. The Church may decline in spirituality under our labors. The discipline may not be enforced. *These failures will be passed by unnoticed. But let us fail in the collections, and we are compelled to answer for the default at the bar of Conference. . . .* The discipline does not make it our duty to obtain from the people any definite sum for any object. God does not promise us access to their purses. But the discipline does say that our one work is to save souls. And the word of the Lord says, "That he that goeth forth and weepeth, bearing precious seed, shall doubtless come again with rejoicing, bringing his sheaves with him." I would suggest, then, whether it would not be more appropriate to require every preacher who fails in being instrumental in the conversion of at least fifty souls, to answer for it at the bar of Conference.[168]

168. B. T. Roberts, "Causes of Religious Declension," *NCA* 13, no. 14 (Apr. 6, 1853): 1. The printed

Readers who knew well the Genesee Conference could hardly read the comment about financiers "[wielding] a controlling influence in all our councils" without thinking of prominent men like Thomas Carlton and perhaps John Robie.

Roberts concluded his article, "I do not write in a captious spirit. I love Methodism for what it has done, and what it is capable of doing. I do not think her mission is accomplished. She has not finished her work. But she is neglecting it. I would, if possible, aid in recalling her to the stern toils of the harvest field."

Roberts's charges did not go unanswered. Noting Robie's comments in the February 24 *Buffalo Christian Advocate*, Benjamin wrote, "My first [article] called forth some sneering remarks in the Buffalo Advocate."[169] On April 13 Richard Waite, an older preacher who had just been sent to pastor at Lima because of the death of the preacher there,[170] published a response in the *Northern Christian Advocate*. Roberts's charges would injure both himself and the church, Waite suggested, creating prejudice against the would-be prophet. With heavy sarcasm he added, "It is, however, matter of gratitude that amid the general defection, there is one true man remaining, 'one true amid many false' who, 'having no fear but the fear of God' before his eyes, dares to reprove the general apathy, and like Luther and Wesley, strives to awaken the slumbering church."[171]

Waite saw external causes as the reason for the numerical decline in the Genesee Conference: the Millerite excitement, the California gold rush, the migration of many Catholics to the Genesee area due to the railroad boom. Such factors might mean that in a particular area, population "might outrun the church for a time." But this was no cause for alarm. In fact, within Methodism the Genesee Conference was the "Banner Conference in several respects" (which of course Roberts did not deny).

Waite then attacked Roberts's credibility. How could he, a "junior preacher" with only four years' experience in the conference, know enough of what was going on to make such sweeping claims? "What have been his opportunities for forming an intelligent opinion concerning the spiritual condition of the ninety circuits and stations within our bounds?" It was "preposterous . . . to indulge in these wholesale denunciations of the Church, concerning whose condition he knows so little."[172] Roberts, of course, could form a fairly accurate picture from the tone of conference gatherings and his frequent conversations with other Methodist pastors, and he had long made a point of observing conditions in the conference and the denomination. Still, it is no doubt true, as Zahniser comments, that "Roberts' judgments were somewhat weighted with his Buffalo revival disappointment."[173]

---

text has "deportment" rather than "department" in the above quote, but this appears to be a typo — though "deportment" is possible.

169. BTRD, Feb. 26, 1853 (not Feb. 20, as in Zahniser, p. 58, and BHR, *BTR*, p. 73).

170. See BTRD, Mar. 11, 1853.

171. R. L. Waite, comment in *NCA* 13, no. 15 (Apr. 13, 1853): 1. Quoted in Zahniser, p. 59. Zahniser has Apr. 16, but that is incorrect, since the *Northern Christian Advocate* was published on Wednesdays.

172. Waite in *NCA*, as quoted in Zahniser, p. 60.

173. Zahniser, p. 60.

Waite concluded, "The truth is, Bro. Hosmer, this hue and cry about declension and apostasy is all moonshine. The Genesee Conference is sound to the core."[174]

Thus the issue was joined. Clearly "a war was on in the Methodist press"[175] — had been, in fact, well before Roberts's articles. But his articles did stir things up. A February 21 letter from Benjamin's parents in Gowanda may refer to reaction to his first article. The letter caused him "great uneasiness," he wrote. "In trying to do good I have exposed myself to trouble."[176] Some of Roberts's articles were reprinted in the *Western Christian Advocate,* the Methodist paper published in Cincinnati. John H. Wallace, who initially had helped out in the Redfield revival at Niagara Street, came to Roberts's defense in the May 11 issue of the *Northern Christian Advocate.*[177]

In Mount Holly, New Jersey, Lydia Lane saw the flurry of articles and was alarmed. She wrote to Ellen in June, "I see that Mr. Roberts is assailed on the right, and left, for his plain truth. I think it is wise in him to be silent."[178] Yet (as she said in a later letter), based on her visits to Buffalo, she had to agree with Roberts's critique.[179]

No doubt the controversy surrounding the Redfield revival and Benjamin's articles took its toll on Ellen. Though she doesn't specify the circumstances, Ellen commented in March, "I have been tried in an unexpected manner. I have barely stood. Sometimes I thought I was the same as lost. God forgive if I have done wrong." But then she added, "I am feeling better than I did[;] more resigned to the will of God — how true that we must have no will of our own."[180]

The Issue of Free Seats

When Roberts arrived as pastor at Niagara Street, he found that it was a "stock church" — that is, it was financed partly by annual pew fees. The same was now true of all the Methodist churches in Buffalo.[181]

Benjamin saw immediately that this undercut both the spirituality and the stewardship of the church. It was in fact a form of merchandising that visibly reinforced economic distinctions in the congregation and was an affront to the poor. Benjamin was of course already well aware of this system of "pewed churches" that was becoming increasingly common in Methodist city churches, but this was his first time to confront it directly. He later wrote that while pastoring at Niagara Street,

---

174. Waite in *NCA,* as quoted in Zahniser, p. 60.

175. Zahniser, p. 60. Zahniser interprets Roberts's second article as a response to Waite, but in fact the second article appeared before Waite's comments were published.

176. BTRD, Feb. 21, 1853.

177. Zahniser, pp. 61-62.

178. LBL to ELR, June 2, 1853, quoted in Zahniser, p. 61.

179. LBL to ELR, July 19, 1853, cited in Zahniser, p. 62.

180. ELRD, Mar. 1853 (exact date not given).

181. BHR, *BTR,* pp. 74-78.

"my attention was drawn to the evils of the pew system. I saw that the house of God MUST BE FREE for all who choose to attend, if the masses would be reached and saved. I began to write and preach upon the subject."[182] He "felt deeply the need of a free church" in Buffalo. "Hundreds did not attend public worship because they could not afford to hire a seat."[183]

Benjamin addressed the matter from the pulpit on Sunday, June 5, showing "that the pewed system was unscriptural." This was probably not the only time he dealt with the issue. He preached "upon the Church — its foundation, &c." on Sunday afternoon, April 3, and such preaching may have been part of his effort to change the thinking of his congregation.[184]

If the pew system was unscriptural and an offense to the poor, then the Niagara Street Church needed to get rid of it. Roberts attempted to accomplish this in a couple of ways. In his 1865 article "A Running Sketch" he says, "I offered to see the debt paid off if they [the Niagara Street congregation] would make the house free. The offer was declined."[185] His plan, apparently, was to lead a fund-raising campaign to retire the debt of several thousand dollars so the congregation wouldn't have to depend on the pew rental income. For whatever reason — perhaps due in part to the controversy over the Redfield revival — the church, or its leaders, refused. It is not clear just when Roberts made this proposal, though presumably it was early in 1853.[186]

Roberts then tried another approach. He thought perhaps he could convince the congregation to build a new building with free seats (and presumably sell the old one). This was a bold plan, and the congregation would need some convincing. It presupposed aggressive evangelism and the winning of many poor or common folk to Christ — and also the assumption that a growing congregation if it practiced biblical stewardship could pay the added cost. That is precisely what Roberts intended. Over several months in the spring and summer of 1853 he worked to convince the church that this was the right thing to do, and had some success.

Benjamin's diary reveals the situation he was facing and his attempts to change it. He met with the stewards on February 18, 1853, and noted that while current expenses were "nearly paid up," still for the previous period "our expenses have exceeded our income by over one hundred dollars."[187] He spent part of Tuesday, March 29, trying to find a lot where a new building might be built. "I fear that our Trustees will neither do nor let be done. We need a free Methodist Church here very much."[188] This seems to be the first occurrence in his diary of the phrase "free Meth-

182. B. T. Roberts, "A Running Sketch," p. 6.

183. [B. T. Roberts], "Niagara Street M.E. Church," p. 257.

184. BTRD, June 5 and Apr. 3, 1853.

185. B. T. Roberts, "A Running Sketch," p. 6.

186. It could have been some months earlier, in the fall shortly after Roberts arrived. If so, the church's hesitancy to approve Roberts's plan would be understandable since they were still just getting acquainted with him.

187. BTRD, Feb. 18, 1853.

188. BTRD, Mar. 29, 1853.

odist Church." As in his third *Northern Christian Advocate* article, written just four days earlier, "free Methodist" here means nothing more than a local Methodist Episcopal church with free seats, though it would eventually become the name of a separate denomination.

This same day, March 29, Roberts noted that he received a letter from Bishop Beverly Waugh (who, as senior Methodist bishop, was now president of the Missionary Society) "favorable to my appointment to Bulgaria."[189] Missionary work was still on Benjamin's mind. He had written to Bishop Waugh on March 12, offering himself for the Bulgaria mission.[190] Although the Methodist Episcopal Church didn't begin missionary work in Bulgaria (then a Turkish province) until 1857, mission work had been authorized in November 1852, with the goal of "resuscitating the old Oriental Churches within the Turkish empire" — that is, helping renew the Bulgarian Orthodox Church.[191] No doubt something had been said about the proposed Bulgaria mission during the missionary rally at the Niagara Street Church in January, and Roberts was interested. The Missionary Society was looking for suitable candidates, and so Roberts wrote to Bishop Waugh. Wade Barclay, in his *History of Methodist Missions,* says, "No candidates were found during the next two years."[192] Benjamin and Ellen were not accepted as suitable candidates, apparently because of Ellen's poor health, though there may have been other factors as well.[193] Years later Ellen wrote, "[W]e would have been sent to Bulgaria, but Mr. Roberts was strongly in favor of going out as an evangelist and the Board wished him to teach a school. He felt that he could not do this."[194]

Benjamin continued his efforts to persuade the Niagara Street congregation to build a new building with free seats. He noted on Saturday, June 4, "I have visited and talked a good deal in favor of building a free Church. Sentiments in favor of the enterprise are becoming current. Bro. Thomas is noncommittal. Jane Evans favors the enterprise very decidedly."[195] When Roberts preached the next afternoon on

---

189. BTRD, Mar. 29, 1853.

190. BTRD, Mar. 12, 1853. Since Bulgaria was at this time under Turkish control, Roberts's interest may have been related to his reading of a biography of Muhammad during this same period, even though the Methodist mission would be directed toward the Greek Orthodox, not the Islamic, population.

191. Minutes of the General Missionary Committee, Nov. 8, 1852, quoted in Barclay, *Widening Horizons,* p. 1018.

192. Barclay, *Widening Horizons,* p. 1018.

193. Benson Roberts says Benjamin's offer was not accepted because of "the ill health of his wife" (BHR, *BTR,* p. 74; cf. Zahniser, p. 64). Benjamin received another letter from Bishop Waugh on Apr. 18 and wrote to him on May 31 (BTRD, Apr. 10 and May 31, 1853). Whether Roberts's articles in the *Northern Christian Advocate* also entered into consideration is unknown. Lydia Lane, though a strong advocate of missions, didn't think their going to the mission field was a good idea, according to a letter she wrote to Ellen on June 10, 1853 (Zahniser, p. 65).

194. Carpenter, p. 126.

195. BTRD, June 4, 1853. "Brother Thomas" here probably is Eleazar Thomas, presiding elder of the Buffalo District.

"church building," arguing that the pew-rental system was unbiblical (as noted above), he felt he made a good impression.[196]

These efforts were in preparation for a church society meeting on Monday, June 6, "to consider the propriety of building a free church."[197] Roberts spent most of the day visiting, then led the society meeting in the evening. Attendance was good, he noted, and several of the members "spoke in favor of [a] free church." These included Sister Perce, presumably the wife of Hiram Perce, one of the trustees, and Charles Wormwood, another trustee, who "took ground in favor of the enterprise and made a good speech." It appears that Eleazar Thomas, the presiding elder, also attended this meeting; Roberts says, "Bro. Thomas also made a speech in favor of the free Church plan." Some of the trustees were present but, other than Wormwood, "did not say much."[198]

A vote was taken, and the church voted in favor of building a free church.[199] Roberts seemed to be winning the battle, but he still had to win over the trustees, whose backing, due to their position and financial means, would be decisive.

In describing the June 6 meeting, Roberts noted that "Even Robie said he thought the current was running strongly in favor a free Church." Robie, editor of the *Buffalo Christian Advocate,* hadn't been won over to Roberts's position. Rather, Roberts notes, "His idea seems to be that there ought to be free Churches for the poor, as they are not permitted to have a right in the more expensive edifices."[200] In other words, Robie may have thought: "Well, we have some prospering Methodist churches in Buffalo with rented pews, and if we're also going to reach the poor, maybe there should be some free churches for them." This still allowed, in effect, for segregation by socioeconomic status, which Roberts strongly opposed.

Roberts did all he could to encourage the proposed building plan. On June 12 he preached from Haggai 2:4, "Be strong, all ye people of the land, saith the LORD, and work: for I am with you." "I spoke encouragingly of our Church enterprise," Roberts noted.[201]

Benjamin held another society meeting on June 13, a week after the first one. Apparently the issue had been referred to the trustees for their input. "The trustees brought in a report in favor of doing nothing," Roberts reported. The majority of

---

196. BTRD, June 5, 1853.

197. BTRD, June 6, 1853. Roberts's diary entries for June 6, 7, and 8 read as a continuous narrative describing the June 6 meeting. A number of diary pages are blank about this time (presumably due to the disruption of the Robertses' move to their own house), and apparently Benjamin used the space of three consecutive days to document this important meeting. In contrast, see BHR, *BTR,* p. 77, and Zahniser, pp. 63-64.

198. BTRD, June 8, 1853 (assuming "Bro. Thomas" refers to the presiding elder, not to a Niagara Street church member).

199. BTRD, June 6, 1853. Roberts writes, "Voted in favor of free Church," but there follows a word that is illegible. It could conceivably mean that the church voted in favor of a free church committee. Benson Roberts reads it simply as "Voted in favor of free church" (BHR, *BTR,* p. 77).

200. BTRD, June 7, 1853. Robie likely made this comment to Roberts in an otherwise unrecorded conversation about this time.

201. BTRD, June 12, 1853.

members thought the church should move ahead with the project, however. Eleazar Thomas warned of "pushing the Trustees to extremity." But after extended discussion, the church voted not to adopt the trustees' recommendation and instead appointed a committee to secure pledges toward a new building. "Bro. Bond stood up like a man and turned the tide of influence" in the church meeting, Benjamin noted — but Bond was not a trustee.[202]

The fund-raising effort was initially successful; "a good proportion of the amount necessary" was pledged.[203] But in the end nothing came of Roberts's efforts to build a "free" church in Buffalo, even though the majority of the congregation supported him. Had he remained longer at the church, he might have been able to win over the remaining trustees. But the summer camp meeting season had come and the end of the conference year was approaching. Roberts later wrote that though a good proportion of the needed money had been pledged, "at the end of the first year, through the influence" of the half-dozen or so who opposed him, "we were removed, and a man of the other party sent in our place."[204]

According to Ellen Roberts, Thomas Carlton was in Buffalo in June "when our people were trying to build a free church" and added fuel to the opposition. Carlton alleged that "the free seat system did not work well in New York" and that the Allen Street Church had recently been repaired and the pew-rental system introduced, Ellen reported, but she disputed this. "I told Mr. Roberts I did not believe they had ever rented the seats" at Allen Street. But in Buffalo "all our churches are stock churches, and several of the . . . preachers in this Conference say they would never build a church upon any other plan."[205]

Through the summer Benjamin, however, was still rather encouraged with the prospects. He wrote to his father on August 8,

> I believe the people are looking with more and more favor upon the principles I feel compelled to advocate. Yesterday I preached a sermon on the duty of the church to spread Christianity in this City which I should judge produced a deep impression. The Lord graciously assisted me. I have no doubt but that the church and congregation with the exception of perhaps half a dozen are anxious that we should return. Still I should be unwilling to, unless a different policy can be pursued. Till our exclusive church system is abolished in this City we cannot do much towards infusing the Spirit of Christianity among the masses.[206]

Here is the true spirit of B. T. Roberts. Not content with merely building up his own congregation, he had a passion to "spread Christianity" throughout the city; to "[infuse] the Spirit of Christianity among the masses." But to accomplish this the

202. BTRD, June 13 and 14, 1853.
203. WAS, p. 105.
204. WAS, p. 105. Roberts was succeeded by H. Ryan Smith, who served for two years.
205. ELS (apparently), perhaps to LBL, undated, quoted in BHR, BTR, p. 78.
206. BTR to TR, Aug. 8, 1853, quoted in BHR, BTR, p. 78.

"exclusive church system," which was a barrier and affront to the poor, had to be "abolished" (another form of abolitionism!). This passion to carry the good news beyond the believing community to those who most needed it, as Jesus did (seen also in Roberts's lifelong missionary interest), goes to the heart of Roberts's experience and understanding of the gospel. It is perhaps the deepest unifying theme in Roberts's life and ministry.

A Home of Their Own

At the same time Benjamin was working to convince his people to build a new church building, he was looking for a house to buy. Apparently the one at 46 South Division Street was not fully adequate. Also, Roberts was probably thinking long-term, viewing a home of their own as an investment. He knew he and Ellen would not be in Buffalo longer than the three-year limit for Methodist pastors (unless he was assigned to another Buffalo church). Still, he probably would not have considered buying a house halfway through the conference year unless he expected to be returned for a second year.

On February 23, 1853, Benjamin and Ellen went to look at a house on Palmer Street, and the next day did more house hunting. Over the next several weeks Benjamin kept watching for available property; he noted on Saturday, April 2: "Run about as usual to find a house to live in. It seems as if this engaged much of my time." He attended an auction of houses on April 6 but felt the prices were too high.[207]

Benjamin and Ellen finally decided that the house at 29 Palmer Street was a pretty good deal. "The house is a good one, well finished," Benjamin noted, on a twenty-five-by-eighty-nine-foot lot. On April 8 he agreed to pay Daniel Wiswell, the owner, $2,200 for the house (about $66,000 in today's dollars), with a $600 down payment and four annual payments of $400 each.[208] He hoped to get the cash from his father, who apparently owed him the $125 he had received from the sale of Bill and might lend him some additional funds. But when Benjamin went by train to see his father in Gowanda the next week, he found that Titus had just bought a dairy farm and was short of cash.[209]

Fortunately Brother Benson, one of the supportive members at Niagara Street, agreed to lend Roberts the $600 for the down payment, on a three-month note. With

---

207. BTRD, Feb. 23 and 24; Apr. 2 and 6, 1853.

208. BTRD, Apr. 8, 1853.

209. BTRD, Apr. 14, 1853. In February Titus had given Benjamin two signed notes totaling $178, perhaps representing the $125 from the sale of Bill and possibly some harness or other items Titus had sold for his son, and/or some interest on the principal. Apparently Benjamin had in effect lent this money to his father (probably as an investment, as Titus was frequently buying and selling property), and now expected to collect the funds and borrow the balance of what he needed for the down payment. Benson Roberts notes, "The sale of [Benjamin's] horse, Bill, for $125, aided much towards this first investment in property rendered almost necessary by scarcity of houses to rent." BHR, *BTR*, p. 76.

this cash Benjamin bought the Palmer Street house on April 15. A few days later he bought two bedsteads and seven chairs for the new house for $7.75.[210] Benjamin and Ellen, along with Georgie and Mary, moved to the Palmer Street house later in the month.[211] The house was located two blocks east of Niagara Street, about six blocks northwest of the Niagara Street church building.[212]

This was the first house Benjamin and Ellen had owned. They had moved into the South Division Street house late in October 1852, and now, six months later, they were moving again. But this time it was their own home. "[I] like living up here much better than down town," Ellen commented. "Feel quite well and happy." She noted that "Georgie runs about out-of-doors some," even though he still wasn't very well. "I feel the presence of God and that he will do all things well."[213]

Ellen occasionally had some help with the housework from a hired girl. Toward the end of the conference year in Buffalo she discovered that a girl she had recently hired was stealing from her, so she let her go.[214]

Finances had been tight all year — even though, as Benson Roberts noted, B. T. was "serving a large city church with a fairly prosperous congregation."[215] Ellen wrote to her aunt Lydia, "We have never been obliged to practice more economy, or as much as since we came to Buffalo. We barely live on our allowance and that is all. I have had no new clothes to speak of, save a bonnet. I made three of my dresses over this Spring." But she was not complaining. "I am thankful for what we have of the comforts of life."[216]

Someone gave Benjamin a $20 gift on April 4, and he used it for new clothes. "I never have been so destitute for clothes before," he noted. A gift of $5 for performing a wedding on Saturday morning, July 9, was helpful, permitting Benjamin to buy a dozen Testaments and settle an old bill.[217] At the end of the conference year, on September 5, Benjamin paid off the $600 down payment loan he had gotten from Brother Benson. Apparently he hadn't been able to pay it on July 15 when it came due, and got it extended another three months. Now he paid off the loan, including $50 interest.[218] He calculated that that left him with a total indebtedness of

---

210. BTRD, Apr. 15 and 19, 1853, and "Cash Account," p. 207 of diary.

211. They probably moved during the week of Apr. 25; Benjamin does not record his activities from Apr. 25 to May 14, likely because of the disruption due to the move. The notes on slavery that cover the spaces for Apr. 25-29 were probably written in July, when he was reading on that subject.

212. Gerber, *American Pluralism*, 1836 and 1855 maps of Buffalo, following p. 109. Palmer Street, only about four blocks long, ran parallel to Niagara Street, two blocks farther inland from Lake Erie. The Roberts house was eight blocks from the lake and from the Erie Canal, which here ran along the lake shore. The street name was later changed to Whitney Place (the present name).

213. ELRD, May 1853 (exact date not given). She also noted, "Mary has gone home" — apparently for a visit to her family in Windsor; she was back again in mid-June.

214. ELR to LBL, Oct. 3, 1853, quoted in BHR, *BTR*, p. 82.

215. BHR, *BTR*, p. 76.

216. ELR to LBL, apparently written about June 1. Quoted in BHR, *BTR*, p. 76.

217. BTRD, Apr. 5 and July 9, 1853.

218. BTRD, Sept. 5, 1853. Thus Benjamin paid about 8.33 percent for what amounted to a five-

"some $3,000 for the year," the bulk of which was the $1,600 he still owed on his house.[219]

Last Months in Buffalo

Benjamin and Ellen attended the camp meeting at Hamburg, twelve miles south of Buffalo, in June. Brother Benson from Niagara Street took them down in his carriage, and the Bensons cared for Georgie and Mary in their Buffalo home while Benjamin and Ellen were away. "It was a most glorious meeting, I found it good to labor for others," Ellen wrote. "The Lord gives strength."[220]

After camp meeting Benjamin went to Lima to fulfill his responsibilities as a member of the Board of Visitors to Genesee Wesleyan Seminary. He spent four days there at the end of June, though on the Sunday, June 26, he went up to Henrietta, near Rochester (East Genesee Conference), and preached twice for Joseph Tinkham, the pastor.[221]

Roberts sat in on the Genesee Wesleyan student examinations on Saturday, talked to various faculty members on Monday, and heard some lectures on Tuesday and Wednesday. In general, the school seemed to be prospering. The examinations went well. "The Classes especially of Tefft [Benjamin Tefft, the president] and Alverson appeared to good advantage." (Professor James Alverson had been Roberts's science teacher at the school eight years earlier.) But Roberts found "a great deal of bitterness among different members of the faculty," with rivalries and factions forming. He was generally impressed with E. R. Keyes's address "The Conditions of Progress" and a lecture by Rev. Joseph Cummings of Boston, who reminded him of Stephen Olin. Benjamin was given the task of writing up the committee report, which he worked on Tuesday afternoon and finished Wednesday morning. He then traveled back to Buffalo by train Wednesday afternoon.[222]

Benjamin was glad to be back home. He worked hard Friday and Saturday getting ready for the Sunday services. "Find my mind very much dissipated by my long

---

month loan. In a letter to his father, Aug. 8, 1853, he wrote, "I sent word to Bro. Gordon of Rushford that I wanted to borrow some money, and he came out immediately, the next day after you were here, and brought me three hundred dollars. He says I can have it till the first of June and longer if he can get along without it. This I have appropriated to the payment of the bank note. . . . I send you a note for that which you so kindly lent me." BTR to TR, Aug. 8, 1853.

219. BTRD, Sept. 5, 1853. It is not clear what Benjamin's other debts were, but they must have consisted chiefly in money he had borrowed. Despite his indebtedness, however, Roberts (who was always careful about his finances) was gradually increasing his equity. He bought Bill, his horse, in 1849 for $70 and sold him three years later for $125; then he apparently invested that money with his father and later put it toward the Palmer Street house, which presumably was appreciating in value. The house purchase also relieved Benjamin and Ellen of the $15 or so they were paying monthly in rent.

220. BTRD, June 15, 1853; ELRD, June 1853 (exact date not given).

221. BTRD, June 24-29, 1853.

222. BTRD, June 25-29, 1853.

absence from my study," he commented. "I need constant study to keep in good mental condition."[223]

In mid-July Benjamin and Ellen made a three-day trip down to Gowanda, leaving Georgie at home with Mary and borrowing Brother Newton's horse and buggy.[224] They found their family and friends in Gowanda doing well. "Most every one is buying land and getting rich," Benjamin commented. He and Ellen visited his sisters Florilla and Caroline. Benjamin noted that David Brown, Caroline's husband, who ran a store in Gowanda, had been made postmaster.[225]

Before returning to Buffalo, Benjamin visited little Willie's grave and put down fresh sod. "Dear little fellow[,] we miss him greatly," he wrote.[226]

As the summer ended, Roberts was thinking of the annual conference sessions, to be held in early September at Batavia. On July 10 he had preached on sanctification "to about our usual congregation," and on September 4 he preached a sermon on Methodism from "Go out and compel them to come in" (Luke 14:23) — another indication of how he viewed the church's mission.[227]

Benjamin could look back over his year in Buffalo with some satisfaction. Despite conflict and opposition, the church had grown. Judging by the progress he was making, it seems likely that the church would have flourished had he been left at Niagara Street. Attendance was increasing. In his diary Roberts frequently noted positive signs — good Sunday congregations; a "very good prayer meeting" on Thursday evening, April 21; a full house at the Sunday evening prayer meeting on April 24.[228] For the year, total membership grew from 135 to 150 — the only year between 1848 and 1857 that the church showed any significant gain.[229]

Ellen apparently was well liked by the Niagara Street people. Back east, Thomas Carlton's wife told Harvey Lane, Ellen's cousin, "that *Mrs.* Roberts was liked by the people where they were stationed, . . . was liked as a *Lady* and a Christian, everywhere." Reporting this to Ellen, her aunt Lydia added, "It is well *you* stand so high" — implying that the Carltons and others found Ellen acceptable, even if they had problems with her husband.[230]

---

223. BTRD, July 1, 1853.

224. Why not take Georgie with them while visiting the toddler's grandparents? Most likely Benjamin wanted to give Ellen a break from child care.

225. BTRD, July 12 and 13, 1853. David Brown served as Gowanda postmaster for eight years (1853-61), then moved with his family to nearby Collins, where he farmed, and later (1871) to Otto, where he operated a gristmill. His Gowanda store burned in the 1856 fire. He and Caroline (who died in 1868) had one son and four daughters. William Adams, ed., *Historical Gazetteer and Biographical Memorial of Cattaraugus County, N.Y.* (Syracuse: Lyman, Horton and Co., 1893), p. 934.

226. BTRD, July 14, 1853.

227. BTRD, July 10 and Sept. 4, 1853. Benjamin's diary is blank for most of July and all of August, and Ellen's has no entries for either month.

228. BTRD, Apr. 21 and 24, 1853.

229. In fact, according to the minutes, Niagara Street showed a loss every year during this period except for the year Roberts was there and the 1854-55 year, when there was a gain of seven.

230. LBL (Mount Holly, N.J.) to ELR (Buffalo), 1853, quoted in Zahniser, p. 68.

Roberts later summarized his year at Niagara Street: "God kept us from compromising, and gave us a good revival of religion. The members generally were quickened and many sinners were converted," despite the opposition of a few.

Benjamin added that under the next pastor, "The people were finally persuaded that what they needed was a more imposing church edifice."[231] After Roberts left, considerable expense was put into remodeling the Niagara Street building, giving it a tall spire and a more impressive facade, as contemporary pictures show.[232] A large organ and tall Gothic pulpit chairs were added.[233] Bishop Janes came for the rededication service in November 1858.[234]

Various public fund-raising events, including a clambake, were held. But the church experienced only small growth and made little progress financially, even though a long-standing mortgage holder forgave the $3,000 owed him.[235] Roberts later commented, "All the money was raised that could be raised by selling the pews, by taxing the members to the utmost of their ability, and by making one of the largest liquor dealers in the city trustee and treasurer."[236] Sandford Hunt, the historian of Buffalo Methodism, wrote, "[A] heavy weight seemed to rest on the church, and there was no substantial gain. Some of the men most relied upon died, others moved from the city, and dark days were experienced. Many of the subscriptions remained unpaid, and a heavy debt confronted the church."[237]

The Niagara Street Church closed in 1861. Roberts noted in the *Earnest Christian*,

The city papers contain the announcement that Dr. Smith, the [Niagara Street] pastor, having obtained leave of absence, there will be no service in this church for the present.

The fact is, the church is closed: not from choice but from necessity. The society has struggled manfully with a heavy debt as long as they were able. A receiver has been appointed: the church edifice has passed into his hands, and has been closed by his direction. We sincerely regret the sad fate of this, the oldest Methodist Episcopal church in this city.[238]

---

231. *WAS*, p. 105.

232. A drawing of the original building, decorated with a picture of a fancy horse-drawn American Express wagon filled with men in top hats passing by on Franklin Street, is found in the booklet *History of Asbury Methodist Episcopal Church*, located in the Western New York Conference Archives, Buffalo. A picture of the remodeled building, the height of its facade doubled by the imposing spire, is printed in Hunt, *Methodism*, following p. 34.

233. *WAS*, p. 105.

234. Hunt, *Methodism*, p. 43.

235. Hunt, *Methodism*, p. 43.

236. *WAS*, p. 106.

237. Hunt, *Methodism*, p. 43.

238. [B. T. Roberts], "Niagara Street M.E. Church," pp. 256-57. "It is understood that the claims against [the property] at present amount to $10,000!" Roberts reported, and he warned: "Let Churches learn to keep out of debt . . . depend on God . . . and not lean upon preachers who would lead them away from the cross" (p. 258).

Hunt notes that the Niagara Street property "was sold for enough to meet liabilities, and subsequently was purchased for a Jewish tabernacle, but has since been taken down, and the Masonic Temple now stands on this old sacred ground."[239] Hunt was writing in 1892. In the late twentieth century this part of Niagara Street was closed off, and today a massive commercial building stands on the site.

These years following Roberts's departure were the final seven lean years of the Niagara Street Church. It was the time as well when Roberts himself was passing through his greatest crisis. But Benjamin and Ellen's year in Buffalo had been fairly positive. Clarence Zahniser nicely summarizes: "That year's pastorate gives a glimpse of the man fasting and praying, studying 'as usual' in the mornings, . . . calling on his members, laboring in the jail and occasionally at the hydraulics [waterworks area]; preaching in his stock church and working for a free church; writing for the church paper to correct what he considered current errors; encouraged and discouraged; denounced and lauded; having little to get along on and yet buying a house which afterward became the means for the first free church in Buffalo."[240]

Roberts came close to winning the battle at Niagara Street. It is breathtaking to think how history would have been different had he remained a second year and succeeded in building a *free* Methodist church in the heart of Buffalo.

1853 Annual Conference

The Genesee Conference held its 1853 annual sessions at Batavia, about midway between Buffalo and Rochester, September 7-15. For the first time the conference was chaired by Matthew Simpson, an Ohio native who was elected Methodist bishop at the 1852 General Conference at age forty. B. T. Roberts had been present in Boston when Simpson was elected bishop (as noted previously). More an academician than a pastor, Simpson had served for nine years as president of Indiana Asbury University and then four years as editor of the *Western Christian Advocate* (Cincinnati) before being elected bishop.[241] He is probably best known today as the editor of the 1,000-page *Cyclopedia of Methodism* (1878), which went through several editions. In fact, it was Simpson's *Cyclopedia* article on the Free Methodist Church that prompted Roberts to write *Why Another Sect*.

---

239. Hunt, *Methodism*, p. 44. Conable wrote in 1876, "At this time [1866] the new and costly [i.e., newly remodeled] Niagara-street Church, Buffalo, was involved in extreme financial embarrassment, growing out of great monetary disasters in the city and the death of some of the prominent members, and Conference adopted a resolution of deep sympathy with the brethren of that Church, and promised to assist them, financially and otherwise, with all their power. It may be added, that the Niagara-street Church, to the great injury of the cause of Methodism and the bitter regret of all, was finally lost. That once Christian temple of worship is now only a Jewish Synagogue" (Conable, p. 667).

240. Zahniser, p. 65.

241. *COM*, p. 801. See George R. Crooks, *The Life of Bishop Matthew Simpson of the Methodist Episcopal Church* (New York: Harper and Brothers, 1890).

Benjamin went to Batavia a couple of days early to examine the first-year Course of Study students as part of his responsibilities as a member of the examining committee.[242]

He found Bishop Simpson's opening remarks at conference on Wednesday morning "very appropriate." He also appreciated James Fuller's sermon on the need for revivals and how they could best be promoted.[243]

Bishop Waugh was present on Sunday and preached in the morning. Bishop Simpson's sermon Sunday afternoon from John 17:21, "That they all may be one," was especially memorable. Simpson preached in a huge tent, and a large crowd from the town attended. Roberts wrote, "This was a powerful, spiritual, sermon. It carried the immense audience completely away."[244]

Issues of alleged ministerial misconduct were again percolating at this annual conference. The case of D. C. Houghton was resolved, as noted earlier.[245] Benjamin mentions a "consultation" he had concerning "the impeachment of Hastings" and adds, "May the will of the Lord be done" — but it is unclear what this refers to.[246] John Wallace drew up a bill of charges against Thomas Carlton that on Saturday, September 10, Roberts presented to Eleazar Thomas, presiding elder of the Buffalo District. Wallace apparently charged Carlton with dishonesty for telling people in Buffalo that the New York City Methodist churches were all going to the pew-rental system.[247] Thomas refused to act on them, however. Zahniser comments that Thomas "suppressed them, probably realizing the futility of presenting them, inasmuch as Mr. Carlton had already been elected head of the Book Concern."[248]

"Conf. business advances slowly," Benjamin noted on Friday, September 9. There were the usual rounds of addresses and anniversaries, including those of the Sunday School Union and the Tract Society. Roberts noted on Friday night, "The evening was cold, and the meeting rather dry."[249]

What to do with Roberts was a conundrum to the conference leadership. "They seem afraid to send me away, and afraid to send me back," Benjamin wrote to Ellen.[250]

242. BTRD, Sept. 5, 1853.

243. BTRD, Sept. 7, 1853.

244. BTRD, Sept. 11, 1853; Conable, p. 607. Conable was similarly effusive: "Every one was completely overwhelmed and carried away, and melted down before the Lord, by the extraordinary eloquence of the speaker," whose "fame . . . as a pulpit orator had preceded him."

245. BTRD, Sept. 13, 1853.

246. BTRD, Sept. 7, 1853. Roberts's entry is cryptic: "Had a consultation with 1 & 2 & 3 in reference to the impeachment of Hastings." What this means, and who Hastings is, is unclear. He was not a minister in either the Genesee or East Genesee Conference.

247. BTRD, Sept. 8, 1853 (entry apparently written on Sept. 10). Roberts's diary seems to read, "Charges duly made out and signed by Bro. Wallace were presented by me on Sat. to Bro. Thomas," but the word after "presented by" is nearly illegible and possibly has some other meaning. Cf. Zahniser, p. 67.

248. Zahniser, p. 67.

249. BTRD, Sept. 9, 1853.

250. BTR to ELR, Sept. 9, 1853, quoted in Zahniser, p. 66.

Most of the Niagara Street people hoped he would return, but his few opponents were influential and vocal.

At the beginning of conference, Thomas sounded out Roberts about his options. If he were returned to Niagara Street, what would Roberts do with the church members who opposed him? Thomas wanted to know. Roberts said he would "turn them all out of the church."[251] This put Thomas in a predicament, as he wanted to keep Roberts at Niagara Street but also wanted to keep the peace. Benjamin wrote to Ellen, "[Thomas], I believe, likes me, and my principles, and my unbending course, but he wants to please." He was somewhat exasperated with Roberts's uncompromising attitude, but Benjamin felt he had to be true to his convictions. He told Ellen, "Bro. Thomas feels tried with me for my opposition to his measures but I cannot help that. When there is so much managing I feel free to express my opinion when it is called for."[252]

Thomas tried to work out a compromise. He and Carlton made a trip to Buffalo to see if they could get consensus (presumably among the Niagara Street trustees) to build a new "stock church" for those who favored that approach and thus allow Roberts to turn Niagara Street into a free church. Nothing came of this, however, and in his letter Benjamin told Ellen to put up a To Rent sign and to try to rent their house for $130 per year.[253]

When the appointments were read at the close of conference on Thursday, September 15, Roberts found that he was appointed to Brockport, about fifteen miles east of Albion. This was not a total surprise, given the difficulties at Niagara Street, and he was at peace about it. He noted in his diary, "I am appointed to Brockport. H. R. Smith succeeds me at Niagara St. I have never felt less anxiety about my appointment, or prayed more. I receive it gratefully as from the Lord. Reached home about 5 P.M."[254]

251. As reported by Ellen, ELR to LBL, Oct. 3, 1853. Quoted in BHR, *BTR*, p. 80.
252. BTR to ELR, Sept. 9 and 12, 1853, quoted in Zahniser, pp. 66-67.
253. BTR to ELR, Sept. 12, 1853; Zahniser, p. 66.
254. BTRD, Sept. 15, 1853.

CHAPTER 15

Revival in Brockport

*"The Lord is at work and we are hoping to see a thorough and extensive revival
of religion."*

B. T. Roberts, 1853[1]

*"It seems to me grace never did more for anyone than it has for me. I love the
work in which we are engaged."*

Ellen Roberts, 1854[2]

Brockport, like Lockport and Middleport, was among the string of towns that lined
the Erie Canal from Rochester to Buffalo. Incorporated in 1829, Brockport had a
population of around two thousand when Roberts was assigned there as pastor.[3] Its
initial growth spurt was due to the fact that the Erie Canal temporarily ended at
Brockport while engineers figured out how to cut through the "great stone ledge"
near Lockport. "Great markets were opened for farm produce, and when the canal
was completed and fully opened, the village continued to derive its wealth from it,"
one author noted. "The entire area of Brockport, Sweden, Clarkson, Parma and
Hamlin was peopled by men and women of good, solid stock, who applied themselves diligently to the hard work of farming." The Brockport Academy was estab-

---

1. BTR (to TR?), Nov. 28, 1853, quoted in BHR, *BTR,* p. 84.
2. ELR to LBL, Jan. 1854 (exact date not given), quoted in BHR, *BTR,* p. 86.
3. Blake McKelvey, "The Genesee County Villages in Early Rochester's History," *Rochester History*
47, no. 1-2 (Jan./Apr. 1985): 25. The population was reported as 2,245 in 1860, according to *French's Gazetteer,* cited by McKelvey.

lished in 1848, five years before Roberts's arrival; it later became Brockport Teachers College and is today part of the State University of New York (SUNY) system.[4]

Methodists came to the Brockport area well before the village was incorporated. They organized a church and in 1828 erected "a very commodious, well-finished brick" building.[5] The Brockport ME Church reported 203 members in 1836 but in recent years had declined. Total membership stood at 108 when Roberts was appointed to Brockport in the fall of 1853.[6]

The people at Brockport received Benjamin and Ellen warmly. When they arrived by train from Buffalo on Thursday afternoon, September 22 (together with Mary and Georgie), they found a brother from the church waiting for them. He took them to his home until they could move into the parsonage, next door.[7]

Packing up for the move from their house in Buffalo had been something of an ordeal for Ellen. Eight months pregnant and not feeling well, she had been confined to bed for several days. She wrote to her aunt Lydia, "I was not able to walk across the room without severe pain. I could but wonder as I looked around me . . . how the work of packing and moving and getting settled again was going to be accomplished without my help, or over-seeing. I felt that the Lord could give me strength to at least attend to things, if He saw best, and if not I must be resigned. That day [Monday, September 19] I did wonders for me, and felt better than I had in weeks, and I was able to do a great deal every day before we left Thursday afternoon."[8]

Many of the Niagara Street people were sad to lose their pastor and his wife. "The people of our church manifested a great deal of feeling at our leaving and the sisters expressed a great deal of sympathy for me and were very kind," Ellen noted. "But though I love some of them very much and found them far more congenial than I have found them elsewhere, yet I have left Buffalo with scarcely a regret." She was surprised that she felt "so cheerful and happy" about moving to Brockport, as she knew no one there.[9]

It turned out that the Brockport parsonage was a fine house — "the best one we have lived in," with "a fine, large garden spot." The congregation had furnished most

4. Howard C. Hosmer, *Monroe County (1821-1971): The Sesqui-Centennial Account of the History of Monroe County, New York* (Rochester, N.Y.: Rochester Museum and Science Center, 1971), pp. 61, 159, 202. Hosmer notes that the Erie Canal made the village of Brockport, "and the Johnston Harvester Company made [Brockport] famous." By 1871 "the huge Johnston factory . . . was manufacturing 500 harvesting machines a year and shipping them to a number of European countries and England as well as South America, Africa and New Zealand" and was "Monroe County's biggest industry" (pp. 159, 160). This company was not started until some years after Roberts's pastorate there.

5. George Peck, *Early Methodism Within the Bounds of the Old Genesee Conference from 1788 to 1828* (New York: Carlton and Porter, 1860), p. 471.

6. The total in 1853 included ninety-one members, sixteen probationers, and one local preacher. Roberts's predecessor at Brockport was Samuel Church, a man in his early fifties, who had been there just one year.

7. ELR to LBL, Oct. 3, 1853, quoted in BHR, *BTR*, p. 81.

8. ELR to LBL, Oct. 3, 1853, quoted in BHR, *BTR*, p. 80.

9. ELR to LBL, Oct. 3, 1853, quoted in BHR, *BTR*, pp. 80-91.

of the house with new furniture. The town was pleasant, abounding in "shade and fruit-trees," Ellen noted, "but our house, parsonage-like, has not the sign of one [tree] about it, nothing but two lilac bushes."

Since the Brockport parsonage was furnished, Benjamin and Ellen sold the furniture they had bought for their Buffalo house — "without loss I think," Ellen wrote to Lydia Lane. "We have never met with so much kindness as we have received here, and so much cordiality," she reported. "We found the sisters had cleaned the parsonage," and when their goods came on Friday "some brethren came in and helped unpack, and the sisters washed and put up the dishes, put down two carpets and corded two bed-steads that evening." Saturday morning the sisters "brought us bread, biscuits, butter, milk, cake, pie, peaches and grapes, etc., so we took possession of our new home and ate our first meal here Saturday afternoon. . . . Before we had been here a week we were quite comfortably settled."[10]

Ellen, however, was far from well, and was near full term in her pregnancy. Benjamin wrote his father on October 18, "Ellen has been very sick since we came here."[11] "I have no help yet but Mary and Mr. Roberts," she told her aunt Lydia. "We have sent to Rochester for a girl," she said, noting that Rochester was only seventeen miles away by train. "The Lord has been so much better to me than I expected that I believe he will still take care of me, and provide somebody in time of need. I feel thankful for good spirits, and that I am not homesick nor lonely in the least."[12]

Two weeks later, on Saturday morning, October 8, Ellen delivered a fine baby boy. His parents named him Benson Howard — Benson, no doubt in appreciation for all the kindnesses Brother and Sister Benson had shown them in Buffalo.[13] This would be the son who, as Zahniser notes, "was probably the nearest to [his parents] in subsequent years."[14]

But Ellen continued very ill. She grew worse, and Benjamin, "becoming greatly alarmed," took the train to Rochester and located a homeopathic doctor. Under this physician's care Ellen improved. One of the sisters of the church cared for baby Benson in her home while Ellen recovered.[15]

This seems to be the occasion Ellen later referred to in writing about her "religious experience."

> The Lord suffered me to come once to the borders of the grave, and I saw *work, work* in the vineyards of the Lord — souls perishing. I promised the Lord that if he would spare my life, I would *live to work* for Him. The things of this world were as the smallest dust compared to the great work of saving souls. I was brought

---

10. ELR to LBL, Oct. 3, 1853, quoted in BHR, *BTR*, p. 81.

11. BTR to TR, Oct. 18, 1853.

12. ELR to LBL, Oct. 3, 1853, quoted in BHR, *BTR*, p. 82.

13. BTR to TR, Oct. 18, 1853. Benjamin's diary is blank from Sept. 17 to Oct. 28 except for an entry on Oct. 18 indicating that he bought half a hog.

14. Zahniser, p. 69.

15. BTR to TR, Oct. 18, 1853.

where I could see only eternity and souls going to hell. My family cares were out of sight; I was conscious that I was at death's door. Oh! such fountains of living water as I saw and my soul panting to get to them; but I felt I would rather live to work, and began to recover.[16]

Ellen did recover sufficiently to participate actively in the life of the church over the next few months.

Despite the health problems, Benjamin and Ellen were pleased with Brockport and its people. "We like it here very much," Benjamin told his father. The church fixed his "claim," or salary, at $500, plus the parsonage — "the same as we had at Buffalo," Benjamin noted, "but living will be much cheaper here than there."

Sunday congregations were large and seemed to be increasing. But though the people were friendly, Benjamin felt they needed revival. "The church is badly backslidden but we are expecting to see a thorough breaking down and an extensive revival."[17] After getting acquainted with his congregation, he concluded that only two were "clearly justified." He was surprised by the degree of worldliness in the church, including the wearing of jewelry and feathers. "I was never among such a company of Methodists." He responded by reading to the church the disciplinary rules on dress.[18]

Revival at Brockport

His first Sunday morning at Brockport Benjamin preached from Ezekiel 33:7, "I have set thee a watchman unto the house of Israel; therefore thou shalt hear the word at my mouth, and warn them from me." As in former appointments, he was in effect announcing his mission at Brockport. In the evening he preached on grace, from Romans 5:2.[19]

Roberts felt he must direct his preaching first to the church, before trying to win new converts. "For eight weeks he preached to the church without inviting a sinner forward."[20] There was little response at first, and some opposed his efforts. But then the people began to yield. In a letter on Monday, November 28, Benjamin wrote, "The cause of the Lord is still advancing among us. The interest is increasing. Many of the members are getting broken down. I have never known a church in a worse spiritual condition than this has been. Besides a general declension there are old quarrels of years standing in the way. But the Lord is at work and we are hoping to see a thorough and extensive revival of religion. I have felt at times almost discouraged but the Lord has graciously sustained me."[21]

---

16. Ellen L. Roberts, "Religious Experience," *EC* 2, no. 9 (Sept. 1861): 284.
17. BTR to TR, Oct. 18, 1853.
18. BHR, *BTR*, p. 83.
19. BHR, *BTR*, p. 83. The second Sunday he preached on Rom. 15:30 and John 17:23.
20. BHR, *BTR*, p. 83.
21. BTR to LBL, Nov. 28, 1853 (RFP, Microfilm Reel 33). Benjamin begins this letter, "Ellen's eyes

During one evening service Benjamin "got on his face in the altar and stayed there waiting on God, while the meeting went on," till he received the assurance that God would give victory.[22]

Before long Benjamin's prayers were answered dramatically. After nine weeks of seeking God, one of the members, E. S., received the witness of the Spirit. Other members were reclaimed or awakened, and word started to get around town. When Roberts finally extended the invitation to sinners, "the altar was filled."[23]

Revival was under way. Sinners were being converted. In early January 1854, Benjamin decided to hold a protracted meeting, with services every night and most afternoons, to extend and deepen the work. He invited Fay Purdy to come and help; Purdy assisted with the meetings from Sunday, January 15, through Wednesday evening of the same week. The effort was undergirded with prayer, including special prayer meetings at daylight.[24]

"The town was stirred" by the revival, according to Benson Roberts. By early January over twenty had been converted. Among the notable conversions was that of William Cusick, a blacksmith who was invited to the meetings by Frank Smith, one of the members. Cusick later became a Free Methodist "firebrand" for the gospel, lighting revival fires in Ohio, Michigan, and farther west.[25] Frank and Emeline Smith (probably the E. S. referred to above) experienced a deeper work of the Spirit in their lives that led them later to work effectively at Water Street Mission in New York City, which became famous through the conversion and ministry of Jerry McAuley.[26] Benjamin later said Emeline Smith "was one of the first women called to public labors among us. She helped inaugurate the movement which has opened the door for women to labor in public extensively in most of the churches."[27]

Just as the Bensons had been such a help in Buffalo, so the Smiths and Brother and Sister Mix were a great encouragement to Benjamin and Ellen at Brockport. The people at Brockport had heard of Roberts before he was appointed, and at confer-

---

are still too weak to allow of her writing, so she wishes me to send you a few lines for her. Mary has gone to school; Maggy is washing; Georgie is running out doors; and the baby is lying on my lap while I write. . . . The young woman who had taken care of him has left, and I take care of him nights. He drinks his milk out of a cup, requiring it usually about twice in the night."

22. BHR, *BTR*, p. 83.

23. BHR, *BTR*, p. 84.

24. BHR, *BTR*, pp. 84-86. The revival seems to have begun in late fall or early winter, before Roberts began the "protracted meeting." It is not clear to what extent he conducted extra meetings in late 1853, in addition to the normal round of Sunday services and prayer meetings, before the special effort in January.

25. BHR, *BTR*, pp. 84, 401. On Cusick, see also Hogue, *HFMC*, 2:36-37, 49, 61; Edward Payson Hart, *Reminiscences of Early Free Methodism* (Chicago: Free Methodist Publishing House, 1903), pp. 182-87.

26. BHR, *BTR*, p. 85. In some sources "Emeline" is spelled "Emiline." On McAuley (1839-84), see R. M. Offord, ed., *Jerry McAuley: An Apostle to the Lost* (New York: American Tract Society, 1907).

27. B. T. Roberts, "The Editor's Travels," *FM* 21, no. 23 (June 6, 1888): 8.

ence Brother Mix had come up to Benjamin and told him the church wanted him as pastor.[28] Sister Emeline Smith became a close friend to Ellen.[29]

Toward the end of January Benjamin wrote his father, "I have only time to say the Lord is reviving His work most powerfully among us. We are enjoying a revival of the old-time Methodist stamp. I should think that over twenty have passed from death unto life, many of them heads of families. I never witnessed a meeting of greater power. Convictions are deep and pungent and conversions clear." He noted that he preached three times on Sunday, "and the Lord owned His truth." "The work is going on with increasing interest."[30]

Both the town and the church were surprised by the manifestations that accompanied the revival. Seekers were slain in the Spirit and would "cry aloud for mercy," Benjamin noted. "At first some were tried with the noise, many of the church members never having witnessed anything like it. But all agree that God is at work in great power."[31] Ellen wrote to Lydia Lane, "We have had some of the most interesting meetings I ever was in. A good many have been reclaimed and over twenty converted. Last Friday evening there were five slain under the power of God. This is something new for Brockport, and many of the Methodists look on in amazement." A "Baptist backslider" was converted, went home, and started to praise the Lord there. "God came down upon him and he fell to the floor powerless. The family were greatly alarmed, the children cried, his wife thought he was dying and sent in great haste for Mr. Roberts," who apparently went and assured them that all was well.[32]

Ellen was well enough to witness the revival and participate to some degree. "I am able to attend the meetings every evening, and most of the time in the afternoons," she told her aunt Lydia. "It seems to me grace never did more for anyone than it has for me. I love the work in which we are engaged. I love the cross. I am thankful to be permitted to do anything for my Lord and Master who has done so much for me. I know I am perfect weakness, but Christ is strong. I feel His presence and power in my heart, and my soul hungers and thirsts for entire conformity to His will."[33]

Ellen was apparently referring to this period when some years later she wrote of being "in meetings from December till March" after recovering from serious illness.

28. ELR to LBL, Oct. 3, 1853, quoted in BHR, *BTR*, p. 82.

29. Five letters from Emeline Smith to Ellen Roberts preserved in the Marston Memorial Historical Center, all apparently from March or April 1860, record Emeline's struggles to find her place in ministry and in relation to her family responsibilities, since she had small children. After she had found it necessary to confront one of the brothers during a class meeting she was leading, she wrote, "When I came to speak to him the Lord held me to dealing with him just as [I] had done with the rest. I was enabled to feel for a few moments, the dignity with which I was invested, while standing up in the name & cause of my master. All fear & shrinking was completely removed." Emeline Smith (Brockport) to ELR, Mar. 28, 1860[?].

30. BTR to TR, Jan. 22 (i.e., 23?), 1854, quoted in BHR, *BTR*, p. 87.

31. BTR to TR, Jan. 22 (i.e., 23?), 1854, quoted in BHR, *BTR*, p. 87.

32. ELR to LBL, Jan. 1854 (exact date not given), quoted in BHR, *BTR*, pp. 85-86.

33. ELR to LBL, Jan. 1854 (exact date not given), quoted in BHR, *BTR*, p. 86.

"We saw many souls saved and sanctified." On one occasion she was "especially blessed." She writes that following "a season of powerful temptation, I felt such an overwhelming sense of nearness to Christ as took my physical strength away. This manifestation humbled me in the dust, and greatly increased my confidence and faith, and gave me greater power to resist the enemy."[34] This was one of several occasions when she was "slain in the Spirit."

The revival spread beyond Brockport to some of Benjamin's outlying preaching points — Clarkson, Redmonds Corners, "the Irish settlement."[35] Benjamin was seeing in Brockport what he had hoped to see in Buffalo.

For whatever reason, this time Roberts did not call on John Wesley Redfield to come and help. Perhaps he had concluded that Redfield was a polarizing influence and that the revival at Brockport could go on just as well without him.[36]

The revival effort, combined with his usual pastoral work, absorbed virtually all of Benjamin's time and energy. Uncharacteristically, his diary is blank from January 2 until March 8, when Ellen left to visit George and Lydia Lane at Mount Holly, New Jersey. (Two weeks later he went repeatedly to the train station, hoping to meet Ellen on her return, and was a bit irked not to find her. "She did not come[,] as might have been expected from the propensity in women to stay over the time when visiting," he grumbled. The next day he learned that Ellen had decided to make a quick visit to Middletown, Connecticut. He met her unexpectedly at the train station on Saturday, March 25, just as he was about to go to Rochester to look for a hired girl. "I had the unspeakable pleasure of meeting my dear wife," he noted in his diary. "She is very tired, having traveled all night. Her eyes do not seem any better.")[37]

Roberts took in many new members as a result of the revival. He received five on probation on March 12 and noted, "This makes fifty-four that have joined on probation, all but sixteen heads of families."[38] Gaining family heads, and thus in most cases whole families, spoke well for the future of the church.

Pleased as he was with the revival at Brockport, Benjamin was concerned about his old charge at Caryville, where things were not going well.[39] In late March and early April he preached a two-week revival at Caryville, spending the weekdays there

---

34. Ellen L. Roberts, "Religious Experience," p. 284.

35. BHR, *BTR*, p. 85.

36. In Roberts's accounts of Redfield's ministry at Niagara Street there is no hint, however, that he was at all dissatisfied with the evangelist's work.

37. BTRD, Mar. 22 and 25, 1854.

38. BTR (Brockport) to ELR (Mount Holly), Mar. 13, 1854.

39. Benson Roberts writes, "The pastor who succeeded [Benjamin] lived on his farm some twenty miles away, and was at Caryville only on Sundays. Of course the church [had] run down on his hands, yet he was one of the most ready to oppose by his pen, efforts made by others to arouse and awaken the church" (*BTR*, p. 89). H. M. Ripley succeeded Roberts at Caryville in September 1849 and in turn was succeeded by Richard L. Waite in 1850. Waite served for two years and then was appointed to Alden in the Buffalo District. J. K. Cheeseman served at Caryville, 1852-53, and E. Smith Furman, 1853-55 (*Minutes*, Genesee Conference, 1847-55). Benson Roberts seems to be referring to Waite, who, as noted in the previous chapter, wrote critically of B. T. Roberts.

but the Sundays at Brockport. "I found the [Caryville] church greatly backslidden," he wrote to George Lane. "They have had no revival since I left there." He preached first on justification, and "there soon was a breaking down among the members." Two local preachers confessed their backslidden condition and found grace. "The members no sooner humbled themselves before God, than deep conviction seized many of the unconverted and a general interest was awakened." On Roberts's last night there some thirty people came forward for prayer and "six or seven found peace in believing."[40]

Roberts's evangelistic success at Brockport and Caryville made him think about going into full-time revivalism. He was discovering that he was a very effective revival preacher. He wrote to Ellen from Caryville on April 5, "I shall get home just as soon as the Lord will let me leave here. My health is very good, and I enjoy myself very well. I should like to be in protracted meetings all the while if I could get humility enough to be successful. I find my heart needs a constant watching at this point."[41]

As usual, Benjamin was earnest in his own spiritual quest, seeking to be all that God wanted of him. He continued to devote himself to his studies and noted on Saturday night, March 11, "I have commenced this [day to] seek earnestly a higher state of religious experience than I ever enjoyed before."[42] At the beginning of his 1854 diary he had inscribed in Greek, Σεαυτὸν ἁγνὸν τήρει — "Keep yourself pure" (1 Tim. 5:22). Clearly Benjamin's understanding of holiness was dynamic rather than static; it allowed for continuing growth in grace, and was not satisfied to rest on past experiences.[43]

Roberts's studies during this time included a number of books, as well as consistent reading of the Hebrew Bible.[44] He noted on March 22, "Finished the 31st chap of Deut. in Hebrew to day." Two weeks earlier he had "recommenced" his study of German. Among the books he read in the first half of 1854 were the autobiography of the Methodist circuit rider and missionary James Finley,[45] the two-volume *Life and Letters of Stephen Olin*, Blair's *Rhetoric*,[46] Bledsoe's *Theodicy*,[47] Austen Layard's *Discov-*

---

40. BTR to GL, Apr. 7, 1854, quoted in BHR, *BTR*, pp. 89-90.

41. BTR (Caryville) to ELR (Brockport), Apr. 5, 1854, quoted in BHR, *BTR*, p. 92.

42. BTRD, Mar. 11, 1854.

43. Though Roberts, like Phoebe Palmer and many others of the time, used the language of "state of grace," the word "state" here can be understood as roughly synonymous with "experience," and was not understood in a "static" sense — though in fact the language did lend itself more to static than dynamic conceptions.

44. Douglas Cullum lists Roberts's reading by year, 1852-55, noting which readings were part of the ME Course of Study. Douglas Russell Cullum, "Gospel Simplicity: Rhythms of Faith and Life among Free Methodists in Victorian America" (Ph.D. diss., Drew University, 2002), pp. 373-82.

45. W. P. Strickland, ed., *Autobiography of Rev. James B. Finley; or, Pioneer in the West* (Cincinnati: Methodist Book Concern, 1854), 455 pages. Finley, a member of the Cincinnati Conference, was a pioneer circuit rider and missionary among the Wyandot Indians.

46. Probably Hugh Blair, *Lectures on Rhetoric and Belles Lettres*, 2 vols. (London: W. Strahan, T. Cadell, 1783), in one of its American editions. Some thirty-seven American editions were published between 1784 and 1853. Hugh Blair, D.D., was "one of the ministers of the High Church, and Professor of Rhetoric and Belles Lettres in the University, of Edinburgh," according to the title page of the 1783 edition.

47. Albert Taylor Bledsoe (professor of mathematics and astronomy, University of Mississippi), *A*

eries in the Ruins of Nineveh and Babylon; with Travels in Armenia, Kurdistan and the Desert,[48] and selections from Wesley's *Works.*[49] Most of these were new books, just published. Benjamin had bought Layard for two dollars in Rochester when he saw Ellen off to New Jersey on March 8.[50]

Later in the year Roberts began reading Tytler's *General History*, which was one of the books listed in the *Discipline* for the third year of the Course of Study.[51]

In reading Olin's *Life and Letters*, Roberts was once again impressed with the character of the great man. "Am greatly pleased with the absence of worldly motives in his choice of this Denomination," he wrote. "He was truly a great pious man. Strong in his attachment to the Church of his choice, but free from all bigotry."[52] Here was an ideal Roberts felt he could emulate.

Roberts was a lover of books. Fortunately George Lane was occasionally able to supply him with books. Though retired and living in New Jersey, Lane helped secure good literature for Benjamin and at times sent him books at his own expense. Benjamin wrote his uncle on April 7 to thank him for the books he had sent back with Ellen. "Please accept my warmest thanks. I prize them highly. There was but a single book among the whole that I previously had and this one I can very easily exchange. They came very opportunely. My library needed replenishing, but I did not know how it was to be replenished. I bought last year a house and lot in Buffalo which I am anxious to pay for. I feel as if I ought to do it for the sake of my family. This used all my means so that I cannot buy books as I would."[53]

Benjamin added a comment about the Book Concern and about Robie's *Buffalo Christian Advocate*. Thomas Carlton had decided to open a book depository in Buffalo to make Methodist literature more easily available in western New York. Benjamin noted, "Robie is to publish his paper over-head, having his office in the depository. This is one way to make the church responsible for an irresponsible paper. It is more an organ of masonry and oddfellowship, to both of which societies the editor belongs, than of Methodism. I should not be at all surprised if an effort should be made to have this Conference adopt it. If we take the paper we shall have to take the editor with it."[54]

Theodicy; or, Vindication of the Divine Glory, as Manifested in the Constitution and Government of the Moral World (New York: Carlton and Phillips, 1854).

48. First published in London in 1853 in a two-volume edition.

49. BTRD, Mar. 19 and Apr. 28, 1954.

50. BTRD, Mar. 8, 1854.

51. BTRD, Sept. 28, 1854; *The Doctrines and Disciplines of the Methodist Episcopal Church* (New York: Lane and Scott, 1849), p. 217. Presumably this was Alexander Fraser Tytler, *Elements of General History, Ancient and Modern to Which is Added a Succinct History of the United States, by an American Gentleman* (Concord, N.H.: J. F. Brown, 1849); cf. Cullum, "Gospel Simplicity," p. 379. Later Roberts quoted from Tytler in an 1861 article: "Free Churches," *EC* 2, no. 1 (Jan. 1861): 17.

52. BTRD, Apr. 29 and 30, 1854.

53. BTR to GL, Apr. 7, 1854, quoted in BHR, *BTR*, p. 90.

54. BTR to GL, Apr. 7, 1854, quoted in BHR, *BTR*, p. 90.

Life and Ministry in Brockport

Benjamin's ministry at Brockport was fruitful and busy. His ministry seems to have been appreciated. At the New Year's Eve watch-night service, he noted, "The church covenanted to begin to live anew for God." In March the sisters of the church presented him with a "fine overcoat." He seems to be describing his spirits, rather than the weather, when he wrote on Friday, March 17, "Rose this morning in the sunshine. But soon a dark cloud obscured the light until night when it broke away." He was missing Ellen, who was still in New Jersey; he wrote to her that evening. He notes that on Sunday, March 19, he preached "in the morning on Eucharist." He kept up his pattern of extensive visitation; on Monday, March 20, he called on seven of his parishioners even though he "felt poorly" due to a cold he was having trouble shaking.[55]

About this time Benjamin bought a cow to help with the family's nutrition.[56] He spent most of Tuesday, March 21, getting fodder; Brother Perry brought him a load of straw.[57] The cow proved to be a bit of a trial, however, occasionally wandering away. She "went off" on Friday afternoon, April 14, and Benjamin searched for her until nine o'clock without finding her. He noted on Saturday, "Searched almost all day for my cow. Found her at last across the canal. She had evidently got lost and could not find her way home." The summer was very dry, and on June 16 Benjamin walked the cow five miles to William Thorpe's farm where he pastured her for a small weekly sum. Toward the end of July Roberts noted, "Went to see my cow. It is a very dry time and the pastures are failing generally."[58]

Roberts hosted the district preachers association meeting on April 18-20 (Tuesday through Thursday).[59] Presumably the preachers met at the Brockport Methodist Episcopal Church. About twelve of the district preachers were there, along with most of their wives. Preachers attending included Asa Abell, Joseph McCreery, Philo Woodworth, Josiah Mason, John Lanckton, John Jenkins, and others — about two-thirds of the Methodist preachers of the district. Roberts wrote an essay in preparation for the meeting.[60]

---

55. BTRD, Jan. 1; Mar. 15, 17, 19-20, 1854.

56. Benjamin notes on Mar. 21, 1854, "Worked most of the day to get fodder for my cow." There are several references in his 1854 diary to his cow. Ellen noted in Feb. 1857, "Our cow died this morning" (ELRD, Feb. 9[?], 1857). Benjamin and Ellen may possibly have owned different cows at different times during this period.

57. BTRD, Mar. 21, 1854. He notes on the same date, "Janette left to day. She has acted of late as if possessed. I fear she has gone over to the evil one." Apparently Janette was a hired girl who worked briefly for the Robertses. It was four days later that Roberts started for Rochester to find a new girl and ran into Ellen at the train station.

58. BTRD, Apr. 14-15, June 16, July 24, 1854.

59. See Conable's comments on such "District Meetings" or "Ministerial Associations," pp. 569-70.

60. BTRD, Apr. 15 and 18, 1854. Roberts doesn't indicate the subject of his essay; it may well have concerned the Kansas-Nebraska Act.

The preachers association conducted its "usual business," but there was one special item. On Thursday McCreery presented "an able petition on the Nebraska bill." Illinois senator Stephen A. Douglas had introduced the Kansas-Nebraska Act in January, and the law, which effectively annulled the Missouri Compromise of 1820, was being hotly debated in Congress. The act proposed to give the new territories of Nebraska and Kansas "popular sovereignty," opening the possibility to slavery in the areas. This outraged abolitionists and encouraged proslavery elements, who hoped to extend slavery to new states. William Lloyd Garrison condemned the legislation and the politics behind it in a lecture at Broadway Tabernacle in New York City on February 14.[61] McCreery's petition was a strong protest against the proposed law.[62] Despite the popular outcry in the North, however, the law passed Congress a few weeks later (toward the end of May) and was signed into law by President Franklin Pierce. Far from resolving anything, the law merely hastened the onset of civil war.

The "anti-Nebraska" movement of early 1854 prompted by Douglas's legislation is a reminder of the critical times in which Roberts was now living and ministering. Henry Mayer notes:

> "The vectors that produced the 1854 Kansas-Nebraska Act and the portentous outcry of opposition can be traced ultimately to the imperative of economic growth. The country had never known such boom times."[63]

Fueled by profits from Southern cotton and the California gold rush, railroads built tens of thousands of miles of new track throughout the Midwest, as far as the Mississippi River and beyond. America was industrializing, finding new applications for improved iron and steel in its growing cities and in the manufacture of tools, farming implements and machines, and small arms. Agricultural yields increased dramatically, as B. T. Roberts could see for himself. Though the nation was still 75 percent rural, cities like New York, Philadelphia, and Buffalo were growing rapidly, fed by economic growth and massive German and Irish immigration. Mayer adds,

> Given the momentum of economic development, the territorial question could not remain dormant. Not only did population pressures in the heartland accelerate the need for opening the remainder of the Louisiana Purchase, but ambitious plans for transcontinental railroads also necessitated midcontinent territorial organization, unless the route was to be a southwestern one stretching from New Orleans across Texas and New Mexico and on to San Diego. For the Democrats'

---

61. Henry Mayer, *All on Fire: William Lloyd Garrison and the Abolition of Slavery* (New York: St. Martin's Press, 1998), p. 438.

62. BTRD, Apr. 20, 1854. Roberts doesn't say whether the preachers adopted the petition or not (presumably they did), nor to whom it was sent. The association set July 18 as the time for its next meeting.

63. Mayer, *All on Fire*, p. 434.

heir apparent, Senator Stephen A. Douglas of Illinois, a northern or central rail-road became not only a matter of personal interest, given his involvement with major investors and land speculators, but a crucial element in his vision of the booming Mississippi Valley as the economic and political center of the Union. In moving to organize the region west of Iowa and Missouri as the Nebraska Terri-tory, an area that extended from the 36°30′ line north to the Canadian border and west to the Rocky Mountains, Douglas attempted a subtle sleight-of-hand that, once exposed, turned into a blatant change of policy that set the collision course toward civil war.[64]

Douglas got Southern support for the bill by adding in Kansas and including the provision that new states formed from the Nebraska Territory would be orga-nized "with or without slavery, as their constitutions may prescribe." Thus the bill amounted to a "silent repeal" of the Missouri Compromise and the restriction of slavery to below 36°30′.

The Monday following the preachers association meeting, Benjamin went to Buffalo to take care of some personal business matters. The trip gave him the oppor-tunity to see Loren Stiles and other Buffalo friends, including the Bensons. He paid Daniel Wiswell $128 on the house mortgage. Roberts's $400 annual payment would have been due about this time; whether he was unable to pay the full amount or had already paid some on it is unclear.[65]

A few weeks later Benjamin had a scare about his father's health. Early on Wednes-day, May 10, he got a letter from Florilla saying Titus Roberts was quite ill. Benjamin started immediately for Gowanda. Arriving at his parents' home at 7:00 P.M., he found his father "better than I expected to find him." But he stayed nearly a week with his folks, helping them and also preaching three times on Sunday. He preached morning and evening at the Methodist church (on "the strait gate" and "Draw nigh to God"), and in the afternoon at the Presbyterian church. After the evening service he noted, "A good degree of interest was manifested. Religion is very low."[66]

Titus Roberts was, as usual, involved in several business deals. Benjamin accom-panied him to see a farm he had bought five miles south of Gowanda, and "went round" with him as Titus collected signatures on a petition to alter the site of a road. Benjamin also wrote up an agreement for the dissolution of the business partnership between Titus and his son-in-law William Smallwood.[67]

On Friday Benjamin again visited the grave of "our dear little Willie. Ma and I planted myrtle," he noted. "There was a violet in blossom upon the grave."[68]

---

64. Mayer, *All on Fire*, p. 435.

65. BTRD, Apr. 24-25, 1854. Roberts sent William Gordon $21 on May 20, and on July 7 sent him $200 more (which he borrowed from Reuben Robles the day before). (BTRD, May 20, July 6-7, 1854.) Presumably these payments related to the $300 Roberts borrowed the previous August.

66. BTRD, May 10 and 14, 1854.

67. BTRD, May 11 and 13, 1854.

68. BTRD, May 12, 1854.

Benjamin returned to Brockport on Monday, May 15. "Grandpa Ellis" (Elnathan Ellis, Sally Roberts's father) took him to Silver Creek where he caught the stagecoach for Buffalo.[69] Grandpa Ellis was then seventy-seven; he died the next year.[70]

Back home in Brockport, Benjamin continued to think about his father — his health, his many business dealings, and his priorities. Titus Roberts turned fifty-one on June 14. Benjamin wrote him in July,

> I have felt much solicitude for you since I was at home. I am very anxious that you should pass the remainder of your days on earth in the enjoyment of much happiness and much of the presence of the Lord. I have not a doubt but that you may do a great deal of good and win many souls to Christ, by living in constant and entire consecration to him. I could not help, when at home last, being impressed with the idea that you were troubled greatly about your business, perhaps more than is really necessary. Do you not think that if you were to give up your business wholly to the Lord, and be willing even to die poor if it be the Lord's will, that even your business might not go any worse than it will by your troubling yourself too much about it?

Benjamin suggested that Titus sell his business and "devote [himself] fully to the work of saving souls," and even take an appointment in the fall, if one should open up in the conference. "[I]f you should enter upon the discharge of the duty to which God has called you, and go out in His name, <u>He</u> would take care of all your interests and you would find yourself free from [financial] embarrassment sooner than by continuing as at present," Benjamin argued. "You will, I trust forgive me if I have said too much. My love for you is my only apology, if any is needed."[71] Titus, however, had faced this issue years before, when Benjamin was a child, and had concluded that his call was not to the preaching ministry. His son wasn't so sure, but perhaps he was in a sense projecting his own sense of call onto his father.

Immediately after returning from Gowanda, Benjamin set out his garden — potatoes, sweet corn, beets, cabbage, carrots, pumpkins, squash, cucumbers, lima beans. The fruit of his labor would provide much of the family diet in the fall and winter. Meanwhile he continued his studies and his visitation, sometimes accompanied by Ellen, though at times he felt he "did not accomplish much." Little Georgie, now almost two and a half, was growing and thriving, keeping Ellen busy. Benjamin spent most of Monday, May 22, building a fence to keep Georgie in the yard. "A hopeless effort!" he concluded.[72]

Roberts raised money for the repair and remodeling of the church basement in order to provide additional rooms. Some people gave willingly to the project; others

---

69. BTRD, May 15, 1854.

70. Elnathan Ellis died on Oct. 8, 1855. Smail, p. 63.

71. BTR to TR, July 22, 1854.

72. BTRD, May 16-29, 1854.

did not. He tried repeatedly to get something from Brother and Sister Hovey, who were well-to-do, but without success. Sister Hovey had her reasons for not giving, Benjamin noted wryly: (1) There are already "Men enough to do it." (2) Heaven is not bought with money. (3) "Charity begins at home." (4) They were unable to give. (5) They gave earlier when the building was constructed.[73]

Roberts frequently mentions the Tuesday evening class meeting. It's not clear how many class meetings the Brockport congregation had, but Roberts apparently led the Tuesday night class at the church building. Only a few attended on May 2, but Benjamin noted that about thirty attended a week later, and the meeting was "profitable." Twenty-six attended the following week. He noted on May 23, "Class met this evening in the new rooms. They are very neat and pleasant. A good attendance, and we had good meetings." Again he said on June 6, "Good class meetings in the evening."[74] These diary entries, and a reference to a "general class meeting" on Tuesday, June 13, seem to indicate that two or more classes met simultaneously at the church building on Tuesday nights, with Roberts conducting a "general" or combined meeting (as prescribed by the *Discipline*) periodically.

Benjamin also gave some attention to building a Sunday school at Brockport. In May he organized a Sabbath school board.[75] He continued his studying and, of course, his Sunday preaching. He noted on June 11, "Had a good time preaching in the morning an off hand discourse. In the afternoon had a poor time preaching an elaborate sermon."[76] The church seemed to be doing well. Benjamin wrote his father in July, "Our meetings are attended with more than usual interest for this season of the year. Some are crowding on to the higher walks of Christian experience."[77]

Though Roberts was always busy, he often was dissatisfied with his time use. He noted on Saturday, July 8, "I find constant occasion to reproach myself for the very little I accomplish. My time is greatly broken in upon and for the want of methodical distribution of my time I do but little. Lord help me to redeem the time."[78]

Roberts was always concerned about his people — their lives generally, their spiritual growth, and their level of discipleship. He wrote on June 14, "Mrs. M. I learned to my great sorrow was at the Circus last evening. Betsey C. [Coats] lives at a Tavern and is low in religion, I fear."[79]

In the midst of his pastoral duties, Roberts continued his intellectual pursuits. He was interested especially in education and its relationship to Christian disciple-

---

73. BTRD, May 30, 1854.

74. BTRD, May 23; May 2, 9, 16; June 6, 1854.

75. BTRD, May 22, 1854. The board met a week later, on Monday, May 29, and adopted a constitution (BTRD, May 29, 1854).

76. BTRD, June 11, 1854.

77. BTR to TR, July 22, 1854.

78. BTRD, July 8, 1854.

79. BTRD, June 14, 1854.

ship, as his writings show. In June he was again working on an article for the *Northern Christian Advocate*. Tuesday, July 11, he went to Rochester to attend the University of Rochester commencement and the inauguration of Martin Brewer Anderson as the school's first president. Roberts listened with some interest to Dr. Anderson's address entitled "End and Means of a Liberal Education."[80] Baptists had founded the university and Rochester Theological Seminary in 1850. Anderson had a long tenure, serving well into the 1880s, and thus was president of the university during the years that Roberts established Chili Seminary in nearby North Chili.[81]

It seems to have been of his time in Brockport that Roberts later reflected:

> Because God calls a man to preach, that is no reason why he should never work with his hands. As a rule it will help him preach to work with his hands several hours a day. It will give him greater bodily and mental vigor. On one of the most important, able and liberal appointments we ever had, we got another horse and put with ours, and drew up our wood for the year. We sawed and split it in the winter. In the summer, we made, with our own hands, a good garden which contributed materially to our support. Yet we had, we presume, on an average a meeting a day through the year. We had appointments week day evenings at the school-houses round about. God gave us powerful revivals. We did not break down under it, but grew in grace, and in bodily strength. Spirituality and industry go well together.[82]

Ellen Tries the Water Cure

Ellen continued to suffer from ill health. It is not clear what the trouble was, though she mentions stomach problems and dyspepsia (poor digestion or indigestion), conditions usually aggravated by stress.[83] She tried various means to improve her health. On June 16, a Friday, she "rose at 4 and rode 3 miles & back on horseback," Benjamin noted.[84]

80. BTRD, June 17 and 19; July 11, 1854.

81. Martin B. Anderson, editor of the Baptist *New York Recorder,* was appointed president of the university in 1853. The university had an enrollment of 163 (all males) by 1856. Blake McKelvey, *Rochester on the Genesee: The Growth of a City* (Syracuse: Syracuse University Press, 1973), pp. 60, 66, 69, 76, 117-18; Hosmer, *Monroe County,* p. 53.

82. [B. T. Roberts], "Editorial Notes," *FM* 20, no. 36 (Sept. 7, 1887): 1.

83. ELR (Geneva, N.Y.) to BTR, July 27-28, 1854. Dyspepsia is defined as "Imperfect or painful digestion; not a disease in itself but symptomatic of other diseases or disorders. It is marked by vague abdominal discomfort, a sense of fullness after eating, . . . heartburn, nausea and vomiting, and loss of appetite. These symptoms may occur irregularly and in different patterns from time to time" and "are increased in times of stress." Clayton L. Thomas, ed., *Taber's Cyclopedic Medical Dictionary,* 18th ed. (Philadelphia: F. A. Davis, 1997), p. 589. Since it may be caused by a variety of conditions ranging from ulcers to constipation, adhesions, and nervous tension, it "can be treated only by treating the disorder which is causing it. In many cases, proper diet is part of the treatment." *The World Book Encyclopedia* (Chicago: Field Enterprises, 1976), D:322.

84. BTRD, June 16, 1854.

The summer of 1854 was extremely hot and dry. In mid-July Ellen decided to try the water cure at the newly opened Geneva Hygienic Institute in Geneva, New York, about seventy miles east of Brockport at the northern tip of Seneca Lake in the Finger Lakes region.[85] She and Emeline Smith traveled to Geneva on Tuesday, July 18. Ellen returned two and a half weeks later, somewhat "improved in health." Sister Dodge kept house for Benjamin, Georgie, Benson, and Mary while Ellen was away.[86]

The Geneva Hygienic Institute (popularly known as the Geneva Water-Cure) had been established by Dr. Amos Bird Smith just a few months earlier and soon became a "flourishing institution." Smith took over the old Geneva Hotel, built in the 1790s, and turned it into a sanitarium.[87]

Born in 1819, Smith was a medical doctor with a successful practice in Ovid, New York. After serious health problems he was "constrained to renounce the allopathic, and to adopt as preferable, the homoeopathic theory of medicine,"[88] and this led to his move to Geneva. An 1873 biographical sketch of him noted:

> [Dr. Smith] makes it a prominent object to interest his patients in the laws of health, and thus to enable them, as far as possible, to render medical service unnecessary. Frequent lectures are delivered by him in the institute on hygiene with this object in view, and also upon cognate subjects. In the treatment of patients, he relies not only upon homoeopathic remedies, but upon a careful adaptation of diet to the condition of the patient, and upon the use of various forms of exercise, voluntary and involuntary. . . . He makes frequent use of electric baths, and of the galvanic battery. . . .
>
> Dr. Smith . . . heats his establishment by a steam apparatus of his own contriving, and a large part of the cooking is performed by steam. He has given . . . close investigation to the subject of alimentation, and hygiene generally, embracing the kinds of food and mode of preparation, and ventilation and heating, the treatment of tumors, etc.

85. Dr. Amos Bird Smith's Hygienic Institute used the water from Geneva's mineral spring for therapeutic purposes. Ellen doesn't give the name of the water cure or the doctor, but presumably the physician was Dr. Bird, as this was the only water cure in Geneva. This same year (1854) a male patient paid six dollars a week for a "'pleasant' third-story room fronting Pultney Park" in Geneva. Jane B. Donegan, *"Hydropathic Highway to Health": Women and Water-Cure in Antebellum America* (Westport, Conn.: Greenwood Press, 1986), p. 187. See John Quincy Adams and Robert S. Breed, comps., *Historic Geneva* (Geneva, N.Y.: Geneva Historical Society, 1929), p. 30, and, more generally, "Brief History of Water-Cure," in *The American Water-Cure Almanac for 1858* (New York: Fowler and Wells, 1858), pp. 4-6.

86. BTRD, July 18 and Aug. 4, 1854.

87. "Geneva Hygienic Institute," *Geneva Gazette*, Nov. 14, 1879; "Old Landmark Sold: Hygienic Institute Passes into New Hands — Was Built in 1796," *Geneva Advertiser-Gazette*, Nov. 19, 1914. Photocopies of these two articles (with no indication of page numbers) are part of a collection on the Geneva Water-Cure at the Geneva Historical Society, Geneva, N.Y.

88. Egbert Cleave, *Cleave's Biographical Cyclopædia of Homœopathic Physicians and Surgeons* (Philadelphia, 1873).

The writer adds that the "ruling motive of Dr. Smith in all his practice and influences, is to do good as a Christian Physician, rather than to advance his own pecuniary interests," and that Dr. Smith endeavored "to induce to such habits of life as will promote general health and happiness."[89] This was the environment in which Ellen sought help from the water cure.

Ellen seems to have enjoyed her time at Geneva and to have benefited from the rest and the treatments she received. She wrote to Benjamin on Thursday evening (July 27), "They are singing around in their rooms to-night which sounds like Camp-Meeting. Our Methodist preacher is a singer." She added, "Now I can write no more till morning for it is so dark, and since I cannot sleep in the daytime I get very sleepy by eight o'clock and generally retire at that time."[90]

Benjamin and Ellen wrote to each other every other day or so while she was in Geneva. On Friday, July 28, after ten days at the water cure, she reported,

> The Doct. says you can cure your throat by the use of cold water. I spoke to him about Georgie, [and] he asked why I did not bring him along, said they would not have charged except a little for his board. Said he must live plain &c. I mean to talk with him again about him before I leave.
>
> I am pleased to hear the children keep as well as usual. My Bensie I presume has forgot me. I dreamed I had him in my arms last night. I am so glad he eats again.
>
> I mean to be a real hydropathist when I get home and let you duck and douse me, I dare say you will "delight to do it." I eat nothing in the bread line but graham. My stomach surely feels better than it has done in a long time.
>
> I hope I may be cured, and I believe I am on the right track. The Doctor says dieting is the only way to cure dyspepsia. This is office day and I mean to find out what he thinks of me in full, whether he thinks I could be benefitted for the future by returning, and if he cannot prescribe a course for me to pursue at home. It does seem to me as if I could not possibly leave home again. My husband and children are dearer to me than ever, and I feel as if I must be with them and devote myself to them.

Ellen wrote this while waiting to see the doctor. She added, "I have a head-ache to-day, had it yesterday also. I think my baths do not agree with me so well these cooler days."[91] Benjamin and Ellen believed God could heal people directly, but they also believed in proper medical care. They were interested too in more "natural" forms of healing, such as homeopathy and hydropathy.

Ellen's letters to Benjamin from Geneva show again the deep love and understanding that marked their marriage. In her July 27-28 letter she made a tiny circle of words in the upper left corner of the first page that read "for thee many kisses." She

89. *Cleave's Biographical Cyclopædia of Homoeopathic Physicians and Surgeons.*
90. ELR (Geneva, N.Y.) to BTR, July 27-28, 1854.
91. ELR (Geneva, N.Y.) to BTR, July 27-28, 1854.

began her letter, "<u>You are so good to me</u>, if I could only repay your goodness, and kindness I would be so happy, but it seems to me I never can. I am sure a more <u>loving</u>, <u>affectionate</u>, <u>kind</u> being could not be found than is my husband."[92] She reflected back over their five years together, and over their courtship after she first met him in Middletown.

> The pure, deep, unwavering love you express for me and have ever manifested toward me, since first I saw you <u>is all reciprocated,</u> I am sure it is. My heart is full of the purest affection and fondness for you, and admiration too, and it knows no change save that of increase. How I thank my God for giving you to me, and how I thank you for ever loving me. Well do I remember the joy, yes, the <u>bliss</u> I felt when first I found that you loved me. I thought it hardly possible that my love for you was reciprocated. Darling many many times have you made me weep for you before I was your wife, and my heart has overflowed with gratitude a thousand times since for <u>so precious</u> so valuable a gift as <u>thou art to me</u>.

Ellen also shared with Benjamin a sort of spiritual self-assessment. After mentioning the question of what to do with the children during the approaching camp meeting, she wrote, "I want to be ready and willing to work for others. I feel an abiding trust and confidence in God and a resting of my all on Christ yet I have not that sensible comfort and presence of God which I have had. I will try this day to ask and look for a clearer witness that I am right. I believe God is willing to give it to me and also to show me the reason why I do not enjoy it. Pray for me."[93]

Ellen returned home on Friday, August 4.[94] While she probably benefited from the time of rest and reflection the water cure provided, her health problems continued. Much later Benjamin commented that his wife "was for many years under the care of different doctors," and though she "went to a celebrated Water Cure" she "grew no better, but rather worse. At the Bergen camp meeting, some twenty-five years ago, she was healed in answer to prayer. She has remained well ever since."[95] Since Benjamin was writing this in 1885, the time of Ellen's healing must have been in 1859 or perhaps 1860, about the time the Free Methodist Church was organized. Thus Ellen apparently continued in frail health during the Brockport and Albion years, and on through Benjamin's two trials and eventual expulsion from the ME Church.

In Brockport Benjamin again needed a horse for transportation. So while Ellen was away at Geneva he bought a three-year-old bay mare from Brother Stickney for eighty-five dollars. He paid twenty-five in cash and gave a note for the balance. He also bought a box-shaped buggy for seventy dollars, and began training the horse.

92. ELR (Geneva, N.Y.) to BTR, July 27-28, 1854. Ellen may have been feeling a twinge of guilt for having temporarily left Benjamin and the two little boys.

93. ELR (Geneva, N.Y.) to BTR, July 27-28, 1854.

94. BTRD, Aug. 4, 1854.

95. [B. T. Roberts], "To a Skeptic," *EC* 49, no. 3 (Mar. 1885): 91. Ellen also testified to this significant healing. See chapter 24.

Hitching the horse to the buggy for the first time, he noted: "She drove off as steady and nice as could be wished for."[96]

Starting the Bergen Camp Meeting

August 1854 was again camp meeting season. Roberts played a key role in organizing a camp meeting near the village of Bergen, eight miles south of Brockport. This was the origin of what would become in a few years the famous and controversial Bergen camp meeting. In June he and Brother Mix had gone "to see about a campground," and on July 27 he wrote to Rochester, ordering a quantity of tents.[97]

This first Bergen camp meeting began on Wednesday evening, August 9.[98] Many of the people, including Benjamin, Ellen, and Georgie, arrived during the day.[99] "There were four tents from Brockport besides the boarding tent," Roberts noted. "Over 30 tents put up the first day." More arrived later, and by Sunday there was a "large multitude."[100] People came in their carriages and buggies, or took the New York Central Railroad to Bergen and then rode by carriage to the campground, four miles away.[101]

Benjamin noted on Monday, "There are about 40 tents on the ground[,] all cloth. It is the largest Camp Meeting I have ever attended. The trees of the woods are large and dense and the appearance fine and imposing." The main problem — other than some rowdies who showed up on Friday and had to be arrested — was the dust. "We suffer from the dust," Roberts noted. "It is so dry that the leaves, being trod upon break up into fine dust."[102]

Nevertheless, it was a great camp, lasting nearly a week. "The Camp Meeting commenced in power," Benjamin wrote after the first full day. "Many of the people are strong and more backslidden."[103] The crowd included "some of the best Methodists in this region I ever met," Benjamin noted. "They keep the fire burning the year round whether the preacher enjoys religion or not."[104] Benjamin had written his father that "Dr. Redfield and Bro. Purdy and Bro. Gorham, one of the editors of the

96. BTRD, July 27–Aug. 1, 1854.

97. BTRD, June 19 and July 27, 1854.

98. BHR, *BTR*, p. 95.

99. BTRD, Aug. 9, 1854. Apparently Ellen left eight-month-old Benson with Mary or one of the Brockport sisters while she and Benjamin were away. The previous Sunday, Aug. 6, Benjamin went out to the campground to preach; apparently an afternoon rally had been planned as a sort of kickoff and advertisement for the camp meeting. He notes, "In the afternoon I went up to the camp ground to preach but the rain had dispersed the congregation. We had however a good meeting in the School house" (BTRD, Aug. 6, 1854).

100. BTRD, Aug. 9 and 13, 1854.

101. BTR to TR, July 22, 1854; cf. BHR, *BTR*, p. 96.

102. BTRD, Aug. 11, 14, and 15, 1854.

103. BTRD, Aug. 10, 1854.

104. BTR to TR, Aug. 17, 1854.

'Guide to Holiness,'" all "Champions for the old paths," were expected.[105] But of these preachers it appears that only Fay Purdy actually attended.[106]

There were four sermons on Sunday, beginning with John Wallace and Roberts in the morning. Benjamin preached at 10:00 from Ezekiel 33:11, "Say unto them, As I live, saith the Lord God, I have no pleasure in the death of the wicked; but that the wicked turn from his way and live: turn ye, turn ye from your evil ways; for why will ye die, O house of Israel?" Asa Abell preached at 2:00 and Sheldon Baker, the pastor at Kendall, at 4:00 P.M.[107]

"The meeting increases in interest," Roberts noted on Tuesday, the last full day. "A great multitude" gathered for the closing service that evening at which Daniel B. Lawton, preacher at West Barre in the Niagara District, "preached with power." The next morning all packed up their tents and prepared to head home. "Camp meeting broke up with shaking hands and parting words. It was very affecting. Some wept and some shouted."[108] Overall, Benjamin was pleased with the meeting. "There were a goodly number of conversions, but the greatest work was in the church," he reported to his father. "Formalists were aroused, backsliders reclaimed and believers sanctified. O, I wish you could have been there."[109]

Benjamin, Ellen, and Georgie were back home in Brockport by early afternoon. On Saturday Benjamin took the train to Rochester "to settle for the tents."[110]

When they returned from the Bergen camp, Benjamin and Ellen found that little Benson was not well. "Bensie has been running down for two weeks with diarrhea," Benjamin noted. "He has grown very poor. We can check it for a little time but it comes on again bad as ever. He cries a great deal." He eventually recovered, though Benjamin noted again in November, "Bensie is quite unwell."[111]

During the three weeks between the Bergen camp meeting and the beginning of annual conference, Benjamin checked possible sites for a permanent location for future camps. He bid unsuccessfully on one piece of ground, and with Brother

105. BTR to TR, July 22, 1854. Benjamin urged his parents to attend the camp and arranged a tent for them, and was disappointed that they did not come. BHR, *BTR*, p. 96.

106. Roberts does not mention Redfield or Gorham in his diary account of the revival. Barlow W. Gorham, originally from Connecticut, was a preacher in the Wyoming Conference (comprising parts of New York and Pennsylvania), and did participate in later Bergen camp meetings (Hogue, *HFMC*, 1:127). He had been converted in a camp meeting (1832), and this same year (1854) he published *The Camp Meeting Manual* (Boston, 1854) in which he argued that Methodists were "silently and gradually" moving away from camp meetings (p. vii, cited in D. Gregory Van Dussen, "The Bergen Camp Meeting in the American Holiness Movement," *Methodist History* 21, no. 2 [Jan. 1983]: 71). An early supporter of Phoebe Palmer, he became known as an evangelist, singer, and songwriter, and coedited the *Guide to Holiness* from 1854 to 1863. See "Gorham, B. W.," in Kostlevy, pp. 117-18.

107. BTRD, Aug. 13, 1854. Presumably the "S. Baker" in Roberts's diary refers to Sheldon Baker, the only Baker in the Genesee District, though there were several Bakers in the conference.

108. BTRD, Aug. 15-16, 1854.

109. BTR to TR, Aug. 17, 1854.

110. BTRD, Aug. 19, 1854. Since Roberts had to wait until 2:40 for the train back to Brockport, he "[w]ent down below the falls and bathed in the Genesee river."

111. BTRD, Aug. 23 and Nov. 21, 1854.

Andross looked at another. One site Roberts examined was a twenty-acre property near Bergen.[112] No purchase was made at this time, however; it was not until May 1856 that twenty-five acres of heavily forested land were bought as a campground.[113] Still, the history of the Bergen camp meeting and the later controversy over the grounds — "the story in microcosm of the 'Genesee conflict' and the even wider confrontation between those who wanted rigorously to maintain the old Methodist ways"[114] — begins here, as early as 1854. The reason this annual camp meeting developed at Bergen, rather than somewhere else, was that Roberts was appointed in 1853-54 to nearby Brockport, largely as the result of the revival controversy at Niagara Street the previous conference year.

End of the Conference Year

As the 1854 annual conference approached, Roberts wrapped up the church finances for the year and also conducted a number of baptisms. "The Church is gaining in spirituality and power," he noted on August 24. At the official meeting on Friday, September 1, the church voted to ask for Roberts's return and also petitioned (probably at Roberts's suggestion) that John Wallace be appointed presiding elder of the district. The next day Roberts noted, "The Conf. year is closing up well. Out of 66 who have joined on probation during the year we have had to drop but ten."[115] Conference records show that Roberts reported a total membership of 161 (including 27 probationers and 2 local preachers) — nearly a 50 percent increase over the previous year's total of 108. Numerically speaking, this was Roberts's most successful year so far. He expected to be reappointed to Brockport; he wrote his father, "I think it probable that we shall return here another year. The people desire it and it may be best."[116]

His report in hand, Roberts set out on Monday, September 4, to attend the Genesee Conference annual sessions at Warsaw, New York.[117]

112. BTRD, Aug. 24 and 31, 1854; also, on Aug. 25: "We have been promised the refusal of 20 acres for a camp ground, in Bergen 8 miles south of Brockport." It is not clear whether this is the same property, owned by Joseph Staples, that Roberts and Andross looked at on Aug. 31, though it seems likely that it was.

113. *WAS*, p. 313.

114. Van Dussen, "Bergen Camp Meeting," p. 77.

115. BTRD, Aug. 24, Sept. 1 and 2, 1854. Roberts noted on Sunday, Sept. 3, "A pleasant day. Preached in the morning on 'The Church.' In the afternoon [on] Methodism. Baptized 4 adults and 2 children of Bro. Andross. Recvd 8 in full connexion."

116. BTR to TR, Aug. 17, 1854.

117. BTRD, Sept. 4, 1854.

1854 Annual Conference

The 1854 annual conference met September 6-14 in Warsaw under the leadership of Bishop Edmund Janes. Conable notes that many of the preachers came by rail as the new Attica and Hornellsville Railroad passed near Warsaw. Roberts arrived on the morning of the fifth to help supervise ministerial candidates' examinations, as he had done a year earlier.[118]

Roberts boarded with local families during the conference, as did most of the preachers. The Tuesday night before sessions began he and another preacher went "up on the hill" and stayed overnight at "Bro. Smallwoods" — probably Michael Smallwood, who likely was the father of Benjamin's brother-in-law William Smallwood.[119] It is not clear where he stayed during the conference itself, though on Monday night, the eleventh, he accompanied William Kendall to Kendall's parents' home in Covington, about twelve miles from Warsaw, and spent the night there. While there Benjamin borrowed $200 from Kendall's father for a two-year period.[120]

Where the preachers boarded during conference had in fact become an issue. Benjamin noted on September 12 that Isaac C. Kingsley, the presiding elder in the Olean District (where conference was to be held the next year), "guaranteed that none should be obliged to go out of the village" for lodging. Roberts felt that secret society influence was at work in assigning lodging at Warsaw. "There is an evident leaning to Odd Fellowship. Out of 30 [preachers] sent out of the village to board there is but a single O.F." — implying that preachers who were Odd Fellows were given preferential treatment and housed in the village, probably in the homes of other Odd Fellows.[121] It is uncertain how Roberts got this information, but clearly he was very sensitive to the issue, partly as a matter of justice, and had checked into it. He himself stayed in Warsaw.

Under Bishop Janes's "prompt and energetic" leadership, the conference conducted its usual business.[122] Most of the committees were constituted by choosing one preacher from each of the five districts. Samuel K. J. Chesbrough, later a prominent defender of Roberts, was elected a trustee of Genesee Wesleyan Seminary. Conable notes that the average salary of appointed pastors in the conference during

118. Conable, p. 612.

119. Michael Smallwood was "an Englishman [living] on East Hill" in Warsaw. His home was a hiding place for slaves in the Underground Railroad. See Helene C. Phelan, *And Why Not Every Man? An Account of Slavery, the Underground Railroad, and the Road to Freedom in New York's Southern Tier* (Almond, N.Y.: Helene C. Phelan, 1987), p. 80. Born in Yorkshire, England, Smallwood (1808-70) was probably the father of William Smallwood, Florilla Roberts's husband.

120. BTRD, Sept. 11 and 12, 1854.

121. BTRD, Sept. 11 and 12, 1854. Similarly Benjamin wrote his father after the conference, "Out of thirty preachers who were stationed to board out from one to four miles from the town there was but a single Odd-Fellow, and he was not known as such. I boarded in the village." BTR to TR, Sept. 18, 1854. Quoted in BHR, *BTR*, pp. 98-99; cf. Zahniser, p. 73.

122. Conable, p. 611.

the year (not including housing) was about $420.[123] Thus Roberts's salary of $500 was somewhat above average.

Thomas Carlton was present and gave his report as book agent. He also delivered a package to Benjamin from the Lanes — "a shawl and one or two other small articles," Benjamin reported to Ellen.[124]

The Sunday during annual conference was always a high day of worship and preaching, with large crowds. On Sunday afternoon, September 10, Roberts heard his former Wesleyan University classmate Dr. Daniel Steele at 1:30 and Dr. John Price Durbin at 2:30. He liked Steele's sermon, and this time was more impressed with Dr. Durbin: "He preached with more unction and power than at any time before when I have heard him."[125]

When the 1854-55 appointments were given out, Roberts was returned to Brockport for a second year, as he expected. Kendall was stationed nearby at Albion, where he had a very successful year. Wallace was also appointed to the district but as preacher at Kendall, not as presiding elder, as Roberts had hoped.[126] Instead Eleazar Thomas, Roberts's former presiding elder in both the Rushford and Buffalo Districts, was named presiding elder. He was a good man, but Roberts felt he was too compromising; Benjamin was losing confidence in him.[127] Benjamin wrote somewhat sarcastically to Ellen during the conference, "If we cannot have a thorough going Methodist let them send us who they please, Parsons, or Fuller or any good Mason or Odd Fellow."[128]

In discussing the appointments, Conable commented on the Genesee District, which included Brockport and to which he himself was appointed this year, after serving in the Niagara District.[129] He writes: "In 1854 the Genesee District was strongly manned," and lists the appointments, including Roberts. He then comments on this "strong" group of preachers: "Besides the constitutional and natural peculiarities of these men, there were beginning to be more and more manifest among them differences as to their tastes, prejudices, and preferences concerning questions of Church polity and Conference administration; touching methods of conducting revival meetings, and many matters of expediency and propriety in promoting the cause of Christian holiness: all claiming to be Methodists, to be sure."

Conable no doubt made this comment in light of later conflict and controversy,

---

123. Conable, pp. 612, 614.

124. BTR to ELR, Sept. 9, 1854, quoted in Zahniser, p. 72.

125. BTR to ELR, Sept. 11, 1854, quoted in Zahniser, p. 72.

126. *Minutes*, Genesee Conference, 1854.

127. Zahniser, pp. 72-73.

128. BTR to ELR, Sept. 9, 1854, quoted in Zahniser, p. 72.

129. After serving a year at Somerset, in the Niagara District, Conable was in 1854 appointed to Clarkson in the Genesee District and served there one year. *Minutes*, Genesee Conference, 1852-55. Being in the same district and serving a church only about two miles from Brockport, Conable would have known Roberts personally. He was nine years older than Roberts (Ray Allen, *A Century of the Genesee Annual Conference of the Methodist Episcopal Church, 1810-1910* [Rochester, N.Y.: By the Author, 1911], p. 78).

though his reference to "questions of Church polity and Conference administration" and "methods of conducting revival meetings" reflects also issues that Roberts had raised in his articles and that were being discussed in the *Northern Christian Advocate*. Conable adds, "J. M'Creery was then stationed at Yates, in the Niagara District, and Loren Stiles at Lockport" (also in the Niagara District)[130] — the point being that the next year both McCreery and Stiles, largely sympathetic to Roberts, were appointed to the Genesee District and were thus associated together as growing "differences" roiled the district and the conference.

Roberts gave his own evaluation of the conference and the 1854-55 appointments in a letter to his father after returning home. "'Safe men' happen to be all the rage just now. The great question seems to be not what is right but what is 'expedient.' Odd-Fellowship and worldly policy bore sway," he wrote. "You could see it in everything."[131]

---

130. Conable, p. 618.
131. BTR to TR, Sept. 18, 1854, quoted in BHR, *BTR*, p. 98; cf. Zahniser, p. 73.

The Bergen Camp Meeting

"I must live more as in the presence of God and do nothing at any time inconsistent with my calling."

B. T. Roberts, 1855[1]

"I will take [the power to reach people for Christ] with suffering if I can have it in no other way."

Ellen Roberts[2]

Benjamin and Ellen began their second year at Brockport with the memory of the first Bergen camp meeting fresh in their minds. Issues surrounding the camp meeting, and the controversy it eventually engendered, marked their continuing ministry in Brockport. The camp meeting controversy was part of the complex of issues that led to the formation of a new denomination. It was during this year that charges of "Nazaritism" first surfaced — the beginning of a three-year struggle and controversy that would finally lead to the expulsion of Roberts, McCreery, and others from the Methodist Episcopal Church.

Second Year at Brockport

The 1854 annual conference adjourned at midmorning on Thursday, September 14, and Benjamin returned to his church and family in Brockport to begin his second year.

1. BTRD, July 28, 1855.
2. Ellen L. Roberts, "Religious Experience," *EC* 2, no. 9 (Sept. 1861): 284.

Roberts immediately jumped back into his pastoral work, visiting, studying, and preaching. He sold his "horse and buggy and cutter to Bro. Selleck" for $200.[3] He may have needed the money in part to settle the balance on the annual payment on his Buffalo house.[4]

Benjamin noted in his diary on September 22, "Met in the eve. with the choir."[5] This is the only time in his diary that he says anything about a choir in the Brockport church. However, in writing later about William Kendall's ministry at Brockport the following year (1855-56), he mentioned Brockport's "popular choir" and that they "insisted on having their own leader, tunes, and instrumental accompaniments." When Kendall came, he opposed this. "He had been accustomed to congregational singing, and in his efforts to introduce it here, he was violently opposed" by the choir. Kendall eventually got rid of the choir, however, "giving the people of God the enjoyment of their own rights, in singing his praises 'in the great congregation.'"[6] Apparently Roberts tolerated the choir while at Brockport, or at least was unsuccessful in ending it.

As the conference year began, Ellen was about five months pregnant. Benjamin noted on November 8 that he "[w]ent down to Clarkson and got Mary to work for us" — either Ellen's niece, Mary Swezey, or a different Mary.[7] Again Benjamin was concerned with providing help for Ellen in managing the household.

About this time Benjamin and Ellen considered moving to a different house, though it is not clear why. Benjamin noted on October 20, "Went to Bro. Peake's to see about moving. The owners of the house are unwilling that we should move."[8] So they continued living in the parsonage.

Slavery still troubled Roberts. It wasn't a remote issue. Shortly after conference "a negro man from Canada" took tea with Benjamin and Ellen, and a few weeks later Benjamin noted, "A dead colored child about a year old and a living one about 7 or 8 were put off the emigrant train a few rods from the station [in Brockport]. The live child stood shivering over the dead one." Such incidents brought the human face of slavery home to Benjamin. He studied and spoke on the issue, giving a lecture on slavery on Sunday evening, October 1.[9] He spoke again on slavery at Sweden on October 11 and in the Presbyterian church in North Bergen on Tuesday evening, Octo-

---

3. BTRD, Sept. 22, 1854.

4. The $200 from this deal, plus the $200 borrowed from Brother Kendall ten days earlier, could have constituted the $400 annual payment on the house in Buffalo — but he had paid $128 on the house in April, as already noted. He may have been late in paying the full amount, as the anniversary of the house purchase was in April, and as noted, he also had other debts.

5. BTRD, Sept. 22, 1854.

6. "Rev. Wm. C. Kendall, A.M. — Labors," EC 2, no. 11 (Nov. 1861): 335.

7. BTRD, Nov. 8, 1854.

8. BTRD, Oct. 20, 1854. Though the Brockport parsonage was the "best one" the Robertses had lived in to date, the summer had been extremely hot and the house had no shade trees, and it was located next to the church building. These or other factors may have played a part in their thinking about moving.

9. BTRD, Sept. 16 and Oct. 1 and 13, 1854; cf. Sept. 28, 1854. Presumably the lecture was given in the Brockport Methodist Episcopal Church building, but Roberts doesn't say.

ber 31. "Audience rather small, but had a very good time," he noted after the October 31 meeting.[10] Benjamin apparently considered it his duty to raise consciousness about the slavery issue whenever and wherever he could.

The fall political campaign was heating up, and Roberts noted that five candidates were running for governor. "The Know Nothings are spreading all over the country."[11] Later he noted on election day, November 7, that "The Know Nothings confound the Politicians."[12] The anti-Catholic, anti-immigrant American Party, popularly called the Know-Nothings because of their secret meetings and claim to "know nothing" about the party, was active particularly in the 1854 state elections.[13] The Know-Nothings won the 1854 election in Massachusetts and polled large numbers in New York and Pennsylvania, but soon split over slavery and declined rapidly.[14]

Like many in western New York, Roberts initially was attracted to the Know-Nothing cause, seeing it as potentially a potent force against slavery. He later admitted that he briefly joined with the Know-Nothings. When in 1858 he was charged with hypocrisy for "appear[ing] before the public as a champion against secret societies" while at the same time being a Know-Nothing, Roberts said that though he had briefly been a member of the secret organization, he left when he saw the direction it was headed and that he could not influence it toward the defense of human freedom.[15] Though it

---

10. BTRD, Oct. 11 and 31, 1854.

11. BTRD, Oct. 14, 1854.

12. BTRD, Nov. 7, 1854.

13. In his biography of William Lloyd Garrison, Mayer writes: "Two strong new party coalitions developed in the aftermath of the Missouri Compromise repeal to compete for the loyalties of disaffected Democrats and take the place left by the impotent and scattered Whigs. One grouping — the explicitly anti-Nebraska free-soil coalition — gradually took on the name 'Republican' as an indication of its commitment to free institutions and focus upon the containment of slavery. The other grouping — emerging from clandestine social lodges opposed to the rising tide of immigration and Catholicism — took on the name 'American' as symbolic of its appeal to traditional Unionist patriotism. It focused upon a grab bag of popular issues, especially nativist protective measures and reform of the political machinery that might unite the old Whig elite and anti-Irish Democratic mechanics against an outside enemy. . . . The challenge for the Americans (or the 'Know-Nothings,' as they were nicknamed for their once-secret character) would be to build a national following without becoming divided over the slavery question." Mayer adds, "Garrison and the abolitionists wasted little time on the Know-Nothings, even though the party scored its most stunning triumph in a fusion effort that secured it the Massachusetts governorship and control of the state legislature in 1854-55. No one could have predicted that a party 'burrowing in secret like a mole in the dark' and relying upon the invidious object of 'proscribing men on account of their birth and peculiar religious faiths' could have so sudden and complete a success, Garrison wrote. Such a whirlwind would prove no more than a 'temporary excitement,' he was confident, but to the degree that it eroded old party discipline and lured politicians and votes out of their accustomed paths, the populist insurgency would be a work of 'beneficent destruction'" (Henry Mayer, *All on Fire: William Lloyd Garrison and the Abolition of Slavery* [New York: St. Martin's Press, 1998], pp. 450-51). Garrison's analysis proved to be quite accurate.

14. As Holt notes, the rise of the Know-Nothings and of the Republican Party hastened the demise of the old Whig Party. Michael F. Holt, *The Rise and Fall of the American Whig Party: Jacksonian Politics and the Onset of the Civil War* (New York: Oxford University Press, 1999), p. 805.

15. Zahniser, pp. 97-98.

is not certain exactly when Roberts had this brush with Know-Nothingism, it most likely was at this time, during the fall 1854 political campaign, when the movement had its broadest popular appeal.[16]

Like many Protestants of the time, Roberts probably shared something of the Know-Nothings' anti-Catholicism, but for him slavery was a much bigger issue. In October Roberts was reading Alessandro Gavazzi's *Life and Lectures,* which included such lectures as "The Blindness of Popery" and "The Present War of Popery against Protestantism."[17] Gavazzi "is fearless in his denunciation of popery," Benjamin noted.[18] But he seems to have been more impressed with the author's fearlessness in addressing the issue than with the issue itself, though he probably sympathized with the author's positions.

The rise of the Know-Nothings was aggravated by economic conditions and competition for jobs. Michael Holt notes, "the last six months of 1854 and the first five months of 1855 witnessed a sharp economic recession that aggravated tensions between native-born and foreign workers."[19] Roberts took note of the economic conditions, which in December were aggravated by heavy snows. He noted on December 7, "The storm continues. What will become of the poor? Flour is $11.00 per. bbl.[,] corn 7/1 pr. bushel. Wood $3.00 per cord, potatoes 6/- pr. bushel. They have put down wages of laborers on the R.R. to 6/- pr. day."[20]

Meanwhile Roberts continued visiting his members and prayed for them and their families. One of his members, Sister Buckley, had an unconverted husband — "a man of talent but of depraved habits," Benjamin noted; "a generous soul, needs greatly to be converted." "Must labor for his conversion," he noted after one visit in the home.[21]

Benjamin had occasionally preached at Holley, a village five miles west of Brockport that had no Methodist church. On Sunday evening, October 8, he preached at the Holley Presbyterian Church. Two weeks later he again preached on a Sunday evening in Holley and noted: "Propose to hold a protracted meeting there." He began the revival effort on Tuesday of that week, apparently in the Presbyterian church. Ellen accompanied him. Benjamin preached the first night from Habakkuk 3:2, "O LORD, revive thy work in the midst of the years, in the midst of the years make known; in wrath remember mercy."[22]

16. This is the only reference I have found to the Know-Nothings in Roberts's diary. Roberts may well have voted for Know-Nothing candidates in 1854.

17. Alessandro Gavazzi, *Father Gavazzi's Lectures in New York, . . . also, the Life of Father Gavazzi, Corrected and Authorized by Himself* (New York: De Witt and Davenport, 1853).

18. BTRD, Oct. 18, 1854.

19. Holt, *Rise and Fall,* p. 805.

20. BTRD, Dec. 7, 1854. Benson Roberts translates this entry, "flour is eleven dollars a barrel, corn eighty-seven cents a bushel; they have put down the wages of laborers on the railroad to seventy-five cents a day." BHR, *BTR,* p. 100. Benjamin apparently uses both dollar and British pound designations; Benson puts all the prices in dollars.

21. BTRD, Oct. 6 and 3, 1854.

22. BTRD, Oct. 8, 22, and 24, 1854.

The protracted meeting in Holley continued for several weeks. Benjamin held meetings afternoons and evenings and called in the mornings, Benson Roberts notes. But he did not preach at Holley every night, nor was he there continuously, as he had to attend to his church and family in Brockport. Other preachers assisted, including William Kendall, Eleazar Thomas, and Mr. Copeland, the Presbyterian preacher.[23]

The Holley effort was not an outstanding success, but there was some fruit. Elizabeth Mallory and a Miss Johnson were converted, among others. Friday evening, November 3, was "a meeting of great interest" with "several forward." In the Sunday evening service a young woman started forward to the altar but "lost her strength and fell" (was slain in the Spirit). "This seemed to deter others from coming forward," Benjamin thought.[24]

The meeting at the Holley Presbyterian Church continued until winter set in. Friday evening, November 10, Benjamin observed, "The meeting moves on slowly. The Churches are twice dead. The doctrine of 'once in grace always so' is having its legitimate effect. Preached in the evening from <u>Strive</u> to enter in at the strait gate." Several days of snow the first week in December made it impractical to continue the special meetings. Roberts noted on Wednesday, December 6, "It has snowed and blowed since Sunday. The snow is on a level about eighteen inches deep. We have not in years had such a snow storm. 3 locomotives came along drawing one train."[25]

At Brockport Benjamin ended 1854 with a watch-night service, as usual. "Had a very good meeting last evening but I began it too soon," he observed the next day.[26]

A Daughter Is Born

As 1855 began, Ellen Roberts was anticipating the birth of her fourth child. Though William had died in infancy three and a half years earlier, Georgie was now almost three and Benson was fifteen months old.

For the first and only time, a girl was born into the Roberts family. Ellen gave birth to Sarah Georgiana in the Brockport parsonage on January 16, 1855.[27] She was named, no doubt, for Lydia Lane's daughter Sarah who had died in 1851, and for her uncle, George Lane. Benjamin noted in his diary, "Mrs. R was taken sick last night and this morning at about six gave birth to a fine little girl. We are very thankful for a daughter." He went over to Holley and got Sister Wright to come and care for Ellen.[28]

With three small children to care for, Ellen now had her hands full, and she continued in somewhat frail health. In early May Benjamin commented, "[Ellen's]

23. BHR, *BTR*, p. 99; BTRD, Oct. 30, Nov. 6 and 8, 1854.
24. BTRD, Nov. 3, 5, 8, and 9, 1854.
25. BTRD, Nov. 10 and Dec. 6, 1854.
26. BTRD, Jan. 1, 1855.
27. Smail, p. 12; BHR, *BTR*, p. 100; Carpenter, p. 46.
28. BTRD, Jan. 16, 1855.

health is poor. She is suffering from general debility of the whole system." Later in the month, on his return from Caryville, he noted that Ellen had "suffered much . . . from Neuralgia" while he was away.[29]

Roberts's Studies and Writing

Benjamin did a considerable amount of reading and writing during the cold winter days of early 1855. He spent part of January 2 "reading and writing," and again on January 4, "Wrote some, and read a little." On April 13 he "Wrote most of the day."[30]

Roberts was concerned with his own intellectual and spiritual development as well as the welfare of the church and issues that were affecting society. "What was for public good interested his efforts, whether it was lecturing against slavery or spiritualism, or working for the cause of temperance," his son observed.[31]

On New Year's Day Benjamin began reading Lydia Maria Child's biography of Isaac Hopper, *Isaac T. Hopper: A True Life*, which had first been published in 1853.[32] Hopper (1771-1852) was a noted Quaker abolitionist whose home in New York City was a refuge for fugitive slaves and a way station on the Underground Railroad.[33] The book was primarily a compilation of the stories of fugitive slaves that Hopper had published in newspapers under the title "Tales of Oppression." Roberts finished the book two and a half weeks later. He was impressed by Hopper: "His was a life abounding in good works. He was the friend of the oppressed."[34]

Roberts's reading during this period included also some of Jonathan Edwards's *Works* and a history of Turkey by Goodrich.[35] In April he was reading Andrew Jackson Davis's *Principles of Nature, Her Divine Revelations, and a Voice to Mankind,* and later prepared a lecture on Spiritualism.[36] Davis, the "Poughkeepsie Seer," was at the time becoming a leading figure in American Spiritualism. In 1845, at age nineteen, Davis gave over 150 lectures in New York City in a trance state. He later published his visions, blending together science, mysticism, and Scripture. He pictured a multisphered world and "described a progression of higher and higher Harmony, which any soul would follow as it left earth and experienced each sphere in turn.

29. BTRD, May 4 and 21, 1855.

30. BTRD, Jan. 2 and 4, Apr. 13, 1855.

31. BHR, *BTR*, p. 100.

32. L. Maria Child (author of "Over the River and through the Woods"), *Isaac T. Hopper: A True Life* (Boston: John P. Jewett and Co., 1854; 1st ed. 1853).

33. Edwin G. Burrows and Mike Wallace, *Gotham: A History of New York City to 1898* (New York: Oxford University Press, 1999), p. 561.

34. BTRD, Jan. 19, 1855.

35. BTRD, Jan. 12 and 31, 1855. See Charles Augustus Goodrich, *The Universal Traveller: Designed to Introduce Readers at Home to an Acquaintance with the Arts, Customs, and Manners of the Principal Modern Nations of the Globe* (Hartford: H. E. Robins and Co., 1849).

36. BTRD, Apr. 4, 1855. See Andrew Jackson Davis (1826-1910), *Principles of Nature, Her Divine Revelations, and a Voice to Mankind* (New York, 1847).

Thus Davis promised ultimate happiness for all, and did so within a system of belief expressed in a vocabulary consonant in form with the laws of science and progress." But his system "reduced the Bible to a mythological text, Jesus to a great human reformer, and divine revelation (aside from his own) to a nullity," notes Robert Abzug.[37]

Roberts wasn't impressed with Davis's visions. "It is astonishing that such pretensions will be listened to by any sane person," he concluded. He gave a lecture on Spiritualism to "a very large audience" at Albion on Sunday evening, July 29, after the evening service at Brockport. On August 6 he prepared his lecture for publication; "Dr. Briggs of Albion wishes to publish it." In April he had written and delivered a lecture on the related topic of "spirit rapping," and on August 7 he apparently prepared this lecture also for publication.[38]

For Roberts, Spiritualism wasn't mere curiosity; it was a pastoral concern. In May he heard that one of his flock, Sister Latta, was dabbling with it. He called on her but found that "she has renounced spiritualism or rather says she has not believed in it though she has attended the circles."[39]

As usual, Roberts's reading during this period was wide-ranging. He read newspapers, Methodist publications, and books on various topics.[40] In April he was reading a book by Lardner, and in July he notes, "Read in Wilkes Exploring Expedition."[41]

On May 22 Benjamin set off on a ten-day trip to New York City, Brooklyn, and Philadelphia. The reason for the trip is not clear, but it gave him a chance to visit the Methodist Book Room and, no doubt, acquire some new publications. A couple of days after his visit to the Book Room he was reading the recently published *Sketches of Western Methodism* by James Finley, whose autobiography he had read earlier.[42]

Benjamin also visited the Lanes in Mount Holly on this trip. He attended a Methodist preachers meeting in Philadelphia and visited there the grave of

37. Robert H. Abzug, *Passionate Liberator: Theodore Dwight Weld and the Dilemma of Reform* (New York: Oxford University Press, 1980), pp. 249-50.

38. BTRD, Apr. 4 and 29; July 29; Aug. 6 and 7, 1855. It appears the lecture on "spirit rapping" was a different one from the one on Spiritualism. (Note Lydia Lane's reference to "spirit rapping" earlier.) Whether these lectures were in fact published or not is uncertain.

39. BTRD, May 3, 1855.

40. See, for example, BTRD, Feb. 17, Apr. 13, May 25, June 28, 1855.

41. BTRD, Apr. 17, May 8, July 16, 18, 1855. Roberts doesn't further identify Lardner or the particular book he was reading. The Reverend Dionysius Lardner published a number of books on popular topics during this period. Roberts may well have been reading his *Railway Economy: A Treatise on the New Art of Transport* (first published in New York in 1850), or possibly the same author's much-reprinted *Popular Lectures on Science and Art*, 14th ed. (New York: Greeley and McElrath, 1852). Douglas Cullum suggests that another possibility is *The Works of Nathaniel Lardner*, 10 vols. (London: W. Ball, 1838). Douglas Russell Cullum, "Gospel Simplicity: Rhythms of Faith and Life among Free Methodists in Victorian America" (Ph.D. diss., Drew University, 2002), p. 379.

42. BTRD, May 22–June 1, 1855. Cf. James B. Finley, *Sketches of Western Methodism: Biographical, Historical, and Miscellaneous, Illustrative of Pioneer Life*, ed. W. P. Strickland (Cincinnati: Methodist Book Concern, 1854). The book includes a chapter on the Western Methodist Book Concern in Cincinnati.

Benjamin Franklin. He did some sightseeing in New York, including a visit to the remarkable Crystal Palace, which had been built for the 1853 New York World's Fair.
Benjamin notes in his diary that he "Called at Dr. Palmer's" in New York — presumably Walter and Phoebe Palmer's home — but doesn't elaborate.[43]

Opposing the Circus

Concern for the public good, in Roberts's mind, included the issue of public enter-
tainments, as well as hot topics like slavery and Spiritualism. He continued to be
strongly opposed to circuses.[44] On May 13, 1855, the Sunday School Association of
the Brockport ME Church, apparently under Benjamin's leadership, appointed a
committee "to request that no circus be permitted in the village." The next morning
Roberts went to see the village trustees, urging them not to license any circuses. They
promised not to, "provided the Justices would not." So a few days later he called on
the justices at nearby Clarkson. "Succeeded well with most," he reported.[45]

Several weeks later, however, the Brockport trustees allowed Dan Rice's circus to
perform in the village. Roberts considered this a violation of the trustees' word. On
Thursday, July 5, he noted, "The Trustees of the village after promising not to license
any Circus provided the Justices would not, have suffered Dan Rice to come in and
exhibit to day. So we are to have the youth corrupted by this pest."[46] Rice, then about
thirty-two (the same age as Roberts), was born in New York City as Daniel McLaren.
He was just becoming famous as a clown, comedian, and circus entrepreneur. Rice
popularized the Uncle Sam costume and did other characterizations. With his trick
horse, Excelsior, and homespun commentary on current events, Rice entertained
crowds in many small towns and cities.

Rice had already achieved some notoriety in the Brockport area. In 1850 he had
been arrested and jailed briefly in Rochester. He wrote a song about the incident that
became a hit and made Rochester's "Blue Eagle Jail" (as Rice called it) nationally famous.[47] Roberts may not have known, however, of Rice's family background. He was
actually the grandson of a Methodist preacher from the New York City area by the
name of Crum.[48]

---

43. BTRD, May 23-31, 1855. Roberts stayed with a Brother McCrossan in Brooklyn, and on Tuesday, May 29, "Married Thomas Watson and Christina [McCrossan?]." This marriage was possibly the
main reason for Roberts's trip to New York.

44. See the discussion in chapter 13.

45. BTRD, May 13, 14, 17, and July 5, 1855.

46. BTRD, July 5, 1855.

47. Howard C. Hosmer, *Monroe County (1821-1971): The Sesqui-Centennial Account of the History
of Monroe County, New York* (Rochester, N.Y.: Rochester Museum and Science Center, 1971), p. 84;
John C. Kunzog, *The One-Horse Show: The Life and Times of Dan Rice, Circus Jester and Philanthropist*
(Jamestown, N.Y.: John C. Kunzog, 1962), pp. 71-78. Cf. David Carlyon, *Dan Rice: The Most Famous
Man You've Never Heard Of* (New York: Public Affairs, 2001).

48. Kunzog, *One-Horse Show*, p. 1. The preacher's daughter, Elizabeth Crum, eloped with Daniel

Prompted by the Rice incident, Benjamin obtained on Saturday, July 7, "a writing from the Clarkson Justices to the effect that they would license no more Circuses."[49]

Roberts's efforts proved ineffective, however. Just the next week he noted, "There has been one Circus in the place and is to be another."[50] And a couple of weeks later he recorded, "Two young girls about 12 years of age, one a daughter of Bro. H. Peck were enticed away by one of the Circus Co. (Spalding & Rogers) and went to Rochester to day, unknown to their parents. The Father of one of them followed and brought them back."[51]

Why did Roberts oppose circuses and traveling entertainers? In his day circuses were not the family-oriented shows they later became. Circuses in America began in the 1820s, when Benjamin was a young lad. As Jack Larkin notes, during this period "circus audiences were not . . . gatherings of families with excited children in tow, but adult and primarily male. The shows were clearly part of a masculine world whose boundaries were defined by liquor and the possibility of violence." Church leaders often opposed them as a menace to public morals. P. T. Barnum in the late 1830s remarked on opposition from preachers and churches. Nevertheless, such shows continued to grow in popularity, satisfying the public appetite for entertainment that in the next century would be met by radio, movies, and television. As Larkin observes, circuses and "traveling exhibitions" of all kinds "brought brief glimpses of the unfamiliar, the exotic, the grotesque into thousands of rural communities, often oddly and offhandedly expanding Americans' knowledge of the world beyond."[52]

Circuses, in effect, competed with churches for the public's attention. In this area Roberts was fighting a losing battle, but he continued to voice his convictions.

The 1855 Bergen Camp Meeting

At the same time that Roberts was working to ban circuses, he was getting ready for the second Bergen camp meeting. Monday afternoon, May 14, he went to the Methodist preachers meeting at Scottsville, south of Rochester, where an extended discussion was held about changing the date of camp meeting. "Concluded not to change

---

McLaren. She later gave birth to baby Daniel. Her father got the marriage annulled, and later Elizabeth remarried. Through his stepfather's influence young Daniel became adept at handling horses, which led eventually to his circus career. Daniel early began using the name Rice instead of McLaren (Kunzog, pp. 1-10; Carlyon, *Dan Rice*, pp. 11-12). See also Earl Chain May, *The Circus from Rome to Ringling* (New York: Dover Publications, 1963), pp. 59-67.

49. BTRD, July 7, 1855. Apparently the justices of the town of Clarkson had jurisdiction over Brockport, though Brockport was actually in the town of Sweden.

50. BTRD, July 9, 1855. Roberts adds, "Went to day to see Mr. Fellows [probably one of the village trustees] about keeping it out."

51. BTRD, July 23, 1855.

52. Jack Larkin, *The Reshaping of Everyday Life, 1790-1840* (New York: Harper and Row, 1989), pp. 284, 297, 209.

it," Roberts noted.[53] This referred to the camp meeting held at Bergen in June (the second annual Bergen camp meeting). This discussion at the district preachers meeting shows that the Bergen camp meeting was in fact the regular camp meeting of the Genesee District.[54] Camp meetings were generally held in each district under the supervision of the district's presiding elder. It is clear, however, that Roberts took the lead in organizing the 1855 camp. In early 1855 there had been a leadership change in the district. Eleazar Thomas, the presiding elder, was transferred to California, and Dr. Samuel Luckey, sixty-four and recently retired as editor of the *Christian Advocate and Journal* in New York City and now living in Rochester, was appointed in his place. Luckey had been the first principal of Genesee Wesleyan Seminary.[55] Coincidentally, he was also the uncle of Joseph McCreery, Jr.[56]

Luckey probably had some prior acquaintance with Roberts and would have known the Lanes while serving as editor and presiding elder in New York City. As presiding elder of the Genesee District, he relied some on Benjamin for leadership, at the end of March sending him to Sweden to conduct the quarterly meeting in his place.[57] A "man of more than ordinary power of intellect, . . . thoroughly acquainted with the history and economy of the church," according to Bishop Simpson, Samuel Luckey was much appreciated by Roberts.[58]

The 1854 Bergen camp meeting had been held in August; in 1855 the dates were June 13-20. On June 5 Benjamin went to Bergen and arranged to hold the gathering in woods owned by a Mrs. Reed.[59] The next morning he and two other men "worked hard" clearing out the undergrowth so the camp could be held.[60]

Benjamin attended the camp meeting from Wednesday evening, June 13, through its close the following Wednesday morning. It is not clear from his diary whether Ellen also attended, though she probably did; Benjamin noted the day before camp was to begin, "Laura came to stay through the Camp Meeting."[61] Probably Laura, whoever she was, either stayed with the two boys while Ellen and baby Sarah were at camp meeting or she accompanied the family to camp to assist with the children.

---

53. BTRD, May 14 and 15, 1855. Roberts traveled with F. W. Conable, then the preacher at nearby Clarkson, later the historian of the Genesee Conference.

54. This is confirmed by Conable, p. 620.

55. Conable, p. 616; *COM,* 553. Thomas served a number of years in California but in 1873 was killed by the Modoc Indians while serving on a government peace commission. Conable, p. 617; *COM,* p. 859.

56. *WAS,* pp. 138-39. McCreery's mother, Jane Luckey McCreery, apparently was the sister of Samuel Luckey. See genealogical records, Joseph McCreery, Jr., MMHC.

57. BTRD, Mar. 31, 1855.

58. *COM,* p. 553.

59. BTRD, June 5, 1855; BHR, *BTR,* p. 100. Van Dussen says the Bergen camp meeting met the first two years (1854 and 1855) in "Asa Abell's forest," but this may not be accurate. D. Gregory Van Dussen, "The Bergen Camp Meeting in the American Holiness Movement," *Methodist History* 21, no. 2 (Jan. 1983): 78.

60. BTRD, June 6, 1855.

61. BTRD, June 12, 1855.

The 1855 Bergen camp meeting, like the first one a year earlier, was a great success. Conable refers to it as "a large camp-meeting," with "thousands attending" on Sunday. Luckey told Roberts it was the best he had ever attended. "Bro. Abel says he never was at a better one," Roberts noted.[62]

Camp meeting was a busy time, with four or five sermons a day, different preachers taking turns. In addition to the district preachers, Seymour Coleman of the Troy Conference and B. W. Gorham of the Wyoming Conference, coeditor of Phoebe Palmer's *Guide to Holiness,* attended and preached. The Genesee District preachers had earlier voted to invite Coleman as a guest preacher.[63] Both Coleman and Gorham were known as strong advocates of holiness, and Coleman later served on the National Camp Meeting Committee that helped promote the holiness cause.[64]

"Father" Coleman (as he was called) preached four times during the camp meeting.[65] Gorham preached twice. Dr. Luckey was featured Saturday afternoon, and John Wallace started off on Sunday morning. Several of Roberts's colleagues in the district preached during the week of meetings, including McCreery, Kendall, Conable, and James Fuller. Roberts was to have preached at ten o'clock on Tuesday, the last day, but the services were rained out — though the campers managed to assemble in the tent in the evening to hear Father Coleman preach the closing sermon, despite the rain.[66]

Wallace was stationed this year at Kendall, about twelve miles north of Brockport, near Lake Ontario. He seems to have been something of a favorite of Roberts during this period. Together with Redfield, he had helped Roberts in the Niagara Street special meetings in January 1853, as noted earlier. It is not clear what Roberts's role was in arranging the preaching schedule at the Bergen camp meeting; no doubt he had a hand in it, at least. But it is noteworthy that Wallace was one of the preachers scheduled for Sunday morning. Conable says of Wallace,

> This man was a profound thinker and theologian, a man of great strength in the pulpit — logical, close, practical, powerful. He would flay a man alive, he would pound him into a pomace, he would crush him to atoms, and then he seemed to know how to gather up the bleeding, quivering mass, and present the poor victim of his power to be healed and restored. He was an unmerciful disciplinarian, one of those who, governing inflexibly by the letter of the old Discipline, would almost break up a society for a lace veil, or some little conformity to fashion, when many others, as true lovers of Methodism as himself would claim to be, would counsel

62. Conable, p. 620; BTRD, June 20, 1855.

63. Conable, p. 620.

64. On Coleman, see Hogue, *HFMC,* 1:90, 1:275-76. He is pictured with other members of the National Camp Meeting Committee in A. McLean and J. W. Eaton, eds., *Penuel; or, Face to Face with God* (New York: W. C. Palmer, 1869), opposite the title page, and a summary of his sermon at the 1867 Vineland, N.J., camp meeting is printed on pp. 30-35.

65. Conable says three times, but Roberts records four times in his diary.

66. BTRD, June 14-19, 1855; Conable, p. 620.

forbearance and gentleness of pastoral dealing. This man, professing "flaming purity," to use a phrase of his own, and a perfect "war horse" in the battle for holiness, to use a representation of him by one of his admirers, was of a character to make disciples of some particular temperaments and prejudices, and really was the leader in a "proposed" and attempted "reform" movement, which had its development and culmination in the Genesee Conference during this period.[67]

While this is a one-sided view, and Roberts would have disagreed, Conable's evaluation does give a sense of the situation in the Genesee Conference at this time.

The camp meeting "broke up in the usual form" on Wednesday morning, Roberts noted, "with a great deal of feeling." The next day Roberts had the tents hauled to Rochester, where he had rented them, and went there himself to pay for them.[68]

It appears that Roberts was the main initiator in the 1855 Bergen camp meeting, as he had been the previous year. Yet Conable, who reports a number of details about the camp, never mentions him. Conable does note that "The leading object of this camp-meeting was the promotion of the work of entire holiness in the Church."[69] He used the occasion of the Bergen camp meeting to assess the holiness emphasis of the time.

Conable writes, "It was a great meeting, closing with an address from the venerable presiding elder, a love-feast of striking testimonies, a procession and the parting hand, and the doxology and benediction." He then adds:

It was thought by some . . . that many came too near falling into the error of taking holiness "out of its proper connections;" that in their zeal for entire holiness they were almost impatient of hearing any thing on the subject of repentance, justification, regeneration, adoption, as if these things did not form the very basis of a complete Christian character; that they labored too exclusively to bring Church members into the right position, to the proportionate neglect of the great work of bringing unconverted sinners to Christ; and further, that some had fallen into the damaging mistake of thinking and speaking of some matters of experience, of obligation and duty, belonging to the life and character of all the children of God, as such; as if such things pertained only to the state of those who had received the "second blessing," who had advanced to the high state of entire sanctification; and it was also thought that some were urged to profess Christian perfection quite too early after their conversion. . . . On the other hand, it was thought that the work of God, in the conversion of sinners, the reclamation of back-sliders, and the sanctification of believers, being essentially one, could always be carried forward in harmony, according to the particular moral state of each and all the persons concerned. As was always the case, there were some who thought and said too little

---

67. Conable, pp. 625-26. Wallace was later expelled from the church on a morals charge. Reinhard discusses his case; see James Arnold Reinhard, "Personal and Sociological Factors in the Formation of the Free Methodist Church, 1852-1860" (Ph.D. diss., University of Iowa, 1971), pp. 67-70.

68. BTRD, June 20 and 21, 1855.

69. Conable, p. 620.

respecting the claims of the higher life, of the deeper, richer experiences of spiritual religion.[70]

Conable noted that this was the period when Phoebe Palmer's *Guide to Holiness* and other writings had considerable influence — and that some regarded them "as presenting views in harmony with the Wesleyan standards, on the subject of the 'interior life;' while others still regarded them as teaching error in matters of doctrine and Christian experience."[71] Clearly the differences and polarization within the Genesee Conference were due in part to the larger doctrinal question regarding holiness. But they took particular shape and sharpness in this conference due to the specific blend of issues, personalities, and social dynamics there.

The Bergen camp meeting, with its thousands attending, was a potential power center for reform and revival within Methodism. Roberts wanted to see its influence extended and deepened, and still hoped to find permanent grounds. On July 7 he went with Brother Hand from the church "to find a Camp ground that could be bought," but was unsuccessful.[72]

With the Bergen camp meeting over, Roberts continued his ministry at Brockport during the closing months of the conference year. He gives a glimpse of family life when he notes, "On Wednesday eve. at family prayer our Mary was greatly blessed and she still goes on her way rejoicing."[73] Presumably this was Mary Swezey, Ellen's niece, who was still living with the Robertses.

Benjamin attended a couple of other camp meetings over the summer. At the end of June he visited the Niagara District camp meeting at Newfane, then went on to Buffalo to check on his house there and pay the taxes.[74]

Roberts notes that on Sunday, July 1, he spoke on temperance at the Presbyterian church. Toward the end of July he got a letter from Bishop Osman Baker "proposing to me to go to California as a missionary." While nothing came of this, Roberts noted a few days later, "I must live more as in the presence of God and do nothing at any time inconsistent with my calling."[75] He felt the situation in his own conference was so critical that he should remain in Genesee. As he wrote to his father, "I cannot think of going to California, at any rate until I see this fight through."[76]

---

70. Conable, pp. 620-21.

71. Conable, p. 621.

72. BTRD, July 9, 1855.

73. BTRD, June 22, 1855.

74. BTRD, June 25-27, 1855. He writes, "Saw about my house. Paid the tax for 1853, contrary to law," but doesn't explain.

75. BTRD, July 1, 25, and 28, 1855.

76. BTR to TR, July 31, 1855, quoted in BHR, *BTR*, p. 105.

The Death of a Daughter

In July, just a few weeks after the Bergen camp meeting, Joseph McCreery and William Kendall decided to hold another camp meeting. This one would be in August near Albion, about twenty miles northwest of Bergen. Kendall and McCreery enlisted Roberts's help, and Benjamin noted a few days later, "Went to Rochester to see about getting cart, tents, and bought some groceries."[77]

Benjamin traveled to Carlton, seven miles north of Albion, to attend this camp meeting on Wednesday, August 15, leaving Ellen and the family at home. The camp apparently lasted for about a week. Seymour Coleman was again one of the preachers. Other preachers included Fay Purdy, A. A. Phelps, F. W. Conable, J. M. Fuller, and McCreery. Roberts himself preached at 10:00 on Thursday morning from the text, "Pure religion and undefiled before God" (James 1:27).[78] The camp probably wasn't as large as the Bergen meeting, though it was "more marked by the power of God," according to Benson Roberts. Benson described the camp meeting as "remarkable for the out-pouring of the Spirit. God's people were being awakened by the faithful labors of zealous earnest Christian ministers who at the expense of popularity were holding fast for old time Methodism with its essential characteristics of power and holy living. . . . There were manifestations of the presence of the Spirit of a marked character. At different times without waiting for an invitation to an altar, people all around the ground knelt where they were, seeking God."[79]

Benjamin returned home on Saturday to conduct Sunday services at Brockport. With her husband and Mary at home to look after baby Sarah and the two boys, Ellen went to the camp meeting Saturday afternoon to spend the weekend. Benjamin returned to the camp on Monday, "announcing all well" at home, and so Ellen decided to stay an extra day.

Purdy preached on Sunday, encouraging believers to "seek the power that would enable [them] to work for souls." Ellen was especially touched. "I want something I never had," she said, kneeling in prayer right where she was. "Such a weight of divine presence and glory rested upon her as to cause her to lose sight of all earthly things till the next day," Benson Roberts reported. And on Monday she "received a wonderful baptism."[80] Recounting her "religious experience" six years later, Ellen elaborated:

> I was conscious [that] I needed . . . something I never had possessed — a power to reach souls — a love for them. As I began to pray for it, the Lord by His Spirit asked me if I would take it *with suffering*. I had always shrunk from suffering for Christ, — especially I felt I could not endure to lose another of my children, (we then had three.) But I felt I cannot live without this power — and my hungering

77. BTRD, July 11 and 16, 1855.
78. BTRD, Aug. 15-21, 1855; BHR, *BTR*, p. 101.
79. BHR, *BTR*, p. 101.
80. BHR, *BTR*, p. 101.

was so intense it seemed to me I could not live thus. I said I will take it with suffering if I can have it in no other way. Then it was said to me, "I may take one of your children," — I hesitated a moment and thought *they* will be safe[—]this world is full of unsaved souls — I must have more power to reach them. I said "any way." I confessed publicly my want — began to look up and believe for all I needed — the power began to come. I was laid on the ground, and my whole being, soul and body, began to melt before the coming of the Lord, like wax before the fire. I saw a little what Jesus suffered for sinners — all I could bear — and I could have wept my life away at the sight. Then my soul was filled with a love for them, which it did seem for a while would consume my life. For hours I could not move — I could only weep, and was "lost in wonder, love and praise." For days after, I felt as solemn as the grave — it was all *eternity* to me.[81]

Early the next morning — Tuesday, August 21 — Ellen started for home. She took a stagecoach to Albion to catch the train for Brockport. But on the way the stage was met by a messenger with urgent news: one of her children had suddenly taken ill and was barely alive. Struck by this blow, Ellen dropped to her knees in the stagecoach, asking God's help. Meanwhile the messenger hurried on to the campground to tell Benjamin.[82]

Which child? Probably Benson, Ellen thought, since he had recently been seriously ill. When the train pulled into Brockport about 9:00 A.M., Ellen rushed home and anxiously asked Mary how Benson was. "Why, Aunt, it is not Benson, it is Sarah," Mary replied. To her shock, Ellen learned that her darling eight-month-old daughter had died just hours earlier.[83]

Benjamin also rushed home as soon as he got the news. That night the stricken father scratched in his diary, "Our dear Sarah was died [*sic*] this morning." He wrote no more in his diary for the rest of the year.[84] Benjamin, accompanied perhaps by Ellen, made his forlorn way to Gowanda to lay Sarah's body in the Presbyterian cemetery, next to Willie's.[85]

The blow fell heavily on both parents. Ellen was crushed, but found strength in God. Seth Woodruff, one of the kindly members of the Brockport church, came to comfort the grieving couple. A man of "great heart" and "large body and commanding voice," he entered the parsonage and "in his deep and solemnly sympathetic tone said 'Glory to God.'" Somehow the words spoke to Ellen. "The cloud lifted and it seemed easier to say amen to God's will, even though His will was the death of a tenderly loved and cherished child."[86]

---

81. Ellen L. Roberts, "Religious Experience," p. 284.

82. BHR, *BTR*, pp. 101-2; Ellen L. Roberts, "Religious Experience," p. 284.

83. BHR, *BTR*, p. 102.

84. BTRD, Aug. 21, 1855. The only other entry is a list of contributions for parsonage repair in the space for Dec. 1-4.

85. Presumably Benjamin himself took the body to Gowanda; Ellen may have accompanied him.

86. BHR, *BTR*, p. 102.

It is not clear what caused Sarah's death, nor whether Mary, Ellen's niece, was in any way responsible. Ellen may have felt some guilt for having left the baby at home with Mary, but she seems to have blamed neither herself nor Mary. Rather, she saw God's hand at work.

Though the tragedy of Sarah's death under such circumstances was a blow for Ellen, she felt that her weekend camp meeting experience had prepared her. She later noted that during this period she had "suffered much from poor health again, and began to feel an intense longing after God and a power to work for him which I had never had." She had gone to camp meeting "for the benefit of soul and body," desiring a fresh touch from God, and received it. When she dedicated her children to God at the camp meeting, she "thought it was only a test." But now she realized that "God had taken me at my word." Ellen recounts:

> I reached home, and found my youngest, our only daughter, a corpse. I could only groan, and for a few moments the anguish of soul and body was all I could endure. It seemed, while I looked at my loss, as if every joint of my body would be dislocated. — I looked to Jesus, and instantly the calmness of heaven came over me, and in that hour I seemed permitted to talk with Him as with a friend. I saw my little Sarah an angel in heaven, for six hours, by an eye of faith, as plainly as I ever saw her when living with my natural eye. While I looked to Jesus and saw her forever safe, and nothing for me here but the work of saving souls, I was powerfully blessed, and not only comforted, but my soul triumphed in Jesus. It was life, life and nothing like death about the house to me. Often I was overpowered with a sense of the presence of God and the heavenly host. When friends came in I had no disposition to speak of myself; but, oh! how I longed for them to get to Jesus and be saved. Sometimes it seemed as if the Lord permitted me to think of my Sarah and weep for her — but I knew when I was grieving the Spirit, and I dared not grieve to excess. Never did I so love souls, never did I know as then the power of grace.[87]

Some months later Benjamin wrote to his father, asking him to arrange for a tombstone for Sarah's grave, inscribed as follows:

> Sarah G. daughter of Rev. B. T. and E. L. Roberts died Aug. 21st 1855, aged seven months and five days. Gone to Jesus.[88]

Bereaved of little Sarah, Benjamin and Ellen were left with their two boys, George and Benson, now three and a half and almost two. Strengthened by her deeper sense of God's presence, Ellen was able to face the challenges that she and Benjamin increasingly encountered. Her heart probably echoed the sentiment Phoebe Palmer expressed in *The Way of Holiness*, which Ellen no doubt had read: "I

---

87. Ellen L. Roberts, "Religious Experience," pp. 284-85.
88. BTR to TR, May 9, 1856.

have sometimes thought that our heavenly Father has taken special pains to teach us, that our little ones are not our own."[89]

The death of these little ones — first William Titus, now Sarah — left its mark on Benjamin as well. Six years later when his sister Florilla Smallwood's little child Charlie died, he wrote in the *Earnest Christian*,

> Has death ever come to your family circle, and suddenly nipped a fair bud of promise? If so, life wears a more solemn aspect than it ever did before. Eternity seems near. Earthly good is of but little account. The heavenly home is clothed with new attractions. The dust of two of our loved children already waits in the village grave-yard the voice of Jesus, in its resurrection power. A few days ago all that was mortal of little Charlie, my beloved sister's sweet child, was laid by their side. He went, not heeding the tears of the stricken ones.

> Thou wast indeed a shining gem for heaven,
>   Nor less a solace of thy parents' woes;
> To-day, for one bright moment kindly given;
>   To-day, gone upward from a world of foes!

> 'Tis well with thee, for now thy peaceful breast,
>   Shall never feel what thousand breasts have riven;
> An angel laid thy little frame to rest,
>   And bore thy spotless soul away to heaven.[90]

---

89. Phoebe Palmer, *The Way of Holiness, with Notes by the Way* (New York: G. Lane and C. B. Tippett, 1848), p. 253 (reflecting on her own daughter Sarah's sixth birthday).

90. [B. T. Roberts], "Death," *EC* 2, no. 10 (Oct. 1861): 324. Roberts does not give the source of the poem; it could conceivably be his. According to Kysor, Charlie Smallwood died on Aug. 23, 1861 (Kysor, p. 29; cf. Smail, p. 10).

PART II

LIMINALITY
(1855-60)

CHAPTER 17

The Rise of Nazaritism

*"Their preaching of the gospel of peace is always attended or followed by jeal-
ousies, heart burnings, and fanatical dissentions."*

John E. Robie, 1855[1]

*"What we call religion they call fanaticism; what they denominate Christian-
ity, we consider formalism."*

B. T. Roberts, letter to Bishop Thomas Morris, 1856[2]

"The Methodists were not then, as now, rich and influential," wrote Gilbert Haven,
editor of *Zion's Herald,* in 1871.[3] He was referring to the American Methodism of two
generations earlier, around 1830. The marked shift he observed goes far to explain
the tensions in the Genesee Conference in the 1850s.

B. T. Roberts was just as aware of this shift as was Haven, his former classmate at
Wesleyan University. Though other factors were at work, the rising social status of
urban Methodists was fueling the fires of conflict in western New York.

Things definitely were heating up in the Genesee Conference. The 1855 annual
sessions were to be held August 29 to September 6 in Olean, near the conference's
southern border. Since the 1856 General Conference was approaching, that year's an-

---

1. [John E. Robie], "Another Secret Society — the Nazarites," *Buffalo Christian Advocate,* July 19,
1855, p. 2.

2. BTR (Albion, N.Y.) to Bishop T. A. Morris, Nov. 15, 1856.

3. Gilbert Haven and Thomas Russell, *Life of Father Taylor, the Sailor Preacher* (Boston: Boston
Port and Seamen's Aid Society, 1904), p. 107.

nual conferences took on added import because General Conference delegates were to be elected.

Roberts knew exactly what was at stake in the conference and in the denomination generally. A letter to his father on July 3, 1855, shows that he was deeply involved in conference politics, working to ensure that genuine "old-line Methodists" would be elected to General Conference. This was a defensive move, because Benjamin had reason to believe that Thomas Carlton, James Fuller, and other influential preachers had already drawn up a slate of preferred delegates.

Benjamin wrote his father, "Carlton & Co. will put forth every exertion to elect pro-slavery, odd-fellow, formalist delegates. We want to elect men who are in favor of the life and power of godliness, of returning to the old paths, and of getting slavery out of the church. We have most of the old men and young men with us, and think we can safely count on from eight to ten majority."[4]

This is a significant comment: it shows that Roberts was counting potential votes, and that the division was developing along generational lines. Roberts, at thirty-two, was forming an alliance with other young preachers and also with conference veterans such as Asa Abell, who was fifty-eight.[5]

Benjamin added, "Fuller is going around the conference saying that we have formed a secret society to put down odd-fellowship in the conference. This is not true. It has been the case under the odd-fellow reign that if a minister was true to his vows and endeavored to carry out the discipline he was crushed. We are determined that this shall be done no longer. But we will stand by one another in doing our duty."[6]

James Madison Fuller, forty-seven, was serving as agent for the Methodist Tract Society rather than being assigned to a church. In this capacity he visited the various churches of the conference. He was a prominent figure, having several times served as conference secretary.[7]

Baby Sarah's death came in the midst of this brewing controversy, just as the conference year was ending. Benjamin grieved the loss but continued his preparation for annual conference and the struggle to maintain Methodist faithfulness.

Just at this time the controversy over "Nazaritism" broke out.

---

4. BTR to TR, July 3, 1855, quoted in BHR, *BTR*, p. 103.

5. Ray Allen, *A Century of the Genesee Annual Conference of the Methodist Episcopal Church, 1810-1910* (Rochester, N.Y.: By the Author, 1911), p. 66. Abell later joined the Free Methodist Church about six months after it was formed. See B. T. Roberts, "Albion Quarterly Meeting," *EC* 2, no. 3 (Mar. 1861): 97-98, where Roberts gives a brief sketch of Abell.

6. BTR to TR, July 3, 1855, quoted in BHR, *BTR*, pp. 103-4.

7. Allen, *Century*, p. 87; *Minutes*, Genesee Conference, 1850-54.

The Beginning of "Nazaritism"

Joseph McCreery, Jr., was nine years older than Roberts. This year he was serving at Yates, in the Niagara District, but the previous year he had been at West Carlton, Genesee District.[8]

When McCreery arrived at Yates in the fall of 1854, he found the church "very much run down in spirituality," needing both discipline and revival. Like Francis Asbury when he assumed leadership of American Methodism in the 1770s, he enforced Methodist discipline, reading and explaining the General Rules. He promoted congregational singing and got rid of the church choir — "Drove out the doves who were billing and cooing in the gallery," he said. In the winter, with "snow-banks higher than the fences," he conducted a revival that attracted people from miles around.[9] The church grew; McCreery took in over forty probationary members, increasing total membership from 147 to 199 during his year at Yates.[10]

McCreery had collaborated with Roberts in revival work, and Roberts respected his spirituality and his preaching. McCreery became, however, the lightning rod in the Nazarite controversy that complicated Roberts's reform efforts and precipitated his eventual expulsion from the Methodist Episcopal Church.

On July 24, a few weeks before the 1855 annual conference, Benjamin wrote to his father, "I wish you would get Robie's paper of last week (date July 19th) and read an article, editorial, headed 'Another Secret Society' — 'The Nazarites.'"[11] A few days earlier Roberts had attended the district quarterly meeting at Albion, and there he apparently first saw the article that Robie had published a few days earlier in the *Buffalo Christian Advocate*. Roberts noted in his diary, "Robie had in his paper . . . a most slanderous attack upon the Nazarites and Bro. McCreery in particular."[12] This is Roberts's first use of the term "Nazarites" in his diary.

Who in the world were the Nazarites? McCreery coined the term, picking up the idea of the Nazirite vow in the Old Testament.[13] He likely had in mind, in particular, Amos 2:11 — "I also raised up prophets from among your sons / and Nazirites from among your young men" (NIV).[14] (McCreery consistently used the

---

8. The next year (1854-55) he served at Parma, Genesee District, between Brockport and Rochester (*Minutes*, Genesee Conference, 1853-55). His father, Joseph McCreery, Sr., had also been a Methodist preacher; he was located in 1836 (Allen, *Century*, p. 105). See photo of Joseph McCreery, Jr., in Hogue, *HFMC*, 1:8a.

9. *WAS*, p. 140.

10. *Minutes*, Genesee Conference, 1854, 1855.

11. BTR to TR, July 24, 1855; cf. BHR, *BTR*, p. 104.

12. BTRD, July 21, 1855.

13. See Num. 6; Judg. 13 and 16. God had told Samson's mother, "You will conceive and give birth to a son. No razor may be used on his head, because the boy is to be a Nazirite, set apart to God from birth, and he will begin the deliverance of Israel from the hands of the Philistines" (Judg. 13:5 NIV).

14. In the *Documents of the Nazarite Union* McCreery also refers to Neh. 10 as a biblical precedent (p. 10; see below).

spelling "Nazarite" rather than the biblical "Nazirite" — probably because "Nazarite" is closer to "Nazarene.")[15]

Sometime in 1854 or 1855 McCreery proposed a Nazarite union among preachers in the Genesee Conference who were "in favor of old line Methodism."[16] Clearly discussions had been going on for some time among McCreery, Roberts, and others about how best to influence the church to return to its roots. These discussions prompted McCreery to propose his "union" of reform-minded preachers. In an April 1855 letter McCreery reportedly said that discussions had been going on for about two years, "but no practical, initiatory steps were taken, till last August [1854], when *eleven* of the preachers on Genesee District agreed to walk in the 'old paths,' and to spread the thing through the Conference as far as possible." In another letter McCreery had said, "The origin of the Band was at the Genesee District camp-

15. See James Alan Revell, "The Nazirites: Burned-Over District Methodism and the Buffalo Middle Class" (Ph.D. diss., University of New York at Buffalo, 1993). In this dissertation Revell elected to use the biblical spelling, "Nazirite," rather than the spelling McCreery used.

16. [Joseph McCreery, Jr.], *Documents of the Nazarite Union, of the Genesee Conference of the M.E. Church* (Brockport, N.Y.: Wm. Haswell, Book and Job Printer, 1856), p. 3. This is the earliest printed form of the "Nazarite Documents" I have located, and is the same edition used by James Reinhard in his dissertation. (See James Arnold Reinhard, "Personal and Sociological Factors in the Formation of the Free Methodist Church, 1852-1860" [Ph.D. diss., University of Iowa, 1971], p. 34.) This seems, in fact, to be the original edition of the Nazarite Documents as such, although "fly sheets" had been circulated earlier, according to F. G. Hibbard. Hibbard wrote in 1859, "The only publications which have emanated from [the Nazarites] are mostly in the form of 'fly sheets,' and we believe, mostly anonymous," prior to 1856. "In 1856, they revised, it would seem, their policy and the result was published in a pamphlet at Brockport." [F. G. Hibbard], "Genesee Conference Matters — Nazarite Union," *NCA* 19, no. 1 (Jan. 5, 1859): 2. (This article was the lead editorial.) At least two printings of the Nazarite Documents seem to have been issued by the Brockport printer, William Haswell, in 1856, as MMHC has in its files a second title page (only) with slightly different wording: *Nazarite Documents: Comprising the Obligations, Practical Propositions, Lamentations, Recommendations, &c. of the Nazarite Union, of the Genesee Conference of the M.E. Church* (Brockport, N.Y.: Wm. Haswell, Printer, 1856). Hogue implies, however, that the Nazarite material read before the 1855 Genesee Annual Conference was in fact the pamphlet *Documents of the Nazarite Union*, which would seem to mean that the pamphlet had already been published in the summer of 1855. Perhaps there was in fact an earlier 1855 edition, but more likely the documents read at the conference were the fly sheets that had been circulated before the pamphlet was published, together with other handwritten material. The question seems to be resolved and the matter accurately summarized by Roberts in *WAS:* "Rev. Joseph McCreery wrote several letters to different preachers [in early 1855, apparently], proposing that they work in harmony in their efforts to persuade the people to return to the old paths of Methodism. There, in all probability, the matter would have rested; but some of these letters were shown to the editor of the *Buffalo Advocate,* who made the most of them, and stirred up some excitement. Anticipating that the subject would be brought up at Conference, the Rev. J. McCreery prepared a statement of the whole affair, including copies of the letters he had written. This he read to the Conference at Olean in 1855. This 'Document' or 'Roll,' as it was called, was greatly misrepresented. To correct these misrepresentations it was published by Rev. Wm. C. Kendall" (pp. 62-63). The implication seems to be that McCreery's statement before the Olean conference consisted of handwritten documents, and that the printing arranged by Kendall (perhaps with Roberts's help, since it was done in Brockport) was the 1856 pamphlet, *Documents of the Nazarite Union.*

meeting, just before Conference."[17] In other words, the key conversations that gave rise to what was later called Nazaritism occurred during the first Bergen camp meeting in August 1854.[18] Apparently McCreery was delegated (or designated himself) to test the waters, to find out which Genesee Conference preachers were sympathetic to this reform effort. He wrote to one of the conference preachers in May 1855, "I am charged during the present [conference] year with the general correspondence on the subject, with the largest discretion of solicitation."[19]

In light of later events, it is notable that the rise of Nazaritism was linked with the story of the Bergen camp meeting.

A number of years later, McCreery, in an important reminiscence, gave a full explanation of how Nazaritism and the name Nazarite arose. In August 1879 he sent a long letter (8,300 words) and some additional "reminiscences" to Roberts, knowing that Roberts had just completed his book *Why Another Sect.* In considerable detail McCreery explained how and why Nazaritism was created. In 1893 James Mathews published a "Memorial Sketch" of McCreery in the *Earnest Christian* that also employed McCreery's account. Mathews quotes McCreery as follows:

> The name Nazarite came in this wise: The old Methodist movement in the [Genesee] Conference had become a power in the land, as some of us proposed it should, and must of necessity have a name of some sort. In some places the pilgrims were called Kendallites, in other places, Robertsites, in other places, Stilesites, along the Ontario Lake shore some were called McCreeryites, while in Illinois they were called Redfieldites — so we had a variety of ites — the opponents representing the pilgrims as followers of men instead of principles. I considered the matter over in my own mind, and concluded that as we must be called some kind of "ite," we would have our say as to what kind of "ite" it shall be. I consulted only Bros. Coleman, Kendall, and G. W. Estes, and we concluded that Nazarite was the most significantly appropriate both to our principles and our relation to the Church. My leading idea from the very start had been to conform the movement to original Methodism in all respects, polity included if necessary; and as original Methodism was virtually an *ecclesia in ecclesiam* or an ascetic Order of

17. Both letters (Apr. 25, 1855, to Rev. John B. Wentworth, and Jan. 5, 1855, to Rev. Schuyler Parker) are quoted "from [Genesee] Conference documents" by F. G. Hibbard in "Nazaritism — Its Judicial History," *NCA* 19, no. 45 (Nov. 9, 1859): 2.

18. Conable says, "Nazaritism may be said to have had its incipiency about 1853, though there were always those in the Church saying 'the former days were better than these,'" and adds that "Nazaritism in fact, if not in name, originated with a few ministers of the Genesee Conference — J. H. Wallace, B. T. Roberts, J. M'Creery, Jun., and others." Conable, p. 628. This is essentially correct.

19. Quoted in Hibbard, "Nazaritism," p. 2. This May 29, 1855, letter was sent to "Rev. G. DeLaMatyr." Gilbert DeLaMatyr, John B. Wentworth, and Schuyler Parker, the recipients of these three letters (according to Hibbard), were at the time preachers in the Buffalo and Wyoming Districts, not the Genesee District. Wentworth was the preacher at Pearl Street, Buffalo. Thus presumably McCreery was attempting to network throughout the Genesee Conference, not just in the Genesee District. (Wentworth was the same age as Roberts, and DeLaMatyr a couple of years younger. Parker was a bit older, closer in age to McCreery. Cf. Allen, *Century,* pp. 82, 110, 128.)

Piety within the English Church, so we might be the same style of Methodists within the Methodist Episcopal Church. In such a case the name Nazarite would be most appropriate that came to my mind. So the name was agreed upon at a Camp meeting at Carlton, in 1855.[20]

McCreery relates how he and Kendall, "to encourage uniformity in singing," drew up and printed "a selection of twenty-seven hymns and tunes, and the same number of books and tracts," which they entitled *Nazarite Selection of Hymns and Books.*[21]

Now — July 1855, almost a year after the first Bergen camp meeting — John Robie triggered the Nazarite controversy with his broadside in the *Buffalo Christian Advocate.* Entitled "Another Secret Society — the Nazarites," the article bears quoting at some length, as it shows both the issues and the tenor of the emerging debate.

Robie began, "The world is afflicted with moral as well as physical epidemics. The last moral contagion which has swept over our country is the mania for secret association. Whatever plan or measure is proposed, to carry out which requires concert and co-operation, becomes, under the influence of the present popular desire for mysterious and hidden association, a signal for the formation of another secret society, with its signs, pass-words, and grips." He feared, he added, that "the present strong proclivity to mystery will 'run the thing into the ground.'"[22]

Thus far Robie was quite right. The organization of brotherhoods and secret fraternities of all sorts became almost a mania during this period. The Masons were mushrooming, and hundreds of other lodges and fraternities were springing up. The number of Masonic lodges in New York State grew from 79 in 1840 (about 5,000 members) to 432 in 1860 (about 25,000 members).[23] Odd Fellowship was established in America in 1819 and also grew rapidly. Nationally Odd Fellow membership

---

20. James Mathews, "Memorial Sketch of Rev. Joseph McCreery," *EC* 66, no. 1 (July 1893): 8-9. McCreery's much longer letter to Roberts, written from Alma City, Nebr., is dated Aug. 7, 1879. It is not clear whether Mathews is quoting a different McCreery document or whether he had a copy of the Aug. 7 letter to Roberts and condensed it for his "Memorial Sketch" of McCreery. McCreery's sometimes colorful letter, too long to reproduce here, goes into considerably more detail, citing precedents from church history including the rise of Methodism in the 1740s and the formation of the Wesleyan Methodist Connexion in 1843. McCreery wrote: "I then said [to Coleman and Estes], That as we must be called some kind of <u>ite</u> I propose we take our choice as to what kind of <u>ite</u> it shall be. 'Your enemies will see to that' said Father Coleman. 'You will have to wear the badge they see fit to put upon you!' 'I'll have a voice in that matter' said I. [']They shall give us the name I choose. I'll spread the plaster and they shall stick it on!' It was finally concluded that the name Nazarite was expressive of our ascetic Style, and also of our relation to the M.E. Church, being to all intents and purposes a religious Order within the Church. Thus the name was agreed upon by us three."

21. Mathews, "Memorial Sketch," p. 8.

22. [Robie], "Another Secret Society," p. 2. Though unsigned, the article clearly was Robie's, as was widely recognized in the Genesee Conference.

23. Peter Ross, *A Standard History of Freemasonry in the State of New York Including Lodge, Chapter, Council, Commandery and Scottish Rite Bodies,* 2 vols. (New York and Chicago: Lewis Publishing Co., 1899), 1:486. The Masons declined precipitously after the Morgan affair of 1826 and the Anti-Masonic movement that followed, but then grew rapidly.

climbed from 30,000 in 1843 to 200,000 in 1860.[24] And then there were the Knights of Pythias, Ancient Order of Foresters, Improved Order of Red Men, even the Sons of Temperance. Many aspiring middle-class businessmen and professional men managed membership in multiple lodges; John Walter of Rochester, for instance, in addition to being a Master Mason, was a Knight Templar Mason, Chivalric Mason, Royal Arch Mason, and a member of the Improved Order of Red Men, Knights of the Maccabees, and the Union League Club![25]

As Robie knew, many Methodist pastors and businessmen were themselves becoming Masons or Odd Fellows. A Masonic newspaper editor claimed in 1826, perhaps with some exaggeration, that "the greatest portion of the Methodist preachers in the New-England Conference are zealous and good Masons." Historian Steven Bullock points out one advantage of lodge membership: Methodist preachers often "used fraternal ties to ease the difficulties of a system that assigned clergy to a different location every few years."[26]

Robie was right also about the growing "popular desire for mysterious and hidden association" and "strong proclivity to mystery." Mark Carnes argues convincingly that fascination with ritual and mystery was at the heart of the "epidemic" (as Robie called it) of secret societies. Carnes gives the phenomenon an anthropological twist: "The fascination for fraternal ritual suggests that even as the emerging middle classes were embracing capitalism and bourgeois sensibilities, they were simultaneously creating rituals whose message was largely antithetical to those structural relationships and values."[27] Both Roberts's opposition to secret societies and Robie's attack on the Nazarites should be understood within this context.

Though Robie himself was said to be a member of four secret societies,[28] on this point he feigned neutrality. He was not opposed to "secret orders . . . founded on a proper basis," he said, but felt that "the religious world" was not "the proper field for the operation of secret organizations." In other words, secret societies were fine in the world, but not in the church. Here Robie is building up to his at-

24. Mark C. Carnes, *Secret Ritual and Manhood in Victorian America* (New Haven: Yale University Press, 1989), p. 29; Albert C. Stevens, ed., *The Cyclopaedia of Fraternities,* 2nd ed. (New York: E. B. Treat, 1907), pp. 257-58.

25. Ross, *Standard History,* 2:138-39. See the further discussion of Freemasonry and other secret societies in chapter 34.

26. Steven C. Bullock, *Revolutionary Brotherhood: Freemasonry and the Transformation of the American Social Order, 1730-1840* (Chapel Hill: University of North Carolina Press, 1996), p. 177. As source for the comment about the New England Conference, Bullock cites "Methodism and Freemasonry," *Masonic Mirror: and Mechanic's Intelligencer* 2 (May 6, 1826): 150 (Bullock, pp. 177, 366).

27. Carnes, *Secret Ritual and Manhood,* p. 32. Carnes adds, "This concurs with anthropologist Victor Turner's belief that social life is a dialectical process whereby society fits individuals into structures and defines their appropriate roles, yet these individuals, longing for a deeper and less restrictive range of experience and meaning, unconsciously react against the structures by participating in what he calls 'liminal rituals,' the symbols of which are in opposition to existing hierarchies and rules" (p. 32).

28. BTR to TR, July 24, 1855; cf. BHR, *BTR,* p. 104.

tack on the Nazarites; he passes over the question of church members being lodge members.

Robie then gets to the point:

We have learned, from a reliable source, and have sufficient evidence placed in our hands to prove, that there exists, among the ministry of a certain Protestant sect of Western New York, a secret religious organization, where one would be least suspected. The purpose of this Jesuitical order we will not at this time attempt to explain; but the consequences of it, unless its progress shall be arrested, and its existence blotted out, it takes no prophet's eye to foresee. — Incurable ministerial factions and ruined churches must otherwise be the inevitable result. This order has been designated by various appellations; but the authorized cognomen is, "THE NAZARITE BAND!" It is to be hoped that those who have assumed this solemn and suggestive title have weighed well what they are doing, and what the solemn imposition of this name upon themselves implies. To us it appears like impious mockery; and if "any good thing can come out of THIS Nazareth," then can a clean thing come forth from an unclean. We know well the men who are the originators of this singular movement, and have been watching their down-sittings and up risings for a long time. Our editorial secret draw [i.e., drawer] contains the record of many curious facts relating to the ministerial career of some of these eminent and most notable characters.

We learn that this society is constituted by three degrees, or "divisions." Into the third, or highest, are admitted only the leading spirits of the order, or those whom it is supposed will heartily favor the purpose of the order. The first degree, it would appear, is so indefinitely constituted that one may get into it, and not be himself aware of the fact. It is only required of the candidate that he express his approbation of certain men and measures, and forsooth he straightway becomes a Nazarite, and that before he knows it. He is, after this, carefully approached, and his opinions drawn out with respect to certain other measures, and if he can be "trusted," is advanced! There are many considerations which give this new organization a novel, not to say ludicrous, aspect. One is, that its originators have heretofore made themselves somewhat notorious by their blazing hostility to secret societies. They have published and spoken great and hard things. They have for years been bent on giving both lay and clerical Odd Fellows and Masons "particular jesse." Indeed, it is a main purpose of this Nazarite Band to oppose the influence which, it is alleged, "secular secret societies" are seeking to exert in religious affairs. Another beautiful feature of this new order is the peculiarly lovely personal and religious characteristics of those by whom it was conceived and brought forth. Their character is a strange compound of sanctity and slander, of pompous humility and humble pride, of peccability and perfection. Their preaching of the gospel of peace is always attended or followed by jealousies, heart burnings, and fanatical dissentions. Peevish and fretful tyrants at home, they have a very ardent charity for the "dear sisters" abroad, some of whom "they lead about." Without any remarkable "sanctity of manners undefiled," their professions reach to heaven, and clothe them with the most spotless garment of assumed purity. As a specimen of this class, we would refer the reader to a certain individual living in Orleans County, called, according to the Nazarite nomenclature, BANI, who is, we are informed, the high priest of this new profession. He has been especially famous, for some months past, for having seized a certain "calf by the horns." He declares it to be "the golden calf," but is probably mistaken. He has always been famous — ever since he has been at all — for eccentric stupidity and brilliant folly, which some few have mistaken for genius, but which the great majority of sensible people regard as the attributes of the genus donkey. To this dark, sepulchral and owlish gentleman we may pay a little more attention on some subsequent occasion. We hope this delectable "Band," having taken the steps and positions they have, will be prepared to face the music, and not, by backing out, attempt to evade the legitimate consequences of their abortive jealousy and spleen. Until we find time to give a more complete expose of their forms and plans, we leave our compliments with them, and hope the leaders of this movement will bring their purposes to so ripe a head that the people, wherever plagued with their mischievous propensities, will pass upon them the verdict which their temerity and folly deserve. Religious Jesuits are awful beings![29]

All the preachers in the Genesee Conference would know that the "certain individual living in Orleans County" was Joseph McCreery, then stationed at Yates in the county's northwest corner. The bitterness of Robie's attack on McCreery, surpassing even his usual sarcasm, suggests a surprising level of personal animosity. The prose was inflammatory, going well beyond the issue at hand to indulge in personal attacks on McCreery (and, by implication, Roberts and others). Presumably Robie included Roberts among those preachers who had "made themselves somewhat notorious by their blazing hostility to secret societies" and had "published and spoken great and hard things." Using the label "Jesuitical" played to anti-Catholic prejudice. Labeling the reformers "fanatical" and smearing their character ("a strange compound of sanctity and slander"), Robie went far beyond anything Roberts had written. The charge that McCreery and his associates were "fretful tyrants at home" while manifesting "a very ardent charity for the 'dear sisters' abroad" suggested not only hypocrisy but also constituted a sly hint at sexual impropriety. It's easy to see why Roberts called Robie's editorial "a most slanderous attack."

Obviously some of the Nazarite documents had fallen into Robie's hands. Probably some of the fly sheets that McCreery had circulated, as well as copies of related correspondence, were given to him by one or more of the conference preachers who

---

29. [Robie], "Another Secret Society." See Zahniser, pp. 74-77. Apparently Robie had access to an earlier form (or collection) of Nazarite documents than was published in 1856. The term "Bani" does not occur in the 1856 publication, but apparently in the original version McCreery had suggested using the biblical names Tirshatha and Bani (from Neh. 10) for the main leader and the scribe of the Nazarite Union — in other words, using secret names for officers, as many secret societies of the time did. See Conable, p. 632.

had received them.[30] McCreery later said he had arranged for a copy of the *Nazarite Selection of Hymns and Books* to be dropped off at the Methodist Book Depository in Buffalo, and that "the next week the Buffalo *Advocate* came out against the 'Nazarites.'" It was largely this negative publicity that made the term "Nazarite" more widespread, McCreery noted. Attacks on the Nazarites continued "for several years, till in a short time all the pilgrims from New York to St. Louis were called 'Nazarites.' The name was meekly borne by most, but chafed a few wonderfully. Dr. Redfield said they might call him anything but a 'formalist.'"[31]

Robie's article set the stage for a showdown at the approaching annual conference, as he intended. His editorial, though intemperate, was very clever. McCreery, Roberts, and others had opposed secret societies — especially the Masons and Odd Fellows, which some Methodist preachers were joining. Now McCreery made rather a mess of things by proposing a Nazarite union that looked enough like a secret society that Robie could attach that label to it. By creating Nazarite documents and letting them fall into the hands of people like Robie, McCreery complicated Roberts's reform efforts and fueled the controversy already brewing in the conference. Clearly Robie intended to turn the anti–secret society argument of Roberts and others on its head, accusing the reformers of doing the very thing they condemned. And he probably succeeded with many readers of the *Buffalo Christian Advocate* who were unacquainted with McCreery, Roberts, and their like-minded colleagues.

Roberts was disturbed by Robie's piece, but he thought it would backfire. He wrote his father, "Show this article to Bro. Newton and Father Evarts. It will help on our cause very much. Bro. McCreery, who is particularly specified[,] is one of our most devoted and successful ministers. Such gross abuse and slander will hurt most those it was designed to benefit." He added, "You can tell Father Evarts there is no secret society, as this article alleges, we are simply agreed in trying to return to the old paths."[32] "Bro. Newton" (Alonzo Newton), a year older than Benjamin, was Titus Roberts's pastor in Gowanda at the time. "Father Evarts" was Rinaldo M. Evarts, sixty-six, a superannuated preacher then living near Gowanda; Benjamin had helped secure conference support for him.[33] Both Newton and Evarts represented potential votes in the upcoming annual conference.

---

30. Very likely Robie was a main source of the Nazarite materials that came into the hands of the conference leadership, together with his close ministerial friends in the conference, including whoever the "reliable source" was who "placed in [his] hands" the information on the Nazarites.

31. Quoted in Mathews, "Memorial Sketch," p. 8.

32. BTR to TR, July 24, 1855; cf. BHR, *BTR*, p. 104.

33. *Minutes*, Genesee Conference, 1853, 1854; Allen, *Century*, pp. 85, 107. Benjamin wrote his father that the conference leadership "wished to put Father Evarts off last year with nothing and Bro. Kingsley and myself had to fight hard to get any thing for him" (BTR to TR, July 31, 1855). Conference records show that Evarts received eighty-five dollars from the superannuated preachers fund that year, less than half the amount he received two years previously. Proper care of superannuated or "worn-out" preachers was a continuing concern with Roberts. Evarts died at Leon, N.Y., near Gowanda, in 1865.

Benjamin wrote to his father a week later, commenting further on the controversy and the approaching annual conference.

> Robie is desperate. This is a good symptom. He sees his craft is in danger. The whole <u>policy</u>, wire pulling faction is greatly and properly alarmed. The Lord will give us the victory. I should like very much to have you see Father Evarts and have him on hand at Conf. Every O.F. [Odd Fellow] that can put in a vote will be there, and the lovers of Methodism must rally. . . .
>
> I hope no one will be frightened by the hue and cry about a secret society. This ado is out of character in men who belong to the Masons, Odd Fellows, &c.[34]

Benjamin thought Robie's blast in the *Buffalo Christian Advocate* might lead to legal action. He told his father, "Bro. McCreery will probably prosecute Robie for libel; though perhaps not till after conf. Two of our best Lawyers here say it is clearly a libel. But I do not know but it is best to let him hang himself."[35]

Was there in fact a "secret society" called the Nazarite Union or Nazarite Band? That became a huge question. Years later Roberts devoted a whole chapter to it in *Why Another Sect,* maintaining that "no such organization ever existed."[36] Similarly, Bishop Wilson T. Hogue in his 1915 *History of the Free Methodist Church* wrote that the Nazarite Union "never had any existence, but was wholly a fictitious affair."[37]

Roberts's comment in his July 24 letter to his father is important: "[T]here is no secret society, as this article alleges, we are simply agreed in trying to return to the old paths." That was the crux of the matter. No society, secret or otherwise, had been organized; there was no Nazarite Band. Yet clearly Roberts and his like-minded colleagues had, as he said, "agreed" to work together to bring reform, to try "to return to the old paths." There was no secret society, but there *was* a definable network. Zahniser says that in light of all the evidence, "the truth of the matter seems to be that these men did act together in concert in order to preserve what they considered old line Methodism, but without organization. The coincidence of the publication of the Nazarite Documents by Mr. McCreery and their circulation, together with the knowledge that there was a solidarity in the accomplishment of their ends, probably produced the conviction in the Conference that such an organization did exist."[38]

According to Roberts, Kendall, pastoring at Brockport in 1855-56 following Roberts's two years there, had a hand in issuing the Nazarite documents. It seems to have been Kendall who actually arranged the publication in Brockport in 1856 of the *Documents of the Nazarite Union.* Roberts wrote after Kendall's death that Kendall

---

34. BTR to TR, July 31, 1855. Part of this letter is quoted (with minor errors) in BHR, *BTR,* pp. 104-5.

35. BTR to TR, July 31, 1855.

36. *WAS,* p. 23.

37. Hogue, *HFMC,* 1:48.

38. Zahniser, p. 78.

fully endorsed the sentiments of the "Nazarite Roll," read at the Olean Conference, and inasmuch as many false reports were afloat concerning it, he judged best
to have the entire document published, that nothing might be hid or misunderstood. He accordingly procured the necessary papers and ordered a thousand copies published, believing it would encourage those under spiritual bondage in
other parts of the work, and stimulate them to a like return to the old paths. Although it was well known there was no *organization* of Nazarites, he was not
afraid or ashamed to declare that he belonged to the band so-called, because he
had for his object in all his labors the restoring of the life of godliness to the
Church, and in *no other way* than that he stood committed everywhere to keep to
the Bible and Methodist Discipline.[39]

McCreery began his *Documents of the Nazarite Union* with a preface consisting
of what he called "Extracts from the minutes of a primary consultation of several
preachers in favor of old line Methodism."[40] What was this "primary consultation,"
or preliminary discussion? Did such a meeting occur, or was this a fiction? If it actually occurred, this lent credence to charges that a secret Nazarite organization had
been or was being formed.

McCreery later testified (at the 1858 Genesee Annual Conference) that he created all the Nazarite documents, including the preface. "The Preface to the pamphlet is a mythical concern altogether," he said. Thus McCreery claimed, apparently,
that the so-called primary consultation never took place, and the preface containing "Extracts from the minutes of a primary consultation of several preachers" was
a fiction. This is what Hogue concluded. Hogue published in full the Nazarite documents as appendix C in his *History of the Free Methodist Church*, labeling them "A
Fiction."[41]

But did this "primary consultation" in fact take place, or not? There seem to be
three possibilities: (1) It did take place, and the extracts are what they claim to be.
(2) It did not take place, and the extracts are an invention. (3) Some degree of consultation did take place, and the extracts are McCreery's composite summary of one
or more meetings or conversations, but not in fact "extracts from the minutes" of a
particular consultation.

There are reasons to believe that these extracts are not wholly fictitious — that
the third possibility is closest to the truth. The five-page extract reads like a report of
an actual meeting. Six specific persons are indicated, though identified by initials
only. A plausible reason to take the document as not entirely fictitious is McCreery's
statement (quoted earlier) that some "practical, initiatory steps were taken" at the
August 1854 Genesee District camp meeting "when *eleven* of the preachers on
Genesee District agreed to walk in the 'old paths,' and to spread the thing through

39. "Rev. Wm. C. Kendall, A.M. — Labors," *EC* 2, no. 11 (Nov. 1861): 336.
40. [McCreery], *Documents*, preface, pp. 3-8.
41. Hogue, *HFMC*, 1:59; 2:376-409. Hogue's appendix C is identical to the 1856 publication of the
Nazarite Documents.

the Conference as far as possible."[42] In other words, it seems certain that McCreery, Roberts, and others *did* meet together at the time of the first Bergen camp meeting and, in effect, plotted strategy. Was this possibly the "primary consultation" McCreery mentions?

One way to check is to identify the preachers who supposedly participated in the "primary consultation." McCreery begins his "extracts" of the meeting as follows:

> Br. R. stated that, in his opinion, it had become necessary to have a closer union among ourselves in respect to the observance of the rules and customs of the Church. Especially as in certain quarters there seemed a set purpose to ignore the discipline and to bring in innovations upon the time-honored customs of the Fathers. The evil results of this were everywhere manifest. Isolated and individual effort in resistance had been tried, but with little success. . . . Either a vigorous and united effort at resistance must be made, or it were as well to give up at once and let the current of events keep on its "progress."[43]

Clearly "Br. R." is B. T. Roberts. The remarks sound like his and represent his views. Significantly, Roberts is portrayed as the initiator of the reform effort. Though of a quieter, more thoughtful temperament than McCreery, Roberts was the clear leader. Thus this document is important evidence for Roberts's leadership role, even if this consultation never actually took place.

In addition to "Br. R.," McCreery identifies five other preachers by initials (Brothers W., H., M., K., and E.), and quotes or summarizes their views. Presumably "Br. W." is John H. Wallace, "Br. M." is McCreery, and "Br. K." is Kendall.[44] It is uncertain who "Br. H." and "Br. E." are. Roberts mentions no preachers with these surname initials in his diary account of the first Bergen camp meeting. "Br. E." could have been T. W. Eaton, the preacher this year at nearby West Carlton, and "Br. H." may signify the supernumerary preacher Amos Hard.[45] In McCreery's "Extracts" "Bro. H." says, "I have . . . kept the faith . . . , and I shall keep it to the end, which is not far off. . . . I am a disabled soldier; I can only hobble along in the ranks."[46] This would fit Amos Hard, then in ill health and listed among the "superannuated or worn-out preachers."[47]

---

42. Hibbard, "Nazaritism," p. 2.

43. [McCreery], *Documents*, p. 3.

44. Wallace preached during the 1854 Bergen camp meeting, as previously noted, and no doubt McCreery and Kendall were also there. By far the longest section of the preface is attributed to "Br. M.," as one might expect if McCreery was the author, in effect quoting himself.

45. *Minutes*, Genesee Conference, 1854. Amos Hard later was one of seventeen signers of a document certifying that no Nazarite Union ever existed. See Hogue, *HFMC*, 1:51, and *WAS*, p. 25.

46. [McCreery], *Documents*, p. 5.

47. *Minutes*, Genesee Conference, 1854. If Allen is correct in his *Century of the Genesee Annual Conference* (p. 91), Hard was born in December 1812 and was thus only forty-one at this time. This is possible, but Allen's dates may be incorrect (though Conable also gives the birth year as 1812). According to Allen, Hard died in 1877. On Amos Hard, see *WAS*, pp. 32-33; Hogue, *HFMC*, 1:122, 262, 299; Marston, p. 321.

On balance, it appears that McCreery's preface was not entirely an invention. There probably was a sort of "primary consultation" or preliminary discussion among several of the conference preachers at the time of the 1854 Bergen camp meeting, and probably B. T. Roberts took the lead in convening it and in proposing "a closer union" in order to reform the church and stop its drift. McCreery participated and may well have taken notes. Thus McCreery's preface probably gives a fairly accurate picture of the initiatives that led to the Nazarite controversy, even though no Nazarite Union was ever actually organized. If this is the case, McCreery's statement that the preface was "a mythical concern altogether" is a bit misleading.

A section of the Nazarite documents is entitled "Nazarite Union" and is marked "Historic Circular." Probably these several pages constitute in essence the first pamphlet or fly sheet that was circulated in late 1854 or early 1855 proposing a "Nazarite Union" and thus are the heart of the Nazarite proposal.[48] The "Historic Circular" contains two key sections, entitled "Nazarite Obligation" and "Practical Propositions." They read as follows:

Nazarite Obligation

1. — I will observe and enforce the Rules of the Methodist Episcopal Church to the best of my ability, and under all practicable circumstances.
2. — I will steadfastly resist all departures from them, or from the religious customs derived therefrom.
3. — I will steadfastly oppose the introduction or continuance among us of any religious practice or custom or of any institution foreign to, or at variance with the Discipline of the Church.
4. — And I will encourage and sustain, in the disciplinary execution of the above purpose, in preference to all others, those covenanting together in this obligation.

Practical Propositions

1. — To restore the observance of the Rules requiring attendance on Class.
2. — To restore the observance of the Rules requiring family prayer.
3. — To restore the observance of the Rules requiring quarterly fasts.
4. — To restore the observance of the Rules requiring singing by the congregation.
5. — To restore the custom, in part, of free seats in our houses of worship.
6. — To restore the custom of attendance from abroad upon our Love Feasts.
7. — To restore the custom of Camp Meetings more fully among us.
8. — To restore, generally, simplicity and spirituality in our worship.

---

48. Conable notes that the "Historic Circular" as printed in 1856 had been "revised" from its original form. Conable, pp. 630, 632.

The above is a true copy of the Obligation and Practical Propositions of the Nazarite Union of the Genesee Conference, as revised and approved in the last general consultation.

J. McCREARY [*sic*], Jr.,
Chief Scribe.[49]

These provisions show that McCreery certainly did envision a sort of vow or covenant and also a specific program of reform or restoration.

This review of "Nazarite" origins is important both because it clarifies the actual history and because it shows the key role that McCreery played. Had he not hatched and circulated his elaborate plan for a semisecret Nazarite union, people like Robie, Carlton, and others would have been robbed of much of the ammunition they used quite effectively against Roberts and his colleagues.

Deeper Issues

What are the key issues here? They concern *community identity* — a person's identity within a particular community or communities — and the *nature* of the communities people immerse themselves in. Until the 1830s or so, virtually all Methodists saw and experienced the Methodist Episcopal Church as their primary community of belonging and identity. This identity was rooted in each member's local Methodist class and congregation. This was unquestioned among Methodists. Methodist belonging relativized all other affiliations. Any other group identity was strictly and clearly subservient to one's Methodist identity.

But this sense of "peculiar" or particular identity was eroding by the 1840s and 1850s. Methodists, especially in the cities, were increasingly aware of their roles in the larger society. Other and perhaps competing identities emerged as Methodists joined other groups. It is not coincidental that the secret society controversy emerged just as the Methodist class meeting was declining. One may hypothesize a close negative correlation here: the more Methodists participated in non-Methodist societies, fraternal orders, or other groups, the less they probably participated in the Methodist class meeting. It seems likely that those Methodists who joined lodges already had largely abandoned the class meeting — and conversely, that Methodists who faithfully attended class weren't interested in the Masons or Odd Fellows.

While Roberts, McCreery, and their comrades seem never to have made this argument directly, they did argue for both a proscription of secret societies and a renewed emphasis on the class meeting. In fact, the first recommendation or "practical proposition" of the *Documents of the Nazarite Union* was to "restore the observance of the Rules requiring attendance on Class Meetings." The document laments "the

---

49. [McCreery], *Documents*, p. 11. It is not clear what "the last general consultation" refers to, or whether this was in fact an actual meeting or a fiction.

general neglect of Class Meetings" in the conference that "has been gradually increasing . . . for the last seven years." Only a minority of Methodists were now attending class meetings; in many congregations class "attendance is considered a mere
matter of convenience or inclination." Because of this, a "fearful accumulation of
lifeless membership has gathered upon the surface of the Church." "No other evil
among us is so enormous as this. It is more general than any other." The solution was
to update all the class-meeting record books, and for each preacher to "*insist* on the
attendance of each member at least one-third of the time" at his or her weekly class.
The discipline should be firmly and impartially applied. All who failed to attend
class at least a third of the time would be excluded from the church.[50]

The issue, then, was Methodist solidarity and discipline versus multiple or divided loyalties and social commitments. McCreery and his associates wanted to rein-
vigorate class meetings and discourage lodge membership. His proposed Nazarite
Union would promote those aims.

But what exactly was the status of the proposed Nazarite Union? Was it in fact
"another secret society," as Robie cleverly charged? A key distinction Robie glossed
over was that, unlike the Masons or Odd Fellows, the Nazarite Union was to be an
association *within* the Methodist church existing to reform and promote Methodism, not an external and competing body. McCreery argued, "We hold such a Society
to be no more improper than a 'Preachers' Aid Society' — or a 'Preachers' Anti-
Slavery Society.' This Nazarite Union might appropriately be styled a 'Preachers'
Come-back-to-the-Discipline Society,' for it is that and nothing else."[51] There was
nothing unseemly about forming a distinct group within the Methodist Episcopal
Church for purposes that were entirely consistent with the church's mission and
well-being. McCreery later argued in a somewhat different vein, "People have a right
to belong to the Methodist E. Church, and the Masons, the Odd-Fellows, the Sons of
Temperance, or the Voluntary Order of Nazarites. There is nothing in the discipline
prohibitory against any or all of these. We complain only, of the *perversion* of the
thing to purposes of ecclesiastical intrigue." Further, he quoted an anonymous Mason as saying, "The Lodge is no place for the preachers. We have more than a supply. . . . You complain that you have too many masons among the preachers; we return the compliment by saying we have too many preachers among the masons: and
some of us are with you in your efforts to rid us of them; or at least, to cure them of
mixing it up with church affairs."[52]

50. [McCreery], *Documents*, pp. 19-21. McCreery noted that Sunday school was beginning to
compete with class attendance, partly because it demanded less and partly because some churches
scheduled Sunday school and class meetings at the same hour. "Here is a dilemma to be avoided if possible." Sunday school ought to be in the morning so as not to interfere "with the Sabbath noon Class
Meetings." This shows that some, and perhaps most, class meetings had by this time been moved from
weeknights to Sundays — in itself testimony to a decline in class meeting vitality. (Note the related discussion in chapter 6 regarding class meeting patterns in New York City Methodism in the 1840s.)

51. [McCreery], *Documents*, p. 10.

52. "Jonadab," *Nazarite Review of the Pastoral Address of the Genesee Conference of the M.E. Church*

The issue was one of different types and levels of community, and of possibly competing forms of community and commitment. As a matter of church life, this is the old *ecclesiola in ecclesia* question (small church within the church), and the related issue of the appropriateness of specialized orders within the larger church. This is an issue of ecclesiology and also of missiology.[53] Class meetings were *ecclesiola* forms within the church. The proposed Nazarite Union would also be a distinct group within the church, a sort of order, but operating at the conference rather than congregational level. By contrast, the Odd Fellows and other secret fraternities functioned largely outside the churches and thus raised the issue of competing loyalties and conflicting time and financial commitments. Roberts's attitude toward the Odd Fellows was similar to that of his friend William Kendall, who regarded "All minor societies [as] mere stepping stones to masonry," which was "a society only fit for worldly men."[54]

Showdown at Olean

Robie's article on the Nazarites six weeks before annual conference was followed a week later by a second brief piece. Apparently McCreery responded in some way to Robie's July 19 article, denying the charges. Robie replied in the July 26 *Buffalo Christian Advocate*:

> We learn that "BANI" denies that the NAZARITES are an organized band, as we asserted them to be in our last week's issue. We would remind this very conscientious and notable individual of the importance of keeping truth on his side, as far as circumstances will permit; and not, by gratuitous and voluntary denials of facts, place himself in a very embarrassing position and one in which honest men seldom find themselves. Bani, it is not right, it is decidedly wrong, to make statements which you know to be false, and you must not do so any more. That "the end justifies the means" is still a very dangerous and heretical doctrine; nor has it become any more safe or truthful as a principle of action, since you assumed the cloak of the Jesuit and invented that wonderfully ingenious machinery of "Nazariteism." For the present we are content to leave this denial of Bani's as a

---

(n.p., n.d.), p. 14. This pamphlet seems to have been written by McCreery. L. R. Marston, in a face sheet to the photocopy of the pamphlet in MMHC, writes, "The content and style of this anonymous polemic clearly point to the unpredictable Rev. Joseph McCreery as the author." Marston notes that this copy of the pamphlet was made from the original at Drew University.

53. Missiologist Ralph Winter has discussed this issue in terms of modality and sodality structures — the modality being a particular church or congregation, which by definition is concerned with all aspects of believers' lives, while the sodality is a specialized, high-commitment group concerned specifically and exclusively with a particular mission or ministry. Ralph D. Winter, "The Two Structures of God's Redemptive Mission," *Missiology* 2, no. 1 (Jan. 1974): 122-24. See also Howard A. Snyder, *Signs of the Spirit: How God Reshapes the Church* (Grand Rapids: Zondervan, 1989), chap. 2.

54. "Rev. Wm. C. Kendall, A.M. — Labors," p. 336.

simple question of veracity between him and ourself. And, leaving the matter there we have no fears about how this question will be decided in the minds of those persons who may chance to be acquainted with that individual.[55]

Hogue later wrote of Robie's accusations, "Their spirit is bitter, their language coarse, vulgar, and unbrotherly, and their declarations are false." Hogue considered Robie's second piece "evasive" because he accused McCreery of untruthfulness rather than accepting his denial that a Nazarite organization actually existed and therefore "making some sort of apology or defense."[56] In the propaganda war now under way, McCreery and Roberts were at a disadvantage because Robie both owned and edited the *Buffalo Christian Advocate* and could publish anything he wanted. Roberts complained that Robie was operating without any accountability. Meanwhile, Roberts wrote in his diary on Saturday afternoon, July 28, "I must live more as in the presence of God and do nothing at any time inconsistent with my calling." That evening he added, "Have succeeded better than usual, as above resolved."[57]

With conference approaching, James Fuller apparently began circulating Robie's article "Another Secret Society — the Nazarites" among the conference preachers.[58] Benjamin wrote his father on July 31,

> Bro. Fuller and I have personally always had a good understanding, but he thinks I stand in his way. He wanted to be P.E. on this Dist. last fall, but was not appointed. He wants to go to the General Conf. [as a delegate] but fears I mistrust that the brethren will not send him.
>
> I am not only looking for coldness but that "all manner of evil should be said of me falsely for Christ's sake." The Lord helping me I mean to go straight let it cost what it will.[59]

It was about three weeks after this that little Sarah died. Her death came just a week before Benjamin was to leave for the annual conference in Olean. Roberts was supposed to get to conference early to again serve on the Examining Committee. But with Sarah's death and Benson critically ill, he decided to delay leaving home. He wrote his father on Monday, July 27, "I do not know when I shall be able to go to Conf.[,] probably not till towards the last of the week." He added, "We had a solemn time at the Church yesterday and the year is closing up in a most satisfactory manner."[60]

55. [John E. Robie], editorial comment, *Buffalo Christian Advocate*, July 26, 1855, p. 2. See *WAS*, pp. 61-62, and Hogue, *HFMC*, 1:65.

56. Hogue, *HFMC*, 1:65.

57. BTRD, July 28, 1855.

58. Zahniser (p. 78) says, "Fuller began to circulate this article," but does not give his source.

59. BTR to TR, July 31, 1855.

60. BTR to TR, July 24 and Aug. 27, 1855. He added a note Tuesday noon, the day before conference was to begin: "Benson still continues to improve. He is better every way so far as we can judge than he was yesterday and we hope he may soon recover."

When Benjamin figured Brockport's membership statistics for the year, he recorded a total of 141 members, of which only 8 were probationers. This was a 31 percent increase over 1853, when Roberts began at Brockport, but a 12 percent drop for the year. Roberts doesn't explain the decrease. However, since the total number of full members remained the same (132) and probationers decreased from 27 to 8, it would appear that a number of probationers dropped by the wayside and did not continue on into membership. Of course, some of the 1854 probationers likely did become full members, and probably some new converts were added.[61]

This membership decline at Brockport during the 1854-55 year contrasts with the considerable growth McCreery and Kendall experienced at Yates and Albion. Both led remarkably successful winter revivals. Benjamin had assisted at least once at Albion, preaching on Sunday night, February 12, to "a very large and attentive congregation."[62] A year earlier Roberts conducted a fruitful winter revival at Brockport, and this was reflected in solid membership growth. In the fall of 1854 he preached a revival at nearby Holley, as previously noted, but did not hold a winter revival at Brockport. It is not entirely clear why, though family concerns may have been a factor, as Sarah was born in January. Perhaps Roberts saw the 1854-55 year as a time to consolidate the fruit of the previous year's revival — but in fact, total membership actually decreased. In addition, the last half of the 1854-55 conference year was a time of busyness and great stress, with the controversy over circuses, planning the Bergen camp meeting, Robie's "Nazarite" article, and then Sarah's death. Taken together, these things may have hampered Benjamin's evangelistic and pastoral effectiveness.

The printed conference minutes show that Roberts reported a Sunday school of sixty-eight pupils with eighteen teachers, and that $252.27 was contributed for missions — fourth-highest in the conference, and higher than any of the Buffalo churches, which on average had more members. The minutes also show that Roberts's $600 salary (higher than the conference average of $453) was paid in full.[63]

It is not clear when Benjamin actually went to Olean for conference, but apparently he arrived late.[64] The conference began on Wednesday, August 29, and didn't complete its work until Friday morning, September 7.[65] Bishop Beverly Waugh presided, but Bishop Matthew Simpson was also present and assisted, presiding at most of

---

61. *Minutes,* Genesee Conference, 1853-55.

62. BTRD, Feb. 12, 1854.

63. *Minutes of the Genesee Annual Conference of the Methodist Episcopal Church, 1855* (Buffalo: Reese and Co., 1855), pp. 32-37. This printed edition of the minutes, which is more extensive than the report contained in the combined book of minutes, is cited hereafter as *Minutes of the Genesee Annual Conference* (1855). Kendall also received $600, while McCreery's salary apparently was set at $436, of which he received only $403.

64. Roberts's diary is blank for these dates.

65. *Minutes of the Genesee Annual Conference* (1855), pp. 5-16. The denominational book of minutes lists the dates as Aug. 29–Sept. 6, but the separate printed minutes record an early Friday morning meeting (Sept. 7), beginning at 5:30, at which the minutes were approved and appointments read by Bishop Waugh.

the afternoon sessions.[66] In light of what Simpson later published about Free Methodist origins in his *Cyclopaedia of Methodism,* his participation in the 1855 Genesee Conference sessions, where the Nazarite controversy first arose, is significant.[67]

Due to the efforts of Robie and others, the Nazarite issue was the hot topic at conference. The preachers conducted all their usual business, and on Tuesday morning, September 4, elected General Conference delegates. Not surprisingly, Thomas Carlton was immediately elected, along with Richard L. Waite and Isaac C. Kingsley.[68]

Much time was given to the Nazarite question. The issue came up at the beginning of conference, occupying parts of the first two morning sessions on August 29 and 30 and nearly all of the afternoon sessions both days.

In what may have been a well-orchestrated move, sixty-year-old Israel Chamberlayne introduced a long paper asking for an investigation of Nazaritism. The roll call at the beginning of conference constituted the passing of the character of each preacher, and when McCreery's name was called and the bishop asked, "Is there anything against him?" Chamberlayne rose and made his charges.[69]

Dr. Israel Chamberlayne was a supernumerary preacher of some influence — an author and several-time delegate to General Conference, and thus a good choice to introduce the Nazarite matter. He was later remembered as "distinguished for intellectual strength, . . . a master in logic, [and] sharp as a controversialist."[70] Roberts described him as "a strong man, of a metaphysical turn of mind, cold temperament, and undemonstrative in his manners" who advocated "the 'gradual' theory of holiness."[71] His words carried weight among his peers.

Chamberlayne lived on a farm near Yates and attended the Yates ME Church,

66. *Minutes of the Genesee Annual Conference* (1855), pp. 5-14. It is not clear why Bishop Simpson was present. Simpson presided at some of the sessions in which the Nazarite documents were read. Was he perhaps present specifically because of this issue?

67. "The first time the Genesee Conference came in formal contact with Nazaritism was at its session in Olean, in 1855." Hibbard, "Nazaritism," p. 2.

68. *Minutes of the Genesee Annual Conference* (1855), p. 11.

69. Conable, p. 640; Hibbard, "Nazaritism," p. 2; *Minutes of the Genesee Annual Conference* (1855), p. 5. Roberts says Chamberlayne "arrested the character of the Rev. Joseph McCreery" (*WAS,* p. 142). The annual conference each year was charged with examining and passing the character of each ordained preacher (question 11 in the standing conference agenda, from Wesley's "General Minutes"), and this was done in connection with the reading of the conference roll. Thus Chamberlayne's charges against McCreery when the roll was called was an indictment of McCreery's character and would have to be cleared by conference action before McCreery's character could be passed. The minutes show that the conference spent considerable time on question 11; in fact, it "engaged the attention of the Conference during most of the session" on Tuesday morning, Sept. 4 (*Minutes of the Genesee Annual Conference* [1855], p. 11). Most of this discussion, apparently, concerned McCreery.

70. *COM,* pp. 191, 193; *Minutes,* Genesee Conference (1854). Chamberlayne is an odd case. Though a supernumerary, semiretired preacher, he wielded considerable political influence in the conference. At an earlier time he had served as presiding elder of the Genesee District. His D.D. appears to have been honorary.

71. *WAS,* pp. 140-41.

where McCreery was the preacher this year. Though his wife responded positively to McCreery's discipline and revival efforts, Chamberlayne didn't. He was offended by McCreery's methods and his style, and began building a case against him. Through the 1854-55 conference year he wrote down everything McCreery said that he didn't like, and this document became the basis of his charges at the annual conference. Roberts later wrote that Chamberlayne compiled "a long list of the odd, characteristic expressions, which Mr. McCreery had uttered in the pulpit."[72] An example of the kinds of things Chamberlayne didn't like was McCreery's colorful defense of his ministry at Yates. Chamberlayne quoted McCreery as saying: "Some of the younger boys have taken my mother, the Methodist Church, in her old age, painted her face and curled her hair, hooped her, and flounced her, and jeweled her, and fixed her up, until we could hardly tell her from a woman of the world. Now when I have taken the old lady, and washed her face, and straightened out her hair, and dressed her up in modest apparel, so that she looks like herself again, they make a great hue and cry, and call it abusing mother."[73]

Chamberlayne introduced the Nazarite issue, reading his paper to the conference, including his quotations from McCreery's sermons. He then urged that due to the "extraordinary circumstances of the case," the conference "waive its usual form of business, and call upon its members for all the information in their possession touching Nazaritism." Bishop Waugh agreed to hear the case, and the conference "*Resolved,* That all the papers in hand relating to the Nazarite Society, be now read to the Conference."[74]

Reading and discussing the Nazarite documents took time — part of the morning session, all the afternoon session, and a good share of the next day as well. Bishop Simpson presided at the two afternoon sessions, which were devoted almost entirely to the Nazarite question.[75]

The conference began considering the Nazarite question toward the end of its opening morning session on Wednesday, September 29. The minutes note, "The remainder of the Session was occupied in the reading and discussion of certain papers, relating to an alleged secret organization among some of the preachers, termed the Nazarite Band." The proceedings continued throughout the afternoon.[76]

McCreery freely admitted being the source of the whole Nazarite affair, and in fact himself read before the conference the Nazarite documents he had written.[77] Presumably McCreery read the "Historic Circular" that later was printed as part of the *Documents of the Nazarite Union,* and perhaps some other papers.

---

72. *WAS,* p. 141.

73. McCreery, as quoted by Chamberlayne, apparently. The passage is quoted in *WAS,* pp. 141-42, and Hogue, *HFMC,* 1:141.

74. Hibbard, "Nazaritism," p. 2.

75. *Minutes of the Genesee Annual Conference* (1855), pp. 5-7.

76. *Minutes of the Genesee Annual Conference* (1855), pp. 5-6. Conference opened at 9:00 A.M. this first day and at 8:00 on most subsequent days.

77. *WAS,* p. 142.

This business occupied the conference also for most of the afternoon session on Thursday, August 30. After the documents were read and discussed, "a motion was made to sustain the statements made in Dr. Chamberlayne's paper," according to Hibbard. Dr. Jesse T. Peck, who was visiting the conference on behalf of the Methodist Tract Society, "took a deep interest in the matter" and was invited to give his views, which he did at length.[78] Peck, a supporter of Phoebe Palmer and a future bishop, the following year published *The Central Idea of Christianity*, advocating holiness.[79] But Peck feared anything that might lead to schism. In his 1856 book he advised holiness people to "permeate the entire church" and not organize separate organizations within it, which would be "highly dangerous" and could lead only to "invidious distinctions," "jealousies, heart-burnings and divisions."[80] No doubt he had the Genesee Conference case in mind.

Peck, a peacemaker and a strong advocate of holiness, apparently thought that Chamberlayne's proposed censure was too harsh — and perhaps missed the point. He proposed a different resolution, "intended to be the mildest form of admonition" possible. Carlton introduced Peck's proposal as a substitute to Chamberlayne's charges, and it was adopted, according to Hibbard, "almost unanimously."[81] The conference actually adopted two resolutions.

Resolved, That, while we doubt not that there is much room for improvement among us in spiritual religion, and in observance of our beloved institutions, we regret that, in view of such deficiencies as may exist, and with the ostensible purpose of returning to first principles, any of our members should have associated together, as we find they have done, under the name of the "Nazarite Band," or other similar appellations, with some forms of secrecy, and with the claim to be peculiar in this respect; and we pass our disapprobation upon such associations, and hereby express our full expectation, that it will be abandoned by all members of this Conference. We especially, but affectionately, condemn the calumnious expressions read in relation to the Methodist Church, and her ministers, within our bounds; and we do hereby submit these views, to the special consideration of all who are concerned in this matter, and expect them, hereafter, to govern themselves accordingly.

Resolved, That the members of this Conference, who are members of Secret

78. Hibbard, "Nazaritism," p. 2. In 1854 Peck had replaced Abel Stevens as secretary and editor of the Tract Society. *COM,* pp. 698-99.

79. In an 1846 letter to Ellen Stowe, Lydia Lane commented that Jesse T. Peck reportedly "experienced the blessing of sanctification" at a recent camp meeting at Watervliet, N.Y. LBL to ELR, Aug. 26, 1846.

80. Jesse T. Peck, *The Central Idea of Christianity* (Boston: Henry V. Degen, 1856), p. 326. See Charles Edwin Jones, *Perfectionist Persuasion: The Holiness Movement and American Methodism, 1867-1936* (Metuchen, N.J.: Scarecrow Press, 1974), p. 7. In his "Appeal to Professors of Perfect Love" in this book, Peck explicitly includes the advice, "Beware of schism." "Any organization [within the church] of the friends of holiness as a distinct work, is highly dangerous" (pp. 321, 326).

81. Hibbard, "Nazaritism," p. 2.

Societies, be affectionately advised to abstain from all association with them in future.[82]

It is not clear whether Peck proposed (and Carlton introduced) both resolutions, or only the first, but the two are printed together in the conference minutes.[83] Hibbard writes, "Thus terminated the first Conference discussion and investigation of Nazaritism." He adds that the matter "was complicated at this time with plans and incessant efforts to control Bishops, cabinet counsels, Presiding Elder appointments, appointments of preachers, [and] election of delegates to General Conference."[84] Hibbard's remarks about "incessant efforts" to influence conference politics are overstated, but as already noted, Roberts *was* working hard to help elect General Conference delegates who would be "in favor of the life and power of godliness, of returning to the old paths, and of getting slavery out of the church."[85]

Toward the end of its sessions the conference, having disposed of the Nazarite question, returned to the issue of McCreery's character. The conference "*Resolved, That Brother M'Creery's character now pass, subject to an examination before his presiding elder of any charges that may be preferred against him by Dr. Chamberlayne or any other person.*" Conable notes that the underlying issue here was Nazaritism.[86]

The conference took no more action regarding Nazaritism, except later to pass a motion instructing the secretary to provide "copies of the several papers in his possession, relating to the Nazarite Band" to "any Presiding Elder" who might need them "for judicial purposes."[87] This referred no doubt to the McCreery case, but specifying *any* presiding elder carried ominous overtones of possible proceedings against other preachers.

The only references to Roberts in the conference minutes concern committee assignments, the statistical report, and the appointments. Roberts was again named

---

82. *Minutes of the Genesee Annual Conference* (1855), p. 7. In his article, Hibbard prints the first but not the second resolution, and he emphasizes the words "associated together, as we find they have done," "with some forms of secrecy," and "the claim to be peculiar in this respect," using italics and small caps. But the phrase "the claim to be peculiar in this respect" is obscure. Perhaps Peck meant the Nazarites claimed to be "peculiar" or unique in their efforts to return the church to first principles. Grammatically the statement seems to say the Nazarites were peculiar in having "some forms of secrecy," which of course is absurd, as Roberts later pointed out: "That men who had for years been opposing secret societies, should be charged with making such a 'claim,' seems extremely marvelous. They knew that there were many societies which had 'forms of secrecy.'" *WAS*, p. 40.

83. It is not clear also whether Roberts was present at this, the second day of annual conference, or arrived later.

84. Hibbard, "Nazaritism," p. 2.

85. BTR to TR, July 3, 1855, quoted in BHR, *BTR*, p. 103.

86. Conable, p. 640. Conable records this conference action; oddly, it is not included in the printed minutes. It is corroborated however by Hibbard, who notes, "The case of J. M'Creery was referred to the Presiding Elder, to be adjudicated on the District" (Hibbard, "Nazaritism," p. 2), and accords with Roberts's account of the disposition of the question of McCreery's character in *WAS*, p. 142.

87. *Minutes of the Genesee Annual Conference* (1855), p. 14.

to the Committee on Examination for first-year Course of Study candidates. He was also made one of the Visitors to Genesee College (along with Stiles, Kendall, and others), but not one of the Board of Visitors to Genesee Wesleyan Seminary, where he had previously served. His specific Course of Study committee assignment was to examine the candidates on Wesley's *Plain Account of Christian Perfection*.[88]

When Bishop Waugh read the appointments early Friday morning, September 7, Roberts found that he was being sent to Albion, about fifteen miles from Brockport, where Kendall had served the previous year. Kendall in turn was sent to Brockport; the two colleagues switched places.[89]

It was at this time that the term "Buffalo Regency" or "Regency Party" was first used in conference sessions to designate the preachers who opposed McCreery, Roberts, and their compatriots. The term "Regency" was borrowed from New York State politics.[90] McCreery (who may have coined the term) was using it in correspondence at least by November 1855, and perhaps earlier.[91] Fuller testified during Roberts's trial in 1858: "I first heard the term, Buffalo Regency, used on the Conference floor [in 1855] at Olean, by Rev. L. Stiles, Jr.; I first saw the name, Nazarite Band, in several documents" about that time.[92] And at that trial Stiles said, "It seems myself had the honor of publicly christening this secret clique. I was not aware that in a little speech on the Olean Conference floor [in 1855], I was doing so notable an act. I had frequently heard this name given to this clique on various occasions, but never dreamed that I was to have the distinguished honor of first pronouncing in public the name of 'Buffalo Regency.'"[93]

The 1855 Genesee Annual Conference sessions were a key turning point in Roberts's attempts to change the direction of the conference and return it to "old-line Methodism." As noted earlier, he had told his father: "We have most of the old men and young men with us, and think we can safely count on from eight to ten majority."[94] But that was before Robie's exposé (as he saw it) of the Nazarites on July 19. Whatever sympathy the conference preachers had with Roberts and McCreery's views on holiness and maintaining the distinctives of historic Methodism — and it seems to have been considerable — the alleged forming of a distinct "band" or "union" that had the smell of a secret society was controversial. McCreery did the cause a disser-

88. *Minutes of the Genesee Annual Conference* (1855), pp. 15, 25, 38.

89. *Minutes of the Genesee Annual Conference* (1855), pp. 16, 39.

90. "Buffalo Regency" suggests an unflattering comparison with the "Albany Regency," the New York State political machine engineered by Martin Van Buren that set much of the pattern for U.S. political parties in the 1820s and 1830s. See Samuel Eliot Morison, *The Oxford History of the American People* (New York: Oxford University Press, 1965), pp. 485, 488-90.

91. Joseph McCreery to Rev. H. Hornsby, Nov. 11, 1855, quoted in *WAS*, p. 36. McCreery used the term "Wyoming Regency" (apparently referring to influential preachers of the Wyoming ME Conference) earlier, in an 1852 letter to Roberts. Joseph McCreery, Jr. (Waterport, N.Y.), to BTR, Dec. 27, 1852 (Archives, Roberts Wesleyan College Library).

92. Chesbrough, *Defence*, p. 26.

93. Chesbrough, *Defence*, p. 36.

94. BTR to TR, July 3, 1855, quoted in BHR, *BTR*, p. 103.

vice by drawing up the Nazarite documents and allowing them to be circulated.[95] Thus McCreery, and by extension Roberts and other like-minded colleagues, was put on the defensive. It is not surprising that Benjamin wrote his father on July 31, "I am not only looking for coldness but that 'all manner of evil should be said of me falsely for Christ's sake'" at the annual conference sessions.[96] His prediction that Robie's attack on Nazaritism would backfire proved wrong.

On the crucial issue of General Conference delegates (which Roberts had targeted), the election turned out to be in effect a split decision. If Carlton and his friends backed a prearranged slate, they didn't win entirely. Fuller was not elected.[97] Carlton himself was elected, along with Richard Waite, who shared Carlton's views and had already attacked Roberts in the *Northern Christian Advocate* (as noted in the previous chapter).[98] But the third delegate elected was Isaac C. Kingsley, a close associate of Roberts who later may have become a Free Methodist.[99] If the order of the names reporting the ballot election indicates the order in which the delegates were chosen, we may assume that Kingsley was elected third, after Carlton and Waite, probably receiving the least votes. Roberts and his compatriots thus failed to muster a majority in the delegate election, but did manage to get one of their preferred candidates elected.

If Roberts and his associates had carried the day at annual conference, preventing the censure of Nazaritism and influencing other crucial decisions including General Conference delegate selection, the whole subsequent history would have been different. As it turned out, the same group of preachers that had dominated conference business for a number of years remained in control. Whether this group constituted, or was largely controlled by, a secret union of preachers who held membership in the Masons or Odd Fellows (as Roberts charged) is not entirely clear.

Benson Roberts later wrote that the 1855 conference sessions at Olean "saw two sentiments clearly defined." Though individually preachers held diverse views, these had not yet hardened into factions. But sentiments "that were necessarily antagonistic and inevitably must array their supporters into opposing parties" congealed at the Olean conference. Benson Roberts, obviously sympathetic to his father, outlined these "two sentiments" as follows:

> The one sentiment was liberal in its utterances, its theology was non-Methodistic and anti-Wesleyan. Its adherents saw no necessity for the rigid adherence of the

95. It appears that Roberts himself did not participate in this, and it is not clear to what extent he actually approved or disapproved of McCreery's actions, though he defended McCreery.

96. BTR to TR, July 31, 1855.

97. As noted earlier, Roberts thought Fuller wanted to be elected delegate. Perhaps he would have been elected rather than Kingsley had the so-called Regency Party been stronger. Fuller (1808-91) served for three years as agent of the American Bible Society (according to *COM*) and was a colonel during the Civil War. Later he transferred to Michigan and served as presiding elder in the Detroit Conference. *COM*, p. 385; Allen, *Century*, p. 87; *Minutes*, Genesee Conference, 1847-59.

98. Richard Lynde Waite (1810-97) was thirteen years older than Roberts and two years younger than Carlton. Allen, *Century*, p. 126.

99. Kingsley withdrew from the ME Church in 1860. Allen, *Century*, p. 100.

early Methodists to the wise rules of the discipline upon the subject of worldliness. It was friendly to the world and would have the world friendly to it. Rented pews, church fairs, sociables were quite in favor with these, and as for the class-meeting they made little use of it, or of the prayer-meetings. The other sentiment that had a strong hold on many of the ministers, and more of the laity was staunch in its adherence to old time Wesleyan Methodism, both in doctrine and experience. It believed in the church rules in respect to worldly conformity and in enforcing them. With this sentiment the practice of supporting churches by the sale or rental of pews was at variance. Spiritual life and power were sought and taught as the privilege and duty of God's children.

The adherents of the former opinion were influential men, who stood well with the powers of the church. They held good appointments and high offices, and at this conference it began to be manifest that they would aid to put no one into office who was not in expressed accord with them. Many of this sentiment were members of secret societies, of the odd-fellows mostly. . . . The adherents of the one sentiment were standing and acting together for the sake of place, power, preferment and good livings. This of necessity served to unite the others for the sake of fidelity to the vows, resting upon them as Methodist preachers, to defend the doctrines and preserve the spiritual life of the church. The lines were drawn on the conference floor, the discussions were pointed and the issue was clearly made. At last the time came to adjourn; they separated to their respective appointments but it was with eyes opened to the necessity, and probable cost, of standing by the right, that the minority took their appointments, some on humble circuits in no way worthy of their abilities.[100]

This description well summarizes the range of issues as conference ended and B. T. Roberts went to his new appointment at Albion. It seems true, as Benson Roberts implies, that B. T. Roberts's views were more in line with those of the Methodist people generally than were the views of the more liberal party, with the possible exception of members in the wealthier, more urbane churches in Buffalo.

Seven weeks after the Olean conference, Robie celebrated the squelching of the Nazarites and took major credit for it. In the *Buffalo Christian Advocate* he noted that after his first article, "Some of our readers and friends thought that we were not only too severe, but that the movement was not of sufficient importance to demand the notoriety which we then gave to it." As a sort of vindication, Robie printed in full the anti-Nazarite resolution adopted by the conference, though he made no reference to the resolution against secret societies. Defending his earlier articles, he noted that the conference viewed the Nazarite "movement" as "of a very serious nature." He added,

We exposed the whole matter long before the Conference, and because we did so a prodigious tirade was attempted against us. Preachers looked askant, members

100. BHR, *BTR*, pp. 105-7.

were a good deal troubled, and among the Nazarites a perfect storm of excitement prevailed. — We had slandered, were false-accusers, and were put down among the vilest beings that were suffered to live. And even the Conference, after they had taken up our exposure of the iniquitous faction, permitted some of the Nazarites to have full play upon our paper. We thought this was ill-timed, and especially so, after they had passed a bull of condemnation upon the same thing.

In other words, Robie didn't like the fact that some of the so-called Nazarites (most likely Roberts and others) had criticized the *Buffalo Christian Advocate* before the conference. But, Robie crowed, "We enjoyed the extreme satisfaction of witnessing the blowing up of the Band, and of seeing demonstrated this one thing farther — that some men have position whether they deserve character and place, or not."[101] Robie's final comment is a bit obscure, but it appears to be a slap at people like Kingsley and Stiles, both of whom were now presiding elders, and possibly B. T. Roberts, who since his appointment to Albion was now pastoring one of the largest churches in the conference. In Robie's eyes such men illegitimately held "position" in the conference. And Robie was always sensitive to position.

Did the "Nazarites" Really Exist?

The "Nazarite" commotion in the Genesee Conference leads back to the question: Was there really ever such a thing as the Nazarite Union? Was Roberts correct that "no such organization ever existed"?

Roberts was telling the truth. He marshaled solid arguments and credible witnesses, showing that no Nazarite Union was ever formally organized. But the full story is not quite so black and white.[102] While Roberts, McCreery, and their colleagues never formally organized and did not as a group adopt the name Nazarite, clearly they did develop a close network that operated with some secrecy, or at least discretion, to bring change in the Genesee Conference and to influence annual conference action. And while Roberts seems never to have owned the name Nazarite, McCreery did. Not only did McCreery publish the Nazarite documents, he later

---

101. [John Robie], "The Nazarites, Once More," *Buffalo Christian Advocate*, Oct. 25, 1855, p. 2.

102. Roberts was a stickler for semantic accuracy in such matters. A few years later he roundly criticized F. B. Hibbard, editor of the *Northern Christian Advocate*, for titling a notice about the Bergen camp meeting "Bergen District Camp-Meeting" rather than "Genesee Camp-Ground Association" — the point being that the camp, sponsored by the association, was not strictly a "district camp meeting." Because Hibbard used this "misleading" wording, Roberts and the other campground association trustees wrote, *"No such notice has been published. No such camp-meeting has been appointed"* ("Genesee Camp-Ground Association," *NCA* 18, no. 30 [July 28, 1858]: 1). This article was signed by Roberts and six other trustees. Presumably Roberts wrote it, or at least had a hand in it. Roberts considered such accuracy a matter of fairness and justice (and the lack of it to be slander), as is seen later in his criticisms of Matthew Simpson's account of the organization of the Free Methodist Church with which Roberts begins his book *Why Another Sect.*

published a sixteen-page pamphlet titled *Nazarite Review of the Pastoral Address of the Genesee Conference of the M.E. Church.*[103] Technically McCreery was really the only "Nazarite"; there never was such an organization. But a reforming network to which opponents attached the name Nazarites did exist, and some within this network apparently did self-identify as Nazarites.

The opposition of course had no interest in whether or not the so-called Nazarites had ever formally organized or not. "Nazarite" became a convenient label, just like "Regency," and became politically useful to the "Regency" faction.

103. "Jonadab," *Nazarite Review of the Pastoral Address of the Genesee Conference of the M.E. Church.*

CHAPTER 18

Ministry in Albion

"I want to do what is best for both worlds."

B. T. Roberts, 1855[1]

"Church stock rises in value, as religion becomes fashionable, and the minister of the Gospel popular, among the proud and aspiring."

B. T. Roberts, 1856[2]

Even as the Nazarite issue was brewing and reaching the boiling point, B. T. Roberts continued his ministry as a Methodist preacher. He and Ellen spent two significant years in Albion, New York, just fifteen miles west of Brockport — still on the Erie Canal, and still in the Genesee District. But now his presiding elder was his friend Loren Stiles.

First Year at Albion

Going to Albion meant "a large [Methodist] society" and "a pleasant village," not far from Benjamin and Ellen's prior assignment.[3]

The previous year, under William Kendall, Albion had seen a remarkable increase from 183 to 285 members, despite initial opposition to Kendall's preaching ho-

1. BTR to TR, Oct. 8, 1855.
2. B. T. Roberts, "Free Churches," *NCA* 16, no. 20 (May 14, 1856): 4.
3. BHR, *BTR*, p. 109.

liness and enforcing the Methodist discipline. The 1855 total membership included 99 probationers, indicating considerable evangelistic success.[4] Benjamin later reported at some length on Kendall's year at Albion. He noted that around Thanksgiving time Kendall began holding "extra prayer-meetings, chiefly among the poor. Several were awakened and converted, and meetings were held daily."[5] Kendall "was accustomed to say," Roberts remarked, that "his peculiar mission seemed to be to 'let God loose among the people.'"[6]

Kendall had conducted a stirring winter revival with the help of John Wesley Redfield. In a February 3, 1855, letter to A. A. Phelps,[7] Kendall wrote, "That man of God, Dr. Redfield, is with us. . . . His shots are finding a lodgment in the hearts of the King's enemies. . . . Our official members are our greatest hindrances. Entire holiness is gloriously prevailing. Young converts and little ones are pressing into possession of it, and their influence is being felt."[8]

Roberts summarized, "Perhaps one hundred and fifty were reclaimed and converted in this revival, most of whom were already members of churches. Over one hundred were added to the church, and the church was a new one indeed, — changed from gay, formal worshippers, to plain, active, humble disciples of the meek and lowly Jesus." Roberts said the work at Albion "continued steadily through the entire year, receiving a fresh impulse at the Bergen camp meeting" of 1855, when "some eight tents from Albion" were on the grounds for the first time.[9]

This spurt in growth had made Albion the second-largest church in the conference by the time Roberts arrived in September 1855. Significantly, the largest church was now Lockport, with 301 members, where Roberts and Kendall's friend Loren Stiles had a successful year. Stiles's appointment this year as presiding elder of the Genesee District was in some measure a recognition of his effectiveness. Stiles was a powerful preacher; Sandford Hunt described him as "a fluent extempore speaker of popular address."[10]

Despite the growth at Albion and elsewhere, overall the conference was not growing. It lost 235 members during the 1854-55 conference year, ending with a total membership of 11,335.[11]

---

4. *Minutes*, Genesee Conference, 1854, 1855.

5. "Rev. Wm. C. Kendall, A.M.," *EC* 2, no. 9 (Sept. 1861): 278.

6. "Rev. Wm. C. Kendall, A.M. — Labors — Death," *EC* 2, no. 12 (Dec. 1861): 373.

7. Phelps was a Methodist preacher and was associated with the *Guide to Holiness*. He later became a Free Methodist. See Hogue, *HFMC*, 1:319, 337-41.

8. William Kendall to A. A. Phelps, Feb. 3, 1855, quoted in BHR, *BTR*, p. 108. Kendall goes on to detail the opposition he was getting from some of his established, nominal members, but adds that God was working in power. "Our house [church building] was crammed Sunday night from top to bottom; but salvation came. Last night, also two lost their strength — a thing never before known in Albion until this winter. The people are filled with wonder and dismay."

9. "Rev. Wm. C. Kendall, A.M.," p. 281.

10. Sandford Hunt, *Methodism in Buffalo From Its Origin to the Close of 1892* (Buffalo: H. H. Otis and Sons, 1893), p. 78.

11. *Minutes of the Genesee Annual Conference of the Methodist Episcopal Church, 1855* (Buffalo: Reese and Co., 1855), pp. 32-37.

Benjamin moved with Ellen and their two boys, Georgie and Benson, to Albion right after conference. A week or so later, on Monday, September 17, he wrote his father, "We are getting nicely settled in our new house. We find things more pleasant about the parsonage than usually falls to the lot of the itinerant." He reported that Benson had recovered and the whole family was in pretty good health. This fall there were fewer family health problems. Although Ellen had "an attack of the neuralgia," in November, Benjamin could report that "We are all very well and things are moving on very pleasantly."[12]

Benjamin concluded that he was going to need a horse to adequately care for his charge at Albion, so he asked his father to send a young horse so it could be trained to be "a good family horse." "I shall want you to wait till I can pay you," he added. A week or so later he did get the horse, which, like his earlier one, was named Bill. "I think he will make as gentle and trusty a family horse as need be," Benjamin wrote. "I drove him around by the [canal] boats, [railroad] cars &c. and he appears less scary than any horse I ever used, that was not accustomed to such sights & sounds. . . . I am no more afraid of him than I am of my cow." But as it turned out, Bill consumed twelve quarts of oats a day, and Roberts thought he would sell him and buy "a cheaper horse [that] would do me just as well and get more miles per quart."[13]

Roberts's first year at Albion seems to have passed without major difficulties or major success, despite the Nazarite controversy. He provides few details in his 1856 diary, which is mostly blank.[14] In November he wrote to his parents, mentioning the general quarterly meeting planned for December 6-9 at Albion, and urging them to attend. "We expect the pilgrims here from all over the district," he wrote. "Come out and see and hear for yourself what these 'fanatical' Methodists are." Benjamin added, "We are expecting salvation in the name of the Lord."[15]

In a January 22, 1856, letter to his father, Benjamin comments, "We are having a very good degree of interest in the Church. Sunday night there were seven forward and one converted. We have preaching 3 or 4 evenings in the week." In March Benjamin mentions heavy snows, noting that the snow was about two feet deep, despite some thawing. He added on Thursday, March 20, "The snow has lain on the ground since Christmas. People came to Church with sleighs. I preached in the afternoon to a crowded house on [']Free Churches.'"[16]

A week later he wrote: "A cold snowy blustering day. Old snow deep. Froze all day. Read. Hume, Patriarchal Age. Called."[17]

---

12. BTR to TR, Sept. 17, Oct. 8, and Nov. 16, 1855.

13. BTR to TR, Sept. 17 and Oct. 8, 1855.

14. For whatever reason, Roberts didn't keep a daily record during 1856. He later used many of the blank pages for various notes and lists.

15. BTR to TR, Nov. 16, 1855. Cf. Zahniser, p. 82. Zahniser gives the date as Nov. 14, but Roberts appears to have first written "15" and then changed it to "16."

16. BTR to TR, Jan. 22, 1856; BTRD, Mar. 18 and 20, 1856.

17. BTRD, Mar. 28, 1856. It is not clear whether Roberts is referring here to one book or two. Perhaps two, as the "Patriarchal Age" book was probably George Smith, *The Patriarchal Age: The Hebrew*

Roberts reports a meeting on Thursday afternoon, March 20, which may indicate that a revival series was in progress.[18] Roberts wrote his father on April 17, however: "We have had and still have a good revival influence in the church; but there has not been that general work that we have desired and prayed for. I have received so far about thirty on probation. It has been a very unpropitious winter for holding meetings. We are hoping to see the good work go on all summer."[19]

Meanwhile, Ellen was again pregnant. In January she considered making a trip to New Jersey to visit George and Lydia Lane, who were in poor health, and other friends. "They are very anxious to have her come and offer to pay expenses," Benjamin noted.[20] It is unclear whether Ellen actually made this trip or not.

Overall, the family was in good health throughout the conference year. "The boys are growing finely," Benjamin wrote in January. Little George, who had just turned four, was beginning to imitate his father. He "has quite a notion of preaching," Benjamin wrote, "holding meetings with Benson most every day."[21]

Ellen continued quite well throughout her pregnancy. She gave birth to the couple's third son, Charles Stowe Roberts, on June 12, 1856 — the very day the Bergen camp meeting was scheduled to begin.[22]

Finney and Redfield in Rochester

During Benjamin's first year at Albion, both John Wesley Redfield and Charles G. Finney conducted revivals in Rochester, thirty-five miles away. Rochester had grown to a city of about 50,000, with many churches.[23] Redfield's meetings were held at the First Methodist Episcopal Church (East Genesee Conference) at the invitation of the pastor, Jonathan Watts, in late March and early April 1856. Watts was sympathetic to Redfield and Roberts and, like Roberts, shortly afterward became a corresponding editor of the *Northern Independent*. Despite opposition from the presiding elder, Augustus C. George, and some of the other Methodist preachers in Rochester, Redfield had a moderately successful meeting.[24]

People (New York: Lane and Scott, 1850), which was listed in the third year of the Methodist Course of Study. *Doctrines and Discipline of the Methodist Episcopal Church* (1856), p. 233; see Douglas Russell Cullum, "Gospel Simplicity: Rhythms of Faith and Life among Free Methodists in Victorian America" (Ph.D. diss., Drew University, 2002), p. 376.

18. Roberts mentions an evening service as well, at which Brother Sandford preached. Presumably this was "R. Sanford," possibly one of the Albion trustees Roberts lists and perhaps a local preacher. BTRD, Jan. 23-24, 1856. (Roberts lists forty-three names, together with contributions made, under the heading "Trustees M.E.C. Albion," but certainly not all these people were trustees.)

19. BTR to TR, Apr. 17, 1856, quoted in BHR, *BTR*, p. 110.

20. BTR to TR, Jan. 22, 1856.

21. BTR to TR, Jan. 22, 1856.

22. Smail, p. 15; Carpenter, p. 47.

23. Garth M. Rosell and Richard A. G. Dupuis, eds., *The Memoirs of Charles G. Finney: The Complete Restored Text* (Grand Rapids: Zondervan, 1989), p. 548.

24. Redfield Autobiography, pp. 322-23; Terrill, *Redfield*, pp. 296-97. There were six ME churches

Meanwhile, Finney, then sixty-three, and his wife returned to Rochester for his third revival there. His first, in 1830-31, was one of the most remarkable in American history and helped spread his fame. The 1856 meeting was also a dramatic success. A Presbyterian pastor wrote later that Finney "preached in several of the churches twice or three times every day and Sunday for . . . months. During all this time a prayer meeting was held every day at 10 o'clock a.m., averaging from 800 to 1,000 attendance. The whole population of Rochester rocked as if the city had been shaken by an earthquake. Almost all the churches were opened to Mr. Finney. . . . The number of converts was incredible."[25]

Finney began his meetings on Sunday, December 30, 1855, and continued them until late April, when he became ill. He worked mostly among the Presbyterians, Congregationalists, and Baptists, noting in his memoirs that "the Methodist churches went to work in their own way to extend the work"[26] — referring to the Redfield revival.[27] Finney said there were "many striking cases of conversion," and that the work "excited so much interest that it became the general topic of conversation throughout the city and the surrounding region."[28] A student at the University of Rochester later wrote, "The interest was extraordinary. . . . Scarcely anything else was talked about. The atmosphere was full of a kind of electricity of spiritual power. The daily papers all reported the meetings at great length."[29] One of the many converts was Augustus H. Strong, later president of the theological seminary in Rochester and a noted Baptist theologian.[30]

As the revival continued, Finney wrote, "all classes of persons, from the highest to the lowest, from the richest to the poorest, were visited by the power of this revival and brought to Christ."[31] Many people from surrounding towns traveled to Roches-

---

in Rochester at this time, two in the Rochester District and four in the West Rochester District of the East Genesee Conference.

25. Dr. J. H. McIlvaine, pastor of First Presbyterian Church in Rochester. Quoted in Keith J. Hardman, *Charles Grandison Finney, 1792-1875, Revivalist and Reformer* (Grand Rapids: Baker, 1987), p. 430. McIlvaine says the Finney revival continued "for about eight months"; actually the period was four months.

26. Rosell and Dupuis, *Memoirs*, pp. 551, 548.

27. An Apr. 29 report in the *Independent* noted, "Mr. Finney's audiences have been composed of all sects, though less, perhaps, of Methodists, as they have had latterly effective preaching of their own." The report adds, "The Methodists have been favored for a time with the services of Rev. Dr. Redfield, of New-York; but most of the preaching in the city, besides that of the pastors, has been by Mr. Finney. He has preached seven times each week during the greater portion of seventeen weeks." The reporter said the 1856 Finney revival "resembles the revivals of 1831-2 and of 1839-40 in New-York, Philadelphia, and other cities," but with "nothing of what was then regarded as religious extravagance and emotional excess." H. F., "The Revival at Rochester," *Independent*, May 15, 1856, p. 155. Cf. Rosell and Dupuis, *Memoirs*, p. 548.

28. Rosell and Dupuis, *Memoirs*, p. 550.

29. William C. Wilkinson, quoted in Rosell and Dupuis, *Memoirs*, p. 550.

30. Rosell and Dupuis, *Memoirs*, p. 551. Strong estimated that one thousand people "joined the churches" in Rochester as a result of this revival.

31. Rosell and Dupuis, *Memoirs*, p. 551.

ter to attend the meetings.[32] Benjamin and Ellen may possibly have traveled from Albion to hear Finney (or Redfield) at some point.

Finney's 1856 union revival in Rochester was in many ways as remarkable as his first. He later viewed this awakening as the precursor of the great 1858-59 revival that began in New York City.[33] In contrast, Redfield's meeting was of shorter duration and was confined mostly to one congregation, the First ME Church. Redfield was in Rochester for just three weeks — Monday, March 24, through Sunday, April 13 — toward the end of the four-month Finney revival. He was assisted by Fay Purdy during part of the meeting.[34]

After two weeks of revival effort Redfield wrote, "The church will not get right, but the pilgrims from all churches come in. The altar is frequently filled, and we have some strong conversions. The house [sanctuary] is very large, but will not hold the people. I never saw a greater chance for a great work in any place. But as soon as we get to a boiling point, the moderators put the fires out, and we have to start anew. My only hope is to strengthen the pilgrims, and get them to work for a salvation church."[35]

Apparently the revival did have some impact on First Church. The conference minutes show that the congregation grew from 154 members to 189 that year, and Redfield reported that a number of people were sanctified.[36]

Redfield's efforts included afternoon services, and Terrill reports that Finney occasionally came to hear the Methodist evangelist. "The two men seemed to enjoy each other's society," notes Terrill, and "[bade] each other Godspeed in their mission of calling souls to Christ."[37] At forty-five, Redfield was eighteen years younger than Finney.

Phoebe Palmer's revival ministry was also expanding during this period. During 1855 and 1856 she spoke at about twenty camp meetings, including several in On-

32. One contemporary source said people came from Buffalo, Lockport, Batavia, Brockport, Syracuse, and many other places. Rosell and Dupuis, *Memoirs*, p. 555.

33. Rosell and Dupuis, *Memoirs*, p. 555. Finney wrote in 1859, "It has been supposed that this present movement originated in prayer-meetings established for business men in the city of New York. This is a great mistake. A spirit of revival had been growing for several years in many parts of the United States. . . . In Rochester, Christians of all denominations . . . united in the work, and daily prayer-meetings and preaching were held in the different churches in succession — the meetings moving round from church to church in a circle." Finney, *The Prevailing Prayer-Meeting: A Sermon* (London: Ward, 1859), p. 24, quoted in Rosell and Dupuis, p. 555.

34. Terrill, *Redfield*, pp. 293, 296-99. Purdy left on Apr. 9, Redfield noted, "rather discouraged as to any great results" (p. 299).

35. Terrill, *Redfield*, p. 299. It is interesting to note that in both Redfield's and Roberts's ministries (and in that of many other Methodist preachers of the time) the revivalist mentality had by now so thoroughly penetrated Methodism that going to or gathering around the altar was the assumed way people normally came to God — though conversions also often took place in private homes or in prayer or class meetings.

36. *Minutes*, East Genesee Conference, 1855, 1856; Redfield Autobiography, pp. 322-23; Terrill, *Redfield*, p. 297.

37. Terrill, *Redfield*, p. 297.

tario, Canada. When her mother died toward the end of 1856, Mrs. Palmer felt "a new baptism" for her ministry and rededicated herself to reaching people for Christ. Her ministry grew increasingly effective, as though in anticipation of the great revival of 1858. Charles White notes, "Mrs. Palmer saw greater blessing upon her labors during 1857 than any previous year. In July at Brighton, Ontario, she saw two hundred conversions. . . . In Spencertown the Holy Ghost fell so mightily upon the people that one hundred prostrated themselves in tears before God. But these events were merely the prelude [to her very significant 1857 revival at Hamilton, Ontario, and the events of 1858]."[38]

Roberts's ministry at Albion thus unfolded in the context of an approaching broader spiritual awakening.

Living in Two Worlds

During this conference year Roberts again considered purchasing some land as an investment — either in New York State or farther west on the American frontier. He wrote his father on October 8, 1855, "I must confess that I am a little afraid of dabbling in western lands, so many of our preachers have lost their power thereby. I want to do what is best for both worlds." But he found out that a man near Brockport had a 120-acre farm to sell, and he decided to check that out. As to western lands, he wrote his father, "Perhaps you can find some government land that has been in market for some time which can be bought at a low price. I would make inquiry, and if you find some that you think is good, make arrangement with some one near by to purchase it for you, and I will obtain the money and send it on your return." Titus and Sally Roberts were about to make a trip to the Midwest, apparently to check on land opportunities.[39]

Benjamin wrote his father again on December 29, suggesting that he might be able to use his house in Buffalo as partial payment for a 120-acre farm near Bergen that he had looked at (possibly the same farm he mentioned October 8). The total price was about $5,000 — more than eight times Roberts's annual salary — but he was thinking long-term investment and hoping his father would help. The farm included a brick house, a barn, an orchard, and 40 acres of woods from which trees could be sold for lumber. Benjamin calculated that his Buffalo house would cover $1,500 of the price, and that he could pay off the balance over six years by selling wood (at $2 per cord) and hay (at $10 per ton).[40]

But Benjamin was still ambivalent about buying land. "I do not know as I had

38. Charles Edward White, *The Beauty of Holiness: Phoebe Palmer as Theologian, Revivalist, Feminist, and Humanitarian* (Grand Rapids: Francis Asbury Press/Zondervan, 1986), pp. 44-45.

39. BTR to TR, Oct. 8 and Nov. 16, 1855. They apparently did travel west and, at this or some other time, did acquire some "western" lands, perhaps in Ohio, Indiana, or Illinois. See BTR to TR, Jan. 8, 1856.

40. BTR to TR, Dec. 29, 1855.

better think of buying it at all," he wrote his father on January 8. "I do not wish to do any thing that will embarrass me in the work to which the Lord has been pleased to call me." Yet he continued calculating how he might make the purchase and pay it off. "With ordinary luck I think I could clear [the balance] off in six years. . . . Still I do not know as I had better think any more about it." He added, "I feel greatly obliged to you for the kind proposal you made to put in western land, but it seems to me you had better keep all your land at the west. It will double in value every four years."[41]

Benjamin continued talking with the farm's owner. He wrote his father about it again on January 22. Instead of taking the Buffalo house in partial payment, the owner would accept "300 acres of western land, if it is good and in a good location," for $1,500 ($5 an acre). "Suppose we buy it together," Roberts proposed to his father. "I think we could without much trouble pay [the balance] off from [the produce of] the farm in six years." Benjamin wanted Titus to come and look at the land with him.[42]

As winter warmed into spring, Benjamin apparently dropped the idea of buying land. He and Ellen kept the Buffalo house, which later proved useful to them in ministry. He began focusing on the Bergen camp meeting in June, telling his father on May 9, "We have bought twenty five acres of beautiful woods for a permanent Camp ground."[43] He also busied himself with a series of articles on "free churches."

The Case for "Free Churches"

Benjamin continued writing. In April and May 1856 he published three articles in the *Northern Christian Advocate* under the title "Free Churches."[44] The first appeared in the April 23 issue, and the others on April 30 and May 14.

On biblical, theological, and practical grounds, Roberts argued against renting and selling pews. Partly this was a matter of good stewardship — and thus of discipleship and spirituality. "Let every one give as in apostolic days, according to his circumstances, and the Church can be far more easily sustained than under the pew

41. BTR to TR, Jan. 8, 1855. This comment shows clearly that Roberts was thinking of long-term investment (no doubt as future financial security), both for himself and for his parents.

42. BTR to TR, Jan. 22, 1856. Apparently Roberts reconsidered his father's offer to help finance the purchase using some of his "western land." Benjamin's comments seem to imply that Titus Roberts already had purchased well over 300 acres of land in the West.

43. BTR to TR, May 9, 1856. In this letter Benjamin also comments on the "calamity" that had recently hit Gowanda — a devastating fire that wiped out his brother-in-law's business and much of downtown Gowanda (as noted in chapter 3).

44. These three articles were signed and dated Albion, Apr. 2, 5, and 20, 1856. They appeared in some of the last issues of the *Northern Christian Advocate* that Hosmer edited. (See RFP, Microfilm Reel 11, Frames 2-21, for Roberts's handwritten manuscript of a version of these articles.)

system," he argued. "An average of 10 cts. per member, per week, would amount in a Church numbering 200, to over $1000 per annum."[45]

These forceful, well-written pieces are good samples of Roberts's style and reasoning. Consciously or not, he employed all the elements of the so-called Wesleyan Quadrilateral: Scripture, tradition, reason, and experience. The first article appeals especially to tradition, reason, and experience, while the second and third are based primarily on Scripture.[46]

Roberts had found an article entitled "Free Churches" in the October 1855 issue of the *Church Review* about the practice of pew rental in the Episcopal Church,[47] and this provided much of the ammunition for his first article. He noted that many Episcopal "houses of worship have been made free, in accordance with resolutions passed by their Conventions," and with good results. He cited several examples from the article and noted: "These facts show conclusively, that even in the Episcopal Church, the expenses of public worship can be better met under the free, than under the pew system. How much more among us, with our liberal Evangelism and doctrine of Entire Consecration!"[48]

But Roberts argued more fundamentally that the selling or renting of pews "has always been contrary to the economy of our Church." Over time "the spirit of the world has encroached upon us" so that now, "in all this region, I do not know of a single free church in any of the cities or larger villages." Roberts, however, was "thoroughly convinced that this system is wrong in principle, and bad in tendency. It is a gross corruption of Christianity." He was passionate about this: "I beg the indulgence of expressing myself strongly. I cannot adopt the cautious language of doubt, for I have no misgivings. I do not believe merely, that there should be free churches; but that all churches should be free. Not merely that some unmarketable seats should not be rented or sold, but that no seat in the house of God should be rented or sold."

Roberts advanced several arguments: voluntary offerings were actually more effective in meeting expenses than was the pew system; pew rental or sale introduced "a certain degree of social distinction" in the church; "[v]oluntary contributions for the support of the ordinances of religion" were the biblical and traditional way.[49] Here Roberts cited Mosheim on the way the early Christians combined praying with giving, and thus both the church's ministers were sustained and the poor were fed. "We have gained little and lost much, by the unnatural divorce of praying and giving." Now people give very disproportionately, and for the wrong reasons. "The distribution of the burden is very unequal. Let every one give as in apostolic days, according

45. B. T. Roberts, "Free Churches," *NCA* 16, no. 17 (Apr. 23, 1856): 4, hereafter "Free Churches I."

46. In the first article Roberts says, for example, "But we are not left to mere reasoning. However conclusive that might be, actual experience is far more reliable."

47. "Free Churches," *Church Review* 8, no. 3 (Oct. 1855): 352-66. Unsigned, the article was probably written by the editor, Nathaniel Smith Richardson. It is a review article of several books or pamphlets and published sermons that opposed or discussed pew rental in the Episcopal Church.

48. B. T. Roberts, "Free Churches I," p. 4.

49. These points are all made in the *Church Review* article.

to his circumstances, and the Church can be far more easily sustained than under the pew system." Here Roberts cited the data from the Episcopal Church study.

Roberts concluded his first article: "Thus is the plea of the necessity for pewed churches completely overthrown," even though the system is often urged with great "pertinacity." "From what we sometimes hear, it would seem as if some supposed that the great object of building a church, is that it may be like a theatre, a paying concern."[50]

In the second article, Roberts's argument is essentially a biblical one. "Several precepts of the Bible plainly require that the house of the Lord should be free for all who may wish to assemble there for purposes of worship," he began. The pew system can't be supported without "great violence . . . to the Scriptures." Arguments for the pew system, as for polygamy or slavery, amount to "perversions of the Divine record."[51]

Roberts emphasized his thesis statement: *"The Pew system is condemned in all those passages that forbid the paying of respect to persons."*[52] Though several such passages "readily recur to the mind," he cites specifically only James 2:1-10, which he quotes in full. With its prohibition of showing partiality to the rich, this had become the key text for opponents of renting and selling pews.[53]

The remainder of the article drew out the implications of this passage. To provide better seating for those "whose appearance indicates wealth and pride" than for the poor clearly is sin. "Sin does not cease to be sin because it is reduced to a system and committed unblushingly." Whenever "pews are rented or sold, 'the brethren' virtually say, whoever is able and willing to pay the most, shall have the best seat permanently, for the exclusive use of himself and his family." Even if he is morally corrupt — "an atheist or an infidel, a gambler or a libertine" — it makes no difference. "He has the money, the one thing needful to secure peculiar privileges in a pewed house of worship."

Thus the whole pew-rental system clearly violated Scripture. It necessarily required "respect of persons." Those seating the congregation know that "it will not do to put plainly dressed persons into the pews of those aspiring to 'social position.' Though the Church be not more than half filled, more or less difficulty is always experienced in seating the congregation, so as not to offend the owners of pews."

The teaching in James 2 clearly proscribed the renting of pews, Roberts concluded. "Explain away the force of this portion of Revealed truth, and you may with the same facility make any other portion of the word of God 'of none effect through your traditions.'"[54]

Roberts's third "Free Churches" article was brief but in some ways the most telling. Significantly, he based it directly on the example and teaching of Jesus. *"We are*

---

50. B. T. Roberts, "Free Churches I," p. 4.

51. The reference to polygamy here may have been prompted by the rise of and controversy over Mormonism.

52. B. T. Roberts, "Free Churches," *NCA* 16, no. 18 (Apr. 30, 1856): 4, hereafter "Free Churches II."

53. The *Church Review* article quoted James 2:1-6, 8-9 (p. 355).

54. B. T. Roberts, "Free Churches II," p. 4.

forbidden to make the house of God a house of merchandise," he began.[55] He based his argument on Jesus' cleansing of the temple in Jerusalem — one of the few incidents in Jesus' life found in all four Gospels, Roberts noted. He quoted John 2:13-16, which concludes, "Take these things hence; make not my Father's house an house of merchandise." This argument apparently was suggested to Roberts by the *Church Review* article, which similarly made the connection between Jesus' cleansing of the temple and pew renting and quoted John 2:16.

Roberts wrote, "To the worst of sinners, the Savior was usually mild and forbearing." "Of all the sins that he witnessed, one sin only aroused his holy indignation to acts of violence" — buying and selling in the temple. Roberts gave a brief exegesis of this incident, noting that the animals bought and sold were all "lawful articles of traffic" and "indispensable to the Temple service."

> All this trade was intended to facilitate religious worship. It was carried on with decency and propriety. But the Savior would not tolerate it, however good the intention. He made a scourge of small cords, and by force drove out these buyers and sellers. What would he have done if he had found them selling off parts of the temple itself, by auction, to the highest bidder? — Would the traffic in pews, in the house of his Father, have excited his indignation less than did the traffic in sacrifices? . . . Pews are offered for sale in the market, and advertised in the newspapers, the same as dry goods and groceries. Church stock rises in value, as religion becomes fashionable, and the minister of the Gospel popular, among the proud and aspiring.
>
> This example of Christ could not have been recorded by the four Evangelists to prevent the repetition of the particular offence that he thus strongly condemned, for He knew that the temple would soon be destroyed, and its typical ceremonials be abolished forever. Had his prophetic eye looked down through the vista of succeeding centuries, and rested upon the pew system, the latest corruption of the religion He established, He could hardly have condemned it more strongly than by the words and the accompanying action, "*Make not my Father's house, an house of merchandise.*"[56]

Though Roberts would return to the "free church" issue a year or so later in his "New School Methodism" articles, these three pieces present his most cogent and detailed attack on the merchandising of pews.

1856 Bergen Camp Meeting

As summer approached, Benjamin began planning for the 1856 Bergen camp meeting. The gathering began on Thursday, June 12, and presumably ran for a week. The

---

55. B. T. Roberts, "Free Churches," *NCA* 16, no. 20 (May 14, 1856): 4, hereafter "Free Churches III."
56. B. T. Roberts, "Free Churches III," p. 4.

camp now had a permanent site, the twenty-five acres of "beautiful woods" that Benjamin mentioned to his father on May 9. Benjamin tried to arrange for one of the Methodist bishops to be present to dedicate the grounds on the first day.[57]

This permanent site was indeed a beautiful spot. The editor of the *Brockport Republic* noted, "The camp ground embraces an area of twenty-five acres, all covered by heavy timber, principally beech."[58] B. I. Ives later described it as "one of the most beautiful [groves] that I ever saw." He wrote, "It does appear as though God in his wisdom had designed it to be used only for camp-meeting purposes. Though there are roads running on two sides of the grove, and the land on every side is cleared, this delightful spot of twenty-five acres has, in the providence of God remained untouched. It is well fenced, and no horses are allowed to be hitched within the enclosure."[59]

Many years later Galusha Anderson, a retired Baptist professor and college president, recalled the Bergen camp meeting when writing of his childhood in this area of New York.

> Within the bounds of the neighborhood was a beautiful primeval forest. There, in God's cathedral, whose pillars were the tall, straight trees, under the leafy arches of pendent limbs, the Methodists held in mid-summer their camp-meetings. Most of the people of the neighborhood, without respect to creed, attended them. Denominational walls for the time being were broken down. Christians of different names preached and prayed together, and the forest rang with their songs of praise.
>
> But there too, at times, were enacted the wildest extravagances. Men and women prayed at the top of their voices, and, as the excitement rose, a score at a time would pray, and each would utter his petitions with the full capacity of his lungs, — and that capacity seemed marvelously great, — until bedlam itself seemed to have broken loose. Sometimes persons fell to the ground, became pale and rigid, and were oblivious to all that was passing around them. Hours sometimes elapsed before they awoke to consciousness.
>
> At these meetings much of the preaching was good, many of the exhortations sensible and weighty, but mingled with these were talks that were strange and grotesque.[60]

Such scenes had been normal, not extraordinary, in Methodist and other camp meetings in the previous generation. In fact, it was the decline of this type of camp

---

57. BTR to TR, May 9, 1856.

58. "The Camp Meeting," *Brockport Republic*, June 27, 1861, p. 3; see D. Gregory Van Dussen, "The Bergen Camp Meeting in the American Holiness Movement," *Methodist History* 21, no. 2 (Jan. 1983): 78.

59. B. I. Ives, "Bergen Camp Meeting," *NI*, July 1, 1858, p. 2.

60. Galusha Anderson, *When Neighbors Were Neighbors: A Story of Love and Life in Olden Days* (Boston: Lothrop, Lee and Shepard Co., 1911), pp. 105-6. Van Dussen quotes most of this passage from Anderson ("The Bergen Camp Meeting," pp. 77, 84, 87). Anderson's father owned a farm at Bergen, and here Galusha Anderson spent his early years. Allen Johnson, ed., *Dictionary of American Biography* (New York: Scribner, 1943), 1:264-65.

meeting among the Methodists that alarmed Roberts and that this new, semi-independent camp meeting was intended to reverse.

The purchase of the land and later the formation of the Genesee Camp-Ground Association to promote and oversee the Bergen camp eventually became controversial. Inevitably, the Bergen camp meeting got caught up in the whole Nazarite issue.

The campsite was actually purchased by Roberts and Stiles (presiding elder on the Genesee District) on May 8, 1856. Clearly Roberts took the initiative. On July 18 the twenty-five acres were legally deeded to Asa Abell, Benjamin T. Roberts, and Asa Allis, presumably because all three then resided in the vicinity.[61]

Stiles and Roberts initially gave their personal note for the land, and then raised money to pay off the debt. Benjamin filled the first several pages of his 1856 diary, previously unused, with the names of contributors and the amounts pledged. He listed over a hundred people, most of whom pledged $10 or $5, with pledges totaling about $1,300. Roberts himself pledged $10, as did Thomas LaDue, Kendall, McCreery, Stiles, Abell, and Allis. In the margin Roberts listed several locations (Albion, Brockport, Chili, Rochester, Holley), indicating that he raised funds among Methodists throughout the area.[62]

Roberts wanted the Bergen camp meeting to be decidedly Methodist, but with its own organization, distinct and semi-independent from the conference. For this purpose he organized the Genesee Camp-Ground Association.[63] He got the association legally incorporated, traveling to Albany to have the necessary documents approved by the state legislature. Roberts structured the association in such a way that the Bergen campground would always be under Methodist control. As Zahniser notes, "Expecting always to remain in the Methodist Church, Mr. Roberts put a clause in the charter, placing the camp meeting and ground under the jurisdiction of the Genesee Conference of the Methodist Episcopal Church, and another clause permitting none but members of the M.E. Church to vote for trustees."[64]

Stiles, the presiding elder, tried to get the Genesee Conference at its sessions that fall to take responsibility for the Bergen camp meeting, but the conference refused. Later, as division in the conference became sharper, the intent and control of the Bergen camp meeting became a hot issue.[65]

Roberts's diary is blank for the period of the 1856 Bergen camp meeting. However, Redfield's later recollections of the annual camps at Bergen give the flavor of

---

61. Zahniser, p. 82. Abell apparently owned a farm nearby. It is not clear who Asa Allis was; likely he was a member of a Methodist church in the area. In Roberts's diary, Allis seems to be listed as one of four pledgers from Chili.

62. BTRD, Jan. 1-13, 1856.

63. The National Camp Meeting Association for the Promotion of Holiness (later the National Holiness Association) was formed in 1867 and became the major vehicle of the Holiness movement following the Civil War. This more local campground association that Roberts formed a decade earlier (and presumably others like it) may be seen as a precursor of the later national association.

64. Zahniser, p. 82. This apparently happened in early 1857.

65. Zahniser, p. 82.

what the 1856 gathering would have been like. Terrill's biography of Redfield calls Bergen "a laymen's camp meeting," stressing the participation of Methodists who were not preachers. In a sense this was true, since the camp had an independent board not under the control of the conference (which at this time was composed only of preachers). But clearly Methodist preachers, and especially Roberts, were the key leaders. Redfield's biography says the Bergen camp meeting was "under the charge of laymen, to keep it from being controlled by church officials, who were opposed to its object," and that "the grove in which these camp meetings were held was a magnificent one." The camp "was largely attended, and extensive in its influence. Wonderful were the manifestations of divine power that here took place. Multitudes were converted and sanctified, and many ministers received the baptism of the Holy Spirit."[66]

Over the next few years the Bergen camp meeting played an increasingly important role in the events that led to Roberts's eventual expulsion from the Methodist Episcopal Church. At the same time, it was virtually the prototype of the many camp meetings that marked the early days of Free Methodism.

Looking back on this period from the vantage point of about 1890, Abel Stevens, the Methodist historian, commented somewhat negatively about the role of camp meetings generally within the Methodist movement.

> The camp meeting, borrowed from the Presbyterians of the West, was found to be a great convenience for the characteristically Methodist work of propagandism, especially in the sparsely settled frontier regions; but it was frequently attended by uncontrollable enthusiasm and those physical phenomena which had occurred in the early meetings of English Methodists and were a sore perplexity to John Wesley. . . . They early subsided in England, but lingered long in America and came, at last, to be considered characteristic of Methodist worship. . . . Early in our present period [i.e., the mid-1860s] they began to disappear, and with no diminution, or rather with great augmentation, of the lay zeal and practical energy of the Church.[67]

Clearly Roberts, Redfield, and many others strongly disagreed with such criticism. Roberts believed that the emotional and physical demonstrativeness at camp meetings, revivals, and worship services constituted normal signs of the working of the Holy Spirit and certainly was not "uncontrollable enthusiasm."

66. Terrill, *Redfield*, pp. 294-95.

67. Abel Stevens, *Supplementary History of American Methodism* (New York: Eaton and Mains, 1899; published posthumously), p. 58. By "physical phenomena" Stevens seems especially to have in mind being "slain in the Spirit," for he comments, "Methodist authorities themselves were among the first to define their true nature as abnormal effects of religious excitement on the nervous system, and to give them their scientific name — 'catalepsy'" (p. 58). Catalepsy is defined as "A condition seen in psychotic patients in which generalized diminished responsiveness usually is marked by a trancelike state" (*Taber's Cyclopedic Medical Dictionary*, 18th ed. [Philadelphia: F. A. Davis, 1997], p. 329). Stevens went on to warn, however, that with the diminution of "audible emphasis and physical demonstrations" had come "a new excess" — too many organizations and growing bureaucracy (pp. 58-59)!

End of Roberts's First Year at Albion

Following the Bergen camp meeting Roberts completed his first year at Albion and prepared for annual conference, to be held in early September.

Zahniser says of Roberts's first year at Albion, "Leadership of the so called Nazarite group seemed at that time to pass into the hands of the young man, Roberts. Before this time, he had never been considered the leader of the 'old line Methodists.'" Zahniser refers here to the leadership role Eleazar Thomas had played before he was assigned to California.[68]

In fact, Roberts's emergence as a leader was not so abrupt. It is clear from the articles he published in early 1853, his key role in starting the Bergen camp meeting, McCreery's references to him, and the opposition he was beginning to attract that Roberts was viewed throughout the conference (and beyond, due to the Methodist press) as an emerging leader and reformer well before his assignment to Albion or the Nazarite flare-up at the 1855 annual conference in Olean.

Roberts had written his father in early May, "Things are moving on pleasantly in the Church. Our prayer meetings are well attended and a good degree of interest is manifested." The year turned out to be relatively peaceful both in the church and in Benjamin and Ellen's family, despite the broader conference turmoil.

Total church membership at Albion actually decreased that year, however, from 285 to 257. Yet the number of full members grew from 183 to 217, apparently indicating that Roberts consolidated 30 to 40 of the converts from the previous year's revival into full membership.[69]

68. Zahniser, p. 80.
69. *Minutes*, Genesee Conference, 1855, 1856.

351

CHAPTER 19

The McCreery Case

"[P]rosperity is producing upon us, as a denomination, the same intoxicating effect that it too often does upon individuals and societies."

B. T. Roberts, letter to Bishop Thomas Morris, 1856[1]

"I am the Lord's, soul body and spirit; I have His presence in the midst of multiplied cares."

Ellen Roberts, 1857[2]

A cryptic series of notations occurs in B. T. Roberts's diary for early April 1856. The entries are unlike any others in his diaries, and there are none immediately before or after to help interpret them. They read as follows:

Wednesday, April 2:   At Batavia at 2. P.M. [crossed through]
Thursday, April 3:   At Lima, house of J. P. Kent at 4 P.M. [crossed through]
Friday, April 4:   Batavia, Eagle Tavern, 7. A.M.
Monday, April 7:   At Buffalo at 10. A.M. [crossed through]
Tuesday, April 8:   James Runcie's Store at 8. A.M.
Wednesday, April 9:   At Gowanda at 1. P.M.
Thursday, April 10:   Attica at 2. P.M. Parsonage.
Friday, April 11:   J. P. Kent. Lima 8. A.M.
Saturday, April 12:   Albion 2. P.M.

---

1. BTR (Albion, N.Y.) to Bishop T. A. Morris, Nov. 15, 1856.
2. ELRD, Jan. 1, 1857.

This appears to be a series of appointments. Could they have to do with the Underground Railroad, which was active in western New York throughout this period and had been given added impetus by the Fugitive Slave Law of 1850? Of the cities Roberts lists, at least three — Batavia, Attica, and Buffalo — were "stops" on the Underground Railroad.[3] Buffalo was a key escape route into Canada.

We know that Roberts was keenly interested in the slavery question and occasionally assisted runaway slaves. He used a memorandum page in his 1856 diary to list statistics on slavery, giving the "Total number of slave holders in the U.S." as 347,525 and the "Total No. of slaves" as 3,204,313.[4] Further, Roberts has a note in his diary for January 17, 1856, indicating that Ellen Roberts and L. W. Crandall (apparently a member of the Albion church) each contributed one dollar "For fugitives" and that this was "Pd. to Kent."[5] This could be the J. P. Kent listed on April 3 and 11. Conceivably Roberts could have been helping transport fugitive slaves at this time.

Several things indicate, however, that these entries refer rather to the networking Roberts was doing among conference preachers concerning his reform efforts. Joseph McCreery's examination before his presiding elder was approaching. Benjamin apparently was traveling from April 2 to 12, or possibly from April 4 through 12, making a number of contacts. Since the April 2 and 3 appointments are crossed through, he may have rescheduled these times, as Batavia and Lima are both listed twice. He probably traveled mostly by train.[6]

It appears that Roberts met someone at the Eagle Tavern in Batavia at 7:00 A.M. on Friday, April 4. He probably then returned the eighteen miles straight north to Albion for the weekend.[7]

Who was his contact in Batavia? It is impossible to say. Probably not James M. Fuller, the Methodist preacher in Batavia at the time, for he was not fully sympathetic with Roberts.[8] It may have been Loren Stiles, then the presiding elder of the Genesee District, which included Batavia. Or this might well have been a strategy session involving several colleagues, such as McCreery, Kendall, and others.

On Monday, April 7, Benjamin apparently went to Buffalo. His diary reads "Buf-

---

3. Helene C. Phelan, *And Why Not Every Man? An Account of Slavery, the Underground Railroad, and the Road to Freedom in New York's Southern Tier* (Almond, N.Y.: Helene C. Phelan, 1987), p. 81.

4. BTRD (1856), p. 216. The whole page is full of statistics relating to slavery and slaveholding, including financial data.

5. BTRD, Jan. 17, 1856.

6. Roberts was also writing his "Free Churches" articles at this time, completing the first on Apr. 2 and the second on Apr. 5. If these appointments referred to Underground Railroad activity, presumably Roberts would have been traveling by horse and buggy (or wagon). It would have been difficult though not impossible to travel these distances by horse and buggy, since there was an intervening night between each appointment.

7. Plausibly, Benjamin traveled down to Batavia Thursday evening, stayed there overnight (at the Eagle Tavern?), and had his appointment early the next morning.

8. Fuller, as noted earlier, seems to have been an opponent of Roberts at this time. A meeting with him is not out of the question, but it seems unlikely that Roberts would arrange to meet him at 7:00 A.M. at a tavern rather than at Fuller's home or church facility.

falo at 10. A.M.," but the entry is crossed through, perhaps indicating that the appointment was canceled or rescheduled. He has "James Runcie's Store at 8. A.M." for the next day, April 8. Runcie, a Methodist, ran the Buffalo Trunk Manufactory at 4 East Seneca Street, "under the Methodist Bookstore," where he sold a variety of trunks, satchels, and bags.[9] Though Roberts could have gone to the store on personal business, more likely this also was a rendezvous with like-minded Methodist preachers.

Roberts's next appointment was the following day, Wednesday, at 1:00 P.M. in Gowanda. Probably Benjamin went there to meet his father, and perhaps also the superannuated preacher R. M. Evarts and/or the Methodist preacher in Gowanda, Robert Moran.

Roberts's journey took him the next day, April 10, to Attica, fifty miles back northeast from Gowanda and about ten miles from Batavia. His diary reads "Attica at 2. P.M. Parsonage." The preacher at Attica was Jason G. Miller, five years older than Roberts, who may at this time have been sympathetic with Roberts's reform efforts.[10]

The next day Benjamin went on to Lima, about thirty-five miles farther east. His diary reads "J. P. Kent. Lima 8. AM." Perhaps this was a rescheduling of the April 3 meeting at Kent's home in Lima. John P. Kent, sixty-three, was assigned this year to assist William Buck at Covington, but apparently he had a home in Lima. He was one of several older conference preachers who were sympathetic with Roberts.[11] Benjamin apparently went to Lima to consult with Kent and perhaps other preachers in the area.

Finally, Roberts has in his diary "Albion 2. P.M." for the next day, Saturday, April 12. So he completed his circuit, returning home.

The Saturday meeting at Albion apparently was the last in this series of half a dozen consultations with like-minded Methodist preachers. These appointments show that Roberts was building a network of preachers throughout the conference, continuing his efforts to restore "old-line Methodism," despite the opposition to "Nazaritism." But the immediate objective probably was to spread the word about McCreery's upcoming examination, scheduled for the following week, and to assure a large attendance.

As noted, McCreery's case was left unresolved by the 1855 annual conference, pending "an examination before his presiding elder" of the charges made against

9. James Runcie advertisement, included in the advertising section at the end of *Minutes of the Genesee Annual Conference* (1855). He sold a variety of "Travelling articles," including carpetbags, leather trunks and valises, and "Ladies' Trunks, Bags and Satchels," all "made to order."

10. A "J. Miller" was one of seventeen Methodist preachers "supposed to be prominent in the 'Nazarite organization'" who the next year signed a statement declaring that no Nazarite organization ever existed in the conference (*WAS*, pp. 23-25). However, this more likely was Job Miller (who later became a Free Methodist) rather than Jason Miller. (See Ray Allen, *A Century of the Genesee Annual Conference of the Methodist Episcopal Church, 1810-1910* [Rochester, N.Y.: By the Author, 1911], p. 106.) The next year Jason Miller voted with the majority to convict Roberts.

11. *Minutes*, Genesee Conference, 1855; Allen, *Century*, p. 99. According to Allen, Kent died at Lima in 1880. He was superannuated in 1857. He was another of the seventeen preachers who signed the 1857 statement denying any Nazarite organization.

him.[12] Ironically, his presiding elder now was Loren Stiles, who was appointed at the 1855 conference to replace Samuel Luckey in the Genesee District. McCreery was appointed to Parma, in the same district. Stiles, a close friend of Roberts, was largely sympathetic toward McCreery.

This examination (technically an ecclesiastical juridical proceeding) was held on Tuesday, April 15, 1856, at Lyndonville, near Yates (Niagara District), where Chamberlayne lived and McCreery had previously been the preacher.[13] Roberts noted that Stiles "ordered the trial to be held at Lyndonville, where the alleged offences were committed, and where the witness [Chamberlayne] lived, though it was outside of his district."[14]

Israel Chamberlayne presented two charges against McCreery. Conable reports on the scene: "all told a large company came together, and a protracted season of labor and excitement peculiar to such occasions was expected." But no sooner had the procedure begun than it ended. When the first charge was presented, with its "numerous specifications," Stiles ruled it inadmissible. The prosecution objected and refused to go on, and thus "was the whole affair suddenly and violently estopped."[15]

This was not the result McCreery's opponents anticipated, and Stiles's surprise decision had repercussions at the annual conference sessions in the fall. This was another link in the chain of events that led to McCreery's and Roberts's expulsion from the Methodist Episcopal Church. It was right at this time that Benjamin was writing the three "Free Churches" articles discussed in the previous chapter.

The 1856 Annual Conference at Medina

Bishop Thomas Morris, who had ordained Benjamin in 1852, presided at the 1856 sessions of the Genesee Conference. The conference met September 3-13 in the village of Medina, just ten miles west of Albion, on the Erie Canal.

At the end of the conference Roberts was reappointed to Albion for a second year. However, his new presiding elder in the Genesee District was A. D. Wilbor, a couple of years older than Roberts, who had just returned from two years of ministry in Michigan.[16] In a major political shake-up, Loren Stiles was transferred to the Cincinnati Conference, as was Isaac Kingsley.[17]

Stiles's short-circuiting of McCreery's examination in April had not set well with the preachers who largely controlled conference action. Conable notes, "As naturally might be expected, . . . there was strong opposition to the re-appointment of

---

12. Conable, p. 640.

13. Conable, p. 642.

14. *WAS*, p. 142. Presumably the examination was held at the Yates ME church building.

15. Conable, p. 643; cf. *WAS*, p. 142; Zahniser, p. 79. It is not clear who the prosecutor was.

16. By prior agreement, apparently, Wilbor served the Woodward Avenue ME Church in Detroit for two years, 1854-56. See Conable, pp. 616, 624-25.

17. *Minutes*, Genesee Conference, 1856; Allen, *Century*, p. 129.

Rev. Mr. Stiles to a district, and this being understood by him, he indignantly asked Bishop Morris to transfer him to the Cincinnati Conference, and he was accordingly transferred."[18] In fact, Thomas Carlton and James M. Fuller prosecuted charges against Stiles, accusing him of maladministration in the McCreery case. Roberts, at Stiles's request, acted as his defense counsel, and he was acquitted.[19]

Behind these events, however, lay a good deal of political maneuvering. By this time conference affairs had become highly politicized, and Stiles's transfer was a sign of this. Outside of regular conference sessions, preachers caucused to control the direction of conference action. Evidence presented later supports the claim that, as Zahniser writes, "secret meetings were held at [the 1856] Conference by the so-called 'Regency' group."[20] This group of from twenty to thirty preachers, led apparently by Carlton, Fuller, and a few others, effectively controlled key decisions at annual conference sessions at least from 1856 to 1860. This was the group Roberts and his friends called "the Buffalo Regency."[21]

During the conference sessions at Medina, three such "select meetings" (as Carlton preferred to call them) were held at the home of John Ryan. Presumably Ryan was a local Methodist with whom some of the preachers were lodging during conference. From twenty to thirty preachers attended, and apparently there were a chairman and a secretary.[22] It is not certain which preachers attended, but Carlton and Sandford Hunt later said they had been present.[23]

Roberts and his friends were not fully aware of these meetings until a year or two later. Roberts wrote in *Why Another Sect,*

> That this association was remarkably secret is evidenced by the fact that it had been holding meetings for two years at least [i.e., 1856 and 1857], before its existence was suspected. It was remarked [i.e., noticed] that about thirty men voted solid on all issues touching old or new fashioned Methodism, but this was supposed to be owing to natural affinities and to the influence of the lodge. Those against whom they were plotting, were not wanting in ordinary sagacity; they were on the lookout; yet the meetings held at two successive Conferences were so carefully concealed, that not a whisper was heard concerning them.[24]

The initial target of these "select" conclaves was Stiles and Kingsley, the presiding elders of the Niagara and Genesee Districts, respectively. In retaliation for Stiles's failure to prosecute McCreery (as Carlton and his friends saw it) and thus properly

18. Conable, p. 643.

19. *WAS,* pp. 142-43; Zahniser, p. 79.

20. Zahniser, p. 83.

21. Whether such secret meetings were held as early as the 1855 annual conference is uncertain, but seems likely. In any case, it is clear from the whole narrative that Carlton had long exerted strong behind-the-scenes influence on the affairs of the conference.

22. According to later testimony by Sandford Hunt. See *WAS,* p. 66.

23. *WAS,* p. 66.

24. *WAS,* p. 67.

finish off the previous year's action against the Nazarites, this group of preachers drew up a petition asking the bishop to remove Stiles and Kingsley from the presiding eldership. They included Kingsley because he was known to be sympathetic to Stiles, McCreery, and Roberts. In their petition the preachers told Bishop Morris, in effect (as William Barrett, the preacher at Yates, later testified), "that we would refuse to take work if Brothers Stiles and Kingsley were continued in the Presiding Elders' office."[25]

At this time the conference had five presiding elders, one for each district. The other three were Richard L. Waite, Charles D. Burlingham, and the veteran Glezen Fillmore, nearly sixty-seven years old. Carlton and his associates apparently had no quarrel with these presiding elders (though Burlingham had long been an opponent of secret societies and later fell victim to conference politics). Waite seems to have been closely associated with Carlton, and had taken Roberts to task for his criticisms of the Genesee Conference in the *Northern Christian Advocate* in 1853. Fillmore, Waite, and Burlingham continued as presiding elders for the next two years or so.[26]

Carlton and his allies were successful in their efforts, and Stiles and Kingsley were transferred to the Cincinnati Conference.[27] It appears that this group of collaborating preachers also kept from entering the conference some younger men who shared the views of Roberts, Stiles, McCreery, Kingsley, and Kendall — men who, very likely, were the fruit of the ministry of this evangelistic group of preachers. Roberts says, "Several young men of good abilities, education, and of deep piety, who professed and preached holiness, were compelled to go to other Conferences." This is corroborated by a piece in the *Buffalo Advocate,* probably by John Robie, that said some "hot-heads and fanatics" had "attempted to gain admittance to the Conference" at Medina "but were repulsed at the threshold." The *Buffalo Advocate* celebrated this triumph of "those who now hold the reins [of power in the Genesee Con-

25. Testimony of William Barrett (preacher at Yates, 1855-57) during the 1857 Genesee Conference sessions, as recorded in *WAS,* p. 68. Benson Roberts says, "Thirty-three of the more prominent of the Regency at the Medina conference coerced Bishop Morris by threats of withdrawal, to remove Rev. Loren Stiles and I. C. Kingsley from the presiding eldership and appoint men acceptable to them" (BHR, *BTR,* p. 126). During Roberts's 1858 trial Carlton tried to show through the questioning of witnesses that these meetings concerned merely "the Spiritual interests of the Church" and "the best means of promoting revivals." Chesbrough, *Defence,* pp. 9-10.

26. *Minutes,* Genesee Conference, 1855-58; Allen, *Century,* p. 86. Fillmore was regarded as the founder of Methodism in Buffalo, where four times he was appointed to Niagara Street. He also planted Methodist churches in Rochester. See Sandford Hunt, *Methodism in Buffalo From Its Origin to the Close of 1892* (Buffalo: H. H. Otis and Sons, 1893), pp. 15-17, 106-7. According to Revell, he was a cousin of President Millard Fillmore, who was from Buffalo (James Alan Revell, "The Nazirites: Burned-Over District Methodism and the Buffalo Middle Class" [Ph.D. diss., University of New York at Buffalo, 1993], p. 181).

27. These Regency machinations "resulted in the voluntary withdrawal of both Kingsley and Stiles, who, sensing that one or both of them would be removed from the Cabinet, asked for a transfer to the Cincinnati Conference, which was unhesitatingly granted" by Bishop Morris. "With Kingsley and Stiles withdrawn, the Cabinet (Superintendents) was then left in the hands of 'Regency' men," writes Zahniser (p. 83) — though Burlingham probably should not be counted as among the Regency.

ference], and who mean to live and govern for God and holiness — and respectable position."[28]

Meanwhile the conference still had to resolve McCreery's case, left pending by the abortive hearing in April. "A painful and tedious process was again gone through," Hibbard reported. "Actuated by an earnest desire to pacify and harmonize the elements, and restore brotherly confidence" (as Hibbard saw it), the conference finally adopted a paper, "a sort of pacification bill," prepared by Jason Miller, the preacher at Attica, that put an end to the case.[29] The paper read, in part:

> Whereas, The peace and harmony of this Conference has been greatly disturbed, and is in farther danger, which has partly grown out of a connection with opposition to secret societies, and partly from a shade of difference on the subject of Christian holiness, and partly from a difference of views in carrying on the work of God among us, and partly from personal matters, as also a variety of other things, — now undefinable, and, whereas, these matters have to some extent assumed party forms, . . . and, whereas, the trial of Rev. J. McCreery, Jr., now pending is more or less mixed up with these matters, and as this trial is regarded by some as a persecution and thrust at holiness: and, whereas, this trial is likely to increase rather than allay the animosity and excited state of feeling now existing; and, whereas, our session has been protracted and we have already trespassed upon the hospitality of our kind friends . . . Now, therefore,
>
> *Resolved,* 1st. That we are not opposed to holiness; but on the contrary we cherish the doctrine as taught by the sainted Wesley and the fathers, and we are as much as ever in favor of the life and power of religion.
>
> 2d. That we greatly fear that there are excesses among us, bordering on *fanaticism,* leading to censoriousness and evil speaking. . . .
>
> 3d. That there is no cover or excuse for such evil speaking, and we do hereby deprecate it, come from whatsoever source it may. . . .
>
> 4th. That we put a double watch over ourselves in this regard in the future.
>
> 5th. That Br. M'Creery, in our judgment from a superabundance of proof, both oral and written, has been repeatedly guilty of the crime above named, and under very aggravated circumstances.
>
> 6th. That as an exercise of mercy we dismiss the case of Br. M'Creery, hoping thereby to prove to him and his friends, that there is no vindictiveness or desire to persecute him or them, hoping thus to check this unfounded jealousy and restore peace among us.
>
> 7th. That in our judgment Br. M'Creery has become unduly excited, and under this state of mind has been betrayed into these extravagances, and this is one reason why we deem it advisable to dismiss the case.[30]

28. *WAS,* pp. 69-70; cf. Zahniser, pp. 83-84.

29. F. G. Hibbard, "Nazaritism — Its Judicial History," *NCA* 19, no. 45 (Nov. 9, 1859): 2.

30. There was some merit to this point. McCreery does seem by temperament to have been "excitable," a trait that at times led him into "extravagances."

8th. That we affectionately request the members of this Conference to cease to publish in the secular press or elsewhere, articles relating to or implicating members of this Conference, and we deprecate certain articles published in the *Buffalo Advocate* and in the *Medina Tribune.*[31]

While this action technically put an end to the McCreery case, it certainly did not quell the controversy, which only heated up.

In criticizing "certain articles" recently published in the *Buffalo Advocate* and the local *Medina Tribune,* the resolution was trying to be evenhanded. It was referring particularly to a sarcastic, rather inflammatory article entitled "Nazarite Reformers and Reformation" that had appeared in the *Medina Tribune* on Thursday, September 11, while the annual conference was still in session. It was signed "Junius" and apparently was written by John B. Wentworth, the preacher at Pearl Street, Buffalo.[32]

"Junius" wrote,

Spurious reformers are as plenty as blackberries, and as contemptible as plenty. Incapable of comprehending the moral condition and wants of society around them, and also of understanding the modes or processes by which reformation is to be effected, they believe, or affect to believe, that they are the chosen instruments of some greatly needed social regeneration — whose necessity or possibility, none, beside themselves, are able to discover. Mistaking a desire to do something grand, for a call to a great undertaking; and the wish to be known to fame, for a prophetic intimation of some splendid achievement — they go forth before the world, putting on strange and uncouth airs, which they expect everybody will regard as proof of the "divine fury" with which they are possessed; and repeating nonsensical and clap-trap phrases, which they have mistakingly selected as the watchwords of a reformatory movement. The ridiculous figure they cut excites the laughter and jeers of all — save those who are as addled and silly as themselves. By such, however, they are frequently mistaken for real prophets; and the gaining of a few proselytes always confirms both in their lunacy.

We, of the Genesee Conference, have such a batch of false prophets — such pseudo reformers among us. And such a group of regenerators as the Nazarites compose, we can not believe was ever before brought together by the force of a common belief in a divine call to a great work. Whence, or why the idea ever struck them that *they* were the chosen ministers of a new reformation, will probably never be rescued from the dimness and uncertainty of speculation. They probably feel the motion of something within them — it may have been wind in the stomach — and mistook it for the intimations of a heaven-derived commission, summoning them to the rescue of expiring Methodism, and the inauguration of a new era of spiritual life in the history of the Wesleyan movement.

31. Hibbard, "Nazaritism," p. 2.

32. Reinhard identifies "Junius" as J. B. Wentworth but does not state his evidence for this identification. James Arnold Reinhard, "Personal and Sociological Factors in the Formation of the Free Methodist Church, 1852-1860" (Ph.D. diss., University of Iowa, 1971), p. 24.

Take a look at this knot of men in the light of correctors of spiritual abuses and corruption — and it is under this title that they present themselves in their confederated Nazarite capacity, to the Methodist public. They pretend that many wicked and corrupt practices have grown up in the church — and above all in the ministry, and claim that they have come forward as the champions of primitive and gospel purity, simplicity and holiness. In taking upon themselves this character and office, they not only accuse their ministerial brethren of having "departed from the faith," but also, assume that they themselves are pre-eminent for moral cleanliness and Christian purity. The modesty of these pretensions can not fail to excite the admiration of all. But the truth of these pretensions is what we are more particularly interested in. *Are* these men so much better — morally and religiously — than their compeers, as they would have the world believe?[33] What fruits of transcendent godliness do they exhibit? Their professions indeed are loud and pretentious, but what of their *works?* Does holiness display itself in spiritual pride, in arrogant boastings of goodness, in canting and crabbed long-facedness, in gross and filthy vituperations? In that case the palm of excellence must indeed be yielded to them. Upon what meat, pray, do these Nazarites feed that they have grown good so fast? It was not long since some of them were wallowing in the deepest mire of moral pollution, and it might conduce to the culture of that eminent Christian grace — humility, if they were called more frequently to remember "the hole of the pit from whence they were digged." But now, by the new and "short way" which they have discovered, they have progressed so rapidly as to far outstrip — in all the forms and practices of holy living — those who from childhood have humbly endeavored to obey the commands of Christ, and whose lengthened ministerial experience embraces a period of nearly or quite as long duration as does the natural life of most of these Nazarite Reformers. Could aught but the most brazen effrontery bear out these persons in thus standing out before the most experienced, and able, and pious ministers of the conference, and accusing them of having left the "old paths," of "having ignored the discipline," and of seeking to crush out and destroy the spirituality of the church? Are these unfledged and beardless and brainless boys thus to be allowed to insult the manhood, to question the honesty, and to malign the character of the fathers of the conference? We do not believe that the public sentiment of the Genesee Conference will longer countenance or endure the self-instituted censorship and malignant abuse of some dozen or twenty of its members, who have met together in secret conclave, and voted that they are the embodiment of all the soundness of doctrine, holiness and Methodism that still linger in the body.[34]

To them, religion still appears to be a system of outward forms and symbols, of material ceremonies, and corporal manifestations, of animal influence and

33. The passage beginning "Take a look at" and ending "the world believe?" is found in *WAS*, p. 123, but omitted in BHR, *BTR*.

34. The passage beginning "It was not long since" to the end of the paragraph is found in BHR, *BTR*, pp. 123-24, but omitted in *WAS*.

nervous sensations. With them, a long face and sanctimonious airs answer for inward purity and goodness of heart. In their creed, a high-sounding profession takes precedence of a holy life, and getting happy in a religious meeting is laid down as an indubitable proof of the divine favor. Boisterous shouting and screaming, "thumping of benches, and throwing the arms and legs about,"[35] while engaged in devotional exercises, they call serving God. An observance of certain prudential, disciplinary requirements, they esteem a more important duty than the practice of the precepts contained in the golden rule. They consider plainness in dress of greater moment than uprightness of character. An ornamental ribbon or flower upon a lady's bonnet is — in their eyes, — an enormity greater than the sin of lying: and the wearing a ring or bracelet they think is more dangerous and damning than covetousness or slander; and generally, they preach with more powerful vehemence against superfluity of outward apparel, than against the breach of the Ten Commandments. With them, a broad-rimmed, bell-crowned hat is equivalent to "the helmet of salvation," and a shad-bellied coat [i.e., plain Quaker coat] to the robe of righteousness.

But what *means* do these reformers employ to accomplish their ends? Do they begin by a proclamation of some new truth — which is the invariable and indispensable antecedent of every real reformation? No: But they begin by a corruption of truth already discovered and made known; as, witness their unscriptural and anti-Methodistic interpretation of the doctrine of Christian perfection. Do they proceed by an open and manly avowal of their principles and plans? No: But they meet in secret "consultation" and private caucuses, in which jealousy supplies them inspiration and a desire to injure other men becomes their primitive motive.[36] Do they go forth to the people with words of truth and soberness, striving to make men better by pressing, with fervent eloquence and earnest, rational appeals, the declaration of God's word upon the heart and conscience of the hearers? No; their harangues to the people consist of factious addresses, cant phrases, and rant; of protestations of their own spotlessness, and both open and concealed imputations upon the Christian and ministerial character of their brethren.

JUNIUS[37]

It was difficult to respond to this kind of attack. Benjamin didn't even try. "You cannot argue against a sneer," Benson Roberts later wrote. "The calm tone in which [B. T. Roberts stated] the facts so distasteful and discreditable to the Regency . . . only awakened a spirit of bitter hatred against, and a determination to crush," him.[38]

---

35. The phrase in quotation marks is omitted in *WAS* but included in BHR, *BTR*, p. 124.

36. The passage beginning "Do they begin" and ending "primitive motive" is found in BHR, *BTR*, p. 125, but omitted in *WAS*.

37. Junius [J. B. Wentworth], "Nazarite Reformers and Reformation," quoted in *WAS*, pp. 114-17, and BHR, *BTR*, pp. 122-25. See also Reinhard, "Personal and Sociological Factors," pp. 24-25, and Zahniser, pp. 87-88.

38. BHR, *BTR*, p. 125. Benson Roberts refers here specifically to "New School Methodism"; he dis-

Wentworth's article in the *Medina Tribune* appeared two days before the close of the 1856 annual conference. The ten-day conference had been contentious, with charges and countercharges. Roberts himself took the offensive, bringing a complaint of fraudulent financial practices on the part of three conference preachers who were in business together. Complaints "of a serious character were made against three of the prominent preachers of the so-called regency party," Roberts wrote. The charges involved the financing of real estate transactions. Roberts claimed they had borrowed money from wealthy Methodists to invest in real estate but never repaid the loans. The investments proved to be worthless and the business failed. Benjamin apparently investigated the case, taking affidavits, before presenting it to conference. He felt that fraud was likely involved, and the conference should investigate, since it concerned the character of preachers. Roberts was not prejudging the case, he said, but the conference had a responsibility to look into it. However, he said, "As soon as the complaints were brought before the Conference, one of the leading men of their party, I think it was T. Carlton, moved to lay the whole matter on the table." This was done, and the matter was thus ignored. The same thing happened with a related case. In failing to properly investigate these matters, Roberts later charged, the conference "WAS GUILTY OF COVERING UP FRAUD!"[39]

Loren Stiles similarly reported to the conference that he had documents "calling in question the business integrity and honesty of a member of the Conference" and asked that a committee be appointed to investigate. The conference, however, refused to do so.[40]

Whether these were defensive measures by Roberts and Stiles, or whether the two besieged preachers were solely concerned with the integrity of the ordained ministry, is not entirely clear. Probably both motives were at work. In any case, Roberts reports: "The so-called regency party now became desperate in their measures. The question between the two parties had, to some of the leaders of these parties, become a question of life and death." The Regency group "saw that something must be done to cripple our influence, or they were still in danger of being called to account for their misdeeds." These were the dynamics, Roberts later wrote, that lay behind the 1857 charges against him.[41]

The 1856 annual conference finally adjourned on Saturday, September 13, after Bishop Morris read the appointments in what must have been a moment of high drama. Roberts writes, "When the appointments were read out . . . and it was seen that Brothers Stiles and Kingsley were removed from being presiding elders, and

---

cusses the "Junius" article after quoting Roberts's article, presenting it by way of contrast. However, the "Junius" article actually appeared almost a year before "New School Methodism."

39. *WAS*, pp. 143-49.

40. *WAS*, p. 147.

41. *WAS*, p. 147. "Charges backed up by the most responsible parties, made against some of [the Regency preachers] for dishonest transactions amounting almost to State Prison offences, were summarily dismissed; while men of spotless lives, accused of being Nazarites, were turned out of the church under pretexts so slight as to admit of no defence" (p. 70).

were transferred to another Conference; and . . . that the party known as 'The Buffalo Regency,' had every thing their own way, the hearts of most of those who were in favor of old fashioned Methodism sank within them in discouragement."[42]

William Kendall, however, refused to be discouraged, despite this outcome and his own appointment to North Chili after just one year at Brockport. Some viewed this appointment as a demotion, though North Chili was at the time a fairly prosperous church, not much smaller than Brockport.[43] When the bishop called for someone to close the meeting by starting a song, Kendall, "in clear, triumphant notes," began the Charles Wesley hymn,

> Come on, my partners in distress,
> My comrades through the wilderness,
>   Who still your bodies feel;
> Awhile forget your griefs and fears,
> And look beyond this vale of tears,
>   To that celestial hill.[44]

As Kendall persisted through all five stanzas, the preachers who felt themselves victimized by conference action took heart. Terrill writes, "as they sang they believed, and hope grew strong. Some fell to the floor; some shouted aloud, while Brother Kendall's voice continued still to make the auditorium ring."[45] Roberts says, "By the time the singing was finished we were all ready to go to the ends of the earth, if need be, to proclaim a free and full salvation."[46]

Shortly after conference Kendall or his wife wrote to Redfield, then conducting revivals in Wisconsin. Learning what had happened, Redfield wrote back from Jefferson, Wisconsin, on December 20, 1856:

> My heart almost sinks when I hear that the tried and true are being driven from the field, and weakening the little band who stand for the right [referring probably to the transfer of Stiles and Kingsley to the Cincinnati Conference]. Shall the enemy yet triumph? I am more and more confirmed in the opinion I expressed long ago that amputation alone will save vital piety. It has come to this, a candidate for the presidency of the United States, in order to election, must guarantee the people that he will do his best to crush out the humanitarian spirit that inspires the abolitionists, and offer premiums to its opposite; and in some of our conferences candidates to be received into the ministry, instead of being required

42. *WAS*, p. 74.

43. At the time of the 1856 annual conference, Brockport had 141 members (total) and North Chili 114. Roberts later said that in being moved from Brockport to North Chili, Kendall went "from the best and wealthiest charge to the poorest" in the conference. "Rev. Wm. C. Kendall, A.M. — Labors — Death," *EC* 2, no. 12 (Dec. 1861): 374.

44. *WAS*, p. 75; hymn 657 in *Hymns of the Methodist Episcopal Church* (New York: Hunt and Eaton, 1878).

45. Terrill, *Redfield*, p. 324.

46. *WAS*, p. 75.

to pledge themselves to uphold the doctrines and spirit of Methodism, are required, virtually, to oppose them.

... To be in a minority is to be rebellious, while to be in the majority is to be loyal.[47]

Letter to Bishop Morris

Two months after annual conference, Benjamin wrote to Bishop Thomas Morris regarding Stiles's transfer and the issues of ecclesiastical procedure that it raised.[48] The letter was in response to one Roberts had received from Morris, answering questions Roberts had asked (probably in an earlier letter right after conference) about the transfer of Stiles to Cincinnati. Roberts hoped that the bishop would return Stiles to the conference and reappoint him as presiding elder of the Genesee District, reversing his recent conference appointment. Clearly Roberts questioned the wisdom of removing Stiles. Yet his letter to the bishop is respectful, and formal in style.

The letter is dated November 15, 1856, from Albion. It is important on several counts, particularly because it gives Roberts's assessment of the situation within the Genesee Conference and makes several points that were to appear in his "New School Methodism" articles several months later.[49]

Roberts addressed Bishop Morris as "Dear Father." He began,

Your very kind letter, assigning the reasons why you could not retransfer Rev. L. Stiles to this Conference, and reappoint him to the Genesee District, was duly received. We are satisfied that in this, as in all your official actions, you were actuated by a sincere desire to promote the glory of God and the welfare of the Church over which a kind Providence has given you with your worthy colleagues the superintendence. I do not write to complain of this decision. It may have been the best that could have been made, though present appearances indicate that it will not be promotive of either the peace of this Conference or the prosperity of the district.

47. JWR to Rev. and Mrs. William Kendall, Dec. 20, 1856, quoted in Terrill, *Redfield*, p. 314.

48. In his diary for Apr. 18, 1856, Roberts has "Law Questions Bp Morris Sept. 13th 1856." This may refer to action at the annual conference that concluded on Sept. 13 and at which Bishop Morris had presided. It is not clear, however, why the entry is found on Apr. 18 (just after the hearing regarding McCreery). It is possible Roberts on that date made himself a note to ask some questions of Bishop Morris at the end of the annual conference sessions, perhaps questions of ecclesiastical law that arose in the McCreery case. Possibly on this date Roberts wrote an initial letter to Morris. However, Morris's reply (to which Roberts refers in his Nov. 15 letter) must have come sometime after the close of annual conference on Sept. 13.

49. The letter as quoted here is from Roberts's initial draft, corrected in his own hand, found in RFP Microfilm Reel 10. The letter is printed as an appendix in Zahniser, with some minor errors (pp. 347-49), and a little more than half of it is included as appendix 1 in Revell, "The Nazirites" (pp. 342-43).

Roberts then elaborated forcefully the real situation in the conference, as he saw it.

> You seem to think that the difficulties of our Conference are satisfactorily adjusted. Permit me to say that, in my opinion they were never greater or more serious than at the present time. The Conference is divided. Two distinct parties exist. With the one or the other every preacher is in sympathy [though some try to remain neutral].
>
> The division is not a personal one. It has no personal animosities for its basis. On the contrary, there exists, in the main, a good understanding between those who are found arranged on opposite sides. With few exceptions I believe the preachers cherish mutually confidence and brotherly love.
>
> Nor is this disagreement occasioned wholly by the connection of some with secret societies. Such connection may and doubtless does tend to produce alienation of feeling. Those bound together by the extra ties of a secret brotherhood with its peculiar interests, its attractive mysteries, and its special recognitions, will, according to the inflexible laws which govern the affections, feel a stronger sympathy for each other, than for those to whom they are bound only by the common ties that unite together ministers and members of the same communion. They may not be aware of the existence of this partiality. Or if they are, they may struggle against it. But here, as elsewhere, the law of affinity will prevail. This connection with secret societies, I regard both as an effect and a cause of the division among us. Were it not for Masonry and Odd Fellowship the party leaning on these societies for support would be too insignificant in numbers to effect much mischief. And, on the other hand, many by belonging to these societies are drawn into measures which, if left alone they would never tolerate.

Here Roberts showed insight into the attraction that secret societies had for some, and also into the sociopsychological dynamics at work among the conference preachers.

But secret societies were not the real issue, Roberts argued. "[T]he real difficulty lies deeper. It is far more perplexing," beyond the power of conference resolutions or committee reports. "Nothing short of the Almighty power of the Holy Spirit can ever bring us together. He alone can give us that unanimity of view without which unanimity of action cannot long prevail." Roberts then elaborated in language that he would later use (in part) in his "New School Methodism" article.

> The difference among us is fundamental. It does not relate to things indifferent but to those of the most vital importance. It involves nothing less than the nature itself of Christianity. Our brethren from whom we differ, have a theory of religion as yet clearly defined in the minds of but a few, and therefore not generally understood. . . . This theory is to the effect, that Christianity changes, that we are not to expect it to present the same manifestations now that it did in a less refined age, that we are in the habit of laying too much stress upon mere experience, that it is

now in a transition state, and is about to assume "the benevolent form." According to this view, the model Christian is one who leads a moral, respectable and fashionable life, and contributes liberally to the various objects of benevolence. Any ado about the salvation of souls is not to be tolerated. What we call religion they call fanaticism; what they denominate Christianity, we consider formalism.

Roberts apparently is referring here to articles he had recently read either in the *Buffalo Christian Advocate* or some other Methodist paper. The article "Christianity a Religion of Beneficence Rather Than Devotion," which later figured so prominently in his "New School Methodism" article, did not appear until six months later, however — in May 1857.

Roberts continues his letter to Morris:

Differing thus in our views of religion, we necessarily differ in our measures for its promotion. They build stock churches, and furnish them with pews to accommodate a select congregation; and with organs, melodeons, violins and professional singers to execute difficult pieces of music for the entertainment of a fashionable audience. We favor free churches, congregational singing, and spirituality, simplicity and fervency in worship. We endeavor to promote revivals, such as we remember to have seen in the days of our childhood, under the labors of the fathers;[50] such as have made Methodism the leading denomination of the land; their most talented men I have never known guilty of any such irregularity as being responsible for a revival. We inculcate upon all, the necessity of self-denial, non-conformity to the world, purity of heart and holiness of life: they ridicule singularity, encourage by their silence, and in some cases by their own example, and that of their wives and daughters "the putting on of gold and costly apparel," and treat with distrust all professions of deep Christian experience. When we desire to raise money for the benefit of the Church we appeal to the love the people bear to Christ; they for this purpose have recourse to the sale of pews to the highest bidder, to parties of pleasure, oyster suppers, fairs[,] grab bags and lotteries. In short we rely practically upon the agency of the Holy Spirit for the building up of the Church of God; they appear to us to depend upon the favor of Secret Societies, the patronage of the worldly and the various artifices of human policy.[51]

If this diversity of opinion and of practice among the ministers of our denomination, was confined to this Conference, it would be comparatively unimportant. But unmistakable indications show that prosperity is producing upon us, as a denomination, the same intoxicating effect that it too often does upon individuals and societies. The change by the General Conference of 1852 in the rule of Discipline requiring that "all our Houses of Worship should be built plain and with free seats," and that of the last General Conf. in the rule respecting Dress,

50. Perhaps the most explicit reference to the significant impact that the revival in which his father was converted (and other revivals of the time) had on Roberts.

51. Roberts had first written "the patronage of the rich, and the various artifices of worldly policy," but changed "rich" to "worldly" and "worldly" to "human."

show, that there are already too many among us, who would take down the barriers that have hitherto separated us from the world. The fact that the removal is gradual, so as not to excite too much attention and commotion, renders it none the less alarming.[52]

Whether Roberts received a reply from Bishop Morris to this letter is uncertain; there seems to be no such letter in the Roberts Family Papers. Roberts's letter, however, gives a comprehensive summary of the situation in the Genesee Conference at the beginning of the 1856-57 conference year. This he later spelled out in more detail in "New School Methodism." Clearly the conflict in the Genesee Conference was reaching a critical stage.

Meanwhile other controversies, and especially the slavery issue, were stirring the Methodist Episcopal Church more broadly.

Founding the *Northern Independent*

Controversy over the slavery issue, and especially slaveholding within the church, led to the founding of the *Northern Independent* in late 1856. Up until the 1856 General Conference, which met in Indianapolis in May, William Hosmer (1810-89) had edited the *Northern Christian Advocate,* the official weekly newspaper of western New York Methodism.[53] Hosmer served as full-time editor for eight years, having been first elected by the 1848 General Conference.[54] Previously he had served as a presiding elder in the Genesee Conference. He was a delegate to the General Conferences of 1848, 1852, and 1856.[55]

Hosmer was sympathetic to Roberts and the so-called Nazarites. But it was his outspoken criticism of slavery, and of slaveholding in the Methodist Episcopal Church, that led to his removal as editor of the *Northern Christian Advocate*. Over the four years since the 1852 General Conference, "a warm discussion" was carried on in the Northern Methodist papers over slavery and slave owners in the church. Thomas Bond at the flagship *Christian Advocate and Journal,* as well as the editors of

---

52. BTR (Albion, N.Y.) to Morris, Nov. 15, 1856. The letter ends abruptly here, without a closing, presumably because this copy was the original draft from which Roberts wrote the actual letter that he sent to Bishop Morris.

53. Allen notes, "During the entire life of the East Genesee Conference it was closely related to the Northern Christian Advocate, and half of that time furnished the editor from its membership." Ray Allen, *History of the East Genesee Annual Conference of the Methodist Episcopal Church* (Rochester, N.Y.: By the Author, 1908), p. 33.

54. Emory Stevens Bucke, ed., *The History of American Methodism* (New York: Abingdon, 1964), 2:176. According to Allen, Hosmer began editing the *Northern Christian Advocate* in late 1842, when it was owned by John Robie. Apparently he served as editor from 1842 to 1844, then again from 1848 until 1856. Allen, *History,* pp. 33-34.

55. COM, p. 455; *Minutes,* Genesee Conference, 1847; East Genesee Conference, 1848; Allen, *Century,* p. 95; Allen, *History,* p. 153.

the *Western Christian Advocate* (Cincinnati) and *Pittsburgh Christian Advocate*, defended the continuing membership of Methodists "who happened to own slaves," while Hosmer at the *Northern Christian Advocate* and the editors of *Zion's Herald* and the new *Northwestern Christian Advocate* (Chicago) "condemned all slaveholding and favored excluding from the church all those who would persist in owning slaves."[56] By the time of the 1856 General Conference, Hosmer had become "the most outspoken abolitionist editor" in Methodism.[57] Bond began calling the Methodist abolitionist editors and their followers "Hosmerites."[58]

Hosmer had indeed become known as an abolitionist and author, not only within Methodism but also beyond. He had published several books (largely based on his articles and editorials): *The Young Lady's Book; or, Principles of Female Education* (1851),[59] *The Young Man's Book* (1852), *The Higher Law* (1852), and *Slavery and the Church* (1853).[60] *The Higher Law* was an attack on the Fugitive Slave Law. "The highest principles of the Christian faith have been impugned" by that law, Hosmer argued, and so ministers must speak up. "It is their business to proclaim the Higher Law, and the Higher Law as paramount to all other laws. They are heralds of the kingdom of God, and when that kingdom is contemned, they must appear in its defence, or Christ is betrayed in the house of his friends." Hosmer argued that "Civil government can-

---

56. Bucke, *History of American Methodism*, 2:189.

57. William Gravely, *Gilbert Haven, Methodist Abolitionist: A Study in Race, Religion, and Reform, 1850-1880* (Nashville: Abingdon, 1973), p. 53.

58. Bucke, *History of American Methodism*, 2:189.

59. William Hosmer, *The Young Lady's Book; or, Principles of Female Education* (Auburn, N.Y., 1851). Drawing on "the ethics of the New Testament, and the progressive spirit of the nineteenth century," Hosmer argued that "The intellectual nature of woman calls for its full share of cultivation. Hers must be an intellectual part," as well as moral. He argued for full equality of "woman" so far as her essential nature was concerned: "[W]hatever may be affirmed of the dignity of [man's] nature, the same may also be affirmed of woman. She partakes the same nature, and consequently sustains the same relation to God and to all things of temporal or spiritual importance." However, "nature" appoints to woman a "more secluded and domestic life" than to men; thus a woman "cannot have the same position as the other sex, but she must have one equally honorable." He argued that woman "ought to know that the state of comparative subordination which falls to her lot by the appointment of nature and the customs of society, is not one of real humiliation, but only of temporary and honorable variety, originating necessarily in the present constitution of human nature. This fact, well understood, will prevent all improper desire to rise above her condition, and all those apings of masculine characteristics which she was never intended to possess, and never can exhibit without destroying the loveliness of her appropriate character" (p. 18). Roberts would later take a much more radical stand.

60. William Hosmer, *The Young Man's Book* (Auburn, N.Y., 1852); *The Higher Law, in its Relations to Civil Government: with Particular Reference to Slavery, and the Fugitive Slave Law* (Auburn, N.Y.: Derby and Miller, 1852), and *Slavery and the Church* (Auburn, N.Y.: William J. Moses, 1853). In *Slavery and the Church* Hosmer argued, among other things, that "The exclusion of slavery [and slave-holding from the church] is essential to the evangelization of the world." *The Higher Law* was dedicated "To William H. Seward, Late Governor of the State of New-York, and Now Senator of the United States" (and later Secretary of State under Abraham Lincoln). Seward had said in 1850 that slavery should be banned from new states by "a higher law than the Constitution." John S. Bowman, ed., *Cambridge Dictionary of American Biography* (New York: Cambridge University Press, 1995), p. 661.

not bind the conscience," "release man from his responsibility to God," or "change the nature of vice and virtue." Thus each one must take personal responsibility and decide whether in good conscience he or she can obey the civil law.[61]

In *Slavery and the Church* Hosmer attacked Bond's defense of slavery, arguing that the situation of the Methodist Episcopal Church in the present time was distinctly different from instances of slavery in biblical times. In the present context slavery clearly is a sin, and the Methodist Church has rules against it. "The Church has everything to do with slavery, if slavery is sin. Caesar belongs to Christ. Sins of the State are to be reproved and extirpated as truly as the sins of individuals."[62]

Hosmer's outspoken "antislaveryism" was very evident at the 1856 Methodist General Conference. With other Methodist abolitionists like Gilbert Haven, Hosmer worked to pass a new rule that would forbid "holding or selling a slave or slaves, or buying [one], except to emancipate," and supported a provision that all Methodists who held slaves must free them within three years.[63] Opponents responded that the church should "maintain the Discipline as it is" — or else remove all reference to slavery from the *Discipline* entirely, as the Methodist Episcopal Church, South, had done in 1854. Thomas Carlton apparently supported this more conservative position in order to maintain peace in the church.[64]

The antislavery reforms pushed by Hosmer and others might have passed but for fears of again splitting the church. Bishop Morris gave the episcopal address near the beginning of the conference, and through him the bishops put a damper on any new antislavery action. Morris played down the slavery issue and argued that the General Conference had no power to make the proposed changes unless they were *first* approved by three-fourths of the annual conferences.[65]

After prolonged debate, the General Conference did vote on amending the church's General Rule by prohibiting "the buying, selling, or holding a human being as property," ignoring the bishops' interpretation. The action received a majority vote (102 to 96), but this fell short of the required two-thirds vote and so failed.[66]

The reformers were able to get antislavery men elected as editors of the *Methodist Quarterly Review* and the *Western Christian Advocate*. But, as William Gravely notes, "conservatives brought off a successful coup against William Hosmer," electing F. G.

---

61. Hosmer, *Higher Law*, pp. v, 41, 79.

62. Hosmer, *Slavery and the Church*, p. 199. Hosmer's two books on the slavery controversy have come to be viewed of such significance in the history of American abolitionism that both were republished in 1969 by the Negro University Press.

63. American Quakers, under the prodding of John Woolman and others, had successfully worked through the slaveholding issue half a century or so earlier. Many Quakers who held slaves freed them, often paying reparation or otherwise providing for their former slaves, though some left the Society of Friends rather than complying with the church's decision that slaveholding must end. See John Greenleaf Whittier, introduction to *The Journal of John Woolman* (London: Headley Brothers, [1908]), pp. 10-24.

64. Gravely, *Gilbert Haven*, pp. 51-52.

65. Gravely, *Gilbert Haven*, pp. 52-53.

66. Gravely, *Gilbert Haven*, p. 53.

Hibbard to edit the *Northern Christian Advocate*, even though Hosmer had been recommended for another term by both the paper's publication committee and the spon-
soring annual conferences. "Thus, in refusing to condemn Methodist slaveholding and
by sanctioning racial segregation in the church," the General Conference was in effect a
victory for status quo conservatives against antislavery reformers.[67]

The 1856 General Conference was in fact the high-water mark of the antislavery,
abolitionist effort within the Methodist Episcopal Church. As the vote totals on key
issues show, a majority of the delegates (all of whom were preachers) favored
tougher action against Methodist slaveholding. But they could not muster the necessary two-thirds vote to bring about structural reform.

Hosmer's successor at the *Northern Christian Advocate*, Freeborn Garrettson
Hibbard (1811-95), was also from the East Genesee Conference. Hibbard edited the
periodical for the next four years. In 1859 he published the series of articles on
Nazaritism noted above.[68]

Relieved of his editorship at one periodical, Hosmer immediately founded another: the *Northern Independent*. He took superannuate relationship with the East
Genesee Conference in order to devote full time to his new venture.[69] The first issue
was published on August 14, 1856.[70] The paper declared on its masthead, "No compromise with sin, no silent submission to wrong, in church or state, a bold advocacy
of all the moral issues of the age, and especially of an uncompromising Christianity."[71] Roberts later said Hosmer "was the first one to start a dollar weekly in the
M.E. Church."[72]

Hosmer published the *Northern Independent* in Auburn, New York, where the
Northern Christian Advocate was published. He asked Roberts to serve as a contributing editor, and Roberts consented. The *Independent* lived up to its name, and was
strongly antislavery from the beginning. Reinhard notes, "What Hosmer had done
in the *Northern Christian Advocate*, he did even more ardently in his new business
venture, the *Northern Independent*. Readers, disappointed with the conciliating denominational papers, rejoiced at Hosmer's return to antislaveryism."[73]

Roberts wrote occasionally for the *Northern Independent;* Hosmer called him
"one of the assistant editors."[74] Benjamin's first article seems to have been a piece re-

67. Gravely, *Gilbert Haven*, p. 54.

68. Allen, *History*, pp. 151, 153-54; *COM*, p. 983.

69. *Minutes*, East Genesee Conference, 1856. Hosmer was not, of course, really "superannuated or
worn-out" (he was forty-six and apparently in good health), but this category allowed him to keep his
Methodist conference membership without being assigned as preacher of a local church. By rule, every
Methodist annual conference was required to indicate the assignment or disposition of every preacher
every year (and to pass on his character, as noted earlier).

70. Not Jan. 1857, as reported in Bucke, *History of American Methodism*, 2:346.

71. *NI* 1, no. 2 (Aug. 21, 1856): 1.

72. [B. T. Roberts], "Literary Notices," *EC* 6, no. 4 (Dec. 1862): 188.

73. Reinhard, "Personal and Sociological Factors," p. 108. Not, of course, that Hosmer had left
"antislaveryism." Also, as noted, some of the Methodist papers continued to be strongly antislavery.

74. "Buffalo Advocate vs. Rev. B. T. Roberts," *NI* 2, no. 7 (Sept. 24, 1857): 2.

porting on his trip to Philadelphia that appeared in the April 2, 1857, issue.[75] It is often difficult to identify the authors of items in this journal because many of the articles were unsigned or signed only with an initial.

Benjamin intended to continue writing, however, also for the *Northern Christian Advocate*. The *Advocate* was still the official paper of western New York Methodism, whereas some viewed the *Northern Independent* as a rival, renegade sheet. The *Independent* opened its office in Auburn across town from the *Advocate* office and issued its weekly edition on Thursdays, whereas the *Advocate* came out on Wednesdays.[76] No doubt Roberts read both papers avidly, and he circulated the *Independent* among his people.

Second Year at Albion

When annual conference ended on Saturday, September 13, 1856, Benjamin returned home to begin his second year at Albion. He made almost no entries in his 1856 diary after April, so there are few details for this period. No doubt this was a time of mounting stress for both Benjamin and Ellen.

With three small children, Ellen had her hands full as Benjamin continued his ministry. The winter and spring of 1857 were a busy time. George and Lydia Lane came to visit at the end of 1856 and stayed until mid-March.[77] Ellen wrote on New Year's Day, 1857,

> I am the Lord's, soul body and spirit; I have His presence in the midst of multiplied cares. My Aunt [Lydia] is sick with a cold, my baby [Charles Stowe, then six months old] sick. . . .
>
> The lord blest me this morning, and still more at family prayer this evening, the Spirit said to me while trying to pray "Hitherto ye have asked nothing in my name" &c. I have not in more than a year felt the same desire of power in prayer. Bless the Lord for it.[78]

Ellen took an active part in the life of the church, to the degree she could. Occasionally she exhorted or "tried to say a few words" after Benjamin's sermons. But she sometimes feared she took initiative on her own too much, rather than being led by

---

75. R. [B. T. Roberts], "Trip to Philadelphia — Rev. G. Lane . . . ," *NI* 1, no. 34 (Apr. 2, 1857): 2. Revell says, "The first column that is almost certain to [have been] written by Roberts appears Apr. 2, 1857. Many more follow, though he was never a major contributor" ("The Nazirites," p. 187). The article is dated "New York, March 21, 1856" (evidently a misprint for 1857; Benjamin wrote to Ellen from New York on the same day).

76. Revell says, "The *Northern Independent* was established in Auburn, New York, across town from his [Hosmer's] old office, and the official paper immediately began to lose subscribers" ("The Nazirites," pp. 186-87).

77. Carpenter, pp. 47, 49.

78. ELRD, Jan. 1, 1857.

the Spirit. "I want self out of sight all the time."[79] Always conscientious, Ellen suffered "a severe trial" because she felt she "had not manifested . . . the right spirit" in a particular situation. But she repented and felt God especially present during the prayer time in the evening service on Tuesday, January 13. "He came in power to my heart," she wrote. "I saw so clearly the great need of the church was to get down. We are afraid of getting so low, when we can do no such thing. Christ humbled Himself for us, became a man, obedient unto death, even the death of the cross. A light so bright shown for a moment[,] beamed forth. I screamed, opened my eyes to see where I was and it was gone. It came from above. Glory to God. Sister Annis was blessed — God gave her the evidence of a clean heart. I thank God one soul has come out into a clear light."[80]

Again she wrote on January 28:

> I have of late been troubled to know always whether I yielded to what seemed temptation. I felt when little trials came that I did not bear them just right but could not detect where the wrong lay — today while talking with Sister Huff & Aunt Lydia I saw clearly I believe that it is want of perfect submission, a willingness to be crossed in little things, to give up my will about them when they go contrary to my wishes. Of course if I felt that I could not have them so — then I would have too much feeling about them & be sure to be tried. I thank God I see my error.[81]

After retiring on Sunday night, February 8, Ellen "felt a great deal of the power and presence of God." She "prayed for a deadness" to her own desires and felt God say to her, "Follow me and you will become dead to yourself."[82]

Benjamin continued his ministry in Albion as winter turned to spring. He had a bad cold in early March, his cough making it nearly impossible to preach on Sunday, March 8. But the general class meeting that day, Ellen felt, was excellent. "When the leader came to me," she said, she felt prompted to say that she believed "the Lord would work" among the people of the church and in her own heart, though she knew not how. "And in a manner altogether new the Lord did work in my heart," she wrote. "I fell on my knees and groaned through the remainder of the meeting and felt the Lord there in an unusual degree."[83]

The next evening, George and Lydia Lane left for their home in New Jersey. Benjamin went along to assist them, though still nursing a bad cough. He was gone for two weeks, visiting New York City and Philadelphia as well as the Lane home in New Jersey. He published an account of his trip in the *Northern Independent,* reporting that he "accompanied that venerable servant of God, the Rev. George Lane, and his devoted wife, to their home in Mount Holly." He noted that George Lane was "in

---

79. ELRD, Jan. 11, 1857.
80. ELRD, Jan. 13, 1857; cf. Carpenter, pp. 47-48. Carpenter omits "I screamed."
81. ELRD, Jan. 28, 1857.
82. ELRD, Feb. 8, 1857.
83. ELRD, Mar. 8, 1857.

feeble health and gradually declining," and gave a brief account of Lane's ministerial career, noting that he had been "the second preacher that travelled the Genesee Circuit." Benjamin added, "I confess to a feeling of veneration for these heroes of the cross, who have over-come, in the well-fought battle of life, and are only waiting the Master's summons to enter into the joy of their Lord."[84]

Benjamin wrote Ellen from Mount Holly to report that the Lanes had arrived home safely and that he himself was well, his cough much better. He added, "And now if I could only know that my darling Wife and loved children were well, at home I should be satisfied." But he entrusted them into God's hands. "O, darling, I do love you more than tongue or pen can express," he added. "Kiss the boys for me and tell George he must be very good indeed."[85]

Roberts apparently preached at Mount Holly during his brief visit there. Lydia Lane wrote to Ellen, "Mr. Roberts has much of the Spirit's influence in preaching. Oh what is to be compared to the love of Christ constraining those who are Watchmen on Zion's Walls. One may preach the truth without it, he may be much in earnest and yet if the Spirit of Christ, his yearning pity and tender sympathy does not pervade the soul the word falls powerless, and sinners in and out of the Church are unsaved[,] but when the baptism of the Spirit is realized fully, how easy to preach and to pray, and live, and how it tells upon the Church."[86]

Benjamin took advantage of this trip to do some sightseeing and of course to visit the Methodist Book Room in Manhattan. Since Mount Holly was only about twenty miles from Philadelphia, he went on by train to Camden and by steam ferryboat across the Delaware River to the City of Brotherly Love. Philadelphia is "a great city," he wrote, and Independence Hall well worth seeing. Here "some of the greatest and noblest men that ever sat in council of affairs of State, deliberated and decided questions that will, for all coming time, have a moulding influence upon the destinies of mankind."[87]

A major reason for going to Philadelphia was to hear James Caughey preach. Benjamin had learned that Caughey was then in the city, and he was eager to hear the fiery Methodist holiness evangelist, whose book *Revival Miscellanies* he had read in 1852. He wrote to Ellen on March 17, "I think I shall go to Philadelphia to-morrow to hear Mr. Caughey, and take observations. I hope to be benefited."[88] It is not clear, however, whether Roberts actually heard Caughey.

---

84. R. [B. T. Roberts], "Trip to Philadelphia," p. 2. The article was written Mar. 21, the same date as Benjamin's letter to Ellen cited below, and possibly also written while he was waiting in McCrossan's store. Cf. Carpenter, p. 49.

85. BTR to ELR, Mar. 17, 1857, from Mount Holly, N.J.

86. LBL to ELR, Apr. 21, 1857, from Mount Holly, N.J. It is interesting that Lydia Lane speaks of "the baptism of the Spirit," but also that the Holy Spirit is specifically "the Spirit of Christ," who makes Jesus real to the hearers. Clearly Lydia felt Benjamin exhibited such a presence of the Spirit.

87. R. [B. T. Roberts], "Trip to Philadelphia."

88. BTR to ELR, Mar. 17, 1857, from Mount Holly, N.J. Caughey would soon embark for his second trip to Great Britain.

From Philadelphia Benjamin went back to New York City, arriving on Friday, March 20. He called on "Dr. Peck" — no doubt Jesse Peck, author of *The Central Idea of Christianity*, who had been present at the 1855 Genesee Annual Conference and was now pastor at the Greene Street Church in Manhattan. Roberts presumably wanted to get Peck's counsel about holiness and the situation in the Genesee Conference. He went to hear Peck preach that night (presumably at Greene Street), and Peck invited him to stay the night, which he did. "I met with a cordial welcome, and had a very pleasant visit," he told Ellen.[89]

One of Roberts's reasons for visiting New York City was to see Brother A. McCrossan, a businessman who had a store in the city. Benjamin apparently spent some time with McCrossan at his store on Saturday, and also from there wrote a letter to Ellen. Also, he ran into Thomas Carlton during his customary visit to the Methodist Book Room. "Carlton <u>seemed</u> glad to see me and paid me considerable attention."[90]

Summarizing his New York visit in his letter to Ellen, Benjamin wrote,

> I am a great deal better of my cold, and think and trust that in a few days, by the blessing of the Lord I shall be entirely well. I am enjoying my mind very well and trust that my visit will be made a spiritual blessing to my soul. I can say truthfully
>
> > "My longing heart is all on fire
> > To be dissolved in love."

Benjamin concluded with advice to Ellen to take care of herself. "Ride out as much as you possibly can," and eat well, he said. "I trust you will go to the Springs as often as every other day." He closed the letter, "Kiss the boys. Love to Mary — and my <u>heart</u> for you." The reference to Mary probably indicates that Mary Swezey, Ellen's niece, was still living with the Robertses. Benjamin arrived home, apparently, the next Wednesday, March 25.[91]

As April brought the first signs of spring, Ellen thought of traveling to Illinois to visit her father and her ailing mother, now living at Bonus Prairie, northwest of Chicago. But then Georgie came down with the dreaded scarlet fever, and she herself became ill (though she was able to attend the quarterly meeting at Chili). Just as she and George were recovering, little Charles also got scarlet fever. So she gave up the idea of visiting her parents.[92]

Through all these trials, however, Ellen felt God's constant presence. She wrote after attending the quarterly meeting, "My soul was greatly blessed there, all the

---

89. BTR to ELR, Mar. 21, 1857, from New York City; *COM*, pp. 698-99.

90. BTR to ELR, Mar. 21, 1857, from New York City. Roberts mentions "A. McCrossan" in his diary for Jan. 25, 1859, listing him as one of a number of persons to whom he sent the *Proceedings of the Laymen's Convention*.

91. BTR to ELR, Mar. 21, 1857.

92. Carpenter, p. 49.

time. I felt such a ceasing from Self — such reliance on Christ. It was a season of great comfort and of constant abiding in Christ."[93]

Ellen had peace about not visiting her mother, even though she received word that she was failing. Finally, however, as Charles improved, Ellen felt she had to go see her mother one last time. She left home on Thursday, June 4 — the very day her mother died, she later learned.[94] Traveling to Chicago and on to Bonus Prairie, she arrived to find that her mother had been buried just that morning. Dorcas Stow was sixty-six.[95]

Benjamin wrote to Ellen on Saturday, June 6, a couple of days after Ellen left. Apparently on Thursday he had traveled by train with Ellen as far as Buffalo, said good-bye to her there, stayed overnight at James Runcie's, then taken care of some business the next day and returned to Albion. "I could not get any money in Buffalo, though I have due me there about $70.00," he reported to Ellen, probably referring to the rent on their house at 29 Palmer Street.

In his letter Benjamin also gave an update on the boys: "Charlie [then nearly one] seemed perfectly delighted to see me. He talked and sputtered and laughed aloud, and made every demonstration of joy in his power. George [five and a half] inquired very particularly after you[,] where you were &c. Benson [almost four] was as loving as ever. Charlie slept good last night Mary said."

Benjamin also gave Ellen some advice about saving on train fare when she returned home from Chicago — showing he was not averse to using what influence he possessed to save some money. "If Mr. Spalding [in Chicago?] will not give you a half fare ticket you had better try the agent of the Southern Michigan Line. Tell him who you are — and that I may do something in the way of sending them passengers — that I am assistant Editor of a paper &c." Roberts's fairly new position as a contributing editor to the *Northern Independent* was one he evidently valued.

Benjamin closed his June 6 letter to Ellen: "Find a kiss at the lower corner of this page. George says 'tell Mother we have been good boys and send our love to her.'"[96]

Ellen spent about three weeks at her parents' place, returning home at the end of June. Her mother's passing before Ellen could get there "was a trial almost insupportable to me, but I could not think it happened by chance," she wrote. She found her father, Stoddard Stow, "very poorly in body & broken in spirit," and her sister

---

93. ELRD, Apr. 1, 1857 (approximately); cf. Carpenter, p. 49.

94. BTR to ELR, May [i.e., June] 6, 1857, from Albion, N.Y. The letter is clearly dated "Home. Sat. Morn. May 6th 1857." May 6 was not a Saturday, however, and other evidence confirms that the letter was in fact written on Saturday, June 6, 1857.

95. Carpenter, p. 49; Smail, p. 129. Ellen says, "My dear mother was buried the morning of the day I arrived," apparently meaning that Ellen arrived after the funeral (though conceivably she could have arrived early in the morning, before the funeral). Smail says Dorcas Stowe "died in Chicago but was buried at Bonus Prairie, Illinois, some 50 miles to the west." She was interred at the East Bonus Cemetery, north of Garden Prairie on Woodstock Road ("Boone County IL Cemeteries," copy furnished by the Cemetery Association of Belvidere, Jan. 3, 2002).

96. BTR to ELR, May [i.e., June] 6, 1857.

and brother in deep grief. Yet, "My father said he prayed daily and wanted to be prepared for death. I hope this affliction may be sanctified to them all." This was Ellen's first excursion so far west, and she found the place her father lived "very beautiful" and "very dear to me."[97] Her father passed away about fourteen months after this visit.[98]

The Bergen Camp Meeting Issue

The 1857 Bergen camp meeting was again held in June and again attracted large crowds, despite stormy weather.[99] Ellen did not attend, as she was in Illinois. John Wesley Redfield had gone to Illinois to participate in the St. Charles camp meeting.[100] Roberts may not have attended, perhaps due to Ellen's being away.

The local newspaper, the *Brockport Republic*, reported: "All our village omnibuses, hacks, buggies, gigs, wagons, and horses, were put in requisition" carrying people to the campground as they arrived at Bergen by train or at Brockport via the Erie Canal for the Sunday services.[101] A description of the campground written in 1861 by editor Horatio Beach gives something of the flavor of the gathering: "The center of the grounds were occupied by the tents, sixty-five in number, set . . . in a circle, inclosing the space devoted to holding of the general meetings. In this center space is erected a preachers stand fronting on a large number of seats formed by laying planks across logs."[102]

A local resident, Charles Reed, years later recalled visiting the Bergen camp meeting about this time. At the center of the camp was a large platform "covered by a tabernacle." The weekend attendance was estimated at 2,500. Teams of horses were hitched to poles fastened between trees in an orchard and tied up for half a mile along the roads in all four directions. Some local residents set up stands near the camp entrance to sell popcorn, oranges, ice cream, and other items. One farmer "turned his farm into a livery for good pay," running horse-drawn stages from the surrounding villages to the campground. In the evenings area residents would sit on their porches and listen. Up to a mile away they "could hear the singing and shouting [and] preaching as plain as if there."[103]

97. ELRD, June, 1857.

98. Smail, p. 195. Stoddard Stow was also interred at the East Bonus Cemetery. Cemetery records show that at the end of their lives Stoddard and Dorcas still spelled their name "Stow," not "Stowe," though Stoddard's brother Hiram spelled it "Stowe" ("Boone County IL Cemeteries").

99. *Brockport Republic*, June 19, 1857, p. 2. Apparently the camp was held June 11-18 (based on the date of this report).

100. Terrill, *Redfield*, p. 318.

101. *Brockport Republic*, June 19, 1857, p. 2. See D. Gregory Van Dussen, "The Bergen Camp Meeting in the American Holiness Movement," *Methodist History* 21, no. 2 (Jan. 1983): 78.

102. "The Camp Meeting," *Brockport Republic*, June 27, 1861, p. 3.

103. Recollections of Charles Reed, as recorded in a manuscript by Mrs. George Greenaker. Quoted in Van Dussen, "Bergen Camp Meeting," pp. 88-89.

Almost a year after the 1857 Bergen camp meeting — in June 1858 — a controversy erupted in the pages of the *Northern Christian Advocate* concerning the camp meeting and the association that had been formed to promote it. By this time the camp meeting had become a contentious issue within the Genesee Conference, tangled up with the "Nazarite" issue. Although these articles appeared after Roberts's first trial (to be narrated in the next chapters), they need to be noted here since they relate to the 1857 Bergen camp. The issue focused on the question of oversight authority for the camp meeting (though other issues were necessarily involved). Who was really in charge of the camp meeting? Who was responsible for organizing and overseeing it? Was it really a Methodist Episcopal camp? District camp meetings had always been supervised by the presiding elder, who in consultation with the preachers set the time and place of camp meetings. But now the Genesee Camp-Ground Association had been formed as a legal body, with elected trustees. The association was largely independent of the conference structure, though (as noted earlier) bound to it by a somewhat ambiguous clause in its charter specifying that the association would function "under the jurisdiction of the Genesee Annual Conference of the M.E. Church."[104]

Albert D. Wilbor (a couple of years older than Roberts) was the presiding elder of the Genesee District from 1856 to 1859. In a June 1858 article in the *Northern Christian Advocate,* Wilbor noted that at the 1857 Bergen meeting "a meeting was called of those who were voters, for the purpose of electing a Trustee" to the association. As presiding elder, Wilbor chaired the meeting. Someone moved that the date for the 1858 camp be set. Wilbor "remonstrated" that this would be improper. The decision should be left to the presiding elder and the preachers, in part because the roster of preachers in the district would be somewhat different after annual conference appointments. "[F]or us as preachers or people to appoint the work of our successors was not in accordance" with Methodist practice, he argued. He suggested that the association recommend a preferred date but leave the final decision up to the presiding elder and preachers. "My remonstrances were treated with contempt," Wilbor later reported, "and the meeting proceeded to" set the date of the 1858 camp, "remarks being made which reflected severely upon the integrity of a portion of the ministry, Presiding Elder and all."[105]

Was Roberts present at this meeting? It is not clear that he was, though he later defended the association's action. It seems unlikely that he would have permitted the association to act contrary to his presiding elder's wishes.

Wilbor was upset by this attitude and action, which he considered "disorderly." As presiding elder, he wanted to keep the control of the Bergen camp meeting in his own hands. "I think the Trustees of the 'camp-ground' have overstepped the limits of their power — I hope in regard to most of them, unwittingly." He added, "I am in favor of camp-meetings, when properly appointed and

---

104. A. D. Wilbor, "Genesee District Camp-Meeting," *NCA* 18, no. 23 (June 9, 1858): 2.
105. Wilbor, "Genesee District Camp-Meeting."

conducted, and I cannot but hope that our people will adhere to the order and regulations of our Church."[106]

F. G. Hibbard, editor of the *Northern Christian Advocate,* agreed with Wilbor. "The Presiding Elder has always appointed camp-meetings, in council with his preachers and Quarterly Conferences," he noted. "A camp-meeting is, by usage and consent, a District meeting" under the supervision of "the pastoral authority of the District," and "they alone, therefore, should appoint" such meetings. As Hibbard implicitly acknowledges, the issue was one of "usage and consent," not official regulation.[107]

Hibbard criticized the whole idea of a distinct campground association for introducing "interminable confusion" into the church. "If an association can appoint camp-meetings against the advice of the Presiding Elder, and authority of the District," Hibbard argued, by the same principle it could appoint any other sort of meeting. "Every thing would be done by the associations and primary assemblies of the people. But all history shows that such ultra democracy is only another name for anarchy." The association was a bad precedent. "There is a spirit of disaffection and uneasiness under the ordinary Church restraints which is infusing its virus into many hearts, in this day, in diffuse sections of the country, and deluding many sincere persons." Hibbard concluded that though many of those promoting the Bergen camp meeting were "our personal friends," yet a bad precedent had been set relating "purely and solely to a question of Church order and discipline."[108]

In response to Wilbor and Hibbard, William Cooley defended the Genesee Camp-Ground Association in a June 11, 1858, letter to the *Northern Christian Advocate.* Cooley noted that for years Methodists in the Genesee District had been "greatly in favor" of camp meetings, and such meetings had been held without controversy. The problem now, however, was "a class of preachers" in the conference who opposed camp meetings and had worked to reduce them to just four weekdays, excluding Sunday. The people wanted weeklong meetings "so as to have time to do something for the cause of God," feeling that "they cannot afford to settle in the woods for so short a time as four days."

Cooley's letter illuminates the thinking that went into the forming of the campground association. Clearly the intent of Roberts and others was to guarantee the continuation of weeklong camp meetings even if the presiding elder or some of the preachers opposed them. Cooley wrote, "Last year [1857] the people suspected . . . that there might be a change of preachers on the District this year, so that if the camp meeting was left to come through them, it would come with no Sabbath in it,

106. Wilbor, "Genesee District Camp-Meeting." Wilbor is appealing primarily to precedent, as there do not appear to have been any "regulations" that prohibited independent camp meetings from operating within the denomination.

107. [F. G. Hibbard], "Genesee District Camp-Meeting," *NCA* 18, no. 23 (June 9, 1858): 2. This editorial and Wilbor's article (essentially a letter to the editor) both appeared on the same page of the June 9 issue and with the same headline.

108. [Hibbard], "Genesee District Camp-Meeting," p. 2.

contrary to their wishes in the matter. So they deemed it best to forestall such a result, by fixing the time themselves."

This led to the discussions at the 1857 Bergen camp meeting that Wilbor criticized. Several "speeches were made" when the question of the 1858 camp meeting came up, Cooley noted, and by a vote of about 100 to 3 the group voted to schedule the camp for June 17-24.

Cooley added that though the Methodist people of the district have "a good degree of respect" for church authority, still they "claim some rights in this matter" since they purchased the campground, support the meetings, "and as farmers claim to know when such a meeting will suit their business." He added, "The ground was bought with the expectation that they would enjoy the privilege of having a camp-meeting every year, with a Sabbath in it, as they had for years, or it would not have been purchased. They are unwilling that preachers who oppose camp-meetings, or have but very little sympathy for them, shall meet and vote whether they shall have one or not, and if they do, when and how long."

Cooley noted that it was common practice during a camp meeting to set the time and place of the next one. As to Wilbor's charge that the association trustees had "over-stepped the limits of their power," Cooley pointed out that the conference had "set no limits to them, or given them instructions what to do," and there was no reason why they shouldn't act to promote the Bergen camp meeting. Now, "for the preachers to take camp-meetings . . . entirely out of the hands of the people, will not promote peace and union very much among us." It would put them in a situation similar to that of John Wesley, who "judged it his duty to disregard the order and regulations of his Church . . . when he could not serve God according to his conscience and sense of duty to the perishing around him." This is no time, said Cooley, to obstruct the work "with technicalities and criticisms, when such a multitude of souls are rushing on to death."

Cooley concluded, "The long experience of our Church has proved that these large meetings do much good, and are for the glory of God." It would be unwise to oppose or restrict them. "But, let the opposition to them be what it may, our people cannot and will not give them up. I deeply regret that camp-meetings and holiness should become party questions in any Conference . . . but hope what is really essential to our vitality and power, will remain free from the blight of party spirit."[109]

A few weeks later, following the 1858 Bergen camp meeting, the trustees of the Genesee Camp-Ground Association published a letter in the *Northern Christian Advocate* defending the group's actions. It pointed out that the association was broader than the Genesee District, and included members from several counties. "The Association includes parts of six Districts and two Conferences." Thus the Bergen camp meeting never was simply "a Genesee District camp-meeting."

The letter noted that the camp meeting had been under the direction of the association ever since the "twenty-five acres of beautiful forest" had been purchased,

109. W. Cooley, "Genesee Camp-Meeting," *NCA* 18, no. 25 (June 23, 1858): 1.

and with no opposition from presiding elders. Wilbor had not opposed the camp until at the 1857 meeting his proposals "were voted down by the people. . . . The good brethren never thought that in dissenting in judgment from the Presiding Elder, they were treating him or his remarks 'with contempt,'" the trustees noted. If anyone had departed from "common usage," it was the presiding elder, not the association. The trustees felt they needed to clarify this matter through the pages of the *Northern Christian Advocate* because of the "remarkable course" Wilbor had taken in publicizing the issue in the church paper.

The letter was signed by the trustees: Thomas LaDue, Amos Hard, George W. Holmes, Hartt Smith, Seth M. Woodruff, Benjamin T. Roberts, and Joshua R. Annis.[110] Two of these were Genesee Conference preachers (Hard and Roberts). The rest apparently were Methodist "lay" members.

A couple of weeks later, Wilbor published a long, fair-minded response to these charges, noting that the forming of "independent associations" like the new camp-ground association created some organizational confusion. Such an association is "an anomaly" in church structure, he wrote. "This would be a wheel within a wheel, more puzzling than that revealed in Ezekiel's vision," creating "a kind of independent congregational system" within the denominational structure.[111]

Roberts and his associates seem to have been blind to this organizational issue (which Hibbard also highlighted), seeing the whole matter as one of being either for or against camp meetings (and, by implication, holiness).[112]

The issue that had sparked the controversy, however, was the question at the 1857 Bergen camp meeting of the dates for the 1858 meeting — and, indirectly, the role of the presiding elder in making this decision. The underlying issue, which had not arisen before, was the status and authority of the Genesee Camp-Ground Association within the existing Methodist conference and district structure.[113]

110. [Trustees], "Genesee Camp-Ground Association," *NCA* 18, no. 30 (July 28, 1858): 1.

111. A. D. Wilbor, "The Genesee Camp-Ground Association Once More," *NCA* 18, no. 23 (Aug. 11, 1858): 2. Once again we see the issue of structure, and particularly the *ecclesiola in ecclesia* or modality/sodality tension, arising.

112. In the July 28, 1858, issue of the *Northern Christian Advocate*, Hibbard published an editorial in which he said the matter was "simply a question of order in the Church." A campground association might properly be formed to secure and care for camp meeting property, but when it appointed religious meetings it was encroaching on the pastoral authority of the church — adding "spiritual powers" to "legitimate secular powers." His one point, he said, was that "such meetings should be appointed by the pastoral authority alone, by and with the advice of the Church." [F. G. Hibbard], "Genesee Camp-Ground Association," *NCA* 18, no. 30 (July 28, 1858): 2. (In this issue also, two pieces — the letter from the campground association and Hibbard's editorial — appear with identical headlines.)

113. Wilbor pointed out that the issue in 1857 was different from previous years because previously there had been no campground association. "[T]he meeting last year [1857] was not appointed *precisely* as the one just closed [1858]; for, at that time [1856, when the dates for the 1857 meeting were set] no Association had been chartered; so that whatever power it has now, it had no such power then. And, further, the meeting according to the above showing, was appointed [in 1856] with the consent of the Presiding Elder [Loren Stiles], who was present; but the camp-meeting just closed was appointed

End of Roberts's Second Year at Albion

Following the 1857 Bergen camp meeting, Roberts wrapped up his second year at Albion and prepared for annual conference, scheduled for the end of August at LeRoy.

Despite Benjamin's labors throughout the year, his congregation showed no numerical growth. It ended where it began, with a total of 257 members, though full membership increased from 217 to 230, as a number of probationary members moved into full connection. Four members had died, so these apparently were replaced by new members. Still, as of the 1857 annual conference, Albion was in total membership the fifth-largest of the ninety-five churches in the conference, and in fact was third-largest in full members. The largest congregation was the prosperous Grace Church in Buffalo, with a total membership of 351.[114]

It was toward the end of Roberts's second year at Albion, just a few weeks before the annual conference sessions, that he wrote the two-part article "New School Methodism" — the focus of the next chapter.

[in 1857] in spite of the earnest remonstrance of the Presiding Elder." Wilbor, "The Genesee Camp-Ground Association Once More."

114. The five largest in total membership were Grace Church (351), Belfast (300), Covington (263), West Barre (258), and Albion (257). One needs to remember, however, that of the ninety-five appointments listed in the minutes, some included outlying congregations or preaching points.

CHAPTER 20

"New School Methodism"

". . . nothing less than the nature itself of Christianity."

B. T. Roberts, "New School Methodism," 1857

"My soul is wonderfully nerved up — I feel a confidence in the Lord I never felt before. It seems to me He is working in a way we thought not of."

Ellen Roberts, at the beginning of the
1857 Genesee Annual Conference[1]

"The year 1857 was a memorable one on several counts," noted John Peters in *Christian Perfection and American Methodism*. "A depression gripped the nation. The 'Prayer Meeting Revival' was getting underway — a religious phenomenon, carried on principally by businessmen, which was to sweep from coast to coast within the next two years. And in the Genesee Conference of the Methodist Episcopal Church factional differences were approaching a climax."[2]

By 1857 B. T. Roberts, though only thirty-four, had already been a key figure in these "factional differences" for several years. But the climax came in 1857 and 1858.

The event that led most directly to Roberts's expulsion from the Methodist Episcopal Church was his article "New School Methodism," published in the newly founded *Northern Independent* in 1857, toward the end of his second year at Albion. The article appeared in two parts in consecutive issues on August 20 and August 27.

---

1. ELRD, Sept. 1 (approx.), 1857.

2. John Leland Peters, *Christian Perfection and American Methodism* (New York: Abingdon, 1956), p. 128.

382

Roberts, a contributing editor to the periodical, simply signed the articles "R."[3] In publishing "New School Methodism" Roberts was going against the "affectionate request" of the 1856 annual conference that preachers not publish "articles relating to or implicating members of this Conference"[4] — though Roberts identified no one by name.

Roberts's article attacked pew rental and other departures from "Old School Methodism," including the identification of sanctification with justification. He argued that a "new theory of religion" was being spread in the conference by "a class of preachers," numbering about thirty, "whose teaching is very different from that of the Fathers of Methodism." The conference was divided. "Two distinct parties exist," and the controversy concerns "nothing less than the nature itself of Christianity."[5] Here Roberts makes some of the same points, and uses some of the same language, found in his letter to Bishop Morris of almost a year earlier.[6]

The key theological errors of these New School Methodists, Roberts felt, were two: putting good works in the place of faith in Christ and holding that justification and sanctification were the same. The results of these errors were predictable.

> Differing thus in their views of religion, the Old and New School Methodists necessarily differ in their measures for its promotion. The latter build stock churches, and furnish them with pews to accommodate a select congregation; and with organs, melodeons, violins, and professional singers, to execute difficult pieces of music for a fashionable audience. The former favor free churches, congregational singing, and spirituality, simplicity and fervency in worship. They endeavor to promote revivals, deep and thorough; such as were common under the labors of the Fathers; such as have made Methodism the leading denomination of the land. The leaders of the New Divinity movement are not remarkable for promoting revivals. . . . When these desire to raise money for the benefit of the Church, they have recourse to the selling of pews to the highest bidder; to parties of pleasure, oyster suppers, fairs, grab bags, festivals and lotteries: the others, for this purpose, appeal to the love the people bear to Christ. In short, the Old School Methodists rely . . . upon the agency of the Holy Ghost, and the purity of the Church. The New School Methodists appear to depend upon the patronage of the worldly, the favor of the proud and aspiring; and the various artifices of worldly policy.

3. [B. T. Roberts], "New School Methodism," *NI* 2, no. 2 (Aug. 20, 1857): 2; [B. T. Roberts], "New School Methodism," *NI* 2, no. 3 (Aug. 27, 1857): 2.

4. F. G. Hibbard, "Nazaritism — Its Judicial History," *NCA* 19, no. 45 (Nov. 9, 1859): 2.

5. [B. T. Roberts], "New School Methodism," Aug. 20, 1857, p. 2. All subsequent quotations from "New School Methodism" are taken from the article's original appearance in the *Northern Independent* and are marked part I or part II to distinguish the Aug. 20 and Aug. 27 installments.

6. See the discussion in the previous chapter; compare "New School Methodism" with Roberts's Nov. 15, 1856, letter to Bishop Thomas Morris (printed in Zahniser, pp. 347-49 [with some minor errors] and in part in James Alan Revell, "The Nazirites: Burned-Over District Methodism and the Buffalo Middle Class" [Ph.D. diss., University of New York at Buffalo, 1993], pp. 342-43).

The special mission of Methodism, Roberts says, is "not to gather into her fold the proud and fashionable, the devotees of pleasure and ambition, but, 'to spread Scriptural holiness over these lands.'"

Roberts here says nothing specifically about the gospel for the poor, though he warns that "prosperity is producing upon us, as a denomination, the same intoxicating effect, that it too often does upon individuals and societies."[7] His main concern in "New School Methodism" is the drift away from historic Methodism in both doctrine and practice.

Roberts began "New School Methodism" with an analogy from nature, making an essentially sociological point about the Methodist Episcopal Church as a denomination. "The best seed sown, from year [to year] on poor soil, gradually degenerates. The acorn from the stately oak, planted upon the arid plain, becomes a stinted shrub. Ever since the fall, the human heart has proved a soil unfavorable to the growth of truth. Noxious weeds flourish everywhere spontaneously, while the useful grains require diligent cultivation."[8]

Methodism, Roberts argued, was not exempt from the same dynamic. "As a denomination, we are just as liable to fall by corrupting influences, as any were that have flourished before us. We enjoy no immunity from danger."[9]

Old and New School Methodism

This "New School"/"Old School" language among Genesee Methodists was borrowed from the Presbyterians. Due to a split in 1837, American Presbyterians were divided into two separate denominations, New School and Old School. The division wasn't healed until after the Civil War. New School Presbyterians generally endorsed revivalism, abolitionism, and broad-based social reform efforts, while Old School Presbyterians were concerned with the doctrinal compromise they felt inevitably accompanied these involvements. Old School Presbyterians, adhering strictly to the Westminster Confession, thought their New School brethren were too influenced by Charles Finney and Arminian theology; in fact, some scholars have called New School Presbyterians the "Methodist" wing of Presbyterianism.[10]

---

7. [B. T. Roberts], "New School Methodism," part II.

8. [B. T. Roberts], "New School Methodism," part I. The original article has "sown, from year, on poor soil"; this was corrected to "from year to year" in WAS, p. 85. The original article and its reprint in WAS have the word "stinted" rather than "stunted"; in BHR, BTR (p. 112), in Hogue, History (1:96), and in Marston (p. 573) this is changed to "stunted."

9. [B. T. Roberts], "New School Methodism," part I.

10. Specifically, Donald Dayton and George Marsden. S. R. Pointer notes that "New School Presbyterianism . . . was not perceptibly different from the broader evangelical movement that nurtured it until it was attacked by Old School Presbyterians in the 1830s. Until then, it was part of an evangelical phalanx that shared a common commitment to evangelism through revivals and to Christianizing America through moral reform. Perhaps the best early representative of the New

This Presbyterian conflict did not have a direct parallel within Methodism, however. In fact, what Roberts called Old School Methodism (which he defended) was closer to New School Presbyterianism in its advocacy of revivalism and abolitionism — though perhaps more like Old School Presbyterianism in its concern with doctrinal integrity.[11] There is some irony, therefore, in applying "Old School" to those Methodists who were at key points in sympathy with the New School Presbyterians.

Roberts's "New School Methodism," however, was provoked by an article entitled "Old and New School Methodism" that appeared three months earlier in the *Buffalo Advocate,* not by the Presbyterian debates.[12] (The article was unsigned; it was likely written by John B. Wentworth, though perhaps by John Robie or Thomas Carlton.) This was one of several substantial articles published in the Buffalo paper in the spring of 1857 that clearly marked out a different course for Methodism.

In "New School Methodism" Roberts specifically attacked three *Buffalo Advocate* articles — "Old and New School Methodism" and two others: "Creed Tests of Orthodox Piety" in the April 16 issue and especially "Christianity a Religion of Beneficence Rather Than of Devotion" in the May 14 issue.[13] The points he makes in "New School Methodism" can be fully understood only in the context of these articles.

"Creed Tests of Orthodox Piety" was signed "W." and probably was written by Wentworth, the preacher at Williamsville, near Buffalo. Wentworth (1823-93) was the same age as Roberts. Much of his ministerial career was spent in the Buffalo area, where in later years he exerted "a commanding influence." Sandford Hunt wrote, "His solid logic in the pulpit, and his uncompromising maintenance and defense of everything peculiar to Methodism, soon won for him a place in the first rank of the preachers in the city."[14]

School spirit was Lyman Beecher," the father of Henry Ward Beecher and Harriet Beecher Stowe. S. R. Pointer, "New School Presbyterians," in *DCA,* pp. 819-20.

11. In theological stance, Old School Methodists occupied a middle ground between Old School Presbyterians (doctrinally very conservative) and New School Methodists (moving in a distinctly liberal, revisionist direction). In terms of polity, evangelism, and church practice, the Old School Methodist ethos was much like that of the New School Presbyterians.

12. [J. B. Wentworth?], "Old and New School Methodism," *Buffalo Advocate,* May 21, 1857, p. 2. As noted below, this article charged the Nazarites with being "new school" in contrast to historic "old school" Methodism. (At the end of 1853 or beginning of 1854, the *Buffalo Christian Advocate* discontinued listing volume numbers, giving only a whole number for each issue, and with the Apr. 2, 1857, issue it dropped "Christian" from its name.)

13. Reinhard refers to these as "Three pro-Methodism, antireformer articles, probably by Wentworth (signed W.)" (p. 25). Actually only the first, "Creed Tests of Orthodox Piety" (Apr. 16), was signed "W."; the others were unsigned. Wentworth may in fact have written all three articles, but this is not certain. All three appeared on page 2 (essentially the editorial/opinion page) of the *Advocate.* See Reinhard's discussion, "Wentworth vs. Roberts," in James Arnold Reinhard, "Personal and Sociological Factors in the Formation of the Free Methodist Church, 1852-1860" (Ph.D. diss., University of Iowa, 1971), pp. 21-28.

14. Sandford Hunt, *Methodism in Buffalo From Its Origin to the Close of 1892* (Buffalo: H. H. Otis and Sons, 1893), p. 78. See Ray Allen, *A Century of the Genesee Annual Conference of the Methodist Episcopal Church, 1810-1910* (Rochester, N.Y.: By the Author, 1911), p. 128.

"Creed Tests of Orthodox Piety" was a substantial, well-written essay occupying two long columns in the *Buffalo Advocate*. Wentworth raised the question: What is the central principle or "essential idea" that gives "the Christian movement" its "distinctive character"? In what may have been a jab at Jesse Peck's recently published *The Central Idea of Christianity*, Wentworth wrote: "It is of the last importance . . . that that which is *in truth* the essential idea of Christianity should be recognized and set up as the standard of orthodox piety in the organized Church of Christ."

For too long, Wentworth argued, Protestantism has made "certain dogmatical Creeds . . . the prime test of Christian character." But this is a perversion of the original Protestant impulse. Essentially, Christianity "is not a collection, or a proclamation, of abstract doctrines, of cold formulas of theoretical divinity," but rather is "a system of spiritual forces — acting upon the heart and actuating the life." True Christianity is ethical, finding its "fullest expression in modes of practical living, rather than in modes of speculative thinking." "Christ never taught that by assent to certain doctrines of theoretic divinity, men became his disciples." Rather, true discipleship is a matter of self-denial and love for God and neighbor.

"But this style of orthodoxy, our creed-mongers cannot endure," Wentworth charged. "To the most of us, it is a more gratifying task to reprehend and convict a brother for heresy, than to forego our own selfish pleasures for the sake of increasing a brother's happiness. By detecting an error in the opinions of another, we gratify our love of victory and our sense of superiority."

An overemphasis on creeds breeds "bigotry and intolerance"; "zeal all the more fiery for being spurious." Further, such emphasis on correct doctrine "greatly retards the progress of religious knowledge and the evolution of Christian truth." Wentworth (assuming he was the author) perhaps was thinking of himself when he added, "The ban of excommunication is pronounced against those audacious individuals who dare think for themselves in matters of religion." In a passage Roberts later quoted, he added, "No matter how holy and blameless a man's life may be, — if he has the temerity to question any tenet of 'Orthodoxy,' he is at once, in due ecclesiastical form, consigned to the Devil — as a heretic and infidel. Thus are the fetters of a spiritual despotism thrown around the human Reason."[15]

By itself, this article probably would not have called forth a response from Roberts. He likely would have agreed, in general, with the emphasis on self-giving and loving service. The error was in setting this in opposition to orthodox doctrine, and in implying that the essence of Christianity was simply the following of Jesus' teachings and example, with no reference to justification or sanctification. In Wentworth's scheme the Christian faith was essentially a life of good works — and by implication, seemingly a form of salvation *by* works. Also, the negative comments about "orthodoxy" and "creed tests" were likely veiled attacks on those Methodists who were promoting a renewed emphasis on entire sanctification, or Christian perfection.

The second article, "Christianity a Religion of Beneficence Rather Than of Devo-

---

15. W., "Creed Tests of Orthodox Piety," *Buffalo Advocate*, Apr. 16, 1857, p. 2.

tion," was similar in tone but marked a sharper departure from traditional Methodism. Here the author set up a contrast not between doctrine and practice, but between devotion and practice. Though unsigned, the tone and style point to Wentworth.[16]

The emphasis here, as in the former article, was on the ethical following of Jesus Christ. The most offensive passage to Roberts was the claim that Christianity "has none of those features which must distinguish a religion grounded on the idea, that to adore the Divine Character is the most imperative obligation resting upon human beings." The author contended that real Christianity did not teach "that the Great Jehovah is so affected with the infirmity of vanity, as to receive with *peculiarly* grateful emotions the attentions and offerings which poor human creatures may offer to Him in worship."

Citing the story of the rich young ruler, the author said: "The great condition upon which one becomes a participant of the Gospel salvation, is — some practical exhibition of self-abnegation, of self-sacrifice for the good of others." He then took a swipe at "the excitation of the religious sensibilities and the culture of emotional piety," arguing that the essential thing is "the development of genial and humane dispositions and the formation of habits of active, vigorous goodness." The writer may have had McCreery in mind when he wrote:

> Certain professors [of religion] are regarded as preeminently holy, and are looked upon as models of excellent sanctity, because of their zeal and vehemence in prayer and exhortation, — whose splenetic tempers and general censoriousness of spirit and language ought to put the seal of reprobation upon their example, and cause all to regard them as children of the Devil. These prayer-meeting saints soon become inflated with a sense of their own superior excellence; — their loud and painful and long-continued supplications to the Deity, they begin to think, have made them His especial favorites; they make sounding professions of "holiness," and put on sanctimonious airs; they grow proud of what they imagine are their spiritual attainments; and look down with contempt upon their more plodding and humble fellow disciples, who are striving — without any formal profession of "perfection" — to emulate the example of Christ by doing good both to the bodies and souls of men.

The writer concluded, "We would not, however, be understood as intending to undervalue prayer and the oblations of piety. The worship of God is, indeed, a high and holy duty, which no Christian can intermit without falling into condemnation and a snare: But it should be used as a means, not pursued as an end." Christians should "pray, in order that they may be empowered to follow the example of Christ, who devoted his life to relieving the wants and woes of men and in going about doing good."[17]

---

16. On the other hand, since it is the lead editorial, it could have been written by Robie himself (as Roberts seems to have assumed).

17. [J. B. Wentworth?], "Christianity a Religion of Benevolence Rather Than of Devotion," *Buffalo Advocate*, May 14, 1857, p. 2.

This article is even more explicit than the former that Christianity consists essentially in the human decision and effort to follow Jesus' example, rather than being fundamentally a life of faith, worship, and devotion.

"Old and New School Methodists" appeared a week later and may, for Roberts, have been the final straw. This was a briefer piece (a little more than one full column). Essentially it was an attack on emotional excess in religion, aimed squarely at the Nazarites, though without using that name.

Since its beginning, said the writer, Methodism has had to deal with the threat of fanaticism. Most of the article in fact consisted of quotations from John Wesley in which Wesley, in his controversy with George Bell and Thomas Maxfield, criticized such behaviors as "loud shouting, horrid, unnatural screaming, repeating the same words twenty or thirty times, jumping two or three feet high, throwing about the arms and legs, both of men and women, in a manner shocking not only to religion but to common decency." Such fanaticism has now arisen among us, the author said. "We have an instance in point, in Western New York. — For several years past there has been considerable uneasiness apparent among quite a number of ministers and laymen" there. This group is marked "by many strange freaks of mind and body."

In a clever move, the author called those who promoted such "fanaticism" a "new school" of Methodists. He detected, he wrote, "a disposition to break away from the old landmarks, which we love so well and have always sustained, and inaugurate a *new school* branch of the Church. This we very much dislike, and think that it augurs no good to the peace and prosperity of Methodism." Roberts, of course, saw the matter as just the reverse. It was he and his colleagues who were trying to preserve "old-time Methodism"; it was those promoting Christianity as essentially "a religion of beneficence" who were the doctrinal innovators — the real "New School Methodists."

The author of "Old and New School Methodists" concluded with a call to action: "We have but a word to add to the above exposure of fanaticism among professing Christian men and women. Has not the time come when the evil should not be blinked at longer, and have not the staid, solid, and pious members of the *old school* branch of the Church a duty to do in the premises?"[18]

"New School Methodism" was Roberts's response to these attacks and doctrinal innovations.[19] He first sent his article to the *Northern Christian Advocate,* the official Methodist paper, but Hosmer's successor there, F. B. Hibbard, refused to print it. In a letter dated August 10, 1857, Hibbard wrote,

> I return your communication as you requested, not feeling it prudent to publish. I presume you can not see things as I do from my stand point. Your communication would involve me in hopeless controversy, which would make me much trouble and perplexity, with no hope, as I view it, of doing substantial good to the

18. [Wentworth?], "Old and New School," p. 2.

19. Though the third article supplied Roberts's title, Roberts especially took issue with the first two articles.

church, or cause of Christ. I do not speak this against your article considered by it-self, but of the controversy which your article would occasion. Your article appears to me to be written in as mild and candid a tone as such facts can be stated in.... I could not feel justified in taking sides in the question that now unhappily divides the Genesee Conference.[20]

Benjamin immediately sent it to Hosmer at the *Northern Independent.* The 3,000-word essay is brief enough, and so strategic in terms of the events that followed, that it is worth including here as it first appeared.[21]

New School Methodism.
Doctrines — Creeds — Worship of God — "Vanity of Jehovah" — Chief Christian Grace — Condition of Salvation — Holiness — Design of means of Grace — Church Wrong.

The best seed sown, from year [to year], on poor soil, gradually degenerates. The acorn from the stately oak, planted upon the arid plain, becomes a stinted shrub. Ever since the fall, the human heart has proved a soil unfavorable to the growth of truth. Noxious weeds flourish everywhere spontaneously, while the useful grains require diligent cultivation.

Correct principles implanted in the mind need constant attention, or monster errors will overtop them, and root them out. Every old nation tells the tale of her own degeneracy, and points to the golden age when truth and justice reigned among men.

Religious truth is not exempt from the liability to corruption. "God will take care of his own cause," is a maxim often quoted by the cowardly and the compromising, as an apology for their base defection. When His servants are faithful to the trusts reposed in them, it is gloriously true; when they waver, His cause suffers. — The Churches planted by the Apostles, and watered by the blood of the martyrs, now outvie heathenism itself in their corruptions. No other parts of the world are so accessible to gospel truth as those countries where the Romish and Greek Churches hold dominion.

As a denomination, we are just as liable to fall by corrupting influences, as any were that have flourished before us. We enjoy no immunity from danger. Already there is springing up among us a class of preachers whose teaching is very different from that of the Fathers of Methodism. They may be found here and there throughout our Zion; but in the Genesee Conference they act as an associate body. They number about thirty. During the last session of this Conference they held several secret meetings in which they concerted a plan to carry their measures and spread their doctrines. They have openly made the issue in the Conference. It is divided. Two distinct parties exist. With the one or the other every

---

20. F. G. Hibbard (Auburn, N.Y.) to BTR, Aug. 10, 1857, as quoted in *WAS,* pp. 96-97. Roberts italicizes the sentence beginning "Your article appears to me . . ."

21. The part that immediately follows, part I, contains about 1,800 words; part II, 1,190 words.

preacher is in sympathy. This difference is fundamental. It does not relate to things indifferent, but to those of the most vital importance. It involves nothing less than the nature itself of Christianity.

In showing the doctrines of the New School Methodists, we shall quote from "The Advocate" of the sect, published at Buffalo. This is the organ of the party. It is sustained by them. They act as its agents. Where their influence prevails, it is circulated to the exclusion of other religious papers. Its former title was, *"The Buffalo Christian Advocate."* But since its open avowal of the new doctrines, it has significantly dropped from its caption, the expressive word *"Christian."* This omission is full of meaning. It is, however, highly proper, as we shall see when we examine its new theory of religion. We commend the editor for this instance of honesty. It is now simply *"The Advocate;"* that is, the *only* Advocate of the tenets it defends.

The New School Methodists affect as great a degree of liberalism as do Theodore Parker and Mr. Newman. They possess "charity" for every body except their brethren of the Old School. — In an article on "Creeds," published in "The Advocate" of April 16th, under the signature of W. the Rev. writer, a prominent New School minister, lays it on to "the sects whose watchword is a Creed," in a manner not unworthy of Alexander Campbell himself. He says, "No matter how holy and blameless a man's life may be, if he has the temerity to question any tenet of orthodoxy, he is at once, in due ecclesiastical form, consigned to the Devil — as a heretic and infidel. Thus are the fetters of a spiritual despotism thrown around the human reason. * * * *[22] And so it has come to pass, that in the estimation of the multitudes — the teachings of Paul are eclipsed by the theories of Calvin, and the writings of John Wesley are held in higher veneration than the inspired words of St. John." Is not that a modest charge?

But their theory of religion is more fully set forth in the leading editorial of "The Advocate" for May 14th, under the title — *"Christianity a religion of beneficence rather than of devotion."* Though it appears as editorial, we have good reason to believe that it was written by a leading New School member of the Genesee Conference. It has not been disavowed by that party. Though it has been before the public for months, no one has expressed a dissent from its positions. It is fair to suppose, that it represents the views of the leaders of this new movement.

It says, "Christianity is not characteristically, a system of devotion. *It has none of those features* which must distinguish a religion grounded on the idea, that to adore the Divine character is the most imperative obligation resting upon human beings. It enjoins the observance of but very few sacred rites; nor does it prescribe *any particular mode* for paying homage to the Deity. It eschews all exterior forms, and teaches that 'they who worship God must worship him in spirit and in truth.'"[23]

The Old School Methodists hold, that "to adore the Divine character" is the

---

22. The ellipses here and elsewhere in the article, reproduced as in the original, indicate material that Roberts deleted in quoting from the *Buffalo Advocate*.

23. Roberts adds the italics for emphasis.

most imperative obligation resting upon human beings — that Christianity has *all* of ["]those features that must distinguish religion grounded on this idea."[24] That he who worships God rightly will, as a necessary consequence, possess all social and moral virtues; that the gospel does not leave its votaries to choose, if they please, the degrading rites of heathenism, or the superstitious abominations of Popery; but prescribes prayer and praise, and the observance of the sacraments of baptism and the Lord's supper, "as particular modes for paying homage to the Deity;" that there is no necessary antagonism, as Infidels and Universalists are wont to affirm, between spiritual worship and the forms of worship instituted by Christ.

The following sneer is not unworthy of Thomas Payne himself. It falls below the dignity of Voltaire. "Christianity in nowise gives countenance to the supposition, that the Great Jehovah is so affected with the infirmity of vanity, as to receive with *peculiarly* grateful emotions, the attention and offerings which poor human creatures may pay directly to him in worship."

The above may be sufficient to show what Christianity is not, in the opinion of these New School divines. Let us now see what it is. "The characteristic idea of this system is benevolence; and its practical realization is achieved in beneficence. It consecrates the principles of charity, and instructs its votaries to regard good works as the holiest sacrifice, and the most acceptable which they can bring to the Almighty. * * * * Whatever graces may be necessary to constitute the inner Christian life, the chief and principal one of these, is *love to man.* * * * The great condition upon which one becomes a participant of the gospel salvation, is — some practical exhibition of self-abnegation, of self-sacrifice for the good of others. *Go sell all that thou hast, and give to the poor,* were the *only* terms of salvation which Christ proposed to the young man, who otherwise, was not far from the kingdom of heaven."

The Old School Methodists hold that benevolence is only *one of the fruits* of true religion, but by no means the thing itself. In their view, "The principal grace of the inner Christian life" is LOVE TO GOD, and "the most acceptable sacrifice we can render HIM, is a broken and contrite heart.["] They teach that the great condition upon which one becomes "a participant of the gospel salvation" is FAITH IN CHRIST — preceded by repentance. They read in the gospel that the young man referred to, was commanded by Christ to *"come, take up the cross and follow me."* The giving of his goods was only preparatory to this.

The New School Methodists hold that justification and entire sanctification, or holiness, are the same — that when a sinner is pardoned, he is at the same time made holy — that all the spiritual change he may henceforth expect, is simply a growth in grace. When they speak of "holiness," they mean by it the same as do evangelical ministers of those denominations which do not receive the doctrines taught by Wesley and Fletcher on this subject.

---

24. The quotation mark after "idea" is in the original; deleted in *WAS*, p. 88. However, I have supplied an additional quotation mark before "those" since this is a quotation from the article Roberts is criticizing. The original article has "distinguish a religion," not "distinguish religion."

According to the Old School Methodists, merely justified persons, while they do not outwardly commit sin, are conscious of sin still remaining in the heart, such as pride, self-will, and unbelief. — They continually feel a heart bent to back-sliding; a natural tendency to evil; a proneness to depart from God, and cleave to the things of earth. — Those that are sanctified wholly are saved from all inward sin — from evil thoughts, and evil tempers. No wrong temper, none contrary to love remains in the soul. All the thoughts, words, and actions are governed by pure love.

The New School ministers have the frankness to acknowledge that their doctrines are not the doctrines of the Church. They have undertaken to correct the teachings of her standard authors. In the same editorial of "The Advocate" from which we have quoted so largely, we read: "So in the exercises and means of grace instituted by the Church, it is clearly apparent that respect is had, rather to the excitation of the religious sensibilities, and the culture of emotional piety, than the development of genial and human[e] dispositions, and the formation of habits of active, vigorous goodness."[25]

Here the evils complained of are charged upon *the exercises and means of grace, instituted by the Church.* They do not result from a perversion of the means of grace, but are the effects *intended* to be produced in their institution. It is THE CHURCH, then, that is wrong — and so far wrong that she does not even *aim* at the development of proper Christian character. "The means of grace," in the use of which an Asbury, an Olin, a Hedding, and a host of worthies departed and living, were nurtured in spiritual manhood, must be abolished; and others, adapted to the "development of genial and human[e] dispositions," established in their place. The Lodge must supersede the class and the love-feast; and the old fashioned prayer meeting must give way to the social party! Those who founded or adopted "the exercises and means of grace, instituted by the Church" — Paul and Peter, the Martyrs, and Reformers, Luther and Wesley, Calvin and Edwards — all have failed to comprehend the true idea of Christianity — for then [i.e., these] all held that the sinner was justified by *Faith in Christ,* and not by "some practical exhibition of self-abnegation." The honor of distinctly apprehending and clearly stating the true genius of Christianity, was reserved for a few Divines of the nineteenth century!

In our next, we shall show the usages and results, so far as developed, of New School Methodism.

R.

Here Roberts reverses the terminology employed in the "Old and New School Methodists" article, claiming that he and those like him are really the Old School Methodists while the New School is departing wholesale from historic Methodism.

Roberts was right about the change in name of the *Buffalo Christian Advocate.* With the April 2, 1857, issue the word "Christian" was dropped and the weekly pa-

25. Roberts here and again in the next paragraph corrects "human" to "humane," as in the original article, in *WAS,* p. 91.

per became simply the *Advocate*. Later, about 1862, when Robie was away serving in the Civil War and W. H. DePuy was briefly editor, it was renamed the *Christian Advocate*.[26]

Perhaps the most notable thing about part I is that it focused primarily on theological issues. The main problem with New School Methodism was that it shifted the foundation of Christianity from justification by faith to salvation by works, in the process collapsing sanctification into justification. Its conception of God was essentially Deist, and the Christian faith was reduced to pure humanism (though Roberts did not use these terms).[27] Thus New School Methodism represented a sharp departure from the long history of Christian orthodoxy.

The second part of Roberts's article appeared in the next issue of the *Northern Independent* a week later, on August 27, 1857.

New School Methodism.

USAGES — RESULTS.

Differing thus in their views of religion, the Old and New School Methodists necessarily differ in their measures for its promotion. The latter build stock churches, and furnish them with pews to accommodate a select congregation; and with organs, melodeons, violins, and professional singers, to execute difficult pieces of music for a fashionable audience. The former favor free churches, congregational singing, and spirituality, simplicity and fervency in worship. They endeavor to promote revivals, deep and thorough; such as were common under the labors of the Fathers; such as have made Methodism the leading denomination of the land. The leaders of the New Divinity movement are not remarkable for promoting revivals; and those which do, occasionally, occur among them, may generally be characterized as the editor of *"THE ADVOCATE"* designated one which fell under his notice, as *"splendid revivals."* Preachers of the old stamp urge upon all who would gain heaven, the necessity of self-denial — non-conformity to the world; purity of heart and holiness of life; while the others ridicule singularity, encourage by their silence, and in some cases by their own example, and that of their wives and daughters, "the putting on of gold and costly apparel," and treat with distrust all professions of deep Christian experience. When these desire to raise money for the benefit of the Church, they have recourse to the selling of pews to the highest bidder; to parties of pleasure, oyster suppers, fairs, grab bags, festivals and lotteries: the others, for this purpose, appeal to the love the people bear to Christ. In short, the Old School Methodists rely for the spread of the gospel upon the agency of the Holy Ghost, and the purity of the Church. The New School Methodists appear to depend upon the patronage of the worldly, the favor of the proud and aspiring; and the various artifices of worldly policy.

26. Buffalo Historical Society, *Publications* (Buffalo, 1915), p. 211; letter to the author from JoAnn Pearson, Special Collections Librarian, Buffalo and Erie County Public Library, Feb. 12, 2001.

27. The question arises whether the author Roberts here criticizes had been influenced by Emerson or other Transcendentalists.

If this diversity of opinion and of practice among the ministers of our denomination, was confined to one Conference, it would be comparatively unimportant. But unmistakable indications show that prosperity is producing upon us, as a denomination, the same intoxicating effect, that it too often does upon individuals and societies. The change, by the General Conference of 1852, in the rule of Discipline, requiring that all our houses of worship should be built plain, and with free seats; and that of the last General Conference in the section respecting dress, show that there are already too many among us, who would take down the barriers that have hitherto separated us from the world. The fact that the removal is gradual so as not to excite too much attention and commotion, renders it none the less alarming.

Every lover of the Church must feel a deep anxiety to know what is to be the result of this new order of things. If we may judge by its effects in the Genesee Conference, since it has held sway there, it will prove disastrous to us as a denomination. It so happened, either by accident, or by management, at the division of the Genesee Conference, eight years ago, that most of the unmanageable veterans, who could neither be induced to depart from the Heaven honored usages of Methodism, by the specious cry of "progress," nor to wink at such departures, by the mild expostulations of Eli, "Why do you thus my sons?" had their destination upon the east side of Genesee River. The first year after the division, the East Genesee Conference had twenty superannuated preachers; the Genesee Conference, but five. — "Men of progress" in the prime of life, went west of the river, and took possession of the Conference. For the most part, they have borne sway there ever since. Of late, the young men of the Conference, uniting with the fathers, and thus united, comprising a majority of the Conference, have endeavored to stop this "progress" away from the old paths of Methodism. But the "progressives" make up in management what they want in numbers. Having free access at all times to the ears of the Episcopacy, they have succeeded, for the most part, in controlling the appointments to the Districts and most important stations. If, by reason of his obvious fitness, any impracticable adherent of primitive Methodism has been appointed to a District or first class station, he has usually been pursued, with untiring diligence, and hunted from his position before his constitutional term expired.

In the bounds of the Genesee Conference, the people generally are prepossessed in favor of Methodism. During the past eight years there have been no external causes operating there against our prosperity, that do not operate at all times and in all places. Within this period, the nominal increase of the Church in that Conference has been but seven hundred and eighty. — The East Genesee Conference has had an increase, within the same time, of about two thousand five hundred. In order to have simply kept pace with the population, there should have been within the bounds of the Genesee Conference, one thousand six hundred and forty-three more members than there [are] at present.[28] That is in eight years,

---

28. In *WAS*, p. 95, Roberts corrects the text by adding "are."

under the reign of New Divinity, the Church has suffered, within the bounds of this one Conference, a relative loss of fifteen per cent in members.

The Seminary at Lima, at the time of the division second to none in the land, has, by the same kind of management, been brought to the brink of financial ruin.

We have thus endeavored to give a fair and impartial representation of New School Methodism. Its prevalence in one Conference has already, as we have seen, involved it in division and disaster. Let it generally prevail, and the glory will depart from Methodism. She has a special mission to accomplish. This is, not to gather into her fold the proud and fashionable, the devotees of pleasure and ambition, but "to spread scripture holiness over these lands." Her doctrines, and her usages, her hymns, her history, and her spirit, her noble achievements in the past, and her bright prospects for the future, all forbid that she should adopt an accommodating, compromising policy, pandering to the vices of the times. — Let her go on, as she has done, insisting that the great cardinal truths of the gospel shall receive a living embodiment in the hearts and lives of her members, and Methodism will continue to be the favored of Heaven, and the joy of the earth. But let her come down from her position, and receive to her communion all those lovers of pleasure, and lovers of the world, who are willing to pay for the privilege, and it needs no prophet's vision to foresee that Methodism will become a dead and corrupting body, endeavoring in vain to supply, by the erection of splendid churches, and the imposing performances of powerless ceremonies, the manifested glory of the Divine presence, which once shone so brightly in all her sanctuaries.

"Thus saith the Lord, stand ye in the ways and see, and ask for the old paths, where is the good way, and walk therein, and ye shall find rest for your souls."

R.[29]

In this second part of the article Roberts thus returned to several of the themes he had written about previously, including the relative lack of numerical growth in the Genesee Conference. As usual, he makes his case clearly and concisely. Though strongly worded with some occasional light sarcasm, the tone of the piece is very mild compared with the harsh attacks upon him and the so-called Nazarites in the *Buffalo Christian Advocate.*

The content of the article makes it clear that in writing it, Roberts essentially revised and expanded his November 15, 1856, letter to Bishop Morris.

Reaction to "New School Methodism"

Roberts's article brought swift reaction. The Regency group "laid hold on this as a weapon to be used against its author," wrote Benson Roberts.[30] But Benjamin re-

---

29. Roberts reprinted "New School Methodism" in its entirety in *WAS*, pp. 85-96, with a few minor corrections and changes in punctuation.

30. BHR, *BTR,* p. 111.

ceived positive as well as negative response. A prominent preacher in the Oneida Conference wrote him, "If you had belonged to our Conference we would have given you a vote of thanks for writing that article," and a presiding elder of the same conference wrote on September 1, "I am gratified with your exposure of the 'New Divinity' that is cursing our church. It is creeping into our Conference and doing immense mischief. Keep the monster in the light."[31]

The first installment of "New School Methodism" appeared just six days before the 1857 Genesee Conference began its annual sessions in LeRoy, sixteen miles south of Brockport, on Wednesday, August 26. The second part was published in the issue dated the next day, August 27. Although many members of conference may not have yet seen the second installment, probably most had read, or at least heard about, the first.

William Kendall noted in his diary the day before conference opened: "Our Conference is in a very disturbed state. Two classes[,] one called Nazarites, the other Buffalo Regency. The former [are] for the old 'land marks' of Methodism[,] the other for policy & progress. The Naz[arite]s are going to try to elect B. T. Roberts to the Secretaryship. Bros. Stiles & Kingsley transferred & are again with us."[32]

The presiding bishop this year was Osman C. Baker, though Bishop Beverly Waugh led the opening communion service on Wednesday morning.[33]

One of the first items of business, as usual, was the election of a secretary. The balloting mirrored the deep division in the conference. James M. Fuller was elected, receiving (according to Kendall) forty-five votes, while B. T. Roberts received forty. The attempt to elect Roberts as secretary, however, and the vote he received, showed the prominent place he held generally in the conference and especially among the group of preachers who shared his views.[34]

Carlton, Fuller, and their associates discovered that their political maneuvering the previous year had produced a reaction among the churches. Hibbard says "a few members" of the conference spread the word "to the popular masses" through "fly sheets, . . . newspaper articles," and "various and unintermitted private communications."[35] As a result, apparently, over 1,500 Methodists petitioned the bishop for the return of Stiles and Kingsley. Stiles was accordingly transferred back to the Genesee Conference and sent to Albion, replacing Roberts.[36] Kingsley, however, though (ac-

31. Quoted in *WAS*, p. 97.

32. WCKD, Aug. 25, 1857.

33. WCKD, Aug. 26, 1857.

34. Kendall gives the vote as 45 for Fuller and 40 for Roberts (WCKD, Aug. 26, 1857), but see Zahniser, p. 98. According to C. D. Burlingham (in testimony at Roberts's 1858 trial), Fuller got 43 or 44 votes, while Roberts got 41 or 42 — to the best of Burlingham's recollection (Chesbrough, *Defence*, p. 75). Fuller served as secretary of the annual conference sessions in 1850, 1851, and 1852, but not in the years 1853-56.

35. [F. G. Hibbard], "Nazaritism — Its Judicial History" [Part II], *NCA* 19, no. 46 (Nov. 16, 1859): 2. Hibbard says, "As the spirit of schism and insubordination developed, the number adhering to the Nazarite party grew less," but this is by no means obvious.

36. Thus Kendall, Roberts, and Stiles served successively at Albion.

cording to Kendall) present at the 1857 Genesee Conference sessions, remained in the Cincinnati Conference.[37]

The Regency group now took steps against Roberts at the 1857 conference, much as they had a year earlier against Stiles and Kingsley. It is clear that Roberts's article was the immediate cause. Roberts wrote that his opponents "saw that something must be done to cripple our influence, or they were still in danger of being called to account for their misdeeds." He noted, "My article on 'New School Methodism' had just been published, and the charges against me were based on that."[38]

The Regency preachers brought charges against Kendall as well, apparently because of his uncompromising promotion of holiness.[39] Just prior to the 1857 annual conference Kendall had attended two camp meetings, one in the Niagara and one in the Wyoming District, and at both he spoke out boldly for holiness. At the Niagara District camp, following a sermon that taught that a person is entirely sanctified at the point of conversion, Kendall gave an exhortation upholding the traditional Methodist position that entire sanctification is a distinct experience subsequent to conversion. "I occupied forty-five minutes" in exhortation, he wrote A. A. Phelps, "while the Regency preachers prayed God to have mercy on me." At the Wyoming camp Kendall preached a holiness message. "The presiding elder and two preachers then exhorted against me," Kendall wrote. "Some of the preachers roar against me 'like the bulls of Bashan.' I know not but they will gore me, tear the ground, or something, at conference. I do not expect to remain at Chili."[40] The presiding elder was Richard Waite, who clearly was on the Regency side.[41]

The wheels of ecclesiastical machinery were put in place, and soon the trial of Benjamin Titus Roberts before the Genesee Conference was under way.

Meanwhile, Ellen Roberts was at home at Albion, praying for the conference and wondering what would happen. Kendall's wife, Martha, and another friend, Sister Shaffer, stayed with Ellen for a day or so at the beginning of the annual conference sessions; Mrs. Kendall then went on to LeRoy to sit in on the sessions.

Ellen wrote in her diary that she and her two friends had

a powerful time while pleading for the Baptism of power and the Holy Ghost to rest upon Mr. R. and some others at Conference. My soul is wonderfully drawn

---

37. *WAS*, p. 147; *Minutes*, Genesee Conference, 1857; Allen, *Century*, p. 100; cf. Zahniser, p. 93. Allen notes regarding Kingsley, "To Cincinnati by transfer 1856. To Genesee by transfer, and to Cincinnati by transfer, 1857" (p. 100) — apparently meaning that the bishop initially acceded to the petition and intended to bring Kingsley back to Genesee, but for whatever reason he remained instead in the Cincinnati Conference. The Genesee Conference minutes of both 1856 and 1857 state, "Isaac C. Kingsley, transferred to Cincinnati Conference."

38. *WAS*, p. 148.

39. Benson Roberts says one bill of charges was brought against Roberts and two against Kendall. BHR, *BTR*, p. 126.

40. William C. Kendall to A. A. Phelps, Aug. 21, 1857, quoted in Terrill, *Redfield*, p. 322.

41. *Minutes*, Genesee Conference, 1856, 1857.

out to pray for my Husband that He may stand for the truth unflinchingly and endure hardness as a good soldier.

"I will not fear though an host encamp against me." "It is better to trust in the Lord than to put confidence in princes." My soul is wonderfully nerved up — I feel a confidence in the Lord I never felt before. It seems to me He is working in a way we thought not of. . . . I know the Lord is there and with my Husband. It will not be what we have endured but what we have <u>failed to endure</u> that will cause <u>regret</u> when we come to the close of life.[42]

42. ELRD, Sept. 1 (approx.), 1857 (slightly corrected). Cf. Carpenter, p. 50.

CHAPTER 21

Roberts's First Trial

"I tried to do my duty faithfully, and the Lord blessed me in it, and blesses me since."

B. T. Roberts, after his 1857 trial[1]

"The Lord will go with us according to His promise."

Ellen Roberts, after Benjamin's 1857 trial[2]

The annual conference sessions began at LeRoy on August 26, 1857. As best he could, Benjamin kept Ellen informed of what was happening.

For somewhat different reasons, both Roberts and Kendall were the targets of Regency action at the 1857 conference, as noted in the previous chapter. The focus of the so-called Nazarite controversy now shifted from McCreery to Roberts and Kendall.

Roberts made a remark during one of the sessions that the Committee on Education was "packed." Samuel Church later mentioned this remark to H. Ryan Smith, a Regency pastor. Smith replied, "One more such statement will blot Roberts out." And he warned Church, "You had better take yourself out of the way, or you will be crushed."[3]

---

1. BTR to TR, Oct. 1, 1857, quoted in BHR, *BTR*, p. 142.

2. ELRD, Sept. 1857 (precise date of entry not given).

3. Written testimony of Samuel C. Church, Caryville, N.Y., Oct. 20, 1857, quoted in *WAS*, p. 170. Kendall noted in his diary for Thursday, Aug. 27, "Things <u>seem</u> to go harmoniously, but fires slumber beneath. Quite a little trifle over Bro. Chamberlayne's relation. He makes a full statement of his case. His [superannuated] relation continues." WCKD, Aug. 27, 1857.

Roberts himself took initiative to call A. D. Wilbor, his presiding elder, to account for what he felt was a case of maladministration. On Friday, August 28, Roberts "prefer[red] a charge against A. D. Wilbor of maladministration in case of Resolutions passed in the Brockport quar[terly] Con[ference]," Kendall noted. This provoked considerable discussion that continued during the Saturday sessions. Roberts made "a stirring speech," Kendall wrote.[4]

Several secret meetings of the so-called Regency preachers were held during the 1857 conference sessions at LeRoy, as had happened a year earlier. This time the meetings were held at night in a rented hall. Thomas Carlton later testified that he attended some of these meetings, and that attendance "ranged from thirty to sixty."[5] De Forest Parsons, preacher in 1856-57 at Wilson, by his own testimony chaired the meetings.[6] The minutes of the September 3 meeting, two days before the end of conference, later came into Roberts's hands, and he printed them in *Why Another Sect:*

Le Roy, Sept. 3, 1857.

Meeting convened according to adjournment; Brother Parsons in the chair. Prayer, by Brother [James] Fuller. Brethren present pledged themselves by rising, to keep to themselves the proceedings of this meeting.

Resolved, That we will not allow the character of Rev. B. T. Roberts to pass until he has had a fair trial. Passed. Moved, That we will not pass the character of Rev. W. C. Kendall, until he has had a fair trial. Passed.

Moved, That Brother Carlton be added to the committee on Brother Kendall's case. Passed.[7]

4. WCKD, Aug. 28 and 29, 1857.

5. In a pamphlet published shortly after the 1857 conference, George Estes, a Methodist from Brockport, said the Regency group held "private caucuses" on Thursday, Friday, and Saturday evenings of the first week of conference (i.e., Aug. 27-29) "in a room over Bryant & Clark's book-store" at LeRoy, and that there the bill of charges against Roberts was decided upon. The chairman of the meeting (apparently Parsons), "One of the chiefs of the Regency," asked, "What shall be done in the case of Bro. Roberts? All in favor of his prosecution raise your hands!" The vote at first was thirty in favor, but after subsequent exhortations that the preachers "must be united enough *to carry the matter through,*" on the third vote a sufficient number was achieved to assure the outcome, all but one voting in favor. Thus the number present must have been around fifty-five or sixty. Estes says this information was "related by one present." The pamphlet is printed in BHR, *BTR*, pp. 127-34. Cf. Conable, pp. 645-46; F. G. Hibbard, "Nazaritism — Its Judicial History" [Part II], *NCA* 19, no. 46 (Nov. 16, 1859): 2.

6. *WAS*, pp. 66-67, 147-48.

7. *WAS*, p. 65. This is the only source for this document that I have found (other than Chesbrough's *Defence,* discussed below). The original does not appear to be among the Roberts papers. Given the evidence of a high level of integrity and accuracy in Roberts's writings, there is no reason to doubt the accuracy of Roberts's citation. It however remains perhaps an open question whether these minutes were authentic or spurious, and what their source was (i.e., who gave them to Roberts). They appear to be authentic; however, note the discussion below. At his 1858 trial Roberts said the authenticity or accuracy of these minutes was never challenged by the prosecution. See Chesbrough, *Defence,* p. 47.

The Charges

Charges were in fact brought against Roberts on Wednesday afternoon, September 2 — the day before the date of the above minutes. Reuben Foote, the preacher at Aurora in the Buffalo District, entered the charges on the floor of the conference when Roberts's name came up for the passing of his character.[8] Earlier, in the morning session, the conference took action after considerable discussion "not to entertain the charge" against A. D. Wilbor.[9] Meanwhile charges were brought against Kendall the previous day by Chauncey Baker, Kendall's successor at Brockport. Kendall was "no longer useful as a traveling preacher," the charges claimed, because of his insistent holiness preaching.[10] "The design is to locate me," Kendall noted in his diary.[11]

The charges against Roberts all related to the "New School Methodism" articles. The bill of charges read as follows:

CHARGE AGAINST REV. B. T. ROBERTS

I hereby charge Rev. B. T. Roberts with unchristian and immoral conduct.

1. In publishing, in the *Northern Independent,* that there exists, in the Genesee Conference, an associate body, numbering about thirty, whose teaching is very different from that of the fathers of Methodism.

2. In publishing, as above, that said members of the Genesee Conference are opposed to what is fundamental in Christianity — to the nature itself of Christianity.

3. In classing them, in the above-mentioned publication, with Theodore Parker and Mr. Newman, as regards laxness of religious sentiment.

4. In charging them, as above, with sneering at Christianity in a manner not unworthy of Thomas Paine, and that falls below that of Voltaire.

5. In charging them, as above, with being heterodox on the subject of holiness.

6. In asserting that they acknowledge that their doctrines are not the doctrines of the Church, and that they have undertaken to correct the teachings of her standard authors.

7. In charging them, as above, with attempting to abolish the means of grace — substituting the lodge for the class-meeting and love-feast, and the social party for the prayer meeting.

---

8. Manuscript Minutes of the Genesee Annual Conference, Sept. 2, 1857, *Journal of the Genesee Annual Conference of the Methodist Episcopal Church, Vol. IV,* p. 310, Western New York Conference Archives, Buffalo, hereafter Manuscript Minutes.

9. WCKD, Sept. 2, 1857.

10. "Rev. Wm. C. Kendall, A.M. — Labors — Death," *EC* 2, no. 12 (Dec. 1861): 374. "[Kendall] himself was presented with two bills of charges, to prove that he was 'no longer useful as a traveling preacher;' which bills however were laid over to be tried at the *next conference.*"

11. Kendall wrote, "I receive a bill of 1. Charge & 13 spec-s [specifications]. Bro. C. S. Baker in the P.M. wishes to withdraw the former bill. . . . He presents me with another of three spec-s. My friends urge me to defend myself. The design is to locate me." WCKD, Sept. 3, 1857.

8. In representing, as above, the revivals among them are superficial,[12] and characterizing them as "splendid revivals."

9. In saying, as above, that they treat with distrust all professions of deep religious experience.

Reuben C. Foote
Le Roy, Sept. 1, 1857.[13]

Presumably Foote, and those who acted with him, selected what they found most offensive in Roberts's article. The last two items make it clear that whoever wrote the charges had seen the second as well as the first installment of "New School Methodism." There is some irony in the fact that a select group of preachers should accuse Roberts of "immoral and unchristian conduct" for charging that such a group existed! Of course, the Regency group was specifically contesting that any such group of preachers held teachings "very different from that of the fathers of Methodism." The wording of the charge, however, implies that no such "associate body, numbering about thirty," really existed, when in fact it did.

The conference voted to entertain the charges and to hear the case the next morning. James Fuller and Israel Chamberlayne were appointed to assist Foote in prosecuting the case, while Samuel Church and John Bowman were named to assist Roberts with his defense. Later in the session Bishop Baker, at Roberts's request, appointed a committee of three to go to Buffalo to take testimony in the case — Samuel Luckey, John Timmerman, and William Barrett.[14]

The Trial

With Bishop Baker in the chair, Roberts's trial was no doubt conducted according to the disciplinary rules for trials that Baker himself had elaborated in his *Guide-Book in the Administration of the Discipline of the Methodist Episcopal Church*. This manual had been issued two years earlier by Carlton and Phillips, the Methodist publishers. Baker's guidebook specified how charges were to be drawn up, how witnesses were to be examined, and what procedures were to be followed. One could argue, however, that both Roberts's 1857 trial and his 1858 trial violated Baker's own princi-

12. So Hibbard; Conable, "that the revivals among them are superficial"; Roberts, "the revivals among them as superficial" (see next note).

13. Hibbard, "Nazaritism," part II. The bill of charges is printed also in Conable, pp. 643-44 (apparently quoting from Hibbard), and in *WAS*, pp. 150-52.

14. Manuscript Minutes, Sept. 2, 1857, pp. 310-12. The committee traveled to Buffalo, took testimony, and reported back, though it was no doubt a futile exercise, as the outcome of the trial was predetermined. George Estes charged that when the committee arrived at the *Buffalo Advocate* office, they found that "an emissary from the conference had been sent on before them to take charge of the *Advocate* office" and that this person refused access to any articles or papers or to allow any testimony to be given (BHR, *BTR*, p. 130). Presumably Roberts wanted evidence from the *Buffalo Advocate* office that would support the charges he made in "New School Methodism."

ple that "There should be a perfect correspondence between the charge and the specifications." Baker wrote, "If the charge is immorality, no specifications should be given under it which involve only an imprudence; and if the charge is imprudent conduct, no specification should be given which involves an immorality."[15] Clearly it was a stretch to label Roberts's conduct "unchristian and immoral."

Roberts's case was not actually taken up until midmorning on Friday, September 4, the last full day of conference. It was delayed a day to give time for the special committee to gather its evidence in Buffalo and report back.[16] Martha Kendall had now arrived at conference, and in a letter to Ellen Roberts wrote, "The house was crowded to overflowing and well filled on the side nearest Br. R. with our spiritual men, who for many days . . . have been praying for Br. R. and Mr. K., whose case comes after."[17]

When the charges were read, Benjamin (then thirty-four) arose and addressed the conference: "I have no intention to misrepresent any one. I do not think I have. I honestly think that the men referred to, hold just the opinions I say they do. But if they do not, I shall be glad to be corrected. If they will say they do not, I will take their word for it, make my humble confession, and, as far as possible, repair the wrong I have done. I will publish in the *Northern Independent,* and in all the church papers they desire me to, from Maine to California, that I have misrepresented them."[18]

The conference was not really interested in the accuracy of Roberts's charges, however, but in the fact that his article further stirred the pot of controversy. Roberts later wrote, "They went on with the trial. There was little to do, as I admitted that I wrote the article."[19] Hibbard says Roberts "consented that extracts from a copy of ['New School Methodism'], issued in circular form among the members of the Conference, should be presented in evidence."[20] Apparently Roberts's accusers had gone to the trouble to have these extracts of his article printed up.

Though Benjamin acknowledged that he had written the article, he nevertheless, in lawyerly fashion and at the urging of his friends, laid out a full defense.[21] Hib-

---

15. Osman C. Baker, *A Guide-Book in the Administration of the Discipline of the Methodist Episcopal Church* (New York: Carlton and Phillips, 1855), p. 92.

16. Manuscript Minutes, Sept. 4, 1857, p. 319. Kendall noted on Thursday, Sept. 3, "The commission not yet returned." WCKD, Sept. 3, 1857.

17. M. F. Kendall to ELR, Friday noon (Sept. 4), 1857 (RFP, Microfilm Reel 22). Mrs. Kendall says Benjamin "only arrived from Buffalo last night, and entered on the case today," apparently indicating that he had accompanied the special committee to Buffalo. Mrs. Kendall took extensive notes and gave a fairly detailed account of the trial. At one point she wrote, "Bp is a Mason," apparently meaning that Bishop Baker belonged to the Masonic lodge.

18. *WAS,* pp. 148-49. This of course is Roberts's recollection twenty years later, but he may have kept notes at the time.

19. *WAS,* p. 149.

20. Hibbard, "Nazaritism," part II. Hibbard reprints these extracts.

21. Kendall noted, "Bro. Roberts' case comes on. Great unfairness. Bro. R____ declines proceeding. By solicitation of friends makes a plea in his defense." WCKD, Sept. 4, 1857.

bard wrote, "The only defence which Mr. Roberts set up in the case was the effort to prove the allegations contained in the specifications to be true."[22] In fact, Roberts made several key points — though no doubt many of his hearers considered them irrelevant. He complained that the indictment did not quote his exact words, which would be required in a legal libel case, and in summarizing his points it actually misconstrued them. "[I]f you make a man responsible for the construction which his enemies put upon his words, you might condemn any man that ever wrote," he argued. For example, the charge said Roberts claimed that "there exists in the Genesee Conference an associate body numbering about thirty, whose teaching is very different" from historic Methodism. But Roberts pointed out that he had said only that certain ministers "act as an associate body," and they might *act* as such without formally *existing* as an association. (He added later, in *Why Another Sect,* "It was true that they had [at the time] a regularly organized 'associate body,' but I did not know it, or even suspect it, and so I did not say it.")[23]

Roberts also pointed out that he had not explicitly charged these ministers with "being heterodox," as stated in the indictment. "[S]aying they mean by 'holiness' the same as 'evangelical ministers' of the other Protestant churches generally do, is by no means charging them with being 'heterodox on the subject of holiness.'"

Roberts cited a number of similar examples. He had not charged, he said, that these ministers were attempting to abolish the means of grace and substitute the lodge for the class meeting and love feast, but only "that this would be the logical result of the teachings that I was reviewing."[24] But he also argued that the charges he made in his article were in point of fact true.

In conducting his own defense, Roberts questioned one or more witnesses. Conable, who was present, gives the following account that, though one-sided, says something about Roberts's persistence. Roberts asked a witness a question, which the chair ruled irrelevant.[25] "This ruling led [Roberts] to change the form of the question, while it remained the same in fact, and again it was objected to; so the question was verbally modified with a strange pertinacity again and again, until [Roberts] refused to proceed further, hastily took up his papers and withdrew from the Conference room."[26] At some point during the proceedings Roberts commented, "Some of us will die hard."[27]

Roberts's case was taken up again in the evening session, after other business had been completed. When it came time to vote, the prosecution, for whatever reason, withdrew the fourth charge (the one referring to Paine and Voltaire). Rob-

---

22. Hibbard, "Nazaritism," part II.

23. *WAS,* p. 152.

24. *WAS,* p. 153.

25. The Estes pamphlet implied that the prosecution objected to Roberts's questioning because it could have led to the uncovering of the secret meetings a year earlier. BHR, *BTR,* pp. 129-30.

26. Conable, p. 645.

27. As quoted in a letter following conference from William Kendall to Roberts, cited in Terrill, *Redfield,* p. 325.

erts himself was not present at this point — it was getting late, and he went to bed![28]

The vote proceeded, and all the remaining charges were sustained. The preachers voted by standing. The result suggested the depth of division in the conference: 52 to 43, with several preachers abstaining.[29] Thus Benjamin Roberts stood convicted before the conference of "unchristian and immoral conduct" for publishing his article "New School Methodism."[30] Kendall noted in his diary, "The Regency are determined to crush the cause of Jesus. God forbid!"[31] C. D. Burlingham's later characterization of the conference action is accurate: "The ostensible cause of [Roberts's] condemnation was the alleged slanderous essay; but, the *real* cause was the prejudice excited against him by the incessant declamations on the alleged *'evils of Nazaritism,'* which it was assumed Mr. Roberts was laboring to foster and promote."[32]

Bishop Baker asked what penalty the conference wished to impose, "gently suggesting," said Conable, that they show mercy.[33] A motion was made that the conference call Roberts in to be reprimanded by the bishop and "cautioned to observe a better course in future." This was vigorously debated, some preachers arguing that "*expulsion* alone would suffice to stop this habit of wholesale slander against the leading men of the Conference."[34] Eventually the motion carried, however, and Bishop Baker summoned Roberts back before the conference.[35]

Receiving the summons, Benjamin got dressed and returned to the conference floor, where Bishop Baker administered the reprimand.[36] With that, Roberts's character was passed.[37] According to Benson Roberts, James Fuller said rather lamely that Roberts's return to the conference floor after retiring proved his fanaticism, for "none but a fanatic would rise from his bed to receive a reproof." "So little conception had these men of Christlike humility," Benson Roberts wrote.[38] (Benjamin later said Baker in his reprimand mentioned nothing about pursuing "a better course in

---

28. Chesbrough, *Defence*, p. 44.

29. Zahniser, p. 95; BHR, *BTR*, p. 135. Zahniser (depending apparently on the Estes pamphlet) says, "Several members of the Conference were absent and several did not vote." Total conference membership at the time was about 106. Estes, who apparently was present for the voting, listed the names of the 52 preachers who "as near as can be ascertained" voted against Roberts. The list included Israel Chamberlayne, Glezen Fillmore, A. D. Wilbor, Philo Woodworth, Richard L. Waite, Thomas Carlton, James M. Fuller, W. H. DePuy, D. F. Parsons, J. G. Miller, F. W. Conable, and J. B. Wentworth. Estes claimed also that the slavery question was a key underlying issue. BHR, *BTR*, pp. 131-32.

30. Manuscript Minutes, Sept. 4, 1857, p. 323; Hibbard, "Nazaritism," part II; Conable, p. 645.

31. WCKD, Sept. 4, 1857.

32. Pelatiah [Charles D. Burlingham], *An Outline History of the Genesee Conference Difficulties: Their Nature, Origin, Causes, Influence and Remedy* (n.p., 1860), p. 11. See BHR, *BTR*, p. 137.

33. Conable, p. 645.

34. Hibbard, "Nazaritism," part II.

35. Manuscript Minutes, Sept. 4, 1857, p. 323.

36. Roberts "Is sentenced to a reproof & caution by the Bishop," Kendall noted. "God blesses him." WCKD, Sept. 4, 1857.

37. Manuscript Minutes, Sept. 4, 1857, pp. 323-24; Conable, p. 645.

38. BHR, *BTR*, p. 138.

the future," so far as he could remember, even though that's what the minutes record.)[39]

Roberts accepted the reprimand, but not its justice. He informed the conference that he intended to appeal the case to the next General Conference.[40] He told Kendall, "It is an honor to be denounced by those men."[41]

The proceedings against Roberts took so long that the conference ran out of time to deal with Kendall's case, which was postponed to the 1858 conference sessions.[42] Kendall noted in his diary, "My character passes with charges against me. Strange work this."[43] The charge against Kendall however had to do not so much with his character as with his "acceptability." Conference finally adjourned at 1:30 A.M. with the reading of the appointments.[44]

Zahniser says regarding these proceedings, "With the express action of the Conference in 1855, instructing its members not to carry on this program of 'stigmatizing' its members, it is not surprising that the author of 'New School Methodism' had action brought against him. From Mr. Roberts' viewpoint, he was defending the truth; from the standpoint of the Conference majority, he was furthering the divisive spirit which they had been ineffectually trying to suppress."[45]

Benson Roberts commented that fundamentally "the whole procedure" showed "the growing influence of a man, whose sole offence was the exposure of their own unfaithfulness and inefficiency."[46]

During the whole period of the Nazarite controversy, slavery continued to be a hot and divisive issue within the Genesee Conference, as it was within the denomination more broadly. The division in the conference on this issue paralleled the Regency/Nazarite polarization. The so-called Nazarites were for the most part strongly abolitionist, while the Regency preachers reflected the dominant attitude within the denomination — that slavery (and slaveholding), though an evil, should not be actively opposed because the issue was so divisive. The Regency preachers either ignored it altogether or took an ameliorative approach. Many in the conference supported the American Colonization Society, as noted earlier.

Was slavery an underlying issue, or even *the* underlying issue, in the Nazarite controversy? William Hosmer, editor of the *Northern Independent,* was sure it was. Hosmer wrote in 1859, "If we had not had a strong pro-slavery party here, we never should have heard this interminable uproar about 'Nazarites.'"[47] The Nazarite con-

39. Chesbrough, *Defence,* p. 44.

40. Manuscript Minutes, Sept. 4, 1857, p. 324; Conable, p. 645.

41. William Kendall to BTR, Sept. 16, 1857, quoted in Terrill, *Redfield,* p. 325.

42. Zahniser, p. 96; BHR, *BTR,* p. 126. Kendall's character was passed, however, at the afternoon session on Sept. 4 (Manuscript Minutes, Sept. 4, 1857, p. 320).

43. WCKD, Sept. 4, 1857.

44. WCKD, Sept. 5, 1857.

45. Zahniser, p. 91.

46. BHR, *BTR,* p. 140.

47. William Hosmer, *NI* 3 (June 20, 1859): 2, quoted in Zahniser, p. 98.

troversy was really created by the dominant party as a check on the abolitionism sentiment, Hosmer argued.

No doubt slavery was an underlying issue. But the basic cause of the Nazarite controversy, and of the action against McCreery, Roberts, and Kendall, was closer to home. It concerned essentially the issues Roberts raised in "New School Methodism" — mixed together, of course, with conference politics and, no doubt, personality factors. While Roberts and McCreery were actively abolitionist, there is hardly a hint of the slavery issue in "New School Methodism" or the documents surrounding Roberts's 1857 trial. For Hosmer, however, slavery *was* the overriding issue, and he devoted much of the *Northern Independent* to discussing it. Understandably, he tended to see everything else in terms of this. But in the Nazarite controversy it wasn't the immediate or key issue.[48]

At the close of conference Roberts found that he was being sent to Pekin, in the Niagara District, about twenty miles north of Buffalo and only ten miles from Niagara Falls. "Mr. Roberts was demoted from a larger appointment . . . to Pekin, a country charge," Zahniser comments.[49] No doubt that is how the appointment was viewed by many at the time, including Roberts. Yet the Pekin congregation was a substantial church, with 160 members (including probationers).[50]

Kendall was appointed to West Falls, southeast of Buffalo — "a starvation appointment some 70 miles away," he wrote.[51] Thus Kendall was "transferred from the best and wealthiest charge to the very poorest."[52] Though North Chili was far from the largest church in the conference, it apparently was quite prosperous economically. North Chili had 117 members at the close of Kendall's year there, while West Falls had just 64.[53] Kendall went to his new appointment "full of joy" and looking "to Jesus for success," but only after a spiritual struggle. Near the close of conference Kendall was in his room crying, "face swollen and red with weeping," groaning over harsh treatment that was "provoked by nothing more than his unshaken purpose to keep his ordination vows as a minister of the cross of Christ." But God was able to "withdraw the arrows that had wounded his sensitive, guiltless soul, and so heal the wounds that his mourning was turned into joy."[54]

Roberts's two years at Albion were now at a close. Statistically, his Albion ministry had not been a resounding success. While he consolidated the gains of earlier re-

48. Contrary to Zahniser's perspective. See Zahniser, pp. 97-99.

49. Zahniser, p. 96.

50. *Minutes,* Genesee Conference, 1857.

51. WCKD, Sept. 5, 1857.

52. "Rev. Wm. C. Kendall, A.M. — Labors — Death," p. 374.

53. In calling North Chili "the best and wealthiest charge" in the conference, the *Earnest Christian* article may be engaging in a bit of hyperbole. The reference could be construed as referring back to Kendall's ministry in Albion in 1854-55, but in context it seems to mean Kendall's immediately prior appointment to North Chili (1856-57). North Chili had a total membership of 114 in 1856 and 117 a year later, when Kendall left.

54. "Rev. Wm. C. Kendall, A.M. — Labors — Death," p. 374. This article was probably written by Martha Kendall, though possibly by Roberts.

vival, the total membership in 1857 was the same as a year earlier: 257. Full membership, however, increased from 217 to 230, despite four deaths. Still, Roberts left Albion in 1857 with 28 fewer members than when he arrived two years earlier.[55]

Reactions to Roberts's Trial

People who knew B. T. Roberts and had been blessed by his ministry were outraged at his trial and conviction. George W. Estes, a prominent member of the Clarkson circuit, near Brockport, was present at conference when Roberts was condemned, and shortly afterward published his own account. In a widely circulated pamphlet, Estes copied the offending extracts from "New School Methodism" and the charges against Roberts and gave a rather inflammatory description of the trial, including the names of the preachers who "as near as can be ascertained" voted against Roberts. He charged that "the influence of the book concern" could be seen in the proceedings, since some of the preachers owed money to Thomas Carlton, the Methodist book agent, and so felt obligated to vote with him.[56] Estes wrote,

> So, brethren in the membership of the Genesee Conference, you see we have a clique among us called the Buffalo Regency — conspiring and acting in secret conclave to kidnap or drive away, or proscribe and destroy, by sham trials, and starvation appointments, every one who has boldness to question their supremacy in the Conference. By threats of insubordination, and farcical outcries of strife and division, they frighten the episcopacy to give them the presiding-eldership power, with its patronage of appointments, and having that, of course they command the Conference vote, so far as they dare for fear of the people. We are fast losing our best men. The fearless champions of true Methodism are being cloven down, one after another, in our sight; and we sit loyally still, and weep and pray, and pay our money, yet another and another year, hoping the thing will come to an end.[57]

Estes concluded his pamphlet by saying he would never give "a cent of my money" in support of the preachers who had voted against Roberts. Withholding funds was the only mechanism available to church members in the face of this injustice, he said. "The remedy of every member is within his own reach. For one, I shall apply that remedy."[58]

55. The next year, under Loren Stiles, total membership at Albion increased to 268. Little can be concluded from these numbers, however, because of unknown factors such as possible transfers or removals from membership.

56. George Estes's pamphlet, quoted in BHR, *BTR*, p. 132. The pamphlet is reprinted in BHR, *BTR* (pp. 127-34), and in *WAS* (pp. 160-68).

57. Estes pamphlet, quoted in *WAS*, pp. 166-67.

58. Estes pamphlet, quoted in *WAS*, p. 167.

This pamphlet was published without Roberts's knowledge or consent, but it further fueled the controversy.[59] Hibbard called it "objectionable and destructive." The conference was "flooded with [Estes's] pamphlet," he wrote, which made "the most unworthy and unfounded allusions to the decisions of the LeRoy Conference." Hibbard charged:

> The Nazarite preachers generally were exceedingly cautious in the circulation of this pamphlet, its circulation being secured mainly by means of certain obscure persons and Nazarite females who had consented, on the ostensible plea of love for "holiness and old-fashioned Methodism," to give aid. . . . The publication, in part, accomplished its purpose. Many of the laity throughout the Conference territory were poisoned by its statements, and joined in its tirade of abuse against the leading ministry and the governmental action of Conference.[60]

Meanwhile Roberts returned to Albion, wrapped up his ministry there, and toward the end of September moved with his family to Pekin. There he began what would be his last year as a preacher in the Methodist Episcopal Church. On September 6, the day after his return from conference, Benjamin preached from 1 Peter 1:7, "the trial of your faith, being much more precious than of gold." He "had great liberty in preaching," Ellen reported. "I bore the cross after preaching [i.e., exhorted] and was helped and blessed." She felt assured that, though "leaving a pleasant home and dear friends" at Albion, still "The Lord will go with us according to His promise." "Grace triumphs in my heart. Hallelujah!"[61] In fact, Ellen had a dream that she and Benjamin would be sent to "Poplarville," and on learning of the Pekin appointment she felt this was the place she dreamed of.[62]

Roberts's Year at Pekin

As it turned out, Roberts's appointment to Pekin, though probably intended and perceived as a demotion, was pivotal in the events that led to the formation of the Free Methodist Church — if for no other reason than that it brought him into acquaintance with old Isaac Chesbrough and his son, S. K. J. (Sam) Chesbrough, and their wives. In many respects the Chesbroughs deserve to be seen as the founders of the new denomination almost as much as Roberts because of their key role in turning Roberts's trial and expulsion into the raw material of a new movement.

Isaac Chesbrough owned a prosperous farm two miles from Pekin. With his large wagon and strong horses he would pick up people along the way as he went to church

---

59. *WAS*, pp. 160, 168.

60. Hibbard, "Nazaritism," part II.

61. ELRD, Sept. 1857 (precise date of entry not given). Cf. Carpenter, p. 52. Carpenter gives the date of these entries as Sept. 21 (a Monday), but Ellen seems to be referring to the days immediately following annual conference.

62. ELRD, Sept. 1857 (precise date of entry not given).

and take them to service with him.[63] Samuel was a businessman with (like Roberts) an entrepreneurial streak. He and his wife Ann had been living in Niagara Falls but had just moved back to Isaac's farm near Pekin. Some years earlier, in 1850, about two years after Sam and Ann were married, Sam had spent eight weeks in New York City on business with his father, and there attended Phoebe Palmer's Tuesday meetings. Apparently he entered into the experience of holiness during this period.[64] Samuel Chesbrough was thus predisposed to have a positive relationship with Roberts.

The Pekin congregation, knowing little or nothing of Roberts, was not thrilled to learn that their new preacher had just been convicted of "unchristian and immoral conduct." Ann Chesbrough recalled, "Our society was considered the strongest outside the city of Buffalo. The question arose, why should they send such a man to our place?"[65] To anyone unfamiliar with the case, the charge naturally carried overtones of moral failure. But Isaac, a leading member at Pekin and a fairminded man with wide business experience, said, "It can do no hurt to hear him once, any way." He sent Samuel to the train depot with a horse-drawn wagon to meet Benjamin and Ellen and their family when they arrived. "Bring Brother Roberts here to my house," he told Sam. "I am going to look into this matter for myself."

The Chesbroughs were reassured by this initial encounter. Ann recalled, "Brother and Sister Roberts inquired as to whether we were saved and sanctified, or just how we were in the sight of God. He questioned us closely, so it made a lasting impression on my mind."[66]

After Roberts's first sermon the next Sunday, Chesbrough became a staunch supporter of the new preacher. He told his son Samuel, "Well, Sam, I know nothing about the man, but I do know that what we have heard to-day is Methodism as I used to hear it in the Baltimore Conference, and as I have not heard it preached in western New York."[67]

The Chesbroughs were equally pleased with Ellen. Samuel wrote later, "I was impressed by her neat and plain attire, as well as by the meek and quiet spirit she manifested, and I was drawn towards her. I also compared her in dress to my mother; they both bore the stamp of a true Baltimore Methodist."[68] Ann said Ellen was "plain and ladylike, and carried an air of devotion and purity all the time. Holiness was written upon [her] every movement." She added, however, "I liked the plain, simple dress *on her,* but I would not follow her example under any consideration."[69]

63. BHR, *BTR*, pp. 146-47.

64. Ann E. Chesbrough, "Experience of Mrs. Ann E. Chesbrough," in *A Sermon by Rev. W. T. Hogue Preached at the Fiftieth Anniversary of the Marriage of Rev. Samuel K. J. and Mrs. Ann E. Chesbrough, February 6, 1898* (Chicago: Free Methodist Publishing House, 1906), pp. 46-47.

65. Ann Chesbrough, "Experience," p. 49.

66. Ann Chesbrough, "Experience," p. 50.

67. *WAS*, p. 155; BHR, *BTR*, 141; Zahniser, p. 99.

68. S. K. J. Chesbrough, "A Tribute to the Memory of Mrs. Ellen L. Roberts," *EC* 95, no. 3 (Mar. 1908): 81.

69. Ann Chesbrough, "Experience," pp. 50-51.

Benjamin, Ellen, and the children were soon settled into the parsonage, which Benson later remembered as a "country parsonage" with a "large garden terminating at the edge of a steep bluff, on the side of which was a mysterious cave."[70] Pekin "is a very small ill-looking town," Ellen reported — quite a contrast to New York City! — "but my home looks very pleasant to me — pleasanter because we all love the Savior and are trying to serve Him."[71] Benjamin wrote to his father, "We have a good parsonage, a good new church, and strong membership . . . composed mostly of substantial farmers." He added, "Our people receive us cordially, and I trust we shall have a prosperous year."[72]

But Benjamin had no intention of giving up the broader fight in the conference and the denomination. In fact, he was thinking of publishing a compilation of his writings. In a letter he received during conference, his father cautioned him about his writing. Benjamin replied, "I shall write nothing for publication but that you would, with a knowledge of the facts, approve. Before I publish the book I spoke of, I shall rewrite the whole, and read it to Brothers Kent and Abell, and also Brother Gulick, perhaps."[73] Benjamin trusted the advice of such veteran preachers as John Kent and Asa Abell, who were old enough to remember early American Methodism in the days of Francis Asbury.

Benjamin added, in his letter to his father,

> I want very much to see you and have a long talk about conference matters. I can only say that the course I have taken has secured for me the approbation of those who fear and love the Lord above the praise of men. Sister Kent, who was present till nearly the close of conference, indorsed fully my course, and exhorted me to firmness and constancy.
>
> I often wished that you were there, as I knew you would feel greatly afflicted at the reports that would reach you. I send you a pamphlet by Brother Estes, of Clarkson, who was present at conference and gives a true and faithful report as I believe of the matter.
>
> I have not felt better at the close of a conference for three years than I have done since our last session. I tried to do my duty faithfully, and the Lord blessed me in it, and blesses me since.[74]

The Pekin Methodists were good people, but Benjamin soon concluded their Christian experience was very shallow.[75] He told Ellen, "These people do not under-

---

70. BHR, "My Mother," *EC* 95, no. 3 (Mar. 1908): 69.

71. ELRD, Sept. 1857 (precise date not given).

72. BTR to TR, Oct. 1, 1857, quoted in BHR, *BTR*, p. 142.

73. BTR to TR, Oct. 1, 1857, quoted in BHR, *BTR*, p. 142.

74. BTR to TR, Oct. 1, 1857, quoted in BHR, *BTR*, p. 142. The date of this letter shows that Estes's pamphlet was published almost immediately after the annual conference at LeRoy.

75. Roberts's predecessor at Pekin (1855-57) was Sandford Hunt, and before that D. F. Parsons had served one year. Both were Regency preachers who in 1857 voted against Roberts. Hunt later wrote *Methodism in Buffalo From Its Origin to the Close of 1892*. During this three-year period (1854-57) total

stand what is meant by giving up the world and being thoroughly saved." Since there was to be a district quarterly meeting at Pekin, Benjamin decided to invite Methodists from Brockport and elsewhere who were "clearly saved of God" to come as "personal examples of God's power to save." A number of people came in response to the summons, and the gathering was "a meeting of marked power" that roused the Pekin congregation.[76] According to Benson Roberts, "Many of the ladies, members of the [Pekin] church, [despite their Methodist membership] vows to [observe] plainness of dress, came to church, their silk gowns so distended with crinoline that their dresses would reach across the aisle; and the high, poke bonnets [bonnets with large projecting brims], then in vogue, were veritable flower gardens, the enormous spaces were so filled with artificial flowers. A salvation that involved plain dressing was not inviting to such, and the seekers ceased to come."[77]

At first it seemed that the "object lesson" of inviting plain saints from elsewhere had failed. Before long, however, people began to seek God "with serious purpose," resulting in a "thorough and lasting" work.[78]

One of the Pekin Methodists who was clearly converted and sanctified was Ann Chesbrough, Samuel's wife. Years later she wrote, "Thank God! Brother Roberts was permitted to be in the Methodist Episcopal church one more year, or my soul must have been lost." In one of his early sermons at Pekin, Benjamin preached on the letter in Revelation to the church in Ephesus, warning about those who had lost their first love: "Remember therefore from whence thou art fallen, and repent, and do the first works; or else I will come unto thee quickly, and will remove thy candlestick out of his place, except thou repent" (Rev. 2:5). Mrs. Chesbrough recalled that Roberts "showed how many good qualities a member of the church could have and be without saving grace. There I sat in all the paraphernalia of the world, nothing *cheap* and *common,* but the richest and best I could find." She realized that she had no assurance of salvation. "Heaven and hell were before me. It was my last call. The choice must be made then and there. . . . The altar call was made and I went forward with sinners under the first call."[79]

After some days of seeking, Ann Chesbrough was converted during the special meetings at Pekin. She noted, "A girl of ill-repute went to the altar with me, night after night." Some of the more respectable church members were scandalized; they thought Sister Chesbrough was "a good Christian" who should "be ashamed to be seen going to the altar with that girl." But Ann recalled, "I said to myself if there was

---

membership at Pekin declined from 175 to 160, and full members, excluding probationers, from 164 to 134.

76. BHR, *BTR,* p. 143.

77. BHR, *BTR,* pp. 143-44.

78. BHR, *BTR,* p. 144. It is not clear just when this quarterly meeting at Pekin was held. Ellen speaks of such a meeting in May 1858 (Carpenter, p. 60), but the meeting Benson Roberts describes seems to have been in the fall. Perhaps two quarterly meetings were held at Pekin. Generally the quarterly meetings were held in January, April, July, and October, though sometimes in the subsequent months.

79. Ann Chesbrough, "Experience," pp. 51-52.

any mercy for me, there was for the girl. It helped me instead of hindering." She realized that she had "never dreamed" that "pure religion . . . would make the slightest difference in my external life." Now she saw that she must live a plain and simple life. "Under the spirit of awakening the world and worldly things were given up and put away. The blessed Spirit went right through my wardrobe item by item."[80]

She said, "Brother Roberts preached holiness in every sermon," and eventually she sought and found this deeper experience. Her description is illuminating:

> I saw the necessity of my being sanctified holy. . . . [I] earnestly sought until I received, without the shadow of a doubt, the witness of the Spirit it was done. All I saw in the way was my opposition to demonstrations, shouting and falling under the power of God as sister Roberts did and her servant, Mary Shultz. . . . I remember saying to myself Sister Roberts is delicate and easily overcome and Mary is ignorant and doesn't know any better, but I was strong physically and knew enough not to be affected in any such way.[81]

The next night when Ann again went to the altar, "the work was done for time and for eternity."

> I arose and went just as near the altar as I could get in the middle aisle of the church, I fell upon my knees, bowing my head as usual, when God said, lift up your head and pray. I obeyed in an instant, straightened up and looking to Jesus, these words were put in my mouth, "Lift the veil," words I had never uttered. These three words were all my prayer. Every time I repeated them the more lost I became to everything of this world, and the heavens parted and my body was prostrated under the power of God. I was as stiff as if in death, except my tongue, that moved as the Spirit gave utterance. First I prayed for the *cold-hearted professors* who sat in their seats opposing the work of God, mostly my more intimate friends. They thought me crazy. . . . Then my praying ceased — no more burden. The Savior says, "Sink away into my will." My tongue was stiff and I lay there three and a half hours. I knew everything going on, the testimonies and singing, all was harmony and heavenly to my soul. If the whole universe had gazed upon me it would have made no difference. It seemed as if I was suspended somewhere between heaven and earth. Words fail me in the attempt to describe that wonderful baptism of the Spirit and the clear witness to the blessing of entire sanctification.[82]

Clearly this was a very "Pentecostal" experience and was not especially unusual at the time, at least among "old-time" Methodists. The only difference between this

---

80. Ann Chesbrough, "Experience," pp. 52-53.

81. Ann Chesbrough, "Experience," p. 55. "Mary Shultz" was perhaps Mary Swezey, Ellen's niece, though possibly a different girl then living with and working for the Roberts. The fact that Mrs. Chesbrough would refer to Mary as Ellen's "servant" hints perhaps at Ann's class background.

82. Ann Chesbrough, "Experience," pp. 56-57. Although this is a recollection some forty years after the fact, and therefore possibly subject to some distortion in detail, still the vividness of the recollection is impressive.

and later twentieth-century Pentecostal experience, it would seem, is that there is no explicit mention here of speaking in tongues, though Ann's "tongue . . . moved as the Spirit gave utterance."

During Roberts's year at Pekin there was a growing spirit of revival. Benjamin engaged aggressively in evangelism, carrying the good news beyond the church building to the surrounding area. He asked George Carl, a man reclaimed from a backslidden condition during the Pekin revival, for help in finding another preaching point. Mr. Carl secured the Stone Schoolhouse some five miles southeast of Pekin, an area where many of the residents were Lutherans.[83] In late spring Roberts held successful meetings at the Stone Schoolhouse, and about forty people were converted. "It was a glorious work," noted Ellen.[84] Carl later recalled, "Brother Roberts often told me this was one of the best revivals he ever held. The work continued to go. . . . Lutherans, Presbyterians, Baptists and Methodists were all blessed together and shouted the praises of God."[85]

At times Benjamin engaged also in open-air preaching. During warm weather he regularly held Sunday afternoon services in a grove of trees. "Hundreds attended that no house [of worship] in the vicinity could accommodate," he noted.[86] In early January he and Ellen attended a four-day meeting at the nearby Ridgeville ME Church. Ellen reported, "The [second] morning we had something of a break in the prayer-meeting. I was enabled to look to God in faith and He came in power to my soul."[87]

Ellen did her best to help with the ministry, though she still battled her natural shyness in giving any kind of public witness. Benson later said, "At this time, my mother was much abroad with my father in religious work, and yet her family was well cared for. Some she took with her, but none were left except with proper care."[88] Ellen accompanied Benjamin back east to Parma to attend the quarterly meeting of the Genesee District in early October. Benjamin preached, and Ellen said, "The Lord blessed me in trying to say a few words." She reflected on Saturday, October 31, "I am buffeted and seemingly driven backwards in my attempts to get nearer to Jesus," and on Sunday: "I have been shut up a good deal. Some little liberty in class, greatly tried fearing I was not led by the Spirit afterwards."[89]

As the new year began, Ellen rededicated her life to God. She wrote in her diary,

---

83. BHR, *BTR*, p. 144; Carpenter, p. 52; Zahniser, pp. 100-101.

84. ELRD, after entry for Mar. 23, 1858, but apparently written somewhat later, summarizing earlier events (slightly corrected). Her entry reads: "After closing our protracted effort at the church last spring we had meetings in a school-house five miles out. Some 50 were converted — it was a glorious work. Most of them remain faithful." George Carl reported the number of conversions as "between thirty and forty."

85. George Washington Carl, recollection published in *FM*, Aug. 9, 1910, pp. 504-5.

86. B. T. Roberts, "Out Door Meetings," *EC* 2, no. 5 (May 1861): 161.

87. ELRD, Jan. 2, 1858.

88. BHR, "My Mother," *EC* 95, no. 3 (Mar. 1908): 69.

89. ELRD, Oct. 7 and 31; Nov. 1, 1857.

I covenant anew with my God to be His, to lay in His hands as clay in the hands of the Potter — to be led by His spirit — to have a single eye for His glory — to seek to please Him — to cease from my own works — to be more careful in the government of my tongue. . . . Also to remember not to think of myself "more highly than I ought to think, but soberly, according as God hath dealt" &c. . . .

Lord help me to cease looking behind and around me. Enable me to get into the mountain.

I also covenant to be more frequent in reading the Bible — to pray more in secret — to examine my own heart <u>daily</u>.[90]

Ellen felt that God especially blessed her during an evening meeting at the parsonage in early January. "There was a getting hold and holding on to the Lord in prayer. I saw how great a loss those sustain who live without holiness."[91] On Friday evening, January 15, she said a few words before the preaching, and though she "did not have much liberty," when she sat down "the Lord began to come in power" and God spoke to her own heart. "I took hold by faith and believed, now is the time for me to receive what I have long desired, this dying to self and sinking into Jesus, and losing self in Christ. I believed and oh what a sense of eternal things rested upon me. Oh what peace followed, what resting in Christ, what solemnity."[92]

Ellen was maintaining a close walk with God, but she still struggled spiritually from time to time — often, it seems, due partly to her retiring temperament.[93] She also felt that she should keep up her diary. She wrote around April 1858, "I have from time to time felt it a <u>duty</u> to keep a diary but it is also a cross. I bear it for a little, then cease to do it. While giving myself anew to God last night I promised to use my pen in this and other ways as the Lord directed. There are many things in the past summer and fall I ought to have recorded — the dealings of God with me — his grace manifested to me in trials &c."[94]

Ellen was particularly blessed during the love feast and the celebration of the Lord's Supper at the quarterly meeting at Albion in mid-January.

I prayed in faith for Jesus to meet me in power at the Sacrament. And as I went to take the wine I could not raise my hands to take it, while the Savior said to me,

---

90. ELRD, Jan. 1, 1858 (slightly corrected).

91. ELRD, Jan. 4 (or possibly 9), 1858 (slightly corrected).

92. ELRD, Jan. 15, 1858 (slightly corrected). Cf. Carpenter, p. 54. Carpenter incorrectly gives the date as Jan. 9 because here, as elsewhere, she conflates diary entries.

93. In the Methodist culture of the time it was accepted and expected that the preacher's wife (in particular) would exhort or testify in public meetings from time to time. In some ways this put a unique burden on the wife, as compared to her husband. It was always appropriate for the preacher to speak, and he was regularly scheduled to preach. But the wife had to discern when it was or was not appropriate to say a special word, to sense the leading of the Spirit in this matter. This seems to have been an ongoing struggle for an introvert like Ellen, at least at this period.

94. ELRD, after entry for Mar. 23, 1858, but apparently written somewhat later (slightly corrected).

"This is the blood that is to keep you," and as I took it my strength gave way, but I soon recovered and testified it was victory through the blood. And as I knelt in my seat these words came to me, "because He lives we shall live also." It came to me so powerfully during preaching that "one" (that had faith in God) "shall chase a thousand and two put ten thousand to flight." As I left the church it seemed as if I could run through a troop and leap over a wall.[95]

In late January 1858 Benjamin fell ill. Then he and Ellen received word that William Kendall was very sick (apparently with typhoid fever) and not expected to live. Benjamin wanted to go to West Falls to see him, but was too sick himself. "It seems as if [Kendall] could not be spared," Ellen wrote. But a few days later she and Benjamin learned that Kendall had passed from this world. "What a blow!" said Ellen, stunned.[96] Benjamin's dear friend died on February 1.[97]

Kendall had requested that Benjamin preach his funeral. The service was delayed until Thursday, February 11, and held at Covington, south of LeRoy — Kendall's hometown. Benjamin and Ellen set out from Pekin on Wednesday and started for home on Friday, staying overnight with friends en route both Wednesday and Friday nights.[98]

The funeral itself was a time of triumph, despite the deep sense of loss. "Mr. Roberts could not preach much, his feelings were such," Ellen said. He preached from Revelation 7:13, "What are these which are arrayed in white robes?" "The congregation was deeply moved. Some wept, some shouted," noted Ellen. "It seemed like triumph rather than death."[99]

At the graveside the congregation sang "On Jordan's Stormy Banks I Stand" and "Heaven, Sweet Heaven." Ellen felt "as if it was the verge of Heaven."[100]

Benjamin had planned to travel to West Falls to preach a memorial in Kendall's pulpit on Sunday, February 21, but since he couldn't find a replacement for himself, he remained in Pekin. He and Ellen did go a couple of weeks later, and Benjamin honored his friend by preaching a memorial sermon based on 1 John 1:7, "if we walk in the light, as he is in the light." God's Spirit was powerfully felt. "It was all light in the House and I never felt so much of the Spirit in a church before," Ellen said. "It came down in floods of light, life and power. A season of prayer [followed] and all prayed for mercy aloud, yet there was no confusion. How abundantly my soul was blessed in talking."[101]

Meanwhile the prospects at Pekin were heartening. "Our meetings increase in

---

95. ELRD, Jan. [17], 1858 (slightly corrected).
96. ELRD, Jan. 28 and Feb. 2, 1858.
97. "Rev. Wm. C. Kendall, A.M. — Labors — Death," pp. 375-77.
98. Carpenter, pp. 56-57.
99. ELRD, entry dated Feb. 10, 1858, but covering Feb. 10-13 (slightly corrected).
100. ELRD, Feb. 10 (i.e., 11), 1858.
101. ELRD, Feb. 20 and Mar. 8, 1858 (slightly corrected). The memorial service seems to have been held on Monday evening, Mar. 8.

interest," Ellen noted; "we are seeing some inquire after salvation." She felt the Lord showed her that "this work is going to spread here. The work of holiness."[102]

John Wesley Redfield and his wife (plus their little terrier Jack) spent several weeks with the Robertses in the spring, and this was an encouragement to Benjamin. Redfield's visit "served to strengthen Mr. Roberts in his adherence to the Scripture line of truth and power in religion."[103] Benson Roberts, then four years old, later remembered fondly "the visit of that great man, who was a delightful companion to children." Benson recalled the evangelist brewing root beer from sassafras and various other roots and "herbs of unsuspected virtues" and taking him fishing out on the Niagara River. Together they climbed the high, rocky riverbanks at Lewiston, a few miles below Niagara Falls.[104]

Although Redfield wasn't directly involved in the Nazarite controversy since he was not affiliated with the Genesee Conference, he was aware of it from the beginning. Through his contacts with Kendall he learned of the "Nazarite Call" as early as 1856.[105] Redfield played a key role in disseminating information about the Nazarite controversy in northern Illinois and in St. Louis. In an August 1858 letter from Elgin, Illinois, Redfield remarked, "I have circulated the Nazarite documents wherever I could, and though some of the preachers try hard to poison the minds of the people against the Nazarites, yet it [*sic*] is taking with all who go for the life and power of salvation."[106]

As the year wore on, Roberts's pastoral efforts began to bear fruit. A number of nominal members were soundly converted, and the class meetings began to function again. Benjamin wrote to his father on Monday, March 1, 1858, "Yesterday was a time of power, such as was never seen here before. In the class-meeting, where six to twelve attended when we came, some forty or fifty were present. The spirit of the Lord came down upon the people and there was a breaking down such as was greatly needed."[107]

Roberts also promoted and developed a network of evening class meetings that met in homes "every night in the week at various points on the charge."[108]

Roberts's comment about the Sunday class meeting is revealing, because it shows the priority he put on the class, and that though the Sunday class had become a fairly large gathering in the church building, still he maintained a network of small weeknight home fellowships where the individual accountability was higher. Thus Roberts's passion for "old-time Methodism" included the vital role of class meetings.

Like many evangelical Methodists who were shaped by the revivals of the 1830s,

---

102. ELRD, Feb. 16 (approx.) and 21, 1858.

103. BHR, *BTR*, p. 145.

104. BHR, *BTR*, p. 145.

105. Redfield Autobiography, p. 324.

106. JWR (Elgin, Kane Co., Ill.) to "Brother and Sister Hicks" (Syracuse), Aug. 26, 1858 (RFP, Reel 22).

107. BTR to TR, Mar. 1, 1858, quoted in BHR, *BTR*, pp. 145-46.

108. *WAS*, p. 158 (quoting S. K. J. Chesbrough; see below).

Roberts had come to put much stock in demonstrative worship experiences where there was a general "breaking down." Yet this did not replace the daily life of covenant discipleship that marked early Methodism. Roberts valued both, and in fact probably would hardly have recognized or acknowledged the distinction.[109]

By March Roberts was conducting protracted meetings at Pekin, services every night. Probably Redfield assisted with these meetings. "A good work is in progress, from ten to twenty forward each night," Benjamin wrote on March 10.[110] Most of Roberts's people were farmers, and he used an agricultural analogy: "The church here was in the condition of a farm that has been surface-tilled until it is worn out, and instead of grain, it bears sorrel and weeds. I am trying to put the plough in deep. The Lord helps me and I have no fears for the results."[111]

Fallout from the Trial

As word of Roberts's censure at the 1857 annual conference spread, so did his celebrity. Invitations came from around the conference and beyond. But Benjamin knew his first duty was at home. He told his father, "Though I feel an interest in the work generally, which perhaps few of the preachers do, yet my first duty is here. I have had calls to go to Attica, Lancaster, Yates, Caryville, the Congregational Church at Le Roy, and other places."[112]

During the year George Estes followed up his pamphlet with a second one — this one a reprint of Roberts's "New School Methodism," prefaced by the account of the 1857 trial that he printed in his first pamphlet. Again, the pamphlet was issued without Roberts's knowledge or consent. It was circulated widely, however, and became the basis for his second trial at the 1858 annual conference.[113]

The 1858 conference sessions were scheduled to begin on October 6, a month later than usual. As he ended his year (effectively thirteen months) at Pekin, Roberts again prepared his statistical report. Total membership had climbed 16 percent, from 160 to 185. More significantly, full membership actually dropped from 134 to 123, while probationers increased from 24 to 60. Apparently a number of full members either left the church or had their membership discontinued, while a substantial number of new converts came into the church. All in all, a very successful year.[114]

109. Roberts may have not understood, however, the degree to which the Methodist class meeting had already departed from its original pattern. As noted in the discussion of Ellen's experience of New York City Methodism in the 1840s, this transition had pretty well occurred a decade or more before Roberts began his preaching ministry.

110. BTR to TR, Mar. 10, 1858, quoted in BHR, *BTR*, p. 146.

111. BTR to TR, Mar. 1, 1858, quoted in BHR, *BTR*, p. 146.

112. BTR to TR, Mar. 10, 1858, quoted in BHR, *BTR*, p. 146.

113. BHR, *BTR*, pp. 147-49.

114. *Minutes*, Genesee Conference, 1857, 1858. Five deaths also enter into the equation. The most likely scenario is that some of the 24 probationers from 1857 moved into full membership; some of them, as well as some full members, were discontinued; and 50 to 70 new converts were added. Proba-

As the conference year ended, Samuel Chesbrough sent a testimonial to the *Northern Independent,* commending Roberts's ministry.

It can not be denied that we received to our church as our pastor, a man whom *The Advocate* informed us was tried and found guilty of "immorality;" and judging from the articles which have appeared from time to time in that paper, it would seem that his opposers think "if we let him alone, all men will believe on him;" and the only way to destroy his usefulness is to pursue him with "slanders and persecutions." A recent article in *The Advocate,* which descends to language unbecoming one Christian speaking of another, is hardly worth noticing, as the shafts hurled at Brother Roberts fall far below him. . . .

In view, then, of all these things, the grand question to be answered is this: Has the church prospered under his labors, and has God honored his labors by bestowing his blessing upon them? We feel glad to say that the church, has prospered, through the blessing of God, during the year. . . .

. . . Notwithstanding the many reports which have circulated to the contrary, God has been at work among the people. Between fifty and sixty have professed conversion; about forty of whom have joined on probation. The preaching has been plain, simple and pointed, and in accordance with the doctrines and discipline of the Church. The consequence has been, very many of the members of the Church have been seen at the altar of prayer, some for justification, some for sanctification. Quite a number have publicly professed to have received the blessing of sanctification. Without an exception, every aged member in our Church has rejoiced to see the return of the days of Wesleyan Methodism, with its uncompromising and earnest spirit.

When Brother R. came among us, our Sunday noon class numbered about fifteen; now the average attendance is, and has been for some time, from seventy-five to eighty. Our prayer-meetings and week evening class meetings, and they occur every night in the week at various points on the charge, have been better sustained through "haying and harvesting," and have been more interesting than for years past. The Sunday School has also reached a point in attendance and interest never before attained in its history. There are scores in the Church to-day, who feel to thank God for having sent him among us.[115]

1858 Bergen Camp Meeting

In the midst of this volatile context the summer Bergen camp meeting was a resounding success. The meeting began on Thursday, June 17, and ended on Friday

---

bly around 30 left the church because they were unhappy with Roberts, while about twice that number were added.

115. Quoted in *WAS,* pp. 156-58. The testimonial is signed "S. K. J. Chesbrough. South Pekin, Sept. 24, 1858."

morning, the twenty-fifth. The Reverend B. I. Ives of the Oneida Conference, one of the evangelists, said it was the largest he had ever attended. Cloth tents numbered 104, some of them very large. Ives estimated the Sunday attendance at five thousand.[116] Over thirty preachers from Genesee and other conferences attended, as well as many local preachers. The preachers included several from East Genesee, William Reddy and Ives from Oneida, and B. W. Gorham of the Wyoming Conference, as well as Loren Stiles and others from the Genesee Conference. Samuel Church and Asa Abell, veteran Genesee preachers and former presiding elders, led the meetings, and "both appeared very much at home in that kind of business," noted Ives.[117] No doubt much of the organization work for the camp was done by Roberts, even though he was now based over fifty miles away.

Two things that especially impressed Ives were "the number of intelligent business and influential men" who were present with their families and the deep sense of God's presence, manifested in a "spirit of prayer and labor for the conversion of sinners, and the sanctification of believers." All were seeking and sensed the glory of God. "So much was this the case that when strangers came upon the ground, they were led to say, . . . 'God is here,' 'there is power here,' 'what awful power,' 'there appears to be a stream of holy fire and power encircling this camp ground.' . . . There appeared to rest upon *all*, as they came within the circle of tents, a holy impression that God was there in awful power, to awaken, convert, purify, and save souls."[118]

Conversion and sanctification were strongly urged at the camp, and with good success. Reddy noted, "The doctrine of sanctification after the John Wesley standard, the definite way of seeking the blessing, the spontaneous confessions of having obtained it, on the part of intelligent and mature persons, the duty of exemplifying it by self-denial and universal obedience, the keeping of the rules of the Discipline, . . . the patient and loving endurance of opposition and persecution for Christ's sake, if need be, were all earnestly taught and enforced, and many were the witnesses."[119]

Ellen Roberts reported her own experience at Bergen. She noted on June 18, "While Bro. Stiles was preaching the power of God came down all over the ground — I felt while here at one time as if in the suburbs of glory — at another such a dying to every thing." She was feeling the weight of Benjamin's troubles with the conference, but the Bergen camp meeting was an encouragement. "I saw it is my privilege to esteem the reproach of Christ greater treasures than the wealth of Egypt. . . . I have in the past dreaded extreme poverty, but while here I saw God could enable me to glory in <u>necessities also</u> when they come."[120]

The love feast on Wednesday morning, the last full day, was a high point for El-

---

116. B. I. Ives, "Bergen Camp Meeting," *NI*, July 1, 1858, p. 2.

117. Ives, "Bergen Camp Meeting." Cf. *WAS*, p. 121. Ives said, "No doubt there would have been a much larger number of ministers in attendance, had it not been that the Commencement exercises at Lima came off at the same time."

118. Ives, "Bergen Camp Meeting."

119. Quoted in *WAS*, p. 119.

120. ELRD, June 18, 1858.

len, as for many others. It was, Ives said, "a time of salvation power and glory."[121] This was a common sentiment; Reddy remarked, "I heard old Methodists from Boston and from Connecticut say, with streaming eyes and bounding hearts, 'This is as it used to be forty years ago.'"[122] Ives noted that "some of the old veterans of the cross" made comments such as, "This reminds me of the early days of Methodism in this country," and "This is such camp-meetings as we used to have thirty, or forty, or fifty years ago." Yet Ives saw "nothing that appeared like 'wild-fire,' or mere 'animal excitement,' during the entire meeting. The motto was 'order and power.' And all the people of God seemed to be baptized with the real old-fashioned 'Jerusalem fire.'"[123]

The contrast between "Old School" and "New School" Methodism — between old-time camp-meeting Methodism and the urbane "religion of beneficence rather than devotion" — could hardly have been more stark. But long before the 1858 annual conference sessions it was clear which kind of Methodism would win out in the body of preachers who made up the Genesee Conference.

By this time the Bergen camp meeting itself had gotten caught up in conference politics. Was the camp, and especially the Genesee Camp-Ground Association that sponsored it, an instrument of the Genesee Conference? Or was it independent, possibly even schismatic? A flurry of articles in the *Northern Christian Advocate* and the *Northern Independent* traded charges and countercharges. The ensuing struggle for the control of the camp meeting eventually led to its demise.

End of Roberts's Year at Pekin

As the end of the conference year approached, it became increasingly clear that the annual conference sessions in October would prove decisive for Roberts's ministry and the "Nazarite" controversy. Ellen grew increasingly apprehensive about what lay ahead. During a love feast at Gasport in July (probably the quarterly meeting for the Niagara District), the Lord showed her for "the second time that there was some severe trial ahead, and it was connected with my Husband and I thought he was going to die." Later she and Benjamin attended a camp meeting at Hamburg, and again, though she felt God very near, "I saw the same trial ahead and it seemed as though my dear Husband was going to die."[124] To lose a child or one's partner was, naturally enough, the greatest trial Ellen could imagine.

Benjamin was always a networker. It appears that during all this period he kept up close contacts and maintained relationships throughout the conference. In Au-

---

121. Ives, "Bergen Camp Meeting."

122. Quoted in *WAS*, p. 118.

123. Ives, "Bergen Camp Meeting." Ives's report was in part a propaganda piece promoting camp meetings and defending them against their critics. He closed his article, "I pray God that we may have more of this in all of our Churches. Praise God for camp-meetings, and let all the people say, Amen."

124. ELRD, July 1858 (exact date not given). Ellen adds (regarding the time of the Gasport meeting), "Mr. Roberts is very unwell — has a cough & bad cold."

gust he and Ellen traveled back to Brockport and spent a few days there, and Ellen's diary shows they visited other places.[125]

Friday, October 1, was a fast day in preparation for annual conference. Though few attended the prayer service at Pekin, God's presence was very near. "What power we had in praying for my dear companion," Ellen wrote. "We all felt God would go with him, and the Red Sea would be divided."[126]

125. ELRD, 1858.
126. ELRD, Oct. 1, 1858.

CHAPTER 22

Tried and Expelled

"Such are the surrounding influences of this trial, . . . that its results upon the interests of our Church must inevitably be wide spread and lasting for good or evil."

Loren Stiles, in his defense of B. T. Roberts[1]

"[W]e shall yet praise God to all eternity for this trial. . . . A fire is being kindled that is going to burn on."

Ellen Roberts[2]

Osman C. Baker was again the presiding bishop as the Genesee Conference met October 6-22, 1858, at Perry, New York, forty miles southwest of Rochester. The sessions were held in the sanctuary of the Perry Methodist Episcopal Church (Wyoming District), where William Tuttle was the appointed preacher. Bishop Matthew Simpson was to have presided but was unable to, due to illness. However, Bishop Edmund S. Janes presided at a number of the sessions, including Roberts's trial (though Baker was also present much of the time).[3] James B. Fuller was again elected secretary, while J. B. Wentworth was assistant secretary.[4] The unusual prolongation of the conference — two and a half weeks — was due primarily to the "Nazarite" controversy and Roberts's trial.

1. Quoted in Chesbrough, *Defence,* p. 41.
2. ELR to TR, Nov. 13, 1858.
3. Manuscript Minutes of the Genesee Annual Conference for 1858, hereafter Manuscript Minutes, 1858; Chesbrough, *Defence,* p. 10. Roberts's trial began on Oct. 13.
4. Manuscript Minutes, 1858, Oct. 6, 1858, p. 328.

423

Benjamin left Pekin and traveled the seventy or so miles to Perry on Monday, October 4. Ellen attended most of the conference as well, and Benjamin's father Titus was also present.[5]

Ellen journeyed to Perry on Friday and Saturday in the company of "Brother C." (probably Samuel Chesbrough).[6] When she saw Benjamin, he reported that the conference had "rejected Bro. Warner and Foster" — Frank M. Warner and Isaac Foster, admitted as probationary members of conference (i.e., ministerial candidates) in 1856 and now up for admission as full members.[7] Apparently Warner and Foster were presumed to be favorable to Roberts and McCreery, and their admission into full conference membership would give the Nazarite side another two votes.

Benjamin said Warner had been rejected for urging people to seek holiness and Foster for a remark about presiding elders. Ellen reflected, "I felt as if their [the conference leadership's] hands were laid on me, and began at once to see the nature of the trial which I had seen ahead at different times through the summer. Mr. R. seems burdened — and surely I feel so."[8]

Benjamin and Ellen attended the conference services on Sunday, the tenth, hearing again the celebrated Dr. John Durbin preach. But in the evening they went to nearby Burke Hill, where Benjamin had been invited to preach.[9]

The process in 1858 was much like that a year earlier. When in due course Roberts's name came up for the examination of his character, charges of "unchristian and immoral conduct" were again lodged against him. This occurred on Wednesday, October 13.

William Kendall Remembered

The case against William Kendall had of course been short-circuited by Kendall's untimely death eight months earlier. Instead of trying Kendall, the conference honored him! Roberts was appointed to preach his funeral sermon. With this assignment, and as a member of the Committee on Memoirs, Roberts prepared to honor the life and ministry of his friend, fully aware of the irony of being entrusted with this assignment while dire charges were pending against him. The memorial service

5. Titus Roberts was present at least for the trial. Benjamin wrote later, "I feel so thankful to the Lord for permitting you to be at the conference, to see and hear for yourself." BTR to TR, Nov. 2, 1858, quoted in BHR, *BTR,* p. 181.

6. ELRD, Oct. 8, 1858. It is not clear who cared for the Roberts children while Ellen was attending conference (or earlier, when she went to Illinois), or whether they accompanied her. Her niece Mary may still have been living with them, helping out with the household management.

7. ELRD, Oct. 8, 1858.

8. ELRD, Oct. 8, 1858.

9. ELRD, Oct. 10, 1858. Ellen commented that Durbin "had much to say about a period in his life when he was a man of one business & aim — and how he was blest at that time — I kept wondering how it was now — yet it is evident."

on Wednesday, October 13, the night before Roberts's trial commenced in earnest, was "a blessed time," Ellen said. "God [was] there."[10]

And so the case against Kendall was closed. The 1858 conference, instead of trying and expelling Kendall, adopted a tribute to him. The tribute — probably written, or at least edited, by Roberts — said, in part:

> He fell at his post, in the midst of one of the most promising revivals that ever attended his labors. It was remarked by his presiding elder, Rev. G. Fillmore, that notwithstanding all his previous ministerial success, he had never known a time when there was such a prospect before him of extensive usefulness as when he was taken sick; and he had never known an instance where a preacher had so interwoven himself into the affections of all the people.
>
> It may be said of Brother Kendall, he fell a martyr to his work.[11]

Conference had already been in session a week when Roberts's case came before the body on October 13. However, a copy of the charges was handed to him on Monday morning, the eleventh.[12] This time the charge of "unchristian and immoral conduct" was brought by David Nichols, a fifty-three-year-old preacher under appointment to assist Alfred W. Luce at Covington.[13] Nichols's accusation, with several "specifications," was read. When a motion that the charge not be entertained was lost, the conference on motion voted to pursue it.[14]

Ellen was present for much of Benjamin's trial, seated beyond the bar of the conference with the preachers' wives and others who had come to watch and listen. She wrote in her diary, "When they first took up Mr. R's case it seemed as if I could not stand it. . . . I asked God to give me nerves like <u>steel</u> and make me like brass that I might sit there unmoved and hear it all. Bless His name, He has done it." Yet she was troubled about "my Husband's being expelled which it seems probably he will be." She opened her Bible to the second chapter of Daniel and was comforted. Daniel 2:44 assured her, "In the time of those kings, the God of heaven will set up a kingdom that will never be destroyed, nor will it be left to another people. It will crush all those kingdoms and bring them to an end, but it will itself endure forever."[15]

10. Manuscript Minutes, 1858, p. 334; ELRD, Oct. 13, 1858.

11. Quoted in *WAS*, pp. 79-80.

12. ELRD, Oct. 11, 1858. Ellen wrote, "My heart aches over such pursuing the innocent. But I must not complain. . . . my trust is in Jesus. He will sustain." Cf. Carpenter, p. 64; Carpenter mistakenly has "punishing" rather than "pursuing."

13. *Minutes*, Genesee Conference, 1857, 1858; Ray Allen, *A Century of the Genesee Annual Conference of the Methodist Episcopal Church, 1810-1910* (Rochester, N.Y.: By the Author, 1911), p. 108.

14. Manuscript Minutes, 1858, p. 361.

15. ELRD, Oct. 11, 1858.

The Trial Begins

As was true the previous year, the proceedings were orchestrated by behind-the-scenes meetings of the group of preachers Roberts and others called the Buffalo Regency — though this was hardly necessary, given the results of the previous year's conference. Many local Methodists were stirred up in defense of Roberts, but only ordained preachers had a seat at the annual conference. And it was now clear that in this clergy group Roberts and his colleagues, whether "Nazarites" or not, were in the minority.

The charges brought against Roberts were extensive:

CHARGES. — I hereby charge Benjamin T. Roberts with unchristian and immoral conduct.

SPECIFICATIONS.

First, Contumacy [i.e., stubborn disobedience]: In disregarding the admonition of this Conference, in its decision upon his case at its last session.

Second, In re-publishing, or assisting in the re-publishing and circulation of a document, entitled "New School Methodism," the original publication of which had been pronounced by this Conference "unchristian and immoral conduct."

Third, in publishing, or assisting in the publication and circulation of a document, printed in Brockport, and signed, "George W. Estes," and appended to the one entitled "New School Methodism," and containing among other libels upon this Conference generally, and upon some of its members particularly, the following, to wit:

1. "For several years past there has been the annual sacrifice of a human victim at the Conference."
2. "No man is safe who dare even whisper a word against this secret inquisition in our midst."
3. "Common crime can command its indulgences; bankruptcies and adulteries are venial offences; but opposition to its schemes and policies is a mortal sin — a crime without benefit of clergy."
4. That "the same fifty men who voted Bro. Roberts guilty of unchristian and immoral conduct, voted to re-admit a brother for the service performed of kissing a young lady."
5. That "Bro. Roberts' trial was marked by gross iniquity of proceedings."
6. That "on the trial, a right which any civil or military court would have allowed him, was denied."
7. That "a venerable doctor of Divinity read the 'Autodafe' [i.e., 'auto-da-fé' (literally, 'act of the faith'), a term for public condemnation borrowed from the Spanish Inquisition] sermon, wherein he consigned in true Inquisitorial style Bro. Roberts body and soul to hell."

426

8. That "this venerable 'D.D.' is quite efficient in embarrassing effective preachers in their work and pleading them to hell for the crime of preaching and writing the truth."[16]

9. That "there is a clique among us called the Buffalo Regency, conspiring and acting in secret conclave, to kidnap, or drive away, or proscribe and destroy, by sham trials and starvation appointments; every one who has the boldness to question their supremacy in the Conference."

10. That "the fearless champions of Methodism are being cloven down one after another in our sight."

11. That "the aforesaid members of this Conference are a 'monster power,' which is writhing its slimy folds around the Church of God and crushing out its life."

Signed, David Nichols.

Perry, Oct. 11th, 1858.[17]

Obviously George Estes's colorful pamphlet had given the Regency preachers some choice ammunition! The case against Roberts really boiled down to one accusation, however: that Roberts was responsible for the Estes pamphlet and thus had violated the admonition given him a year earlier.

The trial proceeded immediately. Bishop Janes asked Benjamin if he was "now ready to enter upon his defence," and Roberts said he was.[18]

No doubt by prearrangement, Nichols immediately asked that James Fuller assist with the prosecution, and the bishop agreed.

Roberts's early legal training now came in handy. Knowing the "court" was stacked against him, he tried several legal maneuvers to ensure a fair trial. First, he requested that Rev. B. I. Ives of the Oneida Conference, who was present, be permitted to assist him in his defense. But the bishop ruled it against the *Discipline* and "general usage" to have counsel from another conference. Well, Benjamin responded, would he then transfer Brother Ives to Genesee so he could serve? Bishop Janes responded, "Our authority [as bishop] to transfer grows out of our authority [to] make appointments. The Discipline does not authorize me to make appointments to act as counsel." Defeated on that point, Roberts asked Loren Stiles to assist with his defense.[19]

Knowing that ecclesiastical courts were not subject to the strict legal standards of civil courts, Roberts offered to have the matter tried as a civil case. If the com-

---

16. A reference to Chamberlayne's charges against McCreery in 1856.

17. *WAS*, p. 169. The charge is printed also in Chesbrough, *Defence,* pp. 9-10. This seventy-seven-page publication was based on "notes and testimony" that Chesbrough recorded during the trial. In reporting the trial Chesbrough said he "took it [testimony] down with care at the time it was given; and we have, also, compared it with the same testimony taken down by another, and found complete agreement" (p. 71).

18. Manuscript Minutes, 1858, p. 361.

19. Manuscript Minutes, 1858, pp. 361-62; *WAS*, p. 170.

plaint before the conference would be withdrawn, he said, he would be willing to take the matter to a law court where witnesses would be required to testify under oath and costs for damages could be assessed. The bishop refused to allow this request even to be entered into the minutes.[20]

Roberts then asked for a change of venue. This request was "unusual," he said, but not unreasonable, given the circumstances. Citing pertinent provisions in civil law, he asked that the bishop transfer him to the Oneida Conference to be tried there. Roberts elaborated,

> Such is the state of party feeling in this Conference, that a fair and impartial trial is entirely out of the question. It cannot be had. Men have ceased to act from the convictions of their own judgment; the voice of justice cannot be heard amid the clamor of partizan strife. The party opposed to me, by threatening to make disturbance, have obtained the control of four out of five of the districts; this has given them a clear majority in the Conference. Questions are not decided according to their merits, but according to their party bearings. The secret meetings keep them together; as the leaders go all go.[21]

Roberts said the outcome of the trial probably "had already been decided in the secret meetings of those who comprise a majority of the Conference. I know it will be denied; it has been repeatedly denied that my case was prejudged last year."

Roberts said, "I look upon this whole matter, last year and this, as a wanton persecution" intended to "cripple my influence to the fullest extent possible."

Roberts denied having anything to do with the Estes tract — though he tacitly admitted that he helped circulate it. He said the pamphlet

> was written and published without my knowledge or consent. It contains some things that I never approved of. It went into circulation without my agency. . . . If there is any crime involved in this circulation, most of the preachers in the Conference have been equally guilty with myself. I am willing to bear my own sins, but I do not consent to be made a scape-goat, to bear the sins of this Conference.
>
> Whoever I should be tried by, if at all, it certainly should not be by them. . . . It is time that a stop be put to these partizan prosecutions.[22]

No, said the bishop; there could be no transfer to another conference. "The Discipline makes every preacher responsible to his Conference for his moral and ministerial character and conduct," and "we cannot transfer men under charges of immorality."[23]

Benjamin was nothing if not persistent. He tried another tack, moving that the case be referred to a committee for investigation. Roberts cited a provision added to

---

20. Chesbrough, *Defence*, pp. 10-11. The minutes in fact do not record this request.
21. Chesbrough, *Defence*, p. 11. Chesbrough says he quotes Roberts "in substance."
22. Chesbrough, *Defence*, p. 12.
23. See *WAS*, p. 171.

the *Discipline* at the 1856 General Conference that permitted an annual conference to appoint a select committee to try a case, rather than having it heard by the whole conference.[24] He saw that the outcome was now inevitable, and he would prefer (he told the conference) to have the matter decided by such a small group "that its members would feel a personal responsibility for their action," even if the group consisted of his strongest opponents, rather than by the whole conference where preachers "could hide behind one another."[25] He added, "In large bodies reason and judgment often give place to party zeal and prejudice. I would rather be tried by a committee composed entirely of men of the opposite side, than by the Conference in its present condition. I would be willing to leave it to the presiding Elders, though all but one are opposed to us. I would have the trial go on now, in just as public a manner as though it were before the entire Conference."

In conclusion Roberts noted that it is "a well established principle, prevailing wherever the right of trial by jury prevails, that no one can sit as judge or juror in a case in which he is personally interested." No man should be a judge in his own case, Roberts argued, citing legal precedents. If this is the case in common law, "shall the plainest principles of justice be set aside in an Ecclesiastical investigation?" If the case is decided by the whole conference, Roberts argued, it will certainly be "by a party vote."[26]

This attempt also failed, though it kicked up some discussion. Fuller said a committee would be just as partisan as the conference — though Roberts admitted that; his point was personal responsibility, not impartiality. Alfred Kendall said, with some insight, "Can we do less than grant the request of Bro. Roberts? Nine or twelve old members would certainly give a more judicious and impartial verdict than the Conference, in the present state of party feeling."[27]

Old Samuel Luckey, well respected in the conference and the denomination generally, spoke in favor of sending the case to a committee. "It should have gone to one in the first place," he said. "It never ought to have been brought here in its present form." But H. Ryan Smith spoke against a committee trial. "I do not believe that a majority of this Conference can be brought to do wrong. Party lines are clearly drawn, yet I mean to do right."[28]

Now Thomas Carlton weighed in. "Reference has been made to secret meetings, and the trial of last year. I did not attend a *secret* meeting at LeRoy. We had *select*

24. Roberts referred specifically to part I, sect. 2, second paragraph of the answer to question 5: "But should the Conference, having jurisdiction in any of the foregoing cases, judge it expedient to try the accused by a select number, it may appoint not less than nine, nor more than fifteen of its members for that purpose who, in the presence of a bishop or a chairman which the President of the Conference shall appoint, and one or more of the Secretaries of the Conference, shall have full power to consider and determine the case according to the rules which govern annual conferences in such proceedings." *The Doctrines and Discipline of the Methodist Episcopal Church, 1856* (Cincinnati: Swormstedt and Poe, 1859), p. 93.

25. *WAS*, pp. 171-72.

26. Chesbrough, *Defence*, pp. 13-14.

27. Manuscript Minutes, 1858, p. 362; Chesbrough, *Defence*, p. 14.

28. Chesbrough, *Defence*, p. 14.

meetings, but there were no votes taken to condemn Bro. Roberts. The vote was that Bro. Roberts should have a fair trial. Reflections [i.e., negative charges] have been made upon this Conference. The trial should be public, in this Church. It should not go to a committee."[29]

Roberts insisted that he wanted a public trial, even if by committee. A committee would feel duty bound to pay careful attention to the evidence, but if the case is heard before the whole conference, "many of the members will, I fear, do as some did last year, be absent while the testimony is being taken, but be on hand to vote." (Chesbrough noted that this prediction was fulfilled; while witnesses were being examined, "some of the preachers were away in the woods gathering chestnuts, others were lounging about the door, and in the lecture room. But care was taken to have them present in time to vote.")[30]

As to secret meetings, Roberts said: "I am sorry to hear it repeatedly said by brethren of the other side, that they had no secret meetings at LeRoy. What do they mean? How can they hazard such assertions?" Someone had given him a copy of the September 3, 1857, meeting at LeRoy, quoted earlier, and Roberts now produced these minutes and read them before the conference. "Thus, it seems that secret meetings were really held," he said. "This secret Conclave assumed to act in a judicial manner upon the cases of absent brethren. The promise to give them 'a fair trial,' means the same as the promise of the [U.S.] Administration to give the people of Kansas a fair election, under border ruffian sway. What right had this Conclave to say that any Brother should have a trial at all?"

Such dealings make a fair trial impossible, Roberts argued.

C. D. Burlingham supported Roberts; "fifteen impartial men can be found," he said. He had been "astounded" after the 1857 conference to learn of the secret meetings held there. "The provision of the discipline, authorizing a committee, was made . . . for the very purpose of meeting such cases," he said. "The Conference should grant the request." Sam Church concurred. "Bro. Roberts has been tried by us once; he feels afflicted about that trial. Let us grant his request."[31]

The preachers voted 48 to 39 against trial by committee, however. Roberts's request was denied.[32]

Following these maneuvers, the conference adjourned for the day. The next day, Thursday, was taken up mostly with other business, including the ordination of Francis Burns, an African American, as the first bishop of the Liberia Annual Conference. Both Bishop Janes and Bishop Baker participated in the ordination.[33]

The conference took up Roberts's case again the next morning (Friday, October

---

29. Chesbrough, *Defence*, p. 14 (italics added to bring out what was probably Carlton's meaning).

30. Chesbrough, *Defence*, pp. 14-15.

31. Chesbrough, *Defence*, pp. 15-16.

32. Chesbrough, *Defence*, p. 16.

33. Manuscript Minutes, 1858, pp. 363-64; *COM*, pp. 147-48. Burns had gone as a Methodist Episcopal missionary to Liberia, and in January 1858 the Liberia Annual Conference elected him as their first bishop. Burns returned to the United States for his episcopal ordination.

15), following other business. As the trial progressed, Ellen wrote, "Not a nerve moves. If we are turned out I'll not shrink a hair's-breadth from suffering His will."[34] Roberts immediately filed two objections, for the record:

1. I object to any member of this Conference sitting as Juror upon this trial, who feels himself personally involved or in his individual character libeled by the article complained of.
2. I object to any person sitting upon this trial as Juror, who has taken any action, or participated in any action upon the case, in any secret or public meeting, or who has expressed an opinion in regard to the merits of the case.
   [Signed] B. T. Roberts

These "exceptions" were duly copied into the conference minutes.[35] Bishop Janes commented, "[W]hatever may be our convictions in the case, we judge we have no authority to say that any member of the Conference shall not sit or vote."[36]

The prosecution now began, led by Fuller. The prosecution defined "contumacy" as "stubbornness, with reference to submission to proper order or authority."[37] Fuller referred to the minutes of the 1857 conference where Roberts's trial and reprimand were recorded, and then introduced the Estes pamphlet into evidence. John Bowman and Loren Stiles were called as witnesses regarding the circulation of the tract. Roberts later noted that the prosecution made no effort to prove that the Estes pamphlet was slanderous or its charges untrue.[38] They focused rather on its publication and circulation.

Bowman testified that Roberts had indeed circulated the Estes pamphlet. Roberts said Bowman responded as follows when shown the pamphlet:

I have seen this document entitled, "New School Methodism," and "To whom it may concern," signed "Geo. W. Estes," before. I first saw it on the [railway] cars between Medina and Lockport. Brother Roberts presented it to me; several were presented in a package; there were, I think, three dozen. Brother Roberts desired me to leave a portion of them at Medina, conditionally. He requested me to circulate them; he desired me to leave a portion of them with Brother Codd, or Brother Williams of Medina, provided I fell in company with them. I put a question to him whether they were to be distributed gratuitously or sold. He said he would like to get enough to defray the expense of printing, but circulate them any how; he desired me not to make it known that he had any agency in the matter of circulating the document, if I could consistently keep it to myself.[39]

34. ELRD, Oct. 14 [i.e., 15?], 1858. The diary entry appears to refer to Friday the fifteenth, not Thursday the fourteenth.
35. Manuscript Minutes, 1858, p. 367. Cf. Chesbrough, *Defence*, p. 16.
36. Chesbrough, *Defence*, p. 16.
37. Chesbrough, *Defence*, p. 30.
38. *WAS*, p. 172.
39. *WAS*, pp. 173-74; Chesbrough, *Defence*, pp. 17-18.

The prosecution established that several of the numbered statements quoted in the "Specifications" (above) were indeed found in the Estes pamphlet (which wasn't hard to do). Fuller then "withdrew" items 6, 7, 10, and 11, which were essentially redundant, and the conference adjourned its morning session.[40]

When the conference reconvened at two o'clock, Fuller took further testimony from Stiles regarding Roberts's alleged "contumacy." With this, the prosecution rested its direct presentation of evidence.

Roberts's Defense

Benjamin now launched his own defense. His principal argument was that he was not responsible for the Estes pamphlet; that he had seen it only "some time after it was published"; that George Estes himself freely acknowledged sole responsibility for it.[41]

It was probably at this point that Roberts called upon Estes to testify.[42] The Brockport-area businessman and Methodist local preacher testified forthrightly that Roberts had not published, assisted in publishing, or helped defray the expense of producing the pamphlet. The reprinting of "New School Methodism" in the pamphlet was done without Roberts's knowledge or consent, and Roberts had nothing to do with those parts of the pamphlet written by Estes himself. So far as he knew, Estes said, Roberts was not even aware that the pamphlet was to be published.[43]

When Fuller saw he could not establish any direct link between Roberts and the Estes pamphlet, he shifted the argument by redefining a key term. The charges accused Roberts of "re-publishing, or assisting in the re-publishing and circulation" of "New School Methodism" in the form of the Estes pamphlet. Fuller now redefined "publish" to mean simply "to make public," and began to use the phrase "circulating, and thereby publishing." Roberts exposed this stratagem as a hole in the prosecution's case, a tacit admission that they could not prove a key point.[44]

In fact (according to Roberts), the prosecution brought the Brockport printer who produced the Estes pamphlet to Perry to testify, but when he stated that Roberts had nothing to do with the pamphlet, the prosecution did not call him as a witness.[45] Later in the trial Roberts noted that the printer had traveled to Perry "as quick as he could come, changing horses by the way, but, after being closeted with the counsel, was sent back, without being called upon the stand, or any intimation being given to us that he was present. I suppose they found out the facts in the case

---

40. Manuscript Minutes, 1858, pp. 367-68.

41. WAS, p. 168.

42. The manuscript minutes do not record that Estes testified, but it is clear from other accounts of the trial that he did. The minutes do not give a complete record of all who gave testimony.

43. Chesbrough, *Defence*, pp. 30-31, 48.

44. Chesbrough, *Defence*, p. 48.

45. WAS, p. 173.

— that I had nothing to do whatever, directly or indirectly, with publishing the pamphlet. But this makes no difference with them; they set their wits to work and called in the help of legal technicalities [i.e., redefining the term 'publish']."[46]

To rebut the charge of contumacy, Roberts called A. D. Wilbor (his presiding elder in the Genesee District), Samuel Hopkins (a young preacher assisting Asa Abell at Parma), and Samuel Smith (another young preacher, stationed at Scottsville). To further establish that he was not responsible for the Estes pamphlet, Roberts called several more witnesses — Joseph McCreery, Sandford Hunt, John Bowman, and James Fuller among them. With that, the conference adjourned for the day.[47]

The conference took up Roberts's case when it reconvened the next morning (Saturday) at eight o'clock. Following worship and the reading of the minutes, Roberts resumed his defense, calling more witnesses. First, however, Fuller requested that Thomas Carlton be appointed to assist him as counsel for the complainant, and this was granted by Bishop Janes.[48] It may be that Fuller found the case was getting more complicated than he had anticipated, and Carlton was the brains behind the whole affair.

Roberts called seven witnesses during the morning session, including the veteran Glezen Fillmore, Fuller (for the second time), and De Forest Parsons, who had chaired the secret Regency meetings the year before.[49] Under questioning by Roberts, Fuller acknowledged that at the 1856 conference he had said he would not serve under either Stiles or Kingsley and "heard others say what would amount to about the same."[50]

One of the witnesses was William C. Willing, and his cross-examination by Carlton brought one of the sharpest exchanges in the trial. Carlton's aim was to rebut the language in Estes's pamphlet.

Willing acknowledged that he had participated in the "select" meetings at both the 1856 and 1857 conferences. Carlton asked, "Did you ever hear in any of those meetings . . . any threats of proscription, or that of any being sent to starvation or hard appointments?"

Willing: "I heard nothing of the kind."
Carlton: "Were there any inquisitorial powers exercised in those meetings?"

Here Roberts objected. The question was improper, he said, because "if answered it would make the witness a judge of opinions, and not a narrator of facts. Let the witness tell what did take place, and then it will be for the Court to decide, and not for the witness, whether such action is 'inquisitorial' or not."

---

46. Chesbrough, *Defence*, p. 48.

47. Manuscript Minutes, 1858, pp. 369-70. At the close of this session Bowman, who may have been uneasy in conscience about his role in the trial, "requested leave of absence, but his request was not granted" (p. 370).

48. Manuscript Minutes, 1858, p. 370.

49. Manuscript Minutes, 1858, pp. 370-71.

50. Chesbrough, *Defence*, p. 23. It is not clear whether this testimony came at this point or earlier, but the context suggests it likely occurred here.

Carlton: "Mr. President: I insist that the question shall be answered. It is perfectly proper. We are charged with having exercised 'inquisitorial powers,' and we want the witness to say whether we did or not. If a man was charged with murder, it would be perfectly proper to ask the witness whether he saw the murder committed or not."

Roberts: "Mr. President: I am surprised to hear one occupying the position of the counsel, making such remarks. If a person were on trial for murder, the witness would be asked, not if he saw the murder committed, but what did he see done, that led to the death of the victim; and then it would be for the Court to determine whether such action constituted murder, manslaughter, or justifiable homicide."

Outdone, Carlton apparently withdrew the question.[51]

In his testimony Parsons admitted chairing the select meetings at LeRoy and acknowledged, in rather vague terms, that there had been some discussion about Kendall and Roberts. Stiles questioned Parsons and asked whether in these meetings most of the time was spent in "promoting the Spirituality of the Church, and the enforcement of the discipline," or in "other matters." Parsons replied evasively, "My judgment is, that as much of the time was spent in considering those things which pertain to the peace and prosperity of the Church, as when we are in Conference."[52]

At some point Roberts called on Carlton himself to testify.[53] Carlton acknowledged that he had attended three of the "select" meetings during the 1856 conference and some of the meetings at LeRoy the following year. "I should think there might have been 60 at one of those meetings, at another, about 40; they ranged from 30 to 60," he said.[54]

The Saturday afternoon and Monday sessions were taken up with other business, so Roberts's trial was not resumed until Tuesday morning, October 19. Roberts now asked that a delegation be sent to East Pike to take testimony regarding the ninth numbered item under the third specification — the issue of the Buffalo Regency and its secret meetings. Bishop Janes granted the request and the committee, consisting of Bowman, C. D. Brooks, and E. S. Furman, was excused to take the requested testimony.[55] Presumably this committee reported back later during the conference, but without any significant effect.

Meanwhile Roberts called three more witnesses — Alfred Kendall, Jesse Murdock, and C. D. Burlingham. Kendall testified that he had heard Gilbert De La Matyr, in a conversation some weeks before the 1857 annual conference, make "re-

---

51. Chesbrough, *Defence,* p. 20. Chesbrough records this exchange, noting at the end, "Question waived," apparently meaning that Carlton dropped the matter.

52. Chesbrough, *Defence,* pp. 20-21.

53. According to Chesbrough, *Defence,* p. 21. This is not clear from the manuscript minutes.

54. Chesbrough, *Defence,* p. 21.

55. Manuscript Minutes, 1858, pp. 378-79. This required traveling about fifteen miles southwest to East Pike.

marks about sacrificing, or expelling" Roberts and "some of his friends" who were "leading Nazarites." "I have always understood that he [De La Matyr] was identified with what is known as the Regency party; from his remarks I should conclude this to be the fact." But he admitted that he had no direct knowledge of "any organization, known as Buffalo Regency." He said that in this conversation remarks were made about "preachers holding meetings off from their own charges," and specifically about "meetings held by Bro. Roberts and others."[56]

Murdock, the next witness, was not a conference preacher but was a member of the Methodist church at West Carlton, Genesee District, where Albert Plumley was the preacher. Shortly before the last Bergen camp meeting, he said, Plumley had told him that "three or four would probably have to be turned out" of the conference, including Roberts and McCreery. Plumley thought that expelling Roberts and McCreery "would put a stop to the trouble."[57] (In the afternoon session Plumley corroborated this conversation but said he never stated that Roberts or others should be expelled; he said only that "we would not have peace until their removal" and "if that was the only thing that would settle our troubles, the sooner we were parted the better.")[58]

At this point Roberts rested his direct testimony, though reserving the right to later call witnesses who were then absent.[59]

The time had come for the prosecution to begin its rebuttal. Carlton (or perhaps Fuller; it is not clear who was prosecuting at this point) presented as testimony material on several pages of the conference journal (book of minutes). This material referred back to sessions before 1857 and was probably introduced to show that Roberts had long exhibited a pattern of "contumacy" or insubordination. Before the morning session ended the prosecution recalled Stiles for further testimony.[60]

Bishop Janes was again in the chair when conference reconvened at 3:00 P.M. After other business, Roberts's case was resumed. Carlton (or Fuller) continued the rebuttal, calling Wilbor and others to testify. The prosecution also introduced into evidence a document from the 1855 annual conference. Presumably this was McCreery's "Nazarite" pamphlet. Roberts admitted its "genuineness and authenticity."[61]

The prosecution now rested, "unless new matter should be introduced by the defense." Roberts then took up his rebuttal, calling William Barrett, the preacher at West Barre in the Niagara District, as a witness.[62] Barrett testified that at the 1856 conference he had seen the petition calling for the removal of Stiles and Kingsley as

56. Chesbrough, *Defence*, p. 22.
57. Chesbrough, *Defence*, p. 23.
58. Chesbrough, *Defence*, p. 25.
59. Manuscript Minutes, 1858, pp. 379-80.
60. Manuscript Minutes, 1858, p. 380. The material from the conference journal was introduced under the first specification, which was the accusation of contumacy.
61. Manuscript Minutes, 1858, p. 381.
62. Manuscript Minutes, 1858, p. 382.

presiding elders and understood its sense to be "that we would refuse to take work if Bros. Stiles and Kingsley were continued in the Presiding Elder's office."[63]

By this time it was late in the afternoon. The conference recessed and reconvened at 6:30.

In the evening session Roberts continued his defense. He argued that the statement quoted in the fifth point of the third specification, that his 1857 trial had been "marked by gross iniquity of proceedings," was in fact true. He introduced corroborating evidence and called on McCreery, J. P. Kent, and John W. Reddy as witnesses.[64] Kent testified that at his request he had received from Roberts a copy of the Estes pamphlet. Roberts "said he did not circulate them, but had no objection to my seeing the one that he had." Reddy corroborated Murdock's testimony that Albert Plumley had said there probably would be expulsions at the annual conference. "Bro. Plumley said he thought there would be a secession; that if two or three of the leading men upon the Nazarite side were expelled from Conference, a portion of the people would go with them."[65]

The conference reconvened the next morning, October 20, at eight o'clock — half an hour earlier than usual. It was now beginning its third week of deliberations. Nearly the whole morning and afternoon sessions were taken up with the trial. Roberts called three more witnesses — R. E. Thomas, Samuel C. Church, and E. S. Furman — before resting his case. Roberts was seeking to further document the political maneuverings against Kingsley and Stiles at the 1856 conference. At that conference John Bowman had spoken in support of Kingsley on the floor of the conference.[66] Church and others testified that Bowman later said a Regency preacher told him he "would rue it" if he didn't retract what he said about Kingsley. Church testified, "Bro. Bowman said to me that a certain member of the Conference, at the [1856] Medina session, said to him, that if he would go before the Conference and take back what he said in Bro. Kingsley's favor, he might expect fair weather or a pleasant time; if not, he could give him no assurance of what would take place."[67]

At some point Stiles, in defending Roberts, pointed out that probably a third to a half of the conference had a hand in circulating the Estes pamphlet, so it was unjust to bring this charge solely against Roberts. The prosecution replied disingenuously,

---

63. Chesbrough, *Defence*, p. 22.

64. Manuscript Minutes, 1858, pp. 382-83.

65. Chesbrough, *Defence*, pp. 18, 23.

66. John Bowman is a very interesting case. He seems to have wanted to keep on good terms with both sides but to have been manipulated and used by the Regency party. John Wesley Redfield wrote in a letter about 1858, "I learn that De Puy and Bowman are to emigrate to this country [Illinois] this year" (Terrill, *Redfield*, p. 344). Terrill adds the note, "Mr. Bowman, at a national camp meeting held subsequent to this, . . . confessed that his course in the Genesee Conference difficulties was wrong" (p. 344). Bowman in fact transferred to Upper Iowa in 1862 (Allen, *Century*, p. 72).

67. Chesbrough, *Defence*, p. 25. In his testimony Bowman was evasive, but admitted that someone came to him after his comments supporting Kingsley and said people "might get a wrong impression as to the efficiency of Br. Kingsley" from Bowman's remarks, and that "We should all suffer in common, in consequence of having an inefficient Presiding Elder." Chesbrough, *Defence*, p. 24.

"What have we to do with others? He is the man. The question is not, Have *others* circulated these documents? but, Has Bro. Roberts circulated them."[68]

Roberts now rested his case. From a comment that Roberts made later, it appears that the chair asked him to end his defense due to the already overextended length of the conference.[69]

The prosecution (Carlton, Fuller, or both) cross-examined four witnesses and then rested its case. This left only the final pleadings. Fuller made the plea for the prosecution, and the conference adjourned for the noon recess.[70]

Stiles's Defense of Roberts

When conference reconvened at 2:00 P.M., Loren Stiles, suffering from a severe cold, rose in Roberts's defense. He spoke at some length; his plea takes up thirteen pages of small print in Samuel Chesbrough's account of the trial. Stiles's address is the only major business recorded in the minutes of the afternoon session. Roberts later wrote, "My friend, Loren Stiles, assisted me most heartily" with the trial "and made an eloquent plea in my defense."[71]

Stiles's speech was indeed eloquent. He carefully reviewed all the charges, showing that none was proven. He complained that the charge of "unchristian and immoral conduct," "the highest grade of crime known in our ecclesiastical courts," was out of all proportion to the alleged offense and clearly was "calculated to reflect unfairly and unjustly" upon Roberts, whether or not he was found guilty.[72]

Stiles also pointed out the absurdity of charging Roberts with libel on the basis of statements in Estes's pamphlet that Roberts himself never made, published, or endorsed. "[W]e do not now and never have endorsed *all* the sentiments in the Estes pamphlet," he noted.[73] Stiles also mocked the prosecution for taking a long time to prove that there was no literal "Inquisition" in the conference (responding to Estes's statement that "No man is safe, who dares even whisper a word against this secret Inquisition in our midst"). "Well, who ever dreamed there was?" asked Stiles. Estes obviously was speaking figuratively, not literally. But who could deny "the spirit of Inquisition" in the conference when a presiding elder went "around with his little common-place book, picking up the little confidential whisperings, uttered in social chit-chat," and building a case out of them?[74]

---

68. According to Stiles, in his summation. Chesbrough, *Defence*, p. 40.

69. In his later summation Roberts said that had he "been permitted to go on," he would have presented further evidence. Chesbrough, *Defence*, p. 48.

70. Manuscript Minutes, 1858, pp. 384-85.

71. *WAS*, p. 172. Stiles's plea is published also in Elias Bowen, *History of the Origin of the Free Methodist Church* (Rochester, N.Y.: B. T. Roberts, 1871), pp. 57-82.

72. Chesbrough, *Defence*, pp. 29-30.

73. Chesbrough, *Defence*, p. 32.

74. Chesbrough, *Defence*, p. 33. Here Stiles refers to evidence brought to conference to bar the admission of a young ministerial candidate, not to the Roberts case itself.

Stiles also referred to Estes's remark about a certain "venerable D.D." who is "quite efficient in embarrassing effective preachers in their work and pleading them to hell for the crime of preaching and writing the truth." Without naming him, Stiles pointed out that at "Three successive Conferences at least, preceding the present," Dr. Israel Chamberlayne had "been chief agent in bringing 'Bills of Information' and 'Bills of Charges' against effective preachers," causing "no small embarrassment in the way of the effective" preachers "whose labors have year after year been followed by extensive revivals."[75]

Stiles also charged Roberts's opponents with deviousness in saying their clandestine meetings were only "select," not "secret." "These men have solemnly testified here . . . that they positively were not in any *secret* meetings, but that they were in *select* meetings." The evidence shows, Stiles said, "that these meetings bore all the essential characteristics and attributes of strictly secret meetings. Yet they were not *secret*, only *select* meetings! Here surely is a distinction without a difference." Stiles said that after the last annual conference one preacher "positively denied that the Regency men had had a single *secret* meeting." But an hour later another preacher Stiles met on the train home said he himself was in "a *secret* meeting of those men." Stiles wondered how the two statements could be reconciled. But the trial has made it clear, he said: "These were not *secret*, but only *select* meetings."

Stiles challenged the idea that these "select" meetings were innocent, informal times of prayer and discussion about how to promote the spiritual welfare of the church. All was done "in a business like manner." True, he said, "those of us who are uninitiated, cannot comprehend fully why a Chairman and Secretary should be necessary in a meeting for talking on the subject of holiness, or of prayers, or why these meetings should be held within closed doors, or why minutes of the same should be kept, . . . or why a door keeper should be necessary; and yet such is the evidence in the case."[76]

Stiles went out of his way to make it clear that though one of the witnesses had implicated the bishops — reportedly saying, "Those men must be sacrificed and they will be; I know the minds of the leading men in this Conference on this point, and also of the Bishops" — Roberts and Stiles believed the bishops were in no way involved, but had maintained strict impartiality. "If we had no other evidence of the impartiality of the Bishops in our Conference issues," Stiles said, "the total absence of the slightest appearance of favoritism" during the trial was sufficient proof.[77]

What about the so-called "evils of Nazaritism"? Stiles reiterated that there never was a Nazarite organization, but he also denied that those called Nazarites were fanatics. "We know positively that the charges of excesses and extravagances in religious devotions, imputed to [the so-called Nazarites], are absolutely and grossly

75. Chesbrough, *Defence*, pp. 35-36.
76. Chesbrough, *Defence*, p. 37.
77. Chesbrough, *Defence*, p. 38.

false and slanderous. . . . Talk about the *evils* of Nazaritism! Sir, the time has come among us, when evil is put for good, and good for evil."[78]

Roberts was singled out by the Regency, Stiles charged, "simply and solely, because he 'Has the boldness to question the supremacy in our Conference,' of this Buffalo Regency clique." Roberts got himself into difficulty "simply because he has the manliness, integrity and boldness to question the supremacy of, and hurl defiance at a secret power in our Conference, which marks every man as a victim who does not submit to its arbitrary rule."[79]

In summation, Stiles said: "There is not, then, as all must see, the slightest ground upon which to base a pretext for the conviction of the defendant; and his conviction under these circumstances would be an outrage on justice, scarce ever paralleled in the history of ecclesiastical jurisprudence." He warned that the trial's impact would reach far beyond the present moment: "It will be well for us to remember that whatever may be the action of this Conference in this case, that after we have passed upon it, it is to go before the tribunal of the Church and the world. Whatever may be our decision, their verdict will, doubtless, be that of acquittal. . . . The people are watching with intense interest our action in this case."

There was such extensive interest in the trial, Stiles said, "that its results upon the interests of our Church must inevitably be wide spread and lasting for good or evil."[80]

Stiles ended on a personal note.

Bro. Roberts is well known to be an ardent lover of, and zealous defender of, the Methodist Episcopal Church. From a special intimacy with him for years past, I know as but few others do, how deep and ardent are his attachments to our Church. I know he loves it as he loves his life, and is willing to suffer and die in its service. His labors in this Church of his choice have been remarkably blessed of the Lord, since he entered its ministry. Wherever he has labored, God has given him seals of his ministry, and favor with the people. The past year has been one of marked success in his ministry. The people expect and desire his return. It is well known that he has so endeared himself to the people of his several charges, as but few among us have ever done. To all appearances, as bright a future of usefulness and of ministerial success lies before him, if permitted to labor on uninterruptedly, as that of any man in our Conference. Now, can it be possible, with the evidences of the innocency of the defendant which we have before us, that we, as a Conference, shall dare in any way, to peril his career of usefulness, by pronouncing Conference censure upon him, for a single act, even if said act be admitted to have transpired, of which, if he be blameworthy at all, he only stands in equal condemnation with, perhaps, half of the members of this Conference? If from the evidences and the facts in the case we now have before us, Benjamin T. Roberts is

78. Chesbrough, *Defence*, p. 39.
79. Chesbrough, *Defence*, p. 40. Stiles is referring here to the language in the Estes pamphlet.
80. Chesbrough, *Defence*, p. 41.

worthy of Conference censure in any degree, then, we ask, emphatically, where is the man among us who is guiltless? "Let him who is without sin cast the first stone."[81]

With that, Stiles sat down. The reaction of the audience is not recorded, but the conference soon adjourned its afternoon session. All that remained now was Roberts's and Fuller's final pleas.

The evening session began at 6:30. After some other business Roberts made his closing plea. "God was with him," Ellen recorded. "There was conviction of his innocence all through the house."[82] Chesbrough records the substance of Roberts's plea in a twelve-page summary.[83]

Roberts began by thanking Bishop Janes for his fairness. "Whatever the result may be, I shall always cherish for you, sir, the liveliest feelings of gratitude for the kindness you have manifested to me personally."[84]

Addressing the "Fathers and brethren of the Conference," Benjamin first expressed his disappointment that the trial had not been referred to a committee. But he reminded all the preachers that "the same responsibility rests upon you personally" that would were each one deciding the case alone.

Roberts explained that he and Stiles had called so many witnesses and gone into such detail not just as a matter of defense, "but because we would have your eyes open to the state of things" in the conference. Roberts was concerned that many preachers, unaware of the political maneuverings, might innocently side with the Regency party. Therefore, "For their sakes we have opened the secret chambers of iniquity, and permitted you to see men professing godliness — the accredited ministers of Jesus Christ — plotting under the pledge of secrecy, and in the guise of devotion to the Church, the overthrow of their unsuspecting brethren."[85]

Roberts pointed out:

This trial grows out of the one of last year. I am charged with "contumacy," in disregarding the action of this Conference at its last session. I do not know in what way I disregarded its action. When friends came in the dead of the night and informed me of the action of the Conference in my case, I arose from my couch, put on my apparel and repaired with all haste to the Conference room, and received, with resignation, the reproof that the Bishop was directed to administer. If there was any admonition to pursue a better course in the future, I am sure I never heard of it until this present trial commenced. I was not present when the vote was taken, but I have enquired of several reliable brethren who were, and they think there was no such addition to the reproof. But it so stands upon the Journal,

81. Chesbrough, *Defence*, p. 41. Here again Stiles is tacitly admitting that Roberts may have to a limited degree helped circulate the Estes pamphlet.

82. ELRD, Oct. 20, 1858.

83. Roberts's plea is published also in Bowen, *History*, pp. 82-105.

84. Chesbrough, *Defence*, p. 43.

85. Chesbrough, *Defence*, pp. 43-44.

and such we must presume to be the action of the Conference.[86] But be that as it may, I have honestly endeavored to do better than I have ever done before. I have tried to be instant in season and out of season, always abounding in the work of the Lord. I have gone, "not only to those who wanted me, but to those who wanted me most" [here quoting Wesley]. The Lord has been pleased to own my unworthy, though sincere efforts, to promote His cause, to a greater degree than in any former period of my ministry. He has permitted me to see many souls rejoice in a present, free and full salvation, who one year ago were walking in the ways of sin and death. I believe in growing in grace; and it appears to me that I have grown in grace the past year; and if spared I will endeavor to in the year to come.

If the want of a cordial acquiescence in the justice of the decision of last year be contumacy, then I am contumacious. I always felt that that trial was a farce, and that decision an outrage. Fifty-two men voted me guilty of "immoral and unchristian conduct," when I knew I was not guilty. Galileo was once compelled by a council that claimed as much wisdom and infallibility as this body of ministers can, to retract his statement that the earth moved instead of the sun. But after his retraction, he was heard to say in an under tone, "but the earth does move after all." Their saying that our planet stands still, did not make it so. Voting a man immoral, does not render him immoral. . . . Nor could I ever persuade myself that those who voted me guilty of immorality, in reality believed this to be the case. I made no retraction nor apology. No effort was put forth to explain away the force of what I had written. I constantly affirmed that I believed it to be true, and I offered to prove it if a fair chance was given me; yet these same men who voted me guilty of immorality, voted to pass my character, and sent me forth to preach the Gospel. I must believe then, *that they voted me guilty when they did not believe this to be the case; or, it is their deliberate judgment, expressed in the most solemn manner, that immorality does not unfit a man for being a Minister of Jesus Christ.*[87]

In reporting these remarks by Roberts, Sam Chesbrough inserts a footnote: "The man who figures most conspicuously in the prosecutions against Mr. Roberts said last year, after he had put forth the most strenuous exertions to convict him of immorality, 'I believe if there is a good man in the Conference that enjoys Religion, it is Bro. Roberts.'"[88] Presumably Chesbrough is referring to James Fuller, though he could possibly have meant Chamberlayne or Carlton.

Roberts went on to defend his "New School Methodism" article, "the ostensible cause of the trial last year; as also of the present one." The article was published in good faith, he said, as a response to various Regency preachers who "from time to time" had

---

86. It seems likely that the words "and cautioned to observe a better course in the future" were part of the motion, as recorded (presumably by Fuller) in the minutes, but that Bishop Baker did not use these words in giving his reprimand — even though the minutes say Baker reprimanded Roberts "in accordance with the above motion." Chesbrough adds here a footnote: "The Secretary is one of the strongest partisans of the Regency faction in the Conference" (Chesbrough, *Defence*, p. 44).

87. Chesbrough, *Defence*, pp. 44-45.

88. Chesbrough, *Defence*, p. 44.

published "very unfair accounts" of the division in the Genesee Conference. There had been no reply to these articles, so that "Many began to think they must be true, or a contrary statement would be made." Roberts felt he had to set the record straight.

> I found in *"The Advocate"* of the Buffalo Regency two articles written by the literary champion of the party, on the doctrines which constitute, as I believe, the real issue in this Conference. I waited some six or eight weeks and no one expressed a dissent from the views thus publicly put forth: on the contrary, I heard that the articles were endorsed by leading men of the party. I thought, then, that I should be treating them with greater fairness by giving their views in the language of one of their own writers than in any other way; I quoted a paragraph at the time and showed wherein we differed.[89]

Roberts first showed his "New School Methodism" article to Asa Abell, Edwin S. Furman, and John Bowman, Benjamin said, all of whom judged it "a just statement of the differences" in the conference.[90] He saw nothing amiss in the article, and still felt his condemnation at the 1857 annual conference was totally unjustified. "If it be a sin to question the righteousness of a verdict bringing me in guilty of 'immoral and unchristian conduct,' for publishing what was never published — a verdict agreed upon in the secret conclave of an opposing party — I trust it is not a mortal sin. Ever since that verdict was rendered, I have thought that it was utterly wrong and wicked, admitting of no apology or palliation."[91]

Here Roberts is referring to material in the Estes pamphlet for which he was in no way responsible. The material Estes appended to the extract from "New School Methodism," he said, "contains some things that I never approved of, and which I have always regretted were ever published." He added, "The opposing counsel has labored earnestly to give the term 'publishing' the technical signification of 'making public,' using many times the phrase 'circulating, and thereby publishing.' But this, I am certain is not the sense in which the term was used when the charges were framed. They expected to prove that I had something to do, in some way, with publishing the document, that is, in issuing it from the press."

Thus, said Roberts, the only remaining basis for conviction was the alleged circulation of the Estes pamphlet. Had he been permitted to continue, he would have shown that "there are but few preachers in the Conference, that have not circulated it more or less."

Roberts pointed out that he had tried unsuccessfully to clear his name over the course of the conference year.

> The Buffalo *Advocate,* and the *Christian Advocate and Journal,* have published to the world, that I was found guilty of "immoral and unchristian conduct;" and,

89. Chesbrough, *Defence,* p. 45.
90. Chesbrough, *Defence,* p. 45. Chesbrough adds a footnote (perhaps by Roberts) indicating that John Bowman "was well qualified to judge, having been identified with the Regency party."
91. Chesbrough, *Defence,* p. 48.

when a friend of mine sought to make an explanation, through the columns of the *Advocate and Journal,* he was refused permission. Could any thing be more natural than that I should desire to have my friends read the article for which I had been condemned, that they might judge for themselves, whether there was any thing that should occasion them to withdraw their confidence? It was, undoubtedly, a conviction of the propriety of this, that excited the unfounded suspicion that I had something to do with the republication of *New-School Methodism.*[92]

Roberts did not try to defend Estes's pamphlet. But he did point out that John Wesley himself had used strong, forthright language in defending the early Methodists when they were attacked. Here Roberts quoted several passages from Wesley's *Works.*

But had he in fact circulated the Estes pamphlet, as alleged? Roberts now turned to this issue directly. Even on this charge, he said, the evidence was "totally insufficient" to warrant a conviction. Benjamin reviewed the testimony of J. P. Kent, who said Roberts had told him he "did not circulate" the pamphlet, and of R. Wilcox, a local deacon in the Pekin church who testified that he never saw the pamphlet until he was on his way to conference. So, Roberts said, "This shows that I could not have been very industrious in circulating it."[93]

Roberts then dealt directly with Bowman's damaging testimony that he had received copies of the pamphlet from Roberts while both were traveling on the train. Roberts never directly denied that he had given copies of the pamphlet to Bowman, but he did show that extensive testimony during the trial cast great doubt on Bowman's credibility. "From [Bowman's] testimony, supposing it to be correct — and it is all there is to prove that I had any agency in the circulation of this 'document' — it does not appear that a single copy ever became public through my instrumentality," since Bowman testified that he never circulated the copies he was given. "The most that can be made of it is that I *once* made an attempt to circulate it, but was unsuccessful."[94]

In any case, Roberts argued, one witness was insufficient to convict. Church law is clear that "the testimony of two or more witnesses" is required. "In this case, there is the testimony of only one witness; and that has been impeached."[95]

Roberts also rejected the argument of the prosecution that since Roberts had gone "into the merits of the case, and showed that many things in the pamphlet are true, therefore he ought to be condemned," whether or not he actually circulated the pamphlet. "This is strange logic," Roberts declared. If convicted, he should be convicted according to the charge brought, not for something different.[96]

---

92. Chesbrough, *Defence,* p. 49.
93. Chesbrough, *Defence,* p. 51.
94. Chesbrough, *Defence,* p. 51.
95. Chesbrough, *Defence,* p. 53.
96. Chesbrough, *Defence,* p. 54. Chesbrough adds a footnote from Roberts: "Since the trial I learn that some who voted against me, attempted to rescue themselves on the ground that we attempted a

Roberts concluded his defense with these words:

Finally, brethren, allow me to say that I do not affect any indifference as to the results of this investigation. I have an ardent attachment for the Church of my
choice. I love her doctrines, her usages, and her aggressive spirit. If I have erred at
all, it has been occasioned by loving the Church too much, rather than too little.
Any departure from the landmarks of Methodism has awakened jealous solicitude, and called forth whatever influence I possessed, to persuade our people to
"ask for the old paths, that they might walk therein." It has been my offense not to
have labored altogether in vain. We have been favored by the Great Head of the
church, with revivals, deep and powerful, such as have given to our beloved Zion
her present position among the Churches of the Lord.

It would be our delight to continue to toil in the same blessed work, with
what little ability and energy the Lord has been pleased to endow us with. This,
above all others, is the service that I delight in, and to which I feel God has specially called and commissioned me from on high. I do not feel that my work is
done, nor my commission from the Lord revoked. I love the Methodist Episcopal
Church; no one has ever heard me say aught against her; and I should esteem it
my highest privilege to be permitted to put forth mightier efforts than I have ever
done, to build up her walls and enlarge her borders.

We are hastening to a great impartial tribunal, before which all actions must
pass in review, and all secrets be revealed. There the deliberations of this hour, and
the motives by which we are governed, will be disclosed before an assembled universe. Remember it is written: "With what judgment ye judge, ye shall be judged;
and with what measure ye mete, it shall be measured unto you again."[97]

Roberts's defense was now ended, and following his speech the session was adjourned. Ellen later reported that Israel Chamberlayne said Roberts's defense was (in
her words) "the most logical, finished, defence he ever heard," and that Roberts was
"the best debater in conference."[98] Benjamin felt that he had in fact made a thorough
and convincing defense.

The hour was still early, and there would have been time for the vote. But his opponents "did not dare to take the vote that evening" right after his final defense, he
said, for fear of losing. Instead, "they adjourned — held their secret meeting — and
worked their courage up to the point where they could come into Conference the

---

vindication of the statements of the pamphlet. They say if we had made no defence we would have
been acquitted. Yet these same men voted against us last year when we did not examine a single witness! . . . If this information be correct it would seem that I was convicted of 'unchristian and immoral
conduct,' not for 'publishing and circulating' the pamphlet, but for attempting to bring to light the secret doings of the Regency party!"

97. Chesbrough, *Defence*, pp. 54-55.

98. ELR to Titus and Sally Roberts, Nov. 1858 (exact date not given), quoted in BHR, *BTR*, p. 183.
"All say that they never saw anyone have a better spirit than he had in all he did at conference," she
added.

next morning" assured of a conviction.[99] Ellen wrote, similarly: "They did not dare to reply and take the vote that night but retired early, to strengthen themselves for the next morning."[100]

That night Ellen had a dream of sailing through a terrible storm in a boat laden with many people. In "the direction in which we were going it was calm, the sky so blue and the water so clear. There was another boat and it was going with all speed in the direction of the storm till it was lost to our sight in the fog, rain, and commotion. I thought we went ashore to wait until the storm had passed."[101]

The conference reconvened for its twenty-fifth session at 8:00 A.M. the next day (Thursday, October 21). Bishop Janes again presided.[102] Roberts's case was resumed, and the minutes note, "Bro. Roberts again briefly addressed the Conf. in his defence." Following this Fuller "made the closing plea in behalf of the Complainant." Ellen wrote, "Fuller made another harangue." Roberts left the sanctuary before the voting began. The time for decision had come.[103]

The conference voted that "the vote be taken by rising and being counted," and proceeded to vote on the three specifications against Roberts. The first specification was sustained, 62 to 29, and the other two by similar margins (61 to 29 and 62 to 27). Finally, the overall charge was voted upon and sustained by a vote of 62 to 32. For the second time, Benjamin Roberts stood convicted by his conference of "unchristian and immoral conduct."[104]

Fuller immediately moved that Roberts "be now expelled from the Conference and from the Methodist Episcopal Church." The motion carried, but by a smaller margin — 54 to 33. It is not clear how many preachers were present at this point, but, assuming some were present who did not vote, the number concurring to expel Roberts must have been just slightly over a majority.[105]

Benjamin was now called back before the conference. Bishop Janes instructed the secretary to read to him the minute of the action just taken. No doubt Benjamin was not surprised. But he immediately gave notice that he would appeal to the 1860 General Conference.[106]

Ellen reports,

99. *WAS,* p. 176.

100. ELRD, Oct. 20, 1858.

101. ELRD, Oct. 20, 1858 (slightly corrected). Carpenter, p. 66.

102. The minutes state, "Bishop Baker Janes in the Chair." Apparently both were present, and Baker, an expert in Methodist church law, may in fact have been present for much of Roberts's trial, though Janes presided.

103. Manuscript Minutes, 1858, p. 388; ELRD, Oct. 21, 1858; Carpenter, p. 66.

104. Manuscript Minutes, 1858, pp. 388-89. Years later Roberts wrote, "We were expelled on a charge of 'Unchristian and immoral conduct' for publishing an article which we proved that we never published. The specifications alleged that there were things in the article which are not in it. A tribunal governed by the principles of justice would have thrown the complaint out of court at once." [B. T. Roberts], "Holiness Sects," *EC* 47, no. 6 (June 1884): 187.

105. Manuscript Minutes, 1858, pp. 388-89.

106. Manuscript Minutes, 1858, p. 389.

Soon as the vote was taken the preachers and people who enjoyed salvation left the house [i.e., sanctuary] — some in silence, some in tears. I had not tears to shed though I had some strange feelings. It seemed as if we were turned out on a great common where the fences were all down and I had a lost feeling till Jesus told me he would be a pillar of cloud by day & fire by night.

We went to Brother Handley's to dinner [i.e., lunch] — and had a blessed season of prayer after dinner.[107]

That night when Ellen went to bed her feelings overwhelmed her. "I wept before the Lord."[108]

In the afternoon session Joseph McCreery's case was taken up. By this point Bishop Baker had resumed the chair. In a repeat of the Roberts case, H. Ryan Smith (then the preacher at Medina) charged McCreery with "unchristian and immoral conduct." Jason G. Miller was appointed to assist Smith. McCreery said he was ready, and the trial commenced. McCreery later wrote, "The defendant [McCreery] declined any counsel. He had not been summoned to his *real* trial which had been going on in secret for several nights past in the Odd Fellows Hall, in Perry, and did not think it worth while to trouble any one to act as counsel in a judicial farce."[109]

In his defense McCreery pointed out (as had Roberts and Stiles) that many conference preachers had a hand in circulating the Estes pamphlet. In fairness, "New School Methodism" needed to be circulated, he argued, to counter the one-sided reports of the 1857 trial that had appeared in the *Buffalo Christian Advocate.* When McCreery called Sandford Hunt to testify and asked him if he had seen the report of the 1857 trial in the *Buffalo Christian Advocate,* the prosecution objected, "We are not trying newspapers here."

No, McCreery replied. "But we are doing the next thing to it — we are trying a pamphlet." The biased report in the *Buffalo Christian Advocate* justified "pamphlet truth as an antidote." McCreery continued,

> The trial of Brother Roberts had become a notorious newspaper fact. The *Buffalo Advocate* had published *ex parte* reports, white-washing one side, and blackballing the other. And when it was asked, as it was concerning one guilty of something like the same crime, eighteen hundred years ago, "Why, what harm hath he done?" the only response of this organ of the Genesee Conference Sadducees was: *unchristian and immoral conduct!* On this text, furnished by a judicial trickery of the lowest grade, the changes were rung; while *the thing he did* was carefully kept out of sight. Truth demanded the re-publication of "New School Methodism," that people might know what sort of writing it was that was so criminal. And a justifiable curiosity demanded a faithful expose of the several Carltonian modes

107. ELRD, Oct. 21, 1858 (slightly corrected).
108. ELRD, Oct. 21, 1858.
109. *WAS,* p. 179.

of reasoning employed by the masters of this judicial ceremony, to bring the Conference to this strange verdict of *"Immorality,"* in the case.[110]

Though the prosecution's objection was sustained, McCreery had made his point.

McCreery's trial continued throughout the afternoon and was commenced again after supper. In the evening session Bishops Janes and Baker alternated in the chair. The meeting began with a devotional period led by Sheldon Baker. He read from Hebrews 12, including the passages, "Consider him who endured such opposition from sinful men, so that you will not grow weary and lose heart," and "See to it that no one misses the grace of God and that no bitter root grows up to cause trouble and defile many" (Heb. 12:3, 15 NIV). Ellen was present and reported that when Baker came to the sixteenth verse he "shut the book, evidently greatly confused — there was great uneasiness among the preachers while he was reading."[111]

McCreery's case was taken up, and the conference prepared to vote. Before the vote was taken, however, Chamberlayne asked to be excused from voting.

The conference voted, and the charge against McCreery was sustained by a 51 to 17 vote. McCreery was then expelled from the conference and church by a vote of 50 to 17. McCreery reported later that some 53 preachers "did not vote at all," so that out of a total of 120 preachers, less than half — just 50 — determined the outcome. It is not clear precisely how many preachers were present for this vote, or earlier for the vote against Roberts. The 53 nonvoting members mentioned by McCreery may have included some preachers who were not then present at conference. McCreery scored the "large number" of timid preachers, fearful of the political repercussions, "who would not vote wickedly, and dare[d] not vote righteously."[112]

Following the vote, McCreery was called in and the results read to him. Like Roberts, he gave notice that he would appeal to the next General Conference.[113] McCreery later wrote that the Regency preachers considered bringing charges also against Asa Abell, but that they couldn't muster enough support against this respected veteran. Thomas Carlton "was at the bottom of all this trickery," wrote McCreery, "all the while [remaining] as sober and solemn as a saint," but he "did not think it wise to attack [Abell] seriously." "The character of Bro. A. was merely arrested, slurred a little, and allowed to pass."[114]

As a countermove, Roberts had earlier brought charges against David Nichols. This case was still pending, so was now taken up by the conference. Since Roberts had now been expelled, Jason Miller presented the case. After the charge and specifications were read, the conference disposed of it by adopting the following resolution:

---

110. *WAS*, pp. 183-84.

111. ELRD, Oct. 22, 1858.

112. *WAS*, p. 185.

113. Roberts included an account of McCreery's trial in *WAS*, pp. 178-85.

114. *WAS*, p. 180. Asa Abell's character was passed on the next-to-last day of conference. Manuscript Minutes, 1858, p. 395.

Whereas Bro. T. Carlton and G. Fillmore have stated to this Conf. that the matters complained of against D. Nicholls [sic], were adjudicated, according to the rule of Discipline applicable to such cases, under the administration of Bro. Fillmore, Presiding Elder, more than six years since, — therefore

Resolved, that the Charge and Specification be not entertained.[115]

The conference held its final sessions on Friday, October 22. Bishop Baker presided. The case of Amos Hard now came before the body. Hard, sympathetic to Roberts, was in danger of being caught up in the anti-Nazarite tide. Someone had charged him with helping to circulate the Estes pamphlet. Hard denied this, disavowing "all the statements [in the tract] reflecting on the official action of the Conf. on the Christian and moral character of its members." With that the charges were withdrawn, his character passed, and he was "continued superannuated."[116] Ellen reported that the conference "disposed of Bro. Hard's case by getting him to confess a little — Oh, how I wanted then to be in his place. I'd have stood up like a man and died before I yielded a hair's breadth."[117]

Before the conference finally adjourned later in the day, after dark, it unanimously adopted a resolution thanking "the citizens of Perry and vicinity" for their hospitality during the "unusually protracted" conference.[118] As Benjamin left the conference Bishop Janes cordially shook his hand and said, "Do not be discouraged, Brother Roberts — there is a bright future before you yet."[119]

Benjamin and Ellen Roberts, Joseph McCreery, and a group of their friends and supporters held a brief service in the local Baptist church building later in the evening. The place was crowded, Ellen reported. Benjamin spoke and McCreery made a few remarks. Then the meeting adjourned, and at nine o'clock Benjamin and Ellen began the long journey home.[120]

Finally, after two and a half weeks, the 1858 annual sessions of the Genesee Conference were over. On balance, it is hard to conclude that Roberts's trial was anything other than a farce. It had all the trappings and procedure of a formal trial, and Roberts conducted his defense with great seriousness and considerable skill, drawing on his earlier legal training. He did his best, but he knew he would almost certainly be convicted. In a sense the trial was a charade, because it wasn't really about whether Roberts had republished "New School Methodism." It was really about his audacity in challenging the direction that the conference, in the sway of the Regency preachers, clearly was headed.

Some Genesee Conference preachers later justified Roberts's conviction on the basis that, even if Roberts was not actually guilty of the charges brought against him,

---

115. Manuscript Minutes, 1858, p. 394. A case against J. B. Wentworth brought by William Cooley was similarly disposed of.

116. Manuscript Minutes, 1858, p. 396.

117. ELRD, Oct. 22, 1858.

118. Manuscript Minutes, 1858, p. 398.

119. WAS, p. 186.

120. ELRD, Oct. 22, 1858; Carpenter, p. 67.

still he was a troublemaker who needed to be dealt with. According to C. D. Burlingham, some preachers had said: "Well, if the charges were not sustained by sufficient proof, the Conference served [Roberts and McCreery] right, for they are great agitators and promoters of disorder and fanaticism." "Why not try them for promoting disorder and fanaticism?" Burlingham asked. "Because the failure of such an effort to convict would have been the certain result."[121]

This point of view — that Roberts and McCreery were troublemakers and had to be disposed of in one way or another — gives some credibility to McCreery's perspective on the trials. In his long retrospective letter to Roberts in 1879, McCreery argued that it was a mistake to have Loren Stiles defend Roberts. Stiles made a "poor and indiscreet defense" of Roberts, McCreery said, "chiefly deprecatory and apologetic." Stiles's defense may have been well reasoned, but reason wasn't what was called for. McCreery argued that if Asa Abell had been Roberts's counsel at the first trial in 1857 "and had stormed and raged, as at a campmeeting," Roberts "would have been acquitted. Those who did not vote at all would have voted and a proper verdict of acquittal would have been the result." What was needed was a stirring, emotional defense that would have roused the indifferent and the fence-sitters, giving them the courage to oppose the conference's political machine. "The timid and conciliatory members would have been carried on the side of truth and right, and the whole ultimate result of the matter would or might have been changed."[122] An acquittal in 1857 would have meant no trial the following year.

McCreery had a point. Political machinations had predetermined the outcome of both the 1857 and 1858 trials. The rational arguments raised in Roberts's defense were thus largely pointless. In 1857 Roberts was convicted by less than half the preachers, due to absences and abstentions. An emotional camp meeting–like defense of Roberts in 1857 might well have so aroused timid or uncertain preachers that they would have come to his defense. It would have stirred up the crowd of church members sitting in on the conference sessions, adding to the pressure to oppose conference politics. But now, of course, with the 1858 trial, the deed was done; Roberts was expelled; the what-ifs were pointless.

Roberts himself, reflecting on his trial and expulsion twenty years later, wrote: "In looking back upon the action of the Conference, I can account for it only on the theory that the leaders of the so called Regency party did not feel safe as long as we remained in the Conference." Roberts was reasonably popular among the preachers and "on good terms socially" with them all, he said.[123] But he had the audacity to challenge the power structure of the conference.

---

121. Pelatiah [Charles D. Burlingham], *An Outline History of the Genesee Conference Difficulties: Their Nature, Origin, Causes, Influence and Remedy* (n.p., 1860), pp. 40-41; *WAS*, p. 177.

122. Joseph McCreery (Alma City, Nebr.) to BTR, Aug. 7, 1879. McCreery saw Stiles as a compromiser and man-pleaser who in the end did more harm than good. Speaking of Stiles and some other preachers, McCreery asserted, "It was a defection in our own ranks that took us unawares, and nothing but the power of God among the laity saved the cause."

123. *WAS*, pp. 177-78.

Roberts was trying to turn back the tide of change in the church, and his opponents considered him enough of a threat that he must be stopped. It is a tribute to his influence and effectiveness that people like Fuller and Carlton felt they must mount a concerted attack against him. Roberts was a persuasive writer and an effective revivalist, and the combination of his writings and the growing influence of the Bergen camp meeting signaled potential trouble.

In a sense, Roberts's opponents were right. It is not fanciful to think that if Roberts, Stiles, Kingsley, and men like them had not been stopped, the drift of the Genesee Conference might have been reversed and Methodism in the area might have regained its earlier movemental dynamic — a movement "preaching the gospel to the poor" and "spreading Scriptural holiness" throughout the region, perhaps effectively reaching the new immigrant populations in the growing cities.

Sociologists Roger Finke and Rodney Stark argue in *The Churching of America* that Roberts's protest was essentially on target. Roberts was "entirely correct that the Methodists [of his time] were no longer the church of the Wesleys or of Bishop Asbury," and also that "the glory of the Methodist 'miracle' was not based on appealing to the 'proud and fashionable'" but on reaching the poor. However, Finke and Stark believe Roberts "was wrong to suppose that he could generate a return to higher tension Methodism."[124] My view is that what Roberts set out to do was not impossible; it was not predestined to fail. On both sociological and spiritual grounds, one can imagine plausible scenarios in which he might have succeeded, and the energy of what was already an incipient movement (mislabeled "Nazaritism" by its opponents) conserved to the Methodist Episcopal Church.

Fallout from Roberts's Trial and Expulsion

When the annual sessions of the Genesee Conference ended late Friday, October 22, Benjamin Roberts found himself without a church, without a denomination, without a ministerial assignment or income, and without a home. Fortunately, he and Ellen still owned the house in Buffalo they had bought five years earlier.

Benjamin and Ellen reached Pekin about 9:00 A.M. Saturday, after traveling most of the night and getting a few hours' rest at the home of some friends en route. Arriving back at the parsonage, Ellen was surprised to find that she felt more like laughing — "the laugh of an innocent child that has <u>no care</u>" — than like crying. "Jesus was with me," she said. "All day these words kept ringing in my ears, 'Care of all the churches.' I do not know what it meant, but am sure it meant something."[125]

We can imagine the scene as Benjamin and Ellen arrived home at the Pekin parsonage that Saturday morning. The weary parents probably embraced Benson,

---

124. Roger Finke and Rodney Stark, *The Churching of America, 1776-1990: Winners and Losers in Our Religious Economy* (New Brunswick, N.J.: Rutgers University Press, 1992), pp. 150-53.

125. ELRD, Oct. 22, 1858 (slightly corrected).

Georgie, and Charles in turn as the boys excitedly danced around them. Benjamin slumped into a chair and told Mary the news, recounting the highlights of his trial. He and Ellen had immediate decisions to make, but Benjamin did not feel discouraged. George and Benson, at six and five, listening curiously, were barely old enough to understand what was going on. Benson had had his fifth birthday while Benjamin and Ellen were away at conference. Little Charles was only two.

Benjamin and Ellen attended services at Pekin the next day, Sunday. Because Benjamin had been ousted from the church, Brother Wilcox, probably one of the two local preachers at Pekin, led the service and preached. "The dear young converts' hearts were full of grief," Ellen wrote. During the general class meeting Benjamin spoke a few comforting words; "it was like pouring oil upon the troubled waters," said Ellen. "The Lord blessed me as I told them I felt it an honor to be the companion of the first minister turned out of conference for Christ's sake. After some other remarks I fell powerless."[126]

The next day Benjamin wrote his father, "It is perfectly wonderful how God sustained me at Perry. I am looking to Him still, and feel confident that He will cause good to come out of this affair, both to myself, to the church, and the world."[127]

But what should Roberts and McCreery do now? Benjamin later observed: "We were both [young], full of life, and energy, and anxious to save our own souls and as many others as we could. Neither of us had any thought of forming a new church — we had great love for Methodism, and unfaltering confidence in the integrity of the body as a whole. We did not doubt but that the General Conference would make matters right. But we did not like to stand idly waiting two long years. We took advice of men of age and experience, in whom we had confidence."[128]

Roberts was determined to remain in the Methodist Episcopal Church and continue his ministry. He hoped the 1860 General Conference would resolve the matter in his favor. He immediately asked William Reddy, a presiding elder in the Oneida Conference, for advice. Just a week after his expulsion he received an encouraging reply:

Dear Brother Roberts:

Let me freely speak to you. The General Conference will not be under such an inflammation as was the Genesee Conference, and I think they will judge righteous judgment. At all events, I am glad you exercise your rights and have appealed; and I am glad you appealed from last year's sentence, because this year's is founded on the last.[129]

But what should Benjamin do in the meantime? He could try to get back into the church by becoming a probationary member of a local congregation, perhaps at Pekin. But Reddy advised against this. Just "remain where you are until the appeal is

---

126. ELRD, Oct. 24, 1858.
127. BTR to TR, Oct. 25, 1858, quoted in BHR, *BTR*, p. 180.
128. *WAS*, pp. 185-86.
129. William Reddy to BTR, Oct. 29, 1858, quoted in *WAS*, p. 187.

decided," he suggested. Roberts was still under God's call to preach. "The Genesee Conference has said you should not preach under their authority; but you have not lost your Christian character" nor forfeited your "commission from God," he wrote. Reddy added,

> I would then go on and *preach* and labor for souls, and promote the work of the Lord, under the *avowed declaration* that you do it, not as by the authority of the M.E. Church, but by virtue of your divine call. Then, whoever invites your labor or comes to hear you, they alone are responsible. You violate no church order, for you are not now under church authority. You are simply God's messenger. I would not exercise the functions of a *minister,* for that implies church authority and order, and that you have not. I would not officiate at meetings nor administer the sacraments, *as a minister.* But I would preach because God calls — I would receive the sacrament of the supper, if invited and *permitted,* because *Christ commands. . . .* This very course, I doubt not, will increase sympathy for you, and *increase your influence,* and if you are restored, will put you on higher ground than ever. Meantime I would avoid reference as far as possible to your *opposers* and oppressors, as though you were fighting *them. . . .*
>
> I do not see why you may not, in that way, promote the work of real *holiness,* and the salvation of sinners. Go where you are invited, and where the door opens, *not in the name of the M.E. Church,* but simply as *a man of God to preach the Gospel.* Who shall forbid your doing this?
>
> But keep yourself from appearing to set yourself in array against the authority and order of the M.E. Church, *while you claim the constitutional rights* of an expelled member. I believe God will bring you out like gold, tried in the fire.[130]

Amos Hard, however, reported to Benjamin that during the conference sessions he had asked Bishop Janes whether it would invalidate an expelled member's appeal to the General Conference if he joined the ME Church on probation. Bishop Janes replied, "I do not think it would."[131]

On November 2, the day after receiving Reddy's letter, Benjamin wrote his father, "I wish to act safely, judiciously; and if I take a little time to make up my mind what to do, it will be better than to make a misstep. I am seeking the wisdom that comes from above."[132]

By the end of the week, however, Benjamin had made up his mind. Taking the advice of several friends, he decided to rejoin the church as a probationary member at Pekin. So the next Sunday, November 7, he again became a member of the Methodist Episcopal Church.[133] The Pekin brothers and sisters received him

---

130. Reddy to BTR, Oct. 29, 1858, quoted in *WAS,* pp. 187-89.

131. *WAS,* p. 186; Zahniser, p. 118.

132. BTR to TR, Nov. 2, 1858, quoted in BHR, *BTR,* p. 182.

133. Ellen records, "Benjamin joined the church here last Sabbath, the first Sunday Brother Burlingham was here, and they voted almost unanimously to give him license to exhort." ELR to TR, Nov. 13, 1858, quoted in BHR, *BTR,* p. 185.

gladly, and the newly assigned preacher, C. D. Burlingham, promptly gave Roberts an exhorter's license.[134] Ellen, however, had doubts. Benjamin's rejoining the church "seemed like child's-play to me," she wrote. "I doubt whether the Lord was pleased with it."[135]

Joseph McCreery took a similar course, joining on probation at Spencerport. Roberts thought these steps would offer some protection to other Methodist preachers who might invite him or McCreery to speak in their churches. "Our holding a relation to the church would, it was thought, shield them from censure."[136]

In his defense, Roberts cited a ruling by Bishop Osman Baker: "When a member or preacher has been expelled, according to due form of discipline, he can not afterward enjoy the privileges of society and sacrament, in our church, without contrition, confession, and satisfactory reformation; but if, however, the society become convinced of the *innocence* of the expelled member, he may again be received on trial, without confession."[137]

Roberts was here quoting exactly from Bishop Baker's 1855 *Guide-Book in the Administration of the Discipline of the Methodist Episcopal Church*, so he was on solid ecclesiastical ground in rejoining the church as a probationary member — though Baker revised the wording in his 1862 edition![138] Roberts being immediately granted an exhorter's license is more questionable, however, if understandable under the cir-

---

134. The Methodist *Discipline* specified that one of the duties of a preacher "in charge of circuits or stations" was "To license such persons as he may judge proper to officiate as exhorters in the Church, provided no person shall be so licensed without the consent of the leaders' meeting, or of the class of which he is a member, where no leaders' meeting is held; and the exhorters so authorized shall be subject to the annual examination of character in the Quarterly Conference, and have their license annually renewed by the Presiding Elder, or the preacher having the charge, if approved by the Quarterly Conference." Matthew Simpson noted in his *Cyclopaedia of Methodism* that "The duties and privileges of an exhorter are to hold meetings for prayer and exhortation whenever an opportunity is afforded, subject to the direction of the preacher in charge," and that the office "also furnishes a sort of probation to the ministry, by preparing the way for the more efficient discharge of its functions" (*COM*, p. 352). Obviously the exhorter's license was never intended as authorization to serve as a preacher and evangelist throughout the church, as Roberts was doing. But in his unique circumstances, this was the only official step open to him.

135. ELRD, Nov. 7, 1858. B. T. should have listened to his wife. In hindsight, he probably would have been wiser to wait until his case had been acted upon by General Conference.

136. *WAS*, p. 189.

137. *WAS*, p. 189.

138. Osman C. Baker, *A Guide-Book in the Administration of the Discipline of the Methodist Episcopal Church* (New York: Carlton and Phillips, 1855), p. 159. Significantly, in his 1862 revised edition Baker has "convinced of the *innocence* of an expelled lay member" — the words "the expelled member" being changed to "an expelled lay member," thus implicitly excluding a case such as Roberts's, involving a preacher (Osman C. Baker, *A Guide-Book in the Administration of the Discipline of the Methodist Episcopal Church*, rev. ed. [New York: Carlton and Porter, 1862], p. 170, italics in original). This change presumably reflects Roberts's case and its disposition at the 1860 General Conference. The implication would be that whereas "an expelled lay member" might properly be received again into membership by a local congregation that was convinced of his/her innocence, an expelled preacher could not be.

cumstances. Normally such a license would be given to a full member, not a probationer. Though the Methodist *Discipline* did not specify that exhorters had to be full
members, this apparently was generally assumed.[139] In fact, in Bishop Baker's
Guide-Book it was explicit: "No person can be licensed as an exhorter who is not a
member in full connexion."[140] Since this stipulation is in the *Guide-Book,* not in the
Discipline, Burlingham and the Pekin society were not technically in violation of the
Discipline in giving Roberts an exhorter's license. But they took a step that inevitably
would raise questions.

Roberts, however, now felt free to preach wherever doors were opened. He and
McCreery "went out," Benjamin said, "holding meetings as providence opened the
way. There was a deep, religious interest wherever we went, and many, we trust, were
converted, and many believers sanctified wholly, and the people generally awakened
to a sense of their eternal interests."[141]

Benjamin and Ellen now began a new, liminal phase in their ministry and life
together. For almost two years Benjamin would function as evangelist-at-large, a reformer seeking to find his place and platform of ministry.

The Roberts family moved out of the Pekin parsonage on Saturday, November 6
— feeling, Ellen said, "that we were indeed pilgrims and sojourners." Isaac
Chesbrough invited them to stay with him and his family temporarily. "[We] do not
yet see where the Lord would have us go," wrote Ellen.[142] "Our goods are in Brother
Chesbro's barn, and our little family scattered around among the people. . . . If we
knew where to go, we have no furniture, and as yet nothing to buy any with."[143]

Ellen found it something of a trial to live temporarily with the Chesbroughs, as
there was little opportunity for ministry. However, she accompanied others to a
meeting at the nearby schoolhouse on a cold Friday night, November 12. At first she
had a "dull time" at the meeting, but then "the Spirit began to come and I prayed till
I lost my strength." She "rose & had a good time talking," feeling that God had spoken through her. Later at the Chesbroughs she and others had a prayer time that
went until 1:00 A.M. "[I]f the Lord ever helped me to pray he did in that hour," she
wrote in her diary. "Brother C. was never so melted before or so blessed. Sister C. was
greatly blessed, also Sis. H. How near Jesus came. A blessed time." Later, however,
when Ellen went to her room, she was conscience-stricken to discover that little
Charlie had fallen out of bed and onto the floor. "[T]he dear child had got out of bed

---

139. See *The Doctrines and Discipline of the Methodist Episcopal Church. 1856* (Cincinnati:
Swormstedt and Poe, 1859), p. 66.

140. Baker, *Guide-Book* (1855), pp. 71-72. The *Guide-Book* also specifies, "It is not contemplated
that an exhorter will attempt to preach," and that exhorters "should not hold meetings beyond the
limits of the charge which recommended their license, unless they go forth to break up new ground, or
are invited to another charge by the requisite authority of the Church."

141. *WAS,* p. 190.

142. ELRD, Nov. 5, 1858; Carpenter, p. 68; BHR, *BTR,* p. 184.

143. ELR to TR, Nov. 13, 1858, quoted in BHR, *BTR,* p. 184. (Benjamin and Ellen often abbreviated
"Chesbrough" as "Chesbro.")

& could not find his way back — he was very cold & seemed frightened," she wrote. "I felt at one time strongly drawn to go and see to him during the evening — I <u>ought</u> to have done so."[144]

Ellen was convinced that God was at work in the midst of all their trials. She wrote to Titus and Sally Roberts,

> I feel assured God has permitted [Benjamin's] enemies to push him out where he can do more for the cause of God than he has ever done, and if he follows on in the Divine order he will have a closer contest with the enemy — more glorious victory, more souls, and more scandal and reproach, but in the end a more abundant entrance, a brighter crown, and a place nearer the throne. Yes, I believe, my dear father and mother, we shall yet praise God to all eternity for this trial; and I believe souls now unsaved will praise God in eternity for the doings of this conference. A fire is being kindled that is going to burn on, a stone set in motion that will roll on.[145]

The next Sunday (November 14) was the quarterly meeting, held at Pekin. Benjamin was away, visiting the saints and speaking at Brockport and Albion, exercising his exhorter's license. At first Ellen wasn't sure she could or should attend the quarterly meeting, under the circumstances, but she felt God showed her she must. She would have to listen to a sermon by the presiding elder, Philo Woodworth, who apparently had voted with the majority to expel Roberts and McCreery.[146] Ellen decided that "to have grace patiently to endure him would be more acceptable in [God's] sight than to go elsewhere to meeting. I did not leave," she wrote, but "it was a trying sermon."[147]

Benjamin reported to Ellen that he had had a good time at Albion and Brockport, "exhorting the people." During the week Benjamin also visited the Methodist Book Room in Buffalo and there ran into two of the conference preachers, Brother Smith and Merrill Ripley. Benjamin told them he had rejoined the church and been given an exhorter's license, and was ready to hold protracted meetings if they wished to invite him.[148]

Friends at both Albion and Brockport offered lodging for the Roberts family, but Benjamin and Ellen were undecided. Ellen wrote in her diary, "We do not see yet where we are to live. Some say Brockport; some Albion; some Batavia, and they want

---

144. ELRD, Nov. 12, 1858 (slightly corrected).

145. ELR to TR, Nov. 13, 1858, quoted in BHR, *BTR,* p. 185.

146. Estes in his pamphlet listed Woodworth as one of those who had voted to convict Roberts in the 1857 trial. *WAS,* p. 164.

147. ELRD, Nov. 14, 1858.

148. ELR to TR, Nov. 13, 1858, quoted in BHR, *BTR,* p. 184. Ellen doesn't give Smith's first name, but most likely it was Griffin Smith. Of the three Smiths then under appointment in the Genesee Conference, Griffin Smith was the only one serving in the Buffalo District. He was assigned to the Riverside Church, Buffalo. Another possibility is Sumner C. Smith, then stationed at Warsaw, about forty miles east of Buffalo. *Minutes,* Genesee Conference, 1858.

us at Allegany — but I cannot see the Lord in either place. We have about concluded to stay in a part of Bro. C.'s [Chesbrough's] house until spring."[149]

Benjamin, Ellen, and the family did stay with the Chesbroughs awhile longer. Soon however Ellen began to experience some depression. "I feel . . . such desolation & sorrow of spirit as I cannot describe — and do not understand," she wrote.[150]

Before the end of November the Lord showed Benjamin and Ellen where they should go: Buffalo. "You cannot live among the pilgrims," God told her. "This had not occurred to me," Ellen reflected, but she said, "Thy will be done" — and instantly Buffalo came to mind. She wrote in her diary, "[God] said to me, 'There will be a terrible cross in living where I want you to,' and then B. [Buffalo] came up before me and my soul was at rest about where we must live — even though the cross rested heavily upon me. I said, 'How could we live there, we've nothing to live on,' and the answer came, 'the earth is the Lord's and the fulness thereof.' . . . Mr. R. feels much as I do about going to Buffalo to live."[151]

"Father" Isaac Chesbrough also concluded that God would have Benjamin and Ellen go to Buffalo, and they began to make plans accordingly.[152]

Meanwhile, doors of ministry began opening for Roberts. Ellen said of Benjamin,

> He seems, since conference, to be commissioned anew to preach the Gospel. He never had so many calls, and I think he never preached with so much of the Divine assistance. It seems to me that never since I have known him has he had so much of the Spirit of His Master as now, and it is wonderful how many friends that last conference has made him. It is, I know, all of the Lord. . . . I believe fully that the Lord was in his writing those articles which caused such commotion, and if there had not been truth in them they would not have raised the stir they did.[153]

As Benson Roberts noted, the effect of Roberts's and McCreery's expulsions "was not a loss of public confidence in the Christian character of the accused ministers, but rather an increase of their influence and an augmented desire to hear what manner of men these were." As word of the trials and expulsions filtered out, "a wave of indignation spread throughout [the Genesee Conference], reaching into adjacent conferences." Invitations came to join other conferences. Benson Roberts reports that Benjamin was invited to join the New York Conference and be appointed to the historic Sands Street Church in Brooklyn, "one of the most important in the city" with a membership of nearly five hundred and a large Sunday school. But Benjamin

149. ELRD, Nov. 16(?), 1858 (slightly corrected). Cf. Carpenter, p. 69. Carpenter adds, as part of this entry, "A home at Mount Holly, New Jersey, has been offered by Aunt Lydia." This sentence is not found in Ellen's diary, but Lydia Lane did make such an offer about this time (as noted in the next chapter).

150. ELRD, Nov. 19, 1858.

151. ELRD, Nov. 22, 1858 (slightly corrected).

152. BHR, *BTR*, p. 186.

153. ELR to Titus and Sally Roberts, Nov. 1859 (exact date not given). Quoted in BHR, *BTR*, p. 183.

felt it was his duty to remain in his home area, assisting those "who were fighting so nobly for vital godliness."[154]

Benjamin began speaking around the conference as invitations came. He preached at Brockport on Friday evening, November 26, and at Clarkson and Holley the following Monday and Tuesday nights. Ellen exhorted after Benjamin's sermon at Clarkson.[155]

Benson Roberts records that in the final months of 1858 Benjamin preached at Yates, Albion, Benton's Corners, Brockport, Clarkson, Sweden, Somerset, Charlottesville, Youngstown, County Line, Kendall, Holly, Gowanda, Collins, Allegany, Olean, Hinsdale, and Pekin, among other places. "Most of the traveling was with his own horse," Benson says, in spite of wintry weather and bad roads, though no doubt some travel was by train.[156]

No longer a Methodist Episcopal minister, Roberts went out and bought a copy of the *Daily Memorandum Book for 1859*, a pocket diary published by Francis and Loutrel in New York City, rather than using the standard Methodist pocket diary. Perhaps sensing the historical significance of this stage in his life, he became much more consistent in his diary entries.[157]

As Benjamin went about preaching, the Chesbroughs and others began organizing. A laymen's convention was called, to convene on December 1. By no means had the conference trials and expulsions put an end to the Nazarite issue. They merely stirred up a hornet's nest.

Retrospective: A Decade of Methodist Pastoral Ministry

B. T. Roberts's expulsion from the Methodist Episcopal Church in 1858 abruptly ended a decade of ministry as a Methodist itinerant preacher. He was twenty-five when he began his first appointment at Caryville in the fall of 1848, unmarried and fresh out of the university. In this ten-year period he served seven churches, all in the Genesee Conference.

The preceding chapters have told the story of these years of ministry, noting how Benjamin ministered, the challenges he faced, and how Ellen labored at his side. We have also noted the degree to which these churches grew during the time Roberts served them.

---

154. BHR, *BTR*, pp. 165-66. Popularly known as the Sands Street Church because of its location, this was actually the First Methodist Episcopal Church of Brooklyn, one of the larger churches in Methodism. It was, however, at this time in the New York East Conference, not the New York Conference. See *Minutes,* New York East Conference, 1857, 1858.

Had Roberts gone to another ME conference (and not run into ecclesiastical roadblocks in the process), conceivably there never would have been a Free Methodist Church, though by this time some kind of rupture in the Genesee Conference was probably inevitable.

155. ELRD, Nov. 26, 29, 30, 1858.

156. BHR, *BTR*, p. 187; Zahniser, p. 122.

157. BTRD, 1859, title page. I have not located any Roberts diaries for 1857 and 1858.

How successful was Roberts's preaching and pastoral ministry from a statistical standpoint? Without question many lives were transformed, stirring revivals were held, and members were added. Much of that success is impossible to evaluate statistically. However, it is possible to analyze the degree to which these churches grew during the years of Roberts's ministry.

Utilizing the annual published minutes of the Genesee Conference, we can draw some conclusions about the evangelistic effectiveness of Roberts's ministry in the Methodist Episcopal Church from 1848 to 1858. One way to do this is to create a hypothetical model of a church that Benjamin served for ten years. This can be done by averaging the statistics of the churches he actually served. The average size of the seven churches Roberts served was 163 when he began his one- or two-year ministry and 170 when he left. Roberts averaged 4.3 new members per year, or 6.1 per church. On average, the churches he served grew 6.6 percent per year.

Using these numbers, we can imagine Roberts being assigned to a church in 1848 with 163 members. If he served the same church for ten years (not possible, of course, in the Methodist system of his time), and the church sustained an average annual growth rate of 6.6 percent, the church would have had 310 members at the end of his decade of service. It would have grown 89.5 percent over the ten years. It would have not quite doubled, but would have doubled by the following year if Roberts's ministry continued and growth remained the same.

This is not dramatic growth, but it does indicate effective ministry. Most pastors today who saw their church grow from 163 to 310 members in ten years would feel they were reasonably successful.

Of course, membership statistics don't reveal, and sometimes mask, the level of real discipleship. And in Roberts's case, the statistics obscure his actual effectiveness since he often found the membership rolls inflated. If the "cleansing of the rolls" that Roberts had to do at Caryville, Pike, Rushford, and other places could be factored in, the growth of the churches he served would appear rather dramatic.[158]

This analysis is only illustrative, but it does give some idea of the degree to which the churches Benjamin served actually grew under his ministry. Membership statistics are an unreliable measure of church health, however, for several reasons — and particularly in the Methodist tradition of this period when the preacher changed every year or two. An incoming preacher might reap the benefits (statistically) of a revival under the previous pastor, or conversely find that the congregation had declined but the membership roll remained the same. Similarly, if a preacher had a particularly successful year, some of the results might not show up in the statistics until a year later (particularly in the category of full membership).

In sum, Roberts's ten-year ministry in the Methodist Episcopal Church was ef-

---

158. The actual initial base of members in most of the churches Roberts served was substantially less than the official number. Thus the real growth rate was considerably higher than the statistics show. Since we don't know how many names of inactive members were removed from the rolls of the various churches Roberts served, we can't calculate the effective growth rate.

fective statistically as well as in other ways. Lives were transformed and the church built up spiritually in each place he served. In addition, Benjamin had a growing ministry through the preaching he did elsewhere and through the growing body of articles he published.

CHAPTER 23

Laymen's Conventions

"They preach the doctrines of the Methodist church, as we used to hear them preached years ago; and through their instrumentality many have been made to rejoice in the enjoyment of a PRESENT AND FULL SALVATION.*"*

1858 Genesee Conference Laymen's Convention[1]

"We will not 'secede.' We are Methodists from conviction. . . . We say to our people everywhere, 'Cling to the Church.'"

B. T. Roberts, 1859[2]

Nearly two years passed from the time of B. T. Roberts's expulsion from the Methodist Episcopal Church in 1858 to the founding of the Free Methodist Church in 1860. This liminal period brought questions Benjamin and Ellen had never faced before. Where did they belong? Where did they fit? Having spent nearly all their lives within Methodism, they now faced an in-between time, without a church home and looking to an uncertain future.

One can see throughout this two-year period — and to some degree earlier — several distinct but interrelated dynamics at work within Genesee Conference Methodism that help clarify later outcomes. All these had their bearing upon Roberts, the "Nazarite" issue, and the eventual formation of the Free Methodist Church.

---

1. *The Proceedings of the Laymen's Convention of the M.E. Church, Genesee Conference, Held at Albion, December, 1858* (Buffalo: Commercial Advertiser Steam Press, 1859), p. 11.

2. B. T. Roberts, "Secession — Bishop Simpson," *NI* 4, no. 15 (Nov. 17, 1859). Cited in Marston, p. 234.

First was Methodist growth in the cities and the accompanying rising prosperity of urban Methodists. Many Methodists were rapidly accommodating to emerging middle-class values — what some have called Methodism's "embourgoisement."

A second key dynamic was slavery. Increasingly slavery was a live and agitated issue within American society generally. It was still unresolved within Methodism, despite the north-south split of 1844.

The other two issues were more internal to the Genesee Conference. One was the "Regency"/"Nazarite" split over secret societies, pew rental, and the proper role of revivals and of demonstrative worship. The other (fourth) dynamic was a growing socioeconomic and cultural cleavage between the cities (particularly Buffalo) and the rural and village areas where support for "old-line Methodism" was strongest. The Regency/Nazarite division was in part a city/rural split, as suggested by the epithet "Buffalo Regency." It was also to some degree a generational tension, reformers like Roberts, Stiles, and Kendall generally being relatively young and men like Carlton and Robie representing the next-older generation, men in their prime and in control.

Underlying these issues, and a contributing factor in ecclesiastical politics, was the growing institutionalization of the Methodist Episcopal Church. While growing denominational apparatus appeared to be a sign of denominational strength and success, this clergy-dominated institutionalization was in some tension with growing "lay" self-awareness in the church and the broader American cultural value of participatory democracy.

Meanwhile, events in the Genesee Conference left many Methodists scratching their heads. Lydia Lane, who dearly loved the Methodist Episcopal Church, was particularly puzzled. She wrote Ellen on October 28, 1858, just a week after Benjamin's trial:

> My ever very dearest Ellen
>
> How shall I begin to write this letter? One half [of what] I feel, <u>words</u> cannot convey to you. When I read of your sorrows and trials last evening the very depths of my soul were stirred, and the tears seemed to come up from my inmost heart. And when I prayed for you there was such an assurance that your case was noticed and cared for, by the Lord, as I cannot express. There seemed a sacredness in my grief about you, that I have not felt in any sorrow since my darling Sarah died. . . . I know how treachery and such deep-laid plots are almost always sure to prevail, and yet when it came, though I had feared the worst I found I had not really expected it. . . . I know there is danger of wrong feeling toward the Church, and you and Mr. R. will have to watch constantly over your own spirits in this time of sore trial, and so much I watch also. — It is dreadful to me, to harbor the thought that the Church is corrupt, and then the question comes up, what has Mr. Roberts done, that he should be so injured. I love the Church and feel we all owe much to the Church, and I have asked the question mentally[,] would the Bishops and all the Church turn against Mr. Roberts and suffer his usefulness to be hindered, and

himself and his family thrown upon the world without support, when he has tried to do good, and to build up the waste places of Zion. If that "fly sheet" was the trouble was it not before the world nearly two years since, and if Mr. Roberts was unfit to be in the Church why was the matter left for so long a time? and why was <u>he</u> chosen to preach bro. Kendall's funeral sermon, and that unanimously, if he was so unfit even for Church membership.

Lydia felt Ellen and Benjamin's duty was "very plain, in one sense" — to leave their opponents alone "to contend among themselves, and follow the Lord fully," knowing that he would "fight for you." Lydia added,

> I am very glad if <u>Bishop Janes</u>, acted honorably toward Mr. Roberts, I thought you had always supposed he was secretly working in favor of the other side. I hope he was all that he professed to be, and I have no reason to suppose he was not. . . .
> . . . If it was any inducement I would urge you to go and take possession of our house in Mount Holly. Every thing in the way of furniture is there and you might, be very comfortable if you had any kind of business there to make it desirable. But I fear (because I do not want to part with you) that you will go away <u>West</u> where I shall never see you again. . . . I feel so glad that Mr. Roberts' Father stands so firmly by him in this trial.

Lydia's advice to Benjamin and Ellen was: "Cleave to the Church though it has smitten you. Mr. Roberts must come back, and stand again on Zion's walls, and there do battle for God and souls. Let him not think of an independent organization, this will do harm. Let him quietly wait, and see the salvation of God."[3]

No doubt this was good advice, but it was not in Roberts's nature to wait (humbly or otherwise). He was an activist, with a strong sense of the duty to preach. Though he was of course waiting for the 1860 Methodist General Conference to resolve his case, these two years were filled with active ministry.

As her letter shows, Lydia Lane was frankly puzzled that the church she loved could take such action. Zahniser wrote, "Mrs. Lane felt keenly the struggle between loyalty to the organization" and loyalty to Benjamin and Ellen, "hardly supposing that the Church with its bishops could go wrong, and yet wondering from what she knew of the problem why such an action would be taken." Zahniser added, "This is the initial quandary" anyone faces "in weighing the evidence presented by both sides of the controversy. If one reads the *Northern Independent,* it was an 'inquisition;' if one reads the *Northern Christian Advocate,* it was a matter of necessary church administration."[4]

If Lydia Lane was mystified at the Genesee Conference's action in expelling Roberts, so were many of the thirteen thousand Methodists scattered throughout the conference.[5] A good number who knew the situation intimately, like George

---

3. LBL to ELR, Oct. 28, 1858 (from Wilkes-Barre, Pa.).

4. Zahniser, p. 117.

5. At this time the Genesee Conference had a total membership of 12,907 (up 1,303 from the previous year), while the East Genesee Conference's total was 21,764.

Estes and Isaac and Samuel Chesbrough, were irate. Since as "laymen" they had no voice in conference affairs, a number of these loyal Methodists decided to take action themselves, calling a laymen's convention.

The Laymen's Convention at Albion

More than any other event, it was B. T. Roberts's expulsion from the Methodist Episcopal Church that led to the formation of the Free Methodist Church twenty-two months later. A key development was a series of laymen's conventions in 1858, 1859, and 1860. The first was held at Albion on December 1, 1858.

Though these conventions were triggered primarily by the Roberts and McCreery trials, they can also be seen as part of a broader "lay" movement within Methodism that was seeking increased participation of members and more democratic process in the church. Instituting "lay" representation in annual and general conferences was a particular focus. A number of Methodist Laymen's Conventions were held in various places during the 1850s.[6]

Calling the first Genesee Conference Laymen's Convention seems to have been "Father" Isaac Chesbrough's idea. He discussed the possibility with Roberts, C. D. Burlingham, and his son Samuel Chesbrough, all of whom concurred with the idea.[7] Isaac Chesbrough, Roberts noted, "was always ready to succor the distressed, to encourage the desponding, and to stand by the oppressed. He saw quickly through mere pretensions, abhorred hypocrisy and shams, and was not afraid to act up to his convictions."[8]

Though responding to his own sense of outrage and injustice, Chesbrough was not alone in feeling that something must be done. Roberts noted, "These violent expulsions naturally created intense excitement all over the Conference. Articles upon the subject appeared in many of the papers, religious and secular, nearly all, except those written in the interests of the majority, condemning the action of the Conference. Quarterly conferences and official boards passed resolutions expressing their sense of the great wrong which had been committed."[9]

Chesbrough had no trouble getting signatures for the convention call. When printed up, the call bore the names of "over one hundred of the leading men of twenty-two circuits and stations" of the Genesee Conference. It is not clear what Roberts's role was; he may have helped circulate an initial draft of the call, collecting signatures. The convention was to be held Wednesday and Thursday, December 1 and 2, 1858, at Kingsland Hall in Albion.[10]

---

6. See Donald B. Marti, "Rich Methodists: The Rise and Consequences of Lay Philanthropy in the Mid-Nineteenth Century," in *Rethinking Methodist History,* ed. Russell E. Richey and Kenneth E. Rowe (Nashville: Kingswood, 1985), pp. 164-65.

7. Zahniser, p. 123; BHR, *BTR,* p. 167.

8. *WAS,* p. 191.

9. *WAS,* p. 191.

10. *WAS,* p. 192; BHR, *BTR,* p. 168; Zahniser, p. 123.

Chesbrough made it clear that the expulsion of Roberts and McCreery from the Genesee Conference had triggered the proposed convention. The call read:

GENESEE CONFERENCE LAYMEN'S CONVENTION

There has been manifested for several years past, a disposition among certain members of the Genesee Conference, to put down, under the name of fanaticism, and other opprobrious epithets, what we consider the life and power of our holy Christianity. In pursuance of this design, by reason of a combination entered into against them by certain preachers, the Rev. Isaac C. Kingsley, and Rev. Loren Stiles, Jr., were removed from the Cabinet at the Medina Conference; and the last conference at Perry, after a trial marked by unfairness and injustice, expelled from the conference and the church two of our beloved brethren, Benjamin T. Roberts, and Joseph McCreery, — for no other reason as we conceive, than that they were active and zealous ministers of our Lord Jesus Christ, and were in favor with the people, contending earnestly for those peculiarities of Methodism which have hitherto been essential for our success as a denomination; and have also dropped from the conference two worthy, pious and devoted young men, viz., Frank W. Warner, and Isaac Foster, who, during their conference probation, approved themselves more than ordinarily acceptable and useful among the people; and also at the last session of the conference removed from the Cabinet Rev. C. D. Burlingham, the only remaining presiding elder who opposed their sway. For several years past they have also, by consummate "clerical diplomacy," removed many of our worthy members from official relation to the church, for no other reason than that they approved of the principles advocated by these brethren.

Therefore in view of these facts, and others of a similar nature, we, the undersigned, hereby invite all our brethren who, with us, are opposed to this proscriptive policy, to meet with us in convention at Albion, on Wednesday and Thursday, December 1st and 2nd, to take such action and adopt such a course as the exigencies of the case may demand. Brethren, the time has come when we are to act with decision in this matter. The convention will commence Wednesday evening at seven o'clock, by holding a layman's love-feast. We hope our brethren who are with us in this matter will attend.[11]

When the date came, 195 Methodists from 47 of the conference's 100 circuits showed up at Albion — including Titus Roberts from Gowanda. These were *"representative men,"* Elias Bowen wrote, "all of them citizens of distinguished intelligence and piety, whose names and social position alone had great weight with the community."[12] Ellen Roberts also attended; it is unclear whether or not B. T. Roberts was there as an observer.

11. BHR, *BTR*, pp. 167-68; Hogue, *HFMC*, 1:195.
12. Elias Bowen, *History of the Origin of the Free Methodist Church* (Rochester, N.Y.: B. T. Roberts, 1871), p. 155. *Representative Men* was the title of a book of essays published by Ralph Waldo Emerson in 1850.

The convention began Wednesday evening with a love feast held at the Albion Methodist Episcopal Church, where Stiles was in his second year as preacher.[13] It was a "glorious time," Ellen Roberts reported; "God was in our midst."[14]

After the love feast the crowd walked over to Kingsland Hall, where the convention proper began at 8:30. The Honorable Abner I. Wood of Parma was elected president. Seven vice presidents were elected: Isaac Chesbrough, George W. Holmes, S. C. Springer of Gowanda, G. C. Sheldon, J. H. Brooks, George Bascom (a merchant from Allegany), and C. Sanford. Chesbrough's son Samuel was elected one of three secretaries, along with W. H. Doyle of Youngstown and J. A. Latta of Brockport. Two committees were chosen: one on resolutions and one on finance. Samuel K. J. Chesbrough chaired the committee on resolutions.

The gathering seems truly to have been a convention of laymen. Of the names listed in the minutes, none can be identified as women (though in most cases initials only are given). Ellen, however, was present at the opening love feast, and it is likely that she and other sisters were present during the sessions, though their names are not listed.[15] It is clear however that the role of women as well as related issues about spiritual gifts were simmering below the surface. Mary Annis of Albion, apparently the wife of lay convention delegate J. R. Annis, wrote to Ellen Roberts after a later convention that some people at Albion "thought it quite improper" for her to attend; the meeting "was not the place for the Sisters[;] it was a business meeting." But, said Mrs. Annis, "I bless the Lord that I went for it needed somebody interested in the case to tell it to the Pilgrims" back home.[16] In fact, the question of the "proper" role of women was an unresolved tension within the movement that became Free Methodism for decades.

The convention continued, with addresses by Isaac and Samuel Chesbrough and others, then adjourned for the night.[17] It reconvened the next morning at 9:00 and met throughout the day, Thursday, December 2. George W. Estes, author of the pamphlet that played such a key role in Roberts's trial, was present and took an active part. In the morning session Estes moved that "none be allowed to speak or vote in the Convention on any question, who is not in sympathy with this Convention and approves of the object set forth in the call." The motion was adopted.

13. BHR, *BTR*, p. 168; Zahniser, pp. 123-24; Hogue, *HFMC*, 1:194. Zahniser implies that the convention met throughout the day on Dec. 1, but in fact it convened at 7:00 P.M. The published minutes list the names of those who signed the call and the roll of those who attended.

14. ELRD, Dec. 1, 1858.

15. *Proceedings*, pp. 3-8. For seventy of the delegates, first names are given — all men's names. Conceivably some of those identified by one or two initials only were women, but this is unlikely. Nor do any married couples seem to be listed. Presumably, however, the total number of people who gathered was well in excess of the 195 who were officially enrolled in the minutes.

16. Mary L. Annis (Albion) to ELR, Dec. 5, 1860. Given the date, Mary was probably referring to the August 1860 convention at Pekin that formally organized the Free Methodist Church. (See chapter 25.)

17. Hogue, *HFMC*, 1:194; *Proceedings*, p. 4. (See also the account of the Laymen's Convention in Bowen, *History*, pp. 155-81.)

The committee on resolutions brought in a long report, some of whose eleven resolutions sparked spirited debate. The longest part of the report was a preamble that rehearsed the events of the past months that had led to the expulsions of Roberts and McCreery. "As members of the Church of Jesus Christ, we have the deepest interest in the purity of her ministers," it began. "To them we look for instruction in those things that affect our everlasting welfare."

The report noted pointedly, "As Methodists, we have no voice in deciding who shall be our respective pastors. Any one of a hundred, whom those holding the reins of power may select, may be sent to us, and we are expected to receive and sustain them." It was entirely appropriate, therefore, for Methodists to be concerned about what was happening within the conference. As biblical precedent, the report appealed to the example of the early apostles who, "enjoying as they did the inspiration of the Holy Ghost, were accustomed, on important occasions, to consult the brethren at large." Thus "reason and revelation both, give us the right to form and express our opinions" on the conduct of ministers who, after all, "are sustained by our contributions." The report continued,

> In theory, at least, we as Protestants, deny the doctrine of infallibility. It is possible for a majority of a Conference to be mistaken; it is also possible that they may take action which is unjust and wicked. We believe that Conferences, as well as other public bodies, may err, and that their acts are proper subjects of criticism, to approve or condemn, as the case may demand; and that individual members, for an honest expression of these convictions, ought not to be rewarded with proscription or excommunication; otherwise concealment and corruption would be the order of the day.
>
> We look upon the expulsion of brothers Roberts and McCreery as an act of wicked persecution, calling for the strongest condemnation. It was also a palpable violation of that freedom of speech and of the press, which is guaranteed by all our free institutions.

The report then summarized the events leading up to the recent trials. The root problem was a division in the conference "growing out of the connection of some with secret societies — a diversity of views upon the doctrine of holiness, and the holding of different views of the standard of justification." Roberts's "New School Methodism" was justified as an effort to counteract departures from "the old landmarks of Methodism."

Reviewing Roberts's recent trial, the resolution noted that "One witness, and one only, Rev. J. Bowman, testified that Brother R. handed him a package of these [Estes's] pamphlets for circulation, but which he never circulated." Even if the charges had been true, they would not have warranted expulsion from the ministry. "But such was the malevolence of those controlling a majority of the votes of Conference, that they could not stop short of the utmost limit of their power. Had they not been restrained by the civil law, the fires of martyrdom might have been kindled in the nineteenth century in western New York."

To the charge of "fanaticism and enthusiasm" often leveled against McCreery and Roberts, the report stated:

> Our means of information are far more reliable than that of those preachers who bring the accusation. We have attended the "camp meetings and General Quarterly meetings," against which a special outcry has been made as the "hot-beds of enthusiasm." We have sat under the preaching of these brethren who are charged with promoting these disorders — have heard some of them by the year. *We know what Methodism is;* some of us were converted, and joined the church under the labors of her honored pioneers. We speak advisedly then, when we say that the charge brought against brothers Roberts and McCreery, and the class of preachers denominated "Nazarites," of promoting fanaticism, is *utterly false and groundless.* . . . They preach the doctrines of the Methodist church, as we used to hear them preached years ago; and through their instrumentality many have been made to rejoice in the enjoyment of a PRESENT AND FULL SALVATION.

The Regency preachers, while they claim to preach holiness, show little fruit in this regard and in fact have "put down the standard of justification far below what Methodism and the Scriptures will warrant." Yet, the report affirmed, "We are true, loyal, God-fearing Methodists. We have not the slightest intention of leaving the church of our choice."

Withholding financial support was the remedy most readily available to these "lay" Methodists. "We are satisfied that no matter how strongly we may condemn the course of the Regency faction, they will not amend, so long as they are sustained. Besides, we cannot in conscience give our money to put down the work of the Lord. Therefore, we wish it distinctly understood, that we cannot pay one farthing to preacher or presiding elder, who voted for the expulsion of Bros. Roberts and McCreery, only upon 'contrition, confession, and satisfactory reformation.'" Here the report pointedly borrowed the language of the Methodist *Discipline* regarding the reinstatement of expelled members.[18]

The report maintained that in taking this action, "We are only exercising our undisputed rights in a constitutional way," and cited passages from such noted Methodist authors as Abel Stevens, John Emory, Thomas Bond, and A. N. Fillmore to show that "the right to withhold supplies, upon good and sufficient reason, is conceded and urged by standard authors of our Church."

The report made it clear that the convention was acting solely at its own initiative. "This Convention originated among ourselves. The first suggestion was made by one of our number. Neither the brethren expelled, nor any of the members of the Conference had anything to do whatever with calling this Convention. We mention this fact, because the insinuation is frequently made, that the people can do nothing except at the instigation of the preachers. We are not papists, requiring to be in-

---

18. *The Doctrines and Discipline of the Methodist Episcopal Church. 1856* (Cincinnati: Swormstedt and Poe, 1859), p. 99.

structed by the priesthood at every turn, what action we shall take, or what papers and books we shall read."

As to those preachers who faithfully do "the work of spreading scriptural holiness," the report promised: "[A]s long as they employ their time and talents in endeavoring to promote the life and power of Godliness, we pledge ourselves to cordially sustain them, by our influence and our means, whether they are in the Conference or not."

The list of specific resolutions then followed:

> *Resolved,* That we have the utmost confidence in Bros. B. T. Roberts and Joseph McCreery, notwithstanding their expulsion from the Conference — ranking them as we do among the most pure and able ministers of the New Testament.
>
> *Resolved,* That we adhere to the doctrines and usages of the fathers of Methodism. . . . but we do not acknowledge the oppressive policy of the secret fraternity in the Conference, known as the Buffalo Regency, as the action of the Church; and we cannot and will not submit to the same. . . .
>
> *Resolved,* That the laity are of some use to the Church, and that their views and opinions ought to command some little respect rather than that cool contempt with which their wishes have been treated by some of the officials of the Conference, for several years past.
>
> *Resolved,* That the farcical cry of disunion and secession is the artful production of designing men, to frighten the feeble and timid into their plans of operation and proscription. We wish to have it distinctly understood that we have not, and never had, the slightest intention of leaving the church of our choice, and that we heartily approve of the course of Bros. Roberts and McCreery in re-joining the church at their first opportunity. . . . Methodists have a better right in the Methodist Episcopal Church than anybody else, and by *God's* grace in it we intend to remain.
>
> *Resolved,* That it is a matter of no small grievance and of detriment to the church of *God* that these [Regency] preachers, in their local, pastoral administration, have deliberately set themselves to exclude from official position in the church, leaders, stewards, and trustees, members of deep and undoubted Christian experience, because of their adhesion to spiritual religious Methodism. . . .
>
> *Resolved,* That we will not aid in the support of any member of the Genesee Conference who assisted, either by his vote or his influence, in the expulsion of Bros. Roberts and McCreery from the Conference and the Church, until they are fully reinstated to their former position; and that we do recommend all those who believe that these brethren have been *unjustly* expelled from the Conference and the Church, to take the same course.
>
> *Resolved,* That we recommend Rev. B. T. Roberts and Rev. J. McCreery to travel at large, and labor as opportunity presents, for the promoting of the work of God and the salvation of souls.
>
> *Resolved,* That we recommend that Bro. Roberts locate his family in the city of Buffalo.

Resolved, That in our opinion Bro. Roberts should receive $1,000 for his support during the ensuing year, and Bro. McCreery should receive $600.

Resolved, That we recommend the appointment of a committee of fifteen to carry out the above resolutions, each of whom shall be authorized to appoint collectors as they may deem necessary; and we also recommend the appointment of a treasurer, to whom all moneys received for the purpose shall be paid, and who shall pay out the same, pro rata, to Bros. Roberts and McCreery, and receive their receipts for the same.

Resolved, That a copy of the foregoing preamble and resolutions be forwarded to the *Northern Independent,* with a request that the same be published.

> S. K. J. Chesbrough, Pekin,
> William H. Doyle, Youngstown,
> George W. Estes, Brockport,
> S. S. Rice, Clarkson,
> John Billings, Wilson,
> Jonathan Handley, Perry,
> Anthony Ames, Ridgeville,
> *Committee on Resolutions.*[19]

This was serious. Going far beyond a moral endorsement of Roberts and McCreery, these stalwart Methodists proposed the withholding of funds from all preachers who had opposed Roberts and McCreery, the commissioning (in effect) of Roberts and McCreery to evangelistic labor, provision for their financial support, and a continuing structure to implement these moves. These "laymen" were proposing to take the obvious steps that were open to them, and in effect to set up an ad hoc, interim (as they saw it) structure to function in the place of the Methodist conference structure in commissioning and supporting two preachers to whom the normal Methodist structure was no longer available.[20]

An implicit ecclesiology (or doctrine of the church) is evident particularly in two statements in this committee report. First, the report begins: "As members of the Church of Jesus Christ, we have the deepest interest in the purity of her ministers." Though these "laymen" were not members of the Genesee Conference (since they were not ordained ministers), they claimed a higher, more inclusive membership, one even broader than the Methodist Episcopal Church: "the Church of Jesus Christ." Second, the report later states, "We look upon the Church as an organization established to aid in securing the salvation of souls, and not mainly to raise money." In this case, "church" clearly means denomination, and specifically the Methodist Episcopal Church. While not spelled out, the operative model here is of the true church of Jesus Christ that transcends denominations, and within that reality,

---

19. *Proceedings,* pp. 8-15.

20. In an ad hoc sort of way, the Laymen's Conventions constituted and set in motion what was in effect an *ecclesiola,* or so-called parachurch, structure.

human-made denominational structures with the functional purpose of "securing the salvation of souls" (an evangelistic function that does not necessarily, however, exclude worship, nurture, and possibly other functions). In effect, the convention is appealing to a broad, fundamental authority derived from membership in the body of Christ as the basis for setting up a substitute, quasi-denominational structure, on pragmatic grounds, to meet an immediate need.

Not all the eleven specific resolutions won immediate support. The first three were passed unanimously, apparently with no debate. When the fourth was read, endorsing Roberts and McCreery's steps in rejoining the church, Brother T. H. Jeffers of Covington objected to the committee on resolutions doing "all the thinking and speaking for us," and there was some discussion about the appropriateness of calling ministers who opposed Roberts and McCreery "designing men." However, the resolution was soon passed unanimously.

The fifth resolution complained of some preachers' actions in removing class leaders, stewards, and trustees "of deep and undoubted Christian experience" for their "adherence to spiritual religious Methodism" and replacing them with others more to their liking. This called forth "a spirited discussion," the minutes noted. Brother Jeffers said he was not personally aware of any such cases, and Brother Dunham of Knowlesville asked whether the resolution called into question the right of preachers to nominate or appoint leaders.[21] George Estes responded that preachers' disciplinary rights were not being questioned, but only their misuse of those rights to get rid of godly leaders. "What is being complained of in this resolution has been done all through this land," Estes said, and he gave some examples from Brockport. T. B. Catton from Perry said the same thing had happened there; the preacher (apparently H. R. Smith) thought "the sort of religion we had was a little too antiquated, or vociferous," so "our class was disbanded, leader and all, and sent off to other classes." There is "a secret inquisition in our midst," he said. Similar reports came from Yates and Batavia. William Jones said that at Batavia the preacher (J. B. Wentworth) maneuvered to remove one of the old-time class leaders, "a man of deep piety, and of substantial social position in the community." He even tried to get the official board to adopt a statement "forbidding the saying 'amen' in meeting."

With this testimony, Brother Jeffers said he was convinced, and apparently this resolution was also adopted.[22]

These deliberations took up the whole morning session. When the convention reconvened at about 1:30, the remaining resolutions were adopted. Brother Jeffers pointed out that it was "a very strong measure" to withhold financial support from preachers. "Sir, is there no other way to meet this difficulty?" He concluded that there wasn't, and said, "I must vote for the resolution."

21. No Brother Dunham is listed in the convention's roll, which suggests that more were present and participated than those officially listed.

22. *Proceedings*, pp. 15-19. The minutes fail to indicate whether the fifth resolution was passed or not, but apparently it was.

When the resolution providing that a copy of the convention's action be sent to the *Northern Independent* came up, someone moved to add, "and *The Northern Christian Advocate.*" Samuel Chesbrough opposed this, however; he said it was now plain that the *Northern Christian Advocate* was "not in sympathy with us" and would not publish the report. "I thank God we have a paper through whose columns we may speak. I hope we will, to a man, sustain the 'Independent.'"

The motion to amend was lost, and now the whole document was adopted. As called for in the resolutions, a treasurer and continuing committee were elected. Isaac Chesbrough was chosen as treasurer. The committee of fifteen (three from each district) included S. K. J. Chesbrough.[23]

The Reverend B. I. Ives of the Oneida Conference, who had taken an active interest in the Bergen camp meeting and the Nazarite controversy, had come to Albion to observe the Laymen's Convention. By invitation he now came forward and addressed the gathering. Ives told of the "rise and progress" of the *Northern Independent* and spoke of the importance of supporting it as an independent voice.[24]

Before adjourning, the convention took several other significant actions. It agreed to hold a subsequent meeting on June 25, 1859, at North Bergen (in conjunction with the Bergen camp meeting) and also appointed a committee "to correspond with brethren in different parts of the work upon the propriety of establishing in the city of Buffalo a periodical devoted to the advocacy of 'Earnest Christianity.'" It is not clear where this idea arose; probably it came out of discussions between Roberts, the Chesbroughs, and perhaps others. In any case, the committee consisted of Roberts, Stiles, Burlingham, Leonard Halstead from Kendall, S. C. Springer from Gowanda, and G. C. Sheldon from Allegany (three "ministers" and three "laymen," signaling the kind of more democratic process that would later mark the Free Methodist Church).[25]

The convention also resolved to immediately "commence a subscription for the support of Bros. Roberts and McCreery, as provided in the ninth resolution." That resolution had specified support of $1,000 for Roberts and $600 for McCreery, which was within the range of average salaries for Methodist preachers in the Genesee Conference at the time — though, of course, Roberts and McCreery had no parsonage provided.[26] Of the $1,600.00 needed, $425.00 was immediately pledged and $97.50 paid in cash.[27]

With that, the convention adjourned. Its resolutions pretty well determined

---

23. *Proceedings*, pp. 20-21.

24. *Proceedings*, p. 21.

25. *Proceedings*, p. 22.

26. The conference minutes for this period published by the denomination do not list preachers' salaries. However, the conference-published *Minutes of the Genesee Annual Conference of the Methodist Episcopal Church,* 1855, cited earlier, does list salaries. Roberts's 1854-55 salary was $600, and McCreery's was $403. At that time the highest salary in the conference was $875 at Swan Street, Buffalo, where Philo Brown was the preacher (pp. 32-35).

27. *Proceedings*, p. 22.

Benjamin's ministry for the next two years. He was to move to Buffalo, begin ministry there but also "travel at large," and take steps to establish a periodical. McCreery's future was more indefinite.

The *Orleans American,* a newspaper published in Albion, reported on the convention and in a December 9 editorial said its "discussions were carried on with animation, in a good spirit, and with marked ability." The body was "composed of able men who had set themselves to work in earnest to correct what they believed to be a great evil in the administration of church affairs. . . . The number in attendance was much larger than we anticipated, all portions of the conference being represented." The editorial remarked on the "large sprinkling of gray heads" in the group, noting that "Prominent among the old men was I. M. Chesbrough, of Pekin, . . . a noble looking old gentleman, formerly from Baltimore."[28]

Roberts lost no time in carrying out the commission of the convention. He noted in *Why Another Sect,* "In accordance with the recommendation of this convention, Brother McCreery and myself went throughout the Conference, in the name of Christ, holding meetings, and laboring for the salvation of souls. But we were careful to state that we claimed no authority from the M.E. Church to hold meetings — that we did as we were doing, at the call of Christ, on our own responsibility as men and Christians."[29]

The Laymen's Convention sparked considerable discussion in the Methodist press, including attacks in the *Buffalo Advocate* and the *Northern Christian Advocate.*[30] In a long editorial in the *Northern Christian Advocate,* F. G. Hibbard said he reserved judgment on the merits of the Genesee Conference expulsions but strongly condemned the Laymen's Convention as the work of "a party in our Church bent on their own measures, deliberately and openly setting at defiance the most solemn judicial acts of the Church." The convention was instigated by "a few laymen, most of whom never heard the testimony, and know nothing of the facts but by hearsay, men strongly prejudiced." Hibbard felt the convention used "insulting language" in its resolutions and manifested an attitude that was "as distinctly contumacious against all Church authority, and revolutionary of all Church government, as actions can be defined to be." The actions "of the Albion Convention and all similar proceedings, are a real repudiation of Church obligation and membership, and must tend inevitably to subvert government, and promote schism and secession." In fact, Hibbard argued, the convention's actions amounted to secession. "They have withdrawn from the Church in fact, though not in form, and they have done it by the very essence and moral of their acts. They have appealed from Church government to a popular and primary and irresponsible assembly of the people, refusing support to the former,

---

28. Editorial, *Orleans American,* Dec. 9, 1858, quoted in *WAS,* pp. 200-201, and Hogue, *HFMC,* 1:203.

29. *WAS,* p. 201.

30. Roberts reported the newspaper charges and countercharges at some length in *WAS,* pp. 202-5.

and giving it to the latter. By the essence and meaning of their acts they belong to a Convention and not to the M.E. Church."[31]

John Robie, who claimed no neutrality regarding Roberts's and McCreery's expulsions, attacked the Albion convention in his usual style and published a long front-page article by "Junius" (probably John B. Wentworth) in the January 27, 1859, issue of the *Buffalo Advocate* entitled "The Genesee Evangelists." "Junius" said of Roberts and McCreery,

> They have determined to perambulate the Conf., at the instance and recommendation of the Albion Convention, and in the character of *Evangelists,* go out among the people exhibiting themselves as great sufferers, if not martyrs, for the Truth.
>
> . . . They are going about through the Conf., and expect to gain the attention and regards of the Methodists of Western New York simply as expelled members of the Genesee Conference. They are depending solely upon the fact of their expulsion to give them notoriety and consideration: For, they have nothing besides this, upon which to rely in their endeavor to gain notoriety and consideration. They cannot expect to attract the notice and secure the regards of the people, by *the display of superior talents:* We do not believe that even *their* egotism could lead them to such a depth of insane self-delusion. — No more can they, by the eminent usefulness of their past lives, or the prestige of place and position heretofore occupied by them.[32]

In the February 3 issue of the *Buffalo Advocate* Robie reprinted Hibbard's editorial on the Laymen's Convention and in an editorial said he would "from time to time, publish articles upon this irregular and fanatical movement" as "Junius" sent in more reports. "Junius" was sure "there are facts in abundance, of a documentary nature, yet lying back, which still more fully demonstrate the iniquitous character of Nazaritism, and the moral obliquity of the motives which actuated its originators." Robie boasted, "We were the first to give notification of the initial plans and policies of Nazaritism, and we calculate still to aid in its demolition among us."[33] Robie also reported, "We learn that the two great leaders of the Nazarites were in Brockport on Sabbath last, and that they constituted two bands, to which twenty-six persons joined. If the report is true, there is a significance in it of a little interest: First, the Band, then the distinct organization."[34]

Roberts quickly responded in the *Northern Independent* to Hibbard's charge that participants in the Laymen's Convention had in effect withdrawn from the Methodist

31. [F. G. Hibbard], "Genesee Conference Matters — Albion Convention," *NCA* 18, no. 51 (Dec. 22, 1858): 2.

32. Junius, "The Genesee Evangelists," *Buffalo Advocate,* Jan. 27, 1859, p. 1. The article continues in similar vein through three long columns. Zahniser quotes part of the above passage but misidentifies the author as Robie and gives the wrong date (Feb. 3 instead of Jan. 29). Cf. Zahniser, p. 127.

33. [John E. Robie], "Articles on Nazaritism," *Buffalo Advocate,* Feb. 3, 1859, p. 2.

34. [John E. Robie], editorial comment, *Buffalo Advocate,* Feb. 3, 1859, p. 2.

Episcopal Church. Turning Hibbard's logic on its head, he wrote: "What then of the preachers who meet in secret societies? Who receive their support, in part, at least from Masonic and Odd Fellow Lodges? What of those who belong to the Sacred Shield of the Conference? According to the logic of this editor, they are no longer ministers of the M.E. Church, but ministers of a secret society. Then when they assumed to act in Conference, their power being usurped, [they] invalidated their action. Hence, we are still preachers of the M.E. Church in full and regular standing!"[35]

In other words, by Hibbard's logic the Regency preachers had seceded from the Methodist Episcopal Church when they joined lodges, so they had no right to vote in the annual conference — and thus Roberts's expulsion was invalid. Roberts had a point, but to the other side secret societies, which weren't churches, didn't seem as much of a threat as did a new structure within the church that *might become* a church.

Second Annual Laymen's Convention

Eleven months after the first Laymen's Convention, the "Second Annual Session" was held on November 1 and 2, 1859. This was actually the third such meeting, but the June gathering during the Bergen camp meeting conducted little or no official business.

The convention again met at Albion, but this time in the sanctuary of the Baptist church. After an opening love feast Tuesday evening, the group organized at 9:00 the next morning and met throughout the day. Abner I. Wood was again elected president and S. K. J. Chesbrough served as corresponding secretary.[36]

This convention adopted a series of resolutions and issued an appeal to the upcoming General Conference. It reaffirmed both its loyalty to the Methodist Episcopal Church and its continuing confidence in Roberts and the other expelled ministers. Noting the expulsions during the conference sessions recently concluded at Brockport, the convention declared:

> Fidelity to God will not allow us to quietly acquiesce in such decisions. It is urged that we must respect the action of the church. But what is the church? Our 13th article of religion says: "The visible church of God is a congregation of faithful men, in which the pure word of God is preached, and the sacraments duly administered." *The ministers then are not "the church."* If ministers wish to have their acts respected, they must, like other men, perform *respectable* actions.
>
> These repeated acts of expulsions, wrong as they are in themselves, deserve the stronger condemnation from the fact, scarcely attempted to be disguised, that THE OBJECT *is to prevent the work of holiness from spreading among us — to put*

35. B. T. Roberts, *NI* 3, no. 22 (Jan. 6, 1859): 3. Quoted in Zahniser, p. 126. It is not clear what the "Sacred Shield" was; apparently it was some form of fraternal organization within the Genesee Conference.

36. "Proceedings of the Laymen's Convention of the Genesee Conference, of the M.E. Church," Albion, N.Y., Nov. 1-2, 1859. Bound with *The Proceedings of the Laymen's Convention of the M.E. Church, Genesee Conference* (cited above), following p. 22. MMHC.

down the life and power of Godliness in our churches, and to inaugurate in its stead the peaceable reign of a cold and heartless formalism, — in short, to do away with what has always been a distinctive feature of Methodism.[37]

The convention recommended that the expelled preachers continue their ministry, and promised to support them. It provided for the organization of "bands" to care for Methodists who had been expelled from their churches and as a method of collecting support for Roberts and the other expelled preachers. Resolutions 5 and 6 read:

> That in order to keep our people who are being oppressed by the misrule of the dominant faction in the Genesee Conference from being scattered, and finally lost to our church, we recommend our brethren in the ministry to gather our people into bands, and to encourage them to union of action and effort in the work of the Lord.
>
> That in each Band and at each preaching appointment, regular and systematic efforts be made by way of band collections and subscriptions, to secure an adequate support for our brethren in the ministry.[38]

It is clear that these were seen as temporary measures designed to hold the expelled Methodists together until General Conference could act. Once the General Conference had resolved the matter, they thought, the abused sheep could be gathered back into the Methodist fold.

Shortly after this second Laymen's Convention Roberts published an article commenting on it and on the Genesee Conference sessions held at Brockport. It was clear at the annual conference, he said, that Bishop Simpson sided with the Regency and had allowed himself to become biased against the Nazarites. Roberts received a letter from "an able lawyer" present at the conference sessions who reported that "he had never before, in all his experience, seen such partiality" in a presiding officer as that exhibited by Bishop Simpson. "The good Bishop was made to believe that the so-called Nazarites, or Old School Methodists of the Genesee Conference, really intended to secede!" But, Roberts added,

> The trouble is, we will not "secede." We are Methodists from conviction. . . . We say to our people everywhere, "Cling to the Church. Do not withdraw, nor suffer yourselves to be withdrawn." The temporary organizations we effect, are necessary to keep our people from being scattered, till the General Conference has had opportunity to correct the wrongs and redress the outrages inflicted upon us. . . . We form no "Free Churches" save where "Free Churches" are needed, and those are ready to come into the Conference as soon as wrongs are made right.[39]

---

37. "Proceedings of the Laymen's Convention of the Genesee Conference, of the M.E. Church."
38. "Proceedings of the Laymen's Convention of the Genesee Conference, of the M.E. Church."
39. B. T. Roberts, "Secession — Bishop Simpson," *NI* 4, no. 15 (Nov. 17, 1859). Cited in Marston, p. 234.

CHAPTER 24

"A Wider Field of Labor"

"Everywhere we go, large and attentive congregations listen to the word with apparently deep interest."

B. T. Roberts, March 1859[1]

"In this city [Buffalo] of fashionable churches, where formality and death reign, we have opened a house of worship, where the seats are free, and the poor have the gospel preached to them."

Ellen Roberts[2]

Even without the action of the Laymen's Conventions and the structure they put in place, B. T. Roberts and Joseph McCreery would probably have engaged in extensive evangelistic and revival efforts following their trials and expulsion. The conventions were helpful, however, in facilitating Roberts's new phase of ministry. Yet the sequence of events, and particularly Roberts's expulsion from the Methodist ministry (in effect, a defrocking), meant that his ecclesiastical status remained murky.

Inside or Outside the Church?

As Roberts launched into wide-ranging public ministry, the question of his ecclesiastical status was still unresolved in the minds of some Methodist preachers.

---

1. B. T. Roberts, statement in *NI*, Mar. 1859.
2. Ellen L. Roberts, "Free Church in Buffalo," *EC* 2, no. 1 (Jan. 1861): 33.

Charles D. Burlingham, Roberts's successor at Pekin, wrote to Bishop Osman Baker for clarification. Ecclesiastically speaking, Roberts was in the unusual situation of facing almost two years of limbo since his General Conference appeal would not be acted upon until May 1860. He had joined the church as a probationary member at Pekin and was given an exhorter's license, as already noted. Benjamin thought these steps were proper — a way to affirm his loyalty to the church while also giving him some ecclesiastical standing as the basis for continuing ministry — but some wondered. Even Ellen had questions, as we have seen.

As the preacher at Pekin, Burlingham no doubt was concerned both about Roberts and that the Pekin congregation do the right thing. Bishop Baker wrote back on February 16, 1859. He was reluctant to express an opinion since "the General Conference alone has power to decide whether a given act of an expelled member cuts off a right to an appeal." He added, "As the appeal has been taken, and Br. Roberts has taken the steps he has, it is for the General Conference to decide" whether Roberts's rejoining the church and functioning as an exhorter would make any difference in the disposition of his case.

The Methodist bishops had just met in Chicago, and while they did not discuss Roberts's case specifically, "the relations of expelled members who had taken an appeal was, among other things, considered," Baker noted circumspectly.[3] But he added,

> Most of the Bishops present expressed, in substance, this sentiment, that the proper course for an expelled member who had taken an appeal was, to remain as he was, until the appellate Court had acted on his case. My private opinion is that the action of the Pekin Society was not in harmony with our usage. Br. R. has appealed to the General Conference — the only Body competent to examine the case & reverse or confirm the decision. Now for a society to act in the premises, without a legal hearing of the case, or any new facts developed, strikes me as very unusual.
>
> I think it would have been better to let the matter take the disciplinary course.
>
> I think also that the office [of exhorter] which Bro. R. holds, according to your exposition of it, is an unauthorized one by the Discipline and usages of the church. An exhorter who is not a member of the Quarterly Conference is an anomaly as I judge. And the relation of a probationer who is requested to speak to the members in class, in a private church capacity is not analogous to giving a probationer a license to hold public meetings, where or when the church is held responsible for those meetings. At least so it seems to me. May divine wisdom guide us.[4]

---

3. It seems unlikely that the bishops could have discussed the question of the status of expelled members who had appealed to the General Conference without having Roberts and McCreery in mind, though there may have been other cases also. Their discussion was probably prompted by Roberts's and McCreery's cases, with which Baker had been intimately involved.

4. Osman C. Baker to C. D. Burlingham, Feb. 16, 1859 (RFP, Microfilm Reel 10). Cf. Zahniser, p. 119, and the earlier discussion of Baker's *Guide-Book in the Administration of the Discipline of the Methodist Episcopal Church* (New York: Carlton and Phillips, 1855) in chapter 22. Somewhat surprisingly, Baker did not specifically raise the point that Roberts was a probationer, not a full member,

In other words, Baker was saying the Pekin church should not have given Roberts an exhorter's license, and anyhow, an exhorter's license is not authorization to preach or conduct services beyond the local church. Baker is suggesting as well that it would have been better had Roberts not tried to get back into the Methodist Episcopal Church before the General Conference heard his case.

This seems to be a fair interpretation of the *Discipline* and Methodist practice. Yet Roberts can hardly be faulted for wanting to reestablish his ties to the Methodist church as quickly as possible and to secure some ecclesiastical standing so he could continue ministering. Perhaps, however, Ellen was right; he should simply have waited for the General Conference to act. But what should he do in the meantime? He was raised in a tradition in which public preaching was understood to be a ministry that required some kind of ecclesiastical credentialing, and he certainly felt called to preach.

It may have been as a result of Bishop Baker's letter that Benjamin published a statement in the *Northern Independent* a few weeks later, making it clear that in his continuing ministry he claimed no ecclesiastical standing.[5] Burlingham apparently gave a copy of Baker's letter to Roberts.[6] Benjamin wrote,

> It seems to be a question among the doctors, whether I belong to the church or not. I did the best I could to stay in; and when I was thrust out without my fault, I tried to get back, and really thought I had accomplished it, but the president of a recent church trial [probably meaning Bishop Baker], which trials, by and by, are becoming quite numerous in the Genesee Conference, decided that I was not a member even "on probation." As this was a "judicial decision," an "act of administration," of course it settles the question. But in or out, I trust I may still be permitted to entertain "a desire to flee from the wrath to come." Our excellent discipline specifies as among the fruits of this desire, "instructing, reproving, and exhorting all we have any intercourse with." This, then, is what I am doing. The Lord has opened a wide door, into which I have entered. I disclaim all authority from man, but simply "instruct, reprove and exhort," because I believe he has called me to it, and he blesses me in it. Everywhere we go, large and attentive congregations listen to the word with apparently deep interest.[7]

If Roberts is responding here to Bishop Baker's letter, his statement is an overinterpretation, or overreaction, since Baker's opinion specifically was not a "ju-

---

when he was given his exhorter's license. Of course, Roberts had been through this process years earlier and was hardly a probationer in the normal sense.

5. Zahniser says, "The question of church membership for Mr. Roberts was settled by the decision of Bishop Baker, and in accordance with it, Mr. Roberts published" his statement in the *Northern Independent* (Zahniser, p. 119). Baker was careful, however, not to give his views in his letter to Burlingham of the status of an episcopal decision nor to deal in any official way with Roberts's case.

6. A copy of Baker's letter to Burlingham is found in the Roberts Papers (as noted above), and is clearly marked "(Copy)." Probably it is not, therefore, in Baker's hand unless Baker himself sent Roberts a copy.

7. B. T. Roberts, statement in *NI*, Mar. 1859, quoted in *WAS*, pp. 201-2, and Zahniser, p. 120.

dicial decision" or "act of administration." However, Roberts may have received some other, official communication.

His statement, however, is full of ecclesiological import. He was facing in 1858 a situation analogous to that faced by John Wesley 120 years earlier. Though not expelled from the Church of England, Wesley was banned from many Anglican pulpits. Where could he preach? Under George Whitefield's influence, he soon went outdoors, though "field preaching" was at first repugnant to him. He was criticized as irregular for not confining himself to one parish. It was this circumstance that led Wesley to say, "I look upon all the world as my parish; thus far, I mean, that in whatever part of it I am I judge it meet, right, and my bounden duty to declare, unto all that are willing to hear, the glad tidings of salvation."[8] In preaching outdoors to the poor, Wesley cited the precedent of Jesus' preaching to the multitudes.[9]

In both Wesley's and Roberts's cases, the ecclesiological issues were the same: Who authorizes authentic gospel ministry, and what does a minister who is clearly called by God do when the exercise of that ministry is denied or restricted? (By implication, also: What is the theological standing of denominational structures that grant such authorization?) Wesley said the demands of the gospel and God's call on his life required him to preach wherever he could, with or without specific ecclesiastical mandate — that in this sense the world was his parish. Later, he argued similarly as he began sending out unordained "lay" preachers who were simply "in connection with" him.

Roberts was forced to a similar conclusion. He knew he was called to preach, and his call was confirmed by the fruit. When official Methodist authorization was withdrawn, he did as Wesley did. He appealed to his own sense of call, the nature and demands of the gospel itself, and the fruit of his labors. He came, in essence, to the position William Reddy had earlier commended to him: he didn't really need Methodist authorization because God had "called and commissioned" him to preach the gospel. He had not forfeited this divine commission, nor had his expulsion by the Genesee Conference invalidated it.[10]

In hindsight, one can see that Reddy's advice was both theologically sound and politically savvy. Roberts's General Conference appeal would probably have received more sympathetic treatment had he not used (or abused, as some may have thought) the route of probationary membership and an exhorter's license. (His reference here to "instructing, reproving, and exhorting all we have any intercourse with" quotes the Methodist General Rules, written by John Wesley and included in all Methodist *Disciplines*.[11] This charge applied to *all* Methodists, not just ordained "ministers," and this apparently was Roberts's point.)

---

8. *The Letters of the Rev. John Wesley, A.M.*, ed. John Telford (London: Epworth Press, 1931), 1:286.

9. See the discussion in Howard A. Snyder, *The Radical Wesley and Patterns for Church Renewal* (Downers Grove, Ill.: InterVarsity, 1980), pp. 31-33, 91-93.

10. *WAS*, p. 187.

11. *The Doctrines and Discipline of the Methodist Episcopal Church. 1856* (Cincinnati: Swormstedt and Poe, 1859), p. 29.

Denied Methodist ministerial status, Roberts now appealed more fundamentally to the gospel itself, and to his status as a simple (albeit Methodist) disciple of Jesus. The underlying ecclesiological issue is one of discipleship, ministry, and authority. Whether Roberts ever seriously reflected further (theologically) on this issue is a question to be investigated later.

"A Wider Field of Labor"

Roberts's expulsion from the ME Church and the pledge of support by the first (1858) Laymen's Convention opened the door to "a wider field of labor," as Benson Roberts later wrote.[12] Benjamin was immediately kept busy as calls came to him. He wrote his father on Saturday, December 11, 1858:

> Friday evening, after the convention, I spoke in the Baptist Church, at Brockport, to a very large congregation; Saturday night at Sweden, Sabbath at Sweden and Brockport; then went to Somerset, some forty-five miles, and held a meeting; thence to Charlottesville, some fifteen miles, on Thursday, and held a meeting in the evening. I am now at Brother Chesbro's, but go this afternoon some twenty miles, to Youngstown, to spend the Sabbath; thence on Monday some fifty miles to Yates, to have a meeting on Monday evening.
>
> The Lord blesses me and the people, and I feel confident that He would not have me hold my peace.

Benjamin added, "Orders for the pamphlet are coming in from all sections, from Indiana, Illinois, Ohio, New York City, and all over. A general interest is felt, and I trust good will result from these trials, severe as they are." Probably the pamphlet referred to is Samuel Chesbrough's seventy-page *Defence of Rev. B. T. Roberts, A.M. Before the Genesee Conference . . .* , which had just been published. Benjamin concluded,

> The sympathies of good men are with us all over the land, and the best of all is, God is with us. We have more to fear from a compromising spirit on the part of those whose sympathies are with us from all other causes combined.
>
> While we stand out decidedly and honestly the Lord will help us. I never so felt my constant need of divine guidance.[13]

Benjamin, Ellen, and the three boys apparently moved back to their house at 29 Palmer Street, Buffalo, in late December 1858.[14] Benjamin's ministry and travels over the next year were extensive. Benson notes that Ellen was "sorely tried in many ways

---

12. BHR, *BTR*, p. 180.
13. BTR to TR, Dec. 11, 1858, quoted in BHR, *BTR*, pp. 187-88.
14. Roberts gives his address as "29 Palmer St., Buffalo N.Y." on the first page of his 1859 pocket diary.

by [Benjamin's] frequent absences, and the hardships of a reduced and an irregular income dependent almost wholly upon public collections." Benson calculated that his father traveled some 860 miles through western New York during the first half of 1859, "much of this with a horse"; he also made a trip to St. Louis. Benjamin was preaching around five times a week.[15]

Such travel and ministry were not easy. Benjamin sometimes suffered from colds and dyspepsia.[16] He recorded, "Tues. morning [March 8, 1859] I started for Varysburgh to fill an appt. on my way home. My horse being sick I was obliged to take stage, hire livery &c. but the roads were so bad that I could not get through, so for the first time since Conf. I had to disappoint a congregation. Yesterday I went 15 miles through the mud some of the time at the rate of 2 miles per hour — took the cars at Attica. Came home, and found, thanks to the kind Heavenly Father, my family well."[17]

As he traveled, Benjamin kept in touch with Isaac Chesbrough, both for advice and because Chesbrough, as the treasurer designated by the Laymen's Convention, was in effect his financial manager. On March 7 Roberts wrote to "Father" Chesbrough reporting a successful meeting at Rushford — which had to be held in the Baptist church building due to the vocal opposition of Jason Miller, the Methodist preacher. Roberts reported that on Saturday evening "the crowd was so dense" that it wasn't possible to take up a collection, but two men were stationed at the door at the end of the meeting to receive contributions, and $25 was collected. "And afterwards in shaking hands &c. enough was handed me to make it up to $30.00 for which you will please give them credit."[18]

Meanwhile the controversy within the Genesee Conference was growing, not subsiding. "Reprisals against those participating in the Albion Laymen's Convention were prompt and severe," Marston notes.[19] Roberts wrote, "To expel members and read them out [as] withdrawn without their consent became the order of the day" in a number of places.[20]

Partly in reaction to the Albion Laymen's Convention, a number of longtime Methodists were in fact expelled by their pastors. In Olean, where the preacher was George Terry, James H. Brooks, Esq., whom the local newspaper called "a man of un-

15. BHR, *BTR*, p. 189. Beginning on Jan. 25, 1859, Benjamin again began writing in his diary with some regularity.

16. Roberts's diary for Jan. 31 notes: "Started early with buggy for Warsaw. From Brockport to LeRoy 17 miles. Dr. Andrews of Bergen gave me prescription for dyspepsia, 1 handful dried peppermint 1 [handful] smartweed[?] 3 table spoons pul.[?] rhubarb, 2 table [spoons] soda. Boil 2 hours, strain, add 1 1/4 loaf sugar, — Scald skins[?] boil down to a quart, and 1/2 pt. best brandy, bottle[.] 1 table spoon 1/2 hour before eating, 1 before going to bed. Dined at bro. Teasdale's. Preached to a full house at Warsaw on the 'Strait gate.['] Staid with bro R. H. Miller [or Mullen]. Had cold, but a free time preaching." On Feb. 5: "Took tea at F. Andrews in Bergen. His prescription for dyspepsia relieves me."

17. BTR to Isaac Chesbrough, Mar. 7 and 10, 1859, from Belfast, N.Y. Cf. BTRD, Mar. 8-9, 1859.

18. BTR to Chesbrough, Mar. 7 and 10, 1859, from Belfast, N.Y.

19. Marston, pp. 212-13.

20. *WAS*, p. 206.

blemished private character" and of "generosity, integrity, honest, and living piety," was expelled for attending the Laymen's Convention. At North Chili, where John Lanckton was the preacher, Claudius Brainard, a prominent member and a conference preacher before locating in 1846, was tried and expelled on February 14, 1859. He reported in the *Northern Independent,* "Yesterday, I was expelled from the M.E. Church, for attending the Laymen's Convention. No other charge was preferred. . . . I shall unite on trial, the first opportunity, with the M.E. Church. It is time the laity were awake to their own rights in the church."[21]

Similar tales came from around the conference. The combination of "wholesale excommunications" and "voluntary withdrawals of those who had lost hope" halted the growth of the Genesee Conference.[22] The conference lost 587 members in 1859 (after gaining 2,161 the previous year) and over a thousand in each of the next two years.[23] Ray Allen observed in 1911 that "the troubles of the Genesee Conference were not cured" by the "surgical operation" of the trials and expulsions. "Following 1859 came the darkest years in her life, and her membership steadily fell year by year until in 1865 it was at the lowest level ever reached."[24]

Founding a "Free Church" in St. Louis

While Roberts and McCreery were ministering in western New York, John Wesley Redfield's evangelistic efforts took him as far west as Illinois and St. Louis, Missouri. Redfield's ministry there turned out to be significant for the birth and growth of Free Methodism. In fact, Redfield's labors in St. Louis led to the founding of the first "free" Methodist (not yet Free Methodist) church in the nation.[25]

Redfield's meetings in St. Louis sparked a significant revival in the Ebenezer Methodist Episcopal Church there. Opposition from the pastor, Dr. Thomas Williams, and some of the members prompted about 90 people to leave the church, however. As a result, Redfield soon found himself, in effect, pastoring a new congregation of about 150 people. He asked Roberts to come to St. Louis to help conserve the fruit.[26]

21. *WAS,* pp. 208-9; Hogue, *HFMC,* 1:210-13; Marston, pp. 212-14. Marston and Hogue spell the name "Brainerd," but the contemporary sources have "Brainard." Hogue says Brainard was a relative of Daniel Steele (1:212).

22. Marston, p. 214.

23. *Minutes,* Genesee Conference, 1859-62. The conference lost 1,274 members in 1860 (-10.3 percent), and approximately 1,120 in 1861 (-10.1 percent). It was thus relatively unaffected by the major nationwide revival of 1857-59 (which originated primarily in New York City), except perhaps in 1858.

24. Ray Allen, *A Century of the Genesee Annual Conference of the Methodist Episcopal Church, 1810-1910* (Rochester, N.Y.: By the Author, 1911), p. 10. The Civil War may also have been a factor in the conference's decline in the years 1862-65.

25. Marston, p. 215.

26. Marston, p. 215; Zahniser, pp. 145-47. Redfield refused to take actual pastoral charge of the church except on a temporary basis and soon continued his evangelistic ministry. Redfield gives an ex-

Ministry beyond western New York was not anticipated by the Laymen's Convention, however. When Roberts reported to Isaac Chesbrough that he had received several telegrams urging him to go to St. Louis, neither "Father" Chesbrough nor Samuel thought this was a good idea. Most of the people he consulted, including Loren Stiles, thought he should go to St. Louis, Benjamin said. "I think it my duty to go."[27] But Sam Chesbrough wrote on March 18, four days after Benjamin left for St. Louis,

> I wish I could look upon Bro. R. going as the call of the Lord. . . . [But] I can not see how it is the duty of Bro. R. to go 3000 miles away and join affinity with strangers [in their] church difficulties. If the Laymen are looked upon for help we need our preachers to stand by us. God will have just as much a call for Bro. R. in New York as St. Louis. And certainly Buffalo needs help. I am not the only one who <u>disapproves heartily of it</u>. . . . I am sorry then that just at this standpoint, one of our "Standard Bearers" has gone to a distant field, and if God blesses him there <u>one</u> week why <u>not six months</u>.[28]

Benjamin spent several days at home in Buffalo before leaving for St. Louis. He had a stack of correspondence to catch up with; he "Paid Mathews for printing my pamphlet $50.00" (apparently referring to Samuel Chesbrough's *Defense of the Rev. B. T. Roberts, A.M. Before the Genesee Conference*); he took care of some work around the house. He noted in his diary on Saturday, March 12, "On the whole this has been a very good week to me. The Lord has showered his blessings upon us. He has given me the victory over many temptations. I must live more wholly for him in time to come than I have ever done."[29]

Sunday, March 13, the day before leaving for St. Louis, Benjamin, Ellen, and the boys went to the morning services at Niagara Street, where Benjamin had served six years earlier. The current preacher, Allan Steele, "read a very good sermon on 'Be thou faithful,'" Benjamin noted. "All the services were conducted with the utmost propriety. House 1/3 or 1/2 full." That evening he "tried to preach at Black Rock in Dr. Rankin's Church" but had "a very dull time," and felt he had spent an "unprofitable Sabbath." It was perhaps as a result of this that he noted in his diary the next day, "This morning the adversary gained some advantage over me — but by grace I am resolved that it shall be for the last time."[30]

Benjamin left for St. Louis at midday on Monday, traveling by train from Buffalo to St. Louis via Cleveland and Cincinnati. From Cincinnati he took the newly opened Ohio and Mississippi Railroad overnight to St. Louis, arriving there at 4:00

---

tended account in Redfield Autobiography, pp. 337-62; cf. Terrill, *Redfield*, pp. 354-80. The controversy over Redfield's ministry and the split in the Ebenezer Church erupted into the pages of the Methodist newspapers.

27. BTR to Chesbrough, Mar. 7 and 10, 1859, from Belfast, N.Y.

28. Samuel K. J. Chesbrough to "My Dear Friends" (apparently Ellen Roberts), Mar. 18, 1859, from South Pekin, N.Y.

29. BTRD, Mar. 10-12, 1859.

30. BTRD, Mar. 13 and 14, 1859.

A.M. on Wednesday, March 16. Redfield came to see him as soon as he learned Roberts had arrived, and was "almost overcome" to see his friend and colaborer. With Roberts in town to look after things, Redfield left two days later for Quincy, Illinois, 130 miles north by boat. Roberts began meeting with the congregation Redfield had formed and started organizing it into a church.[31]

Roberts had never been this far west — or this far south. Here he came face-to-face with slavery as never before. On Saturday he wrote, "Saw a drove of slaves going through the streets on their way probably to the South. This is said to be of frequent occurrence." Roberts noted a few days later, "The blight of slavery extends to every thing. We feel its crushing influence even in our little meetings. God help me to do all I can in behalf of poor suffering humanity."[32]

Similar encounters fueled the outrage that had led to the publication of Harriet Beecher Stowe's *Uncle Tom's Cabin* seven years earlier. Harriet's brother Charles Beecher had visited St. Louis while on a business trip from New Orleans, where he was employed. Either in St. Louis or at some point en route he met a slave trader, originally from New England, who became the model for the infamous Simon Legree in *Uncle Tom's Cabin*. This real-life Legree growled with clenched fist, "I never see the nigger yet I couldn't bring down with one crack." Describing his business model, the Yankee slaver volunteered, "You see, I just put 'em straught through sick or well. When one nigger's dead, I buy another; and I find it comes cheaper and easier, every way." Beecher jotted down the words verbatim and sent them to Harriet in Cincinnati.[33]

Such scenes had their impact on Roberts. The day after he saw the slave gang he interviewed a black woman, "Aunt Clarissa," several of whose children had been sold into slavery. The woman's husband managed to buy his own freedom and built a house for the family — and then died. Her former master then got control of the house and some $400 of the deceased man's cash. Roberts noted that Aunt Clarissa was "in constant fear lest she be sold" back into slavery. He then added immediately, "Church organized in the evening. Free." But there was some "excitement on slavery," as six of the members were in favor of "admitting slaveholders," which Roberts would never agree to.[34]

Roberts and the new congregation had very good services on Sunday, he noted. In the evening he "cried to a great multitude 'Escape for thy life.' The Lord gave me freedom and accompanied the word with the Spirit." Eleven came forward for prayer, three professed conversion, and five joined the church. "It has been a very good day to my soul."[35]

---

31. BTRD, Mar. 14-18, 1859.

32. BTRD, Mar. 19 and 24, 1859.

33. Lyman Beecher Stowe, *Saints, Sinners, and Beechers* (New York: Blue Ribbon Books, 1934), p. 174. The author notes, "Yes, Legree was drawn from life more exactly than any other character. That is perhaps the very reason why he has so often been criticized as unreal and exaggerated" (p. 174).

34. BTRD, Mar. 25, 1859.

35. BTRD, Mar. 27, 1859.

On Monday, March 28, Roberts began calling on "several prominent citizens" of St. Louis, trying to raise money to buy a lot and build a church edifice. He was accompanied by "Brother L. Waite," who seems to have been Roberts's key contact person in St. Louis.[36] Roberts noted that he and Waite "received encouragement that they would aid us in buying a lot and building a free church."[37]

That night the new congregation met under Roberts's leadership to begin a fund-raising campaign. The members pledged $1,500 toward a building, but there was "Some excitement again about slavery," Roberts noted. "A few are greatly afraid of the word 'free' [in the name of the church, in the St. Louis context]. Slavery makes slaves of all. It destroys freedom of Spirit."[38]

Throughout the week Roberts raised funds during the day and conducted services at night. Tuesday night he preached on Revelation 3:18, "I counsel thee to buy of me gold tried in the fire, that thou mayest be rich." There was "a good degree of interest," and several came forward to pray. "O how I need to be entirely free to live close to Jesus. O Lord help me to walk with Thee," he wrote in his diary, concluding his day.[39]

The next day, Roberts notes, he "Called on Mr. O'Fallon[,] the wealthiest man in the city. He owns 40 slaves. All his urbanity could not remove from our mind the impression that he is a robber of men, depriving them of the use of themselves." John O'Fallon, who had become a multimillionaire by the mid-1850s through banking and railroad ventures, was the nephew of William Clark of the famous Lewis and Clark expedition. Apparently Roberts didn't get any money from him.[40]

On Thursday Roberts noted, "Witnessed in St. Louis on the Court House steps the sale of a young man by auction. He was bid off at $915. He was I should judge about 20[?] years of age. This too in the heart of a city claiming to be civilized! Went to visit a slave pen on Locust Street. About 35 colored persons were crowded

36. Roberts refers several times to "Bro. Waite," or "L. Waite, Esq.," in his 1859 diary.

37. BTRD, Mar. 28, 1859. Did Roberts feel any discomfort or ambivalence in asking prominent businessmen to financially assist a local church, given his view that the church should practice responsible stewardship and not rely on the world for support? Or did he perhaps feel that establishing a "free" church was also a political declaration against slavery and slaveholding, and thus deserved public support? (As Roberts wrote in the early Free Methodist *Disciplines,* Free Methodists "do not believe in resorting to worldly policy to sustain the Gospel. . . . The Gospel possesses an inherent power that will not only sustain itself, but make its way through all opposition, wherever its advocates live up to its requirements, and rely on its promises" [*The Doctrines and Discipline of the Free Methodist Church* (Rochester, N.Y.: General Conference, 1870), pp. viii-ix]. Of course, Roberts was specifically denouncing fund-raising programs like "festivals, lotteries, fairs," and above all pew rental.)

38. BTRD, Mar. 28, 1859.

39. BTRD, Mar. 29, 1859.

40. BTRD, Mar. 30, 1859. O'Fallon was born about 1794, so was about sixty-five at this time; William Clark (1770-1838) had been governor of the Missouri Territory from 1813 to 1820. See James Neal Primm, *Lion of the Valley: St. Louis, Missouri,* 2nd ed. (St. Louis: n.p., 1990), pp. 137-49, 208-10. By the 1840s O'Fallon was among the group of prominent citizens who "stood . . . at the peak of the power structure" of the city (p. 191). There is a picture of O'Fallon on p. 216 of Primm's book, and two towns in the St. Louis area bear his name, one in Missouri and one in Illinois.

together in a cell-like room. One was playing on an old fiddle. One young man was as white as many white men. Prayer meeting in the evening. About 75 out. God was with us."[41]

Roberts added the next day, "The anti slavery sentiment of this city seems to be on a pecuniary basis. Men oppose slavery not because it is wrong but because it retards the prosperity of the state. I have heard of a free colored man whose wife is a slave. The free man died leaving some $3000 worth of property. The owner of his wife won possession of the property and keeps her still in the most abject slavery. Many of the negroes specially of the young ones are nearly white."[42]

This time in St. Louis represented, in significant ways, a new chapter in B. T. Roberts's life. He was far away from home, involved now in meeting with Redfield's converts and followers, in consciously seeking to find out more about slavery, and in organizing a "free" church in which slaveholding was strictly forbidden.

This is important for the later history of the Free Methodist Church and particularly for the meaning of "Free Methodist." In western New York, when "free" Methodist churches were later formed, the "free" meant free pews and freedom of the Spirit. In St. Louis, "free" specifically meant freedom from slaveholding and, by implication, freedom for slaves and the end of slavery, as well as freedom from the spiritually numbing influence slavery had in the church. Thus it is accurate historically to say that the "Free" in Free Methodist signifies freedom from slavery, oppression, and racial discrimination, as well as free seats and freedom of the Spirit. Roberts made a point of this in the early Free Methodist *Discipline,* noting: "The first Free Methodist Church ever organized was in St. Louis, a slave-holding city, and at a time when slave-holders were freely admitted to the churches generally. Yet they made non-slaveholding a test of membership, prohibiting, as they have ever done, 'the buying, selling, or holding a human being as a slave.'"[43] Nonslaveholding as a test of membership was a specific prophetic stand against a political, social, economic, and moral evil in St. Louis on the eve of the Civil War.

April 3, Roberts's final Sunday in St. Louis, was "a beautiful day." Roberts noted in his diary, "We had our first Love Feast in our new society. It was a season of refreshing — all felt that God was there." The Lord helped him as he preached from 1 John 5:4. In the afternoon he preached at a colored Baptist church on the kingdom of God from Romans 14:17 — "The kingdom of God is . . . righteousness, and peace, and joy in the Holy Ghost." He preached again at the new "free" church in the evening. He recorded that one was converted and three joined the church that day. "This has been a very profitable and pleasant Sabbath. Our people seem very kind and earnest to gain Heaven."[44]

Benjamin started for home on Tuesday, April 5, 1859, again traveling by train but

41. BTRD, Mar. 31, 1859.
42. BTRD, Apr. 1, 1859.
43. *Doctrines and Discipline of the Free Methodist Church,* pp. v-vi.
44. BTRD, Apr. 3, 1859.

this time going north through Illinois via Alton and Springfield. Probably he traveled as far north as Chicago and there caught a train east.[45]

Roberts's initial fund-raising efforts for the new free Methodist church in St. Louis apparently were not very successful, for a year later the church was still seeking to raise cash to build their own building. The infant church had suffered a serious setback, however, after Roberts left and while Redfield was away ministering in northern Illinois. Redfield reported in his memoir,

> In the fall [of 1859] I was again sent for to visit St. Louis. . . . I found a man [pastoring the new church] who was demanding $1,100 dollars a year, & our people were paying $1,200 more for church rent, & this man had distracted our people & so far disgusted them that many had left, & [he] now spent most [of] his time in a very exceptionable way for a minister of the gospel. My heart was broke to see that little band once numbering about 275 reduced to less than 100 members. I could only weep day & night at the desolation. I tried as long as I could to stem the disaster. . . . [T]his wicked man had completely turned to an enemy the main man [i.e., principal member] who stood by like a man in the hour of trial & but for whose assistance I think I should have left the field [due to the opposition and criticism Redfield had encountered in St. Louis].[46]

The shock and stress of this experience, combined with attacks upon him in some of the Methodist press, brought on a stroke that temporarily paralyzed Redfield — and, as it turned out, proved to be a precursor of a debilitating stroke he suffered about a year later. Terrill wrote, "When Mr. Redfield saw the desolation this [preacher] had caused, he was nearly heart-broken. It so wrought upon his mind as to induce a slight stroke of paralysis. He was now obliged to cease entirely from all public labor for a season, and put himself under medical treatment. By spring he had so far recovered as to be able to preach again."[47]

Redfield then took charge of the church for some months, serving as its pastor. In April 1860 he printed up subscription sheets to aid in securing pledges so the congregation could build its own facility. The text of Redfield's appeal is historically significant because it suggests much about the ethos of early Free Methodism, especially in St. Louis — and about Redfield himself. It reads as follows:

DIME CHURCH

The First Free Methodist Church of St. Louis, organized in 1859, now occupying the Baptist Church, on Sixth St., between Franklin Av. And Wash St., have se-

---

45. BTRD, Apr. 5, 1859. Roberts's diary for the next three days is blank.

46. Redfield Autobiography, pp. 365-66 (slightly corrected).

47. Terrill, *Redfield*, p. 420. Marston was apparently referring to Terrill's account when he wrote, "According to one report, at one time the St. Louis church numbered about 275 members. But a pastor of sensational methods, over-reaching ambition and faulty character scattered many of the flock. About one hundred members survived until Dr. Redfield's return to St. Louis in the fall of 1859." Marston, p. 231.

cured a lot on the corner of Carr and Twelfth Sts., and propose to erect a cheap, plain and large brick Church. Free seats forever, and a free Gospel for all.

Our people, up to their ability, have subscribed from one to ten dimes, to be paid each week till the Church is finished and paid for. The Church will be about 50 to 55 feet by 80 to 85 feet, and capable of seating 800 to 1,200 people, at a cost inside of $6,000. One thousand shares of one dime paid, will complete the whole in ten to twelve months, with what we expect to get in larger sums. We beg of no one out of the Church, but would thankfully receive what is freely offered to build a free house for the long neglected poor.

April, 1860   J. W. Redfield, *Pastor*[48]

The rest of the sheet has spaces for "Subscribers' Names" and "No. [of] Shares."

It is not clear that this campaign, either, was fully successful, but it is clear that by early 1860, well before the denomination was officially organized, there was a Free Methodist church, identified as such, in St. Louis.

Ministry in Buffalo and Western New York

Back home in Buffalo, Roberts ran into renewed opposition from the Regency preachers. He noted on Saturday, April 9, "The regency are exerting their utmost influence to keep me from preaching the Gospel in this City. . . . But I am confident that the Lord wanted us to come here, and He will open the way for me to preach the Gospel in its purity in this City, especially to the poor. O that a double portion of His Holy Spirit might rest upon me."[49]

Benjamin now divided his time between ministry in Buffalo and traveling from place to place in western New York. He wrote his father on June 2, "We have just started out on another preaching tour. Appointments: To-night at Tonawanda, to-morrow night at Akron, Saturday and Sabbath at Caryville, Monday at Batavia, Tuesday at Attica, Wednesday at Varysburgh, Thursday the [ninth] at Rushford, Friday and Saturday, [tenth] and [eleventh], grove meeting at Caneadea, thence back home preaching by the way, once perhaps. I hope to be in Buffalo again by the 14th."[50]

Roberts's diary shows that Joseph McCreery was with him at the weekend grove meeting, along with other preachers, including two from the Wesleyan Methodist Church. "The whole country seemed to have turned out" on Sunday, he noted. "The roads and woods were full of vehicles." Earlier at the love feast (held apparently at

---

48. "Dime Church" subscription sheet. Copy in MMHC. Misprint "monts" corrected to "months."

49. BTRD, Apr. 9, 1859.

50. BTR to TR, June 2, 1859, quoted in BHR, *BTR*, p. 192. Roberts is off by one day in his dates, listing Thursday as the tenth, etc.; hence the corrections indicated. See BTRD, June 2-14, 1859.

the Caneadea Methodist Episcopal Church, where J. W. Reddy was the preacher), "Sister McCreery walked in the aisle — shouted and fell" under the power of the Spirit.[51]

In his June 2 letter to his father, Benjamin added, "Our meetings in Buffalo are increasing in interest, and I dislike to be away, but it seems to be necessary. Nothing is raised for us, only as it is taken up in collections, as we go about. This and the pressing calls seem to indicate that it is the order of Providence that we should keep on the go for the present."[52]

The annual Bergen camp meeting was held June 23-30, 1859. As usual, Benjamin helped with the arrangements. Ellen probably attended with him.[53] The preachers this year included Roberts, Redfield, Daniel Sinclair, and, from the Oneida Conference, B. I. Ives, J. F. Crawford, and A. B. Gregg.[54]

Both Sam and Ann Chesbrough attended. Ann, for whom camp meetings were really a different culture, described the experience.

> I had heard of the Bergen camp meeting, the only camp meeting I knew of anywhere. I wanted to go. So we began to make necessary preparations. It meant much work. All our bread, cakes, pies, doughnuts, everything must be prepared for the week [in advance] at home. My husband prepared the reach, a large, heavy wagon with springs. The tent poles stuck out behind, and it was filled with trunks and boxes of bedding and provisions. Without any backs to our seats, we rode fifty miles, stopping by the roadside to feed the horses and eat our lunch.
>
> . . . The people came hundreds of miles. It was like a little city of tents. I felt God was there as soon as we reached the ground. The first tent we entered struck me rather unfavorably, straw on the ground, no floors or carpets, but I was soon charmed with the simplicity of tent living. Such a sense of holiness as pervaded the grounds I never felt before. It was heaven below. . . . Many were saved and sanctified, the work went on in glorious power and spread in every direction. Not only Methodists but people in every *denomination*, all who received the truth in the love of it were made free indeed, and gave God the glory.[55]

The camp meeting got off to a slow start, but then there was a breakthrough. Benjamin noted on Saturday, the second full day of the camp: "The meeting seemed to be hampered some way till bro. S. K. J. Chesbrough got up and broke through. The Lord blessed him very greatly — he exhorted with power — shouted and jumped. The power of God came down upon the congregation. Some of the

---

51. BTRD, June 12, 1859.

52. BTR to TR, June 2, 1859, quoted in BHR, *BTR*, p. 192.

53. Ellen's 1859 diary has no entries after June 2, but her June 1 entry suggests she was planning to attend the Bergen camp meeting.

54. BTRD, June 23-30, 1859. See the account in *WAS*, pp. 122-24.

55. Ann E. Chesbrough, "Experience of Mrs. Ann E. Chesbrough," in *A Sermon by Rev. W. T. Hogue Preached at the Fiftieth Anniversary of the Marriage of Rev. Samuel K. J. and Mrs. Ann E. Chesbrough, February 6, 1898* (Chicago: Free Methodist Publishing House, 1906), pp. 60-61.

preachers afraid for their lives, endeavored to avoid the scandal of having the C.M. under the control of an expelled minister. But the people insisted that we should be sustained."[56]

Clearly the Bergen camp meeting was growing in its reach and influence. This year some attended from the new "free" church in St. Louis, including Brother and Sister Waite. Sister Osborne came from St. Charles, Illinois, where Redfield had been active, and Brother and Sister Hicks came from Syracuse, which was in the Black River Conference.[57]

An incident occurred at this camp meeting that may help explain the early Free Methodist conviction that a Masonic conspiracy lay behind the Genesee Conference expulsions several months earlier. During the closing love feast on Thursday morning, June 30, Miss Mariet Hardy, then about thirty years old, felt moved of the Spirit to share a word God had given her. There had been "a spirit of uncertainty," she felt, as to the explanation for the conference trials of B. T. Roberts and others. Mariet felt that God gave her the answer. Her daughter related,

> Suddenly the Holy Spirit flashed the light upon Miss Hardy's mind, showing her that organized secrecy, in the form of Free Masonry, was the real cause. She arose and testified to the view she then received.
>
> It was as if a bomb-shell had been exploded in their very midst. Many present, sympathizers with the holiness movement, were Free Masons, and it was hoped they would soon identify themselves with the nucleus of the new church that was rapidly forming. One after another testified, opposing the statements made by Miss Hardy, who had sat down nearly crushed under the opposing influences that she felt.[58]

Others, however, spoke up and affirmed Miss Hardy's witness. And then the Spirit moved dramatically: "Suddenly as if a mighty wind had blown across the vast congregation, beginning near Miss Hardy, an outpouring of the Holy Spirit came, as on the day of Pentecost. She was filled with uncontrollable laughter, others wept, many fell to the ground, some shouted, danced, and leaped for joy. The preachers looked on in wonder, not one in the [preachers'] stand being affected by this mighty outpouring. Thus did the Holy Ghost set his seal upon the truth."[59]

Roberts remarked in his diary, "There has been more accomplished at this meeting than at any meeting I ever attended. Sis Hardy gave a powerful exhortation at the close of the services at the stand."[60]

---

56. BTRD, June 25, 1859.

57. BTRD, June 24, 1859.

58. Emma Freeland Shay, *Mariet Hardy Freeland: A Faithful Witness*, 3rd ed. (Winona Lake, Ind.: Woman's Missionary Society of the Free Methodist Church, 1937; first published in 1913), pp. 113-14.

59. Shay, *Mariet Hardy Freeland*, p. 114. Freeland and her husband became important early leaders and preachers in the Free Methodist Church. Mariet, in particular, was instrumental in the founding of Wessington Springs Seminary in South Dakota. See pp. 163-75.

60. BTRD, June 30, 1859.

Roberts did not comment further on Mariet's "bombshell." Presumably it confirmed what he already believed and had himself said, at least in private. To him, this was no new revelation. But Mariet's testimony must have served to drive deep into the consciousness of the emerging movement the conviction that secret societies played a pernicious, conspiratorial role in removing Roberts from the Genesee Conference.

The Bergen camp meeting concluded with the usual "marching round" and the love feast. About noon B. T. and Ellen Roberts and the others began heading home.[61]

Ellen experienced a remarkable physical healing about this time — probably at this camp meeting.[62] Almost thirty years later she told the story. Her healing came "in the days past when nothing was said upon the subject of healing." She herself had seen only a couple of instances of people healed. Her own healing marked another significant turning point: "It was the dawning of a new life. From that time I had a stronger faith in God and a steadier course heavenward."[63]

Ellen recalled her healing this way: "My health had been poor for ten years [essentially the first decade of her married life with Benjamin] and was gradually growing worse. I had sought relief from earthly physicians and found no permanent help. Then I became convinced that the Great Physician alone could cure me and give me health."

Ellen read in the Gospels that Jesus "healed them that had need of healing" (Luke 9:11), and her faith took hold and she believed that "he who turned not from the leper, the palsied, the lunatic, the importunate widow, and multitudes besides, would also hear [her] cry for help."

She said, "What seemed my privilege now appeared my duty." She must trust God for her physical healing, as she had for spiritual help. By means of "a fuller surrender and a renewed yielding of my all to him," God touched her body. She saw that "work and crosses" lay before her.

> I thought those crosses were in the future — but no, they were right there. I was called upon to take them at once. As I said "yes" to all, and obeyed by taking what seemed to be a step in the dark and unknown, it proved to be a wondrous step into light and liberty. Faith for my body was so easy, and Jesus was my physician from that hour. . . . I began to confess to my friends what the Lord was *doing* for me. I did testify that the healing power rested upon me. The "balm of Gilead" came to my body — my disease was removed. Life and energy, to which I had been a stranger for years, returned.[64]

---

61. Benjamin noted, "The Camp Meeting closed well this morning. It would have been better if we had held the Love Feast before marching round. . . . We started for home about noon." BTRD, June 30, 1859.

62. As noted in chapter 15, B. T. Roberts wrote in 1885 that Ellen "was healed in answer to prayer" while attending the Bergen camp meeting "some twenty-five years ago." [B. T. Roberts], "To a Skeptic," *EC* 49, no. 3 (Mar. 1885): 91. Most likely this was in 1859, though possibly 1860.

63. Mrs. B. T. Roberts, "Healed," *EC* 45, no. 2 (Jan. 1888): 8-9.

64. Mrs. B. T. Roberts, "Healed," pp. 8-9.

Characteristically, Ellen is rather vague as to what "crosses" she was immediately called upon to bear. This may have concerned Benjamin's expanding, largely independent ministry that shortly led to the founding of the Free Methodist Church. In any case, from this point on Ellen had generally robust health for ministry herself and for assisting Benjamin. "In the years that have passed since that time, when attacked by disease, I have gone to the same source for help, and his word has brought health and victory, sometimes gradually but more frequently suddenly. I have found discipline and teaching in affliction of body, but I have found a greater blessing when resurrection power came and lifted me out of the grave of sickness."[65]

Ellen's physical healing came at a strategic time. She would soon be entering into a broader and more demanding ministry as a new denomination and a new magazine were born. Her healing has broader meaning, also: the Free Methodist Church would be born with confidence in God's willingness to heal physically. B. T. and Ellen Roberts did not speak in terms of "the fourfold gospel" as A. B. Simpson and others did a generation later, but they did proclaim Jesus Christ as Savior, sanctifier, and healer.[66] God could and did heal. This was not a question or a point of controversy with the Robertses or within the Free Methodist Church.

A key aspect of Ellen's ministry at this liminal time was her wide correspondence (private and still unpublished) with Methodist or "Nazarite" women who, like herself, made up the movement that would soon give birth to Free Methodism. Emeline Smith wrote, "I cannot find any one throughout this land to whom my heart so instructively turns for counsel & sympathy as to yours," and other sisters wrote similarly.[67] Ellen's quiet, sisterly counsel was probably as important as her husband's more public networking with key male leaders.

Throughout these difficult days Ellen continued her long correspondence with her dear aunt Lydia Lane. Lydia was now nursing her declining husband; the Lanes had moved from Mount Holly, New Jersey, to Wilkes-Barre, Pennsylvania, the area of George's boyhood, and were living in near-poverty. There the venerable George Lane, pioneer circuit rider and former ME book agent, died on May 6, 1859, at age seventy-five.

Three months before his death Lydia wrote to Ellen, describing her uncle's increasing debility. "[Y]our uncle needs all my time, and almost all my strength, and when I can sit down mostly I am so weary, I cannot even write." George was "not sick," she said; "only his mind is almost entirely gone, and I can seldom converse with him only as I would with a child." Yet George still remembered Ellen. One night as Lydia was putting him to bed she mentioned that Ellen by letter sent him her love.

"Thank her kindly for it," George unexpectedly replied.

65. Mrs. B. T. Roberts, "Healed," p. 8.
66. Toward the end of the nineteenth century Simpson began emphasizing what became the motto of the Christian and Missionary Alliance: "Jesus Christ, Saviour, Sanctifier, Healer and Coming King" — the "fourfold gospel." B. T. Roberts affirmed Christ's second coming, but for him this was never a major point of emphasis.
67. Emeline Smith to ELR, July 24, 1861.

"You remember Ellen, do you not," Lydia asked.

"Perfectly," George replied.

"Ellen always loved you a great deal."

"And I have always loved her a great deal," George said.

This was "something so new for him to be able to converse at all," Lydia wrote to Ellen, "that I thought I must mention it."[68]

The first Laymen's Convention had issued a call for a second gathering to meet during the Bergen camp meeting, and this second convention met at 4:00 P.M. on Saturday, June 25.[69] This was not a full-blown convention such as the meeting six months earlier had been and apparently transacted no official business.[70]

Meanwhile Benjamin continued his itinerant preaching throughout western New York. His diary shows that on Sunday, August 14, he preached in a grove meeting at Cayuga Creek, north of Buffalo, on Acts 17:11, "These were more noble than those in Thessalonica, in that they received the word with all readiness of mind, and searched the scriptures daily, whether those things were so," and in the evening "in [the] tent" from Deuteronomy 32:29, "O that they were wise, that they understood this, that they would consider their latter end!" Brothers and sisters were present from the area, including Pekin, Youngstown, and Tonawanda. Roberts noted that just a week earlier "while Bro. Cannon was preaching four or five constables led on by a regency trustee came up and arrested two of our brethren — Bros. Carl and Fairchild — hand cuffed them and took them to jail." When Benjamin got back home the next day, he wrote "an account of the Cayuga Creek outrage" for the *Northern Independent.* "The brethren were arrested on the charge of breaking in windows of the Church though there was not the slightest evidence or even suspicion against them. They are quiet and harmless men as can be found. They are poor and hence could be arrested with impunity."[71]

1859 Genesee Conference: More Expulsions

The expulsions of Roberts and McCreery at the 1858 Genesee Annual Conference caused much more of a stir than the Regency preachers ever expected. Clearly, an incipient movement was under way in reaction to the expulsions. In turn, the Regency response in 1859 was even more drastic as the conference attempted to stamp out "Nazaritism."

68. LBL to ELR, Jan. 8, 1859.

69. Not June 20, as Marston (p. 216) and Zahniser (p. 131) report, based on a misprint in *WAS,* p. 217. See *WAS,* p. 123. June 20 was the Monday before the Bergen camp meeting began, not a Thursday, as given in Zahniser.

70. No minutes seem to have survived, and the minutes of the Nov. 1-2, 1859, Laymen's Convention designate this gathering the "Second Annual Session." See Marston, p. 216.

71. BTRD, Aug. 14-15, 1859.

The Genesee Conference met October 5-17 at Brockport under the leadership of Bishop Matthew Simpson. John Robie reported in the *Buffalo Advocate* that the conference was determined to rid itself of "Nazaritism" and no longer suffer "the disgrace arising from one of the worst scandals which ever pestered a denomination of Christians." "[C]razy men will not be orderly," Robie said. Further expulsions were justified; "having coveted martyrdom, they will have it."[72]

If any of the hundred or so conference preachers thought the Nazarite issue was subsiding, they had only to look at the huge tent meeting that the lawyer-evangelist Fay Purdy conducted on the outskirts of Brockport, not far from where the conference was in session. Purdy's tent seated three thousand, and daily attendance reached as high as five thousand, Hosmer reported in the *Northern Independent*.[73] Not only Genesee Conference Methodists but Methodists from other conferences and some people from other denominations attended. Purdy said he intended the meeting to serve as an olive branch, drawing people together, but Bishop Simpson and the Regency preachers found it divisive and irritating. It was all the more irritating, no doubt, that on Sunday, October 9, Hosmer, Roberts, and D. W. Thurston, a presiding elder from the Oneida Conference, were the featured preachers.[74]

The Regency preachers considered the whole crowd attending this impromptu camp meeting to be Nazarites. But as Hogue notes, the size and diversity of the crowd "clearly showed that 'Nazaritism' was not so nearly extinct as its enemies had hoped and supposed. It was not even weakened, much less destroyed."[75] Many of the people who came for the camp also sat in on the conference sessions (and probably vice versa). Bishop Simpson was not pleased. He wrote his wife on Sunday, "Women have come by troops — one crowd by a canal-boat, others from Utica, and some, it is said, from St. Louis. They are in attendance in the galleries, and some have their knitting busily employed. They are all Nazarites, and use, in their conversation, many epithets denunciatory of the Conference."[76]

The Regency preachers had done their homework, however. Robie, Carlton, Fuller, or others of the Regency group apparently had worked to prejudice Bishop Simpson against the Nazarites, claiming they planned to secede. According to Roberts, Simpson later said he had been given a printed proposal for a new church to be called Associate Methodists. If such a document ever existed, it most likely originated with those who opposed the Nazarites.[77]

---

72. [John E. Robie], "Genesee Conference," *Buffalo Advocate,* Oct. 13, 1859, p. 2.

73. William Hosmer, *NI* 4, no. 10 (Oct. 13, 1859), cited in Marston, p. 217.

74. Marston, pp. 217-18; BTRD, Oct. 9, 1859. It appears from Roberts's diary that he canceled a previously scheduled appointment to preach at the Free Will Baptist Church in South Byron in order to be at Brockport. Hosmer preached in the morning, Roberts in the afternoon, and Thurston in the evening.

75. Hogue, *HFMC,* 1:222.

76. George R. Crooks, *The Life of Bishop Matthew Simpson of the Methodist Episcopal Church* (New York: Harper and Brothers, 1890), p. 359.

77. B. T. Roberts, "Secession — Bishop Simpson," *NI* 4, no. 15 (Nov. 17, 1859). Cited in Marston, p. 234.

On the second day of the conference the Regency preachers introduced five resolutions for dealing with the Nazarite crisis. These were adopted — action that, Roberts felt, preempted the authority of the General Conference since the resolutions were, in effect, new legislation.[78] Among other things, the resolutions stated that "we consider the admission of expelled ministers, whether traveling or local, to our pulpits, and associating with them and assisting them as ministers, until they have, by due process, as described in the Discipline, been restored to the fellowship of the Church, as subversive of the integrity and government of the Church, directly tending to the production of discord and division and every evil work."

The resolutions condemned conference preachers who cooperated with expelled ministers, whether in their own churches, at camp meetings, or on other occasions. The fifth resolution carried the threat that if any conference preacher disregarded these provisions, "he shall be held to answer to this Conference for the same."[79]

After these resolutions were passed (with some opposition),[80] Bishop Simpson addressed the conference, warning against schism and insubordination. Conable records his remarks as follows:

> Brethren, I have been a Methodist from my youth up. I have lived to witness several secessions, but I never heard such doctrines professed by Methodist preachers as have been openly declared on this floor this morning. I have heard brethren declare their right to admit to their pulpits, and associate in labor with them, men who stand expelled from the Methodist Episcopal Church; and I have heard brethren appeal to their right of private judgment in justification of the same, and also of their right to preach when and where they will, and to enter within other men's fields of labor, and work without the consent of the pastor. In all my knowledge of Methodism, I have never heard such doctrines avowed till this morning.[81]

Methodist preachers, Simpson said, had solemnly vowed to obey the disciplinary rules for preachers. They were therefore bound by conscience to yield to the will of the majority in such matters.

> After such vow and covenant to surrender your private will to the judgment of your seniors in the Gospel, a promise made without mental reservation, and freely, I am astonished to hear brethren assert a right of private judgment in regard to the order and manner of their ministerial services, against the judgment and decision of the conference. We are all bound by the covenant, and if any man cannot in conscience follow the judgment and direction of the church, the only

---

78. *WAS*, p. 219.

79. Conable, p. 651; cf. *WAS*, pp. 245-46. According to Conable, the paper containing the resolutions was introduced by Sandford Hunt.

80. Conable says ten to twenty voted against four of the five resolutions. Conable, p. 653.

81. Interestingly, the "doctrines" Simpson refers to are not matters of theology so much as matters of proper structure and administration.

honorable course left for him to pursue is to retire from the Church. I have no doubt that brethren intend right, but they are misled. I have said this as your pastor — your chief pastor, to warn brethren, especially young brethren. You are treading on the verge of a precipice which is crumbling under your feet. By your course you are bringing ruin upon the souls around you. I beg of you to pause where you are. We have all of us work enough to do, and if the circuits are not large enough to fill your hearts and hands and time, let us know and we will make them larger.[82]

It apparently did not occur to Bishop Simpson that if his logic had prevailed in Germany in the 1500s or England in the 1700s, there would never have been a Reformation or a Methodist movement. His argument, to be convincing, had to assume that the conference's decision in expelling Roberts and McCreery was right. And of course, a number of preachers simply couldn't in good conscience accept that. Besides, Simpson's interpretation of the denominational rules is questionable. It is doubtful that even Wesley would have said that Methodist preachers surrendered their right of private *judgment* when they were ordained — though they did in a substantial sense surrender their private *will*.[83] Unwittingly, no doubt, Simpson was articulating a medieval Roman Catholic ecclesiology, not a Protestant or Wesleyan one.

In saying that those who "cannot in conscience follow the judgment and direction of the Church" should leave, Simpson is in effect saying that there is, by definition, no place for reformers in the church. And of course, "the judgment and direction of the Church" in this case meant questionable, highly politicized action of the majority against the minority.

Nevertheless, having established these resolutions, the conference proceeded to try and expel (for "contumacy") four more of its preachers. As Conable says frankly, "The series of resolutions . . . were made a test rule in the examination of character . . . of those who were reported as having disregarded" their provisions. "This proved a very effectual way of settling matters so far as the Conference was concerned."[84]

The preachers thus tried and expelled were Loren Stiles, C. D. Burlingham, William Cooley, and John Wells.[85] Roberts later commented on Stiles's expulsion:

---

82. Simpson, as quoted in Conable, pp. 652-53.

83. Simpson, probably unconsciously, moves in this statement from the "surrender [of] private will" to the total surrender of the "right of private judgment." The two are not the same. Methodist preachers made a commitment of the will to obey the stated rules for preachers (itself an act of judgment), but could not surrender their right of private judgment, which included their consciences, without violating something essential of their very personhood. Thus Simpson's logic falls flat.

84. Conable, p. 653.

85. Burlingham appealed to the General Conference and in the meantime ceased all public ministry. He apparently was the author however of a strongly worded account of the "Genesee Conference difficulties" that was critical of the conference, published in 1860. He later admitted his "errors" and was readmitted into the conference in late 1860 through a rather convoluted process (Conable, p. 653; *Minutes*, Genesee Conference, 1859, 1860; Hogue, *HFMC*, 1:246, 311-13; Marston, p. 218). See Pelatiah [C. D. Burlingham], *An Outline History of the Genesee Conference Difficulties: Their Nature, Origin,*

"Loren Stiles, one of the most eloquent, amiable, gentlemanly and successful preachers in Western New York, was expelled for allowing us to exhort in his church, when we held an exhorter's license; and for preaching on week day nights in a village said to be on another preacher's circuit, though the nearest appointment of this preacher was about three miles from this village."[86]

John Wells was the pastor at Belfast, south of Pike on the Genesee River, where Roberts had preached twice on March 6 and Redfield had preached in July. Roberts had noted in his diary on September 17, 1859, "At Belfast the work of the Lord has gone on with some power since the Laymen's Camp Meeting. Many of the members who have been backslidden in heart for years have come out and again consecrated themselves to God and been restored to his favor."[87] All four expelled preachers had been closely associated with Roberts. The conference also "located" two of the Nazarite preachers, J. W. Reddy and H. H. Farnsworth.[88]

Reporting on the conference actions in the *Northern Independent*, Hosmer was quick to draw parallels with early Methodism. "Methodism grew up in spite of order — not without order in itself, nor contrary to the order of God, but in spite of the order of the established Church, in whose bosom its founder lived and died." He added, "A system which owes its existence to an irregularity of this kind, should be tolerant of irregularities, especially where even prejudice itself can impute no crime."[89]

When the 1859 Genesee Conference adjourned on October 17, the 1860 Methodist General Conference was only about six months away. Roberts still hoped and expected that this supreme governing body would reverse the actions of the Genesee Conference against him. Thus, as Marston notes, "Efforts were now directed to holding together in Bands and Societies the detached groups; to maintaining the cause of reform within the church in places where the reformers still had access; to extending their numbers through evangelism; and to holding their groups in readiness for acceptance by the church when the General Conference should have acted to confirm their rights as loyal Methodists. That General Conference would so act was their confidence. Even in perplexity, they were not in despair."[90]

Causes, Influence and Remedy (n.p., 1860). The copy of this sixty-one-page pamphlet located in MMHC has the name "Rev. C. D. Burlingham" written in under the printed words "By Pelatiah." It is not clear on what basis this work was attributed to Burlingham; however, Hogue says explicitly that this pamphlet was "written and published by the Rev. C. D. Burlingham" (1:24).

86. [B. T. Roberts], "Holiness Sects," *EC* 47, no. 6 (June 1884): 187.

87. BTRD, Sept. 17, 1859. Cf. entries for Mar. 6 and July 14.

88. Wells later joined the Presbyterian Church. See Marston, p. 218.

89. William Hosmer, *NI* 4, no. 10 (Oct. 13, 1859), quoted in Marston, p. 219. Marston suggests, "The Methodist system in the early nineteenth century has been called more autocratic than any other in Protestantism," and discusses this and related issues, noting that the Methodist Protestant Church had its origin in similar expulsions (pp. 219-26). "It is normally thus, that the spirit of earnest Christianity is aroused by Laodicean complacency, and the reformer's zeal disturbs that complacency into vigorous antagonism against the disturber of the peace" (p. 226) — a remarkable comment for one who was at the time himself a bishop.

90. Marston, p. 227.

Throughout the year Roberts had in fact organized several "band societies" or "soul-saving bands" both to consolidate the fruit of his ministry and to extend its evangelistic witness. The parallels to Wesley's forming bands and societies within the Anglican Church in the earliest days of British Methodism are obvious.[91]

Redfield, who by nature was more apocalyptic and iconoclastic than Roberts and who arguably had a broader "on the ground" knowledge of contemporary Methodism, was not optimistic about the upcoming General Conference. He had long thought that eventual separation of the true "pilgrims" from an increasingly compromised Methodism was inevitable. In 1856 he had confided to William Kendall and his wife, "I think the pilgrims will yet have to organize a new church, and yet that will fail, if they do not guard . . . against hard feelings against their oppressors. . . . The opponents of holiness will conquer the pilgrims as long as they remain in the church, as slavery will certainly conquer in the legislation of the church. There is no hope but in getting away from so great a mass of corruption."

Redfield had concluded, "we will never succeed in cleansing the church." He was convinced that "there is no rational hope but in separation; and yet I would by no means hoist the banner of separation, for you cannot then keep out the spirit of carnal warfare, and that will be death to spirituality." If "our darling brethren" remained faithful, eventually "formalists will compel the separation."[92]

Revival in the West

Redfield was reflecting in part his revival experiences in "the West" — Illinois and the St. Louis area, especially. He had conducted a rousing revival at St. Charles, thirty-five miles west of Chicago, in 1856. Many had been converted and many Methodists were led into the experience of holiness. As a result, for the next three years he had a widening ministry in the northern Illinois area, with effective revivals in a number of Methodist churches.

Redfield conducted a particularly remarkable revival in Marengo, Illinois, about thirty-five miles northwest of Chicago, in the winter of 1857-58.[93] Here a number of nominal Methodists and others were converted. Key figures were Mr. and Mrs. Moses L. Hart, Methodists and the parents of future Free Methodist leader Edward Payson Hart. Mrs. Hart had been somewhat acquainted with Redfield and his ministry years earlier in Vermont, and "frequently spoke of him as a remarkable revivalist." In response to a dream in which he "saw Doctor Redfield walking up the aisle of the church," Moses Hart (who had never met Redfield) persuaded the official board

---

91. See BTRD, Jan. 30, Feb. 19, Aug. 22 and 23, Dec. 15, 1859.

92. Redfield to William and Mrs. Kendall, June 2 and July 27, 1856. Quoted in Terrill, *Redfield*, pp. 310-12.

93. Marengo, in western McHenry County, is just a few miles from the area in eastern Boone County where Ellen Roberts's family had settled when they moved west from Windsor, N.Y.

of the Methodist Episcopal church in Marengo to invite Redfield to come and help with a revival already in progress there.[94]

Redfield began his ministry at the Marengo ME Church on Wednesday evening, February 3, 1858. Mrs. Hart entered "into the experience of entire holiness" that first night. Moses Hart, "after a great struggle," also "came out into the experience of 'perfect love'" during this revival. E. P. Hart, then twenty-two, who had made a profession of faith in the revival prior to Redfield's coming, was also deeply affected by Redfield, who stayed in the Hart home during the revival.[95] E. P. Hart later wrote,

> [A]s the members sought and obtained the experience of entire sanctification conviction spread throughout the entire place and the country for miles in every direction. Doctors, lawyers and saloonkeepers were brought under the power of saving grace. As evidence of the genuineness of the work every saloon in the village was closed up. At the close of evening services men going in different directions to their homes could be heard shouting "Glory! Hallelujah!"
>
> People came in wagon loads from eight to ten miles, and in order to secure seats in the church often reached town before dark.[96]

A "large number of the most substantial people in the community" were converted, Hart noted, and a daily 5:00 A.M. prayer meeting continued for over a year. "Doctor Redfield pronounced this revival the most thorough and perfect work in all his labors," Hart was told.[97] One of the converts was twenty-nine-year-old Mrs. Harriet Damon Coon, later a prominent figure in Free Methodism, known affectionately as "Auntie Coon."[98] Joseph Goodwin Terrill, a young man of nineteen, also about this time "received under Dr. Redfield's ministry a baptism with the Spirit" that marked him for life.[99]

These Redfield revivals in "the West" did much to shape later Free Methodism. "Under the Doctor's labors in Illinois a number of men and women were raised up who were afterward to become influential in molding the character of the Free Methodist Church," Hogue noted.[100] Richard R. Blews said of Redfield, "This unique and powerful preacher had a greater influence than any other man upon those who became the founders of the Free Methodist Church."[101]

Eventually opposition to Redfield's ministry arose within the conference, and

94. Edward Payson Hart, *Reminiscences of Early Free Methodism* (Chicago: Free Methodist Publishing House, 1903), pp. 4-5, 10; Terrill, *Redfield*, p. 330.

95. Hart, *Reminiscences*, pp. 7, 14; E. P. Hart, "Obituary" (of Moses L. Hart), *EC* 48, no. 2 (Aug. 1884): 66.

96. Hart, *Reminiscences*, p. 15.

97. Hart, *Reminiscences*, p. 18.

98. E. E. Shelhamer, ed., *Life and Labors of Auntie Coon* (Atlanta: Repairer Office, 1905), pp. 39-45.

99. Hogue, *HFMC*, 1:270.

100. Hogue, *HFMC*, 1:269.

101. Richard R. Blews, *Master Workmen: Biographies of the Later Bishops of the Free Methodist Church during Her First Century, 1860-1960*, centennial ed. (Winona Lake, Ind.: Light and Life Press, 1960), p. 58.

Redfield was not welcome in Methodist pulpits. Wholesale expulsions occurred in 1858 and 1859. The abuse of the rights of Methodist church membership was so flagrant that the 1860 General Conference decreed that no Methodist could be pronounced withdrawn from the church without his or her verbal consent. "[B]efore that restraining action of 1860, many good Methodists suffered the injustice of losing their membership in the church, with no opportunity to defend themselves by exercise of their constitutional right to trial," Marston notes.[102]

At the St. Charles Methodist Episcopal Church, about 60 members were forced out. On their own they formed an independent Methodist "band" that grew in number over the following months. By the end of April 1860 (on the eve of the Methodist General Conference), the group had grown to 112. Finally concluding that there was no hope of reconciliation with the parent congregation, this group on April 27, 1860, organized itself as a "Free Methodist Church." A "Free Methodist Society" was organized about the same time near Elgin, Illinois.[103] These groups, like the new "Free" Methodist Church in St. Louis, were of course independent congregations. The official formation of a Free Methodist denomination was still months away, though clearly the process of forming a new "sect" was already by now well advanced. B. T. Roberts had nothing directly to do with the formation of these new groups in Illinois, but their story quickly became intertwined with his and with developments in western New York.

Growing Ministry in Buffalo

Meanwhile, Roberts continued traveling throughout the Genesee Conference and beyond, preaching and organizing "Salvation Bands" in Syracuse, Rochester, and other places. He was also busy in Buffalo. Early in 1859 he began preaching with some regularity at a small congregation meeting on Thirteenth Street, on the city outskirts but only about three blocks from the Roberts home on Palmer Street.[104]

The Thirteenth Street congregation probably started as a mission outreach of the Black Rock ME Church. It was served regularly by Methodist preachers, though not officially organized as a Methodist Episcopal church — perhaps in part because it met in a building privately owned by Jesse Ketchum, a Congregationalist.[105] In the 1858 Genesee Conference minutes, Thirteenth Street is listed as a preaching point connected with the Riverside (formerly Black Rock) Church. Griffin Smith was the appointed preacher.[106]

102. Marston, p. 229.

103. *WAS*, pp. 274-77; Marston, pp. 229, 232.

104. In his 1859 diary, Benjamin usually refers to this group as "the 13th Street church."

105. Hogue calls it "a Free Methodist Episcopal Church, in which the seats were neither rented nor sold" (*HFMC*, 1:306), though it is unlikely that it officially bore the name Free Methodist. The fact that this group apparently emphasized that it maintained "free seats" likely indicates, however, that it was started partly to protest the pew rental system.

106. *Minutes*, Genesee Conference, 1857-1859. The village of Black Rock was annexed to Buffalo in 1853.

A few months after Benjamin and Ellen moved to Buffalo, someone invited Roberts to preach at a midweek service at Thirteenth Street. This invitation upset Smith and the other Buffalo Regency preachers. But since the building was not under Methodist control and the group was not officially a Methodist congregation, they could not stop him. In fact, Edward Cox, who managed the chapel for Mr. Ketchum, told Smith, "An appointment has been made for Mr. Roberts, and if he chooses to come the doors will be open for him."[107]

Roberts's diary shows that he preached regularly at Thirteenth Street whenever he was in Buffalo. Benson later recalled the "long walk, pleasant in summer, but in winter very tiring," that as a lad he frequently took with his parents "to Jesse Ketchum's church on the suburbs of the city."[108]

The little congregation there began to grow, but so did the opposition. Benjamin noted that on April 30 John Robie and Richard Waite, the Buffalo District presiding elder, called on Ketchum and tried unsuccessfully to get him to ban Roberts from his chapel. The same day Robie and Smith tried to persuade the trustees of the Black Rock Baptist Church not to let Roberts preach there on Sunday — again, with no success. Roberts's diary for Sunday, May 1, notes, "Preached this morning in the Baptist Church at Black Rock. In the afternoon at same place on Holiness." In the evening he preached at Thirteenth Street. "Good congregation and a free time," he noted. "So a door is opened for the Gospel to be preached in Buffalo." His text was Romans 8:9, "But ye are not in the flesh, but in the Spirit, if so be that the Spirit of God dwell in you. Now if any man have not the Spirit of Christ, he is none of his."[109]

With Roberts traveling so much, he needed helpers in Buffalo — and gradually developed some. Samuel Chesbrough had begun to preach occasionally, and Roberts enlisted him from time to time at Thirteenth Street. Benjamin noted on September 1, "Bro. Samuel Chesbrough has preached [at Thirteenth Street] two Sabbaths, with acceptability. The Lord has a work for him to do."[110]

By late 1859 Roberts had effectively become the pastor of this growing congregation. When he formally organized it as a "Free" Methodist church in November, Cox was one of the trustees and Ellen Roberts, it appears, was among the members.[111] The following year when the new denomination was formed, this congregation became the Thirteenth Street Free Methodist Church.[112]

---

107. BHR, *BTR*, p. 217; BTRD, Apr. 12, 1859. There are several references to Jesse Ketchum and Edward Cox in Benjamin's 1859 diary.

108. Benson H. Roberts, "My Mother," *EC* 95, no. 3 (Mar. 1908): 69.

109. BTRD, May 1, 1859.

110. BTRD, Sept. 1, 1859.

111. Cox later was a benefactor of Chesbrough Seminary (now Roberts Wesleyan College); Cox Hall is named for him. Hogue, *HFMC*, 2:307.

112. Marston, pp. 235-36; BTRD, Jan. 20 and Nov. 18, 1859. The Jan. 20 entry actually refers to Nov. 6. It is a list of names, including that of Ellen Roberts, connected with "13th St.," but whether this is a list of members or something else (perhaps a class meeting list) is not indicated. In any case, it identifies Ellen with Thirteenth Street.

During 1859 and 1860 Roberts thus made his base in Buffalo while traveling widely. His vision for his Buffalo ministry was to preach the gospel to the poor in the heart of the city, however, and the Thirteenth Street location wasn't ideal for that. So Roberts began looking for a downtown location. The Regency preachers blocked him from getting the old Swan Street Church building, he said, as well as other properties.[113]

In April of 1860, however, Benjamin found an ideal location. The old Pearl Street Theater, just a block from the Niagara Street Church, was for sale at $3,500. It seated nearly 800 and would be ideal for a central-city ministry. Benjamin wrote his father that he had found "an opening by which we can preach the Gospel in the central portion of the city."

The problem, of course, was money. Benjamin figured he needed $500 to equip the building for church services. "Thus for $4,000 we can get a good brick church centrally located," he told his father. Roberts negotiated for the building and found he could buy it for $1,000 down and yearly payments of $500 or so. It was a good deal, he felt, from both a ministry and a business standpoint. Benjamin probably hoped that his father would contribute something, and he may have.[114]

But where to find the needed $1,500 to get started? Benjamin and Ellen decided to sell their house on Palmer Street, for which they had paid $2,200. Ellen later told the story:

> My husband felt we must get a place for worship in the heart of the city, where the gospel could be preached to the poor. He could see no way of doing it except he gave our home towards it. It was all we had. I looked the matter over. We had three children. I thought of the way the Disciples were led, at that marvelous outpouring of the Spirit, when they "sold their possessions and goods and parted them to all men as every man had need." . . . Let those who have prayed long for blessings not received, begin to feed the poor, clothe the naked, and yield themselves and substance to the Lord as if they meant it, and he will pour them out blessings that will measure beyond their desires and expectations.[115]

It is not clear how much was realized from the sale, but with the proceeds and some pledges from friends Benjamin was able to close the deal on the theater.[116]

Now without a home, Benjamin and Ellen temporarily had Benson and Georgie

---

113. BTR to TR, Apr. 19, 1860, cited in BHR, *BTR*, p. 218.

114. BTR to TR, Apr. 19, 1860, quoted in BHR, *BTR*, p. 218.

115. Ellen Lois Roberts, "Give and Receive," *EC* 44, no. 3 (Sept. 1882): 93.

116. Benson Roberts says, "The proceeds of this sale, applied on the payment, enabled him, with what help was rendered by others, to make secure the purchase of the theatre, which was transformed into a church" (BHR, *BTR*, pp. 218-19). Assuming the house had appreciated and was now paid for (which it should have been, according to the terms of purchase in 1853), Roberts should have realized more than enough from the sale to pay the $1,500. It is not clear whether he in fact received less (perhaps due to some indebtedness on the house), or paid more on the theater than just the down payment. Alternatively, he may have used some of the sale money to help cover living or other expenses.

stay with friends while the couple and little Charlie traveled from place to place in itinerant ministry.[117] Rev. James Mathews wrote later, "Bro. Cox gave my wife and me the use of a house [in Buffalo]. Brother and Sister Roberts put their furniture in it, and we all lived together that winter. They traveled up and down the land coming home occasionally."[118]

It appears that Roberts then bought a house in 1861. A deed dated February 27, 1861, shows that he purchased property on Ninth Street near Maryland Street, and an 1864 receipt for one firkin (about fifty-six pounds) of butter delivered to him at Ninth Street suggests that he and his family were still living there at that time.[119] According to Benson Roberts, "The privations of those days were severe, but I do not remember ever hearing the first word of complaint from my mother, though she was never very strong and there was a family of lively young children to be cared for."[120]

Benjamin proved to be right that a central-city ministry would draw the people. "Soon the church was packed, floor and galleries," Benson wrote. "Many lost souls here found life and salvation. Free churches were an established fact in Buffalo."[121]

The remaining debt on the old theater was a burden, however. Ellen thought Benjamin should do more to raise the necessary funds and retire the debt. In the January 1861 issue of Benjamin's new periodical, the *Earnest Christian,* she published an appeal for help. "In this city of fashionable churches, where formality and death reign, we have opened a house of worship, where the seats are free, and the poor have the gospel preached to them." In Buffalo, schoolhouses were not available for religious meetings, as in rural areas. Thus the "only alternative was to have a church of our own, and this we have; costing less than could be expected, in the central part of the city." For some months the building was unheated, and there were no funds to purchase a new furnace. "[W]e have worshipped there without fires till we could do so no longer, and now the church is warmed in part, and we need means to make it entirely comfortable." The case was urgent, Ellen said, and there were no wealthy members to call on. She urged readers of the *Earnest Christian* to make whatever contribution they could.[122]

Benjamin and Ellen's ministry was becoming both more extensive over a larger area and more intensive in Buffalo. They were being stretched and tested as never before.

---

117. Carpenter says, "The mother placed her older children in the homes of various friends, and taking her younger ones [there were only three children at this time], she and her husband went everywhere preaching the gospel" (p. 73).

118. James Matthews, "Benjamin T. Roberts As I Knew Him," *EC* 65, no. 4 (Apr. 1893): 106. In the sources the name is sometimes spelled "Mathews" and sometimes "Matthews."

119. Deed, RFP, Microfilm Reel 11, Frame 103, dated Feb. 27, 1861; receipt from United States Express Company, dated Jan. 24, 1864, RFP, Microfilm Reel 11, Frame 91. Since the deed does not mention a house but refers only to a "certain piece or parcel of land," Roberts perhaps bought vacant land and had a house built upon it.

120. Benson Roberts, "My Mother," p. 69.

121. BHR, *BTR,* p. 219; cf. Marston, p. 236.

122. Ellen L. Roberts, "Free Church in Buffalo," *EC* 2, no. 1 (Jan. 1861): 33-34.

CHAPTER 25

"Free" Methodists: A Denomination Is Born

"[W]e recommend the formation of Free Methodist Churches."

July 1860 Laymen's Convention, Illinois[1]

"We have . . . an intense desire to see, all over the world, churches in which . . . the Gospel standard of experimental and practical godliness shall be held up, and the Spirit of God be allowed to have free course."

B. T. Roberts[2]

The Free Methodist Church was founded at a time of rapid economic and population growth in the United States. "The country had never known such boom times," notes Henry Mayer. Cities were growing; New York and Brooklyn reached a combined population of over one million; Chicago had emerged as a great railroad hub.

Financed by a half billion dollars in California gold and the profits from the annual export of one billion pounds of cotton, railroad lines had advanced more than twenty thousand miles — with another ten thousand under construction — and reached the Mississippi at ten different points. Developments in iron and steel were beginning to give America's cities stronger, higher, and safer cast-iron buildings; Samuel Colt's small-arms factories had perfected a system of production based on the system of interchangeable machine-tooled parts, which led to a boom in toolmaking, clocks and watches, and literally the nuts and bolts of the in-

---

1. *Minutes of the Laymen's Convention, Held in Wayne, Du Page Co., Ill., July 2, 1860*, printed as a one-page, two-sided leaflet. Archives, Roberts Wesleyan College.

2. [B. T. Roberts], "Free Churches," *EC* 2, no. 6 (June 1861): 192.

dustrial revolution; ingenious work in farm machinery had led to vastly increased yields with the aid of John Deere's plow and Cyrus McCormick's reaper and made the midwestern heartland the American breadbasket and butcher shop.[3]

Although 75 percent of the nation's population was still rural, the increasing ethnic inflow and diversity that Roberts saw in New York and experienced in Buffalo were swelling the nation's cities. The result in urban areas was "a bewildering medley of manufacturing, processing, transport, and financial enterprises." Mayer adds, "In 1860 the country would boast a population greater than Britain's — there would be 32 million Americans, including four million enslaved black people and four million foreign-born whites — and an economy growing even faster than its population. The [formerly] rural, craft-based society . . . had become a modern industrial nation; in [about half a century] the United States had doubled and redoubled its population, quadrupled its territorial domain, and septupled its gross national product."[4]

Just in this period, the Free Methodist Church was born.

But when exactly was the first Free Methodist church organized? Little flocks were springing up here and there, some of which would later become Free Methodist congregations. Already a "Free" Methodist church had been formed in St. Louis in March 1859, as noted earlier.

In New York State, however, the congregation first organized as a Free Methodist church was in Albion, where Roberts had ministered from 1855 to 1857. Here the principal actor was not Roberts but Loren Stiles.

Birth of "Free" Methodism in New York

Stiles had been appointed to Albion in 1857 and again in 1858, but was expelled from the Genesee Conference in October 1859, at the end of his second year. Years later a former presiding elder commented that in expelling Roberts and Stiles the Genesee Conference "lost its scholar and its orator. . . . Stiles was the orator, Roberts the scholar."[5]

Stiles's powerful ministry was not squelched by his expulsion. But what could he do, now that he was no longer a Methodist? After all that he, Roberts, and McCreery had been through, he decided that appeals to General Conference were pointless.

The Albion people loved Stiles, and the congregation was much upset when they learned that he had been expelled and that Gilbert Delamatyr had been sent to replace him.[6] At their own initiative, the congregation met and "the great majority"

---

3. Henry Mayer, *All on Fire: William Lloyd Garrison and the Abolition of Slavery* (New York: St. Martin's Press, 1998), p. 434.

4. Mayer, *All on Fire*, p. 435.

5. BHR, *BTR*, p. 215.

6. In the sources, Delamatyr's name is variously spelled Delamater, DeLaMatyr, and De La

voted to leave the Methodist Episcopal Church, organize "under the congregational form of government," and invite Stiles to come as their pastor.[7] Stiles agreed and soon was serving the Congregational Free Methodist Church of Albion.[8] The church began with 185 of the members of the Methodist Episcopal congregation.[9]

The Albion secession actually commenced before the Genesee Conference had completed its 1859 sessions. Stiles was expelled on Wednesday, October 12. That evening the Albion Official Board met and passed a resolution stating that "we cannot in conscience, and will not, receive or support any minister sent to us from Conference by episcopal authority." They wanted to continue to receive "the pastoral and ministerial services" of Stiles and felt the time had come to protest the "outrages upon justice and religious liberty" exemplified in Stiles's expulsion. The Official Board communicated this by letter to Bishop Simpson the next day.[10]

Stiles immediately returned to Albion and met with the Official Board. He consented to serve as pastor of the independent church, and the members promised him a salary of $600. The next evening (Friday) he preached in the sanctuary of the Free Will Baptist Church on James 2:5, "Hearken, my beloved brethren, Hath not God chosen the poor of this world rich in faith, and heirs of the kingdom which he hath promised to them that love him?" After the sermon Stiles announced that a new church building would be erected on a lot across the street from the existing Methodist Episcopal building, adding, "I am to preach there once in two weeks, and elsewhere the remainder."[11] The real secessionists, he said, were those who had already departed from old-line Methodism. Conable quotes Stiles as saying — but does not give his source — the following: "There is a secession already from the church; the regency party are the secessionists. Of this class there are only a few in Albion, and those shall be read out. We are the Church, and I shall excommunicate all the other party. I will here declare the Genesee Conference expelled from the Methodist Episcopal Church. They have already virtually seceded — they have placed a false inter-

---

Matyr. See *Minutes*, Genesee Conference, 1859. Allen gives it as De La Matyr. According to Allen, Delamatyr was five years younger than Stiles. He transferred to the New York East Conference in 1868 and subsequently to the Nebraska, St. Louis, Southeast Indiana, Colorado, and East Ohio Conferences. He died May 17, 1892, in Akron, Ohio. Ray Allen, *A Century of the Genesee Annual Conference of the Methodist Episcopal Church, 1810-1910* (Rochester, N.Y.: By the Author, 1911), p. 82.

7. B. T. Roberts, "Sketch of the Life of Rev. Loren Stiles," in Elias Bowen, *History of the Origin of the Free Methodist Church* (Rochester, N.Y.: B. T. Roberts, 1871), pp. 341-42. This sketch includes a fine engraving of Stiles.

8. *Buffalo Morning Express*, May 21, 1860, quoted in Hogue, *HFMC*, 1:132.

9. "100th Anniversary of Free Methodist Church," *Albion Advertiser*, May 14, 1959, p. 1.

10. Conable, p. 657.

11. Conable, pp. 657-58. Conable quotes Stiles as stating on this occasion that the lot for building the new edifice had already been purchased — which raises the question whether the lot had been purchased earlier, in anticipation of the conference's action, or whether Conable is in fact reporting a later statement by Stiles. If Stiles intended to preach at the new facility only every other week and "elsewhere the remainder," he apparently intended either to establish branch preaching points or to itinerate more broadly in evangelistic work.

pretation on the Bible and on the Discipline, and this is why I and others are out of the Conference and the Church."[12]

Conable here is probably giving a secondhand or thirdhand, and possibly exaggerated, report of what Stiles actually said. But Stiles did believe that the other party were the real secessionists and that he and his "new" congregation were more truly the Methodist Episcopal Church.

Apparently the seceding congregation immediately gave up all claim to the Methodist Episcopal Church property, however. In the Methodist Episcopal Church all church buildings were legally bound to the denomination, not owned outright by the congregation. Where, then, should the new group meet? Though they might have mounted a legal challenge to retain their old building, the congregation decided to build their own facility. Under Stiles's leadership, construction on the new edifice was soon under way. In the meantime, the congregation apparently met in a school building.[13]

More than half the members at Albion went with the new flock, apparently. The Methodist Episcopal congregation survived however under the leadership of Gilbert Delamatyr. Before the split the ME congregation had a total membership of 334. Within months the new congregation apparently had that many and more, reporting 340 members by midsummer.[14] By 1864, with the new denomination organized and several other Free Methodist churches in the surrounding area, the Albion FM congregation had 255 members and was by far the largest church in the Genesee Conference of the new denomination.[15]

A great celebration was held at Albion on Saturday afternoon, May 19, 1860, when the commodious new church building was dedicated.[16] Coincidentally, this was the same day that a delegation from the Republican National Convention in Chicago arrived at Abraham Lincoln's home in Springfield, Illinois, to inform him officially of his nomination for president of the United States. The nomination had occurred the day before.[17]

---

12. Conable, p. 658.

13. Conable says, "The first Sabbath after his expulsion Mr. Stiles and his adherents met at the academy hall" (p. 658). Roberts says those who elected to leave the Methodist Episcopal Church "were so largely in the majority that, according to equity and according to the laws of the State, they were entitled to the church property; but they chose rather to give no cause of complaint" and gave up the building. *WAS*, p. 251.

14. *Minutes*, Genesee Conference, 1859; "100th Anniversary," p. 1. Conable says this large total membership included many people from "adjacent charges who had left their own societies because their own pastors were not Nazarites." Possession of the parsonage was disputed for about a month; Stiles eventually moved out when the trustees of the Methodist Episcopal congregation called a meeting "to take measures for vacating the property," according to Conable (pp. 659-60).

15. *Minutes of the Annual Conferences of the Free Methodist Church for Year Ending Oct. 1864* (Rochester, N.Y.: "Earnest Christian" Office, 1864), p. 18.

16. Marston gives the date as May 18 (a Friday), but the *Buffalo Morning Express* account suggests a Saturday dedication.

17. David Herbert Donald, *Lincoln* (London: Jonathan Cape, 1995), pp. 250-51.

At Albion people from the area and from Methodist congregations in other towns and cities gathered to attend the dedication of the new church facility. A correspondent for the *Buffalo Morning Express* was present and reported:

> The house was crowded to its utmost; some 1,300 being present, and many left unable to get in. The house thus dedicated is a substantial structure, 101 feet by 55. The audience room — the largest in the place — pleasant and commodious, will seat about 1,000 persons. A basement the whole size of the building, entirely above ground, affords pleasant and convenient rooms for class and prayer-meetings, and Sabbath-school. The lecture room in the basement will hold 600 persons. The house is plainly and neatly furnished, and lighted with gas. The cost of the whole has been in round numbers about $10,000. The whole has been paid or provided for.

Elias Bowen of the Oneida Conference preached the dedicatory sermon (on holiness, based on 1 Cor. 6:20), and in the evening B. I. Ives preached from Zechariah 8:23, "We will go with you: for we have heard that God is with you," and helped raise some $4,500 in cash and pledges for the new building. The celebration continued into Sunday, B. I. Ives preaching "with more than his usual power." The *Buffalo Morning Express* reported, "The sacrament was administered to some 440 communicants, and the season was one long to be remembered. In the evening the altar was filled with penitents." In sum, the *Morning Express* reported, "Mr. Stiles has collected a large and intelligent congregation — a devoted, pious, working church, and with their present facilities for doing good, the best results may be anticipated."[18]

It was natural that when the Free Methodist denomination was formed some months later, Loren Stiles would play a key role.

During this same period an independent free church was formed also at Syracuse. Charles Hicks, an attorney and clerk of Onondaga County, as well as a prominent Methodist class leader, was the key figure. Hicks had come into the experience of holiness under John Wesley Redfield and Fay Purdy and maintained an active correspondence with Redfield. Hicks and others formed what they called the Third Methodist Episcopal Church of Syracuse, though it was in fact an independent church. This congregation later became the First Free Methodist Church of Syracuse.[19]

With the emergence of such "free" churches in places like Buffalo, Albion, Syracuse, and St. Louis, by the time of the 1860 Methodist General Conference, the formation of a new denomination was looking more and more inevitable. But much depended on what the General Conference actually decided.

---

18. "Dedication at Albion," *Buffalo Morning Express*, May 26, 1860.
19. Zahniser, pp. 147-48; Hogue, *HFMC*, 1:374-77.

Third Laymen's Convention

The Third Laymen's Convention[20] was held Wednesday and Thursday, February 1 and 2, 1860, just three months after the second convention in Albion. The meeting was prompted partly by the upcoming Methodist General Conference, partly by the quickening pace of events throughout the Genesee Conference.

This time the convention met at Olean, six miles north of the Pennsylvania border, where the Genesee Conference had met in 1855. It did not meet in the Methodist Episcopal church, however. William C. Willing, the appointed Methodist preacher, apparently was not sympathetic with the cause.[21] A member of the church secured an injunction against the meeting, so the convention met instead at the facilities of the Olean Presbyterian Church.[22]

This convention was large and conducted a substantial amount of business. "In some respects it was the most important" of the series of conventions, noted Hogue; the action of this convention "had a very important bearing upon the ultimate formation of the Free Methodist Church."[23] The *Olean Advertiser* printed an extended account; this is the source that later writers have depended upon.[24]

The paper's report said "The Convention was large" but gave no figures. People were present from every church in the conference, Abner Wood again serving as president and Samuel Chesbrough as secretary.[25]

A whole series of resolutions was adopted. The most important were three petitions to General Conference, calling on the quadrennial meeting to address the issues rending the Genesee Conference and also the broader issue of slavery and slaveholding.

Samuel Chesbrough had written a long paper on the Genesee Conference difficulties, and this probably became the basis for some of the action adopted by the convention. The first petition asked the General Conference to investigate the "judicial action" of the Genesee Conference in expelling Roberts and other preachers, and "so to amend the judicial law of the Church, as to secure to the ministers and members the right of trial by an impartial committee."

The second petition showed how seriously this group of western New York Methodists took the issue of slavery on the eve of the Civil War. Noting that many Methodists in the slave states "hold their fellow-beings, and even their brethren in Christ, as slaves," the petition asked the General Conference to ban from church

20. As it was called; technically it was the fourth, as explained earlier.

21. See *Minutes,* Genesee Conference, 1859. The Estes pamphlet listed Willing among those preachers who, "as near as can be ascertained," voted against Roberts in 1857. *WAS,* p. 165.

22. Marston, p. 238; Hogue, *HFMC,* 1:288.

23. Hogue, *HFMC,* 1:287.

24. Hogue prints most of the article in full (*HFMC,* 1:288-93); cf. Marston, pp. 238-40. Apparently no minutes have survived.

25. "Proceedings of the Laymen's Convention," *Olean Advertiser,* Feb. 3(?), 1860. Quoted in Hogue, *HFMC,* 1:288.

membership all "who shall be guilty of holding, buying or selling, or in any way using a human being as a slave."[26]

B. T. Roberts spoke "at some length" in support of this petition. He had always
opposed slavery, he said; his very first speech was against it. "The Genesee Conference, in former days, was thoroughly anti-slavery," but things had changed. The
minutes of the last annual conference failed to print the antislavery committee report, he said; those responsible "were either afraid or ashamed to publish it." Roberts
felt the church had a key role to play in the national debate. The *Olean Advertiser* reported that Roberts's position was that "if the Church would only take hold of the
matter in the right way, and in the right spirit, slavery would soon be extirpated from
the land," and that he personally would work for that as long as he lived.[27] Clearly
Roberts was not anticipating the Civil War and the prospect that slavery itself would
be abolished within five years.

Joseph McCreery and others also spoke in support of the petition.[28]

This group of loyal Methodists also passed a resolution reiterating their "unfaltering attachment to the M.E. Church" even as they protested "its abuses and iniquitous administration." They specified, "Our controversy is in favor of the doctrines
and Discipline of the Church, and against temporary maladministration. And we exhort our brethren everywhere not to secede, or withdraw from the Church, or be persuaded into any other ecclesiastical organization; but to form themselves into Bands,
after the example of early Methodism, and remain in the Church until expelled."[29]

Related resolutions reaffirmed the actions of the previous laymen's conventions,
protested ministerial tyranny in the administration of the church, and particularly
condemned as "an act of outrage upon our rights as members of the Church" the
practice of "reading out members as withdrawn from the Church, without even the
form of a trial, or without even laboring with them," as "many of the Regency
preachers" had done. A preamble to the resolutions noted that the government of
the denomination was totally in the hands of ordained ministers, so church members had little recourse other than to withhold their tithes and offerings. "The Annual Conference, which says, who shall preach and who shall not, is made up of ministers. The Book Agents, wielding a mighty, pecuniary influence, are ministers. The
official editors, controlling the public sentiment of the Church, are ministers."[30]
These statements were probably part of the document drawn up in advance by Sam
Chesbrough.

The convention also passed a resolution, "unanimously adopted by a rising
vote," commending the new "Free Methodist Church of Albion," greeting "her as a
welcome co-laborer in the vineyard of our common Master, and as a worthy member in the sisterhood of Evangelical Churches." Significantly, the convention set up

26. Hogue, *HFMC,* 1:288-89.
27. Roberts, as quoted and paraphrased in the *Olean Advertiser,* in Hogue, *HFMC,* 1:289-90.
28. Hogue, *HFMC,* 1:290.
29. Hogue, *HFMC,* 1:290.
30. Hogue, *HFMC,* 1:290-92.

an "executive council in each District" charged with responsibility for camp meetings, quarterly meetings, and "the general oversight of the work" between sessions of the convention. These councils consisted of a specified list of "laymen and local preachers" and all the "traveling preachers appointed by this Convention." In setting up this structure and giving appointments to the preachers who had been expelled from the ME Church, the convention was providing a temporary functional alternative to the Methodist conference structure.

In several respects these conventions were now functioning as, in effect, an ad hoc provisional denomination (or at least conference), taking on some key functions of a denominational structure. Through the conventions these "laymen" were doing for themselves what the denomination no longer would do. Under the circumstances, it is hard to see how they could have done anything else if they wanted to remain connected in a Methodist way and preserve the fruit of the ongoing ministry of Roberts, McCreery, and others. On the other hand, Methodist Episcopal leaders obviously would view these steps with alarm and consider them de facto schismatic. Significantly, these Methodists who were now taking matters into their own hands (as they were accustomed to do in their business and farming enterprises) were forming a Methodist-like connectional structure that was, however, much more participatory and democratic than was the Methodist Episcopal Church.[31] Here "ministers" and "laymen" had equal voice, and the key leadership arose from a partnership of the two.[32]

What was B. T. Roberts's role in these developments? Was his the invisible hand behind the scenes, orchestrating these moves? It appears not, though he was an active player. Men like Isaac and Samuel Chesbrough, Abner Wood, and S. C. Springer of Gowanda were fully capable of such action and were sufficiently outraged to undertake it. Samuel Chesbrough seems especially to have been a key figure and may in fact be considered a cofounder of Free Methodism. It appears that the relationship between Roberts and the Chesbroughs (and other key leaders) at this point can best be described as a partnership or collaboration, neither side being dominant.

The convention adjourned at the end of its business on the second day to await the outcome of the General Conference. The petitions to General Conference were immediately printed and circulated among western New York Methodists. The resolution calling for a review of the Genesee Conference trials received over fifteen hundred signatures.[33]

---

31. It appears that at this point most of the participants in the Laymen's Conventions were still members of local ME churches, though a growing number were former Methodists who had been expelled or who had withdrawn from the denomination.

32. Of course, personal relational factors probably played as large a role as did these issues of ecclesiastical status. Also, there were now many precedents of less clergy-dominated church structures, including the Methodist Protestant Church and the Wesleyan Methodist Church, formed in 1830 and 1843, respectively.

33. Hogue, *HFMC*, 1:287.

The *Earnest Christian* Founded

One of the resolutions passed by the February 1-2, 1860, Laymen's Convention read, "[W]e are highly pleased with the appearance of the *Earnest Christian*. The articles, thus far, prove it to be just what is needed at this time, when a conforming and superficial Christianity is prevailing everywhere. We hail it with delight among us; and we pledge ourselves to use our exertions to extend its circulation."[34]

The first issue of the *Earnest Christian* appeared in January. Roberts may have arranged for copies of the February issue to be available at the convention. The participants were pleased with this follow-through of one of the suggestions of the December 1858 Laymen's Convention that "a periodical devoted to the advocacy of 'Earnest Christianity'" be established in Buffalo.

The publication was successful and of such significance in the life and ministry of B. T. and Ellen Roberts that the story will be told more fully in the next chapter.

The General Conference of 1860

The 1860 Methodist General Conference convened on Tuesday, May 1, and met until early June. Ironically it met in Buffalo, "the center of Regency strength," as Marston notes.[35] Benjamin and Ellen Roberts were probably present for at least some of the sessions. Both were hopeful that this supreme body of Methodism, with its broader perspective and representation, would overturn the action of the Genesee Conference and Benjamin could then resume his ministry in the denomination.[36]

Others were not so optimistic. Martha Kendall, William Kendall's widow, wrote to Ellen on May 19, when the conference had already been in session for almost three weeks, that she did not share Ellen's "hope of restoration to the church." She wrote, "Surely if they turn us all loose again into the church, there will be a terrible commotion, and many faint hearts will sink under the influence that now reigns. But God will be glorified in either way. I believe, however, that it is God's will to raise up another people whose God is the Lord, and among whom dwelleth righteousness, peace and joy in the Holy Ghost."[37]

The overriding issue at this General Conference was slavery and slaveholding. The treatment of the Genesee Conference appeals was inevitably shaped by this larger debate. The American Anti-Slavery Society, holding its annual meeting in New York City at this same time, in its annual report blasted the Methodist Episcopal Church for its compromising stand, noting that in the denomination "the struggle still goes on between those who wish to banish Slavery utterly from their communion, and those who

34. Hogue, *HFMC*, 1:290.

35. Marston, p. 240.

36. Hogue gives a fairly detailed account of the General Conference action relating to Roberts and the "Nazarite" issues. Hogue, *HFMC*, 1:294-305.

37. Mrs. William Kendall (St. Louis) to ELR, May 19, 1860, quoted in Zahniser, pp. 146-47.

persist in letting it remain therein, though all the while protesting, most of them, that they are by no means Pro-Slavery." The report noted that northern Methodists owned some 30,000 slaves. It quoted a Methodist preacher as saying "Slavery, as it now exists," far from being a sin, actually was "the only thing which had elevated the negro race." The Anti-Slavery Society report went on to cite an antislavery document written by northern Methodists. These antislavery activists reported that in the denomination "we have thousands of Slave-holders; trustees, stewards, leaders, and local preachers, and even travelling preachers have become Slave-holders, in several instances, and are such still, with but little disapprobation, as a general thing, on the part of the Conferences to which they belong. And a portion of the ministry, especially in the Slave States, are strongly opposed to any ecclesiastical action that will exclude Slave-holders from the church, or even condemn the practice of Slave-holding."[38]

The mood and deliberations of the 1860 General Conference showed that this picture was accurate. The conference adopted a relatively innocuous disciplinary statement on the evils of slavery, but antislavery delegates could not muster the necessary majority to put teeth in the General Rule by adding a specific ban on slaveholding.[39] Meanwhile the conference also extensively debated the "lay delegation" issue. In a compromise move the body went on record "favoring lay delegation whenever a majority of the members and ministers desired it." But, as Bishop Simpson later wrote, following the General Conference a "vote of the membership and of the Conferences was . . . taken, and the matter was decided in the negative."[40]

The General Conference delegates from Genesee, men like Thomas Carlton and James Fuller, wanted to maintain the unity and (as they saw it) continuing success of the Methodist Episcopal Church.[41] They had this in common with delegates from other areas who wanted to sidestep the question of slaveholding. Thus a natural partnership was formed. What the abolitionists were to the General Conference "moderates," the Nazarites were to the delegates from Genesee. As Marston notes, "The Genesee Conference and the conferences along the southern border [of the MEC], reversing their historic positions, were united on the major issues of this Conference, slavery and Nazaritism."[42] This combination defeated the adoption of a

---

38. *Annual Report of the American Anti-Slavery Society, by the Executive Committee, for the Year Ending May 1, 1860* (New York: American Anti-Slavery Society, 1861), pp. 274-77. The report mentions William Hosmer and the work of the *Northern Independent*.

39. The *Discipline's* General Rules already prohibited "The buying and selling of men, women, and children, with an intention to enslave them," but did not specifically prohibit slaveholding.

40. *COM*, p. 399.

41. The Genesee Conference delegates were Carlton, Fuller, D. F. Parsons, and H. Ryan Smith; the reserves were Sandford Hunt and Jason G. Miller (Conable, p. 660) — all considered by Roberts to be part of the Regency faction, though at the time of their election only Fuller and Hunt were actually ministering in Buffalo. Carlton, though based in Manhattan, was connected to the Buffalo District (specifically, Grace Church, where Hunt was pastor) through his Genesee Conference membership. Parsons and Smith were at Cambria and Medina, both in the Niagara District, and Jason Miller was stationed at Rushford, Olean District. *Minutes*, Genesee Conference, 1858.

42. Marston, pp. 240-41.

stronger antislavery rule — and also undermined attempts to thoroughly and fairly examine the clergy trials in the Genesee Conference. The *Northern Independent* commented, "It may be that men who, four years ago took the stump to keep slavery out of the territories, have suddenly become convinced that it should be nestled and fostered in the bosom of the Church! We should like to know by what arguments they were converted, and when it was done! Was this part of the scheme to keep slave-holders in the Church? Did the border understand that if they voted as desired by the Genesee delegates, they would reciprocate the favor? Or did the strange coincidence come about by chance?"[43]

Whether or not a deal was actually struck, Carlton as book agent certainly had connections throughout the denomination and was in a position to accurately assess how General Conference action would likely go.

When the Genesee Conference expulsions came before the conference, the issue was referred first to a special committee of forty-seven, one from each conference delegation. The Genesee delegates at first professed to welcome the investigation. Fuller said, "We have done right, and are not afraid to have our conduct looked into. We want the troubles probed to the bottom."[44] But when William Reddy of the Oneida Conference introduced a resolution instructing the committee to probe the matter thoroughly, examining all relevant conference documents, Fuller and the other Genesee delegates balked. They succeeded in getting the proposal tabled by a vote of 97 to 84. A motion was then made to dismiss the special committee and transfer the matter to one of the standing committees. A number spoke in favor of this, and before any opponents could speak, debate was cut off and the committee was dismissed by a 104 to 81 vote.[45]

All the documents relating to the Genesee Conference case were transferred to the committee on itinerancy, which failed to deal with the matter.[46] As Hogue notes, this committee already had a full docket of routine business, and "it is probable that the chief memorial was not even read before that body. Nothing like the full, fair and impartial investigation asked for was had. Instead of such a proceeding, the matter was passed over in the same farcical manner as had characterized the so-called administration of Discipline under the 'Regency' power during the whole period of the Genesee Conference difficulties. This seems to have been what was intended, on the part of the Genesee Conference delegates, from the beginning."[47]

Meanwhile, B. T. Roberts's own 1857 and 1858 appeals to the General Conference (as distinct from the hundreds of petitions asking for an investigation of the trials) were sent to the conference's Committee on Appeals, which functioned as the denomination's appeals court. Here Roberts very nearly won a reversal of his 1857 reprimand when the committee met on May 30. The initial vote to affirm the Genesee

43. *NI* 4, no. 45 (June 14, 1860), quoted in Marston, p. 241.
44. As quoted in Hogue, *HFMC*, 1:295.
45. Marston, p. 241; Hogue, *HFMC*, 1:296.
46. Marston, p. 242.
47. Hogue, *HFMC*, 1:297.

Conference's action was a tie, 19 to 19. Although the committee voted "almost unanimously" not to order a new trial (which would have been rather pointless), yet, as the committee report noted, "On the question of reversing the action of the Conference, eighteen voted in favor and twenty against, a result which, as the General Conference has decided, leaves this decision of the Genesee Conference as the final adjudication of the case."[48] Thus the vote that would have reversed Roberts's 1857 conviction fell just two votes short of passage.

Roberts's 1858 appeal was taken up by the appeals committee on Thursday morning, May 31. That afternoon the committee reported its decision to the General Conference:

> The Committee have considered the second Appeal of B. T. Roberts, who appeals from the action of the Genesee Conference, whereby he was expelled from the ministry and the Church.
>
> The representatives of the Genesee Conference objected to the admission of the Appeal on the ground,
>
> 1. That B. T. Roberts, subsequently to his trial and condemnation, joined the Methodist Episcopal Church as a probationer, and thus, at least, tacitly confessed the justice of the action of the Conference in his case.
>
> 2. That B. T. Roberts, since he was deprived by his expulsion of his ministerial authority and standing, has continued to preach, and has thus rebelled against the authority of the Conference and the Church.
>
> 3. That B. T. Roberts, since he declared his intention of appealing to the General Conference, has connected himself with another organization, contemplating Church ends independent of and hostile to the Church to whose General Conference he now appeals.
>
> The Committee, after hearing the statements and pleadings of the representatives of the parties,
>
> *Resolved,* That the Appeal of B. T. Roberts be not admitted.[49]

The committee's report did not indicate the number of votes for and against.

With this decision, Roberts's last hope of remaining within the Methodist Episcopal Church died. The appeals committee likewise refused to hear the appeals of the other expelled preachers, with one exception. It remanded the case of C. D. Burlingham back to the annual conference, paving the way for Burlingham's reinstatement when the Genesee Conference met in the fall.[50]

---

48. Report of the Committee on Appeals, May 30, 1860 (reported out to the General Conference on Thursday afternoon, May 31), in William L. Harris, ed., *Journal of the General Conference of the Methodist Episcopal Church, Held in Buffalo, N.Y., 1860* (New York: Carlton and Porter, 1860), pp. 252-53. See Marston, p. 242.

49. Report of the Committee on Appeals, May 31, 1860 (reported out on Thursday afternoon, May 31, at the same time the previous action was reported). Harris, *Journal . . . 1860*, p. 253. See also Marston, pp. 578-79.

50. Report of the Committee on Appeals, May 31, 1860; Marston, p. 243.

As the appeals committee report makes clear, it was delegates from the Genesee Conference who managed to convince the committee not even to consider Roberts's appeal. Their reference to "another organization . . . hostile to the Church" was apparently to the Laymen's Conventions.

The charges made against Roberts in the appeals committee by the Genesee Conference representatives were clearly spurious. Benjamin's rejoining of the Methodist Episcopal Church was not at all a tacit admission of "the justice of the action of the Conference in his case"; wise or not, it was simply an attempt to stay connected with the church he loved. Similarly, the reasoning that Roberts's having "connected himself with" the Laymen's Conventions invalidated his appeal is specious, as the Laymen's Conventions were essentially a Methodist Episcopal (though unofficial and ad hoc) body with professed loyalty to the denomination. It was a stretch to say that the Laymen's Conventions were "contemplating Church ends independent of and hostile to" the Methodist Episcopal Church — though they certainly were hostile to the direction the Genesee Conference was heading, and many no doubt saw that a separate denomination might finally be the result if the General Conference failed to act justly. Given the mood and the dynamics of the 1860 General Conference, however, it is easy to see how such contorted logic could be politically persuasive.

A couple of weeks earlier William Hosmer, foreseeing the likely outcome, editorialized in the *Northern Independent*:

> Personally we have always regretted that our brethren, so unwarrantedly expelled, did not see it consistent with duty to refrain from preaching until their appeals could be tried. Not that we doubted their still being empowered by the Great Head of the Church to preach, but that refraining for the time being would enable the General Conference to take hold of their appeals with less embarrassment. . . . Their course, though anomalous, is not without precedent. Luther, after his expulsion, kept on preaching to the end of his life.[51]

In a later editorial Hosmer pointed out that the Committee on Appeals should have judged Roberts's 1858 appeal on its merits, not on the basis of anything he might have done subsequently. The committee had allowed itself to become prejudiced by the Genesee delegates, and in refusing to entertain the appeal, it violated the *Discipline*'s guarantee of fair trial and fair process.[52]

In his 1957 book *Revivalism and Social Reform*, historian Timothy L. Smith gave this reasonably balanced assessment of the 1860 General Conference action regarding B. T. Roberts:

> There is little to substantiate the "official" Methodist version of the controversy. It alleged that the holiness leaders were fanatics who organized a secret society of their own for the purpose of destroying the reputations of other ministers, and

---

51. William Hosmer, editorial, *NI* 4, no. 41 (May 17, 1860), quoted in Marston, p. 243.
52. William Hosmer, editorial, *NI* 4, no. 47 (June 28, 1860), cited in Marston, pp. 243-44.

who conducted camp meetings amid scenes of unrestrained emotionalism. Roberts' later writings on the doctrine of sanctification were certainly far from fanatical. They emphasized the ideal of perfect character, toward which he believed perfect love and all other authentic religious experiences led. . . .

The Free Methodist contention that their exclusion was proof that Wesley's followers had abandoned their founder's cardinal doctrine is, on the other hand, equally inaccurate. A chief concern of the General Conference of 1860 was to keep the "border conferences" in Kentucky, Maryland, West Virginia, and Missouri within the denomination, and hence to contribute — so its leaders hoped — to the campaign to prevent the secession of those states from the national union. Sustaining an appeal from abolitionists, even sanctified ones, would hardly serve this purpose. The motion to dismiss the committee appointed to consider the difficulties in Genesee was, in fact, carried after one of the Buffalo group [Fuller] proclaimed his adherence to states' rights in politics and conference rights in the church, and a delegate from the Baltimore Conference responded with an appeal which set off a wave of speeches in support![53]

Roberts reported the General Conference action in the July issue of the *Earnest Christian,* devoting equal space to the slavery issue and the Genesee Conference appeals. That Roberts was genuinely saddened by the outcome is clear by the tone of his remarks.

> We must confess that we felt greatly disappointed. The hope had been indulged that these difficulties would be investigated with such thoroughness and impartiality, as would entitle the decision to respect. If we have been wrong in our teaching, or spirit or practice, we feel anxious to know it. No person can possibly be so solicitous as we are, to be convinced that we are out of the way, if this is really the case. But such proceedings convince us only that there is in certain quarters a great dread of LIGHT, and that other considerations weigh more heavily with the authorities of the Church than the disposition to do justice, and to judge righteous judgment.
>
> We trust our friends will give us their sympathies and their prayers, and we will do the best we can, under the disadvantageous circumstances we are placed in, to promote the Redeemer's kingdom, waiting for the revelation of the last day to set all right.[54]

In his book *From Age to Age a Living Witness,* Leslie R. Marston commended Roberts for the grace and restraint he showed under pressure. "Thus, with an influential magazine at his command for purposes of demagoguery, were he tempted in that direction as so often is true of reformers, he quietly handled a crisis in his per-

---

53. Timothy L. Smith, *Revivalism and Social Reform: American Protestantism on the Eve of the Civil War* (New York: Harper Torchbooks, 1965; originally published 1957), p. 131. Smith bases his account in part on Hogue, *HFMC,* 1:295-96.

54. [B. T. Roberts], "Appeal Cases," *EC* 1, no. 7 (July, 1860): 227.

sonal and public life, brought on by heavy injustice, with a few direct statements requiring less than one and a half *per centum* of the magazine's space. Such was the composure and the sober sincerity of B. T. Roberts."[55]

A New Denomination Is Born

With this decisive no by the 1860 Methodist General Conference, the organization of a new "Free" Methodist denomination was virtually inevitable. Another Laymen's Convention was held in New York on June 23 in connection with the Bergen camp meeting. And on Monday, July 2, four weeks after General Conference adjourned, "Free" Methodists in "the West" (that is, Illinois) held a Laymen's Convention at Wayne, DuPage County, west of Chicago, in conjunction with the St. Charles camp meeting.[56] The group organized much as had the conventions in New York. Roberts attended and was unanimously chosen president. Delegates were present from several northern Illinois towns and from St. Louis. The fact that Roberts presided at the meeting, that John Wesley Redfield was listed in the minutes as a delegate from St. Louis, and that several other delegates were preachers show that at this point the term "Laymen's Convention" was being used rather loosely.[57] In fact, as the minutes show, this was de facto the organizing convention of a new denomination. July 2, 1860, and Wayne, Illinois, may thus be considered the time and place of the founding of the Free Methodist Church with nearly as much legitimacy as August 23 in Pekin, New York.[58]

This "western" convention took several steps that formally set the Free Methodist Church in operation in Illinois and in St. Louis, Missouri. As Marston notes, "The convention proceeded to transact business much as though it were an annual conference."[59] The convention appointed preachers to eleven assignments, including "Iowa Mission" and "Michigan." Some men were given licenses to preach; a stationing committee was elected; and Redfield's character was passed and he was "appointed as superintendent for our Western work." A motion "to recognize, as valid, the ordination of those ministers ordained by any evangelist who comes among us" (probably referring to Roberts and/or Redfield) apparently passed. Significantly, the motion creating the stationing committee, charged with assigning preachers to their

55. Marston, p. 245.

56. Marston gives the date as July 1 (a Sunday), whereas the minutes specify July 2. The St. Charles camp meeting just west of Chicago became something of an institution within early Free Methodism and continued for a number of decades. See J. G. Terrill, *The St. Charles Camp Meeting* (Chicago: T. B. Arnold, 1883).

57. Of course, the ecclesiastical categories themselves are fuzzy at this point, since Roberts was now an ex-Methodist clergyman, Redfield's role was somewhat ambiguous, and other preachers were probably not yet ordained.

58. *Minutes of the Laymen's Convention, Held in Wayne, Du Page Co., Ill., July 2, 1860.*

59. Marston, p. 250. A full account is given in Terrill, *Redfield*, pp. 449-51.

appointments, specified that it have equal "lay" and clergy representation — three each.

Finally, the convention unanimously elected B. T. Roberts "our General Superintendent for this work." Roberts proposed the following resolution, which was adopted:

> *Resolved*, That our attachment to the doctrines, usages, spirit and discipline of Methodism is hearty and sincere. It is with the most profound grief that we have witnessed the departure of many of the ministers from the God-honored usages of Methodism. We feel bound to adhere to them, and to labor all we can, and to the best possible advantage, to promote the life and power of godliness. We recommend that those in sympathy with the doctrine of holiness, as taught by Wesley, should labor in harmony with the respective churches to which they belong. But when this cannot be done, without continual strife and contention, we recommend the formation of Free Methodist Churches, as contemplated by the late convention held in the Genesee Conference, N.Y.[60]

Only in the sense that this convention included some Methodists who were still active in their local ME congregations and that it had not yet adopted a constitution or discipline was it not now fully a new denomination.

August 23, 1860, is the official date of the formal organization of the Free Methodist Church as a distinct denomination. The June 23 Laymen's Convention took stock of the situation in light of the recent General Conference action (or inaction). It adopted a resolution similar to the one the Illinois convention adopted two weeks later (probably both written by Roberts) affirming "unfaltering attachment to the doctrines and proper usages of the M.E. Church" but advising people to "form themselves into bands and societies, under the name 'Free Methodist Societies,'" if they could not remain within their Methodist congregations "without strife and opposition."[61]

By now it was clear, however, that some more permanent organization was necessary. The June convention took a key step ecclesiologically in voting to recognize "the ordination of the ordained preachers, traveling and local, who have been expelled from the Genesee Conference" and to endorse "their administration of the sacraments as usual." And it created a committee to lay the groundwork for a new denomination — "to prepare some code of General Rules and Regulations [in other words, the basis of a book of discipline], by which the principles, usages and spirit of primitive Methodism be restored and secured."[62] A process was adopted for choosing delegates from existing "Free Methodist" bands and societies to an organizing convention in August.[63]

---

60. *Minutes of the Laymen's Convention, Held in Wayne, Du Page Co., Ill., July 2, 1860.*

61. Quoted in Marston, p. 249.

62. Quoted in Marston, p. 249.

63. Delegates to the recent ME General Conference would of course have seen these steps as confirming precisely what was alleged about the Laymen's Conventions. The irony, however, is that these steps would not have been taken if the General Conference had upheld Roberts's appeals.

Benjamin published a call to the organizing convention in the August issue of the *Earnest Christian*.

A convention will be held at Pekin, for the purpose of adopting a Discipline for the Free Methodist Church, to commence at the close of the Camp Meeting, August 23d. All societies and bands that find it necessary, in order to promote the prosperity and permanency of the work of holiness, to organize a Free Church on the following basis, are invited to send delegates:

1. Doctrines and usages of primitive Methodism, such as the Witness of the Spirit, Entire Sanctification as a state of grace distinct from justification, attainable instantaneously by faith. Free seats, and congregational singing, without instrumental music in all cases; plainness of dress.

2. An equal representation of ministers and members in all the councils of the Church.

3. No slaveholding, and no connection with secret and oath bound societies.

Each society or band will be entitled to send one delegate at least; and an additional one for every forty members.[64]

This statement is significant because it clearly shows which issues Roberts felt were most crucial, and also that Roberts put doctrinal issues first among the several issues cited.[65] While several issues and currents combined to create Free Methodism, in Roberts's mind everything else was secondary to, and flowed from, the doctrinal foundation of the church. For all the emphasis he put on Christian experience, the central anchor was theological and doctrinal. Experience, important as it was, was not automatically self-authenticating.

A total of sixty persons showed up as official delegates when the organizing convention met at Pekin on August 23 (though no doubt many others were present; Roberts estimated the number at eighty). The delegates consisted of forty-five local church members and fifteen preachers. Given the formula for choosing delegates, this total suggests an organized constituency of perhaps 1,000 to 1,300.[66] Marston calls attention to the fact that "the Pekin Convention, which launched a new denomination with a provision for 'equal representation of ministers and laymen in all the councils of the Church,' had three times as many lay as ministerial members."[67] "The West" was represented by Daniel Lloyd from St. Louis and Redfield, both of whom had participated in the July 2 convention in Illinois.[68] Thus the organizing conven-

---

64. [B. T. Roberts], "Notice for Camp Meeting and Convention," *EC* 1, no. 8 (Aug. 1860): 260. Cf. Marston, p. 253; Zahniser, pp. 165-66; BHR, *BTR*, p. 230.

65. See the discussion in Marston, pp. 252-54.

66. Assuming that the "societies" and "bands" represented averaged around twenty to thirty persons each. The formula for representation did not distinguish between "ministers" and "laymen," though probably the fifteen preachers came on their own, not as delegates of societies or bands, while the rest were band or society delegates.

67. Marston, p. 253.

68. BHR, *BTR*, p. 233.

tion represented a somewhat broader constituency than just the Genesee Conference and was more formally structured as an organizing convention than any of the previous gatherings.

Nationally, the storm clouds of civil war were gathering as the Free Methodist Church came into being. Sectional strife was growing as the U.S. presidential campaign heated up, pitting Republican Abraham Lincoln against Northern Democrat Stephen A. Douglas, Southern Democrat John C. Breckinridge, and Constitutional Unionist John Bell. Two weeks before the Pekin convention Lincoln made the one public appearance of his campaign at an immense rally in his hometown of Springfield, Illinois. An "incredible assemblage" estimated at well over fifty thousand greeted Lincoln with "almost frantic enthusiasm."[69] On November 6, ten weeks after the Pekin convention, Lincoln was elected president with a majority of electoral votes but a decided minority of the popular vote. Talk of a Southern Confederacy was in the air.[70]

The Free Methodist organizing convention at Pekin met near the home of Isaac and Samuel Chesbrough. George Washington Carl later recalled that the gathering was held "two miles south of Pekin, in a beautiful little grove on Isaac M. Chesbrough's farm."[71] When the group came together, however, it turned out that not everyone favored immediate organization. Some, including Sam Chesbrough, thought the step was premature. He said years later, "At the time of the convention I was not clear in my mind that the time had come for us to organize, and, therefore, I refused to be a delegate. . . . I took no part whatever in the proceedings. In fact, I was not present on the campground," though he was nearby in his home and could observe what was happening.[72] In fact, as the whole tale shows, the Free Methodist Church was born reluctantly.

An hour or so before the convention was to begin, B. T. Roberts and several others — probably including Isaac Chesbrough, Loren Stiles, and perhaps Redfield — met under an apple tree behind the Chesbrough home to discuss the meeting. Sam Chesbrough, though he didn't participate, watched from his kitchen door. "They were nearly all seated on the grass under the tree, and it was voted that they proceed to organize the church," Chesbrough recalled. "They then arose and went over into the grove, where the convention was held and the child was born and named."[73]

There was considerable discussion in the convention as to whether or not the time had really come to organize a new church. Joseph McCreery, William Cooley, and three other preachers, as well as a few of the other delegates, thought it would

---

69. "Coming Together of the Masses at 'Old Abe's' Home," *Albany (N.Y.) Evening Journal*, Aug. 11, 1860, reprinted in Eric C. Caren, comp., *Civil War Extra: A Newspaper History of the Civil War from Nat Turner to 1863* (Edison, N.J.: Castle Books, 1999), p. 19.

70. E. B. Long with Barbara Long, *The Civil War Day by Day: An Almanac, 1861-1865* (New York: Da Capo Press, 1971, 1985), pp. 2-3.

71. George Washington Carl, recollection published in *FM*, Aug. 9, 1910, p. 505.

72. BHR, *BTR*, pp. 230-31.

73. BHR, *BTR*, p. 231.

be better to wait awhile. If they delayed, "a greater swarm" would later leave the Methodist Episcopal Church and join the new denomination — as one of the delegates, Moses Downing, put it. In the meantime they could continue to form bands.[74] McCreery, Roberts noted, "said that many of the sheep in the Methodist fold had been so starved by the Regency preachers that they were unable to jump the fence, and he wished to remain in a position where he could salt them through the rails."[75]

Redfield, however, who knew the ME Church well, was sure the time had come to act. He stood and said, "Brethren, when fruit is ripe it had better be picked, lest on falling it bruise. In the West we are ready for an organization. If in the East you are not ready, wait until you are."

Roberts responded, "We are ready, and the West and East should move in the matter simultaneously." Roberts's conclusion, as he noted in his diary, was that the Methodist Episcopal Church had "gone so far from its original position, and . . . become so involved in formalism, secret society influence and pro-slaveryism, that there is no hope of its recovery." Since there was "no existing church that makes the salvation of souls its prominent and main work," Roberts concluded: "We then had to form a new church or live outside of any and have no place to put those that God converts through our instrumentality."[76]

When the time came for decision, a strong majority voted to organize "The Free Methodist Church." Roberts reported in the *Earnest Christian*: "When the vote was taken, all but seven — five preachers and two laymen — stood up in favor of organizing immediately."[77] The convention went on to adopt articles of religion based on the existing Methodist Episcopal Church *Discipline* and a Methodistic organizational structure. These actions were based on work that Roberts had done in advance.[78]

Doctrinal Emphases

In preparing the doctrinal basis for the new denomination, Roberts pared down the twenty-five articles in the Methodist *Discipline* to what he felt was essential.[79] He cut

74. BHR, *BTR*, pp. 231-32. Benson Roberts bases this part of his reporting on the recollections of Moses N. Downing.

75. BTRD, Aug. 23, 1860, quoted in BHR, *BTR*, p. 233. In his diary Roberts went on to list the reasons that convinced him the time had come to act.

76. BTRD, Aug. 23, 1860, quoted in BHR, *BTR*, pp. 234-36. See also the accounts in the September 1860 *Earnest Christian* and the recollections of some participants in the Pekin convention in the April 1893 *Earnest Christian*.

77. [B. T. Roberts], "Convention at Pekin," *EC* 1, no. 9 (Sept. 1860): 291.

78. BHR, *BTR*, p. 232; Marston, pp. 254-59.

79. Benjamin wrote in his diary, "The forms of discipline which I had prepared, under, as I believe, the influence of God's spirit, [were] adopted with but slight alterations." Quoted in BHR, *BTR*, p. 235.

out some of the anti–Roman Catholic material, probably not so much because he disagreed with it but because he didn't see it as essential doctrine. Specifically, he omitted the articles "Of Purgatory," "Of Both Kinds" (referring to the Lord's Supper), and "Of the Marriage of Ministers" (concerning clerical celibacy). He also deleted "Of the Rulers of the United States of America," an article early American Methodism had thought best to include in the wake of the American Revolution. The long Methodist Episcopal article "Of the Sacraments" was pared down to just the first paragraph, excising an anti-Catholic section on the correct number of sacraments. On baptism the new *Discipline* retained the Methodist language that "The baptism of young children is to be retained in the Church."[80]

To these articles Roberts added, and the convention adopted, two new ones: a statement on entire sanctification adapted from Wesley's writings and "Future Reward and Punishment" ("drawn from the Bible," Roberts noted). This article, replacing the one on purgatory, was added to guard against the growing threat of universalism.[81] Thus the denomination began with twenty-three Articles of Religion in place of the ME Church's twenty-five articles.

The proposed article on entire sanctification sparked some debate. As adopted, it read:

> Merely justified persons, while they do not outwardly commit sin, are nevertheless conscious of sin still remaining in the heart. They feel a natural tendency to evil, a proneness to depart from God, and cleave to the things of earth. Those that are sanctified wholly are saved from all inward sin — from evil thoughts, and evil tempers. No wrong temper, none contrary to love remains in the soul. All the thoughts, words and actions are governed by pure love.
>
> Entire sanctification takes place subsequently to justification, and is the work of God wrought instantaneously upon the consecrated, believing soul. After a soul is cleansed from all sin, it is then fully prepared to grow in grace.[82]

Loren Stiles essentially agreed, but he thought the "instantaneous" emphasis should be balanced with a recognition of gradual process. He proposed adding a clause "favoring the gradualistic as well as the instantaneous view of entire sanctification," Downing noted. Redfield arose and said, in substance, "Brethren, . . . unless we go straight on the question of holiness in the Discipline we had better halt where

---

80. Marston, pp. 257-59; *The Doctrines and Discipline of the Free Methodist Church Adopted August 23, 1860* (Buffalo: B. T. Roberts, 1860), pp. 17-26.

81. BHR, *BTR,* p. 236. The article reads, "God has appointed a day in which he will judge the world in righteousness by Jesus Christ according to the Gospel. The righteous shall have in heaven an inheritance incorruptible, undefiled, and that fadeth not away. The wicked shall go away into everlasting punishment, where their worm dieth not and their fire is not quenched" — a conflation of Acts 17:31, 1 Pet. 1:4, Matt. 25:46, and Mark 9:48.

82. Marston, p. 258; cf. *Doctrines and Discipline* (1860), p. 22. Marston thoughtfully notes that although this statement was drawn from Wesley, "This procedure has its limitations, for Wesley might have phrased the doctrine differently had he been writing for such a purpose" (p. 258).

we are. The gradualistic theory is what has made so much mischief. We are John Wesleyan Methodists. We must not dodge at that point." The majority agreed, and the article was adopted as Roberts proposed it.[83]

Within a decade the new church came to realize that the word "merely" at the beginning of the article was a poor choice, seeming to undervalue the work of justification. The word was deleted in 1870.[84]

The debate over sanctification as instantaneous or gradual ("crisis" versus "process," as the issue is often framed) has been an ongoing one in Wesleyan theology, dating back even to Wesley's day. It is understandable that these first Free Methodists endorsed holiness as an instantaneous work of grace, precisely for the reason Redfield stated. Yet they also believed in continuing growth in grace, both before and after the crisis of entire sanctification. How to maintain the balance between progressive growth in sanctification and the crisis of *entire* sanctification remained a struggle, or at least a tension, within Free Methodism, as within the larger Holiness movement.

In the twentieth century many Free Methodists came to feel that their forebears had tilted too much toward crisis over process. What would have happened, one wonders, if Stiles's proposal "favoring the gradualistic as well as the instantaneous view" had prevailed? Would the church have maintained a more dynamic, balanced teaching and experience of holiness? Or would it, as Redfield feared, have drifted into a mere nurture model?[85]

Church Organization

"A church that had developed from a lay movement, the origin of which was a protest against ecclesiastical tyranny, would naturally seek to provide greater lay participation in its government," Marston observed.[86] These founders were thoroughgoing Methodists, of course, committed not only to the doctrines but also to the "usages" of "old-line Methodism." Thus in organization, as in doctrine, they simply took over the Methodist system, though making some key modifications. The major reform was in moderating clergy dominance by adopting the principle of equal "lay" and "ministerial" representation at the annual conference and General Conference levels — something many ME Church members had been advocating for years. Roberts himself said, "The deep interest and close scrutiny of the intelligent laymen who were present as delegates, must have convinced any one that that church is a great

83. BHR, *BTR*, pp. 232-33.

84. Marston, p. 258.

85. Almost inevitably, the nurture model tends to put relatively more stress on the church's nurturing environment (Christian education, for example) and on human agency, and relatively less on the direct or immediate action of God's Holy Spirit. See the further discussion in chapter 36, where Roberts's theology is summarized.

86. Marston, p. 256.

loser which excludes them from her councils."[87] It would be another twelve years before the Methodist Episcopal Church would begin to grant "lay" representation in the General Conference, and then only on a limited basis.[88]

The Pekin convention democratized the denominational structure also by replacing the office of bishop with a general superintendent with a limited term; election of district chairmen rather than episcopal appointment of presiding elders; and the choosing of class leaders by congregational election rather than pastoral appointment.[89]

The other major change — stricter membership standards — was consistent with the new denomination's understanding of the church. The Free Methodist Church continued the same membership categories of the ME Church — "full" members and "probationary" members. However, it tightened the requirements in both categories. Probationary members must "give satisfactory evidence of Scriptural conversion," not just manifest a "desire to flee from the wrath to come," as in early Methodism (where Methodism was a renewal movement within the larger Church of England).[90] In other words, conversion was required for church membership, whereas in the historic Methodist pattern conversion was not necessarily assumed and in fact often occurred through class meeting participation.

Full membership required six months of probation (as in the ME Church), during which time the person was to attend class meetings, and approval by a three-fourths vote of the members present. The Free Methodists made the full membership commitment more explicit than in the ME Church by specifying seven questions that are not found in the *Discipline* of the parent body.

1. Have you the witness of THE SPIRIT that you are a child of God?
2. Have you that perfect love which casteth out fear? If not, will you diligently seek until you obtain it?
3. Is it your purpose to devote yourself the remainder of your life wholly to the service of God, doing good to your fellow men and working out your own salvation with fear and trembling?
4. Will you forever lay aside all superfluous ornaments, and adorn yourself in modest apparel, with shame-facedness and sobriety, not with broidered hair,

---

87. [B. T. Roberts], "Convention at Pekin," p. 291.

88. "Lay representation in Annual [as distinct from General] Conference came even later [than 1900], and not for many years would full and equal lay representation be achieved in the Methodist Episcopal Church — a principle that had been firmly established by the Free Methodist Church at its founding." Marston, p. 257.

89. [B. T. Roberts], "Convention at Pekin," p. 291; Marston, p. 257.

90. *Doctrines and Discipline* (1860), p. 32. Marston notes that the 1866 General Conference added the requirement, "consent to be governed by the General Rules." "Thus, even probationary membership was based upon saving faith in Christ and, after 1866, upon a pledge to maintain the church's standard of Christian living. By such safeguards the early church sought to avoid having the church filled with unconverted members, which the reformers claimed had crippled the spiritual life of the parent church." Marston, pp. 259-60.

or gold or pearls, or costly array, but which becometh those professing godliness with good works?[91]

5. Will you abstain from connection with all secret societies, keeping yourself free to follow the will of the Lord in all things?
6. Do you subscribe to our articles of religion, our general rules, and our Discipline, and are you willing to be governed by the same?
7. Have you Christian fellowship and love for the members of this society, and will you assist them as God shall give you ability in carrying on the work of the Lord?[92]

The General Rules referred to were also taken over from the ME Church. However, the Free Methodists wrote into their General Rules the revision that abolitionist Methodists had been unable to pass at the Methodist Episcopal General Conference. The new *Discipline* included a rule against "the buying, selling, or holding of a human being as a slave" in place of the ME wording, "The buying and selling of men, women, and children, with an intention to enslave them," which did not explicitly prohibit slaveholding.[93]

The new *Discipline* also gave instruction for public worship (including "the morning service," "the afternoon service," and "the evening service" on Sundays). It encouraged congregational singing and prohibited "instrumental music or choir singing" in public worship.[94]

Leadership

Who should lead the new denomination? In keeping with his concern for more democratic organization, Roberts proposed a standing committee charged with "the general oversight of all the interests of the church." The convention, however, preferred a general superintendent. They did not want to establish the office of bishop, a position with considerable authority in the ME Church, but they were not as anti-episcopal as the Wesleyan Methodists had been when they organized seventeen years earlier. Then, episcopal opposition to abolitionist activism had been a key factor, but for Free Methodism the tyrants had not been the bishops but the Regency preachers. The Wesleyan Methodists adopted a modified congregational polity, but the Free Methodists were content merely to adapt Methodist Episcopal structure in a more democratic, participatory direction. However, Roberts said flatly, "The episcopacy

91. Based on 1 Tim. 2:9-10 (KJV): Let "women adorn themselves in modest apparel, with shamefacedness and sobriety; not with broided [i.e., braided] hair, or gold, or pearls, or costly array; but (which becometh women professing godliness) with good works."

92. *Doctrines and Discipline* (1860), pp. 32-33.

93. For emphasis, the prohibition against "buying, selling, or holding" a slave was italicized. *Doctrines and Discipline* (1860), p. 29.

94. See the discussion in Marston, pp. 261-63.

and presiding eldership are abolished." He added that in the new structure, "Class leaders and stewards are chosen by the members, and the sacred right of every accused person to an impartial trial and appeal is carefully guarded."[95]

Who should serve as general superintendent? Though Roberts was the obvious choice, he hadn't anticipated quite this turn of events. He wrote in his diary, "To my surprise the choice fell on me. Lord, give me heavenly wisdom to guide me! It was a heavy cross to accept the appointment, but I did not dare to decline, because of the conviction that God called me to this labor and reproach and responsibility. Yet, O, to what calumny it will subject me. Lord, I will take the cross and the shame. Let me have Thy presence and help, O God of power!"[96]

Roberts's enemies had always accused him of prideful ambition and no doubt saw his appointment as general superintendent as confirmation. My assessment is that while Roberts was politically shrewd, and certainly ambitious for the church and the kingdom of God, he was not personally ambitious or out to build his own empire. He must have anticipated that he might be selected for leadership in the new denomination. But I take at face value his proposal for shared, rather than solo, leadership, and his surprise at being chosen to serve as general superintendent. This assessment is consistent with the tenor of Benjamin's diaries and letters over many years, and with the recollections of close associates following his death.

Bishop L. R. Marston's *From Age to Age a Living Witness* reports in considerable detail the organization and early development of the Free Methodist Church. Since this present book is a biography, not a denominational history, it does not retrace early Free Methodist history in depth. Marston covers it admirably, and his book remains an excellent source. I give only as much of the story as is necessary to illuminate the lives and ministry of Benjamin and Ellen Roberts and their roles in the rise of Free Methodism, and refer readers to the standard histories for more detail. However, subsequent chapters will trace the main trajectory of the denomination as a necessary part of the Roberts story.

At the Pekin convention on August 23, 1860, the Free Methodist Church began its life as the newest member of the growing family of Methodist denominations, with its own structure and book of discipline. B. T. Roberts launched upon his role as general superintendent, based in Buffalo but itinerating widely in the interests of the new church. Within weeks of the Pekin convention he published *The Doctrines and Discipline of the Free Methodist Church*, printed at Clapp and Matthews's Steam

---

95. [B. T. Roberts], "Convention at Pekin," p. 291. The Free Methodists initially made some other terminological changes (e.g., "annual convention" for "annual conference"; "general convention" for "general conference"; "chairman of district" rather than "presiding elder"). However, the first (1862) FM General Conference voted to restore the traditional Methodist term "conference" rather than "convention" ("A Synopsis of the Minutes of the General Conferences of the Free Methodist Church," *Minutes of the Annual Conferences, and General Conference, of The Free Methodist Church,* 1870 [Rochester: Earnest Christian Office, 1870], p. 52). The term "chairman of district" was eventually changed to "district elder."

96. BTRD, Aug. 23, 1860, quoted in BHR, *BTR*, p. 235.

Printing House in Buffalo. He prefaced the *Discipline* with a ten-page "Address" entitled "Origin of the Free Methodist Church" that summarized the circumstances leading to the formation of the new denomination. "The Free Methodist Church had its origin in necessity not in choice. It did not grow out of secession" or from attempts to reform church government, the address noted. Rather, the Free Methodists were "thrown out" and, being rebuffed in their attempts to find proper "redress," "had no alternative but to form a new organization." Being "in doctrine, discipline, and spirit . . . Methodists," they could not well join "any other denomination." The key issue "was between dead formalism, and the life and power of godliness." Since this was the central issue, the Free Methodists "could not feel at home with those branches of the Methodist family into whose formation other questions mainly entered" — a reference primarily, it would seem, to the Wesleyan Methodists for whom polity, and particularly anti-episcopacy, was a key issue.[97]

Beginning with the 1866 *Discipline*, this introductory "Address" was replaced by a statement that focused on the character and mission of the denomination. This revised "Address," which (starting with the 1870 *Discipline*) began with the same statement from Wesley that was carried at the beginning of Methodist Episcopal *Disciplines*, said little about the controversy that gave rise to Free Methodism. It did note, however: "The first Free Methodist Church ever organized was in St. Louis, a slaveholding city, and at a time when slaveholders were freely admitted to the churches generally. Yet they made non-slaveholding a test of membership." And it included the declaration that Free Methodists "believe that their mission is twofold — to maintain the Bible standard of Christianity — and to preach the Gospel to the poor."[98]

The Real Nazarites

The few at the Pekin convention who did not agree with the formation of a new denomination banded together separately under the name Nazarite Bands. Thus technically it was only with the organization of the Free Methodist Church in August

97. *Doctrines and Discipline* (1860), pp. iii-xii; see [B. T. Roberts], "Convention at Pekin," p. 292.

98. *Doctrines and Discipline of the Free Methodist Church* (1866), pp. iii-xii; (1870), pp. iii-xii. Thus the 1866 *Discipline* was the first to carry this statement about Free Methodism's "twofold mission." This statement of mission may be compared with that articulated by John Wesley and the first Methodist Conference in 1744, "To reform the nation, more particularly the Church; to spread scriptural holiness over the land," as well as with the mission stated by the Methodist Episcopal Church at its official organization in the United States in 1784, "To reform the Continent, and to spread scriptural Holiness over these Lands." See Wade Crawford Barclay, *To Reform the Nation*, vol. 2 of *Early American Methodism, 1769-1844*, History of Methodist Missions (New York: Board of Missions and Church Extension of the Methodist Church, 1950), pp. 1-2.

The "Address" in the Free Methodist *Discipline* is identical in the 1860 and 1862 editions and is valuable as an account of the history of the "Origin of the Free Methodist Church" (as it is entitled). This historical introduction was later in effect superseded by Roberts's *WAS*.

1860 that a distinct group came into being that avowed the name Nazarite! Summarizing the whole story later, McCreery wrote,

> All the pilgrims considered [the term "Nazarites"] given as a name of reproach, and many got blessed in enduring it, and there was no general fault found with it till the Free Methodist Church was formed, when the pilgrims became gradually divided into the Nazarite party and the Free Methodist party. Rather than have strife and division in our ranks, the Nazarite party, gradually fell into the new Church. About a dozen were obstinate, and some ran wild, while about half the pilgrims did not join the Free Methodists at all. Some fell back into the old Church and some remained out of any church.

McCreery personally felt that the Free Methodist Church had been organized too soon; "the leaven was moved from the old M.E. Church . . . before all that might have been leavened were leavened."[99] He seems to have felt that if the formation of the new denomination had been delayed by about three years, the impact on the Methodist Episcopal Church would have been much greater — and the exodus to form the Free Methodist Church, if it came, would have been correspondingly larger.

Moses Downing said that after the new denomination was organized at Pekin, the "Nazarite faction went to seed completely at a camp-meeting in East Shelby, N.Y." William Cooley and his wife, who initially went with the Nazarites, "seeing fanaticism in some of its wildest features" at this camp meeting, reconsidered their decision and became useful Free Methodists. McCreery also went with the Nazarites at first but later joined the Free Methodists, though apparently with some reluctance.[100] Marston wrote, "It is fairly safe to assume that [in 1860] McCreery yet hoped that some such movement as he earlier had concocted in his highly fanciful imagination might flourish and reform Methodism. At least now he had the name of the organization of which he had dreamed. But in this hope he was to be disappointed, for the Nazarite movement came to naught."[101]

Marston felt, sensibly enough, that this secession of the more extreme element was providential. He wrote that those who left "tended to be the extremists of the reform element, and later harassed the young church by creating fanatical disturbances in Free Methodist meetings and stirring up contention. Their withdrawal to form their own loosely organized Bands was fortunate for the church which, organized as it was with freedom of the Spirit in worship as one of its principles, faced the task of safeguarding against demonstrations 'in the flesh' and under the guise of assumed spiritual freedom."[102]

---

99. Quoted in James Mathews, "Memorial Sketch of Rev. Joseph McCreery," *EC* 66, no. 1 (July 1893): 9.

100. BHR, *BTR*, p. 232.

101. Marston, pp. 329-30.

102. Marston, p. 255.

An Expanding Ministry

Following the Pekin convention, more Free Methodist churches began springing up in New York and in Illinois. In Bonus Prairie, Illinois, Ellen Roberts's brother Charles Stowe became a part of the new Free Methodist church there.[103] Throughout western New York the various bands organized earlier "were coming into the new church, voting to adopt the Discipline put forth by the Pekin Convention." In Pekin the Chesbroughs and others formed the first Free Methodist congregation there. S. K. J. Chesbrough later wrote, "I well remember the Sunday after the organization, when my wife and eighteen others answered the questions in the Discipline which Bro. B. T. Roberts had written on a piece of paper, and formed the first Free Methodist class ever formed under the Discipline."[104]

In November 1860 Roberts led a convention at Rushford, New York, that organized the Genesee Conference (or Genesee Convention, as it was initially called) of the new denomination with two districts.[105] In Buffalo a young preacher named James Mathews was developing the ministry Roberts had begun, holding regular church services and preaching at the Buffalo docks. The theater that Roberts had purchased was fitted out to seat 500 to 600 people. In October it was dedicated as the Second Free Methodist Church of Buffalo, with Loren Stiles and John Wesley Redfield conducting the services. Benjamin wrote,

> We never felt so sensibly that God owned any place as that. His glorious presence has filled the temple every time we have met there for His worship. IT IS FREE. Glory to God! there is one place in the heart of this large wicked city where the poor may have the Gospel preached to them; one place where the auctioneer's voice is not heard converting the house of God into a house of merchandise; one place where the Gospel will, we trust, be preached without fear or compromise, where it will be in order for God's people to get blessed.[106]

A year later Benjamin was pleased with how the work in Buffalo was going. He held a quarterly meeting there on October 19 and 20, 1861, and reported,

> What hath God wrought in this city! We have here, where strong opposition has been urged every possible way, a good society of about seventy members, all

---

103. Joseph Goodwin Terrill, "Experience of Joseph G. Terrill," *EC* 3, no. 2 (Feb. 1862): 57. Terrill wrote, "One evening while praying around the family altar at Bro. Chas. Stowe's, I obtained the victory, and now I triumph in God." This seems to refer to a time in late 1861 and to a Free Methodist context, though the reference is not explicit.

104. BHR, *BTR*, p. 241.

105. [B. T. Roberts], "Free Methodist Convention," *EC* 1, no. 12 (Dec. 1860): 392-93; BHR, *BTR*, pp. 241-43.

106. [B. T. Roberts], "Dedication of the Second Free Methodist Church of Buffalo," *EC* 1, no. 11 (Nov. 1860): 363. Although the *Earnest Christian* report does not explicitly say so, this building was the "converted" Pearl Street Theater mentioned in the previous chapter.

united, and walking in faith and love. They enjoy a constant revival. At the regular meetings, week day evenings, the house is well filled, and Sunday evenings it is crowded, gallery, aisles and porch, and hundreds go away unable to find standing room. Six precious souls have been converted in the past week at our regular meetings. As soon as our church is paid for, we must open another.[107]

This was close to Roberts's ideal for a church — "constant revival," and ministry among the poor. Since the renovated theater building could seat about 600, the crowded Sunday evening services must have had about 600 or 700 in attendance.

Early Free Methodist Growth

Roberts now found himself at the head of a growing movement. "From all directions calls are coming for the establishment of free churches," he reported in the June 1861 *Earnest Christian*. But lack of "suitable preachers, — men of God, of Apostolical zeal and self denial, full of faith and of the Holy Ghost" — meant that many calls could not be met.

"We have no desire to promote secessions except from sin to holiness; nor are we conscious of any, even the slightest, ambition to build up a new denomination," Roberts wrote. But he had, he said,

an intense desire to see, all over the world, churches in which:
1. The Gospel standard of experimental and practical godliness shall be held up, and the Spirit of God be allowed to have free course — to work as He may without opposition from ministers or members; and as a result, salvation from all sin, be the common experience of those professing religion, and:
2. In which all the seats shall be free, and no respect paid to persons on account of wealth or social position.

Here in a nutshell is Roberts's vision for the Free Methodist Church and his rationale for its existence. He added, in a remark that says much about his ecclesiology, "We should very greatly prefer to see the existing denominations come upon this ground, which we believe to be the only position, in these respects, which a Church of Christ has the right to occupy, than to see a new denomination raised up to spread these Scriptural principles. But perhaps the only way to get them there is for those, who have sufficient faith in God to lead the way."[108]

From the first, the new denomination surged with momentum. The 1864 *Minutes of the Annual Conferences* reported three annual conferences (Illinois, Genesee, and Susquehanna) and a total membership of 3,655, with 67 preachers, and church

---

107. [B. T. Roberts], "Ogle Camp Meeting," *EC* 2, no. 11 (Nov. 1861): 355. (To the account of the Ogle camp meeting Roberts appended a report on his subsequent itinerary, mentioning several meetings over the next month or so.)

108. [B. T. Roberts], "Free Churches," p. 192.

property valued at $64,653.[109] Six years later, in 1870, membership had risen to 6,556, the number of preachers had nearly doubled (to 128), church property was valued at $234,700, and two more conferences had been formed (Michigan and Kansas).

Related to this momentum was an accent on the *power* of God. Reporting on the quarterly meeting at Rochester in November 1862, Roberts wrote, "Sunday evening the house was filled with an attentive audience. The awakening power of God was manifested, and three professed to find the justifying grace of God." Immediately following this is a report from William Cooley, who writes, "We had at Nelson a powerful Quarterly meeting. There was great power in the assembly." And T. W. Read wrote from Big Flats, New York (near Elmira): "Praise the Lord! He is sending his Spirit in great power among us. Last evening the slaying power was in our midst. Four holy women, and a brother were prostrated by the power of God for about two hours. Thirteen have professed to be justified, and a number have got the blessing of Holiness. The work is going on in mighty power. Some of the most respectable citizens, heads of families, have been converted, and are now rejoicing in the Lord."[110]

A revival, renewal movement had begun, as reports in the first years make plain. The extent and patterns of Free Methodist growth during B. T. Roberts's lifetime will be discussed later in chapters 32 and 33.

Redfield's Decline

John Wesley Redfield seemed to be in reasonably good health at the time of the Pekin convention, but about ten weeks later, on Tuesday, November 6 — coincidentally, the day Abraham Lincoln was elected president — Redfield suffered a debilitating stroke while ministering in Aurora, Illinois. He was only fifty years old. Redfield was never able to return to active ministry after this, though he kept up to some degree a ministry of correspondence.[111]

In the period just after the Pekin convention, Redfield did all he could to help establish the new denomination. He noted in his memoir that "Bro. Roberts had enlisted to help us" in Illinois but his responsibilities "as the general superintendent of east and west were such that I could not hope much of that kind of attention which was necessary to keep the little church moving." He added, "Before I left Bro. Roberts at Buffalo he incidentally remarked that he was greatly concerned by his fears that the preachers in our new connection would not feel the same anxiety to push the work as he did. I felt sorry for our superintendent, & secretly resolved that he should have no just occasion to find fault with me. So I started to make a visit to all of our societies within a circumference of something like 200 miles [that is, throughout

109. *Minutes of the Annual Conferences of the Free Methodist Church,* 1864 (Rochester: "Earnest Christian" Office, 1864), p. 36.

110. These reports are all included in [B. T. Roberts], "The Work of God," *EC* 4, no. 6 (Dec. 1862): 186-87.

111. Terrill, *Redfield,* p. 453.

northern Illinois]."[112] But then Redfield suffered his stroke and was largely incapacitated.

Realizing that he was probably near the end of his ministry, Redfield began penning his long, 425-page memoir. He reflected on what he saw as the new denomination was emerging, and how it would fare without him. In a passage that is important for understanding Redfield's theology, including his ecclesiology and eschatology, he wrote:

> I am at present unable to preach but very little & am frequently the subject of severe temptations. . . . As I am able I go to visit the societies which God has raised up, & when I witness their spirituality & the numbers of sinners coming home to God, as likewise the faithful labors of God's young ministers who have as by a miracle been raised up to man this infant church, I can only weep tears of gratitude to see the very thing I have so long desired, wept & labored for is really a living fact, & I live to see it. I had labored & wept, groaned & suffered till my load paralyzed me & I was compelled to stop. . . . But now I see that God has taken the thing in hand & has raised up a goodly number of men from among ourselves who prove by their labors & successes that they are chosen instruments — that God has chosen, taught, & fitted them for the work — & I feel assured they under God can do much better than I could if I had the best of health . . . — self sacrificing young men whose hearts are in the work & whose diversities of talents fit them for the multifarious phases of our ever enlarging, pressing fields of labor.
>
> One peculiar feature in this work is that like unto the first beginning of the gospel, a large number of women are evidently commissioned of God to take the vanguard. In [Redfield's revival in] Rochester 6 women led off, & so at nearly all places where we have churches or societies.
>
> I sometimes relieve myself from the tediousness of my crippled condition by counting over the number of our societies & preachers & praying for them & calculating that in long years to come they will increase in number & stature & in favor with God & man, & then looking forward to the day of final reckoning when death shall deliver up the dead, I feel so assured that a host will accumulate & our number shall help to swell the vast retinue from every age & clime to witness the grand coronation & sing the refrain in the unearthly chorus, "Crown Him, crown Him Lord of all." And then my whole soul is dissolved in tenderness & gratitude for a sight of the prospect.
>
> I am strongly impressed that God has had one grand design in raising up this people, & that is to bring the church back to that type of religion which had its inauguration on the day of Pentecost, & that is to give to the world an abiding specimen of what the gospel is to do for men. As long as the world sees only the moral change produced by the gospel they will soon learn to parry its claims, & seeing the deficiency of the gospel to meet the wants of mankind, they will hardly feel to give full credit to the doctrine that sin has been the cause of all moral & physical

---

112. Redfield Autobiography, pp. 366-67 (slightly corrected).

evil & that Christ is a restorer every way capable of completing the task of mending all our derangements. But let an occasional evidence as on the day of Pentecost be given that Jesus can heal our sickness, cast out devils, & call upon the resources of infinite power in pressing need, & then the world will have a perpetual testimony before it that God is God & that the Christian religion in its purity has God's special care & protection.[113]

The Free Methodist Church, in other words, was to be a demonstration project of the power of Pentecost and the promise of the final coming of the kingdom of God. Significantly, Redfield speaks of Free Methodist growth "in long years to come" until, eventually, "the day of final reckoning." He apparently expected history to continue for some considerable time before Christ's return, rather than an imminent second coming. In this sense Redfield's eschatology was not apocalyptic.

Justification for Free Methodism

Twenty-two years after the formation of the Free Methodist Church, B. T. Roberts reflected on the events that led to the new denomination. He wrote, "For striving, in the spirit of love, to bring the church with which we were connected up to [the New Testament] standard, many of us were violently excluded. We looked around for a home. We could find no Church that appeared to us to be even aiming to be what a church of Christ should be." Consequently he and his colleagues "went to work in all humility and dependence on God to establish such a church." Roberts added, "We should be glad to have all true Christians who agree with us as to what a church should be, to unite with us. But if they will not do it, why should we be blamed?"[114]

It does not appear that Roberts ever did in fact seriously consider joining any other denomination, such as the Wesleyan Methodists, though such options must have crossed his mind. Roberts really wanted to restore Methodism to what it had been a generation or two earlier. To that he devoted the rest of his life.

Again in 1884 when Roberts was urged to join forces with a radical holiness group in Texas known as the Revival Methodists, he reflected on how the Free Methodist Church had come into being nearly a quarter-century earlier.

When we and many others were turned out of the M.E. Church for laboring with success, to promote Scriptural holiness we had no thought of forming a new organization. Many of us had such confidence in the integrity of the M.E. Church, as a body, that we had no doubt that the General Conference would candidly investigate matters and redress all wrongs. But when that august body, in direct violation of the Constitution of the church, refused to entertain our appeals, we were, for a

---

113. Redfield Autobiography, pp. 387-88 (slightly corrected). Terrill did not include this passage in his biography of Redfield.

114. [B. T. Roberts], "Union," *EC* 45, no. 1 (Jan. 1883): 31.

while, at a loss what to do. There was no denomination that agreed with us on the issues on which we were thrust out.

Some who had been clearly saved, unconsciously gave way to spiritual pride and self-will. A spirit of fanaticism . . . was exhibited by some. They would neither be instructed nor controlled. No one had any authority over them. In the eyes of the public we were all held responsible for their unscriptural conduct. The conviction was forced upon us that there must be an organization, even if there were not a dozen to join it. We felt clearly called of God to take the stand we then took.[115]

"Many of us were turned out of the M.E. Church under various pretexts," Roberts said, "but in reality for promoting Scriptural holiness."[116]

---

115. [B. T. Roberts], "In a Serious Dilemma," *EC* 47, no. 5 (May 1884): 161. Roberts is responding here to a letter he received from J. M. Cochran of Nailer, Tex., which he quotes. Cochran wrote, "Your name, together with the names of twenty-two other leaders of the Holiness Movement, is now on a prayer list, and prayer is being offered to Jesus every day to bring you into the work" (p. 160). Thus in Cochran's estimation Roberts was one of the leaders of the Holiness movement.

116. [B. T. Roberts], "Holiness Sects," *EC* 47, no. 6 (June 1884): 187.

Titus and Sally (Ellis) Roberts, parents of B. T. Roberts — pioneers and entrepreneurs.

Methodist camp meeting, probably in New York State, 1852. Ellen Stowe attended several such camp meetings in the 1840s, and B. T. Roberts was a promoter of camp meetings. (Reproduced with permission of Drew University Library)

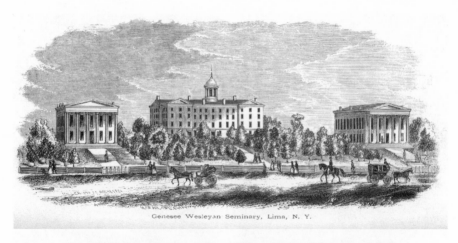

Genesee Wesleyan Seminary, Lima, N. Y.

Genesee Wesleyan Seminary, Lima, N.Y., where B. T. Roberts studied
in 1845 prior to entering Wesleyan University.

AM I NOT A MAN AND A BROTHER

AM I NOT A WOMAN AND A SISTER

American antislavery icon from about 1840, showing both the humanity of slaves
and an awareness of women's rights. B. T. Roberts used the "Am I Not a
Woman and a Sister" slogan in an early poem to his sister Florilla.
(Courtesy of the Boston Athenæum)

Holiness advocate Phoebe Palmer (1807-74) and her physician husband Walter were models for the young Ellen Stowe during her New York City years.

Wesleyan University, Methodism's "flagship" educational institution, Middletown, Conn., 1831. B. T. Roberts graduated from Wesleyan in 1848.

Noted Methodist orator and educator Stephen Olin (1797-1851), much admired by B. T. Roberts, was president of Wesleyan University during Roberts's student years there.

John Wesley Redfield (1810-63), controversial Methodist "lay" revivalist and abolitionist, was virtually the cofounder of the Free Methodist Church.

Young Ellen Stowe had her picture taken in New York City in early 1849 to send to her fiancé, B. T. Roberts.

Buffalo's historic Niagara Street ME Church, shown here with the imposing facade added after B. T. Roberts's 1852-53 pastorate. Expensive renovations put the declining congregation heavily in debt.

Circus entrepreneur and humorist Dan Rice, grandson of a Methodist preacher, popularized the Uncle Sam image. B. T. Roberts called him a "pest" and opposed his circus exhibition in Brockport, N.Y., in 1855.

THE ORIGINAL HUMORIST AS HE APPEAR'D IN HIS
GREAT UNION SPEECH.
Before the **MEDICAL STUDENTS.** Philada. Dec. 20ᵗʰ 1859.

Methodist preacher Joseph McCreery (1814-92) was the key figure in the rise of the "Nazarite" controversy in the Genesee Conference. With B. T. Roberts, he was expelled from the ME Church in 1858.

Influential Genesee Conference preacher and later Methodist book agent Thomas Carlton (1808-74) helped engineer B. T. Roberts's 1857 and 1858 church trials and expulsion from the Methodist Episcopal Church.

William Kendall (1822-58), friend and colleague of B. T. Roberts, would have become a key leader in the Free Methodist Church had he not died before he could be tried and expelled from the Genesee Conference.

Loren Stiles, Jr. (1820-63), eloquent young Methodist preacher, defended B. T. Roberts at his 1858 church trial and was himself expelled in 1859, then helped organize the Free Methodist Church.

S. K. J. (Sam) Chesbrough (1826-1909), farmer, businessman, and later FM preacher; longtime friend and supporter of B. T. and Ellen Roberts. The Free Methodist denomination was organized on his Pekin, N.Y., farm in 1860.

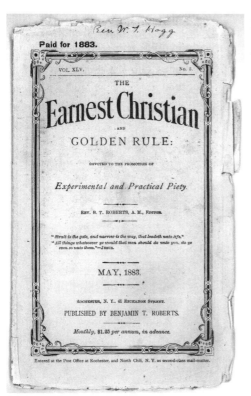

B. T. Roberts founded the *Earnest Christian* in 1860; the periodical survived him, continuing through 1909.

David F. Newton (b. 1796), independent Baptist minister, became associate editor of the *Earnest Christian* in 1862 when he merged his paper, the *Golden Rule*, with Roberts's magazine.

Martha Kendall LaDue.

Mariet Hardy Freeland.

Ellen Lois Roberts

Minerva Wood Cooley.

Ellen Fuller Mathews.

Some key "colaborers" of early Free Methodism — Martha (Wallace) Kendall LaDue,
widow of William Kendall; Mariet Hardy Freeland; Ellen Lois Roberts; Minerva Wood
Cooley; Ellen Fuller Mathews. All were wives of Free Methodist preachers.

Pioneering Free Methodist urban worker and church planter Jane (Shuart) Dunning (1823-90). B. T. Roberts called her "one of the first, ablest and most useful preachers" in Free Methodism.

Clara Leffingwell, after a term with China Inland Mission, founded the Free Methodist mission in China in 1905 and was a correspondent of Ellen Roberts.

Indian Christian reformer and advocate for women's rights Pandita Ramabai and her daughter Manoramabai about the time Manoramabai was a student at Chesbrough Seminary (1898-1900). (Archives, Roberts Wesleyan College)

Benson Howard Roberts and his wife Emma Sellew Roberts successfully served as coprincipals of Chesbrough Seminary (now Roberts Wesleyan College) for a quarter-century.

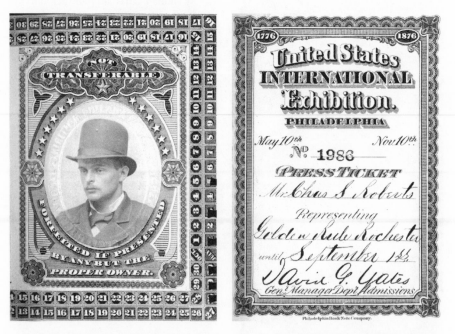

Charles Stowe Roberts attended the 1876 U.S. International Exhibition in Philadelphia, nominally representing his father's magazine, the *Earnest Christian and Golden Rule*.

The second-oldest Roberts son, George Lane Roberts, became an attorney in Pittsburgh after work in Argentina and in Bradford, Pa. B. T. and Ellen's first son and a daughter died in infancy.

B. T. Roberts in the early days of the Free Methodist movement. The engraving first appeared in the *Earnest Christian* in 1865.

FIRST LESSONS

ON

MONEY.

BY

B. T. ROBERTS, A. M.

A man should make it a part of his religion
to see that his country is well governed.
—*William Penn.*

THIRD THOUSAND.

ROCHESTER, N. Y.,
1886.

B. T. Roberts's books *First Lessons on Money* (1886) and *Ordaining Women* (1891) showed his passion for reform in church and society.

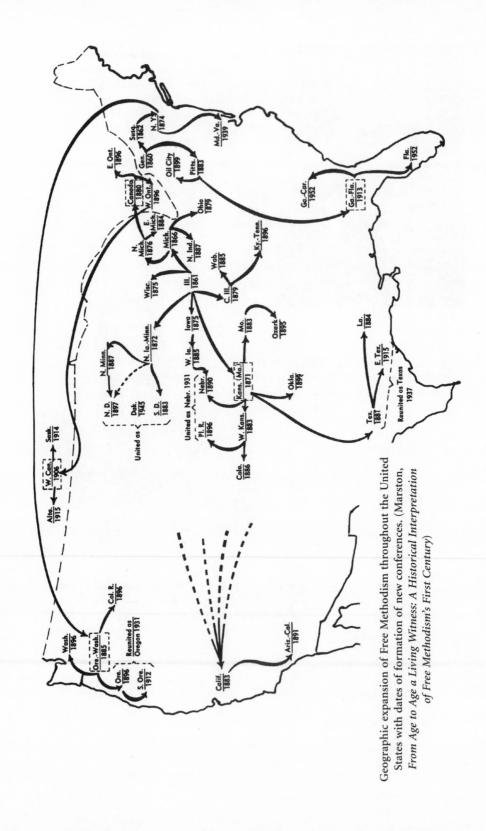

Geographic expansion of Free Methodism throughout the United States with dates of formation of new conferences. (Marston, *From Age to Age a Living Witness: A Historical Interpretation of Free Methodism's First Century*)

B. T. Roberts as general superintendent of the Free Methodist Church.

Fiery Vivian Adelbert Dake
(1854-92), a spiritual son to B. T.
Roberts, founded the controversial
Pentecost Bands missions- and
church-planting movement.

This rare profile view of B. T. Roberts in the early days of Free Methodism
suggests something of his resoluteness.

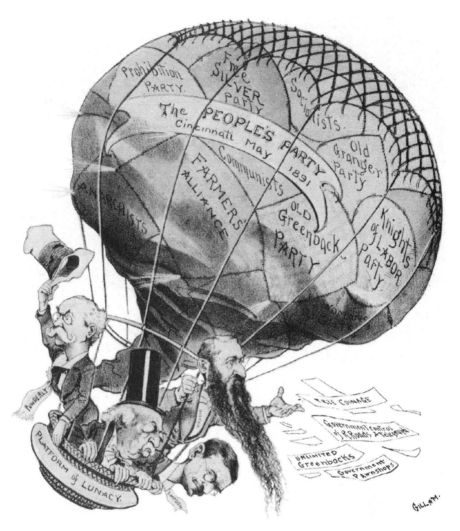

An 1891 Republican cartoon lampooned the new People's Party as an unstable
patchwork of the Farmers' Alliance, socialists, prohibitionists, and other groups.
B. T. Roberts led in founding the first populist Farmers' Alliance.

Urbane ME bishop Matthew Simpson celebrated Methodism's achievements in his monumental 1878 *Cyclopaedia of Methodism.* His account of Free Methodism prompted B. T. Roberts's *Why Another Sect.*

This photo of B. T. Roberts reportedly was a family favorite.

Jerry McAuley (1839-84) founded the famous Water Street Mission in New York City, indirectly the fruit of Free Methodist ministry among New York's urban poor. B. T. Roberts visited the mission on trips to New York.

Hudson Taylor (1832-1905), founder of China Inland Mission, was among the leaders B. T. Roberts met at the 1888 General Missionary Conference in London, England. Taylor's grandson, James Hudson Taylor, became a Free Methodist missionary through contacts with FM missionaries in China.

Chili Seminary (now Roberts Wesleyan College), near Rochester, N.Y., in its early days.

Cox Memorial Hall at Chesbrough (Chili) Seminary, one of the new buildings
erected after a disastrous fire. Completed just months before B. T. Roberts's death,
it became the site of his funeral in 1893, and still stands.

William Taylor (1821-1902), Methodist world missions leader and holiness advocate, influenced Free Methodist missions thinking. B. T. Roberts met him at Ocean Grove, N.J., in 1884.

Alexander and Adelaide Beers, Seattle Seminary (now Seattle Pacific University). Influenced by B. T. Roberts and A. B. Simpson, President Beers maintained a strong missions emphasis at the school.

A. B. Simpson (1843-1919),
founder of the Christian
and Missionary Alliance,
sent his youngest son to
study at Chesbrough Seminary
after becoming acquainted
with B. T. and Ellen Roberts
and the Free Methodists.

B. T. and Ellen Roberts
during his last years.

B. T. Roberts toward the end of his life. This photo was published in the *Earnest Christian* when Roberts died in 1893.

Ellen (Stowe) Roberts in later life. She lived until 1908.

These color portraits of B. T. and Ellen Roberts as a young couple were painted by artist Carlos Stebbins in 1851. Long lost, they were rediscovered in 2002.

The Roberts family tombstone in North Chili, N.Y., where B. T., Ellen, and other family members lie buried. The tombstone mistakenly has B. T.'s birth year as 1824 rather than 1823.

PART III

MISSION
(1860-1908)

CHAPTER 26

The *Earnest Christian* Magazine

"We hope by our catholic spirit, by an uncompromising advocacy of 'righteousness, peace and joy in the Holy Spirit,' to make our magazine a favorite and welcome visitor to every family where pure religion and morality are inculcated."

B. T. Roberts, 1860[1]

"[R]edemption must cover the entire evil resting on our race resulting from the fall."

John Wesley Redfield, in the *Earnest Christian*, 1860[2]

The 1858 Laymen's Convention discussed "the propriety of establishing in the city of Buffalo a periodical devoted to the advocacy of 'Earnest Christianity.'" B. T. Roberts took the discussion seriously; he may in fact have already thought and talked about such a venture. Soon after the convention he began preparations and (as previously noted) in January 1860 launched the *Earnest Christian* as a monthly magazine.

From the first the journal was a success. It developed a wide-ranging constituency that grew with time. Roberts published the magazine until his death in 1893. Under the editorship of his son, Benson, and others, the journal survived him about as long as did his wife — a decade into the new century.

The *Earnest Christian* was never the official organ of the Free Methodist

---

1. [B. T. Roberts], "Object and Scope of This Magazine," *EC* 1, no. 1 (Jan. 1860): 1-2.
2. John Wesley Redfield, "Redemption," *EC* 1, no. 1 (Jan. 1860): 26.

Church[3] and in fact had a significant ministry beyond the denomination. Its founding actually preceded the birth of the denomination, though of course both the magazine and the church arose from the same source. While the *Earnest Christian* initially served some of the functions of a denominational organ, the independent weekly *Northern Independent* better fulfilled that role at first. Later, in 1868, a paper called the *Free Methodist* was started in what Marston termed a "church-related private venture."[4] Through ups and downs this publication eventually became the denominational magazine (and continues today as *Light and Life*).

Roberts initially opposed starting a distinctly denominational magazine, feeling it might be divisive and provoke more controversy. Though the "want of having a medium in which the many misrepresentations of our actions and motives can be corrected, is very generally felt," Roberts noted in the December 1860 *Earnest Christian,* "the financial risk is considerable." "What we need most is, *a general, deep, and thorough revival* of religion. A rehearsal of the wrongs we have suffered, and of the misdeeds of others, will not be very likely to save souls."[5] He did not want to give undue attention to the denomination as such, though he thought that eventually a denominational paper would make sense.[6]

A broadly focused journal "devoted to the promotion of experimental and practical piety" was what was needed now, Roberts felt, and to this he dedicated considerable time and energy. This chapter tells the story of the *Earnest Christian* and, through it, more of the story of Benjamin and Ellen Roberts. We will assess the role and influence of the journal and picture B. T. Roberts as editor and publisher.[7]

Founding a New Religious Journal

In the latter months of 1859 Benjamin began planning for his new periodical. In August he sent a circular letter to a select group of potential sponsors.[8] He asked that they unite to underwrite the venture, but no one responded positively. Roberts explained somewhat ambiguously in 1864 that only "one person that we knew of was willing to assume any such risk. We felt called of God to take it personally and did so cheerfully.

3. In the literature there is some confusion on this point; occasionally one finds the *Earnest Christian* referred to as, or assumed to be, the denominational organ.

4. Marston, pp. 472-73.

5. [B. T. Roberts], "The Weekly Paper," *EC* 1, no. 12 (Dec. 1860): 392.

6. Roberts calculated that $800 to $1,000 would be necessary "to buy type, press, and other fixtures" and begin a publishing operation. "As soon as the Lord puts it into the hearts of those who have the means to supply what is necessary to place the enterprise upon a safe basis, a weekly paper will, we have no doubt, be commenced." [B. T. Roberts], "The Weekly Paper."

7. In tracing the entire history of the *Earnest Christian,* this chapter moves well ahead of the narrative to be covered in subsequent chapters. But the overall history of the magazine forms a fitting backdrop to the continuing unfolding events of Benjamin and Ellen's life together.

8. BTRD, Aug. 9, 1859: "Wrote circular letter about a new paper."

We had means of our own to carry it through one year at least."[9] He perhaps meant that some individual — perhaps Sam Chesbrough or Sam's father Isaac, or possibly Titus Roberts — privately offered Roberts the funds to get the magazine going until it could be self-supporting, though he may have spent some of his own money.

As he began working on the *Earnest Christian,* Benjamin used the blank pages at the beginning of his 1859 diary to record the names of subscribers and donors. He noted under the space for January 2 that Loren Stiles, William Cooley, A. L. Backus, L. T. Halstead, and he himself had each contributed five dollars to become *Earnest Christian* subscribers. The subscription price was one dollar per year.[10]

Benjamin had established a relationship with the Clapp, Matthews, and Company Steam Printing House in Buffalo, where the Buffalo *Morning Express* was published. There he had had Samuel Chesbrough's *Defence of Rev. B. T. Roberts* printed in 1858.[11] He took the first issue of the *Earnest Christian* to them, and Clapp and Matthews became the magazine's printer during the earliest years.

One day Mr. Matthews of Clapp and Matthews told Benjamin good-naturedly, "Mr. Roberts, . . . you do the work of four men. You have too much sense to keep on this way. Pardon me, Mr. Roberts, if I say I think you are foolish. Who cares for all this sacrifice you are making?"

Benjamin replied quietly, "God cares, and I care."

"That's it," replied Matthews. "You are the kind of man we want, and will pay you well. But no, you are a fool for Christ's sake, you say. Well, I don't understand it, but I suppose the world needs such as you to balance the number of stupid fools, so of course you will keep on."[12]

James Mathews (Roberts's young associate in Buffalo, not the printer) helped Roberts put out the first issue of the magazine.[13] Soon Benjamin enlisted other friends and his own family in the laborious task of producing each issue. In those days before typewriters and computers, putting out a monthly journal of thirty-two pages required prodigious effort.

Little George and Benson Roberts were eight and six when Benjamin started the *Earnest Christian,* and as they grew old enough he involved them in the process. "Mailing days were an event each month," Benson later recalled. "My boyhood was closely associated with the publication. How many Saturdays that we would gladly have spent in play were spent in wrapping up the packages that were to go from New York to Illinois, and later to every state in the Union."[14]

---

9. "Price of Subscription," *EC* 8, no. 2 (Aug. 1864): 66-67.

10. BTRD, Jan. 2, 1859. The names may have been entered on that date (a Sunday), but more likely later.

11. BTRD, Mar. 10, 1859.

12. As recalled in 1893 by Rev. James Matthews. James Matthews, "Benjamin T. Roberts As I Knew Him," *EC* 65, no. 4 (Apr. 1893): 106.

13. Matthews, "Benjamin T. Roberts As I Knew Him."

14. Benson H. Roberts, "Changes," *EC* 97, no. 1 (Jan. 1909): 3. B. T. Roberts made considerable use of the post office in connection with the *Earnest Christian,* first in Rochester and then in North Chili. He

A team of people worked together in sending out each monthly issue. Sam Chesbrough helped; "in a great striking hand" he copied out the addresses, assisted by James Mathews, "who wrote a speedy, angular hand, and whose wit would beguile the hours of labor," wrote Benson Roberts. Helpers were "introduced into the mysteries of the mailing room," or the printing office, or the binding room. "And always the dear loving father, when at home, would lead the rest in the swiftness of his pen."[15]

Roberts's M.A. Degree

Alert readers of Samuel Chesbrough's defense of Roberts before the Genesee Conference, published in late 1858, might have noted that Chesbrough identified Benjamin as "Rev. B. T. Roberts, A.M." The *Earnest Christian* also identified Roberts as "A.M." How and when did Roberts become a master of arts, bearing the same degree that John Wesley had and used in his publications?[16]

Securing his M.A. (or A.M.; the two mean the same, master of arts, or in Latin, *Artium Magister*) was part of Benjamin's preparation for the new, expanding role that he saw coming. At this time the master of arts was fairly readily available to nearly any college graduate who had been out of college for three years or more. "In the early nineteenth century, the traditional master of arts degree was routinely given in most colleges after three years to any alumnus baccalaureate with ten dollars and no prison record," as one writer put it.[17] Wesleyan University, Roberts's alma mater, had a policy that stated: "The Degree of Master of Arts, may be conferred in course on every Bachelor of Arts, of three years standing, or more, who has been engaged since his graduation in some literary occupation, and has sustained a good moral character."[18] All that was necessary was to request the degree and pay the stipulated fee. The degree did not require or indicate additional academic work; rather it implied that the person had continued to develop and serve professionally. In fact, Wesleyan University had no graduate degree programs at this time.

---

noted in his diary on June 13, 1874, "News came that Mr A. H. King has obtained an order for the removal of our Post Office to the depot — a distance of about one mile. Wrote a remonstrance against it, and got it in circulation. Wrote to the Post Master General." In September he made a trip to Washington, D.C., to enter a complaint or plea at the general post office there. He noted on Sept. 8, 1874, "Called at General P.O. with Mr. Clapp. They promise to send special agent to investigate our N. Chili P.O. matters. Had a fine view of the capital and other public buildings" (BTRD, June 13 and Sept. 8, 1874).

15. Benson H. Roberts, "Changes," p. 3. Since Benson is reviewing decades of the publishing of the *Earnest Christian*, it is not clear how much of this description applies to the early days in Buffalo and how much to the later years in North Chili.

16. Wesley's publications typically listed him as "John Wesley, M.A."

17. James Edward Scanlon, *Randolph-Macon College: A Southern History, 1825-1967* (Charlottesville: University of Virginia Press, 1983), p. 57.

18. *Catalogue of the Officers and Students of the Wesleyan University, 1853-54* (Middletown, Conn.: W. D. Starr, 1853) p. 21.

Benjamin apparently wrote and applied for the degree in mid-1858 — sometime before his second trial and expulsion from the ME Church. Perhaps he included a record of his published writings as evidence that he had been engaged in "some literary occupation." In any case, the Wesleyan University Board of Trustees granted Roberts the master of arts degree on August 4, 1858, a couple of months before his trial and expulsion from the ME Church. At the same time, it granted M.A. degrees to seventeen 1855 graduates who now qualified according to the three-years rule.[19]

Benjamin could have applied for the degree several years earlier. In fact, his classmate William Kendall did so, receiving his M.A. in 1851.[20] Why did Roberts wait until 1858? Probably because he saw no need of the degree until his troubles with the Genesee Conference heated up. Whether or not he foresaw, as early as mid-1858, that he would be engaged in independent ministry or editing a magazine, he apparently viewed the degree as a useful credential, given his uncertain circumstances. When he started the *Earnest Christian,* he would have seen his degree as appropriate for the literary work he was doing.

There is another angle as well. Roberts may have been smart enough to realize that a further conference conviction and possible expulsion from the denomination might make his alma mater hesitant to award him the degree. After all, a condition for awarding the M.A. was that the candidate "has sustained a good moral character" — and just a few months before he was awarded the degree he had been convicted of "unchristian and immoral conduct"! Getting the M.A. degree (perhaps before the Wesleyan University trustees had heard about his 1857 conviction) was a way for Benjamin to safeguard his public reputation. It was a shrewd move.[21]

Curiously, more than a century later the editor of the *Free Methodist,* Dr. Byron Lamson, wanted to find out how Roberts had gotten his master's degree and what it meant. He wrote to Wesleyan University and received a reply from John W. Spaeth, Jr., the university archivist, dated November 17, 1966. Mr. Spaeth explained the process and cited the August 4, 1858, Wesleyan University Board of Trustees minutes.[22]

B. T. Roberts thus began his career as magazine editor with master's degree in hand. Throughout his publishing career he always listed himself as "B. T. Roberts, A.M."

---

19. Minutes, Board of Trustees, Wesleyan University, Aug. 4, 1858. Located in the Archives and Special Collections of Wesleyan University. The minutes state that Roberts was granted "the degree of A.M. in course," meaning it was granted according to the catalogue provision stated above and was not an honorary degree.

20. Frank W. Nicolson, ed., *Alumni Record of Wesleyan University, Middletown, Conn.,* centennial (6th) ed., 1931 (Middletown, Conn.: Pelton and King, 1931), p. 124.

21. Alternatively, the Board of Trustees may have been aware of Roberts's conviction but may have realized that it was really a political, not a moral, matter.

22. John W. Spaeth, Jr., Middletown, to Dr. Byron S. Lamson, the *Free Methodist,* Winona Lake, Ind., Nov. 17, 1966. Copy in Archives and Special Collections, Wesleyan University. Mr. Spaeth wrote, "Why the action in the case of Roberts was so long delayed I do not know, but it seems likely, on the face of it, that he failed to apply for the award [i.e., the degree] earlier. I can think of no other reason."

The First Issue

The *Earnest Christian* would be a substantial monthly magazine, not a weekly newspaper. It joined a crowded field of religious monthlies and quarterlies — as distinct from numerous weekly papers like the *Christian Advocate* and the *Northern Independent*. These weekly newspapers, which were regional, except for the *Christian Advocate and Journal* (published in Manhattan), enjoyed a wide circulation. The *Northern Christian Advocate* claimed 10,400 subscribers in 1859 and pronounced itself "the largest in Western N.Y."[23]

Three hundred or more religious journals were being published in the United States when the *Earnest Christian* began in 1860, and that number rose to 650 by 1885. A few of the monthly periodicals reached a circulation of 10,000, but most were much smaller.[24] The average circulation of monthly periodicals in 1860 (general-interest as well as religious) was about 12,000.[25] In this environment the *Earnest Christian* did remarkably well, its circulation quickly rising to over 6,000 by 1866.[26] In some ways it had a ready-made market, since Methodists in this period led all other denominations in the number and variety of periodicals and in their circulation. But by the same token it faced considerable competition.

The leading holiness periodical of the time was the *Guide to Holiness*, associated with the ministry of Phoebe Palmer. It was founded in 1839 by Timothy Merritt, then the associate editor of the *Christian Advocate and Journal* in New York City. It often carried articles by Palmer and reports of her ministry. Its circulation and influence grew as Mrs. Palmer became better known. After the Civil War Dr. and Mrs. Palmer bought the magazine and she took over as managing editor. The magazine continued for some decades after her death in 1874, finally ceasing publication about 1901.[27] Thus its history roughly parallels that of the *Earnest Christian*, though it was started about twenty years earlier.

The *Guide to Holiness* reached a circulation of around 5,000 by the early 1850s, but this shot up to over 12,000 in the wake of the 1858 revival and Phoebe Palmer's growing influence. Circulation had reached 16,000 by the time the *Earnest Christian* was launched in 1860, but dropped by 3,000 or so during the Civil War (just as the *Earnest Christian* was growing). But later, after the Palmers bought the *Guide* and

---

23. *NCA* 19, no. 48 (Nov. 30, 1859): 2.

24. Frank Luther Mott, *A History of American Magazines*, vol. 3, *1865-1885* (Cambridge: Harvard University Press, 1957), pp. 66-67.

25. Mott notes that although figures are often unreliable, "according to the eighth [U.S.] census, the average circulation of the quarterlies in 1860 was about 3,370; that of the monthlies about 12,000; while the weeklies, including newspapers . . . an average of about 2,400 copies" (for all periodicals, not just religious). Frank Luther Mott, *A History of American Magazines*, vol. 2, *1850-1865* (Cambridge: Harvard University Press, 1957), p. 10.

26. "To Our Subscribers," *EC* 11, no. 5 (May 1866): 162.

27. Charles Edward White, *The Beauty of Holiness: Phoebe Palmer as Theologian, Revivalist, Feminist, and Humanitarian* (Grand Rapids: Francis Asbury Press/Zondervan, 1986), pp. 92-94.

merged it with another popular holiness magazine, the periodical more than doubled its circulation, peaking at 37,000 in 1870.[28] Roberts may have modeled the *Earnest Christian* to some degree on the *Guide to Holiness.* The two monthly magazines looked similar, both printed in two columns on pages that were nearly the same size, and both normally had thirty-two pages. The *Earnest Christian* was organized differently, however, and treated a broader range of subjects.

Without the ministry of a nationally known revivalist like Phoebe Palmer to build on, the *Earnest Christian* never rivaled the *Guide to Holiness* in circulation. Yet it developed and extended a wide-ranging ministry for many years, surviving both the Civil War and the expansive postwar period when hundreds of magazines were launched but most quickly failed.[29]

With the first issue in January 1860, Roberts set the pattern that would remain through most of the years of the journal's publication: a magazine of thirty-two pages (with very few exceptions), nine and one half inches by six inches (slightly less when bound and trimmed in annual volumes). The magazine was printed clearly and attractively on good-quality paper, two columns per page, with generous margins. From the beginning Roberts numbered the pages consecutively throughout each volume, giving the first page of the first number of each volume the number five, thus allowing four pages for a title page and index when the volumes were bound.[30] The volume title page and index were included at the end of the last issue of each volume — at the end of the December (and after 1861, also the June) issue. The title page and index were then placed at the beginning when the volumes were bound.

Roberts thus from the first intended that the *Earnest Christian* become a useful collection of bound volumes as the years passed. He often included a fine engraved portrait as the frontispiece of bound volumes, both to increase their attractiveness and usefulness and as an incentive for purchase. Among the portraits included were those of John Wesley Redfield (1864), Roberts himself as a young man (1865), D. F. Newton (1866), Loren Stiles (July 1868), Elias Bowen (1871), Joseph Mackey (1875), Claudius Brainard (1892), and Joseph McCreery (July 1893). Generally the lead article was by or about the person pictured. Roberts put a notice at the very end of the December 1861 issue, "We will bind the 'Earnest Christian' in good style for forty cents a volume."[31]

The layout, organization, and content show careful attention to detail, revealing much about Roberts's character and personality.

---

28. White, *Beauty of Holiness,* pp. 92-93. W. B. Rose noted in the November 1909 issue of the *Earnest Christian* that the *Guide to Holiness* "had at one time a list of 32,000 subscribers." "Publisher's Note," *EC* 97, no. 11 (Nov. 1909): 32.

29. White, *Beauty of Holiness,* p. 93.

30. In the bound volumes, either no page numbers appear on the title page and index, or they are numbered with small Roman numerals. This pattern was followed consistently, with only occasional, slight variation.

31. [B. T. Roberts], "Missing Numbers," *EC* 2, no. 12 (Dec. 1861): 384.

People who encounter the *Earnest Christian* today are apt to find it only in bound volumes. However, the magazine was mailed each month in a separate cover slightly larger than the inside pages. The cover included a table of contents and some "Editorial Notes" or "Literary Notes" as well as advertising on its two inside pages, and the back cover featured display ads. A number of issues in 1883, for instance, carried a full-page advertisement for a grain-binding machine called "The Minneapolis" ("The Most Perfect Twine Binder"), manufactured by the Minneapolis Harvester Works in Minnesota, on the back cover. Other issues carried back-page ads for the Erie Railway ("Now known as the New York, Lake Erie & Western Railway"), Warren's Food Flour, the Cunningham Bicycle, and Mr. J. C. McKinney, a real estate agent in Ellis County, Texas. Roberts devised a system to keep track of subscription dates, printing "Paid for 1883" or "Paid to July 1883" (or whatever the year) at the top of the front cover.

The journal began simply as the *Earnest Christian*, though the title page of the first bound volumes reads *The Earnest Christian: Devoted to the Promotion of Experimental and Practical Piety*. Roberts listed himself as "B. T. Roberts, A.M., Editor." All the volume title pages carried Matthew 7:14, printed as "*Strait is the Gate, and Narrow is the Way that leadeth unto Life.* — JESUS." This was one of Roberts's favorite verses, and from it he preached many times. He discussed the meaning of this verse in an 1884 editorial, "Few Saved." It is very important, he wrote,

> that we heed the exhortation of our Savior, *Strive to enter in at the strait gate.* Every word is emphatic. The word translated *Strive*, is, in the original, ἀγωνίζεσθε, from which comes our word agonize. It was used by the classic Greeks to express the efforts which the most powerful men put forth in their athletic contests to win the victory. It denotes the highest pitch of exertion of which one is capable. There is nothing possible for us to do towards securing the salvation of our souls but is included in the word STRIVE. It means repent thoroughly of all your sins. Make restitution to those you have wronged, to the utmost of your ability. Cry unto God with your voice, and present to him a broken heart and a contrite spirit. Trust in the death and intercession of Christ to procure you every grace you need. Seek until you find, and then strive to keep, the witness of the Spirit that your sins are forgiven you. Make it a study how to please God in every thing.[32]

Roberts introduced the first issue with a brief piece entitled "Object and Scope of This Magazine." He began,

> There are many sincere and earnest persons throughout the land, anxiously inquiring "for the old paths." Dissatisfied with being outer-court worshippers, they are desirous of "dwelling in the secret place of the Most High."

---

32. B. T. Roberts, "Few Saved," *EC* 48, no. 6 (Dec. 1884): 168. This is what Roberts meant by *earnest* Christianity.

Upon their minds God often lets the light from Heaven shine. They see that repentance is something more than a vague conviction that the past life has not been entirely right. Conversion as they view it, illuminated by the Spirit, is a work far more radical than is implied in simply a "change of purpose." At times they are tremblingly alive to the fact, that a religion of fashion and parade, of pomp and show, and circumstance, cannot save their souls. The Holy Ghost presses home the truth that Christ's disciples are characterized by self denial, humility, and love.

It is for this increasing class of persons that we write — for those who are IN EARNEST to gain Heaven, and anxious to know the conditions upon which eternal happiness can be secured.[33]

Roberts said the magazine would emphasize "Experimental Religion, as the foundation and life of practical piety" and including "baptism with the Holy Ghost." He expanded on what he meant by "experimental religion":

We shall insist upon a *conversion* that makes a man willingly part with his sins — that makes the proud humble, the churl liberal, the selfish generous, the slaveholder anxious "to break every burden and to let the oppressed go free;" . . .

The doctrine of Christian Holiness, as taught by Wesley and Fletcher, being, as we conceive, plainly enforced by the Word of God, . . . will occupy a prominent place in our columns.

The claims of the neglected poor, the class to which Christ and the Apostles belonged, the class for whose special benefit the Gospel was designed, . . . will be advocated with all the candor and ability we can command. In order that the masses, who have a peculiar claim to the Gospel of Christ may be reached, the necessity of plain Churches, with the seats free, of plainness of dress, of spirituality and simplicity in worship, will, we trust, be set forth with convincing arguments.

Roberts promised to "keep free from controversy," to "avoid all offensive personalities," and when correction or reproof were called for, to write "with all possible mildness, and in the spirit of candor and love." He added, *"In short our object is to publish a revival journal;* our aim shall be to set up the Bible standard of religion. We hope by our catholic spirit, by an uncompromising advocacy of 'righteousness, peace and joy in the Holy Spirit,' to make our magazine a favorite and welcome visitor to every family where pure religion and morality are inculcated."

Benjamin concluded with an appeal for subscribers. "From all parts of the country we have received encouraging promises of support," he wrote. "Let us have, at the outset, a large list of subscribers."[34]

33. [B. T. Roberts], "Object and Scope," p. 1.
34. [B. T. Roberts], "Object and Scope," pp. 1-2.

The Gospel for the Poor

In this first issue Roberts underscored the key importance of free churches and the gospel to the poor, highlighted in his opening article, through a long, four-and-a-half-page essay that immediately followed his introductory piece. Entitled simply "Free Churches," this article was based in part on the first of his three 1856 *Northern Christian Advocate* articles of the same title. Roberts incorporated several paragraphs from the earlier article (with some revision), changing the first-person singular "I" to the editorial "we."[35]

This appropriation of his earlier writing shows, significantly, that his central focus remained unchanged, despite the trauma of his 1857-58 ordeal. His passion was still the gospel for the poor. The 1860 article is more fully elaborated theologically, however, and more specifically christological than the earlier, 1856 version.

This key essay reveals Roberts's passion for reaching the poor. It functioned practically as a manifesto for the Free Methodist Church, formed several months later. It became, in fact, the basis of the statement in early Free Methodist *Disciplines* that Free Methodists "believe that their mission is twofold — to maintain the Bible standard of Christianity, and to preach the Gospel to the poor."[36]

Roberts argued that the church has a special and specific commission from Jesus Christ to preach the gospel to the poor. He maintained that if Christianity prevailed in its purity, it "would bring Paradise back to earth." But it is being corrupted by a number of things, and in particular the growing practice of pew rental. This practice is "wrong in principle, and bad in tendency." Not some but "*all* churches should be free," he said; "our houses of worship should be, like the grace we preach, and the air we breathe, free to all." Then Roberts gave his central argument:

Free Churches are essential to reach the masses.

The wealth of the world is in the hands of a few. In every country the poor abound.... Sin has diffused itself every where, often causing poverty and suffering.

God assured his ancient people, favored above all others with precautions against want, that "the poor shall never cease out of the land." These are the ones upon whom the ills of life fall with crushing weight. Extortion wrings from them their scanty pittance. The law may endeavor to protect them; but they are without the means to obtain redress at her courts. If famine visits the land, she comes unbidden to their table, and remains their guest until they are consumed.

---

35. For example, in his 1856 article Roberts had written, "I am thoroughly convinced that this system is wrong in principle, and bad in its tendency. . . . I beg the indulgence of expressing myself strongly." In the 1860 *Earnest Christian* article Roberts wrote, "We are thoroughly convinced that this system is wrong in principle, and bad in its tendency. . . . We claim the indulgence of expressing ourself strongly." See B. T. Roberts, "Free Churches," *NCA* 16, no. 18 (Apr. 30, 1856): 4, discussed earlier. Also, see Roberts's handwritten manuscript (RFP, Microfilm Reel 11, Frames 2-21), which appears to be his reworking of his 1856 articles for the 1860 *Earnest Christian.*

36. *The Doctrines and Discipline of the Free Methodist Church* (Rochester, N.Y.: General Conference, 1870), p. ix.

The provisions of the gospel are for all. The "glad tidings" must be pro-claimed to every individual of the human race. God sends the TRUE LIGHT to illu-minate and melt every heart. It visits the palace and the dungeon, saluting the kind and the captive. The good news falls soothingly upon the ear of the victim of slavery, and tells him of a happy land, beyond the grave, where the crack of the driver's whip, and the baying of blood-hounds are never heard. The master is as-sured, that though he be a sinner above all other sinners, yet even he, by doing works meet for repentance, may be forgiven, and gain heaven. To civilized and savage, bond and free, black and white, the ignorant and the learned, is freely of-fered the great salvation.

But for whose benefit are special efforts to be put forth?

Who must be *particularly* cared for? Jesus settles this question. He leaves no room for cavil. When John sent to know who he was, Christ charged the messen-gers to return and show John the things which they had seen and heard. "The blind receive their sight, and the lame walk, the lepers are cleansed, and the deaf hear, the dead are raised up," and as if all this would be insufficient to satisfy John of the validity of his claims, he adds, "AND THE POOR HAVE THE GOSPEL PREACHED TO THEM." This was the crowning proof that He was the ONE THAT SHOULD COME. It does not appear that after this John ever had any doubts of the Messiahship of Christ. He that thus cared for the poor must be from God.

In this respect the Church must follow in the footsteps of Jesus. She must see to it, that the gospel is preached to the poor. With them, peculiar pains must be taken. The message of the minister must be adapted to their wants and condi-tions. The greatest trophies of saving grace must be sought among them. This was the view taken by the first heralds of the cross. Paul wrote to the Corinthians, "for ye see your calling, brethren, how that not many wise men after the flesh, not many mighty, not many noble, are called. But God hath chosen the foolish things of the world to confound the wise; and God hath chosen the weak things of the world to confound the things which are mighty; and base things of the world, and things which are despised, hath God chosen, yea, and things which are not, to bring to naught things that are: that no flesh should glory in his presence."

Similar statements in regard to the rich are not to be found in the Bible. On the contrary, the Apostle James asks the brethren, "do not rich men oppress you, and draw you before the judgment seats? . . ." He also refers to it, as an undeniable fact, that the poor are elected to special privileges under the gospel dispensation. "Hearken my beloved brethren, hath not God chosen the poor of this world rich in faith, and heirs of the kingdom which He had promised to them that love him?"

Thus the duty of preaching the gospel to the poor is enjoined, by the plainest precepts and examples. This is the standing proof of the Divine mission of the Church. In her regard for the poor, Christianity asserts her superiority to all sys-tems of human origin. The pride of man regards most the mere accidents [i.e., sec-ondary circumstances] of humanity; but God passes by these, and looks at that which is alone essential and imperishable. In his sight, position, power, and wealth, are the merest trifles. They do not add to the value or dignity of the possessor. God has magnified man by making him free and immortal. Like a good father, he provides for all his family, but in a special manner for the largest number, and the most destitute. He takes the most pains with those that by others are most neglected.[37]

Here Roberts quotes three paragraphs from Dr. Stephen Olin, "that great, good man." More important than questions of polity, Olin had argued, is preaching the gospel to the poor: "There can be no [church] without a gospel, and a gospel for the poor." If a church's ministers "preach a saving gospel to the poor, . . . that is enough. It is an Apostolic church." Roberts then applied this principle to the question of pew rental.

> If the gospel is to be preached to the poor, then it follows, as a necessary consequence, that all the arrangements for preaching the gospel, should be so made as to secure this object. There must not be a mere incidental provision for having the poor hear the gospel; this is the main thing to be looked after.
>
> . . . Hence, houses of worship should be, not like the first class car on a European railway, for the exclusive, but like the streets we walk, free for all. Their portals should be opened as wide for the common laborer, or the indigent widow, as for the assuming, or the wealthy.[38]

Roberts was arguing cogently for what twentieth-century liberation theologians called a "preferential option for the poor," though using other language. The gospel was designed for the "special benefit" of the poor, who have a "peculiar claim" to it. The poor have "special privileges" in the gospel, and therefore the church must exert "special efforts" and "peculiar pains" to reach them. As preaching the gospel to the poor was the "crowning proof" that Jesus was the Messiah, so the church's faithfulness in reaching them is the essential sign that it truly is the church of Jesus Christ. Roberts could hardly have been more emphatic.

Roberts's argument here is both christological and ecclesiological. God sent Jesus Christ to preach the gospel to the poor and gave the church the same commission. Roberts went so far as to affirm (quoting Olin) that while issues of doctrine and polity may be matters of legitimate dispute, there can be no doubt about the gospel for the poor. A church that does not preach the gospel to the poor is not the church of Jesus Christ — period.

But what did Roberts mean by "preaching the gospel to the poor"? Clearly he meant primarily evangelism. He understood evangelism, however, as more than the winning of converts, central as that was. As a good Methodist and one committed to Wesley's emphasis on sanctification and discipleship, Roberts understood the gospel to mean salvation from all sin, with inner cleansing and empowerment for Christlike, self-sacrificing service.

37. B. T. Roberts, "Free Churches," *EC* 1, no. 1 (Jan. 1860): 7-8.

38. B. T. Roberts, "Free Churches," *EC* 1, no. 1 (Jan. 1860): 9. This was a theme throughout Roberts's life. In a brief "Free Churches" editorial in 1891 he wrote, "Every house dedicated to the worship of God should proclaim in its every arrangement, that God is no respecter of persons." "Free Churches," *EC* 61 (Mar. 1891): 97.

Over the years Roberts returned frequently to the themes of free churches and the gospel for the poor in the pages of the *Earnest Christian*. Ten years later, in another editorial entitled "Free Churches," he wrote:

Where the object is to *introduce* the Gospel, no one thinks of selling *the right* to join in the public worship of God. But it is too often the case, that when a church has been built up and become financially strong under the free-seat system, a new and elegant house of worship must be erected, and the table of the changers of money introduced, and the seats sold, and God's poor shut out. This is dishonest. . . .

. . . If a Church must preach the Gospel to the poor to gain God's blessing, it must continue to do the same work to keep God's blessing. Turn the poor out of a church, and you turn Christ out. "The poor have the Gospel preached to them." That which is preached to the rich *exclusively* is not the Gospel. It may be faultless oratory, sound philosophy, refined morality, but it is not the Gospel of Jesus Christ. Where Jesus is, the poor hear him saying, "Come unto me, all ye that labor and are heavy laden, and I will give you rest."[39]

Turn the poor away and you turn away Christ, Roberts insisted.

Roberts elaborated his argument further in an editorial entitled "The Rich" in January 1870:

There is no class of society in such imminent danger of eternal damnation as the rich. If any among them are saved, it will be like Lot coming out of Sodom — the exception not the rule. . . . It is not merely *trust* in riches, that renders it so difficult to enter the kingdom of God, but *their possession*. Yet whoever possessed riches, without trusting in them, at least for influence and consideration, if not for salvation? . . .

Jesus forbids his disciples to amass wealth. His language is plain. It requires a great deal of ingenuity to pervert it.

Here Roberts cites the example of John Wesley, quoting some of Wesley's pointed words about the dangers of riches, including his statement toward the end of his life that "they that have most money have usually least grace." Roberts concluded:

Must we take our choice between laying up treasures on earth or treasures in heaven? To do both is impossible. Deliberately take your choice. Not to choose is inevitably to drift into the current of worldliness. — To choose the world, is to choose sorrow, and trouble, and eternal death.

If you resolve to lay up treasures in Heaven, begin at once. Give yourself to God to do good to the utmost of your ability to your fellow-men. Adopt the motto of Wesley, *Gain all you can, save all you can, and give all you can.*

In the light of these truths, we see the utter criminality of the course taken by

---

39. B. T. Roberts, "Free Churches," *EC* 20, no. 4 (Oct. 1870): 128-29.

the popular churches to secure the patronage of the rich. The very vices which ensure their damnation are encouraged. — Their love of distinction is gratified by being able to buy the exclusive right to the occupancy of the best pews in the house; and their pride is strengthened and encouraged by the splendor that surrounds them, and the deference that is paid to them in the house of God. Plain, free churches, are everywhere needed, quite as much to save the rich as to reach the masses and carry the Gospel to the poor.[40]

Roberts was not opposed to the acquisition of wealth if it was legitimately gained and was used for others, not self-indulgently. He wrote in the February 1865 *Earnest Christian: "You cannot at the same time be devoted to the acquisition of wealth and to the service of Christ."* But he added, "A talent for business is as much the gift of God as a talent for preaching." The "ability to get wealth" is to be used "for the good of your race," but not for luxury or "self-aggrandizement."[41]

In dealing with this subject, Roberts often pointed to Jesus Christ as our model and to the example of the early church. Here he linked poverty and community. When the first Christians shared their possessions, Roberts said, they were simply following Jesus' example. He wrote in 1870,

> When we see how the Saviour sanctified Poverty, by eating her bread and drinking her water — walking in her lowliest vales, and choosing His companions from her despised sons — we no longer wonder, that in the palmy days of Christianity, *as many as were possessors of lands or houses sold them, and brought the prices of the things that were sold, and laid them down at the apostles' feet; and distribution was made unto every man according as he had need.* This also helps solve the mystery why the poor are generally so much more willing to receive the gospel in its purity than the rich. They can say, emphatically, *He was one of us.*[42]

The *Earnest Christian* was a holiness journal, committed to promoting the work of the Holy Spirit in people's lives — "experimental and practical piety." In Roberts's mind "practical piety" was inseparable from a committed concern to reach the masses with the gospel. True holiness was seen in the example of Jesus Christ and the experience of the early church.

---

40. B. T. Roberts, "The Rich," *EC* 19, no. 1 (Jan. 1870): 30-31.

41. B. T. Roberts, "Gospel to the Rich," *EC* 9, no. 2 (Feb. 1865): 60-62. This article is built around five main points: (1) "Riches peril the souls of their possessors," (2) "Christians are forbidden to accumulate wealth," (3) "You cannot at the same time be devoted to the acquisition of wealth and to the service of Christ," (4) "The desire for wealth is dangerous," and (5) "The New Testament speaks of rich men as a class as in an almost hopeless condition."

42. B. T. Roberts, "Riches and Poverty of Christ," *EC* 20, no. 2 (Sept. 1870): 72.

Setting the Tone

The content of the very first issue of the *Earnest Christian* was a good indication of Roberts's mind and his main concerns at the time. Significantly, he included two articles by John Wesley Redfield. The first, right after his own opening article, "Free Churches," was entitled "Be Thorough but Be in Haste," and the second, "Redemption," argued that "redemption must cover the entire evil resting on our race resulting from the fall."[43] The inclusion of Redfield's articles was a clear sign of Roberts's respect for the evangelist's ministry and his understanding of the gospel, and witnessed to Redfield's key role in the rise of Free Methodism.

This issue included a total of five editorials and articles by Roberts, plus some material excerpted from other sources. The last page was headed "Literary Notices" (a common feature in subsequent issues as well) and was a review of two books: Elias Bowen's *Slavery in the Methodist Episcopal Church* and a book by G. W. Henry ("Blind Henry") entitled *Shouting: Genuine and Spurious.* Both books had been published the previous year.

The issue also contained an article by Loren Stiles, "Moral Individuality," one by "D." entitled "'Spiritual Manifestations.' A Few Words Respecting Alleged 'Evils' Connected with Certain Meetings," and a somewhat related article, "Shouting among Scotch Seceders," consisting mainly of excerpts from a book by Maxwell Gaddis entitled *Footprints of an Itinerant.*

Roberts also included an account of the expulsions of Stiles, J. A. Wells, William Cooley, and C. D. Burlingham at the 1859 Genesee Conference sessions.[44]

Theologically, a particularly important piece in this first issue was a long article by Leonidas Hamline entitled "The Millennium," reprinted from the *Ladies' Repository.* The article had been published some years earlier — in January 1843, while Hamline was editing the *Ladies' Repository,* before becoming bishop — at the height of the Millerite excitement when many people were expecting the return of Christ within months. Roberts now saw Hamline's article as especially "appropriate to the conflict at present going on in the Church between spirituality and formalism," and therefore worth reprinting.[45]

Hamline argued that the millennium would be "a period of unexampled religious prosperity, in which Christ will have spiritual dominion from sea to sea,"

---

43. John Wesley Redfield, "Be Thorough But Be in Haste" and "Redemption," *EC* 1, no. 1 (Jan. 1860): 11-12, 26-27.

44. [B. T. Roberts], "Persecuted, But Not Forsaken," *EC* 1, no. 1 (Jan. 1860): 15-17.

45. Bishop [*sic*] Hamline, "The Millenium," *EC* 1, no. 1 (Jan. 1860): 21-25. Cf. L. L. Hamline, "The Millenium," *Ladies' Repository, and Gatherings of the West* 3 (Jan. 1843): 2-4. (In both sources "millennium" is spelled with one *n*; I have corrected this to "millennium" in the text.) Hamline was editor of the *Ladies' Repository,* a Methodist magazine primarily for women, published in Cincinnati, from its inception in 1841 until he was elected bishop in 1844. In January 1843, the same month Hamline's article first appeared, William Miller predicted that Christ would return between Mar. 21, 1843, and Mar. 21, 1844. Cf. Reid, *DCA,* p. 740.

rather than a literal reign of Christ upon the earth. He believed "the commencement of this happy period" was "near at hand" — but also that the church faced "perilous times. Dread darkness will go before the sunrise of the millennium." He concluded that "if all the Church were to assume the attitude of a *praying, laboring, suffering* witness for Jesus," the millennium would soon come.

Hamline wrote that "the severest sufferings of the Church will flow from direct and cruel persecution. Let none suppose for a moment that no more trials of this sort await us."[46] It seems to have been Hamline's call for perseverance and aggressive witness in the face of hardship and persecution — as precursors of the coming millennium — that especially attracted Roberts to this article.

It is not clear how many copies of the January 1860 *Earnest Christian* were printed or distributed — perhaps 1,000 to 2,000.[47] Roberts mailed out copies as broadly as he could, both to individuals and to other publications, and received many positive responses. The *Buffalo Commercial Advertiser* described the new magazine as "handsomely printed." Hosmer at the *Northern Independent* thought it had "a fine appearance" and was "well filled," and described Roberts as "a mature scholar and Christian." The Buffalo *Morning Express,* where the *Earnest Christian* was printed, complimented the new periodical for "the ability of its management" and its articles "upon live topics and subjects of great importance."[48] Roberts omitted some of the praise from the *Morning Express* that he found "too complimentary" to print.[49] He saw himself as now having entered into the broad fraternity of editors and publishers.

Roberts's friends and sympathetic ministerial colleagues were especially pleased with the new venture. Dr. Elias Bowen wrote to say that the "first number augurs well for the enterprise," while D. W. Thurston of the Oneida Conference commented, "I have read your magazine with intense pleasure. It is just the thing." Similar comments came from A. A. Phelps, C. D. Burlingham, and others. Stephen S. Rice of Clarkson, who had participated in the Laymen's Conventions, said the *Earnest Christian* was "destined to be a favorite with those who are in favor of *Christianity in earnest,* and are striving to walk in the *narrow way*."[50]

Succeeding monthly issues continued to be well received. Subscriptions came in steadily. Late in the year Benjamin received an effusive letter from a woman "whose writings upon religious experience we used to read with pleasure and profit in other periodicals." This correspondent pronounced the new magazine "unequivocally the

---

46. Hamline, "The Millenium," *EC.*

47. Since Roberts reported at the end of 1862 that he had printed some 3,000 copies of each issue that year, and that this represented significant growth, we may conjecture that he began with a print run of between 1,000 and 2,000 copies.

48. "Notices," *EC* 1, no. 2 (Feb. 1860): 68. Cf. Zahniser, p. 152.

49. Zahniser, pp. 152-53. Zahniser does not give the source of this quote; it is not found on p. 68 of the February 1860 *Earnest Christian,* cited above.

50. "Notices," *EC* 1, no. 2 (Feb. 1860): 68; cf. "The Work of Revival Goes On," *EC* 1, no. 3 (Mar. 1860): 98-100; Zahniser, p. 152.

best religious periodical in the nation."[51] While Benjamin does not give her name, it could conceivably have been Phoebe Palmer.[52]

The response the first year was very encouraging. Roberts continued editing and writing for the magazine over the next years even as his ministry and travel expanded dramatically. Sensitive to possible charges of empire building, however, he kept his roles as editor and as church leader distinct. In the *Earnest Christian* he never referred to his denominational position. Though he printed notices of Free Methodist gatherings, "nowhere does he mention himself as occupying [a church] office, fearing lest he might offend some of his brethren," as Benson Roberts put it.[53]

A Pattern Established

Benjamin was very gratified with the success of the magazine. He reported at the end of the first year, "Its publication was commenced without subscribers, and without contributors, but, as we believed, at the call of God. The success has, so far, exceeded our most sanguine anticipations. But few ministers have acted as agents, or subscribed for themselves. On the contrary many have used all their influence to prevent its circulation. But by the blessing of the Lord it has lived. From the first the subscription list has been steadily increasing."[54]

Looking back almost two decades later, Benjamin wrote: "With the next number our magazine enters upon the 20th year of its existence. It has met with a favor unexpected, and been the means of doing an amount of good which at the first we did not anticipate. To God be all the glory."[55]

The pattern Roberts established with the first issue varied only slightly through the years. A typical issue began with a lead article by Roberts, which might run two, three, or four pages. Often this article was based on a sermon. A miscellany of articles by various contributors followed, often including women as well as men. Occasionally the pieces were unsigned, or excerpted from other religious periodicals such as the *Free Church Record, King's Highway,* or the *Independent.*

From time to time Roberts included selections from favorite authors like Wesley, Fletcher, Finney, Madame Guyon, Spurgeon, even Cotton Mather, Jonathan Edwards, or John Bunyan. Roberts said Bunyan's *Pilgrim's Progress* was "a book that can hardly be read too much."[56] The October 1862 issue carried an article by Horace

---

51. Untitled letters section, *EC* 1, no. 11 (Nov. 1860): 366. Cf. Zahniser, p. 153.

52. The letter is prefaced "District Parsonage, Oct. 10, 1860," which probably indicates a Methodist preacher's wife — someone other than Phoebe Palmer — unless it indicates the place where Palmer was lodging in her travels.

53. BHR, *BTR*, p. 274.

54. [B. T. Roberts], "The Earnest Christian," *EC* 1, no. 12 (Dec. 1860): 394.

55. [B. T. Roberts], "The Earnest Christian," *EC* 36, no. 6 (Dec. 1878): 191.

56. [B. T. Roberts], "The Conflict," *EC* 4, no. 3 (Sept. 1862): 89.

Greeley entitled "The Duty of Hating Evil."[57] In 1891 he published a long article by Harriet Beecher Stowe on Sojourner Truth.[58] About one-third of the January 1874 issue was material reprinted from other publications; this was fairly typical. Often there were articles on holiness or Christian perfection and pieces headed "Experience," accounts of people growing in grace and experiencing entire sanctification. Roberts's reading was rather eclectic and wide-ranging, and this was reflected in writers he occasionally quoted or referred to in his articles — from Fénelon and Saint Francis de Sales to Edward Irving (1792-1834, often seen as a key figure in the later rise of Pentecostalism), for example.[59] A March 1890 editorial entitled "Pure in Heart" consisted mainly of a long quotation from Horace Bushnell.[60]

Often an issue of the magazine would carry a poem or two — though Roberts, who appreciated good poetry, was rather selective in this regard. "We do not like to publish anything that will not bear criticism," he wrote. While prose articles could be edited, that was harder with poetry. So if poems came in that were "unfit for the public," he had no choice, he said, "but to lay them aside."[61]

Normally the *Earnest Christian* carried no artwork except for an occasional portrait. The last seven pages or so were divided between a section headed "Editorial" and one reporting "Correspondence." The editorials, generally brief and unsigned, usually were written by Roberts, though occasionally signed editorials by others appeared. This section often included also notices of revivals, camp meetings, and Free Methodist conferences or other events, as well as "Literary Notices."[62]

The "Correspondence" section consisted of letters of various sorts, often including personal testimonies or the "dying testimonies" of deceased Christians. For years the section filled with the sharing of personal experience was called "Love Feast." The places from which these letters came give an idea of the periodical's wide circulation: Burlington, Iowa; Piermont, New Hampshire; Brooklyn, New York; Puget Sound, Washington Territory; Evansville, Indiana; Whitehall, Illinois; Olivet, Dakota Territory; Lincoln, Nebraska; Danville, Arkansas; San Jose, California; and the states of Kansas, Michigan, Minnesota, and Texas, as well as scores of other places including, occasionally, England or some other country. One letter was sent from a "Cabin on the Prairie."

The number of contributing writers increased through the years. The issues for 1888, for example, carried articles by Mrs. Lucy M. (Sellew) Coleman, Alice C. Phillips, Hannah Pelton, E. H. Tenny, Edward Matthews, A. H. Springstein, A. D.

---

57. Horace Greeley, "The Duty of Hating Evil," *EC* 4, no. 4 (Oct. 1862): 105-6. Roberts does not indicate the source from which this article presumably was reprinted.

58. Harriet Beecher Stowe, "Sojourner Truth," *EC* 61, no. 4 (Apr. 1891): 113-21.

59. B. T. Roberts, "Training Children," *EC* 59, no. 3 (Mar. 1890): 69-74; [B. T. Roberts], "Patience" and "Life," *EC* 59, no. 3 (Mar. 1890): 86-97 and 97-98, respectively.

60. [B. T. Roberts], "Pure in Heart," *EC* 59, no. 3 (Mar. 1890): 96.

61. [B. T. Roberts], "Poetry," *EC* 3, no. 6 (June 1862): 191.

62. Throughout this biography I have generally assumed that unsigned editorials were written by B. T. Roberts unless there is some evidence to the contrary.

Burdick, Mrs. T. S. Hutton, Rev. S. K. Wheatlake, Hattie E. Warner, Mrs. C. S. Chamberlain, Ellen Roberts, Emma Sellew Roberts, and many others. Some of these became regular contributors.

Roberts did his best to maintain high editorial standards, but this was sometimes complicated by his travels. He noted in the November 1861 issue, "We generally read the proof ourself; but last month we were unavoidably absent, and a good many mistakes crept in." One name was misspelled "Corklin" instead of "Conklin," he noted, and in an article by Elias Bowen on sanctification, twice the word "process" appeared where it should have been "progress." These examples give a sense of how carefully Benjamin normally edited the magazine.[63] In March 1874 Benjamin noted in his diary, "Finished reading proof of the April no. of E.C. We have a good number although it is late owing to my being away West."[64]

As the magazine's second year ended, Benjamin felt that God had helped him and that he had grown spiritually. He commented in the December 1861 issue,

> God has enabled us to perform an amount of labor that, a few years since, we would have deemed utterly impossible. All glory be to Him. . . .
>
> The next volume we hope, by the Divine blessing, to make better than either of the preceding. The Providential indications are that we shall be able to devote more time to it than heretofore has been possible. God has given us a deeper personal experience, has made us know more of ourselves and of the power of his saving grace, and we trust we shall be able to help our readers on in their delightful, though often wearisome journey, to the better land.[65]

Roberts varied the periodical's appearance only slightly over the years. He upgraded it beginning with the January 1871 issue, using "new type throughout." The journal's "appearance, in every respect, will be improved."[66]

Merger with the *Golden Rule*

The name of the journal changed to the *Earnest Christian and Golden Rule* in January 1862, when the *Earnest Christian* absorbed the magazine and mailing list of the *Golden Rule*, edited and published by David F. Newton, an independent, older minister based in New York City.[67] It is not clear how many new subscribers this brought to the periodical. However, with this merging of publications Roberts changed the name and added the *Golden Rule's* key verse to the title page: "All things whatsoever

---

63. [B. T. Roberts], "Errata," *EC* 2, no. 11 (Nov. 1861): 356; see also p. 331.

64. BTRD, Mar. 27, 1874.

65. [B. T. Roberts], "'The Earnest Christian,'" *EC* 2, no. 12 (Dec. 1861): 384.

66. "A New Dress," *EC* 20, no. 6 (Dec. 1870): 187.

67. [B. T. Roberts], "The Addition to Our Title," *EC* 3, no. 1 (Jan. 1862): 30; D. F. Newton, "Our Life As It Has Been and Is," *EC* 11, no. 2 (Jan. 1866): 5-7. Benson Roberts described Newton as "a devoted Baptist minister of New York City." BHR, *BTR*, p. 263.

ye would that men should do unto you, do ye even so unto them." (For convenience, I refer to the magazine as the *Earnest Christian* throughout its history, even though the full name after 1861 was the *Earnest Christian and Golden Rule*.)

At this time Roberts also changed the volume numbering system. For the first two years the volumes corresponded to the calendar years, each volume including the twelve monthly issues for that year. But beginning in 1862 each volume contained only six monthly issues, so that each calendar year included two volumes. Roberts explained:

> We have thought it best to make two volumes a year of our Magazine. This will accommodate those whose subscription commences in July. It will also, we trust, help in getting a good list of new subscribers to commence the first of July this year. We need about one thousand. . . .
>
> The terms are only one dollar a year, in advance. Any one sending us four dollars for new subscribers will be entitled to a fifth copy.[68]

This change made little practical difference, because bound annuals continued to be issued. But beginning in 1862 each bound book contained two volumes of 192 pages each rather than just one of 384 pages. Roberts continued to publish an index at the beginning of each volume, so from 1862 on each bound annual contained two title pages and two indexes, one at the beginning and one between the June and July issues (since July began a new volume number). This pattern continued until 1909, long after Roberts's death, when during the magazine's final year the volume numbering reverted to the twelve issues of the calendar year. (This meant that the half-century publication of the *Earnest Christian* totaled 97 volumes rather than 100.)

Roberts first took note of the *Golden Rule* in the January 1861 issue of the *Earnest Christian*. He reprinted an article from Newton's paper and commended the magazine. The December 1860 *Golden Rule*, Benjamin said, was "full of pith and Gospel truth." He added, "If you want a good Sabbath School paper, adapted to old and young, that speaks out fearlessly in favor of a religion that saves men from the love of sin — of slavery, dress, rum, and tobacco — send for the *Golden Rule*. It comes at 50 cents a year for a single subscriber, or 25 cents apiece for a hundred copies, or for Sabbath Schools."[69] And Roberts gave the address in New York City. In the same issue Roberts reprinted a notice that Newton had placed in the December *Golden Rule*, praising Roberts's magazine. The piece gives a sense both of the first year of the *Earnest Christian* and of Newton's style and concerns.

"THE EARNEST CHRISTIAN," edited by B. T. Roberts of Buffalo, N.Y., at one dollar per annum, is at hand, thankfully, joyfully. It speaks out boldly, uncompromisingly, "*all the words of life*." It breathes the true Wesleyan spirit. Rum, tobacco,

---

68. [B. T. Roberts], "The Earnest Christian and Golden Rule. A New Volume," *EC* 3, no. 6 (June 1862): 190.

69. [B. T. Roberts], "Confession of Sin," *EC* 2, no. 1 (Jan. 1861): 34.

novel-reading, picnics, fancy fairs, sabbath desecration, slave-holding, "receive their portion in due season." Free churches, free seats, congregational singing exclusive of fashionable choirs and instrumental music, are warmly advocated. On turning the pages of this beautiful monthly — in pamphlet form — and perceiving the fearless, outspoken freedom of soul, we thanked God and took courage. Surely there are yet "more than seven thousand who have not bowed the knee to Baal."[70]

David F. Newton, Roberts's new associate, was a unique character — something of a maverick. Born in 1796, he was about sixty-six when he became linked with the *Earnest Christian*.[71] Roberts described Newton's writing style as "close [and] pungent." Newton had about twenty years' experience as an editor and brought to the magazine "a sanctified heart [and] good judgment." For the next four years Newton was listed in the magazine as corresponding editor.[72]

According to his own testimony, Newton was born in New Hampshire, "roamed about in early life," and eventually was converted in Virginia. He attended the Oneida Institute near Utica, New York, and later was a student for two years at Lane Seminary in Cincinnati when Lyman Beecher was the president. There his health failed, but he gradually recovered while spending time at Oberlin, Ohio. He does not seem to have been a student at Oberlin College, but while there he did receive "additional light on the 'higher Christian life.'"[73]

Newton was at Lane Seminary (founded in 1829) in about the years 1832-34, apparently. If so, he certainly would have known Theodore Weld, Finney convert and soon to become famous as the North's most effective abolitionist lecturer and organizer.[74] Weld had also been at the Oneida Institute, and it is very possible that Newton was one of the "Oneida boys" who followed Weld to Lane.[75] Newton was not, however, among the seventy-five "Lane Rebels," led by Weld, who left Lane in 1834 to protest the seminary's ban on open debate on the slavery issue.[76] He may have already left Lane by the time of the "Lane Rebellion."

After some months at Oberlin, Newton returned to Cincinnati, married, and settled across the Ohio River in Covington, Kentucky. Here he began the *Golden Rule*

---

70. *EC* 2, no. 1 (Jan. 1861): 36.

71. The library catalogue at Asbury Theological Seminary gives Newton's birth date as 1796 (but gives no year of death).

72. [B. T. Roberts], "Addition to Our Title," p. 30.

73. Newton, "Our Life," pp. 5-6.

74. See chapter 2. Keith Hardman calls Weld "Finney's most famous convert." Keith J. Hardman, *Charles Grandison Finney, 1792-1875, Revivalist and Reformer* (Grand Rapids: Baker, 1987), p. 86.

75. Though Newton was somewhat older than Weld, who was about twenty-nine when he went to Lane. Robert Abzug speaks of "the Oneida boys who followed Weld to Lane." Robert H. Abzug, *Passionate Liberator: Theodore Dwight Weld and the Dilemma of Reform* (New York: Oxford University Press, 1980), pp. 78-79.

76. Lawrence Thomas Lesick, *The Lane Rebels: Evangelicalism and Antislavery in Antebellum America* (Metuchen, N.J.: Scarecrow Press, 1980), pp. 116-66. Lesick lists the "Lane Rebels" on p. 157.

in 1843 or thereabouts. The object of the periodical was "to reprove all sin" and espe-cially "popular sins" such as intemperance, worldly dress, "popish church building and decorating," fashion magazines like *Harper's*, secret societies, and slavery. "While remaining in a slaveholding, tobacco-raising . . . community, we passed through some severe conflicts," Newton noted.[77]

About five years later Newton moved to Cleveland, and in 1854 to New York City, but continued publishing the *Golden Rule*. (He was "driven out of [Kentucky] on account of the strong position he took against slavery," Roberts wrote.)[78] Newton came to realize, however, that he needed a deeper work of God's Spirit in his life. He attended meetings "held exclusively for the higher Christian walks," and was entirely sanctified. He wrote that he "received a new impulse, the baptismal fire, a fresh token of God's redeeming, sanctifying grace." From that point on holiness was a theme of his writings.[79]

Newton also wrote and published at least five books, including one entitled *The Shining Light*, on the use of the Bible, that Roberts advertised in the June 1866 *Earnest Christian*.[80] His fifth book, *A Holiday Present; or, Educating Little Mary for the Heavenly Kingdom*, was published in 1871 and also advertised in the *Earnest Christian*. Roberts wrote, "On whatsoever topic Bro. Newton writes, he is always sound."[81]

One issue on which Roberts no doubt thought Newton was sound concerned the role of women. Arguing in favor of women speaking in public worship, Newton wrote: "The mind of the female is certainly susceptible of all those sensibilities, af-fections, and improvements which constitute the Christian character. And experi-ence has proved that many females have possessed the natural qualifications for speaking in public, the range of thought, the faculty of communicating their ideas in appropriate language, the sympathy with suffering humanity. . . . Then let no stumbling-block be thrown in their way, but let them fill the place that God calls them to fill."[82]

Newton became involved in another (apparently short-lived) publishing ven-ture, a religious paper called the *Flaming Sword*, toward the end of 1862. It was pub-lished by John F. Seaman of Rose, New York, twice monthly. Seaman secured New-ton as editor and hoped to make the paper a weekly. Roberts duly noted the new periodical in the November 1862 *Earnest Christian*. "It is about the size and style that the Golden Rule was before it was merged in the Earnest Christian," he noted, and

---

77. Newton, "Our Life," pp. 6-7.

78. "Literary Notices," *EC* 7, no. 5 (May 1864): 162.

79. Newton, "Our Life," pp. 6-7.

80. "Literary Notices," *EC* 11, no. 6 (June 1866): 191. At that time Newton's address was 189 West Twentieth Street, New York. He also published *Home Thrusts, and Home Thoughts* (New York: By the author, 1864) and *The Sword That Cuts, The Fire That Burns* (1868), mostly compilations of his writ-ings from the *Golden Rule*.

81. [B. T. Roberts], "Literary Notices," *EC* 22, no. 2 (Aug. 1871): 66.

82. D. F. Newton, "Silencing Women in Worshiping Assemblies," in *Home Thrusts*, p. 129.

was "out-spoken and uncompromising," as one would expect, with Newton as editor. Roberts added wryly, "If it meets with success, it can but do good. One must have a good deal of faith, or plenty of money, to commence the publication of a religious newspaper at this time."[83]

Most of the available information on Newton is found in an autobiographical sketch that Roberts published in the January 1866 *Earnest Christian*, accompanied by a portrait of Newton. Apparently Newton ceased serving as corresponding editor about this time, as his name is not listed with Roberts's on the title page from this point on. However, in advertising Newton's book in the June 1866 issue, Roberts called Newton his "beloved associate." Newton continued to contribute occasional articles to the *Earnest Christian* for some time.

It is easy to see how Benjamin could be attracted to Newton. Though not a Methodist, Newton was shaped by many of the same currents that influenced Roberts in his early years. Older than Benjamin's father, Newton was another link to Roberts's abolitionist past. In some ways he was the literary counterpart to Redfield, a rough prophet sprung from the same radical roots that nourished Roberts.

Roberts's primary contact with Newton was literary, though Newton occasionally collaborated in holiness camp meetings where Roberts also was involved. Roberts noted in October 1861 that Newton was present at the Rose and Yates camp meetings in New York in August and, together with Rev. Henry Belden, a Congregationalist also from New York City, "rendered efficient assistance."[84] This may have been when the two first met. Roberts wrote, "As he is not a Methodist, and was not brought up amongst them, we did not know what impression meetings, which some ministers and editors appear to delight to represent in colors as dark as imagination can invent, would have upon his mind. But he is a man of deep experience in the things of God, one of the few who sees and hears for himself, and who has the courage fearlessly to utter his own convictions."[85]

The absorption of the *Golden Rule* into the *Earnest Christian* a few months later may have resulted from conversations Roberts and Newton had at these camp meetings. Newton heartily supported Roberts's ministry, and when Chili Seminary was formed he donated several books to help start the school's library.[86]

---

83. [B. T. Roberts], "Literary Notices," *EC* 4, no. 5 (Nov. 1862): 158.

84. B. T. Roberts, "Pekin Camp Meeting," *EC* 2, no. 10 (Oct. 1861): 323. According to Kostlevy, Henry Belden at this time was serving "as a city missionary in Brooklyn (1856-1866)." An abolitionist, former Presbyterian, and "leading advocate of holiness experience among Congregationalists, Belden was a frequent revival preacher and addressed some of the early National Holiness Association camp meetings" (Kostlevy, p. 18).

85. [B. T. Roberts], "Religious Meetings," *EC* 2, no. 11 (Nov. 1861): 353.

86. Zahniser, p. 252.

The *Earnest Christian* through the Years

The *Earnest Christian* was published in Buffalo from its beginning in 1860 until the Roberts family moved to Rochester at the end of 1864.[87] From that time on it was published in Rochester and (later) North Chili.

As the *Earnest Christian* reached an expanding audience during its early days, Benjamin received more and more letters from across the country. Usually he printed a selection of these at the end of each issue. In April 1863 he received a letter from the noted Methodist evangelist James Caughey, who had made "earnest Christianity" the theme of his ministry. Writing from Quebec on April 14, 1863, Caughey acknowledged receiving Roberts's letter, with two copies of the magazine. Caughey reported on the success of his ministry and commented, "I cannot visit you, my hands being full here at present, and I sail again this summer for Europe, God willing."[88]

By the end of 1862 the number of paid subscribers had climbed to around three thousand. "We commenced without a single subscriber; for the past year we have printed over 3000 copies of our magazine. Suppose that each number is read by three persons, which is a low estimate, this would give us about 10,000 readers." The cost of paper had risen sharply because of the war, but Roberts thought he could continue the magazine at the same price.[89] He frequently urged his readers to send in more subscriptions and to help promote the magazine.

Occasionally the *Earnest Christian* lost subscribers due to controversial articles Roberts included. In early 1861 he published a two-part piece by Elias Bowen entitled "Of Spiritual Gifts." Bowen strongly affirmed that the age of miracles was not past. Christ gave "extraordinary spiritual gifts" not just to the early church; he "bequeathed [them] to the . . . *whole* church, as a *body* . . . as a perpetual inheritance." Bowen agreed with Wesley and others, he said, "that the miracle-working power, or the power of extraordinary spiritual gifts, still resides in the church," though he recognized that it may be abused.[90]

A quarter-century later in "Healing Faith," a lead article, Roberts recalled Bowen's article and the reaction it brought. Some readers took offense at Bowen's affirmation of miracles and saw the article as "proof conclusive of our unsoundness in the faith. Several hundred of our subscribers at once discontinued."[91] Yet overall, circulation continued to rise.

---

87. The November 1864 issue carries this notice: "REMOVAL. We have removed all our business from Buffalo to Rochester. Hereafter the *Earnest Christian* will be published here." *EC* 8, no. 5 (Nov. 1864): 163. The July 1871 issue contained this notice: "The publication office of the *Earnest Christian* will be removed, after this number is issued, to No. 33 Exchange St., one flight of stairs, over the U.S. Express office." [B. T. Roberts], "Removal," *EC* 22, no. 1 (July 1871): 30.

88. "Letter from Rev. J. Caughey," *EC* 5, no. 5 (May 1863): 164.

89. "Close of the Year," *EC* 4, no. 12 (Dec. 1862): 186.

90. E. Bowen, "Of Spiritual Gifts," *EC* 2, no. 1 (Jan. 1861): 5-8 (the lead article). The article was concluded in the February issue, pp. 37-39 (again the lead article).

91. B. T. Roberts, "Healing Faith," *EC* 50, no. 5 (Nov. 1885): 133. Roberts refers to "an original arti-

Roberts reported in January 1866, "Our subscription list has steadily increased from year to year." The truths it proclaimed were having their impact. "We are daily receiving testimonies from those who have been blessed and saved through their influence."[92]

Benjamin found this work fulfilling. "Never before did time seem to fly with so swift a wing. Our labors have been incessant; but they have been pleasant, for they have been labors of love," he wrote in 1862.[93]

With growing subscriptions came the perennial problem of people who failed to send in their dollar to extend the subscription another year. In November 1861 Roberts noted that a number of subscribers, well over two hundred, had not yet paid. "Can you not send the dollar now?" he wrote. "It is a small amount for one to pay, but when we put all together thus owing us, it amounts to $281 — a sum which we very much need to meet obligations *that must be met*."[94]

The magazine soon was going all across the country. "Through the blessing of God, and the kind efforts of our friends, the 'Earnest Christian' has subscribers in all the free states, from Maine to California; and in Canada, England and Scotland," Roberts wrote in early 1863.[95] Circulation continued to expand, so that Roberts could report at the end of 1864, "We now publish 4,500 copies," and he was aiming for 8,000.[96]

By 1866 the subscription list had climbed to 6,000.[97] The magazine probably never reached the 10,000 Roberts aimed for, but it did achieve a circulation of over 7,000 in mid-1868, probably its all-time high. Roberts was gratified. He wrote, "Notwithstanding many unfavorable circumstances and much opposition both open and covert, our circulation has been steadily increasing from year to year, until we now issue monthly over seven thousand copies. We receive letters from all parts of the country. . . . Revivals have been kindled in some places."[98]

Since the bulk of the circulation was in paid subscriptions (presumably bringing in around $6,000 a year), one may assume that actual readership was substantially higher than the number of paying subscribers.

Roberts noted in June 1870 that new subscribers had "been coming in steadily all year," but he did not give circulation numbers.[99] A year and a half later he wrote,

---

cle from the Rev. Elias Bower [Bowen] D.D., on Miracles" published in the *Earnest Christian* about twenty-five years earlier. It is clear Roberts is referring to Bowen's article "Of Spiritual Gifts"; no article by Bowen entitled "Miracles" appeared during the period.

92. "To Our Friends," *EC* 11, no. 1 (Jan. 1866): 34.

93. "Close of the Year," *EC* 4, no. 12 (Dec. 1862): 186.

94. [B. T. Roberts], "To Our Subscribers," *EC* 2, no. 11 (Nov. 1861): 356. The $281 probably indicates close to that number of subscribers who were in arrears; possibly some owed for the previous year (1860, the first year of publication) as well.

95. "How Subscribers Are Obtained," *EC* 5, no. 3 (Mar. 1863): 94.

96. "Close of the Volume," *EC* 8, no. 6 (Dec. 1864): 190.

97. "To Our Subscribers," *EC* 11, no. 5 (May 1866): 162.

98. "New Volume," *EC* 15, no. 6 (June 1868): 187.

99. "A New Volume," *EC* 19, no. 6 (June 1870): 188.

"We feel thankful to God and our friends that our circulation is as good as it is, but it is not what it should be." The impression given is that subscriptions may have declined somewhat.[100]

Financial hard times, such as the economic recessions of 1873 and 1893, no doubt affected the circulation of the magazine to some degree. Roberts reported in January 1873 that more than $1,000 was owed in delinquent subscriptions. He began to publish a "list of premiums" on the back cover as an incentive to those "who feel that they cannot afford to lose the time necessary to canvass for new subscribers" and so need "a little material encouragement" to promote the magazine.[101] "This is a trying year for religious periodicals," he wrote at the end of 1874.[102] Roberts found it necessary to raise the annual subscription price from $1.00 to $1.25.

The magazine seems generally to have operated with reasonable financial stability. It was part of what became a larger publishing operation that included songbooks and other books and pamphlets. Roberts's publishing ventures suffered a setback at the end of 1868, however, when a fire in Rochester destroyed the office of the *Democrat,* where Roberts had much of his printing done. He lost about $800 worth of printing materials. He wrote, "We had stereotype plates, all ready for the press, of a valuable work by Dr. Bowen, on 'The History and Origin of the Free Methodist Church.'" These were lost, along with plates for the Free Methodist hymnbook, *Discipline,* and some tracts. "We had no insurance," he reported.[103] Later, in 1880, Roberts commented that the magazine had been "burned out twice, [but] has never failed of a regular issue."[104]

Occasionally Roberts gave a retrospective glance at the history of the magazine. Looking back after twenty years, he reflected,

> With this number our magazine begins the twenty-first year of its existence. The time seems short and yet what changes has it witnessed. Slavery has been overthrown, and our popular pulpits no longer contend that a Christian may hold slaves.
>
> Other unpopular principles which, from the first issue we have continued to advocate, have been taken up and are now ably presented and defended over the land.

Roberts added that the magazine's "very success" had "crippled our financial ability and weakened us in resources," for now there were "four or five or more" holiness periodicals, not just one. "The patronage which we then enjoyed is divided up with others." Roberts was not complaining, he said; he was glad for the growth in holiness literature. But he reminded the magazine's friends of "the necessity of put-

---

100. "Our Circulation," *EC* 23, no. 1 (Jan. 1872): 31.

101. "Premiums," "New Subscribers," and "Due Us," *EC* 25, no. 1 (Jan. 1873): 35.

102. "To Our Subscribers," *EC* 28, no. 6 (Dec. 1874): 190.

103. "Fire," *EC* 17, no. 1 (Jan. 1869): 32. Presumably by "our Hymn Book" Roberts meant *Spiritual Songs and Hymns for Pilgrims.* Roberts managed to issue Bowen's book in 1871.

104. [B. T. Roberts], "Of Age," *EC* 40, no. 6 (Dec. 1880): 189.

ting forth extra efforts to extend our circulation." He pointed out that unlike other periodicals that had been substantially "aided by donations" in addition to subscriptions, "We have never received any thing in this way."[105]

Similarly Roberts reflected in December 1880 that the *Earnest Christian* "started out with well-defined, clearly-announced principles, and to these principles it has been true in every number. There has been no toning-down, no falling in with the popular theological notions of the day. The leading advocate of holiness, when *The Earnest Christian* was started [Phoebe Palmer's *Guide to Holiness*], had nothing to say against slaveholding as inconsistent with holiness."[106]

In contrast, the *Earnest Christian* had from the beginning insisted that slaveholding was morally inconsistent with Wesleyan holiness. The magazine had been true to its principles, Roberts said. Its originally announced "promises have been fulfilled. Some who have read every number, think it has grown in grace, that it is more radical and outspoken than it was at the outset. God is certainly giving us increasing light, and as he gives us light, we shall let it shine."[107]

In the spring of 1883 Roberts moved his publishing operation from Rochester to North Chili and as a result was able to reduce the *Earnest Christian* subscription price back to $1.00, plus 10¢ for postage. He printed this notice on the inside back cover of the May and June issues:

> We have removed our publishing house to North Chili, Monroe Co., N.Y., where the Seminary is located, and where our family resides. We tried to give our printing material to our last General Conference but as they would not accept it the will of God appeared to be that we should remove it as we have done.
>
> We hope to lessen the cost of publishing so as to furnish at a cheaper rate the best of religious reading.

Before this move the work of the *Earnest Christian* required frequent trips back and forth to Rochester. Benson recalled, "For years we drove ten miles, night and morning, from North Chili to Rochester, fair weather or foul, through mud or snow, sometimes with great glee, and again silent and chilled as we faced the biting west winds that swept on us from the far off continental stretches."[108]

The biggest blow to the *Earnest Christian* came in October 1886, when the Free Methodist General Conference, which decided to purchase the *Free Methodist* and make it officially the denominational magazine, unaccountably elected Roberts as its editor — in addition to his responsibilities as general superintendent and *Earnest Christian* editor. "A large number of subscribers transferred their names" from the *Earnest Christian* to the *Free Methodist* as a result, Benson Roberts later

---

105. [B. T. Roberts], "The Earnest Christian," *EC* 39, no. 1 (Jan. 1880): 32.

106. [B. T. Roberts], "Of Age," pp. 189-90.

107. [B. T. Roberts], "Of Age," p. 190.

108. Benson H. Roberts, "Changes," pp. 3-4. It is unclear whether Benson is referring to daily trips or to the frequent trips that were necessary at the time the magazine was being mailed. He apparently is speaking of the years after 1866 (roughly from the time he was thirteen) and before 1883.

noted.[109] Benjamin put a note "To Our Preachers" in the December 1887 *Earnest Christian,* pleading for their continued support.

> Since the purchase of the *Free Methodist* much of the support which THE EARNEST CHRISTIAN formerly had from the preachers has been withdrawn. If however you consider it an advantage for our people to have a monthly magazine [in addition to the weekly *Free Methodist*], and if you can endorse the truths as therein set forth; we desire to ask you personally not to forget in the midst of your other work to present to the people the claims of THE EARNEST CHRISTIAN. If its publication is continued it will need all the support you can give it.[110]

Despite the fact that Benjamin was now editing two periodicals that to a degree competed with each other for subscribers, the *Earnest Christian* continued with a respectable subscription base. On November 3, 1887, while Benjamin was traveling, Ellen wrote to him and noted, "Benja has been mailing to-day. He says we have thirty-one hundred subscribers."[111]

The fortunes of the *Earnest Christian* and the Free Methodist denomination with its weekly magazine did not run on precisely parallel tracks, however. The *Earnest Christian* reached places the new church had not yet penetrated and, as noted earlier, was never a denominational organ.[112]

The Free Methodist Church grew fairly rapidly during B. T. Roberts's lifetime. If most Free Methodist households had subscribed to the *Earnest Christian,* the magazine would probably have had some 10,000 subscribers by 1895 from that source alone, as total membership then was nearly 30,000.[113] Most Free Methodists, however, opted for only the *Free Methodist,* not both magazines.

Benjamin, often assisted by Ellen, kept up the arduous work of editing the *Earnest Christian* and of managing its publication and distribution to the end of his life. At the beginning of the year when he had a quantity of accumulated issues from the previous year bound, he sometimes made gifts of the bound volumes to friends and family members.[114] When the 1888 bound volume was issued early in 1889, Benjamin sent a copy to his son George, inscribed "George L. Roberts from Father."[115] George was then thirty-seven years of age and living in Bradford, Pennsylvania.

109. [Benson Roberts], "The Subscription List," *EC* 69, no. 1 (Jan. 1895): 36.

110. [B. T. Roberts], "To Our Preachers," *EC* 54, no. 6 (Dec. 1887): 191.

111. ELR to BTR, Nov. 3, 1887.

112. Illustrative of this independence of the *Earnest Christian* is the fact that the denominational histories (Hogue, Marston, McKenna) give it very little attention, although they occasionally use it as a source. Even Zahniser devotes little space to it.

113. *Minutes of the Annual Conferences of the Free Methodist Church 1895* (Chicago: Free Methodist Publishing House, [1896]), p. 216.

114. Apparently Roberts had an overrun of each issue printed so he would have a quantity on hand for binding in January. He noted in the June 1862 issue, "We want, for binding, the 2nd or February number of vol. 1st. of the Earnest Christian. — If any one can procure it for us and forward it by mail we shall be greatly obliged, and will pay for it besides" (p. 190).

115. The inscribed volume is located in MMHC.

B. T. Roberts always sought to write clearly and to edit carefully. In 1884 he commented on the "unnecessary multiplication" of holiness periodicals and complained of editors who "start holiness papers" but "do not seem to have any very clear ideas of their own, or the training and ability to clearly express them if they had." He was particularly offended by a copy of a new paper that landed on his desk, entitled the *Evangelist,* published in Kansas. Roberts quoted exactly a nearly incoherent passage and noted wryly, "The readers are evidently expected to do their own punctuating. Another holiness advocate is got out in doggerel."[116]

Roberts was an excellent writer and editor. When editing the *Free Methodist,* he advised would-be contributors to send in short articles, to the point. He wrote, in words that modeled what he meant:

> CONDENSE! Keep your thoughts to yourself till you have clear ideas on the subject on which you wish to write. Let them settle. Give us the cream. Leave out all introduction — all apologies. Cut out every word that can be spared without obscuring the sense.
>
> Put in all the love and sympathy and kindness you can; and omit all the sentences and words calculated to grate upon the feelings. Smooth friction generates electricity. If you cannot agree with other writers express your disagreement in courteous, chastened language.
>
> Give us short articles full of faith and of the Holy Ghost.[117]

Roberts's use of short, pungent sentences was rather unusual for the time. Like Wesley, his concern was to communicate clearly and simply. In an 1884 editorial entitled "Shining Lights" he wrote, "The Christian is commanded to let his light shine. He must not obscure it, nor cover it up. He must give it a fair chance. This is all the advantage that light demands. You must not blow it to make it more intense. That might put it out. You need not call attention to its presence. Simply let it occupy its natural position and it will, itself, proclaim its existence."[118]

Similarly, Roberts began his 1884 editorial "Losing Holiness" with several short sentences: "Holiness is voluntary. It is a moral state. But a moral action implies freedom of choice. No one is praised or blamed, rewarded or punished for doing that which could not possibly be avoided. But the holy are rewarded, the unholy are punished. Therefore a holy person is holy from choice."[119]

This writing style was intentional, and it seems to have come easily to Roberts. By this time (1884) he had of course honed his style over many years, but even his early writing is generally marked by crispness and clarity — by attention to form as well as to content. Roberts was also fond of one-word titles for editorials — for example, "Honesty," "Zeal," "Reliable," "Vanity," "Death," "Mistaken," "Fanaticism,"

---

116. [B. T. Roberts], "Holiness Sects," *EC* 47, no. 6 (June 1884): 187-88.
117. B. T. Roberts, "Be Short," *FM* 23, no. 17 (Apr. 23, 1890): 8.
118. [B. T. Roberts], "Shining Lights," *EC* 48, no. 4 (Oct. 1884): 128.
119. [B. T. Roberts], "Losing Holiness," *EC* 48, no. 3 (Sept. 1884): 96.

"Formalism," "Universalism," "Wrongs," "Candor," "Work," "Blundering." Editorials were frequently titled simply "Revival" or "Revivals." Sometimes these were reports of revival efforts, but often they were discussions of the nature of or need for revival.

Benson Roberts later gave this assessment of his father as editor: "He possessed, as few do, the power of clear, terse statement which sprang from a mind clear in its conviction and perception of truth." The *Earnest Christian's* "sharp, incisive articles from his skilled pen made its pages sought after."[120] Benjamin's editorials and articles were sometimes reprinted in other publications — particularly, Benson noted, those about free pews. "His editorials on this topic were widely copied by other papers, not always with due credit."[121]

When Benson became editor after Benjamin's death, he felt he was at some disadvantage compared with his father, who traveled widely and had an extensive network of friends, colleagues, and acquaintances. Benson wrote, "The advantage the founder had of constant contact with different minds and the stimulus of new scenes and new problems, was not mine."[122]

The *Earnest Christian* after B. T. Roberts's Death

With considerable help from Ellen, B. T. edited and published the *Earnest Christian* from 1860 until his death in 1893. The entire April 1893 issue was a tribute to Benjamin's life and work. The magazine survived him for about sixteen years, continuing into the twentieth century. His son Benson picked up the editorial responsibilities immediately following his death, listing himself as "Rev. B. H. Roberts, A.M., Editor," and also as publisher.[123] Benson's direct, clear writing style was much like his father's. He was ably assisted by his wife Emma Sellew Roberts, who also served with him as coprincipal of Chesbrough Seminary.

Though circulation had declined substantially in the late 1880s, the magazine continued on for another fifteen years or so after B. T. Roberts's death. Circulation fell off after 1886, Benson noted, not only because of the transfer of subscribers to the *Free Methodist* but also because many other magazines had "come into existence advocating much the same truths."[124] These included such holiness periodicals as Phoebe Palmer's *Guide to Holiness,* "one of the nation's most widely circulated religious monthlies."[125] Also, as noted earlier, the number of religious journals generally in the United States doubled between 1860 and 1885 (though U.S. population was also growing, doubling between 1860 and 1890).

120. Benson H. Roberts, "Changes," p. 4.
121. BHR, *BTR*, p. 540. Benson notes that the *Earnest Christian* was also "among the first of religious papers to openly discountenance and rebuke the use of tobacco."
122. Benson H. Roberts, "Changes," p. 4.
123. The May 1893 issue is the first in which Benson Roberts is listed as editor.
124. [Benson Roberts], "The Subscription List," p. 36.
125. Kostlevy, p. 196.

Benson noted in January 1895, "The hard financial pressure of the past two years also has made itself severely felt."[126] Earlier he had commented, "The pressure of the hard times has made itself felt widely. Scarcely a town or a farm but that has felt it severely." Benson was "gratified at the number of prompt renewals despite this financial pressure."[127]

Benson began offering various premiums to help attract and hold subscribers. Everyone who renewed or subscribed during December 1893 would receive a free subscription to the *Farm Journal,* "a most excellent farmers paper." A copy of *Holiness Teachings* (a collection of B. T. Roberts's writings) would go to all who sent in three new subscriptions with their renewals.[128]

The circulation probably declined to between two thousand and three thousand, but the *Earnest Christian* continued to be published faithfully. The April 1899 issue noted that "several hundred people" were in arrears in their subscriptions — suggesting a total mailing list of perhaps two thousand or more.[129] Benson edited and published the magazine, he said, "always as secondary to other and pressing demands of a semi-secular nature" (referring apparently to his administrative role at Chesbrough Seminary). Benson was assisted by many people, including John Prior, who looked after the actual printing both before and after Benjamin's death, and Miss Adella Carpenter, who handled much of the office correspondence.[130]

The magazine continued the same basic pattern after Roberts's death, though toward the end of the century Benson introduced such innovations as more departments, an expanded list of regular contributors, International Sunday School Lesson notes, and an occasional hymn, with musical notation, on the back page.[131] Ellen Roberts often contributed columns, as did Emma Sellew Roberts. The "Missionary Department" reported on the expanding foreign missions outreach of the Free Methodist Church. Occasionally a sermon or article by B. T. Roberts was reprinted.

Benson noted in early 1909, after Ellen had died, that during his years as editor, "The question often arose, Should THE EARNEST CHRISTIAN be modernized, its scope widened, to insure a larger reading public and an increased income? Should its form be changed, its pages be made more attractive by illustration? But regard for the wishes of my mother helped decide to continue the same form."[132]

Religious periodical publishing declined substantially toward the end of the century and in the early 1900s. Religious papers "found a formidable competitor in the secular press," noted the *New York Tribune* in 1890. Frank Luther Mott comments

126. [Benson Roberts], "The Subscription List," p. 36. See also Hogue, *HFMC,* 2:245.

127. "Renewals," *EC* 68, no. 1 (July 1894): 33.

128. "Renewals — 1894," *EC* 66, no. 6 (Dec. 1893): 191.

129. "Business Matters," *EC* 77, no. 4 (Apr. 1899): 130-31.

130. Benson H. Roberts, "Changes," p. 4.

131. Some of the hymns were by Vivian Dake, with music by Fannie Birdsall, such as "How Vast the Love of God" at the end of the March 1897 issue (reprinted from the songbook *Songs of the Reapers*).

132. Benson H. Roberts, "Changes," p. 4.

on the "decline in both the prosperity and the prestige of the religious press" at this time. In 1904 the editor of *Zion's Herald* observed that "the decline of religious journalism in this country in recent years has been marked by the suspension and consolidation of religious papers." He added, "The old-time religious paper is gone." This general decline was true of Methodist as well as other religious periodicals.[133]

Although in some ways the *Earnest Christian* was a special case because it represented a distinct subculture, it was not totally immune from these broader social currents. It is worth noting, also, that just at this time of decline the Pentecostal movement was being birthed through the Azusa Street Revival in Los Angeles, beginning in 1906.

The End of the *Earnest Christian*

The *Earnest Christian* finally ceased publication with the December 1909 issue. At the time it apparently had around one thousand subscribers, most of whose subscriptions were due to expire with the December issue.[134]

Ellen Roberts passed away on January 28, 1908. The March 1908 *Earnest Christian* was a memorial tribute to Benjamin's lifelong companion, beginning with an article entitled "My Mother" by Benson Roberts. The issue carried an account of Ellen's funeral and tributes by old S. K. J. Chesbrough, Bishop Wilson T. Hogue, David S. Warner, and others, and a selection of Ellen's articles. At the end of that issue Benson briefly reviewed the history of the *Earnest Christian* and of his labors as editor. "It was hardly to be expected that the son would equal the father, who was a man of unusual gifts and attainments," Benson said. He noted that "the Earnest Christian subscription list suffered a marked loss, from which it never recovered in his lifetime, nor later," when Benjamin became editor of the *Free Methodist*. "The Editor would be very glad to receive suggestions from the friends of the Earnest Christian with regard to its future."[135]

The *Earnest Christian* did not cease publication during Ellen Roberts's lifetime, and that was her goal — and probably Benson's as well. Ellen wanted to keep the magazine going as the continuing legacy of her husband.

Benson gave up publishing the magazine after he moved to Pittsburgh. The Free Methodist Church bought the magazine from him later, in 1908, and moved its publication to the new Free Methodist Publishing House in Chicago. Bishop Wilson T. Hogue, who had been instrumental in founding the publishing house, was appointed editor but due to poor health served only until the end of 1909.[136]

133. Frank Luther Mott, *A History of American Magazines*, vol. 4, *1885-1905* (Cambridge: Harvard University Press, 1957), pp. 288-90.

134. W. B. Rose, "Publisher's Note," *EC* 96, no. 12 (Dec. 1909): 29.

135. [Benson H. Roberts], "To the Earnest Christian Readers," *EC* 95, no. 3 (Mar. 1908): 100.

136. [Wilson T. Hogue], "Greetings," *EC* 97, no. 1 (Jan. 1909): 1; Benson H. Roberts, "Changes," p. 3.

By then, however, the magazine was a superfluous adjunct to the denomination's publishing efforts — or at least was perceived as such — since the Free Methodist Publishing House was by this time issuing the *Free Methodist,* the *Missionary Tidings,* and a considerable amount of Sunday school literature and many other publications. The magazine was now an inheritance, not a mission. With the death of Ellen Roberts and the departure of Benson Roberts, it had no real champion.

William B. Rose, the publisher, noted in the December 1909 issue that the magazine was ceasing publication.[137] Thus the magazine survived Ellen's death by only one year. During its final year the journal appeared under the title *The Earnest Christian: An Exponent of Scriptural Holiness and a Guide to Christian Service.* Benson Roberts had continued to serve as corresponding editor, along with John LaDue and Augustin L. Whitcomb. Benson's name was thus associated with the magazine to the very end.

The December 1909 issue of the *Earnest Christian* brought to an end a half-century of uninterrupted publication of the monthly journal. Since its beginning in January 1860, the magazine was published for exactly fifty years — 600 monthly issues, nearly 20,000 pages.[138]

137. Benson H. Roberts, "Changes," p. 3; Rose, "Publisher's Note," p. 29; Richard R. Blews, *Master Workmen: Biographies of the Later Bishops of the Free Methodist Church during Her First Century, 1860-1960,* centennial ed. (Winona Lake, Ind.: Light and Life Press, 1960), p. 120. Blews is off by one year in his dates, giving 1907 as the date of purchase by the denomination and 1908 as the last year of publication.

138. Had B. T. Roberts continued his original plan of one twelve-issue volume per calendar year, the total number of volumes (1860-1909) would have been fifty. In actuality the number of volumes totaled ninety-seven, since in the calendar years 1860, 1861, and 1909 just one twelve-issue volume was published, while two volumes of six issues each were published from 1862 through 1908.

CHAPTER 27

Ministry during the Civil War

"Faith and works must go together. We must not only pray for righteousness to prevail, but do all we can in a Christian manner to make it prevail."

B. T. Roberts, 1862[1]

"I venture the prediction that not many years hence there will not be found 10 apologists for slavery where there are a hundred now."

John Wesley Redfield, 1862[2]

The *Earnest Christian* had been in publication for a little more than a year when the Civil War broke out on April 12, 1861, with the firing on Fort Sumter near Charleston, South Carolina. The early years of the *Earnest Christian* and of the Free Methodist denomination thus coincided with the four years of the Civil War.

Abraham Lincoln was elected president on November 6, 1860. The next day South Carolinians at Charleston raised the state's palmetto flag in place of the Union banner. Crowds in the streets shouted for a Southern Confederacy. The Charleston *Mercury* reported, "The tea has been thrown overboard, the revolution of 1860 has been initiated." The following week, New York financial markets were in turmoil.[3]

Soon one of the bloodiest wars in human history was unleashed. Author Simon Winchester notes that the "inescapable irony of the Civil War" was that it came at a

1. [B. T. Roberts], "The Trip to the West," *EC* 4, no. 1 (July 1862): 30.
2. Redfield Autobiography, p. 298.
3. E. B. Long with Barbara Long, *The Civil War Day by Day: An Almanac, 1861-1865* (New York: Da Capo Press, 1971, 1985), pp. 2-5.

time when military technology had outrun medical technology, resulting in horrific suffering.

> [T]his was a war fought with new and highly effective weapons, machines for the mowing down of men — and yet at a time when an era of poor and primitive medicine was just coming to an end. It was fought with the mortar and the musket and the minié ball, but not yet quite with anesthesia or with sulphonamides and penicillin. The common soldier was thus in a poorer position than at any time before: He could be monstrously ill treated by all the new weaponry, and yet only moderately well treated with all the old medicine.
>
> So in the field hospitals there was gangrene, amputation, filth, pain, and disease. . . . The sounds in the first-aid tents were unforgettable: the screams and whimperings of men whose lives had been ruined by cruel new guns and in ferocious and ceaseless battles. Some 360,000 Federal troops died in the war, and so did 258,000 Confederates — and for every one who died of wounds caused by the new weapons, so two died from incidental infection, illness, and poor hygiene.[4]

Yet in the midst of all the pain and disruption, life went on. Despite the turbulence of the next four years, the *Earnest Christian* continued publication and kept growing. Roberts commented editorially on the progress of the war, and copies of the paper found their way to Union troops. As he received letters from the front or from scattered Union army camps, Benjamin sometimes sent packages of the magazine to the soldiers.

Roberts's lead editorial in the September 1861 issue was entitled "Our Country." He began, "The struggle between the North and South is becoming more and more sanguinary. Already have many brave men met death upon the field of battle, and many a family circle has been made desolate. We have seen the beginning, but when the end shall come God only knows."

Roberts insisted that the fundamental issue was moral, having to do with slavery.

> The offer of freedom should be made at once to every slave in the rebellious states. But for the delicacy in meeting this question this war would never have been upon us.[5] Years ago we should have followed the example of England, and adopted a system of compensated emancipation that would have been alike beneficial to master and slave. But the day for that has gone by. Emancipation by the sword, or inglorious defeat, are the alternatives now presented. Not to choose the former is to make choice of the latter. Indecision is a wrong decision. Upon the issue now presented the North cannot conquer, and what would be the advantage if she should? Disunion is preferable to union with slavery. It is no advantage to the Free States to have plantation tyrants domineering at the seat of government, meeting arguments with bowie knives and revolvers. Contact with slavery has demoralized

---

4. Simon Winchester, *The Professor and the Madman* (New York: HarperCollins, 1998), p. 52.

5. While the word "delicacy" is possible here, one wonders whether Roberts intended "delinquency" and the printer misread Roberts's manuscript, Roberts failing to catch the error.

the public mind. Men seek office — not that they serve their country — but for the opportunity for enriching themselves with plunder. The churches, the guardians of the public conscience, have, to please the slave-power, gradually lowered their tone, until to a great extent, the first principles of morality have been lost sight of. When slaveholders are admitted to Christian ordinances, no class of criminals should be excluded. Look at the system as you may, view it in its own nature or in its effects upon master and slave, and you can but pronounce it in the emphatic language of John Wesley, *"The sum of all villainies."*

Let every lover of his country insist upon emancipation for the slave. Let the government proclaim this policy, and such an enthusiastic support will be given it as will render its arms irresistable — four millions of friends ready to stake their lives upon the issue, will be secured in the heart of the rebellious states.

Roberts ended with an appeal to the U.S. Constitution: "If, as is very clearly demonstrated by passing events, slavery lies in the way of *insuring domestic tranquility, and providing for the general welfare of the United States,* it ought to be abolished, *and government already possesses the power to do it.* Will it be exercised? We trust it may."[6]

Roberts was in Illinois in late September and early October 1861 for the Ogle camp meeting and the meeting of the Western Convention of the Free Methodist Church. On September 26 he preached at Aurora "on the occasion of the National Fast," taking as his text Isaiah 58:6, "Is not this the fast that I have chosen? to loose the bands of wickedness, to undo the heavy burdens, and to let the oppressed go free, and that ye break every yoke?" The sermon echoed Roberts's editorials on the war. "We showed that slavery was an institution contrary to the Bible and bringing upon us the vengeance of Heaven," he reported in the *Earnest Christian.* "We must 'let the oppressed go free' before we can expect God to bless our arms."[7]

Sometime in September or October 1861 Benjamin visited a Union cavalry encampment "raised by a member of congress whose devotion to his country was highly lauded by the papers." Roberts doesn't say where the encampment was, but he was chagrined at the evidence of profiteering he found. "Inferior goods and poor provisions are procured by the contractors at a low rate and furnished by them at the highest price paid for first rate articles," he reported editorially. "This swindling should be stopped."[8]

With this experience fresh in his mind, Roberts published another lead editorial entitled "Our Country" in the November 1861 *Earnest Christian.* He wrote, "Our beloved country is bleeding at every pore. Our solid advantages in men and money and resources of every kind . . . are far superior to those of the rebels; our soldiers manifest the highest degree of courage and endurance; yet thus far, nearly every important advantage appears to have been gained by our enemies." And Roberts ticked off the distressing list of Union defeats: Sumter, Manassas, and Mulligan's surrender at

---

6. [B. T. Roberts], "Our Country," *EC* 2, no. 9 (Sept. 1861): 289.
7. [B. T. Roberts], "Ogle Camp Meeting," *EC* 2, no. 11 (Nov. 1861): 354.
8. [B. T. Roberts], "Our Country," *EC* 2, no. 11 (Nov. 1861): 352.

Lexington, Missouri, on September 20. Union forces are "hemmed in at Washington, and the national Metropolis is little better than in a state of siege."

"There is a Providence in the want of success attending our arms," Benjamin concluded. The Union was failing for two reasons: the war was being waged on the wrong issue (preservation of the Union rather than ending slavery), and it was being "carried on in the wrong way," with too many profiting from it personally. "The great question with many seems to be, how they can make most money out of it, — how they can coin their country's blood into gold to fill their own pockets."

On the first point, Roberts elaborated:

[The war] is waged on the part of the government to restore the Union as it was. But the Union as it was defended and upheld slavery. It turned the Northern soil into a hunting ground for the poor fugitive [through the Fugitive Slave Act], and compelled Northern freemen to refuse to them the common offices of humanity, and to peril their lives when the occasion demanded it, to return them to the house of bondage. . . . The old Union was put to too bad a use for God to permit it to stand. Slavery is the cause of the war. This no one doubts. If we would have peace we must remove the cause of the war. . . . God cannot help us until we espouse the cause of his oppressed. Emancipate the slaves, and tell them to fight for their freedom and we will help them, and the war would soon be ended.[9]

Roberts issued a call to action: "Petitions should be circulated at once and sent to Congress from every neighborhood in the land, asking them to exercise their power by abolishing slavery in all the rebel states."[10] Roberts thus added his voice to the growing chorus calling for the emancipation of the slaves.

In succeeding issues of the *Earnest Christian* Roberts continued to address war issues from time to time. In March 1862, writing yet another editorial entitled "Our Country," he noted that the course of the war had shifted somewhat. "The slaveholders' rebellion, appears at last, to be in a fair way to be crushed. The recent victories are of the most decisive character." Many celebrate, but "many a hearth is made desolate" by death, he reminded his readers. "All this with heavy taxation, for years yet to come is the result of unholy compromises made in behalf of wrong." He did not see the war as glorious.[11]

In the next issue, April 1862, Roberts reprinted from the Rochester *Democrat* a disheartening firsthand report of conditions at a Union prisoner of war camp at Indianapolis. Here five hundred to six hundred rebel soldiers were held, many of them sick and dying. The whole scene was a lesson in human depravity, Roberts said — not only the violence of the war, but the institution of slavery that lay behind it.

What is the cause of all this suffering? . . . What has reduced the common people of the South to a state of semi-barbarism? What has converted fertile plains into

9. [B. T. Roberts], "Our Country," *EC* 2, no. 11 (Nov. 1861): 352.
10. [B. T. Roberts], "Our Country," *EC* 2, no. 11 (Nov. 1861): 352.
11. [B. T. Roberts], "Our Country," *EC* 3, no. 3 (Mar. 1862): 95.

fields of blood, made so many homes desolate, and taxed coming generations with a debt of gigantic proportions? There can be but one answer, SLAVERY HAS DONE THE MISCHIEF. It has robbed four millions of human beings of their God-given rights, and made it a crime to teach them to read the blessed Bible. It has destroyed the freedom of speech and the freedom of the press in one-half of this republic [and corrupted the churches, Congress, and the judicial system]. And now, at last, it has plunged the nation into a bloody, costly, civil war.[12]

Support for slavery in the North, Roberts argued, proved human depravity as much as did the violence of the war or slavery's support in the South. The fact that "sympathizer[s] with slavery" can be found "living amid our free institutions" in the North, and even in the church, is "conclusive proof of the doctrine of total depravity."[13]

By July 1862 the war was again not going well for the North. "The war had changed sharply within a month," E. B. Long notes. "The string of Northern victories had ended." On July 1 President Lincoln called for 300,000 more men in order to (he said) "bring this unnecessary and injurious civil war to a speedy and satisfactory conclusion," and on August 4 he announced a draft of 300,000 (though this draft was not actually carried out).[14]

In his editorials Roberts continued the theme that the real moral issue of the war was slavery. He wrote in the September 1862 *Earnest Christian,*

> The affairs of our poor bleeding country are growing more and more desperate. Many homes are made desolate, and many more yet will be. Under this last levy, many of our finest, noblest, most promising young men have rushed to the call of their country.
>
> O what a pity it is that our rulers cannot rise to the sublimity of the occasion! God is calling, in thunder tones, "Let my people, the oppressed, go free." The call could be obeyed. This war might be ended in a short time by giving liberty to the bondman. It can never, — we are not a prophet, — yet we are entirely confident, that it can never be ended in favor of the North and still preserve the institution of Slavery. It is strange the President does not see this. It is strange that he does not venture himself on the justice of God, and the magnanimity of a liberty-loving people, and surround himself with men that are heartily in favor of human freedom — men who hate slavery and who would be glad to see it die. An earnest proclamation of freedom to the enslaved would enlist at once on our side, four millions of the bone and sinew of the South; it would kindle such an enthusiasm at the North as would sweep all before it; and, above all it would secure the favor of that God who has written the doom of slavery, and who decides the fate of battles. Treasure and blood may, and doubtless will, be poured out like water; but all

---

12. [B. T. Roberts], "Human Depravity," *EC* 3, no. 4 (Apr. 1862): 128.
13. [B. T. Roberts], "Human Depravity," p. 129.
14. Long and Long, *The Civil War,* pp. 234, 236, 247.

will be in vain unless we awake to righteousness, and unloose the heavy burden, and let the oppressed go free.

The time was when emancipation might have been effected peaceably — that time is now past; the time has come when it may be effected by the sword, and the Nation be saved to take rank among the mightiest of earth — a great, united people: that golden opportunity is fast passing away, and unless improved soon, slavery will die, but the greatness and the unity and the glory of the country will also have passed away forever.[15]

Roberts thought it "strange" that "the President does not see" the logic and moral necessity of emancipation. In fact, President Lincoln did see this, but he was fighting a political as well as a military battle and was trying to hold disparate factions in the North, and in his own party, together — waiting for what he felt was the right time to free the slaves. As one historian notes, "Talk of emancipation as part of the war effort was rising in the North, while at the same time there was increased opposition to making it a war against slavery."[16] Horace Greeley, whose sharp pen was often a thorn in Lincoln's side, criticized the president's war policy in the pages of his *New York Tribune*. "All attempts to put down the Rebellion and at the same time uphold its inciting cause are preposterous and futile," Greeley wrote about this time.[17]

What Roberts, Greeley, and the American public did not know was that Lincoln, after deep thought, had already written his Emancipation Proclamation. He presented it to his cabinet on July 22, 1862, but decided to delay announcing it until the Northern armies won some significant victory on the battlefield.[18]

Meanwhile, more bloody battles showed that the war was far from over. Wednesday, September 17, 1862, proved to be the bloodiest day of the Civil War as a Union army of about 75,000 engaged some 40,000 Confederates at the battle of Antietam near Sharpsburg, Maryland. Union forces lost 12,469 men dead or wounded and the Confederates about 11,000.[19] News of the losses sent shock waves throughout the land.

In the wake of Antietam Roberts editorialized: "Whatever the end may be, a most disastrous civil war is upon us. . . . we seem no nearer a favorable termination

15. [B. T. Roberts], "Our Country," *EC* 4, no. 3 (Sept. 1862): 91-92. Presumably by "this last levy" Roberts means the draft Lincoln announced on Aug. 4, though as noted this draft was never actually put into effect.

16. Long and Long, *The Civil War,* p. 246.

17. Long and Long, *The Civil War,* p. 253, citing the *New York Tribune* for Aug. 19, 1862.

18. Long and Long, *The Civil War,* pp. 242-43.

19. E. B. Long says "the exact figures are uncertain" but puts Union casualties at "2010 killed, 9416 wounded, and 1043 missing for a total of 12,469 out of over 75,000 estimated effectives. Confederate losses were estimated at 2700 killed, 9024 wounded, and about 2000 missing for a total of 13,724 out of around 40,000 engaged." Long and Long, *The Civil War,* pp. 267-68. The U.S. National Park Service puts total Union losses at 12,410 and Confederate losses at 10,700. *Antietam,* National Park Service Brochure, 2000.

than we were one year ago." He added, "The real difficulty lies in our disregard hitherto, of the claims of God. . . . To have the favor of God we must listen to his voice and LET THE OPPRESSED GO FREE."

Roberts was heartened by Lincoln's preliminary Emancipation Proclamation, issued on September 22, just days after Antietam. Lincoln was starting to take the "necessary step." Roberts wrote,

> The news of freedom will soon be carried to every plantation — a general uprising will take place — the rebel troops will be called home . . . and in a few months peace will, we trust, again be restored to our distracted country. . . .
>
> The long-wished for Document has at last been issued. God has answered prayer. — Liberty has been proclaimed to the captive, and relief to the oppressed. To the long-enslaved African the year of Jubilee is about to dawn. On the first of January, 1863, the slaves of the rebels are to be set free. . . . Peace on the basis of liberty will be likely to prove permanent, and, once restored, the nation will enter upon an unprecedented career of prosperity. God bless the President and give him success in his endeavors to restore peace to the country and freedom to the enslaved.[20]

Yet in fact, the war was still far from over.

The *Earnest Christian* among the Troops

Roberts was able to minister to Union soldiers indirectly through the pages of the *Earnest Christian* as the magazine went places he himself could not. In the May 1864 issue he reported on the impact the magazine was having among the troops. "In some regiments, good revivals have been enjoyed," he noted. "*Earnest Christian* bands have been organized in some camps," with remarkable results spiritually. Roberts advised readers in the army to lay "denominational distinctions . . . aside, and let those who are in earnest to gain heaven, associate together for prayer, and testimony, and exhortation." He added, "We give thanks to God that the 'Earnest Christian' is permitted to bear a part in diffusing and keeping alive the power of godliness in the army."[21]

The *Earnest Christian* had its most extensive impact in the Eighteenth Regiment of Illinois Infantry, Volunteers, while it was stationed at Little Rock, Arkansas. Some in the regiment had been receiving the magazine and one, James Whiteker, was a licensed Methodist (or Free Methodist) exhorter. In October 1863 eleven soldiers met together "in the woods back of the city" and organized themselves as the "Earnest Christian Band," adopting several rules and disciplines. "Prior to this there had never been a prayer meeting held inside the camp! But we erected a Chapel and

---

20. [B. T. Roberts], "Our Civil War," *EC* 4, no. 4 (Oct. 1862): 122.
21. "Religion in the Army," *EC* 7, no. 5 (May 1864): 161.

commenced a series of prayer meetings, independent of those who held commissions as Chaplains," Whiteker reported. "A revival of religion broke out at once."[22]

This movement began when someone gave Whiteker a copy of the *Earnest Christian*. Through reading it and the Bible, Whiteker was sanctified. Before long "over a dozen [others had] professed the blessing," he wrote. He reported in early 1864, "We are having a glorious revival here. Over 60 souls have been converted," with people coming to God "in the woods, cornfields, cane-brakes and in camps, as well as in the Church." He concluded, "I feel that God has called me to preach the Gospel."[23]

Benjamin Smith, one of the members of this Earnest Christian Band, wrote letters to the magazine several times. In a July 26, 1864, letter he reported that the initial group of eleven quickly grew to twenty-one. "Several had obtained the blessing of 'perfect love' and our souls were full of the love of God." Soon revival broke out in which the members of the Earnest Christian Band were "the principal laborers in the altar and at the class." Smith continued, "It is estimated that there were over *one hundred* souls converted and reclaimed. We again resumed our meetings in the regiment and the Lord powerfully blessed us; soldiers flocked to our meetings from other brigades and divisions encamped at this place, and often the silence of the winter night was broken by a shout of 'Hallelujah to God and the Lamb' from our little cabin."

The Earnest Christian Band grew to sixty. "We found it necessary to form other societies in other brigades and divisions," Smith reported. The work continued to "spread far and wide, sinners were being convicted, mourners converted, and believers sanctified at the time of our going home in consequence of re-enlistment."[24]

Smith and Whiteker reported later, toward the end of 1864, that through other branches of the Earnest Christian Band "organized in other regiments, . . . the work spread until about two hundred souls were converted, and eighteen professed *sanctification*."[25]

As letters came in from soldiers at the front or in various camps, Roberts printed some of them in the *Earnest Christian*. On April 6, 1863, a soldier signing himself "W. W. K." wrote from Jackson, Tennessee, to say that he had received the package of magazines Roberts had sent him. "I wish you to put me down as a recruiting officer for my sweet little friend E.C. [*Earnest Christian*]. I believe I cannot better spend my spare money and time than in the extension of its circulation." He included an order for six copies.[26] In November the same correspondent reported

---

22. J. W. [James Whiteker], "'The Earnest Christian Band,'" *EC* 8, no. 6 (Dec. 1864): 189; B. F. S. [Benjamin F. Smith], "Earnest Christian Band," *EC* 8, no. 1 (July 1864): 34. Smith gives the band's eight rules and lists the names of the eleven soldiers. Whiteker is listed as "class leader."

23. "The Earnest Christian in the Army," *EC* 7, no. 4 (Apr. 1864): 131-32.

24. B. F. S. [Benjamin F. Smith], "Religion in the Army," *EC* 8, no. 3 (Sept. 1864): 95.

25. J. W. [James Whiteker], "'The Earnest Christian Band,'" p. 189; cf. "From the Army. — B. F. Smith," *EC* 8, no. 6 (Dec. 1864): 192. Whiteker reported that "six out of the eleven who organized the 'E.C.B.' one year ago" were still active. He doesn't indicate what became of the other five.

26. "A Word from the Army," *EC* 5, no. 5 (May 1863): 163.

that a "band" of six soldiers was reading the magazine "with pleasure and profit." Its pages were helping them find "a deeper and more thorough work in [their] hearts."[27]

Letters came from other places as well. A soldier with "the 1st brigade of Gen. Logan's fighting division" wrote from Vicksburg, Mississippi, in November 1863 to say that "the *Earnest Christian* is prized highly, and read with deep interest, by many."[28] Isaac Brewster wrote from a Union camp near New Iberia, Louisiana, west of New Orleans: "I have been able to receive the *Earnest Christian* ever since I have been in the war. I send two new subscribers." And William McKearnin wrote from Fort McHenry, Baltimore, saying he was reading the magazine and that "many in the regiment . . . love to read it. Mine [are] read until they are almost worn out."[29]

It is not clear how broadly the magazine spread or was read in the Union army, or whether any copies found their way to the Confederate troops. Probably some soldiers received copies sent to them by family members who were subscribers. Many years later, after World War II, Bishop Leslie R. Marston wrote about the ministry of the *Earnest Christian* among the troops in the Civil War. "How far these Earnest Christian Bands spread through the Union Army we have no way of knowing, but it is clear that some of us during World War II who thought we were establishing a tradition in providing a spiritual service to servicemen were after all only reviving a tradition begun by the founder of *The Earnest Christian* in the Armed Forces more than eighty years earlier."[30]

Roberts and the War

As his editorials make clear, B. T. Roberts viewed the Civil War as, above all, an antislavery crusade. Here the Free Methodist Church could not be neutral. In 1862 when an attempt was made in Illinois to adopt a state constitution that Roberts said would "greatly give the advantage to the Southern or pro-slavery portion" of the electorate, he dismissed the St. Charles camp meeting a day early so the people could go vote against it. He reported in the *Earnest Christian,* "The election to decide upon the adoption of this constitution was to be held on Tuesday of the Camp Meeting. So the meeting was adjourned on Monday, in order to give the voters time to get home and deposit their emphatic protest against this anti-Christian project. Faith and works must go together. We must not only pray for righteousness to prevail, but do all we can in a Christian manner to make it prevail."[31]

27. "Good Accomplished," *EC* 6, no. 6 (Dec. 1863): 186-87.

28. R. T. F., letter dated Vicksburg, Miss., Nov. 15, 1863, *EC* 7, no. 1 (Jan. 1864): 35.

29. "The Earnest Christian," *EC* 7, no. 1 (Jan. 1864): 33-34.

30. Leslie R. Marston, "Service to Servicemen during the Civil War," *FM* 93, no. 3 (Jan. 19, 1960): 3, 15.

31. [B. T. Roberts], "Trip to the West," p. 30.

The Civil War and the slavery questions were moral issues, and Free Methodists could not be neutral.

Throughout the Civil War B. T. and Ellen Roberts of course continued their ministry in behalf of the church. Summer was always camp meeting season, and Benjamin attended many such meetings during the Civil War, usually as one of the main preachers. In 1862, for instance, after returning from Illinois where he preached at the St. Charles camp meeting, Roberts attended the Bergen camp meeting and then one at Union, near Binghamton, and another at Allegany, all in New York State. He probably attended the camp meeting at Lyndonville, northwest of Albion, at the end of August, and in September held a camp meeting at Rose, forty miles east of Rochester.

Partway through the 1862 camp meeting season Roberts reported,

> We have attended, thus far, four Camp Meetings this year, and judge from what we have seen and heard that the work of Earnest Christianity is in an encouraging state. While some turn back, tired of the reproach of Christ, and unwilling longer to bear the afflictions of the Gospel, some, thank God, do hold out from year to year, and some are constantly being won over from the ranks of sin and formalism to the cross of Christ. These are perilous times in which we live, and happy is he who, resisting all influences to the contrary, remains faithful to the grace of God.[32]

The Civil War finally ended when Confederate General Robert E. Lee surrendered the Army of Northern Virginia to General Ulysses S. Grant at Appomattox Court House in Virginia on Palm Sunday, April 9, 1865. Only five days later — Good Friday, April 14 — the Union was jolted by the assassination of Abraham Lincoln. Lincoln did not rise on Easter Sunday, though he did quickly become a sort of national semidivine hero. He had barely begun his second term, having delivered his eloquent "with malice toward none" second inaugural address on March 4.

The Civil War was over but, with Lincoln's death, so was the nation's best hope for healing and a peaceful recovery from war and slavery. Roberts's lead editorial in the May 1865 *Earnest Christian* was titled simply "President Lincoln" and was set off by black bars at the beginning and end. Roberts wrote, "The assassination of President LINCOLN has thrilled the heart of this people with sorrow and indignation. A mighty outburst of sincere, spontaneous grief has filled the land. Public and private buildings covered with solemn drapery, the slow tolling of bells from morning till night, the immense funeral processions, saddened looks and silent tears are but faint indications of the anguish felt by thirty millions of people at the loss of their honored head by the assassin's hand."[33]

Roberts reviewed Lincoln's life, noting that he was "no common man" though his origins were poor. By study, "good habits," and God's blessing "upon his own efforts," he rose to become president. In "a time of great perplexity" Lincoln ably led

---

32. [B. T. Roberts], "Camp Meetings," *EC* 4, no. 2 (Aug. 1862): 61-62; "Notice of Meetings," p. 64.
33. [B. T. Roberts], "President Lincoln," *EC* 9, no. 5 (May 1865): 157.

the nation, gradually weeding out "disloyal and incompetent officers" in the war effort. "God led him on, and crowned his exertions with success. He gave freedom to the slave, and God give victory to his armies, and honor to his name." But then "he who sat highest in the affections of the people, was suddenly smitten down by the hand of the assassin. . . . The nation reeled under the shock, and grief and horror swayed every mind."

Roberts felt that Lincoln's assassination had

again roused the nation to the enormities of slavery. We were fast forgetting its true character. In our rejoicings over victory we were rapidly losing sight of the hellish nature of that vile institution that inaugurated the war and rendered victory necessary. . . . The subdued, but unrepentant traitors and rebels were about to be received back to the Union to be restored to place and power. There was great danger that all our sacrifices of blood and treasure would have been in vain. Just then slavery personified showed its diabolical spirit by employing assassins to do its dreadful work. The deed has been done, the President has been foully murdered. But the nation has been aroused and united as never before. Indemnity for the past is impossible, but [the nation] will insist upon security for the future. It will demand that *traitors be disenfranchised,* and that loyal men, *be they black or white* shall be intrusted with *all the rights of citizens.* There must be a perfect social revolution at the south. The colored man must have a voice in the making of the laws and in the choice of the men who shall administer them, or all our sufferings and sacrifices have been in vain. Let us heed the voice of God and dare to do right.[34]

Unfortunately, with Lincoln's death the best hope for the just recovery and "perfect social revolution" that Roberts envisioned also died. Roberts's warning was well founded.

With other Americans, Free Methodists celebrated the victory in war and then grieved the loss of the president who won the victory. Yet the work of the church went on, and B. T. and Ellen Roberts sought to be faithful to their calling in the critical postwar years.

---

34. [B. T. Roberts], "President Lincoln," pp. 157-58. This editorial was followed immediately by one entitled "Bishop Hamline," commenting on the life and ministry of Leonidas Hamline, who died at Mount Pleasant, Iowa, on March 23.

CHAPTER 28

"On the Cars"

"We have been doing all we could to carry the Gospel to the poor and the out-cast."

B. T. Roberts, October 1862[1]

"You can never conceive how extremely dirty we got on the cars. They burned soft coal and it was fearful."

Ellen Roberts, 1879[2]

As the new Free Methodist denomination grew, B. T. Roberts began to travel widely, promoting its interests and expanding his role as a revivalist and reformer. His widening travels coincided with the rapid growth of the railroad system, and he was often, as he would say, "on the cars." Newly completed trunk lines across New York and Pennsylvania and on west allowed Roberts to travel much farther and faster in the interests of Free Methodism than would have been possible ten or twenty years earlier.

Lee Benson speaks of "the newly consolidated and extended trunk lines in New York, Pennsylvania, and Maryland," constituting the four major railroads "reaching from the seaboard to the Great Lakes or the Ohio River," further opening up the West. "The New York and Erie [railroads] reached the Great Lakes in 1851, the short lines running from Albany to Buffalo were consolidated into the New York Central in 1853, the Baltimore and Ohio reached the Ohio River in the same year, and the

---

1. [B. T. Roberts], "Our Wants," *EC* 4, no. 4 (Oct. 1862): 124.
2. ELR (Alameda, Calif.) to Mrs. Cady, Jan. 9, 1879, quoted in Zahniser, p. 303.

Pennsylvania Railroad had an all rail route from Philadelphia to Pittsburgh in 1854."[3] From these main lines scores of smaller railroads reached out to connect the cities and smaller towns.

Roberts's travels "on the cars" took him repeatedly to New York City as well as to Buffalo, Cleveland, Chicago, St. Louis, Philadelphia, and many points in between. Later he would travel across the continent in the interests of the church. His diaries give the impression that often he rather enjoyed his travels by train from place to place, despite occasional delays, long nights, or missed connections. One early spring day in Kansas he noted, "We went very slow. The train was stopped several times to pick up Prairie chickens which frightened by the train flew against the telegraph and killed themselves."[4]

An incident from early 1865 captures the life and spirit of Benjamin at this time. On Sunday, January 15, Roberts was in New York City. He preached morning and evening, speaking in the morning on "Lay not up treasures on earth." Professor Thomas Upham, the well-known Congregationalist supporter of Phoebe Palmer's holiness teachings, was present and gave his testimony. In the afternoon Roberts visited the Five Points Mission and also a small Moravian church service, which he found "dry and formal."[5]

Just before 7:30 Monday morning Roberts boarded a train bound north for Albany. He found himself seated with a businessman from New York — a Methodist, he learned, who was president of the Shoe and Leather Bank. Roberts says, "I showed him the necessity of Free churches and also the extreme difficulty of a rich man being saved. The Lord reach him."[6]

This Methodist businessman, it turns out, was Andrew V. Stout, then fifty-two, eleven years older than Roberts. He had become president of the Shoe and Leather Bank in 1855 after helping organize the bank three years earlier and serving as its vice president.[7]

Stout's life had been a true Horatio Alger story — demonstrating, in the words of one admiring account, that "courage, patient industry, and business capacity will bring fortune to any honest worker." Born in New York City and left fatherless as a

---

3. Lee Benson, *Merchants, Farmers, and Railroads: Railroad Regulation and New York Politics, 1850-1887* (Cambridge: Harvard University Press, 1955), pp. 9, 250.

4. BTRD, Mar. 12, 1874. Isabella Lucy Bird gives vivid descriptions of the delights, dangers, and annoyances of rail travel in the United States in the 1850s in her book *The Englishwoman in America* (1856; Toronto: University of Toronto Press, 1966). Traveling from Boston to Cincinnati, she speaks of "the chaotic confusion which attends the departure of a train in America"; the hurry and bustle, the dirt and fatigue, the frequent kindness of strangers; the animated political conversations, the immigrants' cars; at the Erie, Pa., station, "numerous immigrants sitting on large blue boxes, looking disconsolately about them; the Irish physiognomy being the most predominant." She describes traveling through stately "primeval woods" in Ohio, occasionally seeing clearings and settlers' rude cabins, and of the train rushing through the midst of a raging forest fire (pp. 106-14).

5. BTRD, Jan. 15, 1865.

6. BTRD, Jan. 16, 1865. Roberts does not identify the man by name.

7. Obituary, "Andrew Varick Stout," *New York Times*, Sept. 6, 1883, p. 4.

child, Stout succeeded first as an educator, then as a businessman and financier. While still a young man he opened a wholesale boot and shoe business that quickly prospered. Stout "was a zealous and earnest Christian, one who carried his religion into his business," and an active Methodist.[8]

The Shoe and Leather Bank was one of many New York banks formed in the early to mid-1800s around different trades and industries, such as the Merchants' Bank and the Chemical Bank. It prospered, and through it and other ventures Stout became wealthy. Through a series of mergers it eventually became a part of Chase National Bank.[9] Though Stout was no doubt a remarkable man, his story was not unlike that of many other Methodist businessmen in New York and elsewhere, such as Daniel Drew and the Harper brothers, who "rose to fame and fortune."

It is unclear how much Roberts conversed with Stout during the fairly long ride along the Hudson River to Albany. But Benjamin learned enough from his conversation to discern that Stout was wealthy, and therefore in need of warning about the danger of riches — all the more, perhaps, because he was a Methodist. Roberts probably didn't know much about Stout or his bank. We aren't informed how Stout took Roberts's admonition. It is of some interest to the larger story, however, that Stout became a significant benefactor of Roberts's alma mater, Wesleyan University, and that Thomas Carlton, one of Roberts's old opponents, sat on the board of (and no doubt profited from) Stout's bank! Stout was a trustee of Wesleyan and in 1876 gave $40,000 to endow the A. V. Stout Professorship of Moral Philosophy there.[10] A chapter devoted to Stout in the 1871 book *Great Fortunes, and How They Were Made* reports, "His fortune is immense, and is used liberally in behalf of the cause of the Christian religion."[11]

Whether Andrew Stout heeded, or even needed, Roberts's exhortation is unknown. Roberts's encounter with Stout illustrates, however, both his perspective on wealth and discipleship and the considerable growth of "rich Methodists" during this period and the challenges and opportunities this presented.[12]

8. James D. McCabe, Jr., *Great Fortunes, and How They Were Made; or, The Struggles and Triumphs of our Self-Made Men* (Cincinnati and Chicago: E. Hannaford and Co., 1871), pp. 130-33. Stout was an active member and trustee of St. Paul's Methodist Episcopal Church (the successor to the Mulberry Street church), whose impressive Gothic structure dominated the corner of Fourth Avenue and Twenty-second Street. See *COM*, pp. 656-57, 836.

9. James Sloan Gibbons, *The Banks of New-York, Their Dealers, The Clearing House, and the Panic of 1857* (New York: D. Appleton and Co., 1859), pp. 9, 428; W. H. Dilliston, comp., *Historical Directory of the Banks of the State of New York* (New York: New York State Bankers Association, 1947), pp. 16, 57, 70.

10. *COM*, p. 836; Carl F. Price, *Wesleyan's First Century with an Account of the Centennial Celebration* (Middletown, Conn.: Wesleyan University, 1932), pp. 134-35; Obituary, "Andrew Varick Stout." Stout was a Wesleyan University trustee in the mid-1860s (probably at the time Roberts met him) and again from 1877 on, and was president of the Board of Trustees for one year (1881) (Price, p. 135). He also served as trustee and benefactor ($40,000) of Drew Theological Seminary. Carlton is listed as a trustee of the Shoe and Leather Bank (271 Broadway) for 1874 in J. Disturnell, comp., *Business Manual, or Monetary Directory* (New York and Philadelphia: n.p., 1874), but it isn't clear when he became a director or how long he served.

11. McCabe, *Great Fortunes*, p. 137. Stout died in 1883.

12. Donald B. Marti, "Rich Methodists: The Rise and Consequences of Lay Philanthropy in the

With the organization of the Free Methodist Church, Benjamin and Ellen Roberts embarked upon the most remarkable and productive period of their long copartnership in ministry. Benjamin's ministry as editor, author, revivalist, and general superintendent and chief strategist for the growing Free Methodist Church was more visible than was Ellen's. But she was occupied also as a busy mother, editorial assistant (in effect) for the *Earnest Christian,* and inner-city worker.

Throughout this busy period Benjamin and Ellen often felt sustained and supported by God's Spirit. But a major part of their fruitfulness during this period was due also to the mutual encouragement they gave one another — as seen, for example, in the constant flow of correspondence between them when Benjamin (or occasionally Ellen) was traveling and far from home.

The thirty-three-year period until Benjamin's premature death in 1893 saw the growth of Free Methodism as a movement — expanding west across the continent, founding churches, starting schools and colleges. This chapter focuses particularly on the first decade following the key events of 1860.

Based in Buffalo (1860-64)

Benjamin's ministry in Buffalo included the supervision of the new Free Methodist congregations there and his editorial work on the *Earnest Christian.* Soon several others were working with him as the first group of Free Methodist pastors and other workers began to form.

On November 8, 1860, the "Eastern Convention" of the Free Methodist Church met at Rushford, New York (as noted in chapter 25). This was in effect the organizing convention of what became the Genesee Conference of the new denomination. It was the beginning of the formation of regional conferences within the larger church body. In this the Free Methodist Church largely duplicated Methodist Episcopal organization, though in a more democratic and participatory form.

Sixteen preachers and thirteen delegates composed the organizing core of the new conference.[13] Roberts himself was enrolled as one of the ordained preachers, along with Loren Stiles, John W. Reddy, and three others. Ten new preachers were "admitted on probation," including Daniel Sinclair, Moses N. Downing, J. B. Freeland, A. A. Phelps, and James Mathews. The conference was organized into two districts, and preachers appointed. Benjamin commented,

---

Mid–Nineteenth Century," in *Perspectives on American Methodism: Interpretive Essays,* ed. Russell E. Richey, Kenneth E. Rowe, and Jean Miller Schmidt (Nashville: Kingswood, 1993), pp. 265-76.

13. [B. T. Roberts], "Free Methodist Convention," *EC* 1, no. 12 (Dec. 1860): 392-93; Hogue, *HFMC,* 1:337; BHR, *BTR,* p. 241. B. T. Roberts (and Benson, using this source) says the convention "was composed of fourteen lay delegates, and fourteen preachers," but Hogue's account, which gives names, seems to be more accurate. Writing in the *Earnest Christian,* B. T. Roberts no doubt wanted to signal the principle of equal "lay" and "ministerial" representation in church government that the new denomination had adopted.

The district chairmen were authorized to employ ten other preachers. Still all the places that called for preachers could not be supplied. Men full of faith and the Holy Ghost, who seek not their own ease or profit, but the salvation of souls, are in great demand. Though in its infancy, the Free Methodist Church could profitably employ a hundred such men. In the work of soul-saving — in trying to reach the masses, and lead them by the way of the Cross to Heaven, there is too little competition among the "leading denominations" of our country.

There appears to be a very general tendency to display. Fine edifices, fine musical instruments, fine singing, and fine sermons, are all the rage. Be it ever the business of the Free Methodists to preach the Gospel to the poor, and hold out to all the self-denying doctrines of Christ.[14]

The convention appointed Mathews to Thirteenth Street, Buffalo, and S. K. J. Chesbrough, assisted by others, to supply the new congregation meeting in the converted Pearl Street Theater, now designated the Second Free Methodist Church in Buffalo. Sam Chesbrough was among a growing number of unordained preachers who served as "supplies" in caring for or establishing new Free Methodist congregations. Benjamin wrote, "The preachers went to their appointments with, we believe, the determination to have revivals of religion."[15]

When the new conference (or "convention," as it was still called) met in annual session a year later, the results were gratifying. Membership (including probationers) had grown to 1,667; church property valued at $24,800 had been acquired; and the number of appointments increased. Four MEC preachers — Asa Abell, Albert G. Terry, Cornelius D. Brooks, and Levi Wood — became Free Methodists, as did John C. Thomas, who came from the Evangelical Lutheran Church.[16]

Meanwhile Benjamin was gratified that the first "free church" he had established in Buffalo in the old Pearl Street Theater (Second FM Church) continued to grow, ministering to a downtown mixed-ethnic neighborhood. Roberts reported in February 1862,

> One year ago last October, the building on Pearl street, near Niagara [Street], was dedicated for a Free Methodist Church. We organized with seven members. The work has been steadily advancing ever since. For nearly a year, scarcely a week has elapsed without some souls being saved. . . . The last quarter, over thirty have been received on probation. We have now 101 members, and a congregation as large as can be crowded into the church [which seated nearly 600], and many go away for want of room. Many of the members profess, and we believe enjoy, the blessing of

14. [B. T. Roberts], "Free Methodist Convention," p. 392. The somewhat appositive use here of "the masses" and "the poor" suggests that in Roberts's mind the two were nearly synonymous, or at least closely related.

15. [B. T. Roberts], "Free Methodist Convention," p. 393; Hogue, *HFMC*, 1:337; BHR, *BTR*, p. 243.

16. BHR, *BTR*, p. 267; [B. T. Roberts], report on "The Genesee Convention," *EC* 2, no. 11 (Nov. 1861): 355. Abell, Terry, and Brooks came from the Genesee Conference of the ME Church, while Wood came from the East Genesee Conference.

holiness. Several Swedes, and a number of Germans, have been converted among us. We have had, at one time, representatives of five different nations at our altar. Salvation is alike precious to all, and all are alike welcome.[17]

During this busy period Roberts, though continuing to travel as Free Methodist general superintendent, found time to open a mission above a saloon in Buffalo's notorious Five Points area. Here, he said, "almost every building . . . has a brothel and a bar."[18] He later described Five Points as "a place which was as near hell as any place I ever saw. Almost every house was a saloon, and it was made up of the worst class of people on earth."[19]

The place was a few blocks from the old Pearl Street Theater, now the Free Methodist church building in downtown Buffalo.

Five Points was at the heart of the busy port area, near the terminus of the Erie Canal where goods were constantly shipped back and forth between canal boats, lake steamers, and the railroads. The young Herman Melville, four years Roberts's senior, visited this area in 1840 and was reminded of Liverpool.[20] Another visitor spoke of the "steam-boat men, sailors, canallers, . . . mingled with some of the wilder young clerks from the forwarding house and 'stores'" who caroused with women of the district. "The captains, pilots, engineers, clerks, and runners of [the] steamboats were characters — generous, impulsive, reckless, extravagant, they formed a very curious society."[21] David Gerber in *The Making of an American Pluralism* says Buffalo's port culture

> joined laborers, sailors, canallers, vagabonds, and travelers to a number of services — cheap lodging houses and eateries, saloons . . . , gambling dens, and broth-

17. [B. T. Roberts], "The Free Church in Buffalo," *EC* 3, no. 2 (Feb. 1862): 63. By "nations" Roberts probably means Germans, Italians, Irish, Swedes, etc. He reported that while "The preacher is supported, and the incidental expenses kept up," a debt of about $1,800 remained on the building and lot. In 1868 the church's trustees decided to sell the building and relocate, due to the poor condition of the old theater building; "it was recorded that they would not hold further meetings in the audience room until repairs were made on the roof" (Wesley R. Wilder, ed., *Genesee Conference History, Free Methodist Church, 1860-1959* [n.p.: n.p, 1958], p. 27). The congregation constructed a new building at the corner of Virginia and Tenth Streets, about six blocks northwest (three blocks east of Niagara Street), and on moving to the new location in 1869 changed the name to First Free Methodist Church. It remained in this location until 1921. On the later history of this congregation, see Wilder, pp. 28-29.

18. [B. T. Roberts], "A Mission Field," *EC* 3, no. 6 (June 1862): 187.

19. B. T. Roberts, "Sermon," *EC* 45, no. 1 (Jan. 1883): 7. The sermon was given at the 1882 FM General Conference.

20. Hershel Parker, *Herman Melville: A Biography*, vol. 1, *1819-1851* (Baltimore: Johns Hopkins University Press, 1996), p. 174.

21. Thomas Low Nichols, M.D., *Forty Years of American Life, 1821-1861* (1864; New York: Stackpole Sons, 1937), pp. 103-4, 100. Nichols tells of Ned Christy, an entertainer in Buffalo's canal district, who "not long afterwards organized the first make-believe negro band of singers and musicians as Christy's Minstrels. . . . A few months afterwards [around 1850] his minstrels were all the rage in New York, where they attracted overflowing houses for years, and made a handsome fortune for Ned Christy" (p. 104); cf. Edwin G. Burrows and Mike Wallace, *Gotham: A History of New York City to 1898* (New York: Oxford University Press, 1999), p. 758.

els. . . . The center of the port culture was what contemporary editors revealingly called "the infected district," a twelve-block area just up from the water, in the middle of which some streets formed a "five points" conjuncture, providing endless opportunities for comparison to the more notorious New York City slum. This area was a particular source of embarrassment for respectable folk, who found it necessary to pass through it when going between the docks, the central business district, and . . . the railroad stations.[22]

Roberts described this area "between the canal and the lake" as one "where Satan reigns supreme," "the very vestibule of hell!" "Here drunkenness, debauchery, gambling, robbery and fighting are the order of the day."[23] He wrote, "In some respects it is a more heart sickening, ruinous place than the noted Five Points of New York. . . . Here sailors and boatmen spend their hard earned wages. Here clerks, and merchants, and mechanics, and young men from the city, and young men from the country lay the foundation of a ruin more terrible than any war or commercial disaster ever wrought."[24]

Benjamin, probably assisted by Ellen and other workers, began ministry at Five Points in the spring of 1862. Ellen had a young baby in her arms, or at home; Samuel Roberts (perhaps named for Sam Chesbrough) had been born on January 19, joining older brothers George (ten), Benson (eight), and Charles (five and a half).[25]

The previous summer (1861) Roberts and his associates (probably including James Mathews)[26] occasionally preached on the dock not far from Five Points. A boatman who attended these meetings was "partially awakened" and later, when he took sick, called "for some of our people to go and pray with him," Roberts wrote. The man was soundly converted. "The noise of singing, and praying, and shouting, brought many in from the adjoining saloons," and Benjamin saw this as a providential opening to begin a mission at Five Points.[27] He reported in June 1862, "We visited among and prayed with [people of the Five Points area], and on looking around, found, over a saloon [on Canal Street] a large hall which apparently stood waiting for us to occupy. We hired it at ten dollars a month — seated it and commenced meetings. We needed no bell — the sound of praise and prayer . . . was sufficient at any time, to draw a large congregation. We have held meetings five Sabbaths and some week days. Five females, and two young men have been clearly saved, as the visible result of these meetings."[28]

---

22. David A. Gerber, *The Making of an American Pluralism: Buffalo, New York, 1825-60* (Urbana: University of Illinois Press, 1989), pp. 14-15.

23. [B. T. Roberts], "A Mission Field," *EC* 3, no. 6 (June 1862): 187; "Canal Street Mission," *EC* 4, no. 5 (Nov. 1862): 155.

24. [B. T. Roberts], "A Mission Field," pp. 187-88.

25. Smail, p. 12; Carpenter, p. 76. The sources give no middle name for Samuel.

26. Benson Roberts says with reference apparently to late 1860, "Meantime Rev. Jas. Mathews was caring for the work in Buffalo, preaching on the docks each Sunday in addition to the regular church services." BHR, *BTR*, p. 240.

27. [B. T. Roberts], "A Mission Field," pp. 187-88.

28. [B. T. Roberts], "A Mission Field," p. 188.

Benjamin and Ellen felt a safe house must be provided for the young women who were converted. So they provided them "a home in our family, until the way is opened for them to take care of themselves in a respectable manner," Benjamin reported. He appealed for Christian sisters to help by taking these young women into their families, "looking after them, caring for them, and helping them on in the way to heaven. . . . Many of them are quite young, and to hear the sad stories of the wrongs they suffered, which brought ruin upon them, would make your hearts bleed."[29]

Roberts's sense of justice and indignation was aroused by the way these girls had been victimized — reminding one of William and Catherine Booth's reaction to a similar situation in London somewhat later. "In the great day of retribution," Benjamin wrote, "the hottest billows of fiery damnation will be reserved for the wretches who [lead] virtuous females into the path of sin."[30]

What did Benjamin mean when he said he and Ellen gave these rescued young women "a home in our family"? Benjamin and Ellen did not have a home of their own in Buffalo at this time. It appears they were sharing a house with other Free Methodist workers, living in a sort of community. Mathews recalled later that after Benjamin and Ellen sold their house they lived with the Mathewses for a time in a house owned by Edward Cox. "Brother and Sister Roberts put their furniture in it, and we all lived together that winter [apparently the winter of 1860]. They traveled up and down the land coming home occasionally."[31] It is not clear where (or with whom) Benjamin and Ellen and their family were living when the Canal Street Mission was started a year or so later.

Since Benjamin was traveling much of this time in the interests of the spreading denomination, it appears that Ellen provided the primary leadership at the Canal Street Mission. Benjamin wrote to her from Spencerport on May 2, 1862, "Darling you have a great work to do for the Lord, and I pray often for you that you may have all the grace you need. . . . Look after your mission and have the brethren get new seats."[32]

Recalling this significant ministry some twenty years later, Benjamin remembered, "When the room was crowded full I have seen them all melted to tears and bowing in prayer. Some of the hardest of them were converted and lived converted lives. You cannot go where the love of God has not gone before you by his blessed Spirit to lead sinners to Christ."[33]

Roberts saw his work in leading early Free Methodism as a form of preaching the gospel to the poor. When the denomination was formed, he wrote that it had become

---

29. [B. T. Roberts], "A Mission Field," p. 188; BHR, *BTR*, pp. 217-19, 308; Zahniser, pp. 208-10.

30. [B. T. Roberts], "A Mission Field," p. 188.

31. James Matthews, "Benjamin T. Roberts As I Knew Him," *EC* 65, no. 4 (Apr. 1893): 106.

32. Quoted in BHR, *BTR*, p. 294.

33. B. T. Roberts, "Sermon," p. 7.

necessary to provide a humble shelter, for ourselves, and for such poor, wayfaring pilgrims as may wish to journey with us to heaven. We are very firm in the conviction that it is the will of the Lord that we should establish free churches — *the seats to be forever free* — where the Gospel can be preached to the poor. . . . We have no men of commanding ability and influence to help on the enterprise — no wealth, no sympathy from powerful ecclesiastical, or political, or secret societies; but all these against us — so that if we succeed, it must be by the blessings of Heaven upon our feeble endeavors.[34]

Benjamin reported in October 1862 that both the Free Methodist church in downtown Buffalo and the Canal Street Mission were progressing. Many had been saved at the "FREE church, where the poor have the Gospel preached unto them"; the congregation now had 106 members, "poor in this world but rich in faith." Meanwhile the mission at Five Points — "a place that is as truly missionary ground as any . . . in India or China" — had already produced good "beyond our anticipations" and promised, "if properly followed up, a rich harvest." Roberts appealed for funds, noting that he had personally spent over sixty dollars on the Five Points work and received gifts of only seventeen dollars. At this point he was carrying the financial load both of this mission in Buffalo and of the *Earnest Christian*. "For all expenses incurred [at Five Points] we alone are responsible," he wrote. "We now find ourselves out of funds with which to pay rent, publish the Earnest Christian, and meet our other necessary expenses. A number of our subscribers have not yet paid for the current volume of the Earnest Christian and Golden Rule. We need it now."[35]

The Canal Street Mission was indeed both a great challenge and a great opportunity. Benjamin was spread too thin, however, to give it much attention. In November 1862 he reported: "We have not been able to give it the personal supervision we desired, our duties calling us away most of the time." But meetings continued, and "at times the Holy Spirit has been poured out in a remarkable manner." Some were converted; "others have been led to abandon the place and seek their livelihood by reputable means." Yet the ministry was "greatly crippled" by the lack of means and workers. Benjamin added,

> We have no doubt that by this time more than twenty females could have been reclaimed from a life of vice, if there had been a place where they could have found a home, and some Christian counsel and help as their cases demanded. But we have not been able to provide one. There are probably but few cities of the size of Buffalo, where prostitution and its kindred vices more abound, and we know of none but that has its Magdalen Asylum where the penitent wanderer may find refuge and assistance. But Buffalo has none. No effort except our feeble one has been made to save those that are ready to perish.

34. [B. T. Roberts], "Convention at Pekin," *EC* 1, no. 9 (Sept. 1860): 292.

35. [B. T. Roberts], "Our Wants," *EC* 4, no. 4 (Oct. 1862): 124. At the same time, Roberts expressed "not the slightest doubt" that the magazine would continue and would receive adequate support. It does not appear that he was in any financial crisis; this was a not untypical fund-raising appeal.

Benjamin went on to appeal for help to establish "a home for those erring ones who would be glad to return to the paths of virtue."[36]

The Traveling Superintendent — the Busy Mother

Growth and revival marked these early days of Free Methodism. As Benjamin took up the reins as general superintendent, he received encouraging reports from various points in the expanding Free Methodist network. Joseph Goodwin Terrill wrote from Ogle, Illinois, in late 1860 to tell of new groups organized and many conversions. Moses Downing reported from West Kendall, New York: "A powerful work of God is in progress. . . . upwards of fifty souls have been converted to God." Amos Curry sent word in January 1861, "The work is going on in power. . . . There is a general awakening all through the community." A. B. Burdick wrote in February, "The Lord is with us in convicting, converting and sanctifying power. We have organized two classes since I last wrote you."[37]

Word of the new movement was broadcast through the monthly issues of the *Earnest Christian*. Benson Roberts noted, "Reports spread all over the land of the work God was doing through these men and women, consecrated even to be thrust out of the church of their choice, because of their stand against formality and worldliness in the church. As a result, letters came from unknown persons in distant regions."[38]

Much of Roberts's work as general superintendent was essentially revival ministry. He held extended meetings in a number of the new Free Methodist churches and spent most of his summers in camp meeting work. In the summer of 1861 he preached at the Bergen and St. Charles camp meetings, among others.[39] Returning from the "West," he reported that after nearly a year of Free Methodism the work was growing steadily. "Nearly every appointment of the Free Methodists has been visited by the outpouring of the Holy Spirit. The number of our members has, we judge, nearly doubled from conversions alone."[40]

The annual Bergen camp meeting in these early years continued to serve as a major focal point of the Free Methodist Church and the larger movement it represented. Benjamin wrote after the 1862 gathering, where over one hundred reportedly were converted:

The Bergen Camp Meeting is *the great* Camp Meeting of Western New York. The saints of God come together here from all quarters, and from great distances. The attendance this year, as usual, was large. There were, it is said by those who

36. [B. T. Roberts], "Canal Street Mission," *EC* 4, no. 5 (Nov. 1862): 155.
37. BHR, *BTR*, pp. 244-51.
38. BHR, *BTR*, p. 255.
39. BHR, *BTR*, pp. 260, 262.
40. [B. T. Roberts], "Visit to the West," *EC* 2, no. 7 (July 1861): 224.

counted them, sixty-six tents on the ground — most of them of large size. The weather was rainy, a portion of the time, but this it was thought had a beneficial effect upon the meeting. Instead of one service at the stand where but few comparatively could take an active part, many were held at the same time in different tents, a good deal of close work could be done, and a much larger number were probably saved than would have been, if the weather had been pleasant.[41]

As opportunities arose, Roberts ventured farther east into areas beyond the bounds of the old Genesee Conference of the ME Church. In 1861-62 he held meetings in New York City and in upstate cities such as Binghamton, Syracuse, Utica, and Rome. His ministry was fruitful, and as a result he organized the second Free Methodist conference in New York State, the Susquehanna Conference, on April 10, 1862, at Union, New York. While this was a natural move and consistent with Roberts's assigned role as general superintendent, it sparked some controversy in the infant denomination. Roberts had not thought to include in the Free Methodist *Discipline* a process for organizing new conferences, and some Free Methodist preachers felt he was usurping undue authority. The controversy erupted in the denomination's 1862 General Conference — its first since the organizing convention of 1860. As a result, a provision was written into the *Discipline* empowering the general superintendent to "form new Conferences in the intervals of General Conference" when necessary, provided he had the concurrence of two-thirds of an executive committee that was formed to work with him.[42]

Despite this controversy over organizing new conferences — and, perhaps, partly because of it — the 1862 General Conference took one action of far-reaching significance. How was the extension of the church beyond its initial borders in New York and Illinois to be planned and financed? At its last Tuesday afternoon sitting the conference passed the following motion: "Resolved that the following brethren, to wit, B. T. Roberts, Joseph Travis, Thomas Sully, be a committee to draft a constitution for a Missionary Society of the Free Methodist Church: And to secure its incorporation by the legislature of New York . . . to receive legacies in different states; . . . The General Superintendent was elected president, Rev. Orson P. Raper, secretary, and Brother C. T. Hicks. . . ."[43]

The vision was missionary, though at this point the focus was almost entirely on North America. As Byron Lamson notes, "The work of the Missionary Society was primarily that of what we now call evangelism and church extension. Twelve years later, the General Conference enlarged the society and changed its name to General

---

41. [B. T. Roberts], "Camp Meetings," *EC* 4, no. 2 (Aug. 1862): 61-62. As noted earlier, in 1858 the total number of tents was 104 (and weekend attendance was estimated at five thousand), and in 1861 there were 65 tents.

42. BHR, *BTR*, pp. 272-75; *The Doctrines and Discipline of the Free Methodist Church* (Rochester: General Conference, 1870), pp. 48-49.

43. Minutes, 1862 General Conference, quoted in Byron S. Lamson, *Venture! The Frontiers of Free Methodism* (Winona Lake, Ind.: Light and Life, 1960), pp. 18-19.

Missionary Board."[44] This laid the foundation for the remarkable foreign missionary expansion of the denomination later in the century.

The adjournment of the 1862 General Conference did not fully settle the
Susquehanna issue, even though it paved the way for its resolution. The final settlement came only after months of stormy wrangling and disagreement instigated by
those who felt Roberts had overstepped his authority. The dispute could well have
split the infant denomination. In the end Benjamin's tact and patience won out,
however, and peace was restored. Roberts met the crisis with "a Christ-like spirit, exemplifying the grace that [he] preached," Benson later wrote.[45]

Other issues were percolating in the denomination, including the question of
the role of women. Over Roberts's objections, the 1861 Genesee Conference took action forbidding "female preaching," though it endorsed other "female labors" such
as "prayer, personal testimony, or exhortation." The conference took the position
that "woman is not designed for the office of the holy ministry" and that public
preaching "clashes with the ordinary duties and relations of the female sex." Clearly
the underlying problem was the issue of authority and office.

Roberts did not agree with this conference action. In time the Genesee Conference had at least a partial change of heart, however, and began licensing women as
local preachers, though not ordaining them.[46]

Nazarite fanaticism on the fringes of Free Methodism was another problem for
a couple of years, though it gradually died out. Commenting on the August 1861
Pekin camp meeting, Benjamin wrote in his diary, "There is among those who set
out with us a class who style themselves Nazarites, in distinction from the Free
Methodists. They are led by the Rev. J. McCreery, William Cooley, A. Reddy and
H. H. Farnsworth. They are pious, devoted, and some of them profess strong faith.
They are — some of them at least — opposed to church organization, especially the
Free Methodist Church."[47]

One Nazarite sister said at a camp meeting service that God told her to say that
Brother Roberts had a devil and that Brother Abell had been preaching for the devil
from the beginning of the camp![48] McCreery, however, and some of the others soon
renounced the fanaticism and became active in the Free Methodist Church (as noted
earlier).

Roberts's handling of these various issues was a test and sign of his character
and his leadership. While some early Free Methodists opposed women preachers,
others with Nazarite leanings felt that women preaching or speaking in public services was evidence of the moving of the Holy Spirit. Roberts shunned both extremes.
Hearing Sister Freeland and Sister Smith speak at the 1861 Pekin camp meeting, he

44. Lamson, *Venture!* p. 19.

45. BHR, *BTR*, p. 290. Benson Roberts presents the Susquehanna Conference issue in some detail
(pp. 276-91).

46. BHR, *BTR*, p. 326; Hogue, *HFMC*, 1:344-45.

47. BTRD, Aug. 16, 1861, quoted in BHR, *BTR*, p. 321.

48. BTRD, Aug. 20, 1861, cited in BHR, *BTR*, pp. 322-23.

was convinced God was speaking through them. "I cannot, to please anybody, lay my hands on those whom God uses for the salvation of souls." Yet he saw the fallacy in the Nazarite position. The Nazarites "appear to seek reproach and to glory in it rather than [seeking] purity and power," he said. "They exalt being 'led by the Spirit' above the Bible, sometimes claiming Divine inspiration for doing things which the Word of God especially forbids."[49]

Roberts saw the need for balance, wisdom, and the guidance of the Holy Spirit in dealing with these issues. Here he was following in the footsteps of John Wesley, who maintained a "dialectical tension," as David Hempton calls it, "between enlightenment and enthusiasm." Hempton shows how Wesley and early Methodism "flirted with the edge of religious enthusiasm, but had some powerful restraining Impulses; it came across to outsiders as fundamentally irrational, but it had deep roots in reasonableness if not rationality."[50] Grounded in Wesley and in Methodist history, Roberts understood this and sought to hold Free Methodism to the same course.

On one of his trips east to New York City in 1862, Benjamin took time to visit Phoebe Palmer's Tuesday Meeting at the Palmer home, as well as other meetings for holiness. Roberts wrote of his visit to "this great and wicked city": "While sin stalks abroad with unblushing air, and the evidence[s] of defection in the churches from the gospel standard are but too apparent, yet there are many who are striving to walk closely with the Lord. Several meetings for holiness are held weekly both in New York and Brooklyn, and they are, we learn, generally well attended."

On Tuesday Roberts went to the Palmers' "spacious rooms at 54 Rivington street" and found a large crowd gathered. He felt "a good spirit prevailed. A large number professed to enjoy the blessing of holiness, and many arose expressing a desire to seek it."[51]

Roberts also attended a Wednesday afternoon holiness meeting at the home of "the Rev. William Belden, a Presbyterian minister, 32 Bond street."[52] Belden was the son of Henry Belden, a Presbyterian and then, after 1844, Congregational minister who was entirely sanctified and became a holiness advocate, and who had some association with Phoebe Palmer as well.[53] (Roberts later recruited him as a trustee for

49. BTRD, Aug. 16 and 19, 1861, quoted in BHR, *BTR*, pp. 321-22.

50. David Hempton, *Methodism: Empire of the Spirit* (New Haven: Yale University Press, 2005), pp. 32-54.

51. [B. T. Roberts], "Holiness in New York," *EC* 3, no. 3 (Mar. 1862): 98.

52. [B. T. Roberts], "Holiness in New York," p. 98. In September 1862 D. F. Newton also reported a meeting "at Rev. Wm. Belden's, No. 32 Bond street," New York. [D. F. Newton], "Meeting for Holiness," *EC* 4, no. 3 (Sept. 1862): 94.

53. In 1862 Roberts published an account of a sister named Margaret that Henry Belden contributed to the *Earnest Christian,* and also another brief piece by Belden. See Henry Belden, "As Ye Go Preach," *EC* 3, no. 6 (June 1862): 169-71; Rev. Henry Belden, "Jesus and I," *EC* 4, no. 1 (July 1862): 27. Belden's personal testimony of entire sanctification is included in Phoebe Palmer, ed., *Pioneer Experiences; or, The Gift of Power Received by Faith* (New York: W. C. Palmer, Jr., 1868), pp. 109-18. See also

Chili Seminary.)[54] On Friday Roberts met with "the pilgrim band of laborers" (that is, the small group of Free Methodists and others who sympathized with Roberts) at Belden's home. Here he found "a greater degree of simplicity, plainness, freedom and power, than in any other meeting" he attended in New York. He also preached in two Methodist Episcopal churches while in the city.[55]

Although Roberts appreciated Phoebe Palmer's ministry, he added a comment that implied some criticism of the kind of professed holiness he saw in New York. "Pride and worldly conformity are utterly inconsistent with real holiness. Whosoever is not sufficiently consecrated to God, to lay aside their 'gold, and pearls, and costly array' for Jesus' sake, may presumptuously talk of enjoying full salvation, but it is impossible for them to exercise saving faith in Christ."[56]

On such visits to New York City, Benjamin often took the ferry across to Brooklyn, then a separate city, where he had friends and contacts, and where the poet Walt Whitman lived. He often saw the scenes Whitman pictured in his poem "Crossing Brooklyn Ferry." Approaching New York from Brooklyn at sundown, Whitman described "the shipping of Manhattan north and west, and the heights of Brooklyn to the south and east." "Ah, what can ever be more stately and admirable to me than mast-hemm'd Manhattan?" Imagining people surveying the scene years later, Whitman wrote,

> Just as you look on the numberless masts of ships and the
>   thick-stemm'd pipes of steamboats, I look'd.
> . . . .
> Look'd on the vapor as it flew in fleeces tinged with violet,
> Look'd toward the lower bay to notice the vessels arriving,
> Saw their approach, saw aboard those that were near me,
> Saw the white sails of schooners and sloops, saw the ships at anchor,
> The sailors at work in the rigging or out astride the spars,
> The round masts, the swinging motion of the hulls, the slender serpentine
>   pennants,

Kostlevy, p. 18; Melvin Easterday Dieter, *The Holiness Revival of the Nineteenth Century* (Metuchen, N.J.: Scarecrow Press, 1980), pp. 38, 80, 120; Richard Wheatley, *The Life and Letters of Mrs. Phoebe Palmer* (New York: W. C. Palmer, 1881; New York: Garland, 1984), pp. 267, 578-79. Henry Belden was born in Connecticut in 1810 and died in New York City on June 24, 1884. Kostlevy says he became pastor of the Free Church in New York City in 1852 and "served as a city missionary in Brooklyn (1856-1866)." In 1862 he participated in the camp meeting at Union, near Binghamton, where Roberts also was present ([B. T. Roberts], "Camp Meetings," p. 62). The August 1884 *Guide to Holiness* noted his death and said his funeral was "conducted at the residence of his son, William Belden, 841, Fifth Ave., New York" (p. 59). Presumably Roberts's references to William Belden are thus to Henry Belden's son, though conceivably there could have been a different William Belden.

54. *The First Annual Catalogue and Circular of the Chili Seminary, 1869-70* (Rochester, N.Y.: "Earnest Christian" Office, 1870), p. 3, and subsequent catalogues.

55. [B. T. Roberts], "Holiness in New York," p. 98.

56. [B. T. Roberts], "Holiness in New York," p. 98. Roberts quoted John 5:44 as the scriptural basis for this statement.

The large and small steamers in motion, the pilots in their pilot-houses,
The white wake left by the passage, the quick tremulous whirl of the wheels,
The flags of all nations, the falling of them at sunset,
The scallop-edged waves in the twilight, the ladled cups,
    the frolicsome crests and glistening,
The stretch afar growing dimmer and dimmer, the gray walls of the granite
    storehouses by the docks,
On the river the shadowy group, the big steam-tug closely flank'd
    on each side by the barges, the hay-boat, the belated lighter,
On the neighboring shore the fires from the foundry chimneys
    burning high and glaringly into the night,
Casting their flicker of black contrasted with wild red and yellow light
    over the tops of houses, and down into the clefts of streets.[57]

This was the scene Roberts witnessed many times during his years of traveling.

As time went on his ministry increasingly took him west as Free Methodism grew and its boundaries expanded. The last few pages of the *Earnest Christian* often contained summaries of these travels.

On a trip to Michigan to attend camp meetings in the summer of 1864 (toward the end of the Civil War), Benjamin stayed overnight at Oberlin, Ohio.[58] He reported in a letter to Ellen,

> The Oberlin people are very strong anti-slavery people, and go all lengths in behalf of the slave. I was at a meeting there yesterday. Heard Professor [John] Morgan preach a very good sermon. Professor [Charles] Finney made a few remarks and prayed. They had a prayer-meeting in the afternoon, but it was all about our national affairs. I do not know but we are too much taken up with our own personal salvation, and fail in taking as deep an interest as we should in the affairs of the day. . . . President Finney and his co-adjutors commenced in the woods with their school twenty-five years ago, and they certainly have done a great work for the world. They have now about six hundred students in the various departments of their school. We must pray more about our contemplated school, and ascertain what the will of the Lord touching it is.[59]

57. Walt Whitman, *Leaves of Grass,* 1892 ed. (New York: Bantam Books, 1983), pp. 128-32. The poem was originally called "Sun-Down Poem" and has been interpreted both literally and metaphorically; see Justin Kaplan, *Walt Whitman, a Life* (New York: Simon and Schuster, 1980), pp. 80, 158, 222. Whitman's years nearly match Roberts's; he was born in 1819 and died in 1892.

58. Roberts stayed overnight at the home of "Miss Rawson, a cousin of sister Newton" (presumably David F. Newton's wife).

59. BTR (Coldwater, Mich.) to ELR, June 2, 1864, quoted in BHR, *BTR,* pp. 348-49. John Morgan, professor of Bible and church history at Oberlin Collegiate Institute, was a close friend of Finney's. He had formerly taught at Lane Seminary in Cincinnati and had supported the antislavery student activism there, costing him his job. Charles E. Hambrick-Stowe, *Charles G. Finney and the Spirit of American Evangelicalism* (Grand Rapids: Eerdmans, 1996), pp. 167, 298; Lawrence Thomas Lesick, *The Lane Rebels: Evangelicalism and Antislavery in Antebellum America* (Metuchen, N.J.: Scarecrow Press, 1980), pp. 119, 138, 171.

It was just at this time that Benjamin and Ellen were thinking of starting the school that was to become Chili Seminary.

Occasionally in his travels "on the cars" Roberts would run into former MEC colleagues. Someone asked him what he did in such circumstances. "I make right for them, shake hands, ask after their health, and act as though nothing unpleasant had ever happened," Benjamin replied.[60]

Although Ellen sometimes traveled with Benjamin, most of the time she was at home in Buffalo or, later, North Chili. In addition to child rearing and caring for Benjamin when he was home, Ellen's major ministry seems to have been handling correspondence. Her diary shows her spending many hours writing letters, probably including assisting Benjamin with the *Earnest Christian* and helping to maintain the expanding Free Methodist network. Her extensive personal correspondence shows that she played a key networking role among women in the stormy days of earliest Free Methodism. Questions of healings, spiritual gifts, and women's preaching were hotly discussed. Ellen stressed openness to the gifts and leadings of the Spirit and encouraged women to speak in public when God prompted them. She was highly valued as a spiritual counselor, and the respect in which B. T. was held gave additional weight to her words.[61]

When Ellen was able to travel with Benjamin, she often assisted him through public words of exhortation or private counsel. Sometimes when they were ministering at camp meetings, Ellen would conduct the class meetings, which presumably were experience meetings held during the camps.[62]

Ellen's work as Benjamin's partner naturally brought an expanding circle of friends into her life. Adella Carpenter noted that Ellen "numbered among her close friends members of many denominations. Rev. and Mrs. William Belden, Rev. Henry Belden, Rev. D. F. Newton, Miss Mary H. Mossman and others shared her hospitality and proved valued friends."[63]

The Passing of Redfield, Stiles, and Isaac Chesbrough

Three figures prominent in the birth of the Free Methodist Church died within months of each other in 1863, when the denomination was about three years old. While one, Isaac Chesbrough, was a patriarch, the other two, Loren Stiles and John Wesley Redfield, were relatively young. One of the imponderables of history is what difference it would have made to the later fortunes of Free Methodism had Stiles and Redfield (and also William Kendall, who died five years earlier) survived for another ten or twenty years. How would they have shaped Free Methodism?

60. BHR, *BTR*, p. 359.

61. This key networking role is borne out particularly in Ellen's 1859-62 correspondence with Martha Frances Kendall, Emeline Smith, Minerva Cooley, Jane Dunning, and others. Letters in RFP.

62. Rev. B. Winget, "Mrs. Ellen L. Roberts," *EC* 95, no. 3 (Mar. 1908): 90.

63. Carpenter, p. 76.

Chesbrough, the father of Samuel K. J. Chesbrough, died early in 1863. Stiles, still pastoring at Albion, died of typhoid fever on May 7. He was only forty-two. William Hosmer of the *Northern Independent* preached his funeral sermon at Albion with "many hundreds standing upon the outside, unable to gain admission."[64]

Six months after Stiles's death — on November 2 — Redfield passed away at the home of Osgood Joslyn, near Marengo, Illinois, where he had been staying since suffering a stroke three years earlier.[65] He was fifty-three. He had been able to write his long, 425-page memoir (in effect, an autobiography) before he died; this became the basis for J. G. Terrill's *Life of Rev. John Wesley Redfield, M.D.*

The last months of Redfield's life were especially sad. After his stroke in late 1860, Redfield gradually deteriorated physically and, eventually, mentally. He suffered great mental and spiritual anguish over the question of why God did not heal him. He occasionally tried to preach but eventually had to give that up altogether. These circumstances put great strain on Mrs. Redfield and on the Joslyn family in Marengo, where he spent his last months.

Ill though he was, Redfield was elected to deacon's orders and ordained in the Free Methodist Church in June 1861 at the Western Convention, held in conjunction with the St. Charles camp meeting. At this time Redfield was "palsied" (i.e., paralyzed) and "almost helpless," wrote Terrill.[66] Roberts, apparently, ordained Redfield, who had been his mentor, at the public ordination service on the last day of the camp. "That day will never be forgotten," Roberts wrote. "The power and the glory of God rested upon the preachers and the people. The influence of that day will, we trust, be felt in eternity."[67] Since Redfield was now essentially incapacitated, the ordination came more as recognition of his completed ministry than as a commission to service. His two decades of revival preaching in the Methodist Episcopal Church had been as an unordained local preacher; now he was an ordained minister in the Free Methodist Church.

The last twenty pages or so of Redfield's memoir, covering 1862 and the first few days of 1863, are full of his anguish and struggle, though they also contain some profound and eloquent reflections on pain and its place in the Christian's life. Redfield meditated deeply on the sufferings of Jesus Christ, and on Job.

In February 1862 Redfield received, he said, "one of my special revelations," instructing him that he must "return to Syracuse N.Y. & repeat my efforts for a special revival of religion after the type of Pentecost."[68] Redfield felt he could not do this in his paralyzed state, yet he felt God was requiring it. This was another test of his obedience. His friends doubted the authenticity of this leading, however, feel-

---

64. [B. T. Roberts], "Death of Rev. Loren Stiles," *EC* 5, no. 6 (June 1863): 187; BHR, *BTR*, pp. 329-30.

65. Terrill, *Redfield*, p. 464.

66. J. G. Terrill, *The St. Charles' Camp-Meeting* (Chicago: T. B. Arnold, 1883), p. 18.

67. [B. T. Roberts], "The Western Convention of the Free Methodist Church," *EC* 2, no. 7 (July 1861): 225.

68. Redfield Autobiography, p. 414.

ing that in his weakened and depressed condition he was beginning to lose touch with reality.

Still, Redfield was sure that God had spoken to him.

I could now in spirit see Syracuse & the dreadful state of death which must be met & contended against. But with the same inner eye I could see a vast cloud & a voice to my inner ear saying to me that Syracuse is the Jerusalem of America, & from that point must salvation go forth to save the nation. Then, said that voice to me, you visited that city about 12 years ago & there saw the first dawning rays of that type of religion which must usher in the Millennium, & after the pattern of Pentecost. But, said the voice, that has nearly all been squandered & is now in disgrace in the eyes of the people. And now I send you again, & as you went through with the breaking-up plow, I now send you with the sub-soil plow, & though you will have severe conflict & must stand alone nearly, yet I will stand by you.[69]

Redfield was able to travel to Buffalo at the end of October 1862, and partly to humor him, Brother Joslyn and Mrs. Redfield took him on to Syracuse. In Buffalo B. T. Roberts discouraged the idea of Redfield's going to Syracuse. Redfield wrote, "Bro. R [Roberts] thought it all wrong & only a whim which was due to my weak & nervous state of mind, & a project wholly preposterous. My wife too was quite sure that my notions were all wrong. But Sister R [Roberts] thought it best to humor the thing, & she gave some hints that there might be more of God in this matter than could be seen by all, & O how much her advice did relieve me, for I had to bear it all alone thus far."[70]

Redfield did spend several weeks in Syracuse. Charles Hicks, however, with whom Redfield had worked a dozen years earlier, refused to even consider beginning any new revival efforts, given Redfield's feeble condition. Redfield was forced, agonizingly, to give up his idea of a new mission to Syracuse. He reflected back over his whole difficult life, and sometimes felt he had been a failure. He wrote at the end of December 1862, while still in Syracuse:

I was tempted & feel grieved as I looked over my past labors, now about 26 years, & have labored without reward, & can count up over 30 M.E. churches which had been built or redeemed through my labors. And now there are young men who were in their swaddling clothes while I was going forth amid scorn & opposition & at my own expense, weeping & bearing precious seed. And now many of them occupy the very pulpits which God helped me to build or redeem, & I must not be allowed to labor in them, though I do it for nothing & the people desire it.[71]

---

69. Redfield Autobiography, pp. 415-16 (slightly corrected; punctuation added).

70. Redfield Autobiography, pp. 416-17 (slightly corrected). See, relatedly, Redfield's Feb. 10, 1862, letter to Ellen Roberts, reprinted in Terrill, *Redfield*, pp. 459-60.

71. Redfield Autobiography, pp. 423-24 (slightly corrected). The last several pages of Redfield's memoir are in diary format, with entries dated. The manuscript ends with Redfield's entry for Jan. 7, 1863, while he was still in Syracuse.

Redfield and his wife returned to Marengo early in 1863. "At last he turned his face toward the West again, weeping as he went," said Terrill. Redfield was showing "evidences of the breaking down of his mind," Terrill thought, "which led many of his friends to distrust his personal convictions of duty." Now back in Illinois, Redfield "said but little now in public gatherings," though in October he was able to attend the Illinois Conference sessions at Aurora, at which B. T. Roberts presided. Redfield and his wife spent his last days at the home of Osgood Joslyn.[72]

"Auntie" Harriet Coon, a strong prayer supporter of Redfield over the years, often spent time with him during his last days. She comforted and encouraged him, often through singing. "He was very sad most of the time," she said, "and talked out his heart — a little of what he was passing through. I encouraged him as best I could. He often asked me to sing some beautiful hymns."[73] Adding to Redfield's distress, he felt an "undue intimacy" had developed between his wife and the man of the house as the two spent long hours together in caring for him.[74]

B. T. and Ellen Roberts were in Marengo the first part of November 1863, following the Illinois Conference sessions, and stayed in the home of Auntie Coon. Mrs. Coon wrote,

> A conference was held at our church in Marengo; the Spirit was poured out upon the preacher and the people; great grace and power rested upon all. Doctor Redfield attended daily; came the six miles over the country in his carriage. The Spirit of God rested upon him in a wonderful way. His face would shine as though he had been in a heavenly world. The last day he attended he wrote five letters and mailed them, and after the afternoon session, was drawn down to our door where Brother and Sister Roberts were staying, and called us all out to tell us "good-by" for the night, saying, "I am somewhat tired, but the Lord willing I will be with you in the morning."[75]

This was on Saturday afternoon, October 31. That evening at the Joslyn home Redfield experienced another stroke. Ellen Roberts and Auntie Coon went out to the Joslyns' and remained with Redfield until he died on Monday morning.[76] Auntie Coon wrote,

> The same spirit that used to be upon him to keep me singing took possession of [the others in the room], and all through that day and night some one kept saying,

72. Terrill, *Redfield*, p. 462; cf. "The Illinois Conference . . . ," *EC* 6, no. 6 (Dec. 1863): 187.

73. [Harriet Arvilla Damon Coon], *Life and Labors of Auntie Coon*, ed. E. E. Shelhamer (Atlanta: Repairer Office, 1905), p. 89. On Coon, cf. Kostlevy, p. 72.

74. [Coon], *Life and Labors*, p. 89. Coon wrote, "His [Redfield's] wife and the man of the house took entire care of him and were together at his bedside every night. It was very apparent to me there was undue intimacy between these two, and I told them so. But they said that they had *faith*, *communion* and *power* such as none of us could understand" (p. 89). Coon talked this over with Redfield, who said he was aware of and disturbed about this.

75. [Coon], *Life and Labors*, p. 92.

76. [Coon], *Life and Labors*, pp. 92-93; Terrill, *Redfield*, p. 464.

"Sing, sing, oh, Sister Coon, sing!" I was singing when he left us, and when he went the palsied limb lifted up and stepped down, as though it was on the streets of gold, and I said, "There, he has done just as he said he should when he reached the city," viz.: "I will make those streets of gold ring with music just as soon as I get there." The house was filled with a heavenly atmosphere. One sister fell, others staggered, some shouted, a few wept, but those who had caused him trouble were saying: "Oh, that I could speak to him once more to ask his forgiveness," but it was too late.[77]

E. P. Hart recalled, "In preaching the doctor had a peculiar way of bringing up and setting down his right foot, and at the same time with a good deal of emphasis shouting, Hallelujah! On the evening of his death, just as the breath left his body, in his characteristic way he brought up his foot and, as some who were looking on said, set it down in heaven."[78]

On a dark, stormy Wednesday, November 4, "the rain falling in torrents," B. T. Roberts preached Redfield's funeral sermon at the Free Methodist church building in Marengo.[79] Roberts preached a "most excellent sermon," said "Mother" Eunice Cobb.[80] Reflecting on the occasion, Hart wrote, "It was a solemn scene as the young preachers gathered around the casket to take the last look at that calm and heavenly face. Standing there with hands uplifted we sang [a hymn] and pledged ourselves anew to God. By a merciful providence the Lord had, as it were, taken the doctor from us by degrees, for during his two years' illness we had learned to look away from the arm of flesh and to trust more fully in God, so his death did not prove a shock or any great hindrance to the work."[81]

Redfield was buried in the Marengo cemetery and his gravestone was inscribed, "He was true to his motto — Fidelity to God."[82]

In announcing Redfield's death in the *Earnest Christian*, B. T. Roberts wrote:

> Dr. Redfield was one of the most remarkable men of the day. His talents were of a high order, and his life was a sacrifice upon the altar of God, for the good of humanity. For over twenty years he has devoted his time to the promotion of revivals of religion, receiving no compensation for his unremitting labors. As a revival preacher, he had no equal in this country. . . . Vast audiences were wrought to the highest pitch of religious excitement under his awful appeals, and wherever he held meetings the country was moved for miles around, and hundreds of converts were added to the church of God.[83]

---

77. [Coon], *Life and Labors*, pp. 92-93.

78. Edward Payson Hart, *Reminiscences of Early Free Methodism* (Chicago: Free Methodist Publishing House, 1903), p. 75.

79. Hart, *Reminiscences*, p. 75.

80. Mary Weems Chapman, *Mother Cobb; or, Sixty Years' Walk with God* (Chicago: T. B. Arnold, 1896), p. 103.

81. Hart, *Reminiscences*, pp. 75-76.

82. Terrill, *Redfield*, p. 464; Hart, *Reminiscences*, p. 75.

83. [B. T. Roberts], "Death of Dr. Redfield," *EC* 6, no. 6 (Dec. 1863): 184-85.

Benjamin arranged to have an expensive steel-plate engraving made of Redfield for the *Earnest Christian*. "We shall take pains to have an excellent likeness," he noted.[84]

The loss of key actors in the early history of Free Methodism — particularly of Kendall, Stiles, and Redfield — took its toll. When Stiles died Roberts wrote in the *Earnest Christian*, "One of the greatest discouragements we have had to meet with, in trying to promote spiritual religion, has been the early removal from the scene of conflict of those who seemed to be most necessary for the advancement of the cause."[85]

As Roberts continued his travels east and west, and sometimes north and south, he was at times involved in wider arenas beyond the Free Methodist Church. Later chapters will record his participation in the National Christian Association and various reform movements.

Shortly after the Civil War ended in 1865, Roberts participated in "a large union prayer-meeting" in New York City that he said he had been "asked to lead."[86] It is not clear exactly when and where this meeting was held, as he did not record it in his 1865 diary (much of which is blank). But the incident gives a picture of his attitude toward the evangelical Christianity of his day. He notes that the meeting opened with "the hymn then so popular, the sentiment of which remains too popular still:

'Nothing either great or small
    Remains for me to do,
Jesus died and paid it all,
    All the debt I owe.'"

Roberts "took the hymn for a text" and made some impromptu remarks on the need for confession and true repentance. Even John the Baptist, he noted, "insisted that his converts should '*bring forth fruits meet for repentance*,'" and both Peter and Paul preached repentance and confession (referring to Acts 2:37 and 19:18-19). After the service a businessman sought out Roberts, asking counsel. This man, Roberts said,

> had professed to be converted last winter when they sang for him the hymn above referred to. But he said, as nearly as he could make out, he had robbed the Government of about thirty thousand dollars! We told him there was no use in his professing to be converted unless he was willing to make restitution. He went away sad, but kept on with his profession. He became a popular worker in the popular revival, and afterward was sent to State prison for a crime committed while engaged in his evangelistic labors.
>
> This telling people who have been guilty of fraud, and dishonesty, and villainy, and even murder, that they can be forgiven and go to heaven by saying they

---

84. [B. T. Roberts], "Death of Dr. Redfield," p. 185.

85. [B. T. Roberts], "Death of Rev. Loren Stiles," p. 187.

86. [B. T. Roberts], "Crime," *EC* 49, no. 1 (Jan. 1885): 27. Since this account is a recollection of events twenty years earlier, Roberts may have misremembered some of the details.

"believe in Jesus," and uniting with the Church, is not only deceiving souls to their eternal undoing, but is encouraging crime in all its dimensions.[87]

Revivals must be genuine or they do more harm than good, Roberts felt.

Ministry in California, 1879

Near the end of 1878 Benjamin and Ellen embarked on a five-month trip to California, their first to the West Coast. The primary purpose was evangelism, following up on Free Methodist contacts there. As early as 1873 G. W. Humphrey of the Genesee Conference and his family had been sent to California "for the purpose of planting churches on the Pacific coast," and a small Free Methodist society was organized in San Francisco in 1875. Humphrey did not remain with the denomination, but a young Methodist Episcopal local preacher named F. H. Horton joined the Free Methodists in San Francisco and became the real pioneer preacher of Free Methodism in California.[88]

Benjamin's West Coast ministry helped lay the foundation for the organization of the California Conference of the Free Methodist Church in 1883, from which came later the Southern California Conference.[89]

Announcing his western trip in the December 1878 *Earnest Christian,* Roberts wrote, "Our object is to hold meetings along on the Pacific coast as the Lord opens the way. We have had many urgent calls which we fear we have neglected too long." He left the management of the *Earnest Christian* "in hands capable of getting it out better than we could do, with the limited time we should be able to devote to it, if we should remain in this part of the country and go about as usual holding meetings."[90] Over the next months Benjamin sent back reports for the magazine. On this trip Benjamin and Ellen were accompanied by two young women, Ida Collins and Mattie McCreery, the youngest daughter of Joseph McCreery (who became Mrs. F. H. Horton).[91]

The trip took the group first to Chicago, where in mid-December Benjamin preached three times and "found a band of devoted, earnest pilgrims" who had started a Free Methodist congregation and were "opening a mission in another part of the city." On December 22 Roberts preached twice in a revival being conducted in a Methodist Episcopal church near Kellogg, Iowa.[92] During the trip to California Benjamin "took a severe cold," he noted, that continued to bother him during his first weeks on the coast.[93]

---

87. [B. T. Roberts], "Crime," p. 27.
88. [B. T. Roberts], "Conferences," *EC* 26, no. 5 (Nov. 1873): 163; Hogue, *HFMC,* 2:140.
89. Marston, p. 430.
90. [B. T. Roberts], "To California," *EC* 36, no. 6 (Dec. 1878): 190.
91. Hogue, *HFMC,* 2:141.
92. [B. T. Roberts], "On the Way," *EC* 37, no. 1 (Jan. 1879): 30-31.
93. [B. T. Roberts], "From California," *EC* 37, no. 3 (Mar. 1879): 94.

Benjamin wrote on December 30, "To-night — Monday — at mid-night we expect to take the train for Omaha; thence via the Union Pacific, through the frost and snow of the Rocky Mountains, to the Pacific coast."[94] This was nine years after the transcontinental railroad was completed; the Union Pacific and Central Pacific had joined their rails at Promontory Point, Utah, on May 10, 1869. Dee Brown notes that most of the early Eastern travelers on the transcontinental railroad "seemed to look upon the necessary transfers in Chicago and Omaha, and Promontory or Ogden, as welcome breaks in an eight- to ten-day adventure."[95]

The journey from Omaha to Oakland, California, took Benjamin, Ellen, and their companions five and a half days. Ellen wrote back to her friend Catherine Cady in North Chili, describing the trip. Traveling through Nevada on January 3, 1879, Ellen saw "mountains piled on mountains, towering to the skies." Benjamin and Ellen had to sleep on the seats as best they could. Ellen wrote that "for five nights I did not take off my clothes"; she and Benjamin "ate [our] meals from a lunch basket, except one meal, and when I landed I felt well and not much tired." She added, "You can never conceive how extremely *dirty* we got on the cars. They burned soft coal and it was *fearful*."[96]

The party reached Oakland late in the afternoon of Saturday, January 4, 1879. They were met by Dr. and Mrs. M. F. Bishop, Free Methodists from northern Illinois, where the Bishop family had been "prominently identified with" Redfield's ministry and the founding of Free Methodism there. Dr. Bishop was the brother of Mattie Hart, E. P. Hart's wife. The Bishops had migrated to California and were part of the Free Methodist society organized in San Francisco in 1875. They had a "comfortable and hospitable home" in the growing town of Alameda, just south of Oakland, and had now started a Free Methodist class at their house. Roberts began his California ministry here. He noted, "Many of the business men of San Francisco reside" in Alameda and Oakland.[97]

F. H. Horton, "the only preacher we have in California on a circuit," Benjamin noted, arranged for Roberts to preach in several locations. Horton had conducted a successful revival in the town of Pacheco, where Roberts preached and held a quarterly meeting with the new Free Methodist congregation. Roberts said "the interest was such that we continued the meetings through the week," and "a few young persons" were converted.[98]

---

94. [B. T. Roberts], "On the Way," pp. 30-31.

95. Dee Brown, *Hear That Lonesome Whistle Blow: Railroads in the West* (New York: Simon and Schuster, 1977), p. 136.

96. ELR (Alameda, Calif.) to Mrs. Cady, Jan. 9, 1879, quoted in Zahniser, p. 303.

97. Hogue, *HFMC*, 1:272, 2:141-42; [B. T. Roberts], "In California," *EC* 37, no. 2 (Feb. 1879): 62. (Roberts in this report gives the arrival date incorrectly as Saturday, Jan. 5, as do the sources that depend on this report, but in a later report he gives the correct date: Saturday, Jan. 4.) The Bishops conducted meetings in their home Sunday mornings and evenings, as well as Tuesday nights, suggesting that they were no longer involved with any FM group in San Francisco itself.

98. [B. T. Roberts], "In California," *EC* 37, no. 2 (Feb. 1879): 62.

Benjamin also preached by invitation at the Alameda Methodist Episcopal Church. He noted, "We have abundant invitations to preach in other churches, but this is not the work which we came here to do." Evangelism was needed — raising up new churches. California was in "great need of earnest Christian effort," but there were many obstacles including "general indifference to religion, such as we never saw elsewhere," and few churches that maintained "the Christianity of the New Testament." "Many of the permanent residents are old miners, who came here to dig for gold," Benjamin observed. "Most of the people came here to make money. That was their object. Of course they cannot look with favor upon any religion that interferes with the purpose that brought them here." But Roberts was optimistic: "we believe that this beautiful land may be redeemed to Christ, because we believe in the Holy Ghost."[99]

Benjamin decided to make San Francisco his base of operations. Some of the Methodist Episcopal pastors were men he had known in the East, and at their invitation he preached at some ME churches, as well as in the jail in Santa Rosa. But his main aim was to conduct a revival. The Free Methodists in Alameda rented the Adventist church building on Eddy Street, San Francisco, for a month, and here Roberts began a protracted meeting. He and Ellen rented a furnished room nearby and set up housekeeping. "It seemed a little awkward at first to have but one room for kitchen, dining-room, study, and bed-room," Benjamin noted, "but we get along finely. Our simple wants are easily met. We feel happy in God, trying the best we can to do his blessed will."[100] Ellen wrote to their son George, "Our room does seem like *home indeed* to us." She and Benjamin took some of their meals in restaurants but found it more homey and economical to cook for themselves. The little Free Methodist community helped by donating food and other things. Ellen wrote, "This is the most of a faith home I ever got into." At one point when they were short on food, Ellen asked God for more provision, and more variety. Her prayer was answered. "Right away there came a basket with a beautiful baked fowl and bread with it, and jelly. Another brought pie and cake and butter, etc."[101]

Benjamin described their situation in a letter to Anna Roberts, George's wife:

You would be amused to see us living in our little room about fourteen feet by fifteen. This answers for cooking, sleeping, writing and all the purposes of a house. Like a good husband as I am, I get up in the morning, make a fire, and put on the tea-kettle. Our water we bring upstairs in a quart pitcher and a three pint tin pail. The most of our wood I bring from a carpenter's shop about a quarter of a mile

---

99. [B. T. Roberts], "In California," *EC* 37, no. 2 (Feb. 1879): 62-63. In this same issue Roberts took note of the organization of "The Christian Mission" in England, under the leadership of William Booth, which was to become the Salvation Army. "Their meetings are of an earnest, lively character, and they evidently give full liberty to the operation of the Spirit of God," Roberts noted. [B. T. Roberts], "The Christian Mission," *EC* 37, no. 2 (Feb. 1879): 64.

100. [B. T. Roberts], "From California," p. 94.

101. ELR (Alameda) to GLR, Mar. 3, 1879, quoted in Zahniser, p. 306.

distant. We are learning and practicing economy. I find, since admitted to the kitchen cabinet, that housekeeping is a great art. What we fail in variety we make up in honey. I got sick of paying a *bit* a pound, so went among the Commission men [i.e., wholesalers] to buy some. The first inquiry was, "How much do you want, two or three tons?" I bought a can of sixty pounds, nice strained honey for 5 1/2 cents a pound.[102]

The revival effort started inconspicuously but began to bear some fruit. "From the first, the congregation was small, but it is steadily increasing, and the interest is rising in every meeting," Benjamin wrote in February. "Our congregations are made up mostly of members of the various churches, among whom are some Christian workers, who have been nobly battling for the purity of the Gospel. The Lord has held us with great stringency to insist upon the New Testament standard of Christianity. We have never felt more of the Spirit than we have here in every service. So far the visible results have been, a few justified, and a few wholly sanctified to God, and a good deal of an awakening among [professing Christians]."[103]

Twenty-seven years later the Pentecostal movement would begin in a similar small revival effort 380 miles south, at Azusa Street in Los Angeles.

In March Benjamin reported, "We are still holding meetings here [in San Francisco] twice a day. The Lord is in every meeting, and some are getting saved, and others are getting helped" in other ways. "The conversions are generally clear, though, with our utmost plainness of speech, we find it difficult to make the people understand what the Bible teaches it is to be a Christian." Roberts felt that due to the Roman Catholic influence people had difficulty understanding what real Christianity was. "Thus many do not see any inconsistency in being very wicked and at the same time claiming to be very religious."[104]

Always interested in social and economic conditions, Roberts took note of developing monopolies in California and the way some businessmen were growing rich through stock speculation and manipulation. Since this was a form of gambling, it was morally wrong. Roberts wrote,

> In San Francisco, as in New York and other cities, the leading business of the leading men appears to be stock gambling. Though some get rich at the business, yet they are like successful robbers, in that what they gain, others lose. . . . in gambling, no value is created. The general wealth is not increased. Money simply changes hands. . . . Its spirit creeps into the local governments, and leads them into extravagant expenditures, which create the necessity for ruinous taxes. It robs churches of their piety, and makes them consecrated avenues to perdition.[105]

102. BTR (Alameda) to AAR, Mar. 3, 1879, quoted in Zahniser, pp. 305-6.

103. [B. T. Roberts], "From California," p. 94.

104. [B. T. Roberts], "In San Francisco," *EC* 37, no. 4 (Apr. 1879): 129 (the word "speach" corrected to "speech").

105. [B. T. Roberts], "Gambling," *EC* 37, no. 3 (Mar. 1879): 95.

Roberts had no objection in principle to capitalizing a mine or railroad through selling stock, but often "in the way it is managed, there is nothing honest about it." He explained how mine owners, for example, manipulated the value of the stock to their own profit. "They are enriched, and others made poor." Similarly with the railroads: "When those in control wish to sell, they run the stock up by various contrivances at their command. When they desire to buy, they run it down."

Benjamin could see in California the same kind of stock manipulation that characterized railroad capitalization in the East. Though he was essentially correct in his analysis, it is interesting that here he identifies the root problem as gambling. "Many churches encourage gambling by adopting various lottery schemes to raise money," he noted, encouraging a culture of gambling.[106] By contrast, in his promotion of the Farmers' Alliance about this time Roberts was advocating essentially a political solution to socioeconomic injustice (see chapter 35). Some Californians who met Roberts, however, were impressed with his economic insight. Ellen wrote to Anna Roberts that people wondered how Benjamin "got so correct an understanding of the stock business."[107] Benjamin said "one of the old Californians" commented that Roberts explained "how stocks are managed here" better than he himself could.[108]

Roberts saw his evangelistic work in San Francisco as strategic for the future of Free Methodism. "How long the Lord would have us hold on here, we do not see at present; but we should be glad, if it is His will, to see a church permanently established in this, the metropolis of our Pacific coast." Roberts however felt the "great obstacle" to this goal was "the enormous valuation put upon real estate in this city."[109] Despite his insistence on "New Testament Christianity," he was not able at this point to conceive of a church-planting strategy that did not depend upon property and buildings.

Benjamin ended the protracted meeting on March 31, 1879, after a two-month effort. He had preached twice daily, except on Saturdays. He pronounced the revival "a decided success." Though many of those who attended were "members of different branches of the Church," still there were "a goodly number of conversions," and several believers received the blessing of holiness.[110]

Roberts next held meetings for six rainy days in the Friends meetinghouse in San Jose, but without much result.[111] This was followed by special meetings in Alameda that were also "slimly attended," except for the last service. Roberts noted that there was considerable public excitement at the time because the state constitution was being voted on. "The political excitement ran high. But the Lord met us in

---

106. [B. T. Roberts], "Gambling," p. 96.
107. ELR (Alameda) to AAR, Apr. 22, 1879, quoted in Zahniser, p. 307.
108. BTR (San Francisco) to GLR, Mar. 22, 1879, quoted in Zahniser, p. 307.
109. [B. T. Roberts], "In San Francisco," p. 129.
110. [B. T. Roberts], "In California," *EC* 37, no. 5 (May 1879): 162.
111. [B. T. Roberts], "In California," *EC* 37, no. 5 (May 1879): 162.

every meeting. . . . A few professed to receive the blessing of holiness, and a few made a start in the divine life, who, we trust, will go on in the service of our Lord."[112]

Roberts commented that the Methodist evangelist William Taylor, "well known for his apostolic labors," had not been notably successful on his last visit to California. Though he "preached the Gospel with great plainness and power," attendance at his meeting gradually declined so that at the end "the attendance was not greater than it was at our meetings." Roberts quoted Charles Finney's remark, "Until we can remove from the minds of men the common error that the current Christianity of the church is true Christianity, we can make but little progress in converting the world." Roberts was especially dismayed at the condition of the Methodist Episcopal churches in the San Francisco area. "In some of the Methodist churches, even the preacher does not kneel in prayer. In addition to an organ, they have quite a band of wind and string instruments to make music. What they lack in not having the old-fashioned, Methodist noise, of shouts and amens, they endeavor to make up by the noise of music, vocal and instrumental. Some of the preachers are laboring with fidelity [however]."[113]

In San Francisco Benjamin also visited a Congregationalist church that was "the richest appearing and apparently most liberal church we were ever in," but was spiritually poor. He wrote,

> It is expensive to keep up expensive churches. The congregation must dress in style. The singing must be artistic and paid for. The preacher must be genteel and have a large salary. . . . The pews [in this Congregationalist church] were rented for an enormous price. Four or five times as much was paid for the rent of a pew for one year, as people in fair circumstances among us pay for building a church, the seats of which are to be forever free. The ordinary plate collection the day we were present must have amounted, we should judge, to at least three hundred dollars. . . . Yet the preacher announced that the church was behind in the current expenses for the year six thousand dollars![114]

By the end of May Benjamin had concluded that it was about time to return east. He was quite frank that "we have not seen all accomplished that we desired," yet he felt led of God and that their time in California had been "a blessing to us, and to many souls. We have tried to do our duty, and we leave results to him."[115] Two years later General Superintendent E. P. Hart and his family moved to Alameda and helped develop Free Methodist work in the area.[116]

On their return trip Benjamin and Ellen spent a Saturday and Sunday in Salt Lake City, giving them a chance to observe this center of Mormonism. In the *Earnest*

112. [B. T. Roberts], "In California," *EC* 37, no. 6 (June 1879): 188.

113. [B. T. Roberts], "In California," *EC* 37, no. 6 (June 1879): 188.

114. B. T. Roberts, "Unloosing Burdens," *EC* 47, no. 4 (Apr. 1884): 103. Although Roberts doesn't here specify the year, he seems to be referring to this 1879 visit to California.

115. [B. T. Roberts], "In California," *EC* 37, no. 6 (June 1879): 188.

116. Hogue, *HFMC*, 2:144-46; Hart, *Reminiscences*, pp. 255-56.

Christian Benjamin described the city and the surrounding area. "This region supports now a population of about a hundred and twenty thousand, from almost all the nations of Europe," he observed. "They are about two thirds Mormons, converted and brought here through the zeal of the missionaries which have been sent out."

On Sunday morning Benjamin and Ellen attended the Methodist Episcopal church, which he found in a sad state; in the afternoon they attended the service at the Mormon Tabernacle. Wanting to understand Mormonism more thoroughly, he and Ellen attended a smaller Mormon meeting in the evening in one of the church's twenty-two "wards" in the city. Here "the distinctive features of Mormonism," including its doctrine of eternal marriage, "were brought out more clearly."

Benjamin was very impressed with the Mormon Tabernacle, "planned and built by Brigham Young."

> For all practical purposes, it is the best planned, best constructed edifice for the convenience of a large audience, that we ever saw. Every thing about it was designed for use and not for ornament. The building is of oval form, two hundred and fifty feet long, and one hundred and fifty feet wide, and seventy feet high from floor to ceiling. . . . The audience room is light and airy, with a high gallery — altogether capable of seating twelve thousand people. When filled, it can be vacated in one and a half minutes. It has an organ thirty by thirty-three feet, and fifty-eight feet high, having about three thousand pipes. It is made from native wood, and is the best piece of machinery for worship, we have ever seen. . . .
>
> The worship was conducted very much as it is in Protestant churches. The singing, we judge, was fully up to that of fashionable choirs, as we could understand scarcely a word that was sung.

Benjamin was impressed with Mormonism as a movement, despite its distorted doctrines. Commenting on its view of "sealed" marriages, he wrote, "Mormonism agrees with false religions generally, in that it ascribes to the priesthood the power to control the everlasting destiny of others. All religions are to be rejected which make our future felicity depend — not upon what we do, but upon what a priest does for us."[117]

Monday morning Benjamin and Ellen continued "on the cars," journeying eastward. Arriving back home on June 4, 1879, they were happy to find the family well. "Our trip across the continent was as pleasant as we could possibly have anticipated," Benjamin wrote.[118]

---

117. [B. T. Roberts], "Salt Lake City," *EC* 38, no. 1 (July 1879): 30-31.
118. [B. T. Roberts], "At Home," *EC* 38, no. 1 (July 1879): 35.

CHAPTER 29

Founding Chili Seminary

"We know of no branch of Christian effort that promises more good for the world than the Christian education of the young."

B. T. Roberts, 1885[1]

"True refinement and scholarly culture were her natural atmosphere."

Adelaide Beers, describing Ellen Roberts[2]

As soon as the Free Methodist Church was organized, if not earlier, B. T. Roberts was thinking about starting a school. It would teach earnest Christianity and raise up men and women who would live out their faith in the world. Young people needed to be well educated, but preferably in an explicitly Christian environment. As he later wrote, "The future of the cause of God will be greatly affected by the training of the rising generation. Let us do all we can to have them trained up aright."[3]

Benjamin's concern for the poor was not unrelated to this educational goal. Ellen Roberts noted that not long after the formation of the Free Methodist Church Benjamin "began to talk about a school, where poor boys and girls could be helped to an education."[4] The matter came up repeatedly, as well, in early official Free Methodist gatherings.

1. [B. T. Roberts], "Camp Meetings," *EC* 50, no. 1 (July 1885): 36.
2. Adelaide L. Beers, "My Spiritual Mother," *EC* 95, no. 3 (Mar. 1908): 75.
3. B. T. Roberts, "Christian Schools," *EC* 47, no. 5 (May 1884): 137.
4. Carpenter, p. 178.

In late 1864 Benjamin and Ellen moved from Buffalo to Rochester in anticipation of founding a school there. Benjamin wanted an institution that would serve the Free Methodist Church and its broader mission beyond itself.[5]

Several months before moving from Buffalo — on Sunday, March 13, 1864 — Benjamin and Ellen's seventh and last child (and sixth son) was born. The parents decided to name him Benjamin Titus, after his father, though soon he was being called Benjie (and later, Benja). At the time of their move to Rochester the Roberts family numbered seven, including the five boys, George, Benson, Charles, Samuel, and Benjamin, Jr., ranging in age from twelve to a few months.[6]

In November 1864 Benjamin bought a house on Asylum Street in Rochester, two blocks south of University Avenue on the city's east side. This property (lots 17 and 18 on Asylum Street) would later serve as down payment for the school property in North Chili. The following March he also bought some property several blocks away on Goodman Street, at the eastern edge of the city. He paid $3,612 for this property, which, it appears, he later sold in two parcels (in 1877 and 1881) for a total of $13,700, realizing a $10,088 gain.[7]

Why did Benjamin and Ellen choose Rochester, rather than Buffalo or some other place, as the site for their school? Rochester was centrally located within the state, and by this time the University of Rochester had achieved a respectable reputation. A piece of land across from the university was for sale, and Benjamin thought this would be a good site for his school. Later, however, he changed his mind and opted for a 145-acre farm in nearby North Chili that became available in early 1866. A "strong Free Methodist society had been formed" there, and it seemed an ideal location. Benson Roberts notes that "a year's residence in the city, and a more careful consideration of the disadvantages of educating young people among all the dissipations of city life, convinced [Benjamin] that it would be better to locate the school in the country."[8]

The Asylum Street property became a $4,200 down payment on the North Chili

5. See the account in BHR, *BTR*, pp. 353-55. Benson says that "Soon after [the move to Rochester] a church building was secured, and the [Free Methodist] society previously formed in Rochester was greatly strengthened," presumably because of B. T. Roberts's presence and leadership (p. 343).

6. Smail, pp. 12, 16.

7. According to a compilation of Roberts's real estate transactions in the Roberts Wesleyan College Archives, on Nov. 16, 1864, Roberts purchased from Harriet J. Denison lots 17 and 18 on Asylum Street, Rochester, for $3,350. Later (April 1866), when he and Ellen moved to North Chili, he sold this property for $4,200, realizing a $850 capital gain. Also, on Mar. 6, 1865, Roberts bought seven and a half acres (it appears) on Goodman Street for $3,612, which he sold in 1877 and 1881. C. Moore, "Benjamin Titus Roberts Purchases and Sales in Rochester" (handwritten inventory, with attached maps and listings of real estate transactions in North Chili), March 1978. Archives, Roberts Wesleyan College. Goodman Street was on the east edge of Rochester, about five blocks from the Roberts house in Asylum Street.

8. BHR, *BTR*, pp. 353-54; Neil E. Pfouts, *A History of Roberts Wesleyan College* ([North Chili, N.Y.: Roberts Wesleyan College, 2000]), p. 10. The Roberts family apparently lived in Rochester for about sixteen months, from November 1864 to April 1866.

farm. Benjamin purchased the farm in both his and Ellen's name for a total cost of $17,000. Benjamin was able to raise some additional funds, and he and Ellen assumed a $10,000 mortgage to complete the deal. The transaction was finalized on April 12, 1866, and Roberts took possession of the farm.[9]

Other Free Methodist leaders were in favor of starting the school but didn't feel they could commit the necessary resources to it, so Benjamin and Ellen acted largely on their own. Two state normal schools were operating in the area, offering free tuition, so little patronage could be expected locally. "The prospect was bright and clear for a failure financially," Benson Roberts wrote. "Thus many of his brethren thought, and there was a consequent holding back."[10]

Roberts succeeded, however, not only in buying the land but in establishing a school, known as Chili Seminary (seminary meaning an academy for general education, not a theological school). He hired Miss Delia Jeffries as the first teacher and began classes in the fall of 1866, and Benjamin himself taught classes. The school began in one of the rooms of the farmhouse.[11]

To govern the school Roberts formed a sixteen-member board of trustees. He served as president of the board for most of the rest of his life. The roster published in the school's first catalogue (1869-70) shows that seven trustees were ministers, including the Presbyterian William Belden from New York City. Joseph Mackey, a New York City businessman acquaintance of Roberts, was also on the board. Others of the first trustees, such as Claudius Brainard, had been active in the Laymen's Conventions. Benson Roberts later served on the board during the time he was principal of the school.[12]

Early Chili Seminary

In many ways the North Chili site seemed ideal for a new educational venture. The large farmhouse (sometimes called the "Rumsey mansion" after the previous owner), built in 1850, stood at the top of a rise on Town Line Road (today Westside

---

9. The Roberts house on Asylum Street was apparently valued at about $7,000. According to Pfouts, Benjamin completed the purchase by assuming "the $2000 lien left by Catherine Rumsey plus an $8000 mortgage she accepted from Gerritt W. Wilcox." Thus the farm "became the personal possession of B. T. Roberts, his wife and heirs. In return, two days later, as prearranged, Gerritt Wilcox received as down payment on that farm, the title of lots #17 and #18 on Asylum Street in Rochester from Roberts, including the Roberts' family home" (*History*, p. 10). Pfouts gives a description of the property and its previous ownership.

10. BHR, *BTR*, p. 356.

11. BHR, *BTR*, p. 356.

12. *The First Annual Catalogue and Circular of the Chili Seminary. 1869-70* (Rochester, N.Y.: "Earnest Christian" Office, 1870), p. 3; *The Annual Circular of the A. M. Chesbrough Seminary. 1891-2* (North Chili, N.Y., [1891?]), p. 5. For a while in the 1870s Richard W. Hawkins, whose writings later proved somewhat controversial in the Free Methodist Church, was also a trustee. See *Catalogue and Circular, The Chili Seminary. 1873-75* (Rochester, N.Y.: "Earnest Christian" Office, 1875), p. 3.

Drive).[13] Nearby were several farm buildings, including a double-winged barn and a "tenant house" across the street that had been the original Rumsey farmhouse. The "Rumsey mansion" served at first as both the Roberts residence and the seminary school building. Later when Benjamin built his own home about three hundred yards south, at the highest point on Buffalo Road, the Rumsey house became Pioneer Hall.[14]

Taking up residence in the large farmhouse in North Chili, Benjamin and Ellen were soon ready to launch their educational venture. Benjamin announced the project in the May 1866 *Earnest Christian*. "Children should have religious training," he began. "Their welfare for both worlds requires it." Scripture should have a prominent place. "The Bible should be the text book of the school-room."

Benjamin gave a brief summary of his educational philosophy. Education should include the body as well as the mind, he wrote. "Children should also be trained up to the practice of labor. Man was made to work" — it was a blessing, not a curse. "Doubtless one reason why the Saviour forbid [sic] Christians to lay up treasures on earth was that he would not have them in circumstances in which they would not deem it necessary for them, or their children, to work."[15]

Roberts then laid out the project:

> A number of persons who are desirous of doing all the good in their power, have undertaken to establish a school, in which all shall be done that can be done, to train up youth to habits of piety, virtue, industry and economy, while they are acquiring, the elements of a sound education. With this object in view, a farm has been purchased, of 145 acres. It is about ten miles west of Rochester, about one mile from Chili Station on the N.Y. Central Railroad. The farm is pronounced, by every one who has seen it, as one of the very best that can be found for this purpose. . . . The design is to have all the scholars work from three to five hours every day. An accomplished farmer will teach the science and the practice of agriculture and horticulture. The cost of the farm is $17,000.00. Very liberal offers have already been made, by prominent men in the community . . . , to assist us in the erection of suitable buildings. We want to raise the money at once, to pay for the farm.[16]

In purchasing the North Chili farm as a site for the new school, Roberts became not only an educator but also a farmer and farm administrator. This is part of the reason he later was strategically involved in the founding of the New York State Farmers' Alliance, as will be narrated in a later chapter. As leader and overseer of the

---

13. The Rumsey house stood near where the present Garlock Dining Commons of Roberts Wesleyan College is now located, according to Pfouts (*History*, p. 10). Zahniser (p. 239) indicates that Benjamin was already familiar with the "old Rumsey farmhouse," having "often been entertained [there] as a Methodist minister."

14. Pfouts, *History*, pp. 9-11.

15. [B. T. Roberts], "A School Project," *EC* 11, no. 5 (May 1866): 160.

16. [B. T. Roberts], "A School Project," p. 161.

school, his work included supervising the farm operation, which helped support the educational enterprise. Roberts noted in 1887 that the farm "is a valuable one of nearly two hundred acres."[17]

Benjamin was serious about the commitment to "teach the science and practice of agriculture." While holding services in Lansing, Michigan, in April 1874, he twice visited the State Agricultural College (later Michigan State University) to see how their farm was run. "They have good buildings," he noted — "apparatus, and tools and other appliances" and "choice blooded stock," well cared for.[18] Roberts noted the varieties of dairy cattle the college had — Alderney, Shorthorn, Devon, Galloway. He arranged to purchase an animal (probably a milk cow). The animal arrived by train a few weeks later and became part of the Chili Seminary herd.[19]

Benjamin himself served initially as principal of the school, and then George W. Anderson was principal from 1869 to 1872. The 1870-71 catalogue listed Roberts as president of the Board of Instruction and "Teacher of Latin, Greek, &c.," as well as president of the Board of Trustees, with Anderson serving as principal.[20]

The seminary's first year was a success, and more space was needed. The second year Roberts arranged to use an old hotel in North Chili. The hotel ballroom was converted into classroom space, and Miss Jeffries and Benjamin were the teachers. "We had, I think, about as many students as we could accommodate in our close quarters," Delia Jeffries said.[21]

These arrangements were temporary until Roberts could erect adequate facilities. Construction on a seminary building soon began, and the building was ready by the fall of 1869. A large crowd came to the dedication on November 16. The dedicatory address was given by President Martin Brewer Anderson of the University of Rochester, whose inauguration Roberts had attended fifteen years earlier. During his address Dr. Anderson turned to Roberts and said, "You, sir, will find many who are willing to sacrifice you on the altar of Christian education."[22]

It is clear that from the beginning Roberts's vision for the school (as for the magazine) was much broader than simply ministry to Free Methodists. It is also clear that the mission to provide "a sound education" including "habits of piety, virtue, industry and economy" out of concern for students' "welfare for both worlds" was a vision for a general liberal arts education from a Christian perspective, not solely biblical or religious training.

Delia Jeffries later recalled Roberts's labors during this period: "With the work on the seminary, looking after the workmen, seeing that all needed material was at

---

17. B. T. Roberts, "A. M. Chesbrough Seminary," *FM* 20, no. 26 (June 29, 1887): 8. The original size of the farm was 145 acres, as noted.

18. BTRD, Apr. 10 and 14, 1874. On Apr. 10 Benjamin also attended a chemistry lecture at the college, pronouncing it "Good."

19. BTRD, May 2 and 7, 1874.

20. *Second Annual Catalogue,* Chili Seminary (1870-71), p. 3; Pfouts, *History,* p. 66.

21. BHR, *BTR,* pp. 356-57.

22. BHR, *BTR,* p. 361.

hand; doing a vast amount of preaching, making long journeys, having the care of a large family, overseeing the farm, editing a monthly magazine, many times I, as I lived in his house, and assisted in mailing the paper, thought he did more work than a man ought to do."[23]

One time Miss Jeffries asked Benjamin, "Is it right for you to do and bear so much? Is it not duty to take things a little easier, and not wear yourself out so fast?"

Roberts replied, "I am bearing double burdens . . . because those whom the Lord calls to come to my help do not respond to His call, thus leaving me not only to bear my own burdens, but also to do the work they leave undone."[24]

Miss Jeffries added, "I do not remember to have heard him speak one unpleasant, hasty or unkind word while I was there." Delia served at the school for several years. When she told Benjamin she would be leaving and getting married, he gave her his blessing, saying, "The Lord bless and help you, and I shall ever pray for your prosperity and happiness in whatever situation you may be placed. Again, I say, the Lord bless you, Delia, abundantly."[25]

At this time North Chili sported a tavern. Benjamin saw this as a bad influence on the town and potentially on the school, and resolved to get rid of it. Finding the business could be purchased for about $500, Roberts organized a temperance rally to drum up support. The Good Templars, a temperance fraternity, showed up in force. But contributions totaled only about $25. Undeterred, Roberts came up with the needed funds elsewhere and bought the tavern himself. "It was closed, and the blight of liquor was in a great measure removed from the community," Benson Roberts wrote.[26] This was another example of B. T. Roberts's entrepreneurial spirit, his activism and determination, and his ability to make things happen.

Roberts purchased the tavern in 1867. Later, in 1872, Anson and Catherine Cady bought the structure. In response to what they felt was God's call, the Cadys moved to North Chili from Lyons, New York, to help with the school. They lived in the former tavern and Mr. Cady managed the seminary farm for Benjamin. The Cadys turned the building into a successful village store "and at times partially a coffee shop" run as a form of witness and outreach. Catherine Cady became especially close to Ellen Roberts.[27]

The finances for running the school turned out to be an ongoing headache for Benjamin. "We are perplexed and embarrassed," he wrote at one point. In 1868 the Genesee and Susquehanna Conferences pledged to raise $2,000 and $1,000 respectively for the school, but only a small fraction of that was actually paid.[28]

---

23. BHR, *BTR*, p. 357.
24. BHR, *BTR*, pp. 357-58.
25. BHR, *BTR*, p. 359.
26. BHR, *BTR*, p. 360.
27. Pfouts, *History*, p. 16; cf. Zahniser, p. 242.
28. BHR, *BTR*, p. 361.

Program and Philosophy

Chili Seminary published its first annual catalogue in 1870, a twelve-page booklet listing all fifty-six students by name and describing the course of study. The school had received its incorporation papers the year before (January 1869) from the New York State Board of Regents, which during this period was standardizing educational programs throughout the state. By the 1870-71 school year Chili Seminary was using the Standardized Regents Examinations provided by the state.[29]

The first catalogue specified two courses of study, a Preparatory Course and a three-year Graduating Course. For a while the school also operated a Primary Department, which explains how Benjamin and Ellen's youngest sons, Samuel and Benjie, could be enrolled in 1870-71 at the ages of six and eight, respectively. In fact, during that year — Benson's last at Chili Seminary — all four of their youngest sons were enrolled. Benson was seventeen and Charles fourteen.[30]

B. T. Roberts became convinced that a dormitory system in which "the scholars from abroad all board in the school buildings . . . divided up into congenial families of about twenty each" was the best arrangement for a Christian school. In this system the students "with a tutor sleep in a large room specially fitted up for a dormitory," rather than being paired in smaller rooms. "They are kept steadily at their work, and if they want any help in their studies it is furnished at once. *They form habits of application.* This is of great importance — not only in study but in all pursuits of life."[31] Roberts noted that both Roman Catholic and Moravian schools used this system with success and benefit.

William Belden's influence was important here. Benjamin explained,

When we started our school at Chili we were entirely unacquainted with the dormitory system.[32] It was proposed by the Rev. William Belden, a Presbyterian minister of New York city, who gave us one thousand dollars and had much to do with helping to found this school. He had given his attention to schools during nearly all his life. He was a teacher for more than forty years. He quite insisted upon this system, and thought a Christian school could not achieve its greatest results on any other plan. After giving it a fair trial we are decidedly of his opinion. We should be quite reluctant to start another school on any other system.[33]

In 1885 the name of the school was changed from Chili Seminary to A. M. Chesbrough Seminary as the result of a $30,000 gift from the estate of Abram

29. Pfouts, *History,* p. 11.

30. *Second Annual Catalogue,* pp. 7, 11-12.

31. B. T. Roberts, "Christian Schools," pp. 135-36.

32. In the sense that Roberts here describes. At Wesleyan University he had shared a small dormitory room with another student.

33. B. T. Roberts, "Christian Schools," p. 137. In this article Roberts deals with two objections to such a dormitory system: that "scholars do not at first like it, because of the restraint it imposes," and the added burden it imposes on teachers.

Merritt Chesbrough, nephew of Isaac Chesbrough. The legacy stipulated that the school buy from B. T. Roberts the farm on which it was located, invest the balance in "good securities" to provide perpetual scholarships for needy students, and rename the school after Mr. Chesbrough.[34] Roberts was pleased with the gift, believing that such endowments were an appropriate way to provide long-term support for Christian education. Noting in 1883 that D. L. Moody had received a gift of $50,000 to help endow his Northfield Seminary, Benjamin commented, "We have faith for the endowment of our salvation schools. God has greatly helped us thus far. The amount of good which they have already done cannot be estimated."[35]

Over the next several years Chili Seminary's academic program evolved and diversified. By 1891-92 the school had a three-year College Preparatory Course, a four-year Academic Course (essentially a high school program), a four-year English Course "for those who do not care to study Latin," and a Christian Workers' Course. The English Course was identical to the Academic Course except that English composition replaced Latin in the first two years. The one-year Christian Workers' Course was not based on the liberal arts but gave "an introduction to studies especially adapted" for "laboring for Christ." The catalogue added pointedly that this course "is open to young men and women alike."[36]

The school year, beginning the first week in September and ending in mid-July, consisted of three fourteen-week terms with a week's vacation between terms. Later the terms were shortened to thirteen weeks and an eight-week summer school was added.[37]

During the early years the school published a statement that well summarizes Roberts's educational philosophy:

---

34. Hogue, *HFMC*, 2:307-8; Pfouts, *History*, pp. 26-27; B. T. Roberts, "A. M. Chesbrough Seminary," p. 8. In announcing the bequest in the *Earnest Christian*, Roberts wrote: "[W]e are happy to announce that the late A. M. Chesbrough, a beloved brother in Christ, of La Salle, N.Y., near Niagara Falls, has left a legacy, for the Seminary, of thirty thousand dollars, on condition that the Seminary bears his name, and that the farm on which the Seminary is located be purchased; the balance invested, and the income both of the farm and of the investment only, be used to aid indigent students." [B. T. Roberts], "Chili Seminary," *EC* 46, no. 5 (Nov. 1883): 162. Roberts published an obituary of Chesbrough in the December 1883 *Earnest Christian*, noting that he was born in Vermont in 1814 and died at his home near Niagara Falls on Oct. 14, 1883. Chesbrough made his money in the construction of the Erie Railroad and through real estate transactions and other investments. "He accumulated a large amount of property by patient industry and judicious investments. No one ranked higher as a man of strictest integrity. He was ever a friend of the poor, always ready to help where there was a prospect of doing good." He was a member of the Methodist Episcopal Church. Roberts noted, "There was no Free Methodist Church at his place, but he frequently attended our Camp Meetings and contributed of his means for the support of the cause." He left about $80,000 to "various benevolent enterprises," including the bequest to Chili Seminary. [B. T. Roberts], "A. M. Chesbrough," *EC* 46, no. 6 (Dec. 1883): 190-91.

35. [B. T. Roberts], "Endowment," *EC* 46, no. 3 (Sept. 1883): 100.

36. *The Annual Circular of the A. M. Chesbrough Seminary. 1891-2* (North Chili, N.Y.: [1892]), pp. 11-14.

37. *First Annual Catalogue*, Chili Seminary (1869-70), p. 10; *Annual Circular . . . 1891-2*, p. 18.

While we cannot prize, too highly, the benefits of MENTAL culture, we should not lose sight of that MORAL and RELIGIOUS culture, which lies at the foundation of correct principles and good character. Education and religion should by no means be separated. Indeed, to divorce them is dangerous, as is proved by the history of the past. Ignorance is the mother of Superstition and Religious Error; and a system of education that does not comprehend the great truths of revelation, fosters skepticism and infidelity in the youthful mind. The teacher who is interested in the moral destiny of a pupil, and also in his usefulness to mankind will labor to show the harmony between science and Christianity — between the discoveries of the one and the doctrines of the other.

While we would eschew anything sectarian, we shall make the word of God this standard: using the Bible as the text-book. Our aim will be especially to impress that great truth, "The fear of the Lord is the beginning of wisdom." Parents and guardians may feel safe in putting their children and wards under our care, for we shall not only be jealous of their mental improvement, but we shall also "watch for their souls as those who must give account."[38]

Benson Roberts later neatly summarized the educational philosophy as "Education for character."[39]

In an 1884 lead article in the *Earnest Christian* entitled "Christian Schools," B. T. Roberts reiterated his understanding of the purpose of Christian education. The "result that is especially aimed at," he said, is "to train these boys and girls up for usefulness and happiness here; and for a glorious immortality hereafter. It is to accustom their minds to profitable thought and investigation; to teach them how to study, to aid them in acquiring a complete mastery over themselves, to imbue them thoroughly with Christian principles, and make them accustomed to Christian practices; in short to do all that can be done to help them to become intelligent, educated, consistent, efficient Christians."[40]

Arguing for "salvation schools," Roberts urged parents to send their children to schools where the instruction was explicitly Christian. "We cannot understand how Christian parents can, of choice, send their children where they will at the best, grow up in pride and worldliness and formality. No literary advantages can compensate for the loss of morality and a Christian character." American history amply demonstrated the importance of such schools, Roberts felt. "The Puritans of New England founded Christian Schools at the first settlement of the country. The great revival that God carried on through the labors of Charles G. Finney led to the establishment of the most thorough reform school [Oberlin College] of the day."[41]

---

38. *First Annual Catalogue*, p. 7.

39. Benson Roberts appears to have been the author of the statement under "Design" in the Chesbrough Seminary catalogue that states, "Earnest effort is made to encourage each student to 'seek first the Kingdom of God.' The whole purpose of this school is expressed in the phrase, 'Education for character.'" The phrase may not have been original with him. *Annual Circular . . . 1891-2*, p. 15.

40. B. T. Roberts, "Christian Schools," p. 135.

41. [B. T. Roberts], "Salvation Schools," *EC* 46, no. 2 (Aug. 1883): 66-67. Interestingly, Roberts makes no mention of the many Methodist schools started in the early 1800s.

Chesbrough Seminary emphasized community — family — and a sound biblical foundation. As articulated in the 1891-92 catalogue,

> All scholars from abroad [i.e., not local residents] live in the School Family. The
> School Family is a distinctive feature of the school. Our students do not "board,"
> they become members of the family comprising Principals, Teachers and
> Scholars. The same principles of association and conduct that regulate every re-
> fined household hold sway here. Each pupil is expected to become interested in
> the welfare of the whole and to submit cheerfully to any self denial rendered nec-
> essary by proper regard for others. Scholars occupy private rooms for which the
> occupants provide all except heavy furniture.[42]

Although standard textbooks were used in the various courses, the whole curriculum and community were infused with Bible study. The catalogue was explicit on this:
"The work of the school is not merely to educate and inform the mind. It is to *train* the
man, his moral and intellectual powers. We hold that the soul is above the body and
mind, that he only does well who does right, that character is to be first in the work of
training, and so Bible Study is systematically pursued. Twice each day all the school
meet for this purpose. It is the intention that the whole Bible be read each school year
by each student. This work is additional to the work in the courses of study."[43]

Students were also required to attend public worship twice on Sundays.[44]

In 1870-71 tuition was $5.00 per term in the Primary Department, $8.00 for the
Preparatory Course, and $10.00 for the Graduating Course. Board was $2.50 per
week ("Tea and Coffee 50 cts. extra"). To keep the school on a sound financial basis,
the catalogue specified that tuition was "payable in advance, and board monthly in
advance."[45] Twenty years later, costs had risen only slightly, with combined board
and tuition listed as $50.00 per term. Laundry ("12 pieces weekly") was an additional
$4.00 per term.[46]

The personal library of Benjamin and Ellen's deceased friend William Kendall
(about forty volumes) and some twenty-five books contributed by S. K. J. Chesbrough
formed the core of the initial seminary library. D. F. Newton also contributed four of
his own books. Other volumes were soon added; by 1871 the library included *Lives of
the Presidents,* the Koran, and eight volumes of the *Earnest Christian.*[47]

---

42. *Annual Circular . . . 1891-2,* pp. 16-17. Each student was to furnish a "mattress or straw tick, one
pillow, three sheets, two pillow slips, comfortable [i.e., comforter] or blankets, white bed spread, tow-
els, soap, napkins, lamp, clothes brush, shoe brush, looking glass, umbrella. Rubber coats and boots are
very desirable for both boys and girls in bad weather of Fall and Winter" (p. 19).

43. *Annual Circular . . . 1891-2,* p. 17.

44. *Second Annual Catalogue,* p. 16.

45. *Second Annual Catalogue,* pp. 13, 15. By 1891-92 this had been changed to read, "It is requested
that payments be made in advance for each term. Unless other arrangements have been made, this is
expected of each." *Annual Circular . . . 1891-2,* p. 19.

46. *Annual Circular . . . 1891-2,* p. 19.

47. *Second Annual Catalogue,* pp. 13-14.

Early enrollments in Chili Seminary looked promising. Fifty-six students came in 1869-70, and this jumped to 102 the next year (55 men, 47 women). Enrollment grew to 140 in 1873-74. Over the next twenty years, however, the number of students seems to have averaged in the 80s and 90s, usually with slightly more men than women. The student body in 1891-92 included a number of students from other countries, and several Christian and Missionary Alliance children. This rather surprising level of internationalization reflected the missionary interest of Free Methodists during this period, and particularly of Emma and Benson Roberts, as will be noted later.[48]

During the early years of Chili Seminary Benjamin assisted with the teaching — a ministry he delighted in. His "habit of making clear statements, and his practical sense, united with his experience, training, and deep sympathy for humanity . . . made him a popular teacher," Benson Roberts wrote. Though most of the students were children or teenagers, some were young men in their twenties with little prior education. Roberts dealt with them patiently. "Where others failed, with these [Benjamin] succeeded."[49]

Benjamin was known to doze off occasionally during class recitations, especially after a busy weekend of preaching and traveling. But students, thinking he was asleep, would be surprised when he snapped to attention to correct an error. Roberts "had the faculty of hearing while apparently asleep, and would greatly surprise [the students] by suddenly correcting the error made, or calling the offender to account for his conduct," Benson recalled.[50]

Benjamin apparently had lost none of his teaching skills over the twenty years or so since he last taught school. He was patient with students and also skilled in helping them learn. Sometimes he taught English grammar, helping students master the intricacies of the language. One boy couldn't understand the difference between an active and a passive verb. Benjamin called the boy to the front and gave him a playful shaking. He asked the young scholar, "What was done to you?"

"I was shaken," the boy replied.

"And what did I do?" the teacher asked.

"You shook me."

That's right, said Benjamin. "That is an active verb." The students all laughed, and the boy caught the difference.

A semiliterate older student, though well skilled with tools, was having trouble understanding basic grammar. Benjamin tried to teach him the basic elements of a sentence — subject, verb, and direct object. This student's work on the school farm was to help with the milking morning and evening. So Roberts used as an illustration, "The cow gives milk." "Cow" is the subject, Benjamin explained, because it does

---

48. *Catalogues,* Chili and Chesbrough Seminary (North Chili, N.Y.), 1869-96; Carpenter, pp. 126-27.

49. BHR, *BTR,* p. 362.

50. BHR, *BTR,* p. 363.

something. "Gives" is the verb, because it tells what is done. "Milk" is the object, telling what is given.

"Repeating this in the quietude of the cow-barn to the boiling of the streams of milk," Benson Roberts writes, "the science of the relations of words began to open" to the student's mind, and he finally grasped what a sentence was.[51]

Many Chili Seminary alumni later testified to the impact B. T. and Ellen Roberts had on their lives. Kittie Wood recalled an incident that happened one summer morning about 1876 when she was a young student at the seminary. She had been converted a few months earlier but now, faced with heavy school responsibilities, Kittie was discouraged and thinking of giving up. As she was walking, along came B. T. Roberts, "satchel in hand," hurrying to the railway station. She wrote, "I was only fourteen, a child, and he was in a great hurry, but he stopped, put his satchel down, shook hands and said, 'Praise the Lord.' It thoroughly broke me down. I went into the school-room, buried my face in my arms on the desk, and with tears, promised God that I would never give up, and, praise God, I never have. I took fresh strength and courage from that day."[52]

Kittie Wood, who was the daughter of Levi Wood, founder of the *Free Methodist*, called B. T. Roberts her "spiritual father" and after his death published a poem in tribute to him.[53]

As years passed and the school grew, some of the graduates returned as teachers. One of these was Lucy Sellew, a cousin of Roberts from Dunkirk, New York. Her fifteen-year-old sister Emma, "a superior scholar," came and taught languages and mathematics for a year at her own expense. Seven years later (in 1877) she became the bride of Benson Roberts.[54]

Though Benjamin was able to secure teachers and other workers for the school, much of the daily burden fell on Ellen, especially when Benjamin was traveling. Ellen described the labors of a busy Saturday in May 1876. Benjamin was away, as were some of the other workers. Early in the morning Ellen learned that one of the farm animals had died, and later that another had strayed off and couldn't be found.

---

51. Benson Roberts gives these examples in *BTR*, pp. 362-63. Benson says, "One of the cows he milked morning and evening was called John H____, from a former owner," and Benjamin actually used this particular cow by name for the example. Benson may himself have been in his father's classes and recalled these examples from his own experience.

52. Kittie Wood, letter from Madras, India, dated Apr. 27, 1893, in "Correspondence," *EC* 66, no. 2 (Aug. 1893): 65. Kittie said she met Roberts "just as I was going into the yard of the district school," rather than of the seminary, which probably means she was going as a teacher, not a student. According to her obituary, "When she was fifteen years of age she taught a country school." "Obituaries," *FM* (Mar. 23, 1926): 14 (obituary of Mrs. Kittie Wood Kumarakulasinghe).

53. Kittie Wood, "A Loving Tribute," *EC* 66, no. 2 (Aug. 1893): 52.

54. BHR, *BTR*, p. 365; Smail, p. 176. Smail says, "Altho a small woman she was in her younger days a competent equestrienne" (p. 176). Lucy Sellew later married J. Emory Coleman, son of FM General Superintendent George W. Coleman, and with her husband was involved in leadership in the FM "seminary" in Evansville, Wis., when the school was founded in 1880. "Mrs. Lucy Sellew Coleman," *EC* 57, no. 2 (Feb. 1889): 65-66.

Threshing had to be done, and Ellen had to arrange for extra workers and teams of horses. "By continued thanksgiving fewer hands in the family did double the amount of work," Ellen said. A noon meal for thirty was served on time.

Visitors came in the afternoon, some seeking help; and in the evening "a sick friend came," Ellen said, "and I found it good to give a cup of cold water in the name of a disciple. Instead of weariness of body and faintness of soul, I felt strength and vigor, and the force of the words of the Psalmist, 'Oh give thanks unto the Lord.'"[55]

Ellen was not alone in running the Roberts household. She had help from students and others from time to time, and in April 1869 Edith Hurlburt moved to North Chili to live with the Roberts family. "I was as clearly called to come as any one was ever led to the foreign field," Miss Hurlburt said. It appears that she came not as a student but as a domestic helper and one of the family. She lived with the Roberts family for many years, apparently right up till the time of Ellen's death. Ellen Roberts was "indeed a mother to me," she said after her passing.[56]

Another helper and member of the Roberts household was Anna Johnston, a single young woman of about thirty-four who joined the household in 1875.[57] Of Scottish and English descent, Anna and her family had immigrated to Canada and then to the Buffalo area, where she probably became acquainted with the Robertses. She remained with the family beyond Ellen's death in 1908 and in fact continued to live in the family residence until her own death in 1926. Anna's life was completely devoted to Benjamin and Ellen, and she was "invaluable in setting them free to attend to God's public work. She was capable and faithful in all her duties" and "knew how to obtain answers to her prayers."[58]

The Roberts household was thus something of a community, even with Benjamin's frequent absences, and was of course intimately interlaced with the larger seminary family.

The school continued to grow, with students coming from other states and even the Far West, boarding at the seminary during the school year. Benson Roberts wrote, "Rich outpourings of the Holy Spirit upon teachers and scholars at times resulted in sending forth as workers in Christ's vineyard many young men and women of unusual spiritual strength and ability, who soon became leaders in various sections of the country. An outcry of fanaticism was raised by some of the fearful ones, but it only proved a means of developing strength on the part of the young to stand true to God and to keep a spirit of freedom where formality would creep in to deaden the soul."[59]

Benjamin's diary relates such a period of revival at the seminary in the winter and spring of 1874. It seems to have begun when Benjamin preached on a Sunday

---

55. Ellen Roberts, "In Everything Give Thanks," *EC* 31, no. 5 (May 1876): 160.

56. Edith Hurlburt, tribute to Ellen Roberts in *EC* 95, no. 3 (Mar. 1908): 84-85.

57. Anna Johnston, tribute to Ellen Roberts in *EC* 95, no. 3 (Mar. 1908): 86; Obituary, Anna Johnston, *FM*, Feb. 22, 1927, p. 14.

58. Obituary, Anna Johnston, p. 14.

59. BHR, *BTR*, p. 369.

evening in mid-February, but there had been a strong sense of God's presence earlier. On Friday evening, January 2, after a sermon by Sam Chesbrough, "the Spirit of testimony rested on the brethren and sisters," Benjamin noted. "It was a blessed meeting. Sis. Emma Sellew was greatly blessed especially after the meeting. Sis. Griswold was also made unspeakably happy in the Lord. Sister Ida Collins in a transport of holy joy ran about the room[,] her eyes closed, praising the Lord."[60]

Benjamin preached Sunday evening, February 15, on "Come out and be separate." Though none came forward for prayer, there "was great solemnity in the house," he said. He noted in his diary, "Emma C. and Ella both gave in clear testimonies. Conviction appeared to be general. When we reached home I found Louise and Bessie both converted and happy in the Lord. Our son Benson [then twenty] was greatly blessed and was rejoicing in the Lord with great simplicity and sweetness, saying 'I am so glad the Lord has come to our house.' 'O Father, don't you feel encouraged?'"[61]

On Monday Benjamin noted, "There was but little done in the Sem. but praying and praising the Lord. In the evening the students were greatly blessed — and the power of the Lord rested upon them all over the house."[62] The next evening at the weekly class meeting "the power and the glory of God rested down upon us," Benjamin noted. "Emma C. especially was blessed in a wonderful manner. Her testimony was with a simplicity and a power, that no words can describe. All were blessed. Ida Collins was wonderfully blessed, and expressed a strong faith that our Sem. building would be enlarged. So many clear, independent testimonies to the power of Christ to save I never heard — not even on a Camp Ground where the strongest pilgrims from all quarters were congregated."[63]

A revival spirit continued for some weeks, though Benjamin was often away on trips. Returning home on a snowy Friday, April 17, Benjamin was encouraged with the progress of the school. He preached that evening on "Grow in grace" and judged the service "a most excellent meeting. They are generally getting on good. I feel so thankful to the Lord for so pleasant a family and so pleasant a home and so prosperous [a] school."[64]

The 1873-74 school year ended in June on a very positive note. Benjamin commented on Wednesday, June 10:

> The closing exercise of the term were all that we could have desired. The attendance was good. The speaking and essays were creditable. Four students, A. V. [i.e., Vivian A.] Dake, A. H. Stilwell, Lucy Sellew and Lida Dunning were awarded Diplomas. At the close of the literary exercises we had a social religious meeting consisting chiefly of speaking & singing. It was simply glorious. I doubt if the like

60. BTRD, Jan. 2, 1874.
61. BTRD, Feb. 15, 1874.
62. BTRD, Feb. 16, 1874.
63. BTRD, Feb. 17, 1874.
64. BTRD, Apr. 17, 1874.

was ever seen at the closing exercises of a literary institution. Ida Collins was greatly blessed. Emma Chesbro committed herself to go through uncompromising for God.[65]

Vivian Dake later became a Free Methodist evangelist and the founder of the Pentecost Bands; Albert Stilwell served as principal of Chili Seminary and then of Spring Arbor, Evansville, and Seattle seminaries, all Free Methodist institutions.[66] Lida Dunning (later Mrs. William Lamont) worked for several years at Providence Mission on West Thirty-seventh Street in New York City, which ministered "especially to the poor and oppressed colored population."[67] Many of the early graduates went on to receive further education at the University of Rochester or elsewhere and became educators, missionaries, church leaders, or businessmen.

B. T. Roberts was able to report in March 1875 that Chili Seminary "thus far has been successful beyond our most sanguine expectations. The possibility of running a school upon purely Gospel principles, has been abundantly demonstrated." God had provided competent and devout teachers and plenty of students; the need was more space. A good spirit prevailed among the students: "The state of religion is most encouraging. Nearly all our students in the Seminary enjoy religion. They take the narrow way, and embrace the Gospel in its simplicity and purity. With one accord they look for the outpouring of the Spirit, and it comes at times, in great power and sweetness among us."[68]

Four of Roberts's sons, including Benson and Benjamin, were students at Chili Seminary, as noted earlier. Later some of Benjamin and Ellen's grandchildren were students as well. In 1891-92, for example, Benson and Emma's daughters Lois and Lucy (then nine and five) were enrolled, as was George's son Hibbert.[69]

As at other schools, the students formed literary societies from time to time, and occasionally these societies issued their own publications. In 1874 a group calling itself the Phoenix Literary Society "sustained two weekly newspapers, called the Students Gazette and the Literary Review," according to a later student publication, though these were "not printed, but were written on foolscap paper." Through the

---

65. BTRD, June 10, 1874.

66. Howard A. Snyder, *One Hundred Years at Spring Arbor: A History of Spring Arbor College, 1873-1973* ([Spring Arbor, Mich.: Spring Arbor College, 1973]), p. 26.

67. Jane Dunning, *Brands from the Burning: An Account of a Work among the Sick and Destitute in Connection with Providence Mission, New York City* (Chicago: T. B. Arnold, 1881), pp. 245, 256; *Catalogue*, Chili Seminary, 1878-79, p. 10. Lida Dunning was the daughter of Mrs. Jane Dunning, superintendent of the mission. Hogue, noting Jane Dunning's and Lida Dunning Lamont's service at Providence Mission, comments, "The work of this mission became quite famous, and its character and effectiveness were acknowledged to be largely due to the influence of the workers chosen from among the Free Methodist people." Hogue, *HFMC*, 2:363. B. T. Roberts's friend and colleague Joseph Mackey was also associated with the work of this mission; see Dunning, pp. 126, 140, 144.

68. [B. T. Roberts], "Chili Seminary," *EC* 29, no. 3 (Mar. 1875): 94.

69. Smail, pp. 15-16. In the 1891-92 catalogue, Hibbert, Lois, and Lucy Roberts are listed under "Intermediate and Select Students." *Annual Circular . . . 1891-2*, pp. 9-10.

entire 1886-87 school year this society managed to sustain a nicely printed four-page student newspaper called *Students' Chronicle*. The first issue (November 13, 1886) announced, "This is an age of progression. We design to take one step ahead [of previous student efforts], and our paper will be printed weekly at the office of the *Earnest Christian*."[70] For a time there was also the B. T. Roberts Literary Society.[71]

As Benjamin and Ellen traveled in the interests of the church, they served as recruiters for the seminary, sometimes offering students lodging in their home. Adelaide Newton, later Mrs. Alexander Beers, recalled meeting the Robertses at a general quarterly meeting at Binghamton in the early 1880s. When Benjamin and Ellen learned that Adelaide wanted to attend Chili Seminary, they invited her to come and live with them. "This was the turning point in my life and proved to be the entrance to privileges in the Gospel beyond anything I had ever dreamed," said Adelaide. Raised in a home that did not encourage her spiritually, she found in Benjamin and Ellen "a father and mother indeed." Ellen, she noted, "began moulding me for service in the Master's vineyard as soon as I entered her home, and continued to be an example and inspiration to me to the hour of her death." She added, "[Ellen] taught me in detail concerning the practical matters of housekeeping; she gave me constant examples in economy of time, strength and money. True refinement and scholarly culture were her natural atmosphere, and these she strove to impart to me. She was ever instructing me in the deeper truths of the Bible, God's leadings and dealings with me; the beautiful chain of Divine providences; the art of simple and loving faith; how to walk and talk with God."[72]

A student from the 1870s, David S. Warner (later a Free Methodist bishop), recalled the intense earnestness of Benjamin and Ellen's ministry as well as their heavy workload. "Coming home from an extended absence," Warner wrote, Benjamin "must plunge into the great volume of work that had been awaiting his return, and occasionally I caught glimpses of him in his study with his pen racing across his manuscript preparing 'copy' for the Earnest Christian." Warner especially remembered Roberts's preaching — "He had the marvelous faculty of preaching in a manner to interest thoughtless boys and girls" — and his singing. Benjamin's "whole-souled singing" deeply impressed Warner. "I can in memory see him now, as, with head thrown back, and eyes closed in his peculiar manner, he sang the song, 'All I want, all I want, all I want, Is a little more faith in Jesus.'"

Warner said a "characteristic sight in those days" was "Brother Roberts hurrying to and from the station, riding in the well-known open buggy behind the chestnut pony driven by one of the boys."

Warner commented, as did others, on the key role of Ellen Roberts. Since Benjamin was often away from home, "much of the care and burden of the Semi-

70. *Students' Chronicle* 1, no. 1 (Nov. 13, 1886): 2.

71. Minute Book, B. T. Roberts Literary Society. Roberts Room, Roberts Wesleyan College Library.

72. Beers, "My Spiritual Mother," p. 75.

nary," including the financial pressures, was borne by Ellen. She assisted Benjamin in his work, "whether as editor, minister, or manager of school interests." Warner especially recalled, as did "hundreds of other students," Ellen's leading of the Tuesday evening class meeting in the seminary dining room. These seem to have been fairly large witness, testimony, and exhortation meetings, rather than class meetings in the original Methodist sense. As different students shared, Ellen would give words of encouragement or instruction. "Her great desire for the young people was that they might be blessed. It was not enough for them to maintain a profession of religion, but they must receive the outpouring of the Spirit again and again."[73]

The Tuesday evening general class meeting, usually led by Ellen, came to be an important part of the seminary's life. Benjamin noted on January 2, 1872, "A large attendance at class-meeting at the Sem. this eve. Some were blessed a good deal." Again on October 22, 1872, he remarked, "It was quite close in the class-meeting at the Sem. this evening till Minnie White — a colored girl spoke. The Spirit came and we had a blessed season. The Lord helped Sister Roberts very much."[74]

The Roberts Home on Buffalo Road

In 1880 B. T. Roberts built a home for his family on the south side of Buffalo Road, just across the street from Chesbrough Seminary. This large "house on the hill" served as the family residence for the remainder of Benjamin's and Ellen's lives. After living in the Rumsey farmhouse for fifteen years, the Roberts family moved into their new home in 1881.[75]

It was a beautiful location, much loved by the family. Buffalo Road was the main road between Rochester and Buffalo. The house occupied "the highest ground the town afforded," giving Benjamin and Ellen a nice view of the seminary. The property included an orchard and garden and a large variety of trees. Adella Carpenter noted that the house "was circled about with apple trees which in spring time made it a bower of pink and white beauty with their bloom." The house became the Roberts family home and headquarters. "Here students and friends visited; here prayer meetings were often appointed." Here Benjamin and Ellen "counseled foreign missionaries on their way to their fields of labor; here committees met to make a new church hymn book." This is the home from which Benjamin was constantly departing on his many trips, and to which he gladly returned. Though Ellen sometimes accompanied him, more frequently she remained at home "looking after seminary affairs" and assisting Benjamin with the *Earnest Christian* and his many other duties.[76]

73. David S. Warner, "A Student's Recollections," *EC* 95, no. 3 (Mar. 1908): 78-79.

74. BTRD, Jan. 2 and Oct. 22, 1872.

75. Carpenter, pp. 79-80; cf. Pfouts, *History*, pp. 25-26. Carpenter says, "From this home, the bodies of both [Benjamin and Ellen] were carried to their places of quiet rest till the resurrection day" (p. 80).

76. Carpenter, pp. 79-80.

Transition in Leadership

Benjamin and Ellen largely directed the school during its first decade, though with various faculty serving brief tenures as principal.[77] In 1876, however, Benson Roberts, just graduated from Dartmouth, took over as principal — the first Chili Seminary graduate to head the school. Already in 1874, when Benson was just twenty, B. T. Roberts had been thinking of the possibility of his son taking on the leadership of the school. He wrote to Ellen from Michigan, "You must work Benson in at the seminary all you can. It occurs to me that the Lord will give him to us for Principal when he gets through college."[78]

Benson and Emma Sellew were married in 1877, after she graduated from Cornell, and together the two served as dual principals during the 1878-79 school year, living "with the staff and the students in the Seminary building." When Benjamin and Ellen moved to their new home on Buffalo Road in 1881, Benson and Emma moved into the Rumsey farmhouse.[79]

Albert Stilwell served as principal for two years while Benson completed his master's degree. Benson and Emma then ably served as coprincipals of Chesbrough Seminary for a quarter-century, from 1881 to 1906.[80] The school prospered under their joint leadership and the general oversight of B. T. Roberts. Though funds were often short, the seminary operated on a sound financial basis. It was clear in its mission, committed both to spiritual nurture and to academic thoroughness. B. T. Roberts promoted the school in his travels and through the pages of the *Earnest Christian*. He assisted it through fund-raising and his own personal funds, sometimes borrowing money to balance the budget. Reporting the completion of a successful school year in July 1884, B. T. wrote, "The wing is finished and the bills are paid, by my obtaining the money on my individual responsibility; so that no one is entrapped but myself. I have paid in all nearly three thousand dollars more than I have received, besides what we have given. But the Lord is putting it into the hearts of one and another to help, and He will bring us through."[81]

Throughout their tenure Benson and Emma Roberts put high value on serious scholarship, as did Benjamin. Probably no phrase better captures the endeavor during its first several decades than Benson's phrase "Education for character." B. T. Roberts was very pleased to see the school continue to develop. He noted in 1891, as

77. G. W. Anderson served as principal, 1869-72, followed by Fidelia F. Clement (1872-73), Clark Jones (1873-74), B. T. Roberts again (1874-75), and Susan E. Ullyette (1875-76). See Pfouts, *History,* pp. 23, 66.

78. BTR (Jackson, Mich.) to ELR, Feb. 28, 1874, quoted in BHR, *BTR,* p. 463.

79. Pfouts, *History,* p. 25.

80. Pfouts, *History,* pp. 25-26, 66; Smail, pp. 15, 176.

81. [B. T. Roberts], "Chili Seminary," *EC* 48, no. 1 (July 1884): 34. Obviously Benjamin had good credit with the bank, based on prior financial dealings. The $3,000 he mentions, a very considerable sum, must have been largely covered by a loan or loans, since it was "besides what we have given," though he may be referring also to other unnamed sources or transactions.

he was raising funds for new buildings, "This school is no longer an experiment. It is a decided success." Many graduates had gone out to make their mark and "bless the world." "Several are [now] in charge of similar institutions."[82]

In the twentieth century the school B. T. Roberts founded evolved into Roberts Wesleyan College. Receiving a charter to offer junior college work in 1945, the school was renamed Roberts Junior College, honoring the founder. Four years later, when the school became a four-year liberal arts college, it was renamed Roberts Wesleyan College.[83]

As Chesbrough Seminary grew and expanded, Free Methodists in other parts of the country and in Canada followed Roberts's example in founding church-related schools. By 1883 Free Methodists had already established schools at Evansville, Wisconsin, and Spring Arbor, Michigan, as well as at North Chili. Roberts viewed these as an extension of the nurturing task of the Christian home. In an *Earnest Christian* editorial entitled "Christian Education," he maintained that such schools "bring together the young people who are Christians and so form a community of young people in which the prevailing sentiment is Christian, where the weak feel the support that comes from a strong public opinion and the knowledge that the influence of authority is behind them to aid and sustain." Roberts continued, "It is a great step towards permanency of Christian character to keep a youth from his fifteenth year to his twentieth in the way of truth. While young he is easily influenced to become a Christian. Encouraged and helped to continue his trust in Christian life until his twentieth year, he now steps out into life avowedly a Christian with all the strength of Christian associations and habits about him. He is free from worldly snares and habits. He is not now likely to depart from the way."

Roberts was confident that Free Methodist schools such as Chesbrough, Evansville, and Spring Arbor were "doing much to encourage the young to become Christians, and to continue in Christian life. They were founded in prayer and are conducted in prayer. They offer to all the help of a Christian family or society."[84]

In launching Chili Seminary, Benjamin and Ellen Roberts laid the foundation for the surprisingly extensive enterprise of higher Christian education that has since marked Free Methodism.[85]

---

82. B. T. Roberts, "Chesbrough Seminary," *EC* 61, no. 4 (Apr. 1891): 101-2.

83. Pfouts, *History*, pp. 95, 117, 125.

84. [B. T. Roberts], "Christian Education," *EC* 45, no. 6 (June 1883): 188-89. Uncharacteristically, the words "Christian" and "Christians" in most instances are not capitalized in this article. I have capitalized them to conform to Roberts's usual style.

85. See Marston, especially chapters 26 and 27, and David L. McKenna, *A Future with a History: The Wesleyan Witness of the Free Methodist Church; 1960 to 1995 and Forward* (Indianapolis: Light and Life Communications, 1997), chapter 13.

CHAPTER 30

Ben and Ellen

"The greatest domestic happiness always exists where husband and wife live together on terms of equality."

B. T. Roberts[1]

"One could not fail to be impressed with the idea that they were working for God, and that they were intensely in earnest in that work."

David S. Warner[2]

In the story of Benjamin and Ellen Roberts, it is his life that naturally gets more attention. Benjamin was the more public figure and wrote and published much more extensively than did Ellen. Yet the key role played by Ellen in everything Benjamin did is evident all along the way.

The partnership of Benjamin and Ellen Roberts — their marriage, their home and family life, and their expanding ministry together — is a story in itself. It includes the growth of the Roberts boys, who reached adulthood between 1870 and 1882, in the middle of Benjamin and Ellen's active ministry. These family dimensions are important to the story, especially given B. T. Roberts's views on the role of women and of the marriage relationship.

1. B. T. Roberts, *Ordaining Women* (Rochester, N.Y.: Earnest Christian Publishing House, 1891), p. 52.

2. David S. Warner, "A Student's Recollections," *EC* 95, no. 3 (Mar. 1908): 78.

The Roberts View of Marriage

In his 1891 book *Ordaining Women* (in some ways a groundbreaking study), B. T. Roberts pictured marriage as an equal partnership. He promoted a model of cooperative mutuality rather than one of hierarchy or male-dominance. Arguing from the creation account in Genesis, he affirmed: "Woman was created, not as the *servant* of man, but as his *companion,* his *equal.*" Genesis 1:26-27 teaches that the "dominion which God gave to man at the creation was a *joint* dominion. It was given to the woman equally as to the man." From this Benjamin concluded, "God created woman a *female man* — nothing more — nothing less. She had all the rights and prerogatives of the man. The dominion given to him was given equally to her."[3]

Roberts noted that in Genesis, "Nothing was said of the subjection of woman before the fall," and that Jesus in his teachings referred back to the prefall state of humankind when speaking of the relationship between men and women (Matt. 19:4). From this Roberts concluded, "Christ *restored the primitive law.* He said nothing about the *subjection of woman — not one word.*" The subjection of woman in society is a consequence of the fall; it is neither God's original intent nor the teaching of Jesus. Therefore it should not be the teaching of the church.

Based on this, Roberts in a remarkable passage gave his view of marriage:

> The greatest domestic happiness always exists where husband and wife live together on terms of equality. Two men, having individual interests, united only by business ties, daily associate as partners for years, without either of them being in subjection to the other. They consider each other as equals; and treat each other as equals. Then, cannot a man and woman, united by conjugal love, the strongest tie that can unite two human beings, having *the same* interests, live together in the same manner?
>
> Christ came to repair the ruin wrought by the fall. In Him, and in Him only, is Paradise *restored.*[4]

Marriage, then, and especially Christian marriage, is a partnership of total equality. No hierarchy; no chain of command. It is like a business partnership in which both parties have equal say. If two men can be in equal partnership with no hierarchy or dominance/submission pattern, why should it be any different in marriage, just because one is male and the other female? Partly because of this affirmation of "the model of the business partnership" as a pattern for marriage, Donald Dayton has argued that *Ordaining Women* should be seen as "one of the most radical of the Evangelical defenses of feminism" in the nineteenth century.[5]

---

3. B. T. Roberts, *Ordaining Women,* pp. 49-50. By "female man" Roberts meant not that women are to be masculine or exhibit male characteristics, but that women are fully human, with all the rights, capacities, and dignities that entails. Thus "man" here means "human" (as it does in Gen. 1:26-27), not "male."

4. B. T. Roberts, *Ordaining Women,* pp. 50-52.

5. Donald W. Dayton, *Discovering an Evangelical Heritage* (New York: Harper and Row, 1976), p. 92.

In sharing their lives together, Benjamin and Ellen shared also this partnership view of marriage, "liv[ing] together on terms of equality." Did they actually live it out? What was their life together really like? How fully did Ellen share in Benjamin's ministry, for instance, and how much did he share in child raising, the care of the home, and the concerns that were dearest to Ellen's heart? How did the marriage fare in the context of Benjamin's expanding ministry, and of Benjamin and Ellen's growing family?

During the early years of their marriage and pastoral ministry, Benjamin at times helped with the housework (though feeling he had "no commission and no taste for such business," as noted earlier). He also did quite a bit of gardening, necessary to their support. Meanwhile Ellen helped with home visitation, did much informal counseling and (especially) praying with people, and not infrequently testified or exhorted in class meetings and public services.

Benjamin's work around the home probably lessened from 1857 on as more of his time was taken up with writing and holding special meetings, and as he became increasingly embroiled in the Genesee Conference controversy. Yet amid all the pressures and changes of his expulsion from the ME Church and the founding of a new denomination, Benjamin and Ellen nurtured a close, affectionate married life. The best evidence of this is their private correspondence when they were separated — letters obviously not intended for the eyes of others then or of biographers later.

B. T. Roberts stressed the importance of Christian family life and of training up children in patterns of godliness. "Too light an estimate altogether is put upon the *form* of godliness," he wrote. Children need to be taught to obey, because in the first instance "Love springs from obedience, and not obedience from love."[6] Young children need to be grounded in godly practices that shape their character and predispose them to follow God's way.

> Take your children with you to church, and as soon as they can, have them take a part in worship. Have them kneel with you at family prayer and frequently take a part in family prayer. Never allow them to eat without a blessing is asked, and have them ask a blessing. Instead of being afraid of formality, you should be careful and make your children formal Christians. This is as far as you can go. You should teach them that this is not sufficient, and that they must ask God to change their hearts. If they have the form of godliness they will be much more likely to seek the power than they will if they despise both the form and the power.[7]

Proper training of children should be the highest priority of Christian parents, Roberts felt. "If there is any one particular above another, in which Christians should not conform to the world," it is this. Still Roberts recognized that "the children of

6. B. T. Roberts, "Training Children," *EC* 50, no. 2 (Aug. 1885): 39.
7. B. T. Roberts, "Training Children," p. 39.

godly parents are, in many cases, ungodly."[8] It was a source of sorrow to Benjamin and Ellen that most of their children did not become committed Christians.

Married Life

Benjamin and Ellen's forty-four years of married life were close and intimate, both physically and emotionally. Their letters show that they sustained a sense of romance over the years. Though they were fully devoted to the church's ministry, and though Ellen sometimes disagreed with Benjamin's decisions, their life together seems to have been consistently harmonious. Ellen's way of dealing with disagreement when it arose, if she couldn't persuade Benjamin otherwise, was to submissively leave matters in God's hands.

Benson Roberts said of Ellen, "My mother was well trained in domestic arts. She knew how the household should be kept. Though she gave herself to other than domestic duties, yet her household was always orderly, never left without proper care, never neglected. If she gave herself to God's work, God always gave her those who would care directly for the domestic duties, and do it, not as 'unto man but unto the Lord.'"

With a family to care for and concerns about the church, the *Earnest Christian*, Chili Seminary and the seminary farm, Ellen had much to think about and to do. Generally, however, she had domestic help. Sometimes this was hired help, but Benson noted that "after she, with my father, gave herself wholly to evangelical work, there was always someone under the roof who was there because God sent them," who became part of the family and helped run the household.

Ellen enjoyed sewing because "it gave her time to think." In his tribute to his mother, Benson wrote:

> I can remember long mornings when she, in her room, was contriving garments for her children out of made-over clothes, or turning a dress for herself, that she might not shame her husband, but appear in a becoming garb before the eyes of the people. I do not remember that I ever saw my mother appear before the family when she was not neatly attired. Her table was always well ordered as became the family of a minister. There might not be much to put upon it, dainties might wholly be lacking, yet the cloth was clean, the table well spread, and those who sat down to it must be in proper trim.[9]

Ellen frequently entertained guests, especially after she and Benjamin had their own home in North Chili. Beginning in 1885, as the denominational foreign missions enterprise developed, this meant sometimes hosting missionaries on their way to foreign fields. Ellen was well prepared for this task; as a young woman she had as-

---

8. B. T. Roberts, "Training Children," p. 37.
9. Benson Roberts, "My Mother," *EC* 95, no. 3 (Mar. 1908): 69-70.

sisted her aunt Lydia Lane in New York City as Mrs. Lane helped newly assigned Methodist missionaries prepare for their departures.

One of the earliest Free Methodist missionaries, Augusta Tullis Kelley, left a vignette of B. T. and Ellen Roberts in this hosting role. She and Walter Kelley were married at the Roberts home in North Chili in April 1885, on the eve of their departure for Portuguese East Africa.

Augusta, or "Gusta," Tullis was a successful, young Free Methodist evangelist from Indiana. At twenty-five she heard B. T. Roberts preach twice at annual conference in Illinois. "Brother B. T. Roberts is an excellent man of God," Gusta wrote then. "He talked to the ministers as a loving father to obedient children." His sermon on 1 Peter 5:10 was "fresh, practical and wholesome. . . . The saints rejoiced, and Brother Roberts was so blest that his face fairly shone."[10]

In 1885 the Free Methodist missions board appointed Walter Kelley to head the first band of missionaries to Africa. Kelley asked Gusta to join him as his wife. In a few weeks the two were married and on their way overseas as part of the team (including G. Harry Agnew, "indomitable hero of Free Methodist Africa Missions")[11] that established Free Methodist work in Africa.

Gusta Kelley tells of her wedding in the Roberts home. She, Walter, and a few others gathered on Tuesday evening, April 21, for the ceremony. "Sister Roberts gave us a hearty welcome. . . . At 6:30 p.m. Brother B. T. Roberts united us in the holy bonds of matrimony. My soul was calm and my whole being composed as I took the sacred vow. Brother Roberts prayed for us in the Spirit, and I believe his prayer was heard. The tea was well prepared under Sister Roberts' excellent management. We felt highly honored when we learned that the tea-set used on the occasion was the one used at the wedding of Brother and Sister Roberts, some forty [sic] years previous."[12]

Ellen and her helpers prepared a fine wedding supper. "Nothing extravagant, but all good. The bride's cake was very nice," Gusta wrote. "The evening was spent in singing and talking." The newlyweds spent the night in the Roberts home and, after an early breakfast with the family, left by train at 8:30 for New York City and their voyage to Africa, via England.[13]

Walter and Gusta Kelley were forced to return home a year later due to ill health; both apparently contracted disease in Africa. Gusta died just a few years later at age thirty-one. Walter served briefly as general missionary secretary for the denomination but had to relinquish his responsibilities for health reasons. His initial call to Af-

---

10. Walter W. Kelley, *Memoirs of Mrs. Augusta Tullis Kelley: Her Experience, Labors as Evangelist and Missionary to Africa with Extracts from Her Writings*, rev. ed. (Chicago: B. T. Arnold, 1889), p. 32.

11. Marston, p. 454.

12. Kelley, *Memoirs*, p. 72. In a letter to a friend, Gusta wrote, "As soon as the bishop pronounced us husband and wife, he said, 'Let us pray.' I wish you could have heard the prayer. I never heard anything like it. It was simple, but so appropriate and good. We were both blest" (p. 74). It is interesting that Gusta refers to Roberts as "the bishop," since his official title at this time was general superintendent.

13. Kelley, *Memoirs*, pp. 74-79.

rica had been prompted by his experience of commanding Negro troops during the Civil War and of teaching his men to read. He hoped to establish a self-supporting mission station in Africa after the model advocated by William Taylor.[14] The Kelleys and other early Free Methodist missionaries show the spirit of B. T. and Ellen Roberts. The expanding corps of Free Methodist missionaries in the 1880s and 1890s was in fact an extension of B. T. and Ellen Roberts's own shared ministry.

Benson Roberts saw his parents involved in many forms of ministry while he was growing up. From the earliest days of Free Methodism and the founding of Chili Seminary on through the beginning and growth of Free Methodist foreign missions, Benson was both observer and participant. And Benson, who after all was a blend of both parents, saw as well the intimate side of Benjamin and Ellen.

Benson saw in his mother what her teenage diaries reveal: a love for nature and the countryside. "She loved to be out under the sky," he said; "she loved the green fields, the cherry trees in blossom, and watched with eagerness the oriole's first appearance."

Ellen showed great wisdom in parenting the Roberts boys, especially during their teen years. At least that was Benson's assessment. He noted that his parents had five "strong-willed boys," themselves "the sons of a man and a woman who possessed no ordinary degree of firmness and resoluteness." Ellen was "a woman who could keep a secret," and her sons confided in her. Her children "knew her great love, and . . . it was not a difficult thing for the son to open his heart to his mother and tell her his longings, of his aspirations, of his difficulties."[15] Here Benson reflects his own struggles as a young man. The other Roberts sons may not have experienced their mother in quite the same way, though they all apparently loved and admired her.

In North Chili the parents involved the Roberts boys in household and farm duties, partly to instill discipline. Ellen noted in March 1867, "The boys with the help of their father have begun to make maple sugar . . . a slow process."[16] Once when Ellen was away from home she wrote to Benjamin, who was also traveling, "Now, dearest, take a little time to talk with your boys when you get home; hear the full story each one has to tell and sympathize with them in their tribulations and then in love and patience be firm and *strict* with them. Make each one behave at prayers and at the table. I will help you all I can when I get home and you may *exhort* me, and see to it that I do the right thing by the children. . . . Kiss the little ones for me."[17]

Benjamin needed the reminder. With his busy schedule and constant travels he was scarcely able to give the boys the attention they needed.

Benjamin and Ellen shared in financial decisions, though here Benjamin clearly took the lead. Ellen to some degree maintained her own funds, or savings, for

14. Byron S. Lamson, *Venture! The Frontiers of Free Methodism* (Winona Lake, Ind.: Light and Life, 1960), pp. 50-62, 93; Marston, pp. 453-54.

15. Benson Roberts, "My Mother," p. 70.

16. ELRD, Mar. 1, 1867, quoted in Zahniser, p. 218.

17. ELR (Williamsburg [Pa.?]) to BTR, undated, quoted in Zahniser, p. 219.

Benjamin noted on March 25, 1869, that he "borrowed $234.60 of my dear wife" to meet a $500.00 payment to the contractor on the seminary building.[18]

Marriage and the Stresses of Ministry

As general superintendent, Benjamin found his labors growing as the church expanded. His duties ranged from presiding at annual conferences and preaching at camp meetings to conducting quarterly meetings and handling a growing flow of correspondence. Often away from home, he kept in touch with Ellen and other family members through a steady stream of letters. Generally when he traveled Ellen remained at home, though she occasionally went to camp meetings with him and twice accompanied him on long trips to the West Coast.

Benjamin's diaries give a sense of his work in behalf of the church and of his relationship with Ellen. He wrote on Monday, January 1, 1866,

> I held yesterday a quarterly meeting at Rose, N.Y. Services commenced at 9 A.M., and continued till nearly 2 P.M. The Lord is with us in power. I preached from Isaiah 35:8 ["And an highway shall be there, and a way, and it shall be called The way of holiness . . ."].
>
> In the evening we held a watch meeting at Clyde. The house was crowded, and continued full till midnight. I preached from Rom. 6:23. . . .
>
> This has been a very good day to my soul. I give myself anew to the Lord, and look for grace to walk with Him all the days of my life.[19]

A week and a half later Benjamin was in Saratoga, New York. The Free Methodists had "rented a hall on Main Street, which will seat about three hundred persons. It is well filled. About thirty profess to have been saved. I preached in the evening to an attentive congregation from the text, 'Escape for thy life.'" On Monday, January 15, a "very cold day," Benjamin preached in the evening at Saratoga "to a large congregation" from "They have healed slightly the hurt of the daughter of my people." He commented, "It was a good meeting. I passed a restless night; went to the depot the next morning before four o'clock to take the cars for home. . . . Found all well at home."[20]

After a few days at home Benjamin left on Saturday, January 20, for Albany, "expecting to preach in the evening, but no appointment was given out." En route to Albany by train he talked with "two dissolute fine-looking young men who have been in the army. They acknowledged their need of religion." Benjamin hoped he made a good impression.[21]

---

18. BTRD, Mar. 25, 1869, quoted in BHR, *BTR*, p. 389.

19. Quoted in BHR, *BTR*, p. 374. Here and in other similar references, I have transposed Roberts's Roman numeral Scripture references to Arabic numerals.

20. These entries are quoted from BHR, *BTR*, pp. 374-75.

21. BHR, *BTR*, pp. 375-76.

On Sunday, February 4, 1866, Benjamin was in New York City where he preached in the morning from "Who can understand his errors?" and in the evening from "the day of salvation." The following Sunday he was in Buffalo, preaching on "Contend earnestly for the faith" and "Now is the day of salvation." Several came forward seeking help and one was converted, Benjamin noted.[22]

Sunday, February 2, 1868, Benjamin and Ellen were involved with the quarterly meeting at North Chili. "A very good love feast," Benjamin reported. "I preached in the morning from 'They shall devour and subdue with sling stones.' The Lord helped, and I was somewhat blessed. But I feel discouraged about the work here, on account of the unwillingness of the members to break down before the Lord. They feel satisfied with themselves."[23]

When not traveling, Benjamin was at home in North Chili attending to the business of the seminary, the denomination, and the *Earnest Christian.* Working at home on February 17, 1869, he "Wrote an article on 'Murmuring' for *The Earnest Christian.*" Ten days later he was at the office "reading proof for *The Earnest Christian.* The last form." He finished in time to catch the three o'clock train for meetings in Syracuse and Utica while Ellen remained at home with the family.[24]

A few weeks later Benjamin went by train to Mechanicville, New York, where he preached at the Methodist Episcopal church from his favorite text, "Straight is the gate." The congregation, Benjamin said, "was good and attentive," but "seemed hardly to know what to make of the truth." The next day (March 9, 1869) he traveled down along the Hudson River to Albany and sat in on a session of the New York state legislature. At a legislative committee meeting he "opposed the enlargement of the boundaries of the city of Rochester." He added that he was "sorely tempted," without explanation. That night at 10:30, after hearing a "studied, eloquent" lecture on "Daniel in Babylon" by the celebrated Methodist pulpit orator William Punshon, Benjamin took the cars for Rome, 110 miles west, arriving at 3:00 A.M. There he attended to a church trial, then returned to North Chili for a meeting of the Chili Seminary Board of Trustees on March 11. Everything "moves off harmoniously," he remarked of the board meeting.[25]

About ten days later Benjamin was ministering on Sunday at Binghamton. On Monday, March 22, he noted, "Rose at three this morning, and took the train for Rochester. Got along well. Found my dear wife at the [*Earnest Christian*] office. Went home at five o'clock and found all well."[26]

Benjamin's diary entries of this type generally exhibit a rather optimistic, upbeat attitude, despite difficulties and pressures. Apparently Roberts was able to function quite effectively while maintaining a very heavy schedule and often getting little sleep. He missed Ellen keenly as he traveled on behalf of the church and looked for-

22. BHR, *BTR,* p. 377.
23. BHR, *BTR,* p. 381.
24. BHR, *BTR,* p. 384.
25. BHR, *BTR,* pp. 385-86.
26. BTRD, Mar. 22, 1869, quoted in BHR, *BTR,* pp. 388-89.

ward to her letters. He wrote to her playfully from Spring Arbor, Michigan, on September 28, 1871, "A good many inquire after you as usual and wonder why you did not come. You see, darling, it is just as I tell you, the people would rather see you than me." A few days later from Jackson, Michigan, on his way to Chicago: "I would like so much to take my course east instead of west; but I can say more heartily than when I left home, 'The will of the Lord be done.'" He added, "God bless you. It seems to me now that I will never leave home without you unless it is an absolute necessity. But I really want to do the will of the Lord." Four days later he was in Galva, Illinois, 170 miles west of Chicago. He wrote to Ellen, "I long to be with you and take care of you. The conference opens well, and I hope we shall get through with the business so that I can start home Monday morning, leaving Chicago in the evening."[27]

Thus Benjamin continued his itinerating ministry, usually with Ellen remaining at home in North Chili looking after the family, the seminary, and the magazine, though occasionally traveling with him and assisting in the meetings. Day by day Benjamin's letters arrived at the Roberts home, postmarked Cincinnati, Kansas, Texas, Missouri, Ohio, Michigan, Chicago, Vermont, New Jersey, Ontario, Wisconsin, and many other places, often posted from train stations along the way. Benjamin wrote from Michigan in February 1872, "My letters seem so poor in comparison with your dear ones that I am quite ashamed to write. I have written you twice." He added two days later, "Your precious letter came last night and I was so glad to hear from you again. Praise the Lord for His kindness to us, and to me especially in giving me such a precious gift as my dear wife."[28]

On March 19, 1872, traveling to Kansas, Benjamin wrote to Ellen from Cincinnati. "I feel troubled about matters at home. And first I want to ask your forgiveness for not giving you a ride to church Thursday night. I am very sorry for it and I will try and do better if you will only forgive me."[29] The following Sunday he wrote,

> I was so glad to get a few lines from you yesterday. You must look up and cast all your care on the Lord. I feel bad at having you so burdened with work and care. I will hasten back as soon as I can; but the calls are so urgent at Missouri and at Evansville, Ind., that I know not how to resist them. I am better of my cold. I was a good deal blessed yesterday in trying to preach. The Lord is answering your prayers for me. Write me at Evansville, Ind.
>
> God bless you, darling one. Pardon these few lines. I have had to snatch every moment to write for *The Earnest Christian*.[30]

Much of Benson Roberts's account of his father's ministry during the 1870s consists of extracts like these from Benjamin's letters to Ellen.

---

27. BTR to ELR, Sept. 28, Oct. 1 and Oct. 5, 1871, quoted in BHR, *BTR*, pp. 412-13.
28. BTR to ELR, Feb. 22 and 24, 1874, quoted in BHR, *BTR*, pp. 415-417.
29. BTR to ELR, Mar. 19, 1872, quoted in BHR, *BTR*, p. 419.
30. BTR to ELR, Mar. 24, 1872, quoted in BHR, *BTR*, p. 419.

Benjamin also kept in touch with his sons by letter when traveling. Occasionally he took one or another of the boys with him on trips. In July 1874 twelve-year-old Sammie, the second-youngest child, accompanied his father by train to churches and camp meetings in Pennsylvania. After a weekend of services in Philadelphia, Benjamin took Sammie to see some of the sights in the historic city. Benjamin commented, "[Sammie] is deeply interested and takes such an intelligent observation of things that it is a real pleasure to take him around. There is much to be seen in Philadelphia that is deeply interesting — Many relics of revolutionary times." That evening father and son took a long overnight ride from Philadelphia across Pennsylvania to Franklin, north of Pittsburgh — well over 350 miles — arriving midafternoon on Wednesday. "The ride over the mountains was grand and inspiring," Benjamin noted. The train connections took them west to Freeport, then north along the Allegheny River. "We followed its windings up to Franklin which we reached about 2.30 P.M." He and Sammie "[w]alked over to the [camp]ground in a hot sun."[31]

Ellen arrived the next day from North Chili, and she, Benjamin, and Sammie stayed at the camp for a week. Sammie heard his father preach several times, and heard sermons by E. P. Hart, Richard Hawkins, Wilson T. Hogg, Samuel Chesbrough, and others. Benjamin, Ellen, and Sammie returned home on Thursday, July 22, traveling all day by train.[32]

Family Crisis

Tragedy struck the Roberts household six months later when Sammie suddenly died. He was barely a teenager — "thirteen years and thirteen days old," Benjamin wrote. "The doctors pronounced his disease the malignant scarlet fever."[33]

Sammie, a student at Chili Seminary, had taken ill on Friday night, January 29, 1875. At first Benjamin and Ellen thought he simply had a cold. But he grew worse, and the illness proved to be virulent scarlet fever — a form of streptococcal infection that, in those days before penicillin, was often fatal. Ellen's own sister had died from scarlet fever years earlier.

The disease was swift and deadly; Sammie died just before noon on Monday, February 1.[34] Earlier that morning Ellen lovingly changed Sammie's clothes. The boy asked about his father, who was away over the weekend holding meetings. A little later Benjamin arrived and kissed his son. Seeing immediately that Sammie was critically ill, Benjamin fell to his knees and pleaded with God for his healing. But a short

---

31. BTRD, July 14 and 15, 1874.

32. BTRD, July 16-22, 1874. Several weeks earlier (Saturday, May 30) Benjamin "went to an artist's and sat for a photograph" by request while he was visiting Utica, N.Y.

33. [B. T. Roberts], "In Deep Affliction," *EC* 29, no. 2 (Feb. 1875): 63.

34. [B. T. Roberts], "In Deep Affliction," p. 63; Smail, p. 12; Carpenter, pp. 77-78, 91. Carpenter gives the year as 1874 and Samuel's age as fourteen, but this is incorrect.

time later Sammie was gone. "You cannot change the mind of the Lord," Ellen thought.[35]

Sammie's death was a heavy blow to Benjamin and Ellen. "We expected that he would live and preach the Gospel when we were gone," Benjamin wrote sadly. "It never occurred to us that there was any danger of his dying. But he has gone. God has taken him. His ways are far above our ways. We bow submissive to His will, and kiss the hand that has so sorely smitten us." Benjamin put a notice of Samuel's death entitled "In Deep Affliction" at the beginning of the editorial section of the February *Earnest Christian,* marked off with wide black lines, and asked for prayer.[36]

Samuel was a child "of remarkable promise," his parents' delight. He early developed a strong Christian commitment, unlike some of the other Roberts boys. Benjamin wrote,

> His intelligence was far beyond his years. Men and women of cultivation loved to converse with him. . . .
>
> He feared the Lord, and lived a life of prayer and faith. His daily life was that of a consistent Christian. In every thing, he was remarkably conscientious. Whenever any business was intrusted to his care, he was always very particular to account for every penny. He was thoroughly unselfish. He had a few dollars in the Bank, which had been given him from time to time, and whenever he saw us in want of money he would beg us to get his money and use it. He literally cared nothing for money.

In other words, Samuel embodied the qualities Benjamin himself most admired. Benjamin remarked also on Sammie's patience. One day the boy came to Ellen and said, "Mother, Benjie plagues me so I am afraid my patience will give out." Someone asked him once what he did when teased by his brothers, and he replied, "I pray just as hard as I can to keep from getting out of patience."[37]

Now the teenage son — and, presumably, hoped-for successor, along with Benson, then twenty-one — was gone.

Ellen's grief was profound. "When I attempt to write to any of my friends my nerves quiver and shake like an aspen leaf," she wrote some weeks after Sammie's passing.[38] She eventually wrote a letter to her friend Martha Kendall LaDue, reflecting on and processing her loss. "God gave me Sammy in answer to prayer," she wrote.

> He has been a blessing to us all. He preached to us all from his birth and to all in the house. He lived a life of faith, always. He reproved, rebuked and exhorted, and always turned me to the Lord if he saw me tempted or troubled. He never made a public profession of religion, but his life was consistent. During his last illness I

35. Carpenter, p. 79.
36. [B. T. Roberts], "In Deep Affliction," p. 63. The February issue was delayed due to Samuel's death.
37. [B. T. Roberts], "In Deep Affliction," p. 63.
38. ELR to Mrs. LaDue, quoted in Carpenter, p. 78 (no date given).

talked with him, and he said that he felt the Lord blessed him; said he prayed. This I knew he did. He seemed to me almost angelic as he lay on the bed the day before he died. This troubled me. I tried to pray and so did others for recovery. And it was as if a hand was laid on our mouths. All I could get any help in asking was, "God bless him, he is in Thy hands." Still I could not think he was going to die. I dared not think it.[39]

For weeks Ellen could not bring herself to visit Sammie's grave. When she finally did, she "knew at once," she said, "if I grieved the Spirit by too great sorrow."[40]

Benjamin and Ellen were left now with four sons: George Lane, Benson, Charles Stowe, and the youngest, Benjamin Titus, who was a lad of ten when his brother Sammie died.

B. T. and Ellen Roberts as Persons

What were Benjamin and Ellen really like, in personality and temperament? A profile emerges from their letters and diaries over the years.

Clearly Ellen was rather introverted, or inwardly focused, compared with Benjamin. Though quite different from each other, Benjamin and Ellen had much in common. This made for a strong, lasting marriage.

One common approach to temperament compares four sets of personality characteristics or tendencies: extraversion/introversion, intuition/sensation, thinking/feeling, and judging/perceiving.[41] How would Benjamin and Ellen Roberts fare on such a grid?

Clearly Ellen was dominantly an introvert, though she learned to function to some degree in a more extraverted manner. By contrast, Benjamin exhibited a blend of introvert and extravert characteristics, but seems to have been more an extravert than an introvert.

"Intuition" versus "sensation" has to do with the way people think and therefore act. The "sensible" person prefers and trusts facts, while the intuitive relies more on imagination and is alert to future possibilities. Here Benjamin and Ellen were much alike. Both were sensible and realistic (in terms of temperament), but both were also attuned to imagination, metaphor, and intuitive insights.

---

39. ELR to Mrs. LaDue, quoted in Carpenter, pp. 78-79. In Carpenter the name is spelled "Sammy," but in Benjamin's diary and most other sources (including Ellen's 1894 diary) it is "Sammie." Ellen noted in her diary on Feb. 1, 1894, nineteen years after the event, "This is the day years ago when Sammie left us."

40. ELR to Mrs. LaDue, quoted in Carpenter, p. 79.

41. The Myers-Briggs Type Indicator, for example, based on the personality theories of Carl Jung, contrasts these four sets of characteristics. In theory, every person exhibits some combination of these tendencies, thus yielding a variety of personality types. See David Keirsey and Marilyn Bates, *Please Understand Me: Character and Temperament Types* (Del Mar, Calif.: Prometheus Nemesis Books, 1978), for a popular presentation of Jung's personality theory and the Myers-Briggs Type Indicator.

Benjamin and Ellen were quite different on the thinking/feeling scale. Benjamin appears to have possessed an equal blend of thinking and feeling traits, while Ellen was almost totally a feeling person. Not that Ellen was irrational or incapable of clear thinking, of course. But she was very much alive to her own feelings and could relate deeply to others at the feeling level.

Benjamin's balance of thinking and feeling traits gave him strength as a leader. He based decisions on both personal and more "objective" factors. Benjamin and Ellen's letters suggest that this personality difference was at times a source of tension.

The "judging" versus "perceiving" distinction essentially boils down to this: "Do I prefer closure and the settling of things or do I prefer to keep options open and fluid?"[42] Benjamin and Ellen were much alike here. Both wanted to see issues settled and decisions made. If this seems stronger in Benjamin, the reason may be the situations he found himself in, first in the ME Genesee Conference with its tensions and controversies, then in the Free Methodist Church, where he was constantly charged with decision making. Benjamin wanted to see issues resolved, but he was intuitively aware of a wide range of factors and was sensitive to relational factors when decisions had to be made.

B. T. Roberts thus seems to have been rather evenly balanced in introversion/extraversion, intuition/sensation, and thinking/feeling. This is no doubt what people sensed when they described him as a "symmetrical man."[43]

Temperamentally, Benjamin and Ellen were well suited for each other. Not only did they have similar Christian commitments and interests, but they were well matched in personality. His more extroverted nature complemented her more inward spirit. While they both liked to see issues resolved, they could and did tolerate, by God's grace, a significant amount of uncertainty about their future. Perhaps most importantly so far as the marriage was concerned, Benjamin's blend of thinking/feeling qualities enabled him to be sensitive to Ellen's needs and moods and helped her gain perspective on herself. Ellen's emotional sensitivity similarly helped temper and season Benjamin's rational, activist side. The harmony in the Roberts marriage thus was due not only to their Christian commitment — central as that was — but also to their compatibility in temperament and character.

Benjamin and Ellen's relationship was not simply a matter of personality traits. They were shaped by the homes and the largely Christian environments in which they were raised. They responded to God's grace and sought to live out the gospel faithfully throughout their lives. Yet personality was a factor in the ways they responded to God's grace, to each other, and to people generally. God used them in the particular ways he did partly because of *who* they were.

Perhaps the real secret of Benjamin and Ellen's marital happiness was that both of them were living for something more ultimate than their own or even each other's self-fulfillment. They were living and working, they believed, for God and his work

42. Keirsey and Bates, *Please Understand Me*, p. 22.
43. Note especially the way he was described by W. T. Hogue in chapter 1 of this book.

in the world, with eternity in view. Their unity in marriage was a unity in mission. So the newsy, endearing letters flowed as the couple was separated by travel. Ellen wrote to B. T. from "Our Room" in their North Chili home in 1887, "My Precious One, You are so dear to me, and when away from you I miss your dear Sweet Spirit which is so heavenly & so kind. I enjoy being <u>alone</u> when you are away" (though generally there was "little opportunity" for that).[44] Once in 1870 Benjamin closed a letter to Ellen, "I feel that if I was with you I should cling to you as I did that memorable night. My <u>darling one</u>, my precious wife. You are every thing to me."[45]

44. ELR (North Chili) to BTR, Nov. 1, 1887.
45. BTR (Chambersburg, Pa.) to ELR (North Chili), Feb. 26, 1870.

CHAPTER 31

George and Benson, Charles and Benjie

"God wants to bring a little heaven down to every house, that all may sit to-gether in heavenly places, where we may have a joy akin to that of heaven."

B. T. Roberts[1]

"I am afraid that I shall never become a Christian."

George Lane Roberts[2]

The story of the four Roberts sons tells a great deal about the parents.

When young Samuel Roberts died on February 1, 1875, Benjamin and Ellen were left with two grown sons and two boys still at home. George, already twenty-three, was far away in Argentina, engaged in educational work. Benson, twenty-one, was a junior at Dartmouth College. Only Charles (eighteen) and Benjie (ten) were still at home. Charles was in his next-to-last year at Chili Seminary.[3]

As they grew and reached manhood, each of the Roberts sons took a different path. Throughout the 1870s and 1880s Benjamin and Ellen watched and counseled their sons as they continued their education and then established their own careers and families.

---

1. B. T. Roberts, "Sermon," *EC* 45, no. 1 (Jan. 1883): 8.
2. GLR to Anna Rice Roberts, June 24, 1877.
3. The catalogue of Chili Seminary for 1878-79 in its "Record of Graduates" lists Charles S. Roberts as a member of the class of 1876 (p. 11).

644

George Lane Roberts

The story of George Lane Roberts, Benjamin and Ellen's oldest surviving son, is a fascinating one. In later years he became an attorney in Pittsburgh, and as a young man he had a significant adventure in Argentina. Early on, however, he rejected the faith of his parents.

Born in 1852, George Lane Roberts was already fourteen when his father founded Chili Seminary. During the family's year or so in Rochester, George (as well as his brother Benson) attended Satterlee's Collegiate Institute, run by LeRoy Satterlee at the corner of Atwater and Oregon Streets, about ten blocks from the Roberts home on Asylum Street.[4] He may also have been a student at Chili Seminary for a year or two. Later George attended the University of Rochester, graduating with a B.A. in 1873.[5]

Early in life George developed an interest in the law, as had his father. In some ways George was much like his father. In December 1869, when just seventeen, he helped B. T. prepare his legal case in the Genesee Camp-Ground Association affair.[6] For years George served occasionally as an informal legal adviser to his father. Unlike his father, however, George did not experience conversion as a young man.

While he was studying at the University of Rochester, George was recruited for an educational venture in Argentina. Around 1870 a young Harvard graduate named George Albert Stearns (apparently known to B. T. Roberts)[7] and a woman named Mary Gorman were invited by Domingo Sarmiento, president of Argentina, to assist the country with educational reforms. Stearns and Gorman began to carefully select a team of young teachers to go to Argentina. Their mission was to lay the foundation

---

4. Alumni Record of George Lane Roberts, University of Rochester; Blake McKelvey, "Rochester's Near Northeast," *Rochester History* 29, no. 2 (Apr. 1967): 4; Blake McKelvey, *Rochester on the Genesee: The Growth of a City* (Syracuse: Syracuse University Press, 1973), 1859 map of Rochester, following p. 80. According to information provided by Barbara M. Purol, librarian, Local History Division, Rochester Public Library, Satterlee's Institute was in existence only from sometime in the 1850s until 1868 (e-mail to author, July 12, 2001).

5. Alumni Record of George Lane Roberts, University of Rochester; Alice Houston Luiggi, *Sixty-five Valiants* (Gainesville: University of Florida Press, 1965), p. 86. George's biographical record at the University of Rochester, 1920, which seems to have been filled out by him, does not mention Chili Seminary. Under "Preparatory schools attended" only "Saterlee's [*sic*] — Rochester, N.Y." is listed, and under "Name of college, university or professional school at which you have studied without receiving a degree," the record says, "None." However, one obituary from a local newspaper says George "received his early education at the seminary," i.e., Chili Seminary. I have not been able to find George's name among lists of early Chili Seminary students.

6. See handwritten sworn affidavit by George L. Roberts, dated Dec. 15, 1871 (RFP, Microfilm Reel 11, Frame 218).

7. George Stearns and George Roberts may have become acquainted when Stearns was a student at the University of Rochester, but Stearns may have known the Roberts family earlier, especially if he was related to Halsey Stearns of Gowanda. In some letters in July 1874, just before he was to depart for Argentina, Stearns gave his return mailing address as "Care Rev. B. T. Roberts, 33 Exchange St.," in Rochester. (See Stearns to Anna Rice, July 17, 1874, RFP, Microfilm Reel 2.)

of a public school system there.[8] Stearns in turn chose George Lane Roberts as his assistant, and these two men, plus a number of young women (eventually numbering over sixty), traveled to Argentina beginning in 1873 to carry out this work.

George Roberts sailed for Argentina almost immediately after graduating from university. Alice Luiggi, in her account of Lane and the other "sixty-five valiants," writes, "When the class of 1873 was graduated at the University of Rochester, George Lane Roberts was probably one of the most envied among his classmates. He had a three-year contract for a job in his pocket, a guarantee of first-class passage to Argentina and back, via Europe, and a salary of $125 a month to commence the day he sailed."[9]

George "seems personable," wrote James Hope, Stearns's father-in-law, after interviewing him for the position. The young Roberts provided a self-description on his application form: "high forehead, dark grey eyes, curved mouth, pointed chin, dark brown hair, oval face, regular nose."[10]

Once in Paraná, Argentina (the former capital, 330 miles up the Paraná River from Buenos Aires), George quickly mastered Spanish — partly because he had to. Stearns appointed him vice principal of the normal school he himself had charge of, and a month later left for an extended period, leaving George to run the school.[11]

George quickly made friends with his students. Luiggi notes, "He had a passion for baseball, which he soon communicated to his Argentine pupils. On the wide waters of the Paraná he taught them the skills he had gained on Lake Ontario as crew chief of the rowing team. He also passed on to them the training his pleasant baritone voice had received in the University choir and glee club, and in turn

8. The story of George Lane's years in Argentina is told in Luiggi, *Sixty-five Valiants*. Domingo Faustino Sarmiento became president of Argentina in 1868 and was himself a scholar and educational reformer. He much admired Abraham Lincoln and the American educator Horace Mann. Luiggi notes, "Sixty-five North American teachers, invited by the Argentine government between 1869 and 1898, . . . founded or rehabilitated eighteen normal schools, each with its model grade school and kindergarten in which normal-school students could observe and practice modern methods of teaching" (p. 68). This was similar to the system that had recently been established in New York State.

One result of this venture was a rise in literacy in Argentina from 20 percent in 1870 to 50 percent twenty-five years later. An Argentine writer commented in 1881, "All over the country in private and public schools are teachers who reflect the lustre of the keen intellects and polished manners of these American women" who helped found and taught in the normal schools (pp. 68-69). Behind this educational venture lay the influence and educational philosophy of Horace Mann (1796-1859), prominent American educator and educational theorist who led in establishing the public school system of Massachusetts. That system became the model for the nation and earned Mann the appellation "father of American public education." John S. Bowman, ed., *The Cambridge Dictionary of American Biography* (Cambridge: Cambridge University Press, 1995), p. 470.

9. Luiggi, *Sixty-five Valiants*, p. 86.

10. Luiggi, *Sixty-five Valiants*, p. 86.

11. Luiggi, *Sixty-five Valiants*, pp. 77, 86. The school, which George Stearns and his wife Adelaide had opened in August 1871, was the "first normal school actually founded in Argentina by a North American" and was in fact established "only twenty-six years after the rich state of New York, with a population many times that of all Argentina, had built its first normal school" (pp. 77-79).

he picked up a store of mournful gaucho ballads whose strains came back to haunt him for years."[12]

George corresponded with his parents during his time in Argentina. B. T. Roberts noted in his diary in January 1874, "Received two letters from George. He is quite well but homesick — has had all his best clothes stolen. He prizes home as never before. Is affectionate — but says nothing about seeking the Lord. But I expect to see him yet a devoted Christian."[13]

A year after George landed in Argentina, several more teachers arrived from the United States. George was especially attracted to one of them: "twenty-year-old-blue-eyed Anna Ackley Rice from Bath, New York, near Rochester." She had graduated from the normal school in Oswego, New York, and had taught a year in Flint, Michigan, and a year in St. Cloud, Minnesota.[14]

George and Anna fell in love almost immediately. Anna wrote back to her sister Mollie on February 9, 1875, telling her all about George and "the great change in me" as a result of meeting him. "Mother always said that my combative tendencies were too much in the ascendant to allow me to get along without quarreling with people, [but these] tendencies have lessened to such a degree within the past four months that I have the name of being the sweetest and most amiable one of the crowd. I don't say this in an egotistical way but only to show what Cupid's arrow can do for a person."[15]

Until she met George, Anna said, she "never believed there was such a thing" as love. Now she was smitten, and her letter to Mollie is full of her admiration for George. "I have the man of my choice — the man who will make me happy — and who will love you all as I do." Anna was concerned about her mother's reaction, however: "I fear she will borrow trouble about it, but I know she would sanction my choice could she know Mr. Roberts."[16]

On Valentine's Day 1875, a Sunday, just four months after her arrival, George Roberts and Anna Rice were married in a Methodist church. The "two were made one — for six short, lovely years."[17]

---

12. Luiggi, *Sixty-five Valiants*, p. 86.

13. BTRD, Jan. 23, 1874.

14. Luiggi, *Sixty-five Valiants*, p. 87.

15. AAR (Paraná, Argentina) to her sister Mollie, Feb. 9, 1875 (RFP, Microfilm Reel 1).

16. AAR to Mollie, Feb. 9, 1875. Anna says, "We did not expect to be married for some time but the director [Stearns] goes to Tucumán [in the northwest interior of Argentina] to start a new school and the people here would make such disagreeable remarks[?] that everybody thinks we had better be married now."

17. Luiggi, *Sixty-five Valiants*, p. 87; cf. Smail, p. 14. The Roberts Family Papers include a May 27, 1874, letter from George A. Stearns to Anna Rice regarding the possibility of her going to Argentina "to assist me in a Normal School now established in the city of Paraná." He warns her of the "inconveniences" that will be involved; "this is <u>pioneer work</u>." The salary, paid by the Argentine government, was $1,200 in gold ($100 monthly) — "about $1350 [in U.S.] currency." Stearns said, "There are three lady teachers going two of whom are already engaged & there is a young man [George L. Roberts] from this country now there. We shall thus have <u>five</u> Americans [initially] for mutual society in case

Anna had never met George's parents; all she knew of B. T. and Ellen was what she heard from George. He and George Stearns painted a very rosy picture of her new in-laws, and Anna looked forward to meeting them when she and George returned to the United States. Shortly after the marriage Anna wrote a very upbeat letter to her sister Mollie. The letter sheds light on the relationship between George and Anna and his parents and also on how Free Methodists were viewed at the time. Looking forward to their return to the United States, Anna wrote:

> George's father is to build a house for us in Rochester. It is to be of brick with bay window, bath room, and all the modern improvements and his father says that in ordinary times it will be worth ten thousand dollars. His father gives him the lot and starts him in business. Besides we shall have about two thousand in cash besides that we save here. I had no idea of getting anything more than we saved when we first were married[,] and now I find myself quite well off in life. George never said a word about his father having money any more than I could infer from his general talk. But Mr. Stearns told the girls that Mr. Roberts is wealthy. And he said to night at the table, "Your father will leave all you boys well off. Besides giving you a good start in business.["] But George says his father will leave all his money to a Seminary he started in Chili. He expects though he will start all of his boys well in business. It will be a splendid thing for George if he begins the publishing business in Rochester for it is a fine business and he cannot help but succeed. You will all say so when you know him. I am so much better off than I ever expected to be and how thankful I should be. Won't we have lovely times furnishing my home, for of course you will help me and can stay at our house all the time if you want to. George says so.
>
> I think he must have a very fine father & mother. I admire them for they are honest sensible refined people. And christians that can be trusted as living up to what they profess. I am already attached to them. He [B. T.] wrote in his last letter something about going to see mother [Mrs. Rice, in Bath, N.Y.]. I expect they are awfully strict Methodists, but they are too refined to be disagreeable about it. George is not of their opinions, but of course respects them & his love for his mother is the most manly trait I know of. He shows his bringing up. His father is the head man of the Free Methodists[,] a kind of a bishop[;] I don't know what is the Methodist language. The free Methodists are more radical than the others and consequently are much stricter. If Mr. & Mrs. Roberts were not just the people I know them to be I should be afraid of them, but as it is I am sincerely glad that they are true, & good — just as they are. You see I am bound to consider myself the most fortunate woman in the world at any rate.

After talking about health problems and the weather, Anna writes again about George and their future:

---

we do not like native society." The trip to Argentina was to be via Europe, and Anna could "spend a month or so in Europe if you desire" (RFP, Microfilm Reel 2).

I am making shirts for George — night shirts — I have four cut & backed ready for the machine and shall finish them in vacation. . . . I am also making him neck ties. He is awfully <u>handsome</u> & <u>nobby</u> [slang: elegant]. He has the handsomest back you ever saw, and he is just spoiling me[,] he is so good. He never spoke a cross word to me in his life and we have never had a sign of a dispute. People say we love each other more than most people do. I know I have found out what happiness is and am perfectly satisfied with woman's sphere. I am awfully economical and at the end of this year I shall see $2400 <u>gold</u> to pay for it — to say nothing of the gold George gave me to buy silver[?] with when we were married. I don't build dreams that I expect to be real but every thing so far [h]as been so much beyond my expectations that I have to guard against having too extravagant air castles.[18]

Anna would soon discover that B. T. Roberts was not wealthy, though he was a good financial manager and was involved in some substantial business transactions because of the development of Chili Seminary and his operation of the *Earnest Christian*. (George Stearns also mistook Roberts's generosity and financial acumen for personal wealth.) Anna's letter suggests, also, that Roberts had offered to help George and Anna get established in Rochester and probably had given some indication to his sons that he would give them what assistance he could.

By October 1876, about a year and a half after the marriage, George had completed his three-year assignment and he and Anna had returned to the United States. Though George and Anna's time in Argentina was brief, they and their colleagues left behind a solid legacy. The larger story of B. T. and Ellen Roberts includes this remarkable fact, that their eldest son and daughter-in-law were among the pioneers of public education in Argentina. Even today among Argentine educators their work of a century ago is still remembered and honored, and Argentina has one of the highest literacy rates in Latin America.[19]

Returning to the Rochester area, George tried his hand at the printing business. This was done apparently with B. T.'s assistance and advice; he was trying to help his son get established economically. But Anna's "air castles" did not materialize. Rather than staying with George, she went to the family home in Bath, south of Rochester, and stayed with her mother, apparently due to her mother's ill health and perhaps also her own. During this period George and Anna constantly wrote letters and postcards to each other, often in Spanish. George called Anna "Mi querida Nita"; sometimes he wrote her twice in one day.[20]

18. AAR (Argentina) to Mollie, apparently mid- to late 1875 (first page is missing). RFP, Microfilm Reel 1.

19. *World Book Encyclopedia* (1976), A:611. On at least three occasions I have spoken with Argentineans and found that they were familiar with the story of the "65 Valiants."

20. See the GLR/AAR correspondence — for instance, GLR (Rochester) to AAR (Bath), June 8, 1877; postcard in Spanish, imprinted "Office of The Earnest Christian, Rochester, N.Y." (RFP, Microfilm Reel 1). Unfortunately the Roberts Family Papers do not include the corresponding letters from Anna to George during this period. It is not entirely clear why Anna during this time remained with her mother. Anna herself may have been suffering from malaria, contracted in Argentina.

George set up shop at 87 State Street in Rochester under the name of G. L. Roberts and Company, "Book and Job Printers, Publishers, &c." His bold business letterhead hopefully promised "Books, Pamphlets, Law Cases, Catalogues, Bill Heads, Circulars, Cards, Etc., Neatly and Accurately Printed, and at Reasonable Rates." Benjamin thought he could get George started by giving him the *Earnest Christian* job. George wrote to his father on August 25, 1877, "The E.C. is ready to print. Shall I have it printed at the Democrat?"[21] Apparently at this point the type composition was being done in George's shop and the printing elsewhere.[22]

The business did not go very well, however, and George quickly became disillusioned with it. At the end of June 1877 he complained to Anna, "We have nothing to do but the E.C."[23] George was troubled too by his separation from Anna. "If I do not hear from you I will remain at home Sunday," he wrote. "But Oh it is so lonesome here that it makes me feel so very blue and sad. Why did we ever come back to this horrid country."[24]

In November B. T. Roberts bought a press for George's business that could print the *Earnest Christian* as well as books. The new $1,500 Campbell Printing Press was guaranteed "to do Book Work of the best quality."[25] Even so, George was not satisfied with the business and eventually decided to leave it.

Meanwhile Benjamin and Ellen also were very concerned about George and Anna living separately, even though this was temporary and the two were only about seventy miles apart. Benjamin wrote to Anna in July 1877 from Austin, Minnesota — a letter revealing his own views of marriage.

> I hope to go home next week and hope to find you there [where George was]. No one can have a higher respect than I have for filial feelings and filial duties [referring to Anna's concern about her mother]; yet it is God's order that conjugal duties should have the precedence. "For this cause shall a man leave his father & mother and shall cleave unto his wife." I would advise the wife and especially the young wife never to be absent from her husband twenty-four hours at a time, unless it is absolutely necessary. If they enjoy happiness in this life it will come from God and from each other. The spell that binds them to each other should never be broken.

21. GLR to BTR, Aug. 25, 1877.

22. George probably had a small press suitable for business cards, pamphlets, etc., but not large enough for the *Earnest Christian* job.

23. GLR (Rochester) to AAR (Bath), June 29, 1977. George added, "I fully agree with you in your opinion of F.M's [Free Methodists] & also the other lot whose camp meeting you attended." He concluded his letter, "You are my guiding star, my guardian angel. And whenever I am tempted to do anything wrong I stop and think[,] can I tell Nita [his pet name for Anna] of this? If I answer no the temptation flees and I escape. How I do love you my sweetest, dearest." George often uses such quasi-religious language in writing of his love for Anna.

24. GLR to AAR, June 29, 1877. This was the second letter George wrote to Anna on June 29.

25. J. R. Campbell to GLR, Aug. 23, 1877; purchase agreement signed by J. G. Campbell on G. L. Roberts and Co. stationery, Nov. 8, 1877 (RFP, Microfilm Reel 9).

Now, darling, do not be tried with me for writing this. I have a very sincere love for you and a great desire that your married life should be unusually happy. That it may be[,] I know that it is necessary that you should cleave to your husband not only in heart but by being with him all you possibly can.[26]

B. T. Roberts had not, of course, fully followed his own advice in his relationship with Ellen, though clearly he disliked being separated from her. And no doubt he had learned from experience.

During these months Anna sometimes had negative feelings toward B. T. and Ellen. She knew they saw her in a sense as an outsider since she apparently made no Christian profession. She may have been reluctant to live with George in North Chili partly because of this.[27] George wrote to Anna on June 28, just a week before the letter from Benjamin to Anna quoted above, "You are real unkind to write so about my folks. Father and Mother both think that you are a noble woman and they love you dearly. Father always sends his love to you when he writes and Mother asks about you every day."[28]

In a letter to Anna about this time George revealed something of his own spiritual journey. George had intellectual (and perhaps other) reasons for not professing faith in Christ. He reports a conversation with a friend of Emma Sellew's in June 1877, just a few months before Benson Roberts and Emma Sellew were married. George wrote, "I have been discussing Theology with Miss Pacunne[,] Emma's friend. She is a Quakeress and of course orthodox. I am afraid that I rather shocked both her & Ben & Emma, who sat inside the parlor spooning. Miss Pacunne talks so nicely that I am sure you would like to talk with her. She admitted that if a person became a Christian it must be a matter purely of Faith. It seems such an unreasonable doctrine that a man must believe just because he wants to believe. I am afraid that I shall never become a Christian."[29]

Even though George did not share his father's faith, he respected him and worked closely with him during these months. As the summer of 1877 wore on, however, George began thinking about moving to Bradford, Pennsylvania, to take advantage of business opportunities due to the oil boom there.

In September Anna wrote to her father-in-law, asking what he thought of this. B. T. replied in a September 22 letter from Osage, Iowa, where he was ministering. Impressed by the prosperous farms and new towns across Iowa, he wrote, "You and George may go into the oil business if you think best — but I think I should prefer a

---

26. BTR to AAR, July 5, 1877.

27. It appears that during these months George was living with his parents in North Chili, though he may have had an apartment in Rochester. If he was with his parents, this may have been another reason Anna was reluctant to join him.

28. GLR to AAR, June 28, 1877. George continues: "Oh Darling[,] I wish that I could make you completely happy. I love you so much and am able to do so little for you. You are my only treasure here. My All. How I do long to see you. If you don't come to me I must go to you. If I possibly can I will be in Bath Saturday night."

29. GLR to AAR, June 24, 1877.

western wheat or stock farm." Benjamin's concern for his daughter-in-law's conversion is evident at the close of the letter, where he writes, "God bless you my dear Daughter and make you His daughter whose blessing maketh rich and addeth no sorrow!" He signed the letter, "Your loving father, B. T. Roberts."[30]

Benjamin was not unaware of the oil boom that had transformed the economy, and the countryside and towns and cities, of northwestern Pennsylvania since Edwin Drake discovered in 1859 at Titusville that he could successfully pump oil from the earth.[31] Bradford quickly became the center of the oil industry — home to such new companies as Kendall, Pennzoil, and Quaker State — and America's first billion-dollar oil field. In 1862 Roberts visited the region and wrote a report for the *Earnest Christian* that he entitled "The Works of God." "About fifty miles south of the city of Erie, in the state of Pennsylvania, are a number of wells from which oil flows as water does from an ordinary spring. . . . They are situated in a narrow valley between two high ranges of hills, on both sides of Oil Creek, a good sized stream, which flows into the Allegany river. . . . They extend up and down the creek a distance of about sixteen miles. There are about two hundred wells from which oil has been or is obtained. They are from five hundred to six hundred feet deep."

Roberts described the technology involved — how the drilling was done and the oil extracted.

> In some cases, when [a well is] successful, the oil, mingled with gas and water, is thrown up in a stream as large as the pipe will allow, and with a violence equal to that with which water is thrown from a fire engine. We saw a well from which, as we were assured by reliable parties who witnessed it, a stream of oil, three inches in diameter, was thrown into the air to a height of seventy-five feet above the ground! . . . One of the proprietors assured us that a single well had yielded them, already, over 70,000 barrels of oil, and it is still flowing. . . .
>
> Many of the wells prove failures, from the beginning; and while some men make fortunes, others lose large amounts.

Roberts noted that already "numerous refineries in all parts of the country" were operating and that this refined oil made "one of the cheapest and best illuminating substances known." (John D. Rockefeller, Sr., was just at this time discovering that oil refining was his pathway to wealth.)

Roberts saw that the oil business was risky, however, not only economically but in human terms as well. "Two disastrous fires have occurred at the wells," he noted.

30. BTR to AAR, Sept. 22, 1877.

31. Ron Chernow notes, "On Sunday, August 28, 1959, Drake's folly was rewarded when oil bubbled up from a well drilled a day earlier. It was less a matter of Drake discovering oil — its existence was scarcely a secret — than of his figuring out a way to tap commercial quantities in a controlled process." Chernow adds, "Drake's feat touched off pandemonium as bands of fortune seekers streamed into Titusville and its pastoral surroundings." Ron Chernow, *Titan: The Life of John D. Rockefeller, Sr.* (New York: Random House, 1998), pp. 75-76. Titusville is about fifteen miles north of Oil City and about sixty miles southwest of Bradford.

Yet he was prepared to admire the wonderful "works of God," who "has adjusted in the secret laboratories of the Earth, chemical processes . . . on a scale of magnificent grandeur" almost beyond belief "which science at best can only faintly imitate."[32] Roberts was not in principle opposed to George entering the oil business, but he was wary of the risks.

George did decide to go to Bradford (about 140 miles southwest of Rochester). He moved in early 1878, found a legal apprenticeship, and began studying law. He also joined the Bradford Oil Exchange, where petroleum was bought and sold, as a way into the oil business.

"Here the bulls and bears of the trade congregate for serious contest, though thus far nobody has been reported slain," reported *Child's Bradford City Directory* for 1879-80.[33]

George found his niche on the legal side of the oil business. Completing his apprenticeship in 1880, he formed a partnership with D. H. Jack, and the two did business initially under the name Jack and Roberts; later, Elliott, Jack and Roberts. In 1881 George secured the position of general attorney of the Buffalo, Rochester, and Pittsburgh Railroad Company.[34]

Anna joined George in Bradford some months after he moved there. He wrote to her in April 1878, "I have made up my mind to build at Custer and I will commence the house just as soon as I can get the lumber."[35] In October he bought 7,410 feet of lumber from Sellew and Popple in Dunkirk, New York, for $77.80 and had it shipped to him in Bradford.[36] His father had perhaps suggested that George make the purchase through his Sellew cousins in western New York, where he probably got a good deal, rather than buying the lumber locally at inflated prices.

Anna apparently moved to Bradford in late spring or early summer, very pregnant. After a year of separation, George and Anna were glad to be together, reestablishing their home. A son, Hibbert Rice Roberts, was born on July 2, 1878.[37]

Sadly, Anna died just two and a half years after Hibbert's birth, reportedly of malarial fever that she probably contracted in Argentina. She passed away at Bradford on January 24, 1881, and was buried in Bath, New York.[38] Shortly after Anna's

32. [B. T. Roberts], "The Works of God," *EC* 4, no. 5 (Nov. 1862): 156-58.

33. Hamilton Child, comp., *Child's Bradford City Directory, 1879-80* (Bradford, Pa.: Era Office, 1879), pp. 28, 56. A city directory for 1880-81 has this entry: "Roberts, Geo. L. law student. 47 Pleasant St." J. H. Lant and Son, *Bradford City Directory, 1880-81* (Bradford, Pa.: J. H. Lant, 1880), p. 57.

34. Alumni Record of George Lane Roberts, University of Rochester Library.

35. GLR to AAR, Apr. 18, 1878.

36. Receipt from Sellew and Popple Co., Dunkirk, N.Y., Oct. 21, 1878 (RFP).

37. Smail, p. 16; ELR to AAR, July 20, 1878. Smail gives the birth year as 1879, but Ellen's letter refers to the arrival of the baby boy, so the date in Smail must be incorrect (unless a boy was born in 1878 and died). In a P.S. to her letter, Ellen writes, "I announced to your Father [B. T. Roberts] the word you sent through George, that he was to name the boy. But as yet I think he is too busy to appreciate the responsibility." B. T. was "working incessantly on his book" in very hot weather, Ellen noted.

38. Death notice in the *Era*, Bradford, Pa. (Jan. 25, 1881).

death, George took little Hibbert to live with Benjamin and Ellen Roberts in North Chili.

After Anna's death George remained single for several years. Eventually he met a young schoolteacher in Bradford, Winifred Murphy, and the two were married on January 4, 1888. The wedding was at Winifred's parents' home in nearby Wilcox, Pennsylvania, and B. T. Roberts assisted in the ceremony.[39] Ellen had been disappointed when George told her Winifred was a Roman Catholic. Ellen broke the news to Benjamin in a letter of November 1, 1887. Miss Murphy, George said, was a "smart and attractive" woman of about twenty-five — and a Catholic. Ellen "felt very bad" about this, she told B. T. "But I am trying to put it away with the other things, which I cannot make as I would wish to have them in this world. It does hurt me terribly. But I have got to trust that with the Lord. I am reminded that I did not want him in South America because it was a Catholic country. I hope you will not feel as bad over it as I have."[40]

George's son Hibbert was nine when his father remarried and had been living with B. T. and Ellen in North Chili; he seems to have remained with his grandparents following George's remarriage.[41] The grandparents effectively became the parents.

George continued his legal career in Bradford for another fourteen years, remaining with the firm Elliott, Jack and Roberts. Through these years George occasionally gave his father legal advice. On February 22, 1893, he wrote concerning a contested will in Nebraska that B. T. had asked advice on (probably concerning a bequest to Chesbrough Seminary).[42] This letter was written only five days before B. T. died, so Benjamin may never have seen it.

In 1895, two years after his father's death, George Roberts moved to Pittsburgh and had a distinguished legal career there.

Benson Howard and Emma (Sellew) Roberts

Of all the Roberts children, Benson Howard, born in 1853, seems to have been most like his father and to have been especially near to his mother. He was the only son to work closely with B. T. in his ministry and was, in effect, his father's successor both at Chesbrough Seminary and in editing the *Earnest Christian*. Benson was really the

---

39. According to a newspaper clipping in the Roberts Wesleyan College Archives, George Roberts and Winifred Murphy were married in her parents' home in Wilcox, a town about thirty miles south of Bradford. "The ceremony was performed by Rev. Father McNeely of Ridgway, assisted by Rev. Dr. Roberts [*sic*] of Rochester, N.Y., father of the groom. The attendance was quite large and the presents numerous and costly." Ridgway is about fifty miles south of Bradford.

40. ELR (North Chili) to BTR, Nov. 1, 1887.

41. Smail, pp. 14, 16.

42. GLR (Bradford) to BTR, Feb. 22, 1893.

only son to follow in his father's footsteps, though he never became a major leader in the Free Methodist Church.[43]

Benson had just turned eleven when the family moved to Rochester in late 1864. During the family's brief time in Rochester Benson, like his brother George, attended Satterlee's Collegiate Institute.[44] Later when Benjamin started Chili Seminary, Benson became one of the first students.

Benson apparently attended Chili from its opening until 1871. In late August 1871 he began the college preparatory course at Oberlin College in Ohio. His second cousin, Emma Jane Sellew, two years younger, also attended Oberlin that year.[45]

Herein lies a love story. Benson and Emma no doubt knew each other to some extent all their lives. As a teenager Emma was already "a superior scholar," Benson said. At B. T.'s request she came from her home in Dunkirk in 1870 and "gave a year of her time as teacher during her sixteenth year, paying all her own expenses."[46] Here she and Benson got better acquainted. Though older, Benson was the student while Emma was the teacher at Chili.[47]

Emma Sellew was born in Gowanda, New York, the daughter of Ashbel Roberts Sellew and Jane Tucker Sellew.[48] Emma's grandmother, also named Emma, was the older sister of Titus Roberts.[49] After the family moved to Dunkirk on Lake Erie, Emma enrolled in the newly chartered State Normal and Training School at nearby Fredonia.[50] She apparently completed just one year at the Normal School, then at fif-

43. At the funeral of Benson Roberts on Mar. 4, 1930, the Reverend John Nesbitt said his "life had in it extraordinary variety but very genuine symmetry." *Memorial Tribute to Dr. Roberts*, prepared by the Women's Bible Class of Catonsville Presbyterian Church of Catonsville, Md. [1930].

44. "Roberts, Benson Howard," in *Who Was Who in America* (Chicago: A. N. Marquis Co., 1943), 1:1039.

45. *Seventy-fifth Anniversary General Catalogue of Oberlin College, 1833-1908* (Oberlin, Ohio: Oberlin College, 1909), p. 821. Emma Jane Sellew (Mrs. Benson H. Roberts) is listed on p. 863. The first (fall) term at Oberlin began the fourth Wednesday in August and ended the fourth Wednesday in November. After a three-month winter vacation, the spring term began the fourth Wednesday in February and ended the fourth Wednesday in May. The summer term immediately followed, ending with commencement at the end of August or beginning of September. Robert Samuel Fletcher, *A History of Oberlin College from Its Foundation through the Civil War*, 2 vols. (Oberlin, Ohio: Oberlin College, 1943), 2:734.

46. BHR, *BTR*, p. 365.

47. Benson says Emma's teaching at Chili was "during her sixteenth year"; she apparently went there in the summer or fall of 1870, just after her fifteenth birthday (thus during her sixteenth year), as she enrolled at Oberlin in 1871.

48. Emma took some pride in her family background. Around 1907 she noted on an alumni information form submitted to Cornell University, in the space marked "Items of Genealogical Interest," that her father "descended fr. Philip of Bordeaux[,] France, a Huguenot Duke (De Saliere) who married the daughter of Duke of Hamilton, His son 'a man of learning' came to Boston." Alumni Record of Emma Sellew Roberts, Division of Rare and Manuscript Collections, Cornell University.

49. Smail, pp. 8, 10, 174-76, 207; Obituary of Emma Sellew Roberts, *FM* 64, no. 13 (Mar. 27, 1931): 14. The obituary gives 1856 as the year of birth, but Smail gives the birth date as June 6, 1855, which is probably correct. Emma's mother came from a Quaker family.

50. Obituary of Emma Sellew Roberts, p. 14; Alumni Record of Emma Sellew Roberts, Cornell University.

teen went to teach at Chili Seminary for a year.[51] Smail describes Emma as "a small woman" and "a competent equestrienne."[52]

Emma and Benson were students together at Oberlin in 1871-72. Here, perhaps, their romance blossomed. Benson was nearly eighteen and Emma was sixteen.[53] They did not marry until several years later, when both were in their twenties and had graduated from college.

At Oberlin Benson was enrolled in the Preparatory Course and Emma, who, though younger, was further advanced in her education, was in the Collegiate Course.[54]

After his year at Oberlin, Benson entered Dartmouth College in Hanover, New Hampshire, as a freshman, while Emma remained a second year at Oberlin.

During the intervening summer of 1872, at age eighteen, Benson personally professed faith in Christ.[55] He had passed through a period of spiritual struggle and doubt, apparently during his year at Oberlin, and was helped by conversations with his mother.[56] "Never can I forget," he wrote years later, "the great wisdom with which she dealt with me, a young man of eighteen years of age, fighting his way Godward through doubt, through unbelief and through great distrust of self." He shared with her his longings, aspirations, and difficulties, "and she with wonderful self-restraint said to him, 'My son, what you need is Christ,' and not much more did she say." Ellen's empathy and listening ear helped. "Her sympathy with [my] struggles was so great that she came to visit [me] when [I] was away at school, and when there, said not too much but just enough to help [me]. She recognized that the Holy

51. The State Normal and Training School in Fredonia opened in 1867, succeeding the earlier Fredonia Academy that existed from 1821 to 1866. The Training School enrolled students from five to fourteen years of age and was designed to provide students in the Normal (teacher-training) School "opportunity for observation and practice in the different grades of instruction." Fourteen was the minimum age for enrolling in the Normal School. (*Circular of the State Normal and Training School at Fredonia, N.Y., for the Year 1868* [Albany, N.Y.: Weed, Parsons and Co., 1868], included as an appendix in John Ford Ohles, "The Historical Development of State University of New York College at Fredonia as Representative of the Evolution of Teacher Education in the State University of New York" [Ed.D. diss., State University of New York at Buffalo, 1964], pp. 397-405.) It thus seems likely that Emma Sellew was enrolled in the Training School in 1868-69 (and quite possibly in the Fredonia Academy before that), then took the first year of instruction (only) in the Normal School before going to teach at Chili Seminary.

52. Smail, p. 176.

53. Sixteen was the minimum age for female students to enroll at Oberlin "unless [the female student was] committed to the special care of some approved resident of the place." Fletcher, *History of Oberlin College*, 2:712.

54. *Seventy-fifth Anniversary*, pp. 821, 863. Oberlin had around thirteen hundred students at the time, the great majority of whom were in the Preparatory Department; the Collegiate Department numbered around two hundred (Fletcher, *History of Oberlin College*, 2:710).

55. Zahniser, p. 301, citing letter, BTR to ELR (Aug. 21, 1872).

56. As young men, Benson and George both struggled with personal and intellectual questions about the Christian faith. That Benson found a deep and satisfying faith in Jesus Christ and George did not suggests that George's pilgrimage might have turned out differently if he, like Benson, could have successfully worked his way through his questions and come to faith.

Spirit was at work, and though deeply interested interfered not with His workings."[57]

After her two years at Oberlin (1871-73), Emma taught languages another two years at Chili Seminary while taking courses at the nearby University of Rochester where she was, according to her obituary, "the first woman student."[58] In September 1875 she entered Cornell University at Ithaca, New York. She graduated with a B.A. (Phi Beta Kappa) in 1877. At Cornell Emma excelled in classical Greek and was chosen to represent the university at the 1877 Greek Intercollegiate Contest.[59]

Meanwhile Benson, after a year at Dartmouth, took his sophomore year at the University of Rochester, then returned to Dartmouth for his junior and senior years, graduating with a bachelor of arts degree in 1876.[60]

Benson immediately began teaching at Chili Seminary, as instructor in languages. In late 1876, not long after returning to teach at the seminary, he was named principal — the first alumnus to serve in that capacity, as noted earlier.[61]

Benson found his true vocation as an educator, though one with pastoral gifts and sensibilities. A former student later wrote of him: "A well-proportioned physique, a princely intellect, a tender heart, . . . a touch of aristocracy that was innate rather than affected, combined to make him a forceful personality. His scholarship was deep and varied, and his discriminating command of the English language in the classroom, on the chapel platform, or editorially, was fascinating and instructive. He possessed instinctively and culturally the schoolmaster's characteristics, and his ability to impart knowledge made him a charming and inspiring teacher."[62]

57. Benson Roberts, "My Mother," *EC* 95, no. 3 (Mar. 1908): 70-71.

58. Neil E. Pfouts, *A History of Roberts Wesleyan College* ([North Chili, N.Y.: Roberts Wesleyan College, 2000]), p. 24; Obituary of Emma Sellew Roberts, p. 14. Before 1900 the University of Rochester did not admit women as officially enrolled students, but by the 1870s some women were being admitted as "special students." Whether Emma Sellew was in fact "the first woman student" at the university is impossible to verify at this point. Nancy Martin, University of Rochester archivist, writes: "As early as the 1870s women were allowed to take courses as 'special students' meaning that they were not bona fide matriculated students. But they were here in classroom. It was only after Susan B. Anthony's great struggle to get women admitted as real enrolled students in the year 1900 that UR can be said to have had women students. In the ancient records of the Registrar there was a volume called 'Special Students' which might have answered this question [whether Emma Sellew was the first woman student or not], but it is missing." Nancy Martin, manuscripts librarian/archivist, Rare Books and Special Collections, Rush Rhees Library, University of Rochester, Rochester, N.Y., e-mail to author, June 20, 2003.

59. Obituary of Emma Sellew Roberts, p. 14; Alumni Record of Emma Sellew Roberts, Cornell University; "Roberts, Emma Sellew," in *Who's Who in New York City and State*, ed. John W. Leonard, 3rd ed. (New York: L. R. Hamersly and Co., 1907), pp. 1110-11. At Cornell Emma was enrolled in the Classical Course.

60. G. W. Garlock, Obituary of Benson Howard Roberts, *FM* 63, no. 16 (Apr. 18, 1930): 254; Class of 1876 Report for 1931, Dartmouth College Library Special Collections; University of Rochester Alumni Records. Benson's decision to attend the University of Rochester in 1873-74 may have been due in part to financial considerations.

61. Pfouts, *History*, p. 25.

62. C. Adam Kress, "Benson Howard Roberts, A.M., D.D.," *FM* 63, no. 16 (Apr. 18, 1930): 246.

Benson Roberts and Emma Jane Sellew were married in Dunkirk on October 16, 1877, about a year after Benson became principal of the seminary. Emma resumed her teaching at Chili Seminary and during the 1878-79 year served as principal along with her husband.[63] On August 29, 1878, Benson and Emma's first child, Howard Passmore, was born.[64]

Benson and Emma's initial tenure as leaders of the school was brief. Benson stepped down in 1879 after a little more than two years as principal, apparently to pursue further education. He was a student at Rochester Theological Seminary in 1879 and received his M.A. from Dartmouth in 1880.[65] Emma also pursued graduate work, receiving her M.A. from Cornell in 1882. Her master's thesis was entitled "The Imitations of Theocritus Found in Virgil's Eclogues," and demonstrated her mastery of classical Greek.[66]

In 1881, as Emma was finishing her master's work, she and Benson began a long tenure — twenty-five years — as coprincipals of Chesbrough Seminary, giving the school stability and outstanding leadership. Throughout the remaining years of B. T.'s life, Benson and Emma continued serving the seminary and were active in the work of the church. Benson eventually was ordained as a Free Methodist preacher; he joined the Genesee Conference in 1889 and was made a deacon two years later. His ordination as elder came in 1893, just months after his father's death.[67]

Pfouts notes that Benson and Emma, serving as coprincipals, initially "resided with the staff and the students in the Seminary building. Shortly thereafter the founder, B. T. Roberts and his family, moved from the Rumsey house . . . to [their new house on] the south side of Buffalo Road opposite the Seminary. . . . That move opened the way then for [Benson and Emma] to move into the Rumsey farmhouse. However, other teachers continued to room and board with the student body for many years."[68]

Benson was concerned that the seminary remain faithful to his father's vision and was pleased when he could report through the *Earnest Christian* that the school was doing well. In April 1883 he commented that the campus had been "greatly favored with the presence of the Lord" in its meetings, and that at an Easter-season afternoon "resurrection service" held in the dining room, the seminary community experienced "the most general baptism we have had yet." He reported, "Every one

---

63. Pfouts, *History*, p. 25.

64. Smail, p. 15; Alumni Record of Emma Sellew Roberts, Cornell University.

65. Benson's obituary in the *Free Methodist* says, "He took his master's degree at Dartmouth in 1880, after which he studied at Rochester Theological Seminary." However, the University of Rochester Alumni Catalog entry, which was approved by Benson (Aug. 6, 1927), indicates that he received his M.A. from Dartmouth in 1880 and was a student at Rochester Theological Seminary in 1879. Alumni Record of Benson H. Roberts, University of Rochester Library.

66. Alumni Record of Emma Sellew Roberts, Cornell University; Alumni Records, Oberlin College Archives, Oberlin, Ohio.

67. Minutes, Genesee Conference, Free Methodist Church, 1889-93.

68. Pfouts, *History*, pp. 25-26.

present was filled with the Spirit, and soon the unconverted began to come in; before we closed there were six seeking pardon. There is power in a risen Saviour."[69]

B. T. and Ellen were very pleased with Benson and his and Emma's leadership at the seminary. In 1884 Ellen wrote to Emma's sister Lucy Sellew Coleman, "Benson enjoys more of the Lord & is more fully saved this Fall, than he has ever been before. It is very blessed to see him doing so well."[70] Benson remained close to his mother, and he and Emma often dropped in on Ellen when B. T. was traveling. Ellen wrote to B. T. in November 1887, "Benson & Emma come at all hours & all times in the day. . . . Benson or Emma often take breakfast & the other meals with us."[71]

Early in their administration at Chesbrough Benson and Emma tried launching a literary magazine (strictly nonfiction!) called *Roberts' Miscellany*. Emma described it as "a monthly magazine for the young."[72] A few numbers were issued in the early 1880s, but the venture didn't attract enough subscribers to make it viable. Benson and Emma tried again in 1886-87 but again couldn't rouse enough interest. In appealing for support in the *Free Methodist* in early 1886, Benson and Emma noted that the magazine was "the only publication devoted to general literature *that excluded fiction*."[73] Again some issues were published, but the endeavor didn't long survive. Appealing for subscribers in March 1887, Benson and Emma wrote, "It is for you to say, as well as for us, whether we shall have for our households and young people a magazine of instructive, interesting and wholesome literature, or drive our children to the reading of pernicious books and papers because we do not furnish them with something better."[74]

There was simply not enough interest in the Free Methodist Church at this time to sustain such a magazine. The need for good literature for the young was to some degree met later when the denomination established a publishing house and began issuing its own Sunday school literature. Benson and Emma's vision of a literary magazine was perhaps more lofty, but was less realistic than weekly Sunday school papers.

Meanwhile, Benson and Emma were raising a family. Howard Passmore, their first child, was born in August 1878 but survived only three years; he died on September 8, 1881.[75] Nearly a year later, in August 1882, a daughter was born and given the

---

69. B. H. R. [Benson Howard Roberts], "Chili Seminary," *EC* 45, no. 4 (Apr. 1883): 131.

70. ELR (North Chili) to Lucy Sellew Coleman (Evansville, Wis.), Nov. 5, 1884.

71. ELR (North Chili) to BTR, Nov. 1, 1887.

72. Alumni Record of Emma Sellew Roberts, Cornell University. Emma listed herself as editor of *Roberts' Miscellany* from 1878 to 1881 — the years of the birth and death of her first son, Howard Passmore. She may have misremembered the years, however; the dates do not correspond to references to the magazine in the *Free Methodist*. The notice in the 1907 *Who's Who in New York City and State* (no doubt submitted by Emma) is more accurate as to dates: "edited Roberts Miscellany [*sic*] for the Young, 1880-82" (p. 1110).

73. B. H. Roberts and E. S. Roberts, "Roberts' Miscellany," *FM* 19, no. 1 (Jan. 6, 1886): 5.

74. [Benson Roberts and Emma Roberts], "Roberts' Miscellany," *FM* 20, no. 10 (Mar. 9, 1887): 3.

75. Smail, p. 15; Alumni Record of Emma Sellew Roberts, Cornell University; grave marker, North Chili, N.Y., Cemetery.

name Lois Ellen, honoring her grandmother, Ellen Lois Roberts. Three other children followed, all born during B. T.'s lifetime: Lucy George on November 15, 1886; Ashbel Sellew on June 26, 1888 (named for his grandfather Sellew); and Edwin Douglas at the end of May 1890. Lucy and Ashbel would, like their parents, eventually become educators, both earning Ph.D. degrees.[76]

Chesbrough Seminary prospered under Benson and Emma's quarter-century joint leadership. They seem to have worked well together as a team. Periodically Benson put notices in the *Earnest Christian* about the school's progress and ongoing needs. Commenting on the opening of the fall term in 1884, he noted the good enrollment and wrote, "The school is in better working order than ever before. We feel that it is just beginning its usefulness." A new Christian workers course was inaugurated.[77]

As coprincipals, Benson and Emma were fulfilling their sense of calling as Christian educators. This included their interest and involvement in the affairs of the Free Methodist Church, especially its missionary outreach. In 1889 Benson was the Free Methodist delegate to the Ecumenical Missionary Conference in London, England.[78]

Emma was a full partner with Benson in running the seminary and in much else that they did. She occasionally preached; the Chesbrough Seminary *Students' Chronicle* noted that on a Friday evening in early 1887 she "preached from [Eph. 2:22], 'in whom ye also are builded together for an habitation of God through the Spirit.'"[79] Back in May 1874 B. T. had recorded in his diary that Emma, then eighteen, received a call to preach.[80]

Benson and Emma's ministry extended well beyond the Free Methodist Church. In the 1890s they became known as speakers at the frequent missionary conventions that A. B. Simpson's Christian Alliance sponsored in various locations. Benson, for instance, spoke on the "witness of the Spirit" at the Old Orchard, Maine, convention in 1891 and on "God's rewards" at the Ninth Annual Convention of the Christian Alliance in New York City in October 1892. At an 1893 convention Emma, in an address entitled "God's Will," affirmed God's healing power. Christians may be assured, she declared, that "Divine healing is purchased for us in the atonement." The Bible clearly teaches that "Christ healed diseases by taking them

---

76. Smail, pp. 15-18; Alumni Record of Emma Sellew Roberts, Cornell University. According to the "Vital Statistics" Emma submitted to Cornell about 1907, Howard Passmore and Lois Ellen were born at Dunkirk (probably at her parents' home), and the other children in North Chili. She gives Edwin Douglas's (she spells it "Douglass") birth date as May 31, 1890; Smail has May 30.

77. B. H. Roberts, "Chili Seminary," *EC* 48, no. 4 (Oct. 1884): 130.

78. "Roberts, Benson Howard," in *Who Was Who in America* (1943), 1:1039.

79. *Students' Chronicle* 1, no. 17 (Mar. 5, 1887): 2.

80. BTRD, May 29, 1874: "At the Seminary we had the very best meeting I ever attended there and one of the best I was ever in. The Lord came in a glorious manner. Preached from Eph 4.15. The Lord graciously and greatly helped. . . . Emma Sellew was wonderfully led out and confessed that she had to preach."

upon Himself, just as He atoned for our sins by taking them upon Himself." God wants however not merely to heal disease but to give us "constant health for work and service. The Holy Ghost dwelling within us ought to have marked effect upon our physical life."[81]

It was partly through these contacts that Chesbrough Seminary became known throughout the Christian Alliance network. Simpson's *Christian Alliance and Missionary Weekly* periodically carried reports from Benson and Emma on the school's progress.[82]

Charles Stowe Roberts and Benjamin Titus Roberts, Jr.

Charles Stowe Roberts, Benjamin and Ellen's fourth (third surviving) son, grew up in North Chili, like his younger brother Benjie. Both he and Benjie were students at Chesbrough Seminary.

One cold, wintry day in January 1874, when Charles was about seventeen and a half, B. T. was at home hard at work on the *Earnest Christian* but apparently also keeping an eye on Charley, who was supposed to be studying. Benjamin was having a frustrating time of it. He wrote in his diary, "I cannot get Charley to study. He learns easily, but as far as application there is none. I do not know what to do for him."[83]

Like most teenagers, however, Charley did eventually learn to study. He finished at Chesbrough and later studied law at the State University of Iowa at Iowa City, graduating in 1879.[84] In the summer of 1876, at age twenty, he spent a few days at the Philadelphia world's fair, using a press ticket showing him representing the "Golden Rule[,] Rochester." B. T. probably arranged for him to go. Charles was one of the ten million people who attended this highly successful centennial celebration of the signing of the Declaration of Independence (officially, the United States International Exhibition). Many new inventions were on display, including the telephone, first publicly exhibited at the fair. Charles's press pass photo shows a dapper musta-

---

81. Reports in the *Christian Alliance and Missionary Weekly* 7, no. 10 (Aug. 28, 1891): 135; 7, no. 13 (Sept. 25, 1891): 204; 9, nos. 15 and 16 (Oct. 7 and 14, 1892; combined issue): 249; 9, no. 23 (Dec. 2, 1892): 363; 11, no. 5 (Aug. 4, 1893): 76-77. In the "Witness of the Spirit" address, "Prof. Roberts" (apparently Benson Roberts) said, "When I was a young man, I thought a little about going to China as a missionary, but my sympathies and those of my friends were not in that direction, and I said, 'Here is my little boy, I cannot leave him and go.' I resisted the direct call of God, and it was not long before that little boy was taken away by God" (7, no. 10 [Aug. 28, 1891]: 135). This apparently refers to the death of Howard Passmore Roberts in 1881.

82. For example, *Christian Alliance and Missionary Weekly* 9, no. 23 (Dec. 2, 1892): 364-65; 11, no. 4 (July 28, 1893): 63; 11, no. 18 (Nov. 3, 1893): 283.

83. BTRD, Jan. 26, 1874. See also chapters 38 and 39.

84. Charles received the bachelor of laws (L.L.B.) degree on June 17, 1879. Program, *Fourteenth Annual Commencement of the Law Department of the State University of Iowa* (June 17, 1879); *Catalogue of the State University of Iowa at Iowa City for 1878-79* (Iowa City: Published by the University, 1879), p. 91. Special Collections, University Libraries, University of Iowa.

chioed young man in tie and top hat, ready to see the sights. Charles does not however seem to have produced any report for the *Earnest Christian and Golden Rule*.[85]

Charles went into business rather than practicing law, however. In 1881 he married Susan Lowden, and to this union were born two sons, Lowden Stowe (born October 20, 1882) and Charles Parraga (born November 20, 1884). Charles and his family lived for a while in Colorado, then for a number of years in Morgan Park, Illinois, on the southwest side of Chicago.[86] Charles was living in Morgan Park at the time of B. T. Roberts's death in 1893.

Benjamin Titus Roberts, Jr. — "Benjie" — eventually became a medical doctor and also lived for a number of years in Morgan Park. After attending Chili Seminary and the University of Rochester, he graduated with a B.A. from Johns Hopkins in 1884. In 1887 he married Sara Kidwell, an Episcopalian, in Baltimore. Benjamin and Sara had only one child, Dorothy, who was born in Morgan Park in 1890 while Benjamin was studying medicine at the Chicago Homeopathic Medical College. Benjamin was still in medical training at the time of his father's death in 1893.[87]

It appears that neither Charles nor Benjamin, B. T. and Ellen's two youngest sons, made any Christian profession, at least in their early years.[88] Neither remained in the Free Methodist Church. B. T.'s sons followed their father in the pursuit of education, and all in different ways exhibited the Roberts entrepreneurial flair. But only Benson seems to have found the depth of faith and spiritual commitment that was the central passion of their parents' lives.

The Death of Titus Roberts

Three deaths in the Roberts family marked the year 1881. As noted above, George lost his wife Anna in January, and in September Benson and Emma lost three-year-old Howard Passmore, their firstborn.

Just four weeks after Anna's death in Bradford, Benjamin's father Titus died at the family home in Gowanda. Titus died on February 22, 1881, at age seventy-seven. He was faithful to God and was loyal to the Free Methodist Church from the time of its organization in 1860 until his death.[89] Since both B. T. Roberts's sisters Caroline

---

85. Press Ticket, United States International Exhibition, Philadelphia, issued to "Mr. Chas S Roberts" (MMHC); Daniel B. Shepp, *Story of One Hundred Years: A Matchless Record of the Greatest Century of Historic Time* (Philadelphia: Globe Bible Publishing Co., 1900), p. 519. The exhibition ran from May 10 to Nov. 10, 1876; the punched press ticket shows Charles attended June 28-30 and July 1, 3, and 5.

86. Smail, pp. 15-16. Morgan Park was later incorporated into Chicago. Smail says Charles lived "in later years in Rochester, NY, where he was a fruit buyer for Curtis Brothers" (p. 16).

87. Smail, pp. 16, 119.

88. It is curious, however, that the lead article in the November 1887 *Earnest Christian*, "Adam Clarke," was apparently written by Benjie. The author identification reads, "By B. T. Roberts, Jr." He would have been twenty-three at the time (though this could have been an earlier school essay). The author identification might be a mistake; however, the index also identifies the author as B. T. Roberts, Jr.

89. Smail, pp. 10-11; A. A. Burgess, Obituary, "Rev. Titus Roberts," *FM* 14, no. 18 (May 11, 1881): 2.

and Florilla had died earlier, Titus's death left only B. T. and his mother Sally surviving of the immediate family.[90]

Word of Titus's death came just as the March *Earnest Christian* was going to press. B. T. was away traveling, so Benson notified his father by telegram and inserted a brief tribute to his grandfather in the issue. Benson wrote,

> My grandfather's house was a favorite place with me to visit. I was always sure of a cordial welcome from grandfather and grandmother. I never had been long in the house, though, before grandfather would say, "How is it? Have you given your heart to Christ? Are you serving him?" and then such an earnest and affectionate appeal to me to determine to serve God at all hazards. Then at family prayers such a fervent prayer would ascend to God for the salvation of all his grandchildren. . . .
>
> He impressed me from my earliest childhood as a man of God, whose business it was to live for God. He ever walked in view of eternity. He was outspoken in defense of his principles and belief, and was a constant worker for the salvation of souls.[91]

For years a class leader and local preacher, Titus Roberts frequently opened the Word before the Gowanda congregation. His pastor at the time of his death, A. A. Burgess, wrote of him, "He has been class leader in our church nearly ever since its organization. He was an excellent leader, always looking after the interest of the little flock that were committed to his care. If any member of his class was absent from any meeting, from sickness or any other cause, Brother Roberts was sure to see him the next day, labor with him earnestly, and pray with him before he left."[92]

In his tribute to his father, Benjamin wrote, "His preaching was of a highly awakening character. He endeavored to promote the Christianity of the New Testament in all of its plainness and simplicity."[93]

Titus Roberts left a one-page handwritten will, executed about three years before his death. He left "all my real estate and also all of my personal property" to his wife Sally but stipulated that following her death his property and possessions be divided in thirds between Benjamin, the children of Florilla, and Caroline's children. The first item in the will, however, was a $1,000 bequest to Sally "to dispose of as she shall see fit . . . it being money that I received from her father's estate."[94]

Benjamin's mother Sally lived the rest of her earthly life in Gowanda — alone, but with her daughters' children in the area. As he traveled in or through western New York, Benjamin would from time to time visit her at the old family home.

90. Florilla Roberts Smallwood died on Aug. 15, 1877, and Caroline Roberts Brown died on Feb. 25, 1868, according to Kysor (Kysor, pp. 27, 29; Kysor has "1968" as Caroline's death year, evidently a misprint for 1868).

91. Benson H. Roberts, "Bereft," *EC* 41, no. 3 (Mar. 1881): 99-100.

92. Burgess, Obituary, "Rev. Titus Roberts."

93. [B. T. Roberts], "Rev. Titus Roberts," *EC* 41, no. 4 (Apr. 1881): 130.

94. Last Will and Testament of Titus Roberts, Oct. 17, 1877. Copy and transcription in Roberts Wesleyan College Archives.

CHAPTER 32

Leading a Movement

"An individual who is holy cannot consistently belong to a Church that despises the poor."

B. T. Roberts[1]

"You must sit down in quietness and think and write and rest."

Ellen Roberts to B. T. Roberts, 1874[2]

Somewhere around 1866 Free Methodism became a movement. In B. T. Roberts's lifetime, however, from late 1860 onward, the denomination struggled with the tension between movement and institution.

Perhaps the Free Methodist Church was in fact born as a movement. Movement dynamics were to some degree already present in the series of Laymen's Conventions that gave birth to the new denomination, in the Nazarite impulse, and in the revivals of John Wesley Redfield — related but not entirely identical phenomena.[3] Some-

---

1. B. T. Roberts, *Holiness Teachings* (North Chili, N.Y.: Earnest Christian Publishing House, 1893), p. 71.

2. ELR to BTR, Oct. 28, 1874, quoted in Zahniser, p. 294.

3. The argument here is that the Free Methodist Church exhibited the characteristics of a social movement, especially during the twenty-year period from 1866 to 1886. By "social movement" I mean "a group of people who are organized for, ideologically motivated by, and committed to a purpose which implements some form of personal or social change; who are actively engaged in the recruitment of others; and whose influence is spreading in opposition to the established order within which it originated." This is the definition given by L. P. Gerlach and V. H. Hine in *People, Power, Change: Movements of Social Transformation* (New York: Bobbs-Merrill, 1970), pp. 370-71. A key feature of a so-

thing was stirring in the Genesee Conference of the ME Church, and more broadly in those places where Redfield was holding revivals. In other words, the formation of the new denomination was not due solely to Roberts's initiatives and concerns; something broader was afoot.

Though the circumstances that gave rise to the Free Methodist Church were mostly internal to the Genesee Conference, they were nourished also by several broader currents within the Methodism of the time. One key factor was the desire of many Methodists for more democracy and less clerical control in church government. Relatedly, many members wanted to preserve the experiential vitality of earlier Methodism, which in New York State was fast fading by the 1850s (though still lively in frontier areas farther west).

Underlying these issues both within Methodism and in the nation at large was the complex evil of slavery, as noted in previous chapters.

The earliest years of the Free Methodist Church may be read as a reaction to these varied currents. Initially the new denomination was largely shaped by these interrelated issues. If Free Methodism was born as a movement, it was at first defined against the larger Methodist and national context, and was in this sense a reaction.

But this is only half the story. The vision of Benjamin and Ellen Roberts was not reactionary, despite what their critics said. B. T. strove mightily to move the denomination away from reaction into mission — the twofold mission of maintaining biblical Christianity and ministering the gospel to the poor. He was not trying to recapture something so much as reconnect with the impulse of early Methodism. His vision was to move in continuity with the renewing work of the Holy Spirit as seen not only in original Methodism but repeatedly throughout church history. Perhaps nothing gives the lie to charges that Roberts was ambitious or a fanatic so much as this clear, positive, consistent focus on mission.

The soundness of Roberts's vision may be debated, and will be evaluated later. But evidence abounds that his vision was positive, not negative. He was not nearly so concerned with building a denomination as he was with the growth of God's kingdom. That he expressed this concern through a new denomination was, so to speak, a historical accident. Or rather, it was a kingdom necessity due to the declension of Methodism, just as original Methodism arose because of spiritual deadness in the Church of England.

The best evidences for Roberts's missionary vision are his founding of the *Earnest Christian,* his passion for preaching the gospel to the poor, and his efforts (not wholly successful) to steer the new denomination away from reaction, fanaticism, personality conflicts, and organizational self-preoccupation. He did his best to focus the new movement on evangelism, church planting, and radical discipleship. Exam-

---

cial movement is that it exhibits significant energy, dynamism, and growth disproportionate to the amount of human effort and skill apparently devoted to promoting it. It seemingly takes on an energy and life of its own. See the discussion in Howard A. Snyder, *Signs of the Spirit: How God Reshapes the Church* (Grand Rapids: Zondervan, 1989), pp. 31-35.

ples of this are his encouragement of Vivian Dake and the Pentecost Bands in the 1880s and his firm support of women in ministry, which for him was a matter of mission.

Roberts initially was quite successful in focusing the new denomination missionally during its early period, especially from about 1866 to 1886. Movement dynamics — growth, vision, adaptability, social energy — are most obvious here. Roberts led the denomination in mission, even while his own vision and ministry were wider than the Free Methodist Church. This twenty-year period from 1866 to 1886 was really the *movement phase* of Free Methodism.[4]

Membership growth is one indicator of this. Using the quadrennial general conferences beginning in 1862 as membership markers, we can picture the denomination's early growth as follows:[5]

Total Free Methodist Membership, 1862-1894

Year	Members	Rate of Growth (by quadrennium)
1862	2,533	—
1866	4,974	96.4%
1870	6,684	34.4%
1874	7,603	13.7%
1878	10,995	44.6%
1882	14,071	28.0%
1886	17,677	25.6%
1890	21,161	19.7%
1894	26,141	23.5%

Initially the Free Methodist Church consolidated at about 2,500 members in 1862, after a two-year shaking-out period. It nearly doubled between 1862 and 1866, then grew by a little over a third in the next quadrennium, to 6,684 members. Growth over the next quadrennium was about 14 percent, to 7,603 in 1874. The most rapid growth period was the sixteen years from 1874 to 1890, when total membership went from 7,603 to 21,161 — about 178 percent growth over the four quadrennia. If

4. Free Methodist history may helpfully be schematized as the movement phase (1860-90), the sect phase (1890-1950), and the denomination phase (1950 to the present). These phases are fairly clearly marked in the church's ethos, self-understanding, institutions, leading personalities, and even in its statistics. See Howard A. Snyder, "A Schema of Free Methodist History," in Howard A. Snyder, "Aspects of Early Free Methodist History" (photocopied manuscript, 1994), pp. 56-57.

5. Membership figures are based on the following sources: *WAS*, p. 320; *BHR, BTR*, pp. 534-35; *Minutes of the Annual Conferences of the Free Methodist Church*, 1864, 1870, 1891, 1895; Hogue, *HFMC*, 2:182, 189; Carl L. Howland, *The Story of Our Church: Free Methodism; Some Facts and Some Reasons* (Winona Lake, Ind.: Free Methodist Publishing House, 1951), p. 129; Elias Bowen, *History of the Origin of the Free Methodist Church* (Rochester, N.Y.: B. T. Roberts, 1871), p. 293. To give a more complete picture I have included preachers, which in the early statistics are generally listed separately. The figures may not be 100 percent accurate, but they are close enough to give a fair picture of trends.

growth had continued at near this rate, the denomination would have had some 2,000,000 members in North America by the time of its centennial in 1960, whereas total North American membership that year was about 60,000 and membership worldwide was about 100,000.[6]

To put the matter a little differently: The denomination doubled in the four-year period between 1862 and 1866, to almost 5,000 members. It doubled again in about eleven years (1877), and a third time in the next twelve years (1889). It then took the denomination nearly thirty-five years, until about 1924, to double a fourth time; it did not reach 40,000 members (in North America, not counting foreign missions) until 1925.[7]

Meanwhile, the church's growth in other lands was extensive and substantial. Free Methodist foreign missions — a particular concern of Ellen Roberts — began in the mid-1880s. Here the movement energy of early Free Methodism seemed to repeat itself, or perhaps was reborn. As denominational growth began to stagnate in North America, it was accelerating in places like South Africa, Japan, and the Dominican Republic.[8]

The Question of Mission

B. T. Roberts and Free Methodism were in a broad sense part of the Holiness movement within American Methodism. This movement was committed to the doctrine and experience of entire sanctification as taught by John Wesley (and as interpreted by the leaders of the nineteenth-century movement).[9]

Roberts shared this concern for sanctification. Not everyone in the movement shared Roberts's particular concern for the poor, however. In general, early Free Methodism espoused a more radical understanding of entire sanctification as well as a more radical commitment to the poor. And, sociologically speaking, the energy that powered early Free Methodism was for the most part separate and distinct from that of the broader Holiness movement that in the 1860s, 1870s, and 1880s was centered mostly within the Methodist Episcopal Church.

Roberts insisted from the beginning that the mission of the Free Methodist Church was "twofold — to maintain the Bible standard of Christianity, and to

---

6. See the similar discussion in Marston, pp. 438-39.

7. Or, calculating back to 1860: The Free Methodist Church more than doubled during its first four years, recording 3,722 members in 1864 (assuming that it started with about 1,800). It doubled a second time in ten years, reaching 7,603 in 1874. It doubled a third time in about nine years (1883), and again in the next sixteen years (1899). Then it took another sixty-one years for the church to double a fifth time; it did not reach 60,000 members (in North America, not counting foreign missions) until 1960.

8. See the discussion of FM missions growth in chapters 37 and 40.

9. See especially Melvin E. Dieter, *The Holiness Revival of the Nineteenth Century* (Metuchen, N.J.: Scarecrow Press, 1980), and Charles Edwin Jones, *Perfectionist Persuasion: The Holiness Movement and American Methodism, 1867-1936* (Metuchen, N.J.: Scarecrow Press, 1974).

preach the Gospel to the poor."[10] He never lost sight of this, even when he became overburdened with more immediate administrative concerns. Commenting in 1862 on the unfortunate location of the FM church building "at one end of the village" of St. Charles, Illinois, he said, "Free churches, of all others, should be in a central position, accessible to the poor from all quarters of the town."[11] Toward the end of that year at the dedication of the Marengo, Illinois, Free Methodist church building, Benjamin noted: "The house was crowded . . . and the seal of Divine approbation was set upon the efforts of God's children, to provide a place where the Gospel could be preached to the poor — a place where the seats are free for all who wish to participate in the worship of God." He added, "Let us have plain, free churches or none."[12]

But what did Roberts really mean by "the gospel to the poor"? We may make several observations about how he understood "the poor" and the church's special mission to them, and relate these to the doctrine of sanctification.

1. By "the poor" Roberts meant "the masses," particularly in distinction from "the rich" who were gaining increased political and economic power in his day. For Roberts "the poor" constituted at once a moral and an economic category. He did not speak of a middle class, but rather saw society as divided largely between rich and poor. His concern seems to have been with those who suffer most, and especially with the victims of political and economic injustice.

2. Roberts's concern with the poor was related to his economic interests and theories. His economics were a part of his theology, as his book *First Lessons on Money* makes clear. In this book he presupposes the interrelationship of economic and spiritual principles and argues that economic justice is a primary duty of government.[13]

3. Roberts's emphasis on simplicity, sobriety, and plainness of dress also needs to be understood in light of his concern for the poor. Donald Dayton insightfully notes,

> Prohibition was urged in part because [drinking] was perceived to generate poverty and to oppress especially the poor. Simple dress was adopted not primarily for modesty or simplicity, but in an effort to make the poor feel comfortable in church if they could not afford fine clothes or jewelry — a consistent Free Methodist dresses down to go to church! Congregational singing and the banishment of musical instruments from worship was an effort to maintain a more populist style against the emerging cultivated tastes for a "higher class" of music represented by choirs and paid musicians.[14]

As this missional accent on the poor faded, plain dress tended to develop into a legalism, a sort of mark of spirituality. Even so, in Free Methodism's first half-century it

10. *The Doctrines and Discipline of the Free Methodist Church* (Rochester, N.Y.: General Conference, 1870), pp. ix-x.

11. [B. T. Roberts], "Trip to the West," *EC* 4, no. 1 (July 1862): 29.

12. [B. T. Roberts], "Dedication," *EC* 4, no. 5 (Nov. 1862): 158.

13. Roberts's *First Lessons on Money* is discussed further in chapter 34.

14. Donald W. Dayton, "Reclaiming Our Roots: The Social Vision of B. T. Roberts" (unpublished manuscript, 1992), p. 9.

also signaled solidarity — solidarity internally with one another, first of all, but also with the poor. Perhaps it is this, more than anything else, that accounts for the remarkable chain of Free Methodist city missions and rescue homes that grew up just before and after 1900. "It was not uncommon for even small Free Methodist congregations to sponsor rescue missions or homes for unwed mothers, hold street meetings, or, at least, circulate religious literature among the poor," notes William Kostlevy.[15]

For the first two or three generations Free Methodism was primarily a church of the poor, or at least of the lower middle class. In many towns and smaller cities its plain wood-frame church building was found on the "wrong" side of the tracks. Kostlevy notes, "Free Methodists were generally lower-middle-class property owners, although poor people did make up a sizeable part of the total Church membership. Among the poor within the Free Methodist congregations, one could frequently include the pastor. The 1906 religious census indicated that Free Methodist pastors, with an annual salary of $370 were, along with Wesleyan Methodist pastors, Salvation Army officers, and the pastors of a number of predominantly African American Churches, the lowest paid clergy in America."[16]

In other words, Free Methodists continued to be, socioeconomically, more a church of the poor than of the rich or the upper middle class. Douglas Strong posits this as one reason for greater sensitivity to the poor: "Since holiness churches were comprised of the economically poor more often than the increasingly-bourgeois mainline Methodist churches, the holiness folks more easily embraced the causes and struggles of their lower class constituency."[17] Yet theologically, Free Methodists gradually forgot Roberts's specific mission to the poor.

4. Roberts's views on wealth, poverty, and preaching to the poor are essentially those of John Wesley and Francis Asbury. He saw himself as a defender of historic Methodism as much as a reformer. His concern was to be Wesleyan, and in fact his writings contain many echoes of Wesley's comments on preaching to the poor and his warnings about the dangers of riches. Roberts was also echoing Asbury, who frequently referred to the Methodist mission to the poor. Asbury wrote in 1789, "To begin at the right end of the work is to go first to the *poor;* these *will,* the rich *may possibly,* hear the truth: there are [some people] among us who have blundered here."[18]

Did Roberts or other early Free Methodists make any specific theological con-

15. William Kostlevy, "Benjamin Titus Roberts and the 'Preferential Option for the Poor' in the Early Free Methodist Church," in *Poverty and Ecclesiology: Nineteenth-Century Evangelicals in the Light of Liberation Theology,* ed. Anthony L. Dunnavant (Collegeville, Minn.: Liturgical Press, 1992), p. 66. Kostlevy details some of this work. See also Howard A. Snyder, "A Heritage of Caring: Early Free Methodist Social Ministry," in Snyder, "Aspects," pp. 53-55.

16. Kostlevy, "Benjamin Titus Roberts," pp. 56-57.

17. Douglas M. Strong, "'The Deliverance of God's Oppressed Poor': The Ambivalent Legacy of Nineteenth Century North American Perfectionist Social Reform" (unpublished Working Group paper, 1992 Oxford Institute of Methodist Theological Studies), p. 3.

18. *The Journal and Letters of Francis Asbury,* ed. Elmer T. Clark, 3 vols. (London: Epworth; Nashville: Abingdon, 1958), 1:601.

nection between entire sanctification and evangelizing the poor? Or do these two concerns run, in effect, on separate tracks?

I cannot find that Roberts made any explicit theological connection between the two themes, other than to claim that both are essential to the gospel of Jesus Christ. Roberts's basic posture was that the Methodist church in his day was departing from historic Methodism, and that both the gospel for the poor and entire sanctification were essential parts of the Wesleyan message. In this sense the question really traces back to Wesley himself. For Wesley, both entire sanctification and ministry to and with the poor were grounded in his theology of God's grace — in salvation that is "free for all and free in all." Thus the conjunction of sanctification and concern for the poor in Roberts was something he inherited, and it was a heritage he was committed to maintain. This is the gospel that must be preached.

There was, however, an inherent if not explicit logical link between Roberts's concern for the poor and entire sanctification. The link was christological: entire sanctification makes the believer like Jesus Christ. The faithful disciple does the works of Jesus — and Jesus preached the gospel to the poor. "An individual who is holy cannot consistently belong to a Church that despises the poor," Roberts wrote.[19] Roberts was emphatic on this point. He wrote in 1881, "St. Paul says, 'Now if any man have not the spirit of Christ he is none of his.' If we have the spirit of Christ we shall do according to our opportunities and circumstances the work that Christ did. His work among men was teaching the ignorant the way of salvation, preaching the gospel to the poor, and relieving the distressed."[20]

To Roberts this was self-evident. Neither he nor other early Free Methodists felt the need to elaborate this connection theologically. Partly for this reason, once Roberts was no longer on the scene the denomination could with little or no sense of betrayal continue to espouse the doctrine of entire sanctification without equally stressing the corresponding accent on the gospel to the poor. The accent on the poor could drop out seemingly without doing any damage to the doctrine of entire sanctification. This is, in fact, what happened in Free Methodism, particularly after Roberts's death in 1893.

Clearly Roberts had a broader theological, reform, and evangelistic vision than did the Free Methodist Church generally. Once the denomination was formed, much energy went into developing denominational structures and patterns. Roberts was severely overworked, and few other leaders in the denomination fully shared his vision. Within thirty years, and particularly after 1890, much of the denomination developed into an inwardly focused counterculture with a considerably lessened reform and evangelistic focus. The disciplines of early Free Methodism often descended into legalisms. Most of the concern with reform and preaching the gospel

19. B. T. Roberts, *Holiness Teachings*, p. 71.

20. B. T. Roberts, preface in *Brands from the Burning: An Account of a Work among the Sick and Destitute in Connection with Providence Mission, New York City,* by Jane Dunning (Chicago: T. B. Arnold, 1881), p. iii.

to the poor either waned or was channeled into the emerging foreign mission enterprise, scattered missions and rescue homes, or into the work of the Pentecost Bands, which in 1895 left the denomination and became an independent movement (as will be noted later).

One who certainly did share Roberts's passion for the poor was John Wesley Redfield, in many respects the cofounder of Free Methodism. A number of the first Free Methodist churches sprang up in places where Redfield held revivals in the late 1850s. As noted earlier, Redfield shared many of Roberts's convictions, including abolitionism, simplicity, and the right of women to preach.[21] Redfield's impact on Free Methodism doubtlessly would have been much greater had he not died in 1863, just as Free Methodism was beginning.

Redfield's biographer, J. G. Terrill, noted that Redfield "labored to bring all to the gospel level by noticing the poor, and especially the colored poor."[22]

Growth and Expansion of Free Methodism

As noted at the beginning of this chapter, the growth of the Free Methodist Church — initially in spite of "strenuous opposition on the part of the parent church," as Benson Roberts noted — was substantial during the early decades. The denomination grew not only in numbers but also in geographic extent.

By the second Free Methodist General Conference, held in Buffalo and Albion in October 1866, the number of conferences had grown to four (Illinois and Michigan, in addition to Genesee and Susquehanna), and there were now 4,974 members.[23] Not surprisingly the Genesee Conference, where Roberts and his associates labored most intensively and where the influx from the ME Church was probably greatest, was the largest, with 2,025 members. The Illinois Conference, growing up in the area where Redfield had held a number of revivals, counted 1,278 members. And there were now 482 Free Methodists in Michigan. Membership requirements were tightened in 1866 by adding a ban on affiliation with secret societies (though this was pretty much assumed already).[24] Clearly this was no inhibition on growth.

Methodist Episcopal preachers who chose to identify with the new Free Methodist Church did so at some cost, both financially and socially. Benson Roberts re-

---

21. In a letter to Ellen Roberts in early 1860, Redfield said he was expecting a great revival and was "sure that God will open this era by means and instrumentalities quite out of the old stereotyped forms. Among these instrumentalities I believe woman is to take a very prominent part." Terrill, *Redfield*, p. 438.

22. Terrill, *Redfield*, p. 259.

23. The 1866 General Conference met first in Buffalo (Oct. 10-13) and then for four more days in Albion (Oct. 15-18). *Minutes of the Annual Conferences, and General Conference, of The Free Methodist Church*, 1870 (Rochester, N.Y.: Earnest Christian Office, 1870), p. 53.

24. BHR, *BTR*, pp. 371-72; Marston, pp. 398-99.

ported that the average FM preacher's salary in 1866 was less than $200 per year in Illinois and about $350 in the Susquehanna Conference. Though a good number of the preachers were young men who were converted through early Free Methodist ministry, Benson Roberts notes that many others were preachers who "had left salaries twice and thrice as great" to become Free Methodists.[25]

After the 1862 General Conference, the Free Methodists followed the Methodist Episcopal Church pattern of quadrennial general conferences. The 1870 General Conference met at Aurora, Illinois, symbolic of the denomination's westward expansion, October 12-21. During the 1866-70 quadrennium the Michigan Conference more than doubled, growing to 1,063 members. The Susquehanna and Illinois Conferences also posted substantial gains, though the Genesee Conference remained pretty much constant. Overall, the denomination grew from 4,889 in 1866 to 6,556 in 1870 (not including preachers, who now numbered 128), a surge of 34 percent (approximately 8 percent per year). The size of the General Conference itself grew, from thirteen delegates in 1862 to thirty in 1870.[26]

In contrast to the previous two General Conferences, the 1870 one was quite harmonious, though it dealt with thorny issues. The body took action (subsequently ratified by the annual conferences) establishing the general superintendency on a permanent basis and specifically forbidding "chewing, snuffing, or smoking tobacco, for the gratification of a depraved appetite." B. T. Roberts was appointed a delegate to the Christian National Anti-Secret-Society Convention to be held in Philadelphia the next June.[27]

The 1870 General Conference also took note of the financial state of the *Free Methodist* magazine — currently operating in the black, with 2,350 subscribers, but carrying a debt of about $1,500. Free Methodist businessman Joseph Mackey (88 White Street, New York City) offered to take over as editor and publisher, assuming "all the liabilities and indebtedness" and publishing "a new paper." His offer was accepted, and Mackey published the paper for a year. The magazine continued under private ownership until 1886, when it was officially taken over by the denomination.[28]

Benson Roberts notes, "From this time the field occupied by the church began to widen." New congregations were organized and new conferences formed as "self-denying men and women . . . pushed out into new fields with the Gospel of salvation from sin, full and free. From the older conferences laborers anointed for God's work began to go forth to spread the news."[29] New conferences included Kansas (1871), Northern Iowa–Minnesota (1872), New York (1874), Iowa (1875), North Michigan

25. BHR, *BTR*, p. 373.

26. BHR, *BTR*, p. 399; *WAS*, p. 320; *Minutes of the Annual Conferences, and General Conference, of The Free Methodist Church*, 1870, p. 55.

27. BHR, *BTR*, pp. 400-401; *Minutes of the Annual Conferences, and General Conference, of The Free Methodist Church*, 1870, pp. 57, 59.

28. BHR, *BTR*, pp. 400-401; *Minutes of the Annual Conferences, and General Conference, of The Free Methodist Church*, 1870, pp. 59-60; Marston, pp. 472, 489.

29. BHR, *BTR*, p. 401.

(1876), Central Illinois (1879), Ohio (1879), Canada (1880), Texas (1881), California (1883), Louisiana (1884), East Michigan (1884), Oregon-Washington (1885), and a number of others.[30]

When the 1886 General Conference met in Coopersville, Michigan, membership totaled 17,114, plus 563 preachers, and there were 479 local preachers. The number of annual conferences had risen to twenty-three.[31]

How did this rapid expansion occur? Free Methodist preacher–evangelist–church planters followed, to some degree, the expansion of the U.S. population westward, but in this period the church actually expanded in all directions, not just west. Taking on the dynamics of a movement, Free Methodism grew largely through revivals and personal evangelism. Much of the energy for this expansion came from the inherent dynamic of the gospel of Jesus Christ, sufficiently freed from ecclesiastical constraints to show its power, as has happened repeatedly throughout church history. But this expansion testifies also to the visionary leadership of B. T. Roberts. Benjamin was able to challenge and send forth workers into the harvest. He was widely respected and admired among the Free Methodism preachers. One young preacher in Illinois, encountering Roberts for the first time and watching him lead the annual conference sessions, said, "He presided like a Bishop and preached like an Apostle."[32]

The *Earnest Christian* also helped in the expansion. In many cases the magazine either had preceded Free Methodist church planters or served as a useful evangelistic and discipling tool as new churches were planted.

The story of Free Methodism's expansion during this period is mirrored in the experience of William Cusick, a Free Methodist pioneer in Michigan and Minnesota. Cusick, from Brockport, New York was converted during B. T. Roberts's ministry there in 1854 and early became a Free Methodist. Cusick was "a blacksmith, without learning but with a warm heart, a lot of sense and the anointing of the Holy Spirit."[33] In short, he was a man God could use, and one whose potential Roberts quickly recognized.

Cusick was ordained as a preacher in the FM Genesee Conference. But Roberts thought he would make a good missionary. In 1869 he suggested that Cusick go to Michigan and gave him fifty dollars out of his own pocket to get him started. Off Cusick went to labor with E. P. Hart and others in the new Michigan Conference, then encompassing all of Indiana and Ohio as well as both peninsulas of Michigan. At the time there were only about three hundred Free Methodists in Michigan.[34]

---

30. Marston, p. 428. Over time conference boundaries and names shifted as conferences expanded, divided, merged, or birthed new conferences.

31. BHR, *BTR,* p. 535.

32. Anson Stedwell, *Itinerant Footprints* (Chicago: Free Methodist Publishing House, 1915), 65.

33. BHR, *BTR,* p. 401.

34. BHR, *BTR,* p. 401; Hogue, *HFMC,* 2:36. Cusick is quoted in Benson Roberts as saying there were "not more than three hundred members in the three states," but Hogue says the 1869 minutes show a total conference membership of 1,073. The 1870 minutes report a total conference membership

Cusick went first to Coopersville, west of Grand Rapids, where two Free Methodist families from western New York had recently settled. His work bore fruit. At the end of the conference year he and his colleague, Charles H. Sage, reported over two hundred new members in the area. Hogue commented, "Mr. Cusick being a man of marvelous evangelistic ability, raised up work eastward from Coopersville, along the line of the Detroit and Grand Haven railroad."[35] At St. Johns, seventy miles from Coopersville, over one hundred were converted and a strong congregation established. From there, Cusick later recalled, the "work spread in different directions; and at the conference that fall, it was divided into three circuits."[36] One of the families converted during the St. Johns revival moved to Ontario, Canada, giving birth to Free Methodism there.[37] And the 1870 Michigan Conference minutes list W. D. Bishop as "Missionary to California."[38]

About this time a former Methodist living some twenty miles from St. Johns was given a copy of the *Earnest Christian*. The man read it and was so impressed that he wrote to Roberts, asking where the nearest Free Methodist church was. Roberts contacted Cusick and Cusick followed up, resulting in the birth of the Free Methodist Church in Grand Ledge, Michigan. Cusick later wrote, "When I left the circuit it contained a membership of two hundred, all resulting from one copy of *The Earnest Christian*."[39] Thus Roberts's ministry, and that of the Free Methodist Church, continued to expand.

Cusick was sent next to Minnesota, and again he was fruitful in evangelism and church planting. At Owatonna, forty miles north of the Iowa border, Cusick arranged for a revival and got Roberts to come as evangelist. "We secured a large hall and [Roberts] preached with great power," Cusick reported. The work continued with a camp meeting the next summer, and under Cusick and Hart's ministry, many were converted. From there the work spread west and north. Cusick was made district chairman, and under his leadership a local preacher, E. L. Smith, carried the work north to Alexandria, Minnesota. Cusick reported,

> The next spring I drove all through that country where there was not a Free Methodist class in all North Minnesota and Dakota. I saw at once that this was a very needy field. There were no schools save in the towns along the railroads. The people were busy taking up claims and improving the lands. . . . I bought a large tabernacle to be used as needed. . . . [I distributed] copies of *The Earnest Christian*

---

of 1,063 (plus 24 preachers), of which 647 seem to have been in Michigan. *Minutes of the Annual Conferences, and General Conference, The Free Methodist Church*, 1870, pp. 32-33.

35. Hogue, *HFMC*, 2:37.

36. BHR, *BTR*, pp. 402, 414-15.

37. As will be noted later, B. T. Roberts organized the Free Methodist Church in Canada at Galt, Ontario, in October 1880. See A. Sims, comp., *Free Methodism in Canada* (Toronto: A. Sims, [ca. 1920]), p. 6.

38. *Minutes of the Annual Conferences, and General Conference, The Free Methodist Church*, p. 33. The 1870 session of the Michigan Conference was held at Springfield, Ohio.

39. BHR, *BTR*, p. 404.

and the *Free Methodist* [two to each family]. I continued this for five or six years, during which times thousands [of the periodicals] were scattered all through the country, by which means an untold amount of good was done.[40]

Roberts returned to Minnesota from time to time to assist Cusick and others with the work. Cusick reported,

> At a camp-meeting held on the bank of the Blue Earth River in [southern] Minnesota, when B. T. Roberts was present a powerful meeting was held. In this place there was a large society of Zinzendorfians [Moravian Brethren], who taught that we received holiness at conversion. Brother Roberts preached five or six sermons on "holiness" of a very excellent character which so shattered the Zinzendorfian theory that many came forward and received the experience. A flourishing class of Free Methodists was established here as a result of that meeting. At Northfield, Motley [in central Minnesota], Alexander [Alexandria?] and Frazier City, Brother Roberts accompanied me where his preaching did much good. Churches have since been built at most of these places. At Long Prairie, at a tent meeting I held, a young man and his sister came forward. They were very much in earnest and soon the young man fell over, which scared the people dreadfully. The most of the community were composed of Baptists. The next night more came out than usual, and the young man came through and was clearly saved. An intelligent Baptist lady who had been present both nights said to me after the meeting, "I was so scared last night that if you hadn't been so calm I should have run. We never saw such things here before." Many were converted here and a large class was organized.[41]

Through pioneers like William Cusick, Edward P. Hart, Joseph Goodwin Terrill, Thomas S. LaDue, C. M. Damon, Jane Dunning, and many others — women as well as men — the Free Methodist Church continued to expand during the 1870s and 1880s, holding revivals, establishing churches, organizing conferences, and founding schools. Meanwhile B. T. Roberts, as general superintendent, served as chief strategist, recruiter and motivator of workers, networker and encourager.

General Conferences of 1874, 1878, and 1882

Free Methodist General Conferences continued to meet quadrennially throughout B. T. Roberts's lifetime. After the first two in 1862 and 1866, subsequent gatherings were held in 1870, 1874, 1878, 1882, 1886, 1890, and, after Roberts's death, in 1894 and 1898.

Benjamin no doubt approached each new General Conference with some ambivalence. The quadrennial gatherings often made decisions that directly affected his

---

40. Quoted in BHR, *BTR*, pp. 406-7.
41. Quoted in BHR, *BTR*, p. 408.

life, sometimes adding additional burdens to the load he already carried. Though each General Conference strongly affirmed his leadership, the conferences occasionally made decisions he thought unwise or that he opposed theologically.

1874: A Second General Superintendent

The fourth General Conference met at Albion, New York, on October 14-27, 1874. Benjamin arrived a day late, so the conference was led initially by Epenetus Owen of the Susquehanna Conference, a veteran Methodist Episcopal preacher who had become a Free Methodist.[42] When Roberts arrived and gave his superintendent's report, he announced that since the last General Conference he had organized the Minnesota, Northern Iowa, and New York Conferences, following the process established by previous General Conferences.

Free Methodist work had begun also in California. "We have received many and urgent calls to send a preacher to the Pacific coast," Roberts noted in a September 1873 *Earnest Christian* editorial. "Free churches are needed in California as well as on this side of the mountains. Even in the land of gold, the poor are found, who cannot afford to buy or rent a seat in the popular churches." In October 1873 George W. Humphrey, a preacher in the Genesee Conference and an Englishman, and his wife went as Free Methodist missionaries to California. Humphrey went largely at his own initiative, but with Roberts's encouragement: "Bro. Humphrey has the necessary faith, experience, tact and energy for pioneer work. He is confident that God will, in a few years, raise up a Conference in that region."[43] A small Free Methodist congregation was organized in San Francisco in 1875. Roberts visited the San Francisco area in 1879 (as noted in chapter 28), and eventually the California Conference was organized in 1883.[44]

The 1874 General Conference for the first time recognized women as evangelists, providing for licensing them as such. Though this was not ministerial ordination and thus not a full endorsement of women in ministry, it was a step in the direction Roberts favored.[45] As general superintendent, Roberts had himself been constituted a Committee on Woman's Work, and he brought in a recommendation for creating the official category of evangelists, no doubt as a way of getting some recognition of women's ministry in the face of opposition to fully ordaining them as preachers and pastors. Evangelists were defined as "a class of preachers called of God to preach the Gospel, to labor to promote revivals of religion and spread abroad the cause of Christ in the land; but not called to a pastoral charge or to government in the Church." Roberts could live with this. Any man or woman who felt so called could be

42. Zahniser, p. 294; Hogue, *HFMC*, 1:373-74; 2:176.
43. [B. T. Roberts], "Mission to California," *EC* 26, no. 3 (Sept. 1873): 97; Zahniser, p. 302; [B. T. Roberts], "Conferences," *EC* 26, no. 5 (Nov. 1873): 163.
44. Hogue, *HFMC*, 2:140; Marston, p. 430.
45. Zahniser, p. 194.

licensed as an evangelist by the quarterly conference, on recommendation of the local church. After four years of successful service an evangelist could be licensed, then, by his or her annual conference.[46]

Hogue commented that this provision

> opened the way for women to occupy the prominent position in the ministry of the Free Methodist Church which they have so long and efficiently held in many of the Conferences, not merely as Evangelists, in the general acceptation of that term, but as Evangelist-pastors. [Although this provision was] somewhat modified by subsequent General Conferences, [this was] merely in the way of amplification, never in the way of restricting woman's labors in the ministry. Woman's sphere of operation in the Free Methodist Church has been constantly enlarged from the beginning.[47]

This is true, and yet opening the way for women officially as evangelists but not as ordained pastors was a halfway measure. Debate over the full ordination of women continued for nearly twenty years. Women often did in fact serve as pastors, as Hogue implies, but officially they did so only as evangelists.

For Roberts personally, the most important action at this General Conference was the adding of a second general superintendent. The Committee on the Superintendency brought in a report commending Roberts and declaring that they were "heartily pleased with the very able and efficient manner" in which he had exercised his duties. Now a second general leader was needed as the church expanded.[48]

The conference concurred and proceeded to cast ballots, without nominations. Of the thirty-four ballots cast, Roberts received twenty-six votes and Edward Payson Hart, twenty. Both were declared elected; a second ballot was unnecessary.

E. P. Hart was a natural choice. Born in Marengo, Illinois, the son of a Methodist class leader, he was converted indirectly through a remarkable revival Redfield conducted there in 1858. Hart early endeared himself to Free Methodist people and preachers and was a key figure in the St. Charles camp meeting, the birth of Free Methodism in Michigan, and the founding of Spring Arbor Seminary (now Spring Arbor University). He was thirty-eight when elected general superintendent.

To Ellen Roberts, Hart's election was a relief. It would take some of the pressure off Benjamin. She wrote to him, "I feel better and better over your being released from so much traveling. It will prove a blessing and help. You must sit down in quietness and think and write and rest. I believe God is in all you felt in reference to this matter."[49]

---

46. Hogue, *HFMC*, 2:178.

47. Hogue, *HFMC*, 2:178-79.

48. Zahniser, p. 294; Hogue, *HFMC*, 2:177.

49. ELR to BTR, Oct. 28, 1874, quoted in Zahniser, p. 294.

1878: The Work Expands

The fifth Free Methodist General Conference met in the Methodist Episcopal church building in Spring Arbor, Michigan, from October 9 to 19, 1878. The second Free Methodist educational institution, Spring Arbor Seminary had been founded just five years earlier. B. T. Roberts and E. P. Hart presided alternately, and both were overwhelmingly reelected. The Committee on Superintendency reported satisfaction with their two leaders' "faithful and efficient" work and indicated that the annual salary of each was $526.15.[50]

This conference was composed of 58 delegates — 33 ordained ministers and 25 "lay" representatives from local congregations. With the addition of Iowa, Wisconsin, and North Michigan, the denomination now had ten conferences, 313 preachers, and 233 local preachers.[51]

This conference took the first steps toward publishing a Free Methodist hymnbook. It was to contain not fewer than 600 hymns and be copyrighted in the name of the Free Methodist Church, but was to place the denomination under no financial obligation. Roberts chaired a committee of fifteen that worked on the project throughout the quadrennium, but the hymnbook was not published until 1883, following the sixth General Conference.[52] In the meantime Roberts continued issuing editions of his earlier compilation, *Spiritual Songs and Hymns for Pilgrims,* to meet the immediate need.[53]

Methodist Bishop Matthew Simpson had published his *Cyclopaedia of Methodism* in 1878 and included in it a two-column article entitled "Free Methodists." Though not polemical in tone and generally accurate, the article was one-sided and alleged that in the denomination's "early history some of its leaders encouraged a spirit of wild fanaticism" leading to meetings marked by "extravagance."[54] Many Free Methodists were unhappy with Simpson's characterization of the denomination, and the 1878 General Conference passed a resolution "That B. T. Roberts be requested to write and publish a full refutation of the untrue statements and misrepresentations" in the *Cyclopaedia of Methodism* article. This action led to the publication of Roberts's *Why Another Sect* the following year.[55]

The conference also passed a resolution requesting that one of the general su-

---

50. Zahniser, pp. 294-95; Hogue, *HFMC,* 2:180.

51. Zahniser, p. 295.

52. Zahniser, pp. 294-95; Hogue, *HFMC,* 2:181-82.

53. Zahniser (p. 282) says Roberts compiled *Spiritual Songs and Hymns for Pilgrims* in 1879, but this is an error; it was first published in 1868. See the discussion in chapter 34. Roberts did publish a "Church Edition" of the book in 1878; see B. T. Roberts, comp., *Spiritual Songs and Hymns for Pilgrims,* "Church Edition" (Rochester, N.Y.: B. T. Roberts, 1878). This edition did not however contain "two thousand and twenty-eight hymns" (Zahniser, p. 282); perhaps Zahniser meant 228.

54. Matthew Simpson, ed., *Cyclopaedia of Methodism* (Philadelphia: Everts and Stewart, 1878), pp. 379-80.

55. Hogue, *HFMC,* 2:182.

perintendents visit the Pacific Coast. This resulted in Roberts's first trip to the Far West the following year.[56]

In the fall of 1880 Roberts traveled to Ontario to organize the Free Methodist Church in Canada. The first Canadian Free Methodist conference met at Galt, Ontario (north of Brantford, about twenty-five miles west of Hamilton), October 21-23, with Roberts presiding. The conference was organized with thirteen circuits and a total membership of 319 and was divided into two districts, London and Toronto.[57] (Earlier, in 1874, Benjamin had spent about a week ministering in the Toronto area as a result of an invitation from Canadian readers of the *Earnest Christian*.)[58]

1882: Further Growth

When the sixth Free Methodist General Conference convened in 1882, B. T. Roberts was fifty-nine and had served as general superintendent for twenty-two years. Clarence Zahniser estimated that this General Conference "marked the peak of [Roberts's] popularity . . . as evidenced by his unanimous reelection, and by the fact that no action was allowed to go directly against him."[59]

The conference convened on Wednesday, October 11, and continued until Monday, October 23. The sessions were held at the South Hill Free Methodist Church in Burlington, Iowa, symbolic of the movement's westward expansion. The number of conferences had grown with the addition of Ohio, Central Illinois, Texas, and Louisiana. The number of ministerial and "lay" delegates was nearly equal: thirty-six to thirty-two.[60]

Up to this time pastoral appointments had been limited to two years. The 1882 General Conference voted that this could be extended to three years in special cases and did some other organizational tinkering. District chairmen were permitted in the interval between annual conferences to divide circuits in two when necessary in order to facilitate growth, provided the pastor and official board concurred.[61]

Roberts and Hart were reelected general superintendents with solid majorities. However, the Committee on Superintendency in its report censured Roberts for a couple of administrative decisions he had made, one of which affected the formula for determining the number of delegates from the Michigan and North Michigan Conferences and the other concerning the admission of a preacher into the Michi-

---

56. Zahniser, p. 295.

57. Sims, *Free Methodism in Canada*, p. 6.

58. BTRD, Feb. 5-11, 1874; *Autobiography of Rev. Charles H. Sage, a Member of the East Michigan Conference, Free Methodist Church* (Chicago: Free Methodist Publishing House, 1903), pp. 81-82. The key contact was Robert Loveless, who lived about thirteen miles north of Toronto.

59. Zahniser, p. 296.

60. Hogue, *HFMC*, 2:182.

61. Hogue, *HFMC*, 2:183.

gan Conference. After extensive debate, Roberts was exonerated of any infraction of the *Discipline*.[62]

Since no denominational hymnbook had as yet appeared, this matter came up again. A Committee on Compiling and Publishing a Hymn Book, replacing the previous committee, was appointed, to be chaired by Roberts. Other committee members were Richard W. Hawkins, Joseph Travis, J. G. Terrill, Moses N. Downing, and William Gould. The conference now mandated that the hymnbook contain at least 800 hymns. Up to this point Free Methodists used the Methodist Episcopal hymnbook of 1849. The conference voted that the new hymnbook should be based on the Methodist Episcopal one and the earlier Methodist hymnbook compiled by John Wesley.

Roberts was to publish the hymnbook at his own expense, however, and therefore it would be copyrighted in his name. The General Conference had more confidence in Roberts's ability to successfully publish and finance the hymnbook personally than it did in the corporate action of the church, which as yet had no denominational publishing operation.[63]

After General Conference the committee went right to work. It met for several days in North Chili at the beginning of 1883. These meetings coincided with "a gracious work" of God's Spirit at the seminary and in the local congregation, with "a general quickening of holiness," Benjamin noted. Terrill preached several evenings while in North Chili for the committee meetings, and his messages were "greatly blessed."[64]

Roberts reported in February that the committee had completed its work: "Copy has been placed in the hands of the printer, and the design is to push it through as fast as it can be done and done well." The committee had selected over 900 "of the choicest salvation hymns," a large number on the subject of full salvation. "A few good temperance hymns" were also included.[65]

The result of these labors was *The Hymn Book of the Free Methodist Church*, published by B. T. Roberts at Rochester later in 1883. The hymnbook was a handsomely bound small volume (without tunes, like the earlier ME hymnbooks), measuring three and one-quarter inches by five inches and containing 868 hymns.[66] The hymnbook's nine divisions reflect the church's, and Roberts's, theology: "Adoration," "Salvation Needed," "Salvation Provided," "Salvation Proclaimed," "Salvation Offered" (made up of invitation hymns, including "Just as I Am"), "Salvation Sought," "Fruits of Salvation," "Eternal Salvation," and "Miscellaneous" (including hymns on missions, Sunday schools, temperance, and marriage). The first section, "Adoration," contained 135 hymns.[67] This hymnbook served the Free Methodist Church for nearly

62. Zahniser, pp. 295-96.

63. Hogue, *HFMC*, 2:184.

64. [B. T. Roberts], "Revivals," *EC* 45, no. 2 (Feb. 1883): 65.

65. [B. T. Roberts], "The Hymn Book," *EC* 45, no. 2 (Feb. 1883): 67.

66. It is not clear whether Roberts was in error in saying over nine hundred hymns had been selected, or whether he later deleted some. More likely the former.

67. *The Hymn Book of the Free Methodist Church* (Rochester, N.Y.: B. T. Roberts, 1883; Chicago: Free Methodist Publishing House, 1906).

thirty years.[68] The organization of the hymnbook contrasted some with that of the large 1849 *Hymns for the Use of the Methodist Episcopal Church,* the hymnbook in use at the time the Free Methodist Church was formed, as also with the 1878 *Hymnal of the Methodist Episcopal Church,* which contained 1,117 selections.[69]

The 1883 Free Methodist *Hymn Book* bore some resemblance to Roberts's 1878 songbook, though it was much larger. Roberts had prefaced his earlier book with the verse "Be filled with the Spirit, speaking to yourselves in psalms and hymns and spiritual songs, singing and making melody in your hearts to the Lord." But the 1883 denominational hymnbook used 1 Corinthians 14:15, "I will sing with the spirit and I will sing with the understanding, also." Overall, the 1883 hymnbook was organized in a more traditional way.

Though Benjamin was frequently traveling while the 1883 hymnbook was in preparation, the project was "an almost steady burden on my mind," he confessed to Ellen. He wrote to her from Missouri in August 1883, "There is an index prepared by Brother Gould. The pages will need to be corrected. I wish you would have Clara make up a book as far as it is printed and from it correct the index. She can sew on that part of the book which I left on my table."[70]

Roberts noted in the hymnbook's preface that the book "embraces some of the choicest hymns in the language. We claim for the hymns that they are orthodox, evangelical, and generally of an elevated style and character." He noted that William Gould had "with much labor" prepared the copy for the press. The book contained many Charles Wesley hymns, including "And Can It Be" (#395), which inexplicably failed to make it into later Free Methodist hymnals. Robert Robinson's "Come, Thou Fount of Every Blessing" was altered to fit better with Wesleyan theology. "Bind my wandering heart to thee" was changed to "Bind my grateful heart to thee," and the lines beginning "Prone to wander, Lord, I feel it" were replaced with:

On the cross he died to save me,
    Rose to plead my cause above;

---

68. Hogue, *HFMC,* 2:184. Marston discusses the development of FM hymnody, pp. 345-48.

69. The 1849 Methodist Episcopal hymnbook containing 1,148 selections had fourteen main divisions, beginning with "The Divine Perfections" and ending with "Time and Eternity" (plus "Introductory to Worship" and "Close of Worship" sections). The 1878 *Hymnal* was organized similarly but a little more simply. Its main sections were "Worship," "God," "Christ," "The Holy Spirit," "The Scriptures," "The Sinner," "The Christian," "The Church," and "Time and Eternity," plus "Miscellaneous," "Doxologies," and "Occasional Pieces and Chants." It is thus a more churchly volume (in the sect-to-church sense) than was the 1883 FM hymnbook, and somewhat more so than the 1849 ME hymnbook. See *Hymns for the Use of the Methodist Episcopal Church* (New York: Lane and Scott, 1849); *Hymnal of the Methodist Episcopal Church* (New York: Hunt and Eaton, 1878).

70. BTR (St. Elmo, Mo.) to ELR, Aug. 18, 1883, quoted in Zahniser, p. 282. Roberts announced in the August 1883 *Earnest Christian* that the new hymnbook was "now on the press." "It is in new type and is being printed on fine paper and in good style." [B. T. Roberts], "The New Hymn Book," *EC* 46, no. 2 (Aug. 1883): 68.

Henceforth all my life I give thee,
Vanquished by such wondrous love.[71]

Though most of the hymns and gospel songs (such as those of Fanny Crosby) were taken over from other hymnbooks, a few were original compositions by Free Methodists, such as Asa Abell's "I Love the Holy Son of God" (#68) and Joseph McCreery's "I Storm the Gate of Strife" (#850) and "Oh! Wondrous Love Divine" (#306).[72]

The hymnbook was eventually published in two editions and sizes. The 1886 General Conference pronounced the selection of hymns "excellent" but recommended that "in future issues greater care be exercised for the avoidance of typographical errors and that [the books] be more substantially bound."[73] Zahniser notes, "The enforced absences of Mr. Roberts were probably too long for him to exercise as close supervision as was necessary in such a work."[74]

The question of whether the denomination should take over the operation of the *Free Methodist* magazine came up again at this General Conference. The magazine was successfully being published in Chicago by a partnership of D. P. Baker and T. B. Arnold, both preachers in the Illinois Conference, and had over three thousand subscribers. About this time Baker, who edited the magazine, retired, and Arnold offered to continue publishing it if the General Conference would elect a new editor. The conference agreed and elected Joseph Travis as the magazine's first denominationally elected editor. With this action the denomination moved one step closer to establishing its own publishing operation.[75]

The denomination's evangelistic and missionary vision continued to expand. The 1882 General Conference discussed missionary outreach at some length, though principally with reference to the extension of the work in North America. A General Missionary Board was formally organized, and C. B. Ebey was elected the denomination's first missionary secretary. All local churches were to receive offerings of not less than twenty-five cents per member for "general missionary purposes." Three years later the General Missionary Board was legally incorporated.[76]

Free Methodism was beginning to grow also on the West Coast. By the late 1870s

---

71. *Hymn Book of the Free Methodist Church* (1883), #671. The hymn is marked, "R. Robinson, Alt." It is not clear who made the alterations; however, the 1878 *Hymnal of the Methodist Episcopal Church* has the original "prone to wander" language (#726), as did the 1849 hymnbook (#901).

72. *Hymn Book of the Free Methodist Church* (1883). Though unsigned, the preface presumably was written by Roberts. As noted earlier, the hymnbook also includes some hymns by Henry Kirke White.

73. General Conference Minutes, Free Methodist Church (1886), p. 42, quoted in Zahniser, p. 283.

74. Zahniser, p. 283. The 1885 edition of the *Hymn Book* carries an 1885 copyright date, but the 1906 edition carries an 1883 copyright. Apparently the hymnbook was first issued in 1883, then again (probably with corrections) in 1885, and possibly again with further corrections following the 1886 General Conference.

75. Hogue, *HFMC*, 2:184-85; Marston, pp. 472-73.

76. Hogue, *HFMC*, 2:185; Marston, pp. 451-52.

the New York Conference was sending missionaries to the Oregon and Washington territories. Evangelistic work there led to the formation of the Oregon and Washington Territory Conference in 1884, which was later divided into the Washington, Oregon, and Columbia River Conferences.[77]

Expansion into Pennsylvania

During this period Free Methodism was expanding south into Pennsylvania as well as westward. The pioneers in western Pennsylvania were three remarkable people, Hiram Crouch, farmer and businessman; his devout and capable wife Anna; and Richard W. Hawkins, a Methodist preacher employed as bookkeeper for the Columbia Farm Oil Company near Oil City.[78]

Hiram Crouch, three years younger than B. T. Roberts, was a prosperous Christian gentleman who experienced entire sanctification under Roberts's ministry in 1859. He and Anna joined the Free Methodist Church in Rochester in 1863. When Roberts started Chili Seminary, Mr. Crouch considered buying a large farm adjoining the seminary property and giving it to the school to help it financially. The oil boom in northwestern Pennsylvania was just then at full tide, however, so he decided instead to invest there, thinking this would eventually bring much greater return for the seminary. Then the speculative bubble burst and he lost nearly all his money. But he and Anna continued strong in faith.

Mr. and Mrs. Crouch had lived for a while "in quite affluent circumstances" in Jamestown, New York, at the southern end of Lake Chautauqua and just eight miles north of the Pennsylvania state line. About the time of Hiram's oil investment, apparently, he and his family moved to the Oil City area and there, probably in 1870, he and Anna met Richard Hawkins.[79] Through the Crouches, Hawkins was led "into the experience of sanctification, and later into the Free Methodist Church, where he was mightily used of God for many years in building up the work in Western Pennsylvania."[80]

Hawkins joined the Susquehanna Conference in September 1870 and soon organized a Free Methodist congregation at Columbia Farm. Hiram and Anna Crouch were charter members of this pioneer Free Methodist congregation in Pennsylva-

---

77. Hogue, *HFMC*, 2:128; Marston, p. 430.

78. Hogue, *HFMC*, 2:64-67; Richard R. Blews and Frances McKay Roggenbaum, eds., *Our Heritage, 1898-1973* (n.p., [1973]), pp. 1-3. This work is a history of the Oil City Conference. Hiram Crouch was born in Connecticut on Dec. 10, 1826, and died in Los Palmas, New Mexico, on Dec. 13, 1910 (Obituary, Rev. Hiram Albert Crouch, *FM* [Feb. 7, 1911]: 94). He and his wife were pioneers of Free Methodism in Colorado as well as in Pennsylvania. Hogue summarizes the Crouches' life and ministry.

79. Apparently both Hawkins and the Crouches lived in or near Columbia Farm, about six miles from Oil City.

80. Hogue, *HFMC*, 2:64, 67.

nia.[81] Out of this pioneering work grew, with time, both the Oil City and Pittsburgh Conferences of the Free Methodist Church.[82]

Hawkins was "a man of pleasing appearance, great refinement, rare intellect, great penetration, fine scholarship, poetic imagination, remarkable oratorical ability, and of extraordinary personal magnetism," according to Hogue.[83] He was a pastor, evangelist, author, and for some time a trustee of Chili Seminary. Among his writings was *The Book of Psalms in Metre*, published in Rochester by George Lane Roberts in 1877.[84] A later book of his entitled *Redemption; or, The Living Way* proved controversial and created something of a headache for B. T. Roberts.[85]

Meanwhile, Free Methodism was growing rapidly in western Pennsylvania. The area was "a fruitful field for Free Methodism," Wilson Hogue noted; it experienced "a degree of success beyond that which has characterized it in many other places." Hogue noted that camp meetings had been particularly effective in western Pennsylvania, "as in most other sections of Free Methodism."[86] Roberts reported that the first Oil City camp meeting, held in the summer of 1871, was "a decided success" and was largely attended even though few Free Methodists lived in the region. An "untold amount of good was done," he said. "Many were saved, and impressions left upon the minds of the people which, we trust will be lasting."[87]

A congregation was soon organized at Oil City. Hogue noted in 1915, "The societies in Columbia Farm and Oil City were centers from which the light was spread in all directions over Northwestern Pennsylvania, until the work in that region now embraces two of the largest Conferences of the connection."[88]

As the work spread south, a congregation was organized at Pittsburgh in 1876-77 by George W. Coleman (later a general superintendent, 1886-1903). A 1973 history of the Oil City Conference reported, "No property — church or parsonage

81. Hogue, *HFMC*, 2:67. In 1861-62 a Free Methodist congregation had been organized at Eldred, Pa., just south of Olean, N.Y., as an outreach from the Genesee Conference, but this congregation did not survive (Blews and Roggenbaum, *Our Heritage*, p. 1). Five years later, in 1875, when Hiram was forty-eight, the Crouches moved to Colorado, partly for health reasons. Hiram "was forty years old when he began to preach, and later was ordained by Bishop [*sic*] B. T. Roberts. While not a member of conference, he has filled regular appointments on circuits and entered open doors wherever opportunity was given" (Obituary, *FM*). Crouch was thus ordained about 1867, before he moved to Pennsylvania.

82. The Pittsburgh Conference, which initially included the Oil City area, was organized in 1883. The Oil City Conference was formed from the Pittsburgh Conference in 1899, though in fact the work in the Oil City area originated earlier than that in the Pittsburgh area.

83. Hogue, *HFMC*, 2:67. Photos of both Hawkins and Hiram Crouch are found in Hogue, facing 2:66.

84. Richard Watson Hawkins, *The Book of Psalms in Metre. A New Version and Revision* (Rochester, N.Y.: G. L. Roberts, 87 State Street, 1877). The fact that this was a "revision" may suggest that an earlier edition had been published.

85. See chapter 38.

86. Hogue, *HFMC*, 2:64, 67-68.

87. [B. T. Roberts], "Oil City Camp Meeting," *EC* 22, no. 2 (Aug. 1871): 66.

88. Hogue, *HFMC*, 2:68.

— was owned up to [this] time by any of the churches in the state. The infant societies worshiped in homes or in rented halls. The new society at Pittsburgh [was] the first to report any church property — a church [building] valued at one thousand dollars."[89]

Free Methodism in western Pennsylvania "was born in the spirit of evangelism and was perpetuated by heaven-born revivals."[90] Hogue summarized the early decades:

> Notwithstanding the disturbance occasioned by the introduction of the heresy and fanaticism [resulting from Hawkins's teaching], the work of God steadily progressed, and spread in all directions. Revival fires were kindled in all parts of the Conference in which multitudes were saved; new societies were organized, new Church buildings erected, "and the work was enlarged and strengthened in a manner almost unprecedented in the history of Free Methodism." There were Pentecostal outpourings of the Holy Spirit on every hand. Nor was the work superficial, but deep and thorough in its character.[91]

One of the marks of this early growth was the number of women appointed to pastoral ministry, even though they could be licensed only as evangelists, not ordained as preachers. Pittsburgh Conference appointments in 1892 included Mrs. N. F. Hibbard, Emma Ellison, and Mossie Lafferty. In the first year of the Oil City Conference (1899-1900), Gertrude Grimm, Helen Critchlow, Kate Baldwin, May Brunner, and Minnie Smith were appointed to pastor local congregations.[92]

As general superintendent, Roberts was responsible for the general oversight of Free Methodist growth in Pennsylvania and elsewhere. Fortunately, the load was lightened somewhat by the election of Hart as a second general superintendent in 1874, and Coleman as a third superintendent in 1886. Both survived Roberts in the general superintendency, providing continuity when Roberts died in 1893.[93]

---

89. Blews and Roggenbaum, *Our Heritage*, p. 4.

90. Blews and Roggenbaum, *Our Heritage*, p. 7.

91. Hogue, *HFMC*, 2:76; cf. Blews and Roggenbaum, *Our Heritage*, p. 7. Hogue does not give the source of the clause he quotes. Blews and Roggenbaum rework Hogue's comment here, substituting "There was an unusual outpouring of the Holy Spirit on every hand" for "There were Pentecostal outpourings of the Holy Spirit on every hand."

92. Blews and Roggenbaum, *Our Heritage*, pp. 7-8. Presumably Mossie Lafferty was a woman. Often, but not always, these women were appointed as "supply" preachers, indicating (in effect) an interim arrangement. Though these particular appointments were subsequent to B. T. Roberts's death, they witness to the ethos of early Free Methodism that he helped create. Yet, since women could not be ordained elders, they were in effect second-class ministers in the church. On women preachers in the Pittsburgh Conference (and, relatedly, the ministry of the Pentecost Bands), see also Arthur D. Zahniser and John B. Easton, *History of the Pittsburgh Conference of the Free Methodist Church* (Chicago: Free Methodist Publishing House, 1932), especially pp. 20-21, 25-36.

93. Marston, p. 426.

Roberts's Publishing Enterprise

Throughout this period, B. T. and Ellen Roberts continued to make North Chili their base of ministry. Since publishing had become a major part of Benjamin's work, in 1883 he set up an expanded printing and publishing operation in North Chili.

As noted in chapter 31, George Roberts's printing business, started with B. T.'s help, had not gone well. Ellen wrote to B. T. in September 1877, "George is having his usual troubles with the press. Let us get done with the world, and only do the one work to which you are called" — apparently referring to George's attempts to get enough outside business to support the shop and Benjamin's involvement with this.[94]

When George moved to Bradford in early 1878, Benjamin apparently kept the shop at 87 State Street and continued to have the *Earnest Christian* set up and printed there. In 1879 he moved the printing business to a better location on Exchange Street, expecting that the annual rent of $200 would be more than covered by job printing. Debts mounted, however, and Benjamin considered selling the business, worth about $3,500, settling his debts, and applying the balance toward his new house in North Chili. At the 1882 Free Methodist General Conference he offered to donate all his printing equipment to the church as the beginning of a denominational publishing house, but the conference turned this down for financial reasons.[95]

Finally, in 1883 Benjamin resolved to move the business to North Chili. Exhibiting again his entrepreneurial flair, Roberts decided that rather than getting out of the printing business, he would actually expand it, put it on a firmer financial basis, and in essence make it an extension of his ministry. He bought a lot in North Chili. He also bought an old wagon shop (then being used as a student dormitory) and had it moved on horse-drawn rollers to the site.[96] He also upgraded his equipment, adding more presses.[97]

The converted wagon shop provided adequate space for what became, in effect, the *Earnest Christian* office and publishing house. Zahniser writes, "The ground floor of the newly purchased building was used as the press room and was heated by the steam from the boiler that ran the presses. The second floor was used as the composing and mailing room. Here not only *The Earnest Christian*, but the books which Mr. Roberts wrote, and the hymn books and Disciplines of the Free Methodist Church were [from this point on] published."[98]

94. ELR to BTR, Sept. 18, 1877, quoted in Zahniser, p. 271.

95. Zahniser, pp. 271-72.

96. Zahniser says "Mr. Roberts 'bought the Hudson place' at North Chili," citing an 1883 letter from ELR to Lucy Coleman, but does not make clear the location nor whether there was a house or other building on this property (p. 272).

97. Zahniser, p. 272. Citing a "Statement from [an] old resident of North Chili" to a Roberts Junior College student, Zahniser writes that Roberts "equipped [the business] with a Campbell-Country press, size 21 1/2 by 38 inches, which cost approximately twelve thousand dollars. Two other small job presses, the one size 14 by 22, and the other 7 by 11, both Colt Armory, were installed" (p. 272).

98. Zahniser, p. 272.

The printing enterprise proved to be a success as it served the seminary, the growing denomination, and the *Earnest Christian*. Several people, probably including seminary students, were kept busy. About a year after the North Chili operation began, Ellen Roberts wrote to her husband, "Ellen is at the office. E. Warner is stitching [books]. Men are printing covers to *The Earnest Christian*. All is quiet and pleasant at Office."[99]

Although the denomination took steps to start the Free Methodist Publishing House in Chicago just three years after Roberts set up his printing enterprise in North Chili, Roberts continued his printing and publishing operation for the rest of his life, the principal focus being the ongoing publication of the *Earnest Christian*. Books such as *Ordaining Women* were issued under the imprint "The Earnest Christian" Publishing House. A publications list included at the end of the August 1886 *Earnest Christian* (which Roberts suggested readers keep for reference) listed some twenty-one books and pamphlets, plus about twenty tracts, for sale. The *Free Methodist Hymn Book* was available in four different versions, including "Large Size, Full Leather," for two dollars. Several of Roberts's own publications were listed, among them *First Lessons on Money, Right of Women to Preach,* and *Conspiracies against Farmers*. Other books for sale included J. A. Wood's *Perfect Love*, William Arthur's *The Tongue of Fire*, David Bernard's *Light on Masonry*, and William Nast's *Introduction to the Gospel Records*.[100]

Roberts's Assessment of Free Methodism

As Free Methodism grew and expanded, the question naturally arose from time to time: Should this small denomination unite with other like-minded Christian bodies to further the work of the gospel?

Roberts addressed this question directly in an *Earnest Christian* editorial entitled "Union" in early 1883. Here Roberts both reveals his sense of what a true church should be and assesses the first two decades of Free Methodism.

Roberts wrote, "We are united in heart to all who love our Lord Jesus Christ in sincerity. Like has an affinity for like." Consequently, he said, "We should be glad to see all such united in CHURCH fellowship. But we should want such a Church to be a Christian Church. It should include all the saved, and none but the saved. It should be made up of those who answer the New Testament description of believers."

After summarizing the events that led to the formation of the Free Methodist Church, Roberts wrote:

> We have encountered the most bitter opposition. The influence of the leading churches has been against us. But God has been with us. We have met, all things

---

99. ELR to BTR, July 1, 1884, quoted in Zahniser, p. 273.

100. "Publications For Sale at The Earnest Christian Office," *EC* 52, no. 2 (Aug. 1886): following p. 68.

considered, with an encouraging degree of success. We should be glad to have all true Christians who agree with us as to what a church should be, to unite with us. . . .

If any one will show us churches that come up to the Gospel standard, we will gladly unite with them. If there are none, can we do any better than go on and do our utmost to hold up the Bible standard of salvation and preach the Gospel to the poor?

Thus Roberts felt that through the first two decades of Free Methodism the work had seen "an encouraging degree of success" — and it continued to be focused on its original mission to maintain biblical Christianity and preach the gospel to the poor. On relationships with other churches, Roberts concluded: "Let us be joined to all the living. But union with death can only promote death. No matter how costly and imposing may be the sepulchres in which the dead are entombed, we should let them alone."[101]

101. [B. T. Roberts], "Union," EC 45, no. 1 (Jan. 1883): 31.

CHAPTER 33

Movement versus Institution

"We must not let the Free Methodist church become a feeble imitation of the M.E. church."

B. T. Roberts, 1885[1]

"You are more sensible, have broader views, less sectarianism about you [than does the Free Methodist Church]."

Ellen Roberts to B. T. Roberts, 1878[2]

Free Methodism under B. T. Roberts's leadership continued to have a movement character well into the 1880s, though counterforces were at work. Debates at the 1886 and 1890 General Conferences, especially, signaled the increasing tension between movement and institution. Yet new impulse came from the Pentecost Band movement. The bands, under Vivian A. Dake, sparked fresh growth, especially in the Midwest, but at the same time heightened the movement/institution tension.[3]

Free Methodism under Roberts's leadership did not grow in a vacuum, of course. The denomination developed, and Roberts exercised his leadership, in the context of broader cultural currents.

1. Thomas H. Nelson, *Life and Labors of Rev. Vivian A. Dake, Organizer and Leader of Pentecost Bands* (Chicago: T. B. Arnold, 1894), p. 80.

2. ELR to BTR, July 3, 1878, quoted in Zahniser, p. 292.

3. Byron Lamson gives a fine profile of the movemental nature of early Free Methodism in his book *Venture! The Frontiers of Free Methodism* (Winona Lake, Ind.: Light and Life Press, 1960), pp. 23-30. Under the heading "Pattern of a Movement," Lamson lists twenty-two key missional characteristics of the denomination in its early years.

Historian Arthur Schlesinger, Sr., called the period from 1875 to 1890 "a critical period in American religion."[4] This was a time of rapid social and religious change in the United States. Change was fueled by massive immigration from Europe, especially from Roman Catholic countries; urbanization and its attendant problems; and rapid industrialization and economic expansion. Writing toward the end of the century, Josiah Strong, later a key figure in the Social Gospel movement, saw several critical "perils" facing the nation: immigration, "Romanism," intemperance, the growth of the cities, and the rapid increase in wealth.[5]

In the Midwest the 1880s and 1890s were a time of flux as the population was shifting farther west and into the growing larger cities. Schlesinger notes that

> in the Middle West the traditional rural culture of America was rapidly dissolving and a new form rising in its stead. . . . in the great triangular central region, extending from Ohio to Missouri and Minnesota and containing nearly one third of all the people in the nation, the migration from the country districts had attained a momentum that was fast giving the city a dominant position in the social organism. In 1880 one out of every five Middle Westerners lived in urban communities of four thousand or more inhabitants, ten years later one out of every three.[6]

This was also a time of rapid church growth, particularly in the cities, and of the rise of new religious movements. Christian Science was born in the East while the Mormons continued their controversial growth farther west. The Salvation Army began work in the United States in 1880, two years after its founding in England. "In ten years it had marched across the continent and was working in practically every large city in the country."[7]

The Free Methodist Church, unlike the Salvation Army, was centered mostly in small-town and rural America, particularly in the Midwest. Here anti-Catholic sentiment was strong, and occasionally showed up in Free Methodist literature of the period. "Cradled in the heart of agricultural America, the anti-Catholic animus was vaguely mingled with the long-standing rural antagonism toward the great cities where, of course, the citadels of Romanism were to be found."[8]

Free Methodism continued to grow, and B. T. and Ellen Roberts were pleased. In a long report in the October 1883 *Earnest Christian,* Roberts noted the spirit of re-

---

4. Arthur M. Schlesinger, Sr., *A Critical Period in American Religion: 1875-1900* (Philadelphia: Fortress, 1967).

5. Josiah Strong, *Our Country: Its Possible Future and Its Present Crisis,* rev. ed. (New York: Baker and Taylor, 1900; originally 1885).

6. Arthur M. Schlesinger, [Sr.,] *The Rise of the City, 1878-1898* (New York: Macmillan, 1933), p. 57.

7. William Warren Sweet, *The Story of Religion in America* (New York: Harper and Brothers, 1930, 1939), p. 526.

8. Schlesinger, *A Critical Period,* p. 32. Free Methodists during this period did have a number of city churches and started rescue missions or other urban ministries in Pittsburgh, Chicago, and other cities.

vival and growth he encountered while holding camp meetings and conferences across the Midwest. On this tour he organized the Missouri and the West Kansas Conferences. Of the camp meeting at Logan, Kansas (north of Hays, about twenty-five miles south of the Nebraska border), Roberts wrote,

> The grove was a narrow fringe of trees on the bank of a small stream.... It was the most densely populated camp ground we ever saw. Tents and covered wagons were packed closely together. There was a large attendance of earnest Christian people. The sessions of the Conference were harmonious and the business was transacted to general satisfaction. The meetings were attended with a great out-pouring of the Spirit. Souls were saved and the Saints were quickened and encouraged. The Conference was held in a region subject to drouth, and in consequence crops often fail. The people are mostly poor and many have not what in older communities are esteemed necessaries of life. Yet *twenty-six hundred* dollars were pledged for the purpose of establishing in their bounds a CHRISTIAN SCHOOL.[9]

Roberts also commented on the "aggressive character" of the Iowa Conference, whose 1883 sessions were held at Oskaloosa. "The Spirit was poured out at all the services," he noted. Roberts encountered there a group of "Salvation Friends" — Quakers who had been influenced by the Holiness movement. Roberts attended one meeting held on the public square at Oskaloosa. He remarked, "There were several hundred of them in attendance.... It was not different in any essential particular from our own meetings. But it seemed odd and good to see and hear the Quakers preaching, testifying, shouting and singing, and inviting sinners forward like Free Methodists."[10]

Working his way east, Roberts conducted the Illinois and Wisconsin Conferences. "The Illinois Conference . . . was one of the best sessions we ever attended. This is the mother conference of the West. Five or six conferences have been formed from it, but it has lost none of its aggressive spirit. Only one preacher, J. G. Terrill, who was in the Conference when it was organized, is now an effective member of it; but it has a very promising class of young preachers. A spirit of harmony and brotherly love prevailed."

Roberts next held the Indiana and Central Illinois Conference at Greenville, Illinois, and commented similarly on its growth: "Four years ago we organized this Conference with four preachers; this year it stationed thirty-nine, all raised up among them. The membership must have nearly or quite doubled the last year. The

---

9. [B. T. Roberts], "Camp Meetings," *EC* 46, no. 4 (Oct. 1883): 128-29. The school in question was Orleans Seminary, founded in 1884 at Orleans, Nebr. This was the forerunner institution of what is now Central Christian College of McPherson, Kans. Marston notes that Orleans Seminary was founded by "pioneering homesteaders" and that a key early leader was C. M. Damon. "Almost from the first this frontier institution suffered from lack of funds, but its loyal friends continued to sacrifice for its maintenance and to send their children to this struggling institution" (Marston, p. 522).

10. [B. T. Roberts], "Camp Meetings," *EC* 46, no. 4 (Oct. 1883): 129.

work is of the most radical character. Preachers and people are consecrated to the work of soul-saving."[11]

A year later Roberts was pleased to report continued growth after conducting the Indiana and Central Illinois annual conference at Evansville, Indiana, October 15-19, 1884. Roberts noted that "A good deal of the presence of the Lord was manifested" and a "gracious revival was begun which we trust will result in the salvation of many." The conference voted unanimously to divide, resulting in the formation of the Wabash Conference the following year.[12]

Reflecting on this growth, Roberts editorialized:

> The work of this Conference is deep and thorough, and where this is the case, preachers are raised up and called by God to supply the needs of the work. A lack of preachers is evidence of a lack of piety.
>
> Everywhere there is a demand for live preachers — men saved from indolence and selfishness, from worldliness and ambition, from prejudice and envy — men full of faith and of the Holy Ghost, men of sense and judgment, who can get along with those who differ from them, and men who can promote revivals and lead believers on to holiness. Such men are wanted whether they have much or little learning. But there is no call for dead preachers.[13]

Revival was reported also in Wisconsin. Kittie Wood — one of the remarkable women evangelists of early Free Methodism — reported in 1884 a stirring revival at Washburn, in far northern Wisconsin on Lake Superior. Miss Wood called the revival the greatest work of grace she had ever witnessed. "The people came in immense crowds — many came ten and fifteen miles to attend the meetings." She reported, "I think I can safely say that from 150 to 200 have been converted — made free after the regular old gospel fashion. There were only two Free Methodists here when we came. Now something over sixty have joined the class."[14]

---

11. [B. T. Roberts], "Conferences," *EC* 46, no. 5 (Nov. 1883): 161.

12. [B. T. Roberts], "Conferences," *EC* 48, no. 5 (Nov. 1884): 163; Marston, pp. 428-29.

13. [B. T. Roberts], "Conferences," *EC* 48, no. 5 (Nov. 1884): 163. Roberts was not of course excluding women in his references to "men."

14. She added, "Philip got blessed one night and jumped most as high as the pulpit." Kittie Wood, "Revivals," *EC* 47, no. 4 (Apr. 1884): 129. Kittie Wood (1862-1926), born in Lockport, N.Y., was the daughter of Levi Wood, founder and first editor of the *Free Methodist*, and his wife Sarah. In the early 1880s she worked part-time in the *Free Methodist* office in Chicago and was heavily involved in city mission work there. In 1885 she and a band of forty other missionaries went to India as "a purely faith mission, the band collecting their own supplies and financing their own mission efforts," not directly sponsored by the Free Methodist Church. Miss Wood served many years in India and Ceylon, part of the time in association with the Salvation Army. She eventually met and married Charles Barr Kumarakulasinghe, a native of Ceylon and a graduate of Oxford University, whose mother was English, and who worked in government service. Kittie continued her missionary work, eventually founding two orphanages in Ceylon. When her husband died she sailed with their three children for America, intending to enroll them (one girl and two boys) in Seattle Pacific College, but a diphtheria epidemic onboard the ship claimed the lives of all three. Kittie spent a year in America raising funds

Roberts's concern was that this movement dynamic would continue. For him, terms like "aggressive" and "radical" signaled both faithfulness to the biblical gospel and genuine movement of the Spirit.

African American Leaders

As a radical movement, Free Methodism here and there attracted African Americans to its ranks. Some of these, both men and women, became preachers or workers in the movement. Many of their stories are now lost, but some have been preserved.

Notable examples include Eliza Suggs and her father, James Suggs (1831-89), who was ordained by Roberts in 1879. Eliza tells the story of her family in a remarkable little book, *Shadow and Sunshine*, published in 1906.[15]

James Suggs and his wife Malinda were both slaves. Born in North Carolina, James was sold at age three, permanently separating him from his parents and twin brother. "In after years he had a faint recollection of his mother, and could remember distinctly the words of introduction with which he was handed over . . . to his new [master]: 'Whip that boy and make him mind.'"[16]

Sold and resold, James ended up in northern Mississippi, owned by a wealthy but kind master named Suggs. Thus James became known as James Suggs. In his teens he married another of Mr. Suggs's young slaves, Malinda Filbrick. Not long afterward he was converted.

Toward the end of the Civil War, with Union forces in the area, James ran away and joined the Union army. After the war he went north, now a free man. As a slave he had been trained as a blacksmith, and he now supported himself through this trade. Soon he was able to bring Malinda and their four children from Mississippi to his new home in Princeton, Illinois.

But God was calling James to preach. He struggled mightily with this, Eliza recalled: "He had worldly ambitions and was making money, and it was hard for him to give up all and follow Christ." Eventually he made a full consecration, giving up his trade. "He began preaching around in school houses. Large crowds gathered to hear him, and from that time on, it was the business of his life to minister Divine truth to dying men and women."[17]

---

for her work, then returned to Ceylon where she continued her missionary work (except for a final trip to the United States about 1911) until her death in 1926. She died and was buried in Ceylon. Throughout her life she maintained her Free Methodist connections, and in fact retained her membership in the North Chili FM Church for nearly forty years. "Obituaries," *FM*, Mar. 23, 1926, p. 14 (obituary of Mrs. Kittie Wood Kumarakulasinghe); cf. Lamson, *Venture!* p. 263.

15. Eliza Suggs, *Shadow and Sunshine* (Omaha: n.p., 1906). This book, now very rare, has achieved some note as one of the earliest books written by an African American woman and has been reissued by the University of Nebraska Press. See www.unl.edu/history/faculty/Dorsey.html (accessed Dec. 17, 2005).

16. Suggs, *Shadow and Sunshine*, p. 13.

17. Suggs, *Shadow and Sunshine*, pp. 14-24, 48-49.

Suggs became a Free Methodist through meeting preachers such as C. E. Harroun, Jr., C. M. Damon, and others. Roberts ordained him deacon in the Illinois Conference in 1879. That same year — "the year of the great drouth and grasshopper scourge" — Suggs went to Kansas as an evangelist, a pioneer in Kansas Free Methodism. In 1884 he was ordained elder by General Superintendent E. P. Hart in the newly organized West Kansas Conference, which at the time included western Nebraska and all of Colorado.[18]

Suggs discovered a "colony of colored people" from the South that had settled in Graham County, northwest Kansas, in a town they called Nicodemus. Finding them "nearly starving, and with scarcely enough clothing to cover their nakedness," Suggs became their advocate. He got encouragement but little help from the state's governor, John P. St. John, so he returned to Illinois to seek aid. The Illinois Conference endorsed his work, commending him as a "person appointed by the Governor of Kansas to raise funds for the colored refugees" there. Soon Suggs was sending "barrel after barrel of clothing" to the struggling black community.[19]

Later Suggs acquired a homestead in north-central Kansas and fetched his family from Illinois. One time after preaching he was arrested and falsely accused of murder, but even in prison he continued preaching. Eventually he was released and resumed his ministry. His evangelistic work "was quite widely known within the bounds of several [Free Methodist] conferences, the Illinois, Iowa, West Iowa, Kansas, West Kansas, and Nebraska conferences, each having claimed some share of his time and labor."[20]

In 1884 Free Methodists established a school at Orleans, Nebraska, about thirty miles north of the Suggs homestead. The Suggs children were among its first students, and in 1886 James moved his family there to be close to the school. He continued his evangelistic work until his death in 1889.[21]

Eliza Suggs, James and Malinda's youngest, was born in 1876 while the family was living in Illinois. As a baby she had soft bones that frequently broke, leaving her crippled, stunted, and unable to walk — apparently an extreme case of rickets, caused by lack of vitamin D. Because of this, people often treated Eliza as a child or a curiosity. But she developed intellectually and spiritually and became active in the temperance movement and in literary pursuits. C. M. Damon, a leader in West Kansas Free Methodism and friend of the family, described Eliza's public ministry:

> Carried in arms or wheeled about in a carriage, her frail hands and well developed head have accomplished wonders, obtaining a fair education, which makes her a valuable asset, sometimes as secretary of religious organizations and work. [At times] she assisted her father . . . in evangelistic work, and she has presided in

---

18. Suggs, *Shadow and Sunshine*, pp. 24-27; Hogue, *HFMC*, 2:84-85.

19. Suggs, *Shadow and Sunshine*, p. 27. Ralph Helsel reports the Illinois Conference action in "The Slave with Two Masters," *Light and Life*, Feb. 1992, p. 17.

20. Suggs, *Shadow and Sunshine*, pp. 29-32.

21. Suggs, *Shadow and Sunshine*, pp. 32-34.

public meetings with marked dignity and ability. Carried on the platform and moved about as occasion required by kind and willing attendants [she would lead meetings;] I have perhaps never seen more clock-like precision than the execution of an interesting program, at which she presided in a public temperance meeting in the M.E. Church, during my last pastorate in Orleans.[22]

James and Malinda Suggs, Eliza, and others in the Suggs family count among the hardy pioneers of Free Methodism in Kansas and Nebraska. Roberts had long championed the rights of African Americans, and the ministry of the Suggs family was part of the fruit of his influence.

Another example is Mrs. Emma (Smith) Ray and her husband Lloyd, both Free Methodist preachers. They served in the late 1800s and early 1900s, as recorded in their autobiography, *Twice Sold, Twice Ransomed*, largely written by Mrs. Ray.

Emma Ray was born of slave parents in Missouri in 1859. "When I was one month old," she writes, "I, my sister, who was one and one-half years old, and my mother, who held me in her arms, were sold at the auction block to the highest bid-der." They were bought by the family of Emma's father's master, so the family was not scattered. Lloyd Ray was born in Texas of a slave mother and a white father.[23]

Lloyd and Emma Ray eventually became revivalists, street preachers, and city mission workers, serving primarily in Kansas and in Seattle, Washington. Emma was also active in the Woman's Christian Temperance Union (WCTU), directing WCTU prison ministry in Seattle. The Rays developed associations with the Free Methodists about 1890 and became workers at Seattle's Olive Branch Mission after it was founded by Free Methodists in 1903. They joined the Free Methodist Church — at-tracted in part by the lively, demonstrative worship — though much of their minis-try remained interdenominational.[24]

Emma and Lloyd Ray devoted over thirty years to ministry. "We have been led to preach in the highways and hedges, [mostly being engaged] in slum work, with the exception of some occasional evangelistic work," Emma wrote.[25] The Rays ap-parently had little or no direct contact with B. T. or Ellen Roberts, but this was just the kind of ministry Roberts supported and encouraged.

Though the Suggses, the Rays, and other African Americans found welcome in Free Methodism, the denomination was not totally free from racism. Amanda Berry Smith, the famous black holiness evangelist, recounts a telling incident. In New York City around 1868, before she was well known, Amanda and a friend were made to

---

22. C. M. Damon, "Personal Reminiscences and Testimony," in Suggs, *Shadow and Sunshine*, p. 8.

23. [Emma Ray], *Twice Sold, Twice Ransomed: Autobiography of Mr. and Mrs. L. P. Ray* (Chicago: Free Methodist Publishing House, 1926), pp. 15, 54.

24. [Ray], *Twice Sold, Twice Ransomed*, pp. 200-211. Olive Branch Mission in Chicago had been organized earlier, in 1876.

25. [Ray], *Twice Sold, Twice Ransomed*, p. 198; Susie C. Stanley, *Holy Boldness: Women Preachers' Autobiographies and the Sanctified Self* (Knoxville: University of Tennessee Press, 2002), pp. 149, 174, 190.

feel unwelcome in a Free Methodist congregation they visited. Amanda told them frankly, "I think you have the spirit of prejudice among you just like other people." However, she commended Joseph Mackey, B. T. Roberts's businessman friend and a prominent member of the congregation. Mackey, "well known all over New York," said Amanda, was "a good friend to the colored people," for years conducting "meetings at the Colored Home in New York. When we went into the [Free Methodist] church he was there, and was so glad to see us. He shook hands, and seated us, and was so kind."[26] Attracted by the Free Methodists' plainness and holiness message, Smith considered joining them but decided against it once she uncovered the prejudice.

These stories show some of the ways Free Methodism both extended and compromised B. T. and Ellen Roberts's gospel populist vision as the church moved from movement to institution.

The 1886 General Conference

The concentration of Free Methodist preachers and delegates at the quadrennial General Conferences unfailingly surfaced whatever controversies and tensions were stirring in the denomination. This was particularly the case in 1886 and 1890, B. T. Roberts's last two General Conferences.

The 1886 conference was held in Coopersville, Michigan. It met October 13-26 under the chairmanship of Roberts and Hart. Ellen Roberts had written Benjamin four weeks before the conference began, urging him to take care of himself. "You must breathe in more life. Take more by faith. The quickening power of the Spirit I trust will keep you fresh and rested," she wrote. "I do not want you to come to the General Conference jaded and worn. I do not expect you will."[27]

The conference voted to elect three, rather than two, general superintendents. On the first ballot Hart and Roberts were reelected with strong majorities — fifty-four and fifty ballots respectively, out of fifty-seven. On the second ballot George Whitefield Coleman, originally from Perry Center, New York, was elected. Coleman was fifty-six at the time. He had been a successful farmer and a local preacher for several years. Roberts recognized his ministerial gifts, and at his urging, Coleman entered itinerant ministry in the FM Genesee Conference in 1863.[28]

---

26. *An Autobiography: The Story of the Lord's Dealings with Mrs. Amanda Smith the Colored Evangelist* (Chicago: Meyer and Brother, 1893), pp. 112-15; see Stanley, *Holy Boldness*, p. 193. Stanley comments that in contrast with Smith's experience, "Emma Ray, an African American member of the Free Methodist Church, never mentioned racism within her denomination. While many women self-published their autobiographies, the Free Methodists published" hers.

27. ELR to BTR, Sept. 22, 1886, quoted in Zahniser, pp. 296-97.

28. Hogue, *HFMC*, 2:188; Richard R. Blews, *Master Workmen: Biographies of the Later Bishops of the Free Methodist Church during Her First Century, 1860-1960*, centennial ed. (Winona Lake, Ind.: Light and Life Press, 1960), pp. 79-82.

Concerned that the Free Methodist Church expand its witness to the nation, Roberts proposed that the denomination start a church in the nation's capital. His recommendation was referred to the committee on church extension. Later a Free Methodist Church was in fact established in Washington, D.C.[29]

The question of the role of women in ministry was still unresolved in the church. The compromise of licensing women as evangelists was really only a half-measure. The 1886 General Conference took a further step in recognizing women's ministry gifts. Women evangelists were made members of the quarterly conferences, to which they would in turn be accountable. William Gould from the New York Conference, among others, vigorously opposed this; it in effect gave women a ruling function in the church, he argued. When the measure passed, Gould resigned as General Conference delegate and was replaced by Joseph Travis, the reserve delegate.[30] The larger issue continued to simmer, however, and the question of women's ordination was hotly debated in the pages of the *Free Methodist* between the 1886 and 1890 General Conferences.

The 1886 convention also took several decisive steps toward establishing what became the Free Methodist Publishing House. It voted to purchase the *Free Methodist* magazine from T. B. Arnold; to have the church Executive Committee function as a publishing committee; and to elect and employ both an editor for the magazine and a financial agent, each at a salary of $1,000. The salaries of the general superintendents were also set at $1,000, plus traveling expenses. The financial agent was to devise a plan for establishing a publishing house.[31]

The *Free Methodist*, including the mailing list, type, furniture, and fixtures of the business, was purchased from Arnold for $8,000. This became the nucleus of the Free Methodist Publishing House. Thus, the reason the Free Methodist Church came to be headquartered in Chicago was simply that that is where Arnold had established his printing business and published the *Free Methodist*.[32]

Arnold agreed to serve as the church's first publishing agent. He was elected by the General Conference and served for two years, until 1888. He hired S. K. J. Chesbrough, then pastoring at Jamestown, New York, to come to Chicago and serve as bookkeeper. When Arnold resigned in 1888, Chesbrough replaced him as publishing agent and served ably in that position for almost nineteen years, being reelected at each General Conference.[33]

Who should serve as editor of the *Free Methodist*, now that it was officially the

---

29. Zahniser, p. 297.

30. Hogue, *HFMC*, 2:186. Prior to this, evangelists were not officially members of the quarterly conferences (as local preachers were), though they were licensed by the quarterly conference upon recommendation of the local church and in that sense already had some amenability to the quarterly conference. See *The Doctrines and Discipline of the Free Methodist Church* (Rochester, N.Y.: B. T. Roberts, 1879), sec. IV (pp. 43-45); sec. XVIII (pp. 84-85).

31. Hogue, *HFMC*, 2:188-89; Zahniser, p. 297.

32. Hogue, *HFMC*, 2:243-44.

33. Hogue, *HFMC*, 2:246.

organ of the denomination? To Roberts's surprise, he was elected editor on the second ballot, receiving thirty out of fifty-four ballots cast. Since he had already been reelected general superintendent, Benjamin arose and said, "Brethren, you have now chosen me to two of the most responsible positions in the Church, and I am ready to resign whichever one you may designate." No one objected to his holding both offices, however, and so Roberts carried out both responsibilities for the next four years. But, as one preacher observed, "By electing him editor [the church] doubled his labor and shortened his days."[34] Wilson Hogue notes that "the burden of these two offices greatly overtaxed [Roberts's] strength, and was one of the things that broke down his health and hastened the close of his career."[35] And Zahniser observes,

> At the preceding General Conference, [Roberts] had come within one vote of being elected to the editorship of *The Free Methodist*. For a long time, it had been felt that his literary culture should have been utilized more fully by the church, and also there was a growing feeling that the church paper had become too political in character, and that Mr. Roberts would curb the increasing tendency. It had always been the position of Mr. Roberts that the church should not align itself with any one political party, but be free to vote for the best candidates for office, regardless of party affiliation.[36]

The political issue was how closely the denomination should align itself with the Prohibition Party. The party had been formed in 1869 and first fielded candidates for U.S. president and vice president in 1872. In the 1880s the party was growing in influence, and it received 271,000 votes in the 1892 general election.[37] With their strong protemperance views, many Free Methodists supported the party. Nevertheless, Roberts and others felt the denomination should not officially commit itself to any particular political organization. This proved to be a hot issue in some General Conference debates. J. G. Terrill recalled after Roberts's death that Benjamin's election as editor in 1886 occurred after a "heated debate" on the subject of temperance. The choice of Roberts "seemed to be a reaction from a tendency to give the church paper too much of a political character," though other influences were also at work.[38]

These debates were another evidence of an underlying movement/institution tension. Making Roberts editor of the *Free Methodist* would have been a way (some must have felt) to more fully "capture" Benjamin and his literary gifts for the denomination and its interests. The *Earnest Christian*, after all, remained an independent paper, controlled solely by Roberts, and through the magazine Roberts still ex-

34. Anson Stedwell, *Itinerant Footprints* (Chicago: Free Methodist Publishing House, 1915), p. 70.

35. Hogue, *HFMC*, 2:189.

36. Zahniser, pp. 297-98.

37. *World Book Encyclopedia* (1976), P:718b.

38. J. G. Terrill, "Some Reminiscences of Rev. B. T. Roberts," *EC* 65, no. 4 (Apr. 1893): 113. See also the discussion in Marston, pp. 400-402.

ercised a broader ministry and had a wider voice. Perhaps some felt Roberts needed some reining in. Whenever conflicts arose and a choice had to be made, however, Roberts consistently came down on the side of movement over institution. This was part of his vision and his charism, as Ellen clearly saw.

These debates, and especially the way Roberts handled them, also reveal much about Roberts's character. Terrill recalled that during the 1886 General Conference B. T. had forcefully supported the seating of a delegate whose right to serve as delegate was disputed by some — even though this person "hotly opposed" Roberts on the political-temperance issue and on women's ministry. Later, walking with Roberts to their boarding place, Terrill said to him, "Do you know what some of your friends think of you?"

"No; what is it?" Roberts asked.

"They think the best way to get a favor of you, would be to become your enemy."

"Is that not a good trait?" Roberts responded.

Roberts "was often severely criticized for that trait in his character," Terrill commented, "perhaps by none more so than by myself, and yet, as I look it over now, it may be there is less to regret on that than on the other side."[39]

Conference over, Benjamin had to assume the heavy duties of editing the weekly *Free Methodist* as well as continuing his work as general superintendent (now, however, assisted by Hart and Coleman) and his editorship of the *Earnest Christian*.

Ellen Roberts had long opposed Benjamin's taking on the *Free Methodist* in addition to his other responsibilities. In 1878, when he apparently had talked about the possibility of editing the paper, she had written him:

> You know I don't want you to take that F.M. paper. . . . I don't want you ever to undertake that. You know it is hard work. You would not be supported in it as well as the present publishers, because you are more <u>sensible</u>, have broader views, less sectarianism about you, etc., etc. I think you have outgrown or grown beyond a <u>Free Methodist Paper</u>. Dearest, don't you think of it. I would rather start or help start another school. Let the rest of the Church have the Paper. You are not good at <u>dunning</u> people. I beg of you do not think of that over night.[40]

On this point Ellen saw more sharply than did her husband. He would have done well in 1886 to have heeded her advice from eight years earlier. But his sense of duty and self-giving got the best of him. He could not do everything, and clearly now, as he began the added responsibility of editing a weekly magazine, he had overreached his limit.

---

39. Terrill, "Some Reminiscences," p. 113.
40. ELR to BTR, July 3, 1878, quoted in Zahniser, p. 292.

A Fresh Impulse: Vivian Dake and the Pentecost Bands

The tension between movement and institution in early Free Methodism was nowhere more sharply felt than in a new surge of energy that appeared in Free Methodism in the mid-1880s. The key figure was the fiery young Vivian Adelbert Dake, son of Jonathan W. Dake, a former Methodist Episcopal preacher in Illinois who became a charter member of the Free Methodist Church in 1860.[41] Vivian A. Dake was a favorite of Roberts — a firebrand something like John Wesley Redfield but with considerably more organizing skill and a gift for putting people to work. Born in 1854, Dake was thirty years younger than Roberts and would have had almost no memory of the Methodist Episcopal Church. Vivian Dake was Roberts's son in the gospel.

Dake started an organization called Pentecost Bands that soon became a movement within a movement — or, perhaps better, an emerging movement within a slowing one.[42]

The odyssey of the Pentecost Bands is the story of a dynamic evangelistic, church-planting, and missionary movement that in the end could not be contained within the denomination that gave it birth. It eventually went independent. Many years later the surviving body united with the Wesleyan Methodist Church.

The Pentecost Bands tapped into and channeled a significant amount of spiritual and social energy within the Free Methodist Church of the late 1880s. Through the bands hundreds of earnest young Free Methodist men and (especially) women, many of them new converts, became gospel workers. They followed the expanding network of railway lines to dozens of towns and villages, holding evangelistic meetings and establishing churches.

Vivian Dake, the firebrand of the bands, was born on February 9, 1854, at Oregon, Illinois, ninety miles west of Chicago. The family later moved farther west to Iowa, which is where Dake's ministry began.[43]

Vivian was a bright child, and musically talented. He was clearly converted at nine years of age, but wandered from God.

In August 1867 Benjamin and Ellen Roberts were in northern Illinois, minister-

---

41. J. W. Dake was a member of the July 1860 Laymen's Convention in Du Page County, Ill. *Minutes of the Laymen's Convention Held in Wayne, Du Page Co., Ill., July 2, 1860.* Printed as a one-page, two-sided leaflet. Archives, Roberts Wesleyan College.

42. Charles Jones includes the Pentecost Bands among several primarily rural holiness evangelistic associations that grew up during the latter part of the nineteenth century. He notes that there were also "several groups specializing in urban evangelism" in the 1880s and 1890s, though "rural evangelists usually steered clear of cities" (Charles E. Jones, *Perfectionist Persuasion: The Holiness Movement and American Methodism, 1867-1936* [Metuchen, N.J.: Scarecrow Press, 1974], p. 69). The Pentecost Bands did have some urban links; most notably with the Vanguard Mission in St. Louis and with Free Methodists in Chicago, where the *Free Methodist* magazine was then being published.

43. Ida Dake Parsons, *Kindling Watch-Fires: Being a Brief Sketch of the Life of Rev. Vivian A. Dake* (Chicago: Free Methodist Publishing House, 1915), p. 18. The chief biographical sources on Dake are this book by his widow and Nelson, *Life and Labors of Rev. Vivian A. Dake, Organizer and Leader of Pentecost Bands.*

ing and raising funds for Chili Seminary. At the St. Charles camp meeting Benjamin took a collection and later recalled, "One of the first to give was a bashful boy of about twelve or fourteen, who had outgrown his clothes." Young Vivian tremblingly put a ten-cent coin into Mr. Roberts's hand. "A thrill went over me like a gentle shock of electricity," wrote Benjamin, "and a voice said, 'If the children take such an interest, the school will be a success.'" Three years later, at a camp meeting in the New York City area, Benjamin told this story, and Ellen added during the meeting, "This boy is the son of a Free Methodist preacher, in poor circumstances, getting a scanty support. Will not some one here send this boy to school?" Mrs. Joseph Mackey of New York City was in the congregation, and at the end of the meeting she told Benjamin and Ellen, "Send for him to go to school, and I will pay his bills."[44]

In February 1872, just turned eighteen, Vivian enrolled in Chili Seminary — "bright, uncultivated, unconverted," but "thirsting for knowledge." He was "wonderfully reclaimed" shortly after classes began.

Dake graduated from Chili Seminary and then studied briefly at the University of Rochester, but soon left to enter the church's ministry.[45] While at the university he kept contact with the Chili community. "While his intellect was being polished at Rochester, his soul was being fed at Chili." He wrote, "I would rather have the gift of devil-dislodging faith than all the learning that can be acquired at earth's schools."[46] Soon he was assisting Roberts with revivals in New York State and helping his father with meetings in Iowa.

Dake married Lenna Bailey of Spring Arbor, Michigan, in 1876, but she died a few months later. In 1878 he married Ida May Campbell, who survived him by a number of years (and wrote his biography). Meanwhile Dake began pastoral and evangelistic ministry in Iowa with considerable success. At age twenty-five he wrote, "I pledge myself to spend [my life] in blowing the gospel trumpet with no uncertain sound."[47] Dake seems to have been unfailingly zealous and self-assured in his ministry. Roberts captured something of Dake's character when he wrote, "His religion was not of the quiet unemphatic kind. The love of Christ was like fire shut up in his bones. With others, he went from house to house wherever it was acceptable, and prayed, and exhorted, and endeavored to win souls to Christ and to help them on in the kingdom of grace."[48]

Dake served a series of circuits in Iowa from 1876 to 1882 and saw considerable evangelistic fruit. He wrote after one revival, "At two-thirty in the morning I took seven more into the church, all young people, most of whom had been saved since the doors were opened in the evening." He was always concerned with involving be-

---

44. B. T. Roberts, "Vivian A. Dake," *EC* 63, no. 3 (Mar. 1892): 95; cf. Parsons, *Kindling Watch-Fires*, pp. 19-20.

45. B. T. Roberts, "Vivian A. Dake," p. 95; Parsons, *Kindling Watch-Fires*, p. 20.

46. Nelson, *Life and Labors*, pp. 23, 21.

47. Parsons, *Kindling Watch-Fires*, p. 25.

48. B. T. Roberts, "Vivian A. Dake," p. 95; Parsons, *Kindling Watch-Fires*, p. 20; Nelson, *Life and Labors*, p. 20.

lievers in ministry. His wife wrote, "He seems from the very first to have taken a stand with the primitive church fathers in getting everybody at work and thus multiplying their talents and usefulness."[49]

Always attracted to the frontier, Dake transferred to the Minnesota and Northern Iowa Conference in 1882, where within a year he was chairman of the conference's three districts. He wrote, "Oh, what openings all through the northwest; beautiful towns springing up all around. Who will enter them?" He soon wore himself out. T. B. Arnold persuaded him in the fall of 1884 to take an extended vacation. But visiting the Michigan Conference, he agreed to accept the Spring Arbor charge. Shortly thereafter, in response to prayer, he was healed: "The power of God struck me and went through my body from my head to my feet, and I was healed. . . . I began immediately to be more active."[50]

The following year, 1885, Dake transferred to the Michigan Conference and was appointed conference evangelist. In July he began organizing what he called Pentecost Bands to assist in the work. He soon moved to Chicago and used the address of the newly established denominational publishing house as his mailing address and unofficial headquarters while itinerating in evangelistic work.

For the next five years Dake was occupied with evangelism and overseeing a rapidly expanding network of bands. At the invitation of friends he made a brief trip to Germany in 1889, organizing a short-lived Free Methodist class in the city of Durrenentzen.

Pentecost Band Work, 1885-92

Holiness "bands" modeled to some extent after Phoebe Palmer's cottage meetings, and tracing indirectly to Methodist classes and bands, were used in the Holiness movement of the 1880s for the promotion of holiness.[51] Bishop William Taylor, in his influential mission work, sometimes organized new converts into self-supporting, self-directing "fellowship bands" for mutual support and evangelistic outreach.[52] Dake was not consciously following such models when he first organized Pentecost Bands, however. Rather, he simply employed a small-group method that was part of the common heritage of Methodist and Holiness peoples. The name Pentecost Band "was suggested to him because it appeared to be a return to primitive Pentecost methods, for in the revival at Pentecost converts as well as preachers engaged in spreading the gospel."[53]

---

49. Parsons, *Kindling Watch-Fires,* pp. 31, 26.

50. Parsons, *Kindling Watch-Fires,* pp. 34-35. Arnold, denominational publishing agent, was a close older friend of Dake.

51. Jones, *Perfectionist Persuasion,* p. 55.

52. E. Davies, *The Bishop of Africa; or, The Life of William Taylor, D.D.* (Reading, Mass.: Holiness Book Concern, 1885), p. 56.

53. Parsons, *Kindling Watch-Fires,* p. 36. Thus for Dake the term "Pentecost" connoted evangelism and revival rather than specifically a "Pentecostal" baptism in the Spirit.

The origin of the Pentecost Band movement actually traces back to 1882. In July of that year Vivian and Ida Dake, with others, began a revival at Mankato, Minnesota. Thomas Nelson relates,

> Soon after this meeting began, [Dake] organized the first Pentecost Band. It was not the result of a sudden impulse on his part, for this matter had been on his heart and prayed over for months. While at Ottumwa, Iowa, some time before, the Lord made His will known to him, giving, as he felt, even the name by which the Band should be called. It was brought about at last by a succession of events, which were clearly from God. It was a most solemn time when brother and sister Dake, brother and sister J. B. Newville, Henrietta Muzzy, Abbie Dunham and J. L. Keene and one of the young converts, covenanted with God to abandon themselves to Him, to spend their lives in the great work of winning souls. God set His seal to the compact, and an especial blessing fell upon all. This was in August, 1882. Mr. D. was unanimously chosen as leader. This first Pentecost Band was ere long dissolved, but again sprang into being and took permanent form in Parma, Mich., in the year 1885.[54]

The Parma Pentecost Band, designated Band No. 1, opened work in Parma (near Spring Arbor) on July 25, 1885. Its ministry began with a street meeting and an evening service. Dake led the opening service and preached, then left the work in the charge of this band of four young women: Carrie Kimball, Emily Nelson, Lizzie Ball, and Mary Primmer. Nelson notes, "As the workers prophesied for the first time in public, the Spirit applied the truth spoken and God set His seal on the work at once, pouring out His Spirit in convicting and converting power."[55] Soon a second band of young women, with Emily Nelson as leader, was holding meetings in nearby Hanover. Two of the members of this band were Bertha Baldwin and Minnie Baldwin (the future Mrs. E. E. Shelhamer), aged eighteen and nineteen.[56]

A little later the first band of men was formed (Edward Foulk, Reuben Schamehorn, George Chapman, and Charles Edinger). Thus Dake quickly established his band pattern: small groups of young men or young women; a high degree of mobility, with bands moving quickly from one site to another, often being replaced by another band; and members of one band, as soon as they had gained a lit-

---

54. Nelson, *Life and Labors*, p. 73.

55. Nelson, *Life and Labors*, p. 102. See the manuscript journal, "North Parma Pentecost Band" (MMHC), which begins with a sort of constitution for the bands and includes the initial minutes of the official board of the Parma Free Methodist circuit. The cover bears the signature of Vivian A. Dake and (in a different hand) the words "Organized Nov. 25, 1885," which perhaps refer to the date of the organization of the Free Methodist society (or may erroneously refer to the date the first Pentecost Band was organized, which was July 25).

56. Bertha B. Smith and Julia A. Shelhamer, *A Remarkable Woman: The Life of Mrs. Minnie B. Shelhamer* (Atlanta: The Repairer, [n.d.]), pp. 26-28. Original edition: Bertha B. Smith, *A Brief Sketch of a Remarkable Life: The Life of Mrs. Minnie B. Shelhamer* (Atlanta: The Repairer, 1903). Julia A. [Arnold] Shelhamer was E. E. Shelhamer's second wife.

tle experience, becoming leaders of new bands. The whole system was set up for mobility, flexibility, and rapid expansion.[57]

Roberts watched these developments with great interest. He wrote on July 31, 1885, "Organize your bands. Push out. Be as aggressive as the Salvation Army, but more holy, more serious and have no nonsense about it. Let the Holy Spirit take the place of tambourines to draw the people. . . . We must not let the Free Methodist church become a feeble imitation of the M.E. church."[58]

Dake saw many gifted young men and women doing little for God while circuit preachers were overworked, Nelson notes. "He was grieved to see many of these young people either leave the church to labor in the Salvation Army, (a work which he did not consider sufficiently deep and thorough, though possessing many admirable traits) or be much of the time void of a clear experience or become entirely backslidden."[59]

Through the Pentecost Bands, Dake opened a reservoir of youthful energy just waiting to be tapped. Especially was this so for women. Within seven years there were over thirty bands operating, with women outnumbering men by nearly two to one. The total number of band workers appears to have been about 125 in 1892.[60]

The primary work of the bands was evangelism and church planting, first in North America and later overseas. Typically a band would ride the railroad into a Midwestern town, rent a vacant store or hall or set up a tent, and hold meetings for several weeks. Door-to-door visitation, tract distribution (especially at railway stations), and street meetings and marches attracted crowds to the evening services. There, demonstrative worship, singing, and fresh personal testimonies and exhortations increased the interest. Often two or even three of the band members would preach or exhort in the same service. Opposition and occasional arrests added an air of excitement. When dramatic conversions occurred, as they often did, the meetings gained even more notoriety. Frequently a small Free Methodist congregation was organized as a result of a revival series, and a church building erected.[61]

The bands were almost entirely self-supporting, living from offerings or gifts of food or clothing generated by their ministry. Workers often lived very sacrificially, especially in the opening stages of a revival endeavor. Anecdotes about band mem-

57. Nelson, *Life and Labors*, p. 87.

58. Nelson, *Life and Labors*, p. 80. At this time the Salvation Army was five years old in the United States.

59. Nelson, *Life and Labors*, p. 80.

60. Nelson lists Band No. 34 as active in 1892 (p. 309), though it is not clear that all thirty-four bands were in operation at the same time. The first issue of the *Pentecost Herald* (April 1894) lists thirty-three active bands, however. Of thirty-three bands that I have been able to identify, based on the names of participants, twenty were female, ten were male, and three were mixed, involving married couples. Of 208 names of band members I have identified as active in the 1880s and 1890s, 128 are female and 80 are male, a ratio of about 62 percent to 38 percent.

61. Often, it appears, there were more converts than the number that became Free Methodist church members. Converts were not always willing to take the narrow way as defined by the Free Methodists.

bers often recall their going without food, or subsisting for days on donations of potatoes or vegetables while holding meetings and visiting house to house. Sadie Cryer wrote in her journal, "As this morning was fast morning, we did not have occasion to think about the empty cupboard." Repeatedly she noted, "We have called at every house in this town." While in Chicago she wrote, "We called at all the saloons on May St. today," and in another place: "With our suitcases strapped to our shoulders and Bibles under our arms we visited from house to house through the snow drifts."[62]

An article on the Pentecost Bands in the 1891 *Encyclopedia of Missions,* apparently from the hand of Dake, gives a good overview of band work. By this date the bands had organized eight new societies in Michigan and twenty-five in Illinois, and bands were also working in Norway, Germany, Africa, and Canada. "The homework is for the purpose of training workers and raising money for the foreign work," the article noted. It explained band work as follows: "A band is composed of four workers, of whom one is a leader and another an assistant leader. They enter into a field where work is needed, hold street-meetings, visit from house to house, hold public services in church, tent, or hall, and throw everything else aside in desperate efforts to 'pluck brands out of the burning.' They are earnest, enthusiastic, and noisy. Their methods may be called shortcuts to win souls."[63]

The article proved controversial in the Free Methodist Church because it made clear the connection between the bands and the Vanguard ministries of C. W. Sherman in St. Louis. The bands cooperated in carrying on a mission training work there, and the *Vanguard* paper, according to the article, "is the organ of the Pentecost Bands."[64]

The flavor of the "radical holiness" of Dake and the Pentecost Bands comes through in the accounts of individual band members such as the manuscript journal of Harmon Baldwin, a brief biography of Minnie Baldwin Shelhamer written by her sister, and a manuscript based on the journal of Sadie Cryer Hill (previously cited).[65]

From early on Dake had a global missionary vision. Shortly after the Free Methodist General Missionary Board was formed in 1882, Dake told the board he felt called to Africa; however, "The church took no action to send him," Byron Lamson notes.[66] Methodist Missionary Bishop William Taylor's foreign mission work was becoming well known and his appeals for U.S. churches to send missionaries, as well as his advocacy of "self-supporting" mission work, were having an impact in Free Methodism as well as elsewhere.

---

62. Gertrude Hill Nystrom, "Mama Married Me" (n.p., 1946; mimeographed manuscript, 88 pages, 1966), pp. 5, 17. This manuscript was serialized in *Sunday* magazine, May 1946–Jan. 1947.

63. Edwin Munsell Bliss, ed., *The Encyclopedia of Missions,* 2 vols. (New York: Funk and Wagnalls, 1891), 2:214-15.

64. Minutes of the Michigan Conference, 1891, p. 99 (Michigan Conference resolution). *Minutes of the Annual Conferences of the Free Methodist Church* (Chicago: Free Methodist Publishing House, 1891).

65. On Harmon Baldwin and Minnie Baldwin Shelhamer (who do not seem to have been siblings; the sources give different sets of parents), see below; Nystrom, "Mama Married Me."

66. Lamson, *Venture!* pp. 129-30.

In October of 1891, against Roberts's advice, Dake began a missionary trip to Africa from which he was not to return. He traveled via England with a side trip to Norway to visit the Ulnesses, Pentecost Band missionaries sent there the previous year.[67]

Dake met Taylor on board the steamship *Kinsembo*, bound for Monrovia, Liberia, in November of 1891 and had several conversations with him. This was only weeks before Dake died of African fever as he was starting his return voyage to the United States.[68] He died in Sierra Leone in January 1892, just a month shy of his thirty-eighth birthday and a little more than a year before Roberts's death.[69]

The main legacy of Vivian Dake's life was the Pentecost Band work and the indelible impression this young zealot made on scores of Free Methodist young people. A secondary legacy was his hymns and poems. His hymn "We'll Girdle the Globe with Salvation" found its way into the 1910 *Free Methodist Hymnal*. Roberts said of this song, "If Adelbert Dake had done nothing but write that piece, his life work would have been a success."[70]

The spirit of Vivian Dake is well captured in the call he issued to his workers as he was about to embark for Europe and Africa in October 1891:

Wanted! ten thousand to labor in every land. Wanted! those who will work without salary. Wanted! those who will take the fare by the way and shout, "Glory to God!" Amen! They are coming; the tread of their feet is heard. There is a call from Jamaica, West Indies. Who will fill it? There are calls from Australia, Tasmania, and New Zealand. Who will go? Calls from Sweden and Germany wait for workers. Now, who wants to go home? Let all the faint-hearted pack their satchels and leave quickly to make room for the Gideons, the Shamgars, the Daniels, the Davids and the Deborahs, the Marys, the Priscillas, and the Dorcases, who are coming. Amen! All hail! With fingers in your ears, eyes on the mark, feet on the thorny path, hands filled with pitchers and lamps, hearts aflame, on to victory! Fellow-workers, I am with you on the battle-field and will be in the triumphal march.[71]

Impact of the Bands

How many new Free Methodist congregations were started by the Pentecost Bands during the late 1880s and early 1890s? The number is unknown, but clearly the bands

67. Roberts wrote, "Contrary to our judgment, and to the earnest protest of many others of his friends he went to Monrovia, Africa — a place known as the graveyard of missionaries. He was in Monrovia four weeks and preached with fidelity and zeal." B. T. Roberts, "Vivian A. Dake," p. 96.

68. Parsons, *Kindling Watch-Fires*, pp. 92-93.

69. B. T. Roberts, "Vivian A. Dake," p. 96. Roberts quotes George G. Brownell, who was with Dake when he died: "He died at Sierra Leone, January 5, 1892, of African fever."

70. Parsons, *Kindling Watch-Fires*, p. 211.

71. Parsons, *Kindling Watch-Fires*, p. 77.

gave an added boost to Free Methodist growth over this period. During the eighties the denomination expanded especially in western Pennsylvania and the Midwest, where the bands were most engaged. The period from 1886 to 1894, when the bands were especially active, was one of significant growth. Bishop L. R. Marston later calculated that the denomination grew 51 percent during those eight years but only 15 percent during the next nine years, through 1903.[72]

The Free Methodist Church had approximately 13,000 members (total) in 1880 and nearly 29,000 in 1900 — an increase in twenty years of more than 120 percent.[73] This was a period of both expansion and consolidation: the formation of over twenty new conferences, the founding of schools, and the beginning of a foreign missions program, but also struggles with organization, finances, and pastoral support. Pioneers were pushing into new areas and urging redoubled efforts in evangelism while others were warning of overextended resources.

Roberts's encouragement of the Pentecost Band work, his quest for increased opportunities for the ministry of women, his own evangelistic and revival ministry, and his relative lack of concern (though clear competence) in dealing with denominational organizational issues reinforce the conclusion that his chief aim was the mission outreach of the Free Methodist Church — preaching the gospel to the poor. In the tension between movement and institution, his passion (and also Ellen's) was mission and movement.

Pioneer evangelist and church planter Charles Sage (1825-1908) caught this spirit of B. T. Roberts during the 1876 North Michigan Conference. When Roberts read the appointments, Sage learned of his new assignment: Canada! Sage went to Roberts and protested, "You have educated and talented men in the east, why did you not send one of them instead of such an ignorant man as I am?"

Roberts "looked at me fatherly," Sage said, and replied, "Brother Sage, we have got the educated and talented men, but they have not got the missionary fire. You will have to go." And go he did, helping raise up the Free Methodist Church in Canada.[74]

---

72. Marston, p. 438; cf. the discussion on FM growth in chapter 32. Thorough research of conference and local church records and histories, plus early FM biographies and Pentecost Band records, probably could yield a fairly accurate tally of churches started by the bands.

73. *Minutes of the Annual Conferences of the Free Methodist Church* (Chicago: Free Methodist Publishing House, 1901), p. 252; Hogue, *HFMC*, 2:182, 189.

74. *Autobiography of Rev. Charles H. Sage, a Member of the East Michigan Conference, Free Methodist Church* (Chicago: Free Methodist Publishing House, 1903), pp. 80-81.

CHAPTER 34

Roberts as Reformer and Theologian

"It has taken the world a long while to understand the Gospel of Jesus Christ; and even now it is but imperfectly understood."

B. T. Roberts, 1891[1]

"I do not know but we are too much taken up with our own personal salvation, and fail in taking as deep an interest as we should in the affairs of the day."

B. T. Roberts, 1864[2]

The year 1886 was something of a turning point in B. T. Roberts's life, and correspondingly in the life of his family. By the fall of that year, with his new responsibilities as editor of the *Free Methodist*, Benjamin was carrying a load greater than he could bear. His health began to deteriorate, his heart showing the strain of overwork.

By late 1886 Roberts had produced a major body of published writing while continuing his correspondence, administrative work, and incessant travel. He had preached perhaps eight thousand times since he was expelled from the Methodist Episcopal Church in 1858. His editorials alone to this point in both the *Earnest Christian* and the *Free Methodist*, if published in the form of collected works, would probably have filled eight or ten hefty volumes.[3]

---

1. B. T. Roberts, *Ordaining Women* (Rochester, N.Y.: Earnest Christian Publishing House, 1891), p. 12.

2. BTR (Coldwater, Mich.) to ELR, June 2, 1864, quoted in BHR, *BTR*, p. 349.

3. A comprehensive, unabridged collection of Roberts's writings, not including his correspon-

What did Roberts believe he was doing through all this effort, all this response to the call of duty?

Roberts saw his work in writing and in leading the Free Methodist Church as service to God and a form of preaching the gospel to the poor. In addition to the heavy denominational administrative load, he and Ellen conducted a ministry to the poor, as already related, and sought to be reformers in other ways. Their work in establishing Chili Seminary following 1866 was part of the picture.

Benjamin's reform efforts were extended through his writing in the *Earnest Christian* and in his books. He addressed issues of economics, women in ministry, temperance, the Civil War, farmers' rights, and other matters. At times he appears to have muted his opinions on some issues, particularly women in ministry, in order not to stir up further controversy within the denomination.

This and the next two chapters examine B. T. Roberts as a reformer and as a theologian, since his reform efforts were theologically based. They assess his spiritual, social, and theological contribution, including his political and economic views, and the theological foundations that underlay all his work.

Roberts's Major Writings

By the fall of 1886, when Roberts at sixty-three assumed the editorship of the *Free Methodist,* he had completed all the books he was to publish during his lifetime except his last and perhaps most important one, *Ordaining Women. First Lessons on Money* was issued early in 1886, before Benjamin took over the *Free Methodist.* Earlier he had published *Fishers of Men* and *Why Another Sect* as well as issuing *Spiritual Songs and Hymns for Pilgrims* and supervising the publication of the 1883 *Hymn Book of the Free Methodist Church.*

Songs and Hymns for Pilgrims

Roberts seems to have first issued this small compilation in 1868. It was thus his first book (not counting earlier FM books of discipline that Roberts edited and published and the annual bound volumes of the *Earnest Christian*).

Songs and Hymns for Pilgrims went through several editions and expansions. Roberts reported in June 1868, "Our New Hymn Book takes well. The pilgrims like it. There are a good many familiar hymns, and other good ones, not generally known." The hymnbook sold for thirty cents.[4] When the plates for the hymnbook were destroyed in the fire at the office of the *Democrat* in Rochester at the end of 1868, Rob-

---

dence or material he edited but including his diaries and all extant sermons, would probably run to about fifteen volumes of three hundred pages each.

4. Brief notice in *EC* 15, no. 6 (June 1868): 185.

erts soon had the book reset with a number of new "valuable additions." Other editions followed; in 1874 Roberts was again advertising a "new edition, 16 pages added."[5]

Roberts prepared this compilation primarily to meet the need for a Free Methodist hymnbook, though he no doubt also had a larger audience in mind. The book was published in his own name; "Free Methodist" did not appear on the cover or title page. In 1875 he published a "revised edition" with the title *Spiritual Songs and Hymns for Pilgrims*, containing 180 selections. An 1878 version was labeled "Church Edition."[6]

This hymnbook (the 1875 revised edition) begins with Charles Wesley's hymn "The Jubilee Trumpet" (though the author is not identified):

> Blow ye the trumpet, blow
>   The gladly-solemn sound;
> Let all the nations know,
>   To earth's remotest bound,
> The year of jubilee is come;
> Return, ye ransom'd sinners, home.

In the later (1883) *Free Methodist Hymn Book*, this Charles Wesley hymn became #310, located in the section entitled "Salvation Offered."

The 1875 edition of *Spiritual Songs and Hymns for Pilgrims* contained many Charles Wesley hymns (including "And Can It Be") and some more recent songs such as "Just as I Am, without One Plea" (written in 1835) and Joseph McCreery's "I Storm the Gate of Strife." Roberts pointedly called his book a "hymn book," not a "hymnal"; when the new *Hymnal of the Methodist Episcopal Church* was issued in 1878, Roberts wrote, "We suppose that, in high-church language, this is meant for a hymn-book." Roberts thought that "hymn-book" was plainer, less pretentious speech.[7]

Fishers of Men (1878)

The first book B. T. Roberts actually wrote, *Fishers of Men*, started out as informal talks to pastors and other workers at camp meetings in the summers of 1876 and 1877. The full title of the book was *Fishers of Men; or, Practical Hints to Those Who Would Win Souls*. It ran to some 330 pages, divided into eighteen chapters and in-

---

5. [B. T. Roberts], "Our Hymn Book," *EC* 17, no. 2 (Feb. 1869): 66; advertisements for *Songs and Hymns for Pilgrims* printed in the inside front and inside back mailing covers of the September 1874 *Earnest Christian*. The advertisement on the inside front cover says, "Contains 128 pages good soul-stirring Songs and Hymns," and the ad inside the back cover says, "new edition, 16 pages added."

6. B. T. Roberts, comp., *Spiritual Songs and Hymns for Pilgrims*, rev. ed. (Rochester, N.Y.: B. T. Roberts, 1875), 176 pages; B. T. Roberts, comp., *Spiritual Songs and Hymns for Pilgrims*, "Church Edition" (Rochester, N.Y.: B. T. Roberts, 1878), 192 pages.

7. [B. T. Roberts], "The Methodist Hymnal," *EC* 36, no. 6 (Dec. 1878): 192. Roberts perhaps was unaware that the term "hymnal" had been around for hundreds of years, though not commonly used among Methodists.

cluding at the end, as a practical aid, an index of biblical "Texts More or Less Illustrated" in the book.[8] The first edition of the book was published by George Lane Roberts during the brief period of his printing business in Rochester.

Fishers of Men has probably been the most reprinted of all B. T. Roberts books — most recently in 1997, in paperback by Light and Life Communications.[9]

Whether Benjamin had in mind the eventual publication of his talks in book form is unclear. However, Joseph Goodwin Terrill, who often heard Roberts speak, suggested that the talks be published.[10] Roberts was "working incessantly on his Book" during the very hot summer of 1878. Ellen noted in July that he wanted to finish the book in time for the annual conferences in September. "There are two chapters more to write & your Father begins one of those this hot afternoon," Ellen wrote to her daughter-in-law Anna Roberts.[11]

Benjamin stated in the preface that the book's purpose was "to encourage all whom God calls, to enter at once upon the work of saving souls." It was directed especially "to young and inexperienced ministers," but by implication the book also had a wider target audience, since "In the work of soul saving, every follower of Christ should bear a part." The book was intended "to stir up Christians to a more lively appreciation of their duties" as well as providing "strong incentives" to do them.[12]

Two things that may at first appear surprising about this book (at least to today's readers) are that Roberts strongly stressed success in ministry and that he defined success almost exclusively in terms of soul winning. "He is a successful minister who is successful in saving souls."[13] In the second chapter, "Success a Duty," Benjamin argued that Jesus' words "Follow me, and I will make you fishers of men" (Matt. 4:19) are God's unfailing promise that he will make every faithful minister successful in this one central task. "[I]n the work of the Lord, success never comes by chance," he wrote. "[I]f the minister of Jesus Christ fails as a minister, it is entirely his fault. His success is guaranteed by the most unequivocal promises." Jesus' words are "a promise of success." Thus, B. T. argued:

> The conditions of success are within the reach of every minister of the Gospel. It is not required that he be a man of great talent or learning. . . . All it requires is the unflinching purpose, the unwavering faith, the abandonment of all for Christ. Many may be incapable of preaching what are called great sermons; but every one can "go forth and weep, bearing precious seed."

8. BHR, *BTR*, p. 517; B. T. Roberts, *Fishers of Men; or, Practical Hints to Those Who Would Win Souls* (Rochester, N.Y.: G. L. Roberts and Co., 1878).

9. B. T. Roberts, *Fishers of Men* (Indianapolis: Light and Life Communications, 1997). This edition reprints an earlier foreword by B. L. Olmstead, former FM editor of Sunday school literature, that notes, "For many years Roberts' *Fishers of Men* has in certain circles been a devotional classic and a practical stimulus to Christian workers."

10. BHR, *BTR*, p. 517.

11. ELR to AAR, July 20, 1878.

12. B. T. Roberts, *Fishers of Men* (1918 ed.), pp. 7-8.

13. B. T. Roberts, *Fishers of Men* (1918 ed.), p. 13.

It is the duty then of every minister of the Gospel to succeed in saving souls. If he does not, he is either out of place, or he does not fill his place. The fault is his [and not due to external circumstances].[14]

If this seems harsh or potentially burdensome, Roberts felt it was simply a matter of biblical logic, a sort of syllogism. God especially calls some people to preach the gospel, and since the heart of the gospel and the greatest human need is salvation through Christ, therefore that is the essential task of ministers. And since Jesus promised that all who faithfully heeded his call would be "fishers of men," any failure in this calling was a sign of unfaithfulness (or, perhaps, a mistaken calling).

Behind this lay a theology of the church and of ministry that Roberts implied in the first chapter and picked up again toward the end of the book.

Two points are worth noting about Roberts's argument. First, Roberts interpreted the call to preach almost exclusively as the call to evangelism. Though the preaching ministry might involve varied duties, the mark of faithfulness was success in soul winning.

Second, Roberts recognized, and emphasized, that all Christians, not just preachers, were called into ministry.

> One of the most hurtful, practical errors of Protestantism is the idea, so widely prevalent, that to do efficient service for Christ, one must be an accredited preacher of the Gospel, and have the pastoral charge of a congregation. This is a great mistake. . . . The Roman Catholics manage things better. If a person wishes to give himself up to doing good, the Church finds something that he can do, and sets him at it, under her authority and control. In furthering her work, she employs every grade of talent. . . . So she has her teachers, and nurses working with her priests. . . . But Protestants recognize only one authorized band of workers — preachers; and practically but one order of preachers — pastors. This is not as Christ intended. He calls others to his work, and he would have the Church recognize the call.[15]

Here, at least in embryo, is the basis of a doctrine of the priesthood of believers understood as a universal call to ministry and tied to an understanding of charismatic gifts (and, therefore, appropriate church structures). Roberts does not here develop this idea, however. Though he cites 1 Corinthians 12:28 about diversity of gifts and says this is "no temporary expedient, but a permanent arrangement," he interprets this exclusively in terms of evangelism. "God has called others than ministers to labor for the salvation of souls."[16] As a practical matter Roberts did recognize other callings, such as teachers and writers. But did he ever lay an adequate theological basis for the ministry of Christians in, for example, the arts or government or the sciences? He in fact affirmed such work as appropriate Christian endeavor. But did he see it as legitimate only if it in some way contributed to evangelism?

14. B. T. Roberts, *Fishers of Men* (1918 ed.), pp. 17-21.
15. B. T. Roberts, *Fishers of Men* (1918 ed.), pp. 39-40.
16. B. T. Roberts, *Fishers of Men* (1918 ed.), p. 40.

It would perhaps be unfair to expect Roberts to deal with fine points of theology in a practical manual for preachers. Yet it is precisely in practical handbooks that such points should be made. The issue here is not peripheral, but foundational: Who is a minister, what is ministry, and in what sense is the church a ministering community? One finds "seed ideas" here that Roberts never fully developed.[17]

Roberts included in *Fishers of Men* practical advice on a number of matters, including preaching and the priority of love and of fervent prayer. His advice to would-be preachers:

> Do not preach too long. No matter how much piety you have, and how sound your doctrines may be, you will weary the people out with long sermons. [Though Paul on one occasion preached long into the night,] even this long sermon was attended with fatal consequences. . . . Paul raised the young man [in Acts 20:9] to life; but these "long preachers" generally leave the people dead.[18]
>
> It is not necessary to put the whole body of divinity, beginning with the fall and ending with the resurrection, into a single sermon. The people may hear you again. If not, they may hear others just as capable of giving instruction. As a rule, long sermons defeat the object of a sermon, which is to lead souls nearer to God. They leave a sense of weariness instead of encouragement. . . . When you can no longer keep the attention of your audience, stop. Or if you see that souls are so awakened as to be likely to commit themselves to seek the Lord — or to seek full salvation, break off at once and get them to act. . . . Better spoil a hundred sermons than lose a soul.[19]

Benjamin prepared much of the manuscript of *Fishers of Men* for press not while sitting alone in his study, but in snatches of time on trains or in stations or as he found time while attending camp meetings and revivals. The book went through three editions during Roberts's lifetime.[20]

Why Another Sect (1879)

A year after *Fishers of Men* Roberts published *Why Another Sect: Containing a Review of Articles by Bishop Simpson and Others on the Free Methodist Church*. As noted earlier, Roberts wrote this at the request of the 1878 General Conference. The book was bound in cloth and sold for $1.15.

Considering the amount of detailed information contained in this 321-page book, it is remarkable that Roberts was able to write, edit, and publish it within twelve months or so of the 1878 General Conference in the midst of all his other duties.

Why Another Sect grew in part out of unsatisfactory correspondence Roberts

---

17. See the fuller discussion in chapter 36.

18. Another rare example of Roberts's wry sense of humor.

19. B. T. Roberts, *Fishers of Men* (1918 ed.), pp. 140-42. It is notable that Roberts speaks of "the whole body of divinity" as "beginning with the fall," not with creation.

20. Zahniser, p. 278. Zahniser discusses reviews of and reactions to the book, pp. 278-79.

had with Bishop Matthew Simpson in late 1878, shortly after Simpson's *Cyclopaedia of Methodism* was published. Since Roberts's initial letter to Simpson is dated September 13, 1878, about a month before the Free Methodist General Conference met, it is likely that he already had the book in mind before the conference recommended its preparation.

Roberts began *Why Another Sect* with a copy of his letter to Bishop Simpson.

Rev. M. Simpson, D.D.,
Bishop of the M.E. Church.

Dear Sir: I think when one makes incorrect statements, he should have the privilege of correcting them. I therefore take the liberty to address you in reference to the article in your "Cyclopedia of Methodism," on the Free Methodist Church. In your preface you say: "The aim has been to give a fair, and impartial view of every branch of the Methodist family. For this purpose, contributors and correspondents were selected, as far as practicable, who were identified with the several branches, and who from their position, were best qualified to furnish information as to their respective bodies."[21]

Either no such selection was made from the Free Methodists, or the information which they furnished, with the exception of the bare statistics, was not given to the public in that article. In either case, what becomes of the claim of fairness?

In this article there are some fifteen statements or re-statements, which are utterly untrue, and some five or six statements which, though in a sense true, yet are, from the manner in which they are made, misleading.

If furnished with proof, satisfactory to candid minds, that these statements referred to are untrue, and misleading, will you correct them in the church-periodicals, and in future editions of your book? If not, will you give the authority upon which the statements complained of, are made?

Yours most respectfully,
B. T. Roberts[22]

Bishop Simpson, then residing in Philadelphia, replied a few weeks later, and Roberts prints his response:

Philadelphia, Oct. 23, 1878.
Rev. B. T. Roberts.

Dear Sir: Returning home from a long tour in the west, I find your letter of September 13, complaining of inaccuracies in the article on Free Methodism, but without specifying what those inaccuracies are.

21. See *COM*, pp. 5-6. Simpson added, "The editor regrets that his efforts were not as successful in reference to some of the branches as he had earnestly hoped" (a statement found both in the original 1878 edition and in later editions).
22. *WAS*, pp. 16-17.

I am not aware of any incorrect statements in the article, but if you will furnish me with corrections and the accompanying proof, I will gladly make any alterations in a future edition, should such edition be called for. I desire to have perfect accuracy in every article, and it will give me as much pleasure to correct, as it can you to furnish the corrections.

Yours truly,

M. Simpson.[23]

Roberts apparently did send Bishop Simpson a list of corrections, but he also went ahead with the book *Why Another Sect*. His motivation was clear: to correct the "untrue and slanderous reports" contained in Simpson's volume, which, after all, claimed "the arch-dignity of an encyclopedia."[24] Roberts wrote, "We do not charge the Bishop with wilfully misrepresenting a single fact. With his motives we have nothing to do. We would not, knowingly, do him the slightest injustice. But false statements, coming from a reputable source, do not need to proceed from malice, to be capable of doing so much harm as to demand correction."[25]

After quoting Simpson's letter, Roberts noted that the bishop did not offer to issue any corrections until and unless a new edition of the *Cyclopaedia of Methodism* was issued. This was unacceptable to Roberts. In the meantime, Roberts wrote, "the article [will] create all the prejudice, and do all the injustice of which it is capable."[26]

Roberts then reprinted the *Cyclopaedia of Methodism* article in full, marking all the inaccurate statements with numbers and all the misleading ones with small letters. *Why Another Sect* is a detailed rebuttal of the inaccuracies and a clarification of the points Roberts found misleading. Roberts also dealt with a number of inaccuracies and misrepresentations contained in F. W. Conable's *History of the Genesee Annual Conference of the Methodist Episcopal Church*, which had been published in 1876.

In fairness to Bishop Simpson (and to the author of the article on the Free Methodists, whether Simpson or someone else), it may be said that the article was reasonably accurate and evenhanded. Most of the inaccuracies were not substantial. The most offensive things in the article were the assertion that a Nazarite "organization" or "association" had existed, and the charge of fanaticism. These charges Roberts answered in great detail. He also showed that the charge that some Free Methodists "claim[ed] the power of healing by the laying on of hands" was untrue. It was true, Roberts said, that "in answer to prayer there have been among us some remarkable cases of healing — but nothing more than has taken place among true Christians in all ages."[27]

---

23. *WAS*, p. 17.
24. *WAS*, p. viii.
25. *WAS*, p. 16.
26. *WAS*, p. 18.
27. *WAS*, p. 305.

As it turned out, the *Cyclopaedia of Methodism* went through several editions, and Simpson did alter the article on Free Methodists somewhat. The 1879 edition carried some minor but significant changes. Since this edition appeared the same year as *Why Another Sect,* Simpson must have based his revisions on Roberts's correspondence rather than on the book. The following changes were made in the 1879 and subsequent editions:[28]

1878 Edition	1879 Edition
They privately adopted a platform, and, in this organization, were known as "Nazarites."	Some of them proposed a platform of protest, from which they became known as "Nazarites."
This organization and its publications containing such charges	These proceedings and their publications containing such charges
Even prior to the trial, some of the ministers had established appointments, and organized societies	Even prior to the trial, some of the ministers had established services and collected congregations

Apparently Simpson took seriously Roberts's point that there never was, formally, a Nazarite organization. When referring to Nazaritism, he removed the word "organization" though he retained the phrase "association of ministers." The rest of the article he left unchanged, including the references to "wild fanaticism" and "extravagance" among the first Free Methodists.

These modest changes could hardly have been expected to satisfy the Free Methodists, for they still painted the denomination's origin in a somewhat negative light.

Since *Why Another Sect* was published at Roberts's own expense, he did not miss the opportunity to append advertisements for *Fishers of Men,* the *Earnest Christian,* and other publications that the Earnest Christian Office handled. He included a four-page, blue-paper supplement, *"The Earnest Christian" Publications,* at the end of the book. Roberts noted that *Fishers of Men* was available for $1.25 postpaid, and he included endorsements from Wheaton College President J. P. Blanchard, editor of the *Christian Cynosure,* and from such periodicals as the *Banner of Holiness* and the *Church Advocate.*

When Benson Roberts came to write his biography of his father years later, he gave this assessment of *Why Another Sect:*

[The book] presents a clear and full statement of the causes that led to the formation of the Free Methodist Church, and it forever disposes of the charge that its origin was due to a factious, selfish, or ambitious spirit. Moreover, it shows not

28. Matthew Simpson, *Cyclopaedia of Methodism* (1878), pp. 379-80; cf. *WAS,* pp. 19-21; Matthew Simpson, *Cyclopaedia of Methodism,* rev. ed. (Philadelphia: Louis H. Everts, 1879); cf. *COM* (1880), pp. 379-80, which is identical to the 1879 edition. Roberts quotes the *Cyclopaedia of Methodism* article accurately except that he has "previous" rather than "prior" and adds some commas to the text.

only the possibility of intolerant religious persecution under the polity and sanction of the Methodist Episcopal Church, but by unimpeached testimony proves that it existed throughout Western New York and Northern Illinois, not to mention other regions, throughout the years 1856-1864. . . . Yet there is not a word of bitterness in the book, no reproaches, no railing, but an equable spirit of manly righteousness, of the type that dares to say, "Thou art the man."[29]

First Lessons on Money (1886)

Roberts's theology and praxis were not confined to personal evangelism or rescue work or denomination building. He called for national economic reform, particularly in light of the disputed monetary question and the amassing of huge sums of capital and political influence by rich businessmen. Roberts's philosophy on such matters was aptly summarized by a quote from William Penn that he included on the title page of *First Lessons:* "A man should make it a part of his religion to see that his country is well governed."

First Lessons on Money was started, Roberts said in his preface, "several years ago when silver was demonetized." The small 160-page book is a tract on national economic policy, but was intended also as a sort of primer on practical financial management. The book is partly an explanation of basic monetary economics, partly a call for fundamental economic reform. His main concern was that "The people should see to it that their representatives in Congress pass laws in their interest, and not in favor of the moneyed class and rich corporations in the injury of community generally."[30] His intended audience was much broader than the Free Methodist Church. It was, in fact, the general U.S. public.

Initially Roberts had not finished the book, he said, because he hoped things would change and the book wouldn't be needed. "But as it has become evident that the money question will not be settled until THE PEOPLE settle it, this unpretending volume has been published in the hope that it may help them to settle it properly and speedily." He then elaborated on his purpose:

> For the last twenty-five years I have mingled freely with the common people, from New England to California, and from Dakota to Texas.
>
> I have witnessed the distress that the bad management of our finances by our National Government has produced, and the injury that has been done by the same cause to our religious and benevolent enterprises.
>
> Some of the views presented are in advance of their times; but we trust they will be seen to be sound.[31]

---

29. BHR, *BTR*, p. 525.
30. B. T. Roberts, *First Lessons on Money* (Rochester, N.Y.: B. T. Roberts, 1886), p. 160.
31. B. T. Roberts, *First Lessons on Money,* pp. iii-iv.

Silver was demonetized (that is, cut free from a standard value as money) by an act of Congress in 1873. Many reformers believed that contributed to the financial panic that year.[32] Benson Roberts wrote that his father

> was so heartily in sympathy with the life of the common people that he could not witness the financial distress that had come upon them through governmental mismanagement, without making such an effort as was in his power for their relief.
>
> The political parties were divided upon the financial question. The demonetization of silver and consequent contraction of currency had brought great distress. The banks and money lenders alone profited by this course.[33]

This was indeed a period of financial uncertainty and widespread corruption in government and business, particularly on Wall Street and in the mushrooming railroad industry. In the 1870s, notes Samuel Eliot Morison,

> The federal government was at the summit of a pyramid of corruption in the Northern states. "Boss" Tweed's gang stealing $100 million from New York City; Jim Fisk and Jay Gould looting the Erie Railroad by stock-watering, and their rival, Cornelius Vanderbilt, doing the same, somewhat more respectably, to the New York Central; Collis P. Huntington buying the California legislature and bribing congressmen to promote transcontinental railroad interests. . . . Well did Mark Twain call this the Gilded Age, for when the gilt wore off one found only base brass; everyone was trying to make a "fast buck." . . .
>
> Stock speculation, over-rapid expansion of the agricultural West, and a world-wide drop in prices brought on the panic of 1873 and a depression which lasted three years.[34]

This was the context in which Roberts had begun *First Lessons on Money.* Though economic conditions had improved somewhat by the time the book was finished and published in 1886, things had actually gotten worse for many common people, and especially for farmers.[35] Financial and monetary issues continued to be

---

32. Richard Hofstadter, *The Age of Reform: From Bryan to F.D.R.* (New York: Random House, 1955), p. 76. Lawrence Goodwyn gives a lucid summary of the issue in *The Populist Moment: A Short History of the Agrarian Revolt in America* (New York: Oxford University Press, 1878), pp. 16-17. He notes that "the importance of the silver provisions in the multi-purpose [1873] bill [was] not widely grasped, even in Congress, and certainly not in the country at large." He adds, "As the depression worsened, prices fell, though neither as swiftly nor as far as wages did. Commodity income for farmers slumped badly. What all this meant was beyond the ken of orthodox financial thinkers of the day, but the facts seemed to be relatively simple: silver suddenly was not worth much and the country was gripped by depression." Roberts seems to have been one of the few who early grasped the economic consequences of demonetization, though the matter was disputed.

33. BHR, *BTR*, p. 526.

34. Samuel Eliot Morison, *The Oxford History of the American People* (New York: Oxford University Press, 1965), p. 732. Morison attributed the corruption in large measure to the Civil War, which, "like every other great war, broke down morals" (p. 732).

35. See the discussion in chapter 35.

hotly contested all through this period, up to and beyond William Jennings Bryan's famous "Cross of Gold" speech at the 1896 Democratic National Convention.

In presenting his economic analysis, Roberts drew on two of the leading young reform economists of the day, Richard T. Ely and Francis A. Walker. Ely (1854-1943) was a professor at Johns Hopkins University (1881-92; one of his students was Woodrow Wilson), and later at the University of Wisconsin. He led in the development of the "new economics," claiming economics was a matter less of fixed laws and more of cultural patterns and government policy. Sharply critical of laissez-faire capitalism, Ely argued that society was an interdependent organism in which the state should play a leading role for the benefit of all. Wise policies would lead eventually, he thought, to a cooperative commonwealth.[36]

A committed Christian, Ely promoted the views of English Christian Socialists and called for the church to take the lead in social reform. "It is the mission of Christianity to bring to pass here a kingdom of righteousness," he wrote in 1889. His first influential book, *The Past and Present of Political Economy*, was published two years before Roberts's book.[37] Ely later played a key role in the rise of the social gospel in America and thus represents a theological link between Roberts and the later social gospel. Robert Handy included Ely with Washington Gladden and Walter Rauschenbusch as seminal figures in the movement, describing Ely as its "most influential lay exponent," one who "played a conspicuous role in the shaping of the social gospel."[38]

When Roberts's *First Lessons on Money* was published in 1886, the young Walter Rauschenbusch was just beginning his five-year pastorate at the Second German Baptist Church in New York City near the notorious "Hell's Kitchen" area. Rauschenbusch was born in Rochester in 1861, just a few years before B. T. and Ellen Roberts moved there. He read Henry George's book *Progress and Poverty* (1879; a book Roberts later reviewed),[39] and in 1886 supported George's bid to become mayor of New York. Rauschenbusch wrote, "I owe my first awakening to the world of social problems to the agitation of Henry George in 1886."[40] Rauschenbusch be-

---

36. L. R. Marston noted that "when Roberts wrote *First Lessons on Money*, Richard T. Ely was a young professor shortly past thirty in Johns Hopkins University, and the alert Roberts already was reading after him." Marston added that had he himself perused Roberts's book at the time of his own college economics course, it "could have eased the shock of [my] plunge into the depths of Ely's *Principles*." Marston, p. 391.

37. *Dictionary of American Biography, Supplement Three, 1941-1945* (New York: Scribner, 1973), pp. 248-51.

38. Robert T. Handy, ed., *The Social Gospel in America, 1870-1920: Gladden, Ely, Rauschenbusch* (New York: Oxford University Press, 1966), pp. 15, 173. Handy quotes John Everett: "There was probably no other man of the period who had as much influence on the economic thinking of parsons and the general religious community" as did Ely (John R. Everett, *Religion in Economics: A Study of John Bates Clark, Richard T. Ely, Simon N. Patten* [New York, 1946], p. 75; quoted in Handy, p. 173).

39. See chapter 35.

40. Walter Rauschenbusch, *Christianizing the Social Order* (New York, 1912), p. 54, quoted in Handy, *Social Gospel in America*, p. 254.

came a professor at Rochester Theological Seminary, his alma mater, in 1897, after Roberts's death. The two men apparently never had direct contact with each other; Rauschenbusch didn't come into national prominence until the publication of *Christianity and the Social Crisis* in 1907.[41] But both were influenced by some of the same authors and currents.[42]

Francis A. Walker's 1878 book, *Money*, was another key source for Roberts. Walker (1840-97) was the son of businessman and economist Amasa Walker, one of the founders of Oberlin College. The younger Walker became a leading economist and statistician. As chief of the U.S. Bureau of Statistics, he reformed the bureau and directed the 1880 census. Influential in Europe, particularly England, Walker became "unquestionably the most prominent and the best known of American writers" on economics, according to an 1897 report. As president of the Massachusetts Institute of Technology from 1881 to 1897, he set the school on a solid basis and saw enrollment triple. Like Ely a reformer and critic of laissez-faire business practices, Walker led in the newer inductive, historical approach to economics.[43]

In *First Lessons on Money*, Roberts quotes Adam Smith's *Wealth of Nations* as well as Ely, Walker, and others. Noting the political influence of money, Roberts protests that money power "controls legislation until it becomes so oppressive that the people rise up against its control. It places men, simply because they are rich, in official positions for which they are totally unfitted." The $308 million then tied up in government bonds should be released for industrial development, he argued. "The resources of this country, to a great extent, are yet undeveloped. There are plenty of men willing to work but no man hires them. The capitalist, who should set the unemployed to building and manning ships, and railroads, and working mines and farms and factories, spends at his office an hour or two a day examining securities, reckoning his interest, and cutting off his coupons" — in other words, making money from money rather than from employment-producing business. Releasing capital for productive industry "would make many homes comfortable that are now destitute. It would increase immensely the wealth of the country, by encouraging labor, the only source of wealth."[44]

Roberts argued that property and business should be spread equitably among the populace for the best interest of all. "Good order and general prosperity prevail in our cities in proportion as the business is divided up among the inhabitants," he wrote. "The greater the proportion of men who work for others, the greater danger there is of riotous disturbances. It is as advantageous to the city, as it is to the coun-

---

41. Rauschenbusch was a student at the University of Rochester (B.A., 1884) and Rochester Theological Seminary, from which he graduated in 1886. Benson Roberts, eight years older than Rauschenbusch, attended both institutions just a few years earlier.

42. On Rauschenbusch see Handy, *Social Gospel in America*, pp. 253-389; Donald K. Gorrell, *The Age of Social Responsibility: The Social Gospel in the Progressive Era, 1900-1920* (Macon, Ga.: Mercer University Press, 1988).

43. *Dictionary of American Biography* (New York: Scribner, 1943), 19:338-44.

44. B. T. Roberts, *First Lessons on Money*, pp. 16, 75-76.

try, to have the property and the business divided up among a large number of owners."[45]

Roberts did not expect total economic equality but did see the Old Testament economy, and particularly the Jubilee laws, as providing principles for economic life.

> It is impossible that there should be an equality of property among a people free to act and possessing an equality of rights. If an equal division of the property of the country were made among the people, there would be great difference in the amounts which different persons would possess in a year afterward. In the old Jewish republic, the greatest possible precautions were taken that each family should possess a competence. The land was divided among them. Every one had a farm, a homestead, in the country. If one was compelled to sell his inheritance, he could alienate it from his family for only fifty years at the longest. At the year of jubilee debts were cancelled and inheritances restored. Yet in their palmiest days they had their poor among them. But they had none, while the republic lasted, enormously rich, and probably none who suffered from poverty. All, while obedient to God, were in comfortable circumstances.[46]

The same year that Roberts published *First Lessons on Money,* he applied the biblical Jubilee principle to a contemporary case in a *Free Methodist* editorial entitled "Indian Lands." Commenting on possible government policy options, he said that to give Indians individual title to their land, as some advocated, would be a disaster. That would entail the right to sell, and whites would quickly swindle Indians out of their land. "The stronger white race would soon dispossess them," reducing them to "a landless, homeless race of vagabonds." Quoting from Leviticus 25, Roberts said the "one system of land tenure" that God prescribes ensures perpetual family access to land, "from generation to generation." Thus the Jubilee system "would be better than that of absolute ownership, for the whites as well as the Indians. But it would be impossible to effect a change in the system of land tenure among the whites of this country. Our present system has prevailed too long to be easily overthrown. But with the Indians it is different. Their lands are still held in common. Let them continue to be. If not divided among the families, . . . then let each have what land he will improve and till."

Concerned citizens, Roberts said, should support such a policy. "Let the dominant race which has dispossessed [the Indians] treat them with justice and magnanimity."[47]

In *First Lessons on Money* Roberts went on to argue that "vast accumulations of fortune in the hands of a few" were detrimental and were bringing civil unrest. "All laws which specially favor the gaining and the holding of great fortunes should be

---

45. B. T. Roberts, *First Lessons on Money,* pp. 122-23.

46. B. T. Roberts, *First Lessons on Money,* pp. 121-22. It is interesting that Roberts describes the OT Hebrew economy as a "republic."

47. B. T. Roberts, "Indian Lands," *FM* 19, no. 20 (Dec. 15, 1886): 8.

changed."[48] He called for regulations on joint stock companies, stock speculation, and monopolies. It should be illegal, for example, for the owners of the New York Central Railroad to own any part of the Erie or the West Shore Railroad. Similarly, laws of inheritance should be much more restrictive: "Our laws should make provision for the breaking up of great estates upon the death of the owners. The steady aim of our Government should be to afford to all, every just and proper facility for acquiring a moderate competence. To do this, the whole bent of our laws must be unfavorable to the acquisition of a vast amount of property by any one person, and to the handing of it down unbroken from generation to generation."[49]

Roberts's next-to-last chapter is entitled "How to Make Money." He lists seven suggestions for making money legitimately: (1) Do not aim at getting rich. (2) Be diligent in business. (3) Be careful about going into debt. (4) Never become responsible for the debts of others. (5) Maintain good habits. (6) Be willing to commence business on a small scale. (7) Be benevolent in the use of money. He concludes with Wesley's three rules on money: "Gain all you can. Save all you can. Give all you can."[50]

Roberts's book amounted to a fairly radical challenge to the dominant business practices of the day. Many of his proposals were however enacted into law over the next generation, including the nation's first antitrust legislation. It is hard to say how much impact the book had generally, or within Free Methodism.[51] It initially sold well; Benson Roberts noted that the book "had a rapid sale and was read widely, especially in the West where the financial distress was felt the most keenly."[52] The book was reprinted at least twice in 1886; the copy I have bears the imprint "Third Thousand."[53]

Women in Ministry

Long before publishing *Ordaining Women* in 1891, B. T. Roberts advocated full equality of women in the church.[54] In 1872 he published a twenty-four-page booklet, *The*

---

48. B. T. Roberts, *First Lessons on Money*, p. 127.

49. B. T. Roberts, *First Lessons on Money*, p. 142. See "Why B. T. Roberts Favored the 'Death Tax,'" *Free Methodist Historical Society Newsletter* 3, no. 1 (Summer/Fall 2002): 1.

50. B. T. Roberts, *First Lessons on Money*, pp. 143-57.

51. See Marston, pp. 391-97.

52. BHR, *BTR*, p. 529.

53. It is not likely that Roberts's modest book had any significant impact on the national debate. I have not found references to it in sources that discuss the economic history of the period, and the book is extremely rare today.

54. Roberts's advocacy of a freer role for women in the church has been noted by several contemporary authors and was the subject of a 1984 thesis by Jack D. Richardson ("B. T. Roberts and the Role of Women in Ministry in Nineteenth-Century Free Methodism" [M.A. thesis, Colgate Rochester Divinity School, 1984], 142 pages). See also David Thompson's reference to Roberts in his "Women, Men, Slaves and the Bible: Hermeneutical Inquiries," *Christian Scholar's Review* 25, no. 3 (Mar. 1996): 326-49. Jean Hall Gramento's 1992 D.Min. thesis contains much useful information on this topic and illuminates Roberts's influence. ("Those Astounding Free Methodist Women! A Biographical History of Free

Right of Women to Preach the Gospel.[55] In announcing the pamphlet Roberts noted that in addition to a "thorough examination" of relevant Scriptures, it also contained "sketches of Mrs. Wesley, Miss Nullis, Sarah Smiley, and Mrs. Van Cott."[56]

As we have seen, "women preachers" were a contested issue within Free Methodism from the beginning. Yet from the beginning Benjamin made it clear which side he was on. In *The Right of Women to Preach the Gospel* he gave scriptural support for full equality of women with men in the life of the church, advancing arguments he would later elaborate in *Ordaining Women*. He began very forthrightly. "The progress of the Gospel is slow," he noted; only "a small proportion of the human family have heard," and fewer have responded. Why is this? "One cause of this comparative inefficiency of the Gospel is found in the proscription of woman — a relic of barbarism — to which enlightened, Christian people still tenaciously cling. That woman is granted many privileges, of which she was once deprived we readily allow. She may write books, edit newspapers, lecture on scientific or literary subjects, have the official charge of a post office; but her right to preach the Gospel is generally denied."[57]

After discussing a number of common objections and examining relevant Scriptures, Roberts concluded:

> The Gospel gives to woman the same religious rights that it does to man. It allows of no distinction on account of sex or social condition. This, Paul plainly asserts. *There is neither Jew nor Greek, there is neither bond nor free, there is neither male nor female: for you are all one in Christ Jesus.* — Gal. iii. 28. The Gospel withholds not a single privilege from any person, because he is a Gentile, or because he is a bondman, or because she is a woman. *One is your Master even Christ: and all ye are brethren.*
>
> We have thus demonstrated from the Scriptures that God has reserved to Himself the right to call a woman, if He choose, to preach the Gospel. He has put no seal upon her lips. He has not forbidden her to advocate the claims of that Gospel to which she owes her elevation in this world, and her hopes of happiness in the world to come. The Bible leaves her just as free to show the advantages of following its divine instructions, with her tongue as with her pen; to a congregation of listening thousands as to an audience of a single person.
>
> The claim of a woman, to be called of God to preach the Gospel, should not

---

Methodist Women in Ministry Including an Extended Bibliography of Free Methodist Women's Studies; With Selected Ecumenical Entries" [D.Min. thesis, United Theological Seminary, Dayton, Ohio, 1992], 155 pages.)

55. B. T. Roberts, *The Right of Women to Preach the Gospel* (Rochester, N.Y.: B. T. Roberts, n.d.). Although the pamphlet bears no publication date, a notice in the June 1872 *Earnest Christian* verifies 1872 as the year of publication. There it is entitled *Woman's Right to Preach the Gospel.* [B. T. Roberts], "Literary Notices," *EC* 23, no. 6 (June 1872): 191.

56. [B. T. Roberts], "Literary Notices," p. 191. Although the notice says "Miss Nullis," the sketch is actually of Miss McKinney, written by I. S. Nullis. See B. T. Roberts, *The Right of Women*, pp. 16-18.

57. B. T. Roberts, *The Right of Women*, p. 1.

then, be rejected because she is a woman. Apply to her the same tests that you apply to man. You judge whether a woman should teach a school, or edit a paper, in the same way that you judge whether a man should do these things. This is proper. Try in the same way her supposed call to preach the Gospel.[58]

The relevant issue therefore is not gender, Roberts argued, but rather calling and gifts. The three key questions, parallel to those asked of men, are: Has she grace? Has she gifts? Has she fruits?[59]

After profiling the ministries of Susannah Wesley, Maggie Newton Van Cott, and others, Roberts concluded with five points of "Advice to Women Who Feel Called to Preach":

1. Never attempt to preach unless *the Spirit is poured out upon you.* Of dry, formal preachers, there are enough already. Give us the truth, burning hot. Do not try to preach like the men. . . .

2. Be content to begin in a small way. Almost every thing that endures has a small beginning. Do not imagine that you need official authority to speak for Jesus. A license would give you neither thoughts nor grace. It simply means that the authorities of the church believe that the person having it is called of God to preach. Show by your labors that you have a divine call, and it will be recognized.

3. Do not take it for granted, because you are called to labor for souls, that you are therefore called to devote your whole time to preaching. This is a mistake which many men actually make; and women are liable to make it. . . .

4. Be truly humble. . . .

5. Aim at direct results. Seek to win the hearts of your hearers to Jesus. Preach the Gospel. Make the people feel that they have souls to be saved. Do not take the time to try to prove that women should be permitted to preach. Your defense will be in doing your work well.[60]

These were B. T. and Ellen Roberts's views. But B. T. was strongly opposed by other leading Free Methodist preachers who had come from the ME Church, including Asa Abell, Loren Stiles, and Levi Wood.[61] This put Roberts in a difficult position. He wanted to maintain unity and the dynamism of the new movement while not compromising his convictions about what was right biblically and best for the church. On this issue he was a minority voice in both the ME and FM denominations. His personal history, including his roots in abolitionism and early revivalism, helps explain his more radical position on women's roles.[62]

---

58. B. T. Roberts, *The Right of Women,* pp. 9-10.
59. B. T. Roberts, *The Right of Women,* p. 10.
60. B. T. Roberts, *The Right of Women,* pp. 22-24.
61. BHR, *BTR,* p. 530.
62. As the quotations above indicate, Roberts clearly saw gender and "social condition" as parallel cases: "The Gospel withholds not a single privilege from any person, because he is a Gentile, or because he is a bondman, or because she is a woman."

Benson Roberts noted that *The Right of Women to Preach the Gospel*

was written at a time when there was much opposition to the public work of women [in the church]. Few women dared to raise their voices in public assemblies. These were subjected to severe and often unkind criticism. It was an unpopular step to champion such an innovation on the supposed rights of mankind. There had been much agitation, in the Genesee Conference [of the Free Methodist Church] especially, against women's preaching though God had blessed the labors of many. . . . In the face of such sentiment [B. T. Roberts] held to the course he believed to be right even though it was not popular [even in his own denomination].[63]

As noted earlier, Benjamin opposed the resolutions introduced at the 1861 session of the Genesee Conference that condemned women's preaching. Even so, "they were passed by a large majority," Benson Roberts noted. Benjamin finally responded in print through his 1872 pamphlet. His arguments had their impact, and no doubt helped account for the prominent place of women in the denomination and in the Pentecost Bands. Benson wrote,

The pamphlet had a wide circulation, was widely quoted and helped to break down the barriers of prejudice. Many a gifted woman whose heart had been enlarged with holy desires to tell men of Christ's love and power to save, struggling with natural timidity and shrinking from hostile criticism has found his kind words of counsel and encouragement a source of lifelong hope and cheer. Many who faltered and hesitated to face the inevitable opposition have been strengthened to obey the heavenly calling. Many souls saved to God through the efforts of these brave evangels will honor his course in having the courage of his convictions.[64]

Ellen Roberts, though never called to preach, was one of those who feared criticism when she did speak publicly in church and who drew strength from Benjamin's encouragement. Another was Emma Sellew, Benson's future wife. Benson was a young man of nineteen at the time *The Right of Women to Preach the Gospel* was issued; five years later he married the intelligent and articulate Emma, one of many young women his father encouraged in their sense of call.

B. T. Roberts encouraged women in ministry and celebrated the lives of women preachers and ministers he saw as models. After Mrs. Jane Shuart Dunning (1823-90) of Providence Mission in New York City died, Benjamin published a lead article about her in the *Earnest Christian*. Dunning was "one of the first, ablest and most useful preachers" of early Free Methodism, he noted. She founded Free Methodist churches in Binghamton, New York, and Dover, New Jersey, before beginning ministry among New York City's poor and destitute.[65] Later she moved to the Great Plains

---

63. BHR, *BTR*, p. 530.
64. BHR, *BTR*, p. 530.
65. B. T. Roberts, "Mrs. Jane Dunning," *EC* 61, no. 2 (Feb. 1891): 37-41.

where in 1885 Roberts heard her preach a stirring Sunday afternoon camp-meeting sermon where she "proclaimed the Word in plainness and power and held the attention of the people." Roberts noted, "She is out on the frontier with her children, and greatly misses the opportunities for usefulness she enjoyed among the denser population of the east."[66]

Roberts found Dunning's preaching to be "clear, plain, evangelical," and noted that through her "Many were converted, and many were sanctified to God." She "was not only a powerful exhorter, but a sound systematic preacher. Some of her sermons were reported by the New York *Sun*."[67]

Debates about women's preaching continued to stir the young denomination, however. Some conferences admitted women into full conference membership, even though only licensed as evangelists, not ordained as "ministers," while others did not. In some conferences women "were continued year after year 'on trial;' the old prejudice still operating to hinder a full recognition of their ministerial services and abilities. In no case were they admitted to ordination," Benson Roberts noted.[68]

The issue continued to boil and simmer for nearly two more decades, leading finally to a showdown at the 1890 General Conference and to Roberts's fuller argument, *Ordaining Women*, in 1891 (discussed further in chapter 38).

Benson noted that on this issue his father "was in advance of his own church." He wrote, "Many who were ready to assign to women the hardest fields of labor within the conference, who were content to have the church reap the benefits of her self-denying toil were ready to block her elevation to that ecclesiastical position, of which her accredited and accepted services were a proper and recognized function."[69]

Benson wrote this at a time (1900) when the denomination still did not fully embrace Roberts's position. Not until 1974 did the Free Methodist Church come to agree with its founder, finally granting full equality to women by simply excising the restrictive wording from the *Discipline*.[70]

66. [B. T. Roberts], "Camp Meetings," *EC* 50, no. 3 (Sept. 1885): 99. The camp meeting was held at Almena, Kans.

67. B. T. Roberts, "Mrs. Jane Dunning," pp. 37-41. Dunning led the Providence Mission for sixteen years, and during this period also had some influence on Jerry McAuley and his mission. She died in Iowa in 1890. Her daughter Frances ("Frankie") was the wife of Rev. C. M. Damon, a Free Methodist pioneer in Minnesota, Nebraska, and Kansas, and her daughter Lida (Mrs. William Lamont) was for a number of years associated with Providence Mission. See Hogue, *HFMC*, 2:360, 363; Kostlevy, pp. 79-80; Dunning, *Brands from the Burning: An Account of a Work among the Sick and Destitute in Connection with Providence Mission, New York City* (Chicago: T. B. Arnold, 1881).

68. BHR, *BTR*, p. 531.

69. BHR, *BTR*, p. 531.

70. David L. McKenna, *A Future with a History: The Wesleyan Witness of the Free Methodist Church; 1960 to 1995 and Forward* (Indianapolis: Light and Life Communications, 1997), p. 256.

Opposing Secret Societies

As noted earlier, fraternal orders of all types became popular in the 1840s and 1850s, especially in New York State. By 1860 there were over four hundred Masonic lodges in the state, and nationally Odd Fellowship had grown to a membership of 200,000.[71] It was not uncommon for a citizen, including many Methodists, to be both a Mason and an Odd Fellow and perhaps even a member of some other secret society like the Improved Order of Red Men.

B. T. Roberts's strong opposition to fraternal orders and secret societies in the 1850s became a fixed part of his social reform agenda. Secret societies were bad for both church and society, he felt.

Roberts opposed fraternal orders on several grounds. One function of such orders, he noted in 1862, was to provide financial assistance in times of distress. Roberts felt that for Christians this contradicted the principle of faith. To "talk about having faith" in God but not really trust God "for food and raiment," Roberts said, "is nonsense. . . . Can any man who relies upon [God's promise of provision] join an association of ungodly men, to provide against possible want?"[72]

Roberts viewed Freemasonry not just as a fraternal order but as "an anti-Christian religion" incompatible with Christian faith and practice. Therefore Christians should give no support to pastors who were Masons. He wrote in 1883, "If a masonic preacher is sent to your church, do not give him your money; and do not even go to hear him preach. The word of God is very plain upon this point. 'But though we, or an angel from heaven, preach any other gospel unto you than that which we have preached unto you, let him be accursed.' Gal. i:8. . . . 'If there come any unto you, and bring not this doctrine, receive him not into your house . . .' [2 John 10]."[73]

For Christians to practice Freemasonry, Roberts said, was idolatry. He was explicit that "The god of the lodge is not the God of the Bible." He quoted from Salem Town's book *Speculative Free Masonry* ("a work that has received the highest endorsement from Masonic authorities") to show that Masonry was in fact an alternate religion. Masonry "offers salvation . . . without Christ. Its baptism is not Christian baptism. The morality which it enjoins upon its adherents is as far below Christian morality as hell is from Heaven. The whole system is an offspring of the old heathen mysteries" — in effect, a mystery religion.[74]

---

71. Peter Ross, *A Standard History of Freemasonry in the State of New York Including Lodge, Chapter, Council, Commandery and Scottish Rite Bodies*, 2 vols. (New York and Chicago: Lewis Publishing Co., 1899), 1:486; Mark C. Carnes, *Secret Ritual and Manhood in Victorian America* (New Haven: Yale University Press, 1989), p. 29; Albert C. Stevens, ed., *The Cyclopaedia of Fraternities*, 2nd ed. (New York: E. B. Treat, 1907), pp. 257-58.

72. B. T. Roberts, "Faith in God," *EC* 3, no. 4 (Apr. 1862): 108.

73. [B. T. Roberts], "The Religion of the Day," *EC* 45, no. 2 (Feb. 1883): 63.

74. [B. T. Roberts], "Idolatry," *EC* 45, no. 5 (May 1883): 134-35. Roberts made essentially the same point, quoting Town, in an 1875 article in response to a reader's question. See [B. T. Roberts], "Ma-

In calling Masonry an anti-Christian religion, Roberts was following the lead of Charles Finney, President Jonathan Blanchard of Wheaton College, and others. Roberts wrote in the *Earnest Christian*, "If masonry be, as is clearly shown by the late President Finney, by President Blanchard and others, and in our tract entitled 'False Religion,' a rival and hostile religion to Christianity, then that holiness is defective which closes its eyes to this great fact and sustains Masonic preachers and churches."[75] The argument was based largely on official Masonic sources, which clearly did present Freemasonry as a religious system based on ancient mysteries — a sort of higher secret wisdom capable of incorporating Christianity as well as other religions. For example, the authoritative *Encyclopedia of Freemasonry and Kindred Sciences* (first published in 1873), by Albert G. Mackey, a thirty-third-degree Mason, is explicit that "Freemasonry may rightfully claim to be called a religious institution"; "it is indebted solely to the religious element it contains for its origin as well as its continued existence." While "the religion of Freemasonry is not sectarian," Mackey wrote, the "tendency of all true Freemasonry is toward religion." He elaborated, "Freemasonry is not Christianity, nor a substitute for it. It is not intended to supersede it nor any other form of worship or system of faith. It does not meddle with sectarian creeds or doctrines, but teaches fundamental religious truth — not enough to do away with the necessity of the Christian scheme of salvation, but more than enough to show, to demonstrate, that it is, in every philosophical sense of the word, a religious Institution."[76]

The ancient Greek and Roman mysteries, Mackey wrote, "have especial interest to us" and may be regarded as "forerunners of Freemasonry."[77] It is a mistake therefore to attempt to Christianize Freemasonry. Mackey considered it "a great error" to call "the Master Mason's Degree a Christian institution." According to the *Encyclopedia of Freemasonry,*

> It is true that [Freemasonry] embraces within its scheme the great truths of Christianity upon the subject of the immortality of the soul and the resurrection of the body; but this was to be presumed, because Freemasonry is truth, and all truth must be identical. But the origin of each is different; their histories are dissimilar. The principles of Freemasonry preceded the advent of Christianity. Its

---

sonry," *EC* 29, no. 5 (May 1875): 160-62. Here his objection to Freemasonry is twofold: it "claims to be a saving religion," and thus is "a rival of Christianity," and it "binds its followers with the most horrible and murderous oaths." Freemasonry rejects Christ and the Bible in the sense that it claims to have a higher truth within which specifically Christian beliefs and doctrines are viewed as "sectarian."

75. B. T. Roberts, "Defective Holiness," *EC* 43, no. 1 (Jan. 1882): 7. This article is reprinted in Benjamin T. Roberts, *Holiness Teachings,* comp. Benson Howard Roberts (North Chili, N.Y.: "Earnest Christian" Publishing House, 1893), pp. 164-70; however, in the above quotation the reprint has "Masonic preachers in its churches" rather than "Masonic preachers and churches" (p. 169), presumably an editorial correction by Benson.

76. Albert G. Mackey, *Encyclopedia of Freemasonry and Kindred Sciences,* revised and enlarged by Robert I. Clegg, 2 vols. (Chicago: Masonic History Co., 1929), 2:846-49, "Religion of Freemasonry."

77. Mackey, *Encyclopedia of Freemasonry,* 2:691-92.

symbols and its legends are derived from the Solomonic Temple and from the people even anterior to that. Its religion comes from the ancient priesthood; its faith was that primitive one of Noah and his immediate descendants. If Freemasonry were simply a Christian institution, the Jew and the Moslem, the Brahman and the Buddhist, could not conscientiously partake of its illumination. But its universality is its boast. In its language citizens of every nation may converse; at its altar men of all religions may kneel; to its creed disciples of every faith may subscribe.[78]

This supposed ancient history was pure fantasy, of course — Freemasonry as a fraternal order developed in England and Scotland in the early 1700s, largely out of medieval guilds of skilled stonemasons employed in building royal castles and the great cathedrals. The first Masonic Grand Lodge was organized in London in 1717 from four smaller local lodges. Freemasonry developed from an actual "operative" craft to a fraternal order of "speculative Masonry as it attracted patrons from the nobility, interested gentlemen, and some clergy. An elaborate history was invented claiming antecedents in King Solomon, the builders of the tower of Babel, even Adam and Noah."[79] Jasper Ridley writes that such Masonic mythology "was absolute nonsense; but it was flattering to the masons, who believed what they wished to believe."[80] Such "ancient" origins became accepted Masonic mythology and theology.[81]

78. Mackey, *Encyclopedia of Freemasonry*, 1:200-201, "Christianization of Freemasonry."

79. Carnes, *Secret Ritual*, p. 22; Jasper Ridley, *The Freemasons: A History of the World's Most Powerful Secret Society* (New York: Arcade Publishing, 2001), pp. 1-46; John J. Robinson, *Born in Blood: The Lost Secrets of Freemasonry* (New York: M. Evans and Co., 1989), pp. 175-87. Ridley (as also a number of other writers) traces the rise of Freemasonry to the semi-itinerant guilds of stonemasons and master masons who built the royal castles and cathedrals of medieval Europe, and Masonic secrecy to the guild secrets that were part of the masons' craft. Robinson disputes this, tracing the Masonic order back to the Knights Templar (that is, the Knights of the Temple of Solomon in Jerusalem), founded in 1118 in the wake of the First Crusade, and to the Peasants' Revolt in England in 1381.

80. Ridley, *The Freemasons*, p. 20.

81. Lynn Dumenil gives a balanced and well-informed summary: "Although Masons have been fond of claiming that their order originated in antiquity, it is probably descended from a medieval English guild of stonemasons. Its recorded history begins in early eighteenth-century London, where the order included not only 'operative' Masons, but also 'speculative' Masons, men who were honorary members rather than craftsmen. Eventually, the speculative Masons predominated, and the brotherhood devoted itself to building 'spiritual instead of material temples.' Speculative Masons, led by noted scientists and clergymen, drew upon the Bible, stonemasons' legends, and geometry and physics (the builders' sciences) to fashion an elaborate Masonic system. The tone of the order reflected Enlightenment thought, with its emphasis on deism, rationalism, science, and man's relationship to nature. Masonry was pictured as a 'progressive science.' As the candidate advanced through the first three degrees — Entered Apprentice, Fellow Craft, and Master Mason — he advanced in his knowledge of Masonry and its moral lessons. Each degree entailed an esoteric quasi-religious initiation ritual. These secret rituals were the central component of Masonry. Through lectures, allegories, and symbols, they imparted Masonry's commitment to equality, charity, fraternity, morality, and faith in God. This form of Masonry spread to America during the colonial period, and by 1800, the order claimed 18,000 Masons and was growing rapidly. In 1825, in New York state alone, there were 20,000 Masons." Lynn Dumenil, *Freemasonry and American Culture, 1880-1930* (Princeton: Princeton University Press, 1984),

Roberts did not devote much time to anti-Masonic or anti-secret-society activity, but in his editorials he often cited lodge membership as one sign of compromised or unfaithful Christianity. And when the antilodge National Christian Association (NCA) was organized by Jonathan Blanchard and others in 1867 at Aurora, Illinois (at the suggestion of Free Methodist preachers C. H. Underwood and N. D. Fanning of the Illinois Conference), Roberts became a supporter of the new movement.[82]

Blanchard, as well as his son Charles Albert Blanchard (who succeeded him as Wheaton president in 1882 and served until 1925), advocated numerous reforms, but especially the antisecrecy cause. With the support of Finney, Oberlin College President James Fairchild, wealthy Chicago businessman Philo Carpenter, and others, the NCA and its fortnightly (later weekly) publication, the *Christian Cynosure*, had some impact in the 1870s and early 1880s.[83] The NCA's declared "business and object" was "to expose, withstand, and remove secret societies, Freemasonry in particular, and other anti-Christian movements, in order to save the churches of Christ from being depraved, to redeem the administration of justice from perversion, and our republican government from corruption."[84]

Over the years the *Christian Cynosure* advocated numerous reforms. In addition to missionary and national news, the paper carried "reformatory articles" concerning tobacco, Sunday amusements, and similar vices. "It argued warmly against the exclusion of Bible reading from public schools and for years took part in efforts to 'Christianize' the constitution of the United States by writing into it a direct recognition of Christianity," Clyde Kilby notes. As it expanded in the 1870s, it advocated "social legislation such as an eight-hour day for laborers" and attacked "such practices as cruelty to animals, the carrying of firearms, and speculation on the Chicago grain market, and such organizations as Communism and Socialism."[85] David F. Newton, Roberts's *Earnest Christian* associate, occasionally contributed to the *Christian Cynosure*.[86]

For a number of years the NCA fielded a team of antilodge lecturers, some full-time. As Kilby notes, the organization "was thoroughly opposed to all secret organi-

---

p. 4. See similarly Steven C. Bullock, *Revolutionary Brotherhood: Freemasonry and the Transformation of the American Social Order, 1730-1840* (Chapel Hill: University of North Carolina Press, 1996), pp. 9-16. Bullock notes the "peculiar combination of modern science and ancient religion" that "lay at the heart of the new Masonic fraternity" as it emerged in the early 1700s. It is in this context that one can understand the Masonic lodge membership of prominent early Americans like George Washington, Benjamin Franklin, and New York Governor DeWitt Clinton. Interestingly, the rise of the Masonic Order in England took place just a generation before the rise of Methodism.

82. Clyde S. Kilby, *Minority of One: The Biography of Jonathan Blanchard* (Grand Rapids: Eerdmans, 1959), p. 171; Carnes, *Secret Ritual*, pp. 72-73. Carnes called the 1867 founding meeting "the first convention since the 1830s . . . to oppose secret societies" (p. 72).

83. Kilby, *Minority of One*, pp. 171-72.

84. "Constitution and By-Laws of the National Christian Association," *Christian Cynosure* 6, no. 35 (June 11, 1874): 13.

85. Kilby, *Minority of One*, p. 172.

86. D. F. Newton, "Satan's Sugar Pills," *Christian Cynosure* 6, no. 35 (June 11, 1874): 2.

zations of whatever kind, including of course the Ku Klux Klan." It "used the word 'Mason' generically to refer to all lodges, from Freemasons proper down to the Independent Harmonial Benevolent Association of German Workers and Virgin Maids of Cincinnati."[87]

Roberts attended several of the annual NCA conventions and was in general a supporter of the organization. He was present at the first annual convention in May 1868; he had printed a notice of the meeting, apparently sent him by Jonathan Blanchard, in the February issue of the *Earnest Christian*. Roberts commented, "This is an important meeting. We want all the saints to pray that the special blessing of God may attend these efforts to arrest one of the most gigantic evils of the day." The notice was headlined "National Christian Convention Against Secret Societies."[88] Subsequently he reported on the convention, noting that "About one hundred and eighty delegates were present, representing thirteen different Denominations."[89]

Benjamin's diary shows that he participated also in the 1874 NCA convention in Syracuse. He arrived in time for the opening session, which began at 8:00 P.M. "Found there Prest. [President Jonathan] & C. [Charles A.] Blanchard, [D. P.] Rathbun, [James P.] Stoddard, [Joseph] Travis and a good representation from our church," Benjamin noted.[90] Rathbun and Stoddard (Jonathan Blanchard's son-in-law) were NCA lecturers; Travis was a Free Methodist preacher from the Illinois Conference. Other Free Methodists present included James Mathews and M. N. Downing.[91]

Roberts noted in his diary, "Their arrangements for speakers having failed, I was called on and made a short speech. It was favorably reported by the papers."[92] The *Christian Cynosure* printed a summary. Roberts said he regarded secret societies as "a great evil." "A good cause does not need a veil to cover it; bad ones do. We tear away the veil and uncover the hidden iniquity." Benjamin revealed that when he was a young schoolteacher, an Odd Fellow had invited him to join the lodge, "as it would be a great help to him in his profession." Roberts was indignant. "Why should not the order be of as much assistance in forwarding so laudable an object without his becoming a member."[93]

Roberts saw trade unions as dangerous, also, because they function as secret societies, "crush merit and elevate men who are unworthy," and are socially disruptive. "This past winter in New York and other cities men have been reduced to starvation because they did not dare go to their work for fear of some trade combination. These

---

87. Kilby, *Minority of One*, p. 173.

88. "National Christian Convention Against Secret Societies," *EC* 15, no. 4 (Apr. 1868): 124.

89. [B. T. Roberts], "Anti-Secret-Society Convention," *EC* 15, no. 6 (June 1868): 186.

90. BTRD, June 2, 1874.

91. "The Sixth Anniversary of the National Christian Association," *Christian Cynosure* 6, no. 35 (June 11, 1874): 4-5.

92. BTRD, June 2, 1874.

93. Speech by B. T. Roberts, as reported in "The Sixth Anniversary," p. 4 (spelling of "vail" corrected to "veil").

unions proclaim a strike and force all outside to obey their dictations. All these combinations should be suppressed by law. . . . [They] are especially dangerous in our own country where they have the greatest liberty to perfect their organization and push forward their schemes of ambition and social disruption."

Roberts cited instances of injustice due to Masonic influence that he had read about and also warned of Communism. "It is high time people were aroused on these questions," he said. "Communism is only another branch of the secret societies. These may repeat the scenes of Paris in New York, Chicago or Syracuse."[94]

At the close of the evening session James Stoddard announced that about a month earlier he had visited Charles G. Finney, "that venerable man of God, . . . now rapidly descending to the close of life," at Oberlin. Finney sent his greetings and words of encouragement.[95] He was then eighty-one and died the following year.

At the business session the next morning, Roberts was elected president of the NCA for a one-year term. His name headed a ballot proposed by the Committee on Nominations (reported by Joseph Travis) that included seventeen vice presidents representing different states, and other officers. Roberts presided for the rest of the convention (which ended about noon the next day, Thursday) and no doubt had some influence in shaping the program and roster of speakers at the next convention.[96]

The convention debated a range of issues, and endorsed woman's suffrage and Jonathan Blanchard's proposal that the "American Party" be organized as "the political agency for carrying out the objects of the National Christian Association." Blanchard recognized that although "this name had once been used by the 'Know-Nothings,'" it was "so broad, all-embracing and significant that it should not be discarded for that reason."[97] One "lady delegate" asked "whether the Convention would recognize female suffrage as part of its platform."[98] The NCA did not agree to include such a call in its platform, but, like Roberts, many NCA speakers supported both woman's suffrage and the ordination of women. Matilda J. Gage, a prominent woman's suffrage leader who with Susan B. Anthony and Elizabeth Cady Stanton composed the *Woman's Declaration of Rights* two years later, addressed the convention on Thursday morning after being introduced by Roberts. "Her arguments were

94. Speech by B. T. Roberts, as reported in "The Sixth Anniversary," p. 4.

95. "The Sixth Anniversary," p. 4.

96. "The Sixth Anniversary," p. 4. Roberts noted in his diary, "To day [I] was elected Prest. of the Convention. Made a few remarks on taking the chair expressive of my dependence on the Lord for help rightly to discharge my duties" (BTRD, June 3, 1874).

97. The American Party was in fact organized about this time. In 1876 Wheaton College professor James Barr Walker ran for president as the American National Party candidate, and in 1880 the American Party candidate was John W. Phelps of Vermont, with Samuel Pomeroy as vice presidential candidate (Joseph Nathan Kane, *Presidential Fact Book* [New York: Random House, 1999], pp. 121-22, 128; Kilby, *Minority of One*, p. 175). Jonathan Blanchard was temporarily an American Party candidate in 1882-83 but withdrew in favor of Pomeroy before the 1884 national election. Kilby says the American Party "was the political offspring of the National Christian Association and to a large extent the creation of Jonathan himself" (p. 190).

98. "The Sixth Anniversary," p. 5.

pointed and drew out frequent applause," the *Christian Cynosure* noted.[99] Mrs. Gage opposed fraternal orders because, she said, these societies "set one sex against another."[100]

The convention passed a series of resolutions, mostly related to Freemasonry but also denouncing the Grange for its secrecy. The convention resolved "That we recognize in the Patrons of Husbandry, or granges, so-called, which are springing up in all parts of our country, children of secrecy, having Masonry and Odd-fellowship as god-fathers and god-mothers, which organizations are most cunningly devised to give speculators at head centers the control of the farming interests of the country."[101]

Though this NCA convention apparently had a fairly good attendance and reported "growing interest in our cause" and the formation of new auxiliaries in several states, Roberts was not especially impressed. He wrote in his diary, "It is very good but is too much of a family matter to make a permanent success I fear. The Blanchards father and son & two or three sons in law run the whole affair."[102] This was not much of an exaggeration; at this time Jonathan Blanchard was lecturer and general agent; his son Charles was corresponding secretary; and his sons-in-law H. L. Kellogg and H. A. Fischer were treasurer and auditor, respectively.[103] Ezra A. Cook, the publisher of the *Christian Cynosure*, was another son-in-law of Blanchard.[104] Roberts saw that the organization was not broad-based enough to be a movement of national significance.

Jonathan Blanchard, born in 1811 and thus twelve years older than Roberts, was however a tie to Roberts's radical roots. Blanchard had been one of "The Seventy" agents associated with Theodore Weld and the American Anti-Slavery Society in 1836-37, and clearly he saw his antisecrecy campaign and the NCA as a continuation of his earlier Christian social reform efforts.[105] Like Roberts he was a reformer, but temperamentally he was more like the fiery Weld than the mild-mannered Roberts. Jonathan's son Charles described him as "a man of oak and iron . . . stormy and tempestuous when the winds are raving." Another said, "Blanchard is one of the old prophets dropped down into the nineteenth century." The *Christian Press* of Cincinnati commented on "his peculiar natural temperament, which leads him to attack whatever appears to him sinful with the whole strength of his nature," and yet recognized Blanchard as "a noble Christian man. . . . He may have great faults, but he

---

99. "The Sixth Anniversary," p. 12.

100. Carnes, *Secret Ritual*, p. 80.

101. "The Sixth Anniversary," p. 13.

102. BTRD, June 4, 1874.

103. "The Sixth Anniversary," p. 5; Kilby, *Minority of One*, pp. 179, 185, 192.

104. *President Blanchard's Autobiography: The Dealings of God with Charles Albert Blanchard, for Many Years a Teacher in Wheaton College, Wheaton, Illinois* (Boone, Iowa: Western Christian Alliance Publishing Co., 1915), pp. 171-72, 193.

105. John Lytle Myers, "The Agency System of the Anti-Slavery Movement, 1832-1837, and Its Antecedents in Other Benevolent and Reform Societies" (Ph.D. diss., University of Michigan, 1960), pp. 32, 401, 567-70.

has also great virtues."[106] When he was running for U.S. president in 1882, at age seventy, he still showed his reforming zeal. He championed woman's suffrage, and the American Party platform, Kilby notes, "began with an acknowledgment of God as the author of civil government, and . . . advocated Sabbath observance, prohibition, withdrawal of charters of all secret societies, civil equality, arbitration between nations to secure permanent peace, use of the Bible in the public schools, discouragement of monopolies, a sound currency, protection of all loyal citizens, justice to the Indians, and the abolition of electoral colleges."[107]

Blanchard in his own career bridged Roberts's youthful abolitionist roots and later reformist involvements. Roberts's activism in behalf of farmers, however (narrated in the next chapter), had considerably more impact than did his anti-secret-society and prohibitionist efforts.

Roberts later attended the 1884 NCA convention, held in Washington, D.C., in February, eight months before the U.S. presidential election. The NCA had recently moved its headquarters to Washington and had acquired a building "within a stone's throw" of the Capitol. Jonathan Blanchard was spending a considerable amount of his time in Washington, hoping to expand the NCA's activities and to start a daily paper.[108]

This NCA gathering was billed as the American Prohibitory Anti-Secrecy Convention. It was an attempt by Blanchard and others to combine the prohibition and antisecrecy forces before the upcoming election. Blanchard had met with Frances E. Willard and other leaders of the Woman's Christian Temperance Union (WCTU), urging a joint effort, but the ladies held back because the WCTU was itself supported by the Knights of Labor and the total-abstinence Good Templars, both of which had vows of secrecy. Roberts spoke positively about the convention but noted, "The absence of those generally recognized as ladies of the Prohibition party was particularly noticeable!" Blanchard had hoped to use this convention as an effective launching pad for his American Party, and in fact this meeting of the NCA seems to have served as the convention of the American Party.[109]

Roberts attended the opening meeting of the convention on Wednesday evening, February 20, in Lincoln Hall, after sitting in on sessions of the U.S. House and Senate earlier in the day. He was unfavorably impressed by the tobacco-smoke-filled House but found the Senate to be "a dignified, orderly body of able men." Of interest to Roberts, the Senate that day was debating "the money question."[110]

Roberts was pleased to hear Frederick Douglass's stirring keynote address at the opening of the convention. Douglass spoke "on civil rights," Roberts noted, giving "a masterly defence of the rights of the colored people." Jonathan Blanchard said, "The

---

106. Kilby, *Minority of One*, pp. 187-88.
107. Kilby, *Minority of One*, p. 190.
108. Kilby, *Minority of One*, pp. 196-97.
109. [B. T. Roberts], "Visit to Washington," *EC* 47, no. 3 (Mar. 1884): 95-96; Kilby, *Minority of One*, pp. 196, 199.
110. [B. T. Roberts], "Visit to Washington," p. 95.

great crowd was entranced by the eloquence of Douglass in spite of his color and the fact that he had recently married a white woman."[111]

The next afternoon Roberts addressed the convention on the subject of prohibition. Presumably this address was essentially the same as the long (seven-page) article entitled "Prohibition" that he made the lead article in the March 1884 *Earnest Christian*. Roberts advocated "suitable enactments by our National and State Governments, to make the manufacture or sale of intoxicating liquors as a beverage, a crime to be punished by adequate penalties." He laid out his case, noting liquor's contribution to crime and social disintegration. "A traffic which tends thus to unloose the bonds of society should be prohibited," he argued, and in fact the "*principle* of prohibition is already adopted by all civilized nations. It only remains to give the principle a universal application."[112]

Roberts based his argument primarily on a social and political analysis, although he also adduced biblical support. "Man has no natural right to injure for the sake of gain, his fellow man, though he consents to, or even solicits the infliction," he reasoned. The "millions of dollars" and extensive employment of men in the liquor trade are in reality "so much money and so much labor taken from wealth producing industries and employed in wealth destroying pursuits."[113]

Roberts urged the audience, "Use all your political influence in favor of prohibition. If you are a voter, see to it that your vote tells in the strongest possible manner, in favor of strict prohibition. Do not tie yourself up to any party — not even to the prohibition party. If either of the great political parties nominate a man in other respects suitable, who can be relied upon to give his influence in favor of prohibition, then give him your unqualified support."

Roberts concluded, "The temperance question is by far the greatest issue now before the people. Let us not be diverted by any frantic, partisan efforts from giving it our hearty support."[114]

It is not clear that Jonathan Blanchard approved of this rather nonpartisan approach just at the time he was attempting to build a political party, or coalition, that was committed to prohibition and antisecrecy (though to other reforms, as well). In fact, this convention nominated Samuel Clarke Pomeroy, former U.S. senator from Kansas, as American Party candidate for president of the United States in 1884, subject to confirmation by a scheduled American Prohibition Convention in June. Pomeroy did run, but he had even less impact than Prohibition Party candidate John Pierce St. John, who polled 150,369 votes. Grover Cleveland was elected president with nearly 5 million votes — 54.6 percent of the popular vote.[115]

111. [B. T. Roberts], "Visit to Washington," p. 95; Kilby, *Minority of One*, pp. 198-99.

112. [B. T. Roberts], "Visit to Washington," p. 96; B. T. Roberts, "Prohibition," *EC* 47, no. 3 (Mar. 1884): 69-73.

113. B. T. Roberts, "Prohibition," 1884, p. 74.

114. B. T. Roberts, "Prohibition," 1884, pp. 75-76.

115. Kilby, *Minority of One*, p. 199; B. T. Roberts, "Prohibition," 1884, p. 96; Kane, *Presidential Fact Book*, pp. 136-37. Unable to secure a union with the Prohibition Party, Blanchard and like-minded ac-

In assessing the Washington NCA convention in the *Earnest Christian,* Roberts said that though there "was quite an attendance from abroad" (i.e., from around the country), "yet it was small to what it should have been." He was hopeful that good would come from it. "The right position was taken on great and pressing questions affecting the prosperity of our people, and the stability of our government. A great and powerful party embracing all the best elements of society should be organized, but whether those who have taken it in hand, possess the organizing ability to do it, remains to be seen."[116]

As it turned out, they did not — though the story of the antisecrecy and prohibition movements does fit into a larger picture of reform ferment that soon gave rise to the Populist movement. One evidence of this linkage is the fact that Frances Willard of the WCTU was often a delegate to Populist conventions.[117]

The influence of the NCA was in fact never very great. Although the organization showed considerable vigor in the 1870s and early 1880s, it soon waned. Subscriptions to the *Christian Cynosure* dropped from 4,650 in 1875 to 2,714 in 1891. Carnes says, "The NCA, already moribund by 1890, faded rapidly after the death of Jonathan Blanchard in 1892."[118] Robert Wayne Smith concluded in 1956, "The opinion of the general public toward secret orders appears to have been altered to no appreciable degree by the persuasion of the National Christian Association."[119]

Nor did NCA efforts apparently have much impact on Freemasonry itself. Masonic membership in the United States continued to grow, from 446,000 in 1870 to 537,000 in 1880 (after doubling between 1860 and 1870). However, membership of native, white, adult males declined from 7.3 percent in 1870 to 6.2 percent in 1880. The percentage dropped further to 5.3 percent in 1890, though total membership still increased. Total Masonic membership did not decline until the 1930s, and in 1970 reportedly stood at 3,763,000 — 7.6 percent of the native, white, adult male population, not much different percentage-wise from when the NCA was organized in 1867.[120]

Though without much ongoing influence, the NCA did continue into the twentieth century. At the 1915 Free Methodist General Conference in Chicago, Charles

---

tivists apparently arranged for a (so-called) American Prohibition Party convention in Chicago in June, still hoping to attract both antisecrecy and prohibitionist voters, and Pomeroy's nomination was confirmed. The Prohibition Party met in July and nominated John Pierce St. John. Four years earlier when Pomeroy ran for vice president with John Wolcott Phelps on the American Party ticket, he and Phelps polled only 700 votes and the Prohibition Party just 10,305 (Kane, pp. 128, 136-37). Compare this history to that of the People's Party, just a few years later (narrated in the next chapter).

116. [B. T. Roberts], "Visit to Washington," p. 96. See the summary in Zahniser, p. 315.

117. Carlton Beals, *The Great Revolt and Its Leaders: The History of Popular American Uprisings in the 1890's* (New York: Abelard-Schuman, 1968), pp. 206, 222.

118. Carnes, *Secret Ritual,* pp. 88, 199.

119. Robert Wayne Smith, "A Study of the Speaking in the Anti-Secrecy Movement, 1868-1882, with Special Reference to the National Christian Association" (Ph.D. diss., State University of Iowa, 1956), p. 232.

120. Dumenil, *Freemasonry,* p. 225.

Blanchard (then president of Wheaton College) brought fraternal greetings on behalf of the association.[121] That same year, in his autobiography Blanchard paid tribute particularly to the Free Methodists and Wesleyan Methodists among those denominations that had consistently supported the NCA over the past fifty years — "churches which may be particularly designated as witnessing churches" in their stand against secret societies.[122]

Temperance and Prohibition

The record of B. T. Roberts's involvement with the National Christian Association shows the close connection in his mind between the antisecrecy and temperance causes. In fact, as noted above, Roberts in 1884 viewed temperance as "by far the greatest issue now before the people."[123] Roberts advocated prohibition (not just temperance) throughout his adult life, though he also cautioned against too narrow a focus and against any official denominational commitment to the Prohibition Party.

The colorful and controversial temperance advocate Carry A. Nation (1846-1911) owed some of her inspiration and zeal to Roberts, at least indirectly. Mrs. Nation probably never met Roberts personally, but in 1891 she was led into a deeper experience of the Holy Spirit by Free Methodist women in Medicine Lodge, Kansas. In her autobiography, *The Use and Need of the Life of Carry A. Nation,* she later wrote: "The Free Methodists, although few in number, and considered a church of but small influence, have been a great power in reform. They were the abolitionists of negro slavery to a man, and now they are the abolitionists of the liquor curse to a man."[124] Mrs. Nation correctly discerned the connection between earlier abolitionism and the prohibition crusade of the 1890s.

Mrs. Nation added that Free Methodists assisted her in one of her infamous "smashings." She was referring to the help of an FM official in closing illegal saloons in south-central Kansas in 1900, after she had "smashed" several drinking establishments in the town of Kiowa using brickbats, cue sticks, billiard balls, and whatever else came to hand. Biographer Fran Grace writes, "Within three months, Nation and her supporters had successfully forced the closure of all saloons in the county — thanks in part to a Free Methodist justice of the peace, Moses Wright." Mrs. Nation

---

121. Hogue, *HFMC,* 2:235.

122. "During the last fifty years we have had in our country a group of churches which may be particularly designated as witnessing churches, The Free Methodist, The Weslyan [*sic*] Methodist, The Reformed Presbyterian, The United Presbyterian, The Mennonite, The German Baptist, The Friends, The Swedish Mission Churches, The Christian and Missionary Alliance, The Reformed Churches, [and] many synods of the Lutheran Church," wrote Blanchard. He was referring to bearing witness in regard to a range of issues, including worldliness, war, and intemperance, in addition to secret societies. *President Blanchard's Autobiography,* p. 197; cf. p. 114; see also Smith, "A Study," p. 233.

123. B. T. Roberts, "Prohibition," 1884, p. 76.

124. (Topeka, Kans.: F. M. Stevens and Sons, 1909), pp. 137-39.

believed in direct action against illegal saloons, sometimes attacking them with her hatchet — "hatchetation," she called it.

Assessing Free Methodist influence on Carry Nation, Fran Grace wrote, "Founder B. T. Roberts unceasingly criticized the prosperity theology common in the Gilded Age. His alternative 'liberation' theology provided Nation with the connection between asceticism and reform." Grace notes that at her death Mrs. Nation left part of her estate to the Free Methodist Church of Oklahoma.[125]

Roberts's position on temperance and prohibition gives some insight into his view of politics and of the Christian's role in society generally. Joseph Terrill wrote of Roberts after his death in 1893:

> His attitude on the temperance question has been greatly misunderstood by many. The frequent discussions I have had with him in the past, enable me to speak with authority as to his views on this subject. He was a prohibitionist of the most radical stamp; but doubted the wisdom of organizing a party on that issue. He was not a party man. He was not a Republican, though often charged with being one. He was a Democrat as to the tariff question, but not on some other questions. He, like many others, thought the Republican party would do the best for temperance.[126]

Terrill once accompanied Benjamin to the polls during a particularly hot election. "The ticket [Roberts] voted was a mixture of the Democrat, the Republican, and the Prohibitionist," Terrill noted. "Third party prohibitionist as I was, we had a spicy discussion over the course he took; but I could not doubt his conscientiousness in the matter."[127]

Roberts did draw parallels between pre–Civil War abolitionism and the later prohibitionist cause. In 1885 he recalled Charles Finney's words a half-century earlier, at the height of the abolitionist movement: "The grace of God will make any man an abolitionist." So today, Roberts argued, "The grace of God will make any man a prohibitionist." But such reforms were penultimate, not ultimate; nothing must distract us from total loyalty to Jesus Christ. "Reform is not our salvation," Roberts wrote. "One may be wholly devoted to the promotion of beneficent reforms and yet not be saved." Reform efforts have their own dangers: "The Christian may be swallowed up in the partisan. He may unconsciously exaggerate facts that favor his

---

125. Howard A. Snyder, review of *Carry A. Nation: Retelling the Life*, by Fran Grace, *Free Methodist Historical Society Newsletter* 2, no. 3 (Winter/Spring 2002): 4. See Fran Grace, *Carry A. Nation: Retelling the Life* (Bloomington: Indiana University Press, 2001). Mrs. Nation (born Carry Amelia Moore in Garrard County, Ky.) was probably the most widely known temperance advocate in the late 1800s and early 1900s. She was active in the WCTU in the 1890s, but Grace says the WCTU "no longer claims her as their own (if they ever did)." In her later years she carried her temperance message to the Chautauqua circuit and the vaudeville stage. Though she and her hatchet were often lampooned in the press, Carry had a clear sense of vocation and was committed to doing God's will as she understood it.

126. J. G. Terrill, "Some Reminiscences of Rev. B. T. Roberts," *EC* 65, no. 4 (Apr. 1893): 112.

127. Terrill, "Reminiscences," p. 112.

position, and suppress those that militate against it, until he has suffered a serious loss of candor and simplicity."[128] It was for this reason that Roberts always opposed committing the Free Methodist Church as a denomination to any one political party or cause.

The Nature of Roberts's Radicalism

Roberts's writings and activities show that he and Ellen were in fact committed to a variety of social reform efforts — women's rights, a sound monetary system, and temperance among them. Benjamin viewed his opposition to the use of tobacco as a social and moral reform as well as a matter of personal holiness.[129] And of course, he worked constantly for the revival and renewal of the church. In Roberts's mind, revival and reform were intimately connected. "A revival of Christianity, if genuine, is always attended with a reformation," he wrote.[130]

Benjamin argued that an uncorrupted Christianity will always transform society, not by targeting specific social maladies but by transforming human hearts — "curing man of his inhumanity to man." Early Christian preachers "never posed as reformers" but "reformed society by converting men and women to God. They reformed the individual," and as "the individual, the unit of society, was sanctified to God, society was reformed."[131] Here Roberts focuses on individual transformation, but as a number of his reform efforts testify, he believed also in corporate action to address corporate ills.

The point was that true, radical Christianity always transformed society. "No other institution that has appeared among men produces such radical changes in society as the religion of Christ. It is revolutionary in its character," he wrote in an 1890 essay entitled "Gospel Reforms." Unleash the gospel, and you unleash reform; "wherever

---

128. [B. T. Roberts], "Turned Aside," *EC* 50, no. 2 (Aug. 1885): 62. Roberts drew a parallel between abolitionism and prohibitionism also in the next editorial in this same issue, entitled "Prohibition." Here he criticized those who were trying to turn camp meetings into promotional meetings for prohibition — at a profit! "Camp Meetings have been the means of doing a great deal of good; but in many instances they have become popularized and secularized, and turned into pleasure resorts, and are run with the main object, apparently, of making money." Some promoters were even trying to "take advantage of the popular feeling in favor of prohibition, to make temperance camp meetings a source of pecuniary profit. . . . Popular speakers and singers are hired to go from place to place to these meetings. A heavy admittance fee is charged, and the whole affair has much the appearance of a theatre in a grove." "The old abolitionists never charged admission to their anti-slavery meetings," Roberts protested. "They took their lives in their hands and advocated truths so unpopular that to be mobbed was, with many of them, a common experience. The temperance cause needs advocates equally devoted"; only such dedication and self-sacrifice "will enlist sympathy and cooperation, and will win the day." [B. T. Roberts], "Prohibition," *EC* 50, no. 2 (Aug. 1885): 63-64.

129. [B. T. Roberts], "Tobacco and Holiness," *EC* 47, no. 4 (Apr. 1884): 126-27. Roberts claimed that the *Earnest Christian* was the first, or one of the first, holiness journals to advocate this "great reform."

130. [B. T. Roberts], "Reformation," *EC* 42, no. 5 (Nov. 1881): 161.

131. B. T. Roberts, "Gospel Reforms," *EC* 59, no. 5 (May 1890): 134-35.

the Gospel plow breaks up the soil, school houses and churches, and colleges and asy-
lums for the insane, the blind and the dumb, spring up in its furrows as if by magic."
The gospel has a built-in tendency "to unsettle every false foundation of the social edifice." Roberts gave a number of historical examples, from the Roman Empire on. If this
was less evident today, he said, it was because "our Christianity has become corrupted."
This was why a revival of biblical Christianity was urgently needed.[132]

In this sense Roberts was, and saw himself as, a radical reformer — though
never primarily a reformer. Still, his radicalism was in some ways different from that
of much late nineteenth-century Free Methodism. In the 1880s and the 1890s the
Free Methodist Church saw itself as a "radical" holiness body. Though maintaining
some irenic contact with the broader Holiness movement, its leaders and writers often warned against too low a standard of holiness — an experience that did not go
deep enough, was not sufficiently world-denying, and compromised with the
amusements and ostentations of the age.[133] The term "radical" had a positive conno-
tation, as suggested by the article "Radical Holiness," reprinted approvingly from the
Christian Witness in the *Free Methodist* in October 1894. Pointing out that "radical"
means "root" and that "Sin has a root in man," the author observed: "We are sometimes charged with being radical on the subject of holiness. We gladly confess judgment, and would justify our position. We firmly believe that we would be radically
wrong not to be radical on this subject."[134] Authors called for "a thorough work" and
warned against "popular holiness." Vivian Dake and the Pentecost Bands were radical in this sense, but also in the sense that Dake argued for aggressive, innovative
measures in evangelism and missions. For him and for people like FM evangelist
E. E. Shelhamer, who started out in the Pentecost Bands, radical holiness had a keen

132. B. T. Roberts, "Gospel Reforms," pp. 133-36. Roberts noted that "the reign of peace" brought
by the gospel has at times overcome war. He added: "Among professedly Christian nations, which still
resort to war, though the Gospel forbids it, atrocities have been greatly mitigated, and terrible as it is, it
has lost many of its most inhuman features" (pp. 134-35).

133. Some sense of Free Methodism's position within the late nineteenth-century Holiness movement can be gained from Charles B. Jernigan's *Pioneer Days of the Holiness Movement in the Southwest*
(Bethany, Okla.: Arnett Publishing Co., 1964). Speaking primarily of Texas and the organization of the
Free Methodist Church there beginning in 1879, Jernigan says, "The Free Methodist church has been
an important factor in conserving the work of holiness in the Southwest, as it was the first church on
the field that stood out clearly for the doctrine of holiness as a second definite work of grace." He continues, "The lives of her people are clean and holy. Her preachers are a set of the most self-sacrificing
men and women that we know. . . . Her doctrines are in perfect keeping with the great holiness movement, and her teachings are safe, and she was originally intended for [i.e., to be] the church home for
the oppressed and despised holiness people, who were not welcomed in other churches on account of
the 'second blessing' for which they stood; and had it not been for their strenuous objections to instrumental music in public worship, and a few other things of minor importance, the great holiness movement would have found a shelter in her folds by the thousands, but after thirty-five years there are less
than that number of Free Methodist churches in Texas" (p. 86). The "few other things" concerned
dress, especially; "talking against cravats, rag roses, and other externals" (p. 99).

134. "Radical Holiness," *FM*, Oct. 3, 1894, p. 6. See also J. B. Chapman, "Radical Holiness," *God's
Revivalist and Bible Advocate* 42, no. 29 (July 17, 1930): 1.

evangelistic edge. Increasingly, however, especially after 1890, "radical" referred to the experience of holiness manifested more in renunciation of "worldliness" in dress, entertainment, and personal behaviors than in a radical commitment to evangelism or ministry to the poor.

This was different from Roberts's focus. His radicalism, as we have observed, was based in a pre–Civil War vision not only of personal holiness but also of the transformation of society by the power of the Holy Spirit poured out in revival.[135] Like John Wesley Redfield, Roberts believed the gospel could both purify the church and reform the culture. Roberts never really gave up this vision, but by the late 1880s it seems not to have been the vision of the denomination generally. Holiness, though "radical," was increasingly understood inwardly and privately — as the character of the church understood in a fairly small range of specific behaviors, with little expectation of present social transformation.

For Roberts, reformation was most fundamentally based on the righteousness and justice of God, and on God's requirement of righteousness on earth. Outer righteousness, and therefore the promotion of righteousness and justice in society, was part of inner holiness. He wrote in 1884, "We must awake to the importance of promoting righteousness. Conversion amounts to nothing unless those converted turn fully to the right in every thing. Wrong principles and wrong practices must be fully and forever forsaken by every one who would become a disciple of Christ. A revival without a reformation is one of Satan's devices to perpetuate his kingdom."[136]

For Roberts, holiness itself created an impulse toward social reform. "One effect of true holiness," he wrote in 1885, "is to make us deeply interested in various benevolent enterprises. It takes us out of ourselves. It enlists our energies in behalf of interests that have no direct bearing on our personal affairs. We give our time and money for that which brings us neither profit nor reputation."[137]

Roberts saw thoroughgoing revival as the primary way to achieve such transformation. Revival meant not simply holding "extra meetings," however, but required a genuine moving of the Holy Spirit, as at Pentecost. "Armful after armful of green wood will not of itself warm a room in a cold day. To do any good it must be brought into contact with enough fire to set it on fire." This is what happened at Pentecost, Roberts believed, and he saw the "revival which began" then as "the model for Christian revivals" ever since. Like Finney, Redfield, and most of the great revivalists of history, Roberts believed that genuine revival and awakening begins with the church and works outward: "An awakening among the professed people of God will be attended by an awakening among sinners."[138]

---

135. It is instructive that Roberts did not make an automatic transference after the Civil War, as many others did, from abolitionism to prohibitionism as the major focus of his reforming concern. The range of his concern was considerably broader, as this chapter and the next show.

136. B. T. Roberts, "Awake!" *EC* 48, no. 2 (Aug. 1884): 39.

137. [B. T. Roberts], "Follow On," *EC* 50, no. 1 (July 1885): 34.

138. [B. T. Roberts], "Revivals," *EC* 47, no. 1 (Jan. 1884): 31. This might be called the "standard model" of Protestant revivalism. Roberts added, "The great revivals under the labors of Wesley were

In one of several editorials on revival (this one in late 1884), Roberts wrote,

Every town in this land needs a revival of God's work. Sin abounds. Sabbath-breaking, intemperance, licentiousness, and dishonesty are increasing with fearful rapidity. Streams of vice, everywhere percolating through the foundations of society, threaten its overthrow. . . .

The Gospel affords the only remedy. It is adequate for the destruction of sin, the curse of the world. By making men holy it makes them happy. By destroying the love of sin it prevents crime.

The power of the gospel must not only be preached; it must be demonstrated. People must be stirred up to repentance. "Curiosity must be excited; the attention must be gained. Religious excitement, which so many professed Christians speak against, must be stirred up, and kept up to a white heat, to see any great amount of good accomplished." Only when people "feel a deeper interest in religion than in anything else" can an effective revival, "with proper management," be carried on. "Multitudes of souls may be saved, and those reached who were thought to be beyond the reach of mercy."[139] For this reason Roberts felt visible manifestations of the Holy Spirit's presence were entirely normal. He wrote in 1891, toward the end of his life, "Where the Holy Spirit works in power upon human hearts, there is a commotion. It matters not what is the denomination. When God, the Holy Ghost, produces a deep inward conviction, there will be some striking outward manifestations. This manifestation will vary in individual cases, but the outward appearance will indicate, even to unbelievers, that God is working within."

To those who viewed such manifestation as unnatural, Roberts wrote, "It is entirely natural where strong excitement prevails: and Christianity is calculated to produce just such excitement. He who believes its tremendous truths strongly and apprehends them clearly, can but be deeply moved."[140]

Roberts, however, abhorred shallow "popular revivals." Surveying the rampant immorality and injustice of American society in 1890, he declared: "To this demoralizing state of society popular revivals have largely contributed. People have been taught that conversion consists in believing that Christ receives them" without thorough reformation of life. Instead people must learn the Jesus way, "that they can never be right with God until they are right with" one another. God-sent revivals "shake society to its foundation," transforming both church and nation. So the great need is for revivals that will "break up conspiracies of the strong against the weak," that will "purify our politics, secure honest dealings between man and man, and render justice possible in our courts." But revivals designed "chiefly at bringing those

---

confined mostly to the members of the established church." In a later editorial he commented that Christians should pray and work ardently "to contribute towards having a revival of religion of the Pentecost type." [B. T. Roberts], "Revived," *EC* 61, no. 1 (Jan. 1891): 29.

139. [B. T. Roberts], "A Revival," *EC* 48, no. 5 (Nov. 1884): 160.

140. [B. T. Roberts], "Commotion," *EC* 61, no. 3 (Mar. 1891): 93.

into the church who can help pay its expenses, and render possible greater and more striking exhibitions of pride are already sufficiently common."[141]

For preachers who claimed not to be revivalists, Roberts had a word of advice: "Become one. You can if you will," if sufficiently consecrated to God and his work. "The baptism of the Holy Ghost would make you a revivalist."[142]

These views on holiness, revival, and reform give a certain prophetic edge to all that Roberts published. He was constantly trying to push the meaning of holiness into life in the public sphere.

The nature of the reforming radicalism of Roberts's mature years is best seen in his most significant explicitly political involvement — the remarkable story of his key role in forming the Farmers' Alliance and thus helping shape the Populist movement, "the largest democratic mass movement in American history."[143]

---

141. [B. T. Roberts], "Revivals," *EC* 60, no. 6 (Dec. 1890): 189. Roberts here gives a litany of the reforms he saw as particularly urgent: ending class distinctions in the church, making the poor welcome by having free seats; driving out secret societies; overthrowing "the liquor power" and abolishing saloons.

142. [B. T. Roberts], "A Revival," p. 160.

143. Lawrence Goodwyn, *The Populist Moment: A Short History of the Agrarian Revolt in America* (New York: Oxford University Press, 1978), p. vii.

CHAPTER 35

Founding the Farmers' Alliance

"Pure religion does not consist in withdrawing from the world, but in keeping one's self unspotted from the world."

B. T. Roberts, 1883[1]

"We should take God's part in the great moral warfare being carried on in the world. We should array ourselves on God's side in every controversy that is carried on between righteousness and iniquity."

B. T. Roberts, 1884[2]

In March 1877 a brief notice appeared in the *Yates County Chronicle* of Penn Yan, New York, and in other newspapers around the state. Headed "State Convention of Farmers," it read:

In a country where laws are made and administered, often according to popular clamor, men of one class, if united, may exert a much more powerful influence than men of a much larger class, if acting in their individual character. Seeing this, all the great interests of the State, except the farming interest, have become thoroughly organized. As a result there is manifest a strong tendency, by our Legislature, to enact laws operating unjustly against farmers. Several such laws are now in force, and others still more unfair are proposed.

We therefore call a convention of the farmers of this State, to meet at Rochester, on Wednesday, March 21st, at ten o'clock in the forenoon, to effect a perma-

<hr />

1. B. T. Roberts, "Singularity," *EC* 45, no. 4 (Apr. 1883): 103.
2. B. T. Roberts, "Abound in Love," *EC* 47, no. 1 (Jan. 1884): 7.

nent organization of the farmers of this State and such other business as the occasion may demand. Special invitation is extended to Grangers and Farmers' Club.[3]

The call was signed by officers of the Western New York and Elmira Farmers' Clubs and the presidents of the New York State and Western New York Agricultural Societies. Few of the thousands of farmers and others who saw it knew that the call was actually written by Free Methodist leader and part-time farmer B. T. Roberts — though a reader of the *Earnest Christian* might have recognized the style.

Here begins a little-known chapter in the Roberts saga: his strategic role in founding the Farmers' Alliance and thus contributing to the rise of the American Populist movement.

Today Populism is often associated with Senator William Jennings Bryan and his failed 1896 presidential bid as the candidate of the Democratic Party (when Republican William McKinley was elected). By then, however, Populism as an active, potent reform movement had already waned. The real story comes earlier. The creative, dynamic, effervescent stage of Populism occurred in the 1870s and 1880s, and the movement started mainly as a farmers movement.

In the decade after the 1877 call, a nationwide farmers movement arose. Kansas farmer and reformer (and later U.S. senator) William Peffer wrote in 1889, "There is a feeling of unrest among the farmers of this country, and they are forming local, county, State, and national associations . . . to improve their condition." Peffer estimated that at least 1 million of the nation's 4.5 million farmers were already thus organized. The movement was still growing, with the prospect of "a general union" of the vast majority of the nation's farmers within a year. Here was "the greatest revolution ever peacefully inaugurated."[4]

Published in *Forum,* a leading general opinion magazine of the time, Peffer's article alerted the nation to the birth of a new political force many urban Americans had never heard of — the Farmers' Alliance movement. The key issue behind the movement, Peffer said, was the growing "influence and power of railroads and banks — one controlling the transportation of the country, the other controlling its money."[5]

The remarkable story of the Farmers' Alliance reaches from Rochester, New York, to Texas and Chicago, and finally to the national elections of 1892 and 1896. And at the beginning, B. T. Roberts played a key role.

As Peffer noted, the new agrarian movement was born in the struggle of farmers against the railroads. Here Roberts had a unique vantage point: he was both a frequent railroad patron and a farmer of sorts. Unlike most farmers, Roberts crisscrossed the country for decades. He knew railroads and the railway business firsthand and also witnessed the varying economic and agricultural conditions

---

3. "State Convention of Farmers," *Yates County Chronicle,* Mar. 15, 1877, p. 2. The original has "Club," but clearly "Clubs" was intended.

4. W. A. Peffer, "The Farmers' Defensive Movement," *Forum* 8 (Dec. 1889): 464, 468.

5. Peffer, "The Farmers' Defensive Movement," pp. 464-65.

throughout the nation. And yet, unlike most railway passengers, Roberts was ever a farmer at heart and was interested in agriculture and farmers' issues on the ground.

Perhaps for these reasons — and certainly as an extension of his concern with righteousness and justice — Roberts early concluded that farmers must engage in political action to protect themselves from growing railroad power. He proposed political action to control the railroads at a time when this idea was novel — not to say radical and abhorrent. As the Farmers' Alliance and then the Populist movement grew, other issues came and went. But the enduring concern was regulation of the railroads, with national monetary policy usually lurking as a related issue.

Farmers' Issues in the 1870s

Like his father before him, B. T. Roberts was a farmer at heart. He liked turning and tilling the soil, whether the loam of upstate New York or the harvest fields of the Lord. Whether writing, traveling, or teaching, his heart was never far from the soil. When "on the cars" he often remarked about the nature of the land or the state of the farms he passed through. In 1889 he noted, "My duties as a minister of the Gospel call me from New York to California — from Minnesota to Louisiana. I mingle freely with the farmers. In all sections I hear the same complaint, — that they can, [only] with difficulty, meet their expenses."[6]

Roberts's initiatives in behalf of farmers in the 1870s are therefore understandable. Farmers' issues brought together several of his passions and gifts: agriculture, justice for the oppressed, strategic activism, and trust in God's guidance and power.

Roberts was most involved in farmers' issues in the 1870s, when agricultural problems became acute in New York and when he himself was overseeing the Chili Seminary farm (as he did until his death), in addition to other duties. But Benjamin was always interested in agricultural matters. In the December 1862 *Earnest Christian* he mentioned the *American Agriculturist* (which had once been edited by Ellen Roberts's cousin Harvey Lane) and commented, "We have long received the *American Agriculturist,* and can testify to its real merits."[7]

For Roberts, the situation facing New York farmers as the railroads grew in power and influence was an issue of basic justice. Roberts possessed uncommonly sharp antennae for all forms of injustice. Several factors in his own life, as well as his faith, his understanding of God, and his reading of Scripture, predisposed him toward this passion. His frontier upbringing in western New York, his early involvement with abolitionism, and his treatment at the hands of the ME Genesee Conference honed his concern with justice and fairness. In his view, injustice was an affront

6. [B. T. Roberts], "Protection of Farmers," *FM* 22, no. 3 (Jan. 16, 1889): 8.

7. [B. T. Roberts], "Literary Notices," *EC* 4, no. 6 (Dec. 1862): 188; cf. Carl F. Price, *Wesleyan's First Century with an Account of the Centennial Celebration* (Middletown, Conn.: Wesleyan University, 1932), p. 64.

to the character of God, the specific teachings of Jesus Christ, and the liberty given us by the Holy Spirit.

Justice therefore lay at the heart of Roberts's activism in behalf of farmers in the 1870s. Though his immediate focus was New York, he knew the issue was a national one and would need to be addressed nationally.

Roberts's location in western New York was a key factor. Its nice variation of soils and climate allowed New York by the mid-1800s to have a rich and diverse agricultural economy. Proximity to mushrooming New York City made upstate and western New York the breadbasket of Manhattan. New York farmers were given a boost also by the Erie Canal, which enabled relatively cheap transport of goods to market, and then by the railroads. New York deserved the nickname "Empire State" for its agriculture as well as its trade and industry. In 1870 New York led the nation in number of farms and value of farm property. It counted a farm population of over one million, almost a quarter of all residents. Farmers were the largest single occupational group.[8]

New York farmers' fortunes boomed during the Civil War and for a while afterward but then declined due to financial conditions and growing competition from the Midwest. "A span of time several years before and after 1865 constituted the real golden age of New York agriculture," financially speaking; "forty-cent butter and two-dollar wheat built the garishly ornate houses that still dot the countryside," notes Lee Benson. But then "economic difficulties set in at an accelerating rate." Though several factors accounted for the problems, the key one was the growth of the railroads.[9]

New York's advantages turned into disadvantages. The railroad boom boomeranged as rails stretched west into Illinois, Iowa, and Nebraska — rich, flat farming lands more conducive to intensive farming than was New York. The railroads discovered they could increase profits by offering low through rates to Midwestern farmers while keeping New York rates high. Farmers in Iowa could send a ton of grain to New York City cheaper than could wheat farmers in the Rochester area, for example. "Illinois agricultural products were shipped from Chicago to the seaboard as cheaply, or more cheaply, than those grown 700 or 800 miles closer to market."[10] Farmers in the Midwest soon had their own complaints, however, as growing railroad power allowed the railroads to dictate rates and conditions. These were the issues Roberts read about in the papers and heard discussed in meetings of the Western New York Farmers' Club in Rochester.

---

8. Lee Benson, *Merchants, Farmers, and Railroads: Railroad Regulation and New York Politics, 1850-1887* (Cambridge: Harvard University Press, 1955), p. 81. Benson is the most important single source on the Farmers' Alliance in New York. Though he does not specifically mention B. T. Roberts, he in fact quotes him, probably unknowingly.

9. Benson, *Merchants, Farmers, and Railroads*, pp. 81-83.

10. Benson, *Merchants, Farmers, and Railroads*, p. 82.

The Granger Response

The Grange movement of the 1860s and early 1870s was the early response to the railroad issue. The focus of the movement is clear from an early account, published in 1873: *History of the Grange Movement; or, The Farmer's War Against Monopolies: Being a Full and Authentic Account of the Struggles of the American Farmers Against the Extortions of the Railroad Companies.*[11] (The word "grange" means a farm with its various buildings and is related to the words "grain" and "granary.")

The National Grange (officially, the Patrons of Husbandry, which still exists) was founded in Washington, D.C., in 1867 to protect the interests of farmers. After a slow start, "the new order swept over the states of the Northwest like a prairie fire," wrote Solon Buck in a classic study.[12] The movement mushroomed to 850,000 members in 21,000 local granges by 1875, and in some places succeeded in passing state laws limiting the rates railroads could charge for farm products. Edward Martin in 1873 spoke of the Grange's "rapid and unprecedented growth," particularly in the Midwest, and noted that "it is now increasing rapidly in the Middle, Eastern, and Southern States. It has become in all respects a national movement."[13]

The first "regular, active, and permanent grange" chartered by the national organization was not in the Midwest, however, but surprisingly in Fredonia, Chautauqua County, New York, only about a dozen miles from Roberts's birthplace. It was organized in 1868 or 1869.[14]

The Grange was structured as a fraternal order. Oliver Kelley, founder of the Patrons of Husbandry, was himself a Mason and felt that a national fraternal order of farmers was the best way to defend farmers' rights. He and some friends developed a secret ritual, complete with signs and passwords. Unlike the Masons, however, the Patrons of Husbandry admitted women to full membership. Joining a local grange, a farmer passed through the degrees of Laborer, Cultivator, Harvester, and Husbandman, and his wife from Maid to Shepherdess, Gleaner, and then Matron. Above these degrees, which were local, three higher degrees were awarded by the state and national organizations.[15]

Although the Grange grew quickly, it also declined rapidly in social and political influence. Yet it was the first phase of the "agrarian crusade" that gave rise to the Populist movement. Buck noted that the Grange "reached its highwater mark in 1874" with over 20,000 local granges, but dropped to about 4,000 locals in

11. Edward Winslow Martin, *History of the Grange Movement; or, The Farmer's War Against Monopolies: . . . with a History of the Rise and Progress of the Order of Patrons of Husbandry . . .* (Philadelphia: National Publishing Co., 1873).

12. Solon Justus Buck, *The Granger Movement: A Study of Agricultural Organization and Its Political, Economic, and Social Manifestations, 1870-1880* (Lincoln: University of Nebraska Press, 1969; originally 1913), p. 45.

13. Martin, *History*, p. 415.

14. Buck, *The Granger Movement*, pp. 45, 49.

15. Buck, *The Granger Movement*, pp. 40-43.

1880.[16] Many Grangers and former Grange members were in the front ranks of the Farmers' Alliance when it formed a few years later.

The Railroad Issue

As B. T. Roberts could see, railroads had quickly become America's first really big business. Farming had been the nation's largest business, but unlike the railroads, farming was highly dispersed and not centrally organized. As the railroads grew and expanded, they rapidly accumulated capital in Eastern centers, while scattered farmers struggled to find enough ready cash to farm profitably.[17]

Railroads amassed enormous economic power and political clout. Until the passage of the federal Interstate Commerce Act in 1887, they were largely unregulated. They were especially influential in New York because of the growing commercial importance and wealth of New York City as America's gateway and business and financial capital, and because many railroad companies were based there.

New York's railroads enjoyed a friendly political environment. In 1850 the state enacted railroad legislation that Lee Benson calls "perhaps the most sweeping legislative endorsement of *laissez faire* [capitalism] in American history." Quickly other states "paid the ultimate flattery to New York doctrines of political economy [and] . . . faith in the wonder-working qualities of the 'natural law of trade'" by copying its free railroad law.[18] The story of the railroads in New York, and of farmers' attempts to bring them to accountability, thus had national implications.

Eastern farmers faced a crisis. "Two major [rail]roads ran through the Empire State and the Erie Canal was a third strong competitor for western freight," Benson notes. Settlement of the fertile Midwest "deprived New York of the comparative productive advantages it possessed when the Genesee Valley had been 'the granary of the country.'" The Civil War brought temporary relief, but the railroad "rate wars of the seventies . . . produced an almost unprecedented situation, for geographic location no longer assured economic advantage."[19]

The postwar period was thus a particularly critical time for the railroads in relation to the larger society. As historian James Ely notes, "The 1870s witnessed the beginning of a sea change in popular opinion regarding the railroads. Calls for more stringent regulation mounted, eclipsing the earlier policy of encouragement and subsidization."[20] Public opinion was shaped by frequent train accidents and by much-publicized struggles for control of particular lines. Ely notes, "The classic bat-

---

16. Solon J. Buck, *The Agrarian Crusade: A Chronicle of the Farmer in Politics* (New Haven: Yale University Press, 1920), p. 60.

17. "As the nation's first big business, railroads were the most visible symbol of the new industrial order." James W. Ely, Jr., *Railroads and American Law* (Lawrence: University Press of Kansas, 2001), p. 84.

18. Benson, *Merchants, Farmers, and Railroads*, p. vii.

19. Benson, *Merchants, Farmers, and Railroads*, p. 80.

20. Ely, *Railroads and American Law*, p. 80.

tle between [Methodist] Daniel Drew and Cornelius Vanderbilt in 1868 for control of the Erie Railroad was marked by pervasive chicanery. Railroad officers amassed personal fortunes, often through shady business practices."[21]

New York farmers complained they were being manipulated by the railroads and punished by discriminatory rates. Frederick P. Root, a prominent Brockport farmer and acquaintance of B. T. Roberts who owned about 800 acres of good farmland, testified before New York's Hepburn Committee investigation around 1879, "[W]hat we complain of is not the competition of the west, but . . . of unequal rates." Root charged, "we pay for the advantages which the west enjoys; . . . a burden . . . amounting to about six millions a year, over and above what we should be charged."[22] A writer in the *Husbandman* of Elmira (unofficial organ of the New York Grange) protested in 1877, "Our people will not submit to extortions and the general destruction of their business simply to gratify railroads in their freedom to carry freights a long distance at a loss and to make up the deficiency out of their patrons who happen to live along their lines."[23]

New York City's merchants also began to complain about the dominance of railroad power. But it was farmers who first and most painfully felt oppressed. A major contest was brewing between the railroads — concentrated in the East but reaching ever farther west — and farmers scattered across the country. As Solon Buck put it, "The farmers had votes; the railroads had money; and the legislators [in various states] were sometimes between the devil and the deep sea in the fear of offending one side or the other."[24]

Complaints about discriminatory rates are understandable, but farmers and merchants may not have fully understood the economics involved. Differences in rates, and specifically the long haul–short haul differential, did not necessarily mean discrimination, the railroads said. Ely puts the matter in perspective:

In fact, there was often a compelling economic justification for long haul–short haul rate differences. Distance was not the determining factor in setting rates. Railroads insisted that competition, not discrimination, was responsible for holding down the cost of long-distance transportation. Moreover, the operating expenses of carrying local freight were proportionally higher than those for long hauls. Short-haul freight was commonly in small quantities, and there was frequently no return traffic, adding to the cost of servicing rural communities.

But economic arguments did not avail in the political arena. It became an idée fixe that long haul–short haul rate differentials were a type of discrimination against merchants and farmers at noncompetitive points.[25]

---

21. Ely, *Railroads and American Law,* pp. 83-84.

22. Frederick P. Root, Hepburn Committee *Proceedings,* 1:1987-88, quoted in Benson, *Merchants, Farmers, and Railroads,* p. 80; cf. p. 95.

23. *Husbandman* 4, no. 117 (Nov. 28, 1877): 4.

24. Buck, *The Agrarian Crusade,* p. 52.

25. Ely, *Railroads and American Law,* p. 82.

Ely points out as well that "merchants and farmers had their own economic agenda, and were quick to invoke the 'public interest' as a cloak." Yet he acknowledges that "rail critics voiced legitimate concerns. Many of the charges flung at the railroads were overstated but not entirely untrue. By the late nineteenth century railroads exercised vast and unchecked power over the economic life of communities along their lines. A deep sense of vulnerability animated allegations of railroad favoritism and demands for some degree of public control."[26]

It was in this context that B. T. Roberts got involved in the farmers-versus-railroads issue.

Roberts's Role in the Farmers' Alliance

The Patrons of Husbandry struggled against the monopolistic growth of the railroads with only mixed results. Farmers' Alliances, however, mounted a more focused and explicitly political campaign.

The story of the rise of the Farmers' Alliance movement is complex. As early as 1891 the first historian of the Farmers' Alliance, Nelson Dunning, wrote, "The origin of the Farmers' Alliance is not so clearly defined as to leave no room for conjecture."[27] Dunning, an editor for the *National Economist*, the National Farmers' Alliance paper, thus signaled the vexing and still disputed question as to just when and where the Farmers' Alliance began.

Many new farmers organizations sprang up across the land in the 1870s, and some took the name Farmers' Alliance. Most of these alliances coalesced into a nationwide Farmers' Alliance movement in the 1880s. Together with other groups, the Farmers' Alliance then birthed the People's (or Populist) Party in 1891. The movement was highly complex and dispersed — which was to be expected if it was truly "populist." Yet the main outlines are clear and well documented.

The New York State Farmers' Alliance played a leading role in the rise of the national movement — a key fact in understanding Roberts's role. Lee Benson concluded in his careful study of railroad regulation in New York, that the Farmers' Alliance "was born in New York and spread out from that state" to the rest of the nation.[28] Key contemporary sources reveal that Roberts played a much more strategic and catalytic role in the rise of the New York Farmers' Alliance than is reported either in the literature on Populism or in prior biographies of Roberts.[29]

---

26. Ely, *Railroads and American Law*, p. 83.

27. N. A. Dunning, ed., *The Farmers' Alliance History and Agricultural Digest* (Washington, D.C.: Alliance Publishing Co., 1891), p. 12; see Peter H. Argersinger, *Populism and Politics: William Alfred Peffer and the People's Party* (Lexington: University Press of Kentucky, 1974), pp. 316-17.

28. Benson, *Merchants, Farmers, and Railroads*, p. 87.

29. In their biographies, Clarence Zahniser and Benson Roberts give only passing, and therefore misleading, attention to Roberts's involvement with the Farmers' Alliance (Zahniser, pp. 256-57; BHR, BTR, p. 529). Benson Roberts, obviously misinformed about the Patrons of Husbandry, says the

Through the *Earnest Christian* and through his travels as Free Methodist general superintendent, Roberts became increasingly well known to the broader public. In the Rochester area, however, he was perhaps best known for his connection with Chili Seminary and his agricultural interests. Zahniser notes his farming background and points out that for many years and until his death Roberts "had charge of the management of the Seminary farm."[30] Benjamin was often directly involved in the farmwork himself. He noted on January 29, 1874, "In the morning we husked corn with the horse power. In the afternoon with the windmill."[31]

Benjamin was in a position to know the economics of farming intimately.

In 1872 he was invited to deliver the annual address at the gathering of the Western New York Agricultural Society during the regional fair at Rochester. The address was given at 2:00 P.M. on Thursday, September 26, "before a large audience."[32] This was one of many events scheduled that day; some 25,000 people flocked to the fair. "Visitors were present from all sections of the country," the *Rochester Evening Express* reported. "The southern counties were largely represented."[33] Though the reporter for the *Rochester Daily Union and Advertiser* felt Roberts's address had "not much in it to admire," it made an impression on some of the hearers.[34]

Roberts headlined his talk "Conspiracies Against Farmers." Soon afterward he issued the address as a pamphlet. No copies seem to have survived; however, Roberts gave a concise summary of the address in the November 1872 *Earnest Christian* in an advertisement for the pamphlet. Roberts outlined "the obstacles which lie in the way of the prosperity of farmers, and hence of the whole country" — particularly "the

---

Farmers' Alliance idea "took root and afterward developed in the formation of the Grange," whereas the Grange was in fact founded before the Farmers' Alliance. Zahniser says erroneously that the Farmers' Alliance "was first organized in Chicago in 1870." Zahniser's source was an editorial by (apparently) B. R. Jones in the Apr. 8, 1891, *Free Methodist* entitled "Farmers' Secret Societies" that was based in turn on an article in the *Christian Cynosure*. This editorial incorrectly says the Farmers' Alliance "was organized in Chicago in 1870"; the correct date for the Chicago organization is 1880, as noted below. (Thus Marston [p. 392], dependent on Zahniser and Benson Roberts, is also incorrect in saying the Chicago organization of the Farmers' Alliance came "two years earlier" than Roberts's organizing activity in New York.)

The *Free Methodist* editorial cited above condemns all farmers organizations pledged to secrecy and says generally of the Farmers' Alliance, "The element of secrecy in this organization is sufficiently prominent to warrant every Christian farmer in keeping aloof from it" — though the editorial notes correctly that the branch of the alliance organized in Chicago "purposely avoided the secret society features which made the grange odious, and was established as an open, free, American society." "Farmers' Secret Societies," *FM* 25, no. 14 (Apr. 8, 1891): 8.

30. Zahniser, p. 256.

31. BTRD, Jan. 29, 1874. He noted a couple of weeks earlier, "To day we finished in the snow drawing in our corn. The work has dragged terribly on the farm this year" due (he implies) to inadequate help. He noted the next day that "Bro. Stearns and Martin came" and offered "to work the farm" for Roberts. BTRD, Jan. 14 and 15, 1874.

32. *Rochester Daily Union and Advertiser* 47, no. 229 (Sept. 27, 1872): 2.

33. "The Western New York Fair," *Rochester Evening Express*, Sept. 27, 1872, p. 1.

34. *Rochester Daily Union and Advertiser* 47, no. 229 (Sept. 27, 1872): 2.

detrimental working of the various combinations and rings by which most all the business of the country, except farming, is controlled." Key problems included "grants to railroads — the bonding system, and the system of National Banks." He argued that "the remedy for these evils, under which the country groans," was within the farmers' reach. His proposed solution was the formation of a politically effective farmers organization — an alliance of farmers.[35]

Roberts sold copies of *Conspiracies Against Farmers* through the *Earnest Christian* at twenty cents each or 100 for ten dollars. According to Zahniser, the pamphlet was "printed by request and attracted wide notice."[36] It was still being advertised in the *Earnest Christian* into the 1890s.

Behind this proposal for a new, more activist farmers organization was Roberts's dissatisfaction with the Patrons of Husbandry. Roberts had three complaints against the Grange: it was a secret society; it was not specifically focused on political action; and it was not sufficiently broad-based to have political clout. A broader alliance of farmers and farm organizations was needed.[37]

In early 1874 Benjamin sent a letter to the *New York Times* about bond financing for railroad construction. The 900-word letter was published on page 2 of the January 29 edition under the title "Town Bonds for Railroads" and was signed "A Farmer."[38]

Here Roberts is concerned with the disparity of power between large railroads and comparatively small towns (that is, townships) and the injustice of a new state law that permitted company agents to bond a whole town for the financing of railroad construction if they could get a majority of landowners to agree. Roberts saw this as unjust and undemocratic on several counts. He wrote, "Shall we adopt the principle that one portion of the inhabitants of a town or city may compel the other portion to take stock in any business enterprise which the majority may at the time pledge to be of public benefit? Railroads are not built for the benefit of the public. They are built and run to make money for those who control them, just as really as a farm is worked to make a living. The benefit which the public desires is purely incidental. For every service the railroad renders us we are required to pay a full equivalent."

Roberts thought the railroads were often underhanded in securing the bonds. He noted that "the towns do not even vote upon the question at all." Rather, paid

---

35. [B. T. Roberts], "Conspiracies Against Farmers," *EC* 25, no. 5 (Nov. 1872): 163. Cf. Zahniser, p. 256. Zahniser, Benson Roberts, and Marston give the title of the address as "A Conspiracy Against Farmers," but B. T. was probably intentional in using the plural form, as he was speaking of multiple conspiracies.

36. Zahniser, p. 256.

37. Compare this with Roberts's reservations about the effectiveness of the National Christian Association in 1884 (noted in the previous chapter).

38. Roberts noted on Jan. 22, 1874, "Wrote an article on New Bonding system and sent to the New York Times. It expresses my opinion on a legalized plan for robbing farmers." On Jan. 30 he wrote, "Saw in N.Y. Times of yesterday an article I wrote on Bonding towns for railroads." BTRD, Jan. 22 and 30, 1874.

agents "go through the town, visiting every farmer they think they can influence, and make such representations as will be most likely to secure his concurrence. They are lavish in their promises, and not at all scrupulous in the means they employ to obtain consent." Once a majority of property owners have signed, the town is bonded. Roberts noted that though women did not have the right to vote, they did have the right to sign such bonding issues; "even women to whom the ballot is denied may have a voice for the purpose of putting bonds upon us." In unusually strong language Roberts wrote, "I emphatically deny the right of any man or set of men to mortgage my farm in this way for the benefit of a grasping money-making, swindling corporation. These corporations well understand how to escape their part of the contract; how to cheat the towns out of the stock for which the bonds were issued. There is a far greater probability that they will do this than there is that the railroad will be built."[39]

This is partly what Roberts had in mind when he spoke of "conspiracies against farmers." The widespread fraud and manipulation in railroad financing during this period gave some point to Roberts's complaints.

Roberts had an opportunity to stump for farmers' concerns during a visit to St. Louis in early 1874. With C. H. Lovejoy, a Free Methodist leader in St. Louis, Roberts attended a meeting of the St. Louis Farmers' Club on Saturday, March 7. Invited to speak, Roberts "urged upon them the importance of a general organization throughout the country," he noted in his diary.[40] This speech, presumably brief, probably covered some of the same ground as his "Conspiracies Against Farmers" address. Possibly he also distributed copies of his pamphlet. It is noteworthy that he saw the need for a *national* organization, not just a local or regional one.

Roberts may not have known that the Patrons of Husbandry had held their seventh annual meeting in St. Louis just weeks earlier, February 4-12. Solon Buck described this convention as "the most representative gathering of farmers which had ever taken place in the United States" and the most important National Grange meeting of the decade. The convention adopted the important "Declaration of Purposes of the National Grange" that included a commitment "to labor for the good of our Order, our country, and mankind" and the widely quoted (ancient) motto, "In essentials, unity; in nonessentials, liberty; in all things, charity."[41]

It is unclear whether Roberts knew, also, that a so-called National Agricultural Congress was formed in St. Louis in 1872, uniting farmers organizations from several southern states. This organization proved ineffectual, however, being "too loosely organized to exert any considerable influence," noted Buck.[42] Roberts wanted to see a national organization that would be sufficiently broad-based and focused to be politically effective.

39. A Farmer [B. T. Roberts], "Town Bonds for Railroads," *New-York Times*, Jan. 29, 1874, p. 2 ("Letters from the People" section).
40. BTRD, Mar. 7, 1874.
41. Buck, *The Granger Movement*, pp. 63-64.
42. Buck, *The Granger Movement*, pp. 78-79.

Roberts continued to believe that some form of vital farmers alliance was needed and from time to time advocated this as opportunities arose. Meanwhile he may have been heartened to learn in October 1876 that the U.S. Supreme Court in considering several so-called Granger cases handed down key decisions that firmly established the right of states to regulate railroads.[43]

National economic conditions soured in the wake of the Panic of 1873 — a crisis brought on largely by scandals in railroad financing schemes. A long period of deflation (falling prices) began, lasting until 1896. For farmers, this was bad news. Many fell into deep debt as their crops brought little income. In February 1876 Roberts remarked in the *Earnest Christian* on the "stagnation of business all over the country" in all economic sectors. "A large proportion of the people are either unemployed or only partially employed."[44]

The depression of the 1870s quickly became "the most precipitant and widespread economic disaster since the birth of the republic," notes Dee Brown.[45] A writer in the *Husbandman* noted in March 1876 that "the general depression of the times is unusually severe, . . . trade is more stagnant, and finances more embarrassed than we are accustomed to witness."[46] Stressed farmers seeking relief began looking for ways to make their voices heard politically.

The New York Farmers' Alliance

In New York State, the most important and immediate response was the Farmers' Alliance, first organized locally in Rochester in March 1875 and then as a statewide organization in 1877. Both the local and the state organization grew out of discussions in the Western New York Farmers' Club — deliberations in which B. T. Roberts played a key role.

---

43. Buck, *The Agrarian Crusade*, p. 59. The issue of the legal accountability of the railroads was new; there had never before been such a concentration of economic power affecting such a vast geographic area, and it had not previously been legally established that state governments had any authority whatsoever over the railroads. Buck notes that these key Supreme Court decisions "established principles which even now are of vital concern to business and politics. . . . the Granger decisions have furnished the legal basis for state regulation of railroads down to the present day. They are the most significant achievements of the anti-monopoly movement of the seventies."

44. [B. T. Roberts], "Business Stagnation," *EC* 31, no. 2 (Feb. 1876): 64. Roberts identified three causes: overproduction, extravagance, and "Conspiracies to keep up prices. It is one of the natural laws of business that prices should be regulated by supply and demand. Interfere with this law, and confusion follows. All the great industries of the day, except the farmers, are combined to give fictitious values to their productions." As we will see, this economic view did not rule out government involvement to deal with such "conspiracies" on the part of businessmen.

45. Dee Brown, *Hear That Lonesome Whistle Blow: Railroads in the West* (New York: Touchstone, 1977), p. 217. In fact, the U.S. economic crisis was part of a worldwide recession, beginning in 1873.

46. Conrad Wilson, "The Farmers and the Rings," *Husbandman* 3, no. 81 (Mar. 22, 1876): 2.

Early Discussions

Upstate New York had a number of farmers clubs and organizations. These included the Western New York Agricultural Society, the Western New York Farmers' Club, and the Elmira Farmers' Club. Several weekly publications also served the large upstate farming community. One of these, the *American Rural Home,* began publication in Rochester in 1871 and regularly reported the meetings of the Western New York Farmers' Club, in addition to its other features. The paper was edited by Alphonso A. Hopkins of Rochester.

The Elmira Farmers' Club, in Chemung County, about one hundred miles southeast of Rochester, became especially influential. Its secretary, William A. Armstrong, edited the *Husbandman,* a widely circulated weekly, and also was secretary of the state Grange. The Elmira club was formed in 1869 by "prosperous businessmen-farmers in Chemung County," notes Benson, many of whom were Grangers. In 1874 some of its members founded the *Husbandman* as the Grange's unofficial organ. Since the paper reported in detail the Elmira Farmers' Club's wide-ranging and informative weekly discussions, the club soon gained a national reputation. The *New York Times* pronounced it "the best club of the kind in existence anywhere." "Letters came in from all over the union and it was a rare issue which contained no controversy," notes Benson. "Its widely scattered circulation and influential class of readers made the *Husbandman* a strategic carrier of ideas" nationally. Importantly, "the concepts, programs, and activities of the New York Grangers received wide publicity and the paper served as a 'carrier' of the New York emphasis on independent political action."[47] What farmers did in western New York could easily have national implications.

Roberts apparently was a member of the Western New York Farmers' Club and as time permitted participated in its meetings. On various occasions he raised the idea of a new organization of farmers. In late 1874 or early 1875 he went to see editor Hopkins to seek his opinion and to urge that the Western New York Farmers' Club issue a call for "a State Convention of farmers."[48]

Roberts promoted the idea of a new organization for farmers whenever he had the opportunity. He was unable to attend the Western New York Farmers' Club meeting in the Supervisors' Room at the Monroe County Court House in Rochester on Wednesday, February 17, 1875, but he sent word urging "his plan for a State Convention" and "sent in a few replies from farmers whom he had addressed upon the subject," noted the *American Rural Home.*[49]

47. Benson, *Merchants, Farmers, and Railroads,* pp. 92-93, 275. Benson cites the *New York Times* comment from the Aug. 9, 1876, issue.

48. At the Feb. 27, 1875, meeting of the Western New York Farmers' Club, Hopkins reported "that Elder Roberts [*sic*] came to him several weeks since to ask his opinion on the project. He thought favorably of such a call, and would like to hear it discussed. This country is great on conventions, and why should not farmers try their hand at it?" "Western New York Farmers' Club," *ARH* 5, no. 9 (Feb. 27, 1875): 1.

49. "Western New York Farmers' Club," *ARH* 5, no. 9 (Feb. 27, 1875): 1.

The farmers discussed Roberts's proposal at the beginning of the meeting. One farmer, Mr. Beckwith, said he thought farmers were generally agreed that it was time "to combine efforts, so that there may be union of action as well as union of interests." William J. Fowler, club secretary, said farmers certainly had "a right to demand . . . equal taxation." "Vanderbilt deducts his tax from the wages of the employes of the New York Central. Manufacturers add their taxes to the prices of their fabrics. Commercial men add their taxes to the prices of the goods they sell." Fowler hoped the proposed convention "would consider the policy of restoring the income tax, the most equitable way of assessing taxes yet devised." After further discussion the club voted to issue a call for a convention.[50]

As a result of this call, a Farmers' Alliance — apparently the first in the nation — was organized in Rochester in March of 1875.[51] Though Roberts's intent was a statewide alliance, this first attempt was essentially local. Root stated in 1890 that this "first organization embraced only Monroe county and [therefore] could be of no general benefit."[52] From the first, however, the intent was political; Root noted, "Its chief object was to effect legislation in the interest of the agriculturist, not by distinct party action, but through each political party to secure nominations and election of candidates pledged to support such just and equal laws as would bear on the interests of agriculture, also to secure equal representation of the farming class in the legislature of the State."[53] Root reported that in reply to his concerns that the proposed alliance "might interfere with the Grange work," Roberts said "it would not be so, for he only proposed to take up their cause where the Grange left it; that the Grange forbade all interference in politics, and this should be strictly political work, but not party."[54]

Roberts was intimately involved in beginning this initial 1875 alliance. Root noted that at the March 1875 meeting at the Rochester Court House, "a committee was appointed to consider and report name, constitution, and by-laws for a farmers' organization" consisting of "Rev. B. T. Roberts, Prof. A. A. Hopkins, F. P. Root,

---

50. "Western New York Farmers' Club," *ARH* 5, no. 9 (Feb. 27, 1875): 1.

51. F. P. Root, "Origin of the Farmers' Alliance," *Cultivator and Country Gentleman* 55, no. 1970 (Oct. 30, 1890): 1016; Root, quoted in Dunning, *Farmers' Alliance History*, pp. 230-31. In his *Cultivator and Country Gentleman* article Root says the call was issued in January and the alliance was organized "Early in February," but in his letter quoted in Dunning he says, "This organization was in February, or the first of March, 1875." As the *American Rural Home* verifies, the call was issued in late February and thus the organization was in March.

52. Root lists a slate of officers for the 1875 organization, with himself as president (Root, "Origin of the Farmers' Alliance").

53. Root, "Origin of the Farmers' Alliance." See Dunning, *Farmers' Alliance History*, pp. 230-31. Root's "Origin" article in the *Cultivator and Country Gentleman* does not mention Roberts, but in a follow-up letter from Root to Dunning, which Dunning quotes, Root reports receiving "a note from Rev. B. T. Roberts of North Chili" in which Roberts "claimed to be the originator of the Alliance; that he circulated the call for the first meeting, and that he framed the constitution and bylaws adopted" (Dunning, p. 230).

54. Root in Dunning, *Farmers' Alliance History*, pp. 230-31.

John R. Garretson, and Jesse Deney [i.e., Dewey]." Root reported that "after considerable discussion" the committee "reported the name of Farmers' Alliance, and constitution and by-laws, which were adopted by the meeting." According to the constitution adopted, Root said, "none but farmers were eligible; but all who were engaged in any branch of husbandry could become members, by the payment of an annual fee."[55]

Roberts continued to urge a truly statewide farmers organization, however, and his efforts finally bore fruit. Monroe County farmers quickly saw the limitations of an essentially local organization, Root said, and "within a short period we issued a call for a meeting for State organization at Rochester," and there "a State alliance was organized on the model of the county alliance."[56]

The New York State Farmers' Alliance originated, like the 1875 effort, in meetings of the Western New York Farmers' Club. On Wednesday morning, February 21, 1877, "a nearly perfect day," Roberts was among a large number of farmers who gathered for the regular club meeting. The members conducted their usual business. One farmer showed grapes he had preserved from the fall harvest and some Northern Spy apples. The secretary distributed packets of barley and oat seeds donated by the U.S. Department of Agriculture for experimental purposes.[57]

At an appropriate point in the meeting, Roberts brought up the question of a statewide farmers organization. The *American Rural Home* reported, "Mr. B. T. Roberts, of Chili, spoke in favor of calling a State Convention of farmers to organize to protect the rights and interests of farmers. All other industries are organized and act upon the Legislature to promote their interests, but farmers, although the largest and most important class, have no influence upon legislators, because they know there is no combination to enforce their wishes."[58]

This was in fact the heart of Roberts's argument, and it kicked off debate. One farmer (Henry Quinby, who had displayed his apples and grapes) said the Grange was already "a powerful organization" and could meet the need. Roberts countered that "the grangers are pledged not to do just what we wish to do — are pledged not to act politically." Others, including Alphonso Hopkins, supported Roberts's idea. One farmer said farmers needed such an organization to help "prevent unjust and unequal taxation." The *American Rural Home* reported, "Some favored county conventions, to send delegates to a State Convention, but Mr. Roberts favored appointing a State Convention, and then sending a call to all the Farmers' Clubs, Granges, &c." Roberts did not want the process to be any more complicated than it had to be.

Another farmer endorsed Roberts's proposal. "We need something more than

---

55. Root in Dunning, *Farmers' Alliance History*, p. 231.

56. Root, "Origin of the Farmers' Alliance." Similarly Root is quoted in Dunning as saying, "soon after a call was issued for a State meeting at Rochester, to organize a State Alliance" (Dunning, *Farmers' Alliance History*, p. 231).

57. "Western New York Farmers' Club," *ARH* 7, no. 9 (Mar. 3, 1877): 1.

58. "Western New York Farmers' Club," *ARH* 7, no. 9 (Mar. 3, 1877): 1. Note the similarity of this summary to the call that was later issued.

talking organizations," he said. "If a man could appear before the Legislature and say that he represented the organized farmers of the State, he would receive the greatest attention." The Grange is not sufficiently representative, he argued.

The merits of beginning with county alliances or an attempted statewide organization were debated back and forth. Hopkins thought it would be better to start at the county level. It would be difficult to rally a large number of farmers to a state convention, he said, and a small turnout for a state convention would look like failure and "be disastrous."

Roberts suggested that the Farmers' Club issue a call for a statewide convention and send it to all granges and farmers clubs. Quinby, however, moved that the chair appoint a committee to study the matter further. The motion carried, and five were selected, with Roberts as chair and including Hopkins and William Fowler. The club then went on to discuss tax issues and the best ways to use manure.[59]

Issuing the Call

The Farmers' Club took up Roberts's proposal at its next meeting two weeks later, on March 7. Though the weather was unpleasant, "an unusual number, including many strangers, assembled to listen to, and take part in the discussions," noted the *American Rural Home*.[60] Apparently the earlier discussion had sparked considerable interest.

Roberts was called upon to report. The committee had agreed on the need for a state convention, he said, and he read out a proposed call that in style and form was quintessential Roberts:

> In a country where laws are made and administered, often according to popular clamor, men of one class, if united, may exert a much more powerful influence than men of a much larger class, if acting in their individual character. Seeing this, all the great interests of the State, except the farming interests, have become thoroughly organized. As a result there is manifest a strong tendency, by our Legislature to enact laws operating unjustly against farmers. Several such laws are now in force, and others still more unfair are proposed.
>
> We therefore call a convention of the farmers of this State, to meet at Rochester, on Wednesday, March 21st, at ten o'clock in the forenoon, to effect a permanent organization of the farmers of this State to *protect* their interests, and to transact such other business as the occasion may demand. Special invitation is extended to grangers' and farmers' clubs. B. T. Roberts, A. A. Hopkins, C. C. Holton, Heman Glass and W. J. Fowler[,] committee.[61]

---

59. This account is summarized from "Western New York Farmers' Club," *ARH* 7, no. 9 (Mar. 3, 1877): 1.

60. "Western New York Farmers' Club," *ARH* 7, no. 11 (Mar. 17, 1877): 1.

61. "Western New York Farmers' Club," *ARH* 7, no. 11 (Mar. 17, 1877): 1.

The proposal was discussed at some length. Frederick Root of Brockport "endorsed heartily the sentiments of the report" and pointed to the good work done by the Patrons of Husbandry. But he doubted that a state convention would succeed. The *American Rural Home* summarized Root's position: "No question but that the interests of farmers are oppressed, and anything that promises relief would receive his concurrence, but he fears little will be accomplished."

What relation would the proposed organization have to the Grange? Some felt the Grange was the proper vehicle to represent the farmers; no new structure was needed. But others pointed out its liabilities, including the fact that it was a secret society. One farmer suggested that the new organization "would help those not united with the grangers." Heman Glass, a member of the committee, said the Grange had "done great good, especially in the West," but "does not accomplish all that this [proposed] movement may." The new organization would be "a working center whose business it shall be to look after farmers' interests in the Legislature." This would take money, but "There is more money and brains among farmers than in any other class." Mr. Lee of the village of Greece pointed to considerable "prejudice among many against the grange," and felt "the new movement [should be] tried."

Was there time to circulate a call for a meeting just two weeks off? Mr. Holton had already been in touch with William Armstrong of the influential Elmira Farmers' Club, and Armstrong said he would present the call and was sure the club members "would cordially respond." Root said he thought the Grange wouldn't oppose it.

When put to a vote, the call was adopted. A committee of seven, chaired by C. C. Holton and including Roberts and Root, was appointed "to obtain signatures to the call" and prepare for the convention.[62]

The *American Rural Home* endorsed the call in its March 17 issue. The purpose of the convention was "to secure an open organization of the farming class, for purposes of improvement and protection. . . . Such an organization is a vital necessity to farmers if they would enjoy all the rights and privileges possessed by other classes, and would wield an influence as strong, in manifold ways, as their numbers and intelligence should command." The editor noted that the convention "is not to be strictly of delegates from Farmers' Clubs and Granges, although these are specially urged and expected to send delegates." Every concerned farmer was invited.[63]

The call went out. Though time was short, the call managed to get into a number of newspapers. As noted above, it appeared in the March 15 *Yates County Chronicle* (Penn Yan, New York, about halfway between Rochester and Elmira) with the headline "State Convention of Farmers" and over the names of the president and secretary of the Western New York Farmers' Club; the secretary of the Elmira Farmers' Club, W. A. Armstrong; and the presidents of the New York State and the

---

62. "Western New York Farmers' Club," *ARH* 7, no. 11 (Mar. 17, 1877): 1.
63. "The Farmers' Convention," *ARH* 7, no. 11 (Mar. 17, 1877): 3.

Western New York Agricultural Societies.[64] The call was identical to that adopted at the March 7 Farmers' Club meeting (quoted above), except that the words "to *protect* their interests, and to transact" after the words "to effect a permanent organization of the farmers of this State" are omitted — perhaps inadvertently; the wording as published is a little awkward. Thus the call in the *Yates County Chronicle* gives the purpose of the convention as "to effect a permanent organization of the farmers of this State and such other business as the occasion may demand" rather than "to effect a permanent organization of the farmers of this State to *protect* their interests, and to transact such other business as the occasion may demand."[65]

The above account shows clearly that the formation of a new political movement of farmers, including its focus and rationale, was largely Roberts's idea and came at his initiative. The call reflects his style and was no doubt written by him, though perhaps revised some by the committee. The fact that the call as originally presented to the Farmers' Club apparently was not modified during debate testifies to its clarity and cogency.[66]

The Alliance Founded

What kind of response would a call given at such short notice receive from farmers statewide? According to the *American Rural Home,* it was very positive: "a large and enthusiastic gathering of farmers, representing Granges, Farmers' Clubs, &c., assembled in State Convention in the Court House" in Rochester at the time appointed.[67] The *Rochester Evening Express* reported, "The Court House was well filled by delegates and representatives from all parts of Western New York, and some from adjoining States."[68] The meeting was covered in some detail by these papers as well as by the *Rochester Daily Union and Advertiser* and the *Husbandman*. Even with "such insufficient notice," the *Husbandman* reported, "the large hall obtained for the meeting was closely packed by a body of very earnest farmers from many counties, including Monroe, Niagara, Erie, Wyoming, Genesee, Ontario, Yates, Orleans, St. Lawrence, Wayne, Chemung, Seneca and Tompkins."[69]

64. Roberts, of course, is not mentioned, since with the vote of the Western New York Farmers' Club on Mar. 7 the call became a document of the club itself.

65. "State Convention of Farmers," p. 2. The call (given in full at the beginning of this chapter) is reprinted in Benson, *Merchants, Farmers, and Railroads,* p. 97, quoting from this source. Since there is no mention of Roberts in Benson's book, the reader would not know of his role in preparing and issuing the call.

66. It is conceivable that the wording change noted above reflects someone's editorial work — someone may have felt that the words "to *protect* their interests" were better left out. But it seems more likely that it was an error made during the printing process.

67. "New York State Farmers' Alliance," *ARH* 7, no. 13 (Mar. 31, 1877): 1.

68. "Farmers in Convention," *Rochester Evening Express* 19, no. 68 (Mar. 21, 1877): 3.

69. "Convention of Farmers," *Husbandman* 3, no. 136 (Mar. 28, 1877): 4. Benson also gives an account of the convention (Benson, *Merchants, Farmers, and Railroads,* pp. 97-98).

The convention met in the large Supervisors' Room of the courthouse. C. C. Holton, chair of the preparations committee appointed by the Farmers' Club on March 7, called the meeting to order and nominated Heman Glass as temporary chairman. Following his election William Armstrong of the Elmira Farmers' Club and P. C. Reynolds, secretary of the Western New York Farmers' Club, were chosen as secretaries. Mr. Glass said he "regarded the call as of no ordinary importance," for he had "expected for years the moment when the farmers of New York would step forward." The *Rochester Daily Union and Advertiser* summarized his comments as follows: "The object of the meeting was to see if there was any way by which the farmers of New York could centralize. The question was should they organize in towns and counties, or use the societies now formed and bring them together under one head. It would be no easy task to bring the farmers to one mind."[70]

The convention proceeded to elect a committee to work out a specific proposal while the convention continued its discussions. A committee of twelve was elected, chaired by Alphonso Hopkins and including Roberts. The committee was broadly representative of western New York counties, including farmers from Chemung, Orleans, Genesee, Seneca, Erie, and Niagara Counties, and from Monroe County, where Rochester and North Chili were located.[71]

Roberts had received a letter from J. L. Cramer, a farmer in Saratoga Springs who was unable to attend the convention. Had the notice come earlier, Cramer said, he would have been there with "a delegation from this section." Roberts gave the letter to one of the secretaries, who read it out. The *American Rural Home* published it in full since it "furnished the key-note of much of the discussion" and apparently expressed Roberts's position as well. Mr. Cramer had written,

> [T]o secure success in this undertaking, the foremost thing . . . is to make the movement a *political one* — that is to say, let farmers all over the State *enfranchise themselves* from the shackles of partizanship, and cease to be either Republicans or Democrats — mere tools in the hands of wily and designing politicians, who have no sympathy with the farmer, and who use him merely to keep themselves in office. . . . Let us who represent the largest producing interest of the country . . . unite for self-protection, and henceforth vote for such candidates only, as shall receive the endorsement of conventions called by ourselves for this purpose. If none but practical farmers are permitted to take part in our councils, and a firm union is secured of those having a common cause and interest, we shall soon become so formidable a power, as not only to control legislation, but have the entire administration of public affairs in our own hands. . . . [T]here will be an uprising in support of justice and the right, that will completely revolutionize the entire country. Let our agricultural papers make the fact known all over the land, that through a system of most nefarious legislation made by, and in the interests of capital, the

---

70. "Farmers in Council," *Rochester Daily Union and Advertiser* 52, no. 68 (Mar. 21, 1877): 3.

71. The accounts in the *American Rural Home,* the *Evening Express,* and the *Daily Union and Advertiser* all give the composition of the committee.

great bulk of taxation is imposed upon farms and other real estate, while the bondholder and stockholder are almost wholly exempt from taxation.[72]

Cramer's letter stated succinctly the central ethos and argument of the coming Populist movement.

At this point in the convention the organizing committee went to another room to work out details while a series of speakers addressed the larger assembly. Victor E. Piolett, president of the Pennsylvania State Grange, who had come from Bradford County, "referred to the recent decision of the Supreme Court of the United States that States have the right to regulate railroad freights and fares. This is a triumph of the Grangers of the West," he noted.[73] He also was "surprised to find a large element among the farmers of Western New York so much opposed to secret societies, that they refused to unite with the 'Patrons of Husbandry.'"[74]

Another speaker was James Shepard of Wyoming County. Farmers had been too passive, he argued; they were too acquiescent to "political managers." "The truth is, we have hooks in our noses, and the lines are in the hands of politicians, who draw us at their will." Shepard complained of discriminatory railroad rates: "Certainly we can all see that there is no propriety in charging as much for carrying a bushel of grain from Buffalo to my house — thirty miles — as from Chicago to New York; yet that is done. The roads, no doubt, carry freight from Chicago to the sea-board at less than cost, and we are taxed on our traffic to make up the loss." Farmers must organize to fight back.[75]

The organizing committee reported late in the morning, recommending "a permanent organization" to be called the New York State Farmers' Alliance. The committee proposed a constitution and slate of officers. Probably the constitution was adapted from the 1875 organization. According to Roberts, it was in fact written by him, apparently with some help from his attorney son, George.[76] Root later reported, "A. A. Hopkins gave name to the organization, of which fact I have personal knowledge, having been a member of the committee with Mr. Hopkins that reported name and constitution for the association."[77] That may very well be; it is not clear that Roberts used this specific name prior to about 1875, though for some years he had advocated the idea. In any case, Roberts and Hopkins had been in dialogue about such an organization since at least early 1875, as noted above.

The convention began discussing the proposal and then recessed for lunch. When the meeting reconvened at 1:30, so many more farmers had come in that not

---

72. "New York State Farmers' Alliance," *ARH* 7, no. 13 (Mar. 31, 1877): 1.

73. "New York State Farmers' Alliance," *ARH* 7, no. 13 (Mar. 31, 1877): 1.

74. "Farmers' State Alliance," *Rochester Evening Express*, Mar. 22, 1877, p. 3.

75. "Convention of Farmers," *Husbandman* 3, no. 136 (Mar. 28, 1877): 4.

76. "Farmers' State Alliance," p. 3; Dunning, *Farmers' Alliance History*, p. 230; BTR to GLR, Mar. 11, 1880, quoted in Zahniser, p. 257. Root says, "The constitution adopted by the Monroe County Farmers' Alliance [in 1875] was also adopted by the State Alliance" (Dunning, p. 231).

77. Root, "Origin of the Farmers' Alliance."

all could find seats.[78] The *Rochester Evening Express* said the afternoon session was "more interesting and more largely attended" than the morning session, and printed a list of 163 delegates.[79]

The proposed constitution "was adopted after considerable discussion and some amendment. As finally approved, it read as follows:

Constitution of the New York State Farmers' Alliance

We, farmers of the State of New York, being convinced that an organization is necessary for the development and protection of our industrial interests, for the purpose of effecting said organization, do adopt the following constitution:

Article I. Section 1. This organization shall be known as the New York State Farmers' Alliance.

Sec. 2. Any delegate from any Grange, Agricultural Society, or Farmers' Club may be a member of this Alliance, on presentation of the proper credentials and the payment of one dollar, at any meeting of the Alliance; membership to continue one year or until his successor is chosen. Every Grange, Agricultural Society or Farmers' Club may send at least one delegate, or such number of delegates as shall not exceed three per cent. of its own membership.

Article II. Section 1. The officers of this Alliance shall consist of a President, a Vice-President from each judicial district of the State, a Secretary, a Treasurer, who shall be elected annually by ballot at the annual meeting, and an Executive Committee of three, who shall be elected, one for one year, one for two years and one for three years, and one thereafter annually, who shall serve three years.

Article III. Section 1. The annual meeting of this Alliance shall be held on the first Wednesday in September.

Sec. 2. Special meetings may be called by the President, with the concurrence of the Executive Committee, whenever deemed desirable.

Sec. 3. Each annual meeting shall determine the place where the succeeding meeting shall be held.

Article IV. Section 1. This constitution may be amended at any annual meeting of this Alliance, notice of said amendment having been given in writing at a previous meeting.[80]

The basis for membership prompted considerable discussion. As finally approved, the constitution restricted membership to delegates from existing farm organizations. Some present, apparently including Roberts, thought there should be provision for individual membership so as to be less restrictive and to provide opportunity for representation from areas where no agricultural organizations existed. But, noted the *Husbandman*, "the argument that the Alliance must be a representa-

---

78. "Convention of Farmers," *Husbandman* 3, no. 137 (Apr. 4, 1877): 4.

79. "Farmers' State Alliance," p. 3.

80. "New York State Farmers' Alliance," *ARH* 7, no. 13 (Mar. 31, 1877): 1. The constitution was printed also in the *Husbandman, Rochester Evening Express,* and *Rochester Union and Advertiser.*

tive body made up by delegates from existing organizations" prevailed. Roberts disagreed and gave notice that at the September meeting he would submit an amendment to change the article that defined membership.[81]

While a nominating committee worked up a slate of officers, Roberts, "Taking the favorable opportunity afforded by delay," introduced two resolutions dealing with monetary and economic policy.[82] These were in part his effort to shape the political philosophy and agenda of the new organization. His first resolution called for permitting only the federal government to issue paper currency.

> Resolved, That, as the right to coin money is a right belonging to the supreme government, if a substitute for that money is allowed[,] the government itself should furnish it and not allow rich corporations to do it for their benefit. The currency issued by the national banks rests for its value solely and exclusively upon the credit of the government. Therefore for the government to pay the national banks thirty millions of dollars interest simply for the privilege of holding their bonds, is in reality to take that amount of money from the people of the country to put into the pockets of the rich. Therefore we ask the national government to furnish a currency adequate to the wants of the country and to make it a legal tender for all dues to the government except for duties.[83]

This was a hot political issue. The so-called Greenback Party had been formed about a year and a half earlier with a platform similar to Roberts's resolution and had nominated the elderly New York businessman-philanthropist Peter Cooper for president of the United States. Republican Rutherford B. Hayes defeated Democrat Samuel Tilden in the November 1876 election, though in fact Tilden got almost 300,000 more votes. Cooper and the Greenback Party polled only about 1 percent of the vote, not enough to affect the outcome.[84] Roberts had some sympathy for the

---

81. "Convention of Farmers," *Husbandman* 3, no. 137 (Apr. 4, 1877): 4. Here, as always (including in the church), Roberts favored the broadest representation and participation possible, though within an agreed-upon covenant or contract. Benson notes that "apparently three considerations caused [the slightly more restrictive basis of membership that was finally approved] to prevail. First, as a delegated body the Alliance would not compete for members and funds with existing groups. Second, it would act as the 'mouthpiece' of all organized farmers within the state and thereby strengthen agricultural influence. Third, if the Alliance could achieve substantial victories it might stimulate unorganized farmers to join constituent societies." Eventually, however, "the Alliance was to suffer from its extremely loose form of organization" (*Merchants, Farmers, and Railroads*, p. 98).

82. "Convention of Farmers," *Husbandman* 3, no. 137 (Apr. 4, 1877): 4.

83. "Convention of Farmers," *Husbandman* 3, no. 137 (Apr. 4, 1877): 4; "New York State Farmers' Alliance," *Rochester Daily Union and Advertiser* 52, no. 69 (Mar. 22, 1877): 2; "Farmers' State Alliance," p. 3.

84. Joseph Nathan Kane, *Presidential Fact Book* (New York: Random House, 1999), pp. 121-22. Cooper received 81,737 votes to Hayes's 4,036,298 and Tilden's 4,300,590. The Prohibition Party candidate got only 9,522 votes. "The Greenbackers believed that the issuance of large amounts of paper money would bring prosperity, especially to the farmer, by raising prices and making debts easier to pay. Many farmers of the West and South joined the party, or promoted its policies in the Republican and Democratic parties." *World Book Encyclopedia*, G:374.

Greenback position, though it is significant that he did not call for the *abolition* of (private) national banks, as some did.

Roberts's resolution was more than the convention could deal with, and action was postponed until the first regular meeting of the Alliance in September. His second resolution, however, was adopted: "Resolved, That the theory that real estate should bear the burden of taxation is unsound. Real estate is unproductive until labor or personal property is added to it. Personal property requires the most protection, secures the largest returns and should bear its proper proportion of taxation."[85]

This also was a much-discussed issue. Farmers complained that in an age of rapidly expanding capital wealth it was unfair for farmland to bear an increasingly disproportionate tax burden, especially given the depressed economic conditions.

Eventually the nominating committee reported and the first officers of the New York State Farmers' Alliance were chosen. Frederick Root was elected president. The secretary was Prof. C. H. Dann and the treasurer was E. S. Hayward. Several vice presidents were also elected, as provided for in the constitution. B. T. Roberts was not one of the officers.[86]

Toward the end of the meeting Roberts moved "that a call be published requesting all the organized agricultural societies in the State to send delegations to the annual meeting of the Farmers' Alliance next September," and his motion was approved. Shortly thereafter the historic convention adjourned.[87]

In organizing the Farmers' Alliance the state's leading farmers were committing themselves to political action in a way they had never done before. The two main differences that set off the Farmers' Alliance from existing farmers organizations were, first, this specific political focus and, second, the broader-based "alliance" approach that sought to enlist farmers and farm organizations in sufficiently large numbers to be politically potent. Root later said, "The course as most approved . . . was to attend primary meetings of each political party [Democratic and Republican], to which they were severally connected, and to urge the nomination of such men as were favorable to our interests; and when each party could succeed in their aim, each would vote their own ticket; but if one failed and the other succeeded, all should turn in and elect the candidate who favored us; otherwise, if neither candidate favored our views, an independent candidate should be nominated."[88]

Thus the intent was to work through the existing political parties (and farmers' own party loyalties) rather than attempting to organize a new party.

Lee Benson helpfully sets this formation of the New York State Farmers' Alli-

---

85. "Convention of Farmers," *Husbandman* 3, no. 137 (Apr. 4, 1877): 4; "New York State Farmers' Alliance," *Rochester Daily Union and Advertiser* 52, no. 69 (Mar. 22, 1877): 2; "Farmers' State Alliance," p. 3.

86. "Convention of Farmers," *Husbandman* 3, no. 137 (Apr. 4, 1877): 4; "New York State Farmers' Alliance," *Rochester Daily Union and Advertiser* 52, no. 69 (Mar. 22, 1877): 2; "Farmers' State Alliance," p. 3.

87. "Farmers' State Alliance," p. 3.

88. Root in Dunning, *Farmers' Alliance History,* p. 231.

ance in context. Much of the "credit" for the rise of the Alliance goes to the presidents of the trunk-line railroads, he suggests. "Severe rate wars in 1875 had only been succeeded by the still more bitter conflicts of 1876 and early 1877. It was not at all accidental, therefore, that the Farmers' Alliance was born in the Rochester Court House, Monroe County, on March 21, 1877. The cattle and wheat growers of western New York, particularly susceptible to competition from the prairies, watched with growing anger as through rates fell and produce from the prairies rushed past their very farmsteads."[89]

Farmers were increasingly alarmed, as evidenced by the large and extensive turnout for the March 21 meeting in Rochester. Benson notes that

> farmers along the line of the New York Central had little doubt that the road was largely responsible for their troubles. Local rates to Rochester (and other points along the main route) were so exorbitant that . . . it cost more to ship [the same goods] from Rochester to New York than from Chicago to New York. The substantial landowners who created the Alliance were scarcely in danger of losing their property, but the large profits of former days had been reduced to the vanishing point if not to actual loss. Accordingly, land values had declined appreciably, and in this respect western New York was hard hit in the late seventies. Although the bulk of the prairie farmers suffered depression more acutely, it may be conjectured that, man for man, farmers in the Genesee Valley probably lost more money, considering their average scale of operations [because] capital investment in a typical New York farm was usually higher than in a typical prairie farm.[90]

With the March 1877 meeting, a statewide Farmers' Alliance had become a reality, just as Roberts had proposed. Turning it into an effective political force was another matter.

From New York to the National Farmers' Alliance

The route from the formation of the New York Alliance to the emergence of a national movement can be clearly traced through the documented activities of the Alliance during the critical formative years from 1877 to 1891.

September 1877 Meeting, Syracuse

As agreed at the Rochester convention, the first annual meeting of the New York Farmers' Alliance was held on Wednesday, September 5, 1877, in Syracuse. September

---

89. Benson, *Merchants, Farmers, and Railroads*, p. 94. Benson perhaps did not know about the earlier 1875 Monroe County Farmers' Alliance.

90. Benson, *Merchants, Farmers, and Railroads*, pp. 94-95.

had been chosen in order to facilitate maximum political influence within the cycle of the political parties, which generally held their nominating conventions in September.[91]

Farm prices had continued to drop over the summer. Accordingly "resentment against cheap western transportation and high taxes [had] increased," Benson notes, by the time of the September meeting. About 120 delegates from twenty-six New York counties attended, though Roberts was not present. The turnout apparently was lower than expected; the *American Rural Home* reported that the meeting, though "a success," was "not largely attended, owing to the fact, we think, that it occurred . . . in the busy season of sowing when farmers are specially occupied and find it difficult to leave home."[92]

Though Roberts was not present to argue for his proposed amendment to the constitution, an amendment offered by E. S. Hayward of Monroe County may have been the same as what Roberts intended. The change, passed unanimously, added the words "or any other association of agriculturists," so that the amended section 2 of article I read, "Any delegate from any Grange, Farmers' Club, or any other association of agriculturists, may become a member of this Alliance."[93]

Harris Lewis of Herkimer County was elected president for the ensuing year; the slate of officers elected in March had been viewed as temporary. Root said Lewis represented "the eastern portion of the State, [thus] making the interest of the alliance extend throughout the State."[94]

The convention adopted a number of resolutions, the gist of which was summarized later by Root: "The objects specially aimed at were (1) a reform in assessment and taxation; (2) equal railroad freights to shippers, . . . (3) the enactment of laws to authorize co-operative farm insurance, together with other reforms in legislation, and to favor equal representation in the law-making power of the State."[95]

The convention issued an address "To the Real Estate Owners of New York" that analyzed the issue of taxation. It noted that "The farmers of New York do not intend always to be heavily assessed upon their freights to pay the deficiencies from ruinous rates on freights 500 to 1,000 miles further west. They are content that railroads should receive a reasonable compensation for the services performed, but they do not intend to make up deficiencies for reckless competition elsewhere."[96]

All this required direct political action, as the farmers well understood. One resolution spelled out the strategy. On returning home, Alliance members were "to or-

91. "Convention of Farmers," *Husbandman* 3, no. 137 (Apr. 4, 1877): 4.

92. Benson, *Merchants, Farmers, and Railroads*, pp. 98-99. See "Farmers' Alliance," *Husbandman* 3, no. 160 (Sept. 12, 1877): 4; "New York State Farmers' Alliance," *ARH* 7, no. 36 (Sept. 15, 1877): 294.

93. "New York State Farmers' Alliance," *ARH* 7, no. 36 (Sept. 15, 1877): 294. Hayward may have served as Roberts's proxy in presenting the amendment that Roberts had given notice of at the March meeting.

94. "New York State Farmers' Alliance," *ARH* 7, no. 36 (Sept. 15, 1877): 294.

95. Root, "Origin of the Farmers' Alliance."

96. "New York State Farmers' Alliance," *ARH* 7, no. 36 (Sept. 15, 1877): 294.

ganize local associations or alliances . . . with a view to exerting their influence most effectively for securing reliable and fit representatives of their communities, as the nominees of their respective parties" and then "to put a series of questions to the several candidates, for the purpose of committing them upon the questions urged by the Alliance."[97] This was essentially what Roberts had been proposing. The Alliance hoped that a number of farmers would be elected to the state legislature. William Armstrong said that although farmers might be inexperienced in lawmaking, they could quickly learn. It would be "well to send farmers to the legislature, for a whole winter might be profitably spent in repealing laws" that were unfair to farmers, "and certainly farmers know enough to do this work; and in the one winter the farmers might learn from the politicians and lawyers enough to enable them to make laws."[98]

In an editorial, Armstrong noted that the convention did not allow itself to get sidetracked by secondary issues. He wrote, "The greenback issue, the remonetization of silver, the labor question and other matters which are agitating the political mind, were wholly ignored. Whatever opinions individuals might have held in regard to these questions, they clearly saw that the Alliance was not the place for presenting them."[99]

Had Roberts been present, he might not have agreed that these issues should be "wholly ignored," though he certainly was concerned for effective political action on issues of most immediate concern. Roberts, after all, though a farmer of sorts, wasn't *primarily* a farmer. He had a broader agenda since his advocacy of farmers' issues grew out of his theology and his understanding of Christian discipleship, as well as his larger national perspective.

December 1877 Special Meeting

The Farmers' Alliance Executive Committee felt the one-day September convention had been too short and perhaps too small. So it called a special meeting for December 20-21 at Syracuse. The state Dairymen's Association was to meet in Syracuse at that time, so many farmers would already be in town, and Harris Lewis was president of both organizations. The Alliance met from noon Thursday through Friday afternoon. About 150 delegates representing sixty local organizations in thirty counties participated.[100]

This time Roberts was able to attend. Though his name is not found in the list of delegates published in the *Husbandman*, the *American Rural Home* reports him taking part in discussions on Thursday evening and Friday morning. Probably he missed all or most of the Thursday afternoon session, arriving in time for the evening session.

97. "New York State Farmers' Alliance," *ARH* 7, no. 36 (Sept. 15, 1877): 294.

98. "The New York State Farmers' Alliance," *Husbandman* 3, no. 160 (Sept. 12, 1877): 4.

99. Editorial, "Farmers' Alliance," *Husbandman* 3, no. 160 (Sept. 12, 1877): 4.

100. Benson, *Merchants, Farmers, and Railroads*, p. 100; "State Farmers' Alliance," *ARH* 8, no. 1 (Jan. 5, 1878): 1-2; "Meeting of the New York State Farmers' Alliance," *Husbandman* 4, no. 176 (Jan. 2, 1878): 2.

In his opening remarks, President Lewis reviewed the purpose and prospects of the Alliance. In present political practice, "Farmers are not quite equal with other classes. The object of the Alliance is to have them become so," he said. In contrast, "Railroad companies are a 'privileged class.' Vanderbilt can, by the stroke of his pen, ruin or build up any commercial or manufacturing interest along the line of his railroad. This can be done and is done by discriminating freight rates."[101] The meeting covered much the same ground on issues and remedies as did the September meeting, probably because a number of new delegates were present who needed to be brought up to speed.

In the Thursday evening session J. G. Shepard of Genesee County read a paper entitled "Assessment and Taxation." Roberts entered the ensuing discussion, endorsing Shepard's paper and arguing that personal property alone should be taxed. Several speakers complained of the present tax structure, based largely on real estate, in which farmers were paying a disproportionate share. "We can't stand this burden of taxation much longer," one speaker said, noting that in Erie County real estate taxes accounted for 93 percent of the tax burden and personal property taxes only 7 percent.[102]

On Friday the convention appointed working committees on taxation, transportation, and insurance. Toward the end of the morning session Roberts "submitted resolutions on Finance, which were tabled without debate."[103] Presumably these were similar to the ones he had offered at the March meeting. The New Yorkers once again considered them peripheral to the business at hand.

Benson points out that the positions taken by the Farmers' Alliance were moderate and not especially radical. On the other hand, the Alliance was proposing "nothing less than to wrest control of the legislature from the omnipotent railroad lobby," though it was not yet sufficiently strong or well organized to accomplish that goal.[104]

The Money Issue

In hindsight, the Farmers' Alliance might have been more effective had it taken up the monetary issues Roberts raised. Benson explains, "As depression became really acute in 1878, hard-pressed farmers looked for relief to a more immediate, direct,

---

101. "Meeting of the New York State Farmers' Alliance," p. 2.

102. "State Farmers' Alliance," *ARH* 8, no. 1 (Jan. 5, 1878): 1. Despite Roberts's reported comment, he did not believe there should be no tax whatsoever on real estate. Rather his view was that "land should not bear the whole, nor even the principal burden of taxation" ([B. T. Roberts], "The Single Tax," *FM* 23, no. 37 [Sept. 10, 1890]: 8). Although Roberts does not directly deal with this question in *First Lessons on Money,* that book should be read in the context of this whole discussion.

103. "State Farmers' Alliance," *ARH* 8, no. 1 (Jan. 5, 1878): 1.

104. Benson, *Merchants, Farmers, and Railroads,* pp. 99, 101. "The aims [the alliance] avowed at the Syracuse meeting and persisted in thereafter can only be described as 'agrarian radicalism' by a most liberal stretch of the imagination" (p. 99).

and time-honored solution — inflation. Undoubtedly, the Alliance suffered from the fact that just as it was improving its organization, economic difficulties increased to the point where its program seemed a mere palliative." Many New Yorkers, including farmers, turned to the Greenback Party for answers. Benson documents a rapid increase in Greenback support from 1876, when Peter Cooper received only two thousand votes in the presidential contest, to 1878 when some Greenback congressional candidates received as high as eighty thousand votes. "In a number of agricultural counties the increase in Greenback strength was marked and the percentages were much above the state levels," Benson notes. "No Greenbackers were elected to Congress or to state offices but a surprising number of local contests were won in the Southern Tier."[105]

Return of moderate agricultural prosperity in New York eventually undercut the Greenback appeal. Benson notes, "As price indexes rose in the later months of 1879, cheap money sentiment suffered severe deflation. The depression rapidly lifted, and for reasons that obviously owed nothing to inflationary doctrines."[106] As to the role of the Farmers' Alliance, Benson observes, "The crude quantity theories of the Greenbackers may have been completely erroneous but at least they were directed to the major problem confronting farmers in the late seventies. Anything less than a rapid rise in commodity prices could have only slightly relieved growing agrarian difficulties by this time, and it should be noted that in respectable circles a good deal of support then existed for paper currency and bimetallic [silver as well as gold] solutions to the depression."[107]

The 1878 Greenback vote thus deflated some of the Farmers' Alliance's immediate appeal. "Greenbackism . . . limited the strength of the Alliance by supplying a competing doctrine and organization." The Alliance failed to gain a strong base in 1878 because it "did not offer [farmers] sufficient incentive to do so."[108] Though not a supporter of the Greenback Party, Roberts was concerned about the currency issue and felt reforms were called for, as noted above. Had the Farmers' Alliance made monetary issues a part of their platform, they might have had broader appeal.

Greenbackism came and went, however, and yet farmers' concerns and the issue of railroad regulation remained. And this meant a growing role for the Farmers' Alliance.

Influence of the New York State Farmers' Alliance

Not only upstate New York farmers but also New York City merchants were adversely affected by the growing clout of the railroads. This led for a time to a political

---

105. Benson, *Merchants, Farmers, and Railroads*, pp. 102-3.

106. Benson, *Merchants, Farmers, and Railroads*, p. 103. Nationally the depression was not over, but things had improved considerably, especially in New York.

107. Benson, *Merchants, Farmers, and Railroads*, p. 102.

108. Benson, *Merchants, Farmers, and Railroads*, p. 103.

marriage of convenience that increased Alliance influence. As early as 1876 A. B. Miller, a prominent New York City merchant and secretary of the Cheap Transportation Association, had written to William Armstrong proposing that the farmers and merchants work jointly against the railroads. Armstrong endorsed the idea in the pages of the *Husbandman*. Benson notes that "the close working relations developed in 1879 between Grange, Alliance, and commercial interests gave the farm groups far more strength and influence than they could have hoped to achieve unaided." As a result, the main political parties became more alert to farmers' issues and some reforms were passed, including in 1879 the legalizing of mutual fire insurance companies, one of the farmers' demands. A small property tax was levied on railroads and other corporations in 1880. Substantial railroad regulation was still some years off, but small steps toward reform had begun.[109] Roberts wrote to his son George on March 11, 1880: "Our Farmers' Alliance that you assisted me to organize has already become a formidable power in the politics of this State. Through their influence a Bill has been introduced into our Legislature requiring the railroads of the state to carry a car load of the same freight between the same places for the same price for all parties. It is making a great stir. The Railroads oppose it with all the influence they can control. But it will ultimately carry, if not this session, yet at a future one."[110] Although the pro rata bill ("the same freight between the same places for the same price for all parties") never did become law, other forms of railroad regulation were on the way.

Benson notes that the state Farmers' Alliance "probably reached its peak influence in 1880. Large and enthusiastic crowds turned out at numerous summer meetings and the Alliance creed was given publicity through other media." Due partly to exposés in the newspapers and the Hepburn Committee's investigations, "railroad control of the legislature was too blatant to be endured without protest." Politicians developed "greater respect for rural sensibilities."[111]

Roberts, of course, had other things to tend to, and apparently had little or no direct involvement with the Alliance once it had been well launched. But he had played a strategic role at a key time.

Though the New York Farmers' Alliance declined in influence after 1880, it was a key link in a larger chain of events. Benson summarizes:

Paradoxically, the Alliance virtually disappeared in 1881 because public sentiment on the transportation question advanced so rapidly. The methods employed by the railroads to block the regulatory measures that were recommended by the Hepburn Committee backfired and resulted in the establishment of the National

109. Benson, *Merchants, Farmers, and Railroads*, pp. 104-7.

110. BTR to GLR, Mar. 11, 1880, quoted in Zahniser, p. 257; note p. 256. This is the only source I have found for the information that George assisted his father in Farmers' Alliance matters. Since George was at the time in the legal side of the oil business in Bradford, Pa., presumably his help was legal advice rather than more direct involvement.

111. Benson, *Merchants, Farmers, and Railroads*, p. 108.

Anti-Monopoly League. . . . Leaders of the Alliance were prominent in the new organization, designed to unite not only farmers and merchants but the "entire people" against corporation supremacy. With the emergence of the League, the Alliance was superfluous and only existed nominally thereafter. Thus, the time span during which the Alliance may be said to have directly and sensibly influenced the thinking of New York farmers is confined to the brief period between the Greenback agitation of 1878 and the formation of the Anti-Monopoly League early in 1881. At best the program had only a limited mass appeal, winning its most enthusiastic acceptance among relatively large-scale landowners and farmers whose holding declined in value as a direct result of western competition. Yet in the long run it made a significant contribution toward arousing farmers to defend their interests. Through its activities the Grange was able to break down the strict taboos against independent political action and achieve a limited influence upon legislation.[112]

Nelson A. Dunning wrote in 1891 that the New York Farmers' Alliance "died almost, if not completely, . . . and is just at the present time being revived. It was never a secret organization, and did not reach a very high position either in effectiveness or utility; but it did, without doubt, lead to the formation of other and stronger organizations, and in this manner became the pioneer in the agricultural alliances of the North."[113]

The New York State Farmers' Alliance thus played a key catalytic and transitional role politically. Noting that it "represented all organized agricultural societies in the state," Benson points out that the Alliance "worked closely with New York City commercial groups, took a sophisticated approach to this relationship, and became a moderately effective instrument for the protection of agrarian interests. Never a mass organization of any size, it was a highly conscious attempt to restore to agriculture some portion of its erstwhile political power. In the process, it attracted nation-wide interest among farm leaders and led to the creation of the National Farmers' Alliance in 1880."[114]

In these ways B. T. Roberts's efforts bore fruit. Benson credits "several noteworthy historical developments" to the Alliance:

1. It helped lead to the establishment of the New York Railroad Commission in 1882.

2. It showed that farmers could more effectively wield political influence through "a single, all-embracing, permanent organization to represent them politically within the existing party structure" than they could through the Grange or through forming a new political party. A "balance-of-power agrarian organization" could work. Benson notes that "The basic concepts developed by the Alliance are extensively practiced today and find their logical outgrowth in the modern farm bloc."

112. Benson, *Merchants, Farmers, and Railroads*, p. 108.
113. Dunning, *Farmers' Alliance History*, p. 232.
114. Benson, *Merchants, Farmers, and Railroads*, p. 110.

3. The Alliance paved the way for the rise and influence of the National Anti-Monopoly League, which succeeded in mobilizing a broader constituency.

4. Most importantly, the New York State Farmers' Alliance triggered a national movement. Benson states flatly, "the Farmers' Alliance, created in the Rochester Court House on March 21, 1877, began the movement bearing that name which eventually swept through the rural districts of the West and South." In June 1879 the secretary of the New York alliance, William J. Fowler, reported that he was getting letters from all across the country asking about the Alliance. "The idea had even crossed the Atlantic," Benson notes; "hard-pressed tenant farmers of England . . . banded together in a 'Farmers' Alliance' to further the interests of agriculture."[115]

It is important to see the rise of the New York Farmers' Alliance in these larger terms, partly because Roberts's own concern was broader than New York. Roberts was not just a New York farmer; he was the leader of a national denomination, traveled widely, and had national and global concerns. It is illuminating therefore to place the role played by the New York State Farmers' Alliance within the larger national context, including the rise of the Populist movement.

The Farmers' Alliance in Texas

Much of the literature on the Farmers' Alliance states that the movement originated in the South or in Texas in 1877 or slightly earlier.[116] As noted earlier, there is perhaps no single origin to the movement. Yet its earliest springs were in New York, not Texas or elsewhere. The reason was largely geographical. The railroads began in the East and then stretched west; not surprisingly, the same was true generally of farmers' political activism. Where the railroads went and gained political and economic dominance, agrarian activism sprouted.

John Hicks, in his classic *The Populist Revolt: A History of the Farmers' Alliance and the People's Party,* wrote that although "the first really effective Alliance organization" was formed in Chicago in 1880, the origins of the Alliance go back to New York. "Ordinarily the date of the founding of the Northern Alliance is fixed at March 21, 1877, and the credit is given to a group of New Yorkers, mainly Grangers, who thought it expedient to create a 'political mouthpiece' through which the Patrons of Husbandry could speak."[117] This of course was the Rochester meeting in which Roberts played a key role.

From farmers' political discussions in western New York in the 1870s one may trace two streams of direct influence. One leads to Chicago and the formation of the National (Northern) Farmers' Alliance in 1880. The other leads to Texas slightly ear-

115. Benson, *Merchants, Farmers, and Railroads,* pp. 108-9, 112.

116. For example, a 2001 source states that the Farmers' Alliance was formed in Lampasas County, Tex., in 1877. See Daniel Pope, ed., *American Radicalism* (Oxford: Blackwell, 2001), p. 170.

117. John D. Hicks, *The Populist Revolt: A History of the Farmers' Alliance and the People's Party* (1931; reprint, Lincoln: University of Nebraska Press, 1961), pp. 97-98.

lier. These were the streams that, with others, converged to birth the Populist Party in 1891.

As noted earlier, the *Husbandman,* founded in 1874, soon developed a national following. This was partly due to editor Armstrong's wide connections; as secretary of the New York Grange he traveled widely, attending many Grange conferences. Also, ex–New York farmers who had moved west kept up with back-home news through the paper. Armstrong printed letters from all over the country; the weekly paper became a sort of national forum on farmers' issues. By early 1878 the paper was running correspondence from some thirty U.S. states and territories. The secretary of the Texas Grange wrote in 1876, "I want to tell you how much real pleasure it is to me to read the *Husbandman,* especially your spicy articles and the proceedings of the [Elmira] Farmers' Club."[118]

Quite naturally, the *Husbandman* thus became "the major carrier of the Alliance concept to both the South and the West," as Benson notes.[119] Through the *Husbandman* Texas Grangers learned of the New York Farmers' Alliance almost as soon as it was formed. It is hardly coincidental, therefore, that a group of farmers organized themselves in Lampasas County, Texas, in September 1877 into a sort of farmers alliance with aims similar to those of the New York Alliance. These farmers, "comparatively poor," organized to "speedily educate ourselves in the science of free government," one of the founders said. The group first called itself the Knights of Reliance but soon adopted the name Farmers' Alliance. Unlike the New York Alliance, and probably due to Grange influence, it organized as a fraternal order, with vows of secrecy. Lawrence Goodwyn notes, "The movement spread to surrounding counties, and in the summer of 1878 a 'Grand State Farmers Alliance' was formed." In a few years the statewide Farmers' Alliance began a "period of spectacular growth" and became a key player in the rise of the Populist movement.[120]

A remarkable part of this story concerns the Colored Farmers' Alliance in Texas, which eventually became part of the larger Southern Alliance movement. This organization "enrolled hundreds of thousands of black farmers across the South," and for a time blacks and whites worked together in the movement despite inbred white racism. Later the Colored Farmers' Alliance assisted in forming the People's Party.[121]

Some sources mistakenly date the original Lampasas County Farmers' Alliance to 1874 or 1875 — thus missing the New York connection and erroneously claiming that the national movement began in Texas. Through careful research into original

---

118. *Husbandman,* May 3, 1876, quoted in Benson, *Merchants, Farmers, and Railroads,* p. 110.

119. Benson, *Merchants, Farmers, and Railroads,* p. 111. Benson adds, "Another important medium through which the Alliance idea was spread was the annual meetings of the National Grange" (p. 111).

120. Lawrence Goodwyn, *Democratic Promise: The Populist Moment in America* (New York: Oxford University Press, 1976), p. 33; cf. Robert C. McMath, Jr., *Populist Vanguard: A History of the Southern Farmers' Alliance* (New York: Norton, 1977), pp. 3-8.

121. Pope, *American Radicalism,* p. 192. Pope's statement that "the bravest accomplishments and the Achilles' heal of Southern Populism both came in the area of race relations" (p. 191) is a balanced assessment.

source documents, including correspondence and diaries, Goodwyn verified that the Lampasas County Alliance was in fact formed in September 1877 — six months *after* the New York group started. Though it is not absolutely certain that the Texas Alliance was inspired by the New York precedent, the sequence of dates, the known influence of the *Husbandman* in Texas, and the adoption of the name Farmers' Alliance strongly support this link — and thus the reach of Roberts's influence.[122]

Lee Benson's research further supports this conclusion. He notes that the "erroneous impression" that "the Farmers' Alliance originated in the Lone Star State" stems largely from Dunning's 1891 *Farmers' Alliance History*. Dunning, an associate editor of the Southern Farmers' Alliance's paper, the *National Economist*, "played up Texas' role in the movement," though he also printed Root's account of the New York Alliance.[123]

The Texas Alliance did however quickly become the spring of a major Farmers' Alliance movement throughout the South. As Robert McMath, Jr., notes, from the "tiny band" of Lampasas farmers "evolved the National Farmers' Alliance and Industrial Union (NFA&IU), often called the 'southern' Farmers' Alliance" to distinguish it from the National Farmers' Alliance, which was primarily a northern movement.[124]

The National (Northern) Farmers' Alliance

Meanwhile, the New York State Farmers' Alliance gave essential impetus toward the organization of the National Farmers' Alliance in Chicago in 1880. This was the second stream of influence flowing from New York. In this sense "the Alliance movement [nationwide] had a single source in the late seventies," though "after 1880 it split into northern and southern wings," notes Benson.[125]

122. Goodwyn, *Democratic Promise*, pp. 33-34. Goodwyn demonstrated conclusively that the 1874 or 1875 date for the Lampasas County organization is wrong. "The tradition that the National Farmers Alliance originated in 1874-75 [via the Texas organization] or that it had connecting antecedents in other regions apparently cannot be sustained" (p. 620). Goodwyn is partly right and partly wrong here; ironically, he seemed to know nothing of the 1875 and 1877 Farmers' Alliance activity in western New York, referring only to the later activity of the Northern Alliance there in 1890. There *were* in fact "connecting antecedents in other regions" — or, more accurately, in New York State, as noted. Goodwyn writes that "Dunning, who cited Texas and New York origins 'in 1874 or 1875,' . . . wrote after the Alliance had become a multi-sectional organization with internal needs for many 'origins.' [Dunning's] needs . . . were not conducive to accuracy, either in terms of geography or the calendar" (p. 620). In fact, though Dunning may have been off by a couple of years with regard to Alliance organization in Texas and thus gives a misleading account as to Alliance origins, his reporting otherwise is fairly accurate. (Goodwyn spells "Farmers Alliance" without the apostrophe.)

123. Benson, *Merchants, Farmers, and Railroads*, pp. 277-78.

124. McMath, *Populist Vanguard*, p. xi.

125. Benson, *Merchants, Farmers, and Railroads*, p. 112. Benson notes the importance of the Grange antecedent. The earlier rapid spread of the Grange was no doubt a key factor in Alliance growth; the national Alliance movement "was to a considerable extent an outgrowth of the Patrons of Husbandry."

Frederick Root wrote in 1890 that from New York the Farmers' Alliance "extended to other States and in 1878 or 1879 a call was made for a national meeting to be held in Chicago" in 1880. "From that time onward the organization spread throughout the West and South until it has become an acknowledged power in the political status of those States," Root said.[126] He probably was unaware of the Texas history tracing back to 1877 but also indebted to New York.

The National (Northern) Farmers' Alliance was in fact organized in Chicago on October 14, 1880, at a convention that brought together about five hundred farmers from many states. The organizing catalyst was Milton George of Chicago, farmer, activist, and editor of the *Western Rural*. In calling for a national organization George had been influenced by the New York State Farmers' Alliance.[127] The constitution adopted by the new body declared that its intent was

> to unite the farmers of the United States for their protection against class legislation, and the encroachments of concentrated capital and the tyranny of monopoly; . . . to oppose, in our respective political parties, the election of any candidate to office, state or national, who is not thoroughly in sympathy with the farmers' interests; to demand that the existing political parties shall nominate farmers, or those who are in sympathy with them, for all offices within the gift of the people, and to do everything in a legitimate manner that may serve the benefit of the producer.[128]

Its aims were thus essentially those of the New York State Farmers' Alliance, transposed onto the national stage.

William J. Fowler of Monroe County (a member of the original 1877 Farmers' Club committee that Roberts chaired) was a featured speaker at the Chicago meeting and was elected president of the new organization. "It was only fitting," Benson comments, "that one of the original founders of the Alliance in New York should . . . [become] the first president of the National Farmers' Alliance."[129]

McMath gives a helpful summary of the complex development of the Farmers' Alliance that shows how the various strands fit together:

> The "southern" Farmers' Alliance was one of three Alliances that flourished in the last two decades of the nineteenth century. A "northern" Alliance, officially entitled the National Farmers' Alliance, was organized in Chicago in 1880 as an outgrowth of a New York state farmers' organization. Under the leadership of Chicago farm journalist Milton George, this group attracted considerable attention

126. Root, "Origin of the Farmers' Alliance."

127. Buck, *The Agrarian Crusade*, pp. 118-19; Benson, *Merchants, Farmers, and Railroads*, p. 113; McMath, *Populist Vanguard*, p. 77. The National Farmers' Alliance was also sometimes called the Northwestern or (as noted) Northern Alliance to distinguish it from the southern Farmers' Alliance and Industrial Union, often simply called the Southern Alliance.

128. Buck, *The Agrarian Crusade*, p. 118.

129. Benson, *Merchants, Farmers, and Railroads*, p. 114.

across the Midwest in the early 1880s. . . . The . . . southern Alliance, was by far the largest of the three Alliances and played a much more important role in the agrarian revolt of the 1890s than either Milton George's group or the black organization. From its Texas base, it spread across the South in the late 1880s, offering farmers salvation through economic cooperation. In 1889 it absorbed the strong state Alliances in Kansas and the Dakotas, and by 1891 it was organized in thirty-two states reaching from California to New York.[130]

The strands of this complex story trace back, as we have seen, to a Free Methodist farmer and churchman who felt good Christians should be good citizens, committed to justice in society — justice for all the people, which is the essence of Populism.

B. T. Roberts continued to speak and write on this and related matters for the rest of his life. He addressed farmers' issues while editor of the *Free Methodist* — for example in an editorial entitled "Protection of Farmers" in the issue of January 16, 1889.[131] In 1877 he corresponded with Peter Cooper, the 1876 Greenback Party U.S. presidential candidate, and in 1890 he reviewed Henry George's influential book *Progress and Poverty: An Inquiry into the Cause of Industrial Depressions and of Increase of Want with Increase of Wealth* (first published in 1879) in the *Free Methodist*. Roberts affirmed George's concerns for economic justice but vigorously disagreed with his "single tax" proposal to base all taxation on real estate.[132]

Birth of the People's Party

The Grange and the Farmers' Alliance together constituted the first stages of that quintessentially American movement called Populism — "the largest democratic mass movement in American history," according to Goodwyn.[133] The height of the movement was the formation of a national People's Party, more commonly called the Populist Party, in Cincinnati in May 1891.[134]

Years after Roberts's death his grandson Ashbel Sellew Roberts and Theodore

---

130. McMath, *Populist Vanguard*, p. xii. McMath, however, apparently was not aware of the New York/Texas connection documented above.

131. Zahniser, p. 260.

132. [B. T. Roberts], "The Single Tax," *FM* 23, no. 37 (Sept. 10, 1890): 8; Zahniser, pp. 257, 262-63. See Marston, pp. 391-93.

133. Goodwyn, *The Populist Moment*, p. vii.

134. Argersinger, *Populism and Politics*, pp. 80-87, gives a fairly detailed account. The Cincinnati convention was preceded by several other related conventions, in particular a convention in St. Louis on Dec. 6, 1889, which united farmers and labor groups into the Farmers' Alliance and Industrial Union, and a convention on Dec. 7, 1890, in Ocala, Fla., attended by representatives of the Southern Alliance, the Farmers' Mutual Benefit Association, and the colored Alliance. These formed part of the stream leading to the founding of the (national) People's Party in 1891. See Frank L. McVey, "The Populist Movement," *Economic Studies* 1, no. 3 (Aug. 1896): 133-209.

Pease wrote about Populism in their *Selected Readings in American History.* They commented, "Neither benevolent organizations like the Grange nor attempts on the part of the state and Federal Government to regulate railroad and warehouse conditions effectively, improved the farmers' condition or allayed their discontent. By 1890 the farmers had turned to politics as an organized group. Out of the Farmers' Alliance developed the Populist Party."[135]

This was written about 1928. Ashbel Roberts probably was unaware of his own grandfather's role in the rise of the Farmers' Alliance. If he had known the full story, he would have understood that in New York and other places farmers were "turning to politics as an organized group" more than a decade before the People's Party was formed in 1890.

The People's Party was the outgrowth of increasing Farmers' Alliance political activity in a number of states — most dramatically, in Kansas. Here the seed planted by Roberts bore unusually vigorous fruit.

Populism in Kansas

The People's Party had its first rise in Kansas as a result of farmers' political activism there. The Farmers' Alliance was organized in Kansas in 1888 as a branch of the Northern Alliance. Kansas alliancemen designated the *Kansas Farmer,* edited by reformer William A. Peffer, as their official paper. Peffer, a figure much like Roberts in his political and reformist views, had earlier been an antislavery and temperance activist and had helped organize the Republican Party in Indiana in 1854. Soft-spoken, thoughtful, and with an impressive beard that reached nearly to his waist, Peffer became the best-known and most influential voice of Populism, first in Kansas and then nationally. Throughout the 1880s Peffer pressed for the formation of a politically effective farmers organization. His concerns were much like those raised earlier by Roberts: railroad regulation, tax reform, and in general, he said, protecting "farmers' interests in their relation to business and government."[136]

For several years Kansas farmers tried unsuccessfully to influence the Republican-controlled legislature toward reform. But it wouldn't budge. Frustrated in the face of worsening economic conditions and political intransigence, farmers in 1889-90 birthed a widespread farmers movement. During "this period of political frustration exacerbated by deepening depression farmers began to organize spontaneously at the grassroots level," notes historian Peter Argersinger. Although the

135. Theodore Calvin Pease and A. Sellew Roberts, eds., *Selected Readings in American History,* enlarged ed. (New York: Harcourt, Brace, 1940; original 1928), p. 586. Pease and Roberts, p. 587, quote H. R. Chamberlain: "The [Farmers'] Alliance [of 1890] is really a combination of older organizations. A Farmers' Alliance was started in Texas in 1873, and another in New York about the same year" (H. R. Chamberlain, *The Farmers' Alliance* [New York, 1891]). This is accurate except for the date; Chamberlain dates the earliest organization of the Farmers' Alliance about four years too early.

136. Argersinger, *Populism and Politics,* pp. 1-12, 20, 105.

Northern Alliance was already active in the state, the farmers decided to affiliate with the seemingly more militant Southern body (the National Farmers' Alliance and Industrial Union).[137]

The Kansas Farmers' Alliance organized very rapidly in late 1889 and throughout 1890. "By late spring [1890] the Alliance claimed 100,000 members in nearly 2,000 local suballiances, with up to fifty new suballiances being established each week." Peffer traveled the state, often speaking to as many as two thousand people daily. A groundswell arose for the formation of a new political party that would counter Republican control of the state and be more effective and reformist than the state's weak Democratic Party. In June the Kansas Farmers' Alliance in district meetings elected a People's State Central Committee and urged other agrarian and labor organizations to join with the Alliance to nominate independent candidates. A key meeting was held in Topeka on June 12, 1890, in which forty-one Alliance delegates and smaller delegations from the Knights of Labor, the Farmers' Mutual Benefit Association, and the Patrons of Husbandry decided to organize a new political party and to nominate a full slate of candidates for state and congressional office, pledged to Alliance principles. To "avoid the transformation of the Alliance directly into a partisan body," Argersinger notes, the convention "decided that the proper name of the new party would be the 'People's Party.'"[138]

Fighting off a Democratic plot to take over the fledgling movement, the new Kansas People's Party held its nominating convention at Topeka on August 13, 1890. For governor it nominated John F. Willits — farmer, prohibitionist, and Alliance leader who had served as a Republican state legislator. It did not nominate a candidate for the U.S. Senate because at this time senators were still elected by state legislatures, but Peffer was its clear choice. The convention did make nominations for other posts, including the legislature. Argersinger notes, "The People's party respected its name by . . . designating a woman, a Negro, a minister, a farmer, and a schoolteacher for its candidates."[139]

An issue in the 1890 state election was whether the prohibition cause would draw off so many reform votes as to undermine the Populist effort. The Populists ar-

---

137. Argersinger, *Populism and Politics*, p. 22. Argersinger notes, "Farm organizations were not new to Kansas, but they had been weak and [politically] ineffective, and when Kansas farmers actively turned to one in 1889 they joined the militant National Farmers' Alliance and Industrial Union. Known better as the Southern Alliance to distinguish itself from the less contentious National (or Northern) Farmers' Alliance, this organization entered Kansas in 1888 prepared to mobilize isolated farmers into a cohesive group to advance agrarian interests" (p. 22). The subsequent history of Populism might have been different had Kansas farmers affiliated with the Northern rather than the Southern Alliance, because later when the issue of a third party arose many Southern alliancemen, traditionally committed to the Democratic Party, refused to endorse the third-party movement and in fact actively compromised and undermined it by promoting a policy of "fusion" between Democrats (who were not really reformers) and Populists. The negative, neutralizing impact of this fusion politics is a major theme of Argersinger's book.

138. Argersinger, *Populism and Politics*, p. 35.

139. Argersinger, *Populism and Politics*, pp. 35-39.

gued that what was at stake was more fundamental than prohibition. "The issue this year is not whether a man shall be permitted to drink, but whether he shall have a home to go to, drunk or sober," one People's Party advocate wrote.[140]

The Kansas election was as hard-fought as its outcome was dramatic. Benjamin Clover, state Farmers' Alliance president, told his constituency shortly before the election, "Remember the interests at stake. Remember the homeless, the sorrowing, the discouraged, the weary, and the heavy laden. The decalogue and the golden rule must have a place in the great uprising; the great J. J. notwithstanding; reform must come from the heart of the common people where the 'higher civilization' always comes from." This was a slap at powerful U.S. Senator John J. Ingalls, who in a *New York World* interview had said, "The purification of politics is an iridescent dream. Government is force. . . . The decalogue and the golden rule have no place in a political campaign. The object is success." Politics is war and talk of reform is mere "sentimentalism."[141]

As soon as the results of the election were known, the *Kansas City Star* pronounced the outcome "a Waterloo to the Republican party." The People's Party won in a landslide, electing five U.S. congressmen and ninety-one state legislators. Although the Populists failed to win the governorship or gain a majority in the state senate, they took control of the lower house with such a majority that they now controlled the election of U.S. senator. When that voting occurred in January 1891, Peffer was elected, sending Ingalls into retirement.[142]

The Populist victory and the election for U.S. senator sparked nationwide interest. *Harper's Weekly,* noting that Senator Ingalls was a major public figure and president pro tem of the Senate, proclaimed: "Kansas is the State in which the revolution wrought by the Farmers' Alliance is most conspicuous." The election of the bearded Peffer immediately thrust him and the Populist insurgence into the national spotlight. People's parties had less success in other states, however; Peffer was one of just two Populists elected to the Senate, although several won seats in the House of Representatives.[143]

Harper's Weekly reported, "The election of Mr. Peffer has been enthusiastically welcomed by Alliancemen in all parts of the country, and has greatly encouraged them in their political action. It is one of the greatest purely political victories they have won, and will doubtless tend to strengthen the third-party movement" within the Farmers' Alliance itself.[144] Back in New York, however, Frederick Root had some misgivings about Farmers' Alliance support for the People's Party. He wrote in December 1890, just before Peffer's election, "What may yet be the outcome of the [Farmers' Alliance] I will not augur, but I believe its end is not far distant, as it has

140. Argersinger, *Populism and Politics*, p. 42.

141. Argersinger, *Populism and Politics*, pp. 30-31, 45.

142. Argersinger, *Populism and Politics*, pp. 46-55.

143. Argersinger, *Populism and Politics*, pp. 47, 80, 106. The other U.S. senator elected by the Populists was James H. Kyle of South Dakota, who however "considered himself an Independent rather than a Populist" (p. 106).

144. Argersinger, *Populism and Politics*, p. 56.

entered on dangerous ground and is advocating impracticable measures. A *class* political party must be of short duration."[145]

Populism's High Tide

Some 1,400 delegates from Farmers' Alliances (including the Colored Farmers' Alliance) and other groups converged on Cincinnati in May 1891 for what was billed as a National Union Conference. "About two-thirds of the states were represented."[146] This convention birthed the People's Party as a national political force. Kansas had 411 delegates, and, says Argersinger, the convention "clearly depended upon them for its direction and motivating force." Senator-elect Peffer was a star figure. "We come here as harbingers of a revolution," he said, "to reestablish the authority of the people."[147]

Although a variety of groups — particularly the Knights of Labor, the Citizens' Alliance (a sort of urban counterpart to the Farmers' Alliance), and the Farmers' Mutual Benefit Association — joined in forming the People's Party, the new national party was as directly an outgrowth of the Farmers' Alliance movement as was the Kansas People's Party. An antagonistic Republican political cartoon of the time depicted a rising balloon patched together from the Farmers' Alliance, the Knights of Labor, the "Old Granger Party," the Prohibition Party, and the "Old Greenback Party," as well as "socialists," "communists," "anarchists," and "woman's rights" elements. Peffer's long beard flows out impressively but ridiculously from the gondola, which bears the label "Platform of Lunacy."[148]

Capitalizing on the momentum of the previous decade, the People's Party tried to mount a national crusade. At a nominating convention in Omaha in 1892, the Populists nominated James B. Weaver of Iowa for president and James G. Field of Virginia for vice president. The party also entered candidates in many state elections. At Omaha it adopted a platform that, notes Argersinger, embodied "Alliance principles on money, land, and transportation and [advocated] the expansion of responsive governmental power to promote the public welfare."[149]

In the general election Weaver and the Republican presidential candidate, Benjamin Harrison, were defeated by Democrat Grover Cleveland, though Cleve-

145. Root, "Origin of the Farmers' Alliance."

146. McVey, "The Populist Movement," p. 138. McVey noted, "The majority of the assembly were farmers, while the remainder consisted of representatives of the various labor societies." The proposal to endorse an eight-hour workday sparked debate and "was adopted only after much objection on the part of the farmer, for he sometimes has to work sixteen hours and never less than twelve, so that he is not naturally in sympathy with the eight hour movement" (pp. 139-40).

147. Argersinger, *Populism and Politics*, pp. 84-85.

148. William A. Peffer, *Populism, Its Rise and Fall*, ed. Peter H. Argersinger (Lawrence: University Press of Kansas, 1992), p. 41. The chapters in this book originally appeared as a series of essays in the *Chicago Tribune* in 1899.

149. Argersinger, *Populism and Politics*, pp. 111-12.

land won with only 46 percent of the popular vote. The People's ticket polled 8.5 percent of the popular vote and won twenty-two electoral college votes.[150] The Populist crusade had failed to win the White House, though a number of Populists were elected to Congress, and Kansas and Colorado chose Populist governors.[151]

By the 1896 election four years later, "free silver" had become such a hot issue that it largely sidetracked Populism's broader agenda. The Panic of 1893 and ensuing depression again brought financial issues to the forefront of public discussion. Many Populists as well as Democrats and some Republicans became convinced the key reform needed was unrestricted coinage of silver. Democrat William Jennings Bryan declared himself the silver candidate and courted his party's nomination. Proclaiming he would never be crucified on a "cross of gold," Bryan won the Democratic nomination. Meanwhile so-called Silver Populists had gained predominance in the People's Party, and a "fusion" ticket resulted, the Populists supporting Bryan. The *Topeka Advocate* warned prophetically that Bryan was really "an enemy to the People's Party" and not a true reformer, and that if the Populists limited their platform to the silver issue, it "would be a backward step" and "absolutely fatal."[152]

Ironically, Bryan is often pictured as the epitome of American Populism and his defeat by William McKinley as the end of Populism.[153] In fact, Populism as a vital movement had already waned by the time Peffer retired from his one term in the Senate in 1897. Despite this and the 1896 presidential defeat, however, many early Populist proposals eventually became law.[154]

The Legacy of Populism

Was the Populist movement finally a success or a failure? Appraisals are mixed. Argersinger notes that "scholars have frequently agreed that [Populism] was ultimately successful if originally rejected."[155] John Hicks wrote in 1930 that to list the Populist demands "is to cite the chief political innovations made in the United States during recent times."[156] In the early 1900s William Peffer noted that though his Pop-

---

150. Cleveland received 46 percent of the vote, Harrison got 43 percent, Weaver received 8.53 percent, and others received about 2 percent. Kane, *Presidential Fact Book,* p. 375.

151. Pope, *American Radicalism,* pp. 170-71.

152. Argersinger, *Populism and Politics,* pp. 199-200, 248. On Bryan, see Michael Kazin, *A Godly Hero: The Life of William Jennings Bryan* (New York: Knopf, 2006).

153. McKinley received just over 7 million votes; Bryan received 6.7 million, including 222,583 People's Party votes. Kane, *Presidential Fact Book,* p. 152.

154. Argersinger writes that Peffer's "six-year term in the United States Senate coincided exactly with the generally recognized birth and death dates of Populism; and with good reason, for he carried the title 'Father of Populism' and was the foremost public representative of the movement in the 1890s" (*Populism and Politics,* p. xii). But Argersinger shows that the Populists had been effectively outmaneuvered politically by 1893.

155. Argersinger, *Populism and Politics,* p. 302.

156. Hicks, *Populist Revolt,* p. 407.

ulist principles were "laughed to death at that time[, they] are now considered respectable"; "the country now hotly demands legislation it abused me for advocating." Peffer supported Theodore Roosevelt's reforms, believing TR was "applying the principles of Populism."[157]

It is true that some of the main reforms pushed by the Populists eventually became law. Yet it is also true, Argersinger argues, that "the transformation of American society promised in original Populism never occurred." The fulfillment was much less than the vision. Populism, and many of the Populists themselves, fell prey to party politics and sectional loyalties. "Populism died because it failed to transcend the American political system. It was killed by those very factors of politics that its founders had intended to kill: prejudice, elite manipulation, corruption." Populists "had hoped to transform politics but had fallen under its dead weight." In the end, Argersinger suggests, its efforts "became more of a struggle for office and power than for reform."[158]

Annie Diggs, a Populist activist in Kansas, later declared that "the memorable revolt of 1890" was triggered by "the discovery that the national machinery of both the Republican and the Democratic parties was set to the service of the privileged classes and of commercial combinations."[159] Though she was speaking of 1890s Populism, her comment was largely valid for the 1870s as well. Many Populists became disillusioned with the possibility of substantial reform by working *through* the existing political parties, as Roberts and other early reformers hoped could happen.

Populism ran aground also through its attempts at "fusion," forming a united front with Democrats against Republicans. Fusion meant too much compromise of original Populist principles. "Fusionists were never as interested in political, or general, reform as in limited measures of economic reform," Argersinger notes. Peffer argued in 1902 that those who wanted (in Argersinger's words) "to compromise issues, restrict their application, emphasize free silver, adopt the unscrupulous methods of the unacceptable old parties, and fuse with the Democrats" had in fact betrayed Populism.[160]

Yet in the broader sense Populism did produce reforms. One of the fruits of its campaign actually happened before the creation of the People's Party. Gradually Congress came to see the need for railroad regulation and in 1887 passed the Interstate Commerce Act. This legislation, Benson notes, "formally signaled the end of *laissez faire* in transportation and presaged its eventual decline in all other important segments of the national economy."[161]

Throughout this whole sequence of events Roberts continued to address farmers' issues from time to time. In his January 1889 *Free Methodist* editorial entitled "Protection of Farmers," he noted that while he did "not, as a rule, take an active part

157. Argersinger, *Populism and Politics*, p. 302.
158. Argersinger, *Populism and Politics*, pp. 303, 305-6.
159. Argersinger, *Populism and Politics*, p. 307.
160. Argersinger, *Populism and Politics*, pp. 310-11.
161. Benson, *Merchants, Farmers, and Railroads*, p. vii.

in politics," yet "on questions which affect the religious as well as the material well-being of the people at large, it is our duty, as a Christian editor, to give audible expression to our opinion." Especially is this the case regarding "measures which have a direct tendency to impoverish the many in order to enrich the few."

Roberts commented on the hard-pressed financial situation of many farmers and the growing number of bankruptcies. Why are farmers in such distress? he asked. Not because of poor crops or poor farming. "The CAUSE OF THE GROWING POVERTY of farmers is not natural but artificial. *It is found in the combinations made by those engaged in other productive industries, and in transportation,* by means of which the proper proportion is destroyed between the prices of what the farmer has to sell and what he wishes to buy. Because of these combinations, and the laws which render them possible, the farmer is compelled to give two days' work of his own, for one day's work of the man who made any article which he buys."[162]

After quoting Adam Smith's statement that labor "is alone the ultimate and real standard by which the value of all commodities can at all times and places be estimated and compared," Roberts states that "THE REMEDY is, to break up, by law, these conspiracies to control prices. They amount to monopolies, and will, unless suppressed, ruin the country."[163]

Several weeks later, in March 1889, Roberts followed up with a related editorial entitled "Killing the Goose." In America, Roberts said, the goose that lays the golden egg is the farmer. "The master who appropriates the golden egg, is *the monopolist,*" whether he be a "great railroad owner," "great manufacturer, doubling his capital from his profits every year," or "an express or telegraph lord."

Roberts then presented an analysis of the 1880 U.S. Census reports. Based on the number of farmers, the value of farms, and total capital invested, he concluded that on average, people engaged in farming received only 62¢ a day. "Out of this is to come the board and clothing! Is it any wonder that farming does not pay?" In contrast, "the net product of the labor of each person engaged in manufactures, . . . amounts to $2.11, a day . . . about three and one-half times as much as a person engaged in farming gets for his labor!"

162. [B. T. Roberts], "Protection of Farmers."

163. [B. T. Roberts], "Protection of Farmers." The Smith quotation is from *The Wealth of Nations,* chapter 5, "Of the Real and Nominal Price of Commodities, or of Their Price in Labour, and Their Price in Money." See Adam Smith, *An Inquiry into the Nature and Causes of the Wealth of Nations,* ed. Edwin Cannan (New York: Modern Library, 1937), p. 33. In a later chapter Smith wrote, "No society can surely be flourishing and happy, of which the far greater part of the members are poor and miserable" (p. 79).

Immediately following Roberts's editorial was another entitled "The President's Cabinet." Here Roberts advised Benjamin Harrison, president-elect, not to "select for his cabinet any man simply because he is rich, and has contributed liberally" to the Republican Party. "One of the strongest evidences of possessing the faculty to govern, is the ability to select competent and trusty subordinates," Roberts wrote. "The people can bear, in patience, to be persistently plundered by rich corporations and 'trusts;' but there they stop. They will not consent to be governed by a plutocracy." [B. T. Roberts], "The President's Cabinet," *FM* 22, no. 3 (Jan. 16, 1889): 8.

Roberts saw this as a great economic injustice. Noting the "depression of farming interests prevail[ing] all over the country," Roberts said the causes were "wholly artificial" and could be addressed by economic reforms. Among other recommendations, he urged lawmakers to "enact such stringent laws against 'Trusts' and combinations to control prices, as would render them impossible."

Roberts concluded his editorial with a warning:

> When Communists seized upon Paris, the farmers rallied to the protection of the property holders, and after terrible fighting, restored order. The help of the farmers will be needed in this country when the hordes of the unemployed, led by socialists and anarchists, constantly increasing in our cities, shall assail with dynamite the palaces of the rich, overthrow civil authority, and seek to divide among themselves the property which has been so unequally and unfairly distributed.
>
> The monopolists should, for their own safety, lift the hand of oppression from the farmers, which is now crushing them into the earth.[164]

It is a mark of how strongly Roberts felt about issues of economic justice that at this busiest, most pressured period of his life he took the time to analyze the U.S. Census reports in order to make his case.[165]

In June 1890 Roberts published a *Free Methodist* editorial endorsing a bill by Senator Leland Stanford of California that would "afford substantial relief" by authorizing limited government loans directly to hard-pressed farmers. "This bill in substance should become a law," Roberts argued. Noting that the U.S. government already loaned money without interest to national banks, he asked, "If it be right for the government to lend to *bankers* how can it be wrong for it to lend to *farmers?*" But farmers would "need to rally and demand [the bill's] enactment."

In an aside, Roberts commented, "It is very remarkable that Senator Stanford, the richest man in the United States senate, a body made up largely of millionaires, should originate and champion such a measure. It shows that wealth does not always benumb the humane feelings and render its possessor insensible to the needs of his fellow men."[166]

These editorials, coming just a few years before his death, show how consistently throughout his life Roberts was passionate about issues of social and economic justice. Given these convictions, it is little wonder that he took the lead in forming the Farmers' Alliances.

---

164. [B. T. Roberts], "Killing the Goose," *FM* 22, no. 12 (Mar. 20, 1889): 8.

165. Roberts cited the Compendium of U.S. Census for 1880, parts 1 and 2, as well as reports from the *New York Tribune* and the *New York Evening Post*.

166. [B. T. Roberts], "For the Farmers," *FM* 23, no. 25 (June 18, 1890): 8.

Assessing Roberts's Role

The documented history of the Populist movement in America reveals that B. T. Roberts played a brief but strategic role in its rise. Several conclusions may be drawn from Roberts's Farmers' Alliance initiatives:

1. Roberts was a key figure in the rise of the Farmers' Alliance in New York State. Would some such organization eventually have been formed without his initiative? Possibly. But Roberts had a catalytic role at a strategic time, helping to inspire, shape, and give a particular direction to the Alliance.

2. Because of the national influence of New York farm leaders, Roberts contributed indirectly to the formation of *both* the Northern and Southern Farmers' Alliances, and thus to the rise of the Populist movement. He would no more have agreed with everything Populism became than did Peffer. But his was one of the voices that inspired the movement.

3. Roberts saw direct political involvement for the sake of enacting just laws as a proper expression of Christian discipleship. He had no problem in cooperating with those who were not explicitly Christian, or with specifically political organizations (as long as they did not have vows of secrecy), in order to achieve political ends. He was not unique in this regard; many Populists were Christians and worked from Christian convictions. As Daniel Pope notes, "evangelical themes infused . . . the Farmers' Alliances, and [the] People's Party" as well as the Knights of Labor and similar groups.[167]

Roberts's involvement with the Farmers' Alliance was different from his support of the National Christian Association in that, unlike the NCA, the Farmers' Alliance was not an explicitly Christian organization or movement. Although his Alliance activities were based in his Christian convictions, he seems to have seen them more as an expression of responsible citizenship than as explicitly Christian ministry.

4. For Roberts the overriding issue was justice. Securing justice in the social and political realm, he felt, was a legitimate end for Christians to pursue. Thus his work for justice for farmers in the 1870s was consistent with his support for the abolition of slavery in the 1840s and 1850s and for other causes such as temperance and women's rights. It paralleled in the political sphere his rejection of pew rental within the church.

It is not inappropriate to call Roberts a Populist. The essence of Populism is that the people (*all* the people, fairly represented, and especially the common people and the oppressed) should control the government and that the test of faithful, legitimate government is the people's general welfare. As the secretary of the Texas Colored Farmers' Alliance wrote in 1890, the Farmers' Alliance was "peculiarly a movement of the people, by the people and for the people."[168] This is nothing more than the ideal enshrined in America's founding documents. By the 1870s and 1880s, however, it sounded radical and even subversive.

---

167. Introduction to Pope, *American Radicalism,* p. 13.
168. Pope, *American Radicalism,* p. 197.

5. Roberts's role in organizing the Farmers' Alliance is an instructive example of leadership and influence. Roberts devoted only a small amount of time to the Alliance and apparently was minimally involved once the movement was launched. It was never his main focus. The fact that he gave it as much attention as he did shows his depth of conviction on the issues. In the midst of a grueling schedule, Roberts took time to attend farmers meetings, agitate for a new organization, and write on farmers' issues. His role in organizing the Farmers' Alliance is a lesson in what can be accomplished through brief, focused, intelligent intervention at a strategic time.[169] It also seems consistent with the philosophy of reform he had articulated several years earlier. He wrote in 1870,

> Political reform is greatly needed. Our Legislatures are utterly corrupt; our administrators of justice are bought and sold far more shamefully, and almost as openly, as the negroes were in the days of slavery. . . .
>
> But if a reform is effected, a few impracticable radicals, who consult only the right, must take the lead; and when the cause becomes popular so that their help is not needed, the co-operation of the leading ministers and churches of the day [and, presumably, citizens generally] may be expected.[170]

In working to establish the Farmers' Alliance, Roberts was addressing a vital issue that continues to be of great relevance. How can power — particularly economic and political power — be harnessed and channeled for the public good — for the benefit of all, especially those with little or no power? How can the people control their political and economic institutions so they exist for the public good and are not exploitive or co-opted for the benefit of special interests? This is the essential focus of Populism. In the twenty-first century it is an issue writ large due to the globalization of business, commerce, and technology. Roberts firmly believed that it is the role of government to regulate business for the common good, and it is the role of citizens to make the government responsive to the people.

Roberts was always concerned with *the people* (the essential meaning of Populism), and especially with people who were poor and oppressed — socially, politically, and economically as well as spiritually. His involvement with the Farmers' Alliance was an expression as much of his theology as of his political philosophy. As important as the question of his role or influence is the simple fact that Roberts was being true to his convictions.

In the end, and in fact from the beginning, Roberts understood that his ministry as a preacher and church leader was ultimately more important and strategic than was political reform. And yet his efforts at political reform were part and parcel of his ministry — his sense of calling as a Free Methodist minister, as a citizen, and as Jesus' disciple responsibly "seeking first" God's kingdom and its justice.

---

169. This account is also instructive in terms of movement dynamics, though this is another matter that can't be pursued here.

170. [B. T. Roberts], "Political Reform," *EC* 19, no. 5 (May 1870): 156.

CHAPTER 36

The Heart of Roberts's Theology

"Is it impossible for Christ to have a pure church on earth?"

B. T. Roberts, 1861[1]

"The Bible lays great stress on plainness, but it lays still greater stress on kindness."

B. T. Roberts, 1884[2]

In 1883 B. T. Roberts succinctly summarized the Christian faith as he had come to understand it.

> Christianity has its doctrines to be believed, its grace to be experienced, and its practices to be obeyed. Each is important. The three combined in due proportion in any person render him a Christian. A preponderance of the one cannot take the place of the others. Common sugar is composed of certain definite proportions of carbon, hydrogen and oxygen. Omit [any one] of these ingredients and you have something else entirely different from sugar in its nature and uses. So one may believe the doctrines of Christianity and still be a mere natural man. His hopes of Heaven are no better than those of a decent infidel. He may believe the doctrines and experience the grace; but if he neglects to obey the precepts he becomes an enthusiast or a fanatic. If he endeavors to obey its precepts without the inward grace he becomes a pharisee. The great mistake that many make is to take a part of Christianity for the whole.[3]

1. [B. T. Roberts], "Receiving Members," *EC* 2, no. 11 (Nov. 1861): 355.
2. [B. T. Roberts], "Consistent," *EC* 47, no. 3 (Mar. 1884): 100.
3. [B. T. Roberts], "Good Manners," *EC* 45, no. 5 (May 1883): 159.

Roberts knew what he believed. Over the years he continued elaborating his theology as he read, traveled, preached, and taught. His views on race, the role of women, economics, farmers' concerns, and other issues were not ad hoc opinions generated on the spot. They were not mere whims or prejudices. Usually they were well-thought-out views that expressed an underlying and deeply held theology. Whether or not his views were always consistent with this theology (at least as viewed today), he believed that all the positions he advocated were the necessary outworkings of fundamental biblical truth — the "Bible standard" as he called it.

Roberts's Theological Foundations

Roberts's principal theological convictions, and their roots in his own experience, are already evident from the story of his and Ellen's life and ministry that has been traced to this point. But how did his whole theology hang together? What were its main foundations and root images? Was there coherence or system to these views?

Roberts's fundamental theology was orthodox at all essential points. He stood in the mainstream of historic Christian orthodoxy on key doctrines such as the Trinity, the sovereignty of God, creation, revelation, the divine-human nature of Jesus Christ, salvation by grace through faith in the sacrificial death and resurrection of Jesus, and the inspiration and authority of the Bible. Blended with these basic doctrines, however, was a set of radical accents that Roberts believed were essential to restore Christianity to its New Testament authenticity and vigor. They were the keys to the church experiencing again the dynamic of early Methodism (and of other renewal movements down through history) and to its redemptive role in society.[4]

These radical accents were not add-ons. They gave a particular cast to all of Roberts's theology, making it distinctive, if not unique. These accents may be summarized in three propositions. Though not stated by Roberts in this form, they seem to have been fundamental convictions.

1. The life and teachings of Jesus Christ, the experience of the New Testament church, and the Bible generally are authoritative and decisively normative for the church in all ages, without compromise. This is what Roberts meant when he said "the Bible is a radical book."[5] Roberts was aware of the hermeneutical questions this raised and dealt with them forthrightly.

2. The church is a community of the redeemed, and as a voluntary human orga-

4. In this connection, note Roberts's reading of and occasionally quoting from both Jonathan Edwards and Charles Finney — for example, in his editorial "Seventh of Romans," *EC* 50, no. 6 (Dec. 1885): 189-90, where Roberts quotes both Edwards, "a man of great talent, of profound learning, and of deep piety, and a Calvinist," and Finney, "a Congregationalist." The two key authors quoted in the introductions to early Free Methodist *Disciplines* were Wesley and Edwards.

5. B. T. Roberts, *Fishers of Men; or, Practical Hints to Those Who Would Win Souls* (Rochester, N.Y.: G. L. Roberts and Co., 1878), p. 8.

nization should be composed of only those who are converted and who experience or are seeking holiness.

3. Based on Jesus' example and teaching, the church's primary mission is to "preach the gospel to the poor" and "to maintain the Bible standard of Christianity." This meant, especially, evangelism among the masses, particularly the poor and oppressed; the building of a community of believers among those who respond; the church's continuing mission to reach the poor; and doctrine tested by Scripture.

4. The normative Christian life is one of holiness — being baptized with the Holy Spirit, living a life of separation from the sins and popular fashions of the world and in union with the church, ready obedience to all Christian duty, and engaging in the church's mission. Holiness meant a deep and abiding sense of God's presence and guidance day by day and the manifestation of the power of the Holy Spirit in times of prayer and public worship.

5. Separation from the world does not mean lack of social or cultural engagement. On the contrary, Christians are to be salt and light, first through the integrity of their lives and witness individually and communally, but also through "mental culture" and their legitimate roles as citizens and actors in the cultural and economic realms. They must be especially sensitive to issues of justice and the poor.

6. On the one hand life is ongoing crisis, both personally and culturally, because of human rebelliousness and satanic opposition to God's purposes. Yet history is a continuing, long-term reality, ultimately in God's hands. Though Jesus Christ might return at any time and believers should live in that expectancy, yet there are continuity and significance in history. One lives in the midst of the present crisis, yet is confident in God's ultimate victory.

This was Roberts's essential theological framework. In many respects it resembles the historic Radical Protestant or Believers' Church view that is found also, in somewhat modified form, in John Wesley and early Methodism.[6]

Roberts's own writings elaborate these points.

1. Jesus and the Bible as Essential Standard

Roberts intended to be radically christocentric and thoroughly biblical. He intended, he said, "to take no position that is not sustained by a fair interpretation of the word of God. To this word we bow with the most cordial submission. If our work may be thought by some to be radical, we beg them to bear in mind that the

---

6. See Howard A. Snyder, *The Radical Wesley and Patterns for Church Renewal* (Downers Grove, Ill.: InterVarsity, 1980), pp. 109-24. All seven elements of the Radical Protestant model that I outline in *The Radical Wesley* are found to greater or lesser degree in Roberts's theology. As one would expect, generally the shades of difference from the Radical Protestant model in Roberts's theology are similar to those in Wesley. However, Roberts's theology was in some ways more apocalyptic than Wesley's (as noted below).

Bible is a radical book."[7] This is a claim about both the content of Scripture and the nature of its authority.

Nature gives us "proofs of the existence of a creative, intelligent Power, by whom all things were made," but Scripture is essential to steer humanity away from polytheism, pantheism, Deism, and other distortions. Biblical revelation alone shows us the true nature of God and therefore of salvation.[8]

Periodically Roberts returned to the theme of biblical radicalism. A lead article in the February 1869 *Earnest Christian* entitled "Radicalism of the Bible" spelled out his view: "The Bible is a Radical book. It never proposes half-way measures. The word radical comes from radix[,] root — and the Bible always goes to the root of the matter." The Bible shows that sin must be abandoned at once, not tolerated over time. Echoing the arguments of earlier abolitionists, Roberts insisted this was true in both a personal and a social sense. "Sin may be deeply planted in the nature, confirmed by indulgence, and strengthened by Legislative enactments. *God shows it no quarter.* Slavery struck its roots deep in the virgin soil of our country; *but God overthrew it.* Intemperance has the high sanctions of law for its support; but itself and the laws by which it is sustained are placed under the ban of the Higher Law. — *Woe unto him that giveth his neighbor drink, that putteth thy bottle to him, and maketh him drunken also.* Hab. ii.15."

Roberts believed divine revelation went to the bottom — the root — of the human predicament. "The Bible, unlike all human schemes, destroys sin, in the very fountains of its existence. It makes the fruit good, by making the tree good." Its radicalism is seen also in the fact that the Bible's "requirements" are not just for the church; Scripture "imposes its commands alike upon all." "God's law is universal. It covers all his creatures."

The Bible therefore calls for radical obedience — no halfway measures. We must be fully "and continuously devoted to the service of God." Quoting both Jonathan Edwards and Stephen Olin, Roberts argued: "To serve God moderately is to serve the devil fully. . . . Lukewarmness is as dangerous as idolatry."[9]

This was the view of the later as well as the earlier Roberts. "Biblical Radicalism," the lead article in the April 1887 *Earnest Christian*, made a similar argument. The Bible proposes a radical solution to the human dilemma. Radicalism "means root work, going to the root of the matter. When applied to sins or wrongs, it means taking them out by the roots. When applied to righteousness it means becoming rooted in its principles." The Bible deals not just with externals but "with first principles." The scriptural way is radical because it requires both inward change and outward conformity to God's law. Roberts applied this both to personal holiness — the "disease" of sin "must be removed" — and to social reform. "Christianity has reformed society wherever it has gone" because it gets to root issues. Christianity

7. B. T. Roberts, *Fishers of Men*, p. 8.
8. B. T. Roberts, "Thoughts of God," *EC* 61, no. 1 (Jan. 1891): 5-8.
9. B. T. Roberts, "Radicalism of the Bible," *EC* 17, no. 2 (Feb. 1869): 37-38.

rooted out slavery not by "direct attack upon the civil institutions" but "by stirring up the consciences of men against every kind of wrong. This is still the true way to reform society."[10]

As noted earlier in discussions concerning the gospel for the poor, much of this radicalism comes from Roberts's focus on the life and ministry of Jesus Christ. Similar to the Radical Protestant tradition and early Methodism, Roberts focused not only on the death and resurrection of Jesus but equally on his life and teachings and on what it meant to follow him faithfully. The church must prioritize ministry to and among the poor because that is what Jesus did. Christians are to follow Jesus' example in living holy lives and in denouncing hypocrisy and injustice.

The roots of this radicalism trace to Roberts's frontier upbringing, to his early exposure to abolitionism and Finneyite revivalism, and to his high regard for and actual engagement with Scripture. It no doubt has some grounding also in what historian Gordon S. Wood has called "the radicalism of the American Revolution" that still shaped the western New York society in which Roberts grew up.[11]

2. The Church as Redeemed, Holy Community

Roberts had a clear, thought-out conception of the nature and mission of the church. At heart this was the ecclesiology he had inherited from the Methodist Episcopal Church, modified to some extent by American democratic ideas and pragmatism. He represented that element within and, later, beyond the ME Church that wanted to see church government made more democratic and responsive to the people. But his fundamental conception of the church was essentially Methodist.

A seemingly small Free Methodist doctrinal shift in 1870 gives insight into his view of the church. The change involved the Articles of Religion. It seems not to have provoked much discussion.[12] Though it involved the change of just one word, it tellingly altered the denomination's declared doctrine about the nature of the church.

---

10. B. T. Roberts, "Biblical Radicalism," *EC* 53, no. 4 (Apr. 1887): 101-5.

11. Gordon S. Wood, *The Radicalism of the American Revolution* (New York: Vintage Books, 1993). Wood writes, "To base a society on the commonplace behavior of ordinary people may be obvious and understandable to us today, but it was momentously radical in the long sweep of world history up to that time" (p. ix). Arguing that the American Revolution was "as radical and social as any revolution in history" — though "in a very special eighteenth-century sense" — Wood says: "By the time the Revolution had run its course in the early nineteenth century, American society had been radically and thoroughly transformed. One class did not overthrow another; the poor did not supplant the rich. But social relationships — the way people were connected one to another — were changed, and decisively so. By the early years of the nineteenth century [i.e., just prior to Roberts's birth] the Revolution had created a society fundamentally different from the colonial society of the eighteenth century" (pp. 5-6). See also Joyce Appleby, *Inheriting the Revolution: The First Generation of Americans* (Cambridge: Harvard University, Belknap Press, 2000), especially chap. 7, "Reform."

12. Neither Marston nor Hogue discuss it, though they do note other (relatively minor) doctrinal changes at the 1870 General Conference. See Hogue, *HFMC*, 2:175-76; Marston, p. 289.

The 1856 *Discipline* of the ME Church (upon which the Free Methodist Articles of Religion were based) stated, "The visible Church of Christ is a congregation of faithful men, in which the pure word of God is preached, and the sacraments duly administered, according to Christ's ordinance, in all those things that of necessity are requisite to the same."[13] This is the classic formulation that John Wesley took over word for word from the Anglican Thirty-nine Articles.

The original Free Methodist statement in 1860 was identical. However, in the 1870 *Discipline* the definition was changed to read "a congregation of pure men" rather than "faithful men."[14] The shift is significant because it locates the purity of the church less in the purity of the gospel preached and more in the purity of the church's members. The church is a community not just of "the faithful," but of "the pure." In Roberts's mind there may not have been a big difference between the two, but clearly he (and whoever else was responsible for this change) wanted to accent that "faithful" meant pure (an inner transformation), not just loyal in religious practice.[15]

This shift is consistent with the more explicit emphasis on entire sanctification that Free Methodists adopted in 1860, compared with the ME Church. It may be thought of, in fact, as the ecclesiological implication or counterpart of the stress on inner cleansing. Although in terms of explicit theology the shift from "faithful" to "pure" is not major — essentially a matter of nuance — it did alter an ancient formula going back to Latin theology and gave a sense of Roberts's theology of Christian experience and of the church.[16]

Roberts and his colleagues were no doubt thinking of holiness when they defined the church as "a congregation of pure men." Yet the statement didn't say "holy men" — probably recognizing that not all Christians have experienced entire sanctification, and yet if they were truly converted they were a part of the church. Presumably a church would be "pure" if those members who had not yet experienced holiness were earnestly seeking it.[17]

This was somewhat different from John Wesley's view. Wesley was perhaps less sanguine that all true Christians could be expected to experience entire sanctification and was more comfortable with the seeming paradox that all Christians should experience holiness and yet many in fact would not. Wesley seems to have been more

13. *The Doctrines and Discipline of the Methodist Episcopal Church, 1856* (Cincinnati: Swormstedt and Poe, 1859), p. 20.

14. *The Doctrines and Discipline of the Free Methodist Church* (Rochester, N.Y.: General Conference, 1870), p. 24 (art. XVI). Compare the 1860, 1862, and 1866 editions.

15. Sociologically speaking, this change is evidence that the Free Methodist Church at this point was more of a sect than was the Methodist Episcopal Church. It is conceivable, however, that Roberts was not himself entirely comfortable with this change. Presumably it was made as a result of General Conference action, but the 1870 General Conference minutes do not record any debate or action specifically on this.

16. See Snyder, *Radical Wesley*, pp. 73-75.

17. The doctrinal formula continued to read "pure men" until the 1951 *Discipline*, when the original wording, "faithful men," was restored.

ready than was Roberts to acknowledge as genuinely part of the body of Christ those professed Christians whose experience fell short of the provisions of grace.

The true church of Jesus Christ is composed of saints, those who are holy or sanctified, Roberts maintained. "The true church is holy; not in name merely, but in reality." This holiness is a matter of life and character, not just belief. It "implies personal purity" and "has to do, not merely with the head, but much more with the affections and the will and the every day life." This, Roberts argued, is clear from the New Testament use of the term "church." He was ready to acknowledge that this did not necessarily mean the consistent holiness of every member — "exceptions there doubtless were," even in the early church — "but the general character of the church was such that they were spoken of, as a body, as possessing a high degree of sanctity."[18] A church is holy if its "general character" is holy, in spite of some "exceptions."

Roberts does not spell out precisely what this means. What percentage of truly holy members (or what other qualities) determines the "general character" of a church? What he seems to have meant is that the church should do its best to maintain a "general character" of holiness; should admit only those who are truly seeking holiness; and to this end should exercise discipline. (The above quotations on the nature of the church in fact introduce the "Discipline" chapter in *Fishers of Men*. The "New Testament idea of the constitution of the church" calls for careful, godly discipline, which "should be exercised by each church as a whole, and not by the ministers alone.")[19]

In an 1875 article Roberts discussed the use of *ekklesia* in the New Testament and, more generally, biblical teachings on the church. He described the church as essentially "those whom Christ has called out of the world and who have obeyed the call." The apostle Paul in 1 Corinthians 1:2 "designates the Church, not by its creed, or officers, or history, but by the character of those of whom it is composed." Noting a number of other passages that speak of the holiness and character of Christians, Roberts concluded:

> These, then, are the persons who, united together for the worship of God and the spread of His kingdom, constitute the Church of Christ. The fundamental thing is — not the creed, nor government, nor history — these may be important — but they are not essential — but the character of its members. . . . This accords, as we understand it, with the definition of "the Church," given in the nineteenth article of the Church of England: "The visible Church of Christ is a congregation of faithful men in which the pure word of God is preached, and the sacraments duly administered."

Weighing the adequacy of this traditional Anglican definition, Roberts wrote: "A congregation of faithful men" implies "those who have those graces of the Spirit, and a life corresponding, which fit men for heaven." He added, "If the congregation is

---

18. B. T. Roberts, *Fishers of Men*, pp. 322-25.
19. B. T. Roberts, *Fishers of Men*, pp. 320-21, 325.

mixed, a part faithful, and a part unfaithful, then the faithful part, however small, constitutes the Church."

Significantly, Roberts finds the Anglican qualification "In which the pure word of God is preached" to be "too exclusive. . . . I would not deny that 'a congregation of faithful men' is a Church, because they may listen sometimes to preaching which is not in every particular 'the pure word of God.'" Similarly with regard to the sacraments being "duly administered," Roberts says, "I could not insist upon this in its full force and meaning. It is important that the sacraments be duly administered, but where is the passage of Scripture that makes this essential . . . ? I would not deny that a congregation of faithful Quakers belong to the Church of Christ, if they love God with all their hearts, and are led by the Spirit, and have come out from the world and are separate." Roberts argued that the "essential thing to the existence of the Church of Christ is the spiritual state of its members," and quoted John Wesley to this effect.[20]

These statements suggest some of what Roberts meant by "maintaining the Bible standard of Christianity and preaching the gospel to the poor." The two accents seem to function as essential ecclesiological marks. The church is an organized but diverse congregation of people who reflect the character of Jesus Christ (love and holiness) and the example of Jesus Christ (ministry to and with the poor).

In this ecclesiology the sacraments play a comparatively minor role. Roberts seldom wrote about the sacraments, although when he was a pastor he occasionally preached on baptism.[21] In the 1890 article "Training Children" he defended infant baptism primarily as an act of dedication. Noting that the "custom of dedicating children to the service of the God that his parents worshipped is of very ancient origin," Roberts wrote, "Christians should solemnly dedicate their children to God in holy baptism. If it is said that this is nowhere commanded in the New Testament, we reply that it is nowhere forbidden. This answer is all sufficient."[22]

In treating of the church, Roberts does not discuss directly the four classic Ni-

---

20. B. T. Roberts, "Who Compose the Church," *EC* 29, no. 4 (Apr. 1875): 101-3.

21. Roberts published a one-paragraph editorial entitled "Sacraments" in 1877 and occasionally wrote on the question of communion wine. See [B. T. Roberts], "Sacraments," *EC* 34, no. 4 (Oct. 1877): 130. While the sacraments "should be held in high esteem" and not neglected, we are not saved by them but solely through Jesus Christ. "The means of grace are all intended to bring us near to God. Christ is our only Saviour."

22. B. T. Roberts, "Training Children," *EC* 59, no. 3 (Mar. 1890): 69. Roberts cites also Abraham's dedication of his children through circumcision (Gen. 17) as precedent. Douglas Cullum gives a helpful summary of sacramental understanding and practice in Roberts and early Free Methodism in his dissertation "Gospel Simplicity: Rhythms of Faith and Life among Free Methodists in Victorian America" (Ph.D. diss., Drew University, 2002), pp. 278-88. Cullum notes, "Early Free Methodist sacramental practices were largely identical to those of the parent denomination. . . . This means that early Free Methodists inherited the tension between a sacramental and an evangelical theology that characterized movements and churches in the Methodist family since the time of the Wesleys. And, like other representatives of nineteenth-century American Methodism, early Free Methodists tended to accent the evangelical side of the equation. Therefore, the preaching of the gospel was almost always given prominence over the sacraments in early Free Methodist worship. Nevertheless, a certain appreciation of the sacraments was a constant feature of Free Methodist piety in the founding era" (pp. 278-79).

cene "marks" or "notes" of the church (one, holy, catholic, apostolic). He stressed holiness, of course, and he implied (following Stephen Olin) that preaching the gospel to the poor was tied up with the church's apostolicity. In his keynote "Free Churches" article in the first issue of the *Earnest Christian* in 1860 (quoted in chapter 26), Roberts maintained that "the duty of preaching the gospel to the poor" is plainly enjoined in the Bible, and that doing so "is the standing proof of the Divine mission of the Church."[23] He was thus making a claim not just about evangelism or about the gospel, but about the nature of the church itself.

An 1884 *Earnest Christian* article shows how preaching the gospel to the poor and maintaining "the Bible standard of Christianity" were for Roberts two sides of the same coin. The pastor of "a large, fashionable church," after hearing about the nature of Free Methodism, asked Roberts, "Is there not danger of making the door narrower than Christ has made it? Of imposing burdens upon the people which Christ does not impose?"

Roberts admitted there was such a danger — though he was not ready to admit, apparently, that the Free Methodist Church actually did this. Rather, "the greater danger [lies] in the opposite direction." Quoting perhaps his favorite verse — "Strait is the gate, and narrow is the way" (Matt. 7:14) — Roberts implied that Free Methodists really did not require anything more than Jesus did. Properly understood, the "New Testament standard of Christianity," though demanding, really brings liberation. "In trying to persuade the people to come to the New Testament standard of Christianity we lighten their burdens," he said. "We endeavor to persuade [people] to renounce all popular, as well as unpopular sins." Sins "tolerated by the popular churches" are what weigh people down: the burden of pride that "leads many into bankruptcy," the financial and health burdens of tobacco, the burden of expensive church buildings. "It is expensive to keep up expensive churches. The congregation must dress in style. The singing must be artistic and paid for. The preacher must be genteel and have a large salary."

This is not the Bible way, Roberts reasoned. Rather, "is it not evident that in trying to persuade the people to return to gospel humility and simplicity and plainness we are seeking to lighten their burdens? We render it possible for every man who will repent of his sins and get saved, to become a respected and respectable member of the church." Roberts concluded with Luke 4:18 (another favorite text): "The Spirit of the Lord is upon me, because he hath anointed me to preach the gospel to the poor."[24]

This is an interesting argument — an attempt to bridge the inclusive and exclusive aspects of the gospel. In the last few decades of Free Methodist history, certainly since the 1960s, majority opinion in the denomination has shifted to the view that the Free Methodist Church should not require more for membership than the New Testament church did. Roberts says, in effect: the New Testament church had high membership standards. Though inclusive in its invitation, it was exclusive in its de-

23. Benjamin T. Roberts, "Free Churches," *EC* 1, no. 1 (Jan. 1860): 7-8.
24. [B. T. Roberts], "Unloosing Burdens," *EC* 47, no. 4 (Apr. 1884): 101-4.

mands. The church today has no license to compromise — to require less than total commitment. And (Roberts implies) the church must make that commitment specific in terms of the "popular sins" of the day.[25] Since holiness is to be the normative experience for Christians, it should be the normal requirement for church membership. If one wants a church with minimal requirements, there are plenty of those around. But they don't lead very deep into the enjoyment and liberty of the gospel. The truly liberating way, the truly fulfilling way, and the way that wins the poor and breaks down class barriers in the new community of the church is the "strait and narrow way" that "leads to life." This was the justification for the Free Methodist Church and, Roberts believed, its essential charism.

Like Wesley, Roberts had a functional view of church order. Despite his lofty view of holiness, he recognized that the church was also an organization, or at least had an organizational dimension. "God has always had a visibly organized church," he argued in 1883. "Wherever two or more individuals act together and each has his allotted duties to perform for the benefit of the whole, there is an organization." The organization of the Christian church began with Jesus Christ himself, who at the beginning of his ministry "began to visibly organize his church." Roberts viewed the statement about apostles, prophets, evangelists, pastors, and teachers in Ephesians 4:11 as Jesus' action in making the church's "organization more complex" in response to the church's growth. He thought the various gifts mentioned in 1 Corinthians 12:28 constituted "eight different classes [or categories] of workers" in the church and that this was a divine "permanent arrangement." Such passages clearly demonstrate "that the Church of Christ is a visible, organized body."[26] (Roberts was here arguing against the "Campbellites" [Disciples of Christ] and others who argued that a truly New Testament church would be nonsectarian and nondenominational.)

Several years earlier Roberts had argued that though the New Testament "does not prescribe any method of Church government," it does give "general principles" for the church's effectiveness and efficiency. Ephesians 4 and 1 Corinthians 12 clearly teach "a variety of officers in the church," and none "of these gifts has been recalled." Thus "whatever form of government be adopted," the church should recognize "all the different kinds of orders or ministers which God has appointed." This was actually a prescription for variety and flexibility, he felt. Traditional Protestantism has often been too restrictive in dividing "the church mainly into two classes — preachers and members." The church would be closer to the New Testament pattern, Roberts implied, if it affirmed a wider variety of ministers and "officers," though he does not spell out the implications of this.[27]

Roberts was explicit that the gift of healing and other spiritual gifts would be found in any spiritually alive church. Jesus gave his disciples a commission to heal,

25. This, of course, John Wesley attempted to do in his "General Rules" for Methodists.

26. [B. T. Roberts], "Church Organizations," EC 15, no. 6 (June 1883): 165-66.

27. B. T. Roberts, "Officers of the Church," EC 29, no. 6 (June 1875): 166-67. Roberts here uses "gifts" and "orders of ministers" interchangeably, based on Eph. 4:11 and 1 Cor. 12:28.

and the "gift of healing was to remain in the Church as a permanent gift," though not all Christians receive it. "The *graces* of the Spirit are for all. The *gifts* of the Spirit, God, in his sovereignty, bestows upon whomsoever he chooses."[28]

Roberts "emphatically" denied that the gift of healing was for the early church only. Healing "was to run down through all ages, to the end of the world." This and other gifts are to be expected when God works in the church. "Dead trees can be sawed into boards of the same size. Dead churches can easily have but one order of ministers. But just as soon as a church gets life enough to let God's order begin to prevail these different classes of ministers [mentioned in 1 Cor. 12] appear. Then some stand out whom God has given the 'gift of healing.' These have appeared from time to time, in the church, in all ages."[29]

In an 1885 editorial entitled simply "Sects," Roberts, with sociological realism, argued the inevitability of sects in a free society and the naïveté of thinking otherwise. "Any religious organization or association composed of Christians, that acts and worships permanently together and does not include *all the Christians* of that place or country is of necessity a sect. There is no possibility of avoiding it. It may claim as its chief feature that it opposes sects. It may call itself by the most *general* name that can be found. That makes no difference. Names do not alter the nature of things."

Denouncing the division of Christianity into sects is therefore nonsensical. "The one who makes opposition to sects the pretext for trying to get up another sect presumes most wonderfully upon the ignorance and the credulity of mankind."[30]

Roberts was prepared in fact to argue that the division of the church "into sects, or sections, or divisions," was actually God's will. "The Christian church itself is but a sect of the Abrahamic church." The very division of the church "tends to promote its unity and efficiency" and also "promote[s] its purity" since the different groups "reform each other." Arguing in a manner somewhat similar to the Moravian leader Nikolaus von Zinzendorf in the previous century, Roberts felt each particular sect had its special contribution to make, like the various divisions in an army.[31] Methodists might disagree with Friends and Baptists on certain points, for example, but they could appreciate their contribution to the gospel — Friends, "in endeavoring to persuade people to be governed by the strictest integrity," and Baptists for their "great work in extending Christ's Kingdom" through aggressive evangelism.[32]

Christianity in fact "exists in its most corrupt forms where there are no sects," Roberts asserted. As new groups arise, they reform and vitalize the church. "The Protestants reformed the Roman Catholic church by coming out from it, as they could not have done by remaining in it," and the history of Methodism and Free Methodism was similar. Division into various groups is actually a sign of life. "Live

---

28. B. T. Roberts, "Healing Faith," *EC* 50, no. 5 (Nov. 1885): 134-35.

29. B. T. Roberts, "Healing Faith," p. 135.

30. [B. T. Roberts], "Sects," *EC* 49, no. 6 (June 1885): 184.

31. See the discussion of Zinzendorf's ecclesiology in Howard A. Snyder, *Signs of the Spirit: How God Reshapes the Church* (Grand Rapids: Zondervan, 1989), pp. 141-57.

32. [B. T. Roberts], "Church Organizations," pp. 166-68.

things never agree in every particular." Yet Christians "in different sects can labor in harmony to try and get men to be holy in heart and in life." "One may belong to a sect without being sectarian."

Roberts thought, therefore: "The true course is that which is generally pursued. When Christians cannot, in conscience, agree with those with whom they are associated, in matters of primary importance, they should separate from them. If they cannot find any with whom they can conscientiously agree they should form a new sect — as the Protestants, Baptists, Friends, Methodists and others have done. This should never be effected unless it becomes strictly necessary."[33]

If this sounds like special pleading or self-justification, it also represents sociological and historical realism. Roberts's views here in fact neatly parallel the sociological argument that Rodney Stark and Roger Finke make in their "religious economy" model of "the churching of America." The greater the freedom and religious variety, the more the vitality and growth.[34] Roberts thought such diversity would ultimately work for the unity and vitality of the church. This is not blanket justification for multiplying sects, however. "No two denominations of Christians should be found in the same country unless there is, on some points at least, a radical difference between them."[35]

Roberts believed that much of the life and vitality of the church hinged on the preaching service, which he viewed as a key battleground. In his 1862 "Free Churches" article he contrasted the formal worship of pew-renting churches with what he evidently saw as the proper, normative pattern. In "a free church" the "members are drawn together by the strong laws of spiritual affinity. This is as it should be. If you wish to kindle a fire you must bring your materials into contact with each other." Switching metaphors, Roberts compared a live church service to a phalanx of soldiers on the field of battle.

> When the soldiers of Jesus are left to arrange themselves according to their own spiritual instincts upon the field of conflict with the powers of darkness [not segregated by assigned pews], the oldest and most devoted will be found nearest the altar; others, anxious to follow them as they follow Christ, will come next, all forming one united, invincible body, ready to do battle under the Captain of their salvation. Nearest to these the most deeply convicted and hopeful of the unconverted take their places. The hymn is given out; the lovers of God, being together, sing his praises "with the Spirit, and with the understanding;" the minister says "Let us pray," and a host of praying souls kneel down and pray with him; their earnest petitions go up with his, and the Holy Spirit comes down upon all their

33. [B. T. Roberts], "Church Organizations," pp. 166-68.

34. See Roger Finke and Rodney Stark, *The Churching of America, 1776-2005: Winners and Losers in Our Religious Economy* (New Brunswick, N.J.: Rutgers University Press, 2005), an updating of their 1992 book; Rodney Stark and Roger Finke, *Acts of Faith: Explaining the Human Side of Religion* (Berkeley: University of California Press, 2000).

35. [B. T. Roberts], "Holiness Sects," *EC* 47, no. 6 (June 1884): 187.

hearts; and by the time the opening services are through, the man of God finds he has a warm and free atmosphere in which to preach. As he commences his sermon, the fire burns with increasing intensity — it goes from heart to heart, the deep-felt "amen" and the stirring shout are occasionally heard; the preacher is carried far beyond himself; the saints of God are blessed — sinners are awakened, and all go away feeling that the Lord has met with his people to-day. Some may seem offended; and threaten never to come again; but they will, in all probability, be found at the next service. This is no overdrawn picture, as many can testify.[36]

On the other hand, Roberts warned that a congregation could be "preached to death" if a pastor did not understand how a church properly functions and tried to accomplish everything through preaching.[37]

A church that faithfully preached and lived out the gospel would grow and have an impact in society. It would proclaim a gospel of holiness and the narrow way, but blessed and empowered by the Holy Spirit, it would move ahead. Any church where the gospel is faithfully preached "will grow in piety, in numbers, and in influence."[38] Especially, it will effectively preach the gospel to and among the poor.

3. Mission to and with the Poor

Roberts's insistence that the mission of the Free Methodist Church was twofold — to maintain the Bible standard of Christianity and to preach the gospel to the poor — was of course a statement about mission as well as about the church. Better: it was an affirmation that in a fundamental sense church and mission are one, especially in their focus upon the poor.

This insistence that the church has a fundamental commission to preach the gospel to the poor was perhaps the most radical note in Roberts's theology, at least in the context of early nineteenth-century Methodism and post–Civil War American society. Everything about the church's evangelistic outreach was to be measured by fidelity to this principle, Roberts felt.

Roberts's insistence on the priority of the gospel to the poor was not simply a call to evangelism. It was a call to be the kind of community Jesus initiated. This is especially clear in the key Stephen Olin quotation that Roberts used in his original 1860 "Free Churches" essay. Roberts quoted at length a sermon by Olin entitled "The Adaptation of the Gospel to the Poor," a sermon Roberts may have heard at Wesleyan University but in any case had read.

There are hot controversies about the true Church. What constitutes it — what is essential to it — what vitiates it? These may be important questions, but there are

---

36. B. T. Roberts, "Free Churches," *EC* 3, no. 5 (May 1862): 134-35.
37. [B. T. Roberts], "Preached to Death," *EC* 45, no. 3 (Mar. 1883): 95.
38. [B. T. Roberts], "Preached to Death."

more important ones. It may be that there can not be a Church without a bishop, or that there can. There can be none without a Gospel, and a Gospel for the poor. Does a Church preach the Gospel to the poor — preach it effectively? Does it convert and sanctify the people? Are its preaching, its forms, its doctrines adapted *specially* to these results? If not, we need not take the trouble of asking any more questions about it. It has missed the main matter. It does not do what Jesus did — what the apostles did. Is there a Church — a ministry — that converts, reforms, sanctifies the people? Do the poor really learn to love Christ? Do they live purely and die happy? I hope that Church conforms to the New Testament in its government and forms as far as may be. I trust it has nothing anti-Republican, or schismatic, or disorderly in its fundamental principles and policy. I wish its ministers may be men of the best training, and eloquent. I hope they worship in goodly temples, and all that; but [more important:] They preach a saving Gospel to the poor, and that is enough. It is an apostolic Church. Christ is the corner-stone. The main thing is secured, thank God.[39]

This Roberts fully affirmed. An apostolic church — a church that does what Jesus did and obeys the commission given to the first Christians — ministers the gospel to and among the poor.

Roberts returned to this theme repeatedly. He wrote in 1864,

The preaching of the Gospel to the poor is the standing miracle which attests to its Divine origin. It is placed by our Saviour in the same class with raising the dead, and cleansing lepers — something which no man acting from the mere promptings of nature ever did, or ever will do. It requires no heaven-born motive to lead one of a literary and serious turn of mind to read, for a good salary, nicely written essays on moral or religious topics, to an audience whose gentility is secured by the high price needed to pay for a sitting; but to go out, without purse or scrip, among the poor and the outcast, and proclaim the Gospel of God in all fidelity, having no dependence for support but the promise, "Lo, I am with you always," is a course of life, which one will not be very likely to pursue until the end of his days, unless he has been sent by God. He who does this, is in the true succession. He walks as Christ walked.[40]

39. Stephen Olin, "The Adaptation of the Gospel to the Poor," in *The Works of Stephen Olin, D.D., LL.D., Late President of the Wesleyan University* (New York: Harper and Brothers, 1852), 1:345. Roberts quotes this passage (and more) from Olin in his original "Free Churches" article. This had been a common Wesleyan emphasis since the days of early British and American Methodism, but by the 1850s it was fading or even under attack. Bishop Thomas Morris (1794-1874), who ordained Roberts, had argued similarly in the 1840s in a sermon entitled "The Privileges of the Poor," based on Matt. 11:5, noting that the answer Jesus sent to John the Baptist "afforded the most conclusive evidence of Messiahship, by showing himself to be the author of the very works which the ancient prophets had foretold Messiah should perform." Thomas A. Morris, *Sermons on Various Occasions* (Cincinnati: Swormstedt and Mitchell, 1845), pp. 172-87.

40. Benjamin T. Roberts, "Gospel to the Poor," *EC* 7, no. 3 (Mar. 1864): 70.

Roberts advanced both a sociological and a theological argument about the priority of the poor — or, perhaps more accurately, a sociotheological argument. "Wesley and Whitefield, going to the collieries and commons, and into the streets and lanes of the cities, proclaiming the Gospel to the neglected masses, . . . did more to rescue England from infidelity than all the learned divines who wrote essays upon 'the evidences of Christianity,'" he said. "In all ages" the poor are most ready to respond to the Gospel. Roberts elaborated:

> If it is the duty of the Church of Jesus Christ to preach the Gospel to the poor, then all the arrangements of the Church must be made with a view to the accomplishment of this end. No incidental provision will answer. It must be aimed at directly. Every thing, in the adoption of prudential regulations, that has a tendency to defeat this, must be thrown out. If the Gospel is placed within the reach of the poor it is placed within the reach of all. . . . Preaching that awakens the attention of the poor, and leads them to Jesus, will interest all classes.

Roberts concluded the article with a Jubilee appeal to Isaiah 61 and Luke 4:

> Let us come back to the spirit of the Gospel. Let us get down so low at the feet of Jesus as to forget all our pride and dignity, and be willing to worship with the lowest of our kind, remembering that we are the followers of Him "who had not where to lay his head." "THE SPIRIT OF THE LORD IS UPON ME, BECAUSE HE HATH ANOINTED ME TO PREACH THE GOSPEL TO THE POOR; *he hath sent me to heal the broken-hearted, to preach deliverance to the captives, and recovering of sight to the blind, to set at liberty them that are bruised, to preach the acceptable year of the Lord.*"[41]

In this discussion Roberts (and Olin) were making two fundamental claims: first, that preaching the gospel to the poor is an essential identifying mark of the church; and secondly, that the genuineness of the church's *apostolicity* may be tested by this mark. Whoever ministers the gospel among the poor "is in the true succession. He walks as Christ walked," Roberts asserted. The church that preaches the gospel to the poor "is an apostolic Church," Olin said. True apostolicity means the church following in the steps of Jesus.[42]

---

41. B. T. Roberts, "Gospel to the Poor," p. 73.

42. The theological significance of Roberts's ecclesiological claim has been highlighted by Donald W. Dayton in "The Wesleyan Option for the Poor," *Wesleyan Theological Journal* 26, no. 1 (Spring 1991): 7-16. Dayton observed, "Roberts seems to be arguing that 'a preferential option for the poor' is defining of the true church — that it belongs to its *esse* rather than to its *bene esse*. As such Roberts has . . . clearly articulated the Wesleyan 'preferential option for the poor,' grounding it theologically in the messianic office of Jesus and making it defining of the church — thus raising it to the level of the *status confessionis* of more confessional traditions" (p. 14). Dayton included Roberts's 1860 "Free Churches" article as an appendix to his essay (pp. 17-22). Significantly, Roberts's appeal here is primarily to Scripture, and particularly to the teaching and example of Jesus Christ. There is no explicit reference to the creeds.

Roberts's passion on this key point has been observed throughout this book. The question should be raised, however: How do the stress on holiness and the accent on the gospel to the poor fit together in Roberts's theology? Is there an essential theological connection?

As noted in chapter 32, Roberts saw holiness and preaching the gospel to the poor as intimately linked. But Roberts seems never to have spelled out this link theologically. A possible criticism of his theology would be this failure to develop a necessary connection between mission to the poor and sanctification. More generally, Roberts did not fully develop this side of his doctrine of redemption. His concern with both the poor and holiness was based in Jesus' redeeming work, but this connection was not clarified. Of course, Roberts's intent on these points was simply to affirm the Methodist tradition that he had inherited, not to do constructive theology.

Significantly, few of his early Free Methodist colleagues (with the notable exception of John Wesley Redfield) apparently stressed preaching the gospel to the poor to the extent Roberts did. This concern was assumed to some degree in early Free Methodism and certainly in Roberts's circles within Methodism prior to 1860. It appears, however, that an explicit, self-conscious commitment to preach the gospel to the poor never penetrated deeply into Free Methodist self-understanding and that the concern waned following Roberts's death.[43]

From the beginning, Free Methodism lived with a certain tension between mission to the poor and to "all classes." A. A. Phelps, for example, in an early article in the *Earnest Christian,* said the new denomination was raised up *"to seek the salvation of all classes,"* to open its "doors alike for the rich and the poor, the black and the white, the educated and illiterate." It is instructive that in an article that he entitled "Mission of the Free Methodist Church," Phelps put no particular stress on the poor.[44] Roberts probably did not disagree with what Phelps said (he published the article, after all). But Roberts never could speak at any length about the mission of the church without especially accenting the poor.

4. The Life of Holiness

Holiness of heart and life was central in Roberts's theology. Yet when he sought a name for his magazine he didn't choose something like *Guide to Holiness* (Phoebe

---

43. This question deserves further research, however. It would require a thorough search of the *Earnest Christian* up to the time it ceased publication, and particularly of the *Free Methodist,* as well as the fairly voluminous Free Methodist missionary and biographical literature. M'Geary's *Outline History* of the denomination says nothing specifically about the gospel to the poor and very little about pew rental, though it gives considerable attention to the secret society issue and some to abolitionism. "The real issue was between worldliness and formality on the one hand and a vital, Spirit-baptized type of religion on the other." John S. M'Geary, *The Free Methodist Church: A Brief Outline History of Its Origin and Development,* 3rd ed. (Chicago: W. B. Rose, 1908, 1910), p. 20.

44. A. A. Phelps, "Mission of the Free Methodist Church," *EC,* Feb. 1861, p. 48.

Palmer's periodical mouthpiece) or *Banner of Holiness*. Instead, he chose the *Earnest Christian*.

Though it is often said that holiness (Christian perfection) was *the* central theme in Roberts's theology, this claim is in fact misleading. "The Bible standard of Christianity" certainly meant holiness, but it meant it in the broad sense of entire Christlikeness and maintaining the truth, justice, and righteousness of the kingdom of God as revealed in Scripture. For Roberts, the gospel for the poor was not a different accent from holiness but an essential part of it.

Benson Roberts, in publishing *Holiness Teachings*, a compilation of B. T. Roberts's editorials, following his father's death in 1893, may have inadvertently contributed to the misperception that holiness was *the* central theme for Roberts. In his preface Benson noted that holiness was "a constantly recurring [not the central] theme" in his father's writing and that B. T. himself had said in the first issue of the *Earnest Christian* that holiness would "occupy a prominent place" (not be the central theme) in the magazine. If *Holiness Teachings* was well received, Benson said, "other volumes on other topics" might follow — but none did. Had Benson published volumes on other subjects — for example, key Roberts themes such as the gospel to the poor, revival, the church, healing, or missions — the dominant perception of Roberts today might be considerably different![45]

Roberts believed in and advocated holiness as the teaching was inherited from John Wesley, Adam Clarke, and John Fletcher and as taught in his day by Phoebe Palmer and others. But it was not holiness for its own sake. It was holiness for the sake of enabling believers to live out the earnest Christianity that the Bible teaches.

Roberts gave attention to both the "crisis" and "process" aspects of sanctification, but (like nineteenth-century Methodist holiness advocates generally) put more emphasis on the crisis of entire sanctification than on the process of growth in holiness throughout life. He did stress that sanctified believers must continue to grow in grace and that entire sanctification was not the beginning point for obedience and holy living; that should mark every stage of Christian life. Growth, taking "advanced ground in Christian experience," is normative Christian experience. "A person clearly converted, and brought by the Spirit of God to see the necessity of going on unto perfection, will, unless he obeys the solicitations of the Spirit, become dry and powerless. One fully sanctified, commanded to 'grow in grace,' and failing to take the advanced steps that God shows him he should, will inevitably become formal, tedious and worse than useless."[46]

Like Wesley, Roberts stressed that entire sanctification was equivalent to the perfecting of love in the believer. "Entire sanctification is but another name for perfect love," he wrote. "One who is sanctified wholly, loves God with all his heart and

---

45. Benson Howard Roberts, *Holiness Teachings: Compiled from the Editorial Writings of the Late Rev. Benjamin T. Roberts, A.M.* . . . (North Chili, N.Y.: "Earnest Christian" Publishing House, 1893), 256 pages. Benson did list at the end of the book several "Earnest Christian Tracts" and B. T. Roberts's books *Fishers of Men* and *Ordaining Women*.

46. [B. T. Roberts], "Spiritual Power," *EC* 2, no. 11 (Nov. 1861): 339.

his neighbor as himself." Yet Roberts was well aware of the risk of self-deception here: "The power of the human heart to deceive itself is seen clearly in the confidence with which some will profess perfect love, while it is apparent to every one but themselves that they sometimes manifest any thing but a loving spirit."[47]

Roberts was explicit that "The perfection which God requires is a perfection of love" — a love that constantly increases. In a brief but pungent 1884 editorial he noted that true perfection is the outworking of having "the love of God shed abroad in our hearts" by the Holy Spirit. "When this is the case — when we love God with all our heart, mind and strength, and our neighbor as ourselves — then have we perfect love. Not that it is incapable of increase. As our capacities enlarge, our love will increase."

Roberts added, "If we have this perfect love to God, it will be manifested — not in words only, but in actions"; in "tender feelings and kind conduct towards our fellow-men." So, he wrote, "Do not profess perfect love, if you are cross, unamiable, and unkind at home. If you have not natural affection, you certainly have not supernatural. If you do not do as well as the brutes, do not profess to be like the angels of God. If you are not kind to her whom you have sworn to cherish, or to those whose protector nature has constituted you, stop your professions at once. You have already sins enough to sink you to hell, without adding hypocrisy to them."[48]

True holiness, Roberts maintained, was manifested in humility and a readiness to admit mistakes. He wrote in 1883, "If overtaken in a fault, or mistaken in our judgment, we must be ready to confess it. Holiness . . . does not imply infallibility. If others think we have been wrong we should candidly look at it and see if we have not been. If in anything we can, in conscience, confess, we should frankly do it. A self-justifying spirit rapidly grows into a Pharisaic spirit. . . . Confessing our faults both evidences and augments our humility."[49]

Don't be discouraged over your mistakes, Roberts urged in an 1890 editorial. "Perfect Love does not secure perfect Knowledge. We know only in part. So we are often mistaken in our opinions and this leads to mistakes in conduct." We should profit from our mistakes and move on. "Because we cannot do as well as we would we must not cease to do as well as we can." He went on to quote Francis de Sales: "It will be a precious imperfection if it makes us acknowledge our weakness and strengthens our humility, our self depreciation, our patience and diligence."[50]

5. Responsible Living in the World

Roberts was particularly concerned that Christians live out holiness in practical ways in society. "The great want of the times," he wrote in 1883, "is men and women

---

47. [B. T. Roberts], "Love," *EC* 50, no. 5 (Nov. 1885): 159.
48. [B. T. Roberts], "Perfection," *EC* 48, no. 4 (Oct. 1884): 127.
49. [B. T. Roberts], "Stand Fast," *EC* 46, no. 1 (July 1883): 8.
50. [B. T. Roberts], "Mistakes," *EC* 60, no. 3 (Sept. 1890): 99.

in every neighborhood who, in every-day life, year in and year out, manifest before the world, practical holiness." Living honest and ethical lives, regardless of how humble their circumstances, such persons are true witnesses of the gospel. "Such persons are needed to keep alive in the minds of the people, the true idea of what it is to be a Christian. They are needed to comfort the afflicted and relieve the distressed. They are needed as friends to be consulted by those in trouble. They are needed to keep before the world examples of holy living. They are needed to point out the way to those who are really in earnest to go to heaven."[51]

Holiness extends to every area of life. Roberts opposed any split-level view that would put spirituality on one plane and business, politics, and economics on another. In an 1891 editorial entitled "Business" he noted, "True consecration takes in one's business. He who serves God in the Church, and serves the devil in his business, does not serve God at all." Both "the nature of the business" and "the manner in which it is carried on" must be examined. "Business is not one thing and religion another. There is not a branch of business into which true religion does not enter and exert a controlling influence."[52]

Christians thus were to be in but not of the world, just as Jesus taught and modeled. They were to live an alternative life, yet to be responsible participants in every legitimate aspect and enterprise of society. Their salt-and-light witness began with the integrity of their lives and their life together in the church but extended to all their legitimate roles as citizens and actors in society. Though concerned about people everywhere, Jesus' followers should have particular regard for justice and the poor.

On this basis Roberts from time to time addressed a range of issues. Although by contemporary standards it seems he gave an inordinate amount of attention to such pet causes as temperance and antisecretism, he did address a broad spectrum of issues. "War," he noted, "is an act of barbarism. When resorted to for the sake of conquest it is no better than organized robbery on a large scale." Strong nations should not dominate weak ones just because they are able to, but should seek equity and justice. "If the world ever reaches true Christian civilization, standing armies will be disbanded and an international tribunal established, by which all disputes between nations shall be authoritatively decided."[53]

Although the pursuit of justice in the world is a consistent theme in Roberts, theologically it is not spelled out in detail. It is seen primarily in the way Roberts wrote about and became engaged in a variety of social, moral, and economic issues. Both Roberts's reform efforts and his personal business dealings were grounded in this conviction of responsible Christian living in the world.

This is why in his book *First Lessons on Money* he was not content to deal with

51. [B. T. Roberts], "A Great Want," *EC* 46, no. 6 (Dec. 1883): 190.

52. [B. T. Roberts], "Business," *EC* 61, no. 3 (Mar. 1891): 94.

53. [B. T. Roberts], "Notes," *FM* 20, no. 9 (Mar. 2, 1887): 1. Note here that patriotism and national sovereignty rank lower, not higher, than international peace and justice, being relativized by the biblical gospel.

issues such as banking or money supply and distribution but also added the chapter "How to Make Money." Its opening paragraph is a concise summary of his understanding of responsible living in the world.

> It is a gross caricature of Christianity to represent that it teaches that happiness in the future world is to be secured by neglecting the duties which we owe to our fellow men in the present world. It teaches quite the contrary. It insists upon the faithful performance of all the duties we owe to others in every relation of life. Nor is the prohibition to lay up for ourselves treasures on earth any exception. We must provide for our own wants, so as not to be chargeable to any; but we must not heap up riches that can do us no good. "But if any provide not for his own, and specially for those of his own house, he hath denied the faith and is worse than an infidel." — 1 Tim. 5:8.[54]

It is proper therefore "for any man to secure a moderate competence" — that is, to have an adequate income and modest standard of living. Yet accumulating riches beyond our reasonable needs is wrong and a moral danger. Echoing Wesley, Roberts wrote: "It is next to impossible for one to have riches and not trust in them."[55]

Roberts and his many successors in Free Methodist higher education felt that the goal of Christian schooling was to prepare youth to function in the world responsibly, making their own way economically, contributing to society, witnessing to the radical power of the gospel, living that out through modesty and simplicity in dress and habits, and maintaining a particular sensitivity to the poor and issues of justice and righteousness.

6. The Crisis and Process of History

Roberts maintained a fine balance between a sense of long-term historical process and apocalyptic crisis. Even though he lived through the near-apocalypse of the Civil War, the earlier abolitionist controversy, and severe economic crises and financial panics, he never adopted the kind of foreshortened apocalyptic worldview found, for example, among the Millerites of the 1840s or among many evangelicals toward the end of the century (as well as today).

Roberts's view of history comes through clearly in some of his editorials during the Civil War. He wrote, for example, in January 1862: "These are historical times in which we live. The world is in motion. Great events are taking place, and greater ones are soon to follow. . . . But God is just the same as ever. His promises are still immu-

54. B. T. Roberts, *First Lessons on Money* (Rochester, N.Y.: B. T. Roberts, 1886), p. 143.

55. B. T. Roberts, "Leaving All," *EC* 49, no. 1 (Jan. 1885): 2. Roberts wrote more explicitly in 1865, "When a competence is secured appropriate *all* the income in doing good." He argued, "A talent to make money should be devoted to the service of God just as much as a talent to preach or write. You have no more right to employ it for your own special advantage in the one case than in the other." [B. T. Roberts], "The True Theory," *EC* 9, no. 3 (Mar. 1865): 94-95.

table . . . though the earth be shaken to its foundations, we have a firm footing. The people never needed to be more earnestly exhorted to live in constant readiness for whatever may transpire than at the present period."[56]

Historic, critical times, yes — and yet Roberts did not speak of an impending apocalypse. He expected history to go on, and the United States to survive the Civil War crisis.

Significantly, Roberts wasn't much interested in the millennial theories and debates that filled the pages of religious periodicals, especially as the end of the century approached. While editor of the *Free Methodist,* he advised would-be contributors: "Now but few read these long continued articles touching the millennium. They are nothing but opinions, and prove nothing; therefore, of what use can they be? . . . Will the millennial theory as ventilated [in such articles] help us to comfort the sick and afflicted ones among us? Will the idea of a Christ coming one thousand years sooner, or later, assist us to lead souls to the Christ who came 1888 years ago?"[57]

Wilson T. Hogg (later Hogue) was one of those who wrote a series of "long continued articles" on millennial theories that ran in the *Free Methodist* in 1888. Under the general title "Premillennialism," Hogg, then a corresponding editor, explained the premillennial theory and why he endorsed it. In his introductory article he noted that he had "received permission from the editor" (Roberts) to publish the series of articles, and that the series was provoked in part by a number of recent articles in the *Free Methodist* that attacked and caricatured "the true theory of Premillennialism." Hogue wrote, "From the study of the Bible alone, I was early led to believe that the second coming of the Lord would be personal and premillennial, although this belief is contrary to my early instruction . . . ; nor have I ever found anything since . . . to unsettle my premillennial views."[58] He found postmillennialism "wholly untenable."[59]

But Roberts himself had little interest in such theories. When he reprinted Leonidas Hamline's article on the millennium in the first number of the *Earnest Christian* in 1860 (which was postmillennial in tone), it wasn't to advance a particular millennial theory but rather to underscore the critical days the church then faced and to exhort the church to faithfulness.[60] As early as 1868 Roberts had written in an article entitled "Christ's Second Coming" that so far as timing was concerned, "we dare not speculate where [the Bible] is silent." He "lack[ed] the temerity," he said, "to pry into mysteries which the word of God assures us are purposely concealed. We have no vanity to gratify by appearing to be wise above what is written. To the law and the testimony." Roberts criticized coupling "the second coming of our Saviour

---

56. [B. T. Roberts], "Our Prospects," *EC* 3, no. 1 (Jan. 1862): 30.

57. B. T. Roberts, "Suggestions to Contributors" (reprinted from the *Free Methodist*), in *Pungent Truths, Being Extracts from the Writings of the Rev. Benjamin Titus Roberts, A.M., While Editor of "The Free Methodist" from 1886 to 1890*, ed. W. B. Rose (Chicago: Free Methodist Publishing House, 1912), p. 106.

58. W. T. Hogg, "Premillennialism. — No. 1," *FM* 21, no. 28 (July 11, 1888): 8.

59. W. T. Hogg, "Premillennialism. — No. 4," *FM* 21, no. 31 (Aug. 1, 1888): 8.

60. See the discussion in chapter 26.

... with other doctrines with which it has no necessary connection, and which we believe to be fundamentally wrong."[61] He was old enough to remember, of course, the mischief caused by the Millerite hysteria in 1843-44.

As the century wore on, Roberts did manifest some heightened expectancy that the end was near. He wrote in January 1887, "Many things look as if we were in the last days. Compare the marks laid down in the Scriptures with the signs of the times." He mentions particularly the increase in spiritism and the "general backslidden condition of the churches." Yet just two months later he speaks of the possibility of an eventual time coming when "the world [might reach] true Christian civilization" and universal peace be achieved through a functioning "international tribunal." As did many evangelical missionary leaders of the time, Roberts saw the likely fulfillment of Matthew 24:14 — the gospel being preached "in all the world for a witness unto all nations" — as a particular "sign that the end is near." Yet the lesson was steady faithfulness, not apocalyptic excitement. "Speculations and disputations as to the time and manner of Christ's coming cannot fit us for his appearing. We must see to it that we have the mind of Christ, that we are meek and lowly in heart, and that like him we are continually going about doing good." He concluded, "Our chief concern should be to see that we are holy in heart and in life and in all manner of conversation. Speculations will not save us; understanding mysteries will not save us; we must have the charity that 'beareth all things, hopeth all things, endureth all things, that never faileth.'"[62]

Roberts's writings confirm Leslie Marston's retrospective analysis. Marston noted in 1860 that Methodism generally, with its accent on God's transforming power in the present order, had put "less emphasis on the time schedule of last things than do those who hold to man's inescapable sinfulness in the present dispensation." Accordingly, the Free Methodist Church has always "included those who could not accept the premillennial position, even when premillennialism was sweeping through the conservative Christian world" at the beginning of the twentieth century.[63] This legacy likewise reflects Roberts's own perspective.[64]

---

61. B. T. Roberts, "Christ's Second Coming," *EC* 16, no. 3 (Sept. 1868): 69-70 — a comment of some interest in the light of the later development of the "fourfold gospel" of A. B. Simpson and others.

62. B. T. Roberts, "The End," *EC* 53, no. 1 (Jan. 1887): 5-9.

63. Marston, p. 298.

64. In an otherwise useful theological study of Roberts, Rick McPeak rather misleadingly describes Roberts's theology as "apocalyptic" and maintains that this is key to understanding his views. McPeak argues, "Roberts' apocalyptic worldview with its dominating metaphor of God as governor drove and directed all of [his] practical reasoning." In fact, however, Roberts's own writings show that in the context of the times, and as the term is generally used, his theology was not apocalyptic. He largely avoided apocalypticism and apocalyptic language. Nor is it clear that "God as governor" (not in itself an apocalyptic image) was a "dominating metaphor" in his theology any more than other images for God's sovereignty and his engagement with human history. McPeak believes that Roberts held to "a dispensational view of history as opposed to the progressive view held by the liberal tradition in American Christianity." This also is misleading. Roberts's theology was dispensational only in the broadest biblical sense. He avoided dispensational theories and his view of history may in fact prop-

Roberts's understanding of history combined crisis and process. Perhaps his classical education and his grounding in Scripture gave him some ballast in the midst of social, political, economic, and ecclesiastical storms. His interest in science and in scientific discoveries is part of the picture, as well. This perspective also reflects, of course, Roberts's fundamental Wesleyan (not to say Edwardean) theology. God is at work in history and will ultimately fulfill his purposes. In the midst of crisis we calmly trust God's guiding hand and through the Spirit we access his power for the present to live holy lives and to be channels of God's saving, liberating power in the world.

Behind this steady confidence in God's handling of history was a conviction of the suprahistorical reality of the kingdom of God and of divine sovereignty. Roberts spelled this out in an unusually lyrical 1881 essay entitled "God's Moral Government." This brief essay (four pages) combines Scripture, poetry, science, and political theory — quoting Isaac Newton, John Milton, and Charles Wesley, among others — in laying out what for Roberts clearly were very deep convictions. He begins with Psalm 145:13, "Thy kingdom is an everlasting kingdom, and thy dominion endureth throughout all generations," and quotes also Nehemiah 9:6, "Thou, even thou, art LORD alone; thou hast made heaven, the heaven of heavens, with all their host, the earth, and all things that are therein, the seas, and all that is therein, and thou preservest them all; and the host of heaven worshippeth thee."

Roberts here articulates his fundamental understanding of God's reign. He has three main points: (1) "God's kingdom is universal in its extent." (2) "It embraces the moral and intellectual as well as the material universe." (3) "God's reign is an eternal one." The same principles work throughout the whole created order because God is fully sovereign. One can reason by analogy from the material to the moral and intellectual realms. There are no self-standing natural laws; rather, "What are called laws of nature are only God's established mode of carrying on the operations of the material world."

Roberts argues,

> [God's] government [and] his dominion [continue] throughout all generations.
>> It began with the first created object.
>> It will continue while eternity rolls its unceasing rounds.
>> We are all subject to the moral government of God.
>> Too many are unmindful of this fact. We hear so much about the mercy of
> God, that we forget that he is a just governor.

---

erly be described as progressive — not of course in a secular evolutionary sense, but in the sense of God progressively working out his purposes in history. McPeak sets up an unnecessary tension between prophetic and apocalyptic accents, and between dispensational and progressive interpretations of history, in a way that obscures the fact that Roberts's theology for the most part bridged these tensions. McPeak does not really substantiate his claims from Roberts's own writings, despite extensive quotations. Rick Hughes McPeak, "Earnest Christianity: The Practical Theology of Benjamin Titus Roberts" (Ph.D. diss., Saint Louis University, 2001).

All people are, universally, responsible before God, who "sets before us motives and then leaves us free to act. We obey or disobey according to the determination of our wills." Thus responsible choice is everything. "Happiness unmixed, eternal is promised on the one hand. Misery unassuaged, unending on the other. Both are rendered more certain than any of the objects for which worldly men live."

God in mercy freely offers salvation to all, without restriction. "A consciousness of the security of his throne disposes him to clemency." If we accept salvation on God's terms, happiness and heaven are ours. But in any case, God's kingdom will triumph. God's army "has always conquered" and "always will"; a "triumph such as imperial Rome never witnessed will be celebrated."[65]

Reflecting on God's "sovereign mercy" thus demonstrated, Roberts quotes the second stanza of Charles Wesley's hymn "Where shall my wondering soul begin":

O how shall I the goodness tell,
    Father, which thou to me hast showed?
That I, a child of wrath and hell,
    I should be called a child of God,
Should know, should feel my sins forgiven,
Blest with this antepast of heaven.[66]

Roberts never spelled out a detailed theology of the kingdom of God and, as noted, generally thought millennial theories missed the point. The important things to know were that God is sovereign, merciful, and just; that he will fulfill his purposes in his way; and that human beings are responsible to obey God and accept his offer of salvation while they have the freedom to do so.

On these points Roberts's fundamental theology is not markedly different from John Wesley's and has significant points of contact with that of Jonathan Edwards. Roberts had an orthodox view of the existence and sovereignty of God, of the moral nature of the universe, and of human probation, responsibility, and gracious possibility.

Nevertheless, when one views his theology in toto, it does seem that for all his avowed intent to follow in the footsteps of John Wesley (and John Fletcher and other Methodist worthies), in some respects his theology represents a narrowing of Wesley's theology — perhaps even a narrowing of Fletcher's thought, for Fletcher was closer to Wesley, both in time and in theology, than to Roberts.

The main contributing influences to this theological narrowing seem to have been Phoebe Palmer and especially Charles Finney, together with the general ethos

65. B. T. Roberts, "God's Moral Government," *EC* 42, no. 4 (Oct. 1881): 101-4. See the related discussion in McPeak, "Earnest Christianity," especially chap. 5. McPeak concludes that God as governor was Roberts's "dominating metaphor." I don't see sufficient evidence throughout Roberts's writings, however, to conclude that this metaphor was more dominant than others. For Roberts it served primarily as an assertion of the sovereignty of God and the nature of God's reign.

66. Charles Wesley, "The Antepast of Heaven," hymn 415 in the 1883 *Hymn Book of the Free Methodist Church* (Rochester, N.Y.: B. T. Roberts, 1883).

of the Methodism in which Roberts was raised (including the influence of Olin and Redfield). From Finney the influence was more indirect than direct, but no less shaping. It came less from Finney's formally articulated theology than from the ethos created by his early revivalism and the theology that undergirded it and was diffused by it.

The Finney-Palmer influence both constricted Roberts's theology somewhat and also intensified it at certain points. Crisis tended to overwhelm process, particularly in Christian experience. It seems to me that this is the legacy Roberts received primarily from the revival and camp meeting tradition that so shaped his early life. In many ways he transcended this, as seen in his longer view of history, his concern with ongoing reforms in society, and his commitment to Christian education and character formation. It is as though his default position was the priority of the immediate, deeply emotional experience of God's Spirit — evidence that God was present and blessing through a strong, almost overwhelming sense of the divine presence.

From this perspective Roberts's theology might be called proto-Pentecostal (in the sense of later Pentecostalism; Roberts would have described it as simply being Pentecostal in the proper biblical sense!). Yet in significant ways Roberts transcended this and exhibited a broader perspective. It is this breadth that gives complexity and nuance to Roberts's theology, and this can easily be missed. This is why it is important to see his doctrinal teaching grounded in the soil of his total life and ministry.

Roberts and the Wesleyan Synthesis

B. T. Roberts believed he was faithfully upholding and continuing the witness of John Wesley and the early Methodists. This was central to his sense of mission. But how Wesleyan was Roberts, in fact, in theology and practice?

Shades of difference between Wesley and Roberts on some points have already been noted, particularly on the doctrine of entire sanctification. Here we may ask about the broader sweep of Roberts's theology compared with that of Wesley.

Much of the dynamic of early Methodism lay in the fact that Wesley developed and maintained a dynamic synthesis, in doctrine and practice, of biblical truth. He held together faith and works, doctrine and experience, the individual and the social, and the concerns of time and eternity.[67] What about B. T. Roberts?

Divine Sovereignty and Human Freedom

Basic to all else in Wesley was his tenacious hold on both the total sovereignty of God and the freedom of human beings to accept or reject God's grace. Wesley af-

---

67. The background of this discussion as it pertains to Wesley is found in Snyder, *Radical Wesley,* pp. 143-52.

firmed that God is sovereign, and everything depends on his initiative and working. But humans, even though sinful, have a measure of God-given freedom. If they turn to God, they can be his coworkers in the concerns of the kingdom. For Wesley, much of this was based in the biblical doctrine of the image of God and in his understanding of God's grace — particularly his stress on "prevenient" grace, that grace of God that goes before us, giving us the capacity, if we will, to turn to God.

Wesley's deep optimism of grace grounded his emphasis on the universal atonement, the witness of the Spirit, and Christian perfection. God's grace so fully abounds that no one can set limits on what the Spirit may accomplish through the church in the present order, both in personal experience and in society. Wesley's view takes the church seriously as agent of gracious transformation in the world.

Roberts was essentially Wesleyan at this point. He had a high view of God's sovereignty but also affirmed human freedom and responsibility. His lifelong emphasis on *duty* can be seen in this context.

Did Roberts put too much stress on human freedom and thus risk the danger of salvation by works? This charge has sometimes been made of Charles Finney, and there is no doubt Roberts was influenced by Finney and by Finneyite revivalism, as noted.

Theologically, Roberts saw all positive human action as enabled by God's grace. Yet it may be that he had such an exalted view of human responsibility that he at times set the bar too high for what people could and should do. One can at times get the impression from Roberts's writings that he believed in sanctification by works, rather than by God's grace enabling and inspiring our works of piety and for justice and righteousness. He was so insistent on full obedience to the radical demands of the gospel that the note of radical grace may at times have been muted. Here we confront of course the enduring law/grace tension inherent in all Christian living that strives to be fully faithful to the Jesus life.[68]

Like Wesley, Roberts saw the church as God's instrument for justice and righteousness in society, not just for individual salvation. While Roberts insisted, as noted earlier, that "Reform is not our salvation," he also insisted that the church, through revival and through Christians acting responsibly in society, was the key to social, political, and economic transformation.

68. Is there some basis here for the later "legalism" of Free Methodist teachings on holiness? Legalism afflicts all earnest Christian traditions; it is not unique to holiness groups. But in the Holiness movement legalism took the form of associating holiness (that is, genuine Christianity) with particular patterns of dress, behavior, and entertainment. Those who knew Roberts described him as a gracious, grace-filled Christian, and this no doubt moderated the strictness he expected to see in all genuine "pilgrims." It appears that as his personal influence waned, however, the radical discipleship emphasis did become less gracious and more legalistic.

Doctrine and Experience

Because of his stress on both divine sovereignty and human freedom, Wesley focused on Christian experience. He looked for moral transformation in believers' lives and behavior. Thus Wesley stressed both doctrine and experience, "faith working by love." If faith didn't produce moral change, including good works, it wasn't genuine. Thus also Wesley's focus on holiness: regeneration began and enabled the process of sanctification, so every believer was morally obligated to "press on to perfection." Justification and sanctification went together.

Wesley's consistent stress on both inward and outward holiness is evidence of this balance of doctrine and experience. An inner experience of God in the soul that does not result in one's "doing all the good one can" is inherently suspect. Wesley's concern for sanctification simply shows that he really believed that doctrine and experience go together. Men and women do not truly *believe* the gospel without a moral change that enables them to *live* the Jesus life. Faith not only believes; it *works* — in both senses.

This balance between doctrine and experience showed itself also in Wesley's dual stress on reason and experience. Faith was rational and reason was its handmaid. A conscious sense of God in the soul and the inner witness of the Spirit were God's gracious gifts, and not at all irrational.

This balanced emphasis gave Methodism historically a strong ethical sensitivity. It underscored the role of the church, for Wesley knew that Christian community was either the environment where grace turned sinners into saints or else a cold, lifeless shell where newborn believers died of spiritual exposure.

In all these respects, Roberts was thoroughly Wesleyan. Here in fact he is perhaps most Wesleyan. The new birth was the beginning of the life of holiness, and its authenticity was to be seen in the genuineness of transformed lives. Roberts emphasized both "inward and outward holiness," even if he did not use that formulation as consistently as did Wesley.

Although in his writings Roberts quite consistently spoke of the ways holiness should shape behavior in all areas, including in the public sphere, his emphasis on plainness of dress (especially for women) and on avoiding popular fashions perhaps set Free Methodism on a course in which these matters eventually became litmus legalisms instead of discipleship disciplines. Yet in Roberts's own lifetime, shared Free Methodist disciplines in dress, entertainment, style of worship, and ministry to and with the poor marked off Free Methodists as "a peculiar people," almost a distinct order, in some ways very similar to early Methodists as well as Quakers and other radical discipleship groups. Regarding dress, Charles Sage wrote, "Brother Roberts used to say that when the sap started in the spring, dead leaves would fall off, so when the Spirit has free course through our spiritual veins all signs of pride fall off."[69]

---

69. *Autobiography of Rev. Charles H. Sage, a Member of the East Michigan Conference, Free Methodist Church* (Chicago: Free Methodist Publishing House, 1903), p. 172.

Roberts's marked sensitivity to ethical and moral issues was thoroughly Wesleyan. His biography makes clear however that this sensitivity was shaped also by the revival impulses, millennial hopefulness, and American democratic idealism that characterized American reform movements in the early 1800s. For these reasons Roberts's reform agenda in nineteenth-century America was in some respects politically more radical than was Wesley's in eighteenth-century England.[70]

Experience and Structure

Wesley, with keen sociological insight, saw the connection between experience and structure. Perhaps no one in church history was more perceptive of the link between Christian experience and appropriate nurturing structures or was so successful in matching church forms to church life (though this is a characteristic of most of the church's greatest reformers). Wesley's system of societies, classes, and bands in large measure formed the genius of the discipline, growth, and enduring impact of Methodism. To these basic structures were added many others, including schools, dispensaries, and loan funds for the poor. For Wesley the class meeting and other key Methodist structures constituted an ecclesiological statement, integrally linked to sanctification and discipleship. Wesley saw that such covenant structures were essential if Christians were to make a successful stand against the world, the flesh, and the devil and to be gospel leaven in society.

Here Roberts missed some essential Wesleyan notes. The record of Roberts's years as Methodist Episcopal pastor shows that he never experienced, and never fully understood, the class meeting and other early Methodist structures in the way Wesley intended, and the way they in fact functioned fifty and a hundred years earlier.[71] The Methodism Roberts inherited had already been altered by the decline of the class meeting and the rise of a revivalist mind-set that was significantly different from Wesley's understanding.

The principal ecclesiological point here is that Roberts did not fully grasp Wesley's conception of the nature of Christian community — of "social Christianity," as Wesley termed it. Roberts, for example, put relatively more emphasis on revival and camp meetings and less on the class meeting. He perhaps had less insight than Wesley on the processes of the development of Christian character and of the necessity of ongoing close community to nurture it. Roberts was not as effective as Wesley in nurturing people into the Christian faith and into ongoing discipleship and in helping believers find a whole range of useful Christian ministries. In these regards he was perhaps more suc-

70. This is true only comparatively, however. Though Wesley was a monarchy man and relatively conservative politically, his opposition to slavery, support of abolishing the slave trade, and critique of the medical profession in his day (for example) really made him a radical reformer.

71. Roberts had read Wesley's sermons, but it is not clear that he paid any particular attention to Wesley's "Plain Account of the People Called Methodists" and similar writings about the prescribed functioning of the class and band system.

cessful in his work with Chili Seminary, which in its early years really functioned as a discipleship community, than he was in the Free Methodist Church generally.

As noted earlier, Roberts simply took over the ecclesiology of the Methodism he inherited, relatively unaware of the ways in which Methodism itself had changed over the previous half-century. For that reason primarily, Roberts never did much work in the area of fundamental ecclesiology.

The Charismatic and the Institutional

Wesley balanced the charismatic and the institutional aspects of church life and experience. Early Methodism was a charismatic church within the institutional church. Wesley intentionally worked to keep the fire of the Spirit burning within the structures of the Anglican Church. Essentially he saw Methodism as *ecclesiola in ecclesia* — the charismatic community (not entirely unstructured) within the institutional church (not entirely devoid of grace).

B. T. Roberts was trying to rescue the church (in his case Methodism, not Anglicanism) from institutionalism and make it charismatic — that is, alive and animated by the Holy Spirit. Since his context was not that of Wesley, who birthed a renewal movement within the institutional church, Roberts had little sense of the need to combine and balance the institutional and charismatic aspects of church life. He in fact became increasingly the victim of denominational institutionalization as his administrative burdens increased. The 1890 FM General Conference may be read as an institutional-charismatic split with Roberts unsuccessfully defending charisma over institution.

Roberts's functional view of church order was much like Wesley's, though formed in a rather different ecclesiological context. Church order was to be seen as secondary to mission. No specific structure was prescribed in Scripture, and structures must yield to the promptings of the Spirit. Wesley reflected more deeply about such questions than did Roberts, but both placed the life of the Spirit and the authenticity of spiritual experience above proprieties of structure. Wesley, however, had a deeper understanding of the need to create or adapt church structures for the sake of mission and discipleship.

Two differences may be noted between Wesley and Roberts here. First, since Wesley had a sense of Methodism as *ecclesiola in ecclesia* within the Church of England, he felt free to develop functional, nontraditional structures as necessary to renew the church and extend its witness. But by Roberts's time Methodism *was* the church. Roberts saw no need for new structures but rather simply urged the faithful use of existing ones. When he later of necessity created new Free Methodist structures, they were essentially identical to the existing Methodist models. Roberts, however, wanted to maintain the same rigor in Free Methodism *as a church* as Wesley did in Methodism as a *movement within* the church. Hence the high membership standards of early Free Methodism.

Second, Roberts was more concerned that church structures be democratic than was Wesley. Here the differing political contexts played a role. As noted in chapter 25, Free Methodist structure was more participatory and democratic than that of the Methodist Episcopal Church. Roberts seems to have grounded the more democratic form of the new denomination more in contextual and pragmatic considerations than in biblical or theological ones, however. This was the form of the church that better fit the American context.[72]

Present and Future Salvation

Finally, Wesley in his theology balanced present and future salvation. Eternal blessedness with God was the goal and the gift to be sought above all else. For Wesley, this was the ultimate meaning of the kingdom of God. And yet Wesley's stress on Christian perfection focused on the *present* reality of the life of God in the human soul. It was a progressive, dynamic concept and experience. He reasoned that if holiness could come at death, God could just as surely enable holy living now.

By stressing "all inward and outward holiness" on biblical grounds, Wesley kept Christian experience from retreating into an inner world divorced from the problems, sufferings, and opportunities of daily life. Holiness involved making a present stand for the righteousness of the kingdom of God, and especially bringing the gospel to the poor.

Here also Roberts was essentially Wesleyan. Like his contemporary William Booth, Roberts was explicit in his concern for salvation for both worlds. With his Wesleyan doctrine of sanctification (though modified in some ways from Wesley, with more emphasis on crisis and less on process), and with his practical turn of mind, Roberts was concerned about the present life and witness of the church within society while clearly focused on the ultimate goal of the kingdom of God in its everlasting fullness. The saga of Roberts's involvement with the Farmers' Alliance is perhaps the best example of this, but there are many others.

Roberts seems to have shifted somewhat in this regard, however. The tone of many of the entries in *Spiritual Songs and Hymns for Pilgrims* (1868) is otherworldly, filled with images of leaving the world behind and journeying to the (heavenly) promised land. This was in the earliest years of the Free Methodist movement. With time, however — as Roberts grew older and as the Free Methodist Church grew in numbers and in institutional complexity — Roberts's view of Christian social and cultural involvement seems also to have expanded. This was not discontinuous with the early Roberts, however; it was in continuity with the character of Methodism that Roberts had learned from Stephen Olin and with his abolitionist, social-reformist roots.

---

72. Impulses toward greater democracy played a role in nearly all the early Methodist schisms and secessions in America, and also to some extent in England.

Roberts was Wesleyan in his fundamental theology and can be understood theologically only in terms of the Wesleyan heritage. The Finneyite revivalist mentality did influence his theology in some ways but did not shift it from its Wesleyan base. In his basic theology and even in his insistence that Christian faith and discipleship are radical, Roberts was actually more truly Wesleyan than was Phoebe Palmer and most other Holiness movement leaders of his day. And he certainly was more Wesleyan than was the main current of the Methodist Episcopal Church that by the 1860s was headed in directions theologically that marked a conscious departure from original Wesleyanism.

Yet Roberts's theology was in some ways narrower and less dynamic than Wesley's. Wesley had some keen theological insights that have been only partially preserved within the later Wesleyan traditions. To this day the full potential of Wesleyan theology has never been realized, it can be argued, due to failure to follow through on key Wesleyan themes.[73] Highlighting these themes also helps us place and profile Roberts's theology.

Four Wesleyan insights are particularly important here. First, Wesley's doctrine of Pentecostal grace, while feeding on Eastern Orthodox sources, overcame the elitism of Eastern spirituality by arguing (biblically) that the fullness of God's grace is available to every human being without distinction. Second, Wesley's theological methodology, emphasizing the created order plus reason, experience, and tradition as necessary adjuncts in interpreting biblical revelation, tended to overcome the persistent spirit/matter dualism of both the Eastern and Western theological traditions.[74] Third, Wesley's doctrine of salvation as effective gracious healing corrected the pessimism of much of the Augustinian theological tradition that has so shaped Protestant theology. Finally, Wesley's stress on "social Christianity" corrected the persistent individualism of the Enlightenment bequest to Western culture.

Where does B. T. Roberts fit on this matrix?

He is strongest on the first point. Here, in fact, Roberts surpassed Wesley. Ever the foe of elitism, Roberts emphasized that God's restoring grace was for everyone — and particularly for the poor, African Americans, women, and others who were oppressed or marginalized. God's grace was for all, not just in the sense of eternal salvation but also in terms of useful, fully Spirit-endowed ministry in the present order.

Regarding the second point: Roberts's articles reveal his Wesleyanism in his use of Scripture, reason, and experience in theological argumentation. Roberts put relatively less stress on the created order as a theological category, however. He did not for example lay the groundwork for an ethic of environmental stewardship, though the resources for that are available in Wesley. He did not put as much stress as did Wesley on salvation as the healing and restoration of the whole created order. At this point

73. This is the gist of my argument in Howard A. Snyder, "The Babylonian Captivity of Wesleyan Theology," *Wesleyan Theological Journal* 39, no. 1 (Spring 2004): 7-34.

74. As noted in "The Babylonian Captivity" essay, this is a critique of the so-called Wesleyan Quadrilateral (Scripture, reason, tradition, and experience), which largely misses Wesley's strong emphasis on the created order, "the wisdom of God in creation."

Roberts (like virtually all his contemporaries) was not as Wesleyan as he might have been. Consequently he did not bequeath to his Free Methodist progeny a broad biblical and theological basis for an ethic of the kingdom of God in all its dimensions.

Roberts did, thirdly, stress salvation as healing, though not to the extent Wesley did. Roberts taught that physical healing by faith is within the economy of present salvation, but he did not use healing metaphors as broadly in portraying salvation as did John and Charles Wesley.

Finally, as already suggested, Roberts did not put as much emphasis on "social Christianity" — the social nature of Christian experience — as Wesley did. He understood this intuitively, perhaps, but did not develop the kind of ecclesiology that made *koinonia* in the biblical sense central to the experience and structures of the church.

Overall, Roberts did not have the breadth of theological insight that Wesley had. Yet he was, and sought to be, Wesleyan in theology and practice, which meant also that his theology fell within the broad current of Christian orthodoxy. But Roberts was also a reformer, a radical seeking expressions of the gospel in which the power of the Holy Spirit would be unleashed in Christian experience and in the world despite compromise in the church and unrighteousness in society.

The Theology of Ellen Roberts

What of Ellen Roberts? Did she develop a theology of her own, or contribute anything substantial to her husband's theological work?

While Ellen Lois Stowe Roberts was no theologian, she of course had a theology. Her convictions were largely those of her husband, though her story reveals some different accents and nuances, partly related to her different life experiences and partly perhaps due to gender and temperamental differences. As the more introspective of the two, Ellen developed a theology that was more intensely experiential and inward-focused.

Ellen contributed occasionally to the *Earnest Christian* and to Free Methodist publications. Most of her writings had to do with holiness and practical Christian living or with missions. An 1890 article entitled "Divine Love," written when she was about sixty-five, well represents her mature experience in contrast to her earlier inner struggles.

> Infinite Love and Wisdom created us, gave us being. Love came to redeem us and fit us for the abodes of the blest, and teach us how to live here as His representatives.
>
> . . . To live out and act out divine love is the most effectual testimony that we have it in our hearts. If we are in communication with The Fountain, or that flowing well of Love, it will flow out naturally, and easily, and its manifestation will be spontaneous and unceasing. There will be no hard work about manifesting it to all.

Love that is begotten of God will lead to acts of self-denial; but they will be easy and pleasant, and often be our sweetest experience.[75]

After her death in 1908 the Free Methodist Publishing House issued a selection of Ellen's writings entitled *Extracts from the Writings of Mrs. Ellen Lois Roberts.* This thirty-one-page booklet gives a sense of key themes in Ellen's faith and thought. Often her pieces were based in her own experience. Topics included "The Lord's Dealings," "God's Will," "In Everything Give Thanks," and "The Spirit's Leadings."[76] Ellen was variously identified as E. L. R., Mrs. Ellen L. Roberts, or Mrs. B. T. Roberts, and some pieces may have appeared anonymously.[77] Adella Carpenter also reprinted a number of Ellen's articles in her book *Ellen Lois Roberts: Life and Writings.*[78]

In "Woman's Foreign Missionary Societies," Ellen traced the rise of the women's foreign missions movement in the eighteenth century, noting when different societies had been formed. Although there were earlier antecedents, Ellen noted, "Woman's [missionary] societies and work in this country were not considered fully launched until 1860-61. There was a loud call for women to come and do what men could not do in getting access to their sisters in the East. Single women who could give all their time to the work were urgently called for. This led to the formation of the Women's Union Missionary Society of America for Heathen Lands, in New York. This undenominational society was the parent of the various denominational boards now found in all Christian bodies."

Ellen noted that the Woman's Foreign Missionary Society of the Methodist Episcopal Church was organized in 1869 and the (Free Methodist) Woman's Foreign Missionary Society in 1894. The point of her piece was to encourage women to continue to be involved in and support missions. It is not possible for the church to "keep the spirit of the home work and neglect or be indifferent to the foreign."[79] After B. T.'s death, Ellen continued his passion for outreach through this focus on global missions.

There seems to have been no substantial theological disagreement between Benjamin and Ellen. Here Ellen largely followed Benjamin's lead, although she also thought for herself, read fairly widely, and probably engaged in theological conversations with her husband. She of course lacked the extensive education Benjamin had. Though Ellen was not raised and nurtured within frontier Methodism as Benjamin was, the Methodism she imbibed from George and Lydia Lane in Manhattan was largely in sync with Benjamin's understandings.

---

75. Mrs. B. T. [Ellen] Roberts, "Divine Love," *EC* 59, no. 6 (June 1890): 169 (a piece not found in Carpenter or in *Extracts,* noted below).

76. *Extracts from the Writings of Mrs. Ellen Lois Roberts* (Chicago: S. K. J. Chesbro, n.d.); Ellen L. Roberts, "The Spirit's Leadings," *EC* 36, no. 6 (Dec. 1878): 183. If all Ellen's published writings were identified and collected into a book, they would constitute a volume of perhaps 80 to 100 pages.

77. Articles in *EC* signed "E. S. R." are by Emma Sellew Roberts, Benson's wife, not by Ellen Roberts.

78. Carpenter, pp. 139-82.

79. Ellen Roberts, "Woman's Foreign Missionary Societies," in *Extracts,* pp. 25-31.

Radical Biblicism versus "America's God"

Though not primarily a theologian or philosopher, B. T. Roberts certainly was a theological practitioner. He devoted himself principally to revival and reform, and increasingly to church and educational administration, rather than to intellectual pursuits. As an engaged and practicing theologian, however, he made some strategic theological moves that have had long-range impact within the tradition he founded.

Mark Noll's comprehensive *America's God: From Jonathan Edwards to Abraham Lincoln* traces the key theological developments in America over the period that included Roberts's own theological formation. At some length Noll analyzes nineteenth-century developments in Methodist theology and especially "the Americanization of Methodism." Noll shows how Methodist theologians progressively adopted republican ideas and commonsense moral reasoning, as did other Protestant traditions in America. He deals with Methodist figures who were key in B. T. and Ellen Roberts's own Methodist upbringing — among them Willbur Fisk, Stephen Olin, Nathan Bangs, Phoebe Palmer, and Daniel Whedon.[80]

Noll notes, "By the era of the Civil War, Methodist theology was dividing in two. A few Methodists [Phoebe Palmer and early leaders in the Holiness movement] were abandoning the quest for intellectual relevance in order to recapture a key conviction of the early movement," namely, experiential holiness. But other Methodists, typified by Daniel Whedon (1808-85), "were abandoning the movement's early convictions in order to become intellectually relevant."[81]

Whedon, says Noll, led Methodist theology "toward a much greater reliance on the deliverances of the moral sense and a much greater willingness to reason from those deliverances, instead of from experiential biblicism." Notably absent from Whedon's thought were "the traditional Methodist keystones of revelation from Scripture and the experience of the Holy Spirit."[82]

In contrast, the Bible and the experience of holiness by the Holy Spirit were precisely what Palmer stressed. "Instead of presenting Methodism in the categories of commonsense moral philosophy," Noll notes, "the teachers of holiness employed, with single-minded thoroughness, the words of Scripture." While this "acted as a prophylactic" against the intellectual currents of the day, it also in the end "rendered the holiness movement largely irrelevant to the nation's larger cultural history."[83] Noll notes, "Phoebe Palmer's holiness theology offered comfort to many in the era of the Civil War but little for the problems leading to the Civil War." She refused to

---

80. Mark A. Noll, *America's God: From Jonathan Edwards to Abraham Lincoln* (New York: Oxford University Press, 2002). On Methodism, see especially pp. 330-64. Noll does not discuss B. T. Roberts or Free Methodism.

81. Noll, *America's God*, p. 362.

82. Noll, *America's God*, p. 355.

83. This of course needs some qualification. By "larger cultural history" Noll means primarily intellectual history. "Cultural relevance" can be measured in many ways.

discuss slavery, viewing it as a divisive issue, and she and Walter spent most of the years of the Civil War on an extended evangelistic tour in England.[84]

But what of B. T. Roberts? Significantly, it is precisely on issues of social justice and cultural accommodation that Roberts distanced himself from Palmer and most of the Holiness movement. Roberts marked out a different path for himself and early Free Methodism. Noll notes that by the 1830s, Methodism, then the largest Protestant denomination in America, was moving into "an era of refinement," though in two "contrasting forms. Those who were busy articulating Methodism in the categories of moral-sense philosophy sought consecrated respectability; those who were busy with the pursuit of holiness sought respectable consecration."[85] Respectability, of course, was the last thing Roberts was interested in. The reasons are clear: his radical biblicism manifested in his emphasis on the poor, the evils of slavery, and the rights of women and all who were oppressed.

Roberts in fact took a path different from either Whedon or Palmer.[86] If he followed Palmer in her biblicism and experientialism, he did not follow her in her openness to cultural accommodation. If on the other hand he rejected the theological and philosophical moves of thinkers like Whedon, he did not veer into anti-intellectualism. Roberts's theology was populist but not anti-intellectual. Though various factors were involved, the principal reason for this was his biblical radicalism that in turn was nurtured, as noted earlier, by his own radical and abolitionist roots and his own experience of God's grace.

Noll maintains that

> Methodist theology was most creative when it was least philosophical. When the Methodists' all-consuming purpose was to evangelize the nation's restlessly mobile lower and middle classes, their theology cut across the grain of dominant American ideologies with unexpected force. Later, as Methodist attention shifted toward the rising middle classes it had recruited so effectively, Methodist theology began to move with the currents of intellectual fashion. Methodists in the age of Asbury believed in human free will because of what they read in the Bible and because of how the Holy Spirit was making the universal effects of Christ's atonement actual in their lives. Methodists in the age of Whedon believe in human free will because of the intuitive deliverances of human consciousness.[87]

B. T. Roberts, however, consciously followed Asbury (and Wesley, and Edwards) here, rather than Whedon, and more than he followed Palmer. The result, for the

---

84. Noll, *America's God,* p. 362.

85. Noll, *America's God,* p. 354, citing Kathryn T. Long, "Consecrated Respectability: Phoebe Palmer and the Refinement of American Methodism," in *Methodism and the Shaping of American Culture,* ed. Nathan O. Hatch and John H. Wigger (Nashville: Abingdon Kingswood, 2001), pp. 281-307.

86. See Kathryn Long's discussion, "The Free Methodist Challenge," in "Consecrated Respectability."

87. Noll, *America's God,* p. 364. In less academic and more pungent language, John Wesley Redfield repeatedly made just these points in his autobiography.

thirty years following 1860, was a dynamic movement that, had it understood and continued Roberts's vision following his death, might well have had a remarkable impact on American culture. Even so, the tradition Roberts launched made and continues to make a substantial global contribution in missions and evangelism, in education, and in works of compassion and mercy, if not so much in concerns of justice and reform.

In the wake of Abraham Lincoln's assassination, Roberts wrote two editorials of note. The first, entitled "President Lincoln" and reflecting on Lincoln's death, was discussed in chapter 27. The second was published a month later (June 1865) and was entitled "Religious Aristocracy." Here the note of biblical populism is especially strong. Common to the ills of both nation and church is the evil of aristocracy, or special-interest elitism, Roberts maintained. The Civil War was brought on by a "social aristocracy" that withheld rights from the people; the church is largely controlled by a "religious aristocracy" that similarly acts oppressively and unjustly. Roberts argued,

> Had our governments, national and state, been true to their own principles and given to every man his rights, without regard to race or complexion, what an untold amount of suffering would have been avoided! It is never safe to withhold from others their God given rights. Yet this is done by the Churches. It is done systematically, and by almost common consent. Christianity greatly suffers in consequence. Our free institutions — our civil and religious liberties, are endangered thereby. A reformation is loudly demanded. The point to which we specially refer is this. THE POOR, AS A BODY, ARE DEPRIVED OF THEIR RIGHT OF HEARING THE GOSPEL. It is theirs by virtue of the common brotherhood of man. The Gospel belongs to man, *as man* — not because he can pay for it — but because he needs it, — therefore it belongs to them. But it is theirs by special bestowment. Jesus said *The poor have the Gospel preached unto them.* This was the crowning proof that he was the Messiah. The Gospel then was especially designed for the poor. It is for all — for it is to be preached to every creature — but their claims are paramount. If there is any preference they must have it.

Significantly, Roberts here does not justify the North and condemn the South. Rather, he brings a different theological analysis to bear, echoing Old Testament prophets and citing Jesus' example. Though Roberts speaks of the "rights" of the poor, his foundation is not a theory of natural rights but rather divine creation and the example of Jesus. In other words, his basis is what may be termed a radical Christ-centered biblicism.

Roberts then sounds many of the keynotes of his life: the apostle Paul showed how "God has chosen the foolish things of the world to confound the wise; and . . . the weak things of the world to confound the things that are mighty." Roberts insists, "A church of which such a description is true could not possibly have founded a religious aristocracy based upon money." Saint James gives the same testimony (James 2:6). Roberts concludes, "To reach the masses we must go among them, as of them, not as patrons. There should be no caste in the house of God. All ye are brethren. The petty distinctions of society have no right among the followers of the despised Nazarene."[88]

In his post–Civil War analysis, Roberts did not echo the voices of most Protestant leaders of the day. Noll maintains that in general "the distinguished theologians of Lincoln's generation" offered very "little of theological profundity concerning the religious meaning of the Civil War."[89] In marked contrast, Abraham Lincoln gave a profound theological interpretation, refusing simply to identify God's purposes with those of the nation.[90] If Roberts's interpretation was different from Lincoln's, it also stood in stark contrast to that offered either by "mainstream" Protestant theologians or by most leaders in the Holiness movement. In his fundamental theology Roberts remained closer to Wesley and Edwards. But in his radical biblicism he was prepared to sound the note of the gospel to the poor, with the implications of that affirmation for politics, economics, social relations, and church life, in ways that went beyond and implicitly critiqued Wesley and Edwards.

For Roberts, these theological convictions were fundamental. They were constant throughout his adult life and continued to be sounded during his closing years.

B. T. and Ellen Roberts entered the last period of their life together united in their faith and their sense of vocation. Their theological convictions were firm. As their grown children left home and started their own careers and families, Benjamin and Ellen increasingly immersed themselves in the work of the Free Methodist Church, the *Earnest Christian*, and Chesbrough Seminary.

---

88. [B. T. Roberts], "Religious Aristocracy," *EC* 9, no. 6 (June 1865): 188-89.
89. Noll, *America's God*, p. 426.
90. See especially Noll, *America's God*, pp. 422-38.

CHAPTER 37

Traveling and Editing the *Free Methodist*

"You talk of hard work; why, bless you, those who work hard for God are so blessed at times they hardly know where they are."

B. T. Roberts, 1883[1]

"I never feel it is the Lord's order for us to be very long separated."

Ellen Roberts, 1888[2]

B. T. Roberts turned sixty on July 25, 1883. Ellen was fifty-eight. Benjamin was beginning the busiest period of his ministry and, as it turned out, the last decade of his earthly life.

Roberts did a considerable amount of traveling during this period, including a trip to England. As Free Methodism and the scope of his own ministry grew, his travels became more extensive. Benson Roberts noted that during the four years his father edited the *Free Methodist* (1886-90), B. T. "made long journeys by sea and land, held his conferences as usual, and at the same time conducted the *Earnest Christian*."[3]

Already Benjamin was beginning to have some health concerns — due largely, it appears, to overwork. After his fall tour of conferences in 1881, he noted that he at first felt "uncommonly well," but then took ill. During his travels, he said, "We had encountered rain about every day for seven or eight weeks. But we had taken a cold bath daily, had escaped taking cold and had come to consider ourselves as well nigh weatherproof. But the first cold blast from the north we encountered, brought out

---

1. B. T. Roberts, "Sermon," *EC* 45, no. 1 (Jan. 1883): 8.
2. ELR to BTR, May 30, 1888, quoted in Zahniser, p. 324.
3. BHR, *BTR*, p. 546.

our old enemy, the malaria, in all its force. Almost at its touch, strength, vigor and flesh were gone. We were helpless."

Through rest and people's prayers, Benjamin began to recover and by mid-November 1881 was "daily gaining strength." But, he said,

> we need a rest — a good, long, quiet rest. Whether we shall be able to take it or not till forced to, is doubtful. For about twenty years we have been doing the work of three men. Our life has been one of ceaseless activity bodily and mentally. We have shrunk from no hardship nor exposure. The wonder is that we have endured it as well as we have. But we are admonished that we must hold up in some directions. But we do not anticipate being inactive. If we go less we will try and write more. Let all the saints pray for us. It still seems to us that we should yet do much work for the Master.[4]

In fact, Roberts kept going — traveling, editing, fund-raising, handling correspondence, dealing with church leadership issues. This chapter focuses especially on the last ten years of his ministry, from 1883 to 1893, giving particular attention to his travels and his editing.

The Free Methodist Church continued to grow throughout the 1880s, and Roberts frequently reported revivals in the pages of the *Earnest Christian*. In January 1883 he mentioned conversions and a revival spirit among Free Methodist work in Texas; in Portland, Oregon; and in Vivian Dake's work in Minnesota. Thomas La Due wrote from Oregon, "The Lord is pouring out his Spirit in power all around our four weeks' circuit, and there are added to us those who are saved." Roberts reported that at Chili Seminary also "there is a general awakening among the students."[5] In February he spoke of "a gracious work . . . going on in the Church and Seminary," with "a general quickening of holiness." In part under the preaching of J. G. Terrill, both seminary and church were sharing "alike in the outpouring of the Spirit."[6]

New York City

Benjamin continued to make trips to New York City from time to time, primarily in the interest of Free Methodist work there. In May 1883 he held meetings at the Free Methodist church in Brooklyn (not yet part of New York City). The meetings ended Sunday evening, May 27, and the next day Roberts crossed the new Brooklyn Bridge back to Manhattan. He was impressed with the bridge, just opened after many years of construction, and with the sight of lower Manhattan and New York harbor.

---

4. [B. T. Roberts], "Sick," *EC* 42, no. 6 (Dec. 1881): 187. I have found no earlier references to Roberts's having suffered from malaria.

5. [B. T. Roberts], "Revivals," *EC* 45, no. 1 (Jan. 1883): 35.

6. [B. T. Roberts], "Revivals," *EC* 45, no. 2 (Feb. 1883): 65. Roberts reported a revival spirit also in several of the local churches.

[The Brooklyn Bridge] is about a mile long and is a wonderful feat of engineering skill. The view from the bridge, of the harbor dotted with vessels from all maritime nations, and of the two cities is grand and imposing.

The bridge was thronged with people of many different nationalities, going in opposite directions. There were men with pipes in their mouths and mothers with babes in their arms. They were there from Europe, Asia and Africa.

Just two days later a panic on the bridge killed twenty people, with many more injured — a cautionary tale, Benjamin thought, reminding us that "We are safe only in the arms of Infinite Love. Death may be lurking near us in our moments of greatest security."[7]

That summer Benjamin attended camp meetings in Michigan, North Chili, and elsewhere, but in July was again back in the New York area, holding meetings in Brooklyn. On July 24, 1883, he attended the funeral of Dr. Walter C. Palmer, widower of Phoebe Palmer, at the Seventeenth Street ME Church in Manhattan. Dr. Palmer had died in Ocean Grove, New Jersey, four days earlier. Roberts noted that Walter and Phoebe Palmer, and also Walter's second wife, Sarah Lankford Palmer (Phoebe's sister), "contributed largely to keep [the doctrine of holiness] before the people — especially the M.E. Church[,] and the prominence now given it is largely owing to their indefatigable labors."[8]

On this New York trip Roberts also visited Jerry McAuley's Water Street Mission, and was impressed. He described McAuley, then about forty-four, as "tallish, raw-boned, Scotch-Irish, shrewd, ignorant, and I believe honest."[9] McAuley had founded his mission about a decade earlier, in 1872. He died a little more than a year after Roberts's visit.[10] Here Frank and Emeline Smith, B. T. and Ellen's friends and former parishioners at Brockport, had been engaged in ministry for a number of years.[11] Indirectly the fruit of Free Methodist ministry among the poor in lower Manhattan, the Water Street Mission became a model for city missions in America and in other countries, making McAuley "one of the most important founders of the modern rescue mission movement," noted Norris Magnuson in *Salvation in the Slums*.[12]

Benjamin also went swimming with friends a couple of times while in the New

7. [B. T. Roberts], "Death on the Bridge," *EC* 45, no. 6 (June 1883): 191.

8. [B. T. Roberts], "Dr. W. C. Palmer," *EC* 46, no. 3 (Sept. 1883): 98. Phoebe Palmer died in 1874, and in 1876 Walter married her sister Sarah.

9. BTR to ELR, July 23, 1883, quoted in Zahniser, p. 315.

10. R. M. Offord, ed., *Jerry McAuley, An Apostle to the Lost* (New York: American Tract Society, 1885, 1907).

11. See [B. T. Roberts], "Missions in New York," *EC* 52, no. 3 (Sept. 1886): 94-97, which includes a long letter from Emeline Smith.

12. Norris Magnuson, *Salvation in the Slums: Evangelical Social Work, 1865-1920* (Metuchen, N.J.: Scarecrow Press, 1977), p. 9; cf. Hogue, *HFMC*, 2:358-61. Hogue says it is "not generally known, that Jerry McAuley and his great work in Water Street Mission were largely the products of Free Methodism," and gives details.

York area. He thought Coney Island "a carnival of hell," but he enjoyed the ocean waves that brought him "life and vigor" (as he told Ellen in letters to her).[13]

Travels in 1884 and 1885

By the 1880s the Ocean Grove camp meeting on the Atlantic coast, about fifty miles south of New York City, had become a popular gathering place for people associated with the Holiness movement. Roberts visited there occasionally, and in the summer of 1884 he and Ellen enjoyed three weeks there — a combination vacation and holiness convention. Someone offered them the use of a tent on the grounds — "Free, with all the convenience for house-keeping," Ellen noted happily. This was a special time for B. T. and Ellen to be away together, though Benjamin was gone most of one week, speaking at a different camp meeting.

Both B. T. and Ellen enjoyed hearing noted speakers at Ocean Grove. A highlight was hearing William Taylor three times on Sunday and Monday, July 20-21. Monday evening Taylor "talked on Africa," Ellen noted; "very interesting. He is a very plain man — mightily in earnest. Mr. Roberts has had a good visit with him to-day." This may have been the only occasion on which Benjamin had face-to-face contact with Taylor.[14]

Ellen, now sixty-four, especially enjoyed the bathing at Ocean Grove. "Oh, this bathing is grand! I am quite courageous in the water," she wrote to Lucy Sellew Coleman. "That bathing at Old Orchard was nothing compared to the bathing here. I feel so well after it." She felt God had opened the way for this respite at Ocean Grove. "I have found Him in bathing in the Ocean, in soul & body."[15]

B. T. made a trip to the American Southwest in October and November 1884, an area he had first visited three years earlier. In 1881 Roberts had organized the Texas and Louisiana Conference in a grove near Corsicana, south of Dallas, with six preachers and fifty-eight members. Now he returned to preside at the fourth annual conference; E. P. Hart had held the conference in the intervening years.[16] Ellen remained at home in North Chili.

13. BTR (Brooklyn) to ELR, July 26, 1883, quoted in Zahniser, pp. 314-15.

14. David Hempton assesses William Taylor's significant ministry during this period in *Methodism: Empire of the Spirit* (New Haven: Yale University Press, 2005), pp. 151, 168-76.

15. ELR (Ocean Grove, N.J.) to Lucy Sellew Coleman, July 22, 1884 (spelling corrected). Ellen added, "I am with Miss Mossman here a good deal and through her I hear from all the faith people on this side & the other side of the Atlantic. There is a great variety of them. All laying great stress on faith-healing."

16. Hogue, *HFMC*, 2:99-100; John S. M'Geary, *The Free Methodist Church: A Brief Outline History of Its Origin and Development*, 3rd ed. (Chicago: W. B. Rose, 1908, 1910), pp. 120-21. Charles B. Jernigan, in *Pioneer Days of the Holiness Movement in the Southwest* (Bethany, Okla.: Arnett Publishing Co., 1964), notes, "In 1879 the great holiness revival broke out in Corsicana, Texas, under the leadership of Dr. Bush, a presiding elder in the Methodist Episcopal church, assisted by Rev. G. R. Harvey, the Free Methodist district elder, and a host of others, both preachers and laymen" (p. 88).

Roberts conducted the Indiana and Central Illinois Conference at Evansville, Indiana, October 15-19, 1884, and was pleased with the rapid growth and the revival spirit. Going on to St. Louis, he left for Dallas on Tuesday morning, October 21, on the Missouri Pacific line. It was a long day-and-night trip of well over six hundred miles. "We felt we could not afford a sleeping car, but passed the night quite comfortably," Benjamin commented. "The morning found us in the Indian Territory," every little while passing "great herds of cattle."[17]

Benjamin noted that the Indian Territory was divided among several Indian peoples — Creeks, Choctaws, Cherokees, and Chickasaws; probably he supplemented what he saw from the train window by reading newspapers. Roberts thought the Indians seemed relatively "prosperous and happy." They had "flourishing schools and churches" but fortunately no saloons, thanks to federal policy. But Roberts's sense of justice was aroused by attempts to wrest control of Indian lands. He deplored "the persistent efforts made to drive, by fraud or force, the Indians from this territory and open it up to the whites. The Indians have a better right to it than the whites have to New York or Illinois, or any of the lands that we possess; and it is shameless for papers to advocate that they be dispossessed, because their lands are desirable. If their lands were a thousand times more valuable than they are, that would be no reason why they should be robbed of their homes."[18]

Roberts traveled to Ennis, Texas, about thirty miles south of Dallas, to hold the Texas and Louisiana Conference. He preached seven times, in addition to conducting the business sessions. "There was a want of harmony," he noted, "but we never saw brethren disagree with a better spirit." ("They have the best spirit in doing improper things of any people that I ever saw," he confided to Ellen.)[19] In three years the conference had grown to 115 members and nine ordained preachers. Though the work had received impetus initially from the 1879 holiness revival in the area, the holiness churches had recently suffered from fanatical elements that had given holiness a bad name. "The doctrine of holiness became as unpopular as it had been popular," said Roberts. Richard Haynes, an engaging Cumberland Presbyterian preacher who had professed sanctification, enjoyed "remarkable success" in the Corsicana area. But becoming "puffed up with spiritual pride," Benjamin said, he began to claim special gifts and to preach extreme doctrines. He exhorted his followers to leave all the organized churches, which had become instruments of Satan. His group became known in the area as the "Corsicana Enthusiasts." The group aroused much local opposition and soon disintegrated, but it cast a shadow on the holiness emphasis. Now Roberts hoped for "a year of prosperity!"[20]

17. [B. T. Roberts], "Conferences," EC 48, no. 5 (Nov. 1884): 163; "Trip to Texas," EC 48, no. 6 (Dec. 1884): 185. Roberts presumably is using the editorial "we" here, though it is possible he was accompanied by one or more others.

18. [B. T. Roberts], "Trip to Texas," p. 185.

19. BTR (Denison, Tex.) to ELR, Oct. 24, 1884, quoted in Zahniser, p. 316.

20. [B. T. Roberts], "Trip to Texas," pp. 185-87; Hogue, HFMC, 2:100. Roberts summarizes the Corsicana fanaticism. He says Haynes "claimed extraordinary spiritual gifts" and that through his "in-

As it turned out, things got worse rather than better. Roberts noted that "Bro. Philip Allen was elected Chairman" and "goes to his work full of faith and courage." But B. T. had observed a "spirit of judging" and was a bit concerned that Allen thought Brother Matterby was "too formal and had not the Spirit."[21]

Not long after Roberts left, a woman evangelist from the North named Mrs. Wheaton arrived in the area and sparked a new wave of fanaticism. "She called all churches Babylon, and cried, 'Come out of her, my people,' until she drew away quite a following." Philip Allen came under her spell, resigned from the Free Methodists, and became part of her group. Jernigan says this group "taught that they did not need to read the Bible, as they had the one who had inspired the Bible in their hearts when they got sanctified. They no longer needed to pray, since they had the very spirit of prayer all the time. . . . They showed deep humility of spirit by laying off all neat and respectable clothing, and wearing overalls at all times." Their people "made tours in other states preaching these fanatical doctrines." Eventually the group "died away, but left much hurt in their wake, and many blighted lives."[22] The Free Methodist work survived, however, and gradually grew.

Following the 1884 annual conference at Ennis, Roberts traveled south twenty miles to Corsicana, "a pleasant city of about three thousand inhabitants" situated on a rise in the prairie. The Free Methodist society there was growing and now had "about forty members, 'poor in this world, but rich in faith.'" Roberts preached nine times to congregations that were small at first but gradually grew. He thought the work still suffered from the earlier Corsicana fanaticism.[23]

Roberts next traveled eastward to Louisiana to attend to Free Methodist work there. In contrast to the bustling but drought-stricken Texas frontier, here he was in the Old South. He traveled by train through Shreveport to Monroe, then forty miles south by buggy to Columbia. "The country is not thriving," Roberts remarked. "A

---

fluence families were separated and the wildest excesses indulged in. With a number of his followers he waited a long time in an upper room expecting to be translated" ("Trip to Texas," p. 186). See also Jernigan, *Pioneer Days*, pp. 150-51; Barry W. Hamilton, "The Corsicana Enthusiasts: A Pre-Pentecostal Millennial Sect," *Wesleyan Theological Journal* 39, no. 1 (Spring 2004): 173-93. Hamilton says the Corsicana Enthusiasts "brought holiness and premillennialism together to form a millennial sect that closely resembled [early] Pentecostalism [in some significant ways]. They blended primitivism, an emphasis on spiritual gifts for all believers, leadership of Christians by impressions, revivalism, divine healing through the Atonement, as well as glossolalia, and thus formed a pre-Pentecostal, ecstasy-seeking sect that sharply distinguished itself from the rest of society. Convinced that the gospel of the New Testament had been restored among them, the enthusiasts pointed to extraordinary manifestations in their midst as incontrovertible evidence that Christ would return at any moment" (p. 176). Hamilton helpfully sets the phenomenon in the context of the rise of premillennialism and its impact on the Holiness movement. See also George McCulloch, *History of the Holiness Movement in Texas, and the Fanaticism which Followed* (Aquilla, Tex.: J. H. Padgett, 1886), for a fairly detailed account.

21. BTR (Denison, Tex.) to ELR, Oct. 24, 1884, quoted in Zahniser, p. 316.

22. Jernigan, *Pioneer Days*, pp. 151-52.

23. [B. T. Roberts], "Trip to Texas," p. 186. It is probably merely coincidental that Corsicana is only 120 miles from Lampasas where the Farmers' Alliance movement in Texas began (as noted in chapter 35) a year or so before the holiness revival in Corsicana.

well informed planter said to me that they were all poorer than they were ten years ago" due to frequent floods and the fact that former slaves were no longer compelled to work so hard. Buildings in the towns and even on the great plantations looked dilapidated. Roberts noted the prevalence of malaria and the high infant mortality rate.[24]

The Free Methodists held a camp meeting "in the hill country among the pines" seven miles from Columbia. Over five hundred people gathered from as far as forty miles away, most coming on horseback but some by ox-drawn wagons. Though Roberts observed that blacks vastly outnumbered whites in the region, he does not indicate whether or to what degree the camp meeting crowd might have been interracial.[25]

Here Benjamin preached numerous times out-of-doors. On Thursday, November 13, he organized the Louisiana Conference (thus separating the work from the Texas Conference, largely because of the 300-mile distance). Free Methodists happened to have work in Louisiana because of the earlier ministry of Philip Allen. Allen had been a Methodist Episcopal Church, South, preacher in Louisiana. After experiencing entire sanctification and beginning to preach the doctrine, he ran into opposition from his own church. Hearing of the Free Methodists, he became one of the founding preachers of the Texas and Louisiana Conference and organized the first Free Methodist Church in Louisiana at Welcome Home, near Columbia. Two other ME, South, preachers who had experienced holiness under Allen's ministry also withdrew due to opposition and organized what they called the Union Methodist Church. The crowd of five hundred or so that now gathered for the camp meeting at Welcome Home was thus largely the fruit of Allen's ministry.[26]

Before organizing the conference Benjamin explained the origins of Free Methodism and urged these folks not to join the denomination unless they clearly felt so called of God — or if they thought connection "with a Church having its seat in the North" would be a problem. If so, they should "go back to their old organization. But without exception," Roberts said, "they desired to be organized." Nine preachers were sent to circuits.[27]

Roberts was concerned especially about the black population of the state. "Schools are sadly needed. I could not learn that there is a single one in the State for the higher education of the colored people. A great work could be done for God by establishing such a school."[28]

During these travels Benjamin kept up a constant, sometimes lighthearted, correspondence with Ellen. He wrote about the landscape, his schedule and meals, farming conditions, mockingbirds (could he bring one home?); about recommend-

24. [B. T. Roberts], "To Louisiana," *EC* 48, no. 6 (Dec. 1884): 187-88.
25. [B. T. Roberts], "To Louisiana," p. 189.
26. M'Geary, *Outline History*, pp. 122-23. Interestingly, Jernigan begins his history of the early Holiness movement in Louisiana with holiness ministry in Shreveport in 1885, not mentioning the prior FM work.
27. [B. T. Roberts], "To Louisiana," pp. 189-90.
28. [B. T. Roberts], "To Louisiana," pp. 189-90.

ing catnip tea to help a colicky baby. Benjamin teased about bringing Ellen "a darkee from Louisiana" to help around the house. Ellen replied in the same vein (or perhaps puzzling over Ben's handwriting), "Was it a darkey or a donkey you asked about?" She wasn't sure if Benjamin was serious or not; she was afraid he was.[29]

Benjamin also wrote Ellen about the U.S. presidential election (which occurred November 4, the day before he left Texas for Louisiana). He hoped Grover Cleveland would lose. If Cleveland won, he told Ellen, "I want you to sell out if you can before I get home. Let's go to England!" When he learned from the papers that Cleveland had in fact been elected, he told Ellen it was "a national calamity and a national disgrace."[30]

"I write every day as a boy whistles going through grave yards, in part at least, to keep my courage up," Benjamin told Ellen. "I get such a longing at times to be at home once more."[31]

His labors in Louisiana finished, Benjamin began the return trip. After three days and "three nights on the cars" traveling fifteen hundred miles, he reached North Chili on Saturday, November 22. "Yet the Lord had so wonderfully kept us that we could not say we were tired." Since June he had attended nine camp meetings and ten annual conferences and "worked hard at each."[32]

Back in North Chili, Benjamin was gratified to find a spirit of prayer and revival. Sunday afternoon was "one of the most glorious scenes we have ever witnessed" as teachers and students prayed together in the seminary dining room, Benjamin said. "Some ten or more were converted or sanctified wholly. . . . We felt abundantly repaid for all our trials and sacrifices to build up a salvation Seminary. It was simply glorious!"[33]

Two years later Roberts made a second trip to Texas and Louisiana (a "journey of over three thousand six hundred miles," he noted) and found the Texas Conference now "harmonious" with a "blessed spirit prevailing." "The work appears to be settling down on solid basis," he noted after presiding at the annual conference sessions at Corsicana in February. He went on to Louisiana but, missing connections with the Free Methodists there, returned to Chicago and, after a weekend of services, went home to North Chili.[34]

Roberts followed a somewhat similar pattern each summer, preaching at camp meetings, holding annual conferences, and overseeing the expansion of the work on the western frontiers. The St. Charles camp meeting near Chicago was often a part of his "western" itinerary. In July 1885 he preached at this camp after a zigzag trip to camps at Hebron, Minnesota; Concord, Indiana; and Evansville, Wisconsin. He re-

29. ELR to BTR, Nov. 4, 1884, quoted in Zahniser, p. 317.

30. BTR (Corsicana, Tex.) to ELR, Nov. 4, 1884; BTR (Marshall, Tex.) to ELR, Nov. 6, 1884; BTR (Welcome Home, La.) to ELR, Nov. 10, 1884. Quoted in Zahniser, pp. 318-20.

31. BTR (Marshall, Tex.) to ELR, Nov. 6, 1884, quoted in Zahniser, p. 318.

32. [B. T. Roberts], "To Louisiana," p. 190.

33. [B. T. Roberts], "To Louisiana," p. 190.

34. [B. T. Roberts], "Southern Trip," *EC* 51, no. 4 (Apr. 1886): 131.

ported that the St. Charles camp meeting was "moving on in glorious power." He wrote, "There are about seven services a day, and the special presence of the Lord is manifested in each one of them. The saints are full of faith and love; the preaching is in the spirit [*sic*]; and frequently the Holy Ghost is poured out in special power upon the people. Every day souls are being converted and sanctified to God."

He added that a "new departure" this year was a meeting held each morning "for the benefit of preachers and Christian workers." Roberts reported a large attendance. The grounds were filled with over seventy tents, and some people had come from great distances.[35]

Such travel was wearing on Roberts, but he generally took it in stride, using his time as productively as possible. Sometimes he rode in relative comfort. Traveling west from Chicago to Kansas City in August 1885, he was surprised at the amenities of the Chicago, Burlington and Quincy Railroad: "The floor was covered with Brussels carpet, the seats were high-backed, upholstered chairs that could be inclined at will, and turned into an easy couch. At each end of the car was a washroom with marble washbowl and clean towel. A gentlemanly porter was in attendance to keep everything in order and render any needed assistance. This car was *free* to all through first-class passengers."[36]

Roberts doesn't indicate whether he himself was traveling first class or not, though he may have been, possibly on a clergy pass.

Getting to specific locations off the main trunk lines could be exasperating, however. Traveling from Orleans, Nebraska, to Neosho Rapids, Kansas — over two hundred miles — proved complicated. "We rode parts of three days and nights. We changed cars six times. The nights were so broken that we could get but little sleep. The days were hot, and the roads dusty." But Roberts experienced such divine help, he said, that "when we reached the seat of Conference on Wednesday, we were ready for duty."[37]

Despite the stresses of travel, church oversight, and health issues, Roberts during this period was generally positive and upbeat in attitude. He wrote toward the end of 1885, "Discouragement is a stranger to us. We are doing the work of God, and we must succeed. Mighty obstacles, like mountains of mist, vanish as we approach them."[38]

An interdenominational General Holiness Assembly was held in Chicago, May 20-26, 1885, and it is likely that Roberts was among the several Free Methodists who attended. Held at the Park Avenue Methodist Episcopal Church, the assembly brought together a number of prominent leaders in the spreading but increasingly diverse Holiness movement. These included George Hughes, editor of the *Guide to Holiness*; J. P. Brooks of Bloomington, Illinois, who until 1883 was editor of the *Ban-*

35. [B. T. Roberts], "Camp Meetings," *EC* 50, no. 1 (July 1885): 35-36.

36. [B. T. Roberts], "Camp Meetings," *EC* 50, no. 3 (Sept. 1885): 98.

37. [B. T. Roberts], "Camp Meetings," *EC* 50, no. 3 (Sept. 1885): 99.

38. [B. T. Roberts], "Discouragement," *EC* 50, no. 5 (Nov. 1885): 162. Though Roberts here uses "we" and is writing primarily to encourage pastors, he seems to be speaking autobiographically.

ner of Holiness, organ of the Western Holiness Association; and S. B. Shaw, president of the Michigan Holiness Association and editor of the *Michigan Holiness Record.*[39]

This gathering was in fact one of a series of general holiness conventions held in 1877, 1880, 1882, and later in Chicago in 1901. These conferences provided opportunities for fellowship and inspiration but failed to bring any real organizational unity or coordination to a movement that was increasingly divided, particularly over the question whether holiness people should remain within their denominations or form new holiness bodies. This of course was a moot point for Free Methodists who already had a quarter-century history as a holiness denomination. As Melvin Dieter notes, however, the Free Methodist Church "was especially active within the [holiness] movement during these fluid years [of the 1880s]; it was young and aggressive and dedicated to a very radical standard of holiness and life."[40] Wilson T. Hogg (Hogue) and Joseph G. Terrill were two of the Free Methodists who were active in the 1885 convention, Hogg serving as assistant secretary.

Roberts was appointed to a committee of nine to plan for the next assembly. Hogg in his report noted, "Rev. Geo. Hughes, editor of the *Guide to Holiness* is the first on said committee, and Rev. B. T. Roberts . . . is second on the list." The committee, however, seems never to have met, and the next convention was not held until 1901, eight years after Roberts's death.

Editing the *Free Methodist*

Roberts's election as editor of the *Free Methodist* in 1886 complicated his and Ellen's lives in multiple ways. For one thing, it meant frequent trips to Chicago, where the weekly magazine was published — over six hundred miles and up to two days by train from their home in North Chili. A major part of Benjamin's reading, correspondence, and editorial work was done "on the cars."

Benjamin received an additional annual salary of $500 for his work as denominational editor, but that much was eaten up by the added expense of travel and lodging. The amount he received did not cover the cost of "living in a very plain manner in Chicago," he noted.[41] In fact, Roberts had himself contributed $500 to help the denomination purchase the magazine.[42]

---

39. W. T. Hogg, "The Holiness Assembly," *EC* 50, no. 1 (July 1885): 21-22; W. T. Hogg, "The Holiness Assembly," *EC* 50, no. 2 (Aug. 1885): 41-43; W. T. Hogg, "The Holiness Assembly. Report on Deliverances," *EC* 50, no. 1 (July 1885): 55; S. B. Shaw, ed., *Echoes of the General Holiness Assembly Held in Chicago, May 3-13, 1901* (Chicago: S. B. Shaw, n.d.), pp. 3-4, 7.

40. Melvin Easterday Dieter, *The Holiness Revival of the Nineteenth Century* (Metuchen, N.J.: Scarecrow Press, 1980), p. 224. Dieter gives a very useful analysis of "the early General Holiness Conventions" (pp. 215-25).

41. Zahniser, p. 289.

42. B. T. Roberts, "A Publishing House," *FM* 19, no. 49 (Dec. 8, 1886): 8. The list of contributors in this article shows that Roberts and T. B. Arnold each contributed $500, presumably their salaries.

In November 1886, about two weeks after General Conference, Benjamin and Ellen traveled by train to Chicago so he could begin his editorial duties. T. B. Arnold met them and showed them the printing operation and editor's office at 104 and 106 Franklin Street. Benjamin was pleased to see that Arnold, as proprietor of the business, conducted a noonday prayer service for the magazine's staff.[43]

Benjamin and Ellen found a two-room furnished apartment "facing west" and set up temporary housekeeping. Ellen wrote to their son George on November 24 that Benjamin was taking to his work "as easy and naturally as if he had always been doing it." She was pleased in one sense — the job would mean less travel (or so she thought). She had come along to take proper care of Benjamin, she told George, and "I am doing it."[44]

During the four years of his denominational editorial labors Benjamin periodically spent time in Chicago, but he and Ellen continued to maintain their home in North Chili where Ellen was quite involved in the seminary's life.

Taking up his editorial duties, Benjamin, in characteristic remarks indicative of his theology, said that under his guidance the magazine would seek to advance both "the peace and prosperity of its readers in this world" and their "eternal happiness in the world to come." It would promote both moral reforms and missionary extension. It would however avoid unnecessary controversy and all personal attacks.[45]

In fact, Benjamin did not measurably cut down on his travel once he became editor and in fact went on an extended foreign trip in 1888. Toward the end of his first year as *Free Methodist* editor he wrote, "I have travelled no less, and preached no less than I did before. But to write as I am doing for the paper, and carry on the correspondence, and do the other work necessarily connected with it, doubles my labor. I have to write on the cars, in the intervals of meetings, and everywhere I go."[46]

Roberts saw that if the denomination was to continue publishing the *Free Methodist* and an expanding range of other literature in Chicago, it should establish its own publishing house. The space on Franklin Street was rented. From the time he began as editor he argued the wisdom of the denomination acquiring its own space. With a twist of humor he wrote in the December 1, 1886, *Free Methodist,*

> Our publishing house needs a local habitation. Rents are high in Chicago. Of all things, to move a printing office is one of the worst. Everything is heavy, from the editor down to bundles of blank paper. Get settled into a place, and landlords keep raising rents. Now is the time to buy a place. Suitable property for our purpose, in a good location, can be bought for twelve thousand dollars — one half down. In a very few years it will be worth double the money. Are there not twelve persons among us who will give one thousand dollars each for this object?[47]

43. *FM* 19, no. 46 (Nov. 17, 1886): 8; Zahniser, p. 290.
44. ELR to GLR, Nov. 24, 1886, quoted in Zahniser, p. 290.
45. B. T. Roberts, "Salutatory," *FM* 19, no. 46 (Nov. 17, 1886): 8.
46. B. T. Roberts, "The Paper," *FM* 20, no. 32 (Aug. 10, 1887): 8.
47. B. T. Roberts, "Notes," *FM* 19, no. 48 (Dec. 1, 1886): 1.

Benjamin reasoned, "A denominational publishing house will contribute materially to preserve among us unity of faith and practice." Taking a long view, he wrote:

> Denominational books tend greatly to the growth of the denomination, and to a steady adherence to the principles which led to the formation of the church. Preachers and people may backslide; but the literature remains to remind them of what they once were. Some will, in reading the lives of the godly, be led to ask for the old paths that they may walk therein. Principles that are worth holding are worth propagating. They are preserved in literature. . . . So books hand down from age to age their record of the thoughts and deeds of their times.[48]

Only after Benjamin's death, however, did the denomination acquire its own building. By action of the 1894 General Conference it purchased the property of the First Free Methodist Church, 14-16 May Street, Chicago, a substantial brick building, and turned it into a publishing and printing establishment. In 1909, a year after Ellen's death, the denomination moved its publishing interests several blocks north to a large new three-story brick building that the church had constructed at 1132-34 Washington Boulevard, at the intersection with May Street, west of the Loop. This served as the denominational publishing house and headquarters until the operations were moved to Winona Lake, Indiana, in 1933.[49] As of 2006, the building at 1132-34 Washington Boulevard was still standing and housed the Museum of Holography (http://holographiccenter.com).

As editor of the *Free Methodist* (work he often enjoyed, despite his overloaded schedule), Benjamin kept the church abreast not only of denominational affairs but also to some degree of broader social currents. He reported or commented especially on moral or reform issues. The items he featured naturally reflected to some degree his own concerns. In late 1886 he reported on "equal suffrage conventions" being held in various places and noted that while in Evansville, Indiana, for annual conference business he attended some sessions of a suffrage convention there and heard Susan B. Anthony and Emma B. Colby speak. Roberts noted that Anthony "is well and favorably known throughout the country as a pioneer in this movement." He said of her two-hour address, "Miss Anthony carried with her the sympathies and the convictions of the intelligent people who listened to her. She spoke briefly of the great progress that the cause had made in the last twenty-five years." Though Benjamin did not directly express his own views on woman's suffrage, readers could sense where he stood.[50]

Benjamin also had some contact with the holiness evangelists Pearsall and Hannah Whitall Smith during this period. On a trip to Philadelphia in early 1888 he called upon the Smiths at their home. By this time Pearsall and Hannah, who were several years younger than Roberts, were well known for their "higher life" ministry

---

48. B. T. Roberts, "A Publishing House," *FM* 19, no. 48 (Dec. 1, 1886): 8.
49. Marston, pp. 479-81. See the photograph in Hogue, *HFMC*, after 2:250.
50. B. T. Roberts, "Equal Suffrage Convention," *FM* 19, no. 48 (Dec. 1, 1886): 8.

in England that birthed the Keswick Conventions, and for Hannah's 1875 best seller, *The Christian's Secret of a Happy Life*. Roberts visited the couple shortly before their permanent move to England.

Roberts had "a short and pleasant visit" with the family. He noted that Pearsall Smith, a Quaker businessman, "was a successful evangelist in this country, and more especially in England and on the continent of Europe, until his health gave out." Roberts thought Hannah's *Christian's Secret of a Happy Life* was "a book that can hardly be read by any one without profit." He found Hannah "still busily engaged in evangelical and reformatory labors."[51] The Smiths' extensive ministry in Europe in the 1870s was a key link between the Holiness movement in the United States and the Higher Life movement in England.[52]

Free Methodist Missions

As he said he would when he began editing the *Free Methodist,* Roberts promoted foreign missions, just as he had for years in the *Earnest Christian.*

Roberts had become particularly interested in Africa, due largely to reports of the explorations of Livingstone and Stanley. In a long (six-page) lead article in the September 1884 *Earnest Christian* entitled simply "Africa," Roberts gave a physical description of the continent and quoted extracts from Stanley's *Across the Dark Continent.* He commented on the slave trade, and on the work of Livingstone and others. "A general interest has been awakened in Africa," he noted. "Ethiopia is stretching out her hands to God." He concluded, "As soon as the funds can be raised for the purpose, we expect to send some men and women of God as missionaries to Africa. We should send out a company of at least six; and more would be better. By settling down within access of each other, they could help each other. To start with we should have at the least three thousand dollars. Inquire of the Lord, what your duty is in relation to this great work."[53]

Two months later, Roberts commented on a missionary rally held at the Illinois Conference sessions at which missionary candidates Robert and Catherine Shemeld were present and gave their testimonies. "He is English, by birth, she German," Roberts noted. Two hundred dollars were raised for their support.[54]

Roberts expected to see great things accomplished for God's kingdom through Free Methodist missions, in Africa and elsewhere. Noting that the Shemelds would soon be sailing for Africa, he wrote, "This, we trust, is but the beginning of a great

51. [B. T. Roberts], "Editorial Notes," *FM* 21, no. 14 (Apr. 4, 1888): 1. Roberts notes that Pearsall Smith "is a man who carries his religion into his business. During the twenty years he has been connected with a large glass manufacturing concern, they have steadily refused to make any ware for the liquor dealers." He died in England in 1899; Hannah lived until 1911.

52. Kostlevy, pp. 237-38.

53. B. T. Roberts, "Africa," *EC* 48, no. 3 (Sept. 1884): 69-75.

54. [B. T. Roberts], "Conferences," p. 162.

work which shall aid materially in the redemption of Africa. It is of great importance that Christianity in its purity should be introduced there at the beginning. Unless a good foundation is laid the superstructure is always in danger."[55]

A few months later he wrote in the *Earnest Christian:* "A wonderful field for missionary effort is opened in the Congo Valley in Central Africa. The Congo river is the second largest in the world. The attention of the civilized world is being directed to this region on account of its great commercial advantages."[56] Henry Morton Stanley, Roberts noted, reported from his explorations that this was the most fertile region in the world, had a population of some ninety million and rich natural resources. Roberts apparently had read a report of "a recent Conference of European nations" at which Stanley had given his glowing and somewhat exaggerated account.

"The people of this region have no regular systematic religion like Buddhism, or Mohammedanism, and therefore are more accessible to the influence of the Gospel. There should be as soon as possible a thousand devoted, saved, Protestant missionaries sent into this region. We have the right kind of men and women ready, but need the money to get them on the field," Roberts concluded.[57]

"For the evangelization of Africa, the Lord is stirring up his people, in all denominations," Roberts reported, noting that the "colored Baptists of Missouri recently pledged over three thousand dollars for the Congo mission." The Free Methodists also were doing their part. The Missionary Board had just appointed Rev. Walter Kelley as superintendent of the FM mission to Africa, "with full authority to select a site and establish a mission." Kelley was an experienced and successful preacher who earlier as a soldier had received "valuable experience as captain of a colored company," Roberts noted.

"We should not send a company of less than four or five. They hope to be able to sail in February," Roberts reported. Part of this group were Robert and Catherine Shemeld, who were to "go to England in advance and attend Mr. and Mrs. Grattan Guinness' training school for missionaries, and get all the help and information they can."[58] The Free Methodists eventually decided on Portuguese East Africa rather than Congo.

55. [B. T. Roberts], "Conferences," pp. 162-63.

56. [B. T. Roberts], "A Great Mission Field," EC 49, no. 1 (Jan. 1885): 28.

57. [B. T. Roberts], "A Great Mission Field," p. 28. In a later editorial Roberts celebrated "the interest that is being excited in all parts of the world for the regeneration of Africa," including that of King Leopold II of Belgium. Roberts noted that Leopold was "deeply interested in the new Congo state that promises so much for the civilization and the elevation of Africa" ([B. T. Roberts], "Africa," EC 49, no. 5 [May 1885]: 158). In 1885 Leopold II made himself king of the independent state of Congo (so-called Congo Free State), partly through the agency of Henry Stanley; only years later did it become clear to the outside world that Leopold's designs and activities were exploitive and oppressive, not benevolent or redemptive. See Adam Hochschild, *King Leopold's Ghost: A Story of Greed, Terror, and Heroism in Colonial Africa* (Boston: Houghton Mifflin, 1998).

58. [B. T. Roberts], "Mission to Africa," EC 49, no. 1 (Jan. 1885): 28-29. Henry Grattan Guinness (1835-1910) founded the East London Institute for training missionaries in 1873. He also founded the Livingstone Inland Mission in the Congo in 1878, and other missions that were amalgamated in 1899

Due to its mid-nineteenth-century founding, the Free Methodist Church was not part of the earliest wave of North American Protestant foreign missions, but it soon developed a missionary vision. Benjamin and Ellen were of course very interested in foreign missions due largely to their formation in the ME Church at a time when Methodist mission work was expanding.[59]

The fact was, of course, that Free Methodist "work in the home land was [itself] purely missionary work," as John S. M'Geary noted in 1908. "In the earlier part of our history as a church the subject of missions to the heathen did not receive much attention" since the focus was on mission in North America.[60] In this the Free Methodist experience largely paralleled that of Methodism half a century or so earlier. The energies of the movement initially were focused on evangelism and church extension, mainly through revivals and camp meetings.

As the Free Methodist Church expanded, however, and a first generation of young people grew up within the denomination, interest in foreign missions blossomed. In significant ways the Pentecost Bands under Vivian A. Dake were the forerunner and harbinger of this, but as early as 1874 church leaders were talking of forming a Free Methodist foreign missions board. The General Missionary Board of the Free Methodist Church was actually organized in 1882 and incorporated in 1885.[61]

Free Methodist missions interest was also quickened by the growing North American Protestant missionary enterprise and the rise of the Student Volunteer Movement (SVM) after 1886, which Free Methodist young people encountered as they attended colleges where the SVM was active. Methodist Episcopal missionary entrepreneur William Taylor also was an influence, as was the rapid growth of China Inland Mission, founded in England by James Hudson Taylor in 1865.[62]

Roberts kept abreast of these developments through his reading, and especially as editor of the *Free Methodist*. To some degree at least he read the *Missionary Review*

---

into the Regions Beyond Missionary Union. In April 1890 Roberts, noting a comment by Stanley about the steadfastness of Ugandan Christians under persecution, observed that "the Africans are capable of making substantial Christians," and added, "Let us bear a part in the conversion of Africa to Christ. As Grattan Guinness said 'the *evangelization* of the world is as necessary as was its redemption.'" [B. T. Roberts], editorial comment, *EC* 59, no. 4 (Apr. 1890): 132.

59. Earlier chapters have noted Benjamin's interest in possibly serving as a foreign missionary and Ellen's involvement with Methodist missions as she was part of the George and Lydia Lane household in New York City.

60. M'Geary, *Outline History*, pp. 165-66.

61. M'Geary, *Outline History*, pp. 166-67; see the earlier discussion in chapters 32 and 33. The 1874 General Conference actually created a General Missionary Board, but a functioning board was not created until 1882. See Marston, pp. 451-52.

62. The *Free Methodist* not infrequently carried articles and reports by or about William Taylor. Some Free Methodists served with the China Inland Mission (CIM), and contact with Free Methodist missionaries in China about 1920 led James Hudson Taylor II (the grandson, not the son, of the CIM founder) to "a rich, personal experience of holiness" and to become a Free Methodist missionary. Ruth Tapper, *Life Stories of Foreign Missionaries of the Free Methodist Church* (Winona Lake, Ind.: YPMS Council, 1935), p. 111.

of the World and other missions publications.[63] He and Ellen were always strong supporters of Free Methodist foreign missions and sought to stimulate missionary interest. Early Free Methodist missionaries knew they were supported in prayer by B. T. and Ellen. When Walter and Augusta Kelley arrived in Portuguese East Africa in June 1885, they recalled Benjamin's prayer at the time of their marriage in the Roberts home in April.[64] After their forty-five-day voyage to Africa, Augusta wrote back that God had answered the prayers "sent up from your family altar, the morning of April 22nd." She added, "Brother Roberts we kept your exhortation about entering Africa through the gates of praise."[65]

Free Methodist missionaries went to India in 1880; Portuguese East Africa, South Africa, and Liberia in 1885; the Dominican Republic in 1889; Japan in 1895; Egypt in 1899; and China in 1904 (but not to Congo until 1935). Though in the earliest days often beset by disease, inadequate funding, early deaths, sometimes unwise strategy, or conflict, Free Methodist mission work took hold around the world. At the time of Free Methodism's centennial in 1960, Bishop Leslie R. Marston could say, "The church's missionary enterprise now surpasses in magnitude the home church of forty years ago, and is increasing much more rapidly than the home church."[66] By the beginning of the twenty-first century, world Free Methodism had far outstripped the North American church.[67]

In 1888, in response to a rather sarcastic piece in the ME *New York Christian Advocate* that the Free Methodist Church was "really too small to do much harm or do much good," Roberts retorted, "Small as we are, and brief as is our history, we have already sent to heathen lands — to places where 'the [ME] Church' has no stations, some twenty-four missionaries."[68]

So far as B. T. Roberts was concerned, foreign missions were the natural extension of Free Methodism's primary mission to maintain the Bible standard of Christianity and preach the gospel to the poor. Benjamin and Ellen Roberts were missionaries at heart.

The 1888 London Missionary Conference

Given Roberts's prominence and missions interest, it was natural that he be selected by the General Missionary Board as one of two Free Methodist representatives at the Cen-

---

63. The *Earnest Christian* occasionally reprinted articles from the *Missionary Review of the World* and similar publications.

64. See chapter 30.

65. "From Brother and Sister Kelley," *EC* 50, no. 3 (Sept. 1885): 97.

66. Marston, p. 466.

67. M'Geary devotes three chapters to early Free Methodist missions. M'Geary, *Outline History,* pp. 163-97; Marston, pp. 451-70; Byron S. Lamson, *Venture! The Frontiers of Free Methodism* (Winona Lake, Ind.: Light and Life Press, 1960). Lamson includes an eighteen-page field-by-field chronology (pp. 248-65).

68. B. T. Roberts, "Another Attack!" *FM* 24, no. 49 (Dec. 5, 1888): 8.

tenary Conference of the Protestant Missions of the World, to be held at Exeter Hall in London, England, June 9-19, 1888. The other was T. B. Arnold, at the time the denominational publishing agent. Both offered to travel at their own expense.[69]

Benjamin was away for seven weeks, including a little over two weeks of ocean travel. He left New York City on Wednesday, May 30, on the steamship *Adriatic* of the White Star Line (the same line that would launch the *Titanic* twenty-four years later) and arrived back in New York on the *State of Nebraska*, a steamer of the State Line, in mid-July.[70] He arranged for others to cover most of his editorial duties while he was away. It appears that Benson took major responsibility for the July and August issues of the *Earnest Christian*.[71] Benson also contributed many of the brief page 1 editorial notes in the *Free Methodist* while his father was traveling.[72] Benjamin, however, sent back to the *Free Methodist* reports of his travels and other material — "far beyond our expectations," noted the office editor.[73]

Before sailing B. T. spent three days in New York City, preaching twice at the Brooklyn Free Methodist Church on Sunday, calling on potential major donors to Chesbrough Seminary, visiting his friends Frank and Emeline Smith at Jerry McAuley's Water Street Mission, and sitting in on some sessions of the Methodist Episcopal General Conference, meeting at New York's Metropolitan Opera House.[74]

The ten-day voyage to Liverpool was mostly smooth. Benjamin suffered almost no seasickness, he noted. He "did not lose a single meal" and slept well except when occasionally disturbed by reveling passengers. He "spent most of the leisure time on deck, reading and conversing, so that the time was profitably spent." He read from his Greek Testament and a history of England. He met and conversed with several others who were bound for the missionary conference, including Dr. George W. Dowkontt, medical director of the International Medical Missionary Society, based in New York City.[75]

69. Marston, p. 563; Zahniser, p. 321; Lamson, *Venture!* p. 144. B. T. Roberts referred to it as "The General Conference of Foreign Missions"; Benson Roberts called it "the first ecumenical missionary conference," which in some respects was true (BHR, *BTR*, p. 547).

70. Zahniser, pp. 325-26, 335. Roberts appears to have traveled alone. He does not mention that Arnold was with him, and his editorial "we" in the *Free Methodist* and *Earnest Christian* seems to refer just to himself.

71. The lead articles of both issues were by Benson Roberts, and Emma Sellew Roberts contributed at least three short pieces.

72. See, for example, page 1 of *FM* 21, no. 25 (June 20, 1888).

73. "Personal Mention," *FM* 21, no. 30 (July 25, 1888): 9.

74. B. T. Roberts, "The Editor's Travels," *FM* 21, no. 23 (June 6, 1888): 8; Zahniser, pp. 321-24. Roberts contacted, or tried to contact, several wealthy potential donors in New York: Mrs. Russell Sage, a noted philanthropist whose multimillionaire husband was prominent in railroad financing (as an ally with Jay Gould) and in stock trading; Mrs. Marshall Roberts, whose husband was a prominent New York City businessman; and "Mr. Depew" — probably Chauncey Mitchell Depew (1834-1928), president of the New York Central Railroad and former attorney for "Commodore" Vanderbilt. Benjamin was not immediately successful. "We must hold on for that fifty thousand dollars from Philadelphia," he wrote Ellen. BTR (New York City) to ELR, May 29, 1888, quoted in Zahniser, p. 324.

75. B. T. Roberts, "The Voyage," *FM* 21, no. 25 (June 20, 1888): 8; Zahniser, pp. 325-27.

Roberts arrived in Liverpool on Friday evening, June 8, and the next morning took a train to London, arriving at St. Pancras station about 3:00 P.M. There he was met by conference representatives who took care of his luggage and put him on a double-decked omnibus that took him directly to Exeter Hall in central London, a YMCA facility that was the conference venue. That evening he attended the opening session of the conference, which was primarily a reception for the delegates; the conference proper began on Monday morning. Sunday morning he went to hear the noted British Wesleyan preacher Mark Guy Pearse at St. James Hall and in the evening attended an Anglican service at St. Mathews, where the rector's warmhearted evangelical message impressed him. Benjamin spent much of the day wandering around central London, judging that he walked in all about six miles.[76]

During the conference he was comfortably entertained at the home of Mrs. I. L. Frere, 30 Palace Garden Terrace — "a high, beautiful street, in an aristocratic part of the city," near Kensington Palace. Mrs. Frere, the well-to-do widow of an Anglican vicar, was "thoroughly evangelical" and "full of missionary zeal," Benjamin wrote to Ellen.[77]

The Centenary Conference on the Protestant Missions of the World, or General Missionary Conference (as it was also called), is best understood in the context of the series of interdenominational Protestant missions conferences beginning in the late 1800s that culminated in the 1910 Edinburgh Conference (and in effect launched the modern ecumenical movement). It was a fairly large conference, with nearly 1,600 people credentialed in various categories and about 1,000 actually attending. It was a predominantly British affair; only 189 of the participants were from the United States, with some also from Canada and the European continent. Many of the participants were themselves missionaries. In terms of number of mission agencies, however, North America was well represented: officially 57 U.S. and 9 Canadian societies were represented plus 18 from continental Europe, while societies from England, Ireland, and Scotland totaled 53. Roberts noted that 317 of the participants were women, 47 of those from the United States, and that a number of the women were missionaries.[78]

Coming toward the end of Queen Victoria's long reign and at the height of the British Empire, the conference may be seen as a marker in the transition from a

76. B. T. Roberts, "To London," *FM* 21, no. 27 (July 4, 1888): 8; B. T. Roberts, "The Mission Conference," *EC* 56, no. 2 (Aug. 1888): 61; Zahniser, pp. 328-29.

77. B. T. Roberts, "To London"; B. T. Roberts, "The Mission Conference," *EC* 56, no. 2 (Aug. 1888): 61; BTR (London) to ELR, June 11, 1888, quoted in Zahniser, p. 328; B. T. Roberts, "General Remarks," *FM* 21, no. 30 (July 25, 1888): 8.

78. B. T. Roberts, "The Missionary Conference," *FM* 21, no. 28 (July 11, 1888): 8; James Johnston, ed., *Report of the Centenary Conference on the Protestant Missions of the World,* 2 vols. (New York: Fleming H. Revell, [1888]), 1:xxiii, xlv; 2:574-96. The official report listed 1,579 participants, including 1,316 "Members, representing fifty-three Societies in Great Britain and Ireland," plus "Delegates" from the United States, Canada, the continent of Europe, and the British colonies (Johnston, 1:xlv).

British-dominated to a largely American-dominated world missions enterprise —
paralleling what was happening politically and economically. (There was a bit of incidental symbolism in the fact that Roberts went to England on a British ship and returned on an American one!)

Many major missionary leaders of the day were present, including James Hudson Taylor; B. La Trobe, secretary of Moravian Missions; and Rev. and Mrs. Henry
Grattan Guinness, Baptists who ran the East London Institute for missionary training. Gustav Warneck, the great German mission historian and missiologist, sent a
paper to be read, though he was unable to attend. Notables from the United States
included Arthur Tappan Pierson, editor of the *Missionary Review of the World* and
instrumental figure in the rise of the Student Volunteer Movement; A. J. Gordon; the
Methodist William Taylor; Washington Gladden, influential pastor of the First Congregational Church in Columbus, Ohio; and the historian Philip Schaff. In later
years some of these, like Pierson and Gladden, would become theological enemies
with the rise of the social gospel and the fundamentalist reaction.

The British viewed the gathering as a "centenary conference" because it celebrated approximately one hundred years of Protestant foreign missions, dated from
the rise of foreign missions interest in England in the late 1780s and the publication
of William Carey's *Enquiry into the Obligations of Christians to use Means for the
Conversion of the Heathens* in 1792. One speaker noted, "This year 1888 may be pronounced the first centenary of modern Missions in their design, while 2nd October,
1892 [commemorating Carey] will be observed as the first centenary in fact." He
noted that 1788 was also the year in which "Wilberforce and Pitt . . . first committed
Great Britain to the abolition of slavery."[79]

Participants saw the conference as "ecumenical" because it attempted to incor-
porate virtually all Protestant mission agencies, with as large a global reach as possible. Though it was hardly "ecumenical" by later standards, it was certainly the most
ecumenical missions conference to date. The conference report said "every *Evangelical Church* in the world, having any agency for the extension of the Redeemer's kingdom, was represented. . . . The countries represented were practically those of the
whole world," making "the Council [*sic*] in the highest sense œcumenical."[80]

The conference was called "to stimulate and encourage all evangelistic agencies,
in pressing forward, in obedience to the last command of the risen Saviour, 'Go ye
therefore, and make disciples of all nations,' especially in those vast regions of the
heathen world in which the people are still 'sitting in darkness and in the shadow of
death,' without a preached Gospel, or the written 'word of God.'" Three key aims
were stated:

79. Johnston, *Report,* 1:151-52; address by Mr. George Smith, "Missions a Hundred Years Ago and
Now." The 1780s were also the period in which Thomas Coke was stirring up global missions interest
within British and American Methodism, having published his *Address to the Pious and Benevolent Proposing an Annual Subscription for the Support of Missionaries* in 1786, four years before Carey's *Enquiry.*
80. Johnston, *Report,* 1:xiii-xiv.

1st. To turn to account the experience of the past for the improvement of the methods of Missionary enterprise in the foreign field.

2nd. To utilise acquired experience for the improvement of the methods for the home management of Foreign Missions.

3rd. To seek the more entire CONSECRATION OF THE CHURCH OF GOD, in all its members, to the great work committed to it by the Lord.[81]

Although the impetus for the conference came from England, American mission leaders were happy to join in. British mission leaders viewed the conference as a successor to an 1878 London meeting, but some American leaders had for years been calling for a first "World's Missionary Council." A. T. Pierson had appealed in 1881 for such a conference, and D. L. Moody's Northfield (Mass.) Convention in 1885 had issued a similar call. Pierson wrote in the April 1888 *Missionary Review:*

> There will be many who will regard this council, now called to meet in June, as the answer to many fervent prayers. This will be an ecumenical council in fact. And think for what purpose they meet who gather there and then! To map out the world — for Christ's war of the ages! To cover every district of earth's surface with the network of missionary effort; to plant the cross in every valley and on every hill; to put the Bible in every hamlet and hut; to prevent all waste of men and material and means; to distribute work equally and equitably; to accelerate the progress of missions so that in the shortest time the witness may be borne to all people and to every soul![82]

Pierson was convinced that God's "plan in this generation" was "the immediate evangelization of the world."[83]

A 1994 assessment of the 1888 London conference by Thomas Askew noted that though this was "the largest, most representative interdenominational, international assembly to date," it has received little attention historically. It is best seen as preparatory to the later New York (1900) and Edinburgh (1910) gatherings. Yet the conference, suggested Askew, "facilitated a heightened level of mutuality among English-speaking mission leaders, elevated British respect for the Americans present, and prepared the way for increased Anglo-American missionary cooperation. By the century's end this collaboration resulted in North America assuming larger respon-

---

81. Johnston, *Report,* 1:viii.

82. A. T. Pierson, *Missionary Review of the World,* April 1888, p. 268, quoted in Todd M. Johnson, *Countdown to 1900: World Evangelization at the End of the Nineteenth Century* (Birmingham, Ala.: New Hope, 1988), p. 28. Johnson devotes a chapter to the 1888 conference, setting it in context.

83. A. T. Pierson, *Missionary Review of the World,* May 1888, p. 332, quoted in Johnson, *Countdown to 1900,* p. 28. In terms of Roberts's own missions interest and formation, it is worth noting that Stephen Olin had made essentially the same point half a century earlier, employing language remarkably similar to Pierson's and to the famous "watchword" of the Student Volunteer Movement. Olin wrote in 1835, *"The Church must familiarize itself with the stupendous apprehension that the world is to be evangelized before another generation shall perish."* Stephen Olin, "Duties of the Church — Missions," *Christian Advocate and Journal* 9, no. 23 (Jan. 30, 1835): 89.

sibilities for supplying money and personnel for overseas missions. In other words, London 1888 marks the coming of age of North American foreign missions after a century of decided British leadership."

Thus, as "a milestone event during the zenith years of the nineteenth-century trans-Atlantic evangelical united front," London 1888 produced two results: "The precedent for decennial missions megaconferences was furthered, and North Americans assumed increased leadership in Protestant foreign missions."[84]

B. T. Roberts judged the London missions conference "one of the most important gatherings of Christians held in modern times," and he was pleased he could attend.[85] Benjamin was an activist, however, and not very content to sit passively through long conference sessions. On June 14 he wrote to Ellen, "The Conference is going on very pleasantly; but I have nothing to do but to listen, and you know I am not used to that."[86] He took some breaks from conference sessions to hear General William Booth speak about Salvation Army mission work on Tuesday evening, June 11, at City Temple and to visit the grave sites of John Bunyan and Susannah Wesley at Bunhill Burying Ground. Saturday and Sunday, June 16-17, were free of major conference activities, and on Saturday he may have visited an art gallery and made a trip to Oxford. On Sunday morning Benjamin, along with many other conference delegates, went to hear Charles Haddon Spurgeon at the Metropolitan Tabernacle. Though about ten years younger than Roberts, Spurgeon was in frail health and used a cane while preaching. Roberts was impressed with his spirituality and eloquence.[87]

Reporting on the missionary conference in the *Free Methodist*, Roberts noted the range of topics discussed: qualifications of missionaries; medical missions; "commerce and Christian missions" (particularly the liquor and opium traffic); the "increase of Mohammedanism, the condition of India, China, Japan, Africa, the isles of the sea, and missions to the Jews"; "the Turkish Empire in Central Asia"; women's

---

84. Thomas A. Askew, "The 1888 London Centenary Missions Conference: Ecumenical Disappointment or American Missions Coming of Age?" *International Bulletin of Missionary Research* 18, no. 3 (July 1994): 113-18. Askew notes that some Anglican mission societies, notably the Society for the Propagation of the Gospel (SPG) and the Society for Promoting Christian Knowledge (SPCK), "were absent by their own choice," and that the Salvation Army did not cooperate; it was having its own international convention the same week. Askew examines the worldview assumptions of the participants and suggests some major conference shortcomings: failure to address underlying theological issues or to provide for any continuing follow-up structure.

85. B. T. Roberts, "The Missionary Conference," p. 8.

86. BTR (London) to ELR, June 14, 1888, quoted in Zahniser, p. 331.

87. Zahniser, pp. 330-31; [B. T. Roberts], "Bunhill Burying Ground," *EC* 56, no. 2 (Aug. 1888): 64; [B. T. Roberts], "Hugh Latimer," *EC* 56, no. 2 (Aug. 1888): 66; B. T. Roberts, "General Remarks," *FM* 21, no. 30 (July 25, 1888): 8. See Johnston, *Report*, 1:453. Benson Howard Roberts visited Spurgeon's tabernacle a year later and described Spurgeon as "a large man with a kindly face and a friendly manner" who from nothing had built "a congregation of five thousand" working people in London. [Benson H. Roberts], "Spurgeon's Church," *EC* 58, no. 4 (Oct. 1889): 129.

work in missions; polygamy. There was considerable discussion also of comity arrangements on mission fields.[88]

The missionary conference had three tracks of parallel sessions each day. Benjamin chose the sessions that most interested him. Two sessions especially sparked his interest: one in which J. Hudson Taylor gave an address on China and one on women's work.

Taylor had spoken in the "Great Missionary Meeting" on Monday evening, June 11, on the condition and need of China, and Roberts was very impressed. This was the first Roberts had heard anything much about the China Inland Mission. The next afternoon he went to the missionary methods section to hear Taylor read his paper, "The Relation of Itinerant to Settled Missionary Work." Again Benjamin was impressed, both with Taylor's work and with his spiritual pilgrimage. Either after this session or at a later point in the conference Roberts met and talked with Taylor, and the two men prayed together.[89]

Roberts went to the session on women's work in the mission field on Wednesday morning, June 13. Papers were presented by Miss C. Rainy of the Free Church of Scotland Ladies' Society for Female Education and by Miss A. K. Marston, a medical doctor working in India with the Zenana Bible and Medical Mission. During the discussion time following the two papers, Roberts spoke briefly on women's role in world mission. The official report of the conference carried his comments:

> I rejoice at the door that is opened for women's work in spreading the Gospel, and I want to say a word to try and open the door wider. My experience in America is like that of many from India. I find the women morally superior to the men; and, if so, I can see no reason at all why they should not be permitted to preach as well as to labour in an inferior position.
>
> My reasons for saying this are based on Scripture and on experience; and not to repeat what has already been said on the sixty-eighth Psalm, and Joel and Acts, we find in the sixteenth chapter of Romans, Paul sends his salutations to a great many women, and amongst others he sends them to "Andronica and Junia." Chrysostom, who understood the Greek language, was a Greek by birth and one of the brightest of scholars, says that Junia in that place is declared by the Apostle to be an Apostle. Our version is "of note among the Apostles," but he says Junia was an Apostle, and was a noted Apostle; and it seems to me that there is very strong ground for women to take an advanced place in spreading the Gospel in heathen lands as well as at home. And so, in experience, we find that some of the most useful labourers in America and in England have been women.[90]

88. B. T. Roberts, "The Missionary Conference," p. 8; "The Mission Conference," *FM* 21, no. 29 (July 18, 1888): 8.

89. Zahniser, p. 329; Johnston, *Report*, 1:172-77; 2:29-34; [B. T. Roberts], "China Inland Mission," *EC* 56, no. 2 (Aug. 1888): 62-63. See J. Hudson Taylor, "China Inland Mission," reprinted in *EC* 56, no. 6 (Dec. 1888): 181-83.

90. Johnston, *Report*, 2:153; cf. Zahniser, p. 332. It is interesting that in this brief speech Roberts appeals to all four elements of the so-called Wesleyan Quadrilateral: Scripture, reason, tradition, and

Benjamin's comments were not unpremeditated; the day before, he had written to Ellen that although he had not yet spoken during the conference, he thought he soon would. Later he told Ellen his remarks were "not worth crossing the Atlantic twice to say," though he thought they did some good. It is indicative of Roberts's keen interest in the right of, and need for, women in public ministry that the one time he spoke during the conference, it was on this subject.[91]

Once the conference was over, Roberts dispatched his final report to the *Free Methodist*. He wrote, "The influence of the conference recently held in London can but be widely felt and far-reaching. The missionaries will be stirred up to do more thorough work. Though no conclusions were formulated and resolutions passed except the resolutions touching on that traffic in liquor and opium, yet convictions were fastened on many minds." He noted that some missionaries thought it was "necessary to tolerate, to a certain extent, polygamy in heathen lands." Roberts disagreed, feeling there were redemptive ways of dealing with the issue without moral compromise.[92]

The conference report itself noted that some "ardent minds" were disappointed that more definitive action didn't come from the gathering. Some wished the conference would have "passed rules to put an end at once to all encroachments of one Society on the territories occupied by another," but of course the gathering was a consultative, not a deliberative, body.[93] The *Evangelical Magazine* gave a fairly balanced assessment, which seems to echo Roberts's view:

> [Conference participants] "were of one mind and one soul" in desire and purpose, to "preach the gospel to every creature." How best this could be done was the dominant thought. Much information was given. Difficulties and obstacles were stated with great candour. Many statements were made of a most encouraging and stimulating character. But the meetings were deliberative, not executive. Therefore it was that many questions of great practical and doctrinal interest were hardly touched, and others were ventilated only, not decided. The conference was not a council, and was too large, miscellaneous and popular to develop into true practical deliberative forms, or to elicit much boldness of speech or freedom of opinion. This, no doubt, was felt by many to be a want, but it was inevitable.[94]

---

experience. Roberts's remarks had to be brief, as discussion comments were not supposed to exceed five minutes.

91. Zahniser, pp. 331-32; B. T. Roberts, "The Missionary Conference," p. 8. In this report Roberts actually quotes an article from the *Christian* that reported on this session, mentioning Roberts's participation in the discussion. This particular session had to be moved from the Annex to the Large Hall because of the crowded attendance (Johnston, *Report*, 2:140).

92. B. T. Roberts, "The Mission Conference," *FM* 21, no. 29 (July 18, 1888): 8; cf. B. T. Roberts, "The Mission Conference," *EC* 56, no. 2 (Aug. 1888): 61.

93. Johnston, *Report*, 1:xxiv-xxv.

94. *Evangelical Magazine*, Aug. 1888, pp. 374-75, quoted in Johnson, *Countdown to 1900*, p. 30.

Todd Johnson's assessment 100 years later (1988) was similar. In not really resolving the cooperation and comity issue, he wrote, "the great London conference failed to achieve one of its major objectives. Because it was hastily organized and because so many speakers were on the platform, there was no opportunity for genuine strategic planning. 'Dividing up the world' [strategically] was pushed aside as the delegates tended to focus on what was being done and not on what remained to be done. Pierson's rallying cry fell on an auditorium of men and women just learning to listen to each other, not on Christians ready to plan the final conquest of the world."[95]

The conference was a great learning opportunity for Roberts, however. "The discussions were carried on largely by missionaries, who have a practical knowledge of the subjects on which they spoke," he noted. "The influence of this Conference can but be wide spread and lasting" and was an impetus to "take hold of the mission cause intelligently, practically and with a deep love for the souls that are perishing for a lack of a knowledge of Christ."[96] Byron Lamson (FM general missionary secretary, 1944-64) suggested that what Roberts learned at the London conference "regarding mission procedures" probably contributed to the set of policies that the FM mission board adopted in 1889. Both Roberts (who was president of the General Missionary Board) and T. B. Arnold, who handled most board business, submitted recommendations as part of the policy formation process.[97]

The conference over, Roberts went to the wool-manufacturing city of Leeds for a few days, where he had some Primitive Methodist contacts; he preached on Sunday, July 1, to a "fair" Primitive Methodist congregation. He went on to Scotland, making brief visits to Edinburgh and Glasgow before sailing from Glasgow on July 6. He expected a direct ten-day passage to New York, but was disappointed to discover there would be a thirty-hour stop at Belfast to take on freight. This gave him the chance however to visit Belfast and see a bit of Ireland. He was eager to get home; he wrote to Ellen, "Darling, you are more to me than all the countries and all the wonders and sights of the world."[98]

Health-wise, the England trip was a good break for Benjamin. He needed the (comparative) rest and exercise. As he started home he told Ellen he felt rested but would be "only too glad to get to work again."[99] In fact, his health was not very good, though he apparently had no particular difficulties in England and did quite a bit of walking.

The journey to England and Scotland was a broadening experience for Benjamin. He was "gratified and surprised," he said, "at the deep spiritual tone and the fraternal spirit manifested by many of the preachers and members of the Church

95. Johnson, *Countdown to 1900*, p. 30.

96. B. T. Roberts, "The Mission Conference," *EC* 56, no. 2 (Aug. 1888): 61-62.

97. Lamson, *Venture!* p. 148.

98. B. T. Roberts, "Primitive Methodists," *FM* 21, no. 36 (Sept. 5, 1888): 8; Zahniser, pp. 334-35; BTR (Ireland) to ELR, July 7, 1888, quoted in Zahniser, p. 335.

99. BTR (Ireland) to ELR, July 7, 1888, quoted in Zahniser, p. 335.

of England." He quoted with apparent approval a sermon by Frederic W. Farrar, canon of Westminster, in which Farrar said he would humbly "stand bareheaded before any true saint of God," whether Romanist, Independent, Quaker, or Presbyterian, and would sooner be around God's throne with them than with those who "have spent their lives in the endless round of outward ordinances" but didn't manifest God's love. "For it is Christ, and Christ alone, . . . not episcopal government, or apostolical succession, or ancient ritual, or the orthodoxy of curiously articulated creeds; it is . . . Christ only, and the innocence which shines in the lives of them that truly believe in Him, which has been the strength of Christianity."[100]

Long-Distance Love

Benjamin and Ellen were seldom separated for such a long period of time — at least not at such great distance! They corresponded constantly, as they did during other separations. "I never feel it is the Lord's order for us to be very long separated," Ellen reminded Benjamin in a letter written the day he sailed for England. But the Lord "can make this time seem short."[101]

As Benjamin embarked, Ellen was concerned about his health and his appearance. He should buy some oranges and lemons, she said. (He did; before going onboard he bought himself "a good chair, lemons, oranges, and bananas," and also "a good waterproof coat" that came in handy in rainy England.) Ellen also suggested that Benjamin, who was growing a bit portly, looked better with his coat unbuttoned — "but keep the fold in the collar just as Taylor H. pressed it." She was a bit concerned to learn there had been "a bad storm on the Atlantic."[102]

Ellen showed remarkable generosity of spirit as she sent Benjamin off to England. She urged him to enjoy himself, to get some rest, and to "not economize on yourself this trip and while in London. Just as far as you can, go and see other places. Do not calculate on bringing home a cent of money but send for more. You always pinch yourself. Don't on this trip."[103] In her May 30 letter she wrote, "The apple blossoms are falling fast, the ground is white in places with the blossoms. The greatest beauty is past. Beauty is short lived any way, wherever we see it. Yet my husband is ever beautiful to me. The soul's eyes see what is far beyond the power of the natural eye to see, or discern. Dearest, I will be with you daily on the Ocean, and Jesus will be nearer than all."

"I live for you mostly," she declared.[104]

---

100. [B. T. Roberts], "Christian Union," *EC* 56, no. 3 (Sept. 1888): 96-97. Frederic William Farrar (1831-1903), a "Broad Church Evangelical," later became dean of Canterbury (1895). He was especially well known for his *Life of Christ* (1874) and *Life and Works of St. Paul* (1879). Roberts doesn't say whether he heard Farrar personally while he was in London or read the sermon in a published source.

101. ELR to BTR, May 30, 1888, quoted in Zahniser, p. 324. Zahniser provides additional details about the voyage and the conference.

102. Zahniser, pp. 322-23.

103. ELR to BTR, May 26, 1888, quoted in Zahniser, p. 325.

Cleverly, Ellen had hidden "little token[s] of remembrance" — love notes — in Benjamin's satchel. The first note, which Ellen marked "First Mail at sea for my husband," read:

My dearest one,
    Be of good cheer. Look up and expect greater blessings of your Father. Do not look behind you, at your home or friends. See God in everything and everywhere.
    I commit you to him who controls the waves and my prayers for your safety will ascend continually. God will bless and care for you.

In the <u>greatest</u> love

ever

Your own,

E.L.R.[105]

Ellen's fifth note was written on tiny gray, diagonally striped notepaper, folded into a miniature linen envelope measuring about one inch by two and a half inches. She wrote, "Dearest One, I shall have hard work not to <u>wish</u> I was with you. But I expect we shall cross the Ocean together some time." In another, longer note Ellen wrote to her nearly sixty-five-year-old husband:

The best of my married life is the <u>oneness of spirit</u> I feel with you. You are my God-given husband and I expect better and better days with you. You are dear and very precious to me. I love you always and with an unceasing love. My love is like a deep <u>well</u>. I cannot show it all. I cannot bring it all to the surface. But I do always feel a <u>deep</u> supply on hand.
    Evermore in deepest, truest, tender love, your

E.L.R.[106]

Benjamin wrote to Ellen, "Darling, your letters are a great comfort to me. They are such beautiful notes — like you."[107]

104. ELR to BTR, May 30, 1888, quoted in Zahniser, p. 324.
105. Quoted in Zahniser, p. 325.
106. Quoted in Zahniser, pp. 324-25.

CHAPTER 38

Weary but Faithful

"Our progress may be steady towards our final, eternal home. As fruit grows and ripens until the time of the harvest, so may we until the Master gathers us into his garner."

B. T. Roberts, 1884[1]

"We should live in constant readiness to exchange worlds."

B. T. Roberts, 1883[2]

With all B. T. Roberts's combined duties, his health began to deteriorate. In the summer and fall of 1888 he conducted nine or ten annual conferences, "largely in the West, on the frontier" — that is, "from southern Kansas to the northern part of Minnesota." This required a good deal of inconvenient north-south rail travel, making rest almost impossible. Thus the conferences that year were "unusually wearisome," even though Roberts found the church growing healthily. "The church was never, as far as we are able to judge, in a state of greater prosperity."

But the same could not be said for Benjamin's health. He was beginning to experience worrisome chest pains. He wrote,

> In going from one conference to another, over three roads, we had to change cars nine times. On four different occasions we had to take local freight trains. Frequently we had to change cars in the night. Once we took a train at seven in the

1. B. T. Roberts, "Abound in Love," *EC* 47, no. 1 (Jan. 1884): 7.
2. [B. T. Roberts], "Death in a Church," *EC* 45, no. 6 (June 1883): 191.

evening — had to change cars at eleven — and at two had to change again and wait till half-past four for our train. This was on Monday after we had preached twice and attended protracted services on the Sabbath. We were so worn out that we spread our overcoat on the floor and laid down and went to sleep.

These exposures have brought on a difficulty we never experienced before. We may feel as well as ever, but if we walk five minutes at an ordinary gait it brings on a pain in the chest, and a shortness of breath, and such a tired feeling through the upper part of the body that compels us to rest.

It was "evidently time to call a halt," Roberts recognized; "it does not appear to us that it would be right for us to continue to hold meetings as we have been doing in the past. Brethren, give us a little needed rest, and we may be able to serve you longer."[3] Yet he still tried to keep his appointments.

At the Canada Conference later that fall he had severe chest pains, and returned home quite ill. Some close friends who were physicians advised him unanimously: Absolute rest! Ellen wrote that the doctors "told him how to care for himself; but in labors abundant and constant, most of the time away from home, it was impossible to follow out their directions. Seeing and feeling the needs of the work, in hope and trust he <u>worked on</u>, often finding relief from suffering by taking his difficulties to the Lord in prayer."[4]

As he traveled, Benjamin's friends and colleagues would from time to time gather around and pray for him, and he would experience some relief. But he really was not well. "For some time his family were not aware how serious his condition was," Benson Roberts commented.[5] Benjamin learned to live with pain, and apparently got some medical help but did not commit himself to the extended rest that likely would have prolonged his life another ten or twenty years.

"It was too much," said Benson Roberts. "The demand upon his strength was greater than one man should be called upon to bear."[6]

Benjamin had written in 1885, "Health of soul, and health of body are preserved in pretty much the same way — by obeying God and trusting him." He advised, "Observe the laws of health. . . . Do not over-work. Do not over-eat. Take regularly all the sleep you need."[7] But Roberts's intense sense of duty to his denominational responsibilities kept him from following his own advice.

In February 1890 Benjamin uncharacteristically put a plea in his own behalf on the editorial page of the *Free Methodist*. "The editor is in great danger of giving out

3. B. T. Roberts, "Conferences," *FM* 24, no. 47 (Nov. 21, 1888): 8.

4. Quoted in BHR, *BTR*, p. 555.

5. BHR, *BTR*, p. 555.

6. BHR, *BTR*, p. 546.

7. B. T. Roberts, "Healing Faith," *EC* 50, no. 5 (Nov. 1885): 137. Like Wesley, Roberts saw the interconnection between physical and spiritual health and believed health was maintained by both spiritual and physical means. He therefore did not hold, as some did, that Christians must forgo all medication. "While, as a rule, we should keep free from the use of medicine, we should also be equally free to use it if necessary," he wrote (p. 137).

utterly from overwork," he wrote. "He is greatly burdened with correspondence. He is in the habit of writing many letters a day; and still unanswered letters get buried on his table." He urged contributors "for a season at least" not to submit belligerent, controversial articles. "With his nervous system overtasked they make him feel like resigning the editorial chair at once. If we cannot have peace, let us have a truce until General conference."[8] The 1890 General Conference was indeed approaching — scheduled for Chicago in October — and the pages of the *Free Methodist* were heating up with articles for and against women's ordination and debating missionary policy, probationary membership, and other issues.

Benjamin was concerned about the health of the denomination, not just his own. In another February 1890 editorial he warned against too much "scattering" — multiplying schools and publications and other enterprises beyond what was wise for a still-small group. "There is a tendency among us as a church," he said, to be "*too scattered*. Many well-begun enterprises languish and die for lack of adequate support." Across the country the church had "so many independent papers" that the denomination struggled to build up its own publishing enterprise. Schools were multiplying "so rapidly as to endanger each other's existence." In foreign missions endeavors in Africa, an "independent adventurous spirit" was undermining a cooperative strategy that would be more effective. We need more strategic, concentrated effort, Roberts argued. "It is just as easy to write a good editorial for fifty thousand readers as for five hundred," he said, and "a good teacher would rather teach a class of thirty than of three. And the class, on the whole, would be better."[9]

"Let us have *no more schools started* till those we have are either paid for and well sustained or abandoned. It looks to us as little less than *wicked* for a conference" to start a new school while in neighboring conferences schools for which "immense sacrifices have been borne" are struggling to find enough students, teachers, and funds.[10] Roberts was not simply being protective of his own school in North Chili or of the *Free Methodist*. He correctly saw that a spirit of independent, individualistic action was undermining effective denominational strategy and growth. The Methodist Episcopal Church had similarly multiplied enterprises two or three generations earlier, but it had a much broader base of support.

Through the late summer and early fall of 1890 Benjamin conducted annual conferences as usual and continued his editorial work. He dreaded the approaching General Conference, not only because of his own weariness but also because of the tough issues that would rack the conference — particularly women's ordination and the relation of the Pentecost Bands to the denomination and its missions program. He could see that the drift of sentiment on these issues was going against him.

As he was conducting annual conferences in Michigan just weeks before General

8. B. T. Roberts, "Controversy," *FM* 23, no. 8 (Feb. 19, 1890): 8.

9. B. T. Roberts, "Scattering and Scattered," *FM* 23, no. 9 (Feb. 26, 1890): 8 (emphasis in original). Relatedly, Benjamin published an editorial expressing his concern about "independent missions" in June 1890. B. T. Roberts, "Independent Missions," *FM* 23, no. 23 (June 4, 1890): 8.

10. B. T. Roberts, "Scattering and Scattered."

Weary but Faithful

Conference, Benjamin received an urgent telegram from North Chili the evening of Thursday, September 11. The large Chesbrough Seminary building, constructed twenty years earlier, had burned down just a day after the start of the fall term.

The fire was discovered just as the last study-hour bell was rung at 7:15 Thursday night. Flames were bursting from the cupola atop the building, and the structure went fast, though there was time to rescue some things from the burning building. "The effects of most of the students were saved, much of the library, and most of the apparatus was saved. The desks, stoves, bedsteads, with other furniture, were destroyed."[11]

Ellen Roberts, at home on the hill across from the seminary, hurried to help. She wrote in her diary, "Memorable night! Seminary burned up. It was a sad sight. Fire started in the attic and was seen first in Cupola. Could not be put out. I felt it had to go as soon as I saw it. A funeral tread came upon me as I walked to the seminary & entered its doors for the last time. It was like seeing one's prayers burned up, almost."[12]

By midnight the brick walls had mostly fallen. Ellen opened her diary a second time and wrote, "My soul is full of groaning — a load is on my heart. Lord help is my prayer. Darkness closes in around us."[13]

In Michigan Benjamin received the news gravely but went on with conference sessions. "The Seminary is burned. Praise the lord, there are no lives lost!" he said. "Great as the loss [is,] it is as nothing compared with the loss of character."[14]

In the following days Ellen busied herself helping Benson and Emma find emergency lodging for the students and prepare to resume classes, using the church building. Only one day of school was lost; classes resumed Monday morning.

Benjamin returned to North Chili "full of zeal and courage to rebuild," despite his physical weakness. Ellen was afraid, she said, that "the work of rebuilding would be too heavy for his advancing years and diminished strength," but he seemed reenergized by the challenge. Fund-raising efforts were successful, and Benjamin lived to see the destroyed building replaced by two new ones: Roberts Hall, a dormitory funded by money "received mainly in small sums," and Cox Memorial Hall, funded by an $8,000 gift from the Robertses' old friend Edward P. Cox of Buffalo.[15] Since Benson and Emma Roberts were the principals of Chesbrough Seminary at the time, the heaviest load following the fire fell on them. Benjamin's skill and networks and his amplified voice through the *Earnest Christian* were key, however, in the rebuilding process. A statement issued by the Board of Trustees five days after the fire, no doubt written by Benjamin and published in the October *Earnest Christian*, called for quick donations. The board resolved to erect "new buildings" as soon as possible. About $15,000 would

11. "A. M. Chesbrough Seminary. Statement of Trustees," *EC* 60, no. 4 (Oct. 1890): 129.
12. ELRD, Sept. 11, 1890. Cf. Neil E. Pfouts, *A History of Roberts Wesleyan College* ([North Chili, N.Y.: Roberts Wesleyan College, 2000]), pp. 30-32.
13. ELRD, Sept. 11, 1890.
14. BHR, *BTR*, p. 561.
15. Carpenter, pp. 82-84; BHR, *BTR*, pp. 560-61; Pfouts, *History,* pp. 32-33, 36.

855

be needed. "Send . . . subscriptions and remittances for this purpose to the treasurer, B. T. Roberts, North Chili, N.Y.," the statement urged. Roberts noted the importance of the seminary: "This school has helped hundreds to an education. They are everywhere in this land. They have come from New York, Ohio, Pennsylvania, New Jersey, Dakota, Wisconsin, Illinois, Iowa, Washington, Texas and Oregon." He continued,

> This work has continued for a quarter of a century. . . . [Graduates] have gone forth to sow the seed all over this land and even in foreign lands. India, Africa, and Ceylon have been the scenes of the labors of its students to spread the Gospel. Many have become efficient workers in Christ's vineyard. Here the poor have been helped, they have been clothed, fed, and taught in things human and divine. . . . Shall not that school *that in proportion to its means has done more than any other school in this land to help the helpless have your help in its hour of need to make it more helpful?*[16]

Even as Benjamin raised funds to rebuild, his attention increasingly turned to the upcoming General Conference. About three weeks after the fire he and Ellen were on their way to Chicago.

The 1890 General Conference

General Conference met October 8-23 in the just-completed edifice of the First Free Methodist Church on May Street, Chicago. The congregation "provided dinner and supper for a large number in the pleasant basement of their new church," Benjamin noted. He and Ellen stayed at the home of Mr. and Mrs. C. Willis Smith and Mrs. Smith's mother, Mrs. Mary C. Baker, office editor of the *Free Methodist*, at 323 South Wood Street, some distance from the conference site.[17]

Well before the conference Benjamin had concluded that he could no longer keep up the pace of the past four years. He asked to be relieved of his editorial duties with the *Free Methodist*. "We have a large number of names to select from," he told the delegates. "I want you to vote for some of them and not vote for me."[18]

The General Conference complied and elected Burton R. Jones of Ohio as editor.[19] One delegate, whose submissions to the magazine had apparently been rejected by Rob-

---

16. "A. M. Chesbrough Seminary. Statement of Trustees," pp. 130-31. See similarly, B. T. Roberts, "Chesbrough Seminary," *EC* 61, no. 4 (Apr. 1891): 101-2.

17. B. T. Roberts, "The General Conference," *FM* 23, no. 44 (Oct. 29, 1890): 8; Zahniser, p. 298. C. Willis Smith, Roberts said, "formerly printed the *Earnest Christian* for us." Mary Baker, office editor of the *Free Methodist* for twenty-three years, provided continuity through times of transition for the magazine. Her husband, Rev. D. P. Baker, had earlier been editor (1874-82) and coproprietor with T. B. Arnold of the magazine before it was bought by the denomination (Marston, pp. 473, 489).

18. Zahniser, p. 291, citing the *General Conference Daily*, Oct. 23, 1890, p. 208.

19. Zahniser, p. 291. Jones served a four-year term and then was elected general superintendent in 1894.

erts as too controversial, remarked that he hoped now the magazine would allow freer expression of opinion. Roberts rose and in his defense said he allowed free expression of a range of views but had rejected only "political or partizan" articles, in keeping with the advice of the previous General Conference. "I have had more trouble in that direction in one week than I have had with *The Earnest Christian* during all the time that I have published it," he said.[20]

The 1890 General Conference was painful for Roberts. Opinion was sharply divided on several key issues, and in the end the conference by narrow margins passed legislation he strongly opposed. Roberts shared the chair with the two other general superintendents, E. P. Hart and G. W. Coleman. The conference consisted of eighty-one voting members. Including the general superintendents, there were forty-three "ministerial" and thirty-eight "lay" delegates, meaning the body was somewhat over-balanced toward clergy representation.[21]

Three issues were especially significant in the longer trajectory of the denomination, and all were of concern to Roberts: the role of the Pentecost Bands, women's ordination, and the case of Richard W. Hawkins. All concerned people close to Benjamin and Ellen, and all involved younger colleagues they had encouraged and mentored in ministry.

The Pentecost Bands

By the 1890 General Conference, Vivian Dake's Pentecost Band movement was deploying more than twenty evangelistic teams and had planted over thirty new Free Methodist churches (as noted in chapter 33). The bands were controversial because of their independence, operating increasingly outside denominational oversight or control. Many also felt their emphasis on the "death route" to the experience of holiness was extreme.[22]

The General Conference eventually adopted four guidelines on the Pentecost Bands issue.

1. Chairmen of Districts [district superintendents], and Evangelists appointed by the General or Annual Conference, may organize Bands for evangelistic work; but no person shall become a member of such a Band without the recommendation of the Society to which he [*sic*] belongs.

---

20. Zahniser, p. 292, citing the *General Conference Daily,* Oct. 24, 1890, p. 213.

21. Hogue, *HFMC,* 2:189.

22. Hogue said that despite the bands' commendable zeal and fruitfulness, they "came at length . . . under Mr. Dake's leadership and tuition, to entertain more strained notions regarding Holiness than the rank and file of the Church could indorse, particularly in what they denominated 'the death route' into the experience; and, when the authorities of the Church sought to regulate their operations somewhat, the 'Bands' began to show increasing tendencies toward independence of Church government, and practically to become a Church within the Church." Hogue, *HFMC,* 2:194.

2. The rules and regulations of such Bands shall be subject to the approval of the Annual Conference to which the Leader belongs, or within the bounds of which he holds his membership.

3. No Evangelist or Band shall appoint or hold meetings where they will interfere with the regular work of any preacher duly appointed to a circuit, or station, or district.

4. Those who labor successfully in a Band for one year may be licensed by the Quarterly Conference from year to year as Band workers.[23]

The annual conferences affected by band work subsequently adopted somewhat more restrictive "Band Rules" that provided, among other things, that bands be known as "Free Methodist Bands," that they operate under the authority and supervision of the conference, and that they promote the *Free Methodist* paper.[24] Dake was left without appointment in 1891 by the Illinois Conference because he would not give assurance that he would operate strictly within the rules, feeling that they would restrict the commission God had given him.[25]

The General Conference action did not of course settle the issue. It actually stirred it up more.

Ordination of Women

The most contentious issue was the ongoing debate about women's ordination. The 1890 General Conference produced what proved to be a decisive vote on the question.

Free Methodists had been of two minds (at least) on the role of women since the beginning. Most seem not to have been opposed to women *speaking* in public in words of testimony or exhortation or even to serving as evangelists. As already noted, the denomination had increasingly recognized the ministry of women as revivalists and church planters. But many opposed permitting women to be ordained as elders, which would grant them equal status and authority with men.

Up to this time the Free Methodist Church had a remarkably large number of women in recognized ministry. Many of these served as licensed evangelists. For example, the Susquehanna Conference in 1895 listed nineteen evangelists, nearly all women. Some were wives of pastors and were themselves appointed to assist in the churches where their husbands were appointed; others were not. That year the conference also listed forty-three ordained preachers, so it had nearly one woman evan-

23. Hogue, *HFMC*, 2:194-95.

24. See, for example, the rules adopted by the Illinois Conference, *Minutes of the Annual Conferences of the Free Methodist Church* (Chicago: Free Methodist Publishing House, 1891), p. 54.

25. Report of Ministerial Relations Committee, Illinois Conference, *Minutes*, 1891, pp. 54-55. The General Conference action apparently would have required the Pentecost Bands to change their name to Free Methodist Bands.

gelist for every two ordained preachers.[26] In many conferences women played key roles as evangelists, preachers, and exhorters, among other involvements — though as preachers they always could expect some degree of opposition, even within Free Methodism. Many of these women remained single, but many others exercised a public preaching ministry both before and after marriage. Free Methodism thus had a significant number of women preachers in its earliest decades, and in the 1880s a new wave of women preachers and evangelists went forth through the Pentecost Bands.[27]

Despite Roberts's unflagging support of the public ministry of women, this remained an unsettling issue in some parts of the denomination. In the interval between the 1886 and 1890 General Conferences, it was clear that the issue needed to be definitively settled. A flurry of pro and con articles on the matter appeared in the *Free Methodist* in 1886, before and after the General Conference that fall. The opposition articles focused not so much on women's preaching but on the question of authority to govern. There were few articles on the subject during the intervening years, but several appeared in 1890 prior to and during the General Conference. As *Free Methodist* editor during this critical quadrennium, Roberts published some ten articles on women's issues — only one written by himself — all supportive of women in ministry, and all but one endorsing women's ordination. At least four were authored by women.[28]

By 1890 the women's ordination debate was complicated and perhaps aggravated by the Pentecost Bands controversy. The majority of Pentecost Band workers were women; they served sacrificially and effectively as evangelists and church planters.

While ordination was the focal issue regarding women's ministry, 1890 General Conference actions show that broader issues of gender and women's roles were also in play. Rev. H. DeForest Gaffin of the North Michigan Conference wanted to change "men" to "persons" in the Articles of Religion; Roberts quashed that idea, suggesting that to be consistent one would "have to change the Bible" as well. Rev.

---

26. *Minutes,* Susquehanna Conference, 1895. The conference also listed twenty-two local preachers, all of whom seem to have been male.

27. See the biographical sketches in Emma Freeland Shay, *Mariet Hardy Freeland: A Faithful Witness; A Biography by Her Daughter* (Winona Lake, Ind.: Women's Missionary Society of the Free Methodist Church [1913], 1937), especially pp. 105-18, and in Jean Hall Gramento, "Those Astounding Free Methodist Women! A Biographical History of Free Methodist Women in Ministry Including an Extended Bibliography of Free Methodist Women's Studies; With Selected Ecumenical Entries" (D.Min. thesis, United Theological Seminary, Dayton, Ohio, 1992), pp. 94-104, and appendix A, "Conference Records of Women Appointed."

28. Women who wrote favoring women's ordination during the quadrennium included Mrs. A. G. Warne, Mrs. Clara L. Wetherald, and Mrs. Mariet Hardy Freeland. Emma Sellew Roberts contributed an article entitled "Help It On!" that appeared during the General Conference. See the extended discussion in Jack D. Richardson, "B. T. Roberts and the Role of Women in Ministry in Nineteenth-Century Free Methodism" (M.A. thesis, Colgate Rochester Divinity School, 1984), especially pp. 111-16, 138-41. Richardson helpfully analyzes this issue during the whole period of Roberts's general superintendency.

Benjamin Winget proposed that licensed evangelists (many of whom were women) be granted seats on local churches' official boards, since by previous action they had been made members of the quarterly conferences. This was approved — another small step endorsing women's ministry. The General Conference also revised the marriage ritual, striking the words "obey and serve him" from the questions asked of the woman. Roberts proposed the alternative reading "comfort him," but in the end the delegates simply mandated that the questions asked the woman be in substance the same as those asked of the man. The fact that this change passed by a comfortable margin (59 to 12) seems to indicate that the issue of authority in marriage wasn't as hot as authority in the church.[29]

It is also of some note that this was the first FM General Conference to seat women as delegates. There were two: Clara Wetherald of the East Michigan Conference and Anna Grant from North Indiana. Mrs. Wetherald, an advocate of women's ordination, was herself a licensed evangelist. She preached several times in different churches during the conference.[30]

The debate on women's ordination was long and complex. Though the fundamental question was simple enough — to ordain or not to ordain — it was complicated by the question whether the conference should take definitive action on such a hot issue without submitting the matter to a vote of all the annual conferences. The *Discipline* required a three-fourths vote of all the members of the annual conferences and a two-thirds General Conference majority to change the Articles of Religion or the General Rules, but ordination requirements fell outside those categories.

The women's ordination issue was debated on and off throughout the two-week conference, sometimes at length. Jack Richardson notes, "It seems to have been common knowledge that Free Methodism's senior but ailing general superintendent would use that occasion to attempt to crown his struggle on behalf of women's full equality by securing ordination for the denomination's women preachers."[31]

Wilson T. Hogg, "of growing influence in the denomination and a prominent pastor in the Genesee Conference"[32] then serving in Buffalo, sought to head off definitive action on women's ordination (which he opposed) by introducing a restrictive resolution early in the conference. Since a simple majority vote could have opened the door to ordaining women, Hogg proposed:

> Whereas, the question of the ordination of women is likely to come up during this conference, and,

29. "General Conference," *FM* 23, no. 43 (Oct. 22, 1890): 3; "General Conference," *FM* 23, no. 44 (Oct. 29, 1890): 3; Zahniser, p. 298; Richardson, "Roberts and the Role," p. 96; Gramento, "Free Methodist Women," p. 81.

30. Gramento, "Free Methodist Women," p. 82. Since they were not elders, women preachers could be elected only as "lay" delegates to annual conferences or General Conference.

31. Richardson, "Roberts and the Role," p. 103.

32. Marston, p. 531. In recounting the General Conference debates, I have used the form "Hogg," since that is the spelling Hogue was still using in 1890. I used the form "Hogue" when citing his *History of the Free Methodist Church.*

Whereas, on the questions involving like radical changes in the polity of the church, we require more than a majority vote in the annual conferences as well as the General conference before they shall become the law of the church,

Therefore, resolved, that it is the sense of this conference that in the interest of unity and harmony among us as a people, a like vote be required on said question before it shall become incorporated in our Discipline.[33]

This was at the third sitting, the morning of Friday, October 10. G. W. Coleman was presiding, so Roberts was free to respond. He moved that the resolution be amended to call for a simple majority, as would be true of other normal business, arguing that the conference had no right to require a higher threshold. "The Discipline is explicit as to what may not be changed without a two-thirds vote," Roberts noted. In fact, he said, "I hold that the ordination of women requires no change of Discipline" at all.[34] He was legally correct on this point, because the *Discipline* did not specifically forbid women's ordination; the provision for ordaining deacons and elders was not gender-specific. What was really at stake was precedent. It appears, however, that a majority, including some who favored women's ordination, believed that women could not be ordained unless the *Discipline* specifically authorized it.

After some discussion, T. B. Arnold, calling the matter "a revolutionary question," moved that it be tabled until the next morning's session, and this was done. Before the session adjourned, however, Roberts offered a carefully worded resolution he hoped would open the door to ordaining women: "Resolved, That the Gospel of Jesus Christ, in the provisions which it makes, and in the agencies which it employs for the salvation of mankind, knows no distinction of nationality, condition or sex; therefore, no person who is called of God, and who is duly qualified, should be refused ordination on account of sex, or race or condition."[35]

The resolution called not for a disciplinary change but rather for an affirmation of principle. Roberts seems to have felt that this would be sufficient — that a declaration of principle would give annual conferences both the authority and the impulse to begin granting qualified women full ordination. Debate on Roberts's resolution was scheduled for the following Wednesday at 10:00 A.M.

The next morning, Saturday, Hogg's tabled motion was considered. Roberts was now in the chair. He ruled that Hogg's resolution was out of order because it required a higher standard for approval than did the *Discipline*. Roberts ruled that the General Conference had no right "by a bare majority vote" to require a two-thirds majority on the women's ordination issue and to require votes in the annual conferences. According to the *Discipline*, that higher threshold was required only for changes in the Articles of Religion or the General Rules.[36]

---

33. "General Conference," *FM* 23, no. 43 (Oct. 22, 1890): 3. Hogue in *HFMC* does not reveal that he was the presenter of this resolution (2:191).

34. "General Conference," *FM* 23, no. 43 (Oct. 22, 1890): 3.

35. "General Conference," *FM* 23, no. 43 (Oct. 22, 1890): 3; Hogue, *HFMC*, 2:191.

36. Hogue, *HFMC*, 2:191.

This ruling touched off debate, and E. P. Hart appealed the chair's ruling. General Superintendent Coleman said the issue "involves a radical change" and therefore should be sent to the annual conferences. "We ought to give the church a voice in this matter." At one point Roberts turned over the chair to Hart so he could argue his case. "Is not this conference the voice of the church?" he asked. He opposed sending the matter back to the annual conferences. This was unnecessarily restrictive. "All restrictions should be, not for forging chains, but for breaking chains." The General Conference is fully representative and should act. "I hold we have no right to send it back."[37]

Actually Roberts was on shaky constitutional and parliamentary grounds here, as some of the delegates pointed out. The *Discipline* did not specify that the General Conference could not require a higher majority on a particular issue when it wished to. R. W. Hawkins put the issue succinctly: "Taking the view Brother Roberts does, this body has the full power to act in a majority; but the point Brother Hart makes is that they have equal power to require a two-thirds vote and that it shall go back to the annual conferences."[38] Roberts, however, was trying to head off any action that would further postpone the full recognition of women as ordained ministers.

The debate showed how deeply divided the General Conference was. Appealing to church tradition, Hawkins said, "From the apostles down we have had a certain order of things. And now we undertake to change this order" by ordaining women.[39]

But others saw things differently and said the time for action had come. W. B. M. Colt insisted, "This question of equal rights is a question that will not down. It keeps coming up. I do hope that this General conference will have the magnanimity to grant the sisters the rights that have been kept from them all down the ages." If the issue is to be sent back to the conferences, he said, Hogg's resolution should read "in the interest of disunion, and inharmony," not "in the interest of union and harmony." (G. P. Wilson responded that it "was not a question of equal rights, but of proper sphere and relation.")[40]

J. M. Reilly complained about the conference's seeming "disposition to stave off this issue." He argued, "We ought not to allow ourselves to adopt political methods to keep the shackles on women and trench upon their liberties. I think that we are perfectly safe in giving to our mothers and daughters the same liberties we have ourselves."[41]

Clara Wetherald opposed sending the issue back to the conferences because some conferences had had "no opportunity to prove the efficiency of women as preachers" and so "will vote against it. Only those conferences where women have labored will not hesitate to pass it." For twenty-four years, she pointed out, she had preached the gospel, but without the ordinary rights of an ordained minister. "There

37. "General Conference," *FM* 23, no. 43 (Oct. 22, 1890): 5; cf. Hogue, *HFMC*, 2:191; Richardson, "Roberts and the Role," p. 97.
38. "General Conference," *FM* 23, no. 44 (Oct. 29, 1890): 2.
39. "General Conference," *FM* 23, no. 43 (Oct. 22, 1890): 5.
40. "General Conference," *FM* 23, no. 43 (Oct. 22, 1890): 5.
41. "General Conference," *FM* 23, no. 43 (Oct. 22, 1890): 5.

are those who have been saved under my labors who have desired to receive the Lord's Supper from my hands; but I could not administer it. God has given us this right, but the conference refuses it."[42]

When Hart's appeal was put to a vote, Roberts's ruling was overturned by a vote of 48 to 28. This meant that Hogg's motion was now properly before the conference. The morning session was now nearly over, however, and Roberts asked that action be deferred until Wednesday morning so Hogg's proposal could be considered jointly with Roberts's resolution supporting women's ordination. Hart concurred, but his words implied a threat: "I think in all fairness this should be deferred until action is had on the question of ordination of women. Let us know what the prevailing sentiment of the church is, and then any of us who are not in harmony may have the privilege of stepping down and out."

"I give notice now that no matter how it is settled I will not step down and out," Roberts responded.

"I might," said Hart.[43]

Both Hart and Coleman, the other two general superintendents, as well as Hogg, opposed Roberts on the women's ordination issue.

The showdown came when, as scheduled, Roberts's resolution and Hogg's proposal came before the General Conference on Wednesday morning, October 15. At Roberts's request, his resolution was amended by adding the provision "This resolution shall not take effect until it is presented to the Annual Conferences, and has received the votes of a majority of all the members present and voting." This was a partial concession on Roberts's part. He knew that a two-thirds vote in the General Conference and a three-fourths majority in all the annual conferences were very unlikely, but a majority at both levels might be achievable. He was willing to compromise by sending the issue to the annual conferences if that secured the adoption of the key enabling action.[44]

The debate consumed the rest of the morning session and the afternoon session as well. Roberts was prepared with a long speech in defense of women's ordination, dealing with a number of problematic Scripture passages and covering much of the ground that was later included in his *Ordaining Women* book. He made the same reference to Chrysostom's opinion that Junia (Rom. 16:7) was an apostle that he cited two years earlier at the London missionary conference.[45] Recognizing that he was facing an uphill battle, Roberts commented at one point that he seemed usually to be about five years ahead of the church on issues coming before it.[46]

---

42. "General Conference," *FM* 23, no. 43 (Oct. 22, 1890): 5.

43. "General Conference," *FM* 23, no. 44 (Oct. 29, 1890): 2-3; Richardson, "Roberts and the Role," pp. 97-98.

44. Hogue, *HFMC,* 2:192.

45. "General Conference," *FM* 23, no. 44 (Oct. 29, 1890): 3-5. Roberts's speech, along with speeches by Hogg, Hart, and Wetherald, has been reprinted in Gerald Coates, ed., *Passion of the Founders* (Indianapolis: Free Methodist Communications, 2003), pp. 107-18.

46. C. B. E. [C. B. Ebey], "The General Conference," *FM* 23, no. 43 (Oct. 22, 1890): 8.

Several other speeches were given. Olin M. Owen, an ardent opponent, asked what would happen if "some little woman" preacher performing baptisms tried to immerse a 250-pound man; "it might be a question as to which one of them would go under the water." (Brother Colt replied that "a little woman would look as well baptizing a large man, as a little man baptizing a large woman.") More substantially, Owen argued that it was "contrary to divine law, physical law, the law of common sense, to place woman in a sphere designed for man." Give woman proper place "in her sphere," but "do not place her as ruler in the church of God."[47]

In the afternoon session Hogg gave a rather lengthy reply to Roberts's address. After Roberts's "able, eloquent and thrilling plea" in the morning session, Hogg said, a delegate had whispered to him, "I'm converted." Well, said Hogg, "I was not converted by that remarkable address, though I was ready to say at its conclusion, 'Almost thou persuadest me to believe' — in the ordination of women."

Hogg argued that even if there were a few exceptional cases in the New Testament, the Bible does not "recognize the general practice of ordaining women permanently to all the functions of the Christian ministry." The case for Junia being an apostle is "certainly ambiguous," he said. In any case, "a discussion about Greek roots and verbs and nouns is an inexcusable waste of time." The general tenor of Scripture, Hogg argued, did not support Roberts's case.[48] Hart also went on record: "Does the New Testament by its teaching authorize the ordination of women? I am ready to answer most unqualifiedly and decisively in the negative."[49]

When Roberts's resolution favoring women's ordination was finally put to a vote, it was narrowly defeated, 41 to 37.[50] But in terms of clergy and "lay" representation, the votes were very lopsided. The "lay" delegates actually endorsed the resolution by a vote of 21 to 15, while the clergy delegates voted against it, 26 to 16. According to the General Conference manuscript minutes, Hart actually ended up voting *for* Roberts's resolution, perhaps won over by Roberts's concession to submit the issue to annual conference vote, despite his personal reservations on the issue.[51] The parliamentary issue had gotten sufficiently complex, however, that delegates

47. "General Conference," *FM* 23, no. 44 (Oct. 29, 1890): 5; *General Conference Daily*, Oct. 17, 1890, pp. 188-89, 124.

48. "General Conference," *FM* 23, no. 44 (Oct. 29, 1890): 5; "General Conference," *FM* 23, no. 45 (Nov. 5, 1890): 2-3.

49. *General Conference Daily*, Oct. 17, 1890, p. 122; Richardson, "Roberts and the Role," p. 99.

50. 1890 General Conference Minutes, Oct. 15, 1890, p. 145. Cf. *General Conference Daily*, Oct. 16, 1890, p. 107; C. B. E., "The General Conference," p. 8; Richardson, "Roberts and the Role," p. 99; Hogue, *HFMC*, 2:192. Hogue erroneously reports the vote as 41 to 38; the *General Conference Daily* and the *Free Methodist* have 40 to 38.

51. The General Conference manuscript minutes list the names of the thirty-seven delegates who voted for and the forty-one who voted against the resolution; by comparing this with the role of delegates, it is possible to identify the clergy and "lay" delegate votes. Those voting yea included Walter A. Sellew, B. R. Jones, W. B. M. Colt, W. W. Kelley, T. B. Arnold, and both women delegates, Clara Wetherald and Anna Grant. The nay votes included G. W. Coleman, S. K. J. Chesbrough, W. T. Hogg, Benjamin Winget, W. R. Cusick, H. D. T. Gaffin, and R. W. Hawkins.

apparently voted for or against the resolution for a variety of reasons. J. G. Terrill, who was not a delegate but was editing the *General Conference Daily,* wrote a day or so after the vote, "There was involved with it other questions, that distracted the minds of some, and caused others to apparently vote contrary to their pronounced positions."[52]

With the defeat of Roberts's resolution, Hogg's resolution was now irrelevant, as there was nothing to send to the annual conferences. It is sobering to realize that if just two or three delegates had been persuaded to vote with Roberts, the outcome, and thus in some measure the whole subsequent history of the denomination, might have been different. On the other hand, if Hogg's restrictive resolution had passed, it is possible that the measure could not have achieved the two-thirds majority that would then have been required, let alone the three-fourths majority in the annual conferences.

Terrill judged that if Roberts had compromised a bit more and allowed his resolution to be linked to Hogg's, support would have been nearly unanimous. "The friends of the measure made the mistake of asking too much at this time."[53] But again, it is questionable whether the measure could have received a three-fourths majority of all annual conference delegates, even if it had achieved a two-thirds majority in the General Conference.[54]

The daylong debate was very taxing for Benjamin. Hogue later wrote,

> During the somewhat long and very heated discussion of the subject, owing to his great weariness and to the intensity of his interest in the question, [Roberts] showed signs of being near a physical collapse, and personal friends had to lead him from the room. It was a pathetic sight to witness as this veteran of many battles was led from the scene of debate looking as though in imminent danger of an apoplectic stroke. Fresh air and the tender ministry of his beloved wife and other

52. *General Conference Daily,* Oct. 17, 1890, pp. 125-26. Terrill wrote, "It is not for those who favor the ordination of women to be discouraged, nor for any who are opposed to it, if there be such, to glory in its defeat. The vote Wednesday evening was not decisive of that question. There was involved with it other questions, that distracted the minds of some, and caused others to apparently vote contrary to their pronounced positions. There are some among us who believe there is nothing natural or scriptural in the way of the ordination of women. But they hold that we are not prepared for it until the church as a body has expressed its opinion on the subject; and they therefore favor its being submitted to the annual conferences; and because the ordination of women is such a wide departure from the custom of the church universal, they think it best that more than a majority should decide it" (pp. 125-26).

53. *General Conference Daily,* Oct. 17, 1890, p. 126; Richardson, "Roberts and the Role," p. 99.

54. If Roberts's resolution had passed, and then Hogg's restrictive resolution had also passed, presumably Roberts's resolution (or something like it) would have had to be voted on a second time with the requirement of a two-thirds majority for adoption. However, if Roberts's resolution had passed and Hogg's had lost, the issue would have gone directly to the annual conferences (unless some other restrictive action was taken).

Benson Roberts gives an account of the debate and vote that is at variance with other accounts and does not seem to be borne out by the facts. See BHR, *BTR,* pp. 557-58.

friends soon revived him, and he was able the following morning to take up his work as usual in the Conference.[55]

The October 15 defeat was not quite the end of the matter. Toward the last of the General Conference, on October 20, Hogg introduced a new resolution, somewhat like his earlier one. He anticipated that the women's ordination question would come up again at the 1894 General Conference, and in the resolution instructed the annual conferences just prior to the General Conference to vote simply yes or no on the question: "Do you favor the ordination of women, on the same conditions as those on which we ordain men?" When the General Conference delegates assemble, Hogg said in his resolution, "it will be very desirable to know the minds of our people at large on the subject." This resolution was adopted, 38 to 32.[56]

The subsequent annual conference votes were revealing. Overall the poll of the twenty-nine conferences showed about 45 percent in favor of women's ordination and 55 percent opposed. In his analysis, Jack Richardson found that among the nineteen conferences from which he was able to ascertain the vote count, 304 voted yes and 370 no. "In ten conferences the majority voted for ordination; in eight conferences the majority opposed ordination; in one conference the vote was tied." This would seem to indicate growing opposition, a fact confirmed by a 65 to 35 vote against ordaining women at the 1894 General Conference.[57]

This is not the whole story, however. In the nine conferences for which separate "ministerial" and "lay" votes are available, the preachers voted 93 to 66 *against* women's ordination while the local church delegates voted 98 to 68 *for* it. It appears that in the denomination generally, opposition was strongest among the clergy. Further, the greatest support tended to be in the Midwest (much of it still the frontier for Free Methodism) and the strongest opposition in the conferences in New York and Pennsylvania and north Michigan.[58]

Though the Free Methodist Church would finally endorse Roberts's position eighty-six years later, he had lost this key battle. Richardson is probably right in his assessment that "Roberts' poor health must have had a bearing upon his decision to press for the ordination of women in 1890. He had good reason to suspect that he could not be counted upon to champion the cause much longer." Yet it is true ultimately that "No one person was more instrumental in bringing about women's ordination in the Free Methodist Church than Benjamin Titus Roberts." Richardson felt that "Far from rejecting Roberts' leadership in the matter of women's full equality, Free Methodism followed Roberts at a reasonable speed as he urged the

55. Hogue, *HFMC*, 2:192.

56. Hogue, *HFMC*, 2:192-93; Richardson, "Roberts and the Role," pp. 99-100.

57. Richardson, "Roberts and the Role," pp. 119-20; Hogue, *HFMC*, 2:196.

58. See the figures in Richardson, "Roberts and the Role," pp. 119, 142. In the 1894 General Conference vote, however, the proportion of yes/no vote of the preachers was about the same as among the conference delegates, whose perspective presumably was closer to that of their preacher colleagues than to that of the membership generally (Hogue, *HFMC*, 2:196).

denomination on a course which would inevitably lead to the ordination of women."[59]

Clyde B. Ebey (later editor of the *Free Methodist*), just after the key vote against ordaining women, called Roberts's speech "one of the finest arguments on record in favor of the ordination of woman to the Christian ministry." Ebey "would have rejoiced," he said, to have seen this "scriptural truth" adopted. "The sentiment is rising as the light increasingly shines in this direction." He added, "It is coming, brethren. Fall in line and help to consummate that which the Lord wills."[60]

The Hawkins Case

At the 1890 General Conference and in the months leading up to it, B. T. Roberts had to confront another issue: controversy surrounding Richard W. Hawkins's 1888 book, *Redemption; or, The Living Way.*[61] In Marston's words, "confusion resulted from [Hawkins's] teaching the redemption of the body in such a way as to lead some into the snare of 'spiritual affinity' and into the license naturally following."[62] Hogue notes that Hawkins "taught the redemption of the body from disease and mortality" and says rather vaguely that Hawkins's

> ability, spirituality, and strong personal magnetism . . . , together with the subtle and specious character of his teaching, combined to bring many most devoted souls under the influence of the error, some of whom made sad shipwreck of their faith. While he gave no intentional encouragement to the "free love" heresy, others who embraced his doctrine did, and, in some cases, families were disrupted by the working of this mischievous leaven. Cases of "spiritual affinity" became far too common, and there grew up in certain quarters, under the pretense of spiritual freedom, a degree of freedom and imprudence between the sexes which could not be justified by any code of ethics or of etiquette. These extremes were not countenanced by Mr. Hawkins, but were indirectly due to his peculiar teaching.[63]

In his book Hawkins defined redemption as "deliverance from all the consequences of sin; the complete transformation of spirit, soul and body into the likeness of Christ; and the transition and translation of the living being from the mortal to

---

59. Richardson, "Roberts and the Role," pp. 102, iii, 2.

60. C. B. E., "The General Conference," p. 8. Ebey was general missionary secretary (1882-90) and later editor of the *Free Methodist* (1903-7). He was also the "prime mover" in establishing what became Los Angeles Pacific College (later merged with Azusa College to form what is now Azusa Pacific University). Marston, pp. 470, 489, 535.

61. Richard Watson Hawkins, *Redemption; or, The Living Way. A Treatise on the Redemption of the Body, including a Doctrinal Outline of Experimental Religion* (Olean, N.Y.: Herald Publishing House, 1888), 507 pages, including index.

62. Marston, p. 295.

63. Hogue, *HFMC*, 2:72-73.

the glorified state and place." Such "translation" could happen here on earth; it did not have to await physical death. There are "two ways into the glorified state," he argued: *resurrection*, "which will be attained unconditionally by all who die in Christ," and *translation*, which might be experienced by those who discerned "that to be translated is according to the will of God concerning them." He argued that, just as justification and sanctification were "provided for in the *atonement*, and received by *grace* through *faith*," as Wesley had taught, so also with this "further work of salvation, in the redemption of the body." In translation "the consequences of sin are removed upon the basis of the atonement, by grace, through faith, by the effectual operation of the Holy Ghost." Christians thus would "be immortalized without dying." Hawkins viewed his understanding as an "advancement . . . in the development of the doctrine and experience of redemption."[64]

Hogue implies that the controversy over Hawkins's teachings arose before the book was published — presumably, in other words, in the early or mid-1880s. Kostlevy notes that in his book Hawkins "insisted on the possibility of the direct spiritual translation of individual Christians to paradise apart from death." Although Hawkins specifically rejected the teaching of "spiritual affinity," which could become a spiritualized rationalization for divorce and remarriage, Kostlevy notes, yet "his view that such a 'heresy' was a special danger to the spiritually advanced angered many" Free Methodists.[65]

Toward the end of its deliberations, the General Conference censured parts of Hawkins's book as "unsound, and unscriptural, and consequently misleading and dangerous." Roberts dissented; he thought the problem could be dealt with adequately if Hawkins simply issued a new edition with a clarifying appendix.[66] Hawkins was "clear and instructive" on justification and sanctification, Roberts felt, and the denomination had taken no doctrinal stand on "translation" of believers' bodies from the physical to the spiritual state, so on this point Hawkins could not be "exposed to ecclesiastical censure," whatever people thought of his views. Roberts agreed that Hawkins's teaching on redemption was "unscriptural" at points, but that this could be corrected. When the Committee on the State of the Work brought in a censure motion asking Hawkins to withdraw his book, Benjamin presented a more conciliatory minority (of one) report calling instead for Hawkins to add an appendix to his book as a means of resolving the issue. The majority report was adopted, however, 35 to 28.[67]

Hawkins did write a brief two-page appendix just a week after the 1890 General Conference and added it to the book. But he felt "sorely afflicted," Hogue notes, by the General Conference censure, and in view of the controversy and the conference action he soon transferred to the Allegheny Conference of the Wesleyan Methodist

64. Hawkins, *Redemption*, pp. 269, 278, 280-81, 284.
65. Kostlevy, pp. 126-27. Cf. Hawkins, *Redemption*, especially pp. 374-94.
66. Marston, pp. 295-96.
67. Hogue, *HFMC*, 2:73-74.

Connection. In 1891 he was elected the first Wesleyan Methodist general missionary superintendent, but he died of influenza two weeks after this appointment became effective, on January 13, 1892.[68]

Hawkins's censure was another blow to Roberts, not only because Hawkins was a capable and articulate leader but also because he had been a friend and younger colleague in the denomination and at the seminary for many years.

Benjamin participated in other discussions and debates throughout the conference. He tried unsuccessfully to change the name of the denomination to Free Methodist Connection. It is unclear why, but he apparently felt that was a more adequate description and would put the denomination "in a more clear light before the people."[69] When a resolution on temperance was presented that endorsed the Prohibition Party, he once again opposed such an explicit commitment. "I like the report very much," he said, but "the clause committing the church to a political party" was wrong. "We have no right to make the church a part of any political party." Here again Roberts's was the minority view; the resolution was passed almost unanimously. Benjamin was not surprised; in his speech against the resolution he recalled that he had once been introduced as "Brother Roberts, who was never in the majority in his life."[70]

Summarizing General Conference action in the *Free Methodist,* Roberts was candid, but took the long view:

> Of the righteousness of some of the acts God will judge. Those who know the facts will form their own opinion. The wisdom of the measures adopted time will determine.
>
> This General conference differed widely, in some respects, from any we ever attended before. But little disposition was manifested to harmonize conflicting views. If a proposed action was found to have a majority in its favor, it was generally pushed through, no matter how large a minority strongly protested against it.
>
> But God has brought us through many perilous places before, and our trust is in him to save us from distraction and give us continued prosperity.[71]

No doubt Roberts would have preferred to see a General Conference process that built some consensus before binding votes were taken. Many of the key issues of long-range consequence were passed by slim margins.

---

68. Marston, p. 296; Hogue, *HFMC,* 2:74-76; Ira Ford McLeister, *History of the Wesleyan Methodist Church of America* (Syracuse: Wesleyan Methodist Publishing House, 1934), pp. 110-11; Obituary of Richard Watson Hawkins, *FM* 25, no. 7 (Feb. 17, 1892): 7. Hawkins's appendix was dated "Olean, N.Y., Oct. 31, 1890." It is not clear whether the book was reprinted at this point or whether the appendix was added to already-printed copies. The copy (with appendix) in the Marston Memorial Historical Center has a publication date of 1888, though the appendix is dated 1890.

69. *General Conference Daily,* Oct. 10, 1890, p. 4; "General Conference," *FM* 23, no. 43 (Oct. 22, 1890): 2.

70. "General Conference," *FM* 23, no. 45 (Nov. 5, 1890): 4.

71. B. T. Roberts, "The General Conference," p. 8.

The Loss of the Pentecost Bands

Roberts still felt considerable affinity for the Pentecost Bands, and especially for Vivian Dake, despite the 1890 General Conference action. The movement became even more controversial, however, in the interim between the 1890 and 1894 General Conferences. And by 1894 both Dake's inspiring leadership and Roberts's moderating influence were gone from the scene.

Vivian Dake's death in 1892 only aggravated the already tense relationship between the bands and the denomination. The bands were inherently controversial simply because of their semiautonomy. As a youth movement they displayed a dynamism and zeal that sometimes clashed with denominational leaders seeking to consolidate and organize on a firmer basis. In addition, there were specific organizational and doctrinal issues.

Dake left Thomas Nelson, one of the band divisional leaders, temporarily in charge of the work when he left for Africa, and Nelson succeeded Dake as head of the bands after the founder's death.[72] Nelson was a member of the Illinois Conference, where he was ordained elder in 1893.[73] Both he and his wife Flora Birdsall Nelson had been active in the bands for several years. His accession to leadership seems to have caused some tension within the bands as well as complicating relations with the denomination.[74]

The controversy clustered around three related issues: the semiautonomy of the bands and their linkages with other "fringe" movements, support of foreign missionary work, and the bands' particular understanding of "radical" holiness. The question of women preachers was not a primary issue since the denomination had for some time had female evangelists and pastors and since Pentecost Band workers were itinerant evangelistic workers who were not seeking ordination.

Would Roberts's experience with the Methodist Episcopal Church be repeated in the case of the Pentecost Bands within Free Methodism? Roberts could see that there were both similarities and differences, and he could see both sides of the three key issues involved.

72. Thomas H. Nelson, *Life and Labors of Rev. Vivian A. Dake, Organizer and Leader of Pentecost Bands* (Chicago: T. B. Arnold, 1894), p. 52.

73. *Minutes*, Illinois Conference, 1893, p. 98.

74. E. E. Shelhamer was, with Nelson, one of several divisional leaders at the time of Dake's death, and some band workers thought he should be Dake's successor. Shelhamer argued for shared leadership among the divisional leaders, however, feeling that no one was qualified to fill Dake's shoes. Nelson was opposed to this and assumed control of the bands. This appears to have been a key factor leading to the Shelhamers leaving the band work in 1895. (Information provided by Esther Shelhamer James, April 1990, based on conversations with her father, E. E. Shelhamer.)

Autonomy and Linkage with Independent Ventures

Though Dake was an ordained elder in the Michigan and later Illinois Conferences from 1885 until his death, the Pentecost Bands had no official linkage with the denomination except through him. Free Methodist preachers often encouraged Dake in his ministry, and band work was generally carried out in cooperation with conference, district, or local leaders. But the movement had no official denominational sponsorship or control. Some band workers were members of a conference or were conference evangelists or workers, which provided for a measure of oversight. But it was Dake, and later Nelson, who made the key decisions. This created a certain uneasiness as the size and breadth of Pentecost Band work increased. In response, Dake argued that his loyalty to the church was not in question, and that the churches organized and turned over to the denomination proved he had no intention of creating a separate church.[75]

The issue was complicated by Dake's free association with many people within and beyond Free Methodism who shared his vision and his brand of radical holiness. Dake began conducting annual Harvest Home camp meetings each July, over the anniversary date of the bands, and these became in effect interdenominational rallies. Up to 3,000 people attended the 1891 Harvest Home gathering.[76] Clearly something was going on here that was broader than the Free Methodist Church itself.

Dake was informally in association with several key figures who headed independent ministries within and beyond the Free Methodist Church. Chief among these were C. S. Hanley, an ordained Free Methodist who published an independent paper called the *Firebrand;* C. W. Sherman of the Vanguard work in St. Louis and at this time a Free Methodist; Solomon B. Shaw, publisher and editor of the *Michigan Holiness Record;* and Robert Lee Harris. Harris, a preacher ordained by Roberts and until 1889 a Free Methodist, later founded the New Testament Church of Christ, one of the antecedent bodies of the Church of the Nazarene.[77]

In his dissertation on Mary Lee Harris Cagle, Stanley Ingersol calls this informal association of independent or semi-independent leaders the Free Methodist Radical Alliance. A key figure initially was Robert Lee Harris (Mary Lee Cagle's first hus-

75. Dake said his policy was "to go upon no circuit unless the pastor and official board desire us to come. We have been at work largely upon new ground," in cooperation with existing Free Methodist circuits. Nelson, *Life and Labors,* p. 470.

76. See the description of the rather remarkable 1890 and 1891 Harvest Home camp meetings in Ida Dake Parsons, *Kindling Watch-Fires: Being a Brief Sketch of the Life of Rev. Vivian A. Dake* (Chicago: Free Methodist Publishing House, 1915), pp. 40-42 and 48-52.

77. Initially, in 1887, the FM General Missionary Board under Roberts's leadership worked out an agreement with Harris for cooperative mission work in Africa. See B. T. Roberts, "The Mission Board," *FM* 20, no. 34 (Aug. 24, 1887): 8. See also [B. T. Roberts], "Robert L. Harris' Mission," *FM* 22, no. 8 (Feb. 20, 1889): 8, and [B. T. Roberts], "Changing the Issue," *FM* 22, no. 13 (Mar. 27, 1889): 8. These two editorials refer to Harris and reply to allegations in the *Vanguard.* In 1886 Benson Roberts published in the *Earnest Christian* an appreciation of Harris's life and ministry to that point; see B. H. R. [Benson H. Roberts], "Rev. Robert L. Harris," *EC* 52, no. 5 (Nov. 1886): 163-64.

band), a Free Methodist from Texas who was intent on missionary work in Africa according to the independent self-support approach advocated by William Taylor.
Ingersol writes, "A central feature of the radical alliance was its members' activities
'on the independent line,' outside normal denominational oversight, though the
radicals maintained nominal commitments to their annual conferences. A leading
figure in the radical orbit was C. W. Sherman of St. Louis, publisher of an independent weekly, *The Vanguard*, who became the chief sponsor of Harris' mission to Liberia. . . . The most sizable component of the alliance was constituted by the Pentecost Bands."[78]

Ingersol bases the term "radical Free Methodist" primarily on "the distinction
[this group] drew between 'radical' and 'popular' holiness, the latter regarded as an
antinomian corruption of the former." Ingersol cites E. E. Shelhamer's *Radical versus
Popular Holiness Contrasted* as an example.[79]

The term "radical Free Methodist" could be somewhat misleading here, however, as Free Methodists generally during this period considered themselves "radical"
and used that term positively, as previously noted. Ingersol rightly points out that
"the radicals [in his sense] differed from mainstream Free Methodists by a matter of
degrees."[80] He describes this coalition as follows:

> The radicals were avidly evangelistic — more so than many in an essentially
> revivalistic-oriented denomination. They maintained rigid standards of dress and
> behavior, reacting to what they perceived as a growing second-generation laxness
> within the denomination, and espousing anew puritanical rules that had shaped
> the church in earlier years. . . . The issue that brought the radicals most directly
> into conflict with church authority was their commitment to independent "faith
> work" in both home and foreign missions. Here they opposed a strong institu-
> tionalizing trend within Free Methodism, arguing that faith missions on "the Pau-
> line plan" was the form of missionary organization truest to the New Testament
> model.[81]

Thus the growing independence of the Pentecost Bands was not incidental; it
was theologically and ecclesiologically based.

Ingersol documents a number of significant linkages between the Pentecost
Bands, figures like Sherman and Shaw, and the beginnings of the New Testament
Church of Christ. A key link was the *Vanguard*, which for a time was the official or-
gan of the Pentecost Bands (as previously noted) and also the missions organ of the
New Testament Church of Christ. Much of the character of the New Testament

78. Robert Stanley Ingersol, "Burden of Dissent: Mary Lee Cagle and the Southern Holiness
Movement" (Ph.D. diss., Duke University, 1989), p. 79.

79. Ingersol, "Burden of Dissent," p. 79. See E. E. Shelhamer, *Popular and Radical Holiness Contrasted*, 2nd ed., rev. (Atlanta: The Repairer, 1906), 159 pages. The first edition of 10,000 copies was entitled *Bible Standard of Regeneration and Holiness*.

80. Ingersol, "Burden of Dissent," p. 80.

81. Ingersol, "Burden of Dissent," pp. 80-81.

Church of Christ was shaped by this "radical Free Methodist" impulse, mediated through the Pentecost Bands. Ingersol documents this influence particularly in terms of the affirmation of the leadership gifts of women.[82]

Support of Foreign Missionary Work

The Pentecost Bands became increasingly controversial as they began sending missionaries to other lands and soliciting support for them among Free Methodists "at home." This was precisely the period when denominationally sponsored Free Methodist missions were being developed, and Dake appeared to be in competition with the denominational program. By 1891 Dake had sent band workers to Africa, Norway, and Germany and was preparing to send them to India, Australia, and England.[83]

Dake's view of foreign missions did tend to align him with the "Free Methodist radical alliance" that Ingersol describes. According to Nelson, Dake "argued that Boards of necessity were slow and cumbersome . . . there was a more expeditious mode of accomplishing the work. He interpreted the action of Paul and Barnabas, as recorded in the thirteenth chapter of Acts to be on this plan. . . . He thought that the annual conferences were better acquainted with the qualifications and experiences of their own respective members than a Board, who perhaps had little personal knowledge of the one professing to be called."[84]

Dake's approach thus clashed philosophically to some degree with that of the denomination, and raised as well the always-sensitive issue of promotion and fundraising. Byron Lamson noted, "In 1890 Dake's bands were a powerful evangelizing agency at home, and a strong force abroad. As yet the denomination had no full-time secretary to promote foreign missions. To an outside observer, Dake might seem to be secretary of evangelism, missionary secretary and general superintendent, all in one package."[85]

Understanding of Holiness

The third issue concerned the doctrine of holiness. This also involved the "radical alliance," including the *Vanguard* and *Firebrand* papers. Dake and others like him

---

82. On the New Testament Church of Christ see, in addition to Ingersol, Timothy L. Smith, *Called unto Holiness: The Story of the Nazarenes; The Formative Years* (Kansas City, Mo.: Nazarene Publishing House, 1962), especially pp. 153-59, 168-71; Charles B. Jernigan, *Pioneer Days of the Holiness Movement in the Southwest* (Bethany, Okla.: Arnett Publishing Co., 1964), pp. 89, 116-17.

83. Edwin Munsell Bliss, ed., *The Encyclopedia of Missions,* 2 vols. (New York: Funk and Wagnalls, 1891), 2:214.

84. Nelson, *Life and Labors,* p. 53.

85. Byron S. Lamson, *Venture! The Frontiers of Free Methodism* (Winona Lake, Ind.: Light and Life Press, 1960), p. 133.

stressed "the death route" in experiencing entire sanctification. Of his own experience Dake says, "I discovered a love for place and position, and that I was not sanctified wholly. After an awful struggle and a death to carnal self, I came out into the blessed light of purity."[86] Necessary to obtain holiness, he said, are "First, light; second, conviction; third, confession; fourth, crucifixion; fifth, saving or appropriating faith."[87] Like many other Free Methodists, Dake criticized "popular holiness" that put such emphasis on faith that it neglected the necessity of crucifixion — facing up to the depths of sin and a total dying to self. Thus Pentecost Band worker Harmon Baldwin (later the author of *Holiness and the Human Element*) could write in his band journal, "Susie Falk was in trouble and seeking holiness. I was led to give some of my experience on that line. God touched me and the fire fell. Kate [his sister, also a band worker] ran and praised the Lord. The old 'death route' is the Bible track. Amen."[88]

It was in part this focus, carried at times to an extreme, that increased the perception that the Pentecost Band movement was moving toward fanaticism. A. F. Curry probably had this tendency in mind when he wrote a brief article entitled "The Death Route" in the June 5, 1895, *Free Methodist*. Curry argued that all Christians die to sin and self in repentance and regeneration, and that the biblical path to holiness is "not death" but "the life route." He asked, "Do we not have to die to our carnal or animal appetites and passions? No. Let no one attempt it. Some have undertaken this way only to drift into fanaticism, if not into scandalous delusions. All you need is to be so 'strengthened with might by his Spirit in the inner man,' that you have complete control of appetite and passion."[89]

This constellation of issues spelled increasing controversy for the Pentecost Bands at just the time Dake disappeared from the scene and leadership fell into the hands of the less charismatic and perhaps less stable and more authoritarian Thomas Nelson. Both the 1890 and 1894 FM General Conferences were urged by some annual conference leaders to rein in the bands.

With Dake's death in 1892, the question of the bands' relationship to the denomination devolved primarily upon Nelson, also a member of the Illinois Conference. In 1893 this conference carefully examined the question of Pentecost Band

---

86. Nelson, *Life and Labors*, p. 468.

87. Parsons, *Kindling Watch-Fires*, p. 176.

88. Harmon Baldwin, Manuscript Pentecost Band Journal, July 23, 1892–Oct. 19, 1894, pp. 14-15 (Aug. 24, 1892). Photocopy in MMHC. See H. A. Baldwin, *Holiness and the Human Element* (Louisville: Pentecostal Publishing Co., 1919).

89. A. F. Curry, "The Death Route," *FM* 28, no. 23 (June 5, 1895): 3. Curry's mention of fanaticism likely is a reference to a particular interpretation of "social purity" that held that sexual union in marriage should be for procreation only ("marital purity"). This was an emphasis of a number of people in Free Methodism and in the holiness "radical alliance" of this period, including H. A. ("Auntie") Coon, by this time an elderly woman who was a holiness worker often used by the Pentecost Bands. Dake says "Auntie Coon's faithful prayers and dealings were of great help to me in this critical hour" when he was seeking holiness (Parsons, *Kindling Watch-Fires*, p. 38). The "marital purity" line was picked up for a while by *Vanguard* and *Firebrand* writers (Ingersol, "Burden of Dissent," p. 224).

work in passing Nelson's character. The conference was sufficiently satisfied with Nelson's promise to confine his labors within the bounds of the conference "as much as possible" that they granted his request to be given the relation of conference evangelist and ordained him elder.[90] Apparently the conference did not insist on further restrictions on the band work nor that they be called "Free Methodist Bands."

A year later the Illinois Conference adopted several resolutions concerning the bands that were conciliatory in tone. It asked the General Conference meeting later that year to recognize the bands "as an evangelistic movement which . . . should be tenderly cared for" and to appoint Nelson as general leader for a term of four years (i.e., until the subsequent General Conference).[91] This action was taken out of recognition that the bands were a denomination-wide movement and needed more general coordination. Significantly, had the proposed action been implemented, the Pentecost Bands would have been established as an auxiliary, or a missions/evangelism sodality, within the denomination.[92]

A cooperative arrangement between the denomination and the bands seemed to be in the making. The action proposed by the Illinois Conference was considered but not adopted, however, by the 1894 General Conference, which approved instead an irenic but rather general statement reaffirming the regulations of 1890.[93] This threw the issue back to the annual conferences; yet, as the Illinois Conference had recognized, the bands were now a denomination-wide movement and could not adequately be dealt with at the conference level. The General Conference missed the chance to recognize the bands as a movement and make structural provision for them.

The result was that the bands soon became an independent organization. Hogue says only that the General Conference action "was unacceptable to Mr. Nelson" and his followers, and that the bands therefore "decided to withdraw from" the denomination.[94] But in fact the church missed its opportunity to provide an official and workable denomination-wide linkage for a denomination-wide movement.

The Pentecost Bands officially withdrew from the Free Methodist Church in February 1895, a few months after the 1894 General Conference.[95] A statement in their paper, the *Pentecost Herald,* headed "Withdrawn," was signed by fifty-eight band members, indicating that around 60 or 70 percent of the workers opted to stay

90. *Minutes,* Illinois Conference, 1893, pp. 98-99.

91. *Minutes,* Illinois Conference, 1894, pp. 76-77. The committee report noted that "there are some eighty or ninety workers composing the Pentecost Bands, and less than fifteen of these workers have a membership within the bounds of this conference, but are distributed throughout the conferences and States."

92. *Minutes,* Illinois Conference, 1894, p. 76.

93. Hogue, *HFMC,* 2:197-99.

94. Hogue, *HFMC,* 2:199.

95. *Discipline of the Missionary Bands of the World* (Indianapolis: General and Editorial Offices [of the Missionary Bands of the World], 1943), p. 13.

with the bands and leave the denomination while a number of others, including the Shelhamers and Harmon Baldwin, stayed in the denomination and left the bands.[96]

From this point on the Pentecost Bands were an independent organization and began establishing their own churches. With time the group became primarily a foreign missions society with a gradually declining home base of congregations in the Midwest. The name was changed to Missionary Bands of the World, Inc., in 1925, and under that name the organization finally united with the Wesleyan Methodist Church in 1958.[97]

During the critical years just before and after Roberts's death, the Free Methodist Church found it difficult to be tolerant of or work out an effective arrangement with the Pentecost Bands. This was due in part to the denomination's small size and the struggles it was then having as a relatively new movement. The denomination was only twenty-five years old when Dake started the bands in 1885 and was still having its own struggles with structure, self-definition, pastoral support, the establishing of educational institutions, and similar issues. Still, both Bishop Marston and Byron Lamson, writing around 1960, considered it highly unfortunate for Free Methodism that the zeal and aggressive evangelizing impulse of the bands, so characteristic of Roberts himself, were lost to the denomination. From his perspective as general missionary secretary for many years, Lamson wrote concerning the loss of the Pentecost Bands: "The rate of church growth suffered a drastic moderation from this time. To the present day, Free Methodism does not have the early evangelistic drive, the sense of mission, the sacrificial concern for saving the lost world that characterized the founders of the movement and that was incarnate in Vivian Dake. In correcting errors and regulating the fiery zeal of youthful Band workers, the church itself seemed to somehow lose its 'first love' for the lost world."[98]

And Bishop Marston commented, "A more moderate course might have conserved to Free Methodism the zeal of this movement which had been fruitful in bringing a considerable harvest into the church."[99]

---

96. "Withdrawn," *Pentecost Herald* 1, no. 11 (Feb. 1895): 2. "In consideration of the growing opposition on the part of the Free Methodist Church generally, to the teachings, the mode of operation, and distinctive nature of the Pentecost Bands; and in consideration of the fact that we cannot fulfill our promise made last Fall to harmonize with the Church without forfeiting the divine favor by changing our views on the conditions of receiving the experience of holiness, by disorganizing the Bands and abandoning what we feel to be a heaven-born evangelism, we have decided to quietly withdraw from the Free Methodist Church."

97. Ira F. McLeister and Roy S. Nicholson, *Conscience and Commitment: The History of the Wesleyan Methodist Church*, 4th ed., rev. (Marion, Ind.: Wesley Press, 1976), pp. 242-43. Another group that merged with the Wesleyan Methodists (1948) was the Hephzibah Faith Missionary Association, whose formation in 1892 was sparked in part by the influence of Vivian Dake and early Pentecost Band workers (McLeister and Nicholson, pp. 224-25; Charles E. Jones, *Perfectionist Persuasion: The Holiness Movement and American Methodism, 1867-1936* [Metuchen, N.J.: Scarecrow Press, 1974], pp. 66-67) — another example of the long influence, through Dake, of B. T. Roberts.

98. Lamson, *Venture!* p. 135.

99. Marston, p. 435.

During the last two years of his life, B. T. Roberts, as well as Ellen, was burdened with this complex of issues — the disappointing outcome of the 1890 General Conference, the death of Vivian Dake, the continuing controversy over the Pentecost Bands. B. T. apparently attended the July 1892 Harvest Home camp meeting near Lincoln, Nebraska, trying to keep contact with the bands in this period just after Dake's death.[100]

Yet B. T. and Ellen Roberts had a life beyond these denominational concerns. Benjamin continued publishing the *Earnest Christian* and was gratified with the ongoing progress of Chesbrough Seminary.

B. T. Roberts's Investments and Business Dealings

Another dimension of Roberts's life concerns his personal financial dealings and investments. This area sheds light on facets of his character that may be overlooked if one focuses solely on his life as a church leader.[101]

Roberts was a practical man, concerned among other things with money and economics. His economic interest was based partly on his understanding of the implications of biblical holiness and partly on pragmatic concerns about his own finances and those of a small denomination and of the seminary at North Chili. His book *First Lessons on Money* gives a good picture of his views in this area, as previously noted.

Like his father, Roberts was an astute businessman, and not averse to taking risks. He was involved at various times in the buying and selling of property, including parcels in Chicago and Aurora, Illinois, and in Iowa. His son Charles was for a while in "City and Suburban Real Estate" in Chicago, and B. T. probably worked with him in acquiring some property.[102]

Roberts also invested in stocks and in mining, in addition to real estate. It is not always clear just what his objectives were in some of these transactions, but generally his investments were intended in one way or another to benefit the denomination, as in his buying of property in North Chili for the Chili Seminary. Presumably he and Ellen were concerned as well to secure their financial future in old age.

Roberts apparently bought some 160 acres of land in Calhoun County, Iowa (then part of the frontier), around 1865. In an October 1872 letter he refers to the deed and says he intends to see the land for himself on a trip to Iowa as part of his travels for the church.[103] Around the same time he invested in a venture with James

---

100. The envelope of a letter, probably from Ellen, postmarked July 30, 1892, addressed to B. T. at Lincoln, Nebr., is directed to "Harvest Home Camp Meeting."

101. There is room for a thorough study here, since financial ledgers and other records exist, principally at Roberts Wesleyan College, that would provide the necessary evidence. See the discussion of Benjamin's will and personal belongings in chapter 39.

102. The envelope of a Sept. 23, 1890, letter from Charles Roberts to BTR has the printed return address, "C. S. Roberts, City and Suburban Real Estate, Room 502 Phenix [*sic*] Building, Chicago, Ill."

103. BTR to ELR (Oct. 1, 1872), cited in Zahniser, p. 301.

Mathews (apparently unsuccessful) involving a patent for a new type of waterproofing blacking, probably for boots.[104]

In 1892, just a year or so before his death, Roberts made some gold mining investments in Colorado. He seems to have invested several hundred dollars in gold claims at Cripple Creek, working through Hiram A. Crouch, Free Methodist pioneer preacher and businessman who went to Colorado from back east.[105] These investments were left in his sons' hands after B. T.'s death, and how they turned out is unclear. A 1903 note to Benson Roberts from a representative of Douglas, Lacey and Company of Batavia, New York, concerning "Dividend Pay Stocks," setting up an appointment in North Chili, suggests that some ongoing income may have been accruing from these or other investments.[106]

Valedictory

The November 5, 1890, issue of the *Free Methodist* was the last that B. T. Roberts edited. He offered a brief final editorial entitled "Valedictory." "Our labor in writing Editorials and Notes for [the magazine] the last four years, has been a labor of love," he wrote. "We have greatly enjoyed writing the truth, as God gave us to see it, plainly and kindly. We have endeavored to be considerate of all, and can confidently say that we have not written a word in malice or ill-will."[107]

Roberts's other editorial in this issue, entitled "Extortioners," complained that trusts and other business combinations were driving up prices in many areas, including food and clothing — even the price of coffins! "Combination destroys competition." Until there is "a change in the civil administration" of the country, Benjamin said, the only choice is "for the people to buy as little as possible and live within themselves. . . . Darn and patch the old clothes instead of buying new ones on credit." "Hire a carpenter to make the coffin; and leave the undertaker to his grave reflections."[108]

Benjamin's editorial labors with the *Free Methodist* were done. As general superintendent he still occasionally contributed to the magazine during the remaining two years of his earthly life, and he continued editing the *Earnest Christian*.

Roberts also continued traveling and holding conferences and revivals over these final months. At the end of March 1891 he journeyed to Verona, Ontario, north of Kingston, to dedicate a new church building. Crossing the partially frozen St.

---

104. These two ventures seem to have been related. See Zahniser, pp. 220-21.

105. RFP, Microfilm Reel 12, Frames 8-40. These properties or claims were not specifically listed as part of Benjamin's personal property when he died. On Hiram Crouch, see the sketch in Hogue, *HFMC*, 2:64-68.

106. Oliver Heinze (Batavia) to BHR (North Chili), Aug. 20, 1903.

107. B. T. Roberts, "Valedictory," *FM* 24, no. 45 (Nov. 5, 1890): 8.

108. B. T. Roberts, "Extortioners," *FM* 24, no. 45 (Nov. 5, 1890): 8. The original has the spelling "competion," obviously a misspelling for "competition."

Lawrence River at the eastern end of Lake Ontario was treacherous; Roberts traversed the three-mile stretch from Wolfe Island to Kingston in an ice boat that had to be poled through thin ice. But the trip was worth the effort; Roberts found a "powerful revival" in progress at Verona. People got blessed at the love feast preceding the dedication service: "Testimonies from full hearts came rushing in. Sometimes six or seven would be on the floor, shouting, leaping, and praising God. There was no confusion, no disorder but all was the blessed harmony of the Holy Spirit." Sinners were converted in the evening service, at which Roberts again preached, and even during the night. Journeying home on Monday, Roberts was glad he had made the arduous trip.[109]

Roberts's 1891 travels spanned the continent, Atlantic to Pacific. Early spring found him in New York City, where he visited Frank and Emeline Smith at the McAuley Mission, and in Brooklyn, where he found a promising revival in progress under the ministry of J. T. Logan. Roberts preached at the McAuley Mission. The ravages of alcohol on promising young men and women Roberts witnessed there reinforced his opposition to liquor and the liquor trade. "You should look upon the person who urges you to drink the inebriating cup, be he parson or physician, as you would upon the assassin who lies in wait to rob and murder you."[110]

Shortly after this eastern trip B. T. and Ellen began a long journey west, crossing the continent. In Los Angeles Benjamin organized the Southern California Conference. The couple then traveled north for the California Conference sessions and were refreshed in the home of General Superintendent and Mrs. E. P. Hart, now living in Alameda. Preaching in San Francisco's Mariner's Church, Benjamin was gratified to meet a number of believers who were converted during his brief ministry in San Francisco in 1879.[111]

Benjamin and Ellen journeyed on north by train to Tacoma, then had a bracing two-hour steamer cruise up Puget Sound to Seattle. "The water was as smooth as that of a deep, quiet river," he wrote. "Mountains capped with snow were in sight. Solemn fir-trees stood as sentinels on the banks."[112]

In Seattle Benjamin held the Washington-Oregon conference. The meetings breathed the spirit of revival; "the Spirit of the Lord was poured out in a remarkable degree." Many were converted, and services were continued after the close of conference business. Benjamin and Ellen stayed an additional week to help out. This conference proved to be a landmark one, for steps were taken to found Seattle Seminary (now Seattle Pacific University). Mr. and Mrs. Nils Peterson, homesteaders on North Queen Anne Hill, Seattle, offered five acres of land for the school, and Benjamin and

---

109. B. T. Roberts, "Dedication," *EC* 61, no. 4 (Apr. 1891): 127-28.

110. B. T. Roberts, "Meetings," *EC* 61, no. 4 (Apr. 1891): 128-29.

111. B. T. Roberts, "Going Preaching," *EC* 62, no. 1 (July 1891): 5-9. Roberts here relates also his brief ministry in Phoenix, Ariz., "a beautiful town of some seven or eight thousand," where he preached by invitation in Methodist Episcopal and Methodist Episcopal Church, South, churches. At Miracopa he gave an impromptu sermon at the invitation of a hotel keeper and Ellen exhorted.

112. [B. T. Roberts], "The Oregon and Washington Conference," *EC* 62, no. 1 (July 1891): 32.

Ellen went out to see the property. Benjamin and Ellen personally selected the site for the first building, which was begun that fall. Nearly $12,000 was pledged to get the school started.[113]

After an initially difficult start due to the financial panic of 1893, Seattle Seminary flourished under the able leadership of Alexander and Adelaide Beers. The two had met and married at Chesbrough Seminary. Seeing his potential, B. T. Roberts recommended Alexander to head the school. The Beerses opened classes in 1893. Initially Alexander and Adelaide served as coprincipals, following the model they saw in Benson and Emma Roberts at Chesbrough. Eventually Alexander served as sole principal while Mrs. Beers continued as a teacher.[114]

Seattle Pacific University is thus another monument to the influence and foresight of B. T. Roberts during his last years. Roberts urged that the school not be narrowly denominational and that it should be able to compete with public education. Seattle Seminary was born with a particular focus on foreign missions, both because Nils Peterson in donating the land stipulated that the school educate and train scholars "for the work of proclaiming the Gospel of the Lord Jesus Christ in foreign countries," and because foreign missions was a passion also of Alexander and Adelaide Beers. As a young man Peterson had reportedly been influenced by missionaries in his native Norway. And Alexander Beers was marked for life by a missionary address he heard A. B. Simpson of the Christian and Missionary Alliance give at Chesbrough Seminary at the dedication of Cox Hall in the fall of 1892, shortly before the Beerses went to Seattle. "While listening to [Simpson's] burning message," Adelaide later wrote, "a flame was kindled in Mr. Beers' heart that was never extinguished to the day of his death." He became "a transformed man — a man with a world-wide vision."[115]

Following the 1891 Washington-Oregon conference sessions in Seattle, Benjamin and Ellen traveled north by steamer to Canada and journeyed east on the Canadian Pacific. They crossed back into the States for a Free Methodist camp meeting near Fargo, North Dakota, then continued on home, arriving in North Chili on July 10. They had been gone since late April and traveled some 6,500 miles. "The Lord graciously preserved us from all evil," Benjamin commented, "provided us with the base of care, kept us from getting over-weary, and greatly blessed us in laboring for the salvation of souls."[116]

113. [B. T. Roberts], "The Oregon and Washington Conference"; Adelaide Lionne Beers, *The Romance of a Consecrated Life: A Biography of Alexander Beers* (Chicago: Free Methodist Publishing House, [1922]), p. 95; Zahniser, p. 270; Donald McNichols, *Seattle Pacific University: A Growing Vision, 1891-1991* (Seattle: Seattle Pacific University, 1989), pp. 9-13; Marston, p. 527.

114. McNichols, *Seattle Pacific University*, pp. 9-13; Norma G. Cathey, ed., *Free Methodist Church Centennial: Pacific Northwest Conference, 1895-1995* (Seattle: Pacific Northwest Conference of the Free Methodist Church of North America, 1995), p. 13.

115. Beers, *Romance*, p. 101; McNichols, *Seattle Pacific University*, pp. 10-13; [B. T. Roberts], "Dedication," *EC* 64, no. 5 (Nov. 1892): 157.

116. [B. T. Roberts], "Reached Home," *EC* 62, no. 2 (Aug. 1891): 63.

Ellen was still concerned about Benjamin's health, and she was alarmed in late 1891 when a letter from J. G. Terrill arrived in North Chili suggesting that B. T. accompany a party of FM missionaries soon to depart for Africa. "This is too much for anything. I think it is <u>worse</u> than presumption. I hope you will abandon such thoughts. I'll not consent — and you will not want to go without it." She added, "You will finish your work quick enough without going to Africa."[117]

In the spring of 1892 B. T. did make a trip south to Spotsylvania, Virginia (near Fredericksburg), where some Free Methodists were operating a school, and on to Savannah, Georgia. While in Georgia he visited the Georgia State Industrial College, a colored school near Savannah. The main reason for the southern trip appears to have been Roberts's health. In this regard he was disappointed. He wrote that though the weather was mild and flowers in bloom, "we cannot recommend anyone to go south for health. The warm, damp air is depressing and it seems as if it must breed malaria." He was encouraged, however, by "signs of prosperity" among the African American population. "Teach the colored people books and trades," he wrote, "and the race problem will solve itself. Give them a chance, and they will not fall behind the whites in intelligence and thrift."[118]

A high point in his life came in October 1892 when three new buildings were dedicated at Chesbrough Seminary in one day — Roberts Hall, Cox Hall, and a two-story dormitory and dining room built as an addition to the farmhouse. The completion of these projects was largely the fruit of Roberts's successful fund-raising efforts after the September 1890 fire. Roberts Memorial Hall (as it was later called) was and is a substantial three-story brick building that, when opened, accommodated about seventy students.[119] Roberts described Edward P. Cox Memorial Hall, "substantially built of stone," as "a beautiful structure, one hundred and twenty-one feet in length," containing classrooms, a laboratory, a general assembly room, a chapel, and additional space upstairs for adding dormitory rooms later. A wealthy patron in Rochester donated "very comfortable, expensive seats" for the building. Total cost of the combined projects was about $30,000; Benjamin was pleased that all but about $5,000 had been raised.[120]

The high point of the day of celebration on Wednesday, October 26, was a stirring missionary address in the afternoon in the Cox Hall chapel by A. B. Simpson, leader of the newly formed Christian Alliance, functioning in this early period as an interdenominational agency promoting, recruiting, and sending missionaries. Benjamin reported that Simpson's address "was full of argument, pathos, and power. A fire was kindled that will be felt to the remote parts of the earth. A strong missionary spirit prevails among the teachers and students of this

117. ELR (North Chili) to BTR (Chicago), Dec. 1, 1891.
118. [B. T. Roberts], "Trip South," *EC* 63, no. 4 (Apr. 1892): 128; [B. T. Roberts], "A College for Colored Men," *EC* 63, no. 5 (May 1892): 158-59.
119. Renovated in 2002-3, Roberts Hall is now the main building of Northeastern Seminary at Roberts Wesleyan College.
120. [B. T. Roberts], "Dedication," *EC* 64, no. 5 (Nov. 1892): 157-58.

Seminary, and it was greatly quickened under the fervent appeals of Mr. Simpson."[121] Roberts spoke the truth; one of those touched that day was Alexander Beers, as noted above.

The Christian Alliance Connection

A. B. Simpson apparently felt a spiritual kinship with B. T. and Ellen Roberts, as well as with Benson and Emma Roberts. He was so favorably impressed with the seminary that in 1891 he sent his youngest son Howard to study there. Missionary Kittie Wood, meeting Simpson in Burma in 1893, learned from him that "he had put his boy in [Chesbrough Seminary], because he felt him safe"; "there was not a better place on earth that he knew of where he could leave him," for "the Spirit for the salvation of the world had been poured out" there.[122]

An informal network of relationships developed between Chesbrough Seminary and Simpson's Christian Alliance and Evangelical Missionary Alliance (combined in 1897 as the Christian and Missionary Alliance). In the early 1890s, as Roberts was (unknown to himself) nearing the end of his life's work, Simpson, twenty years younger and still in his forties, was beginning his most dynamic period of ministry.

The Chesbrough–Christian Alliance connection developed largely through Marcus and Jennie Fuller, Alliance missionaries in India. Marcus reportedly received his call to missionary service through hearing a sermon by Wilson Hogue, and there may have been some Oberlin connections as well.[123] Jennie Fuller spent some months at Chesbrough in 1891 as she enrolled her young son and daughter there, and in February 1892 she published a glowing report of the school in the *Christian Alliance and Missionary Weekly*. Here, she said, students not only receive "a good education" but also are taught "practical religion and a Bible standard of holiness." Fuller pronounced the education "thorough" and thought "very remarkable, the number of [the school's] students that have entered the ministry and other departments of Christian work." She could "heartily recommend" the school to Christian parents,

121. [B. T. Roberts], "Dedication," p. 157.
122. Kittie Wood, "A Letter to the Students of A. M. Chesbrough Seminary," *EC* 66, no. 3 (Sept. 1893): 100. *The Annual Circular of the A. M. Chesbrough Seminary,* 1891-92, lists Howard Simpson of New York City as a student in the Intermediate and Select Studies program. Thus Simpson apparently sent his son to Chesbrough even before his 1892 visit to North Chili. Howard Home Simpson, youngest son of A. B. and Margaret Simpson, was born during the Simpsons' ministry in New York City. A. E. Thompson, *The Life of A. B. Simpson* (Harrisburg, Pa.: Christian Publications, 1920), p. 48.
123. Marcus Bell Fuller (b. 1852) was later editor of the *India Alliance*. His first wife Jennie (née Amanda Jane [Jennie] Frow [1851-1900]) wrote the book *The Wrongs of Indian Womanhood*. He was an Oberlin graduate, as were his wife and daughter. See Hogue, *HFMC,* 2:362; Oberlin College, *Seventy-fifth Anniversary General Catalogue of Oberlin College, 1833-1908* (Oberlin, Ohio: Oberlin College, 1909), pp. 350, 352; "Fuller, Jennie (Frow)," in *Biographical Dictionary of Christian Missions,* ed. Gerald H. Anderson (New York: Macmillan, 1998), p. 231.

she said. "I write this trusting that many parents would be glad to know of a school in sympathy with the four-fold gospel."[124]

Jennie Fuller's article opened the Christian Alliance constituency to Chesbrough Seminary. As noted in chapter 31, reports on the seminary appeared from time to time in the *Christian Alliance and Missionary Weekly* and both Benson and Emma Roberts spoke at Simpson's missionary conferences.

Through these contacts B. T. and Ellen became acquainted with Simpson and the Alliance. B. T. was among those who "spoke with much power and blessing" at the Alliance convention in Chicago in late 1891, along with R. A. Torrey of the Moody Tabernacle, President Blanchard of Wheaton College, and others.[125] Roberts may have attended other Alliance events, and at one of the Alliance's regular Friday Meetings in New York City in April 1892, "Mrs. Roberts, of Chili, was present and gave forth a sounding note of praise in the joy of the Lord." This was probably Ellen Roberts, though it could have been Emma, Benson's wife.[126]

When B. T. Roberts died in 1893, Benson and Emma in their report on Chesbrough in the Alliance weekly noted, "God came very near to us in the fire He allowed us to pass through two years ago; but this Spring He spoke still more loudly to us in taking from our midst the beloved founder of the school, our dear father, Rev. B. S. [*sic*] Roberts. The blow was a severe one and still is keenly felt."[127]

In 1891 B. T. Roberts made a significant and revealing comment about the Alliance. He and Ellen conducted ongoing discussions about how to understand and interpret this new movement. Benjamin never subscribed to the "fourfold gospel" as such, but he appreciated the emphasis on foreign missions and also the stress on healing and sanctification. Though he had some misgivings — this was a movement arising largely from a different tradition — yet overall he evaluated the Alliance positively.

Writing to Ellen from Ocean Grove, New Jersey, in March 1891, Benjamin continued the discussion with Ellen concerning the Alliance. Having finished the letter, he added a small note and stuck it in the same envelope. His comment here to Ellen speaks volumes about his own attitude and his optimism of grace: "One thing more about 'The Alliance.' Do not misunderstand me that I consider them advanced in the life in God, but they are ready for advanced teaching when they come into freedom above people & ch's [churches]. So it seems to me. Some of the leaders are precious. Many of them know little of close walking in God. But then God is overturning, overturning & ere long we will see harmony everywhere. Amen."[128]

---

124. Jennie Fuller, "A Christian School," *Christian Alliance and Missionary Weekly* 8, no. 6 (Feb. 5, 1892): 93.

125. Report on the Chicago Convention, *Christian Alliance and Missionary Weekly* 7, no. 25 (Dec. 18, 1891): 370.

126. "Friday Meeting, New York," *Christian Alliance and Missionary Weekly* 8, no. 18 (Apr. 29, 1892): 282-83.

127. Benson Howard Roberts and Emma Sellew Roberts, "The A. M. Chesbrough Seminary," *Christian Alliance and Missionary Weekly* 11, no. 4 (July 28, 1893): 63.

128. Unsigned note in BTR's handwriting, found in an envelope addressed to ELR from Ocean

*   *   *

During B. T. Roberts's last months, Ellen could see his health was failing. In December 1892 she thought he seemed better, "but towards the end of January, as he again went Sabbath after Sabbath to fill appointments," she said, "I saw another constant manifestation of his disease." She begged him to stay home, but he said he felt duty-bound to continue as long as he could. Ellen thought Benjamin seemed "more heavenly all winter," despite his illness and pain; "he was overflowing with praise, and he ministered the spirit to all at home as fully as in other places." He remarked to Ellen several times, "What a happy life we have had together."[129]

His own mortality was on Benjamin's mind from time to time during the last few years of his life. He wrote in the *Free Methodist,* "If you would die the death of the righteous, you must live his life. Holy living makes easy dying."

He added, "Rivers that flow into the ocean reach it, no matter from what high grounds they may come, on a level with it. Their waters run into the ocean and the waters of the ocean run into them." This was a parable of life and death: if your life "is going out towards God, his life will come into yours and you will become more and more like him, until at last you are swallowed up in the ocean of infinite love."[130]

It can be said of B. T. Roberts, as it was of Jesus, that "he loved the church and gave himself up for her." If he erred in 1886 in accepting the editorship of the *Free Methodist,* it was an error of wisdom and discernment, not of love or intention. When Roberts died in February 1893, he joined history's long procession of prophetic leaders who were misunderstood, underappreciated, or even betrayed by the movements they founded, but who expended themselves beyond their own limits in seeking others' welfare.

Grove, postmarked March 27, 1891 (MMHC). From the context it seems clear BTR is referring to Simpson's Christian Alliance, not some other group.

129. Mrs. B. T. Roberts, "In Loving Memory," *EC* 45, no. 4 (Apr. 1893): 135-36.
130. [B. T. Roberts], "Editorial Notes," *FM* 21, no. 42 (Oct. 17, 1888): 1.

CHAPTER 39

Ellen Alone

"I feel heaven all around me."

Ellen Roberts, near the end of her life[1]

"Pre-eminently she was a holy woman."

Bishop Walter A. Sellew[2]

When B. T. Roberts died on February 27, 1893, he left behind a widow, four grown sons and their wives, and eight grandchildren. George Lane Roberts was at the time forty-one, Benson was thirty-nine, Charles was thirty-six, and Benjamin Titus, Jr., was twenty-eight.

Since the children were now all grown and had their own families, Ellen was alone in a way she had never been before. Yet, living in the house on the hill in North Chili, she was surrounded by a caring community and still had ministry to do at the seminary and through writing and correspondence.

Ellen Copes with Grief

Ellen was deeply shaken by the sudden death of Benjamin in February 1893, but her faith remained strong. "I have been like a clinging vine — now the support is all gone and I lie low, with a sense of being in the world with changed conditions all about me," she wrote several weeks after Benjamin's death. "Many seem to expect me

1. Carpenter, p. 189.
2. Bishop Walter A. Sellew, tribute to Ellen Roberts in *EC* 95, no. 3 (Mar. 1908): 84.

to appear very triumphant. They do not know that it is triumph even to live and endure, meekly, resignedly," she said. "God is near and does not forsake and He does not chide nor reprove. I am silent, silent — such silence as I never knew before. Physically weak, nerves sensitive and shaken."[3]

One of the first things Ellen and her sons had to cope with was the disposal of Benjamin's personal property. Realizing that he was in declining health, Benjamin executed a last will and testament on February 11, 1892, a year before his death. He specified that Ellen was to receive "the use of our homestead" with all its contents and property, including "the cow, horse, fowls, carriages, harnesses and belongings of the barn." He also left her $1,000 cash and the income from an invested $10,000, which would have been adequate to live on.

To Benson he bequeathed his whole printing operation, including printing office and a rented house on the property, with the exception of the plates and copyright of the *Free Methodist Hymn Book* and *Discipline*. This bequest included "the subscription list and good will of the Earnest Christian" and several copyrights, meaning that Benson became the sole proprietor of the magazine and owner of his father's literary remains. Benson also got "his choice of fifty books" from his father's library. The *Discipline* and hymnbook property, plus $500 to be paid after Ellen's death, were transferred to the Free Methodist Publishing House.

Benjamin left some of his books to Chesbrough Seminary and some to Wessington Springs Seminary in South Dakota. He also bequeathed to Chesbrough "such sum as it was owing me at the time the buildings of said Seminary were burned" in 1890 — in other words, he canceled a debt. Significantly, he also gave the seminary his home, which legally was solely in his name. He intended that the homestead be used as a residence for seminary students who were the children of Free Methodist preachers, "my own descendents to have the preference."

Other than cash gifts to Benjamin and Ellen's longtime friends and housekeepers Edith Hurlburt and Anna Johnston and a $200 gift to Clara Russell Freeland, Benjamin left the remainder of his estate to his four sons "to be equally divided between them." This included the $10,000 invested for Ellen's support and the balance of his personal property and real estate (some of which was in the Chicago area). B. T. requested that George divide his share equally with his son Hibbert. Ellen, George, and Benson were appointed as executors.

It was a fair distribution. However, late in the night of February 25, 1893, as Benjamin lay suffering from his heart attack in Cattaraugus, and warned by Dr. Tefft that the end was near, he wondered if he had done the right thing in leaving the house to the seminary instead of to his wife. He wrote a brief codicil to his will, revoking that provision and giving the house to Ellen. This bequest included, he noted, "the garden and all the furniture of the house and tools and live stock in the barn." Dr. E. Amelia Tefft and George G. Grinnell signed as witnesses.[4]

3. ELRD, May 16, 1893, as quoted in Carpenter, pp. 90-91.
4. Last Will and Testament of Benjamin T. Roberts. Archives, Roberts Wesleyan College.

An inventory of all his personal property, presumably compiled just following his death, reveals interesting details about Roberts's life — and the task his family faced when he was gone. He had bought a typewriter, which he kept in his carpeted library/office. He had in his library two desks, one oak and one walnut, and two bookcases containing 350 bound volumes of the *Earnest Christian* and 560 other bound books. Elsewhere in the house and barn he had about 500 more books, not counting 200 hymnbooks, 50 copies of *Fishers of Men*, and 500 copies of *Ordaining Women* in sheets in the book room.

The Roberts home had some ten rooms, excluding kitchen, bathroom, and hall. Ellen had a sewing room. There was an organ in the parlor and hat racks in the hall and bathroom. The dining room was equipped with a table and ten chairs. The parlor and sitting room each contained two rocking chairs. No sofas were listed, but some additional furniture probably belonged to Ellen. Her good china and silver tea set are not included in the inventory. The cellar contained thirty cans of fruit, eight bushels of potatoes, and two barrels of vinegar.

The Roberts barn, according to the inventory, housed three horses, a "top carriage" valued at $22, a buggy, a cutter, and a sleigh, as well as various farm implements and equipment. On his farm Benjamin had at this time nine cows, five calves, a bull, one boar, a dozen chickens, three turkeys, and several horses.[5]

Roberts's printing business was fairly well equipped. His printing office boasted a cylinder press run by steam valued at $100, three smaller presses, twenty-five fonts of type, a stitching machine, and a considerable amount of other equipment.

His total property, including $5,000.00 in bonds and $12,581.52 in notes pertaining to his Morgan Park, Illinois, property, was valued at a little over $20,000.00. The listed values for some of the personal property seem to be merely nominal, however; the books in his library were valued at only about 6¢ each. Other than his home, his printing business, and the property in Illinois, Roberts does not seem at this time to have personally owned any substantial amount of real estate, though he bought and sold property from time to time, mostly in the interests of the seminary.[6]

Roberts had managed well, and had provided a secure future for his wife. Unlike Wesley (who died 102 years before Roberts), it was not Roberts's goal to leave no wealth behind. But also unlike Wesley, Roberts had a wife and family to be concerned about.

Following his death, it took a number of years for his family to wrap up his business and financial affairs. As late as 1898 the Roberts sons were still corresponding about disposing of rented houses and other property in the Chicago area.[7]

Meanwhile, Ellen was gradually adjusting to life without Benjamin. New Year's

5. This may not have included some animals and equipment owned directly by Chesbrough Seminary.

6. "Inventory of All Personal Property" (handwritten journal entry), RFP, Microfilm Reel 11, Frames 193-95 (seven numbered pages). This is preceded by what appears to be a preliminary listing in which some items are higher and many are lower.

7. See RFP, Microfilm Reel 33.

Day 1894, Benson and Emma were away visiting the Sellew family, but Charles and Susan Roberts and their two sons came to visit Ellen in North Chili. She wrote in her diary, "No sense of this being the New Year's day. No gladness because of the return of the day. Am thankful to have Charlie and family here. It relieves me of much of sadness. We have a quiet dinner by ourselves."[8]

Ellen was getting back into the routines of seminary life. Thursday night, January 4, she attended the class meeting at the seminary and found it "excellent." She was able to give a word of exhortation that some found helpful. She wrote, "The spirit of determination was poured in upon me as never before. . . . It came to me that I must be desperately determined that salvation should come to some people. A determined spirit will hold on. I have said, 'I will never let go. I will never give it up.'"[9]

Gradually Ellen resumed an active role also in the *Earnest Christian* office. "It seems good to me to do this," she said as she helped with the monthly mailing. "The names and places are very familiar to me. It is like an old and a tried friend."[10] The Lord "made it very plain" that she should attend the district quarterly meeting at Albion over the weekend of January 19-21, so she went. She was asked to lead one of the sessions and gave a word of exhortation.[11] Some weeks later she agreed to lead the Sunday afternoon meeting in Cox Hall on March 18 and felt that God helped her.[12]

Throughout February 1894, a "memorable marked month," Ellen recalled the events of the previous February, her last days with Benjamin. Other family deaths had also occurred in February. She noted in her diary, "This is the time of year when many [of] our number left this world. Dear Sam[m]ie and Father Roberts and lastly my dear dear Husband."[13] On the anniversary of Benjamin's last trip to Cattaraugus and his death, she wrote, "I could weep bitter tears but dare not. My orders have been to praise God and the best I can I must do it."[14] A day or so later she wrote, "Days of painful memories but I feel forbidden to live them over. To find Jesus, I must not look back. He is risen and thoughts of my departed one must be of his risen life above. In thinking thus and looking thus I have had much of lifting up. God can fill the place only as I obey Him in my thoughts as well as word and deed."[15]

When May 3, 1894, came around, Ellen recalled that she and Benjamin had been married on that date forty-four years earlier. "A happy life we had."[16] God comforted her in multiple ways. Thinking back over her life, she could see that the Lord "pre-

---

8. ELRD, Jan. 1, 1894.

9. ELRD, Jan. 4, 1894, as quoted in Carpenter, p. 91.

10. ELRD, Jan. 15, 1894, as quoted in Carpenter, p. 91.

11. ELRD, Jan. 20 and 21, 1894.

12. ELRD, Mar. 18, 1894.

13. ELRD, Feb. 2, 1894. Samuel Roberts had died on Feb. 1, 1875, and Titus Roberts, Benjamin's father, on Feb. 22, 1881, as previously noted.

14. ELRD, Feb. 24, 1894.

15. ELRD, Feb. 26-27, 1894.

16. ELRD, May 3, 1894.

pared me under my Uncle's roof for the place he had me fill." God would take care of her. On Sunday, May 13, she wrote, "While lying in the hammock, it came to me. 'I will acknowledge Jesus as my husband. I will leave all care with him[,] the kind of care my husband used always to take himself.' A precious sense of relief came to me. The Spirit did indeed answer and witness that it was of Him."[17]

In mid-May Ellen and her friend Catherine Cady spent a couple of days at a holiness and healing conference in Toronto, traveling by train to Buffalo and from there by steamship. At the conference Ellen heard the Swiss Reformed preacher Otto Stockmayer and other Continental advocates of healing preach. Stockmayer, whom A. J. Gordon called the "theologian of the doctrine of healing by faith," traveled extensively and helped influence Andrew Murray to accept the divine healing message.[18] Ellen said Stockmayer "looked so like the Master as he spoke to me." She noted that he and his associates "speak strongly and very decided[ly]" on healing. "To them seeming disease is God's dealing with them."[19]

To Ellen, this emphasis on healing was nothing new; she and Benjamin, like Wesley himself, had always taught that God could and often did heal. Not all Free Methodists agreed with the Robertses, however, in this as in other areas. When Sister Annis died in late 1894, Ellen recalled that this sister had once mentioned to her an incident that had occurred at a district quarterly meeting at Albion in the early days of Free Methodism. "Do you remember how many voted that you were leading souls to perdition because you talked about healing?" Sister Annis asked. Ellen didn't remember, but Sister Annis said "six women and one man" had opposed her. "Praise God!" Ellen said; such opposition "never caused me to withhold testimony."[20] It's unclear just what this incident was, but it shows again Ellen's determination to stand for what she believed was right as well as her belief in divine healing.

Eventually Ellen began again to think more about other people, and of "the best way to lead people on in their experiences." The "definite route is the best," she said. "Will not God witness to His own work in our hearts?" Perhaps reflecting on the sermons she heard at the Toronto conference, she added, "The Wesleyan way of teaching sanctification is to me the most satisfactory."[21]

The 1894 General Conference was approaching, and Ellen felt she should attend. The conference was scheduled for October 10-25 in Greenville, Illinois. The issue "of chief interest" at this conference, Hogue noted, "was the question of ordaining women," since the issue had agitated the annual conference sessions over the qua-

---

17. ELRD, May 11 and 13, 1894.

18. Stanley M. Burgess and Gary B. McGee, eds., *Dictionary of Pentecostal and Charismatic Movements* (Grand Rapids: Zondervan, 1988), pp. 355-56, 361-62. Stockmayer is sometimes viewed as a forerunner of modern Pentecostalism. See, e.g., W. J. Hollenweger, *The Pentecostals: The Charismatic Movement in the Churches*, trans. R. A. Wilson (Minneapolis: Augsburg, 1973), p. 353.

19. ELRD, May 14(?), 1894. Ellen has "P Stockmeyer," presumably Pastor Stockmayer.

20. ELRD, Sept. 2, 1894.

21. ELRD, May 20, 1894, as quoted in Carpenter, p. 93.

drennium. The other controversial issue was again the status of the Pentecost Bands. The 1894 General Conference would now confront these issues in the absence of both B. T. Roberts and Vivian Dake.[22]

Ellen left for General Conference on Thursday, October 4. Benson accompanied her by train as far as Buffalo, where he saw her safely aboard the Grand Trunk Railroad, which took her across lower Ontario to Detroit and then on into the Chicago area sometime Friday. Ellen traveled alone, but of course she was an experienced traveler. All went well except for "a little unpleasant experience" that only served to show her "how God could overrule for good when we make mistakes." Ellen naturally wanted to visit her sons Charles and Benjamin and their families in Morgan Park, south of Chicago, so she disembarked before the train entered the Windy City. The "unpleasant experience" may have been getting off at the wrong station. "I left [the] train at Blue Island Junction. It worked out right for Charlie met me and got a carriage to" Morgan Park. Ellen spent the weekend with her sons before heading south to Greenville. "Found all well. It seems home-like here at Benja's. No dear Father [Benjamin, Sr.] to meet me here. But I am kept."[23]

Tuesday afternoon, October 9, Ellen took the train on into Chicago where Charlie met her after work and put her on an Illinois Central train that would take her to Greenville. Chicago had now become the "world's largest railroad center"; ten trains of various lines made daily trips between Chicago and St. Louis in each direction.[24] As a businessman, Charles no doubt knew the transportation system well, and arranged a private apartment for his mother for the overnight trip to Greenville. "Had an apartment instead of usual berth on Sleeper," Ellen commented. "A new arrangement to me."[25]

Before leaving Chicago, Ellen discovered that T. B. Arnold and his wife Tressa, Chicago Free Methodists who at the time published several Sunday school papers, and Rev. and Mrs. Freeborn D. Brooke were on the same train, also bound for General Conference. They stepped into her apartment to see her. "While I have company the sense of aloneness is painful," she confided to her diary. Still, she had a good sleep and arrived in Greenville at 6:00 A.M.[26]

Ellen reached Greenville Wednesday morning, the day the General Conference convened. This was her first General Conference without Benjamin, and it was difficult for her. She stayed at the home of a local Free Methodist (Sister Davis), and at 2:00 P.M. Wednesday went to the General Conference session, which apparently already had begun. "The Sacrament was being administered. It was a great cross to be

22. Hogue, *HFMC*, 2:196-97.

23. ELRD, Oct. 4, 1894 (apparently written Oct. 7).

24. Albro Martin, *Railroads Triumphant: The Growth, Rejection, and Rebirth of a Vital American Force* (New York: Oxford University Press, 1992), pp. 73-74.

25. ELRD, Oct. 9, 1894. Ellen calls the train the "Chicago Central," but there was no railroad by that name. Presumably it was the Illinois Central.

26. ELRD, Oct. 9, 1894. On Arnold and Brooke, see Hogue, *HFMC*, 2:251-53, 352-53. Arnold had been succeeded by S. K. J. Chesbrough as denominational publishing agent in 1888.

alone to the Sacrament but Jesus lifted my head up and [I] returned to my Seat. Sr. Hart came to get me to sit with her on a nearer seat."[27]

Despite being alone, Ellen found this conference "much like other" recent General Conferences — "Many here whom I know and many I do not know of both preachers and people." She was glad to meet old friends, but thought the conference sessions on Thursday afternoon "rather formal."[28] Following B. T. Roberts's death, the denominational executive committee had appointed Wilson T. Hogg (Hogue) to finish out Roberts's term, so the three general superintendents now were E. P. Hart, George W. Coleman, and Hogg. However, when the election of general superintendents was held, Burton R. Jones was elected rather than Hogg, while Hart and Coleman were reelected. Hogg was elected editor of the *Free Methodist*, replacing Jones.[29]

Hart preached what Ellen called "a memorial sermon" on Sunday morning from the text "He being dead yet speaketh." Presumably the sermon had particular reference to B. T. Roberts. Ellen found it "a trying time" that she had patiently to endure. "A lack of respect to me it seemed," she noted in her diary, without explanation.[30]

Understandably, given her temperament and her loss and the sense from the previous General Conference that in some key areas the denomination was heading in a direction different from what B. T. had envisioned, Ellen felt alone in the crowd during the conference activities. She confided to her diary, "One afternoon in meeting I was led to ask the dear Lord why the alone feeling I seemed to have so much of, not the taking of my dear husband, but the continual finding myself alone in reference to others. He seemed to tell me I was walking with Him. If I walk with Him I walk alone. This brought much of blessing and solid comfort to me. God will see us through. . . . His way is to scatter His children."[31]

A highlight of the 1894 General Conference was the formal organization of the Woman's Foreign Missionary Society (WFMS) of the Free Methodist Church as an auxiliary to the General Missionary Board. This was the beginning of the denomination-wide organization, though some local societies had already been formed. Ellen was elected the first president of the WFMS and served until 1902, by which time the society had some five thousand members in over three hundred local societies.[32]

After attending General Conference Ellen returned to North Chili and resumed her life there and her activities in the seminary, local church, and *Earnest Christian*

27. ELRD, Oct. 10, 1894.

28. ELRD, Oct. 11, 1894.

29. Marston, p. 418; Hogue, *HFMC*, 2:199. As noted in chapter 1, Hogue did not change the spelling of his name from "Hogg" until 1900.

30. ELRD, Oct. 15, 1894.

31. ELRD, Oct. 18, 1894, as quoted in Carpenter, pp. 93-94. Ellen adds in her diary in quotes (perhaps a quote from a sermon, or remembered from Benjamin), "A full, large church is generally a weak church."

32. Hogue, *HFMC*, 2:257-58; Marston, p. 459.

office. In November 1894 she returned to Chicago for another visit with Benjamin, Jr. Arriving home on the morning of November 24, she wrote in her diary, "Benson and Emma and family were at the depot for me. Others were at the house. After dinner all the Seminary folk marched to the door singing. It sounded heavenly. Home seems very good. I can only praise God continually. No trip that I ever took on the [railway] cars seemed so easy as this trip home. Perfectly easy day and night. I was the only lady in the sleeper, but I did not care. I was as contented as could be. Praise God."[33]

At the end of November G. Harry Agnew, early Free Methodist missionary to South Africa, stopped in North Chili on his way back to the field. He held meetings at Chesbrough Seminary, presenting the missionary cause, as he had done some days earlier at Spring Arbor Seminary. Ellen had "a good talk with him and a season of prayer."[34] In December Agnew sailed from New York for South Africa. Shortly after arriving there he married Susie Sherman, daughter of C. W. Sherman of the Vanguard Mission in St. Louis, already on the field. She died, however, just ten months later.[35] Ellen kept Agnew and other Free Methodist missionaries prominent in her personal prayers.

The Thanksgiving celebration on November 29, 1894, was a seminary-wide event. Benson preached, and the whole seminary community had dinner together in Cox Hall. Ellen enjoyed the event. "A grand sight, a good dinner, some pleasant talks after dinner," she noted.[36]

Ellen turned seventy on March 4, 1895. She wrote in her diary on March 7,

I had a glimpse of my privileges in Jesus, which was like a revelation. I could take all by faith, but I must take it definitely, then it was mine, and faith would make it real. No fiction, a reality (things that are not as though they were even now). Oh, what a flash of light. Take all the land you wish to possess, tread on it, praise on it — it will even be "according to your faith." Hallelujah — a citizen of heaven. Not living here. Jesus in us by faith. What a hindrance is our desire to feel everything. I am walking in a new country. All new.[37]

As Ellen grew older, some of her husband's coworkers, even some of his former junior colleagues, began to pass on. Ellen noted on April 20, 1895, that Joseph Goodwin Terrill, then in his midfifties, had died, "victorious in prospect of death."[38] At the time Terrill was serving as general missionary secretary, and he was succeeded in this position by Benjamin Winget.

Always an advocate of missions, Ellen was glad when a local chapter of the

33. ELRD, Nov. 26, 1894, as quoted in Carpenter, p. 94.
34. ELRD, Nov. 27, 1894, as quoted in Carpenter, p. 94.
35. Wilson Thomas Hogue, *G. Harry Agnew, a Pioneer Missionary* (Chicago: Free Methodist Publishing House, 1905), pp. 189-93.
36. ELRD, Nov. 29, 1894, as quoted in Carpenter, p. 94.
37. ELRD, Mar. 7, 1895, as quoted in Carpenter, pp. 94-95.
38. ELRD, Apr. 20, 1895, quoted in Carpenter, p. 95.

WFMS was organized in North Chili in November 1895. The need for such a society "had been on my mind much," she said, and she probably played some role in organizing the local chapter.[39]

Among the missionaries Ellen corresponded with was the remarkable Clara Leffingwell. Ellen noted in 1904 that Miss Leffingwell was "happy in the sending of two missionaries to China. So am I. It is time, full time."[40] A former Chesbrough Seminary student, Miss Leffingwell first served a term with the China Inland Mission (1896-1903), adopting Chinese clothing and becoming Miss Li An Tong. She served in Yunan, southwestern China, surviving the Boxer Uprising of 1900. Her preference was to serve with the Free Methodists, however, so the General Missionary Board deputized her to raise $7,000 to send Free Methodist missionaries to China. Back in the United States, beginning with contacts with her friend Adelaide Beers at Seattle Seminary, Clara traveled across the country, promoting the China mission. She succeeded, but her health gave out. Though she was able to return to China in 1905, departing from Seattle with some of the newly appointed FM missionaries on April 8, she died in China just three months later. Through her efforts, however, Free Methodist work in China began and eventually grew. Ellen Roberts followed all these developments with her concern and prayers.[41]

Ellen began again to speak in services from time to time. After Winget, the newly elected general missionary secretary, preached at North Chili on Sunday, November 24, Ellen exhorted. "I was led to talk after the sermon about our burdens and cares," she wrote. "One way is to take them, move up to them and God will help us through. Unless we take them as part of our inheritance, we will get tired of them, and feel them heavy. Accept them and Jesus will make them lighter."[42]

Catherine Cady continued to be a friend and encouragement to Ellen through these years. The two would pray together, and on December 1, 1895, Ellen wrote, "She prayed for more love. The next morning she came to see me, dripping with love."[43] Sister Cady once wrote of her friendship with Ellen: "I do not remember the first time I ever saw Sister Roberts, but I do remember the first time the Holy Spirit drew me to her and put an untold, undying love into my heart for her. . . . Our fellowship for over forty years has been uninterrupted. She has been true to the Holy Spirit. There has been no policy [i.e., contrivance or insincerity] about her. She has ever been a true friend to me."[44]

---

39. ELRD, Nov. 10, 1895, quoted in Carpenter, p. 95.

40. ELRD, Nov. 10, 1904, as quoted in Carpenter, p. 104.

41. Donald McNichols, *Seattle Pacific University: A Growing Vision, 1891-1991* (Seattle: Seattle Pacific University, 1989), pp. 35-38; Byron S. Lamson, *Venture! The Frontiers of Free Methodism* (Winona Lake, Ind.: Light and Life Press, 1960), pp. 101-6.

42. ELRD, Nov. 24, 1895, as quoted in Carpenter, p. 95.

43. ELRD, Dec. 1, 1895, as quoted in Carpenter, p. 95.

44. Quoted in Carpenter, pp. 95-96.

Ripples

Ellen Roberts's missions interest was extended through her son and daughter-in-law, Benson and Emma Roberts, and through her influence on students.

Of the four surviving Roberts sons, only Benson was now living in North Chili. Benson and Emma continued their shared principalship of Chesbrough Seminary for another thirteen years following B. T.'s death, until early 1906. B. T. and Benson had worked closely together for several years, as noted earlier, and when his father died Benson immediately picked up the editorial responsibilities of the *Earnest Christian* in addition to his work at the seminary. At the time of B. T.'s death all five of Benson and Emma's children had been born (three sons and two daughters), though the first child, Howard, had died, as previously noted. Their youngest child, Edwin Douglas, was just eight months old when B. T. died.[45]

During their quarter-century in North Chili, Emma found time for a variety of social and philanthropic engagements. She was a member of the College Woman's Club in Rochester and a charter member of the whimsically named Woman's Fortnightly Ignorance Club.[46] She continued to read and to write articles, in addition to her teaching and administrative work. She was state evangelist for the Woman's Christian Temperance Union (WCTU) in New York.[47]

Benson shared his wife's missions concern and global perspective. Both he and Emma attended the Ecumenical Missionary Conference in London in 1889, retracing some of B. T.'s steps a year earlier, and Benson was the lone Free Methodist delegate to the Ecumenical Conference of Methodist Churches (forerunner of the World Methodist Conference) in London in 1901.[48] In 1900 Benson and Emma were among several Free Methodists who participated in the great Ecumenical Missionary Conference in New York City, attended by over three thousand missionaries and mission personnel. The conference met from April 21 to May 1 at Carnegie Hall and other venues. There Benson and Emma presumably heard President William McKinley and Governor Theodore Roosevelt (who gave welcoming addresses) and such well-known missionary leaders as J. Hudson Taylor, Robert Speer, A. T. Pierson, H. Grattan Guinness, and John R. Mott. Benson and Emma took with

45. Smail, p. 15.

46. "Roberts, Emma Sellew," in *Who's Who in New York City and State,* ed. John W. Leonard, 3rd ed. (New York: L. R. Hamersly and Co., 1907), p. 1111.

47. Alumni Record of Emma Sellew Roberts, Cornell University. It appears from this source that the WCTU position was in 1907 or earlier — perhaps during the interval between the time of relinquishing the coprincipalship and moving to Pittsburgh, though this was no doubt a part-time assignment.

48. Alumni Records, Benson Howard Roberts, University of Rochester; "Roberts, Benson Howard," in *Who Was Who in America* (Chicago: A. N. Marquis Co., 1943), 1:1039; B. H. R. [Benson H. Roberts], "Sketches of Travel," *FM* 22, no. 46 (Nov. 13, 1889): 8; B. H. R. [Benson H. Roberts], "Spurgeon's Church," *EC* 48, no. 4 (Oct. 1889): 127-28; *Proceedings of the Third Œcumenical Methodist Conference Held in City Road Chapel, London, September, 1901* (New York: Eaton and Mains, 1901); Marston, p. 563.

them some of the Indian girls or young women who were studying at Chesbrough Seminary; they were scheduled to be introduced by Emma at the Woman's Work in Foreign Missions session at the Central Presbyterian Church site on Thursday morning, April 26.[49]

Benson and Emma's missions involvements are another testimony to the outreach and "gospel to the poor" legacy of B. T. and Ellen Roberts. Obviously the influences on Benson and Emma were many, but important among them were the example and heritage they received from their families. Their missionary involvements owe something as well to B. T. Roberts's radical egalitarian and abolitionist roots.

Pandita Ramabai: The Remarkable Indian Connection

Throughout their twenty-five-year tenure as coprincipals of Chesbrough Seminary, Benson and Emma Roberts exhibited the strong foreign missionary interest that had been nurtured by B. T. and Ellen Roberts. Around 1890 Benson and Emma learned of the remarkable work of Pandita Ramabai in India. Over the ensuing decade this interest brought consequences that affected both their lives and those of Ramabai and her daughter, Manoramabai. Here the story of Chesbrough and of B. T. Roberts and his family intersects with that of Pandita Ramabai Sarasvati, "the most widely known and widely acclaimed Indian woman (if not indeed Indian person) of the nineteenth century."[50]

Chesbrough Seminary was an unusually cosmopolitan and international community in the 1890s. The school was linked in multiple ways to the growing foreign missions enterprise of the Free Methodist Church but also with other groups such as A. B. Simpson's Christian Alliance, as previously noted. In 1891-92 the Chesbrough student body included William Warwick from England, George Oberdorf from Germany, George and Mary Lucia Bierce Fuller (children of Marcus and Jennie Fuller, Alliance missionaries in India), Rangit Singh from India, Eduardo Galan from Mexico City, A. B. Simpson's son Howard, and two Japanese students.[51]

Emma Roberts was especially passionate about foreign missions. She served as

---

49. The report of the gathering is *Ecumenical Missionary Conference, New York, 1900,* 2 vols. (New York: American Tract Society, 1900). See especially 2:353-77, which is the daily program, and the list of delegates, missionaries, and honorary members (2:395-418). Other Free Methodist participants were Mrs. Emma Hillmon Haviland, missionary to Africa; Benjamin Winget, general missionary secretary, and his wife; and John S. McGeary, later missionary bishop and general missionary secretary (see Hogue, *HFMC,* 2:211; Marston, pp. 426, 470, 563).

50. Philip C. Engblom, "Translation Editor's Preface," in Pandita Ramabai, *Pandita Ramabai's America: Conditions of Life in the United States,* ed. Robert Eric Frykenberg, trans. Kshitija Gomes (Grand Rapids: Eerdmans, 2003), p. xvii.

51. *Catalogues,* Chili and Chesbrough Seminary (North Chili, N.Y.), 1869-96; Carpenter, pp. 126-27.

associate editor and, later, as editor of the *Missionary Tidings,* the organ of the (Free Methodist) WFMS, which began publication in 1897. When she learned of the work of the Indian educator and reformer Pandita Ramabai, a convert from Hinduism to Christianity, she was intrigued. Emma became active in the Rochester Ramabai Circle, serving as president in 1905-6.[52] It was not lost on Emma that Ramabai was among other things a strong example of female leadership and employed women preachers in her rescue and evangelistic work in India.[53]

Ramabai's connection with Chesbrough Seminary is a little-known but remarkable chapter in both the Roberts family's larger story and her own.[54] One sign of the connection is the fact that Ramabai had two of B. T. Roberts's books in her personal library.[55]

Pandita Ramabai (1858-1922) was born into a high-caste Hindu family. Her father, a distinguished scholar in Sanskrit and Indian literature, took the controversial steps of giving his daughter a classical Hindu education rather than allowing her to become a child bride. Ramabai's parents and sister died of starvation when she was only about sixteen, but she and her brother survived. In 1880 she married Bipin Medhavi, and the next year had a daughter, Manoramabai ("Heart's Delight"; "Mano" for short). In 1882 Medhavi died of cholera, leaving Ramabai, then twenty-three, to support herself and her infant. A brilliant scholar, Ramabai had already become an expert in the Hindu classics, and her learning became the means of her survival.

Through reading the New Testament and contacts with Anglican missionaries,

---

52. "Roberts, Emma Sellew," p. 1111.

53. Emma Sellew Roberts, "Pandita Ramabai and Her Work," *Missionary Tidings* 2, no. 6 (June 1898): 6.

54. Though there has recently been a virtual explosion of scholarly interest in Ramabai in both India and the United States, virtually all her contemporary interpreters misunderstand the Holiness movement context of the later stages of her spiritual pilgrimage, as noted below. See especially Pandita Ramabai, *Pandita Ramabai's American Encounter: The Peoples of the United States (1889),* trans. and ed. Meera Kosambi (Bloomington: Indiana University Press, 2003), and Ramabai, *Pandita Ramabai's America.* Each book is a translation, with commentary, of Ramabai's report on her 1886-88 visit to the United States, published in India in the Marathi language in 1889.

55. The personal library of Ramabai and Manoramabai included Roberts's *Fishers of Men* and the posthumous collection, *Holiness Teachings* (two copies), compiled and published by Benson Roberts in 1893. All are inscribed by Benson Roberts. One copy of *Holiness Teachings* is inscribed "To the Pandita Ramabai With the love of BH and E. S. Roberts, A. M. Chesbrough Seminary, North Chili, N.Y. June 27 1898. May his love and power compass you." The other is inscribed "To Manorama Medhavi, Domini filiae [daughter in the Lord]. Pax gratia que Domini tecum. Natalie die XVII. With the regards of Benson Howard Roberts, AM Chesbrough Seminary." The inscription is undated, but the reference to day of birth suggests it was a birthday gift. The volume *Fishers of Men* is the 1886 revised edition and is inscribed "To the Pandita Ramabai, from BH and ES Roberts, North Chili, N.Y. June 27 1898. 'All things are possible.'" Benson and Emma likely gave Ramabai the two books inscribed to her when Ramabai visited Chesbrough Seminary to enroll Mano there in 1898. See "The Papers, Publications, Pamphlets and Selected Books of Pandita Ramabai (1858-1922)," microfilmed archival collection from the Pandita Ramabai Mission, Kedgaon, India, 2001 (microfiche #1 and subsequent fiches).

Ramabai became intellectually convinced of the truth of the Christian faith. While studying in England in 1883, she (and two-year-old Mano) was baptized in the Church of England. Ramabai later wrote that in England she "found the Christian *religion,* which was good enough for me, *but I had not [yet] found Christ, Who is the Life of the religion,* and 'the Light of every man that cometh into the world.'"[56] However, her writings at the time show that this clearly was a major spiritual breakthrough for her — finding Christian truth after her increasing disillusionment with Hinduism.

Ramabai's passion to improve the lot of Indian women burned even as she continued her studies in England. It was deepened when she saw the rescue work being carried out near London by the (Anglican) Sisters of the Cross. When she witnessed this "work of mercy," she was confronted with a major "real difference between Hinduism and Christianity."[57]

Beginning in 1886, Ramabai spent two and a half years in the United States studying, lecturing, and raising support for her Indian reform work. She brought little Mano with her, but due to her constant travels she soon sent the five-year-old back to England, putting her in the care of (Anglican) Sisters of St. Mary the Virgin there. While in the United States Ramabai published an influential book, *The High-Caste Indian Woman* (1887), which quickly sold over ten thousand copies and earned her some $8,000. She developed an influential circle of well-connected American friends who helped her financially, arranged hundreds of speaking opportunities, and organized the Ramabai Association. Ramabai soon had received donations of over $20,000 to start a child widows home in India, plus pledges of $5,000 per year for ten years from the Ramabai Association.[58]

In America Ramabai paid particular attention to educational and reform movements. She learned of the pre–Civil War abolitionists and immediately saw parallels to the cause of liberating India's child widows. She was deeply impressed with the lives of Harriet Tubman (whose home in Auburn, New York, she visited twice), William Lloyd Garrison, Wendell Phillips, and also Abraham Lincoln — liberators all. She became close friends with Frances Willard, president of the WCTU, who appointed her vice president of the India WCTU. Willard described Ramabai as a "young woman of medium height and ninety-eight pounds"; "delightful to have about; content if she has books, pen and ink, and peace"; "a sort of human-like gazelle; incarnate gentleness, combined with such celerity of apprehension, such swiftness of mental pace, adroitness of logic and equipoise of intention as to make her a

---

56. Pandita Ramabai, *A Testimony of Our Inexhaustible Treasure,* reprinted in *Pandita Ramabai through Her Own Words: Selected Works,* comp. and ed. Meera Kosambi (New Delhi: Oxford University Press, 2000), p. 309.

57. Pandita Ramabai, "A Short History of Kripa Sadan, or Home of Mercy" (Mar. 1903), in Kosambi, *Pandita Ramabai,* p. 279. Kripa Sadan was the rescue home Ramabai established for sexually abused or "fallen" young women.

58. *The Letters of Pandita Ramabai,* comp. Sister Geraldine, ed. A. B. Shah (Bombay, India: Maharashtra State Board for Literature and Culture, 1977), pp. xx-xxi, 192-93.

delightful mental problem. She is impervious to praise, and can be captured only by affection."[59]

Ramabai also paid close attention to the various Christian denominations in the United States, and especially the way they treated women. She commented on the Methodist Episcopal Church General Conference held in New York City in 1888, at which women's rights were an issue. Ramabai spoke caustically of Methodism's failure to open the doors of leadership fully to women and noted that except for a few denominations such as the Quakers, Unitarians, "and a progressive branch of the Methodists," Christian churches "do not allow women the liberty to expound the Scriptures . . . for no other reason than that they are women!" She added, "Women may be as pure as anybody could wish, they may be learned, they may be eloquent and talented, they may be a hundred times superior to male preachers, but their one and only failing is that they are women," and so are not permitted to preach even if called by God. By "a progressive branch of the Methodists" Ramabai may have meant the Free Methodists; at this time Free Methodists had a number of women preachers and evangelists, even though they did not fully ordain women. Ramabai also observed that in America most of the financial support for missions and reform efforts came from the poor and from women.[60]

Now thirty, Ramabai arrived back in India in early 1889. Within months she opened a home and school, the Sharada Sadan ("Home of Learning"), for child widows. Mano returned from England, so mother and daughter were again united. With backing from the Ramabai Association and the support of over four thousand members of some seventy-seven Ramabai Circles in America, and with Hindu as well as Christian support in India, Ramabai's home for high-caste Indian widows flourished. Before long Ramabai also "admitted to her school other girls and women who were not child-widows, but whose life was a drudgery, misery, and a struggle for existence."[61]

Due to devastation of plague and famine, Ramabai vastly expanded her mission. "The Sharada Sadan was now no more an institution meant only for the high-caste Hindu child-widows. It was literally open to all irrespective of caste and creed."[62] In 1898 Ramabai founded her famous Mukti ("Salvation" or "Liberation") mission community at Kedgaon, near Poona, and began taking in hundreds of child-widow famine victims. Unlike her earlier work, Mukti was explicitly Christian. Some of Ramabai's widows had begun asking for Christian baptism, and given her own spiritual pilgrimage and some conversions among her students, Ramabai could no longer maintain her policy of religious neutrality. She could not refuse or discourage

59. Edith L. Blumhofer, "'From India's Coral Strand': Pandita Ramabai and U.S. Support for Foreign Missions," in *The Foreign Missionary Enterprise at Home: Explorations in North American Cultural History*, ed. Daniel H. Bays and Grant Wacker (Tuscaloosa: University of Alabama Press, 2003), p. 158.

60. Ramabai, *Pandita Ramabai's America*, pp. 219, 203-4.

61. Shamsundar Manohar Adhav, *Pandita Ramabai* (Madras: Christian Literature Society, 1979), p. 27. Opened first in Bombay, the Sharada Sadan was moved to Poona in 1891.

62. Adhav, *Pandita Ramabai*, p. 28.

the spiritual quest of these young Hindus who were of course influenced by their teacher's own example. "Ramabai's intentional religious neutrality ultimately yielded to the force of her own goodness."[63]

Advocating for the rights of women and children in India, Ramabai spoke out against both British colonial rule and the oppressions of Hinduism. In a letter published in a Marathi-language magazine in 1886, she wrote, "The British Government is sucking Indian blood and wealth while per force despatching Indian armies to march and fight the British battle in Egypt and ultimately die over there." She complained also of unfair taxation and unjust legal proceedings.[64]

In 1891 or 1892, as her work with child widows was growing, Ramabai had an encounter with God that in some ways resembled John Wesley's Aldersgate experience of 1738. Faith became deeper and more personal, giving her a daily sense of Christ's presence. She came "to know the Lord Jesus Christ as my personal Saviour and have the joy of sweet communion with him," she later wrote.[65] Then in April 1895 she experienced a deeper work of the Spirit at the holiness camp meeting at Lanauli (or Lanowli, between Bombay and Poona) established by the American Methodist evangelist and entrepreneur William Bramwell Osborn, founder of Ocean Grove, New Jersey, and other holiness encampments and one of the founders of the National Camp-Meeting Association for the Promotion of Holiness in 1867.[66] This new experience was influenced partly through Ramabai's reading the autobiography of Amanda Berry Smith, the African Methodist Episcopal holiness evangelist and former slave (who served briefly as a missionary in India). She came "to realize the personal presence of the Holy Spirit" in her life "and to be guided and taught by Him," she wrote. "The Holy Spirit taught me how to appropriate every promise of God in the right way, and obey His voice."[67]

63. Blumhofer, "'From India's Coral Strand,'" p. 163, citing a remark by the noted Oxford University philologist and Sanskrit scholar Friedrich Max Müller. Max Müller (1823-1900) befriended Ramabai in England. His linguistic work was key to establishing the historical links between Indian and European languages and civilizations. See F. Max Müller, *Auld Lang Syne, Second Series: My Indian Friends* (New York: Charles Scribner's Sons, 1899), p. 142.

64. Adhav, *Pandita Ramabai*, p. 37.

65. Ramabai, *A Testimony*, p. 314.

66. Blumhofer, "'From India's Coral Strand,'" p. 164; Padmini Sengupta, *Pandita Ramabai Saraswati: Her Life and Work* (Bombay: Asia Publishing House, 1970), p. 232; Nicol MacNicol, *Pandita Ramabai: A Builder of Modern India* (1926), republished as *What Liberates a Woman? The Story of Pandita Ramabai, a Builder of Modern India* (New Delhi: Nivedit Good Books, 1996), p. 142; Kostlevy, p. 194. Blumhofer dates this experience in 1894, but most sources give 1895.

67. Ramabai, *A Testimony*, p. 316. Cf. Sengupta, *Pandita Ramabai Saraswati*, pp. 231-32; Mary Lucia Bierce Fuller, *The Triumph of an Indian Widow: The Life of Pandita Ramabai*, 2nd ed. (Philadelphia: American Council of the Ramabai Mukti Mission, [1939]), pp. 40-41. Most accounts miss, or misunderstand, the Holiness movement connection here. There was significant Holiness movement influence in India in the 1870s and 1880s, particularly through Methodist missionary and bishop James Thoburn, missionary and church planter William Taylor, and others. In 1880 John Inskip, prominent holiness evangelist and president of the National Association for the Promotion of Holiness, conducted a series of evangelistic and holiness meetings in India in cooperation with William Osborn,

Ramabai developed connections with several American holiness people and also with Christian and Missionary Alliance (CMA) workers in India. Her work at Mukti continued to expand. When the original ten-year mandate of the Ramabai Association ended in 1898, she returned to America to reorganize support. A more explicitly evangelical American Ramabai Association was formed. As Edith Blumhofer notes, Ramabai's "embrace of conversionist Christianity and affinity for aspects of the higher life and holiness movements had brought her into the flow of growing streams of popular Protestantism in the United States. D. L. Moody and his many networks promoted her as ever in their publications, collecting and forwarding funds. . . . She had come around to the conviction that only the gospel could accomplish what she had set out to do."[68]

Manoramabai and Chesbrough Seminary

Ramabai's spiritual pilgrimage in the 1890s complicated her daughter's educational progress. In 1896 Ramabai sent Mano, then fifteen, back to England where in a year and a half she attended four different schools. These changes were dictated by Ramabai and reflected her own spiritual and theological transitions. Sister Geraldine of the Anglican Community of St. Mary the Virgin, who had been Ramabai's principal mentor in England in 1883, complained about "the mismanagement of [Ramabai's] only child's education." She and other Anglican friends constantly tried to strengthen Mano's ties to the Church of England and to steer her away from "dissenting" groups and what Sister Geraldine called "the adulterations of Methodism." But Ramabai told Sister Geraldine in 1896, "I believe in the Universal Church of Christ which includes all the members of His body, and am not particular about others being members of different sects. The dry discussion about sects and differences has never been an attractive one to me since I was converted. And now I enjoy the peace of God which passeth all understanding and do not trouble myself with small matters of opinion and differences."[69]

Sister Geraldine noted that Ramabai finally in 1897 sent Mano "to be trained as a missionary with people at Brighton," England, and "to be prepared to go with her to America early in January 1898."[70] Ramabai brought Mano with her to America in early 1898, along with two high-caste child widows. She had decided to enroll her daughter and these Indian girls in Chesbrough Seminary, which she learned about

---

who had gone to India with William Taylor in 1875. Inskip preached the Methodist doctrine of entire sanctification as "the baptism of the Holy Spirit." Amanda Smith was also ministering in India at this time; Smith and Inskip crossed paths in Bombay in October 1880. See W. McDonald and John E. Searles, *The Life of Rev. John S. Inskip, President of the National Association for the Promotion of Holiness* (1885; reprint, Salem, Ohio: Allegheny Publications, 1986), pp. 328-42.

68. Blumhofer, "'From India's Coral Strand,'" p. 166.

69. *Letters of Pandita Ramabai*, pp. 335, 338.

70. *Letters of Pandita Ramabai*, p. 350.

in India through the Fullers and perhaps others.[71] As Blumhofer notes, the attraction this Free Methodist school "now held for Ramabai revealed her shifting religious sensibilities."[72] Ramabai had finally decided that Chesbrough was the best place for Mano and for selected others of her wards whom she wished to see receive further education.

Emma Sellew Roberts heard Ramabai speak in Rochester on this 1898 trip, but she and Adella Carpenter apparently had had contact with her for some time prior to this. In fact, Ramabai sent three high-caste child widows to study at Chesbrough in the summer of 1897. Now she enrolled two more and her own seventeen-year-old daughter.[73]

This mission accomplished, and with renewed pledges of support, Ramabai returned to India in 1898. Stopping briefly in England en route, she was invited to attend the July Keswick Convention. There in a five-minute address she challenged the four thousand attendees to pray for revival in India, asking them "to pray for an outpouring of the Holy Spirit on all Indian Christians" and "that 100,000 men and 100,000 women from among the Indian Christians may be led to preach the Gospel to their country people."[74]

Mano's education at Chesbrough Seminary, according to Sister Geraldine, "was given to her without cost, as was also that of the five Indian girls with her in the Seminary, by the liberality of Mrs. E. S. [Emma Sellew] Roberts, the Lady Principal."[75] Sadly, some of the Indian girls died while at the seminary; they lie buried in the North Chili cemetery.[76] Mano, however — like her mother, an outstanding student — flourished, completing a three-year course of study in two years. Sister Geraldine wrote,

> [Mano] rose at five and spent her first half hour in prayer and Bible reading before beginning study and thus claimed a daily blessing on her work. She left the

---

71. Mary Lucia Bierce Fuller (1882-1965), a Chesbrough and Oberlin alumna, was especially close to Ramabai and looked upon her as her spiritual mother. She later wrote *The Triumph of an Indian Widow: The Life of Pandita Ramabai*. Of this journey to America Sister Geraldine wrote, "With Miss [Minnie] Abrams' capable help at Mukti, . . . Ramabai felt able to leave [in early 1898]. She had, the year before, sent three of her best pupils to America, and she now took two others with her. In England, she was joined by her daughter Manorama whom she took to America. These six girls were placed under the care of Mrs. Roberts, Principal of the A. M. Chesbrough Seminary, North Chili, N.Y." *Letters of Pandita Ramabai*, pp. 353, 355; Adhav, *Pandita Ramabai*, p. 19.

72. Blumhofer, "'From India's Coral Strand,'" p. 166.

73. Emma Sellew Roberts, "Pandita Ramabai and Her Work," pp. 5-6; Emma Sellew Roberts, "The High-Caste Widows of India at the A. M. Chesbrough Seminary," *Missionary Tidings* 2, no. 6 (June 1898): 7-8. Dyer notes, "When Ramabai went to America in 1898 she took with her several young women who were in moral danger from their relatives." Helen S. Dyer, *Pandita Ramabai: Her Vision, Her Mission and Triumph of Faith* (London: Pickering and Inglis, [1923]), p. 84.

74. Pandita Ramabai, in *Mukti Prayer-Bell* 2, no. 1 (Oct. 1905), quoted in Adhav, *Pandita Ramabai*, p. 216.

75. *Letters of Pandita Ramabai*, p. 351.

76. "Ramabai, Great Native Indian, Sent Daughter to Chesbro," *Pioneer* 3, no. 10 (June 1927): 1. The *Pioneer* was published by A. M. Chesbrough Seminary.

Seminary having gained the goodwill of all her fellow-students and the highest commendation of her teachers for the quiet and unobtrusive influence she had exercised. The five other Indian girls were her special charge while in the Seminary; she overlooked their studies, and was referred to by her teachers if any difficulty arose with regard to them. The examinations shewed that she had gained the first place of the year [1889-90] in the Seminary, and out of some ten subjects she gained honours in all but two. She also took extra science subjects. And to this must be added instrumental music. As a pianist she was brilliant.[77]

Mano completed her course, graduating with honors in June 1900.[78] She intended to go on to Mount Holyoke for her college education but decided instead to return to India to help her mother, who was in urgent need of assistance.[79]

Ramabai's Mukti mission community had expanded rapidly as Ramabai rescued hundreds of starving child widows from a devastating famine that killed an estimated 37 million people. "By the end of 1897, Ramabai has assembled the three hundred famine widows she had set out to find. She now began to develop plans to make Mukti a place for education, vocational training, and the equipping of Indian female village evangelists. The famine widows constituted the nucleus for this experiment," notes Blumhofer.[80] Eventually, as the result of subsequent famines, Mukti grew to a community of about two thousand. Mary Lucia Bierce Fuller, who knew Ramabai well, wrote that as Ramabai took in more and more girls during the 1900 famine, she "finally abandoned her original plan of a school for high-caste widows only, and [took] in girls of all castes, even thieving castes, aboriginals and out-caste

77. *Letters of Pandita Ramabai*, p. 363. Shortly after graduating in June 1900, Mano sailed for England, where she visited Sister Geraldine and others before going on to India. Sister Geraldine notes that in returning to India Mano was commissioned by the American Ramabai Association to take charge of the Sharada Sadan, the residential school that Ramabai had opened in 1889 (p. 364).

78. Benson and Emma Roberts took, or at least intended to take, Mano with them to D. L. Moody's Northfield Summer Conference for a week in August 1898, according to a July 30, 1898, letter in the Roberts Family Papers. Ambert G. Moody (D. L. Moody's nephew) of the Northfield Summer Conferences wrote to Benson Roberts, "We are . . . glad to know that you are planning to come to Northfield for the August Conference for a week at least. We trust that you and Mrs. Roberts will bring the daughter of Pundita [*sic*] Ramabai with you, for the outing can but do her good." A. G. Moody (Northfield, Mass.) to Mr. B. H. Roberts (North Chili), July 30, 1898. RFP, Microfilm Reel 12, Frame 405.

79. Frykenberg misunderstands the Chesbrough Seminary connection. He writes, "Soon after reaching America, Manorama was admitted to a women's college ('seminary') in New York." He doesn't mention the name of the school, or of Emma or Benson Roberts, and misses the Holiness movement context. Chesbrough was not, of course, a college, and was coeducational. Blumhofer does mention the school and B. T. Roberts, but misidentifies Roberts as the founder of the Wesleyan Methodists. Kosambi also mentions the school (misspelling it "Cheseborough") but also is oblivious to the character of the school and its connections. See Frykenberg, "Pandita Ramabai Saraswati: A Biographical Introduction," in *Pandita Ramabai's America*, p. 47; Blumhofer, "'From India's Coral Strand,'" pp. 165-66; Meera Kosambi, "Returning the American Gaze: Situating Pandita Ramabai's American Encounter," introduction to Ramabai, *Pandita Ramabai's American Encounter*, p. 29.

80. Blumhofer, "'From India's Coral Strand,'" pp. 164-65.

scavengers," much to the consternation of even her helpers and the older girls. Ramabai was assisted now by a whole corps of American and English women who "one by one, came to Ramabai's help, never to leave her, some of them, till they died" — the Methodist missionary Minnie Abrams, Mary Macdonald, Lissa Hastie, and many others, some of them medical doctors.[81]

Revival at Mukti

A remarkable revival swept Mukti Mission in 1905. Ramabai noted that the revival grew out of "a special prayer-circle" consisting of "about 70 of us who met together each morning," praying for "the true conversion of all the Indian Christians including ourselves, and for a special outpouring of the Holy Spirit on all Christians of every land." Six months later "the Lord graciously sent a glorious Holy Ghost revival among us, and also in many schools and Churches in this country."[82] Sister Geraldine (based on Mano's letters) described the revival as "a marvellous Pentecostal outpouring of the Holy Spirit," continuing for "more than six weeks." Mano said the revival's outbreak "was manifestly God Himself working," for "no stirring address [had been] delivered at the meeting; nor had there been any special effort to bring conviction of sin." Mano reported that a "large number of girls and women" were converted, and "many have received the cleansing and fulness of the Spirit for life and service."[83]

Three months later Mano wrote to Sister Geraldine,

> I told [in my previous letter] how the Holy Spirit had begun to work in the hearts of the girls in a most marvellous way and how His working led to agony on account of sin, confession and restoration and then intense joy. Perhaps, I did not mention the joy, for I remember that I wrote that letter at the very beginning of this Revival; and for the first few days hardly any joy was seen, but a sense of awe pervaded the atmosphere, and there was deep sorrow for sin. Then came the joy and the baptism of the Holy Ghost and Fire; and what seems to be a special anointing for the Ministry of Intercession.[84]

Reports of revival outbreaks in Korea, Australia, and Wales appear to have helped spark the Mukti revival. Blumhofer writes, "[W]ith reports of the Welsh revival circulating widely, hundreds of Ramabai's two thousand girls manifested unusual concern about sin, crying and praying for forgiveness. The noise of hundreds

---

81. Fuller, *Triumph*, pp. 48-49, 52-55. "No other biographer was more closely and intimately associated with the Pandita" than Mary Lucia Fuller (Adhav, *Pandita Ramabai*, p. 47).

82. Ramabai, *A Testimony*, p. 320. Adhav says this revival "rooted at Mukti in 1905," which began on June 29, spread to a number of other cities and towns including Poona, Bombay, Yeotmal, and Dhokla. Adhav, *Pandita Ramabai*, pp. 21, 230.

83. *Letters of Pandita Ramabai*, pp. 390-91.

84. *Letters of Pandita Ramabai*, p. 391.

praying aloud individually and simultaneously permeated the compound day and night."[85]

Mano probably witnessed somewhat similar scenes, if on a smaller scale, earlier at Chesbrough Seminary. In a circular letter Mano sent out in October 1906, she described the revival. "A realization of the awfulness of sin, and a dread of its results took possession of many. And in almost all parts of Mukti, in the dormitories and school rooms, in the garden, and in the various compounds, there were to be found at all times of the day, souls crying to God for mercy and forgiveness." Then as the Holy Spirit was poured out, the community experienced indescribable joy. "God graciously granted to those who were seeking, the Baptism of the Holy Ghost and Fire, and to those who were willing, a real yearning for the salvation of souls and a special anointing for the ministry of intercession. In a marked way, God has been reminding us of the words of Scripture, 'God hath *chosen* the foolish . . . the weak . . . and base things of this world,' the 'things which are despised . . . yea and the things which are not, to bring to nought things that are: that no flesh should glory in His Presence.'"[86]

Revival of a somewhat different character came in late December 1906 and early 1907. Ramabai called it "another and greater outpouring of the Holy Spirit." Some of the girls "received a definite call to preach the Gospel," and some began "praying in different tongues." Ramabai said she wasn't surprised by the tongues speaking because she had heard that this gift had been given to Christians elsewhere in India.[87] She was a bit surprised, however, when one of the girls, who did not know English, began praying and praising God in English. "She was perfectly unconscious of what was going on, her eyes were fast closed, and she was speaking to the Lord Jesus very fluently in English."[88]

News of Pentecostal revival in India filtered back to Azusa Street and was reported in the *Apostolic Faith,* the monthly paper associated with the Azusa Street revival that began publication in September 1906. A brief piece in the November 1906 issue entitled "Pentecost in India" reported that "the baptism with the Holy Ghost

85. Blumhofer, "'From India's Coral Strand,'" p. 168.

86. Manoramabai, circular letter (Oct. 8, 1906), quoted in Adhav, *Pandita Ramabai,* p. 230.

87. An editorial in the September 1906 *Alliance Witness* spoke of "reports of the revival movement in India" that "frequently read like a continuation of the Acts of the Apostles. Some of the gifts which have been scarcely heard of in the church for many centuries, are now being given by the Holy Ghost to simple, unlearned members of the body of Christ and communities are being stirred and transformed by the wonderful grace of God. Healings, the gift of tongues, visions and dreams, discernment of spirits, the power to prophecy [sic] and to pray the prayer of faith, all have a place in the present revival." Maud Wiest, "Editorials," *Alliance Witness,* Sept. 1906, p. 30, quoted in Gary B. McGee, "'Latter Rain' Falling in the East: Early-Twentieth-Century Pentecostalism in India and the Debate over Speaking in Tongues," *Church History* 68, no. 3 (Sept. 1999): 655.

88. *Mukti Prayer-Bell* 3, no. 4 (Sept. 1907), quoted in Adhav, *Pandita Ramabai,* pp. 218-19. Other girls were said to have spoken in Sanskrit and Kannada. McGee notes that Minnie Abrams testified to speaking in Hebrew and that "Ramabai did not speak in tongues, but commended the experience." McGee, "'Latter Rain' Falling," p. 656.

and gift of tongues is being received there by natives who are simply being taught of God." This referred however to revivals elsewhere in India, not at Mukti.[89] A longer article in the September 1907 issue entitled "Pentecost in Mukti, India" (reprinted from an Indian publication) specifically mentioned Ramabai and her work and the Pentecostal outpouring at Mukti just before Christmas 1906. The report stated that both Ramabai and Minnie Abrams were impressèd by the reports from Azusa Street and had exhorted the Mukti community to "tarry for the promised baptism of the Holy Ghost." Ramabai, the report noted, "fully acknowledged all that God had bestowed through His Spirit in the past; but she discerned there was the deeper fullness of the outpouring of the Holy Ghost accompanied with the gift of tongues which had not yet been received." Gifts of various tongues, interpretation, and healing were part of this movement. The report noted that at Mukti "the girls and women are pressing on to greater things and are believing for the restoration to the Church of all the lost gifts of the Spirit."[90]

Reflecting on the tongues speaking, Ramabai said she "praised God for doing something new for us," but she saw this revival in continuity with the one two years earlier despite its "special features" including "the shaking of the body, and other physical demonstrations, speaking in different tongues, simultaneous prayer, and such other things." Ramabai was very clear that tongues were not "the only and necessary sign" of the Spirit's baptism. She wrote at the height of the 1907 revival, "The gift of tongues is certainly one of the signs of the baptism of the Holy Spirit. There is scriptural ground to hold this belief. But there is no Scripture warrant to think that the speaking in tongues is the only and necessary sign of the baptism of the Holy Spirit."[91] Pentecostal historian Gary McGee notes that "neither Abrams nor Ramabai registered tongues as indispensable to every instance of baptism in the Holy Spirit as did their American counterparts," though both views were represented at Mukti. Ramabai and Abrams held a "more inclusive doctrine" of tongues that was similar to A. B. Simpson's views and less like "that taught at Topeka and Azusa."[92]

Through these revivals at Mukti, Ramabai became something of a bridge figure between the Holiness and Pentecostal movements. Abrams, who was baptized with the Holy Spirit during the 1905 revival, in 1906 published *The Baptism of the Holy*

89. "Pentecost in India," *Apostolic Faith* 1, no. 3 (Nov. 1906): 1. This report quotes Maud Wiest's September 1906 editorial, cited above. A similar report from Sister A. G. Garr, "In Calcutta, India," appeared in the April 1907 issue of the *Apostolic Faith*, p. 1.

90. Max Wood Moorhead, "Pentecost in Mukti, India," *Apostolic Faith* 1, no. 10 (Sept. 1907): 4. See the discussion in McGee, "'Latter Rain' Falling," p. 656.

91. *Mukti Prayer-Bell* 3, no. 4 (Sept. 1907), quoted in Adhav, *Pandita Ramabai*, pp. 219-21, 223. This was also Minnie Abrams's view; like Ramabai, Abrams saw the 1907 revival in continuity with the 1905 one. Simultaneous praying aloud and outbreaks of prayer "all over the church while singing or preaching is going on, putting a stop to all other exercises," had been part of the Mukti community's experience "since the big Revival of 1905," Abrams noted in 1907, as documented in Adhav, p. 225.

92. McGee, "'Latter Rain' Falling," pp. 657-58.

Ghost and Fire, an important book that influenced the beginnings of Pentecostalism in Chile and elsewhere.[93] McGee argues in fact that the 1905 and 1907 revivals at Mukti challenge the common view that modern Pentecostalism traces exclusively to the 1906-9 Azusa Street revival. A Pentecostal revival was already well under way in India before news of Azusa Street arrived. Thus "Early Pentecostalism in India represents an important chapter in the story of modern Pentecostalism that must be examined on its own merits and not just as a spinoff from the Azusa Street revival." Further, McGee argues, the role of glossolalia as understood by Ramabai and others at Mukti calls into question "the dominance of the classical Pentecostal doctrine of speaking in tongues" that portrays tongues speaking as the essential initial evidence of Spirit baptism. As McGee puts it, "Despite claims that Pentecostalism first sprouted in America, the fact that Holiness seed had been scattered on the soil of India has been overlooked." The Mukti revival was nurtured by holiness and Keswickian Higher Life streams, as Ramabai's own story bears out. The language of "Pentecost" and "Spirit baptism" was common in these streams well before Azusa Street. This background is part of the reason that Ramabai and Abrams "did not insist that every Pentecostal had to experience glossolalia."[94]

In the United States, the controversy over tongues speaking split the Holiness movement, giving rise to modern Pentecostalism.[95] It is impossible to know just where B. T. Roberts would have come down on this issue had he lived into the early 1900s. Certainly he would have rejected as unbiblical the view that tongues are the necessary evidence of Spirit baptism. But given his own "Pentecostal" leanings — his emphasis on the baptism and the freedom of the Holy Spirit; on the empowerment of *all* believers, including women, for ministry; plus his emphasis on revival, his passion for world missions, and his support of Vivian Dake's Pentecost Bands — it is at least plausible that he might have embraced the more inclusive view of Ramabai that glossolalia was a legitimate but not the most important gift of the Spirit. If so, he would have been an exception among holiness leaders. But given the climate of controversy over tongues in the United States after 1906, with extreme positions taken by both sides, it is just as plausible that he would have rejected tongues speaking except perhaps as the gift of known languages for missionary purposes.

Manoramabai was familiar with the Free Methodist emphasis on revival and the work of the Holy Spirit due to her years at Chesbrough. Her own spiritual journey in

---

93. G. B. McGee, "Abrams, Minnie F.," in *Dictionary of Pentecostal and Charismatic Movements,* p. 7. McGee notes that through sending a copy of her book "to May L. Hoover (Mrs. Willis C. Hoover) in Valparaiso, Chile, with whom she attended the Chicago Training School for Home and Foreign Missions (Methodist-related), Abrams significantly influenced the beginnings of the Pentecostal movement" in Chile. See also Gary McGee, "'Baptism of the Holy Ghost and Fire!' The Mission Legacy of Minnie F. Abrams," *Missiology,* Oct. 1999, pp. 515-22.

94. McGee, "'Latter Rain' Falling," pp. 648-65.

95. Best documented in Vinson Synan, *The Holiness-Pentecostal Tradition: Charismatic Movements in the Twentieth Century* (Grand Rapids: Eerdmans, 1997), rev. ed. of *The Holiness-Pentecostal Movement in the United States* (1971).

the 1890s essentially paralleled that of her mother. She embraced personal faith in Jesus Christ and the deeper work of the Spirit, sharing with her mother the emphasis on holiness and on the Pentecostal empowerment of the Spirit. In this sense she, like Abrams, was one of the early pioneers of the modern Pentecostal movement.

After graduating from Chesbrough in 1900, Mano worked steadily with her mother for about twenty years. She took an active part in the 1905 and 1907 revivals, as noted. She accompanied Abrams on a voyage to England in 1908, intending to continue on with her to the United States to visit a number of Pentecostal centers. She became seriously ill, however, and returned to India, gratefully experiencing God's healing on the return voyage.[96]

Ramabai expected her daughter to succeed her in directing the mission, but Manoramabai, who had been in declining health for some time, died on July 24, 1921, at age forty. Ramabai herself died only nine months later, on April 5, 1922, at age sixty-four. The work has continued to the present, however. Sometime after Ramabai's death the Christian and Missionary Alliance took over trusteeship of the Mukti Mission "in accordance with Ramabai's will," noted Mary Lucia Bierce Fuller, with the understanding that it would continue as an independent ministry, not as part of the CMA missionary enterprise.[97]

Solving the Puzzle: Why Chesbrough?

At first it seems odd that Pandita Ramabai, with her wide international network of well-placed Christian and reformist leaders, would send her daughter and her choice scholars to the rather obscure Chesbrough Seminary. It is true that Ramabai had a pronounced affinity for America over England; as Meera Kosambi notes, Ramabai viewed the United States as "a more progressive country than imperial Britain and as a more suitable model for a colonized India to follow in its pursuit of freedom and advancement."[98] So Ramabai apparently wanted Mano to be educated and shaped in America. But why Chesbrough?

Ramabai's own spiritual pilgrimage provides some clues. The attraction was at

96. Dyer, *Pandita Ramabai*, p. 133; cf. McGee, "'Latter Rain' Falling," p. 658.

97. Fuller, *Triumph*, p. 49. Information on Pandita Ramabai and Manoramabai is drawn primarily from the following sources, in addition to those already indicated: Eric J. Sharpe, "Ramabai Dongre Medhavi," in *Biographical Dictionary of Christian Missions*, ed. Gerald H. Anderson (New York: Macmillan Reference, 1998), p. 557; Rajas Krishnarao Dongre and Josephine F. Patterson, *Pandita Ramabai: A Life of Faith and Prayer* (Madras: Christian Literature Society, 1963), pp. 33-38; "Ramabai, Sarasvati (Pandita)," in *Dictionary of Pentecostal and Charismatic Movements*, pp. 755-56; "Smith, Amanda Berry," in Kostlevy, pp. 235-36; Basil Miller, *Pandita Ramabai, India's Christian Pilgrim* (Grand Rapids: Zondervan, 1949), pp. 69, 80, 116. See also [Emma Sellew Roberts?], "Pundita Ramabai," *EC* 75, no. 6 (June 1898): 183-85. This issue of the *Earnest Christian* carried a photograph of Ramabai on the front cover.

98. Kosambi, "Preface and Acknowledgements," in Ramabai, *Pandita Ramabai's American Encounter*, p. ix.

several levels. In hindsight, and in light of the growing body of literature on Ramabai, five interlocking factors emerge, all of which have continuing relevance today.

1. *Commitment to social concern and reform issues — particularly women's rights and ministry with the poor and oppressed.* Like her Hindu father, Ramabai was a lifelong reformer. Even before she was a Christian she was an advocate for reform and liberation. Her concern especially was for full equality of women. As Frykenberg notes, Ramabai "stood as a champion of the lowly, the weak, and the poor, particularly downtrodden women and children."[99] She learned of the long-standing Free Methodist commitment to women's equality as well as, no doubt, the church's earlier opposition to slavery and its concern for the poor. It is unlikely that she would have sent Mano to study at Chesbrough if the school had not embraced and lived these values.

2. *Countercultural witness.* While Ramabai openly admired the freedom and relative equality of American society, she was aware of discrimination against women and against African Americans, Native Americans, and other minorities. She also disapproved of American materialism, pride, and the ostentation of the rich. These were all concerns that B. T. Roberts articulated repeatedly.

Ramabai could see that Chesbrough Seminary maintained some critical distance from American culture, even though it was thoroughly committed to a classical quality education. Also, the Free Methodist emphasis on simplicity and plainness in dress and lifestyle would have attracted her — in principle, if not in detail. Ramabai always wore a plain white cotton sari and her hair short, both symbols of her widowhood, and maintained a simple lifestyle, including a vegetarian diet.[100] These of course were reflections of her Indian Hindu culture, but she apparently affirmed them also as Christian values.[101] Like Benson and Emma Roberts, and of course B. T. and Ellen, Ramabai looked on the ostentations of popular American fashion with disdain.

3. *Commitment to a broad liberal arts education for all.* Brilliant and well educated herself, Ramabai wanted her protégés to be thoroughly grounded in history, literature and languages, and the arts and sciences. She apparently became convinced that Chesbrough was committed to serious and rigorous study, within an explicitly Christian context.

99. Frykenberg, "Editor's Preface to the English Translation," in Ramabai, *Pandita Ramabai's America,* p. xi.

100. Clementina Butler, *Pandita Ramabai Sarasvati: Pioneer of the Movement for Education of the Child-widows of India* (New York: Fleming H. Revell, 1922), pp. 88-89.

101. In a standard letter to prospective volunteer workers at Mukti, Manoramabai emphasized, "[O]ur style of living is thoroughly India. Our European workers do not wear the Indian dress, but they dress simply in their own way. Our rooms are very plain." She explained that while "in most Missions where European workers are in charge, the food and manner of living is European, . . . ours is a thoroughly Indian Mission." "The Papers, Publications, Pamphlets and Selected Books of Pandita Ramabai (1858-1922)," microfilmed archival collection from the Pandita Ramabai Mission, Kedgaon, India, 2001.

Ramabai knew that many American reform movements were populist in character — that is, that they were energized by broad-based popular support, worked for the welfare of common people, and believed that the nation's political and economic structures should benefit all the people, not just the wealthy and powerful — the essence of American populism. This populist current found resonance with her own spirit and agenda. She may have been attracted to the fact that Chesbrough was not an elitist school but provided quality liberal arts education for common people and the poor.

4. *Emphasis on Christian mission.* As Ramabai became increasingly evangelical in her outlook, explicit Christian mission became a more central concern. Ramabai approved the strong missions emphasis at Chesbrough, and the fact that it was not narrowly sectarian. Though the major focus of missions at Chesbrough was on Free Methodist work, the mission work of other groups, such as the Christian Missionary Alliance, was also celebrated.

5. Finally — and very importantly in the light of Ramabai's own spiritual journey — was the Free Methodist *emphasis on the baptism of the Holy Spirit,* understood at this point in the Wesleyan Holiness sense, not in the later Pentecostal sense. Experientially at least, by 1895 Ramabai had become a part of the Holiness movement, and she wanted Mano and the other Indian students to come under this influence. She presumably hoped the rising generation of Indian Christian leaders would arrive at the place where she had arrived. Chesbrough Seminary, reflecting the shadow of the now-departed B. T. Roberts, uniquely combined the set of concerns that was closest to Ramabai's heart.[102] Ramabai was always a pilgrim on a journey. Despite the colossal differences of culture, in her pilgrimage she found kinship with the Wesleyan Holiness pilgrim community in North Chili, New York.

Ellen's Last Years

Ellen Roberts lived to see the beginning of a new century, surviving her husband by fifteen years. She stayed active in the work of the church for as long as she could. In her diaries of the early 1900s she occasionally speaks of writing for the *Earnest Christian* and attending to correspondence for the magazine. She attended her Tuesday class meeting except when the weather was too cold, continuing for some time as its leader. She noted on March 12, 1901, when she was nearly seventy-six, that the meeting was "profitable," but since "I do not hear well it seems as if another should be appointed leader of the class."[103]

For years Ellen maintained a wide-ranging correspondence that, as she grew

---

102. Ramabai published *A Testimony of Our Inexhaustible Treasure* in 1907. This remarkable account (running to thirty pages in a recent republication) traces her spiritual pilgrimage. She also describes the 1905 revival and at the end recounts that she had now come to believe firmly in the imminent second coming of Jesus Christ. Ramabai, *A Testimony,* pp. 295-324.

103. ELRD, Mar. 12, 1901; Jan. 21 and 22, 1903; Carpenter, pp. 100-101.

more aged, she only reluctantly gave up. "She understood the well nigh lost art of letter writing," said Benson. Her contacts were mainly within the Free Methodist Church, in which "her whole interests were wrapped up," but she also "had fellowship with many of God's saints in other churches."[104]

Ellen continued to be concerned about the salvation of her children and grandchildren. Reminded in Scripture of God's promises to answer prayer, she wrote, "My family came before me as in a picture and the assurance of the salvation of all."[105]

February 1901 was "a beautiful white month," snow falling every day. "Shut in, but not lonely," Ellen noted. "Peace has reigned. Great peace."[106] In her diary she often commented on spiritual lessons or insights. "Praise God the first thing in the morning before Satan has a chance to say anything. Depression goes out when we give praise," she wrote on March 23.[107]

Ellen began to suffer some from rheumatism and other ailments. She noted on April 27, 1901, "A severe attack of rheumatism in my hip — it makes me feel sick. . . . I feel greatly pressed in spirit — as if the bottom had fallen out of everything. Whether this is wholly physical depression is a question. It seems to me Satan is doing his worst somewhere." Some months later she stayed home from Sunday worship because she "seemed full of rheumatism. Had to wrap and lie down," she noted. "Nothing relieves me but heat when I feel as I do today." In June 1902 she was "quite lame when I walk."[108] On another occasion she felt God's "healing touch in my neck," which had been lame.[109]

Ellen continued her reading. In April 1901 it was the life of Bishop Leonidas Hamline, who had died in 1865. She remembered that "when a girl" (actually at age nineteen) she had heard him preach at the momentous 1844 ME General Conference in New York City. "He was a great Preacher and a very devoted man." In July 1902 Ellen finished reading a biography of Florence Nightingale, "a rare woman." Nightingale, born in 1820, was five years older than Ellen and still living. She died in 1910; thus her life span was very similar to Ellen's. On another occasion Ellen was reading about Madam Guyon.[110]

Ellen also kept up her Bible reading, noting in June 1901 that she was going through Philippians and Colossians. "Blessed Bible! It seems alive to me. As I read the same word over and over, I do not want to pass on to another verse or chapter. I am trying to live by the moment in reference to all temporal matters as well as spiritual."[111]

Prayer also continued to be a central part of Ellen's life; increasingly she felt this

104. Benson H. Roberts, "My Mother," *EC* 95, no. 3 (Mar. 1908): 71.
105. ELRD, Jan. 8, 1901, as quoted in Carpenter, p. 97.
106. ELRD, Feb. 28, 1901, as quoted in Carpenter, p. 98.
107. ELRD, Mar. 23, 1901.
108. ELRD, Apr. 27, 1901; Mar. 9 and June 6, 1902.
109. ELRD, Jan. 21, 1903, as quoted in Carpenter, p. 100.
110. ELRD, Apr. 28, 1901; July 31 and Aug. 1, 1902.
111. ELRD, June 30, 1901, as quoted in Carpenter, p. 99.

was "the most important work left me to do." She noted on April 3, 1902, that she had had a "blessed season of prayer for every member" of the family.[112]

Ellen noted that on February 20, 1902, Benson and Emma left on a trip to the Bahama Islands. Their older children, Lucy and Ashbel Sellew, stayed at the seminary, but eleven-year-old Edwin Douglas stayed with Ellen. "I trust my charge will be a profitable one though it seems new and strange to have so young a member of the family," she noted.[113]

The Bahamas trip temporarily interrupted Benson's daily visits to see his mother. "Year after year . . . always once a day, sometimes twice a day, I found my way across the fields" to see her, Benson said, "because we found delight together and I found counsel."[114] Adella Carpenter generally would stop to see Ellen each day, also, after her duties at the seminary were done. "I was never acquainted with any one who kept the Holy Spirit so constantly and so consciously," Miss Carpenter wrote. "At times, merely to sit down beside her would solve my perplexities before I told her of them."[115]

Ellen continued to write articles as she was able. In March 1902 she said her "constant writing" was giving her "head trouble," and she felt God distinctly told her to stop. "As I obeyed, much of the Lord's presence seemed very near. My head quite relieved."[116]

At the end of December 1902, Ellen mentions receiving a "greeting" from "Bro. Shelhamer and his workers" and notes that "Sr. Coon is with them this winter."[117] E. E. Shelhamer, one of the early leaders of the Pentecost Bands, was at this time pioneering Free Methodist work in Atlanta, Georgia, serving the Pittsburgh Conference as chairman of the Georgia District.[118]

As Ellen grew older and weaker, heaven seemed nearer. She wrote on February 17, 1903, "This has been a memorable day. A day of the Lord's coming. All day I seemed loosed from my body. I have had rest from it. Praise, praise, praise!"[119] On May 3, 1903, her fifty-first wedding anniversary, she wrote, "My married life has been a pleasant and blessed one. My companion has been ten years in glory. I have three dear children there, Willie, Sarah and Samuel. They are safe, praise God!"[120]

Despite physical weakness, Ellen's prayer life continued strong. She prayed for the church, for "all our schools," for missionaries. She noted in her diary on July 30,

112. ELRD, Apr. 3, 1902, as quoted in Carpenter, p. 99.
113. ELRD, Feb. 20, 1902.
114. Benson H. Roberts, "My Mother," p. 71.
115. Adella P. Carpenter, "The Home-Going," *EC* 95, no. 3 (Mar. 1908): 72-73.
116. ELRD, Mar. 15, 1902.
117. ELRD, Dec. 29, 1902.
118. Arthur D. Zahniser and John B. Easton, *History of the Pittsburgh Conference of the Free Methodist Church* (Chicago: Free Methodist Publishing House, 1932), p. 51; C. H. Canon, E. W. Cowsert, and R. L. Page, *History of the Pittsburgh Conference of the Free Methodist Church, Centennial Edition, 1883-1983* (n.p.: Pittsburgh Conference, 1983), p. 25.
119. ELRD, Feb. 17, 1903, as quoted in Carpenter, p. 101.
120. ELRD, May 3, 1903, as quoted in Carpenter, p. 101.

1904, "I never had such a spirit of prayer given me as this night, beyond my power to explain or tell about it, except that God was in it — the Holy Spirit prompted it."[121]

On Sunday, October 30, 1904, well into her seventy-ninth year, Ellen managed to walk to church, but it "tired me much," she said. "I could hear but very little of the sermon. I had no strength or life in me. I lay down for two hours when I reached home. I felt glad that I went. God moves in His own way. He does not explain His ways to us."[122] She had peace and a sense of God's presence. "It means much to have and keep perfect submission. Stillness of the Holy Spirit steals over me to-night. God is here."[123] At the end of the year she wrote, "Praise God for His blessings the past year. Praise Him for health, strength, and life in the degree given to us."[124]

Ellen wrote in a clear hand in January 1905, "My health is quite good I know, but because I cannot do as I once could, I seem to myself like a half invalid. But it is all right. Heaven comes very near sometimes, and Jesus abides with me." She exhorted one correspondent, "Take the cross. Be a true soldier. Let no one take your crown. Live for eternity," adding, "Let God have all there is of you. He can & will make and mould us if we lay in His hands."[125]

It became more and more difficult for Ellen to get out to the regular worship services. She was able to attend on Sunday, November 12, 1905 — "her last going to church," according to Carpenter — and noted, "It is a long time since I attended church; but I praise God He helped me. I felt the heavenly benediction upon me all the time."[126] For several weeks she was ill, unable to leave her bed. She noted on New Year's Day 1906, "This is the longest time I have ever been confined to my room." But she felt God was with her, and wrote, "I believe we may keep much more of heaven within than we have thought possible, amid care and toil and responsibilities."[127]

Ellen welcomed the coming of spring 1906. "The Lord is good; His mercy endures forever. The apple trees never seemed so full of blossoms before, the grass never such a beautiful green."[128] In August her son, Dr. Benjamin T. Roberts, Jr., and his family paid a visit. The day they left to return to Morgan Park, Illinois, Ellen noted, "This morning I have been down stairs — the first time in weeks."[129]

Homegoing

Ellen continued to weaken as the months passed. These were days of "comparative seclusion," though she occasionally got out to visit the sick or went for short walks.

---

121. ELRD, July 30, 1904, as quoted in Carpenter, p. 102.
122. ELRD, Oct. 30, 1904, as quoted in Carpenter, p. 103.
123. ELRD, Oct. 31, 1904, as quoted in Carpenter, p. 103.
124. ELRD, Dec. 31, 1904, as quoted in Carpenter, p. 104.
125. ELR (North Chili) to "Bro. Bristol," Jan. 18, 1905. Archives, Roberts Wesleyan College.
126. ELRD, Nov. 12, 1905, as quoted in Carpenter, p. 104; Carpenter, p. 106.
127. ELRD, Jan. 1 and 3, 1906, as quoted in Carpenter, p. 105.
128. ELRD, May 22, 1906, as quoted in Carpenter, p. 105.
129. ELRD, Aug. 6, 1906, as quoted in Carpenter, p. 105.

Often friends came to visit. "Her days and nights were given to the work of prayer, in the Spirit, for her family, for the school, for the world." One day after reading Psalm 91 she said, "I saw answers to prayer coming down as thick as hailstones, and I was sure I lived to pray."[130]

On Christmas Day 1907 the Chesbrough Seminary students and teachers walked up to the Roberts home and, gathering outside Ellen's window, sang hymns to her. Ellen was cheered. She walked out on the porch and shook hands with each one, exhorting them to be true to God. A few days later she caught a "hard cold," and when someone expressed concern, given her frail health, she told the person, in effect, not to worry. "If I die *there'll be no mistake about it.*" Adella Carpenter said Ellen's "pithy sayings were never more apt and witty than during her last year, her interest in God's cause was never greater, nor her prayers more mighty."[131]

Ellen peacefully breathed her last on Tuesday, January 28, 1908, in her eighty-second year. She died at the home in North Chili that she and Benjamin had shared for a dozen years and where she lived, seldom if ever alone, for another fifteen.[132] She "had lived near heaven's border land for a long time," Adella Carpenter wrote. "Her life often seemed to me like the flickering flame of dying embers, now going, now coming, ready at any moment to cease being forever."[133] Benson said, "For her it was no great change, in a way, for she had walked with God through many of the long years of her life."[134]

It had been clear for some days that Ellen was declining and that the end was near. Many friends came to see her on Monday, the day before she died. One brother said, "Jesus is here," and Ellen replied, "*Certainly* He is."[135]

At one point during the day Ellen seemed to be staring at the ceiling.

"What do you see?" someone asked.

"I am reading," Ellen replied. She said she was "reading all that is written there." Adella Carpenter commented that "God had at other times given her messages in letters of living light, had often brought heavenly scenes before her," and thought that God was now giving her a vision.[136]

Ellen continued to weaken through the afternoon and evening and died about one o'clock Tuesday morning. Six had remained with her through the night — her son Charles and his wife Susan, Adella Carpenter, Edith Hurlburt and Anna Johnston, "the faithful helpers of many past years," and Mr. Prior. Carpenter wrote that after Ellen's passing everyone "knelt and thanked God, amid our tears, for the many years He had given her to us and consecrated ourselves anew to follow her example and her exhortations. The room was filled with heavenly peace. The Spirit

---

130. Carpenter, p. 106.
131. Carpenter, "The Home-Going," pp. 72-73.
132. Carpenter, p. 106; Hogue, *HFMC*, 2:258.
133. Carpenter, "The Home-Going," p. 72.
134. Benson H. Roberts, "My Mother," p. 69.
135. Carpenter, "The Home-Going," p. 73.
136. Carpenter, "The Home-Going," p. 73.

gave me Bunyan's words, 'The name of that chamber is Peace.'" She added, "God has made [Ellen] effectual in aiding multitudes in the way to heaven."[137]

The funeral for Ellen Lois Stowe Roberts, presumably held in Cox Hall on the Chesbrough Seminary campus, was marked by simplicity. Ellen's four surviving sons — George, Benson, Charles, and Benjamin — were present, together with Emma Sellew Roberts (who wrote an account of the funeral) and probably Charles's wife Susan. Five of the grandchildren were also present.[138]

Free Methodist ministers of the Genesee Conference bore the casket, while others walked ahead of it as it was carried into the chapel. Bishop Walter Sellew, Emma's older brother, preached on "heart wisdom" from Psalm 90:12.[139]

William Pearce and David S. Warner, both future bishops, were among the six preachers who bore the casket to the nearby cemetery. As people filtered away following the graveside ceremony, one of Ellen's granddaughters — probably Lois Ellen Roberts, Benson and Emma's daughter, who was named for her grandmother and was then twenty-five — exclaimed, "What an inheritance I have!"[140]

The March 1908 *Earnest Christian* was full of tributes to Ellen Roberts. Benson Roberts praised his mother's gentleness, wisdom, modesty, and sincerity as primary character qualities she exhibited.[141] Emma Sellew Roberts said, "Everyone who met her was impressed with the force of her personality. Her presence was felt even when she was silent, in any gathering."[142] J. T. Logan, editor of the *Free Methodist*, wrote, "Very few are privileged to see so many brought into the fold of God as the result of their labors and as the reward of their faithfulness" as Ellen Roberts was. He was sure that B. T. Roberts "never could have accomplished [his] great work" without her help, encouragement, and devotion to God. Together they labored "to extend the kingdom of Christ in the earth." Ellen, he said, had led "scores of precious souls to the Saviour" and had given them encouragement, counsel, and godly example. She loved the Free Methodist Church, keeping "in close touch with every department" and rejoicing in its growth.

> Before she was removed hence she had the gratification of knowing that there are over nine hundred preachers of the Gospel scattered here and there in this country and in foreign lands, under the auspices of the Free Methodist church, who are proclaiming Scriptural holiness, and a full, free, and present salvation to a dying world, and that there are over thirty-three thousand pilgrims with faces Zionward, battling for the right and contending against the mighty forces of evil; . . . often struggling to keep poverty's gaunt wolves from their doors.[143]

137. Carpenter, "The Home-Going," pp. 73-74.
138. Emma Sellew Roberts, "The Funeral," *EC* 95, no. 3 (Mar. 1908): 74. Emma's account simply says, "The four sons, two daughters in-law, and five grand-children were present."
139. Emma Sellew Roberts, "The Funeral," p. 74.
140. Emma Sellew Roberts, "The Funeral," p. 74.
141. Benson H. Roberts, "My Mother," p. 71.
142. Emma Sellew Roberts, in "A Chapter of Tributes," *EC* 95, no. 3 (Mar. 1908): 85.
143. J. T. Logan, "A Pilgrim Gone Home," *EC* 95, no. 3 (Mar. 1908): 76-78.

Moses Downing, who had been a colleague in pastoral and evangelistic ministry in Buffalo with Benjamin and Ellen in the early days, was convinced that Ellen's "monumental" faith and consistent influence "had more to do with the growth, spirituality and perpetuity of the Free Methodist denomination than will ever be fully known on earth."[144]

Ellen's spiritual discernment, especially with students, is a recurrent theme among those who paid tribute to her following her death. Alexander Beers wrote,

> With a keen sense of spiritual discernment she was always able to help the young Christian into a better and richer experience. This spiritual discrimination was always accompanied by thoroughness of dealing. I regard it as one of the rare privileges of my life to have been favored by having her as my class-leader when I was a student in the A. M. Chesbrough Seminary. The students looked forward to the class-meeting that was to be led by Mother Roberts. She was possessed with a marked degree of heavenly wisdom and much spiritual illumination. . . . She rarely labored with two individuals in the same way. She was quick to recognize the difference of individuality, and could see the peculiar need of each student. At times her words were as gentle as the most loving mother dealing with a discouraged child. Again, her words of reproof and rebuke would flash like lightning, and rarely failed reaching the mark and accomplishing the end. At other times the spirit of exhortation would come upon her, and she was a veritable Deborah leading on the hosts of the Lord to victory. Her counsel was greatly sought by the students and members of the faculty as well.[145]

Wilson Hogue saw Ellen Roberts as a "strong personality" and "a woman of very unusual type"; one of the church's "original and noblest lights." He called Ellen's death "a universal bereavement," the loss of "a woman of much intelligence, sound judgment, rare devotion, deep spirituality, heroic faith, invincible courage, Christlike charity, and unaffected modesty and simplicity."[146] Surely Ellen would have protested, not recognizing herself in this fulsome description. Yet it shows the wide veneration with which Ellen had come to be regarded throughout Free Methodism, particularly by those who knew her well. Bishop Walter Sellew, who knew Ellen better than most, described her as "a holy woman" who "lived for others. Her life was a continual succession of sacrifices for those with whom she was associated. . . . Time, money, conveniences, comforts, and reputation were gladly yielded up to the constantly recurring conditions in which some one must sacrifice or much good would be destroyed and lost forever."[147]

---

144. M. N. Downing, tribute to Ellen Roberts in *EC* 95, no. 3 (Mar. 1908): 87.

145. Alexander Beers, "Sister Roberts' Influence among the Students," *EC* 95, no. 3 (Mar. 1908): 80.

146. Hogue, *HFMC*, 2:258; W. T. Hogue, "A Tribute to the Memory of a Noble Woman," *EC* 95, no. 3 (Mar. 1908): 82.

147. Walter A. Sellew, tribute to Ellen Roberts in *EC* 95, no. 3 (Mar. 1908): 84.

CHAPTER 40

Legacy

"We want this church to promote the kingdom of God."

B. T. Roberts, 1890[1]

"The only way for us to hold our ground is to be as radical as we were at the beginning."

B. T. Roberts, 1890[2]

What legacy did B. T. and Ellen Roberts leave to the Free Methodist Church, and to the world?

Personal legacies may exist in many dimensions. This is the case here. This chapter surveys the Roberts legacy in terms of the Roberts family, the Free Methodist Church, and the wider human family.

The Roberts Sons and Descendants

Ellen Roberts was survived by her four grown sons and their families. The later stories of George, Benson, Charles, and Benjamin, Jr., give some of the dimensions of the Roberts inheritance. More extensive attention to Benson and Emma Roberts,

1. B. T. Roberts, sermon on Rom. 14:18, May Street Free Methodist Church, Chicago, Oct. 12, 1890, as reported by W. W. Kelley in the *General Conference Daily,* reprinted in Gerald Coates, ed., *Passion of the Founders* (Indianapolis: Light and Life Communications, 2003), p. 100.

2. BTR to W. P. Ferries, Nov. 19, 1890, quoted in BHR, *BTR,* p. 560.

who continued on in Christian ministry, will be given after a brief review of the lives and families of the other three sons.

George Lane Roberts

As noted in chapter 31, George Lane Roberts and his second wife Winifred moved from Bradford to Pittsburgh in 1895, and there George had a distinguished legal career. He practiced law in the firm of Roberts and Carter, having entered into partnership with Charles Gibbs Carter. His legal business required considerable travel; George wrote to Benson on May 7, 1901, "I returned from New York last night and go to West Virginia to-morrow morning; will be back here Saturday." In the same letter he added, "I appreciate what you have been doing for Hibbert and hope to be able to reciprocate in the near future."[3] George's son Hibbert, then about twenty-three, had been a student at Chesbrough Seminary.

After nine years in the firm of Roberts and Carter and three years of private practice, in 1907 George became general counsel of the Oil Well Supply Company, Pittsburgh, which eventually became a part of U.S. Steel. He held this position, as well as continuing as general attorney of the Buffalo, Rochester, and Pittsburgh Railroad Company, until his death.[4] The *Pittsburgh Press* noted that George "practiced law here until his death in the state, superior and county courts. He was a member of the United States, Pennsylvania and Allegheny County bar associations, a member of the University club and the Oakmont Country club."[5] George was described in a contemporary book, *Memoirs of Allegheny County*, as "a distinguished attorney" and a member also of the West Virginia bar, since he devoted "a considerable part of his time to practice in that State." This source says George was at the time also president of the Bradford, Bordell and Kinzua railway company.[6]

George Lane Roberts died of pneumonia on February 27, 1924, at the age of seventy-two — "quite well off," according to Smail. He was buried with the Roberts family in North Chili. Winifred had died two years earlier.[7] It appears that in his later years George became an Episcopalian; whether he ever came to a vital Christian faith is uncertain.

George Roberts was survived by his only son, Hibbert Rice Roberts, who, as noted earlier, lived with B. T. and Ellen Roberts after his mother died. Hibbert sur-

3. GLR (Bradford, Pa.) to BHR (North Chili), June 15, 1894; GLR (Pittsburgh) to BHR, May 7, 1901. By the early 1890s George had begun to use a typewriter. George made repeated visits to Sisterville, W.Va. (on the Ohio River, across from the state of Ohio, about fifty miles south of Wheeling). No doubt he was doing legal work for a company that had operations there.

4. Smail, pp. 14-15; Alumni Record of George Lane Roberts, University of Rochester Library.

5. "George L. Roberts," *Pittsburgh Press*, Feb. 28, 1924.

6. *Memoirs of Allegheny County*, pp. 116-17. Photocopy provided by Carnegie Library of Pittsburgh, August 2001.

7. Smail, pp. 14-15.

vived his father by only eight years, dying in 1932 at the age of about fifty-four. He studied medicine, apparently in Rochester, and had a successful medical practice in Rochester.[8] Hibbert was married three times. His first wife, Annie, died without children, and he later married Nellie Luescher, a divorcée. To this union was born one son, George Lane Roberts (1908-60), who became a stockbroker. He was married, but it is unclear whether he and his wife had any children.[9]

According to Smail, Hibbert and Nellie eventually divorced, and he remarried. His third wife was a nurse whose last name was Jones. They had one son, Hibbert Rice Roberts, Jr., who received an M.A. from Cornell and became a teacher in western New York State. Hibbert Rice Roberts, Sr., reportedly died in Los Angeles.[10]

Charles Stowe Roberts

At the time of B. T.'s death, Charles and Susan Roberts were living in Morgan Park, south of Chicago, where Charles was engaged in business. Their two sons, Lowden and Charles, were ten and eight. Charles and his family later moved back to Rochester, where he was employed as a buyer for the Curtice Brothers fruit-preserving company.[11]

Benjamin Titus Roberts, Jr.

Benja and his wife Sara were also living in Morgan Park, Illinois, at the time of B. T. Roberts's death. Their only child, Dorothy, was born just four months before B. T. died. After graduating from the Chicago Homeopathic Medical College in 1896, Benja completed a second medical degree at Rush Medical College in 1899. He practiced medicine for a number of years but, in yet another manifestation of the Roberts family entrepreneurial flair, went into a cosmetics business partnership with C. A. Reed of Oak Park. Eventually he became president of Illinois Cosmetics Company of Chicago, making his home in Oak Park.[12] Sara died in 1934 and Benjamin, Jr., in 1950; they are buried in Forest Home Cemetery, Forest Park, Illinois, along the

---

8. Smail says, "Hibbert Roberts received a good medical education, largely thru his own efforts because of an unsympathetic step-mother" (p. 16). He apparently means that George's second wife, Winifred (whom George married when Hibbert was nine), did not support Hibbert's medical education financially. It does not appear that Hibbert lived with his father and stepmother after his father remarried.

9. According to Smail's research; Smail, p. 16.

10. Smail, pp. 16, 19.

11. Smail, pp. 15-16; cf. Howard C. Hosmer, *Monroe County (1821-1971): The Sesqui-Centennial Account of the History of Monroe County, New York* (Rochester, N.Y.: Rochester Museum and Science Center, 1971), p. 116.

12. Smail, p. 16.

Des Plaines River, west of Chicago.[13] Benja lived longest of the Roberts brothers; he was eighty-six when he died.

Dorothy Roberts, Benja and Sara's daughter, became a high school language teacher. In 1919 she married Elmer S. Smail, also an educator, who in the 1950s compiled the important genealogical collection, "Forebears of Some Roberts Cousins."[14]

Benson and Emma Roberts

By the time Ellen Roberts died in 1908, Benson and Emma Roberts were no longer living in North Chili. They gave up their work as coprincipals of Chesbrough Seminary, and he his editorship of the *Earnest Christian,* in 1906, though Emma continued for a time to edit the *Missionary Tidings.* Benson and Emma moved to Pittsburgh, where they managed the Christian Home for Girls beginning in January 1907. They lived at the home, 424 Du Quesne Way.[15]

It seemed like a strange career move for B. T. Roberts's son and heir, and for Emma. Why they made the move, and what his mother thought of it, is not entirely clear. Presumably Benson and Emma might well have continued in their key roles for many more years. Neil Pfouts, in his history of Roberts Wesleyan College, says only that "In 1906, Benson H. Roberts resigned the Principalship, after having given twenty-five years of service to the Seminary." Benson's resignation included that of Emma as well, as coprincipal. Pfouts also notes that "In 1905 Free High Schools in the State of New York began to cut down on the Seminary's registration. The Trustees became concerned that the State requirements were increasing, and that there was a great need for improved equipment for Science if the Seminary was to retain its standing with the Board of Regents." This may have been a factor in Benson's decision, though the difficulty was not an insurmountable one. The school survived, with increasing enrollments.[16]

Behind Benson and Emma's leaving lay, it seems, some disagreement and conflict over the direction the school should take. One source, based on conversations

---

13. The grave is in Section 57, Lot No. 284, in Forest Home Cemetery, 863 S. Des Plaines Avenue, Forest Park.

14. Smail, p. 16.

15. The Emma Sellew file, Oberlin College Archives, contains an announcement card in Old English script that reads: "The Christian Home for Girls Founded by reason of faith in God and love for humanity through the efforts of Edward M. Sandys [in] 1895 — Rev. Benson Howard Roberts, A.M.[,] Mrs. Emma Sellew Roberts, A.M. announce that they have accepted the office of Managers by request of the Founder and by vote of the Board of Directors[,] January, 1907 — Pittsburg, Pa. 424 Du Quesne Way." Sandys, a Free Methodist preacher in the Pittsburgh Conference, founded the Providence Mission and Rescue Home (originally called Hope Mission) in 1895 (Hogue, *HFMC* 2:72, 78). The Christian Home for Girls developed from the ministry of the Providence Mission and Rescue Home.

16. Neil E. Pfouts, *A History of Roberts Wesleyan College* (North Chili, N.Y.: Roberts Wesleyan College, 2000), pp. 42-43, 51, 59.

with Benson and Emma's grandchildren, says Benson "was dismissed by the [semi-nary's] Board of Trustees. A breach between the Free Methodist Church and the Roberts family occurred at that time which has never been healed."[17] This is not en-tirely accurate, for Benson and Emma continued to maintain contact with Free Methodists. Benson was still a corresponding editor for the *Earnest Christian* during its final year (1909); both he and Emma contributed articles. And Emma wrote some articles for the *Missionary Tidings*. Benson continued his membership in the Genesee Conference of the Free Methodist Church until 1919.

Over time, however, Benson and Emma did have less and less contact with Free Methodists as their lives followed a different path. In the twentieth century, Roberts Wesleyan College reestablished contact with many of the Roberts descendants.

Benson and Emma served the Christian Home for Girls for a little over four years. In January 1908 Emma received a letter from a puzzled editor at Oberlin Col-lege who was working on the seventy-fifth anniversary *General Catalogue of Oberlin College, 1833-1908*. Emma had submitted an information form in which she had listed both her and Benson's employment at Chesbrough Seminary and then at the Christian Home for Girls. The editor read her report and said it appeared to him "that some of the entries must refer to Mr. Roberts rather than yourself. For in-stance, the report states that Mr. Roberts was principal of the A. M. Chesbrough Seminary, while in another part of the report it states that you occupied this posi-tion" — and similarly with regard to the management of the Christian Home. Emma patiently penned an explanation at the bottom of the letter and mailed it back: "Mr. Roberts and I were joint Principals of the A. M. Chesbrough Seminary and are both Managers of the Christian home. You will find full account of Mr. Roberts' work in 'Who's Who in America' and some reports of mine in 'Who's Who in N.Y. State.'"[18]

In 1911 Benson accepted the pastorate of the nondenominational Church of Christ, Union, in Berea, Kentucky, the campus church at Berea College. He and Emma had a fruitful eight-year ministry in Berea. During his tenure church mem-bership grew from 596 to 941. Benson received a salary of $1,400 in 1912 and a little over $1,600 in 1918 (half paid by the college). Emma was active in the church's minis-tries, serving variously as president of the Women's Christian Association "for be-nevolent and religious work" and leading services at Hart's Settlement, part of Union Church's "outlying work."[19] Her obituary noted that she "taught in the col-lege and was active in missionary work among the mountaineers."[20]

At Berea Benson worked to strengthen the sometimes strained relations be-tween the church and town and the college. The campus community appreciated

17. Jean R. Heath, "Memories of the Roberts Family Reunion," June 4, 1980 (photocopy of one typed page), Roberts Wesleyan College Archives.

18. L. D. Harkness to Mrs. Benson H. Roberts, Dec. 29, 1908 (typewritten), with Emma Sellew Roberts's signed note at the bottom. Emma Sellew Roberts Alumni Record, Oberlin College.

19. *Annual Report of the Church of Christ, Union at Berea, Kentucky* for the years 1911 through 1919. Published by Berea College Press, Berea, Ky.

20. Obituary of Emma Sellew Roberts, *FM* 64, no. 13 (Mar. 27, 1931): 14.

Benson's ministry, and Berea College gave him an honorary doctor of divinity degree in 1912. Emma served for a time as a member of the Council of Dean of Women at the college.[21] The president of Berea College during this time was William Goodell Frost, son-in-law as well as namesake of the noted abolitionist William Goodell. When President Frost learned of Benson's resignation from the Union Church pastorate, he wrote to him appreciatively, "I wish you to know that I consider Mrs. Frost and I have greatly profited from your ministry. I have never heard you preach without personal benefit and satisfaction, and beside this we have much enjoyed the friendship and social intercourse with yourself and Mrs. Roberts. Should it be that you do not take other pastoral charge, we would be very happy if you should decide to make Berea an abiding place so that we might be neighbors for the coming years."[22]

In 1919 Benson, at sixty-five, was ready for a new venture. Benson and Emma's second daughter, Lucy George Roberts (who never married), had taught Latin and Greek for some years at Wells and Vassar Colleges after graduating from Mount Holyoke and receiving a Ph.D. from the University of Wisconsin. Out of conversations among Lucy, Benson, Emma, and Lucy's friend and University of Wisconsin colleague Dr. Sarah Morehouse Beach came the Roberts-Beach School for Girls, which opened in 1920 at Catonsville, Maryland, a suburb of Baltimore. The partners acquired a ten-acre estate including a "spacious house with every modern convenience." The school was a success, and Benson served on the faculty until his death in 1930.[23] A photo from the 1920s shows about fifty female students, dressed in white, and their professors arrayed on the front lawn of the Roberts-Beach School.[24]

Benson pastored Presbyterian congregations in the Baltimore area during his time at the Roberts-Beach School. He served the Fallston and Franklinville Presbyterian Church, 1920-22, and the Presbyterian Church at Relay from 1922 until November 1929.[25] Benson's connection with the Presbyterian Church occasioned the break-

21. *Historical Register of the Officers and Students of Berea College from the Beginning to June, 1915* (Berea, Ky.: Berea College, 1916), pp. 30, 50.

22. President William Goodell Frost to BHR, June 14, 1919 (unsigned carbon copy of typed letter), William Goodell Frost Papers, Historical Collections, Berea College. Frost was president of Berea College from 1892 to 1920.

23. Smail, p. 15; "The Roberts-Beach School" (promotional flyer, 1920), Alumni Record of Benson Howard Roberts, University of Rochester. Benson filled out the 1920 "Biographical Record of Graduates and Former Students" form for the University of Rochester. In a later update (Mar. 22, 1923) Benson noted: "1920 Cooperated in establishing Roberts-Beach School — college preparatory school for girls at Catonsville Md., suburb of Baltimore." The school acquired Kenwood, formerly the summer home of John Gill (Baltimore County Public Library Historic Collection Development Project [http://www.bcplonline.org/archive/hcdg3/html], accessed July 12, 2001).

24. Baltimore County Public Library Historic Collection Development Project (http://www.bcplonline.org/archive/hcdg3/html), accessed July 12, 2001.

25. Biographical Record of Graduates and Former Students 1920, University of Rochester, filled out by Benson Howard Roberts. Alumni Records, University of Rochester; Alumni Records for Benson Howard Roberts, Dartmouth College Library.

ing of his last formal tie to the Free Methodist Church. He had kept his Free Methodist membership during his ministry in Pittsburgh and at the Union Church in Berea. When he left Berea for Maryland in 1919, he requested a letter of good standing from the Genesee Conference of the Free Methodist Church, where he was a member. The 1919 minutes show that Benson was "given [a] letter of dismissal to the Presbyterian Church," and on January 22, 1920, he was received into the Presbytery of Baltimore.[26]

Benson died peacefully at his Catonsville home on March 3, 1930, at age seventy-seven, and Emma died less than a year later. Both were interred with other Roberts family members in North Chili. They were survived by their two daughters, Lois Ellen and Lucy George, and their son Ashbel Sellew Roberts. Their first child, Howard Passmore, died as a child (as previously noted), and Edwin, their youngest, serving in the U.S. Navy in World War I, died of influenza at the Great Lakes Naval Station near Chicago in 1918. Lois, a 1904 graduate of Mount Holyoke, married Henry McLellan Hallett; the couple had three children. Smail described her as "an Episcopalian."[27]

Ashbel Sellew Roberts graduated from Cornell in 1910 and completed a Ph.D. at Harvard in 1922. He was professor and head of the history department at Kent State Normal College in Kent, Ohio. With Theodore Calvin Pease of the University of Illinois, he coedited and in 1928 published *Selected Readings in American History* (enlarged edition, 1940), a book referred to earlier (chapter 35) for its references to the Farmers' Alliance. Benson noted proudly in his 1929 class report to Dartmouth, "In Dec. I received a copy of 'Select[ed] Readings in American History, by Pease and Roberts', — Sellew Roberts, Ph.D., Head of History Department in State College for Teachers at Kent, O., — a substantial volume of 800 pages, a compilation of charters, writs, constitutions, proclamations, from 1584 . . . to Coolidge and McNary-Haugen Bill of 1928. Naturally I am pleased to have my son enter the circle of writers."[28]

Memorial tributes to Benson and Emma were effusive. Rev. L. A. Sager wrote of Emma in the *Free Methodist:* "She was always interested in the advancement of women. Her interest in missions centered in India because of the child widows, several of whom she educated at Chili. A worker for suffrage, for prohibition, a believer in peace, a lover of all God's children, her influence was wide and deep as well as lasting."[29] At Benson's funeral in Catonsville the Reverend John Nesbitt, a colleague in the Presbytery of Baltimore, said Dr. Roberts's life "had in it extraordinary variety but very genuine symmetry." The "central thread" in Benson's life, he said, was his vocation as a Christian minister. "His life was energized by that noblest of purposes,

---

26. *Minutes,* Genesee Conference, Free Methodist Church, 1919; "Death of Rev. Benson H. Roberts, D.D.," *Presbyterian* (1930) (Photocopy, Presbyterian Historical Center, Philadelphia). Genesee Conference minutes during this period list Benson first as supernumerary, then as "supplying college church, Berea, Kentucky."

27. Smail, pp. 15, 17, 176; Alumni Records of Benson Howard Roberts, Dartmouth College Library.

28. Alumni Records for Benson Howard Roberts, Dartmouth College Library.

29. L. A. Sager, obituary of Emma Sellew Roberts, *FM* 64, no. 13 (Mar. 27, 1931): 14.

namely, to make vital Christian thinking and Christian living through the Church, the school and the home. His was a full-rounded life. He gave his life in youth to the Master and behold! how our Lord multiplied it, and enlarged it, and extended it."[30]

Benson and Emma were fondly remembered and their lives and influence celebrated by many Free Methodists, especially those who had been their students at Chesbrough. When Benson died, a large funeral service was held in North Chili after the brief service in Catonsville. George Washington Garlock, then president of the seminary and a Chesbrough student during Benson's administration, led the service.[31] In a tribute in the *Free Methodist* Adam Kress, a Latin scholar under Benson and later his longtime secretary at Chesbrough, wrote:

> A well-proportioned physique, a princely intellect, a tender heart, and . . . a touch of aristocracy that was innate rather than affected, combined to make [Benson Roberts] a forceful personality. His scholarship was deep and varied, and his discriminating command of the English language in the classroom, on the chapel platform, or editorially, was fascinating and instructive. He possessed instinctively and culturally the schoolmaster's characteristics, and his ability to impart knowledge made him a charming and inspiring teacher. He could make the poets of ancient Rome pulsate with life, and felt equally at ease in marshaling the kings of Israel and Judah before his class with a realism that made them appear like modern contemporaries. . . . What Thomas Arnold, the famous Headmaster of Rugby, was to that institution, Benson Roberts was to Chesbrough. . . . [He] laid emphasis on Christian character as the goal of all true education. This educational ideal, of which he and his coworkers were such worthy exponents, found its verbal expression in his self-originated phrase, "Education for Character." While this has since become the oft-repeated motto expressive of the educational aim of our denominational schools, its origin may not have been so generally known among us.[32]

The legacy of Benjamin and Ellen Roberts thus includes this array of sons and other descendants — intelligent, educated, self-directed men and women, several of whom became educators, attorneys, physicians, or businesspeople. Interestingly, nearly all of them exhibited in one way or another the Roberts entrepreneurial flair. Yet none remained active in the Free Methodist Church. Of all the Roberts children, Benson most nearly resembled his father and most fully embodied his legacy.

---

30. Memorial Tribute to Benson Howard Roberts, "Prepared by the Women's Bible Class of Catonsville Presbyterian Church . . . as a Memorial Tribute to Dr. Roberts and as an Expression of Sympathy and Affection for Their Beloved Teacher Mrs. Emma Sellew Roberts." Oberlin College Archives.

31. Obituary of Benson Howard Roberts, *FM* 63, no. 16 (Apr. 18, 1930).

32. C. Adam Kress, "Benson Howard Roberts, A.M., D.D.," *FM* 63, no. 16 (Apr. 18, 1930).

The Free Methodist Church after the Death of Ellen Roberts

Surviving her husband by fifteen years, Ellen Roberts witnessed significant developments as the denomination grew and changed. Her life spanned nearly the first half-century of Free Methodism.

Denominational growth was not very impressive after the Roberts era, at least in North America. The mission work, in which Ellen had special interest, continued to make steady gains, however.

When Ellen died in 1908, there were 33,598 Free Methodists in North America (United States and Canada). Local churches numbered 1,214. There were 39 annual conferences, 36 in the United States and 3 in Canada. The average Free Methodist church had about 28 members, but since attendance typically ran twice to three times membership, average worship attendance was probably around 60. Over 43,000 were enrolled in Sunday schools.[33]

Thirty years later, in 1938, the denomination had grown to only 37,740. By 1950 North American membership had reached 51,585, and at its centennial in 1960 the church had about 58,000 members. Total U.S. membership in 2006 stood at about 76,000.[34]

In 1908, growth outside North America was progressing slowly but steadily, laying the foundation for dramatic growth later. The Free Methodist Church then had mission work in India, Japan, China, Ceylon, the Dominican Republic, and several places in Africa, and had 76 foreign missionaries (45 of them women). The 1908 minutes show a total membership in Africa, India, Japan, and China of 1,345.[35] However, a decade later that number had more than doubled to 3,130; the number, adding in members in the Dominican Republic, was 3,296. In 1949, at the time of the Communist takeover in China, Free Methodist membership outside North America totaled 16,365, including 2,849 Chinese. Free Methodists now had work in Brazil, Paraguay, and the Philippines in addition to Africa, India, China, and the Dominican Republic. In 1949 the Free Methodist Church had 198 missionaries, 163 in active service on the field and 35 on furlough.[36]

The Woman's Foreign Missionary Society had nearly 7,000 members in 1908 — an impressive number, amounting to more than 20 percent of total denominational membership.[37] For the better part of a century after Ellen Roberts's death, this group

---

33. *Annual Minutes,* Free Methodist Church, 1908, pp. 310-11. At this time the denomination did not publish worship attendance figures.

34. *Annual Minutes* and *Yearbooks,* Free Methodist Church of North America, 1938, 1950, 1960, 2005.

35. *Annual Minutes,* Free Methodist Church, 1908, p. 357. Numbers for other countries are not given.

36. *Annual Minutes,* Free Methodist Church, 1949, pp. 380, 392. In addition, in North America, there was home mission work in Mexico, the Kentucky mountains, and among Indians in Colorado and Hispanics in Tampa, Fla.

37. *Annual Minutes,* Free Methodist Church, 1908, pp. 310, 368.

(later called the Woman's Missionary Society, now Women's Ministries International) played a key role in fostering missions interest throughout the denomination and in supporting the work by prayer and financial giving. This was an important part of the legacy of Ellen Roberts.

Membership growth, of course, tells only part of the story. In a way that is true perhaps of few denominations (though some parallels with the Moravian Brethren come to mind), the Free Methodist Church has had an influence all out of proportion to its size. Roberts himself noted this in a sort of valedictory sermon he preached at the 1890 FM General Conference, about two and a half years before he died. He preached on Sunday morning, October 12, on Romans 14:17-18, a favorite John Wesley text: "For the kingdom of God is not meat and drink; but righteousness, and peace, and joy in the Holy Ghost. For he that in these things serveth Christ is acceptable to God, and approved of men."

Picking up on the phrase "approved of men" as he concluded his sermon, Roberts spoke of the impact Free Methodist witness was having beyond itself, among other church traditions. Partly this influence came through the circulation of the *Earnest Christian*. Roberts told of a Presbyterian elder whose father was spiritually renewed through reading the paper and whose sister in Mobile, Alabama, took courage to give public witness to her faith even though women speaking in church was not considered proper. "You are doing a great deal more through your influence on other denominations than in your own," this Presbyterian said to Roberts.

The man was right, Roberts suggested. He concluded his message:

We are doing much more in our influence on other churches, than we think. I remember when we started as a church, there was hardly such a thing as a free church in any of our large cities at the east. Soon after I began publishing the "Earnest Christian," there was an appeal in a New England paper for a free church in Boston. I read it over and found that nearly every word of it was from the "Earnest Christian."

The Free Methodists are exerting a tremendous influence on other denominations. If we stick to these principles, and have the joy of the Holy Ghost, you need not stop to answer those that oppose you. You will triumph over all opposition, you will see the kingdom of God built up. We want this church to promote the kingdom of God. I want the King to come in His beauty, but I want just as many as possible prepared for His coming. O God, give us this religion in all its fullness, for Jesus' sake. Amen.[38]

Wilson Hogue picked up the same theme at the end of his 1915 *History of the Free Methodist Church.* Hogue pointed out that Free Methodists were "the first distinctively Holiness Church organized in the United States" and that the *Earnest Christian* in its beginning was "the only publication in this country devoted explic-

---

38. B. T. Roberts, sermon on Rom. 14:18, May Street Free Methodist Church, Chicago, Oct. 12, 1890, in Coates, *Passion of the Founders,* p. 100.

itly to promoting the work of holiness" except for Phoebe Palmer's *Guide to Holiness*. Hogue traced ongoing Free Methodist influence on the Methodist Episcopal Church and other denominations. He noted Dwight L. Moody's baptism with the Holy Spirit through the witness of two Free Methodist women in Chicago; the Free Methodist role in the origins of Jerry McAuley's mission to the poor in New York City; and Free Methodist influence through educational and philanthropic enterprises.[39] History shows clearly that the long legacy of Free Methodist urban ministry traces to the lives and vision of B. T. and Ellen Roberts. There is a direct line of connection, not only through Roberts's writing and his and Ellen's example but also through chains of personal relationship, between the early city ministry of B. T. and Ellen in Buffalo in 1852-53 and 1860-65 and urban ministries in the Free Methodist Church today.

Free Methodists never considered their denomination to be *the* church in an exclusive sense and showed some ambivalence at times, as we have seen, even as to whether the denomination was *a* church, as distinct from a "connection" or "movement" or simply a "band" of pilgrims. Bishop L. R. Marston argued in 1960, perceptively, that the Free Methodist Church never really fit the sect/church typology of Ernst Troeltsch, H. Richard Niebuhr, and others: "Free Methodism, as practically every religious movement, was more concerned with its differences from other groups in its earlier than in its later history. Accordingly it partook more of the nature of the sect-type then than it does now when the church seeks a basis of agreement with other groups within the evangelical family. But even in the beginning it was not fully the sect-type. This is suggested by its early deep concern for social, economic, and political issues."[40]

Free Methodism's concern for liberal arts education underscores the same point. Marston added, "Probably all will agree that during [its first] century the Free Methodist Church has moved farther from the sect-type and nearer the church-type."[41]

This shift can be documented in many ways. One of the clearest evidences is the gradual move away from a specific focus on the gospel to the poor. As noted in earlier chapters, even at the beginning not all Free Methodist leaders were fully in sympathy with this central focus of B. T. and Ellen Roberts. Yet this commitment marked the ethos of the denomination throughout B. T. Roberts's lifetime and even beyond, despite some gradual erosion.

A 1927 denominational pamphlet entitled *The WHAT and the WHY of Free Methodism* testifies to a move away from an explicit commitment to the poor. The

39. Hogue, *HFMC*, concluding chapter, "Influence of the Free Methodist Church beyond the Pale of Its Own Communion," 2:354-65.

40. Marston, p. 566. In the 1940s Marston was one of the founders of the National Association of Evangelicals. See *Evangelical Action! A Report of the Organization of the National Association of Evangelicals for United Action*, compiled and edited by the Executive Committee (Boston: United Action Press, 1942).

41. Marston, p. 567.

pamphlet shifts the emphasis from the poor to "all people." It asks: "What did the leaders of the church in its beginning conceive to be the mission of the Free Methodist Church?" Claiming (somewhat misleadingly) to base its answer on "articles published in the *Earnest Christian* for 1860," the pamphlet states:

> [T]he mission of the Free Methodist Church, negatively considered, was not to
> 1. Aim at numerical enlargement.
> 2. Not one of ecclesiastical rivalry.
> 3. Not comprehended in the idea of carnal warfare.
>
> On the contrary, it was to
> 1. Exemplify an earnest, practical, saving Christianity among its own membership.
> 2. To publish an unmutilated gospel to others.
> 3. To seek the salvation of all classes.
> 4. Specifically, "to spread scriptural holiness over these lands."[42]

Here, in an apparently intentional move, the specific emphasis on the poor drops out — even at a time when Free Methodists still clustered toward the lower end of the socioeconomic scale and counted very few wealthy persons among them.

The current denominational mission statement reads: "The mission of the Free Methodist Church is to make known to all people everywhere God's call to wholeness through forgiveness and holiness in Jesus Christ, and to invite into membership and to equip for ministry all who respond in faith."[43] Here the words "all people everywhere" replace the earlier focus on the poor. The 1974 *Discipline* consigned the original statement that included reference to the mission of preaching the gospel to the poor to a historical section at the end and replaced it with a new introductory section. Yet many Free Methodists and FM ministries continue to stress and to embody this concern, and the last decade or so has witnessed some resurgence of this central Free Methodist passion and charism.

Roberts's Parchments Restored

Two years after Ellen's passing, and ten years after Benson Roberts published his biography of B. T., the Genesee Conference of the Methodist Episcopal Church decided it was time to right an old wrong. The year was 1910 — just over half a century

---

42. Executive Committee of the Free Methodist Church, *The WHAT and the WHY of Free Methodism* (Chicago: Free Methodist Publishing House, 1927), pp. 30-31. The thirty-two-page pamphlet begins with sections reprinted from the Free Methodist *Discipline,* including the introductory section that affirms "preaching Gospel to the poor." Though it claims this statement of mission comes from articles in the *Earnest Christian* in 1860, these points come directly from A. A. Phelps's February 1861 *Earnest Christian* article, "Mission of the Free Methodist Church," not from Roberts. By "an unmutilated Gospel" Phelps meant, he said, "the *anti-slavery* Gospel," among other things.

43. *Yearbook 2005*, p. 2.

since B. T.'s expulsion, and the centennial year of the Genesee Conference. Meeting in Silver Lake, New York, the conference (as L. R. Marston later wrote) "acknowledged error and did what it could to make amends."[44]

Benson Roberts was invited to attend the conference sessions as a fraternal delegate, representing both B. T. and the denomination he founded. In a gracious address he stated, "The child of fifty years, begotten amid the stress and storm of divided opinion and stern antagonisms, of reluctant parentage, greets to-day the mother who has attained the century mark."[45]

Dr. Ray Allen, Genesee Conference secretary and historian, gave an evenhanded review of the events leading to Roberts's expulsion and the formation of the new denomination. The trials and expulsions, Allen said, "might have seemed necessary at the time, but looked at half a century later" they seem "unjust, and therefore exceedingly unwise. Those expelled brethren were among the best men the Conference contained, and scarce anyone thought otherwise even then." Allen noted that the ME General Conference of 1860 "failed to right the wrong, and in the most conspicuous case [that of B. T. Roberts] did not get far enough even to entertain the appeal, because of a technicality."[46] Allen included this assessment as part of his "Historical Sketch of the Genesee Conference" with which he began his book *A Century of the Genesee Annual Conference of the Methodist Episcopal Church.*[47]

Following his address, Allen delivered Roberts's yellowing ordination parchments into the hands of Benson. On the previous day the conference had "voted unanimously and with general applause" to take this action.[48] The credentials of other preachers similarly expelled were also restored.

Wilson Hogue described Benson's address as "dignified, scholarly, eloquent and fearless, yet withal a gentlemanly and convincing justification of the position of his father and others who had been expelled in 1858 and 1859. At the close of the address the members of the Conference were generally bathed in tears, and numerous old-time responses of Amen and Hallelujah were heard."[49] In his address Benson noted the common heritage and common call to mission that rested upon both denominations. Benson — the educator and scholar — said, "The church to-day needs men who know God. The contest is between an intellectual and a spiritual religion, between a religion that is a result of a syllogism and a religion that is a result of experience."[50]

---

44. Marston, p. 246. Cf. Zahniser. pp. 344-46; Hogue, *HFMC,* 2:204.

45. Marston, p. 583.

46. Marston, p. 247.

47. Ray Allen, *A Century of the Genesee Annual Conference of the Methodist Episcopal Church, 1810-1910* (Rochester, N.Y.: By the Author, 1911), pp. 9-10.

48. Report in *FM* (Oct. 11, 1910), quoted in Marston, p. 583.

49. Hogue, *HFMC,* 2:204.

50. Marston, p. 584.

Personal Reflection: An Argument with B. T. Roberts

As this book was being written, five portraits of Benjamin Titus Roberts and three of Ellen Lois Stowe Roberts decorated the space above my computer. Drawn, painted, or photographed at different periods in their lives, the visual and documentary record of B. T. and Ellen Roberts transformed these two almost into living presences to the author. I came to admire them, the more so as I got to know them better with all their strengths and weaknesses, passions and prejudices — above all, their earnestness and integrity in seeking to follow Jesus Christ faithfully.

How does a biographer assess his or her subjects — their lives, theology, and legacy — finally, at the end of this journey? In the case of the Robertses, questions arise. Was B. T. really as "symmetrical" as those who knew him well claimed? Was Ellen an admirable model and mother for Free Methodists?

Actually my admiration for Benjamin and Ellen Roberts grew the more I got to know them. They were remarkable, godly people, sold out to God and for his kingdom. The qualities I most appreciate about B. T. Roberts are his Christ-centered, populist biblicism, his integrity, his courage, his discipline, his skill with language — above all, his compassion. Symmetry, yes, especially in terms of character and learning.[51]

Still, I have some questions for B. T. Roberts.

Benjamin was nothing if not earnest. But can one be too earnest? Does earnestness in Christian faith lead to unhealthy self-preoccupation; to a focus on one's own spiritual state, rather than God? Does it feed an obsessive tendency to look inward rather than outward? Does it put too much emphasis on personal religious experience? Do we, in fact, see these tendencies in B. T. and Ellen Roberts?

I do not fault Roberts's earnestness. "Earnest Christianity" is a wonderful phrase and goal, especially as Roberts meant and understood it. One would hope only, then or now, that it means an earnest focus primarily on Jesus Christ and his reign as biblically revealed, without becoming too preoccupied with one's own emotional or behavioral experience of that reality. Yet the opposite danger is always present: focusing so explicitly on the "objective" gospel that we miss the essential biblical (and specifically Wesleyan) emphasis on personal appropriation by faith of the presence of Jesus Christ and the power of the Holy Spirit in our lives.

B. T. Roberts strove to be symmetrical here. Yet he and his movement were explicitly a reaction, intentionally a corrective, to where Methodism clearly was headed in the 1850s. It is hard to launch, and even harder to maintain, a symmetrical correction; a balanced renewal.

This leads to some more specific questions:

---

51. If Roberts's radical populist biblicism seems more "eccentric" than "symmetrical" today, that perhaps says more about North American Christianity than about either the Bible or Roberts's theology.

- Did Roberts overemphasize manifestations of the Spirit, such as shouting, vocal amens, and being slain in the Spirit, as evidence of the vitality of the church?
- Roberts knew enough history to understand that the life and experience of the church have varied considerably over centuries. Did he however idealize the revivals of Finney's day, making them too much a model for the church in all ages? Relatedly, how deeply did he really understand early Methodism?
- As Roberts often pointed out, the Bible is explicit about simplicity and plainness of dress, especially for women. On the other hand, the New Testament is explicit also in places about women not speaking in church — yet Roberts argued that these passages reflected particular cultural circumstances and were superseded by broader biblical truths. Perhaps Roberts put too much emphasis on dress and adornment, not allowing enough for cultural factors and innocent shifts in styles.
- Why did Roberts almost invariably equate wealth and any lack of austere plainness in dress with pride? Does this hold up logically, and in practice? Couldn't earnest Christians simply adapt to some degree to changing styles without this necessarily being a sign of pride, or of unfaithful compromise with the world?
- Was the issue of secret societies really as important as Roberts made it out to be? Did B. T. perhaps acquire a prejudice in this area due to his early experiences — one that in fact colored and narrowed his reform vision?
- What did Roberts think about the fact that the Free Methodist Church did not follow his lead in some areas, particularly ministry to the poor and the rights of women?

Actually it is pretty clear how Roberts would respond to most of these questions. And I have great sympathy with the impulse behind his concerns. Yet these remain issues — perhaps blind spots — in Roberts's theology. Perhaps if he had applied some of the same rational common sense and biblical argumentation to issues of dress, entertainment, music, and the nature of the church that he did to women's ordination, his theology and insights would be even more relevant today. It seems to me that the specific scope of Roberts's theology was sometimes too narrow, even though his essential vision was comprehensive. His concerns were right and vital, but he often applied key biblical truths rather narrowly to the individual experience of holiness, missing the larger context and reach of application of God's truth. Yet at other times he clearly transcended this.

In other words Roberts, like everyone, reflected his particular experience and cultural context. So the task, as always, is sorting out the ever-abiding from the culturally shifting.

The Free Methodist Church is approaching a century and a half of existence. It is almost twice as old as the Methodist Episcopal Church was when the Free Methodist Church was formed in 1860. It has remained relatively free of divisive disputes over doctrine or polity — though unable to unite with like-minded sister denominations such as the Wesleyan Methodists (now Wesleyan Church) or the Nazarenes.

The Free Methodist Church is part of the not unambiguous legacy of the life and ministry of Benjamin and Ellen Roberts. But that legacy, which here and there continues to stir the global church, is broader than the denomination B. T. Roberts was instrumental in founding. The legacy belongs now to the whole church.

In retrospect, B. T. Roberts's commitment to "maintain the Bible standard of Christianity, and to preach the Gospel to the poor" is more profound than may at first be obvious. Theology must not merely be "biblical" in some general sense; the church is to live "the Bible standard." Roberts's biblical radicalism is central to his whole project. If the church is faithful to the Bible standard, it will indeed preach the gospel to the poor — because biblical faithfulness is a matter of life and mission, not just of correct theology or right belief. Faith without works is dead, and theology without mission to the poor is a betrayal.

The whole history of nineteenth-century Methodist (and in fact American) theology underscores the significance of Roberts's shift in emphasis from "spreading scriptural holiness" to maintaining "the Bible standard of Christianity." Roberts was concerned not solely with scriptural holiness; he wanted to anchor the whole Christian project in Scripture, with central focus on the life, mission, and ethics of Jesus Christ (Roberts's hermeneutical key) and the power and present operation of the Holy Spirit.

When Roberts preached Christ to the urban poor, he understood himself to be maintaining the Bible standard of Christianity. When he advocated holy, ethical living and the avoidance of "popular fashions," he was trying to maintain the Bible standard. When he denounced secret societies and pew rents, he saw this as maintaining the Bible standard. When he defended farmers' rights and supported women's equality, here too he understood himself to be upholding "the Bible standard of Christianity and preaching the Gospel to the poor." It was all of one piece. Whether he was always right on specific applications or not, he was clear on his first and underlying principles. And those are still prophetic.

Theologically, Roberts's biblical radicalism, populism, and "biblical experientialism" (Noll's term for Wesley's theology) are thus more crucial than they may at first seem. As a theological and intellectual project, the Free Methodist Church through Roberts's influence was set on a path that steered it away from the rationalistic, liberalizing currents of nineteenth-century philosophy. True, the denomination and most of its leaders never fully understood the intellectual project (and Roberts may be partly to blame for that). Free Methodists tended to reduce theology to piety, and a piety that was sometimes too otherworldly or that succumbed to legalism. Still the church, educational institutions, and global missions that Roberts directly or indirectly launched were taught to base their faith on the Bible and biblical ethics, not on the deceptive philosophies and ideologies of the age.

It may be, in fact, that the major reason why the Free Methodist Church over a century and a half has not become doctrinally "liberal" or heterodox is Roberts's biblical radicalism. Because of its inborn commitment to Scripture, experience, and traditional Wesleyan categories, Free Methodism did not succumb to the theological drift that the Methodist Episcopal Church experienced between 1830 and 1870. Nor on the other side was it ever fully captured by dispensational fundamentalism, despite significant inroads in the twentieth century.

Viewed historically, the contribution of the Free Methodist Church as an extension of B. T. and Ellen Roberts's legacy lies more in the areas of countercultural witness, missions and evangelism, and education than it does in intellectual leadership or cultural impact. Yet it may still be possible for Free Methodism — especially global Free Methodism — to make key, culture-transforming contributions to American and global intellectual life, if it can combine a faithful biblical radicalism with an astute, informed engagement, without compromise, with the intellectual, cultural, and ideological currents of the day.

Even today, more than a century after his death, B. T. Roberts's still-unfulfilled legacy points in that direction. Is it not true, after all, that the mission of the church is "twofold — to maintain the Bible standard of Christianity, and to preach the gospel to the poor"?

Index

self-assessment of, 282; social development of, 53-54; as teacher of girls'
Sunday School class, 155, 163; theology
of, 598, 820-21; transcontinental travel
of, 604-10, 636; tributes to, 570; views of,
on marriage, 145, 158-59; views of, on
spiritual gifts, 598; work of, with *Earnest
Christian*, 566, 568, 569, 586. *See also*
marital relationship, BTR and ELR
Roberts, Emma Sellew, 557, 568, 622-27,
654-61, 894, 901, 919-23; as coprincipal of
Chesbrough Seminary, 628-29, 658-61,
919-20; death of, 922; at Oberlin College,
657
Roberts, Florilla. *See* Smallwood, Florilla
Roberts
Roberts, George Lane (son), 201, 205-14,
223-27, 244, 258-60, 266, 277, 280-84, 293,
304, 339-40, 373-75, 451, 502-3, 566, 589,
612, 644-54, 885-86, 916-17; birth of, 198;
death of, 917; educational work of, in
Argentina, 645-49; and Farmers' Alliance, 772; illness of, 213, 216-17, 224, 234,
374; legal career of, 645, 652-54; and
marriage to Anna Rice, 647-49; and
marriage to Winifred Murphy, 654; in
oil business, Bradford, Pa., 652-53; in
printing business, 649-51, 684; religious
experience of, 651
Roberts, Hibbert Rice, 625, 886, 917-18;
birth of, 653
Roberts, Hibbert Rice, Jr., 918
Roberts, Howard Passmore, 659, 922
Roberts, Jerusha (Pratt), 16
Roberts, Lois Ellen. *See* Hallett, Lois Ellen
Roberts
Roberts, Lowden Stowe, 662, 918
Roberts, Lucy George, 625, 660, 911, 922; as
founder of Roberts-Beach School for
Girls, 921
Roberts, Nellie Luescher (Mrs. Hibbert R.),
918
Roberts, Polly (Risley), 15-17
Roberts, Sally (Ellis; mother of BTR), 5,
14-25, 31, 33, 40, 168, 175, 179, 187, 210,

223, 252, 276-77, 343, 375, 455; conversion
of, 22; death of, 375
Roberts, Samuel (son), 589, 612, 888; birth
of, 589; death of, 639-41, 644
Roberts, Sara (wife of BTR, Jr.), 918
Roberts, Sarah Georgiana (daughter),
293-94, 298, 302-5; birth of, 293, 327;
death of, 303-5, 310, 326-27
Roberts, Susan (Mrs. Charles S.), 888,
913-14, 918
Roberts, Susannah, 16
Roberts, Thankful, 16
Roberts, Titus (father of BTR), 5, 14-25, 31,
33, 97, 153, 168-69, 175-79, 183, 187, 210,
223-27, 252, 257, 270, 318, 354, 411, 424,
455, 464, 888; business dealings of,
276-77, 343-44; character of, 24-25,
662-63; conversion of, 13, 21-24, 26, 36,
366; death of, 5, 661-63; as local
preacher, 23, 277
Roberts, William (ca. 1660–ca. 1735), 16
Roberts, William Titus (son), 179, 184-89,
201, 224, 233, 244, 260, 277, 293, 303, 305;
death of, 187-88
Roberts, Winifred Murphy, 917
Roberts family life, 630, 635
Roberts Family Papers, xvi-xvii, 367
Roberts household, 622-23; as community,
623
Roberts house in Buffalo, 273, 276, 290, 301,
343, 375, 500-503, 590; in North Chili,
627
Roberts Inn (Pomfret, N.Y.), 17
Robertsites, 313
Roberts Wesleyan College, xi, xvi, 191, 629,
919-20. *See also* Chesbrough Seminary;
Chili Seminary
Robie, John E., 219-22, 229-38, 241, 246, 251,
255, 273, 309, 311, 314, 323, 328, 357-58, 385,
393, 473, 461, 494, 501; description of,
220; influence of, 220, 238; as writer
against Nazaritism, 311-19, 324-27, 332-33
Rochester, N.Y., 5, 8, 11, 33, 37, 135, 167, 170,
190, 214, 220, 231, 259, 262, 265, 267, 271,
273, 279, 284, 296-98, 300, 302, 315,
340-43, 349, 423, 500; growth of, 340